Resources, Pollution, and Environmental Degradation

- Resources are limited and should not be wasted; there is not always more.

- Don't use high-quality energy to do something that can be done with lower-quality energy; don't use a chain saw to cut butter or electricity to heat water or a house.

- Pollution control and waste management methods help treat the symptoms of environmental degradation, but eventually they will be overwhelmed because they only shuffle around the growing outputs of throwaway societies.

- Pollution prevention and waste reduction are the best and cheapest ways to sustain the earth; the best way to reduce pollution and waste is not to produce so much; if you don't put something into the environment, it isn't there.

- Reducing resource consumption and waste production is the most important priority, followed by reusing items, recycling key mineral resources, and buying recycled items (the three Rs of Earth care).

- Don't dilute, disperse, mix, burn, or bury matter, products, or wastes that can be recycled or reused.

- Use locally available perpetual and renewable resources where possible, and use renewable resources no faster than they're replenished by natural processes (concept of sustainable yield).

- Everyone is downwind or downstream from everybody (principle of the global commons).

Economics and Politics

- Everything we have comes from the sun and the earth; the earth can get along without us, but we can't get along without the earth.

- Don't deplete or degrade Earth's physical, chemical, and biological capital, which supports all life and human economic activities; the Earth deficit is the ultimate deficit.

- We cannot have a truly healthy economy in a sick environment.

- Use economic incentives and penalties to change Earth-degrading and Earth-depleting manufacturing processes, products, and businesses into Earth-sustaining ones.

- The market price of a product should include all present and future costs of any pollution, environmental degradation, or other harmful effects connected with it that are passed on to society and the environment (concept of internalizing external costs).

- Anticipating and preventing problems is cheaper and more effective than reacting to and trying to cure them; an ounce of prevention is worth a pound of cure.

- Cost-benefit analysis is useful but will not protect Earth because essential things such as human life, good health, clean air and water, nature's beauty, wildlife, and Earth's natural cleansing, renewing, and recycling processes cannot be reduced to dollars and cents.

- We cannot have economic and military security without environmental security.

- Individuals matter; history shows that the most important changes come from the bottom up, not the top down.

- Every crisis is an opportunity for change.

- Think globally, act locally.

Worldview and Ethics

- The earth does not belong to us; we belong to the earth.

- We should try to understand and work with the rest of nature rather than try to dominate and conquer it.

- Every living species has a right to live, or at least to struggle to live, simply because it exists; this right is not dependent on a species' actual or potential use to us.

- Any chemical that we manufacture should not interfere with Earth's natural biogeochemical cycles in ways that degrade Earth's life-support systems for us or other species.

- Any chemical we manufacture and introduce into the environment should be considered potentially harmful (guilty) until shown to be innocent.

- An action is right when it tends to maintain the ecological integrity, sustainability, and diversity of Earth's life-support systems for us and other species and wrong when it tends otherwise.

- It is wrong for humans to cause the premature extinction of any wild species and the elimination and degradation of their habitats.

- When we alter nature to meet our needs or wants, we should choose the method that does the least possible harm to other living things; in general, in minimizing harm it is worse to harm a species than an individual organism, and still worse to harm a community of living organisms.

- When we alter nature, we should aim to make such changes at nature's rates and in ways that don't disturb natural processes.

- We should protect Earth's remaining wild ecosystems from our activities, rehabilitate or restore ecosystems we have degraded, use ecosystems only on a sustainable basis, and allow many of the ecosystems we have occupied and abused to return to a wild state.

- In protecting and sustaining nature, go farther than the law requires.

- We should leave the earth as good as we found it, if not better.

- It is wrong to treat people and other living things primarily as factors of production, whose value is expressed only in economic terms.

- All people should be held responsible for their own pollution and environmental degradation.

- We can't expect to reduce the dangers from most hazards to zero, but we have an obligation to reduce them as low as possible (concept of risk-benefit analysis).

- We should understand that any system that depends on fallible humans for its design, operation, and maintenance will sooner or later fail (limitation-of-risk-benefit-analysis concept).

- To prevent excessive deaths of people and other species, people must prevent excessive births (birth-control-is-better-than-death-control concept).

- We cannot have peace, justice, a sustainable-Earth, or a sense of pride about our accomplishments as long as people still live in poverty.

- To understand the earth and yourself, take time to experience and sense directly the air, water, soil, plants, animals, bacteria, and other parts of the earth.

- Learn about and care for your local environment.

- The best things in life aren't things; they are love, caring, and joy based on sustaining the earth for ourselves and other species and leaving the earth better than we found it.

FOUR LEVELS OF ENVIRONMENTAL AWARENESS

First Level of Awareness

Pollution and Environmental Degradation

Environmental problems are seen as essentially pollution problems that threaten human health and welfare. Individual environmental problems are solved one by one by waiting until each problem reaches a crisis level. Then it is dealt with by using legal, technological, and economic methods to try to control or clean up pollution instead of preventing it. At this level, it is assumed that growth-oriented, technological societies can continue indefinitely.

There are four major drawbacks to staying at this awareness level. First, it is a human-centered view, not a life-centered view. Second, individuals see their own impacts as too tiny to matter, not realizing that billions of individual impacts acting together threaten the life-support systems for us and other species. Third, this approach seduces people into thinking that environmental and resource problems have quick technological solutions: "Have technology fix us up, send me the bill at the end of the month, but don't expect me to change my way of living." Fourth, it attempts to treat the symptoms of environmental abuse instead of trying to determine and deal with the causes leading to our environmental and resource problems.

Second Level of Awareness

Consumption Overpopulation

The causes of pollution, environmental degradation, and resource depletion are seen as a combination of people overpopulation in poor countries and consumption overpopulation in affluent countries, with the most environmentally damaging populations living in industrialized societies with high rates of resource consumption and waste production. At this level, the answers seem obvious. Stabilize and then reduce population sizes in all countries. Reduce wasteful consumption of matter and energy resources, especially in affluent countries.

At this level, there is little emphasis on transforming political and economic systems in ways that help sustain the earth, or in setting aside or restoring natural systems as wilderness areas, parks, and wildlife preserves. There is little awareness that most protected areas are too small to sustain their natural diversity of organisms and are being rapidly overwhelmed and biologically impoverished by unsustainable use of resources and the pollutants produced by technological, growth-oriented societies. This second level of awareness still views humans as above or outside nature, with an obligation to dominate and conquer it.

Third Level of Awareness

Spaceship Earth

The goal at this level is to use technology and existing economic and political systems to control population growth, pollution, and resource depletion to prevent environmental overload. Earth is viewed as a spaceship, a machine that can be controlled by using advanced technology. If Earth becomes too crowded, the solution is to build space stations for the excess population. If Earth becomes depleted of mineral resources, we will mine other planets. Genetic engineering will be used to control the evolution of life forms and develop organisms that produce more food, clean up oil spills and toxic wastes, and satisfy more of our wants. Because of our ingenuity and power over the rest of nature, there will always be more.

This view of the earth as a spaceship is a sophisticated expression of the idea that technology and human ingenuity can control nature and create artificial environments and life forms to avoid environmental overload. However, this approach can also *cause* environmental overload and resource depletion in the long run, because it is based on the false ideas that we understand how nature works and that there are no limits to the earth's resources and our ability to overcome any problem with technological innovations.

This view calls for sustainable economic development and sustainable societies for humans. Careful analysis reveals that some of the proposals now being made under the guise of sustainability are in the long run unsustainable. The human-centered spaceship worldview is inadequate for dealing with an overpopulated, environmentally stressed, and globally interconnected world based on living by depleting and degrading Earth's natural capital.

Fourth Level of Awareness

Sustainable Earth

The first three levels of awareness are human-centered views in which we shape the world to meet our needs. They do not recognize that the solution to our problems lies in developing an Earth-centered or life-centered worldview based on the principles summarized on the preceding two pages.

At this level, we recognize that we cannot have sustainable or *any* form of economic development or sustainable human societies unless we help sustain the entire earth by working with Earth's natural processes. Respecting and honoring human life is based on respecting the Earth that sustains us and other species. We must do this not only because it helps ensure our survival, but because it is wrong to do otherwise.

Environmental Science

Sustaining the Earth

FOURTH EDITION

G. Tyler Miller, Jr.

Wadsworth Publishing Company
Belmont, California
A Division of Wadsworth, Inc.

SCIENCE EDITOR: Jack Carey

EDITORIAL ASSISTANT: Marlene Zuvich

PRODUCTION EDITOR: Vicki Friedberg

MANAGING DESIGNER: Andrew H. Ogus

TEXT DESIGNERS: James Chadwick and Cynthia Schultz

PRINT BUYER: Barbara Britton

ART EDITOR: Donna Kalal

PERMISSIONS EDITOR: Peggy Meehan

COPY EDITOR: Joan Pendleton

PAGE MAKE-UP: Cynthia Schultz

PHOTO RESEARCHER: Stephen Forsling

TECHNICAL ILLUSTRATORS: Susan Breitbard, Tasa Graphic Arts, Inc., Darwin and Vally Hennings, Marjorie Leggitt, Guy Magellenes, Joan Carol, Raychel Ciemma, Florence Fujimoto, Jeanne M. Schreiber, and John and Judith Waller

COMPOSITOR: Thompson Type/San Diego, CA

COLOR SEPARATOR: Vec-Tron/Schiller Park, IL

PRINTER: Rand McNally/Versailles, KY

COVER DESIGN: Andrew H. Ogus

PART OPENING PHOTOGRAPHS:

Part 1: Brian Parker/Tom Stack & Associates

Part 2: Los Angeles Convention & Visitors Bureau

Part 3: Thomas Kitchin/Tom Stack & Associates

Part 4: Errol Andrew/FPG International

Part 5: California Energy Commission

COVER PHOTOGRAPH: Northern spotted owl in an old-growth forest in the Pacific Northwest, © Tom and Pat Leeson/ Photo Researchers, Inc. The spotted owl, which is endangered because of logging, is an indicator of the health of vanishing old-growth forests in the United States. The owl is being used by environmentalists as a way to protect remaining old-growth forests from essentially irreversible destruction and degradation. This controversy is often framed as jobs versus the owl, but the real issue is people versus the earth, which sustains all economies and all life. If we don't protect remaining old-growth forests and other ecosystems from ourselves and help people whose jobs are threatened make a transition to Earth-sustaining jobs, we will have neither forests nor jobs in the future.

Printed in the United States of America

2 3 4 5 6 7 8 9 10 — 97 96 95 94 93

Library of Congress Cataloging-in-Publication Data
Miller, G. Tyler (George Tyler), 1931–
    Environmental science : sustaining the earth / G. Tyler
Miller, Jr. — 4th ed.
        p.   cm. — (Wadsworth biology series)
    Includes bibliographical references and index.
    ISBN 0-534-17808-1
    1. Human ecology.   2. Environmental
protection.   3. Natural resources.   4. Pollution.   I. Title.
    II. Series.
GF41.M538   1992
363.7—dc20   92-17936

BOOKS IN THE WADSWORTH BIOLOGY SERIES

Resource Conservation and Management, Miller

Living in the Environment, 7th, Miller

Biology: Concepts and Applications, Starr

Biology: The Foundations, 2nd, Wolfe

Biology: The Unity and Diversity of Life, 6th, Starr and Taggart

Dimensions of Cancer, Kupchella

Evolution: Process and Product, 3rd, Dodson and Dodson

Introduction to Cell Biology, Wolfe

Molecular and Cell Biology, Wolfe

Oceanography: An Introduction, 4th, Ingmanson and Wallace

Oceanography: An Invitation to Marine Science, Garrison

Plant Physiology, 4th, Devlin and Witham

Exercises in Plant Physiology, Witham et al.

Plant Physiology, 4th, Salisbury and Ross

Plant Physiology Laboratory Manual, Ross

Plants: An Evolutionary Survey, 2nd, Scagel et al.

Psychobiology: The Neuron and Behavior, Hoyenga and Hoyenga

Sex, Evolution, and Behavior, 2nd, Daly and Wilson

HOW I BECAME INVOLVED In 1966, when what we now know as the environmental movement began in the United States, I heard a scientist give a lecture on the problems of overpopulation and environmental abuse. Afterward I went to him and said, "If even a fraction of what you have said is true, I will feel ethically obligated to give up my research on the corrosion of metals and devote the rest of my life to environmental issues. Frankly, I don't want to believe a word you have said, and I'm going into the literature to try to prove that your statements are either untrue or grossly distorted."

After six months of study I was convinced of the seriousness of these problems. Since then I have been studying, teaching, and writing about them. I have also attempted to live my life in an environmentally sound way — with varying degrees of success — by treading as lightly as possible on the earth (see pp. 409–410 for a summary of my own progress in attempting to work with nature). This book summarizes what I have learned in 27 years of trying to understand how various parts of the earth are connected.

MY PHILOSOPHY OF EDUCATION I agree with Norman Cousins's statement: "The first aim of education should not be to prepare young people for careers, but to enable them to develop a respect for life." If we accomplish this, things we now dream and hope for can become possible.

In our lifelong pursuit of knowledge, I believe we should do four things: The first is to question everything and everybody, as any good scientist does. Second, I believe each of us should develop a personal list of principles, concepts, and rules to use as guidelines for making decisions. This list should be continually evaluated and modified as a result of experience. The purpose of our lifelong pursuit of education should really be to learn as *little* as we can — to learn how to sift through mountains of facts and ideas to find the few that are useful and worth knowing. We need a wisdom revolution not an information revolution.

This book is full of facts and numbers, but I hope readers will remember that facts are merely stepping-stones to ideas, laws, concepts, principles, and connections. Most statistics and facts are human beings with the tears wiped off and living things whose lives we are threatening.

Third, I believe that interacting with what we read makes learning more interesting and effective. When I read, I mark key passages with a highlighter or pen. I put an asterisk in the margin next to something I think is important and double asterisks next to something that I think is especially important. I write comments in the margins, such as *Beautiful, Confusing, Bull, Wrong*, and so on. I fold down the top corner of pages with highlighted passages and the top and bottom corners of especially important pages. This way, I can flip through a book and quickly review the key passages. I urge you to interact in such ways with this book.

Finally, I believe that we have an ethical obligation to act on the always incomplete and usually controversial knowledge we have. We should not be mere toe-dippers, who refuse to jump into the dirty, difficult, uncertain, and challenging sea of life. I believe that my readers should see how I have struggled as a questioner and learner and passionate doer — however imperfectly.

KEY FEATURES This book is designed to be used in introductory courses on environmental science. It treats environmental science as an *interdisciplinary* study, combining ideas and information from natural sciences such as biology, chemistry, and geology and social sciences such as economics, politics, and ethics to present a general idea of how nature works and how things are interconnected. It examines how the environment is being used and abused, and what individuals can do to protect and improve it for themselves, for future generations, and for other living things.

The book uses basic scientific laws, principles, and concepts to help us understand environmental and resource problems and the possible solutions to these problems. I have introduced only the concepts and principles necessary to understanding material in this book and have tried to present them simply but accurately. Key laws, principles, and concepts are summarized inside the front cover.

My aim is to provide an accurate and balanced introduction to environmental science without the use of mathematics or complex scientific information. To help make sure the material is accurate and up to date, I have consulted more than 10,000 research sources in the professional literature. This and previous editions have also been reviewed by more than 200 experts and teachers (see list on pp. ix–x).

The book is divided into five major parts (see Brief Contents). After Parts One and Two are covered, the rest of the book can be used in almost any order. In addition, most chapters and many sections within these chapters can be moved around or omitted to accommodate courses with different lengths and emphases.

After looking at the Brief Contents I urge you to read the list of laws, concepts, and principles given inside the front cover and the four levels of environmental awareness summarized on the page after these principles. In effect, it is a three-page summary of the key ideas in this book, based on what I have learned so far.

Then I suggest that you turn to the back of the book and read the three-page epilogue, which summarizes the major themes of this book.

Students often complain that textbooks are difficult and boring. I have tried to overcome this problem by writing in a clear, interesting, and informal style.

I also relate the information in the book to the real world and to our individual lives, in the main text and in various kinds of boxes sprinkled throughout the book. The *Spotlights* (38) highlight and give further insights into environmental and resource problems. The *Case Studies* (41) give in-depth information about key issues (and how to apply concepts). The *Pro/Con* discussions (16) outline both sides of controversial environmental and resource issues, while each *Guest Essay* (9) exposes readers to an individual environmental researcher or activist's point of view. *Individuals Matter* (15) give examples of what we as individuals can do to help sustain the earth.

The book's 374 illustrations are designed to present complex ideas in understandable ways and to relate learning to the real world. They include 223 four-color diagrams, 151 carefully selected color photographs, and 38 maps to provide a geographical perspective.

MAJOR CHANGES IN THIS EDITION The book has been thoroughly updated and revised throughout. Many new topics have been added, and the coverage of some other topics has been expanded. Among these are Earth capital, exponential growth, pollution prevention and waste reduction, evaluation of the Spaceship-Earth worldview, the nature of science and environmental science, the five kingdom classification of organisms, net primary productivity, the concept of an ecological niche, mangrove swamps, coral reefs, homeostasis, coevolution, sustainable-Earth economies, environmental careers, chemical hazards, tropical deforestation, loss of biodiversity, megadiversity countries, Japan's global environmental impact, old-growth forests and deforestation in the United States, sustainable-Earth forestry, the Clean Air Act of 1990, water crises in the Middle East, the dangers of lead, hazardous waste, drift-net fishing, farm subsidies, the Bhopal tragedy, wildlife extinction, wildlife poaching in the United States, world conservation strategy, the ecological importance of bats, solar envelope houses, geologic processes and plate tectonics, and the nature of sustainable-Earth societies.

In this edition there are 7 new Spotlights, 7 new Case Studies, 2 new Pro/Con discussions of controversial issues, 4 new Guest Essays, 12 new photographs, 12 new diagrams, and 2 new tables.

WELCOME TO CONTROVERSY A theme of this book is that most (perhaps all) environmental and resource problems and their possible solutions are interrelated. I point out many of these connections and give cross references to other sections of the book where related ideas are discussed. Environmental and resource problems are considered on a local, national, and global scale.

There are no easy or simple answers to these problems and challenges. We will never have scientific certainty or agreement about what we should do, because science provides us with probabilities not certainties, and advances through continuous controversy. When we see scientists arguing, this is science at work—science at its best. Furthermore, despite considerable research, we still know relatively little about how nature works at a time when we are altering nature at an accelerating pace. The complexity of environmental issues we face and their importance to our lives and to the lives of future generations of humans and other species make them highly controversial.

Intense controversy also arises because environmental science questions the ways we view and act in the world around us. It asks us to rethink our worldviews, values, and lifestyles and our economic and political systems. This often can be a threatening process.

In this book I present pros and cons on key issues. My goal is to encourage readers to think critically and make up their own minds. However, just as an economist writing an economics text is pro-economics, I am passionately pro-Earth for us and other species. I believe that we must change the ways we think and act, as our ancestors in earlier periods of cultural change and transition had to.

Despite great uncertainty, we cannot put off making these difficult decisions. Because our impacts on the environment are growing so rapidly, time may be our scarcest resource. Many environmentalists believe that we have only a decade or two in which to drastically change the way we are treating the earth and thus ourselves. They believe that denial and delay are recipes for disaster in a time of rapid change.

I wish everything was more certain, but it isn't. Making difficult choices without ever having enough information is what being human is all about. Waiting for more information before acting on an important issue is a way of acting by default—not to decide is to decide.

Yet this book offers a realistic but hopeful view of the future. Much has been done since the mid-1960s, when many people first became aware of the resource and environmental problems we face. But the 1960s, 1970s, and 1980s were merely a dress rehearsal for the much more urgent and difficult work we must do in the 1990s and beyond. This book suggests ways that each of us can help sustain the earth. It's a scary and exciting time to be alive.

STUDY AIDS Each chapter begins with a few general questions to give readers an idea of what they will be learning. Answering these questions after completing the chapter also serves as a general review of the material. When a new term is introduced and defined, it is printed in **boldface type**. There is also a glossary of all key terms at the end of the book.

New to this edition are factual recall questions (with answers) listed at the bottom of most pages. Readers might cover the answer on the right-hand page with a piece of paper and then try to answer the question on the left-hand page. These questions are not necessarily related to the chapter in which they are found.

Each chapter ends with a set of discussion questions designed to encourage readers to think critically and to apply what they have learned to their lives. Some ask readers to take sides on controversial issues and to back up their conclusions and beliefs. Experiments, individual projects, and group projects also appear at the end of each chapter. These items are marked with an asterisk (*). Many new ones have been added to this edition.

Readers who become especially interested in a particular topic can consult the list of further readings for each chapter, given at the back of the book. The Appendix contains a list of publications to help keep up to date on the book's material and a list of some key environmental organizations.

This book is also designed for future reference. I hope readers who value what they've learned from it will add the book to their personal library or give it to someone else who wants to learn about sustaining the earth.

HELP ME IMPROVE THIS BOOK Let me know how you think this book can be improved, and if you find any errors, please let me know about them. Most errors can be corrected in subsequent printings of this edition, rather than waiting for a new edition. Send any errors you find and your suggestions for improvement to Jack Carey, Science Editor, Wadsworth Publishing Company, 10 Davis Drive, Belmont, CA 94002. He will send them on to me.

SUPPLEMENTS New for this edition is an expanded *Instructor's Manual and Test Items Booklet*, written by Jane Heinze-Fry (Ph.D. in science and environmental education). For each chapter, there are objectives; key terms; multiple-choice test questions with answers; projects and field trips; term-paper and report topics; and filmstrips, slide sets, videos, films, and computer programs.

A set of master sheets for making overhead transparencies, which includes all line art, is available to adopters.

The new *Critical Thinking Software Tools and Workbook* is a special educational version of STELLA® II software (with an accompanying workbook) that helps students understand the hows and whys underlying ecosystem dynamics, waste management, ozone depletion, and other environmental concepts and issues. Stu-

dents control the learning process as they build a model, incorporate assumptions into their model, and then, through simulation and animation, discover the dynamic implications of their assumptions. Alternately, instructors can lead the class in the construction of a model. The workbook contains exercises to guide students through the software, providing yet another avenue for learning.

Finally, a new *Laboratory Manual* has been written by C. Lee Rockett (Bowling Green State University) and Kenneth J. Van Dellen (Macomb Community College). The *Laboratory Manual* grew out of an extensive survey to determine the most important lab exercises to be included.

ANNENBERG/CPB TELEVISION COURSE This textbook is being offered as part of the Annenberg/CPB Project television series *Race to Save the Planet*, broadcast on PBS.

Race to Save the Planet is a 10-part public television series and a college-level television course examining the major environmental questions facing the world today, ranging from population growth to soil erosion, from the destruction of forests to climate changes induced by human activity. The series takes into account the wide spectrum of opinion about what constitutes an environmental problem, as well as the controversies about appropriate remedial measures. It analyzes problems and emphasizes the successful search for solutions. The course develops a number of key themes that cut across a broad range of environmental issues, including sustainability, the interconnection of the economy and the ecosystem, short-term versus long-term gains, and the trade-offs involved in balancing problems and solutions.

A *Study Guide* available from Wadsworth Publishing Company integrates the telecourse and my texts (*Living in the Environment* and *Environmental Science*).

For further information about available television course licenses, duplication licenses, and off-air taping licenses, contact PBS Adult Learning Service, 1320 Braddock Place, Alexandria, VA 22314-1698, 1-800-ALS-ALS-8.

For information about purchasing videocassettes, the Faculty Guide, and other print material, contact the Annenberg/CPB Collection, P.O. Box 2284, South Burlington, VT 05407-2284, 1-800-LEARNER.

ACKNOWLEDGMENTS I wish to thank the many students and teachers who responded so favorably to the seven editions of *Living in the Environment*, the three editions of *Environmental Science*, and the first edition of *Resource Conservation and Management* and offered many helpful suggestions for improvement.

I am also deeply indebted to the reviewers who pointed out errors and suggested many important improvements in this and earlier editions, and to those who wrote guest essays for this edition. Any errors and deficiencies left are mine.

The members of Wadsworth's talented production team, listed on the copyright page, have also made important contributions. I especially appreciate the competence and cheerfulness of my production editor, Vicki Friedberg. My thanks also to Wadsworth's dedicated sales staff.

Special thanks go to Jack Carey, Science Editor at Wadsworth, for his encouragement, help, friendship, and superb reviewing system. It helps immensely to work with the best and most experienced editor in college textbook publishing.

I also wish to thank Peggy Sue O'Neal, my earthmate, spouse, and best friend, for her love and support of me and the earth. I dedicate this book to her and to the earth that sustains us all.

G. Tyler Miller, Jr.

General Changes and Improvements

- Updating and revising material throughout the book. Because of rapid changes in data and information, a textbook in environmental science needs to be updated every two years.

- Adding 7 new *Spotlights*, 7 new *Case Studies*, 2 new *Pro/Con* discussions of controversial issues, 4 new *Guest Essays*, 12 new photographs, 12 new diagrams, 2 improved diagrams, and 2 new tables. See individual chapter changes.

- Adding or expanding coverage of many topics, including Earth capital, exponential growth, pollution prevention and waste reduction, evaluation of Spaceship-Earth worldview, nature of science and environmental science, five kingdom classification of organisms, net primary productivity, ecological niche, mangrove swamps, coral reefs, homeostasis, coevolution, sustainable-Earth economies, environmental careers, chemical hazards, tropical deforestation, loss of biodiversity, megadiversity countries, Japan's global environmental impact, old-growth forests and deforestation in the United States, sustainable-Earth forestry, Clean Air Act of 1990, water crises in the Middle East, the dangers of lead, hazardous waste, drift-net fishing, farm subsidies, Bhopal tragedy, wildlife extinction, wildlife poaching in the United States, world conservation strategy, ecological importance of bats, solar envelope house, geologic processes and plate tectonics, and nature of sustainable-Earth societies. See individual chapter changes.

- Adding factual recall questions (with answers) at the bottom of most pages.

- Simplified and revised summary of laws, concepts, and principles inside the front cover.

- Adding one or more experiments, individual projects, or group projects at the end of most chapters. These items are marked with an asterisk (*).

- New and expanded *Instructor's Manual*.

- New *Laboratory Manual*.

- Special educational version of Stella® II software for developing critical thinking.

Part One
Humans and Nature: An Overview

Chapter 1 Population, Resources, Environmental Degradation, and Pollution
2 color photos; new Spotlight: The Nature of Exponential Growth; expanded discussion of Earth capital, exponential growth, environmental degradation, and pollution prevention; Guest Essay by Jessica Tuchman Mathews

Chapter 2 Cultural Changes, Worldviews, Ethics, and Environment
New discussion of Spaceship-Earth worldview, expanded discussion of sustainable-Earth worldview, Guest Essay by Peter Montague

Part Two
Scientific Principles and Concepts

Chapter 3 Matter and Energy Resources: Types and Concepts
2 new diagrams, 1 improved diagram, new section (3-1) on nature of science and environmental science, expanded discussions of energy resources and nature of sustainable-Earth societies

Chapter 4 Ecosystems: What Are They and How Do They Work?
1 new diagram, introduction of five kingdom classification of organisms, expanded discussions of net-primary productivity and ecological niche

Chapter 5 Ecosystems: What Are the Major Types and What Can Happen to Them?
1 new color photo; 1 new diagram; new discussions on homeostasis and stability of living systems and coevolution; expanded discussions of ecological importance of oceans, mangrove swamps, and coral reefs

Chapter 6 Human Population Dynamics: Growth, Urbanization, and Regulation
Extensive updating of population and urbanization data

Chapter 7 Environmental Economics and Politics
New Spotlight: Environmental Careers, expanded discussions of sustainable-Earth economies and making sustaining the earth profitable, Guest Essay by Claudine Schneider

Chapter 8 Hazards, Risk, and Human Health
New Pro/Con: Is Risk Analysis a Form of "Legalized" Murder?, new table ranking ecological and health risks, expanded discussion of chemical hazards

Part Three
Air, Water, and Soil Resources

Chapter 9 Air Resources and Air Pollution
1 new figure, discussion of Clean Air Act of 1990

Chapter 10 Climate, Global Warming, Ozone Depletion, and Nuclear War: Ultimate Problems
1 new figure, extensive updating of information

AUTHORS OF GUEST ESSAYS

Lois Marie Gibbs, Director, Citizens' Clearinghouse for Hazardous Wastes; **Garrett Hardin**, Professor Emeritus of Human Ecology, University of California, Santa Barbara; **Edward J. Kormondy**, Chancellor and Professor of Biology, University of Hawaii-Hilo/West Oahu College; **Amory B. Lovins**, Energy Policy Consultant and Director of Research, Rocky Mountain Institute; **Jessica Tuchman Mathews**, Vice President, World Resources Institute; **Peter Montague**, Senior Research Analyst, Greenpeace, and Director, Environmental Research Foundation; **Norman Myers**, Consultant in Environment and Development; **David Pimentel**, Professor of Entomology, Cornell University; **Claudine Schneider**, former Congresswoman, Rhode Island

CUMULATIVE REVIEWERS

My thanks to the following people who over the years have contributed to the development of *Environmental Science*:

Barbara J. Abraham, Hampton University; Donald D. Adams, State University of New York at Plattsburgh; Larry G. Allen, California State University, Northridge; James R. Anderson, U.S. Geological Survey; Kenneth B. Armitage, University of Kansas; Gary J. Atchison, Iowa State University; Marvin W. Baker, Jr., University of Oklahoma; Virgil R. Baker, Arizona State University; Ian G. Barbour, Carleton College; Albert J. Beck, California State University, Chico; W. Behan, Northern Arizona University; Keith L. Bildstein, Winthrop College; Jeff Bland, University of Puget Sound; Roger G. Bland, Central Michigan University; Georg Borgstrom, Michigan State University; Arthur C. Borror, University of New Hampshire; John H. Bounds, Sam Houston State University; Leon F. Bouvier, Population Reference Bureau; Michael F. Brewer, Resources for the Future, Inc.; Mark M. Brinson, East Carolina University; Patrick E. Brunelle, Contra Costa College; Terrence J. Burgess, Saddleback College North; David Byman, Pennsylvania State University, Worthington-Scranton; Lynton K. Caldwell, Indiana University; Faith Thompson Campbell, Natural Resources Defense Council, Inc.; Ray Canterbery, Florida State University; Ted J. Case, University of San Diego; Ann Causey, Auburn University; Richard A. Cellarius,

Evergreen State University; William U. Chandler, Worldwatch Institute; F. Christman, University of North Carolina, Chapel Hill; Preston Cloud, University of California, Santa Barbara; Bernard C. Cohen, University of Pittsburgh; Richard A. Cooley, University of California, Santa Cruz; Dennis J. Corrigan; George Cox, San Diego State University; John D. Cunningham, Keene State College; Herman E. Daly, The World Bank; Raymond F. Dasmann, University of California, Santa Cruz; Kingsley Davis, Hoover Institution; Edward E. DeMartini, University of California, Santa Barbara; Thomas R. Detwyler, University of Wisconsin; Peter H. Diage, University of California, Riverside; Lon D. Drake, University of Iowa; T. Edmonson, University of Washington; Thomas Eisner, Cornell University; David E. Fairbrothers, Rutgers University; Paul P. Feeny, Cornell University; Nancy Field, Bellevue Community College; Allan Fitzsimmons, University of Kentucky; Kenneth O. Fulgham, Humboldt State University; Lowell L. Getz, University of Illinois at Urbana-Champaign; Frederick F. Gilbert, Washington State University; Jay Glassman, Los Angeles Valley College; Harold Goetz, North Dakota State University; Jeffery J. Gordon, Bowling Green State University; Eville Gorham, University of Minnesota; Michael Gough, Resources for the Future; Ernest M. Gould, Jr., Harvard University; Peter Green, Golden West College; Katharine B. Gregg, West Virginia Wesleyan College; Paul K. Grogger, University of Colorado at Colorado Springs; L. Guernsey, Indiana State University; Ralph Guzman, University of California, Santa Cruz; Raymond Hames, University of Nebraska, Lincoln; Raymond E. Hampton, Central Michigan University; Ted L. Hanes, California State University, Fullerton; William S. Hardenbergh, Southern Illinois University at Carbondale; John P. Harley, Eastern Kentucky University; Neil A. Harrimam, University of Wisconsin, Oshkosh; Grant A. Harris, Washington State University; Harry S. Hass, San Jose City College; Arthur N. Haupt, Population Reference Bureau; Denis A. Hayes, environmental consultant; John G. Hewston, Humboldt State University; David L. Hicks, Whitworth College; Eric Hirst, Oak Ridge National Laboratory; S. Holling, University of British Columbia; Donald Holtgrieve, California State University, Hayward; Michael H. Horn, California State University, Fullerton; Mark A. Hornberger, Bloomsberg University; Marilyn Houck, Pennsylvania State University; Richard D. Houk, Winthrop College; Robert J. Huggett, College of William and Mary; Donald Huisingh, North Carolina State University; Marlene K. Hutt, IBM; David R. Inglis, University of Massachusetts; Robert Janiskee, University of South Carolina; Hugo H. John, University of Connecticut; Brian A. Johnson, University of Pennsylvania, Bloomsburg; David I. Johnson, Michigan State University; Agnes Kadar, Nassau Community College; Thomas L. Keefe, Eastern Kentucky University; Nathan Keyfitz, Harvard University; David Kidd, University of New Mexico; Edward J. Kormondy, University of Hawaii-Hilo/West Oahu College; John V. Krutilla, Resources for the Future, Inc.; Judith Kunofsky, Sierra Club; E. Kurtz; Theodore Kury, State University of New York at Buffalo; Steve Ladochy, University of Winnipeg; Mark B. Lapping, Kansas State University; Tom Leege, Idaho Department of Fish and Game; William S. Lindsay, Monterey Peninsula College; E. S. Lindstrom, Pennsylvania State University; M. Lippiman, New York University Medical Center; Valerie A. Liston, University of Minnesota; Dennis Livingston, Rensselaer Polytechnic Institute; James P. Lodge, air pollution consultant; Raymond C. Loehr, University of Texas, Austin; Ruth Logan, Santa Monica City College; Robert D. Loring, DePauw University; Paul F. Love, Angelo State University; Thomas Lovering, University of California, Santa Barbara; Amory B. Lovins, Rocky Mountain Institute; Hunter Lovins, Rocky Mountain Institute; Gene A. Lucas, Drake University; David Lynn; Timothy F. Lyon, Ball State University; Melvin G. Marcus, Arizona State University; Gordon E. Matzke, Oregon State University; Parker Mauldin, Rockefeller Foundation; Theodore R. McDowell, California State University; Vincent E. McKelvey, U.S. Geological Survey; John G. Merriam, Bowling Green State University; A. Steven Messenger, Northern Illinois University; John Meyers, Middlesex Community College; Raymond W. Miller, Utah State University; Rolf Monteen, California Polytechnic State University; Ralph Morris, Brock University, St. Catherines, Ontario, Canada; William W. Murdoch, University of California, Santa Barbara; Norman Myers, environmental consultant; Brian C. Myres, Cypress College; A. Neale, Illinois State University; Duane Nellis, Kansas State University; Jan Newhouse, University of Hawaii, Manoa; John E. Oliver, Indiana State University; Eric Pallant, Allegheny College; Charles F. Park, Stanford University; Richard J. Pedersen, U.S. Department of Agriculture, Forest Service; David Pelliam, Bureau of Land Management, U.S. Department of Interior; Rodney Peterson, Colorado State University; William S. Pierce, Case Western Reserve University; David Pimentel, Cornell University; Peter Pizor, Northwest Community College; Mark D. Plunkett, Bellevue Community College; Grace L. Powell; James H. Price, Oklahoma College; Marian E. Reeve; Carl H. Reidel, University of Vermont; L. Reynolds, University of Central Arkansas; Ronald R. Rhein, Kutztown University of Pennsylvania; Charles Rhyne, Jackson State University; Robert A. Richardson, University of Wisconsin; Benjamin F. Richason III, St. Cloud State University; Ronald Robberecht, University of Idaho; William Van B. Robertson, School of Medicine, Stanford University; C. Lee Rockett, Bowling Green State University; Terry D. Roelofs, Humboldt State University; Richard G. Rose, West Valley College; Stephen T. Ross, University of Southern Mississippi; Robert E. Roth, The Ohio State University; David Satterthwaite, I.E.E.D., London; Stephen W. Sawyer, University of Maryland; Arnold Schecter, State University of New York at Syracuse; William H. Schlesinger, Ecological Society of America; Stephen H. Schneider, National Center for Atmospheric Research; Clarence A. Schoenfeld, University of Wisconsin, Madison; Henry A. Schroeder, Dartmouth Medical School; Lauren A. Schroeder, Youngstown State University; Norman B. Schwartz, University of Delaware; George Sessions, Sierra College; David J. Severn, Clement Associates; Paul Shepard, Pitzer College and Claremont Graduate School; Frank Shiavo, San Jose State University; Michael P. Shields, Southern Illinois University at Carbondale; Kenneth Shiovitz; F. Siewert, Ball State University; E. K. Silbergold, Environmental Defense Fund; Joseph L. Simon, University of South Florida; William E. Sloey, University of Wisconsin, Oshkosh; Robert L. Smith, West Virginia University; Howard M. Smolkin, U.S. Environmental Protection Agency; Patricia M. Sparks, Glassboro State College; John E. Stanley, University of Virginia; Mel Stanley, California State Polytechnic University, Pomona; Norman R. Stewart, University of Wisconsin, Milwaukee; Frank E. Studnicka, University of Wisconsin, Platteville; William L. Thomas, California State University, Hayward; Tinco E. A. van Hylckama, Texas Tech University; Robert R. Van Kirk, Humboldt State University; Donald E. Van Meter, Ball State University; John D. Vitek, Oklahoma State University; Lee B. Waian, Saddleback College; Thomas D. Warner, South Dakota State University; Kenneth E. F. Watt, University of California, Davis; Alvin M. Weinberg, Institute of Energy Analysis, Oak Ridge Associated Universities; Brian Weiss; Raymond White, San Francisco City College; Douglas Wickum, University of Wisconsin, Stout; Charles G. Wilber, Colorado State University; Nancy Lee Wilkinson, San Francisco State University; John C. Williams, College of San Mateo; Ray Williams, Whittier College; Samuel J. Williamson, New York University; Ted L. Willrich, Oregon State University; James Winsor, Pennsylvania State University; Fred Witzig, University of Minnesota, Duluth; George M. Woodwell, Woods Hole Research Center; Robert Yoerg, Belmont Hills Hospital; Hideo Yonenaka, San Francisco State University; Malcolm J. Zwolinski, University of Arizona

BRIEF CONTENTS

DETAILED CONTENTS

PART ONE

Humans and Nature:

An Overview

The environmental crisis is an outward manifestation of a crisis of mind and spirit. There could be no greater misconception of its meaning than to believe it is concerned only with endangered wildlife, human-made ugliness, and pollution. These are part of it, but more importantly, the crisis is concerned with the kind of creatures we are and what we must become in order to survive.

LYNTON K. CALDWELL

CHAPTER 1

POPULATION, RESOURCES, ENVIRONMENTAL DEGRADATION, AND POLLUTION

General Questions and Issues

1. How rapidly is the human population increasing?

2. What are Earth's principal types of resources? How can they be depleted or degraded?

3. What are the principal types of pollution, and how can pollution be controlled?

4. What are the relationships among human population size, resource use, technology, environmental degradation, and pollution?

We must stop mortgaging the future to the present. We must stop destroying the air we breathe, the water we drink, the food we eat, and the forests that inspire awe in our hearts. . . . We need to prevent pollution at the source, not try to clean it up later. . . . It's time to remember that conservation is the cheapest and least polluting form of energy. . . . We need to come together and choose a new direction. We need to transform our society into one in which people live in true harmony—harmony among nations, harmony among the races of humankind, and harmony with nature. . . . We will either reduce, reuse, recycle, and restore—or we will perish.

REV. JESSE JACKSON

COMPLEX MIX OF interlocking problems are reaching crisis levels on the beautiful blue, white, and green planet that is the only home for us and a rich diversity of other life forms. One problem is population growth. Unless death rates rise sharply from disease, famine, or global nuclear war, the world's population is projected to double to 10.8 billion by 2045 and could almost triple to 14 billion before leveling off by the end of the next century.

Each year more of the world's forests, grasslands, and wetlands disappear, and deserts grow in size as more people increase their use of the earth's surface and its resources. Vital topsoil is washed or blown away from farmland and cleared forests (Figure 1-1) and then clogs streams, lakes, and reservoirs with sediment. In many areas, water occurring underground is withdrawn faster than it is replenished. Every hour, as many as six of Earth's wild species are driven to permanent extinction by human activities.

By burning one-time deposits of fossil fuels and cutting down and burning forests faster than they are replenished, we add carbon dioxide to the lower atmosphere. As we increase the concentrations of carbon dioxide and several other heat-trapping gases in the lower atmosphere, Earth's climate may become warmer through an enhanced *greenhouse effect*, or *heat-trap effect*, within the next 40 years. If such a rapid change in Earth's climate takes place, it will disrupt our ability to grow enough food, alter water distribution, and make some densely populated areas uninhabitable from either lack of water or flooding due to rising sea levels.

Figure 1-1 Severe soil erosion on a hillside in Spain. Removal of forest cover often leads to this type of erosion. Wildlife habitat is lost and eroded, and streams in the land below can be polluted with eroded sediment.

Our burning of fossil fuels is also the greatest source of the air pollution that threatens trees, lakes, and people and causes extensive water pollution and land disruption. The oil that runs cars and heats homes and that is used to produce food and most of the products we use will probably be depleted within 50 years. So far, we are doing little to reduce waste of this vital resource and to phase in substitutes.

Chemicals we add to the air are drifting into the upper atmosphere and depleting ozone gas, which protects us and most other forms of life by filtering out most of the sun's harmful ultraviolet radiation. In the lower atmosphere, those same chemicals trap heat and help intensify the planet's natural heat-trap effect.

Toxic wastes produced by factories and homes are accumulating and poisoning the air, water, and soil. Agricultural pesticides contaminate the groundwater that many of us drink and some of the food we eat.

The most important fact of our existence is that *the resources keeping us alive, supporting our lifestyles, and driving the world's economies come directly or indirectly from the sun and from Earth's air, water, rocks, fossil fuels, soil, and tens of millions of wild species that make up Earth's* **natural capital**.* Deplete this capital or global and national treasure and we change from a sustainable to an unsustainable lifestyle. Get too greedy and we'll soon be needy.

The bad news is the growing evidence that we are depleting Earth's natural capital at unprecedented and accelerating rates by living in ways that are eventually unsustainable. The good news is that we can help sustain Earth for human beings and other species indefinitely by learning how to live off the interest from the natural capital provided for us and other species by the sun and the earth.

We can do this if enough of us change the way we view and act in the world, as summarized in the quote that opens this chapter. This cultural change begins by understanding that we can't get along without Earth, but Earth can easily get along without us. Our power to destroy other species and our own species is now so great that we must make peace with the planet, try to understand and cooperate with its magnificent rhythms and cycles, and repair much of the damage we have inflicted on our only home. The best news is that living sustainably and in touch with the earth is one of the most meaningful and joyful things we can do.

This book is an introduction to **environmental science**, the study of how we and other species interact with each other and with the nonliving environment of matter and energy. The two main goals of environmental science are to learn how Earth works and how to sustain it so we and other species can exist and flourish indefinitely.

---

*Boldfaced terms are also defined in the Glossary at the back of the book.

1-1 Human Population Growth

RATES OF CHANGE: LINEAR AND EXPONENTIAL GROWTH Things such as car speed, population size, resource use, and pollution can increase in two major ways: linearly (arithmetic growth) or exponentially (geometric growth). With **linear growth**, a quantity increases by some fixed amount during each unit of time: 1, 2, 3, 4, 5, and so on. For example, suppose you start your car and accelerate it by 1.6 kilometers (1 mile) an hour every second. After 60 seconds of such linear growth, you would be traveling at 97 kilometers (60 miles) per hour. After 2 minutes, your speed would be 193 kilometers (120 miles) per hour.

With **exponential growth**, a quantity increases by a fixed percentage of the whole in a given time period. With exponential growth, a quantity can increase by doubling: 1, 2, 4, 8, 16, 32, and so on. The higher the percentage growth, the less time it takes for the quantity involved to double.

For example, if you doubled the speed of a supercharged car every second, it would take you only 5 seconds to reach a speed of 103 kilometers (64 miles) per hour, and 1 second later you would be traveling 206 kilometers (128 miles) per hour. If you had a magic motor, after 30 seconds you would be traveling at 1.6 billion kilometers (1 billion miles) per hour. After 44 seconds, your speed would be 27 trillion kilometers (17 trillion miles) per hour! Another example of the astounding power of exponential growth is given in the Spotlight on p. 4.

$C \approx 6.70 \times 10^8$ mph

THE J-SHAPED CURVE OF HUMAN POPULATION GROWTH Plotting the estimated number of people on Earth over time gives us a curve with the shape of the letter J (Figure 1-2). This increase in the size of the human population is an example of exponential growth taking place over time at several different rates.

The slow, early phase of exponential growth is represented by the long horizontal part of the composite curve plotted in Figure 1-2. As the base of people undergoing growth has increased, the number of people on Earth has risen sharply and the curve of population growth has rounded the bend of the J and headed almost straight up from the horizontal axis (Figure 1-2).

This growth means that it has taken less time to add each new billion people. It took 2 million years to add the first billion people; 130 years to add the second billion; 30 years to add the third billion; 15 years to add the fourth billion; and only 12 years to add the fifth

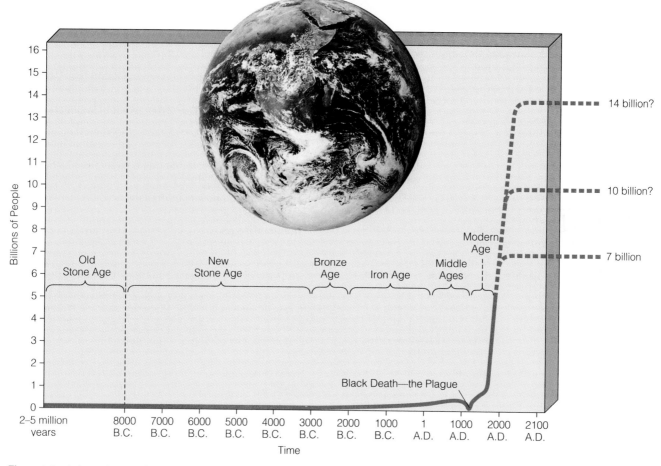

Figure 1-2 J-shaped curve of past exponential world population growth with projections to 2100. This curve is a composite of exponential growth taking place over time at several, mostly increasing, rates. (Data from World Bank and United Nations)

SPOTLIGHT The Nature of Exponential Growth

A major shortcoming of the human race is our failure to understand the implications of exponential growth. We can use a fable to help understand this type of growth.

Once there were two kings who enjoyed playing chess, with the loser giving a prize to the winner. After one of their matches, the winner asked the losing king to place a grain of wheat on the first square of the chessboard, two on the second, four on the third, and so on. The number of grains was to double each time until all 64 squares were filled.

The losing king didn't understand about exponential growth and was delighted to get off so easy. He agreed to the proposal. It was the biggest mistake he ever made.

The winning king wanted the losing king to start with one grain of wheat and double it 63 times. This amounts to one less than 2^{64} grains of wheat. This may not seem like much, but it's actually more than 500 times all the wheat harvested in the world this year. It's probably larger than all the wheat that has ever been harvested!

From this example, we can understand some of the properties of exponential growth. It is deceptive because it starts off slowly. However, a few doublings lead quickly to enormous numbers, because after the first doubling each additional doubling is more than the total of all preceding growth.

Doubling time is the time it takes (usually in years) for the quantity of something growing exponentially to double. We can calculate doubling time in years by using the **rule of 70**. This involves divid-

ing the annual percentage growth rate of a quantity into 70 (70/percentage growth rate = doubling time in years). In 1992, the world's population grew by 1.7%. If that rate continues, Earth's population will double in 41 years (70/1.7 = 41 years) — more growth in this short period than has occurred in all of human history.

One of our biggest challenges is that most of the environmental problems we face — population growth, excessive and wasteful resource use, wildlife extinction, and pollution — are growing exponentially at high rates. As a result, we have little time to make drastic changes in the way we use technology and the ways we treat the earth and thus ourselves.

Q: How many people are there in the world?

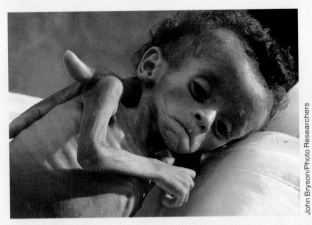

Figure 1-3 This Brazilian child is one of the estimated 1 billion people on Earth who suffer malnutrition caused by a diet without enough protein and other nutrients needed for good health.

Figure 1-4 One-sixth of the people in the world have inadequate housing or no housing at all. These homeless people in Calcutta, India, are forced to sleep on the street.

In mid-1992, the world's population of 5.4 billion people grew exponentially at a rate of 1.7%. This means that by mid-1993 there will be 92 million more people to feed, clothe, and house (5.4 billion people × 0.017 = 92 million)—an average increase of 1.8 million people a week, 252,000 a day, 10,500 an hour. At that rate, it takes about

- 5 days to add people equal to the number of Americans killed in all U.S. wars

- 4 months to add people equal to the 30 million people killed in all wars fought since 1945

- 9 months to add 75 million people—the number killed in the bubonic plague epidemic of the fourteenth century, the world's greatest disaster

- 1.8 years to add 165 million people—the number of people killed

in all wars fought during the past 200 years

- 2.7 years to add 256 million people—the population of the United States in mid-1992

- 12 years to add 1.17 billion people—the population of China in mid-1992

These figures give you some idea of what it means to go around the bend of the J curve of exponential growth. This enormous increase in population is happening when

- One out of five persons, including one out of three children under the age of 5, is hungry or malnourished (Figure 1-3)

- One out of five persons lacks clean drinking water and bathes in water contaminated with deadly, disease-causing organisms

- One out of five persons has inadequate housing and an estimated 150 million people—100 million of them children—are homeless (Figure 1-4)

- One out of three persons has poor health care and not enough fuel to keep warm and cook food

- More than half of humanity lacks sanitary toilets

- One out of four adults cannot read or write, including one out of three in poor countries (one out of two in Africa) and one out of five in the United States

- Every day, at least 40,000 children under the age of five die in poor countries of conditions that could be prevented or cured at a cost of about $5 per child a year

billion. With present growth rates (see Spotlight above), the sixth billion will be added during the 10-year period between 1987 and 1997, and the seventh billion is expected to be added 9 years later in 2006.

POPULATION GROWTH IN THE MORE DEVELOPED AND LESS DEVELOPED COUNTRIES Virtually all economies in the world today seek to increase their **economic growth**: an increase in the capacity of the economy to provide goods and services for final use. Such growth is usually measured by an increase in

a country's **gross national product (GNP)**: the market value in current dollars of all goods and services produced by an economy for final use during a year. To show how the average person's slice of the economic pie in an economy is changing, economists often calculate the **per capita GNP** (per person): the GNP divided by the total population.

The United Nations broadly classifies the world's countries as more developed and less developed according to their degree of economic growth and development. The **more developed countries (MDCs)** are

A: Approximately 5.4 billion in mid-1992 (0.1 billion added per year)

Chapter 1   5

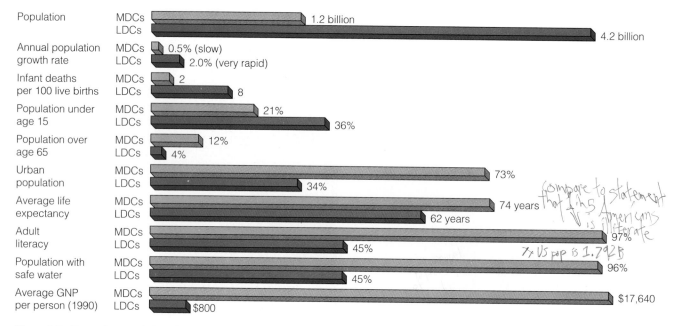

Figure 1-5 Some characteristics of more developed countries (MDCs) and less developed countries (LDCs) in 1992. This simple classification does not reveal the variations in per capita GNP among MDCs and LDCs. Also, per capita GNP does not tell us how the wealth of a country is distributed among its population. Most LDCs, such as moderately industrialized Mexico and Brazil, consist of small islands of affluence in a vast ocean of poverty. Another problem is that most governments use GNP and per capita GNP as measures of the well-being of their people when these indicators measure only the speed at which an economy is running. (Data from United Nations and Population Reference Bureau)

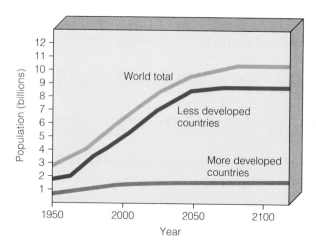

Figure 1-6 Past and projected population size for MDCs, LDCs, and the world, 1950–2120. (Data from United Nations)

highly industrialized, and most have high average GNPs per person. They include the United States, Canada, Japan, the Commonwealth of Independent States (CIS),* Australia, New Zealand, and all countries in Eu-

rope. These MDCs, with 1.2 billion people (22% of the world's population), command about 80% of the world's wealth, use about 80% of the world's mineral and energy resources, and generate most of the world's pollution and wastes.

All remaining countries are classified as **less developed countries (LDCs)** with low to moderate industrialization and low to moderate GNPs per person. Most are located in the Southern Hemisphere in Africa, Asia, and Latin America. The LDCs contain 4.3 billion people or 78% of the world's population, but they have only about 20% of the world's wealth and use only about 20% of the world's mineral and energy resources. Figure 1-5 shows some general differences between MDCs and LDCs. Most of the projected increase in world population will take place in LDCs, where 1 million people are added every 4.3 days (Figure 1-6). How the earth will accommodate the rapid exponential growth in population and resource use now taking place in poor and rich nations is one of the most important questions we face.

1-2 Resources and Environmental Degradation

TYPES OF RESOURCES A **resource** is anything we get from the living and nonliving environment to meet our needs and wants. *Material resources* are those

---

*The Commonwealth of Independent States is a loose federation of 11 independent republics — Russia, Armenia, Ukraine, Belarus, Kyrgyzstan, Turkmenistan, Moldova, Tajikistan, Uzbekistan, Kazakhstan, and Azerbaijan — that constitute much of what was the Soviet Union. At the time this book was written, Georgia, Estonia, Latvia, and Lithuania were not part of the commonwealth. We have made every effort to supply the most current information available; however, because of economic and political uncertainty, the composition of this alliance may change.

Q: Where does everything that supports your life come from?

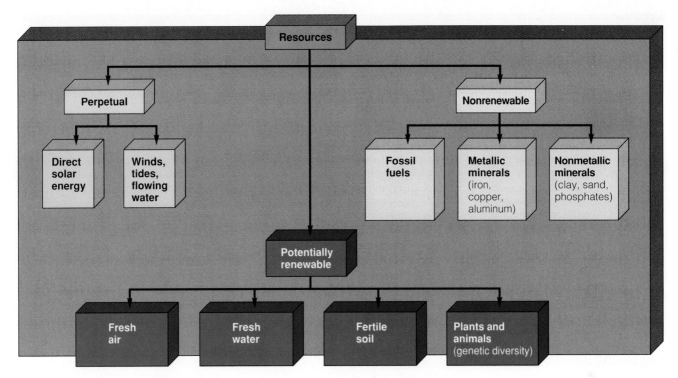

Figure 1-7 Major types of material resources. This scheme isn't fixed; potentially renewable resources can be converted to nonrenewable resources if used for a prolonged time faster than they are renewed by natural processes.

whose quantity can be measured. Some, such as fresh air, fresh water, fertile soil, and naturally growing edible plants, are directly available for use.

Most material resources, such as petroleum (oil), iron, groundwater (water occurring underground), and modern crops, aren't directly available, and their supplies are limited. They become resources only when we use our ingenuity to make them available at affordable prices. Petroleum, for example, was a mysterious fluid until we learned how to find it, extract it, and refine it into gasoline, home heating oil, road tar, and other products at affordable prices. On our short human time scale, we classify material resources as nonrenewable, perpetual, and renewable (Figure 1-7).

Solitude, beauty, knowledge, and love are *nonmaterial*, or *intangible resources*. In theory, they are unlimited, but their availability can be reduced or destroyed in an increasingly crowded and degraded environment.

NONRENEWABLE MATERIAL RESOURCES **Nonrenewable**, or **exhaustible**, **resources** exist in a fixed amount (stock) in various places in Earth's crust and have the potential for renewal by geological, physical, and chemical processes taking place over hundreds of millions to billions of years. Examples are copper, aluminum, coal, and oil. We classify these resources as exhaustible because we are extracting and using them at a much faster rate than the geological time scale on which they were formed. Instead of being physically exhausted, nonrenewable resources become **economi-**

cally depleted to the point where it costs too much to get what is left (typically when 80% of their total estimated supply has been removed and used).

Some nonrenewable material resources can be recycled or reused to extend supplies—copper, aluminum, iron, and glass, for example. **Recycling** involves collecting and reprocessing a resource so that it can be made into new products. Aluminum beverage cans can be collected, melted, and converted into new beverage cans or other aluminum products. Glass bottles can be crushed and melted to make new glass bottles or other glass items. **Reuse** involves using a resource over and over in the same form. Glass bottles can be collected, washed, and refilled many times.

Other nonrenewable resources, such as fossil fuels (mostly coal, oil, and natural gas), can't be recycled or reused. When burned, the useful energy in these fuels is converted to waste heat and exhaust gases that can pollute the atmosphere and the soil, water, and wildlife when they fall or are washed out of the air.

Often we can find a substitute or a replacement for a scarce or expensive nonrenewable material resource, but some materials have properties that can't easily be matched. In other cases, replacements may be inferior, too costly, or too scarce.

PERPETUAL AND POTENTIALLY RENEWABLE MATERIAL RESOURCES A **perpetual resource**, such as solar energy, is virtually inexhaustible on a human time scale. Not wasting energy and living off vir-

Earth's organisms are classified into different **species**, groups of organisms that resemble one another in appearance, behavior, chemical makeup and processes, and genetic structure. Organisms that reproduce sexually are classified as members of the same species if they can actually or potentially interbreed with one another and produce fertile offspring.

Over billions of years, the formation of new species and the extinction of species that could not adapt to changing environmental conditions have produced the planet's most valuable resource: **biological diversity**, or **biodiversity**. It is made up of three related concepts: genetic diversity, species diversity, and ecological diversity.

Genetic diversity is variability in the genetic makeup among individuals within a single species. **Species diversity** is the variety of species on Earth and in different parts of the planet such as forests, grasslands, deserts, lakes, and oceans (see photo on p. 1 and Figure 1-8). **Ecological diversity** is the variety of forests, deserts, grasslands, streams, lakes, and other biological communities that interact with one

another and with their nonliving environments.

We don't know how many species exist on Earth, but biologists estimate that there are probably 40 to 100 million different species. So far, biologists have classified fewer than 1.7 million species. They know a fair amount about roughly one-third of these species and the detailed roles and interactions of only a few.

We are utterly dependent on this mostly unknown biological capital. The priceless diversity within and among species has provided us with food, wood, fibers, energy, raw materials, industrial chemicals, and medicines and contributes hundreds of billions of dollars yearly to the world economy.

Earth's vast genetic library of life forms also helps provide us and other species with free resource recycling and purification services and natural pest control. Every species here today represents stored genetic information that allows the species to adapt to certain changes in environmental conditions. We can think of biodiversity as nature's "insurance policy" against disasters.

Extinction is a natural process, but since agriculture began about

10,000 years ago, the rate of species extinction has increased sharply as human settlements have expanded worldwide. There is evidence that we are bringing about the greatest mass extinction since the end of the age of dinosaurs, 65 million years ago.

No one knows how many species we are eliminating, but biologists estimate that each day at least 10, and probably 140, species are becoming extinct because of our activities. Biologists warn that if deforestation (especially of tropical forests), destruction and degradation of topsoil, and destruction of wetlands and coral reefs continue at their present exponential rates, this extinction rate could rise sharply by early in the next century and then climb even more.

This catastrophic loss of biological diversity cannot be balanced by formation of new species because it takes between 2,000 and 100,000 generations for a new species to evolve. Genetic engineering is not a solution to this biological holocaust because genetic engineers do not create new genes. They transfer genes or gene fragments from one organism to another and thus de-

tually inexhaustible solar energy in the form of heat, wind, flowing water, and renewable wood and other forms of biomass (tissue from living organisms that can be burned or broken down to provide energy) is a sustainable lifestyle. Depending on indirect solar energy stored in essentially one-time deposits of fossil fuels, or uranium used to fuel nuclear power plants, is sooner or later an unsustainable lifestyle.

A **potentially renewable resource** theoretically can last indefinitely without reducing the available supply because it is replaced more rapidly through natural processes than are nonrenewable resources. Examples are trees in forests, grasses in grasslands, wild animals, fresh surface water in lakes and streams, most groundwater, fresh air, and fertile soil. The planet's most valuable resource is its diversity of potentially renewable forms of life (see Spotlight above).

The highest rate at which a potentially renewable resource can be used without reducing its available supply throughout the world, or in a particular area, is called its **sustainable yield**. If this natural replacement rate is exceeded, the available supply of a potentially renewable resource begins to shrink — a process known as **environmental degradation**.

Several types of environmental degradation can change potentially renewable resources into nonrenewable or unusable resources:

- Covering productive land with water, concrete, asphalt, or buildings to such an extent that crop growth declines and places for wildlife to live (habitats) are lost

- Cultivating land without proper soil management so that crop growth is reduced by soil erosion and depletion of plant nutrients

Q: At current growth rates, how many years does it take to add 1 billion people?

Figure 1-8 Two of Earth's diversity of species. On the left is the world's largest flower, called the flesh flower (*Rafflesia*), growing in a tropical rain forest in Sumatra. The flower of this leafless plant can have a diameter as large as 1 meter (3.3 feet). It is the only part of the plant found above the ground. This plant gives off a smell like rotting meat to attract flies that pollinate its flower. Its lurid colors also imitate those of a carcass lying on the forest floor. On the right is a cotton top tamarin, another resident of a tropical rain forest.

pend on natural biodiversity for their raw material.

Prematurely eliminating many of Earth's species for our own short-term economic gain is not only shortsighted, but also wrong. It will reduce the ability of our species and other species to survive. What do you think should be done to protect Earth's precious biodiversity from us?

- Irrigating cropland without sufficient drainage so that excessive buildup of water (waterlogging) or salts (salinization) in the soil decreases crop growth

- Removing water from underground sources (aquifers) and from surface waters (streams and lakes) faster than it is replaced by natural processes. Water scarcity is emerging on every continent

- Removing trees from large areas (deforestation) without adequate replanting so that wildlife habitats are destroyed and long-term timber growth is decreased

- Depletion of grass by livestock (overgrazing), eroding soil to the extent that productive grasslands are converted into unproductive land and deserts (desertification)

- Eliminating or severely reducing the populations of various wild species by destruction of habitat, commercial hunting, pest control, and pollution

- Polluting renewable air, water, and soil so that they are unusable for various purposes

Table 1-1 summarizes the status of key life-sustaining resources. One reason for environmental degradation and ways to manage potentially renewable resources are discussed in the Spotlight on page 10.

TYPES OF RESOURCE SCARCITY **Absolute resource scarcity** occurs when supplies of a resource are insufficient or too expensive to meet present or future demand. For example, the world's affordable supplies of nonrenewable oil may be used up within the next 50 years. The period of absolute scarcity and increasing cost of oil may begin between 1995 and 2010.

Relative resource scarcity occurs when enough of a resource is still available to meet the demand, but its distribution is unbalanced (see Case Study on p. 12).

Table 1-1 Health Report for Some of Earth's Vital Resources

Land

Productive Land	About 8.1 million square kilometers (3.1 million square miles) of once-productive land (cropland, forests, grasslands) have become desert in the last 50 years. Each year, almost 61,000 square kilometers (23,500 square miles) of new desert are formed.
Cropland Topsoil	Topsoil is eroding faster than it forms on about 35% of the world's cropland—a loss of about 24 billion metric tons (26 billion tons) of topsoil a year (Figure 1-1). Crop productivity on one-third of Earth's irrigated cropland has been reduced by salt buildup in topsoil. Waterlogging of topsoil has reduced productivity on at least one-tenth of the world's cropland.
Forest Cover	Almost half of the world's original expanse of tropical forests has been cleared. Each year, about 171,000 square kilometers (66,000 square miles) of tropical forest are destroyed and another 171,000 square kilometers (66,000 square miles) are degraded. Within 30 to 50 years, there may be little of these forests left. One-third of the people on Earth cannot get enough fuelwood to meet their basic needs, and many are forced to meet their needs by cutting trees faster than they are being replenished. In MDCs, 312,000 square kilometers (120,400 square miles) of forest have been damaged by air pollution. Furthermore, many remaining areas of diverse, ancient forests are being cleared and replaced with more vulnerable tree farms that greatly reduce wildlife habitats and biodiversity.
Grasslands	Millions of hectares of grasslands have been overgrazed; some, especially in Africa and the Middle East, have been converted to desert. Almost two-thirds of U.S. rangeland is in fair to poor condition.

Water

Coastal and Inland Wetlands	Between 25% and 50% of the world's wetlands have been drained, built upon, or seriously polluted. Worldwide, millions of hectares of wetlands are lost each year. The United States has lost 56% of its wetlands and loses another 150,000 hectares (371,000 acres) each year.
Oceans	Most of the wastes we dump into the air, water, and land eventually end up in the oceans. Oil slicks, floating plastic debris, polluted estuaries and beaches, contaminated fish and shellfish are visible signs that we are using the oceans as the world's largest trash dump.
Lakes	Thousands of lakes in eastern North America and in Scandinavia have become so acidic that they contain no fish; thousands of other lakes are dying; thousands are depleted of much of their dissolved oxygen because chemicals produced by human activities have entered the water.

Data from Worldwatch Institute and World Resources Institute

SPOTLIGHT The Tragedy of the Commons and Management of Potentially Renewable Resources

One situation that can cause environmental degradation is the use of **common-property resources** that are owned by no one and available for use by everyone. Most are potentially renewable. Examples are clean air, fish in parts of the ocean not under the control of a coastal country, migratory birds, Antarctica, gases of the lower atmosphere, and the ozone content of the upper atmosphere.

Abuse or depletion of common-property resources is called the **tragedy of the commons**. It occurs be-cause each user reasons, "If I don't use this resource, someone else will. The little bit I use or the little bit of pollution I create is not enough to matter."

When the number of users is small, there is no problem. Eventually, however, the cumulative effect of many people trying to maximize their use of a common-property resource depletes or degrades the usable supply. Then no one can make a profit or otherwise benefit from the resource. Therein is the tragedy.

One solution is to reduce popu-lation size and resource use to the point where potentially renewable common-property resources are used at rates below their estimated sustainable yields. Such reduction isn't easily achieved because people don't like to be told how many children they can have or what types and amounts of resources they can use.

Another approach is to determine what is everyone's fair share of a common-property resource and then regulate access to the resource to ensure that annual sustainable

Water (continued)

Drinking Water   In LDCs, 61% of the people living in rural areas and 26% of urban dwellers do not have access to safe drinking water. Each year, 5 million die from preventable waterborne diseases. In parts of China, India, Africa, and North America, groundwater is withdrawn faster than it is replenished by precipitation. In the United States, one-fourth of the groundwater withdrawn each year is not replenished. Pesticides contaminate some groundwater deposits in 38 states. In MDCs, hundreds of thousands of industrial and municipal landfills and settling ponds, several million underground storage tanks for gasoline and other chemicals, and thousands of abandoned toxic waste dumps threaten groundwater supplies.

Air

Climate   Emissions of carbon dioxide and other gases into the atmosphere from the burning of fossil fuels and other human activities may raise the average temperature of Earth's lower atmosphere several degrees between now and 2050. This rapid enhancement of Earth's natural heat-trap effect would disrupt food production and water supplies and possibly flood low-lying coastal cities and croplands.

Atmosphere   Chlorofluorocarbons released into the lower atmosphere are drifting into the upper atmosphere and reacting with and gradually depleting ozone faster than it is being formed. The thinner ozone layer will let in more ultraviolet radiation from the sun. This will cause increases in skin cancer and eye cataracts, and our immune-system defenses against many infectious diseases will be weakened. Levels of eye-burning smog, damaging ozone gas, and acid rain in the lower atmosphere will increase, and yields of some important food crops will decrease.

Biodiversity

Wildlife   Each year at least 4,000, and probably 51,000, species become extinct, mostly because of human activities; if deforestation (especially of tropical forests), desertification, and destruction of wetlands and coral reefs continue at present rates, at least 500,000 and perhaps 1 million species will become extinct over the next 20 years.

People

Environmental Refugees   Worldwide, an estimated 16 million people have lost their homes and land because of environmental degradation. These people are now the world's largest class of refugees.

Poverty   At least 1.2 billion people — about one of every five — live in absolute poverty. During the 1980s, this group increased by 200 million people.

---

yields are not exceeded. The difficulty is getting the users to agree on what their fair share is.

One problem with all these approaches is that it is very difficult and expensive to make reliable estimates of the sustainable yield of a forest, grassland, or the population of a wild animal species. Even if we could do so, sustainable yields can and often do change because of changes in short-term weather, long-term climate, and unpredictable interactions with humans and other species. These uncertainties

mean that it is best to use a potentially renewable resource at a rate well below its estimated sustainable yield. This is rarely done because of the strong drive for short-term economic growth and profit regardless of the future consequences.

Another guideline for the management of potentially renewable common-property resources, such as national forests owned jointly by the public, is the **principle of multiple use**. According to this principle, these resources should be used for a variety of purposes, such as timber-

ing, mining, grazing, recreation, wildlife preservation, and soil and water conservation.

The problem with multiple use is that resource managers find it difficult to balance the competing uses because of strong pressures to use these resources for short-term economic gain. Often the result is that one use, such as timber cutting in national forests, becomes dominant. How do you think we should deal with the problem of the "tragedy of the commons"?

Everything runs on energy. It's the key that unlocks all other material resources. For most people in MDCs and an increasing number in LDCs, oil is the main source of energy used to help us promote economic growth and dominate the earth. When the price of oil rises, so do the prices of other forms of energy and most things we use.

When adjusted for inflation, oil has been cheap since 1950 (Figure 1-9). Its low price has encouraged MDCs and LDCs undergoing economic growth to become heavily dependent on — indeed, addicted to — this important resource. Low prices have also encouraged waste of oil and discouraged the search for other sources of energy.

The relative scarcity of oil between 1973 and 1979 was caused by several factors. One was rapid economic growth during the 1960s, stimulated by low oil prices. Another factor was the growing dependence of the United States and many other MDCs on imported oil (Figure 1-10).

A third factor was that between 1973 and 1979, the Organization of Petroleum Exporting Countries (OPEC)* was able to control the world's supply, distribution, and price of oil. About 67% of the world's known and economically affordable oil deposits (proven reserves) are in the OPEC countries, compared with only 4% in the United States.

*OPEC was formed in 1960 so that LDCs with much of the world's known and projected oil supplies could get a higher price for this resource and stretch remaining supplies by forcing the world to reduce oil use and waste. Today its 13 members are Algeria, Ecuador, Gabon, Indonesia, Iran, Iraq, Kuwait, Libya, Nigeria, Qatar, Saudi Arabia, United Arab Emirates, and Venezuela.

In 1973, OPEC produced 56% of the world's oil and supplied about 84% of all oil imported by other countries. In 1973, Arab members of OPEC reduced oil exports to Western industrial countries and banned all shipments of their oil to the United States because of its support of Israel in its 18-day war with Egypt and Syria.

This embargo lasted until March 1974 and caused a fivefold increase in the average world price of crude oil (Figure 1-9). The increase contributed to double-digit inflation in the United States and many other countries, high interest rates, soaring international debt, and a global economic recession. Americans, accustomed to cheap and plentiful fuel, waited for hours to buy gasoline and turned down thermostats in homes and offices.

Despite the sharp price increase, U.S. dependence on imported oil increased from 30% to 48% between 1973 and 1977. OPEC imports increased from 48% to 67% during the same period (Figure 1-10). This increasing dependence was caused mostly by the government's failure to lift controls that kept oil prices artificially low and thus encouraged energy waste and greatly increased oil consumption.

The artificially low prices sent a false message to consumers and set the stage for the second phase of the oil distribution crisis of the 1970s. Available world oil supplies decreased when the 1979 revolution in Iran shut down most of that country's production. Waiting lines at gas stations became even longer, and by 1981 the average world price of crude oil had risen to about $35 a barrel.

A combination of energy conservation (using energy more efficiently), substitution of other energy sources for oil, and increased oil production by non-OPEC countries

led to a drop in world oil consumption between 1979 and 1989. Because supply exceeded demand, the price of oil dropped from $35 to around $18 per barrel between 1981 and 1989. This oil glut meant that the price of crude oil (and gasoline) today, adjusted for inflation, is about the same as it was in 1974 (Figure 1-9). Also, gasoline in the United States today costs less in real terms (correcting for inflation) than it did in 1950 and in 1974.

Because of its enormous use and unnecessary waste of oil, the United States has gone from being the world's largest oil exporter to being the world's largest oil importer. *The United States will never again be self-sufficient in oil.*

Countries such as Japan, France, and the United States that rely on oil imports from the highly unstable Middle East are especially vulnerable to temporary supply disruptions or the threat of such disruptions. In 1990, the world was taught another harsh lesson about its addiction to oil, especially imports from the Middle East. The invasion of Kuwait by Iraq during the summer of 1990 sent oil prices soaring from around $18 to $40 a barrel within a few months, with the price falling to below $18 in March 1991 after the war ended.

This temporary price rise was due not to an actual or a relative shortage of oil, but rather to the *possibility* of a future relative shortage of oil should war break out in the Middle East and cause the disruption of oil flows from Saudi Arabia. As Christopher Flavin and Nicolas Lenssen put it, "Not only is the world addicted to cheap oil, but the largest liquor store is in a very dangerous neighborhood."

Most resource analysts expect that some time between 1995 and 2010 we will enter a period of in-

Q: How long does it take to add people equal to all those killed in all wars fought since 1945?

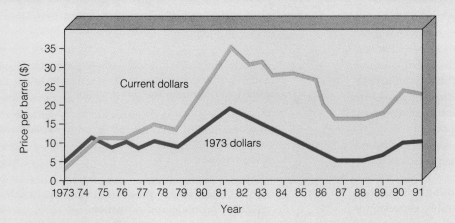

Figure 1-9 Average world crude oil prices between 1973 and 1991. (Data from Department of Energy and Department of Commerce)

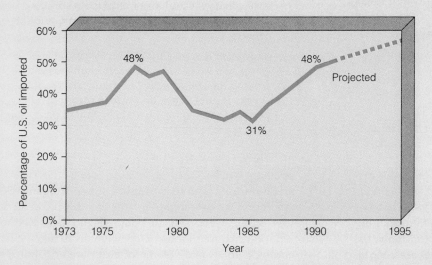

Figure 1-10 Percentage of U.S. oil imported between 1973 and 1991 with projections to 1995. (Data from U.S. Department of Energy and Spears and Associates, Tulsa, Oklahoma)

creasing absolute scarcity of oil, when the world's demand for oil will exceed the rate at which remaining supplies can be extracted. During this period, OPEC countries are projected to increase their share of the world's oil market to at least 60%, dominate world oil markets, and raise prices even more than in the 1970s.

The U.S. Department of Energy and most major oil companies project that sometime between 1995 and 2000 the United States could be dependent on imported oil for 60%

to 70% of its oil consumption — much higher than in 1977 (Figure 1-10). This would drain the already debt-ridden United States of vast amounts of money, leading to severe inflation and widespread economic recession, perhaps even a major depression.

The first step in dealing with this addiction is to admit that we are "oilaholics." The next step is to begin withdrawal and recovery by changing our oil-wasting lifestyles to kick this Earth-degrading addiction.

What do you think should be done to reduce our addiction to oil? What have you done to reduce your own addiction to oil?

WHAT IS POLLUTION?   Any undesirable change in the characteristics of air, water, soil, or food that can adversely affect the health, survival, or activities of humans or other living organisms is called **pollution**. Most pollutants are unwanted solid, liquid, or gaseous chemicals produced as by-products or wastes when a resource is extracted, processed, made into products, and used. Pollution can also take the form of unwanted energy emissions, such as excessive heat, noise, or radiation.

A major problem is that people differ in what they consider an acceptable level of pollution, especially if they have to choose between expensive pollution control and losing their jobs. As philosopher Georg Hegel pointed out, the nature of tragedy is not the conflict between right and wrong, but the conflict between right and right.

SOURCES OF POLLUTION   Pollutants can enter the environment naturally (for example, from volcanic eruptions) or through human activities (burning coal). Most natural pollution is dispersed over a large area and is often diluted or broken down to harmless levels by natural processes.

We have been overloading and disrupting this natural dilution, breakdown, and recycling of chemicals essential for life, with the pace picking up sharply during the past 50 years. Most serious pollution from human activities occurs in or near urban and industrial areas, where large amounts of pollutants are concentrated in small volumes of air, water, and soil. Industrialized agriculture is also a major source of air, water, and soil pollution.

Some pollutants contaminate the areas where they are produced. Others are carried by winds or flowing water to other areas. Pollution does not respect the state and national boundaries we draw on maps, as demonstrated by the release of massive amounts of radioactive particles into the atmosphere from the Chernobyl nuclear power plant in 1986.

Some of the pollutants we add to the environment come from single, identifiable sources, such as the smokestack of a power plant or an industrial plant, the drainpipe of a meat-packing plant, the chimney of a house, or the exhaust pipe of an automobile. These are called **point sources**.

Other pollutants enter the air, water, or soil from dispersed, and often hard-to-identify, sources called **nonpoint sources**. Examples are the runoff of fertilizers and pesticides from farmlands into streams and lakes and pesticides sprayed into the air or blown by the wind into the atmosphere. It is much easier and cheaper to identify and control pollution from fixed point sources than from widely dispersed nonpoint sources.

EFFECTS OF POLLUTION   Pollution can have a number of unwanted effects:

- *Nuisance and aesthetic insult* — unpleasant smells and tastes, reduced atmospheric visibility, and soiling of buildings and monuments

- *Property damage* — corrosion of metals, weathering or dissolution of building and monument materials, and soiling of clothes, buildings, and monuments

- *Damage to plant and nonhuman animal life* — decreased tree and crop production, harmful health effects on animals, and extinction

- *Damage to human health* — spread of infectious diseases, irritation and diseases of the respiratory system, genetic and reproductive harm, and cancers

- *Disruption of natural life-support systems at local, regional, and global levels* — climate change and decreased natural recycling of chemicals, reduced energy inputs, and a decrease in the biodiversity needed for good health and survival of people and other forms of life

Three factors determine how severe the effects of a pollutant will be. One is its *chemical nature* — how active and harmful it is to specific types of living organisms. Another is its **concentration** — the amount per volume unit of air, water, soil, or body weight. One way to reduce the concentration of a pollutant is to dilute it by adding it to a large volume of air or water. Until we started overwhelming the air and waterways with inputs of pollution, dilution was the solution to pollution. Now it is only a partial solution.

A third factor is a pollutant's *persistence* — how long it stays in the air, water, soil, or our bodies. **Degradable**, or **nonpersistent**, **pollutants** are broken down completely or reduced to acceptable levels by natural physical, chemical, and biological processes. Those broken down by living organisms (usually specialized bacteria) are called **biodegradable pollutants**. Human sewage added to a river or the soil is biodegraded fairly quickly by bacteria as long as it is not added faster than it can be broken down.

A major problem is that many of the substances and products we have made and introduced into the environment in large quantities often take decades or longer to degrade. Examples of these **slowly degradable**, or **persistent**, **pollutants**, are the insecticide DDT, most plastics, aluminum cans, and chlorofluorocarbons (CFCs) — chemicals widely used as coolants in refrigerators and air conditioners, spray propellants (in some

Q: How many children under age 5 die each day in poor countries of causes that could be prevented?

countries), and foaming agents for making plastics such as Styrofoam.

Nondegradable pollutants cannot be broken down by natural processes. Examples are the toxic elements lead and mercury. The best ways to deal with nondegradable pollutants are not to release them into the environment, to recycle them, and to remove them from contaminated air, water, or soil (an expensive process).

A serious problem is that we know little about the potential short- and long-range harmful effects of 80% of the 70,000 synthetic chemicals in commercial use on people and other species. Even our knowledge of the effects of the other 20% of the chemicals we have introduced into the environment is limited, mostly because it is quite difficult, time consuming, and expensive to gather this data. We are running a gigantic and exponentially increasing chemical experiment on ourselves and other species with very little knowledge of the possible long-term effects.

POLLUTION PREVENTION **Pollution prevention**, or **input pollution control**, prevents potential pollutants from entering the environment or sharply reduces the amounts released. This approach is summarized in biologist Barry Commoner's **law of pollution prevention**: If you don't put something into the environment, it isn't there. Pollution prevention is achieved by

- Evaluating the potential environmental harm of a chemical or technology before it is widely used by assuming it is guilty (potentially harmful) until proven innocent

- Recycling and reprocessing hazardous chemicals within industrial processes to keep them from entering the environment

- Redesigning technologies so that potential pollutants are not used or produced

- Reducing unnecessary and wasteful use of matter and energy resources

- Switching from reliance on nonrenewable and potentially polluting fossil fuel and nuclear energy resources to perpetual and renewable energy resources from the sun, wind, flowing water, renewable trees (wood), and heat from Earth's interior (geothermal energy)

- Making products that can be recycled or reused, that have long useful lives, and that are easy to repair

POLLUTION CLEANUP **Pollution cleanup**, or **output pollution control**, deals with pollutants after they have entered the environment. So far, most improvements in environmental quality in the United States and other MDCs have been based on using pollution cleanup.

Relying mostly on pollution control causes several problems. One is that, as long as population and resource use continue to increase, pollution cleanup is only a temporary bandage. For example, adding catalytic converters to cars has helped reduce air pollution; but as the number of cars has increased, this cleanup approach becomes less effective

A second problem is that cleanup often removes a pollutant from one part of the environment and causes pollution in another part. We can collect garbage; but garbage must be burned (perhaps causing air pollution and leaving a toxic ash that must be put somewhere), dumped into streams, lakes, and oceans (perhaps causing water pollution), buried (perhaps causing soil and groundwater pollution), recycled, or reused.

Both pollution prevention and pollution cleanup are needed, but environmentalists urge that we place primary emphasis on pollution prevention because it works better and is cheaper than pollution cleanup. As Benjamin Franklin reminded us long ago, "An ounce of prevention is worth a pound of cure." Currently, about 99% of environmental spending in the United States is devoted to pollution cleanup and only 1% to pollution prevention.

As you make decisions about what things to buy and about proposed solutions to an environmental or resource problem, ask yourself, Is this a prevention (input) or a cleanup (output) approach? Our motto should be: *Pollution cleanup is better than doing nothing, but pollution prevention is the best way to walk more gently on the earth.*

Relationships Among Population, Resource Use, Technology, Environmental Degradation, and Pollution

1-4

ONE MODEL OF ENVIRONMENTAL DEGRADATION AND POLLUTION According to one simple model, the total environmental degradation and pollution—that is, the environmental impact of population—in a given area depends on three factors: the number of people, the average number of units of resources each person uses, and the amount of environmental degradation and pollution generated when each unit of resource is produced and used (Figure 1-11).

Overpopulation occurs when people exceed the **carrying capacity** of an area: the number of people that can be supported in an area given its physical resource base and the way those resources are used. Overpopulation is a result of growing numbers of people, growing affluence (resource consumption), or both.

We know from studying other species that when a population exceeds or *overshoots* the carrying capacity of its environment, it suffers a *dieback* that reduces its population to a sustainable size. The crucial question is, How long will we be able to continue our exponential

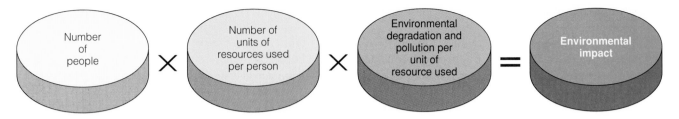

Figure 1-11 Simplified model of how three factors affect overall environmental degradation and pollution, or the environmental impact of population.

growth in people and resource use on a finite planet and crowd out or eliminate other species that we depend upon without suffering overshoot and dieback? No one knows the answer to this, but it is a question that warning signals from the earth (Table 1-1) are forcing us to consider seriously.

Differences in the importance of the factors shown in Figure 1-11 lead to two types of overpopulation: people overpopulation and consumption overpopulation (Figure 1-12). **People overpopulation** exists where there are more people than the available supplies of food, water, and other important resources can support at a minimal level (Table 1-1). In this type of overpopulation, population size and the resulting degradation of potentially renewable soil, grasslands, forests, and wildlife resources tend to be the key factors determining total environmental impact (Figure 1-12). In the world's poorest LDCs, people overpopulation causes premature death for at least 20 million, and perhaps 40 million, people each year and absolute poverty for 1.2 billion people.

Industrialized countries have a second type of overpopulation: **consumption overpopulation**. It exists when a small number of people use resources at such a high rate that significant pollution, environmental degradation, and resource depletion occur. With this type of overpopulation, high rates of resource use per person, and the resulting high levels of pollution and environmental degradation per person, are the key factors determining overall environmental impact (Figure 1-12).

By controlling at least 80% of the world's wealth and material resources, people in MDCs presently enjoy an average standard of living at least 18 times that in LDCs. This high standard of living by the world's 1 billion overconsuming meat eaters, car drivers, and throwaway consumers is the major cause of the world's pollution, environmental degradation, and poverty (or underconsumption).

Using the model in Figure 1-12, one can conclude that the United States has the world's highest level of consumption overpopulation. With only 4.7% of the world's population, it produces about 21% of all goods and services, uses about one-third of the world's processed mineral resources, uses about one-fourth of the world's nonrenewable energy, and produces at least one-third of the world's pollution and trash.

According to biologist Paul Ehrlich, "A baby born in the United States will damage the planet 20 to 100 times more in a lifetime than a baby born into a poor family in an LDC. Each rich person in the United States does 1,000 times more damage than a poor person in an LDC."

MULTIPLE-FACTOR MODEL   The three-factor model shown in Figure 1-11, though useful, is too simple. The principal causes of the environmental, resource, and social problems we face are much more complex. They include:

- *Unsustainable population growth resulting in people overpopulation and consumption overpopulation* (Figure 1-12).

- *Population distribution* — the population implosion or urban crisis.

- *Overconsumption and wasteful patterns of resource use, especially in industrialized countries* — throwaway mentality, planned obsolescence, producing unnecessary and harmful items, very little recycling and reuse of essential resources, unsustainable industrialized agriculture, and unsustainable industrial production.

- *Belief that technology will solve our problems* — failure to distinguish between forms of technology that reduce or prevent pollution and unnecessary resource waste and help sustain Earth's life-support systems and those that without proper control can degrade Earth's life-support systems.

- *Poverty* — failure of the world's economic and political systems to achieve a fairer distribution of the world's land, food, shelter, health care, education, employment, wealth, energy and mineral resources, and political power.

Q: What are proven reserves of a nonrenewable resource such as oil or copper?

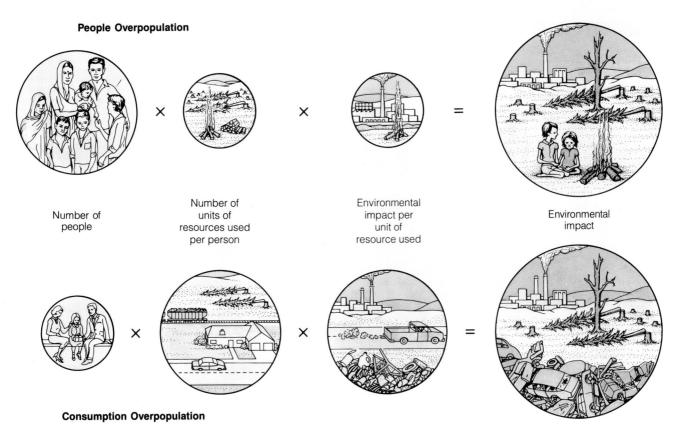

People Overpopulation

Number of people × Number of units of resources used per person × Environmental impact per unit of resource used = Environmental impact

Consumption Overpopulation

Figure 1-12 Two types of overpopulation based on the relative importance of the factors in the model shown in Figure 1-11. Circle size shows relative importance of each factor. People overpopulation is caused mostly by growing numbers of people. Consumption overpopulation is caused mostly by growing affluence (resource consumption).

- *Oversimplification of Earth's life-support systems —* especially excessive reduction of biological diversity.

- *Crisis in political and economic management —* overemphasizing all types of economic growth instead of encouraging sustainable forms of economic growth such as pollution prevention and cleanup, recycling, reuse, and waste reduction; treating problems in isolation rather than as an interacting set.

- *Failure to have market prices represent the overall environmental cost of an economic good or service to society and to Earth's life-support systems.*

- *Human-centered (anthropocentric) worldview and behavior instead of Earth-centered (biocentric) worldview and behavior —* attempting to dominate and alter nature to suit our purposes rather than working with nature.

These and other factors interact in complex and largely unknown ways to produce the major environmental, resource, and social problems the world faces (Figure 1-13). *The population, energy, poverty, pollution, urban, war, and environmental degradation crises we face are* *interlocking parts of an overall crisis.* We can stabilize world population only when poverty is sharply reduced worldwide. As long as LDCs are burdened by enormous debts, they will feel driven to pay the interest on these debts by depleting and degrading their natural resources, mostly for export to MDCs.

We cannot solve pollution problems by continuing to rely mostly on pollution cleanup and waste management instead of on pollution prevention and waste prevention. We cannot sustain the earth for ourselves and other species by continuing forms of economic growth based on depleting Earth's natural capital, which supports all life and economic activities.

The way out is for us to act together to formulate interdisciplinary, integrated approaches to the problems we face at the local, national, and global levels (see Guest Essay on p. 19). Treating each problem in isolation in a world where everything is connected to everything else is a recipe for disaster.

EVERYTHING YOU DO MATTERS The most important message of this book is that *we can deal with the*

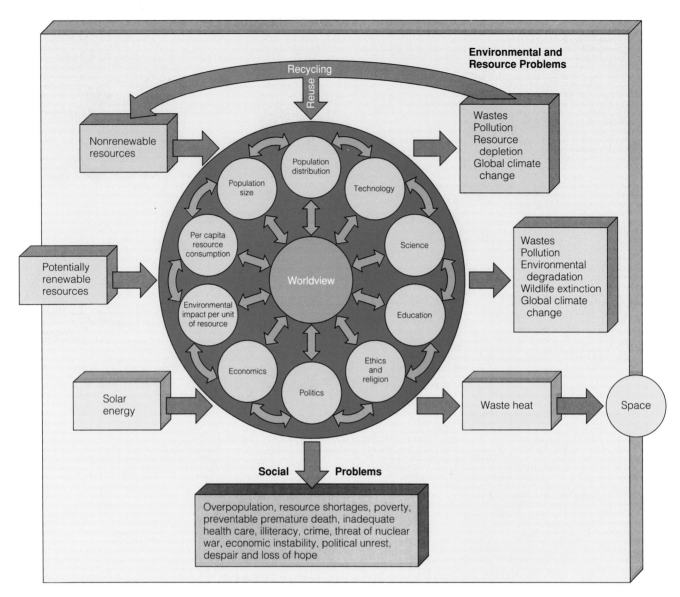

Figure 1-13 Environmental, resource, and social problems are caused by a complex, poorly understood mix of interacting factors, as illustrated by this simplified model.

problems we face and begin to turn things around within this lifetime. It will not be easy, painless, or without controversy, but it can and must be done.

The key to dealing with these problems is recognizing that *individuals matter.* Billions of individual actions contribute to the environmental and resource problems we face and to the solutions to these problems. Throughout this book you will find a number of boxes, titled Individuals Matter, that suggest what you can do to help sustain the earth.

History shows that significant cultural changes are brought about by individuals from the bottom up. Anthropologist Margaret Mead has summarized our po-

tential for change: "Never doubt that a small group of thoughtful, committed citizens can change the world. Indeed it is the only thing that ever has."

The choice is ours. We can continue to walk hard on the earth and thus ourselves or we can learn to walk more gently on the earth.

What's the use of a house if you don't have a decent planet to put it on?

HENRY DAVID THOREAU

Q: What percentage of Earth's proven reserves of oil are in OPEC countries?

Jessica Tuchman Mathews

Jessica Tuchman Mathews is currently vice president of the World Resources Institute, a highly respected center for policy research on global resource and environmental issues. Dr. Mathews has served as director of the Office of Global Issues on the President's National Security Council and on the editorial board of The Washington Post. *In 1989, she published an influential article in* Foreign Affairs *calling for nations to redefine national security in terms of national and global environmental security.*

National security and *national sovereignty* must be redefined during the 1990s to accommodate new global environmental realities, just as they were during the 1970s to accommodate global economic realities.

Intricately interconnected effects of the way we live — the buildup of greenhouse gases, the depletion of the ozone layer, and the loss of tropical forests and species — are shifting the center of gravity in international relations. These phenomena threaten national securities, defy solution by one or a few countries, and render national borders irrelevant. By definition, then, they pose a major challenge to national sovereignty.

They also compound the difficulty of ensuring security in an international order already in flux as the bipolar order that emerged from World War II gives way to multipolarity. One of the few things that is clear about the post–cold-war era we're entering is that national security will increasingly depend on how resource, environmental, and demographic issues are resolved. It is no coincidence that control of Persian Gulf oil was central to this era's first international crisis.

Regional environmental decline is already threatening well-being and thereby political stability in many parts of the world. Eastern Europe's horrendous environmental degradation is undercutting attempts to rebuild shattered economies: for instance, 95% of the water in Poland's rivers is unfit for human consumption, land is being withdrawn from cultivation because of contamination with toxic heavy metals, and air pollution causes heavy economic losses due to health costs and lost productivity. In the developing world, natural resources such as farm-

land, forests, and fisheries are being laid waste while the number of people these resources must sustain is expected to grow by nearly 1 billion during the 1990s.

The fallout from global environmental trends goes far beyond economic and political arrangements. Unless the community of nations finds ways to reverse these trends, they will eventually shake not just the security of states, but also the foundations of life.

Ozone Depletion

People living in South America and Australia are already exposed to dangerous levels of ultraviolet radiation as the Antarctic ozone hole breaks up each spring. The U.S. Environmental Protection Agency announced in 1991 that the ozone layer is thinning much faster than expected over the northern hemisphere's middle latitudes, where most of the industrial world's population lives. Increased exposure to ultraviolet radiation from ozone depletion in the upper atmosphere is expected to increase skin cancer, cataracts, and immune system damage and to damage terrestrial and marine ecosystems, thereby threatening the world's food supplies.

Climate Change

Despite remaining uncertainties about the extent and timing of enhanced greenhouse warming, most scientists agree that it will usher in adverse changes the world over in the next century. The rate of change is critical, and unless nations can substantially slow the present rate of greenhouse gas emissions, change could be catastrophic for some. If climate models are correct, nations will have to adapt to rising sea levels, changing rainfall patterns, and temperatures higher than the world has seen for 2 million years. Adaptive mechanisms will be costly, and the gap between rich and poor countries will almost certainly widen. Sea-level rise calls into question some nations' very existence. Most wildlife and their habitats will adapt or perish on their own, beyond the reach of human intervention.

Tropical Forest and Species Loss

Tropical forests are being cleared at the rate of about 17 million hectares (42 million acres) a year, or 50% faster than only a decade ago. Since these forests are home for more than half of Earth's species, tropical deforestation is the main force behind a species extinction rate that is unmatched in 65 million years. These interlocking losses are eroding tropical countries' economic prospects and shredding the planet's biological heritage. Deforestation in the tropics, and elsewhere, also contributes to an enhanced greenhouse effect, though far less than fossil-fuel use. In turn, greenhouse warming is expected to amplify species loss over the coming decades.

(continued)

Dealing with these global environmental problems will require a higher and higher level of collective international cooperation and management. Fortunately, nations are beginning to act as though they understand their mutual interest in cooperation, as demonstrated most spectacularly by the agreement reached by 93 nations meeting in London in June 1990 to phase out emissions of ozone-destroying chemicals. This updated the Montreal treaty developed in 1987.

Turning this mutual interest into effective international management remains an elusive goal. Progress does not lie in a vain attempt to apply uniform environmental standards to nations whose members differ by 100-fold in per capita income and have vastly different cultures, climates, religions, resources, and attitudes toward nature. Instead, it lies in institutional innovations as sweeping as those that inaugurated the post–World War II period we're now emerging from.

The new international system must be designed to catalyze cooperation. Instead of the glacial pace required to negotiate treaties that set particular performance standards, we need fluid international processes that respond quickly to changes in scientific understanding and that set all nations moving in the same direction at whatever pace is realistic for each nation's circumstances.

Scientific theory and economic, political, and environmental concerns are all in a constant state of flux. Only a new institutional agility can keep international environmental governance closely attuned to these changing realities and ensure the best possible outcome.

Guest Essay Discussion

1. Do you agree that national security and national sovereignty must be redefined to include national and global environmental security? Explain.

2. What changes in the current international interactions between nations do you believe must be made to catalyze cooperation between nations on global environmental problems? How would you bring about these changes?

DISCUSSION TOPICS

1. Do you favor instituting policies designed to reduce population growth and stabilize (a) the size of the world's population as soon as possible and (b) the size of the U.S. population as soon as possible? Explain. What policies do you believe should be implemented? How many children do you plan to have?

2. Explain why you agree or disagree with the following proposition: High levels of resource use by the United States and other MDCs is beneficial. MDCs stimulate the economic growth of LDCs by buying their raw materials. High levels of resource use also stimulate economic growth in MDCs. Economic growth provides money for more financial aid to LDCs and for reducing pollution, environmental degradation, and poverty.

3. Do you believe that all automobiles, vans, and light trucks sold in the United States should be required to achieve at least 21 kilometers per liter (50 miles per gallon) by 2003? Explain. Do you believe that all houses and buildings should be required to meet stringent insulation, heating efficiency, lighting, and other standards designed to greatly reduce unnecessary energy waste? Explain.

4. Do you believe that a high disposal tax should be placed on all throwaway items to discourage their use? Explain.

5. Would you support greatly increasing the amount of land protected from development as wilderness, even if the land contained valuable minerals, oil, natural gas, timber, or other resources?

*6. Make a list of the resources you truly need. Then make another list of the resources that you use each day only because you want them. Then make a third list of resources you want and hope to use in the future.

---

*Discussion Topic items preceded by an asterisk are laboratory exercises or individual or class projects.

Note: Near the end of this book is a brief list of key references for each chapter. For a more comprehensive set of references, see Further Readings in the expanded version of this book: *Living in the Environment*, 7th ed. (Belmont, Calif.: Wadsworth, 1992).

CHAPTER 2

CULTURAL CHANGES, WORLDVIEWS, ETHICS, AND ENVIRONMENT

General Questions and Issues

1. What major cultural changes have taken place during the 40,000 years that our species, *Homo sapiens sapiens*, has lived on Earth, and what effects have these had on Earth's life-support systems?

2. What worldview leads to the throwaway societies found in most of today's industrialized countries?

3. What worldview leads to a sustainable-Earth society, and how can we achieve such a worldview?

A continent ages quickly once we come.
ERNEST HEMINGWAY

OSSIL EVIDENCE SUGGESTS that the most recent form of our species, *Homo sapiens sapiens*, has lived on Earth for only about 40,000 years, a brief instant in the planet's estimated 4.6-billion-year existence. During 30,000 of the 40,000 years our current species has been around we survived as mostly nomadic hunter-gatherers. Since then, there have been two major cultural shifts, the Agricultural Revolution, which began 10,000 to 12,000 years ago, and the Industrial Revolution, which began about 275 years ago.

These cultural revolutions have given us much more energy (Figure 2-1) and many new technologies, which we've used to alter and control increasingly larger parts of the earth to meet our basic needs and rapidly expanding list of wants. By expanding food supplies, increasing average life spans, and improving average living standards, each of these shifts led to sharp increases in the size of the human population (Figure 2-2). These cultural shifts have also led to the J-shaped curves of exponentially increasing resource use, pollution, and environmental degradation we are experiencing today (Table 1-1).

Members of a rapidly growing environmental movement that began in the United States in the 1960s believe there is an urgent need to make a new cultural change before we are overwhelmed by rapid exponential growth in people, pollution, and environmental degradation. At this turning point, called a *sustainable-Earth revolution*, we are called upon to halt population growth and alter our lifestyles, political and economic systems, and the way we view and treat the earth to help sustain Earth for us and other species.

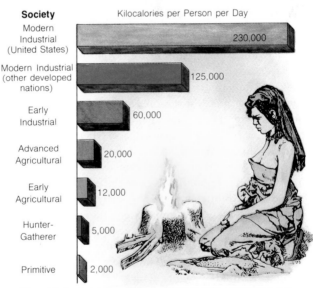

Figure 2-1 Average direct and indirect daily energy use per person at various stages of human cultural development. A *calorie* is the amount of energy needed to raise the temperature of 1 gram of water 1°C (1.8°F). A *kilocalorie* is 1,000 calories. When we refer to food calories expended during exercise, we're referring to kilocalories.

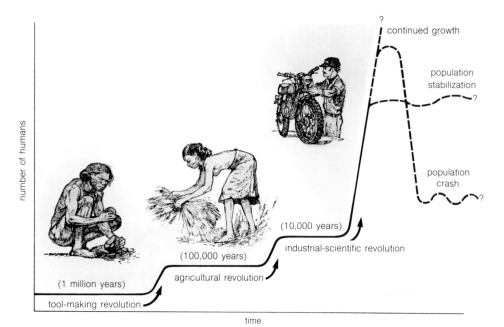

Figure 2-2 We humans have expanded Earth's carrying capacity for our species through technological innovation, leading to several major cultural changes, and by displacing and reducing the populations of other species that compete with us for resources and that provide us with resources. Dashed lines represent possible future changes in human population size: continued growth, population stabilization, and continued growth followed by a crash and stabilization at a much lower level. This generalized curve (a plot of the logarithm of population size versus the logarithm of time) is plotted by a different mathematical method from that used in Figure 1-2 (a plot of population size versus time).

| 2-1 | **Major Cultural Changes** |

HUNTING AND GATHERING SOCIETIES Archaeological evidence suggests that during about three-fourths of our 40,000-year existence, we were **hunter-gatherers** who survived by gathering edible wild plants and by hunting and killing wild animals (including seafood) from the nearby environment (Figure 2-3). Evidence indicates that our hunter-gatherer ancestors lived in small groups of rarely more than 50 people who worked together to get enough food to survive. If food became scarce, they picked up their few possessions and moved to another area.

Our hunter-gatherer ancestors (and those still living this way today) survived only by having expert knowledge about their natural surroundings. They learned to anticipate the seasons—when the fish would run, when animals would emerge from hibernation, when edible berries would ripen, and when migrating animals would come and go—and they learned how to find water, even in the desert. They discovered that a variety of plants and animals could be eaten and used as medicines. By using stones to sharpen and shape sticks, other stones, and animal bones, they made primitive weapons for killing animals and tools for cutting plants and scraping hides for clothing and shelter. These dwellers in nature had only two energy sources: sunlight captured by plants, which also served as food for the wild animals they hunted, and their own muscular power (Figure 2-1).

In most cases, males and females shared work, food, and power in these social groups. Men did the hunting, and women did most of the gathering. Women could not hunt because they had to carry their nursing infants and young children with them. Thus, cooperation with one another and with nature has been the dominant force during three-fourths of the time our current species has existed.

Groups made conscious efforts to keep their population size in balance with available food supplies. Population control practices varied with different cultures, but they included abstention from sexual intercourse, infanticide, abortion, late marriage, and feeding infants with breast milk as long as possible (a practice that provides some degree of birth control by inhibiting ovulation). Infant deaths from infectious diseases and infanticide (killing the newborn) led to an average life expectancy of about 30 years. This kept the world's hunter-gatherers from undergoing rapid population growth (Figure 2-2).

Archaeological evidence indicates that hunter-gatherers gradually developed improved tools and hunting weapons. Some people learned to work together to hunt herds of reindeer, woolly mammoths, European bison, and other big game. They used fire to flush game from thickets toward hunters lying in wait and to stampede herds of animals into traps or over cliffs. Some also learned to burn vegetation to promote the growth of food plants and plants favored by the animals they hunted.

Advanced hunter-gatherers had a greater impact on their environment than early hunter-gatherers, especially in using fire to convert forests into grasslands. There is also evidence that they contributed to, and perhaps even caused, the extinction of some large game animals in different parts of the world.

Because of their small numbers, nomadic behavior, and dependence on their own muscle power to modify the environment, however, their environmental impact

Q: What percentage of Earth's proven reserves of oil are in the United States?

Figure 2-3 Most people who have lived on Earth have survived by hunting wild game and gathering wild plants. These !Kung bushmen (left) in Africa are going hunting. The man (right) is digging for roots in a tropical forest in the Amazon basin of Brazil.

was fairly small and localized. Both early and advanced hunter-gatherers were examples of *people in nature*, who trod lightly on the earth because they were not capable of doing more. These dwellers in the land survived by being keenly aware of their intimate dependence on nature and by learning to work with nature and with one another.

THE AGRICULTURAL REVOLUTION   About 10,000 to 12,000 years ago a cultural shift, known as the **Agricultural Revolution**, began at several places in the world. It involved a gradual shift from small nomadic hunting-and-gathering bands to settled agricultural communities, where people survived by learning how to breed and raise wild animals and how to cultivate wild plants near where they lived.

Archaeological evidence indicates that plant cultivation probably began in tropical forest areas. People discovered that they could grow various wild food plants by digging holes with a stick (a primitive hoe) and placing roots or tubers (fleshy stems of plants usually found underground) of these plants in the holes.

To prepare for planting, they cleared small patches of forests by **slash-and-burn cultivation** — cutting down trees and other vegetation, leaving the cut vegetation on the ground to dry and then burning it (Figures 2-4 and 2-5). The ashes that were left replaced plant nutrients in the nutrient-poor soils found in most tropical forest areas. Roots and tubers were then planted in holes dug between tree stumps.

These early growers also used **shifting cultivation** (Figure 2-4). After a plot had been planted and harvested for several years, few if any crops could still be grown. By then, either the soil was depleted of nutrients or the patch had been invaded by a dense growth of vegetation from the surrounding forest. When yields dropped, the growers shifted to a new area of forest and cleared a new plot. The growers learned that each aban-

doned patch had to be left fallow (unplanted) for 10 to 30 years before the soil became fertile enough to grow crops again. By doing this they practiced sustainable agriculture.

These growers practiced **subsistence farming**, growing only enough food to feed their families. Their dependence on human muscle power and crude stone or stick tools meant that they could cultivate only small plots; thus, they had relatively little impact on their environment.

About 7,000 years ago, the invention of the metal plow, pulled by domesticated animals, allowed farmers to cultivate larger plots of land and to break up fertile grassland soils, which previously couldn't be cultivated because of their thick and widespread root systems. In some arid (dry) regions early farmers further increased crop output by diverting water from nearby streams into hand-dug ditches and canals to irrigate crops.

The gradual shift from hunting and gathering to farming had a number of significant effects:

- Using domesticated animals to haul loads and do other tasks increased the average energy use per person (Figure 2-1).

- Population increased, mostly because of a larger, more reliable supply of food (Figure 2-2).

- People controlled and shaped more of Earth's surface to meet their needs by clearing increasingly larger areas of land and by building irrigation systems to transfer water from one place to another.

- People began accumulating material goods. By necessity, nomadic hunter-gatherers had to travel with few possessions, but farmers living in one place could accumulate as much as they could afford.

- Urbanization — the formation of villages, towns, and cities — began because a small number of

A: 4%. The United States uses about 30% of global oil production each year.

Chapter 2   23

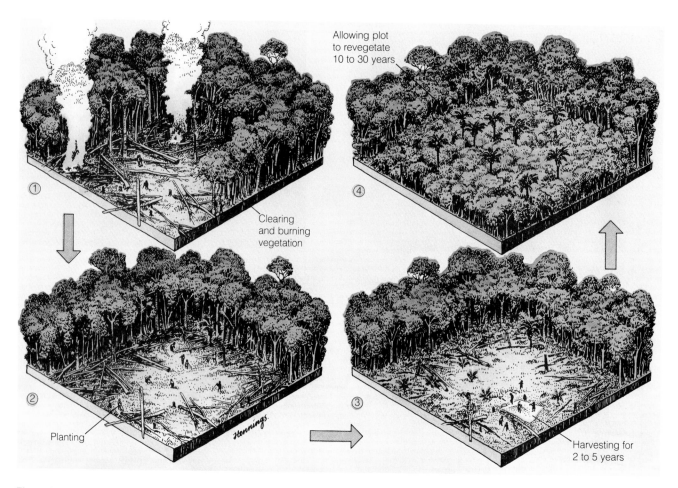

Allowing plot to revegetate 10 to 30 years

Clearing and burning vegetation

Planting

Harvesting for 2 to 5 years

Figure 2-4 The first crop-growing technique was probably a combination of slash-and-burn and shifting cultivation in tropical forests. This method is sustainable only if no more than a small portion of the forest is cleared and only if each plot, when abandoned, is left unplanted for 10 to 30 years so soil fertility can be restored. This form of agriculture can be sustained indefinitely if population levels are low.

farmers could produce enough food to feed their families, plus a surplus that could be traded to other people. Many former farmers moved into permanent villages. Some villages gradually grew into towns and cities, which served as centers for trade, government, and religion.

- Specialized occupations and long-distance trade developed as former farmers in villages and towns learned crafts such as weaving, toolmaking, and pottery to produce handmade goods that could be exchanged for food.

- Conflict increased as ownership of land and water rights became a valuable economic resource and as human numbers grew and societies confronted one another. Armies and their leaders rose to power and took over large areas of land. These rulers forced powerless people—slaves and landless peasants—to do the hard, disagreeable work of producing food and constructing irrigation systems, temples, and other projects.

- Competition between people for land, water, and power led to male-dominated societies still in ex-

istence today. To survive, females had to give up the shared power they had in most cooperative hunter-gatherer societies to male warriors who could protect them and their children from aggressors. Men were taught not to show their emotions and inner feelings, since this would make them seem weak and ineffective as warriors.

- Our unwinnable and self-destructive war against the rest of nature began. The survival of wild plants and animals, once vital to humanity, no longer seemed to matter. Wild animals, competing with livestock for grass and feeding on crops, were killed or driven from their habitats. Wild plants invading cropfields were a threat to be eliminated.

The growing populations of these emerging civilizations needed more food and more wood for fuel and buildings. To meet these needs, people cut down vast areas of forest and plowed up large areas of grasslands. Such extensive land clearing destroyed and degraded the habitats of many forms of plant and animal wildlife, causing or hastening their extinction.

Q: How much of the oil used in the United States is imported?

Figure 2-5 Slash-and-burn subsistence farming in a small patch of cleared tropical rain forest in Costa Rica. The family using this patch will be able to grow crops for a few years before the plant nutrients in the nutrient-poor soil are depleted. Then the family will move to another part of the forest and repeat this process.

Jack Swenson/Tom Stack & Associates

Many of these cleared lands were poorly managed, resulting in greatly increased deforestation, soil erosion, salt buildup in irrigated soils, and overgrazing of grasslands by huge herds of sheep, cattle, and other livestock. These unsustainable practices helped convert fertile land to desert. The topsoil that washed off these barren areas polluted streams, lakes, and irrigation canals, making them useless. The gradual degradation of the vital resource base of soil, water, forests, grazing land, and wildlife was a major factor in the downfall of many great civilizations. These people squandered the natural capital they inherited. There is evidence that we may be repeating this mistake on a much larger scale (see Table 1-1).

The gradual spread of agriculture meant that most of the world's human population shifted from hunter-gatherers *in nature* to shepherds, farmers, and urban dwellers *against nature*, who viewed their role as learning to tame and control wild nature and to gain power and wealth by controlling other humans. Many analysts believe that this cultural change in how people viewed their relationship to nature and each other is a major cause of today's resource and environmental problems.

THE INDUSTRIAL REVOLUTION The next great cultural change, known as the **Industrial Revolution**, began in England in the mid-1700s and spread to the United States in the 1800s. It greatly increased the average per capita energy consumption and thus our power to alter and shape the earth to meet our needs and wants and fuel economic growth (Figure 2-1). This led to greatly increased production, trade, and distribution of goods.

The Industrial Revolution arose as a response to absolute resource scarcity in England caused by the overuse and depletion of wood for fuel and construction. People began burning surface deposits of coal as a substitute for wood. The availability of coal led to the invention of coal-powered steam engines to pump water and perform other tasks.

People invented an increasing array of new machines powered by coal and later by oil and natural gas. Thus, the Industrial Revolution represented a shift from dependence on renewable wood and flowing water as principal sources of energy to dependence on nonrenewable fossil fuels (first coal, then later oil and natural gas).

Increased agricultural production, plus the concentration of factories in cities, freed farm workers to move to the cities for work. Many found jobs in the growing number of mechanized factories. There they worked long hours for low pay in boring assembly-line jobs. Most factories were noisy, dirty, and dangerous places to work. Other workers toiled in dangerous and unhealthy coal mines. With more income and a more reliable supply of food, the size of the human population began the sharp exponential increase we are still experiencing today (Figures 1-2 and 2-2).

After World War I (1914–18), more efficient machines and mass production techniques were developed, forming the basis of today's advanced industrial societies in the United States, Canada, Japan, and western Europe. These societies are characterized by

- Greatly increased production and consumption of goods, stimulated by mass advertising to create artificial wants (the consumer society) and encourage economic growth and the creation of more jobs

A: About 50%

- Greatly increased dependence on nonrenewable resources such as oil, natural gas, coal, and various metals

- A shift from dependence on natural materials, which are environmentally harmless or are broken down and recycled by natural processes, to dependence on synthetic materials, which break down slowly in the environment and often are toxic to humans and wildlife

- A sharp rise in the amount of energy used per person for transportation, manufacturing, agriculture, lighting, and heating and cooling (Figure 2-1)

Advanced industrial societies benefit most people living in them. These benefits include

- Creation and mass production of many useful and economically affordable products

- A sharp increase in average agricultural productivity per person because of advanced industrialized agriculture, in which a small number of farmers produce large amounts of food

- A sharp rise in birth control and average life expectancy from improvements in sanitation, hygiene, nutrition, and medicine, taking place first in MDCs and, to a lesser extent, more recently in most LDCs

- A gradual decline in the exponential rate of population growth in MDCs because of improvements in health, birth control, education, average income, and old-age security (Figure 1-6)

Along with their many benefits, industrialized societies have intensified many existing resource and environmental problems and created new ones (Table 1-1 and Figure 1-12). Industrialization has greatly intensified the view that our role is to conquer nature, a worldview that began to take hold with the invention of agriculture. Domination of Earth is viewed as progress.

MAKING A NEW CULTURAL CHANGE Most environmentalists believe that there is an urgent need to begin shifting from our present array of industrialized and partially industrialized societies to a variety of *sustainable-Earth societies* throughout the world. Dealing with the environmental and resource problems we face will involve much controversy and require us to make some trade-offs and significant changes in our worldview, economic and political systems, and lifestyles.

Emphasis will have to shift from pollution cleanup to pollution prevention (see Guest Essay on p. 33), from waste disposal to waste prevention and reduction, from species protection to habitat protection, and from increased resource use to increased resource conservation.

Existing economic and political systems will need to be used to reward Earth-sustaining economic activi-

ties and discourage those that harm the earth. We must recognize that short-term economic greed eventually leads to long-term economic and environmental grief.

We will have to allow parts of the world we have damaged to heal, help restore severely damaged areas, and protect remaining wild areas from any form of destructive development. Governments will have to cooperate to deal with a host of global and regional environmental problems (see Guest Essay on p. 19).

The Agricultural Revolution took place over the course of 10,000 years and the Industrial Revolution over more than 200 years. Because of the exponential growth of population, resource consumption, pollution, and environmental degradation, we have only a few years to bring about a sustainable-Earth revolution. Making this transformation of our worldviews, lifestyles, and economic and social systems in such a short time is the greatest challenge our species has faced.

2-2 The Throwaway and Spaceship-Earth Worldviews in Industrial Societies

CULTURAL CHANGES, WORLDVIEWS, AND ETHICS Your decisions and actions are built around your **worldview** — how you think the world works and what you think your role in the world should be — and your **ethics** — what you believe to be right or wrong behavior. Regardless of what you say you believe, how you act in the world reveals your true beliefs.

Worldviews are based on the cultures in which people are raised and educated and on their progress through various levels of environmental awareness, summarized in "Four Levels of Environmental Awareness" on the page opposite the title page of this book. Conflicts about how serious the world's present and projected environmental and resource problems are and what should be done about them arise mostly out of differing worldviews or differences in what people hold to be sacred truths.

When European settlers moved to North America they found a vast continent with seemingly unlimited resources. It is not surprising that they had a **frontier worldview** in which they viewed their role as expanding their use of the continent's resources. Resource conservation was not important because there was always more.

This worldview was in sharp contrast to that of many of the Native Americans whose land was taken over and whose cultures were fragmented or destroyed as European settlers spread across the continent. Although there were exceptions, the cultures of most Native Americans were based on a deep respect for the land and its animals. This way of viewing the earth is

Q: Will the United States ever again be self-sufficient in oil?

revealed by a medicine woman in California's Wintu tribe:*

The white people never cared for the land or deer or bear. When the Indians kill meat, we eat it all up. When we dig roots, we make little holes. When we build houses we make little holes. . . . We don't chop down trees. We only use dead wood. But the white people plow up the ground, pull down the trees, kill everything. The tree says: "Don't. I am sore. Don't hurt me." But they chop it down and cut it up. The spirit of the land hates them. . . . The white people destroy all. They blast rocks and scatter them on the ground. The rock says: "Don't. You are hurting me." But the white people pay no attention. . . . How can the spirit of the Earth like the white man? . . . Everywhere the white man has touched the Earth it is sore.

THE THROWAWAY WORLDVIEW The important successes of the Industrial Revolution have given most people in MDCs the idea that there are no limits to human ingenuity, Earth's resources, and the ability of Earth's air, water, and soil to absorb our wastes. Most people in today's industrialized societies have a **throwaway worldview**, which is based on several beliefs:

- We are apart from nature.

- We are superior to other species.

- We know what we are doing.

- Our role is to conquer and subdue wild nature and use nature for our purposes.

- Resources are unlimited because of our ingenuity in making them available or in finding substitutes—there is always more.

- There is an "away" to throw things to.

- Science and technology can solve any problem that comes up.

- The more we produce and consume, the better off we are. All economic growth is good and more economic growth is better. There are no limits to economic growth.

- The most important individual or nation is the one that can command and use the largest fraction of the world's resources. Possession of more and more things is the source of happiness.

---

*Many environmental textbooks and articles illustrate Native American views about land and nature by quoting from a letter that Chief Seattle of the Dwamish tribe of the state of Washington allegedly wrote to President Franklin Pierce in 1865. Historical research, however, has revealed that he never wrote a letter to President Pierce. The famous and inspiring letter that is often attributed to Chief Seattle was written in the winter of 1971–72 by Ted Perry, a screenwriter, for a film called *Home*, shown on U.S. national television in 1972. While some of the ideas in this speech were based on Chief Seattle's speeches, its content should be viewed as closer to a summary of the more modern sustainable-Earth worldview.

You may not accept all these statements; but most people in today's industrialized societies act as if they did, and that's what counts.

This worldview has led to the throwaway lifestyles found in most MDCs. If there is always more, why go to the trouble and expense of picking up, recycling, or reusing what we dump into the environment? If Earth's resources, coupled with our ingenuity, are unlimited, why attempt to regulate population growth, discourage the production and consumption of anything people are willing to buy, and face up to the problem of a fairer distribution of wealth built upon exploiting Earth's resources? If life will always get better because of our ingenuity, why should we make sacrifices now for future generations whose lives will be better anyway?

If the air, water, and soil can handle all the wastes we dump into them, why worry about pollution? Even if we do pollute an area, we can invent a technology to clean it up or we can move somewhere else. So don't worry, don't get involved, be happy. We will always be able to use technology to save us from ourselves.

Those who say there are limits to economic growth are sometimes derided as gloom-and-doom pessimists, but many analysts fear that continuing devotion to the seductive throwaway, or there-will-always-be-more, worldview will turn out to be a fatal attraction. Catholic theologian Thomas Berry calls the industrial-consumer society built upon the throwaway worldview the "supreme pathology of all history":

We can break the mountains apart; we can drain the rivers and flood the valleys. We can turn the most luxuriant forests into throwaway paper products. We can tear apart the great grass cover of the western plains, and pour toxic chemicals into the soil and pesticides onto the fields, until the soil is dead and blows away in the wind. We can pollute the air with acids, the rivers with sewage, the seas with oil—all this in a kind of intoxication with our power for devastation. . . . We can invent computers capable of processing ten million calculations per second. And why? To increase the volume and speed with which we move natural resources through the consumer economy to the junk pile or the waste heap. Our managerial skills are measured by our ability to accelerate this process. If, in these activities, the topography of the planet is damaged, if the environment is made inhospitable for a multitude of living species, then so be it. We are, supposedly, creating a technological wonderworld. . . . But our supposed progress toward an ever-improving human situation is bringing us to a wasteworld instead of a wonderworld.

THE SPACESHIP-EARTH WORLDVIEW A modified version of the throwaway worldview is the **Spaceship-Earth worldview** in which Earth is viewed as a spaceship—a machine that we can understand, dominate, and change at will by using advanced technology. This view is a sophisticated expression of the basic idea found in the throwaway worldview—that through technology and human ingenuity we can control and manage nature and create artificial environments and life-forms to avoid environmental overload and provide a good life for everyone.

If resources become scarce or a substitute can't be found, we can get materials from the moon, asteroids, or other planets in the "new frontier" of space. We can use genetic engineering to control the evolution of life-forms and develop organisms that produce more food, clean up oil spills and toxic wastes, and satisfy more of our unlimited wants. We can also use space as the ultimate waste dump.

If Earth becomes too crowded or too polluted, we will build stations in space for the excess population. Never mind that to do so we would have to send off 252,000 people a day—10,500 an hour—just to keep Earth's current population of 5.4 billion from rising. Assuming that each spaceship could carry 500 people (compared with about 6 people on today's spaceships), 21 such larger ships would have to be launched every hour, without stop. Never mind that the pollution from these ships would worsen conditions and deplete the ozone layer for the 5.4 billion people left behind on a dying planet. Never mind that we don't know how to build a space station that could sustain even 6 people indefinitely, much less 92 million more people each year. Never mind that the materials used to build these stations would deplete resources for the billions of people left behind on Earth.

This outlook is an upside-down view of reality. It thinks of Earth as a spaceship—a simple, unsustainable, human creation. This is a simplified, arrogant, and dangerous view for a species that doesn't even understand what is going on in a pond or in the first few millimeters of topsoil. This worldview, like the throwaway worldview, can lead to environmental overload and resource depletion because it is based on two false ideas—that we understand how nature works and that there are no limits to Earth's resources and our ability to overcome any problem with technological innovations.

2-3 A Sustainable-Earth Worldview

WORKING WITH THE EARTH Critics of the prevailing throwaway and Spaceship-Earth worldviews believe we should ask several crucial questions. Is what we are doing really progress? Can we sustain what we are doing? Should we sustain what we are doing? What kinds of growth are useful and sustainable and what kinds are harmful and unsustainable? If we end up eliminating or killing off large numbers of our own species and millions of other species, is that success?

A small but growing number of people have a **sustainable-Earth worldview.*** They believe that Earth does not have infinite resources and that ever-increasing production and consumption will put severe stress on the natural processes that renew and maintain the air, water, and soil and support Earth's variety of potentially renewable plant and animal life. They believe that if we want to solve the world's gravest problems—war, poverty, pollution, and environmental degradation—the first step is to change our destructive throwaway and Spaceship-Earth worldviews by thinking differently.

People with a sustainable-Earth worldview believe that nature exists for all of Earth's living species, not just for us. This life-centered approach sees human beings as part of nature—not apart from nature and not conquerors of nature. People with this worldview emphasize

- Seeing the world as an integrated, interconnected, interdependent whole rather than as a fragmented collection of parts.

- Seeing our most fundamental value as maintaining the integrity, good functioning, and sustainability of Earth's life-support systems for us and other species now and in the future. This begins by recognizing that the interconnected and interdependent life-support systems of the planet have little to do with our geographic and geopolitical boundaries.

- Building societies and personal relationships that emphasize cooperation over competition and domination.

- Protecting Earth's biodiversity by interfering with nonhuman species only to meet important needs.

- Concentrating on pollution prevention and waste reduction and converting to more environmentally benign technologies.

- Not wasting nonrenewable minerals, fossil fuels, and water.

- Greatly increasing our dependence on perpetual solar energy and decreasing our use of fossil fuels and nuclear power.

- Achieving sustainable use of potentially renewable cropland, forests, and grasslands by using these resources more slowly than they can be renewed and by placing primary emphasis on sustaining the fertility of Earth's topsoil.

---

*Others have used the terms *sustainable worldview, conserver worldview, holistic worldview,* and *deep ecology worldview* to describe this idea. I add the word *Earth* to make clear that it's all of Earth's life-support systems and life, not just human beings and their societies, that must be sustained.

Q: What percentage of environmental spending in the United States is devoted to preventing pollution?

- Protecting the world's remaining wild areas from development and pollution and restoring many of the areas we have damaged.

- Converting the world's existing economic systems, all based on ever-increasing economic growth with little concern for possible long-term consequences, to systems that reward Earth-sustaining forms of growth.

- Halting human population growth to prevent a massive dieback; then encouraging a slow population shrinkage toward an optimum level that can allow every person an opportunity for a decent life without impairing the ability of Earth to sustain human and nonhuman life in the future.

This worldview is based on the following general beliefs and guidelines:

- We can never completely "do our own thing"; everything we do has mostly unpredictable present and future effects on other people and other species (*first law of ecology*).

- We are part of nature; all living species are interconnected and interdependent (*second law of ecology, or principle of interdependence*).

- Nature is not only more complex than we think but also more complex than we can ever think; it is a myth that with enough science and technology we can understand and manage planet Earth (*principle of complexity*).

- The earth does not belong to us; we belong to the earth; we are just one particular strand in the web of life; in the words of Aldo Leopold, each of us is "to be a plain member and citizen of nature" (*principle of humility*).

- Our role is to understand and work with the rest of nature, not to conquer it (*principle of cooperation*).

- Every living species has a right to live, or at least to struggle to live, simply because it exists; this right is not dependent on its actual or potential use to us (*respect-for-nature principle*).

- Something is right when it tends to maintain the ecological integrity, sustainability, and diversity of Earth's life-support systems for us and other species and wrong when it tends otherwise; the bottom line is that Earth is the bottom line (*principle of sustainability and ecocentrism*).

- The best things in life aren't things (*principle of love, caring, and joy*).

- It is wrong for humans to cause the premature extinction of any wild species and the elimination and degradation of their habitats (*preservation of wildlife and biodiversity principle*).

- When we alter nature to meet what we consider to be basic needs or nonbasic wants, we should choose the method that does the least possible harm to other living things; in minimizing harm, it is in general worse to harm a species than an individual organism and still worse to harm a community of living organisms; when damage cannot be avoided, it should be minimized and repaired (*principle of minimum wrong*).

- When we alter nature we should make such changes at nature's rates and in nature's ways (*principle of sustainable change*).

- Resources are limited and must not be wasted (*principle of limits*).

- No individual, corporation, or nation has a right to an ever-increasing share of Earth's finite resources. As the Indian philosopher and social activist Mahatma Gandhi said, "The earth provides enough to satisfy every person's need but not every person's greed" (*principle of enoughness*).

- It is wrong to treat people and other living things primarily as factors of production, whose value is expressed only in economic terms (*economics-is-not-everything principle*).

- Everything we have or will have comes from the sun and the earth; the earth can get along without us, but we can't get along without the earth; an exhausted planet is an exhausted economy; short-term greed leads to long-term economic and environmental grief (*respect-your-roots*, or *Earth-first principle*).

- We should leave the earth in as good a shape as we found it, if not better (*rights-of-the-unborn* or *leave-it-better-than-you-found-it principle*).

- All people should be held responsible for their own pollution and environmental degradation; dumping our wastes in another area or country is the equivalent of using chemical warfare on the people or other species receiving our wastes (*responsibility-of-the-born principle*).

- We must protect Earth's remaining wild systems from our activities, rehabilitate or restore natural systems we have degraded, use natural systems only on a sustainable basis, and allow many of the systems we have occupied and abused to return to a wild state; as David Brower said, "The wild places are where we began. When they end so do we" (*principle of Earth protection and healing*).

- In protecting and sustaining nature, go farther than the law requires (*ethics-often-exceeds-legality principle*).

- To prevent excessive deaths of people and other species, people must prevent excessive births (*birth-control-is-better-than-death-control principle*).

- Put the poor and their environment first, not last; help the poor sustain themselves and their local environment, and do this with love, not condescension; we cannot have peace, environmental

The essence, rhythms, and pulse of the earth within and around us can only be experienced at the deepest level by our senses and feelings — our emotions. We must listen to the soft, magnificent symphony of billions of organisms expressing their interdependency. We must pick up a handful of soil and try to sense the teeming microscopic life-forms in it that keep us alive. We must look at a tree, a mountain, a rock, a bee and try to sense how they are a part of us and we are a part of them.

Michael J. Cohen urges each of us to recognize who we really are by saying,

I am a desire for water, air, food, love, warmth, beauty, freedom, sensations, life, community, place, and spirit in the natural world. These pulsating feelings are the Planet Earth, alive and well within me. I have two mothers: my human mother and my planet mother, Earth. The planet is my womb of life.

We need to stop attaching more feelings of survival and happiness to dollars that we can't eat, breathe, and drink than to the sun, land, air, water, plants, bacteria, and other organisms that really keep us alive. We need to recognize that our technological cocoon and our feeling of self-importance as a species have given us an incredibly distorted picture of what is really important and joyful.

If we think of nature as separate from us and made up of disjointed parts to be manipulated by us, then we will tend to become people whose main motivation with regard to each other and to nature is also manipulation and control. That is an unsatisfying, empty, and joyless way to live.

We need to understand that although formal education is important, it is not enough. Much of it is designed to socialize and homogenize us so that we will accept and participate in the worldview that our role is to conquer nature and to suppress and deny the deep feelings of guilt we have about doing so. We can no longer wage a war against nature and ourselves and justify it in the name of progress.

The way to break out of this mental straitjacket is to experience nature directly, so that you truly feel that you are part of nature and it is part of you. As philosopher Simone Weil observed, "To be rooted is perhaps the most important and least recognized need of the human soul."

To be rooted, you need to find a *sense of place* — a stream, a mountain, a yard, a neighborhood lot, or any piece of the earth you feel truly at one with. It can be a place where you live or a place you occasionally visit and experience in your inner being. When you become part of a place, it becomes a part of you. Then you are driven to defend it against damage and to heal its wounds.

Experiencing nature allows you to get in touch with your deepest self, which has sensed from birth that when you destroy and degrade the natural systems that support you, you are attacking yourself. Then you will love the earth as an inseparable part of yourself and live your life in ways that sustain and replenish the earth and thus yourself and other living things. This is true progress. This is living life at its fullest.

---

justice, or a sense of pride about our accomplishments as a species as long as anyone still lives in poverty (*eliminate-the-poverty-trap principle*).

- To love, cherish, celebrate, and understand the earth and yourself, take time to experience and sense the air, water, soil, trees, animals, bacteria, and other parts and rhythms of the earth directly (*direct-experience-is-the-best-teacher principle*).

- Learn about, love, and care for your local environment and live gently within that place; walk lightly on the earth (*love-your-neighborhood principle*).

ACHIEVING A SUSTAINABLE-EARTH WORLD-VIEW
Achieving a sustainable-Earth worldview involves working our way through four levels of environmental awareness summarized on the page opposite the title page. Sustaining the earth requires not only a new way of thinking but also a new way of feeling based on listening to and experiencing the earth and ourselves with our senses and our hearts (see Spotlight above).

BECOMING EARTH CITIZENS
Sustaining the earth means that all of us, especially those with an affluent lifestyle, must adopt a simpler, less consumptive, Earth-caring lifestyle. Helen and Scott Nearing offer the following ten tips for doing this:

1. Do the best you can, whatever arises.

2. Be at peace with yourself.

3. Find a job you enjoy.

4. Simplify your life. Live in simple conditions: housing, food, clothing.

5. Contact nature every day. Feel the earth under your feet.

6. Exercise physically through hard work, gardening, or walking.

Q: How much of the world's resources are used by the 1.2 billion people in MDCs?

Figure 2-6 A growing number of people are pledging allegiance to the planet that keeps them alive. Some display the Earth Flag as a symbol of their commitment to sustaining the earth. (Courtesy of Earth Flag Co., 33 Roberts Road, Cambridge, MA 02138)

7. Don't worry. Live one day at a time.

8. Share something every day with someone.

9. Take time to wonder at life and the world. See some humor in life where you can.

10. Be kind to all creatures, and observe the one life in all things.

Many people now see themselves as members of a global community with ultimate loyalty to the planet, not merely a particular country (Figure 2-6). These Earth citizens urge individual citizens to think globally and act locally to sustain the earth (see Individuals Matter on p. 32). They are the earth's true heroes. They are guided by historian Arnold Toynbee's observation: "If you make the world ever so little better, you will have done splendidly, and your life will have been worthwhile," and by George Bernard Shaw's reminder that "indifference is the essence of inhumanity."

Instead of succumbing to despair and denial, we should rejoice at living during a pivotal time in human history—a unique window of opportunity to grow up as a species by making a new cultural change. If we don't do the job now, future humans and other species will have to exist on a planet that we have impoverished.

Can we do it? Yes. If we care enough to make the necessary commitment and in the process discover that caring for the earth is a never-ending source of joy and inner peace. We have an opportunity to participate in a sustainable-Earth revolution that makes every day an Earth Day. No goal is more important, more urgent, and more worthy of our time, energy, creativity, and money.

So long as we are under the illusion that we know best what is good for the earth and for ourselves, then we will continue our present course, with its devastating consequences on the entire earth community. . . . We need not a human answer to an earth problem, but an earth answer to an earth problem. . . . We need only listen to what the earth is telling us. . . . The time has come when we will listen, or we will die.

THOMAS BERRY

In the late fifteenth century, Jambeshwar, the son of the leader of a village in northern India, renounced his inheritance and set out to teach people to care for their health and the environment. He developed 29 principles for living and founded a Hindu sect, called the Bishnois, based on a religious duty to protect trees and wild animals.

In 1730, when the Maharajah of Jodhpur in northern India ordered that the few trees left in the area be cut down, the Bishnois forbade it. Women rushed in and hugged the trees to protect them, but the Maharajah's minister ordered the work to proceed anyway. According to legend, 363 Bishnois women died on that day.

In the 1960s, people in the villages located in the foothills of the Himalaya mountain ranges of northern India faced disaster from severe deforestation, torrential floods, and landslides. Over two decades, the slopes of many of the mountains had been cleared of most trees.

This deforestation occurred because of intensive commercial logging combined with the needs of a growing population for firewood and land for cultivation. Men were being forced to leave the village to find work in other parts of the country. Women were having to travel farther every day in search of firewood.

In 1973, some women in the Himalayan village of Gopeshwar started the modern Chipko (an Indian word for "hug" or "cling to") movement to protect the remaining trees in a nearby forest from being cut down to make tennis rackets for export. It began when Chandi Prasad Bhatt, a village leader, urged villagers to run into the forest ahead of loggers and "hold fast," or "chipko," to protect the trees (Figure 2-7), thus carrying on the tradition started several hundred years earlier by the Bishnois.

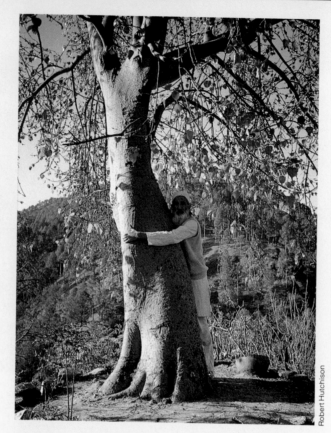

Figure 2-7   Leader of the Chipko movement protecting a tree in northern India from being cut down for export to industrialized countries. This is another example of a successful grassroots group dedicated to helping sustain the earth. Women are the driving force of this movement.

Robert Hutchison

When the loggers came, local women, children, and men rushed into the forests, flung their arms around trees, and dared the loggers to let the axes fall on their backs. This successful movement spread rapidly as their action inspired the women of other Himalayan villages to protect their forests. As a result, the commercial cutting of timber in the hills of the Indian state of Uttar Pradesh has been banned.

Since 1973, the Chipko movement has widened its efforts. Now the women who still guard trees from loggers also plant trees, prepare village forestry plans, and build walls to stop soil erosion.

The spreading actions of such Earth citizens should inspire us to help protect the earth. Sustaining the earth will come mostly from the bottom up, not from the top down. It will happen because of the daily actions of ordinary people who collectively force leaders to get on the bandwagon or lose their power.

Q: How much of the world's population is in the United States?

Peter Montague

Peter Montague is senior research analyst for Greenpeace and director of the Environmental Research Foundation in Washington, D.C. The Foundation conducts studies of various environmental problems and provides the general public with information about environmental problems and the technologies and policies that might contribute to their solution. He has served as project administrator of a hazardous waste research program at Princeton University. Prior to that he taught undergraduate and graduate courses in environmental impact analysis in the School of Architecture and Planning at the University of New Mexico. He is the coauthor of two books on toxic heavy metals in the natural environment and is editor of Rachel, *a highly informative and readable newsletter on environmental problems with emphasis on hazardous waste.*

Environmentalism as we have known it for the past 23 years is dead. The environmentalism of the 1970s advocated strict numerical controls on releases of *dangerous wastes* (any unwanted or uncontrolled materials that can harm living things or disrupt ecosystems) into the environment. Industry's ability to create new hazards, however, quickly outstripped governments' ability to establish adequate controls and enforcement programs.

After 23 years of effort by government and by concerned citizens (the environmental movement), the overwhelming majority of dangerous chemicals are still not regulated in any way. Even those few that *are* covered by regulations have not been adequately controlled.

In sum, the *pollution management* approach to environmental protection has failed and stands discredited; *pollution prevention* is the way of the future and is our only hope. An ounce of prevention really *is* worth a pound of cure.

Here, in list form, is the new environmentalism that is emerging:

1. All waste disposal—landfilling, incineration, deep-well injection—is polluting because disposal means dispersal into the environment. Once wastes are created they cannot be contained or controlled because of the scientific laws of matter and energy [Chapter 3]. The old environmentalism failed to recognize this important truth and thus squandered enormous resources trying to achieve the impossible. We in the United States presently spend about $90 billion per year on pollution control. Yet, the global environment is increasingly threatened by a buildup of heat because of heat-trapping gases we emit into the atmosphere; at least half the surface of the planet is being subjected to an influx of damaging ultraviolet radiation from the sun as a result of ozone-depleting chemicals we have discharged into the atmosphere; and vast regions of the United States, Canada, and Europe are suffering from loss of forests, crop productivity, and fish, as a result of acid rain (caused by releases of sulfur and nitrogen compounds, chiefly by power plants and automobiles) and other air pollutants. Soil and water are dangerously polluted at thousands of locales where municipal garbage and industrial wastes have been (and continue to be) dumped or incinerated; thousands of such sites remain to be discovered, according to U.S. government estimates.

2. The inevitable result of our reliance upon waste treatment and disposal systems has been an unrelenting buildup of exotic synthetic toxic materials in humans and in other forms of life worldwide. For example, breast milk of women in industrialized countries like the United States is so contaminated with pesticides and industrial hydrocarbons that, if human milk were bottled and sold commercially, it would be subject to ban by the Food and Drug Administration (FDA) as unsafe for human consumption. If a whale today beaches itself on the shores of the United States and dies, its body must legally be treated as a "hazardous waste" because whales contain PCBs (polychlorinated biphenyls—a class of industrial toxins) at levels that exceed threshold concentrations for classifying a waste as legally "hazardous."

3. The ability of humans and other forms of life to adapt to changes in their chemical environment is strictly limited by the genetic code each form of life inherits. Continued contamination occurring hundreds of times faster than we can adapt will drive humans to increasingly widespread sickness, to degradation of the species, and ultimately to extinction.

4. Damage to humans (and to other forms of life) is abundantly documented. Birds, fish, and humans in industrialized countries like the United States are enduring steadily rising levels of cancer and other serious disorders attributable to pollution. An astonishing 88% of children under 6 years old in the United States

(continued)

have sufficient toxic lead in their blood to cause them to perform below par on standardized tests of physical, mental, and emotional development. If we will but look, the handwriting is on the wall everywhere.

To deal with these problems, industrial societies must abandon their reliance upon waste treatment and disposal and upon the regulatory system of numerical standards created by government to manage the damage that results from relying on waste disposal instead of waste prevention. We must — relatively quickly — move the industrialized and industrializing countries to new technical approaches accompanied by new industrial goals — namely, clean production or zero discharge systems.

The concept of "clean production" involves industrial systems that avoid or eliminate dangerous wastes and dangerous products and minimize the use of raw materials, water, and energy. Goods manufactured in a clean production process must not damage natural ecosystems throughout their entire life cycle, including **(a)** raw materials selection, extraction, and processing, **(b)** product conceptualization, design, manufacture, and assemblage, **(c)** materials transport during all phases, **(d)** industrial and household usage, and **(e)** reintroduction of the product into industrial systems or into the environment when it no longer serves a useful function.

Clean production does not include "end-of-pipe" pollution controls such as filters or scrubbers or chemical, physical, or biological treatment. Measures that pretend to reduce the volume of waste by incineration or concentration, mask the hazard by dilution, or transfer pollutants from one environmental medium to another are also excluded from the concept of "clean production."

A new industrial pattern, and a new environmentalism, is thus emerging. It insists that the long-term well-being of humans and other species must be factored into our production and consumption plans. These new requirements are not optional; human survival depends upon our willingness to make, and pay for, the necessary changes.

Guest Essay Discussion

1. Do you agree with the author that the pollution management approach to environmental protection practiced during the past 23 years has failed and must be replaced with a pollution prevention approach? Explain.

2. List key economic, health, consumption, and lifestyle changes that a switch from pollution management to pollution prevention would have on you and on any child you might choose to have.

DISCUSSION TOPICS

1. Make a list of the most important benefits and drawbacks of an advanced industrial society such as the United States. Do you feel that the benefits outweigh the drawbacks? Explain. What are the alternatives?

2. Governments are in the process of virtually eliminating the world's remaining hunter-gatherers and other indigenous peoples, who have lived gently on the land for centuries and who can teach us much about how to live sustainably. This cultural extinction is being done in the name of "progress" by taking over their lands for crop growing, timber cutting, cattle grazing, mining, building hydroelectric dams and reservoirs, and creating other forms of economic development. Some believe that the world's remaining tribal and indigenous people should be given title to the land they and their ancestors have lived on for centuries, a decisive voice in formulating policies about resource development in their areas, and the right to be left alone by modern civilization. We have created protected reserves for endangered wild species, so why not create reserves for these endangered human cultures? What do you think? Explain.

3. What is your worldview?

4. Do you agree with the principles and guidelines of the sustainable-Earth worldview given in Section 2-3? Explain. Can you add others? Which ones do you try to follow?

5. What obligations, if any, concerning the environment do you have to future generations? List the most important environmental benefits and harmful conditions passed on to you by the last two generations.

PART TWO

Scientific Principles and Concepts

Animal and vegetable life is too complicated a problem for human intelligence to solve, and we can never know how wide a circle of disturbance we produce in the harmonies of nature when we throw the smallest pebble into the ocean of organic life.

GEORGE PERKINS MARSH

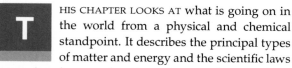

CHAPTER 3

MATTER AND ENERGY RESOURCES: TYPES AND CONCEPTS

General Questions and Issues

1. What is science? Environmental science?

2. What are the principal forms of matter? What is matter made of? What makes matter useful to us as a resource?

3. What are the principal forms of energy? What energy resources do we rely on? What makes energy useful to us as a resource?

4. What are physical and chemical changes? What scientific law governs changes of matter from one physical or chemical form to another?

5. What are the three principal types of nuclear changes that matter can undergo?

6. What two scientific laws govern changes of energy from one form to another?

7. How can we waste less energy? How much net useful energy is available from different energy resources?

8. How are the scientific laws governing changes of matter and energy from one form to another related to resource use and environmental disruption?

The laws of thermodynamics control the rise and fall of political systems, the freedom or bondage of nations, the movements of commerce and industry, the origins of wealth and poverty, and the general physical welfare of the human race.

FREDERICK SODDY
(NOBEL LAUREATE, CHEMISTRY)

THIS CHAPTER LOOKS AT what is going on in the world from a physical and chemical standpoint. It describes the principal types of matter and energy and the scientific laws governing changes of matter and energy from one form to another. Chapters 4 and 5 examine what is going on in the world from an ecological standpoint, based on how key physical and chemical processes are integrated into the biological systems we call life.

3-1 Science and Environmental Science

WHAT IS SCIENCE? **Science** is an attempt to discover order in nature and then use that knowledge to make predictions about what will happen in nature. In this search for order, scientists try to answer two basic questions: *What happens in nature over and over with the same results? How or why do things happen this way?*

To find out what is happening, scientists collect **scientific data**, or facts, by making observations and taking measurements. Collecting data, however, is not the main purpose of science. As the French scientist Henri Poincaré put it, "Science is built up of facts, but a collection of facts is no more science than a heap of stones is a house."

Data are the stepping stones to **scientific laws**, which summarize what happens in nature over and over in the same way. Examples are the law of conservation of matter and the two energy laws discussed in this chapter.

Once a scientific law has been formulated, scientists try to explain how or why things happen the way the laws describe. They make a **scientific hypothesis**, an educated guess that attempts to explain a scientific law or certain scientific facts.

Then they test the hypothesis by making more observations and taking more measurements. If many experiments by different scientists support the hypothesis, it can become a scientific theory. In other words, a **scientific theory** is a well-tested and widely accepted scientific hypothesis. The *atomic theory*, the idea that all matter is composed of atoms, is an example.

The ways scientists gather data and formulate and test scientific laws and theories are called **scientific methods**. Discovering and formulating scientific laws and theories may require logical reasoning, but it also requires imagination and intuition. As Albert Einstein once said, "Imagination is more important than knowledge, and there is no completely logical way to a new scientific idea."

Thus, intuition, imagination, and creativity are as important in science as in poetry, art, music, and other great adventures of the human spirit. Science, at its best, is an adventure that helps awaken us to the wonder, mystery, and beauty of the universe, the earth, and life.

Science is often held up as being value-free and neutral. But scientists are ordinary human beings with conscious and unconscious biases, values, opinions, and financial and other needs that can influence what questions they ask of nature, how they design experiments, and how they interpret the results. Open publishing of results and mutual criticism among scientists help to correct for biases more than in other professions, but they do not remove them.

ARE SCIENTIFIC THEORIES AND LAWS TRUE?
A favorite debating and advertising trick is to claim that something "has not been scientifically proved." But scientists don't establish absolute proof or truth.

Science is the acceptance of what works and the rejection of what does not. That's why scientific theories may be modified, or even discarded, because of new data or more useful explanations of the data. It's also why advances in scientific knowledge are often based on vigorous disagreement, speculation, and controversy.

Scientific laws and theories are based on statistical probabilities, not on certainties. Scientists trying to find out how oak trees grow cannot study any more than a minute fraction of Earth's oak trees. The growth of oak trees is affected by numerous variables—factors that vary from site to site. Scientists can study only a small number of the thousands, perhaps millions, of possible interactions of these and other variables.

ENVIRONMENTAL SCIENCE: A HOLISTIC SCIENCE
For the past 250 years, scientists have studied nature mostly by examining increasingly lower levels of organization of matter (Figure 3-1). This approach is called *reductionism*. It is based on the belief that if we can understand subatomic particles, then we can go back up the ladder of organizational levels and understand atoms, then molecules, and so on to organisms, communities, ecosystems, the ecosphere, and eventually the universe. It is based on examining the world in isolated fragments.

The reductionist approach has helped us learn much about nature, but in the last few decades we have learned that it has a basic flaw. Each higher level of organization of matter has properties that cannot be predicted or understood merely by understanding the lower levels that make up its structure. Even if you learn all there is to know about a particular tree, you will know only a small part of how a forest works. Reductionism does not tell us about the whole, or about the interaction between the parts or the interaction with other parts of the environment. Even if reductionism did work, the natural world is so incredibly complex that it is the height of arrogance to think we have or will

ever have enough knowledge to wisely manage even a single natural resource, much less the entire planet.

The science of ecology has shown the need for combining reductionism with *holism* (sometimes spelled wholism)—an attempt to describe all properties of a level of organization, not merely those based on the lower levels of organization that make up its underlying structure. This approach also attempts to understand and describe how the various levels of organization interact with one another and with their constantly changing environments. This challenging and incredibly difficult task requires interdisciplinary research and cooperation. Unfortunately, such research is rare, because most of the jobs and grants in the scientific disciplines reward those who do disciplinary research.

Environmental science is a holistic physical and social science that uses and integrates knowledge from physics, chemistry, biology (especially ecology), geology, resource technology and engineering, resource conservation and management, demography (the study of population dynamics), economics, politics, and ethics.

SCIENCE, TECHNOLOGY, AND THE FUTURE
Our challenge is to learn how to use scientific knowledge and technology to sustain the earth for humans and other species and to improve the quality of life for all people—not to plunder the planet for short-term economic gain. This means that scientists and technologists need to consider the possible short- and long-range implications of their research, air these thoughts, and engage the public and decision makers in an ongoing debate about the ends that science should serve.

It's also important for nonscientists to have a basic knowledge of how nature works, because most decisions about how to use science and technology are made by nonscientists, usually with advice from scientists. Decision makers in business and government must have enough general knowledge of science and technology to be able to ask tough questions of scientists and engineers, evaluate the answers, and make difficult decisions, often with incomplete scientific information.

3-2 Matter: Forms, Structure, and Quality

NATURE'S BUILDING BLOCKS: CHEMICAL AND PHYSICAL FORMS OF MATTER
Matter is anything that has mass (the amount of material in an object) and takes up space. Matter is found in three *chemical forms:* **elements** (the distinctive building blocks of matter that make up every material substance), **compounds** (two or more different elements held together in fixed propor-

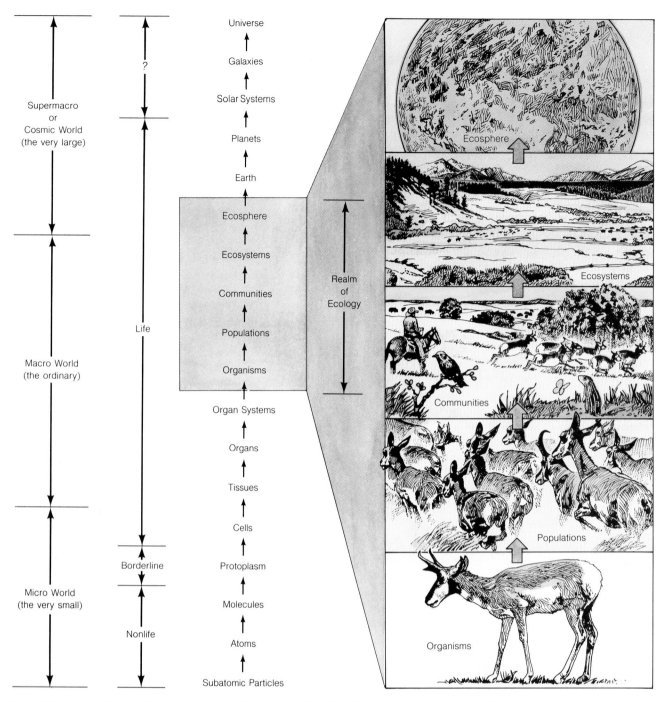

Figure 3-1 Levels of organization of matter, according to size and function. This is one way scientists classify patterns of matter found in nature. Part of this chapter is devoted to a discussion of the three lowest levels of organization of matter—subatomic particles, atoms, and molecules—that make up the basic components of all higher levels. Chapter 4 discusses the five levels of organization of matter (shaded in purple and illustrated)—that are the primary concerns of ecology.

tions by attractive forces called *chemical bonds*), and **mixtures** (combinations of elements, compounds, or both).

All matter is built from the 109 known chemical elements. Ninety-two of them occur naturally, and the other 17 have been synthesized in laboratories. Each of these elements has a size, an internal structure, and other properties uniquely different from the others, just as each of the 26 letters in the English alphabet is differ-

ent from the others. Examples of these basic building blocks of all matter include hydrogen (represented by the symbol H), carbon (C), oxygen (O), nitrogen (N), phosphorus (P), sulfur (S), chlorine (Cl), fluorine (F), bromine (Br), sodium (Na), calcium (Ca), and uranium (U).

Some elements are found in nature as molecules, or combinations of their atoms. Examples are the nitrogen

Q: In terms of resource use and environmental impact, what is the most overpopulated country in the world?

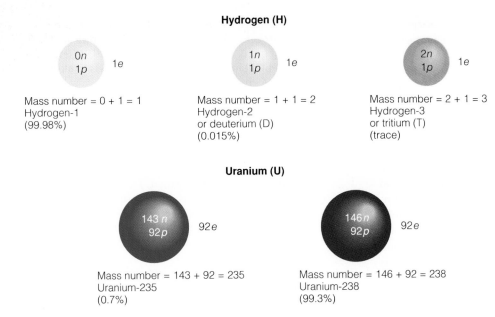

Hydrogen (H)

$0n$
$1p$ $1e$

Mass number = 0 + 1 = 1
Hydrogen-1
(99.98%)

$1n$
$1p$ $1e$

Mass number = 1 + 1 = 2
Hydrogen-2
or deuterium (D)
(0.015%)

$2n$
$1p$ $1e$

Mass number = 2 + 1 = 3
Hydrogen-3
or tritium (T)
(trace)

Uranium (U)

$143\,n$
$92p$ $92e$

Mass number = 143 + 92 = 235
Uranium-235
(0.7%)

$146\,n$
$92p$ $92e$

Mass number = 146 + 92 = 238
Uranium-238
(99.3%)

Figure 3-2 Isotopes of hydrogen and uranium. Note that all isotopes of hydrogen have an atomic number (number of protons in their nuclei) of 1 and those of uranium an atomic number of 92. However, the isotopes of each of these elements have different mass numbers because their nuclei contain different numbers of neutrons. Figures in parentheses show the percent abundance by weight of each isotope in a natural sample of each element.

and oxygen gases, making up about 99% of the volume of air we breathe. Two atoms of nitrogen (N) combine to form a nitrogen gas molecule with the shorthand formula N_2 (read as "N-two"). The subscript after the symbol of the element gives the number of atoms of that element in a molecule. Similarly, most of the oxygen gas in the atmosphere exists as O_2 (read as "O-two") molecules. A small amount of oxygen, found mostly in the second layer of the atmosphere (stratosphere), exists as ozone molecules with the formula O_3 (read as "O-three").

Elements can combine to form an almost limitless number of compounds, just as the letters of our alphabet can be combined to form the almost 1 million words in the English language. So far, chemists have identified more than 10 million compounds.

If you had a supermicroscope with which to look at the world's elements and compounds, you would discover that they are made up of three types of building blocks: **atoms** (the smallest unit of an element that can exist and still have the unique characteristics of that element), **ions** (electrically charged atoms), and **molecules** (combinations of atoms held together by chemical bonds). Since ions and molecules are formed from atoms, atoms are the ultimate building blocks for all matter.

If you increased the magnification of your supermicroscope, you would find that each of the world's different types of atoms is composed of a certain number of *subatomic particles*. The main building blocks of an atom are positively charged **protons** (represented by the symbol p), uncharged **neutrons** (n), and negatively charged **electrons** (e). Many other subatomic particles have been identified in recent years, but they need not concern us at this introductory level.

Matter is also found in three *physical forms:* solid, liquid, and gas. Water, for example, exists as ice, liquid water, and water vapor. The differences among the three physical states of a sample of matter are the relative degree of ordering between the atoms, ions, or molecules that make up their structure.

ATOMS AND IONS   Your supermicroscope would show that each atom of an element consists of a relatively small center, or **nucleus**, containing protons and neutrons, and one or more electrons in rapid motion somewhere around the nucleus. We can describe electrons only in terms of the probability that they might be at various locations outside the nucleus.

The distinguishing feature of an atom of any given element is the number of protons in its nucleus, called its **atomic number**. The simplest element, hydrogen (H), has only 1 proton in its nucleus, and its atomic number is 1. Carbon (C), with 6 protons in its nucleus, has an atomic number of 6. Uranium (U), a much more complex atom, has 92 protons in its nucleus and an atomic number of 92 (Figure 3-2).

Atoms normally have the same number of positively charged protons and negatively charged electrons and thus do not carry an electrical charge. For example, an uncharged atom of hydrogen has one positively charged proton in its nucleus and one negatively charged electron outside its nucleus. Similarly, each atom of uranium has 92 protons in its nucleus and 92 electrons outside (Figure 3-2).

Protons and neutrons have essentially the same mass and are assigned a relative mass of 1. Each electron outside the nucleus is assigned a relative mass of 0 because its mass is almost negligible compared with the mass of a proton or a neutron. Thus, the approximate relative mass of an atom is determined by the number of neutrons plus the number of protons in its nucleus. This number is called its **mass number**. An atom of hydrogen with 1 proton and no neutrons has a mass number of 1; an atom of uranium with 92 protons and 143 neutrons has a mass number of 235 (Figure 3-2).

Although uncharged atoms of an element must have the same number of protons and electrons, they may have different numbers of uncharged neutrons in their nuclei and thus different mass numbers. These different forms of an element are called **isotopes** of that element and are identified by attaching their mass numbers to the name or symbol of the element; for example, hydrogen-1, or H-1; hydrogen-2, or H-2 (common name, deuterium); and hydrogen-3, or H-3 (common name, tritium). A natural sample of an element contains a mixture of its isotopes in a fixed proportion or percent abundance by weight (Figure 3-2).

Atoms of some elements can lose or gain one or more electrons to form **ions**: atoms or groups of atoms with one or more net positive ($+$) or negative ($-$) electrical charges. For example, an atom of sodium (Na) can lose one of its electrons and become a sodium ion with a positive charge of one (Na^+). An atom of chlorine (Cl) can gain an electron and become an ion of chlorine with a negative charge of one (Cl^-). The number of positive or negative charges on an ion is shown as a superscript after the symbol for an atom or a group of atoms. Examples of other positive ions are calcium ions (Ca^{2+}) and ammonium ions (NH_4^+). Other common negative ions are nitrate ions (NO_3^-), sulfate ions (SO_4^{2-}), and phosphate ions (PO_4^{3-}).

COMPOUNDS Most matter exists as **compounds** — combinations of atoms, or oppositely charged ions, of two or more different elements held together by chemical bonds. Water, for example, is a *molecular compound* made up of H_2O (read as "H-two-O") molecules, each consisting of two hydrogen atoms chemically bonded to an oxygen atom. Sodium chloride, or table salt, is an *ionic compound*, consisting of a network of oppositely charged ions (Na^+ and Cl^-) held together by the forces of attraction that exist between opposite electric charges.

Table sugar, vitamins, plastics, aspirin, penicillin, and many other materials important to you and your lifestyle have one thing in common. They are *organic compounds*, containing atoms of the element carbon, usually combined with each other and with atoms of one or more other elements such as hydrogen, oxygen, nitrogen, sulfur, phosphorus, chlorine, and fluorine.

The following are examples of the millions of known organic compounds:

- *Hydrocarbons* — compounds of carbon and hydrogen atoms. An example is methane (CH_4), the principal component of natural gas.

- *Chlorinated hydrocarbons* — compounds of carbon, hydrogen, and chlorine atoms. Examples are DDT ($C_{14}H_9Cl_5$), an insecticide, and toxic PCBs (such as $C_{12}H_5Cl_5$), used as insulating materials in electric transformers.

- *Chlorofluorocarbons* (CFCs) — compounds of carbon, chlorine, and fluorine atoms. An example is Freon-12 (CCl_2F_2), used as a coolant in refrigerators and air conditioners, as an aerosol propellant, and as a foaming agent for making some plastics.

- *Carbohydrates* (simple sugars) — certain types of compounds of carbon, hydrogen, and oxygen atoms. An example is glucose ($C_6H_{12}O_6$), which most plants and animals break down in their cells to obtain energy.

All other compounds are called *inorganic compounds*. Some of the inorganic compounds you will encounter in this book are sodium chloride (NaCl), water (H_2O), nitrous oxide (N_2O), nitric oxide (NO), carbon

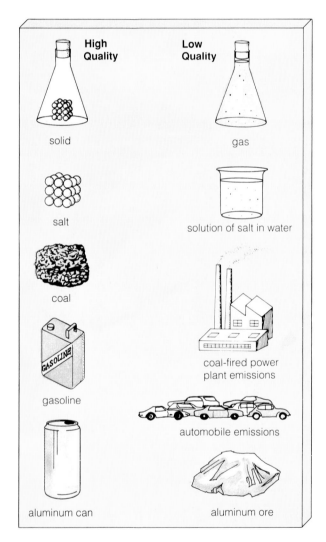

Figure 3-3 Examples of differences in matter quality. High-quality matter is fairly easy to get and is concentrated. Low-quality matter is harder to get and is more dispersed than high-quality matter.

Q: How many people would have to be sent into space each day to keep Earth's population from increasing?

monoxide (CO), carbon dioxide (CO_2), nitrogen dioxide (NO_2), sulfur dioxide (SO_2), ammonia (NH_3), sulfuric acid (H_2SO_4), and nitric acid (HNO_3).

MATTER QUALITY **Matter quality** is a measure of how useful a matter resource is, based on its availability and concentration (Figure 3-3). **High-quality matter** is organized, concentrated, and usually found near the earth's surface. It has great potential for use as a matter resource. **Low-quality matter** is disorganized, dilute, or dispersed and is often found deep underground or dispersed in the ocean or in the atmosphere. It usually has little potential for use as a matter resource.

An aluminum can is a more concentrated, higher-quality form of aluminum than aluminum ore with the same amount of aluminum. That's why it takes less energy, water, and money to recycle an aluminum can than to get aluminum from ore and make a new can.

3-3 Energy: Types, Forms, and Quality

TYPES OF ENERGY Energy, not money, is the real "currency" of the world. We depend on it to grow our food, run factories, keep us and other organisms alive, and to warm and cool our bodies and the buildings where we work and live. We also use it to move people and objects from one place to another, change matter from one physical or chemical form to another, and to raise the temperature of a sample of matter.

Energy is defined as the capacity to do work by performing mechanical, physical, chemical, or electrical tasks or to cause a heat transfer between two objects at different temperatures. Forms of energy include light (a form of radiant energy), heat, chemical energy stored in the chemical bonds holding elements and compounds together, moving matter, and electricity.

Scientists classify energy as either kinetic or potential. **Kinetic energy** is the energy that matter has because of its motion and mass. Examples include a moving car, a falling rock, a speeding bullet, heat, and the flow of water or charged particles (electrical energy).

Heat refers to the total kinetic energy of all the randomly moving atoms, ions, or molecules within a given substance, excluding the overall motion of the whole object. **Temperature** is a measure of the average speed of motion of the atoms, ions, or molecules in a sample of matter at a given moment. A substance can have a high heat content (much mass and many moving atoms, ions, or molecules) but a low temperature (low average molecular speed). For example, the total heat content of a lake or an ocean is enormous, but its average temperature is low. Other samples of matter can have a low heat content and a high temperature. For example, a cup of hot coffee or a burning match has a much lower heat content than an ocean or a lake, but it has a much higher temperature.

Radio waves, TV waves, microwaves, infrared radiation, visible light, ultraviolet radiation, X rays, and gamma rays are forms of kinetic energy traveling as electromagnetic waves and known as **electromagnetic radiation**. These forms of radiant energy make up a wide band or spectrum of electromagnetic waves that differ in their wavelength (distance between each peak or trough) and energy content (Figure 3-4).

Cosmic rays, gamma rays, X rays, and ultraviolet radiation have a high enough energy content to knock

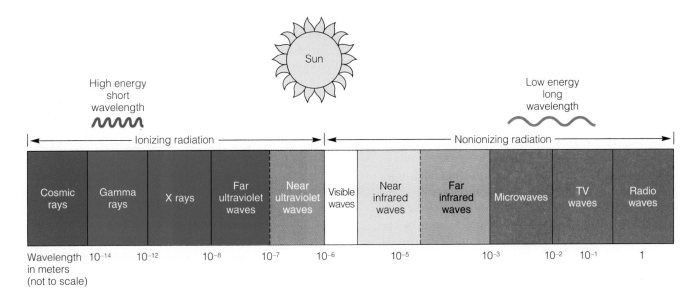

Figure 3-4 Electromagnetic spectrum of different types of kinetic energy traveling as electromagnetic waves that differ in their wavelength (distance between each peak or trough) and energy content.

A: About 258,000 a day (10,800 per hour)

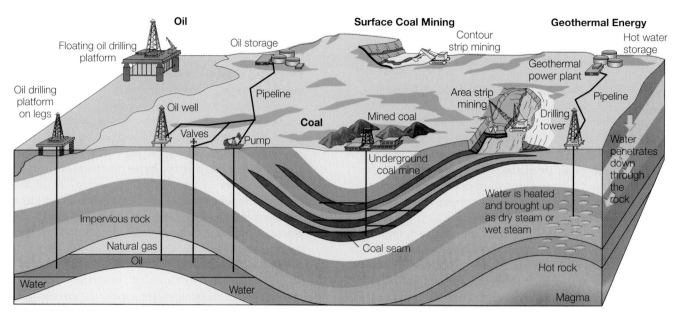

Figure 3-5 Important energy resources we obtain from Earth's crust are geothermal energy, coal, oil, and natural gas. Uranium ore is also extracted from the crust and then processed to increase the concentration of uranium-235 (Figure 3-2), which can undergo nuclear fission (Figure 3-11) in nuclear bombs and warheads and in nuclear reactors used to produce electricity.

electrons from atoms and change them to positively charged ions. The resulting highly reactive electrons and ions disrupt millions of organic compounds in living cells, interfere with body processes, and cause many types of sickness, including various cancers. These potentially harmful forms of electromagnetic radiation are called **ionizing radiation**.

The other forms of electromagnetic radiation do not have enough energy content to form ions and are called **nonionizing radiation**. There is now some controversial evidence that long-term exposure to nonionizing radiation emitted by radios, TV sets, the video display terminals of computers, overhead electric-power lines, electrically heated water beds, electric blankets, and other electrical devices may also damage living cells.

Potential energy is stored energy that is potentially available for use. A rock held in your hand, a stick of dynamite, still water stored in a reservoir behind a dam, and nuclear energy stored in the nuclei of atoms all have potential energy. Other examples are the chemical energy stored in molecules of gasoline and in the carbohydrates, proteins, and fats of the food you eat.

ENERGY RESOURCES USED BY PEOPLE *The direct input of perpetual solar energy alone supplies 99% of the energy used to heat Earth and all of the buildings we have constructed.* Were it not for this direct input of energy from the sun, the average temperature would be −240°C (−400°F), and life as we know it would not have arisen. This input of solar energy also helps recycle the carbon, oxygen, water, and other chemicals we and other organisms need to stay alive and healthy and to reproduce.

Broadly defined, **solar energy** includes perpetual *direct* energy from the sun and a number of *indirect* forms of energy produced by the direct input. Indirect forms of solar energy include wind, falling and flowing water (hydropower), and biomass (solar energy converted to chemical energy stored in the chemical bonds of organic compounds in trees and other plants).

Passive solar energy systems capture and store direct solar energy and use it to heat buildings and water without the use of mechanical devices. Examples are a well-insulated, airtight house with large insulating windows that face the sun and the use of rock, concrete, or water to store and release heat slowly.

Direct solar energy can also be captured by *active* solar energy systems. For example, specially designed roof-mounted collectors concentrate direct solar energy; pumps transfer this heat to water, to the interior of a building, or to insulated storage tanks of stone or water to store and release heat slowly. We have also learned how to make solar cells that convert solar energy directly into electricity in one simple, nonpolluting step. We also use wind turbines and hydroelectric power plants to convert indirect solar energy in the form of wind and falling or flowing water into electricity.

The sun's input of 99% of the energy used to heat the earth and make it livable is not sold in the marketplace. The remaining 1% of the energy we use to supplement the solar input is *commercial energy* sold in the marketplace. Most of this commercial energy is obtained from mineral resources in the earth's crust (Figure 3-5), with most of it produced by the burning of nonrenewable fossil fuels (Figure 3-6).

Q: Adjusting for inflation, how does the price of gasoline in the United States in 1992 compare with its price in 1950? In 1973?

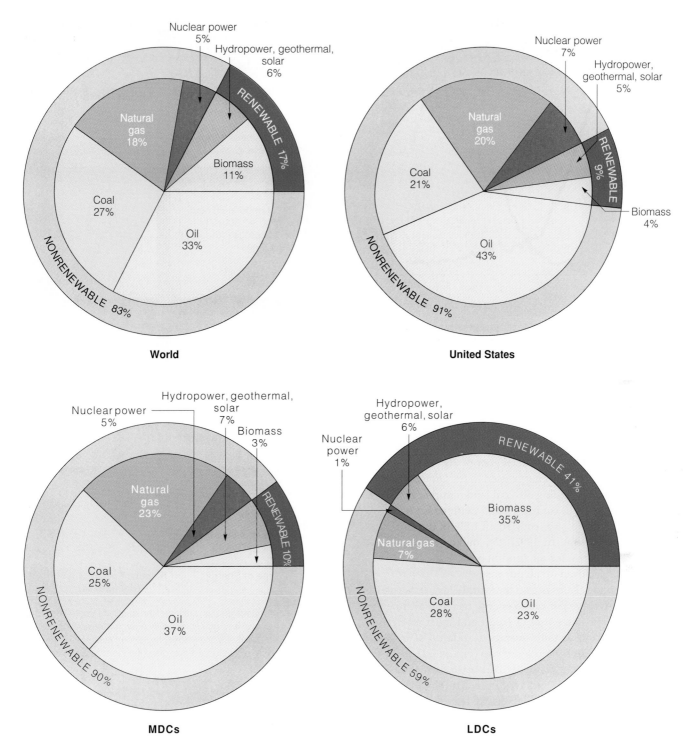

Figure 3-6 Commercial energy use by source in 1988 in the world, MDCs, LDCs, and the United States. This amounts to only 1% of the energy used in the world. The other 99% of the energy used to heat Earth comes from the sun and is not sold in the marketplace. (Data from U.S. Department of Energy, British Petroleum, and Worldwatch Institute)

MDCs and LDCs differ greatly in their sources of energy (Figure 3-6), the total amount used, and the average energy used per person. The most important supplemental source of energy for LDCs is potentially renewable biomass—especially fuelwood—the main source of energy for heating and cooking for roughly half the world's population (Figure 3-6). One-fourth of the world's population in MDCs may soon face shortages of oil, but half the world's population in LDCs already face a fuelwood shortage.

The United States is the world's largest user of energy. With only 4.7% of the world's population, it uses

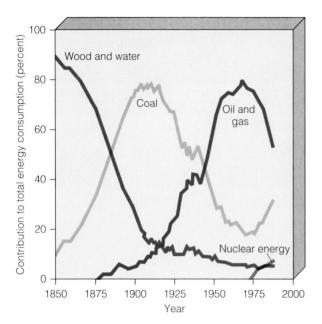

Figure 3-7 Shifts in the use of commercial energy resources in the United States since 1850. Shifts from wood to coal and then from coal to oil and natural gas have each taken about 50 years. Affordable oil is running out, and burning fossil fuels is the primary cause of air pollution and projected warming of the atmosphere. For these reasons, most analysts believe we must make a new shift in energy resources over the next 50 years. (Data from U.S. Department of Energy)

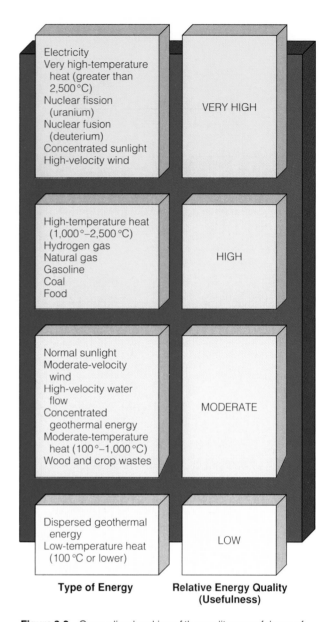

Figure 3-8 Generalized ranking of the quality or usefulness of different types of energy. *High-quality energy* is organized or concentrated and has great ability to perform useful work. *Low-quality energy* is disorganized or dispersed and has little ability to do useful work.

25% of the world's commercial energy. By 1988, about 83% of the commercial energy used in the United States was provided by burning oil, coal, and natural gas (Figures 3-6 and 3-7). In contrast, India, with about 16% of the world's people, uses only about 1.5% of the world's commercial energy. In 1992, 256 million Americans used more energy for air conditioning alone than 1.2 billion Chinese used for all purposes.

The United States is also the world's largest waster of energy. Average per capita energy use in the United States is about twice that of Japan and most western European countries with average standards of living similar to those in the United States (Figure 2-1).

To bring the energy use of LDCs up to current levels of MDCs by 2025 would require a fivefold increase in present global commercial energy use. Many scientists believe that even a doubling of energy use based mostly on nonrenewable fossil fuels will seriously disrupt Earth's already-damaged life-sustaining processes. This explains why our top priorities should be to waste less energy by greatly improving energy efficiency and to greatly increase our use of perpetual and renewable forms of energy.

ENERGY QUALITY Energy varies in its quality, or ability to do useful work. **Energy quality** is a measure of energy usefulness (Figure 3-8). **High-quality energy** is organized or concentrated and has great ability to perform useful work. Examples of these useful forms

of energy are electricity, coal, gasoline, concentrated sunlight, nuclei of uranium-235, and heat concentrated in a fairly small sample of matter so that its temperature is high.

By contrast, **low-quality energy** is disorganized or dispersed and has little ability to do useful work. An example is heat dispersed in the moving molecules of a large sample of matter such as the atmosphere or a large body of water so that its temperature is relatively low. For instance, the total amount of heat stored at a relatively low temperature in the Atlantic Ocean is greater than the amount of high-quality chemical energy stored in all the oil deposits in Saudi Arabia. However, this

Q: How much of the commercial energy used in the world comes from nonrenewable resources?

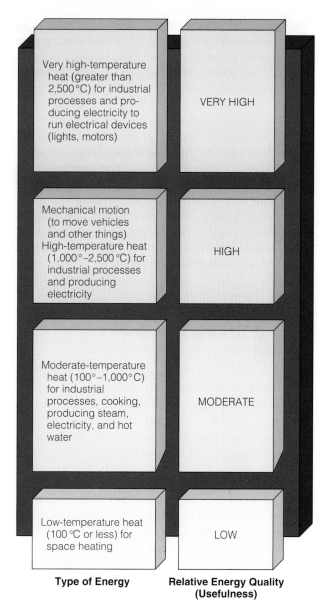

Type of Energy	Relative Energy Quality (Usefulness)
Very high-temperature heat (greater than 2,500 °C) for industrial processes and producing electricity to run electrical devices (lights, motors)	VERY HIGH
Mechanical motion (to move vehicles and other things) High-temperature heat (1,000°–2,500 °C) for industrial processes and producing electricity	HIGH
Moderate-temperature heat (100°–1,000 °C) for industrial processes, cooking, producing steam, electricity, and hot water	MODERATE
Low-temperature heat (100 °C or less) for space heating	LOW

Figure 3-9 General quality of energy needed to perform various energy tasks. To avoid unnecessary energy waste, it's best to match the quality of an energy source (Figure 3-8) to the quality of energy needed to perform a task — that is, not to use energy of a higher quality than necessary. This saves energy and usually saves money.

heat is so widely dispersed in the ocean that we can't do much with it. This dispersed heat, like that in the air around us, can't be used to move things or to heat things to high temperatures.

We use energy to accomplish certain tasks, each requiring a certain minimum energy quality (Figure 3-9). Electrical energy, which is very high-quality energy, is needed to run lights, electric motors, and electronic devices. We need high-quality mechanical energy to move a car, but we need only air at a low temperature (less than 100°C) to heat homes and other buildings. It makes sense to match the quality of an energy source (Figure 3-8) to the quality of energy needed to perform a particular task (Figure 3-9). This saves energy and usually saves money (see Guest Essay on p. 58).

Unfortunately, many forms of high-quality energy do not occur naturally. These include a sample of matter at a high temperature, electricity, gasoline, hydrogen gas (a useful and clean-burning fuel that can be produced by passing electricity through water), and concentrated sunlight. We must use other forms of high-quality energy, such as fossil, wood, and nuclear fuels, or devices such as solar collectors or solar cells, to produce, concentrate, and store them or to upgrade their quality so they can be used to perform certain tasks.

3-4 Physical and Chemical Changes and the Law of Conservation of Matter

PHYSICAL AND CHEMICAL CHANGES Elements and compounds can undergo physical and chemical changes; each change either gives off or requires energy, usually in the form of heat. A **physical change** is one that involves no change in chemical composition. For example, cutting a piece of aluminum foil into small pieces is a physical change. Each cut piece is still aluminum.

Changing a substance from one physical state to another is also a physical change. For example, when solid water, or ice, is melted or liquid water is boiled, none of the H_2O molecules involved is altered; instead the molecules are organized in different spatial patterns.

In a **chemical change**, or **chemical reaction**, there is a change in the chemical composition of the elements or compounds involved. For example, when coal burns completely, the carbon (C) it contains combines with oxygen gas (O_2) from the atmosphere to form the gaseous compound carbon dioxide (CO_2). In this case energy is given off, making coal a useful fuel (C + O_2 → CO_2 + energy).

This reaction shows how the burning of coal or any carbon-containing compounds, such as those in wood, natural gas, oil, and gasoline, adds carbon dioxide gas to the atmosphere. As the concentration of carbon dioxide in the lower atmosphere increases, this heat-trapping gas could warm the lower atmosphere, enhance Earth's natural greenhouse effect, and possibly bring about changes in global climate, water distribution, and food production.

THE LAW OF CONSERVATION OF MATTER: THERE IS NO AWAY Earth loses some gaseous molecules to space, and it gains small amounts of matter from space, mostly in the form of occasional stony or metallic bodies (meteorites) and the fallout of small amounts of cosmic dust. These losses and gains of matter are minute compared with Earth's total mass.

This means that *Earth has essentially all the matter it will ever have*. In terms of matter, Earth is essentially a closed system. Fortunately, over billions of years, natural processes have evolved for continuously cycling key chemicals back and forth between the non-living environment (soil, air, and water) and the living environment.

You, like most people, probably talk about consuming or using up material resources, but the truth is that we don't consume any matter. We only use some of Earth's resources for a while. We take materials from the earth, carry them to another part of the globe, and process them into products. These products are used and then discarded, reused, or recycled.

In making and using products, we may change various elements and compounds from one physical or chemical form to another, but we neither create from nothing nor destroy to nothingness any measurable amount of matter.* This fact, based on many thousands of measurements of matter undergoing physical and chemical changes, is known as the **law of conservation of matter**: *In all physical and chemical changes, we can't create or destroy any of the atoms involved. All we can do is rearrange them into different spatial patterns (physical changes) or different combinations (chemical changes).*

The law of conservation of matter means that there is no "away." *Everything we think we have thrown away is still here with us in one form or another*. We can collect dust and soot from the smokestacks of industrial plants, but these solid wastes must then go somewhere. We can remove substances from polluted water at a sewage treatment plant, but this produces a gooey, often toxic, sludge. The sludge must either be burned (producing some air pollution), buried (possibly contaminating underground water supplies used for drinking water), or cleaned up and applied to the land as fertilizer (dangerous if the sludge contains nondegradable toxic metals, such as lead and mercury). High smokestacks can reduce some types of local air pollution but cause acid deposition that kills trees and aquatic life in distant downwind areas. Banning DDT in the United States and still selling it abroad means that it comes back to us as DDT residues in imported coffee, fruits, and other types of foods.

We can make the environment cleaner and convert some potentially harmful chemicals into less harmful, or even harmless, physical or chemical forms. Nevertheless, the law of conservation of matter means that we will always be faced with the problem of what to do with some quantity of wastes. By placing much greater emphasis on pollution prevention and waste reduction, however, we can greatly reduce the amount of wastes we add to the environment.

We need to recognize that most of what we call wastes are really wasted resources. They are potential resources that we are not recycling, reusing, or converting to useful raw materials or products. In a world with more and more people rapidly converting the world's resources to trash and waste heat, waste production is an outmoded and dangerous concept. Using our economic and political systems to reward resource conservation, pollution prevention, and waste reduction instead of resource waste is the key to making the transition from a throwaway society to a sustainable-Earth society.

3-5 Nuclear Changes

NATURAL RADIOACTIVITY   In addition to physical and chemical changes, matter can undergo a third type of change, known as a **nuclear change**. It occurs when nuclei of certain isotopes spontaneously change or are forced to change into one or more different isotopes. The three principal types of nuclear change are natural radioactivity, nuclear fission, and nuclear fusion.

The law of conservation of matter does not apply to nuclear changes because they involve conversion of a small but measurable amount of the mass in a nucleus into energy. This type of change is governed by the **law of conservation of matter and energy**: In any nuclear change the total amount of matter and energy involved remains the same.

Natural radioactivity is a nuclear change in which unstable nuclei spontaneously shoot out particles (usually alpha or beta particles), energy (gamma rays), or both at a fixed rate. An isotope of an atom that spontaneously emits fast-moving particles, high-energy radiation, or both from its unstable nucleus is called a **radioactive isotope**, or **radioisotope**.

Radiation emitted by radioisotopes is damaging ionizing radiation. The most common form of ionizing energy released from radioisotopes is **gamma rays**, a form of electromagnetic radiation with a high energy content (Figure 3-4). High-speed particles emitted from the nuclei are a different form of ionizing radiation, with enough energy to hit other atoms and dislodge one or more of their electrons to form positively charged ions. The two most common types of ionizing particles emitted by radioactive isotopes are high-speed **alpha particles** (positively charged chunks of matter that consist of two protons and two neutrons) and **beta particles**

---

*According to modern physics, we may be converting a tiny amount of matter into energy when a chemical reaction takes place. However, the amount is so minute that it cannot be detected by even the most sensitive measuring devices.

Q: How much of the commercial energy used in the United States comes from nonrenewable resources?

(high-speed electrons). Figure 3-10 shows the relative penetrating power of alpha, beta, and gamma ionizing radiation. You are exposed to small amounts of harmful ionizing radiation from natural sources and from human sources.

NUCLEAR FISSION: SPLITTING NUCLEI **Nuclear fission** is a nuclear change in which nuclei of certain isotopes with large mass numbers (such as uranium-235, Figure 3-2) are split apart into lighter nuclei when struck by neutrons; this process releases more neutrons and energy (Figure 3-11). Each fission produces two or three neutrons. Each of these neutrons, in turn, can cause an additional fission. For these multiple fissions to take place, there must be enough fissionable nuclei present to provide the **critical mass** needed for efficient capture of these neutrons.

These multiple fissions taking place within the critical mass represent a **chain reaction** that releases an enormous amount of energy (Figure 3-12). Living cells can be damaged by the ionizing radiation released by the radioactive lighter nuclei and by high-speed neutrons produced by nuclear fission.

In an atomic or nuclear fission bomb, an enormous amount of energy is released in a fraction of a second in an uncontrolled nuclear fission chain reaction. This reaction is initiated by an explosive charge, which suddenly pushes two masses of fissionable fuel together from all sides, causing the fuel to reach the critical mass needed for a chain reaction.

In the nuclear reactor of a nuclear electric power plant, the rate at which the nuclear fission chain reaction takes place is controlled, so that under normal operation only one of each two or three neutrons released is used to split another nucleus. In conventional nuclear fission reactors, nuclei of uranium-235 are split apart and release energy. The heat released is used to produce high-pressure steam. The steam is used to spin turbines, which run generators that produce electricity.

NUCLEAR FUSION: FORCING NUCLEI TO COMBINE **Nuclear fusion** is a nuclear change in which two nuclei of isotopes of light elements, such as hydrogen (Figure 3-2), are forced together at extremely high temperatures until they fuse to form a heavier nucleus, releasing energy in the process (Figure 3-13). Temperatures of at least 100 million °C are needed to force the positively charged nuclei (which strongly repel one another) to join together.

High-temperature fusion is much harder to initiate than fission, but once started, it releases far more energy per unit of fuel than fission. Fusion of hydrogen nuclei to form helium nuclei is the source of energy in the sun and other stars.

After World War II, the principle of *uncontrolled nuclear fusion* was used to develop extremely powerful hy-drogen, or thermonuclear, bombs and missile warheads. These weapons use the D-T fusion reaction, in which a hydrogen-2, or deuterium (D), nucleus and a hydrogen-3, or tritium (T), nucleus are fused to form a larger, helium-4 nucleus, a neutron, and energy (Figure 3-13).

Scientists have also tried to develop *controlled nuclear fusion*, in which the D-T reaction is used to produce heat that can be converted into electricity. Despite more than 40 years of research, however, this process is still at the laboratory stage. Even if it becomes technologically and economically feasible, it probably won't be a significant source of energy until 2100 or later, if ever.

3-6 The First and Second Laws of Energy

FIRST LAW OF ENERGY: YOU CAN'T GET SOMETHING FOR NOTHING   After making millions of measurements, scientists have observed energy being changed from one form to another in physical and chemical changes, but they have never been able to detect any creation or destruction of energy.

This information is summarized in the **law of conservation of energy**, also known as the **first law of energy** or **first law of thermodynamics**. In physical and chemical changes, no detectable amount of energy is created or destroyed; but in these processes energy can be changed from one form to another. This law does not apply to nuclear changes, where energy can be produced from small amounts of matter. This law means that *energy input always equals energy output: We can't get something for nothing in terms of energy quantity.*

SECOND LAW OF ENERGY: YOU CAN'T BREAK EVEN   Because the first law of energy states that energy can be neither created nor destroyed, you might think that there will always be enough energy; yet, if you fill a car's tank with gasoline and drive around, or if you use a flashlight battery until it is dead, you have lost something. If it isn't energy, what is it? The answer is energy quality (Figure 3-8).

Millions of measurements by scientists have shown that in any conversion of energy from one form to another, there is always a decrease in energy quality or the amount of useful energy. This summary of what we always find occurring in nature is known as the **second law of energy**, or the **second law of thermodynamics**: When energy is changed from one form to another, some of the useful energy is always degraded to lower-quality, more-dispersed, less-useful energy. This degraded energy is usually in the form of heat that flows into the environment and is dispersed in the random

Figure 3-10 The three principal types of ionizing radiation emitted by radioactive isotopes vary considerably in their penetrating power.

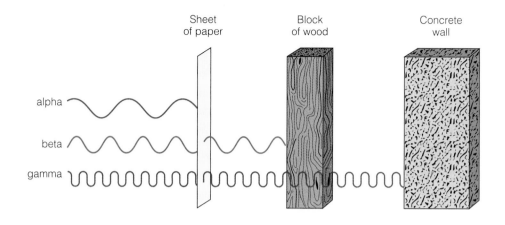

Figure 3-11 Fission of a uranium-235 nucleus by a slow-moving neutron.

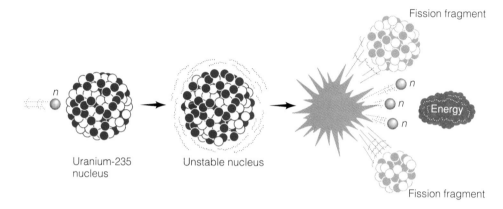

Figure 3-12 A nuclear chain reaction initiated by one neutron triggering fission in a single uranium-235 nucleus. This shows only a few of the trillions of fissions caused when a single uranium-235 nucleus is split within a critical mass of uranium-235 nuclei. The elements shown as the fission fragments produced in this nuclear fission chain reaction are only two of many possibilities.

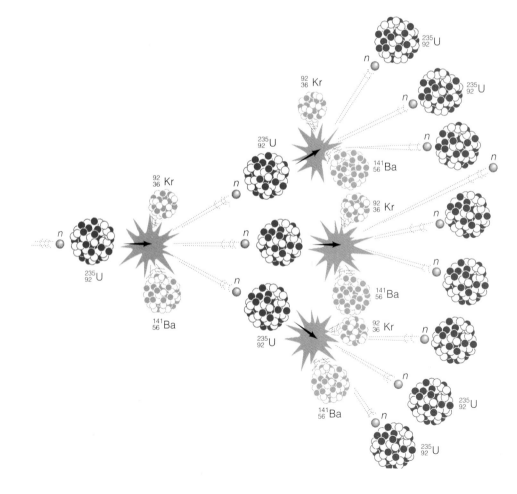

Q: How much of the commercial energy used in the United States is wasted?

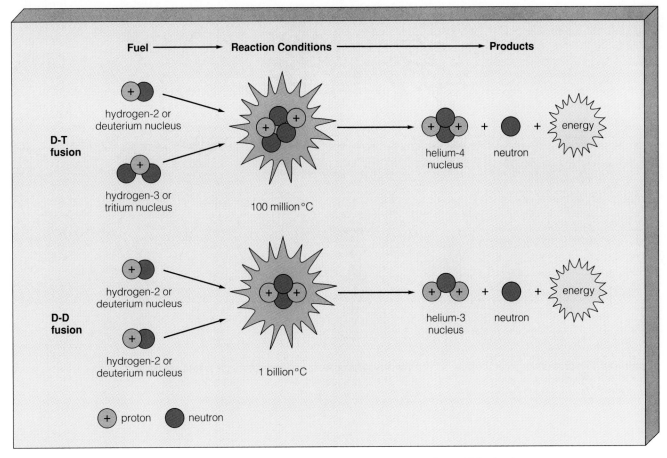

Figure 3-13 The deuterium-tritium (D-T) and deuterium-deuterium (D-D) nuclear fusion reactions, which take place at extremely high temperatures.

motion of air or water molecules at a relatively low temperature.

In other words, according to this law of degradation of energy quality, *we can't break even in terms of energy quality.* The more energy we use, the more disordered low-grade energy (heat) we add to the environment. No one has ever found a violation of this fundamental scientific law.

Consider three examples of the second energy law in action. First, when a car is driven, only about 10% of the high-quality chemical energy available in its gasoline fuel is converted into mechanical energy to propel the vehicle and into electrical energy to run its electrical systems. The remaining 90% is degraded to low-quality heat that is released into the environment and eventually lost into space. Second, when electrical energy flows through filament wires in an incandescent light bulb, it is changed into a mixture of about 5% useful radiant energy, or light, and 95% low-quality heat that flows into the environment. What we call a light bulb is

really a heat bulb. A third example of the degradation of energy quality in living systems is illustrated in Figure 3-14.

The second energy law also means that *we can never recycle or reuse high-quality energy to perform useful work.* Once the concentrated, high-quality energy in a piece of food, a gallon of gasoline, a lump of coal, or a piece of uranium is released, its degraded, low-quality heat becomes dispersed in the environment. We can heat air or water at a low temperature and upgrade it to high-quality energy, but the second energy law tells us that it will take more high-quality energy to do this than we get.

LIFE AND THE SECOND ENERGY LAW Life represents a creation and maintenance of ordered structures. Thus, you might be tempted to think that life is not governed by the second law of thermodynamics.

However, to form and preserve the highly ordered arrangement of molecules and the organized network

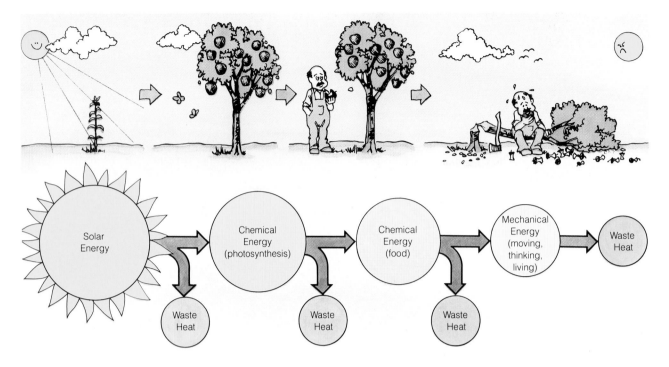

Figure 3-14 The second energy law in action in living systems. When energy is changed from one form to another, some of the initial input of high-quality energy is degraded, usually to low-quality heat, which is added to the environment.

of chemical changes in your body, you must continually get and use high-quality matter resources and energy resources from your surroundings. As you use these resources, you add disordered, low-quality heat and waste matter to your surroundings.

For example, your body continuously gives off heat equal to that of a 100-watt light bulb; this is the reason a closed room full of people gets warm. You also continuously give off molecules of carbon dioxide gas and water vapor, which become dispersed in the atmosphere.

Planting, growing, processing, and cooking the foods you eat all require high-quality energy and matter resources that add low-quality heat and waste materials to the environment. In addition, enormous amounts of low-quality heat and waste matter are added to the environment when concentrated deposits of minerals and fuels are extracted from the earth's crust, processed, and used or burned to heat and cool the buildings you occupy, to transport you, and to make roads, clothes, shelter, and other items you use.

Because of the second energy law, the more energy we use (and waste), the more disorder we create in the environment. This is the reason that reducing energy waste and switching from harmful nonrenewable energy resources to less harmful renewable and perpetual energy resources is the key to a sustainable future for us and other species.

3-7 Energy Efficiency and Net Useful Energy

INCREASING ENERGY EFFICIENCY You may be surprised to learn that only 16% of all commercially produced energy that flows through the U.S. economy performs useful work or is used to make petrochemicals, which are used to produce plastics, medicines, and many other products (Figure 3-15). This means that *84% of all commercial energy used in the United States is wasted*. About 41% of this energy is wasted automatically because of the energy-quality tax (degradation of energy quality) imposed by the second energy law, but 43% of the commercial energy used in the United States is unnecessarily wasted.

One way to cut much of this energy waste and save money is to increase **energy efficiency** (see Guest Essay on p. 58). This is the percentage of total energy input that does useful work and is not converted to low-quality, essentially useless heat in an energy conversion system. The energy conversion devices we use vary considerably in their energy efficiencies (Figure 3-16).

We can save energy and money by buying the most energy-efficient home heating systems, water heaters, cars, air conditioners, refrigerators, and other household appliances available. The initial cost of the most energy-efficient models is usually higher, but in the long

Q: How much of the energy input of an incandescent light bulb is converted to light?

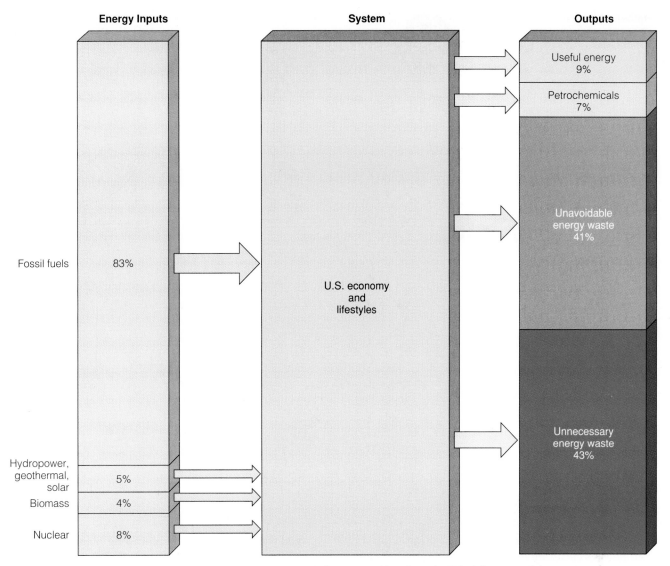

Figure 3-15 Flow of commercial supplemental energy through the U.S. economy. Note that only 16% of all commercial energy used in the United States ends up performing useful tasks or is converted to petrochemicals. The rest either is automatically and unavoidably wasted because of the second law of energy (41%) or is wasted unnecessarily (43%).

run they usually save money by having a lower **life-cycle cost**: the initial cost plus lifetime operating costs.

The net efficiency of the entire energy delivery process of a heating system, water heater, or car is determined by finding the efficiency of each energy conversion step in the process. These steps include extracting the fuel, purifying and upgrading it to a useful form, transporting it, and then using it.

Figure 3-17 shows how net energy efficiencies are determined for heating a well-insulated home (**1**) passively with an input of direct solar energy through windows facing the sun and storing this heat in rocks or water for slow release and (**2**) with electricity produced at a nuclear power plant, transported by wire to the home, and converted to heat (electric resistance heating). This analysis shows that the process of converting

the high-quality nuclear energy in nuclear fuel to high-quality heat at several thousand degrees, converting this heat to high-quality electricity, and then using the electricity to provide low-quality heat for warming a house to only about 20°C (68°F) is extremely wasteful of high-quality energy. Burning coal, or any fossil fuel, at a power plant to supply electricity for space heating is also inefficient. By contrast, it is much less wasteful to use a passive or active solar heating system to obtain low-quality heat from the environment, store it in stone or water, and—if necessary—raise its temperature slightly to supply space heating or to provide household hot water.

Using high-quality electrical energy to provide low-quality heat for heating space or household water is like using a chain saw to cut butter or a sledgehammer to

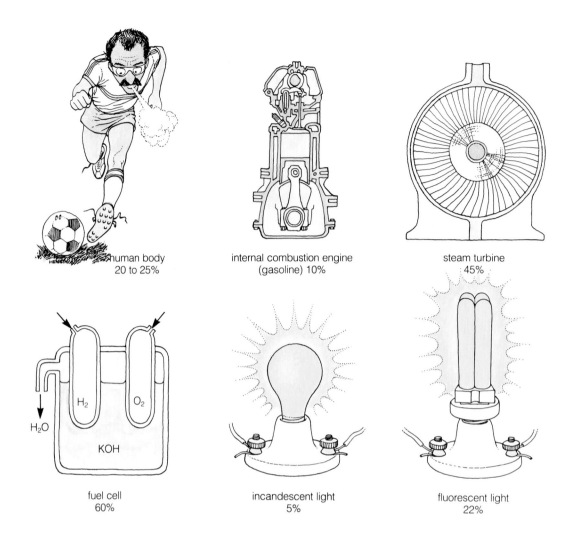

Figure 3-16 Energy efficiency of some common energy conversion devices.

human body
20 to 25%

internal combustion engine
(gasoline) 10%

steam turbine
45%

fuel cell
60%

incandescent light
5%

fluorescent light
22%

kill a fly. A general rule of energy use is the *principle of matching energy quality to energy tasks:* Don't use high-quality energy to do something that can be done with lower-quality energy (Figures 3-8 and 3-9).

Figure 3-18 lists the net energy efficiencies for a variety of space-heating systems. It shows that the two most wasteful (least efficient) and most expensive ways to heat a house are with electricity produced by nuclear power plants and with electricity produced by coal-fired power plants. A heat pump is an efficient way to heat a house as long as the outside temperature does not fall below −15°C (5°F); but when it does, these devices begin using electric resistance heating, the most expensive, energy-wasting way to heat any space. Heat pumps are useful for space heating in areas with warm climates; but in such areas their main use is for air conditioning. The air conditioning units with most heat pumps are much less energy-efficient than many stand-alone units. Most heat pumps also require expensive repair every few years.

A similar analysis of net energy efficiency shows that the least efficient and most expensive way to heat water for washing and bathing is to use electricity produced by nuclear power plants. Indeed, we save money

and waste less energy by not using high-quality electricity produced by any type of power plant to heat water for washing and bathing.

The most efficient method is to use a tankless instant water heater fired by natural gas or liquefied petroleum gas (LPG) (Figure 3-19). Such heaters fit under a sink or in a small closet and burn fuel only when the hot-water faucet is turned on. They heat the water instantly as it flows through a small burner chamber and provide hot water only when, and as long as, it is needed. In contrast, conventional natural gas and electric resistance heaters keep a large tank of water hot all day and night and can run out after a long shower or two. Tankless heaters are widely used in many parts of Europe and are slowly beginning to appear in the United States. A well-insulated, conventional natural gas or LPG water heater is also efficient.

Using electricity to heat space or water by any method is extremely wasteful of energy and money because it involves using high-quality heat produced at a power plant to provide moderate-quality heat (Figure 3-8). In 1990, the average price of obtaining 250,000 kilocalories for heating space or water in the United States was $5.50 using natural gas, $5.55 using kerosene, $6

Q: How much of the energy input of a screw-in fluorescent light bulb produces light?

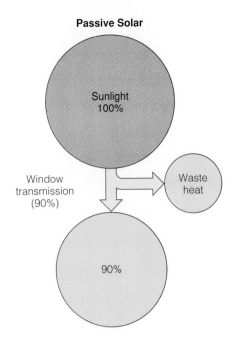

Passive Solar

Sunlight 100%

Window transmission (90%)

Waste heat

90%

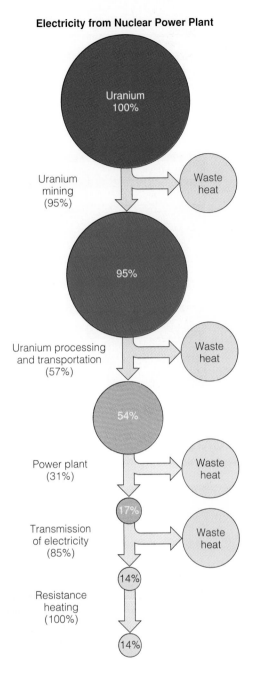

Electricity from Nuclear Power Plant

Uranium 100%

Uranium mining (95%)

Waste heat

95%

Uranium processing and transportation (57%)

Waste heat

54%

Power plant (31%)

Waste heat

17%

Transmission of electricity (85%)

Waste heat

14%

Resistance heating (100%)

14%

Figure 3-17 Comparison of net energy efficiency for two types of space heating. The cumulative net efficiency is obtained by multiplying the percentage shown inside the circle for each step by the energy efficiency for that step (shown in parentheses). Usually, the greater the number of steps in an energy conversion process, the lower its net energy efficiency. With passive solar heating, only about 10% of the incoming solar energy is wasted. By contrast, about 86% of the energy used to provide space heating by electricity produced at a nuclear power plant is wasted.

using fuel oil, $8 using propane, and $23 using electricity. If you like to throw away hard-earned dollars, then use electricity to heat your house and bath water.

If engineers were asked to invent three devices that would waste enormous amounts of energy, they would probably come up with these:

- The incandescent light bulb (which wastes 95% of its energy input)

- A car or truck with an internal combustion engine (which wastes 90% of the energy in its fuel)

- A nuclear power plant producing electricity to heat space or water for washing and bathing (which wastes 86% of the energy in its nuclear fuel; Figure 3-17)

These devices were developed and widely used during a time when energy was cheap and plentiful. As this era draws to a close, we will have to replace or greatly improve the energy efficiency of these and other energy conversion items (see Guest Essay on p. 58).

USING WASTE HEAT We cannot recycle high-quality energy, but we can slow the rate at which waste heat flows into the environment when high-quality energy is degraded. For instance, in cold weather, an uninsulated, leaky house loses heat almost as fast as it is produced. By contrast, a well-insulated, airtight house can retain most of its heat for five to ten hours, and a well-designed, superinsulated house can retain most of its heat up to four days.

A: 22% (over 4 times as much as an incandescent bulb)

Net Energy Efficiency

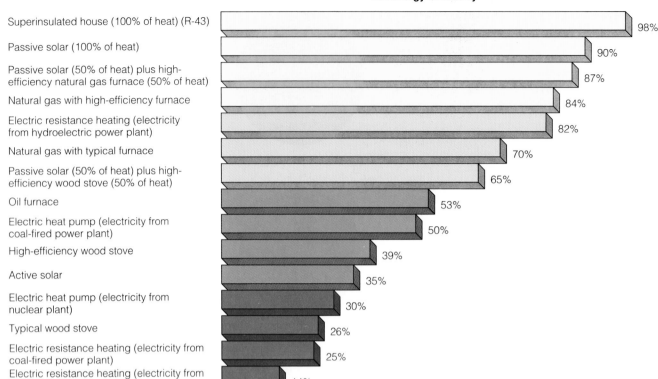

Superinsulated house (100% of heat) (R-43)	98%
Passive solar (100% of heat)	90%
Passive solar (50% of heat) plus high-efficiency natural gas furnace (50% of heat)	87%
Natural gas with high-efficiency furnace	84%
Electric resistance heating (electricity from hydroelectric power plant)	82%
Natural gas with typical furnace	70%
Passive solar (50% of heat) plus high-efficiency wood stove (50% of heat)	65%
Oil furnace	53%
Electric heat pump (electricity from coal-fired power plant)	50%
High-efficiency wood stove	39%
Active solar	35%
Electric heat pump (electricity from nuclear plant)	30%
Typical wood stove	26%
Electric resistance heating (electricity from coal-fired power plant)	25%
Electric resistance heating (electricity from nuclear plant)	14%

Figure 3-18 Net energy efficiencies for various ways to heat an enclosed space such as a house. From this information, we see that the most energy-efficient way to heat space is to build a *superinsulated house*. Such a house is so heavily insulated and airtight that even in areas where winter temperatures fall to − 40°C (− 40°F), all of its space heating can usually be supplied by a combination of passive solar gain (about 59%), waste heat from appliances (33%), and body heat from occupants (8%). Passive solar heating is the next most efficient and next cheapest method of heating a house, followed by one of the new, high-efficiency natural gas furnaces. The most wasteful way to heat an enclosed space is to use electric resistance heating with the electricity provided by coal-burning or nuclear power plants.

Figure 3-19 Two LPG tankless instant water heaters that I use to provide backup hot water and space heating in my office (see Spotlight on p. 409). The unit on the right provides hot water for washing and bathing. Roof-mounted solar collectors (Figure 17-24) preheat water stored in an insulated tank — a discarded conventional water heater wrapped in extra insulation. When I turn on a hot water faucet the solar-heated water flows through the instant heater. If a sensor indicates that the water is below 49°C (120°F), the instant heater comes on to raise the water temperature to that level. About 50% to 60% of my space heat is provided passively by solar energy. The rest is provided by a combination of active solar collectors and the tankless water heater shown on the left. Roof-mounted solar collectors store heat in a well-insulated tank — another discarded conventional water heater wrapped in extra insulation. When the thermostat calls for heat, this solar-heated water is pumped through the instant heater and then through a coil and back to the tank it came from. A fan blows air over the coil and transfers hot air through heating ducts, as with a conventional forced-air space-heating system. Any heat not extracted from the hot water by the coil is returned to the insulated tank for reuse in this closed-loop system.

Evan Kruppenbach

Q: How much of the energy in gasoline is used to move a motor vehicle powered by an internal combustion engine?

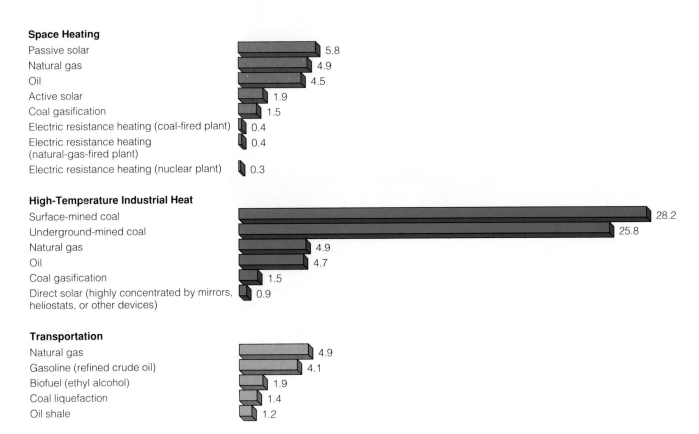

Figure 3-20 Net useful energy ratios for various energy systems over their estimated lifetimes. (Data from Colorado Energy Research Institute, *Net Energy Analysis*, 1976, and Howard T. Odum and Elisabeth C. Odum, *Energy Basis for Man and Nature*, 3rd ed., New York: McGraw-Hill, 1981)

In some office buildings and stores, waste heat from lights, computers, and other machines is collected and distributed to reduce heating bills during cold weather and is exhausted to reduce cooling bills during hot weather. Waste heat from industrial plants and electric power plants can be distributed through insulated pipes and used as a district heating system for nearby buildings, greenhouses, and fish ponds, as is done in some parts of Europe.

Another way to use waste heat produced by industrial plants burning coal or other fuels to produce heat or steam is **cogeneration**, the production of two useful forms of energy such as steam and electricity from the same fuel source. Waste heat from coal-fired and other industrial boilers can be used to produce steam to spin turbines and generate electricity at half the cost of buying it from a utility company. The electricity can be used by the plant or sold to the local power company for general use. Cogeneration is used in many industrial plants throughout Europe. If all large industrial boilers in the United States used cogeneration, there would be no need to build any electric power plants through the year 2020.

NET USEFUL ENERGY: IT TAKES ENERGY TO GET ENERGY The usable amount of high-quality energy obtainable from a given quantity of an energy resource is its **net useful energy**. It is the total useful energy available from the resource over its lifetime minus the amount of energy used (the first energy law), automatically wasted (the second energy law), and unnecessarily wasted in finding, processing, concentrating, and transporting it to users. For example, if 9 units of fossil fuel energy are needed to supply 10 units of nuclear, solar, or additional fossil fuel energy (perhaps from a deep well at sea), the net useful energy gain is only 1 unit of energy.

We can express this relationship as the ratio of useful energy produced to the useful energy used to produce it. In the example just given, the net energy ratio would be 10/9, or 1.1. The higher the ratio, the greater the net useful energy yield. When the ratio is less than 1, there is a net energy loss over the lifetime of the system. Figure 3-20 lists estimated net useful energy ratios for various alternatives to space heating, high-temperature heat for industrial processes, and gaseous and liquid fuels for vehicles.

Currently, oil has a relatively high net useful energy ratio because much of it comes from large, accessible deposits such as those in Saudi Arabia and other parts of the Middle East. When those sources are depleted, however, the net useful energy ratio of oil will decline and prices will rise. Then more money and high-quality fossil fuel will be needed to find, process, and deliver

A: About 10% (the other 90% is given off to the environment as waste heat)

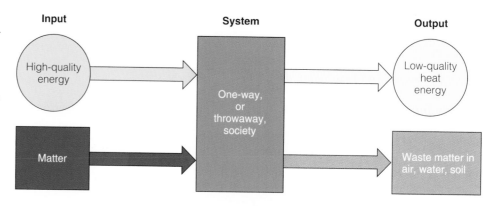

Figure 3-21 The one-way, or throwaway, society of most industrialized countries is based on maximizing the rates of energy flow and matter flow, rapidly converting the world's high-quality matter and energy resources into trash, pollution, and low-quality heat.

new oil from widely dispersed small deposits and deposits found deeper in the earth's crust and in remote, hostile areas like Alaska, the Arctic, and the North Sea—far from where the energy is to be used.

Conventional nuclear fission energy has a low net energy ratio because large amounts of energy are required to extract and process uranium ore, to convert it into a usable nuclear fuel, and to build and operate power plants. Additional energy is needed to take nuclear plants apart after their 25 to 30 years of useful life and to store the resulting highly radioactive wastes for thousands of years.

3-8 Matter and Energy Laws and Environmental and Resource Problems

THROWAWAY SOCIETIES Because of the law of conservation of matter and the second law of energy, resource use by each of us automatically adds some waste heat and waste matter to the environment. Your individual use of matter and energy resources and your addition of waste heat and waste matter to the environment may seem small and insignificant. But you are only one of the 1.2 billion individuals in industrialized countries using large quantities of Earth's matter and energy resources at a rapid rate. Meanwhile, the 4.2 billion people in less developed countries hope to be able to use more of these resources. Each year there are 92 million more users of Earth's energy and matter resources.

Today's advanced industrialized countries are **throwaway societies**, sustaining ever-increasing economic growth by maximizing the rate at which matter and energy resources are used and wasted (Figure 3-21). The scientific laws of matter and energy tell us that if more and more people continue to use and waste more and more energy and matter resources at an increasing rate, sooner or later the capacity of the local, regional, and global environments to dilute and degrade waste matter and absorb waste heat will be exceeded.

MATTER-RECYCLING SOCIETIES A stopgap solution to this problem is to convert from a throwaway society to a **matter-recycling society**. The goal of such a shift would be to allow economic growth to continue without depleting matter resources and without producing excessive pollution and environmental degradation. As we have learned, however, there is no free lunch when it comes to energy.

The two laws of energy tell us that *recycling matter resources always requires high-quality energy, which cannot be recycled*. In the long run, a matter-recycling society based on indefinitely increasing economic growth must have an inexhaustible supply of affordable high-quality energy. The environment must also have an infinite capacity to absorb and disperse waste heat and to dilute and degrade waste matter. There is also usually a physical limit to the number of times a material, such as paper fiber, can be recycled before it becomes unusable.

Shifting from a throwaway society to a matter-recycling society is only a temporary solution to our problems in a world built on the goal of ever-increasing economic growth. We should recognize that the main purpose of the shift to a matter-recycling society is to give us more time to shift to a sustainable-Earth society.

Experts disagree on how much high-quality energy we have, mostly in the form of fossil and nuclear fuels. However, supplies of coal, oil, natural gas, and uranium are clearly finite. Affordable supplies of oil, the most widely used supplementary energy resource, may be used up in several decades.

"Ah," you say, "but don't we have a virtually inexhaustible supply of solar energy flowing to Earth?" The problem is that the amount of solar energy reaching a particular small area of the earth's surface each minute or hour is low, and it is nonexistent at night.

With a proper collection and storage system, using passive and active systems to concentrate solar energy

Q: What is the most inefficient and costly way to produce electricity for heating water or an interior space?

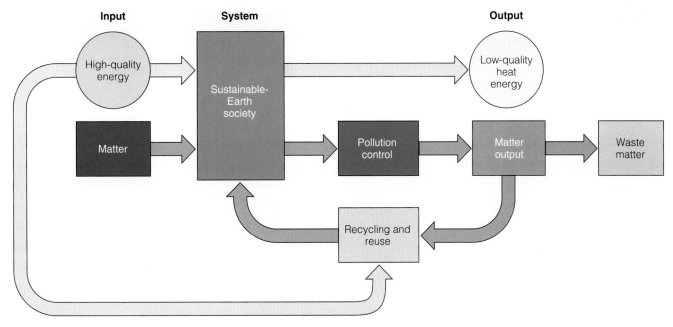

Figure 3-22 A sustainable-Earth society, based on energy flow and matter recycling, reuses and recycles renewable matter resources, wastes less matter and energy, reduces unnecessary consumption, emphasizes pollution prevention and waste reduction, and controls population growth.

slightly to provide hot water and to heat a house to moderate temperatures makes good thermodynamic and economic sense. But to provide the high temperatures needed to melt metals or to produce electricity in a power plant, solar energy may not be cost-effective. Why? Because it has a very low net useful energy ratio (Figure 3-20). It takes a lot of energy to concentrate and raise its quality to a high level.

Suppose that affordable solar cells, nuclear fusion at room temperature, or some other breakthrough were to supply an essentially infinite supply of affordable useful energy. Would that solve our environmental and resource problems? No!

Such a breakthrough would be important and useful. However, the second energy law tells us that the faster we use more energy to transform more matter into products and to recycle those products, the faster large amounts of low-quality heat and waste matter are dumped into the environment. Thus, the more we attempt to "conquer" Earth, the more stress we put on the environment. Experts argue over how close we are to reaching overload limits, but the scientific laws of matter and energy indicate that such limits do exist.

SUSTAINABLE-EARTH SOCIETIES The three scientific laws governing matter and energy changes indicate that the best long-term solution to our environmental and resource problems is to shift from a throwaway society, based on maximizing matter and energy flow (and, in the process, wasting an unnecessarily large portion of Earth's natural resources), to a **sustainable-Earth society** (Figure 3-22).

A sustainable-Earth society would do the following:

- Use energy more efficiently and not use high-quality energy to do things that require moderate-quality energy (Figure 3-9). This is an important first step that buys us time, saves us money, and reduces pollution. Unless we stop population growth and lower the rate at which we use matter and energy resources, however, we'll eventually be back where we started as long as more people use more energy.

- Shift from exhaustible and potentially polluting fossil and nuclear fuels to less harmful perpetual and renewable energy obtained from the sun and from Earth's natural cycles and flows.

- Recycle and reuse most (at least 80%) of the matter we now discard as trash.

- Reduce use and waste of matter resources by making things that last longer and are easier to recycle, reuse, and repair. Our lifestyle motto should be: *Throwaway no, recycle yes, reuse is better, and reduced use is best.*

- Bring human population growth to a halt to reduce stress on Earth's life-support systems.

- Emphasize pollution prevention and waste reduction instead of pollution cleanup and waste management.

Amory B. Lovins

Physicist and energy consultant Amory B. Lovins is one of the world's most recognized and articulate experts on energy strategy. In 1989 he was the first recipient of the Delphi Prize for environmental work; in 1990, the Wall Street Journal *named him as one of the 39 people in the world most likely to change the course of business in the 1990s. He is director of research at Rocky Mountain Institute in Old Snowmass, Colorado, a nonprofit resource policy center, which he and his wife, Hunter, founded in 1982. He has served as a consultant to 190 utilities, private industries, and international organizations and to many national, state, and local governments. He is active in energy affairs in 31 countries and has published several hundred papers and a dozen books, including* Soft Energy Paths *(New York: Harper Colophon, 1979) and the nontechnical version of that work with senior coauthor L. Hunter Lovins,* Energy Unbound: Your Invitation to Energy Abundance *(San Francisco: Sierra Club Books, 1986).*

The answers you get depend on the questions you ask. But sometimes it seems so important to resolve a crisis that we forget to ask what problem we're trying to solve.

It is fashionable to suppose that we're running out of energy and that the solution is obviously to get lots more of it. But asking how to get more energy begs the question of how much we need. That depends not on how much we used in the past but on what we want to do in the future and how much energy it will take to do those things.

How much energy it takes to make steel, run a sewing machine, or keep you comfortable in your house depends on how cleverly we use energy; and the more it costs, the smarter we seem to get. It is now cheaper, for example, to double the efficiency of most industrial electric motor drive systems than to fuel existing power plants to make electricity. (Just this one saving can more than replace the entire U.S. nuclear power program.) We know how to make lights five times as efficient as those presently in use and how to make household appliances that give us the same work as now, using one-fifth as much energy (saving money in the process).

Ten automakers have made good-sized, peppy, safe prototype cars averaging 29 to 59 kilometers per liter (62 to 138 miles per gallon). We know today how to make new buildings and many old ones so heat-tight (but still well ventilated) that they need essentially no energy to maintain comfort year-round, even in severe climates. (In fact, I live in one.)

These energy-saving measures are uniformly cheaper than going out and getting more energy. Detailed studies in more than a dozen countries have shown that supplying energy services in the cheapest way — by wringing more work from the energy we already have — would let us increase our standard of living while using several times less total energy (and electricity) than we do now. Those savings cost less than finding new domestic oil or operating existing power plants.

However, the old view of the energy problem included a worse mistake than forgetting to ask how much energy we needed: It sought more energy, in any form, from any source, at any price — as if all kinds of energy were alike. This is like saying, "All kinds of food are alike; we're running short of potatoes and turnips and cheese, but that's okay; we can substitute sirloin steak and oysters Rockefeller."

Some of us have to be more discriminating than that. Just as there are different kinds of food, so there are many different forms of energy, whose different prices and qualities suit them to different uses [Figure 3-8]. There is, after all, no demand for energy as such; nobody wants raw kilowatt-hours or barrels of sticky black goo. People instead want energy services: comfort, light, mobility, ability to bake bread, ability to make cement, hot showers, and cold beverages. We ought therefore to start at that end of the energy problem and ask, "What are the many different tasks we want energy for, and what is the amount, type, and source of energy that will do each task most cheaply?"

Electricity is a particularly special, high-quality, expensive form of energy. An average kilowatt-hour delivered in the United States in 1991 was priced at about 7¢, equivalent to buying the heat content of oil costing $116 per barrel — more than six times the average world price in 1991. The average cost of electricity from nuclear plants (including fuel and operating expenses) beginning operation in 1988 was 13.5¢ per kilowatt-hour, equivalent on a heat basis to buying oil at about $216 per barrel.

Such costly energy might be worthwhile if it were used only for the premium tasks that require it, such as lights, motors, electronics, and smelters. But those special uses, only 8% of all delivered U.S. energy needs, are already met twice over by today's power stations. Two-fifths of our electricity is already spilling over into uneconomic, low-grade uses such as water heating, space heating, and air conditioning; yet no matter how efficiently we use electricity (even with heat pumps), we can never get our money's worth on these applications.

Q: What are the two most energy-efficient ways to heat interior space?

Thus, *supplying more electricity is irrelevant to the energy problem that we have*. Even though electricity accounts for almost all of the federal energy research and development budget and for at least half of national energy investment, it is the wrong kind of energy to meet our needs economically. Arguing about what kind of new power station to build — coal, nuclear, solar — is like shopping for the best buy in antique Chippendale chairs to burn in your stove or brandy to put in your car's gas tank. *It is the wrong question*.

Indeed, *any kind of new power station is so uneconomical that if you have just built one, you will save the country money by writing it off and never operating it*. Why? Because its additional electricity can be used only for low-temperature heating and cooling (the premium "electricity-specific" uses being already filled up) and is the most expensive way of supplying those services. Saving electricity is much cheaper than making it.

The real question is, What is the cheapest way to do low-temperature heating and cooling? The answer is weatherstripping, insulation, heat exchangers, greenhouses, superwindows (which have as much insulating value as an outside wall of a typical house), window shades and overhangs, trees, and so on. These measures generally cost about half a penny per kilowatt-hour; the running costs *alone* for a new nuclear plant will be nearly 4¢ per kilowatt-hour, so it's cheaper not to run it. In fact, under the crazy U.S. tax laws, the extra saving from not having to pay the plant's future subsidies is probably so big that by shutting the plant down society can also recover the capital cost of having built it!

If we want more electricity, we should get it from the cheapest sources first. In approximate order of increasing price, these include:

1. Converting to efficient lighting equipment. This would save the United States electricity equal to the output of 120 large power plants plus $30 billion a year in fuel and maintenance costs.

2. Using more efficient motors to save half the energy used by motor systems. This would save electricity equal to the output of another 150 large power plants and repay the cost in about a year.

3. Eliminating pure waste of electricity, such as lighting empty offices at headache level. Each kilowatt-hour saved can be resold without having to generate it anew.

4. Displacing with good architecture, and with passive and some active solar techniques, the electricity now used for water heating and space heating and cooling. Some U.S. utilities now give low- or zero-interest weatherization loans, which you need not start repaying for ten years or until you sell your house — because it saves the utility millions of dollars to have available the electricity you don't use instead of building new power plants. Most utilities also offer rebates for buying efficient appliances.

5. Making appliances, smelters, and the like cost-effectively efficient.

Just these five measures can quadruple U.S. electrical efficiency, making it possible to run today's economy, with no changes in lifestyles, using no thermal power plants, whether old or new and whether fueled with oil, gas, coal, or uranium. We would need only the present hydroelectric capacity, readily available small-scale hydroelectric projects, and a modest amount of wind power. If we still wanted more electricity, the next cheapest sources would include:

6. Industrial cogeneration, combined-heat-and-power plants, low-temperature heat engines run by industrial waste heat or by solar ponds, filling empty turbine bays and upgrading equipment in existing big dams, modern wind machines or small-scale hydroelectric turbines in good sites, steam-injected natural gas turbines, and perhaps recent developments in solar cells with waste heat recovery.

It is only after we had clearly exhausted all these cheaper opportunities that we would even consider:

7. Building a new central power station of any kind — the slowest and costliest known way to get more electricity (or to save oil).

To emphasize the importance of starting with energy end uses rather than energy sources, consider a sad little story from France, involving a "spaghetti chart" (or energy flowchart) — a device energy planners often use to show how energy flows from primary sources via conversion processes to final forms and uses. In the mid-1970s, energy conservation planners in the French government started, wisely, on the right-hand side of the spaghetti chart. They found that their biggest need for energy was to heat buildings; and that even with good heat pumps, electricity would be the least economical way to do this. So they had a fight with their nationalized utility; they won, and electric heating was supposed to be discouraged or even phased out because it was so wasteful of money and fuel.

Meanwhile, down the street, the energy supply planners (who were far more numerous and influential in the French government) were starting on the left-hand side of the spaghetti chart. They said: "Look at all that nasty imported oil coming into our country! We must replace that oil. Oil is energy. . . . We need some other source of energy. Voilà! Reactors can give us energy; we'll build nuclear reactors all over the country." But they paid little attention to what would happen to that extra energy and no attention to relative prices.

Thus, the two sides of the French energy establishment went on with their respective solutions to two different, indeed contradictory, French energy problems: *more energy of any kind* versus *the right kind to do each task in*

(continued)

the most inexpensive way. It was only in 1979 that these conflicting perceptions collided. The supply side planners suddenly realized that the only thing they would be able to *sell* all that nuclear electricity for would be electric heating, which they had just agreed not to do.

Every industrial country is in this embarrassing position (especially if we include as "heating" air conditioning, which just means heating the outdoors instead of the indoors). Which end of the spaghetti chart we start on, or *what we think the energy problem is*, is not an academic abstraction: *It determines what we buy*. It is the most fundamental source of disagreement about energy policy.

People starting on the left side of the spaghetti chart think the problem boils down to whether to build coal or nuclear power stations (or both). People starting on the right realize that *no* kind of new power station can be an economic way to meet the needs for low- and high-temperature heat and for vehicular liquid fuels that are 92% of our energy problem.

So if we want to provide our energy services at a price we can afford, let's get straight what question our technologies are supposed to provide the answer to. Before we argue about the meatballs, let's untangle the strands of spaghetti, see where they're supposed to lead, and find out what we really need the energy *for*!

Guest Essay Discussion

1. The author argues that building more nuclear, coal, or other electrical power plants to supply electricity for the United States is unnecessary and wasteful. Summarize the reasons for this conclusion, and give your reasons for agreeing or disagreeing with this viewpoint.

2. Do you agree or disagree that increasing the supply of energy, instead of concentrating on improving energy efficiency, is the wrong answer to U.S. energy problems? Explain.

Because of the three basic scientific laws of matter and energy, we are all dependent on each other and on the other living and nonliving parts of nature for our survival. Everything is connected to everything else, and we are all in it together. In the next chapter, we will apply these laws to living systems and look at some biological principles that can teach us how to work with the rest of nature.

The second law of thermodynamics holds, I think, the supreme position among laws of nature. . . . If your theory is found to be against the second law of thermodynamics, I can give you no hope.

ARTHUR S. EDDINGTON

DISCUSSION TOPICS

1. Explain why we don't really consume anything and why we can never really throw matter away.

2. A tree grows and increases its mass. Explain why this isn't a violation of the law of conservation of matter.

3. If there is no "away," why isn't the world filled with waste matter?

4. Use the second energy law to explain why a barrel of oil can be used only once as a fuel.

5. Explain why most energy analysts urge that the basis of any individual, corporate, or national energy plan should be improved energy efficiency. Is it an important part of your personal energy plan or lifestyle? Why or why not?

6. Explain why using electricity to heat a house and to supply household hot water by resistance heating is expensive and wasteful of energy. What energy tasks can be done best by electricity?

7. **a.** Use the law of conservation of matter to explain why a matter-recycling society will sooner or later be necessary.
   b. Use the first and second laws of energy to explain why, in the long run, a sustainable-Earth society, not just a matter-recycling society, will be necessary.

*8. You are about to build a house. What energy supply (oil, gas, coal, or other) would you use for space heating, cooking food, refrigerating food, and heating water? Consider the long-term economic and environmental impact. Would you decide differently if you planned to live in the house for only 5 years instead of 25 years? If so, how?

CHAPTER 4

ECOSYSTEMS: WHAT ARE THEY AND HOW DO THEY WORK?

General Questions and Issues

1. What fundamental natural processes keep us and other organisms alive?

2. What is an ecosystem, and what are its major living and nonliving components?

3. What happens to energy in an ecosystem?

4. What happens to matter in an ecosystem?

5. What roles do different organisms play in an ecosystem, and how do organisms interact?

If we love our children, we must love the earth with tender care and pass it on, diverse and beautiful, so that on a warm spring day 10,000 years hence they can feel peace in a sea of grass, can watch a bee visit a flower, can hear a sandpiper call in the sky, and can find joy in being alive.

HUGH H. ILTIS

WHAT ORGANISMS LIVE in a field or a pond? How do they get enough matter and energy resources to stay alive? How do these organisms interact with one another and with their physical and chemical environment? What changes might this field or pond undergo through time?

Ecology is the science that attempts to answer such questions about how nature works. **Ecology** is the study of how organisms interact with one another and with their nonliving environment of energy and matter (Figure 4-1). Scientists usually carry out this study by examining different **ecosystems**: communities with groups of different species interacting with one another and with their nonliving physical and chemical environment.

This chapter will consider the principal nonliving and living components of ecosystems and how they interact. The next chapter will consider principal types of life zones and ecosystems and the changes they can undergo because of natural events and human activities.

4-1 Earth's Life-Support Systems: An Overview

THE BIOSPHERE AND THE ECOSPHERE Several important, interacting parts play a role in sustaining life on Earth (Figure 4-2). You are part of what ecologists call the **biosphere**—the entire realm where life is found. It is a relatively thin, 20-kilometer (12-mile) zone of life extending from the deepest ocean floor to the tops of the highest mountains.

Figure 4-1 Ecology is a study of how organisms interact with other living things and with nonliving things such as sunlight, air, water, and soil. This arctic fox, with its winter coat that helps hide it in the snow, and other animals depend on sunlight, water, plants, and decomposers (mostly bacteria and fungi) for their survival. When the snow melts during the brief arctic summer, the fox's coat turns brown so it can blend into its environment.

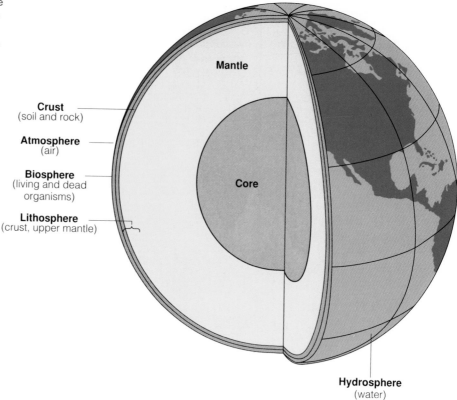

Figure 4-2 Our life-support system: the general structure of the earth. The atmosphere is composed of several layers. The innermost is called the *troposphere*, and the second layer is known as the *stratosphere*.

Earth's collection of living organisms (found in the biosphere) interacting with one another and their non-living environment (energy and matter) throughout the world is called the **ecosphere**.* If Earth were an apple, the ecosphere would be no thicker than the apple's skin, existing between the molten heat of Earth's interior and the lifeless cold of space. *The goal of ecology is to learn how this thin global skin of air, water, soil, and organisms works and how it sustains itself.*

ENERGY FLOW AND MATTER CYCLING Life on Earth depends largely on two fundamental processes (Figure 4-3):

- The *one-way flow of high-quality (usable) energy* from the sun, through materials and living things on or near the earth's surface, then into the environment (mostly as low-quality heat dispersed into air or water molecules at a low temperature), and eventually into space as infrared radiation

- The *cycling of matter* required by living organisms through parts of the ecosphere

THE SUN: SOURCE OF ENERGY FOR LIFE The source of the energy that sustains life on Earth is the sun. It lights and warms Earth and supplies the energy used by green plants and some bacteria to synthesize the compounds that keep them alive and serve as food for almost all other organisms. Solar energy also powers the recycling of key forms of matter and drives the climate and weather systems that distribute heat and fresh water over Earth's surface.

The sun is a gigantic fireball composed mostly of hydrogen (72%) and helium (28%) gases. Temperatures and pressures in its inner core are high enough that the hydrogen nuclei found there undergo nuclear fusion to form helium nuclei (Figure 3-13) and constantly release enormous amounts of energy.

This gigantic, faraway nuclear fusion reactor radiates energy into space as a spectrum of electromagnetic radiation (Figure 3-4). These forms of radiant energy travel outward in all directions through space and make the 150-million-kilometer (93-million-mile) trip to Earth in about 8 minutes.

About 34% of the solar energy reaching the lower atmosphere (troposphere) is immediately reflected back to space by clouds, chemicals, and dust and by the earth's surface of land and water (Figure 4-4). Most of

---

*Many sources use the term *biosphere* in this way. I use the term *biosphere* to indicate where Earth's life is found and the term *ecosphere* to represent the interaction of the biosphere (life) with the energy and matter in the surrounding nonliving environment.

Q: What is the most energy-efficient fuel for powering a motor vehicle?

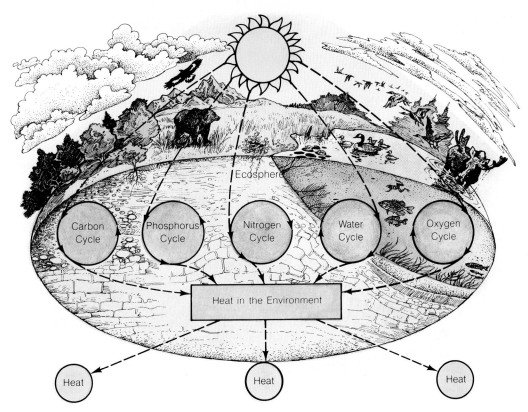

Figure 4-3 Life on Earth depends on the cycling of critical elements (solid lines around the circles) and the one-way flow of energy from the sun through the ecosphere (dashed lines). This greatly simplified overview shows only a few of the many elements that are recycled.

Ecosphere

Carbon Cycle

Phosphorus Cycle

Nitrogen Cycle

Water Cycle

Oxygen Cycle

Heat in the Environment

Heat

Heat

Heat

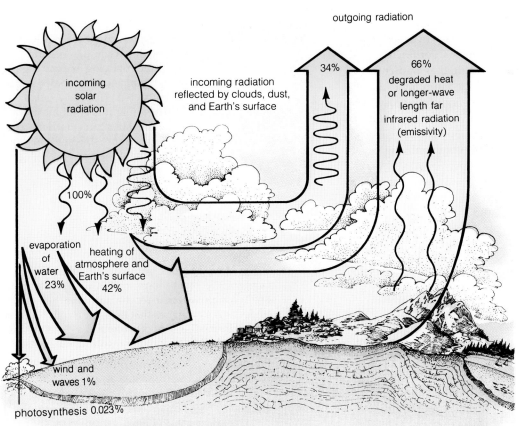

Figure 4-4 The flow of energy to and from Earth.

outgoing radiation

incoming solar radiation

incoming radiation reflected by clouds, dust, and Earth's surface

34%

66% degraded heat or longer-wave length far infrared radiation (emissivity)

100%

evaporation of water 23%

heating of atmosphere and Earth's surface 42%

wind and waves 1%

photosynthesis 0.023%

the remaining 66% warms the troposphere and land, evaporates water and cycles it through the ecosphere, and generates winds. A tiny fraction (0.023%) is captured mostly by green plants and by some bacteria and is used in the process of photosynthesis to make organic compounds that plants and the organisms that feed on them need to survive.

Most of the 66% of solar radiation not reflected away is degraded into lower-quality infrared radiation (which we experience as heat) as it interacts with the earth (Figure 4-4). The rate at which this heat flows through the atmosphere and eventually into space is affected by the presence of heat-trapping gases, such as water vapor, carbon dioxide, methane, nitrous oxide, and ozone.

Our activities add large quantities of carbon dioxide and several other heat-trapping gases to the troposphere. Computer models of Earth's climate systems suggest that this enhancement of Earth's natural greenhouse effect could alter the planet's climate patterns, disrupt food growing patterns and wildlife habitats, and possibly raise average sea levels.

BIOGEOCHEMICAL CYCLES Any element an organism needs to live, grow, and reproduce is called a **nutrient**. About 40 elements are essential to organisms, although the number and types of these elements can vary with different organisms. These nutrient elements are usually found in various compounds.

Most of Earth's chemicals do not occur in forms useful to the planet's living organisms. Fortunately, elements and their compounds required as nutrients for life on Earth are continuously cycled in complex paths through the living and nonliving parts of the ecosphere and converted into useful forms by a combination of biological, geological, and chemical processes.

This cycling of nutrients from the nonliving environment (reservoirs in the atmosphere, the hydrosphere, and Earth's crust) to living organisms, and back to the nonliving environment, takes place in **biogeochemical cycles** (*bio* standing for "life," *geo* for "earth," and *chemical* for the changing forms of matter in the cycle). These cycles, driven directly or indirectly by incoming energy from the sun, include the carbon, oxygen, nitrogen, phosphorus, sulfur, and hydrologic (water) cycles (Figure 4-3).

Thus, a chemical may be part of an organism at one moment and part of the organism's environment at another moment. For example, one of the oxygen molecules you just inhaled may be one inhaled previously by you or your grandmother, by King Tut thousands of years ago, or by a dinosaur millions of years ago. Similarly, some of the carbon atoms in the skin covering your right hand may once have been part of a leaf, a dinosaur skin, or a layer of limestone rock.

<table>
<tr><td>4-2</td><td>

Ecosystems: Types and Components

</td></tr>
</table>

THE REALM OF ECOLOGY Ecology is concerned primarily with interactions among five of the levels of organization of matter shown in Figure 3-1: organisms, populations, communities, ecosystems, and the ecosphere. An **organism** is any form of life. All organisms are classified into species that make up the planet's biodiversity (see Spotlight on p. 8).

The smallest living unit of an organism is the **cell**. All cells are encased in an outer membrane or wall. Each cell contains genetic material in the form of DNA and other components that perform specialized functions necessary for life. Organisms such as bacteria consist of only one cell, but most organisms contain many cells.

Cells are classified as eukaryotic or prokaryotic on the basis of their internal structure. All cells, except bacteria, are **eukaryotic**. They have a *nucleus*, a region of genetic material surrounded by a membrane. Membranes also enclose several other internal parts of a eukaryotic cell. Bacterial cells are said to be **prokaryotic** because they don't have a distinct nucleus. Other internal parts are also not enclosed by membranes.

In this book, Earth's organisms are classified into five major kingdoms:

- **Bacteria** are prokaryotic, single-cell organisms. Many are **decomposers**, which get the nutrients they need by breaking down complex organic compounds in the tissues of living or dead organisms into simpler, inorganic nutrient compounds. Others, such as cyanobacteria (formerly called blue-green algae), use sunlight to combine inorganic chemicals to make the organic nutrient compounds they need (*photosynthesis*). Some combine inorganic chemicals without the presence of light to make the organic nutrients they need (*chemosynthesis*).

- **Protists** are eukaryotic, mostly single-cell organisms such as diatoms, amoebas, some algae (golden brown and yellow-green), protozoans, and slime molds.

- **Fungi** are eukaryotic, mostly multicelled organisms such as mushrooms, molds, and yeasts. They are decomposers that get the nutrients they need by secreting enzymes that break down the organic matter in the tissue of other living or dead organisms. Then they absorb the resulting nutrients.

- **Plants** are eukaryotic, mostly multicelled organisms such as algae (red, blue, and green), mosses, ferns, flowers, cacti, grasses, beans, wheat, rice, and trees. These organisms use photosynthesis to produce organic nutrients for themselves and for other organisms feeding on them. Water and other

Q: What percentage of the matter thrown away as trash could be recycled and reused?

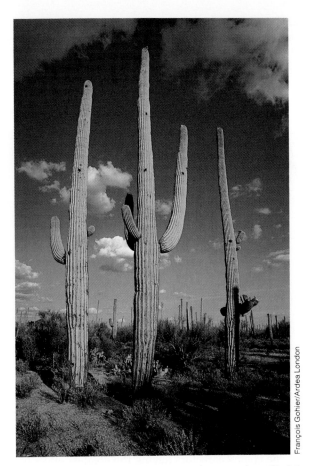

Figure 4-5 These saguaro (pronounced sa-*wa*-ro) cacti in Arizona are succulent green plants that store water and produce food in the fleshy tissue of their stems and branches. They reduce water loss in the hot desert climate by having no leaves and by having pores (stomata) that open only at night. Their thorns help keep predators away.

Figure 4-6 This peacock, exhibiting its courtship display, is a vertebrate because it has a backbone. This display can also be used to scare off predators.

Figure 4-7 This cobalt blue sea star found on a barrier coral reef in Indonesia has no backbone and is classified as an invertebrate. Other invertebrates are insects, crabs, jellyfish, sponges, and mollusks.

inorganic nutrients are obtained from the soil for terrestrial plants and from the water for aquatic plants. Some plants are **evergreens**, which retain some of their leaves or needles throughout the year. Examples are ferns, tall broadleaf trees that thrive in warm-moist rain forests, and cone-bearing trees (conifers) such as firs, spruces, pines, redwoods, and sequoias. **Deciduous plants**, such as oak and maple trees, survive during dry seasons or cold seasons by shedding their leaves. **Succulent plants**, such as desert cacti (Figure 4-5), survive in dry climates by having no leaves, thus reducing the loss of scarce water. They store water and use sunlight to produce the food they need in the thick fleshy tissue of their green stems and branches.

■ **Animals** are eukaryotic, multicelled organisms such as sponges, jellyfish, arthropods (insects,

shrimp, lobsters), mollusks (snails, clams, oysters, octopuses), fish, amphibians (frogs, toads, salamanders), reptiles (turtles, lizards, alligators, crocodiles, snakes), birds, and mammals (kangaroos, bats, cats, rabbits, elephants, whales, porpoises, monkeys, apes, humans). They get their organic nutrients by feeding on plants (**herbivores**), other animals (**carnivores**), or both (**omnivores**). Some animals, called **vertebrates**, have backbones (Figure 4-6), and others, called **invertebrates**, have no backbones (Figure 4-7). Some are cold-blooded (invertebrates, fish, amphibians, and reptiles), and others have warm blood (birds and mammals).

A **population** is a group of individuals of the same species occupying a given area at the same time (Figure 4-8). The place where a population (or an individual organism) lives is its **habitat**. Examples of populations

Figure 4-8 Population of monarch butterflies hibernating during winter in Michoacán, Mexico.

Frans Lanting/Bruce Coleman Ltd.

are all sunfish in a pond, gray squirrels in a forest, white oak trees in a forest, people in a country, or people in the world.

Populations of all species occupying a particular place make up what is called a **community** or **biological community**. What constitutes a community depends on the size of the place on which we wish to focus. For example, we could study an entire forest, a patch of the forest, or a single tree or log as a community.

An **ecosystem** is a community of different species interacting with one another and with the chemical and physical factors making up its nonliving environment. An ecosystem is an ever-changing (dynamic) network of biological, chemical, and physical interactions that sustain a community and allow it to respond to changes in environmental conditions. Like that of a community, the size of an ecosystem is arbitrary and is defined in terms of what system we wish to study. All of Earth's ecosystems together make up the **ecosphere**.

Climate—the general patterns of weather conditions, seasonal variations, and weather extremes of an area over a long time—is the primary factor determining the types and abundance of life, especially plants, found in a particular land area. Biologists have divided the terrestrial portion of the biosphere into **biomes**, large ecological regions inhabited by certain types of life, especially vegetation (Figure 4-9).* Examples of these large-scale vegetational zones are forests, deserts, and grasslands.

Each biome consists of large numbers of ecosystems whose communities have adapted to smaller differences in climate, soil, and other environmental factors within the biome. Marine and freshwater portions of the biosphere can also be divided into life zones, each made up of numerous ecosystems. Principal terrestrial

---

*Some sources call biomes major terrestrial ecosystems, but most classify them as large life or vegetation zones made up of many different smaller ecosystems.

and aquatic life zones and ecosystems are discussed in more detail in Chapter 5.

ABIOTIC COMPONENTS OF ECOSYSTEMS Ecosystems consist of various nonliving (abiotic) and living (biotic) components. Figures 4-10 and 4-11 are greatly simplified diagrams showing a few of the components of ecosystems in a freshwater pond and in a field.

The nonliving, or **abiotic**, components of an ecosystem include various physical and chemical factors. The physical factors having the greatest effect on ecosystems are

- Sunlight and shade
- Average temperature and temperature range
- Average precipitation and its distribution throughout each year
- Wind
- Latitude (distance from the equator)
- Altitude (distance above sea level)
- Nature of soil (for terrestrial ecosystems)
- Fire (for terrestrial ecosystems)
- Water currents (in aquatic ecosystems)
- Amount of suspended solid material (for aquatic ecosystems)

The chemical factors having the greatest effect on ecosystems are

- Level of water and air in soil
- Level of plant nutrients dissolved in soil moisture in terrestrial ecosystems and in water in aquatic ecosystems
- Level of natural or artificial toxic substances dissolved in soil moisture in terrestrial ecosystems and in water in aquatic ecosystems
- Salinity of water for aquatic ecosystems
- Level of dissolved oxygen in aquatic ecosystems

BIOTIC COMPONENTS OF ECOSYSTEMS Organisms that make up the living, or **biotic**, components of an ecosystem are usually classified as *producers* and *consumers*, based on how they get the food or organic nutrients they need to survive (Figures 4-10 and 4-11).

Producers—sometimes called **autotrophs** (self-feeders)—can manufacture the organic compounds they need as nutrients from simple inorganic compounds obtained from their environment. In most terrestrial ecosystems, green plants are the producers. In aquatic ecosystems, most of the producers are *phytoplankton*, consisting of various species of floating and drifting bacteria and protists.

Most producers make the organic nutrients they need through **photosynthesis**. Although hundreds of chemical changes take place in sequence during photo-

Q: Upon what two processes does life on Earth depend?

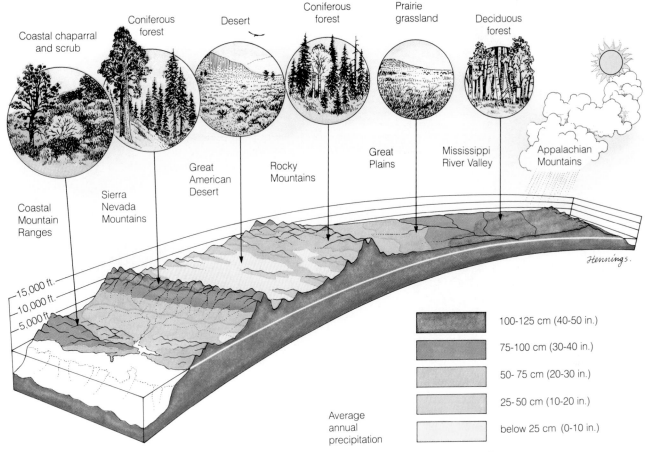

Figure 4-9 Gradual transition from one major biome to another along the 39th parallel crossing the United States. These transitions are caused primarily by changes in climate, which are due mainly to differences in average temperature and average precipitation.

Average annual precipitation

100-125 cm (40-50 in.)

75-100 cm (30-40 in.)

50- 75 cm (20-30 in.)

25- 50 cm (10-20 in.)

below 25 cm (0-10 in.)

synthesis, the overall net chemical change can be summarized as follows:

carbon dioxide + water + **solar energy** → glucose + oxygen

Some producer organisms, mostly specialized bacteria, can extract inorganic compounds from their environment and convert them into organic nutrient compounds without the presence of sunlight. This process is called **chemosynthesis**. For example, in the pitch-dark environment around hydrothermal vents in some parts of the deep ocean, specialized producer bacteria carry out chemosynthesis by converting inorganic hydrogen sulfide to organic nutrients used by the bacteria and organisms feeding on them.

All other organisms in ecosystems are **consumers**, or **heterotrophs** (other-feeders), which cannot synthesize the organic nutrients they need and which get their organic nutrients by feeding on the tissues of producers or of other consumers. There are several classes of consumers, depending on their food sources.

- **Primary consumers** feed directly on plants (*herbivores*) or on other producers.

- **Secondary consumers** feed only on primary consumers. Most secondary consumers are animals, but some are plants such as the Venus flytrap, which traps and digests insect prey.

- **Tertiary or higher-level consumers** feed only on animal-eating animals (carnivores).

- **Omnivores** ("everything eaters") can eat both plants and animals. Examples are pigs, rats, foxes, cockroaches, and humans.

- **Detritivores** (decomposers and detritus feeders) live off **detritus**, parts of dead organisms and cast-off fragments and wastes of living organisms (Figure 4-12). **Decomposers** digest detritus by breaking down the complex organic molecules in these materials into simpler inorganic compounds and absorbing the soluble nutrients. Decomposers consist of various bacteria and fungi—mostly molds and mushrooms (Figure 4-13). Bacteria and fungi decomposers in turn are an important source of food for organisms such as worms and insects living in the soil and water. **Detritus feeders**, such as crabs, carpenter ants, termites, and earthworms, extract nutrients from partly decomposed particles of organic matter.

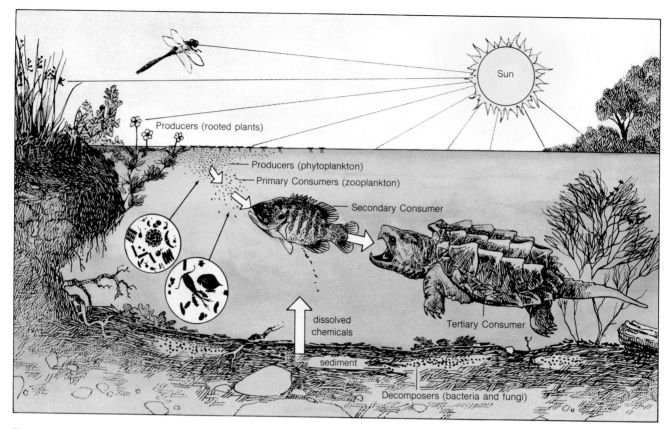

Figure 4-10 Some principal components of a freshwater pond ecosystem.

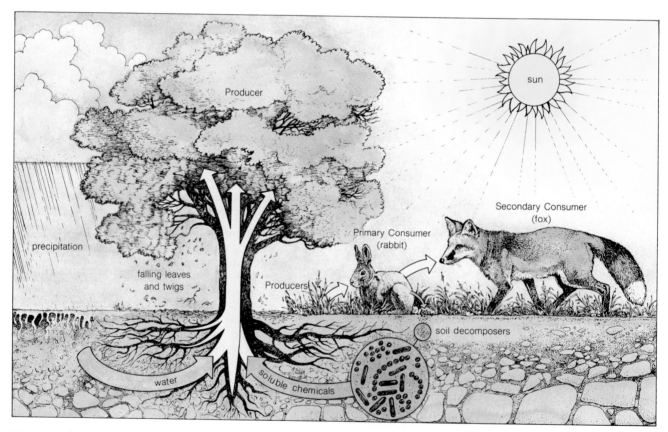

Figure 4-11 Some principal components of an ecosystem in a field.

Q: What five levels of the organization of matter are the focus of ecology?

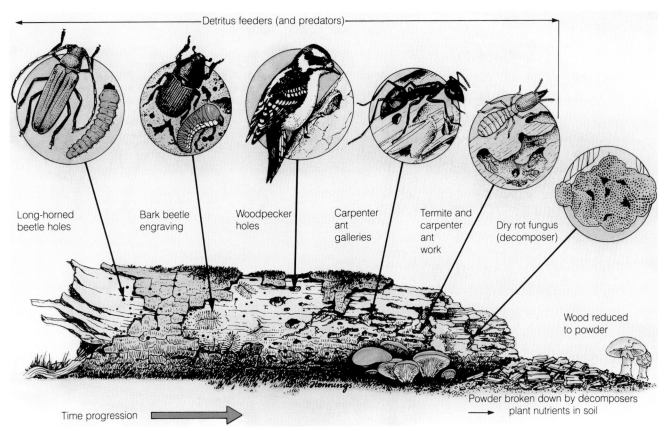

Long-horned beetle holes

Bark beetle engraving

Woodpecker holes

Carpenter ant galleries

Termite and carpenter ant work

Dry rot fungus (decomposer)

Wood reduced to powder

Time progression

Powder broken down by decomposers plant nutrients in soil

Henning

Figure 4-12   Some detritivores, called *detritus feeders*, directly consume fragments of this log. The woodpecker shown in this diagram is not a detritivore. In its search for insects, it pecks out fragments of organic matter that are consumed by detritivores. Other detritivores, called *decomposers* (mostly fungi and bacteria), digest and break down complex organic chemicals in fragments of the log into simpler inorganic nutrient chemicals.

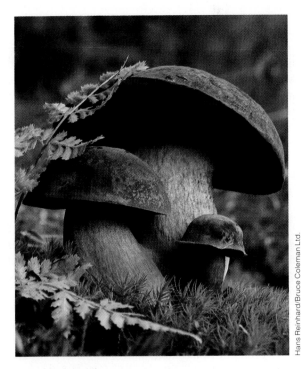

S. Flegler/Visuals Unlimited

Hans Reinhard/Bruce Coleman Ltd.

Figure 4-13   Two types of decomposers are shelf fungi (left) and *Boletus luridus* mushrooms (right).

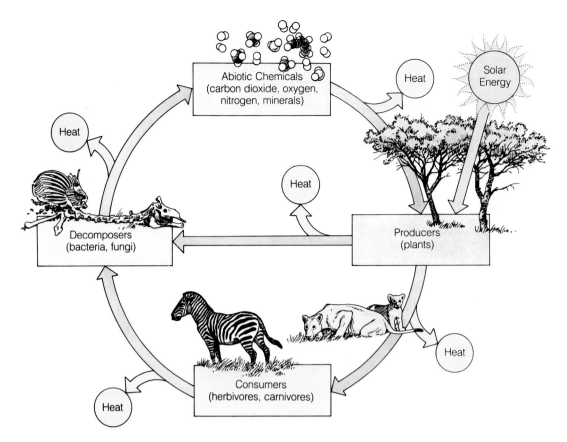

Figure 4-14 The principal structural components (energy, chemicals, and organisms) of an ecosystem are connected through the functions of energy flow and matter recycling. There is a one-way flow of energy from the sun through the living components of an ecosystem and back into the environment as heat. Because of the second energy law, the quality of this energy is degraded as it flows through the ecosystem (Figure 3-14). Nutrients are transferred from one organism to another and modified as needed. Decomposers break down the complex organic matter accumulated in organisms into simpler inorganic compounds that may be used by producers to begin the cycle again.

The chemical energy stored in glucose and other organic nutrient compounds is used by producers and consumers to drive their life processes. This energy is released by the process of **aerobic respiration**, in which aerobic organisms use oxygen produced in their cells or transferred to their cells from their environment to break down the glucose and organic nutrient compounds they synthesize (producers) or eat (consumers) back into carbon dioxide and water. The hundreds of chemical changes taking place in sequence during this complex process can be summarized by the following overall net chemical change:

glucose + oxygen → carbon dioxide + water + **energy**

Although the detailed steps in the complex processes of photosynthesis and aerobic respiration differ, the net chemical change for aerobic respiration is the opposite of that for photosynthesis.

The survival of any individual organism depends on *matter flow* and *energy flow* through its body. However, the community of organisms in an ecosystem survives primarily by a combination of *matter recycling* and a *one-way flow of energy* (Figure 4-14).

Figure 4-14 shows that decomposers are responsible for completing the cycle of matter in this life-and-death cycle by breaking down the organic compounds in detritus into inorganic nutrients that can be used by producers. Without decomposers, the entire world would soon be knee-deep in plant litter, dead animal bodies, animal wastes, and garbage. Figure 4-14 also shows that the ecosphere and its ecosystems need only producers and decomposers to exist. This means that we and all other consumers, except decomposers, are an unnecessary part of the ecosphere.

TOLERANCE RANGES OF SPECIES TO ABIOTIC FACTORS The reason that organisms don't spread everywhere is that populations of species have a particular **range of tolerance** to variations in chemical and physical factors, such as temperature, in their environment (Figure 4-15). The tolerance range includes an optimum range of values within which populations of a species thrive and operate most efficiently. This range also includes values slightly above or below the optimum level of each abiotic factor — values that usually support a smaller population size. When values exceed

Q: How do most producer organisms get the nutrients they need?

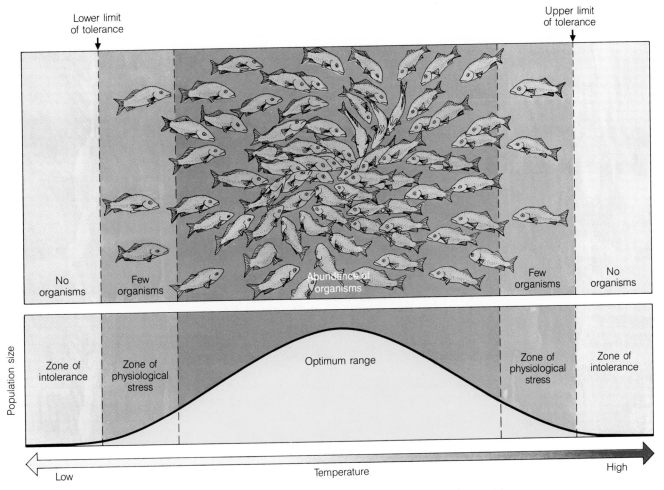

Figure 4-15 Range of tolerance for a population of organisms of the same species to an abiotic environmental factor—in this case, temperature. Individual organisms within a large population of a species may have slightly different tolerance ranges because of small differences in their genetic makeup, health, and age. For example, it may take a little more heat or a little more of a poisonous chemical to kill one fish or one person than another.

the upper or lower limits of tolerance, few if any organisms of a particular species survive.

These observations are summarized in the **law of tolerance**: *The existence, abundance, and distribution of a species in an ecosystem are determined by whether the levels of one or more physical or chemical factors fall within the range tolerated by the species.* A species may have a wide range of tolerance to some factors and a narrow range of tolerance to others. Most organisms in a species are least tolerant during juvenile or reproductive stages of the life cycle. Highly tolerant species are likely to be able to live in a range of habitats with different conditions.

Some species can adjust their tolerance to physical factors such as temperature if exposed to gradually changing conditions. For example, you can tolerate a higher water temperature by getting into a tub of fairly hot water and then slowly adding hotter and hotter water.

This adjustment to slowly changing new conditions, or **acclimation**, is a useful protective device. However, there are limits to acclimation and it can be dangerous. With each change, the species comes closer

to its limit of tolerance. Suddenly, without any warning signals, the next small change triggers a **threshold effect**, a harmful or even fatal reaction as the tolerance limit is exceeded—much like adding the single straw that breaks an already overloaded camel's back.

The threshold effect partly explains why many environmental problems seem to arise suddenly even though they have been building for a long time. For example, one or more tree species in certain forests begin dying in large numbers after prolonged exposure to numerous air pollutants. We usually notice the problem only when entire forests die, as is happening in parts of Europe and North America. By then, we're 10 to 20 years too late to prevent the damage. The threshold effect also explains why we must emphasize pollution prevention to keep thresholds from being exceeded.

LIMITING FACTORS IN ECOSYSTEMS Another ecological principle related to the law of tolerance is the **limiting factor principle**: *Too much or too little of any abiotic factor can limit or prevent growth of a population of a species in an ecosystem even if all other factors are at or near*

A: They produce them through photosynthesis.

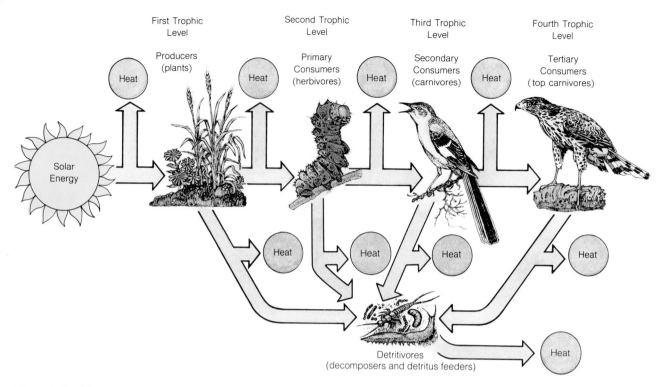

Figure 4-16 A food chain. The arrows show how chemical energy in food flows through various trophic levels, with most of the high-quality chemical energy being degraded to low-quality heat in accordance with the second law of energy.

the optimum range of tolerance for the species. A single factor found to be limiting the population growth of a species in an ecosystem is called the **limiting factor**.

Examples of limiting factors in biomes and terrestrial ecosystems are temperature, water, light, and soil nutrients. For example, suppose a farmer plants corn in a field where the soil has too little phosphorus. Even if the corn's needs for water, nitrogen, potassium, and other nutrients are met, the corn will stop growing when it has used up the available phosphorus. In this case, availability of phosphorus is the limiting factor that determines how much corn will grow in the field. Growth can also be limited by the presence of too much of a particular abiotic factor. For example, plants can be killed by too much water or by too much fertilizer.

In aquatic ecosystems, **salinity** (the amounts of various salts dissolved in a given volume of water) is a limiting factor. It determines the species found in marine ecosystems, such as oceans, and in freshwater ecosystems, such as streams and lakes. Aquatic ecosystems can also be divided into surface, middle, and bottom layers or life zones. Three important limiting factors determining the numbers and types of organisms found in these different layers are temperature, sunlight, and **dissolved oxygen content** (the amount of oxygen gas dissolved in a given volume of water at a particular temperature and pressure).

4-3   Energy Flow in Ecosystems

FOOD CHAINS AND FOOD WEBS *There is no waste in functioning natural ecosystems.* All organisms, dead or alive, are potential sources of food for other organisms. A caterpillar eats a leaf; a robin eats the caterpillar; a hawk eats the robin. When the plant, caterpillar, robin, and hawk die, they are in turn consumed by decomposers.

The general sequence of who eats or decomposes whom in an ecosystem is called a **food chain** (Figure 4-16). These relationships show how energy is transferred from one organism to another as it flows through an ecosystem.

Ecologists assign every organism in an ecosystem to a **trophic**, or feeding, **level** (from the Greek *trophos*, "nourishment"), depending on whether it is a producer or a consumer and depending on what it eats or decomposes (Figure 4-16). Producers belong to the first trophic level; primary consumers, whether feeding on living or dead producers, belong to the second trophic level; secondary consumers (meat eaters) are assigned to the third trophic level, and so on. A special class of consumers, detritivores, obtain energy and materials from detritus accumulated from all trophic levels.

Q: How much of the available high-quality energy is transferred from one trophic level to another in a food chain or food web?

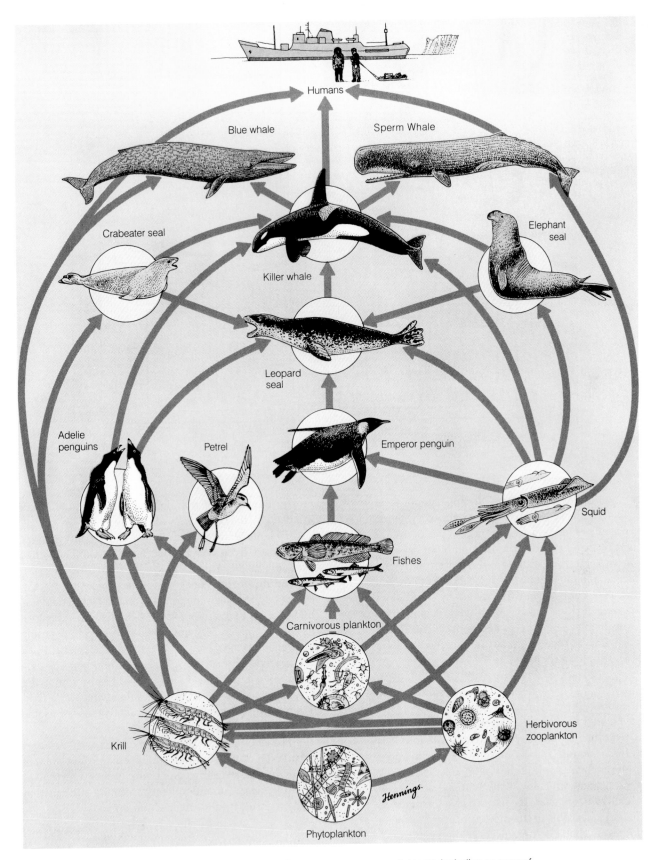

Figure 4-17 Greatly simplified food web in the Antarctic. There are many more participants, including an array of decomposer organisms.

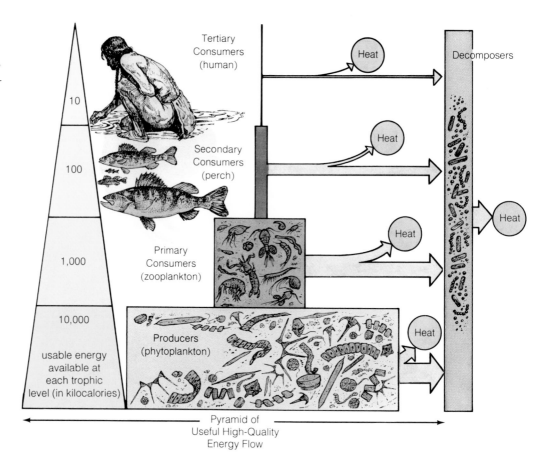

Figure 4-18 Generalized pyramid of energy flow, showing the decrease in usable high-quality energy available at each succeeding trophic level in a food chain or web. In this diagram, it is assumed that there is a 90% loss in usable energy with each transfer from one trophic level to another. In nature, such losses vary from 80% to 95%.

Tertiary
Consumers
(human)

Heat

Decomposers

Heat

Secondary
Consumers
(perch)

Heat

10

100

Primary
Consumers
(zooplankton)

Heat

1,000

Heat

10,000

Producers
(phytoplankton)

usable energy
available at
each trophic
level (in kilocalories)

Pyramid of
Useful High-Quality
Energy Flow

You will have a hard time finding simple food chains like the one shown in Figure 4-16 in ecosystems. Most consumers feed on two or more types of organisms and in turn are fed on by several other types of organisms. Some animals feed at several trophic levels. This means that the organisms in most ecosystems are involved in a complex network of many interlinked feeding relationships called a **food web**. A simplified food web in the Antarctic is diagrammed in Figure 4-17 on p. 73. Trophic levels can be assigned in food webs just as in food chains.

ENERGY FLOW PYRAMIDS **Biomass** is the organic matter produced by plants and other photosynthetic producers. In a food chain or web, biomass is transferred from one trophic level to another. Before it is transferred, some of this biomass is broken down by the producers, with some of the energy released as heat to the environment. This means that the amount of high-quality energy available to primary consumers is less than that available to the producers. Also, some of the biomass available to organisms at the next trophic level is not eaten or is not digested or absorbed.

An additional loss of high-quality energy in biomass occurs at each successive trophic level. This reduction in high-quality energy available to organisms at each successive trophic level in a food chain or web is

mostly the result of the inevitable energy-quality tax imposed by the second law of energy.

The percentage of available high-quality energy transferred from one trophic level to another varies from 5% to 20% (that is, a loss of from 80% to 95%), depending on the types of species involved and the ecosystem in which the transfer takes place. The pyramid-shaped diagram in Figure 4-18 illustrates this loss of usable high-quality energy at each step in a simple food chain, assuming a 90% loss in usable energy with each transfer from one trophic level to another. The **pyramid of energy flow** in Figure 4-18 shows that the greater the number of trophic levels or steps in a food chain or web, the greater the cumulative loss of usable high-quality energy.

The energy flow pyramid explains why a larger population of people can be supported if people eat at lower trophic levels by consuming grains directly (for example, rice→human) rather than eating animals that feed on grains (grain→steer→human).

PRODUCTIVITY OF PRODUCERS The *rate* at which an ecosystem's producers capture and store a given amount of chemical energy as biomass in a given length of time is called the ecosystem's **primary productivity**. The actual amount of energy depends on the balance between the rate at which biomass is produced by an

Q: What are the three most productive types of ecosystems?

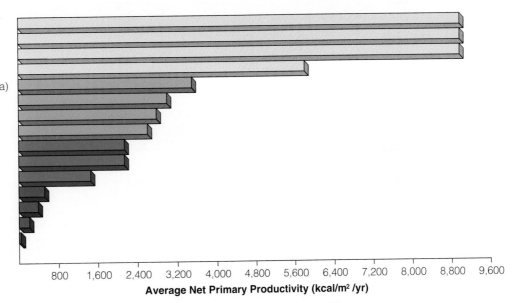

Type of Ecosystem

Estuaries
Swamps and marshes
Tropical rain forest
Temperate forest
Northern coniferous forest (taiga)
Savanna
Agricultural land
Woodland and shrubland
Temperate grassland
Lakes and streams
Continental shelf
Tundra (arctic and alpine)
Open ocean
Desert scrub
Extreme desert

800 1,600 2,400 3,200 4,000 4,800 5,600 6,400 7,200 8,000 8,800 9,600

Average Net Primary Productivity (kcal/m² /yr)

Figure 4-19 Estimated annual average net productivity of producers per unit of area in principal types of life zones and ecosystems. Values are given in kilocalories of energy produced per square meter per year.

ecosystem's producers and the rate at which the producers use some of this biomass (usually by aerobic respiration) to stay alive. The difference in these two rates is an ecosystem's **net primary productivity**.

net primary productivity	=	rate at which producers produce chemical energy stored in biomass through photosynthesis	−	rate at which producers use chemical energy stored in their biomass through aerobic respiration

Net primary productivity is usually reported as the energy output of a specified area of producers over a given time.

Net primary productivity can be thought of as the basic food source or "income" of the consumers in an ecosystem. Ecologists have estimated the average annual net primary production per square meter of producers for the principal terrestrial and aquatic ecosystems. Figure 4-19 shows that ecosystems and life zones with the highest average net primary productivities are estuaries, swamps and marshes, and tropical rain forests; the lowest are tundra (arctic grasslands), open ocean, and desert.

You might conclude that we should clear tropical forests to grow crops and that we should harvest plants growing in estuaries, swamps, and marshes to help feed the growing human population. Wrong. One reason is that the plants—mostly grasses—in estuaries, swamps, and marshes cannot be eaten by people, though they are extremely important as food sources and spawning areas for fish, shrimp, and other forms of aquatic life that provide us and other consumers with

protein. So we should protect, not harvest or destroy, these plants.

In tropical forests, most of the nutrients are stored in the trees and other vegetation rather than in the soil. When the trees are cleared, the low levels of nutrients in the exposed soil are rapidly depleted by frequent rains and by growing crops. Thus, food crops can be grown only for a short time without enormous, expensive inputs of commercial fertilizers. So we should protect, not cut down, these forests.

We are already consuming, diverting, and wasting about 27% of the world's potential net primary productivity and about 40% of that produced on land. Earth's remaining net primary productivity is used to support all of Earth's other species, which are also a vital form of Earth capital that keeps us alive. What will happen if we double the human population within the next 40 years and in the process eliminate much of the planet's biodiversity by using 54% of the world's potential net primary productivity and about 80% of that produced on land?

4-4 Matter Cycling in Ecosystems

BIOGEOCHEMICAL CYCLES Nutrients, the chemicals essential for life, are cycled in the ecosphere (Figure 4-3) and in mature ecosystems in biogeochemical cycles (Figure 4-20). In these cycles, nutrients move from the environment, through organisms, and then back to the environment. All are driven, directly or indirectly, by energy from the sun and by gravity.

A: Estuaries, swamps and marshes, and tropical rain forests

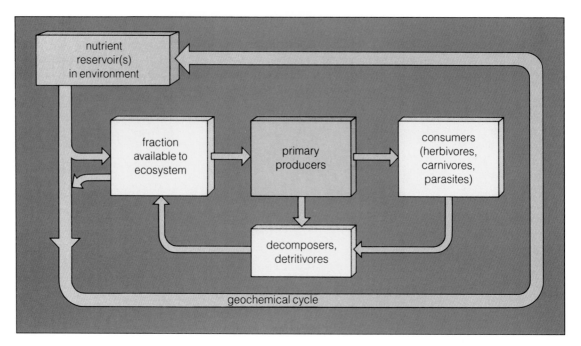

Figure 4-20 Generalized model of nutrient cycling in a mature ecosystem. Nutrients move from the environment, through organisms, and back to the environment in biogeochemical cycles. Some nutrients are lost in mature ecosystems, but most are recycled. Younger, developing ecosystems gain many of their nutrients from other ecosystems and lose many of their nutrients to other ecosystems. (Used by permission from Cecie Starr, *Biology: Concepts and Applications*, Belmont, Calif.: Wadsworth, 1991)

There are three types of interconnected biogeochemical cycles. In *gaseous cycles*, nutrients circulate mostly among the atmosphere, the hydrosphere (water), and living organisms. In most of these cycles elements are recycled rapidly, often within hours or days. The principal gaseous cycles are the carbon, oxygen, hydrogen, and nitrogen cycles.

In *sedimentary cycles*, nutrients circulate mostly among the earth's crust (soil, rocks, and sediments on land and on the seafloor), the hydrosphere, and living organisms. Elements in these cycles are usually recycled much more slowly than those in atmospheric cycles because the elements are tied up in sedimentary rocks for long periods of time, often thousands to millions of years, and some don't have a gaseous phase. Phosphorus and sulfur are two of the 36 or so elements recycled in this manner.

In the *hydrologic cycle*, water circulates among the ocean, the air, the land, and living organisms. This cycle also distributes heat from the sun over the planet's surface.

CARBON CYCLE Carbon is the basic building block of the carbohydrates, fats, proteins, nucleic acids such as DNA and RNA, and other organic compounds necessary for life. The carbon cycle is based on carbon dioxide gas, which makes up only about 0.03% by volume of the lower atmosphere and is also dissolved in water.

Producers absorb carbon dioxide from the atmosphere (terrestrial producers) or water (aquatic produc-

ers) and use *photosynthesis* to convert the carbon in carbon dioxide into carbon in complex organic compounds such as glucose. Then the cells in oxygen-consuming producers and consumers carry out *aerobic respiration*, which breaks down glucose and other complex organic compounds and converts the carbon back to carbon dioxide in the atmosphere or water for reuse by producers.

This linkage between photosynthesis in producers and aerobic respiration in producers and consumers circulates carbon in the ecosphere and is a major part of the global **carbon cycle** (Figure 4-21). Oxygen and hydrogen, the other elements in glucose and other organic nutrients, cycle almost in step with carbon.

Figure 4-22 shows other parts of the global carbon cycle in terrestrial ecosystems and marine ecosystems. It reveals that some of Earth's carbon is tied up deep in the earth for long periods in fossil fuels—mostly coal, petroleum, and natural gas—until it is released to the atmosphere as carbon dioxide when fossil fuels are extracted and burned. Carbon dioxide is also released to the atmosphere by aerobic respiration and by volcanic eruptions, which release carbon from rocks deep in the earth's crust.

In marine ecosystems, some organisms take up dissolved CO_2 molecules or carbonate ions (CO_3^{2-}) from ocean water and form slightly soluble calcium carbonate ($CaCO_3$) to build shells and rocks and the skeletons of marine organisms from tiny protozoans to corals. When the shelled organisms die, tiny particles of

Q: How much of the world's net primary productivity on land is used by the world's 5.4 billion people?

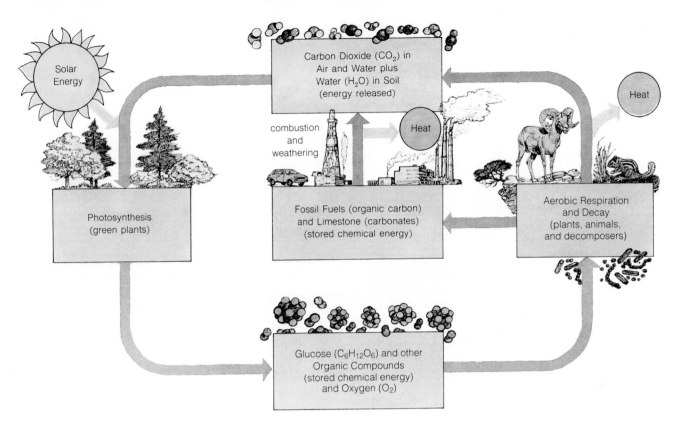

Figure 4-21 Simplified diagram of a portion of the gaseous carbon cycle, showing matter cycling and one-way energy flow through the processes of photosynthesis and aerobic respiration. Photosynthesis takes in carbon dioxide and releases oxygen, and aerobic respiration takes in oxygen and releases carbon dioxide. This cyclical movement of matter through ecosystems and the ecosphere is also an important part of the oxygen and hydrogen cycles.

their shells and bone fall slowly to the ocean depths and are buried over eons of time in bottom sediments (Figure 4-22).

Carbon in these deep ocean sediments reenters the cycle very slowly when some of the sediments dissolve and form dissolved carbon dioxide gas that can enter the atmosphere. Long-term geologic events can also bring bottom sediments to the surface, exposing the carbonate rock to chemical attack and conversion to carbon dioxide gas.

Especially since 1950, as world population and resource use have increased rapidly, we have intervened in the carbon cycle in two primary ways:

■ Removal of forests and other vegetation without sufficient replanting, which leaves less vegetation to absorb CO_2.

■ Burning carbon-containing fossil fuels and burning wood faster than it is regrown (Figure 4-22). This produces carbon dioxide that flows into the atmosphere. Some scientists project that this carbon dioxide, along with other chemicals we're adding to the atmosphere, could enhance Earth's natural greenhouse effect, alter climate patterns, and disrupt global food production and wildlife habitats.

NITROGEN CYCLE Organisms require nitrogen in various chemical forms to synthesize proteins, nucleic acids such as DNA and RNA, and other nitrogen-containing organic compounds. The nitrogen gas (N_2) that makes up 78% of the volume of the lower atmosphere cannot be used directly as a nutrient by multi-cellular plants or animals. Fortunately, nitrogen gas is converted into water-soluble ionic compounds containing nitrate ions (NO_3^-) and ammonium ions (NH_4^+), which are taken up by plant roots as part of the **nitrogen cycle**. This gaseous cycle is shown in simplified form in Figure 4-23.

The conversion of atmospheric nitrogen gas into other chemical forms useful to plants is called **nitrogen fixation**. It is carried out mostly by certain kinds of bacteria (mostly cyanobacteria) in soil and water and by rhizobium bacteria living in small swellings called nodules on the roots of alfalfa, clover, peas, beans, and other legume plants (Figure 4-24).

Plants convert inorganic nitrate ions and ammonium ions obtained from soil water into proteins, DNA, and other large, nitrogen-containing organic compounds they require. Animals get their nitrogen-containing nutrients by eating plants or other animals that have eaten plants.

Figure 4-22 Simplified diagram of the global gaseous carbon cycle. The left portion shows the movement of carbon through marine ecosystems and the right portion its movement through terrestrial ecosystems. (Used by permission from Cecie Starr, *Biology: Concepts and Applications*, Belmont, Calif.: Wadsworth, 1991)

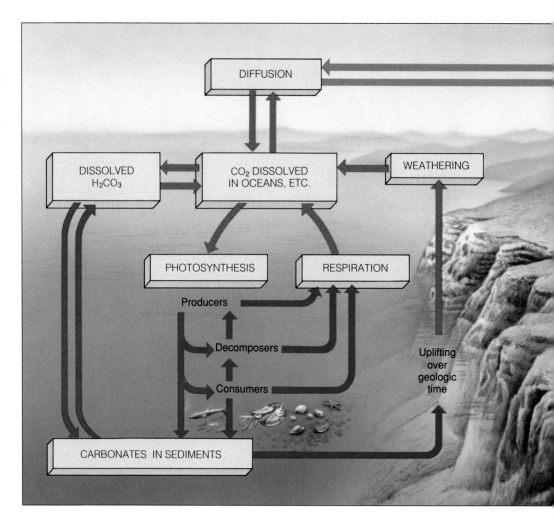

After nitrogen has served its purpose in living organisms, armies of specialized decomposer bacteria convert the nitrogen-containing organic compounds found in the wastes, cast-off particles, and dead bodies of organisms into simpler inorganic compounds such as ammonia gas (NH_3) and water-soluble salts containing ammonium ions (NH_4^+). Other specialized groups of bacteria then convert these inorganic forms of nitrogen back into nitrite (NO_2^-) and nitrate (NO_3^-) ions in the soil and then into nitrogen gas, which is released to the atmosphere to begin the cycle again.

We intervene in the nitrogen cycle in several ways:

- Emission of large quantities of nitric oxide into the atmosphere when wood or any fuel is burned. Most of this NO is produced when nitrogen and oxygen molecules in the air combine at the high temperatures involved when fuels are burned. The nitric oxide then combines with oxygen gas in the atmosphere to form nitrogen dioxide (NO_2) gas, which can react with water vapor in the atmosphere to form nitric acid (HNO_3). This acid is a component of acid deposition, which is damaging trees and killing fish in parts of the world.

- Emission of the heat-trapping gas nitrous oxide (N_2O) into the atmosphere by the action of certain bacteria on commercial inorganic fertilizers and livestock wastes.

- Mining mineral deposits of compounds containing nitrate and ammonium ions for use as commercial inorganic fertilizers.

- Depleting nitrate ions and ammonium ions from soil by harvesting nitrogen-rich crops.

- Adding excess nitrate ions and ammonium ions to aquatic ecosystems in runoff of animal wastes from livestock feedlots, runoff of commercial nitrate fertilizers from cropland, and discharge of untreated and treated municipal sewage. This excess supply of plant nutrients stimulates rapid growth of algae and other aquatic plants. The breakdown of dead algae by aerobic decomposers depletes the water of dissolved oxygen gas, killing great numbers of fish.

PHOSPHORUS CYCLE Phosphorus, mainly in the form of certain types of phosphate ions (PO_4^{3-} and HPO_4^{2-}), is an essential nutrient of both plants and an-

Q: How much of Earth's tropical forests have been cleared?

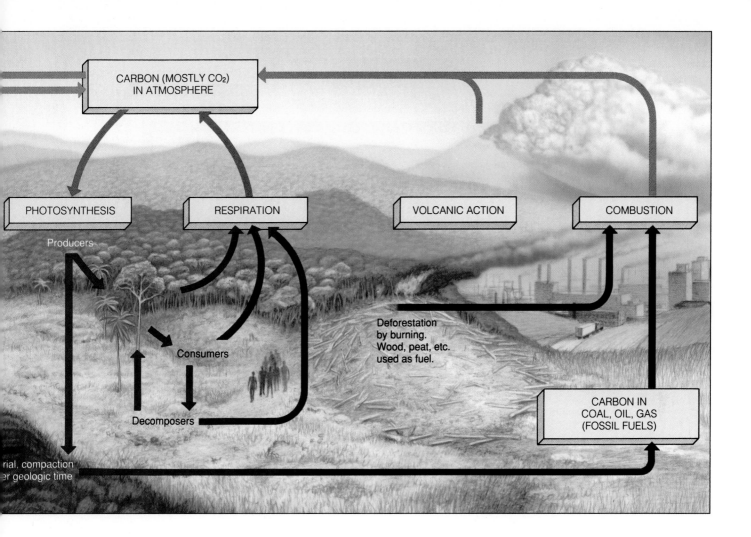

CARBON (MOSTLY CO₂)
IN ATMOSPHERE

PHOTOSYNTHESIS

Producers

RESPIRATION

VOLCANIC ACTION

COMBUSTION

Consumers

Decomposers

Deforestation
by burning.
Wood, peat, etc.
used as fuel.

CARBON IN
COAL, OIL, GAS
(FOSSIL FUELS)

rial, compaction
er geologic time

imals. It is a part of DNA molecules, which carry genetic information; ATP and ADP molecules, which store chemical energy for use by organisms in cellular respiration; certain fats in the membranes that encase plant and animal cells; and bones and teeth in animals.

Various forms of phosphorus are cycled mostly through the water, Earth's crust, and living organisms by the sedimentary **phosphorus cycle**, shown in simplified form in Figure 4-25. In this cycle, phosphorus moves slowly from phosphate deposits on land and shallow ocean sediments to living organisms and back to the land and ocean.

Phosphorus released by the slow breakdown, or weathering, of phosphate rock deposits is dissolved in soil water and taken up by plant roots. Wind can also transport phosphate particles long distances. Most soils contain only small amounts of phosphorus because phosphate compounds are only slightly soluble in water and are found in few kinds of rocks. Thus, phosphorus is the limiting factor for plant growth in many soils and aquatic ecosystems.

Animals get their phosphorus by eating producers or by eating animals that have eaten producers. Animal

wastes and the decay products of dead animals and producers return much of this phosphorus to the soil, to streams, and eventually to the ocean bottom as deposits of slightly soluble phosphate rock.

Some phosphate is returned to the land as guano — the phosphate-rich manure produced by fish-eating birds such as pelicans, gannets, and cormorants. This return is small, though, compared with the much larger amounts of phosphate transferred from the land to the oceans each year by natural processes and human activities.

Over millions of years, geologic processes may push up and expose the seafloor. Weathering then slowly releases phosphorus from the exposed rocks and allows the cycle to begin again.

We intervene in the phosphorus cycle chiefly in two ways:

- Mining large quantities of phosphate rock to produce commercial inorganic fertilizers and detergent compounds.

- Adding excess phosphate ions to aquatic ecosystems in runoff of animal wastes from livestock

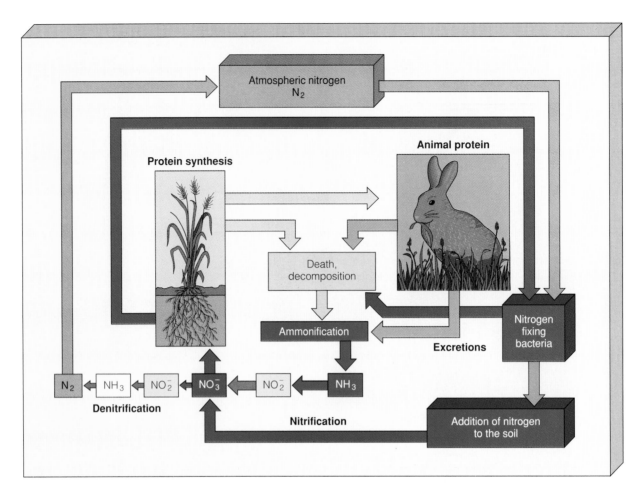

Figure 4-23 Simplified diagram of the gaseous nitrogen cycle. (Used by permission from Carolina Biological Supply Company)

E. R. Degginger

Figure 4-24 Plants in the legume family have root nodules where rhizobium bacteria fix nitrogen by converting gaseous nitrogen (N_2) in the atmosphere into ammonia (NH_3), which in soil water forms ammonium ions (NH_4^+) that are taken up by the roots of plants. This mutualistic interaction between these plants and bacteria benefits both species. The bacteria capture atmospheric nitrogen and convert it into a form usable by the plants, and the legume provides the bacteria with sugar.

feedlots, runoff of commercial phosphate fertilizers from cropland, and discharge of untreated and treated municipal sewage. As with nitrate and ammonium ions, an excessive supply of this nutrient causes explosive growth of cyanobacteria, algae, and various aquatic plants that disrupt life in aquatic ecosystems.

HYDROLOGIC CYCLE The **hydrologic cycle** or **water cycle**, which collects, purifies, and distributes Earth's fixed supply of water, is shown simplified in Figure 4-26. The hydrologic cycle is linked with the other biogeochemical cycles, because water is an important medium for the movement of nutrients into and out of ecosystems and organisms.

Solar energy and gravity continuously convert water from one physical state to another and move water among the ocean, the air, the land, and living organisms. Incoming solar energy evaporates water from oceans, streams, lakes, soil, and vegetation into the atmosphere. Winds and air masses transport this water vapor over various parts of Earth's surface. Decreases in temperature in parts of the atmosphere cause the water vapor to condense and form tiny droplets of water in the form of clouds or fog. Eventually these

Q: How much of Earth's surface is covered by oceans?

Figure 4-25 Simplified diagram of the sedimentary phosphorus cycle. (Used by permission from Cecie Starr, *Biology: Concepts and Applications*, Belmont, Calif.: Wadsworth, 1991)

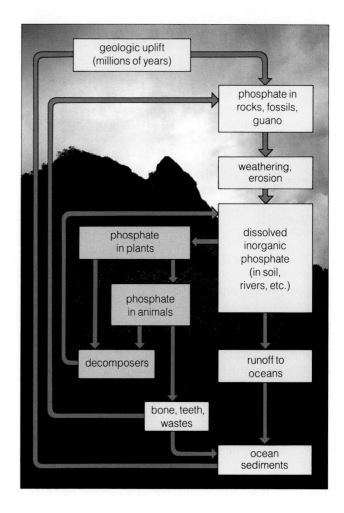

droplets combine and become heavy enough to fall to the land and into bodies of water as precipitation (dew, rain, sleet, hail, snow).

Some of the fresh water returning to Earth's surface as precipitation becomes locked in glaciers. Much of it collects in puddles and ditches and runs off into nearby lakes and into streams, which carry water back to the oceans, completing the cycle. This runoff of surface water from the land helps replenish streams and lakes and also causes soil erosion, which moves various chemicals through portions of other biogeochemical cycles.

A large portion of the water returning to the land seeps into or infiltrates surface soil layers, and some percolates downward into the ground. There it is stored as groundwater in the pores and cracks of rocks. This underground water, like surface water, flows downhill and seeps out into streams and lakes or comes out in springs. Eventually, this water evaporates or reaches the sea to begin the cycle again.

We intervene in the water cycle in two main ways:

- Withdrawing large quantities of fresh water from streams, lakes, and aquifers. In heavily populated or heavily irrigated areas, withdrawals have led to

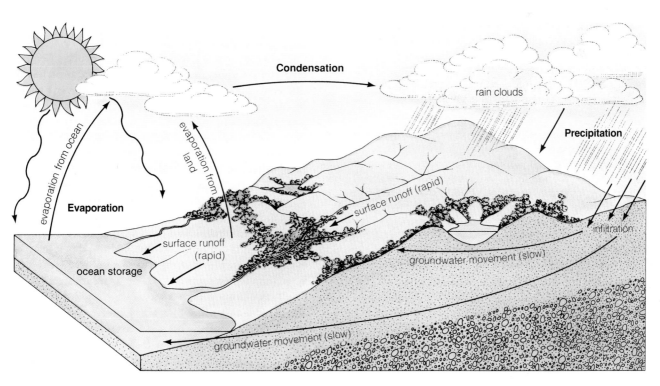

Figure 4-26 Simplified diagram of the hydrologic cycle.

groundwater depletion or intrusion of ocean salt water into underground water supplies.

■ Clearing vegetation from land for agriculture, mining, roads, parking lots, construction, and other activities. This reduces seepage that recharges groundwater supplies, increases the risk of flooding, and increases the rate of surface run-off, which increases soil erosion and landslides.

<table>
<tr><td>4-5</td><td>

Roles and Interactions of Species in Ecosystems

</td></tr>
</table>

TYPES OF SPECIES FOUND IN ECOSYSTEMS If you observe various ecosystems, you will find that they can have four types of species:

■ **Native species**, which normally live and thrive in a particular ecosystem.

■ **Immigrant, or alien, species**, which migrate into an ecosystem or which are deliberately or accidentally introduced into an ecosystem by humans. Some of these species are beneficial, while others can take over and eliminate many native species.

■ **Indicator species**, which serve as early warnings that a community or an ecosystem is being degraded. For example, the present decline of migratory, insect-eating songbirds in North America indicates a loss of habitat in their summer homes in North America and in their winter homes in the rapidly disappearing tropical forests in Latin America and the Caribbean Islands. Some indicator species, such as the brown pelican and the American bald eagle, feed at high trophic levels in food chains and webs. This makes them vulnerable to high levels of fat-soluble toxic chemicals such as DDT, whose concentrations are increased in the tissues of organisms at each successive trophic level.

■ **Keystone species**, which play roles affecting many other organisms in an ecosystem. Generally, keystone species play a more important role in marine ecosystems than in terrestrial ecosystems. The loss of a keystone species can lead to sharp population drops and extinction of other species that depend on it for certain services. An example is the alligator (see Case Study on p. 83).

NICHE The **ecological niche**, or simply **niche**, (pronounced "nitch") of a species is its total way of life or its role in an ecosystem. It includes all physical, chemical, and biological conditions a species needs to live and reproduce in an ecosystem.

Some species, called **specialists**, have narrow niches. They may be able to live in only one type of habitat, tolerate only a narrow range of climatic and other environmental conditions, or use only one or a few types of food. The giant panda, for example, has a highly specialized niche because it gets 99% of its food by consuming bamboo plants. The destruction of several species of bamboo in parts of China, where the panda is found, has led to the animal's near extinction.

In a tropical rain forest, an incredibly diverse array of species survive by occupying a variety of specialized ecological niches in distinct layers of the forest's vegetation (Figure 4-28). The widespread clearing and degradation of such forests is dooming millions of specialized species to extinction.

Other species, called **generalists**, have a broad niche. They can live in many different places, eat a variety of foods, and tolerate a wide range of environmental conditions. Examples of generalist species are flies, cockroaches, mice, rats, white-tailed deer, raccoons, and human beings.

Is it better to be a generalist than a specialist? It depends. When environments have fairly constant conditions, such as in a tropical rain forest, specialists have an advantage because they have fewer competitors (Figure 4-28). But when environments are changing rapidly, the adaptable generalist is usually better off than the unadaptable specialist.

COMPETITION BETWEEN SPECIES FOR LIMITED RESOURCES As long as commonly used resources are abundant, different species can share them. This allows each species to come closer to occupying its **fundamental niche**: the full potential range of the physical, chemical, and biological factors it could use, if there is no competition from other species.

In most ecosystems, each species faces competition from one or more other species for one or more of the limited resources (such as food, sunlight, water, soil nutrients, or space) it needs. Because of such **interspecific competition**, parts of the fundamental niches of different species overlap significantly. However, experiments have shown that no two species can occupy exactly the same fundamental niche indefinitely in a habitat where there is not enough of a particular resource to meet the needs of both species. This is called the **competitive exclusion principle**.

When the fundamental niches of two competing species overlap, one species may occupy more of its fundamental niche than the other species by producing more young, getting more food or solar energy, defending itself better, or limiting or preventing the other species from using a resource. This may cause a species to be eliminated from an area or force an animal species to migrate to another area.

Another way in which the degree of fundamental niche overlap is reduced is by **resource partitioning**, the process of dividing up resources so that species with similar requirements use the same scarce resources at different times, in different ways, or in different places. In effect, they "share the wealth," with each

Q: How much of Earth's wetlands have been destroyed or polluted?

People tend to divide plants and animals into "good" and "bad" species and to assume that we have a duty to wipe out the villains or to use them up to satisfy our needs and wants. One species that we drove to near extinction in many of its marsh and swamp habitats is the American alligator (Figure 4-27).

Alligators have no natural predators except people. Hunters once killed large numbers of these animals for their exotic meat and for the supple belly skin used to make shoes, belts, and other items. Between 1950 and 1960, hunters wiped out 90% of the alligators in Louisiana. The alligator population in the Florida Everglades also was threatened.

People who say "So what?" are overlooking the key role the alligator plays in subtropical, wetland ecosystems such as the Everglades. Alligators dig deep depressions, or "gator holes," which collect fresh water during dry spells. These holes are refuges for aquatic life and supply fresh water and food for birds and other animals.

Large alligator nesting mounds also serve as nest sites for birds such as herons and egrets. As alligators move from gator holes to nesting mounds, they help keep waterways open. They also eat large numbers of gar, a fish that preys on other fish. This means that alligators help maintain populations of game fish such as bass and bream.

In 1967, the U.S. government placed the American alligator on the

Figure 4-27 The American alligator is a keystone species in its marsh and swamp habitats in the southeastern United States. In 1967, it was classified as an endangered species in the United States. This protection allowed the population of the species to recover to the point that its status has been changed from endangered to threatened. Because of its thick skin, speed in the water, and powerful jaws, this species has no natural predators except humans.

Luther C. Goldman/U.S. Fish and Wildlife Service

endangered species list. Averaging about 40 eggs per nest and protected from hunters, by 1975 the alligator population had made a strong comeback in many areas — too strong, according to some people who found alligators in their backyards and swimming pools.

The problem is that both human and alligator populations are increasing rapidly, and people are taking over the natural habitats of the alligator. A gator's main diet is snails, apples, sick fish, ducks, raccoons, and turtles, but a pet or a person who falls into or swims in a canal, a pond, or some other area where a gator lives is subject to being attacked.

In 1977, the U.S. Fish and Wildlife Service reclassified the American alligator from endangered to

threatened in Florida, Louisiana, and Texas, where 90% of the animals live. In 1987, this reclassification was extended to seven other states.

As a threatened species, alligators are still protected from excessive harvesting by hunters, but limited hunting is allowed in some areas to keep the population from growing too large. The comeback of the American alligator is an important success story in wildlife conservation.

---

competing species occupying a **realized niche**, which is only a part of its fundamental niche.

For example, hawks and owls feed on similar prey, but hawks hunt during the day and owls hunt at night. Where lions and leopards occur together, lions take mostly larger animals as prey and leopards take smaller ones. Some species of birds, such as warblers, avoid competition for food by hunting for insects in different parts of the same coniferous trees in New England forests.

PREDATION AND PARASITISM The most obvious form of species interaction in food chains and webs is **predation**: An individual organism of one species, known as the **predator**, feeds on parts or all of an organism of another species, the **prey**, but does not live on or in the prey. Together, the two kinds of organisms involved, such as lions and zebras, are said to have a **predator-prey relationship**. Defined broadly, predator-prey relationships include carnivore-prey, herbivore-plant, and parasite-host interactions. Examples of pred-

A: 25% to 50% (56% in the United States)

Figure 4-28 Stratification of specialized plant and animal niches in various layers of a tropical rain forest. These specialized niches allow species to avoid or minimize competition for resources with other species and lead to the coexistence of a great diversity of species. This niche specialization has been promoted by adaptation of plants to different levels of light available in the forest's layers and hundreds of thousands of years of adaptation and evolution in a fairly constant climate.

ators and their preys are shown in Figures 4-10, 4-11, 4-16, and 4-17).

Some predators hunt and kill live prey. Other predators, called **scavengers**, feed on dead organisms that were either killed by other organisms or died naturally. Vultures, flies, and crows are examples of scavengers. Sharks are one of the most important predators in the world's oceans (see Case Study on p. 85).

Prey species have various protective mechanisms. Otherwise, they would easily be captured and eaten. Some can run, swim, or fly fast; and others have highly developed sight or a sense of smell that alerts them to the presence of a predator. Some have thick or tough skins (alligator, Figure 4-27), shells (turtles), or bark (giant sequoia); and others have spines (porcupines) or thorns (cacti, Figure 4-5). Still others have camouflage coloring (stone plant, which looks like a gray stone) or the ability to change color (chameleon) so that they can hide by blending into their environment.

Some prey species give off chemicals that smell (skunks and skunk cabbages) or taste bad to their pred-

ators (buttercup) or irritate (bombardier beetles) or poison them (poison arrow frogs). Some prey species attempt to scare off predators by puffing up or spreading their wings (the peacock, Figure 4-6). Other prey gain some protection by living in large groups (schools of fish, herds of antelope).

Predators also have a variety of methods that help them capture prey. Some carnivores, such as the cheetah, catch prey by being able to run fast, and others have keen eyesight (American bald eagle). Other carnivores cooperate in capturing their prey by hunting in packs, as spotted hyenas, African lions, wolves, jackals, and Cape hunting dogs do. Like prey species, some predators use camouflage to hide and wait for unsuspecting prey or to blend into their environment (arctic fox, Figure 4-1). Many predators attack prey that is young, old, weak, sick, crippled, or in some way disabled. This natural weeding out of diseased and weak individuals also benefits the prey species by preventing the spread of disease and leaving stronger and healthier individuals for breeding. Other predators, such as hu-

Q: How many species are there on Earth?

Sharks have lived in the oceans for more than 450 million years, long before dinosaurs appeared. There are now about 360 species of sharks, whose size, behavior, and other characteristics differ widely (Figure 4-29).

Sharks range in size from the dwarf-dog shark (0.1 meters or 6 inches long) to the whale shark—the world's largest fish at 18 meters (60 feet). The whale shark, like two other large shark species—the basking shark and the megamouth shark—are harmless to people because they feed on microscopic diatoms and plants and small aquatic animals such as zooplankton and shrimp. Various shark species are the key predators in the world's oceans, helping control the numbers of many other ocean predators.

Some sharks can detect the scent of decaying fish or blood even when it is diluted to only one part per million parts of seawater. They can probably hear underwater sounds that originate as far as 3 kilometers (2 miles) away and can tell the direction from which underwater sounds are coming. They also sense weak electrical impulses radiated by the muscles and hearts of fish, making it difficult for their prey to escape detection.

Every year, we catch and kill more than 100 million sharks, mostly for food and for their fins. Other sharks are killed for sport and out of fear. Sharks are vulnerable to overfishing because it takes most species 10 to 15 years to begin reproducing, and they produce only a few offspring.

Figure 4-29 This blue shark and other types of sharks are key predators in the world's oceans. This is one of only a small number of shark species that occasionally attack swimmers. These sharks prefer deep water and are a potential threat only to people swimming from boats in deep water.

Howard Hall/Earth Images

Influenced by movies and popular novels, most people see sharks as people-eating monsters. This is far from the truth. Every year, a few types of shark—mostly great white, bull, tiger, gray reef, blue, and oceanic whitetip—injure about 100 people worldwide and kill about 25. Most attacks are by great white sharks, which often feed on sea lions and other marine mammals and sometimes mistake human swimmers for their normal prey, especially if they are wearing black wet suits.

In a typical year, only about 10 or 12 shark attacks occur in U.S. waters (most off Florida and southern California), with only one or two of those attacks being fatal. If you are a typical ocean-goer, you are more likely to be killed by a pig than a shark and thousands of times more likely to be killed when you drive a car. For every shark that injures a person, we kill 1 million sharks.

Sharks help save human lives. In addition to providing people with food, they are helping us learn how to fight cancer, bacteria, and viruses. Their highly effective immune system allows wounds to heal quickly without becoming infected, and their blood is being studied in connection with AIDS research. A chemical extracted from shark cartilage is being used as an artificial skin for burn victims.

Sharks are among the few animals in the world that almost never get cancer and eye cataracts. Understanding why can help us improve human health. Chemicals extracted from shark cartilage have killed cancerous tumors in laboratory animals, and someday they could help prolong your life or the life of a loved one.

Sharks are essential to the world's ocean ecosystems. Although they don't need us, we need them.

---

mans, have invented weapons and traps to capture prey.

Another type of predator-prey interaction is parasitism. A **parasite** is a consumer that feeds on another living organism (its **host**) by living on or in its host organism for all or most of the host's life. Parasitism is a special form of predation in which the predator (parasite) is much smaller than its prey (host) and either lives on or within its living prey. The parasite draws nourishment from and gradually weakens its host. Parasitism may or may not kill the host. Tapeworms, disease-causing organisms (pathogens), and other parasites live inside their hosts. Lice, ticks, mosquitoes, mistletoe plants, and lampreys (Figure 4-30) attach themselves to the outside of their hosts.

Some parasites can move from one host to another, as dog fleas do. Others may spend their adult lives attached to a single host. Examples are mistletoe, which

Figure 4-30 Parasitism. Sea lampreys are parasites that use their suckerlike mouths to attach themselves to the sides of fish on which they prey. Then they bore a hole in the fish with their teeth and feed on its blood.

Figure 4-31 Mutualism. These oxpeckers are feeding on the ticks that infest this endangered black rhinoceros in Kenya. The rhino benefits by having these parasites removed from its body, and oxpeckers benefit by having a dependable source of food. This and other species of rhinoceros face extinction because they are illegally killed for their horns and because of loss of habitat.

feeds on oak tree branches, and tapeworms, which feed in the intestines of humans and other animals.

MUTUALISM AND COMMENSALISM **Mutualism** is a type of species interaction in which both participating species generally benefit. The honeybee and certain flowers have a mutualistic relationship. The honeybee feeds on a flower's nectar and, in the process, picks up pollen and pollinates female flowers when it feeds on them. Other examples are the mutualistic relationships between rhinos and oxpeckers (Figure 4-31) and between legume plants and rhizobium bacteria that live in nodules on the roots of these plants (Figure 4-24).

In another type of species interaction, called **commensalism**, one species benefits, while the other is neither helped nor harmed to any great degree. In the open sea, certain types of barnacles live on the jawbones and outer coverings of whales. The barnacles benefit by having a safe place to live and a steady supply of the plankton on which they feed. The whale apparently gets no benefit from this relationship, but it suffers no harm from it either.

This chapter has shown that the essential feature of the living and nonliving parts of individual terrestrial and aquatic ecosystems and of the global ecosystem, or ecosphere, is interdependence and connectedness. Without the services performed by diverse communities of species, we would be starving, gasping for breath, and drowning in our own wastes. We have also seen how some species survive by avoiding competition and by entering into nondestructive relationships (mutualism and commensalism) with other species — lessons that the human species could learn from. The next chapter shows how this interdependence is the key to understanding Earth's principal types of life zones and ecosystems.

We sang the songs that carried in their melodies all the sounds of nature—the running waters, the sighing of winds, and the calls of the animals. Teach these to your children that they may come to love nature as we love it.

GRAND COUNCIL FIRE OF AMERICAN INDIANS

DISCUSSION TOPICS

1. **a.** A bumper sticker asks, "Have you thanked a green plant today?" Give two reasons for appreciating a green plant.
    b. Trace the sources of the materials that make up the sticker and see whether the sticker itself is a sound application of the slogan.
    c. Explain how decomposers help keep you alive.

2. **a.** How would you set up a self-sustaining aquarium for tropical fish?
    b. Suppose you have a balanced aquarium sealed with a clear glass top. Can life continue in the aquarium indefinitely as long as the sun shines regularly on it?
    c. A friend cleans out your aquarium and removes all the soil and plants, leaving only the fish and water. What will happen?

3. Using the second law of energy, explain why there is such a sharp decrease in high-quality energy as energy flows through a food chain or web. Doesn't an energy loss at each step violate the first law of energy? Explain.

4. Using the second law of energy, explain why many poor people in less developed countries exist mostly on a vegetarian diet.

5. Using the second law of energy, explain why, on a per weight basis, steak costs more than corn.

CHAPTER 5

ECOSYSTEMS: WHAT ARE THE MAJOR TYPES AND WHAT CAN HAPPEN TO THEM?

General Questions and Issues

1. What are the principal types of biomes, and how does climate influence the type found in a given area?

2. What are the basic types of aquatic life zones and ecosystems, and what major factors influence the kinds of life they contain?

3. What are the principal effects of environmental stress on living systems?

4. How can populations of species change and adapt to natural and human-induced stresses?

5. How can communities and ecosystems change and adapt to small- and large-scale natural and human-induced stresses?

6. What impacts do human activities have on populations, communities, and ecosystems?

When we try to pick out anything by itself, we find it hitched to everything else in the universe.

JOHN MUIR

HE BIOSPHERE CONTAINS an astonishing variety of life zones and ecosystems, some found on land and others in Earth's waters. Each realm of life contains characteristic communities of species adapted to certain environmental conditions, especially climate. The different communities vary in the average productivity of the producer organisms that directly or indirectly support other forms of life (Figures 4-19 and 5-1).

Organisms, populations, communities, and ecosystems are always changing and adapting in response to major and minor changes in environmental conditions caused by interactions between organisms (Section 4-5), disruptions such as climate change and floods, and human actions such as land clearing and emissions of various pollutants. Understanding how organisms, populations, communities, and ecosystems adapt to stress and recognizing the limits of those adaptations can help us to sustain rather than continue to degrade and destroy these living systems.

5-1 Biomes: Life on Land

EFFECTS OF PRECIPITATION AND TEMPERATURE ON THE DISTRIBUTION OF TERRESTRIAL PLANTS Why is one area of Earth's land surface a desert, another a grassland, and another a forest? Why are there different types of deserts, grasslands, and forests? What determines the types of life you would expect to find in these biomes if they were undisturbed by human activities?

The general answer to these questions is differences in **climate**: the average weather of an area. It is the general pattern of atmospheric or weather conditions, seasonal variations, and weather extremes in a region over a long period—at least 30 years. The two most important factors determining the climate of an area are the temperature, with its seasonal variations, and the quantity and distribution of precipitation over each year.

Figure 5-2 shows the global distribution of the main types of climate based on these two factors. Figure 5-3 shows the distribution of eleven principal **biomes**—ecological regions with characteristic types of natural vegetation we would expect to find if the land in these areas has not been disturbed by human activities. By comparing these two figures, you can see how the world's principal biomes vary with climate. With respect to plants, *precipitation generally is the limiting factor that determines whether most of the world's land areas are desert, grassland, or forest.*

Average precipitation and average temperature, along with soil type, are the most important factors

Figure 5-1 The biosphere. Three years of satellite data were combined to produce this picture of Earth's biological productivity. Rain forests and other highly productive areas appear as dark green, deserts as yellow. The concentration of phytoplankton, a primary indicator of ocean productivity, is represented by a scale that runs from red (highest) to orange, yellow, green, and blue (lowest).

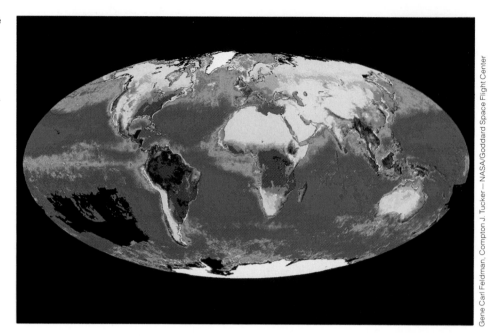

Gene Carl Feldman, Compton J. Tucker—NASA/Goddard Space Flight Center

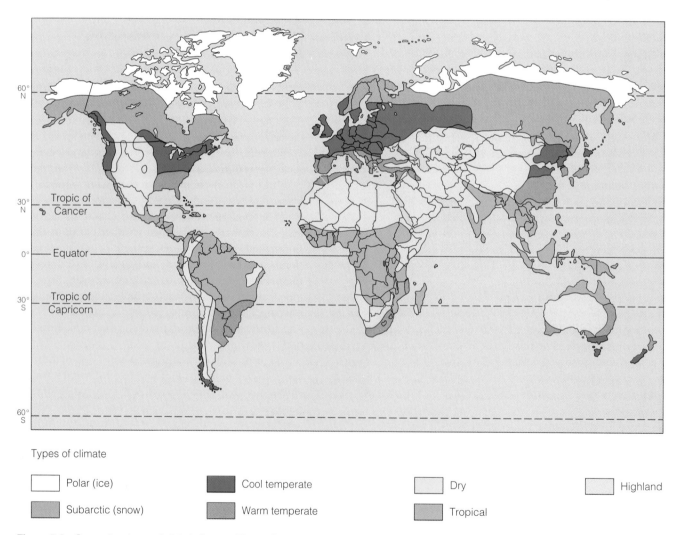

Types of climate

☐ Polar (ice)   ■ Cool temperate   ☐ Dry   ☐ Highland

■ Subarctic (snow)   ▨ Warm temperate   ▨ Tropical

Figure 5-2 Generalized map of global climates. These climates are dictated mainly by two variables: the temperature, with its seasonal variations, and the quantity and distribution of precipitation over each year.

Q: How many of Earth's species have been identified?

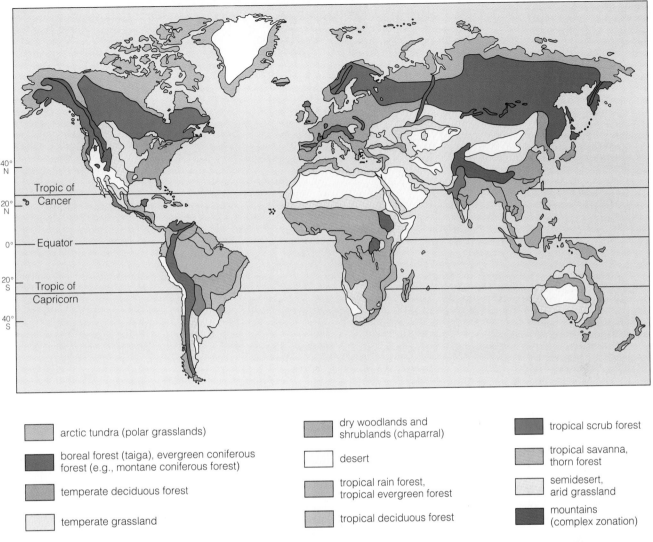

arctic tundra (polar grasslands)

boreal forest (taiga), evergreen coniferous forest (e.g., montane coniferous forest)

temperate deciduous forest

temperate grassland

dry woodlands and shrublands (chaparral)

desert

tropical rain forest, tropical evergreen forest

tropical deciduous forest

tropical scrub forest

tropical savanna, thorn forest

semidesert, arid grassland

mountains (complex zonation)

Figure 5-3 Earth's principal biomes. This map indicates the main types of natural vegetation we would expect to find in different land areas, mostly because of differences in climate. Each biome consists of large numbers of ecosystems whose communities have adapted to smaller differences in climate, soil, and other environmental factors within the biome. This map does not show what we actually find in different parts of the world because people have removed or altered much of this natural vegetation. (White areas are covered in ice.)

determining the particular type of desert, grassland, or forest in a particular area. Acting together, these factors lead to tropical, temperate, and polar deserts, grasslands, and forests (Figure 5-4).

Climate and vegetation both vary with **latitude** (distance from the equator) and **altitude** (height above sea level). If you travel from the equator toward either of Earth's poles, you will encounter increasingly cold and wet climates (Figure 5-2) and zones of vegetation adapted to each climate (Figure 5-5). Similarly, as elevation or height above sea level increases, the climate becomes colder and is often wetter. If you climb a tall mountain from its base to its summit, you will find changes in plant life similar to those you would find in traveling from the equator to one of Earth's poles (Figure 5-5).

DESERTS *Tropical deserts*, such as the southern Sahara and the Namib in Africa, make up about one-fifth of the world's desert area (Figure 5-6). They typically have few plants and a hard, windblown surface strewn with rocks and some sand. In *temperate deserts* (Figure 5-7), such as the Mojave in southern California, daytime temperatures are hot in summer and cool in winter. In *cold deserts*, such as the Gobi lying beyond the Himalaya south of Siberia, winters are cold and summers are warm or hot. In mostly semiarid zones between deserts and grasslands we find *semidesert* dominated by thorn trees and shrubs adapted to a long dry season followed by brief, sometimes heavy, rains.

Plants and animals in all deserts are adapted to capture and conserve scarce water. Some are evergreens with wax-coated leaves that reduce the amount of wa-

Figure 5-4 Average precipitation and average temperature act together over a period of 30 years or more as limiting factors that determine the type of desert, grassland, or forest biome found in a particular area. Although the actual situation is much more complex, this simplified diagram gives you a general idea of how climate determines the types and amounts of natural vegetation you would expect to find in an area that has not been disturbed by human activities.

Figure 5-5 Generalized effects of latitude and altitude on climate and biomes. Different biomes with similar types of vegetation occur primarily as a result of changes in climate in traveling from the equator toward Earth's poles or up mountain slopes on land undisturbed by our activities. Similar types of animals live in each of these vegetation belts or life zones by adapting to similar environmental conditions.

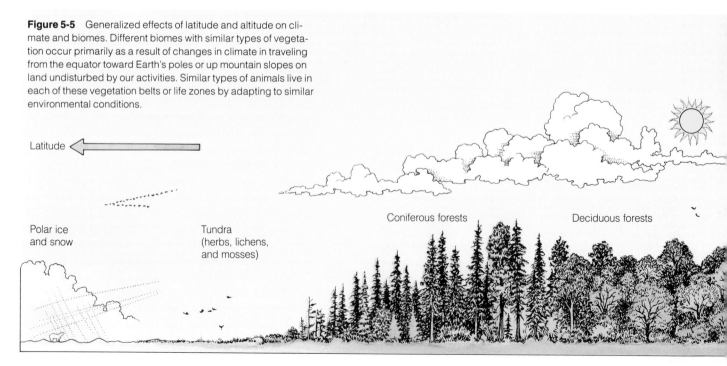

Q: What percentage of all species that have ever lived have become extinct?

ter lost by evaporation (creosote bush). Certain desert plants get water through roots that reach deep into the soil to tap groundwater (mesquite), while fleshy-stemmed, short (prickly pear) and tall (saguaro, Figure 4-5) cacti have widespread shallow roots to collect water that is stored in the succulent tissues of these plants.

Most desert animals escape the daytime heat by staying underground in burrows or under rocks or in crevices during the day and being active at night. Desert animals also have special adaptations to help them conserve water (Figure 5-8). Insects and reptiles have thick outer coverings to minimize water loss through evaporation. Some desert animals become dormant during periods of extreme heat or drought.

The slow growth rate of plants, low species diversity, and shortages of water make deserts quite fragile. For example, vegetation destroyed by human activities such as livestock grazing and driving of motorcycles and other off-road vehicles may take decades to grow back. Vehicles can also cause the collapse of some underground burrows that are habitats for many desert animals.

GRASSLANDS *Tropical grasslands* are found in areas with high average temperatures and low to moderate average precipitation. They occur in a wide belt on either side of the equator beyond the borders of tropical rain forests (Figure 5-3).

Figure 5-6 Tropical desert. The Namib Desert of southwest Africa. Few of the world's deserts are covered with vast expanses of sand and dunes as shown in this photograph. Most deserts are covered with rock or small stones.

Figure 5-7 Temperate desert in Arizona. The vegetation includes creosote bushes, ocotillo, saguaro cacti, and prickly pear cacti. After a brief and infrequent rain, the ground is covered with a variety of wildflowers. Most animals escape the hot days by living underground and coming out at night.

Altitude

Mountain
ice and snow

Tundra (moss,
lichen, herbs)

Coniferous
forests

Deciduous
forests

Tropical forests

Tropical
forests

Figure 5-8 This nocturnal kangaroo rat in a California desert is a master of water conservation. It comes out of its burrow only at night, when the air is cool and water evaporation is slow. This animal stores dry seeds in its burrow, and these absorb some of the moisture lost in the animal's exhaled breath. Instead of drinking water, it gets the water it needs from recycled moisture in the seeds it eats and from metabolic water produced by aerobic respiration of the sugars in the seeds. It also conserves water by excreting hard, dry feces and thick, nearly solid urine.

A: 98% to 99%

Chapter 5   91

Figure 5-9 African elephant on the Serengeti Plain in Tanzania. The Serengeti is an example of one type of tropical grassland, called a tropical savanna. Most savannas consist of open plains covered with low or high grasses and occasional small, mostly deciduous trees or shrubs, such as palm, acacia, and baobab. These plants shed their leaves during the dry season and thus avoid excessive water loss. Many savanna animal species are threatened with extinction because people kill them for their beautiful coats (cheetah), ivory tusks (elephant), or horns (rhinoceros, Figure 4-31).

Figure 5-10 A patch of tall-grass prairie temperate grassland in Mason County, Illinois, in early September. Grasses in this type of biome may be more than 2 meters (6.5 feet) high. Only about 1% of the original area of tall-grass prairies that once thrived in the midwestern United States and Canada remain. Because of their highly fertile soils, most have been cleared for crops such as corn, wheat, and soybeans, and for hog farming.

Figure 5-11 Sheep grazing on a temperate grassland (short-grass prairie) in Idaho. Grasses in this biome are less than 0.6 meter (2 feet) high. Precipitation is too light and soils are too low in some plant nutrients to support taller grasses. These grasslands are widely used to graze unfenced cattle and, in some areas, to grow wheat and irrigated crops.

A grassland that has scattered trees is called a *savanna* (Figure 5-9). Most are tropical savannas found between deserts and tropical forests, although some temperate savannas do occur. Tropical savannas are found in areas with warm temperatures year-round, no winter, two prolonged dry seasons, and abundant rain the rest of the year.

Temperate grasslands are found in the large, interior areas of continents, especially North America, South America, Europe, and Asia (Figure 5-3), where winters are bitterly cold with hard frosts and summers are hot and dry. Types of temperate grasslands are the *tall-grass prairies* (Figure 5-10) and *short-grass prairies* (Figure 5-11) of the midwestern and western United States and Canada, the *pampas* of South America, the *veld* of southern Africa, and the *steppes* that stretch from central Europe into Siberia. In these biomes, winds blow almost continuously and evaporation is rapid. As long as it is not plowed up, the soil is held in place by a thick network of grass roots, but because of their highly fertile soils, many of the world's temperate grasslands have been cleared of their native grasses and used for growing crops (Figure 5-12). Overgrazing, mismanagement, and occasional prolonged droughts lead to severe wind erosion and loss of topsoil, which can convert these fertile grasslands into desert or semidesert.

Polar grassland, or *arctic tundra*, is found in areas south of the Arctic polar ice cap (Figure 5-3). During most of the year, this treeless plain is bitterly cold with icy, strong winds and is covered with ice and snow. Winters are long and dark, and average annual precipitation is low and occurs mostly as snow. The arctic tundra is carpeted with a thick, spongy mat of low-

Q: What two countries have the world's largest populations?

Figure 5-12 Replacement of a temperate grassland with a monoculture cropland near Blythe, California. When the tangled network of natural grasses is removed, the fertile topsoil is subject to severe wind erosion unless it is kept covered with some type of vegetation. If global warming accelerates as projected over the next 50 years, many of these grasslands are expected to become too hot and dry for farming, thus threatening the world's food supply.

Figure 5-14 Arctic tundra is a fragile ecosystem, as shown by this degradation of tundra soil on Victoria Island, Northwest Territories, Canada. Vehicles have broken the thin layer of vegetation and soil that covers the permafrost (ice) and shields it from the sun. Some of the permafrost melts, and the tire tracks turn into thin ribbons of water and ice. Such tracks can mar the terrain for decades.

Figure 5-13 Polar grassland (arctic tundra) in Alaska in summer. During the long, dark, cold winter this land is covered with snow and ice. Its low-growing plants are adapted to the lack of sunlight and water, to freezing temperatures, and to constant high winds in this harsh environment. Below the surface layer of soil is a thick layer of ice, called permafrost, which remains frozen year-round.

growing plants such as lichens (mutually beneficial associations of algae and fungi), sedges (grasslike plants often growing in dense tufts in marshy places), mosses, grasses, and low shrubs (Figure 5-13). Most of the annual growth of these plants occurs during the three to four months of summer when there is sunlight almost around the clock.

One effect of the extreme cold is **permafrost**—a thick layer of ice beneath the soil surface that remains frozen year-round. During the summer, water in the surface layer of soil thaws, but the permafrost layer below remains frozen and prevents water melted at the surface from seeping into the ground. During this period, the largely flat tundra turns into a soggy landscape dotted with shallow lakes, marshes, bogs, and ponds. Hordes of mosquitoes, deerflies, blackflies, and other insects thrive in the shallow surface pools. They serve as food for large colonies of migratory birds, especially waterfowl, which migrate from the south to nest and breed in the bogs and ponds.

The low rate of decomposition, the shallow soil, and the slow growth rate of plants make the arctic tundra perhaps Earth's most fragile biome. Vegetation destroyed by human activities can take decades to grow back (Figure 5-14). Buildings, roads, oil and natural gas pipelines, and railroads must be built over bedrock, on insulating layers of gravel, or on deep-seated pilings. Otherwise, the structures melt the upper layer of permafrost and tilt or crack as the land beneath them shifts and settles.

FORESTS *Tropical rain forests* are a type of evergreen broadleaf forest (Figure 5-15) found in areas near the equator (Figure 5-3), where hot, moisture-laden air rises and then dumps its moisture. They have a warm annual mean temperature that varies little daily or seasonally, high humidity, and heavy rainfall almost daily.

The almost unchanging climate in rain forests means that water and temperature are not limiting factors as they are in other biomes. In this biome, nutrients

Figure 5-15 Tropical rain forest in Monteverde Cloud Forest Reserve in Costa Rica. Life in these storehouses of biodiversity exists in several layers, populated mostly by species with specialized niches (Figure 4-28). Although tropical forests cover only about 6% to 7% of Earth's land surface, they are habitats for 50% to 80% of Earth's species.

Brian Rogers/Biofotos

from the often nutrient-poor soils are the principal limiting factors.

A mature rain forest has a greater diversity of plant and animal species per unit of area than does any other biome. These diverse forms of plant and animal life occupy a variety of mostly specialized niches in distinct layers, based mostly on their ability to thrive with different levels of sunlight (Figure 4-28).

Rain forests are deceptively fragile. Left to themselves, tropical rain forests can sustain themselves indefinitely; but if you clear large areas, you end up with patches of grassland and, eventually, desert. Most of the nutrients in this biome are in the vegetation, not in the upper layers of soil as in most other biomes. As a result, once the vegetation is removed, the few nutrients in these soils are quickly leached out, and the runoff carries them away in solution. This means that regenerating a mature rain forest on large cleared areas is almost impossible on a human time scale.

These forested storehouses of Earth's precious biodiversity (see Spotlight on p. 8) are being cleared or degraded at an alarming rate to harvest timber, to mine minerals, and to plant crops and graze livestock on unsustainable soils. If the clearing and degradation of tropical rain forests continue at the present rate, within 50 years only a few scattered fragments of these diverse biomes will remain. Also gone forever will be hundreds of thousands of species with highly specialized niches in these forests.

Burning and clearing the vegetation from large areas of these forests also releases enormous quantities of carbon dioxide into the atmosphere and decreases the number of plants removing this gas from the atmosphere as part of the global carbon cycle (Figure 4-22). This deforestation could enhance Earth's natural greenhouse effect, cause rapid warming of the troposphere, and disrupt regional and global water and food supplies.

Temperate deciduous forests grow in areas with moderate average temperatures that change significantly during four distinct seasons (Figure 5-3). These areas have long summers, cold but not too severe winters, and abundant precipitation, often spread fairly evenly throughout the year. This biome is dominated by a few species of broadleaf deciduous trees, such as oak, hickory, maple, poplar, sycamore, and beech. These plants survive during winter by dropping their leaves and going into an inactive state (Figure 5-16).

Temperate deciduous forests have nutrient-rich soil (helped by decomposition of the annual fall of leaves) and valuable timber. All but about 0.1% of the original stands of temperate deciduous forests in North America have been cleared for farms, orchards, timber, and urban development. Some have been converted to intensely managed *tree farms* or *plantations*, where a single species is grown for timber, pulpwood, or Christmas Trees (Figure 5-17).

Evergreen coniferous forests, also called *boreal forests* (meaning "northern forests") and *taigas* (meaning "swamp forests"), are found in northern regions with a subarctic climate (Figures 5-2) in an almost unbroken belt just south of the Arctic tundra across North America, Asia, and Europe (Figure 5-3). Winters are long and dry, with light snowfall, and temperatures range from

Q: What continent has the world's highest population growth rate?

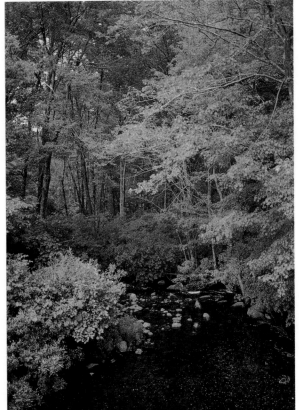

Figure 5-16 Temperate deciduous forest in Rhode Island during winter, spring, summer, and fall (clockwise from top left).

Paul W. Johnson/Biological Photo Service

Figure 5-17 Tree farm, or plantation, in North Carolina. Converting a diverse temperate deciduous forest to an even-aged stand of a single species (monoculture) increases the production of wood for timber or pulpwood but results in a loss of biological diversity. Such monocultures are more vulnerable to attacks by pests, disease, and air pollution than are the more diverse forests they replaced.

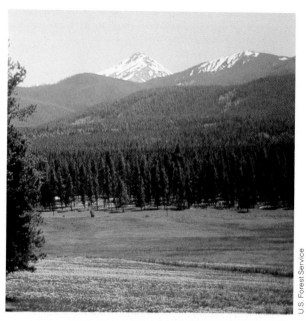

Figure 5-18 Evergreen coniferous forest (taiga or boreal forest) in Washington. Many of these ancient forests and the temperate rain forests found along the West Coast from Canada to northern California have been clear-cut and replaced with tree plantations. There is intense pressure to clear-cut many of the remaining stands of these forests located on publicly owned land in the national forests.

cool to extremely cold, with temperatures low enough to snap steel. Summers are short, with mild to warm temperatures, and the sun typically shines 19 hours each day.

These forests are dominated by a few species of coniferous evergreen trees such as spruce, fir, cedar, hemlock, and pine (Figure 5-18). The tiny, needle-shaped, waxy-coated leaves of these trees can withstand the intense cold and drought of winter. Plant diversity is low in these forests because few species can survive the winters, when soil moisture is frozen.

Beneath the dense stands of trees, a carpet of fallen needles and leaf litter covers the nutrient-poor soil, making the soil acidic and preventing most other plants from growing on the dim forest floor. During the brief summer the soil becomes waterlogged. Wet bogs, or muskegs, are found in low-lying areas of these forests.

Loggers have cut the trees from large areas of taiga in North America, and many of these remaining ancient forests may soon be cut. Most of the vast boreal forests that once covered Finland and Sweden have been cut and replaced with even-aged tree plantations. Industrial activities in and around the taiga are increasing the number of trees being killed or degraded by fires and by acid deposition and other forms of air pollution.

5-2 Life in Water Environments

WHY ARE THE OCEANS IMPORTANT? As land-lubbers, we tend to think of Earth in terms of land, but Earth is largely a water planet. A more accurate name for the planet would be Ocean, because oceans cover more than 70% of its surface (Figure 5-19).

The oceans play key roles in the survival of virtually all life on Earth. Because of their size and currents, the oceans mix and dilute many human-produced wastes flowing or dumped into them to less harmful or even harmless levels, as long as they are not overloaded. Because solar heat is distributed through ocean currents and because ocean water evaporates as part of the global hydrologic cycle (Figure 4-26), oceans play a major role in regulating Earth's climate. They also participate in other important biogeochemical cycles.

By serving as a gigantic reservoir for carbon dioxide (Figure 4-22), oceans help regulate the temperature of the troposphere through the greenhouse effect. Oceans provide habitats for about 250,000 species of marine plants and animals, which are food for many organisms, including human beings. They also serve as a source of iron, sand, gravel, phosphates, magnesium, oil, natural gas, and many other valuable resources.

MAJOR OCEAN ZONES Oceans have two principal life zones: coastal and open sea (Figure 5-20). The

Q: Worldwide, what is the average number of children per woman?

Figure 5-19 The ocean planet. About 97% of the volume of Earth's water is in the interconnected oceans that cover 90% of the surface of the planet's mostly ocean hemisphere (left) and 50% of the surface of its land-ocean hemisphere (right).

Ocean hemisphere

Land-ocean hemisphere

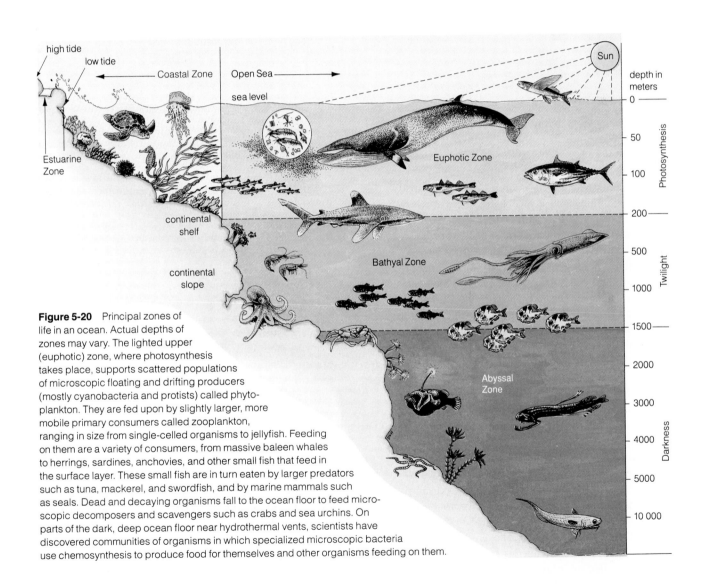

Figure 5-20 Principal zones of life in an ocean. Actual depths of zones may vary. The lighted upper (euphotic) zone, where photosynthesis takes place, supports scattered populations of microscopic floating and drifting producers (mostly cyanobacteria and protists) called phytoplankton. They are fed upon by slightly larger, more mobile primary consumers called zooplankton, ranging in size from single-celled organisms to jellyfish. Feeding on them are a variety of consumers, from massive baleen whales to herrings, sardines, anchovies, and other small fish that feed in the surface layer. These small fish are in turn eaten by larger predators such as tuna, mackerel, and swordfish, and by marine mammals such as seals. Dead and decaying organisms fall to the ocean floor to feed microscopic decomposers and scavengers such as crabs and sea urchins. On parts of the dark, deep ocean floor near hydrothermal vents, scientists have discovered communities of organisms in which specialized microscopic bacteria use chemosynthesis to produce food for themselves and other organisms feeding on them.

Figure 5-21 Salt marsh on Cape Cod off the coast of Massachusetts. These and other temperate coastal wetlands trap nutrients and sediment flowing in from rivers and nearby land and thus have a high net primary productivity. They also filter out and degrade some of the pollutants deposited by rivers and land runoff.

Figure 5-22 Mangrove swamp in Gambia. Since the mid-1960s, some tropical coastal countries have lost half or more of their mangrove forests because of industrial logging for timber and fuelwood, conversion to ponds for raising fish and shellfish (aquaculture), conversion to rice fields and other agricultural land, and urban development. The worst destruction has taken place in Asia, especially in the Philippines, Indonesia, and Java.

coastal zone is the relatively warm, nutrient-rich, shallow water that extends from the high-tide mark on land to the gently sloping, relatively shallow edge of the *continental shelf*, the submerged part of the continents. The coastal zone, representing less than 10% of the world's ocean area, contains 90% of all ocean species and is the site of most of the large commercial marine fisheries. This thin zone is the source of most of the oceans' net primary productivity per unit of area (Figure 5-1).

The sharp increase in water depth at the edge of the continental shelf marks the separation of the coastal zone from the **open sea**, which is divided into three zones based primarily on the ability of sunlight to penetrate to various depths (Figure 5-20). This vast zone contains about 90% of the world's ocean area, but has only about 10% of all ocean species.

THE COASTAL ZONE: A CLOSER LOOK The coastal zone includes a number of different ecosystems with the world's highest net primary productivities per unit of area (Figure 4-19). An **estuary** is a partially enclosed coastal area at the mouth of a river where its fresh water, carrying fertile silt and runoff from the land, mixes with salty seawater. In these areas, temperature and salinity levels vary widely because of seasonal variations in stream flow and the daily rhythms of the tides.

A **wetland** is an area of land covered all or part of the year with salt water (called a **coastal wetland**) or fresh water (called an **inland wetland**, excluding lakes, ponds, and streams). About 5% of all wetlands in the United States are coastal wetlands. The other 95% are inland wetlands.

Coastal wetlands extend inland from estuaries. In temperate areas, coastal wetlands usually consist of a mix of bays, lagoons, salt flats, mud flats, and salt marshes (Figure 5-21), where grasses are the dominant vegetation. In coastal areas with warm tropical climates, we find saltwater swamps dominated by mangrove trees, species of trees and shrubs that can live partly submerged in the relatively salty environment of coastal swamps (Figure 5-22). These swamps have the highest net primary productivity per unit of area of any terrestrial or aquatic ecosystem.

The coastal zones of warm tropical and subtropical oceans often contain coral reefs (Figure 5-23). They are formed by massive colonies containing billions of tiny coral animals, called polyps, which secrete a stony substance (calcium carbonate) around themselves for protection. When the corals die, their empty outer skeletons form layers that cause the reef to grow. The resulting maze of cracks, crevices, and caves provides shelter for huge numbers of various marine plants and animals, including many colorful fish (Figure 5-23). Coral polyps are colorless, but they harbor in their tissues armies of green and brown algae that give these reefs their vibrant colors. In this mutualistic relationship, the algae are provided a habitat, and in turn they provide the polyps with sugar nutrients through photosynthesis.

Despite their size, coral reefs are very sensitive and vulnerable ecosystems, existing within a narrow range of temperature, nutrient, and light conditions. Coral reefs are being destroyed or damaged in 93 of the 109 countries where these ecosystems are found.

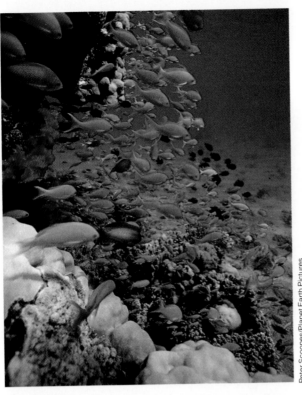

Figure 5-23 Coral reef in the Red Sea. These incredibly diverse and productive ecosystems are being destroyed and degraded at an alarming rate.

Figure 5-24 Rocky shore beach in Acadia National Park, Maine. Organisms of most seashores must be able to withstand the tremendous force of incoming waves and the pull of the outgoing tide. Coasts like this one provide rocks to which organisms can attach themselves.

Some coasts have steep *rocky shores* pounded by waves (Figure 5-24). Other coasts have gently sloping *barrier beaches* at the water's edge. If not destroyed by human activities, one or more rows of natural sand dunes on such beaches (with the sand held in place by the roots of grasses) serve as the first line of defense against the ravages of the sea (Figure 5-25). Such beaches, however, are prime sites for human developments (Figure 5-26).

Along some coasts (such as most of North America's Atlantic and Gulf coasts), we find *barrier islands*: long, thin, low offshore islands of sediment that generally run parallel to the shore. These islands help protect the mainland, estuaries, lagoons, and coastal wetlands by dispersing the energy of approaching storm waves.

People build cottages, hotels, casinos (Atlantic City), and other structures on barrier islands (Figure 5-27) and barrier beaches (Figure 5-26), even though they are the most dynamic places on Earth. Their low-lying beaches are constantly shifting, as a result of the actions of gentle waves, currents, and storms. Sooner or later, many of the structures we build on low-lying barrier islands and gently sloping barrier beaches are damaged or destroyed by flooding, severe beach erosion, and wind from major storms (including hurricanes).

When coastal developers remove the dunes or build behind the first set of dunes, minor hurricanes and sea storms can flood and even sweep away houses and other buildings. Coastal dwellers mistakenly refer to these human-assisted disasters as natural disasters and expect federally supported insurance and disaster aid to allow them to rebuild in these highly vulnerable areas and await the next disaster.

Along some steep, western coasts of continents, almost-constant trade winds blow offshore and push surface water away from the shore. This outwardly moving surface water is replaced by an **upwelling** of cold, nutrient-rich bottom water which supports large populations of plankton, fish, and fish-eating seabirds. Although they make up only about 0.1% of the world's total ocean area, upwellings are highly productive (Figure 5-1). However, changes in climate and ocean currents that take place every few years (the El Niño effect), coupled with overfishing, can reduce their high productivity and cause sharp drops in the annual catch of some important marine fish species. Because of their immense value to us and other species, coastal zones need to be protected and managed in ways that sustain their productivity (see Case Study on p. 103).

FRESHWATER LAKES AND RESERVOIRS **Lakes** are large natural bodies of standing fresh water formed when precipitation, land runoff, or flowing groundwater fills depressions in the earth. Lakes normally consist of four distinct zones (Figure 5-28), which provide a variety of habitats and ecological niches for different species.

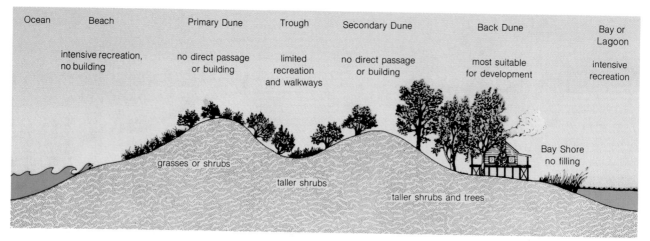

Ocean | Beach | Primary Dune | Trough | Secondary Dune | Back Dune | Bay or Lagoon

intensive recreation, no building | no direct passage or building | limited recreation and walkways | no direct passage or building | most suitable for development | intensive recreation

grasses or shrubs

taller shrubs

taller shrubs and trees

Bay Shore no filling

Figure 5-25 Primary and secondary dunes on a gently sloping beach play an important role in protecting the land from erosion by the sea. The roots of various grasses that colonize the dunes help hold the sand in place. Ideally, construction and development should be allowed only behind the second strip of dunes, with walkways to the beach built over the dunes to keep them intact. This helps protect structures from being damaged and washed away by wind, high tides, beach erosion, and flooding from storm surges. This type of protection, however, is rare, because the short-term economic value of limited oceanfront land is considered to be much higher than its long-term ecological and economic values.

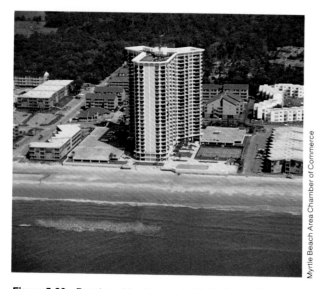

Myrtle Beach Area Chamber of Commerce

Figure 5-26 Developed barrier beach, Myrtle Beach, South Carolina. Note that the protective dunes have been eliminated.

G. H. Demetrakas/O. C. Camera

Figure 5-27 Developed barrier island, Ocean City, Maryland (Fenwick Island), is host to 8 million visitors a year. To keep up with shifting sands, officials must spend millions to pump sand onto the beaches and to rebuild natural sand dunes; they may end up spending millions more to keep buildings from sinking. There is no effective protection against flooding and damage from severe storms. Within a few hours, a barrier island may be cut in two or destroyed by a hurricane. If global warming raises average sea levels as projected sometime in the next century, most of these valuable pieces of real estate will be underwater.

A lake with a large or excessive supply of nutrients needed by producers is called a **eutrophic** ("well-nourished") **lake** (Figure 5-29). These lakes have a high net primary productivity and are often shallow. A lake with a small supply of nutrients (mostly nitrates and phosphates) needed by producers is called an **oligotrophic** ("poorly-nourished") **lake** (Figure 5-29). Because of its relatively low net primary productivity, such a lake is usually deep and has crystal-clear blue or green water. This type of lake is often deep with steep banks. Many lakes fall somewhere between the two extremes of nutrient enrichment and are called **mesotrophic lakes**.

Eutrophication (pronounced, *yoo-tro-fuh-kay-shun*) refers to the physical, chemical, and biological changes that take place after a lake receives inputs of nutrients and silt from the surrounding land basin as a result of natural erosion and runoff over a long period of time. Some lakes naturally become more eutrophic over time, but others do not because of differences in the surrounding waterbasin.

Near urban or agricultural centers, the input of nutrients to a lake can be greatly accelerated by human

Q: What is the average number of children per woman in the United States?

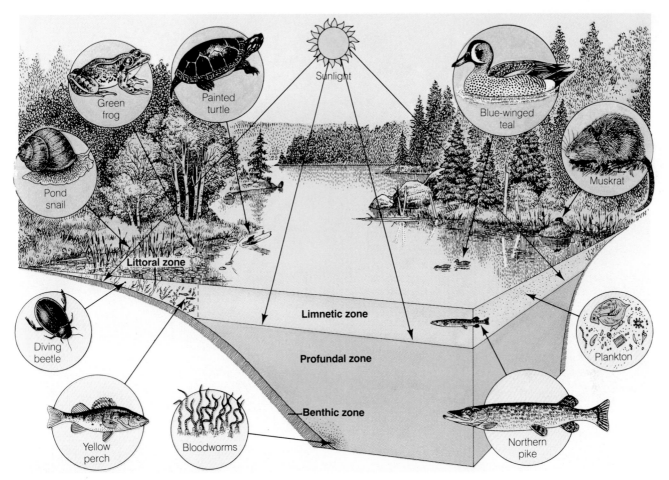

Figure 5-28 The four distinct zones of life in a lake. The *littoral zone* includes the shore and the shallow, nutrient-rich waters near the shore, in which sunlight reaches the bottom. It contains a variety of floating and drifting producers (phytoplankton), rooted aquatic plants, and other forms of aquatic life, such as frogs, snails, and snakes. The *limnetic zone*, like the euphotic zone of the ocean (Figure 5-20), is the open-water surface layer that gets enough sunlight for photosynthesis. It contains varying amounts of phytoplankton, plant-eating zooplankton, and fish, depending on the supply of nutrients available to producers. The *profundal zone* is the deep, open water where it is too dark for photosynthesis. It is inhabited by fish adapted to its cooler, darker water. The *benthic zone*, at the bottom of a lake, is inhabited mostly by large numbers of decomposers (bacteria and fungi), detritus-feeding clams, and wormlike insect larvae. They feed mostly on plant debris, animal remains, and animal wastes that descend from above.

activities, a process known as **cultural eutrophication**. It is caused mostly by nitrate- and phosphate-containing effluents from sewage treatment plants, runoff of fertilizers and animal wastes, and accelerated erosion of nutrient-rich topsoil.

Reservoirs are normally large, deep, human-made bodies of standing fresh water. Large reservoirs are frequently created by building dams to collect water running down from mountains in streams (Figure 5-30). Often artificial reservoirs are wrongly called lakes.

Reservoirs store water, which can be released in a controlled manner to produce hydroelectric power at the dam site, provide irrigation water on dry land found below the dam, prevent or reduce flooding in land below the reservoir, and provide water carried by aqueduct to towns and cities. Reservoirs are also used for recreation such as swimming, fishing, and boating.

FRESHWATER STREAMS Precipitation that doesn't infiltrate the ground or evaporate remains on the earth's surface as **surface water**. This water becomes **runoff**, which flows into streams and eventually downhill to the oceans to continue circulating in the hydrologic cycle (Figure 4-26). The entire land area that delivers the water, sediment, and dissolved substances via small streams to a major stream (river), and ultimately to the sea, is called a **watershed**, or **drainage basin**.

The downward flow of water from mountain highlands to the sea takes place in three phases in a *river system* (Figure 5-31). Because of differences in environmental conditions in each phase, a river system consists of a series of different ecosystems.

As streams flow downhill, they become powerful shapers of land. Over millions of years, the friction of moving water levels mountains and cuts deep canyons.

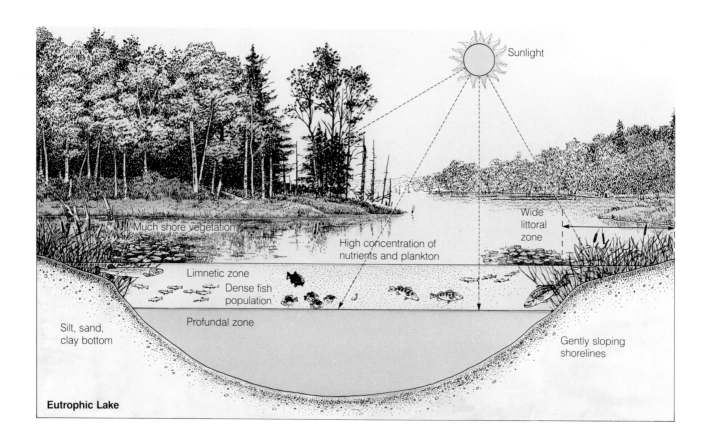

Eutrophic Lake

Sunlight

Much shore vegetation

High concentration of nutrients and plankton

Wide littoral zone

Limnetic zone

Dense fish population

Profundal zone

Silt, sand, clay bottom

Gently sloping shorelines

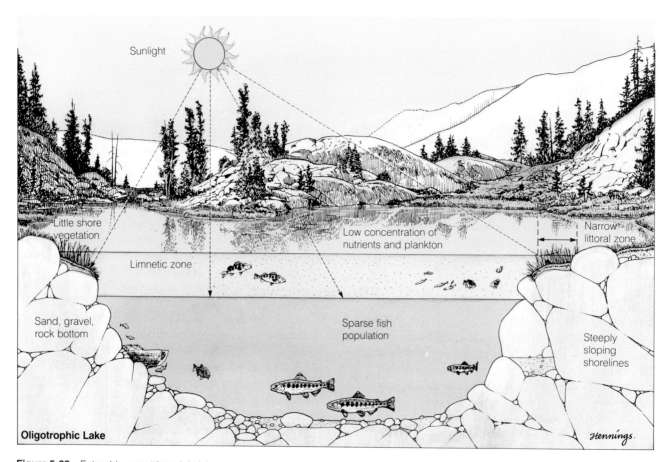

Oligotrophic Lake

Sunlight

Little shore vegetation

Limnetic zone

Low concentration of nutrients and plankton

Narrow littoral zone

Sand, gravel, rock bottom

Sparse fish population

Steeply sloping shorelines

Hennings

Figure 5-29 Eutrophic, or nutrient-rich, lake and oligotrophic, or nutrient-poor, lake. Mesotrophic lakes fall between these two extremes of nutrient enrichment.

Q: How many people were added to the U.S. population (including legal and illegal immigrants) in 1992?

Many people view estuaries and coastal wetlands (Figures 5-21 and 5-22) as desolate, mosquito-infested, worthless lands. They believe these ecosystems should be drained, dredged, filled in, built on, or used as dumps for human-generated pollutants and waste materials.

Nothing could be further from the truth. These highly productive areas supply food and serve as spawning and nursery grounds for many species of marine fish and shellfish. They are also breeding grounds and habitats for waterfowl and other wildlife, including many endangered species.

Coastal areas also dilute and filter out large amounts of nutrients and waterborne pollutants, helping protect the quality of waters used for swimming, fishing, and wildlife habitats. It is estimated that 0.4 hectare (1 acre) of tidal estuary substitutes for a $75,000 waste treatment plant and has a total land value of $83,000 when its production of fish for food and recreation is included.

By comparison, 0.4 hectare (1 acre) of prime farmland in Kansas has a top value of $1,200 and an annual production value of $600.

Estuaries, coastal wetlands, barrier islands, and the natural sand dunes found on most gently sloping barrier beaches help protect coastlines and land behind them from storms and flooding. They absorb damaging waves caused by violent storms and hurricanes, and coastal wetlands serve as giant sponges to absorb floodwaters.

They are also among our most densely populated and most intensely used and polluted ecosystems. Nearly 55% of the area of estuaries and coastal wetlands in the United States has been destroyed or damaged. California has lost 90% of its original coastal wetlands.

These ecosystems are particularly vulnerable to toxic contamination because they trap pesticides, heavy metals, and other pollutants, concentrating them to very high levels. On any given day, one-third of U.S. shellfish beds are closed to commercial or sport fishing because of contamination.

Fortunately, about 45% of the area of estuaries and coastal wetlands in the United States remains undeveloped. Each year, however, additional areas are developed or severely degraded, especially in the southeastern United States, where 83% of the remaining wetlands in the lower 48 states are found. Wetlands fare no better in LDCs. In India and Bangladesh, for example, firewood gatherers have reduced vital mangrove swamps by more than 90%.

In our desire to live near the coast and use coastal resources, we are destroying the very things that make coastal areas so enjoyable and valuable. An urgent environmental priority should be to protect remaining unspoiled estuaries, coastal wetlands, beaches, and coral reefs around the world from destruction and degradation and to manage those we have developed sustainably.

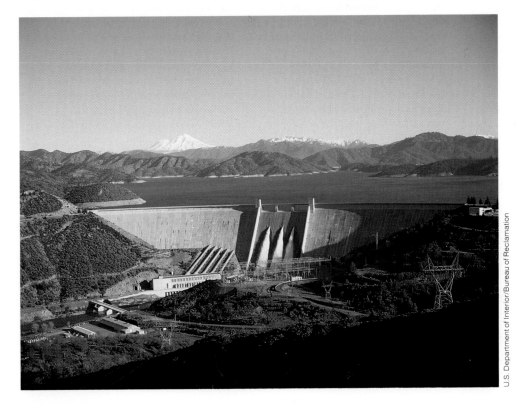

Figure 5-30 Reservoir formed behind Shasta Dam on the Sacramento River north of Redding, California. This reservoir and dam are used to produce electricity (hydropower) and to help control flooding in areas below the dam by storing and releasing water slowly. Water flowing through the base of the dam drives turbines that spin generators and produce electricity. About 13.5% of the electrical power used in the United States is produced by large hydroelectric power plants like this one.

U.S. Department of Interior/Bureau of Reclamation

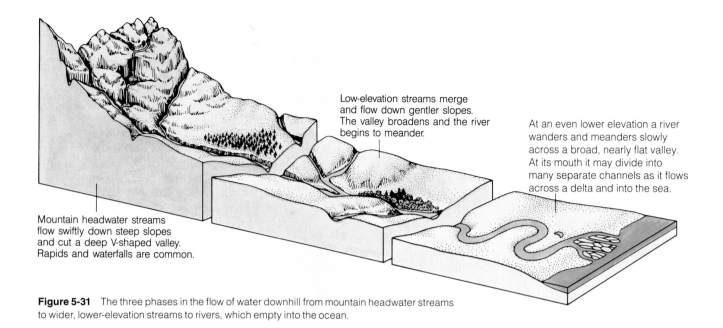

Low-elevation streams merge and flow down gentler slopes. The valley broadens and the river begins to meander.

At an even lower elevation a river wanders and meanders slowly across a broad, nearly flat valley. At its mouth it may divide into many separate channels as it flows across a delta and into the sea.

Mountain headwater streams flow swiftly down steep slopes and cut a deep V-shaped valley. Rapids and waterfalls are common.

Figure 5-31 The three phases in the flow of water downhill from mountain headwater streams to wider, lower-elevation streams to rivers, which empty into the ocean.

SPOTLIGHT Why Are Inland Wetlands So Important?

Inland wetlands, including seasonal ones, provide habitats for a variety of fish, waterfowl, and other wildlife, including many rare and endangered species. Wetlands near rivers help regulate stream flow by storing water during periods of heavy rainfall and releasing it slowly. This helps reduce riverbank erosion and flood damage. These inland wetlands also improve water quality by filtering, diluting, and degrading various sediments, disease-causing bacteria, and toxic pollutants as water flows through. Seasonal wetlands can purify water more efficiently than can deep, stagnant swamps.

By storing water, many seasonal and nonseasonal wetlands allow increased infiltration, thus helping recharge groundwater supplies. Inland wetlands are used for recreation, especially waterfowl hunting, and to grow crops such as blueberries, cranberries, and rice (which feeds half the world's people). They also play significant roles in the global cycles of carbon, nitrogen, and sulfur.

Because people are unaware of their ecological importance, inland wetlands often are dredged or filled in and used as croplands, garbage dumps, and sites for urban and industrial development. They are viewed as wastelands and threats to public health.

Since 1780, about 53% of the original coastal and inland wetlands in the continental United States have been destroyed. About 95% of remaining U.S. wetlands are inland wetlands, usually on or adjacent to agricultural property. Attempts have been made to slow the rate of inland wetland loss, but each year about 121,000 hectares (300,000 acres) are destroyed. About 80% of this loss involves draining and clearing for agricultural purposes. Iowa has lost 99% of its inland wetlands and Nebraska 91%. Other countries have similar losses.

The goal of current federal policy is no net loss of the function and value of wetlands, but this stated goal is deceptive because the policy allows destruction of existing wetlands as long as an equal area of the same type of wetland is restored or created. Exceptions are also allowed. As a result, at least 14 hectares (34 acres) of U.S. wetlands are being destroyed every hour. Wetland restoration and creation is desirable but cannot duplicate the complex ecological services supplied by natural wetland ecosystems with any scientific certainty. The result is a net loss of wetland function and value.

In 1991, President Bush yielded to pressure from real estate developers, mining companies, and oil companies and proposed that wetlands be redefined in a way that would allow as much as one-third of the country's remaining wetlands (mostly seasonal wetlands) in the lower 48 states to be vulnerable to development. He also supported industry efforts to strip the EPA of its current role (through the Clean Water Act) in approving or vetoing wetland development permits. Future permits would be reviewed only by the Army Corps of Engineers, which is not charged by law with protecting water quality or aquatic ecosystems.

The United States urgently needs a better system for protecting and managing its wetlands, both coastal and inland. The immediate goal of such a program should be to prevent further loss of the country's natural wetlands by strengthening, not weakening, wetland protection laws. The long-term goal should be to restore the quantity and quality of the country's wetlands.

Q: How many teenage women (ages 15 to 19) become pregnant each year in the United States?

The rock and soil the water removes is then deposited as sediment in low-lying areas.

INLAND WETLANDS   Lands covered with fresh water all or part of the year (excluding lakes, reservoirs, and streams) and located away from coastal areas are called **inland wetlands**. They include inland bogs, marshes, prairie potholes, swamps, mud flats, floodplains, wet meadows, and the wet arctic tundra (Figure 5-14) during summer. Some of these wetlands are covered with water year-round. Others, such as prairie potholes and the edges of lakes, streams, and swamps, are seasonal wetlands that are underwater or soggy for only a short time each year. Fully submerged and seasonal inland wetlands are important ecosystems that are rapidly being destroyed and degraded (see Spotlight on p. 104).

5-3   Responses of Living Systems to Environmental Stress

HOMEOSTASIS AND STABILITY OF LIVING SYSTEMS   To survive, you must maintain various internal conditions such as temperature and blood pressure, within certain tolerable ranges (Figure 4-15) in the face of a harsh and often fluctuating external environment. This state of dynamic balance is called **homeostasis**: the maintenance of constant internal conditions despite fluctuations in the external environment.

Organisms, populations, communities, and ecosystems have some ability to withstand or recover from externally imposed changes or stresses—provided those stresses are not too severe. In other words, they have some degree of *stability*.

This stability, however, is maintained only by constant dynamic change. Although an organism maintains a fairly stable structure over its life span, it is continually gaining and losing matter and energy. Similarly, in a mature tropical rain forest, some trees will die, and others will take their place. Some species may disappear, and the number of individual species in the forest may change. Unless it is cut, burned, or blown down, however, you will recognize it as a tropical rain forest 50 years from now.

It's useful to distinguish between three aspects of stability in living systems. **Inertia**, or **persistence**, is the ability of a living system to resist being disturbed or altered. **Constancy** is the ability of a living system, such as a population, to maintain a certain size or keep its numbers within certain limits. **Resilience** is the ability of a living system to restore itself close to an original condition after being exposed to an outside disturbance that is not too drastic.

Table 5-1 Changes Affecting Ecosystems		
Natural Changes		
Catastrophic	Drought	
	Flood	
	Fire	
	Volcanic eruption	
	Earthquake	
	Hurricane	
	Disease	
Gradual	Changes in climate	
	Immigration and emigration of species	
	Adaptation and evolution of species as a response to environmental stress	
	Changes in plant and animal life (ecological succession)	
Human-Caused Changes		
Catastrophic	Deforestation	
	Overgrazing of grasslands	
	Plowing of grasslands	
	Soil erosion	
	Using pesticides	
	Excessive or inappropriate use of fire	
	Release of toxic substances into the air, water, or soil	
	Urbanization	
	Mining	
Gradual	Salt buildup in soil from irrigation (salinization)	
	Waterlogging of soil from irrigation	
	Compaction of soil from agricultural equipment	
	Pollution of surface waters (streams, lakes, reservoirs, wetlands, oceans)	
	Depletion and pollution of underground aquifers	
	Air pollution (can also be catastrophic)	
	Loss and degradation of wildlife habitat (can also be catastrophic)	
	Killing of undesirable predator and pest species	
	Introduction of alien species	
	Release of toxic substances into the air, water, and soil	
	Overhunting	
	Overfishing	
	Excessive tourism	

TYPES AND EFFECTS OF ENVIRONMENTAL STRESS   Ecosystems are affected by a number of natural and human-caused changes, which are summarized in Table 5-1. Some of these changes are gradual, and some are sudden or catastrophic.

Table 5-2 summarizes what can happen to organisms, populations, communities, and ecosystems as a

Table 5-2 Some Effects of Environmental Stress

Organism Level

Physiological and biochemical changes
Psychological disorders
Behavioral changes
Fewer or no offspring
Genetic defects in offspring (mutagenic effects)
Birth defects (teratogenic effects)
Cancers (carcinogenic effects)
Death

Population Level

Population increase or decrease
Change in age structure (old, young, and weak may die)
Survival of strains genetically resistant to stress
Loss of genetic diversity and adaptability
Extinction

Community-Ecosystem Level

Disruption of energy flow
   Decrease or increase in solar energy input
   Changes in heat output
   Changes in trophic structure in food chains and food
   webs

Disruption of chemical cycles
   Depletion of essential nutrients
   Excessive addition of nutrients

Simplification
   Reduction in species diversity
   Reduction or elimination of habitats and filled
   ecological niches
   Less complex food webs
   Possibility of lowered stability
   Possibility of ecosystem collapse

result of environmental stress in which one or more environmental factors fall above or below the levels tolerated by various species (Figure 4-15). The stresses that can cause the changes shown in Table 5-2 may result from natural hazards (such as earthquakes, volcanic eruptions, hurricanes, droughts, floods, and fires) or from human activities (industrialization, warfare, transportation, urbanization, and agriculture).

5-4   Population Responses to Stress

CHANGES IN POPULATION SIZE, DISTRIBUTION, AND STRUCTURE Populations undergo changes in their size, density, dispersion, and age distribution in response to changes in environmental conditions, such as an excess or a shortage of food or other critical nu-

trients. These changes in the properties of populations are called **population dynamics**.

Changes in the *birth rate* (number of live births in a population per unit of time), the *death rate* (number of deaths in a population per unit of time), or both, are the principal ways that populations of most species respond (usually involuntarily) to changes in resource availability or other environmental changes (Figure 5-32).

Members of some animal species can avoid, or reduce the effects of, an environmental stress by leaving one area (emigration) and migrating to an area (immigration) with more favorable environmental conditions and resource supplies. Plants can migrate to other areas, but that often takes decades or centuries.

The structure of the population in terms of the numbers of individuals of different ages and sex may change. Old, very young, and weak members may die when exposed to an environmental stress. The remaining population is then better equipped to survive such stresses as a more severe climate, an increase in predators, or an increase in disease organisms.

J AND S CURVES: IDEALIZED MODEL OF POPULATION DYNAMICS With unlimited resources and ideal environmental conditions, a species can produce offspring at its maximum rate or **biotic potential**. Such growth starts slowly and then increases rapidly to produce an *exponential growth curve*, or J-shaped curve of population growth that grows steeper with time (Figures 1-2 and 5-33). Almost any kind of organism would be capable of increasing its population to crowd out the entire world if given ample food, water, space, and protection from its enemies.

But unlimited growth *doesn't* occur, because environmental conditions are less than ideal and resources are normally limited. No matter how rapidly a population may grow, it will eventually reach some size limit imposed by shortages of one or more limiting factors, such as light, water, space, and nutrients.

Environmental resistance consists of all the limiting factors jointly acting to limit the growth of a population. They determine the **carrying capacity (K)**, the number of individuals of a given species that can be sustained indefinitely in a given area. The carrying capacity for a population is not fixed and can vary over time because of changes in seasons, climate, and other environmental conditions.

Because of environmental resistance, any population growing exponentially at, or below, its biotic potential starts out slowly, goes through a rapid growth phase, and then levels off and fluctuates slightly above and below its carrying capacity. A plot of this type of growth yields an *S-shaped curve* (Figure 5-33, left). Sometimes a population undergoing rapid growth suffers a dieback or population crash (Figure 5-33, right), unless large numbers can migrate to an area with more

Q: What percentage of the world's population is under age 15?

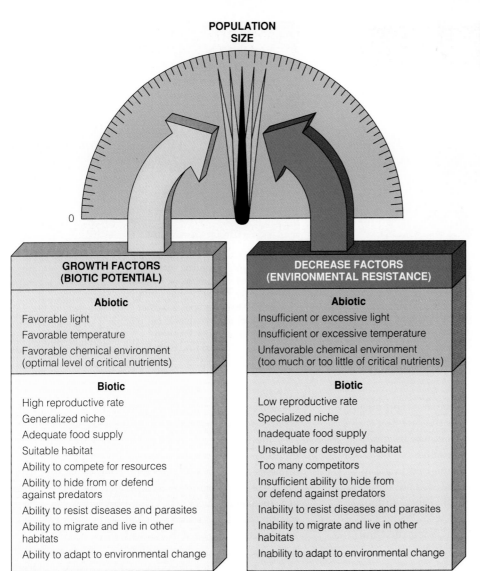

Figure 5-32 Population size is a balance between factors that increase numbers and factors that decrease numbers.

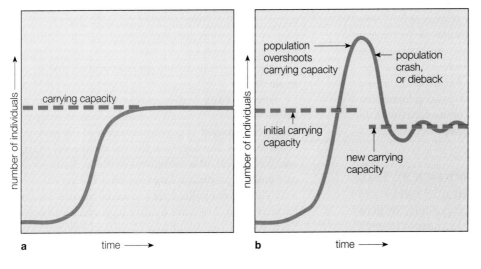

Figure 5-33 (**a**) Idealized S-shaped curve of population growth. (**b**) Overshoot and die-back when a rapidly expanding population temporarily overshoots the carrying capacity of its environment or when a change in environmental conditions lowers that carrying capacity. The population size may fall roughly to the size supported by the area's carrying capacity. If the excess population destroys or degrades vegetation, soil, or other resources, the carrying capacity of an area may be lowered. Then the population dieback or crash is more severe. These idealized curves only approximate what goes on in nature.

J. A. Bishop and L. M. Cook

Figure 5-34 Two varieties of peppered moths found in England in the 1800s. In the mid-1800s, before the Industrial Revolution, the speckled light-gray form of this moth was prevalent. These moths, active at night, rested on light-gray speckled lichens on tree trunks during the day. Their color helped camouflage them from their bird predators. A dark-gray form also existed but was quite rare. However, as the Industrial Revolution proceeded during the last half of the 1800s, the dark form of this moth sharply increased in frequency, especially near industrial cities. The soot and other pollutants from factory smokestacks began killing lichens and darkening tree trunks. In this new environment, the dark form blended in with the blackened trees and the light form was highly visible to its bird predators. Through natural selection, the dark form began to survive and reproduce at a greater rate than its light-colored kin. (Both varieties appear in each photo. Can you spot them?)

favorable conditions. A crash occurs when a reproducing population of a species overshoots the carrying capacity of its environment or when a change in conditions suddenly lowers the carrying capacity.

Crashes have occurred in the human populations of various countries throughout history. Ireland, for example, experienced a population crash after a fungus infection destroyed the potato crop in 1845. Because of this prolonged disaster, about 1 million people died and 3 million people emigrated to other countries.

In spite of such local and regional disasters, the overall human population on Earth has continued to grow (Figure 1-2). Humans have made technological and cultural changes that have extended Earth's carrying capacity for their species (Figure 2-2). These changes include developing methods of increasing food production, controlling disease, and using large amounts of energy and matter resources to make normally uninhabitable areas of Earth habitable. A crucial question is how long we will be able to keep increasing the carrying capacity for humans on a planet with finite resources that we are depleting and degrading at a rapid rate.

NATURAL SELECTION AND BIOLOGICAL EVOLUTION A population of a particular species can undergo changes in its genetic composition, or gene pool, that enable it to adapt better to changes in environmental conditions. This can happen because not all individuals of a population have exactly the same genes. Individuals with a genetic composition that allows them to survive changes in environmental conditions generally produce more offspring than those that don't have

these traits, and they pass these traits on to their offspring, a process known as **differential reproduction**.

The process by which some genes and gene combinations in a population are reproduced more than others is called **natural selection**. Charles Darwin, who proposed this idea in 1858, described natural selection as "survival of the fittest." That phrase has often been misinterpreted to mean survival of the strongest, biggest, or most aggressive. Instead, *fittest* means that individuals in a population with the genetic traits best able to survive and reproduce under existing environmental conditions tend to outreproduce and replace less successful individuals (Figure 5-34).

The change in the genetic composition of a population resulting from differential reproduction of genetic types (genotypes) and natural selection (after the population has been exposed to new environmental conditions) is called **biological evolution**, or simply **evolution**.

Species differ widely in how rapidly they can undergo evolution through natural selection—depending on the amount of genetic diversity in the gene pool of the species, the degree of the environmental change, and how rapidly the change takes place. Some species can quickly produce a large number of tiny offspring with short average life spans (weeds, insects, rodents, bacteria), and they have a fairly high genetic diversity. Such species can adapt to a change in environmental conditions through natural selection in a relatively short time.

For example, when a chemical is used as a pesticide to reduce the insect population in an area, a small number of resistant individuals usually survive. They can

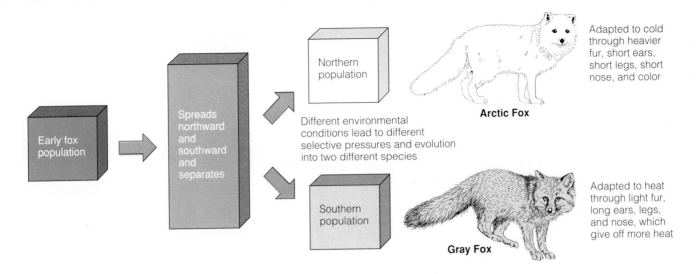

Figure 5-35 Speciation of an early species of fox into two different species as a result of migration of portions of the original fox population into areas with different climates. See Figure 4-1 for a photograph of an arctic fox with its white winter coat.

then rapidly breed new populations with a larger number of individuals genetically resistant to the toxic effects of the chemical. Thus, in the long run, our present chemical approach to pest control usually increases, not decreases, the populations of species we consider pests. As one observer put it, "I hope that when the insects take over the world, they will remember that we always took them along on our picnics."

Other species, such as elephants, horses, tigers, sharks, and humans, have long generation times and a small number in each litter and may have only low to moderate genetic diversity. This means that they cannot produce a large number of offspring rapidly. For such species, adaptation to an environmental stress by natural selection typically takes thousands to millions of years. If they cannot adapt or evolve into a new species because of lack of time or low genetic diversity, they become extinct.

Over a long period of time, interacting species in an ecosystem exert selective pressures on each other that can lead each to undergo various adaptations. Evolution resulting from such interactions between species is called **coevolution**. For example, plants may evolve defenses, such as camouflage or unpleasant or poisonous chemicals, against efficient herbivores. This, in turn, can lead their herbivore consumers to evolve ways to counteract those defenses. Animals may also evolve adaptations such as poisons to help protect them from their predators. Through coevolution, animals may also develop camouflage for protection or to make them more effective predators. Coevolution enhances or leads to mutualism (Figure 4-31), commensalism, and other cooperative relationships between species.

SPECIATION AND EXTINCTION Earth's estimated 40 to 100 million species are believed to be the result of a combination of two processes taking place over billions of years. One is **speciation**: the formation of two species from one species as a result of divergent natural selection in response to changes in environmental conditions. The other is **extinction**: A species ceases to exist because it cannot genetically adapt and successfully reproduce under new environmental conditions. It may no longer exist in any form, or it may evolve into a new, genetically modified species better adapted to new environmental conditions.

Biologists estimate that 98% to 99% of all the species that have ever lived are now extinct. However, the fact that we have an estimated 40 to 100 million species on Earth today means that speciation, on average, has kept ahead of extinction.

Speciation can occur from changes within a single genetic line over a long period of time, often because of long-term changes in climate. It can also take place by the gradual splitting of lines of descent into two or more new species in response to new environmental conditions. This type of speciation is believed to occur when members of a particular species become distributed over geographical areas with different climates, food sources, soils, and other environmental conditions for long periods — typically for 1,000 to 100,000 generations (Figure 5-35).

Populations of some animal species may split up and live in areas with quite different environmental conditions when part of the group migrates in search of food (Figure 5-35). Populations may also become separated by physical barriers caused by earthquakes, continental drift, and other geological events, or by accidental or deliberate transplantation of a few individuals to new areas by humans. Winds can transport the seeds of plant species to new areas with different environmental conditions.

If we compress the development of Earth's different forms of life through biological evolution to a 24-hour time scale, then our species, *homo sapiens sapiens*, appeared less than 1 second before midnight. Agriculture began only one-fourth second before midnight and the Industrial Revolution has been around for only seven-thousandths of a second. Despite our brief instant on Earth, we are now in the process of hastening the extinction of more of the earth's species in a shorter time than at any other time in Earth's 4.6-billion-year history. One of our key goals should be not to reduce by our actions the *genetic diversity, species diversity,* and *ecological diversity* that make up this biological part of Earth's natural capital (see Spotlight on p. 8).

5-5 Community-Ecosystem Responses to Stress

RESPONSES TO SLIGHT AND MODERATE STRESS
Communities and ecosystems are so complex and variable that ecologists have little understanding of how they maintain some degree of inertia and resilience and also undergo continual change in response to changes in environmental conditions. A major problem is the difficulty of conducting controlled experiments. Identifying and observing even a tiny fraction of the interacting variables in simple communities and ecosystems is virtually impossible. Greatly simplified ecosystems can be set up and observed under laboratory conditions, but extrapolating the results of such experiments to much more complex natural communities and ecosystems is difficult, if not impossible.

At one time it was believed that the higher the species diversity in an ecosystem, the greater its stability. According to this idea, an ecosystem with a diversity of species has more ways to respond to most environmental stresses because it does not "have all its eggs in one basket." Research indicates that there are numerous exceptions to this intuitively appealing idea.

Part of the problem is that there are different ways to define stability and diversity. Does an ecosystem need both high inertia and high resilience to be considered stable? Evidence indicates that some ecosystems have one of these properties but not the other. For example, California redwood forests and tropical rain forests (Figure 5-15) have high species diversity and high inertia. This means they are hard to alter significantly or to destroy. However, once large tracts of these diverse ecosystems are cleared or severely degraded, they have

---

SPOTLIGHT Ecosystem Interference Is Full of Surprises!

Malaria once infected nine out of ten people in North Borneo, now known as Brunei. In 1955, the World Health Organization (WHO) began spraying dieldrin (a pesticide similar to DDT) to kill malaria-carrying mosquitoes. The program was so successful that the dreaded disease was almost eliminated from the island.

Other, unexpected things happened, however. The dieldrin killed other insects, including flies and cockroaches, living in houses. The islanders applauded, but then small lizards that also lived in the houses died after gorging themselves on dead insects. Then cats began dying after feeding on the dead lizards. Without cats, rats flourished and overran the villages. Now people were threatened by sylvatic plague carried by the fleas on the rats. The situation was brought under control when WHO parachuted healthy cats onto the island.

Then roofs began to fall in. The dieldrin had killed wasps and other insects that fed on a type of caterpillar that either avoided or was not affected by the insecticide. With most of its predators eliminated, the caterpillar population exploded. The larvae munched their way through one of their favorite foods, the leaves used in thatched roofs.

In the end, the Borneo episode was a success story; both malaria and the unexpected effects of the spraying program were brought under control. However, it shows the unpredictable results of interfering in an ecosystem.

---

such low resilience that they may never become such forests again because the soil nutrients and other environmental conditions needed for recovery are no longer present.

On the other hand, grasslands, with a much lower species diversity than most forests, burn easily and thus have low inertia. However, because most of their plant matter consists of roots beneath the ground surface, these ecosystems have high resilience, which allows them to recover quickly. A grassland can be destroyed only if its roots are plowed up and wheat or some other crop is planted in its soil (Figure 5-12).

Another difficulty is that populations, communities, and ecosystems are rarely, if ever, at equilibrium. Instead, nature is in a continuing state of disturbance and fluctuation. The size and other properties of undisturbed populations and communities vary between some limits but rarely remain at some constant level. When disturbed, these systems may change and oper-

canopy

lower
canopy trees

tall shrub
understory

| annual weeds | perennial weeds and grasses | shrubs | young pine forest | mature oak-hickory forest |

Time⟶

Figure 5-36 Secondary ecological succession of plant communities on an abandoned farm field in North Carolina over about 150 years.

ate within a new set of limits, rather than returning to some "perfect" equilibrium state.

Clearly, we have a long way to go in understanding how the factors involved in natural communities and ecosystems interact and change in response to changes in environmental conditions. Because of our limited understanding of how nature works, we are often unable to predict the short- and long-term beneficial and harmful effects of simplifying an ecosystem by the intentional or accidental removal or addition of a species (see Spotlight on p. 110).

RESPONSES TO LARGE-SCALE STRESS: ECOLOGICAL SUCCESSION One characteristic of most communities and ecosystems is that the types of species present in a given area are usually changing in response not only to small and moderate changes in environmental conditions but also to quite severe changes. The process by which gradual changes occur in the composition of species making up a community or ecosystems is called **ecological succession**, or *community development*.

Ecologists recognize two types of ecological succession: primary and secondary. Which type takes place depends on the conditions at a particular site at the beginning of the process. **Primary succession** in-

volves the development of biotic communities in an area with no true soil. Examples of such areas include the rock or mud exposed by a retreating glacier or a mudslide, cooled lava, a new sandbar deposited by a shift in ocean currents, and surface-mined areas from which all topsoil has been removed. After such a large-scale disturbance, life usually begins to recolonize a site. First, a few hardy **pioneer species**, often microbes, mosses, and lichens, invade the environment. They are usually species with the ability to quickly establish large populations in a new area.

The more common type of succession is **secondary succession**, which begins in an area where the natural vegetation has been removed or destroyed but where the soil or bottom sediment has not been covered or removed. Examples of areas that can undergo secondary succession include abandoned farmlands (Figure 5-36), burned or cut forests, heavily polluted streams, and land that has been flooded naturally or to produce a reservoir or pond. Because some soil or sediment is present, new vegetation can usually sprout within only a few weeks.

Ecological succession can result in a progression from immature, rapidly changing, unstable communities to more mature, self-sustaining communities when this process is not disrupted by large-scale natural

Table 5-3 Ecosystem Characteristics at Immature and Mature Stages of Ecological Succession		
Characteristic	**Immature Ecosystem**	**Mature Ecosystem**
Ecosystem Structure		
Plant size	Small	Large
Species diversity	Low	High
Trophic structure	Mostly producers, few decomposers	Mixture of producers, consumers, and decomposers
Ecological niches	Few, mostly generalized	Many, mostly specialized
Community organization (number of interconnecting links)	Low	High
Ecosystem Function		
Food chains and webs	Simple, mostly plant → herbivores with few decomposers	Complex, dominated by decomposers
Efficiency of nutrient recycling	Low	High
Efficiency of energy use	Low	High

events or human actions. It is tempting to conclude that succession proceeds in an orderly, predictable sequence, with each successional stage leading predictably to the next, more stable stage until an area is occupied by a stable, mature or climax community. Research has shown that this is not necessarily the case. The exact sequence of species and community types that appear during primary or secondary succession can be highly variable. Immature ecosystems and mature ecosystems have strikingly different characteristics, as summarized in Table 5-3.

5-6 Human Impact on Ecosystems

HUMAN BEINGS AND ECOSYSTEMS In modifying ecosystems for our use, we simplify them. For example, we plow grasslands and clear forests. Then we replace the thousands of interrelated plant and animal species in those ecosystems with greatly simplified, single-crop ecosystems (Figures 5-12 and 5-17), or monocultures, or with structures such as buildings, highways, and parking lots. A monoculture of plants is an unstable and vulnerable system that lacks the checks and balances of a natural diverse ecosystem.

A serious problem is the continual invasion of monoculture crop fields by unwanted pioneer species, which we call *weeds* if they are plants, *pests* if they are insects or other animals, and *pathogens* if they are harmful microorganisms such as bacteria, fungi, and viruses. Weeds, pests, or pathogens can wipe out an en-

tire monoculture crop unless it is artificially protected with pesticides such as insecticides (insect-killing chemicals) and herbicides (plant-killing chemicals) or by some form of biological control.

When rapidly breeding insect species develop genetic resistance to certain chemicals in pesticides, farmers must use ever-stronger doses or switch to a new product. As a result, the rate of natural selection of the pests increases to the point that eventually these chemicals become ineffective. This process illustrates biologist Garrett Hardin's **first law of ecology**: *We can never do merely one thing. Any intrusion into nature has numerous effects, many of which are unpredictable.*

Cultivation is not the only way people simplify ecosystems. Ranchers, who don't want bison or prairie dogs competing with sheep for grass, eradicate those species as well as wolves, coyotes, eagles, and other predators that occasionally kill sheep. Far too often, ranchers allow livestock to overgraze grasslands until excessive soil erosion converts these ecosystems to simpler and less productive deserts.

The cutting of vast areas of diverse tropical rain forests is causing the irreversible loss of vital biodiversity. People also tend to overfish and overhunt some species to extinction or near extinction, another way of simplifying ecosystems. The burning of fossil fuels in industrial plants, homes, and vehicles creates atmospheric pollutants that return to Earth as acidic compounds in fog, rain, and solid particles. These chemicals simplify forest ecosystems by killing or weakening trees, and they simplify aquatic ecosystems by killing fish.

It is becoming increasingly clear that the price we pay for simplifying, maintaining, and protecting such

Q: How many motor vehicles are there in the world?

Table 5-4 Comparison of a Natural Ecosystem and a Simplified Human System

Natural Ecosystem (marsh, grassland, forest)	Simplified Human System (cornfield, factory, house)
Captures, converts, and stores energy from the sun	Consumes energy from fossil or nuclear fuels
Produces oxygen and consumes carbon dioxide	Consumes oxygen and produces carbon dioxide from the burning of fossil fuels
Creates fertile soil	Depletes or covers fertile soil
Stores, purifies, and releases water gradually	Often uses and contaminates water and releases it rapidly
Provides wildlife habitats	Destroys some wildlife habitats
Filters and detoxifies pollutants and waste products free of charge	Produces pollutants and waste, which must be cleaned up at our expense
Usually capable of self-maintenance and self-renewal	Requires continual maintenance and renewal at great cost

SPOTLIGHT Nature's Secrets for Sustainable Living

Nature is sustained by several processes:

- Relying on abundant, nonpolluting, and inexhaustible solar energy by using plants to capture solar energy and convert it to chemical energy used to keep plants and plant-eating animals alive.

- Using biological, chemical, and geological processes to gain resources and dispose of waste by recycling vital nutrients.

- Relying on renewable resources by having soil, water, air, plants, and animals that are renewed through natural processes.

- Biodiversity — evolving a variety of species (species diversity), ge-

netic variety within species (genetic diversity), and ecosystems (ecological diversity) in response to environmental changes over billions of years and as a mechanism for responding to future changes.

- Adaptation in which natural populations can change their genetic makeup in response to changes in environmental conditions.

- Population control in which the birth rates, death rates, age distribution, and migration patterns of natural populations respond to changes in environmental conditions.

- Resource conservation. There is little waste in nature. Organisms

generally use only what they need to survive, stay healthy, and reproduce.

Understanding and mimicking these secrets does not mean that we should stop growing food, building cities, and making other changes that affect Earth's biological communities. We do need to recognize, however, that such human-induced changes have far-reaching and unpredictable consequences. We need wisdom, care, and restraint as we alter the ecosphere (see Guest Essay on p. 114).

---

stripped-down ecosystems is high: It includes time, money, increased use of matter and energy resources, reduced biodiversity, and loss of natural landscape (Table 5-4). The challenge is to maintain a balance between simplified, human ecosystems and the neighboring, more complex (mature) natural ecosystems on which our simplified systems and other forms of life depend.

SOME ENVIRONMENTAL LESSONS It should be clear from the brief discussion of principles in this chapter and Chapter 4 that living systems have six key features: *interdependence, diversity, resilience, adaptability, unpredictability,* and *limits* (see Spotlight above).

In addition to the first law of ecology, our actions should take into account the **second law of ecology** or

Edward J. Kormondy

Edward J. Kormondy is chancellor and professor of biology at the University of Hawaii–Hilo/West Oahu College. He has taught at the California State University at Los Angeles, the University of Southern Maine, the University of Michigan, Oberlin College, and Evergreen State College. Among his many research articles and books are Concepts of Ecology *and* Readings in Ecology *(both published by Prentice-Hall). He has been a major force in biological education and for several years was director of the Commission on Undergraduate Education in the Biological Sciences.*

Energy flows — but downhill only in terms of its quality; chemical nutrients circulate — but some stagnate; populations stabilize — but some go wild; communities age — but some age faster. These dynamic and relentless processes are as characteristic of ecosystems as are thermonuclear fusion reactions in the sun.

Thinking one can escape the operation of these and other laws of nature is like thinking one can stop Earth from revolving or make rain fall up. Yet we have peopled Earth only for hundreds of millions to endure starvation and malnutrition; deliberately dumped wastes only to ensure contamination; purposefully simplified agricultural systems only to cause widespread crop losses from pest invasions. Such actions suggest that we believe energy and food automatically increase as people multiply, that things stay where they are put, that simplification of ecosystems aids in their productivity. Such actions indicate that we have ignored basic, inexorable, and unbreakable laws of ecosystems. We have proposed, but nature has disposed, often in unexpected ways counter to our intent.

We proposed more people, more mouths to be fed, more space to be occupied. Nature disposed by placing an upper limit on the rate at which plants can produce organic nutrients for themselves and for the people and other animals that feed on them. It also disposed by using and degrading energy quality at and between all trophic levels in the biosphere's intricate food webs and by imposing an upper limit on the total space that is available and can be occupied by humans and other species.

Ultimately, the only way there can be more and more people is for each person to have less and less food and fuel energy and less and less physical space. Absolute limits to growth are imposed both by thermodynamics and by space. We may argue about what these limits are and when they will be reached; but there are limits and, if present trends continue, they will be reached. The more timely question then becomes a qualitative one. What quality of life will we have within these limits? What

principle of interrelatedness: *Everything is connected to and intermingled with everything else; we are all in it together.* The bad news about this is that intruding into an ecosystem can have harmful and often unpredictable consequences. The good news is that by understanding some of these connections we can promote, even amplify, changes that reduce the effects of our actions or help heal the harmful results of past intrusions. Another cardinal rule is the **third law of ecology:** *Any substance that we produce should not interfere with any of Earth's natural biogeochemical cycles.*

We also have an obligation to work with nature to repair many of the wounds we have already inflicted. This is the goal of the emerging science and art of *rehabilitation and restoration ecology.* But our primary goal should be to reduce the destruction and degradation of wild natural systems instead of having to depend on

expensive, incomplete, and time-consuming ecosystem rehabilitation and restoration. We must learn much more about how nature works and sustains itself, sensing in nature fundamental rhythms we can trust and cooperate with even though we will never fully understand them.

What has gone wrong, probably, is that we have failed to see ourselves as part of a large and indivisible whole. For too long we have based our lives on a primitive feeling that our "God-given" role was to have "dominion over the fish of the sea and over the fowl of the air and over every living thing that moveth upon the earth." We have failed to understand that the earth does not belong to us, but we to the earth.

ROLF EDBERG

Q: What percentage of the world's cars are found in the United States?

kind of life do you want? What quality of life will future generations have?

We proposed exploitative use of resources and indiscriminate disposal of human and technological wastes. Nature disposed and, like a boomerang, the consequences of our acts came back to hit us. On the one hand, finite oil, coal, and mineral resource supplies are significantly depleted — some nearing exhaustion. On the other hand, air, water, and land are contaminated, perhaps beyond restoring.

Nature's laws limit each resource; some limits are more confining than others, some more critical than others. Earth is finite, and its resources are therefore finite.

Yet another of nature's laws is that fundamental resources — elements and compounds — circulate, some fully and some partially. They don't stay where they are put. They move from the land to the water and the air, just as they move from the air and water to the land. Must not our proposals for using resources and discharging wastes be mindful of ultimate limits and Earth's chemical recycling processes? What about your own patterns of resource use and waste disposal?

We proposed simplification of our agricultural systems to ease the admittedly heavy burden of cultivation and harvest. Nature has disposed otherwise, however. Simple ecosystems such as a cornfield are youthful ones and, like our own youth, are volatile, unpredictable, and unstable. Young ecosystems do not conserve nutrients, and agricultural systems in such a stage must have their nutrients replaced artificially and expensively by adding commercial inorganic fertilizers. Young agricultural systems essentially lack resistance to pests and disease and have to be protected artificially and expensively by pesticides and other chemicals. These systems are also more subject to the whims of climate and often have to be expensively irrigated. Must not our proposals for managing agricultural systems be mindful of nature's managerial strategy of providing biological diversity to help sustain most complex ecosystems? What of your own manicured lawn?

The take-home lesson is a rather straightforward one: We cannot propose without recognizing how nature disposes of our attempts to manage Earth's resources for human use. We are shackled by basic ecological laws of energy flow, chemical recycling, population growth, and community aging processes. We have plenty of freedom within these laws, but like it or not we are bounded by them. You are bounded by them. What do you propose to do? And what might nature dispose in return?

Guest Essay Discussion

1. List the patterns of your life that are in harmony with the laws of energy flow and chemical recycling and those that are not.

2. Can you think of other examples of "we propose" and "nature disposes"?

3. Set up a chart with examples of "we propose" and "nature disposes," but add a third column titled "we re-propose," based on using ecological principles to work with nature.

DISCUSSION TOPICS

1. Since the deep oceans are vast and located far away from human habitats, why not use them as a depository for essentially all of our radioactive and other hazardous wastes? Give your reasons for agreeing or disagreeing with this proposal.

2. Why are coastal and inland wetlands and coral reefs considered to be some of the planet's most important ecosystems? Why have so many of these vital ecosystems been destroyed by human activities? What factors in your lifestyle contribute to the destruction and degradation of wetlands?

3. Someone tells you not to worry about air pollution because through natural selection the human species will develop lungs that can detoxify pollutants. How would you reply?

*4. What type of biome do you live in or near? What effects have human activities had on the characteristic vegetation and animal life normally found in this biome? How is your own lifestyle affecting this biome?

*5. If possible, visit a nearby lake. Would you classify it as oligotrophic, mesotrophic, or eutrophic? What are the primary factors contributing to its nutrient enrichment? Which of these are related to human activities?

CHAPTER 6

HUMAN POPULATION DYNAMICS: GROWTH, URBANIZATION, AND REGULATION

General Questions and Issues

1. How is population size affected by birth rates, death rates, fertility rates, and migration rates?

2. How is population size affected by the percentage of males and females at each age level?

3. How is the world's population distributed between rural and urban areas, and how do transportation systems affect population distribution and urban growth?

4. What methods can be used to regulate the size and the rate of change of the human population?

5. What success have the world's two most populous countries, China and India, had in trying to control the rate of growth of their populations?

We shouldn't delude ourselves: the population explosion will come to an end before very long. The only remaining question is whether it will be halted through the humane method of birth control, or by nature wiping out our surplus.

PAUL H. EHRLICH

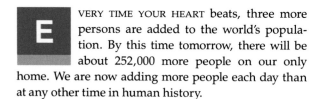

VERY TIME YOUR HEART beats, three more persons are added to the world's population. By this time tomorrow, there will be about 252,000 more people on our only home. We are now adding more people each day than at any other time in human history.

The reason that the world's population continues to grow exponentially by 1 billion people every ten years is simple. There are about 3 births for each death, with 1.6 births for each death in MDCs and 3.3 births for each death in LDCs.

We have brought death rates and birth rates down, but death rates have fallen more sharply than birth rates. If this continues, one of two things will probably happen during your lifetime: the number of people on Earth will at least double before population growth comes to a halt, or the world will experience an unprecedented population crash, with hundreds of millions of people — perhaps billions — dying prematurely.

6-1 Factors Affecting Human Population Size

BIRTH RATES AND DEATH RATES   The **birth rate**, or **crude birth rate**, is the number of live births per 1,000 persons in a population in a given year. The **death rate**, or **crude death rate**, is the number of deaths per 1,000 persons in a population in a given year. Figure 6-1 shows the crude birth rates and death rates of various groups of countries in 1992.

When the birth rate of an area is greater than the death rate, its population grows (assuming no net migration in or out of the area). When the death rate equals the crude birth rate, population size remains stable. This condition is known as **zero population growth (ZPG)**. When the death rate is higher than the birth rate, population size decreases.

The annual rate at which the size of a population changes is usually expressed as a percentage.

$$\text{annual rate of population change (\%)} = \frac{\text{birth rate} - \text{death rate}}{1,000 \text{ persons}} \times 100$$

$$= \frac{\text{birth rate} - \text{death rate}}{10}$$

The annual rate at which the world's population was growing decreased from a high of 2% in the mid-1960s to 1.7% today, but the base of the population undergoing this exponential growth increased by more than 2 billion during this period (Figure 1-2). This 15% drop in the annual exponential growth rate is good news; however, it's like learning that a truck heading straight at you has slowed down from 161 kilometers (100 miles) per hour to 137 kilometers (85 miles) per hour while its weight has increased by two-thirds.

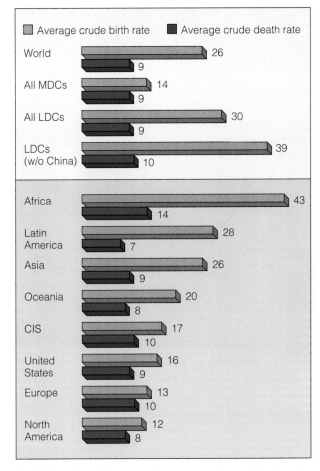

Figure 6-1 Average crude birth rates and crude death rates of various groups of countries in 1992. (Data from Population Reference Bureau)

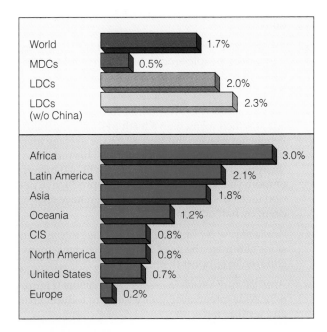

Figure 6-2 Average annual population change rate in various groups of countries in 1992.

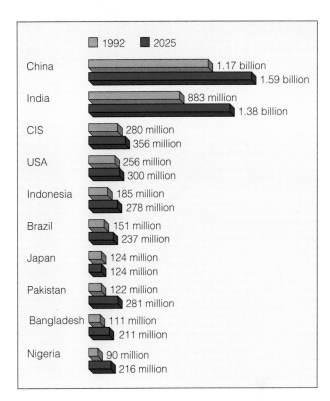

Figure 6-3 The world's ten most populous countries in 1992, with projections of their population size in 2025. (Data from World Bank)

Figure 6-2 gives the annual population change rates in major parts of the world. An annual population growth rate of 1% to 3% may seem small, but such exponential rates lead to enormous increases in population size over a 100-year period (see Spotlight on p. 4).

The impact of exponential population growth on population size is much greater in countries with a large existing population base. In sheer numbers, China and India dwarf all other countries, making up 38% of the world's population (Figure 6-3). One in every five people in the world is Chinese, and 59% of the world's population is Asian.

FERTILITY RATES Two types of fertility rates affect a country's population size and growth rate. **Replacement-level fertility** is the number of children a couple must have to replace themselves. The actual average replacement-level fertility rate is slightly higher than two children per couple (2.1 in MDCs and as high as 2.5 in some LDCs), mostly because some female children die before reaching their reproductive years.

The most useful measure of fertility for projecting future population change is the **total fertility rate (TFR)**: an estimate of the average number of children a woman will have during her childbearing years. In 1992, the average total fertility rate was 3.4 children per woman for the world as a whole, 1.9 in MDCs, and 3.8 in LDCs (4.4 if China is excluded). Population experts

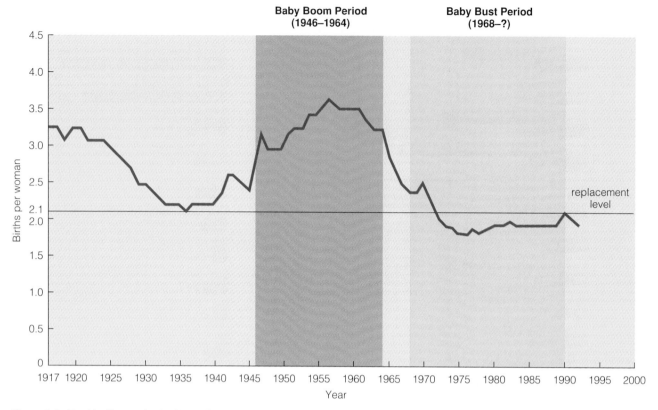

Figure 6-4 Total fertility rate for the United States between 1917 and 1992. (Data from Population Reference Bureau and U.S. Census Bureau)

expect TFRs in MDCs to remain around 1.9 and those in LDCs to drop to around 2.3 by 2025. That is good news, but it will still lead to a projected population of around 9 billion by then.

Since 1972, the United States has had a total fertility rate at or below the replacement level (Figure 6-4). A total fertility rate below replacement level doesn't necessarily mean that a country's population has stabilized or is declining (see Case Study on p. 119).

FACTORS AFFECTING BIRTH RATES AND FERTILITY RATES The following are the most significant factors affecting a country's average birth rate and total fertility rate:

- *Average levels of education and affluence.* Rates are usually lower in MDCs, where both of these factors are high.

- *Importance of children as a part of the family labor force.* Rates tend to be low in MDCs and high in LDCs (especially in rural areas).

- *Urbanization.* People living in urban areas tend to have fewer children than those living in rural areas, where children are needed to help in growing food, collecting firewood and water, and other survival tasks. People living in urban areas also often have better access to family planning.

- *High costs of raising and educating children.* Rates tend to be low in MDCs where raising children is much more costly because they don't enter the labor force until their late teens or early twenties.

- *Educational and employment opportunities for women.* Rates tend to be low when women have access to education and to paid employment outside the home.

- *Infant mortality rates.* In areas with low infant mortality rates, people tend to have fewer children because they don't need to replace children who have died.

- *Average marriage age* (or more precisely, the average age at which women give birth to their first child). People have fewer children when the average marriage age of women is 25 or higher. This reduces the typical childbearing years (ages 15–44) by ten or more years and cuts the prime reproductive period (ages 20–29), when most women have children, by half or more.

- *Availability of private and public pension systems.* Pensions eliminate the need for parents to have many children to support them in old age.

- *Availability of reliable methods of birth control* (Figure 6-5). Widespread availability tends to reduce birth and fertility rates.

- *Religious beliefs, tradition, and cultural norms that influence the number of children couples want to have.*

Q: What percentage of the world's population own cars?

The population of the United States has grown from 4 million in 1790 to 256 million in 1992 — a 64-fold increase. The total fertility rate in the United States has oscillated wildly (Figure 6-4). At the peak of the post–World War II baby boom (1946–64) in 1957, the TFR reached 3.7 children per woman. Since then, it has generally declined and has been at or below replacement level since 1972.

Various factors contributed to this decline:

- Widespread use of effective birth control methods (Figure 6-5).

- Availability of legal abortions.

- Social attitudes favoring smaller families.

- Greater social acceptance of childless couples.

- Rising costs of raising a family. It will cost $86,000 to $168,000 to raise a child born in 1992 to age 18.

- Increases in the average marriage age between 1958 and 1990 from 20.1 to 23.9 for women and from 22.8 to 26.2 for men.

- An increasing number of women working outside the home. By 1992, more than 70% of American women of childbearing age worked outside the home and had a childbearing rate one-third the rate of those not in the paid labor force.

The United States has not reached zero population growth (ZPG) in spite of the dramatic drop in the average total fertility rate to below the replacement level. The main reasons for this are

- The large number of women (58 million) born during the baby-boom period (Figure 6-4) still moving through their childbearing years

- High levels of legal and illegal immigration

- An increase in the number of unmarried young women (including teenagers) having children

(continued)

Extremely Effective

Total abstinence — 100%
Abortion — 100%
Sterilization — 99.6%
Hormonal implant (Norplant) — 99%

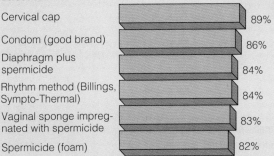

Highly Effective

IUD with slow-release hormones — 98%
IUD plus spermicide — 98%
IUD — 95%
Condom (good brand) plus spermicide — 95%
Oral contraceptive — 94%

Effective

Cervical cap — 89%
Condom (good brand) — 86%
Diaphragm plus spermicide — 84%
Rhythm method (Billings, Sympto-Thermal) — 84%
Vaginal sponge impregnated with spermicide — 83%
Spermicide (foam) — 82%

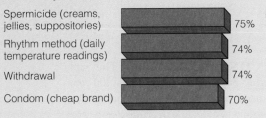

Moderately Effective

Spermicide (creams, jellies, suppositories) — 75%
Rhythm method (daily temperature readings) — 74%
Withdrawal — 74%
Condom (cheap brand) — 70%

Unreliable

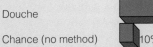
Douche — 40%
Chance (no method) — 10%

Figure 6-5 Typical effectiveness of birth control methods in the United States. Percent effectiveness is based on the number of undesired pregnancies per 100 couples using a method as their sole form of birth control for a year. For example, a 94% effectiveness rate for oral contraceptives means that for every 100 women using the pill regularly for one year, 6 will get pregnant. The failure rates shown are for the United States. Failure rates tend to be higher in LDCs because of human error and lack of education. (Data from Alan Guttmacher Institute)

In 1992, the U.S. population grew by 1.25%. This added 3.2 million people: 2.0 million more births than deaths, 1.0 million legal immigrants, and at least 0.2 million illegal immigrants.

Given the erratic history of the U.S. total fertility rate (Figure 6-4), no one knows whether or how long it will remain below replacement level. The Census Bureau and the World Bank have made various pro-

jections of U.S. population growth, assuming different average total fertility rates, life expectancies, and net legal immigration rates (Figure 6-6).

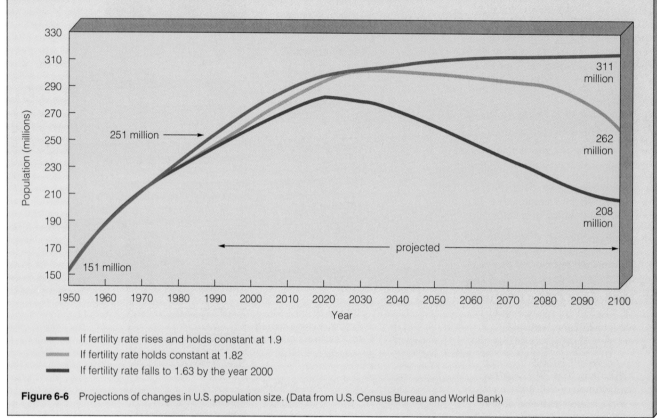

Figure 6-6 Projections of changes in U.S. population size. (Data from U.S. Census Bureau and World Bank)

FACTORS AFFECTING DEATH RATES The rapid growth of the world's population over the past 100 years has not been caused by a rise in crude birth rates. Rather, it is due largely to a decline in crude death rates, especially in the LDCs (Figure 6-7).

The principal interrelated reasons for this general drop in death rates are

- Better nutrition because of increased food production and better distribution

- Fewer infant deaths and increased average life expectancy because of a reduction in the incidence and spread of infectious diseases from improved personal hygiene, sanitation, and water supplies

- Improvements in medical and public-health technology, including antibiotics, immunization, and insecticides

Two useful indicators of overall health in a country or region are **life expectancy**—the average number of years a newborn infant can be expected to live—and the **infant mortality rate**—the number of babies out of every 1,000 born that die before their first birthday (Figure 6-8).

In 1992, average life expectancy at birth ranged from a low of 40 years in Guinea in western Africa to a high of 79 years in Japan, followed by Sweden (78). In the world's 41 poorest countries, mainly in Asia and Africa, average life expectancy is only 47 years.

Between 1900 and 1992, average life expectancy at birth rose sharply in the United States from 42 to 75; yet, in 1992, people in 18 countries and colonies had an average life expectancy at birth one to three years higher than that of people in the United States.

Because it reflects the general level of nutrition and health care, infant mortality is probably the single most

Q: What percentage of the cars carrying people to and from work in the United States have only one passenger?

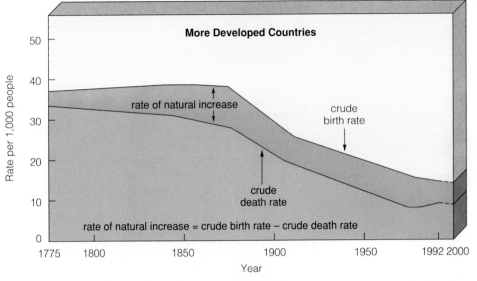

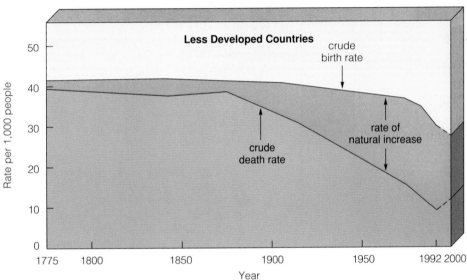

Figure 6-7 Changes in crude birth and death rates for MDCs and LDCs between 1775 and 1992 and projected rates (dashed lines) to 2000. (Data from Population Reference Bureau and United Nations)

important measure of a society's quality of life. A high infant mortality rate usually indicates insufficient food (undernutrition), poor nutrition (malnutrition), and a high incidence of infectious disease (usually from contaminated drinking water).

Although the infant mortality rate in the United States is low by world standards, it is among the highest in the developed world, with 29 other countries having lower rates. Several factors keeping the U.S. infant mortality rate higher than it could be are

■ Lack of adequate health care for poor women during pregnancy and for their babies after birth

■ Drug addiction among pregnant women

■ The high birth rate for teenage women in the United States (see Case Study on p. 122)

MIGRATION The annual rate of population change for a particular country, city, or other area is also affected by movement of people into (*immigration*) and out of (*emigration*) that area:

$$\text{population change rate} = \left(\begin{array}{c} \text{births} \\ + \\ \text{immigration} \end{array} \right) - \left(\begin{array}{c} \text{deaths} \\ + \\ \text{emigration} \end{array} \right)$$

Most countries control their rates of population growth to some extent by restricting immigration. Only a few countries annually accept a large number of immigrants or refugees. This means that population change for most countries is determined mainly by the differences between their birth rates and death rates.

Migration within countries, however, especially from rural to urban areas, plays an important role in the population dynamics of cities, towns, and rural areas.

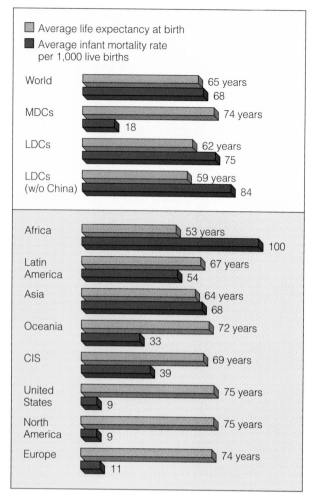

Figure 6-8 Average life expectancy at birth and average infant mortality rate for various groups of countries in 1992. (Data from Population Reference Bureau)

This migration affects the way population is distributed within countries, as discussed in Section 6-3.

6-2 Population Age Structure

AGE STRUCTURE DIAGRAMS Why will world population probably keep growing for at least 60 years after the average world total fertility rate has reached or dropped below the replacement-level fertility of 2.1? The answer to this question lies in an understanding of the **age structure**, or age distribution, of a population: the percentage of the population, or the number of people of each sex, at each age level.

Demographers make a population age structure diagram by plotting the percentages or numbers of males and females in the total population in three age categories: *prereproductive* (ages 0–14), *reproductive* (ages 15–44), and *postreproductive* (ages 45–85+). Figure 6-9

The United States has the highest teenage pregnancy rate of any industrialized country, ten times higher than Japan's, two times higher than Canada's, and two to five times higher than that of most European countries. Every year in the United States, approximately 1 million teenage women — one in every nine between ages 15 and 19 — become pregnant. About 83% of these pregnancies are not planned. About 590,000 of these young women give birth. The remaining 410,000 have abortions, accounting for almost one of every four abortions performed in the United States. Teenage pregnancies cost state and federal governments at least $21 billion a year.

Babies born to teenagers are more likely to have a low birth weight — the most important factor in infant deaths — thus increasing the country's infant mortality rate. The United States has developed the medical technology for saving low-weight babies, but babies of poor teenage women with no health insurance often do not have access to these expensive, life-saving procedures.

Why are teenage pregnancy rates in the United States so high? UN studies show that U.S. teenagers aren't more sexually active than those in other MDCs, but they are less likely to take precautions to prevent pregnancy.

In Sweden, which has a much lower teenage pregnancy rate than the United States, every child receives a thorough grounding in basic reproductive biology by age 7. By age 12, each child has been told about the various types of contraceptives.

Polls show that 87% of Americans favor sex education in the schools, including information about birth control, and school clinics that dispense contraceptives with parental consent. Many analysts urge that effective sex education programs be developed in which U.S. children are made aware of the values of abstinence and the various types of contraceptives by age 12 and that school-based health clinics be opened in all junior and senior high schools. These proposals are vigorously opposed by groups who fear that early sex education will lead to increased sexual activity. What do you think should be done about sex education and teenage pregnancy?

shows the age structure diagrams for countries with rapid, slow, and zero growth rates.

Mexico and most LDCs with rapidly growing populations have pyramid-shaped age structure diagrams (Figure 6-9, left). This means that these countries have a high ratio of children under age 15 to adults over age 65. In contrast, the diagrams for the United States and

Q: What percentage of Americans use public transportation to get to and from work?

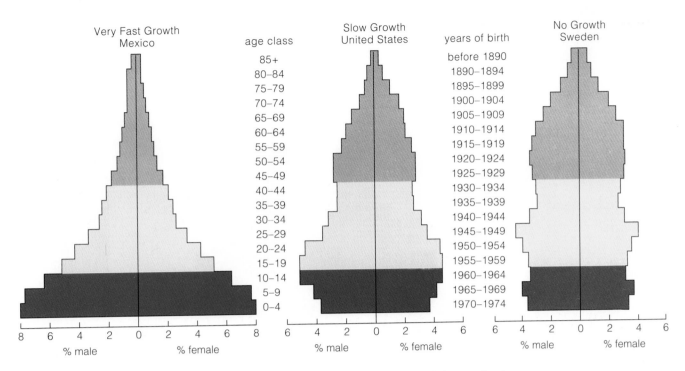

Figure 6-9 Population age structure diagrams for countries with rapid, slow, and zero population growth rates. Bottom portions represent prereproductive years (0–14), middle portions represent reproductive years (15–44), and top portions represent postreproductive years (45–85+). (Data from Population Reference Bureau)

most other MDCs undergoing slow or no population growth have a narrower base (Figure 6-9, middle). This shows that such countries have a much smaller percentage of population under age 15 and a larger percentage above age 65 than countries experiencing rapid population growth.

MDCs, such as Sweden and Denmark, that have achieved or nearly achieved zero population growth have roughly equal numbers of people at each age level (Figure 6-9, right). Hungary and Germany, which are experiencing a slow population decline, have roughly equal numbers of people at most age levels but lower numbers under age 5.

AGE STRUCTURE AND POPULATION GROWTH MOMENTUM Any country with a large number of people below age 15 has a powerful built-in momentum to increase its population size unless death rates rise sharply. The number of births rises even if women have only one or two children, because the number of women who can have children increases greatly as females reach their reproductive years.

In 1992, one of every three persons on this planet was under 15 years old and half the world's population was under age 24. In LDCs, the number is even higher—36% compared with 21% in MDCs. Figure 6-10 shows the powerful momentum for population growth in LDCs because of the large numbers of people under age 15 who will be moving into their reproductive years. If each female in this group has only two children, world population will still grow for 60 years un-

less deaths rise sharply. Instead of having two children, women in LDCs now have an average of 3.8 children (4.4 children if China is excluded).

This explains why population experts project that the world's population will not level off until around the middle of the next century and perhaps not until the end of the next century. The key question is whether it will peak at 7 billion, 10 billion, or 14 billion (Figure 1-2).

The powerful force for continued population growth, mostly in LDCs, will be slowed only by an effective program to reduce birth rates or by a catastrophic rise in death rates. Greatly increasing efforts to reduce birth rates now could bring the projected peak population down to 7 billion instead of 10 billion, or even 14 billion. Many analysts consider this one of our most urgent challenges.

MAKING PROJECTIONS FROM AGE STRUCTURE DIAGRAMS A baby boom took place in the United States between 1946 and 1964 (Figure 6-4). This 80-million-person bulge, called the *baby-boom generation*, will move upward through the country's age structure during the 80-year period between 1946 and 2045 as baby boomers move through their youth, young adulthood, middle age, and old age (Figure 6-11). By 2030, when all living members of the baby-boom generation are senior citizens, about 21% of the projected population will consist of people 65 and older, compared with 14% today.

Today, baby boomers make up nearly half of all adult Americans. In sheer numbers, they dominate the

A: 7%

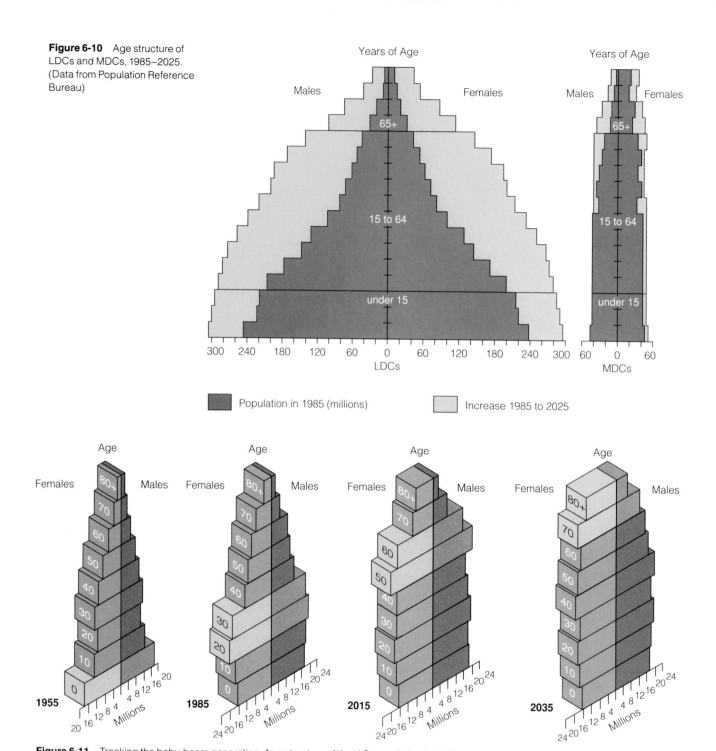

Figure 6-10 Age structure of LDCs and MDCs, 1985–2025. (Data from Population Reference Bureau)

Population in 1985 (millions)   Increase 1985 to 2025

Figure 6-11 Tracking the baby-boom generation. Age structure of the U.S. population in 1955, 1985, 2015, and 2035. (Data from the Population Reference Bureau and U.S. Census Bureau)

population's demand for goods and services. Companies not providing products and services for this aging bulge in the population can go bankrupt. Young people making career choices should also consider these demographic facts of life. Baby boomers, who made up an estimated 60% of registered voters in 1992, will play an increasingly important role in deciding who gets elected and what laws are passed between now and 2030.

During their working years, baby boomers will create a large surplus of money in the Social Security trust fund. However, unless changes in funding are made, the large number of retired baby boomers will quickly use up this surplus by 2048. Elderly baby boomers will also put severe strains on health care services.

The economic burden of helping support so many retired baby boomers will be on the *baby-bust generation*, the much smaller group of people born between 1968

Q: What percentage of the U.S. working population lives within biking distance of work?

and 1992, when total fertility rates fell sharply (Figure 6-4). Retired baby boomers may use their political clout to force members of the baby-bust generation to pay greatly increased income, health care, and Social Security taxes.

In many respects, the baby-bust generation should have an easier time than the baby-boom generation. Much smaller numbers of people will be competing for education, jobs, and services. Labor shortages should also drive up their wages, but three out of four new jobs available between now and 2010 will require education or technical training beyond high school. People without such training may face economic hard times.

The baby-bust group may find it hard to get job promotions as they reach middle age because most upper-level positions will be occupied by the much larger baby-boom group. Many baby boomers may delay retirement because of improved health and the need to build up adequate retirement funds. From these few projections, we see that any baby-boom bulge or baby-bust indentation in the age structure of a population creates a number of social and economic changes that ripple through a society for decades.

6-3 Population Distribution: Urbanization and Urban Growth

THE WORLD SITUATION Economic, environmental, and social conditions are affected not only by population growth and age structure but also by how population is distributed geographically in rural or urban areas. An **urban area** is often defined as a town or a city with a population of more than 2,500 people, although some countries set the minimum at 10,000 to 50,000. A country's **urbanization** is the percentage of its population living in an urban area. **Urban growth** is the rate of growth of urban populations. Urban populations grow in two ways: by natural increase (more births than deaths) and by immigration (mostly from rural areas).

Several trends are important in understanding the problems and challenges of urbanization and urban growth:

- The percentage of the population living in urban areas increased from 14% to 43% (73% in MDCs and 34% in LDCs) between 1900 and 1992. It is projected that by 2020, almost two out of three people will be living in urban areas.

- The number of large cities is increasing rapidly. Today, 1 of every 10 persons lives in a city with a million or more inhabitants, and many of these live in *megacities* with 10 million or more people. The United Nations projects that by 2000, there will be 26 megacities, more than two-thirds of them in LDCs. At that time the world's two largest

cities will be Mexico City, with a projected population of 26.3 million, and São Paulo, Brazil, with 24 million people.

- LDCs, with 34% urbanization, are simultaneously experiencing high rates of natural population increase and rapid and increasing urban growth, four and a half times as fast as in MDCs. LDCs are projected to reach 58% urbanization by the year 2020, with their urban populations almost tripling from 1.4 billion to 3.9 billion between 1990 and 2020—the greatest mass migration in history.

- In MDCs, with 73% urbanization, urban growth is increasing at lower rates than in LDCs.

- The distribution of people living in absolute poverty is shifting from rural to urban areas at an increasing rate.

THE WORSENING SITUATION IN LDCS The largest and most rapid rural to urban migration is taking place mostly in LDCs. Yet, these countries can't provide adequate services, shelter, and jobs for a third to a half of their present urban populations (see Case Study on p. 126).

People are pulled to urban areas mostly in search of jobs and a better life. Other factors push rural people into urban areas. Modern mechanized agriculture decreases the need for farm labor and allows large landowners to buy out small-scale, subsistence farmers who cannot afford to modernize. Without jobs or land, these people are forced to move to cities. Urban growth in LDCs is also caused by government policies that distribute most income and social services to urban dwellers at the expense of rural dwellers—policies that both push and pull people into the cities.

For most of the rural poor migrating to urban areas in LDCs, as well as for the urban poor in MDCs, the city becomes a poverty trap, not an oasis of economic opportunity (see Case Study on p. 127). Those fortunate enough to get a job must work long hours for low wages. To survive, they often have to take jobs that expose them to dust, hazardous chemicals, excessive noise, and dangerous machinery.

Worldwide, an estimated 150 million are homeless (Figure 1-4). The United Nations estimates that at least 1 billion people—19% of the world's population—live in crowded, often wretched, inhumane conditions in slums of central cities and in the vast squatter settlements that often ring the outskirts of most cities in LDCs. In squatter settlements (Figure 7-1), people generally live illegally on public or private land that no one else wants to live on because it is too wet, too dry, too steep, too hazardous (subject to landslides, flooding, or fumes from industrial plants), or too polluted (city dumps). Most of the squatters live in shacks made from corrugated metal, plastic sheets, cardboard, discarded packing crates, or whatever building materials they can come up with.

A: More than 50%

Brazil, the largest country in South America, ranks fifth in land area in the world and eighth in population (Figure 6-12). In 1992, its population of about 151 million was expanding by 1.9%, adding 3 million people a year. It is encouraging that between 1965 and 1992, Brazil's total fertility rate fell from 6.8 to 3.1. As in most LDCs, however, a large share of Brazil's population (35%) is under age 15. This explains why the country's population is projected to reach 237 million by 2025.

Brazil's gross national product averages almost $2,680 per person, making it a middle-income developing country. This average is deceiving because most of the country's wealth is concentrated in the hands of a small fraction of the population. Most other people are poor and must survive on an average income of only several hundred dollars a year. About 70% of the country's rural families are landless.

Brazil has fueled much of its recent economic growth by borrowing abroad. It now has the largest foreign debt of any LDC. This heavy burden of debt pushes the country to expand its exports of timber, minerals, and other resources to pay the interest on its debt and, in the process, deplete and degrade its natural resource base. This is leading to widespread deforestation and degradation of Brazil's tropical forests in the Amazon basin (Figure 6-12). Brazil is like a family giving the appearance of affluence by living off credit cards and having to use much of its capital and income to finance its debt.

Brazil is divided geographically into a largely impoverished tropical north and a temperate south, where most industry and wealth are concentrated. The Amazon basin, which covers about one-third of the country's territory, remains largely unsettled. This is changing as landless poor migrate there, hoping to grow enough food to survive, and as its tropical forests are cut down for grazing livestock, timber, and mining or are flooded to create large reservoirs for hydroelectric dams.

With 74% of its population living in urban areas, Brazil is more than twice as urbanized as most LDCs. Attracted by the prospect of jobs, many of the rural poor in the north and northeast have flooded into Rio de Janeiro and São Paulo in the south. These modern cosmopolitan centers are surrounded by mostly illegal squatter settlements where the poor try to survive (see Figure 7-1) and by widespread poverty in rural areas. By 2000, São Paulo is expected to be the world's second most populous city.

As a safety valve for its exploding population, the Brazilian government has encouraged migration to the Amazon basin, with economic aid from international lending agencies such as the World Bank. This policy is supported by wealthy Brazilians, who want to diffuse pressures for more equitable land distribution, and by wealthy ranchers, who until 1990 received government subsidies to establish cattle ranches by clearing tropical forests.

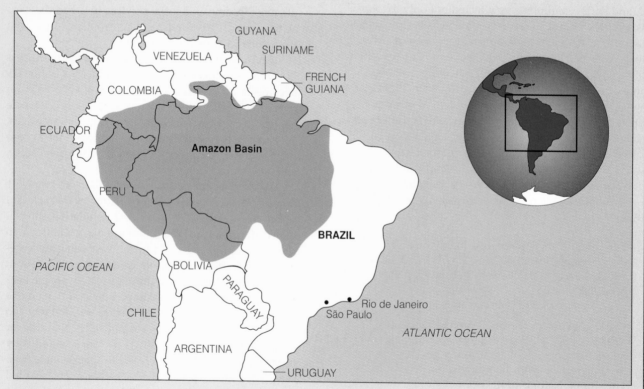

Figure 6-12 Where is Brazil?

Q: What percentage of Americans walk or use a bicycle to get to and from work?

In 1992, Mexico's (Figure 6-13) population was 88 million and was growing exponentially at 2.3% a year. Between 1965 and 1992, Mexico's average total fertility rate dropped from 6.7 to 3.8, but because 39% of Mexico's population is under age 15 (Figure 6-9), its population is projected to reach 143 million by 2025. Annual per capita income is $2,490, but this gives a distorted view because much of the wealth is in the hands of a few.

In 1992, the population of Mexico City, the capital of Mexico (Figure 6-13), was 22 million — the most populous city that has ever existed. Every day, an additional 2,000 poverty-stricken rural peasants pour into the city, hoping to find a better life.

The city suffers from severe air pollution, high unemployment (close to 50%), deafening noise, congestion, and a soaring crime rate. One-third of the city's people live in crowded slums (called barrios) or squatter settlements, without running water or electricity.

With at least 5 million people living without sewer facilities, huge amounts of human waste are left in gutters and vacant lots every day.

When the winds pick up dried excrement, a "fecal snow" often falls on parts of the city. About half of the city's garbage is left in the open to

(continued)

United Nations

Figure 6-14 The air in Mexico City ranks with the dirtiest in the world. This is due to a combination of topography, a large population, industrialization, large numbers of motor vehicles, and too little emphasis on reducing rural-to-urban migration and preventing and controlling pollution. Breathing the city's air has been compared to smoking two packs of cigarettes a day. This photo was taken during the morning of a bright, sunny day.

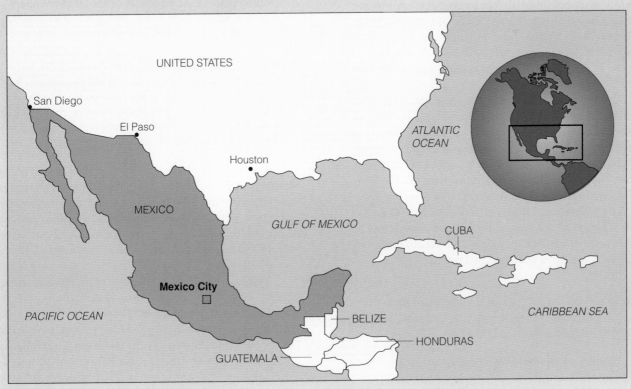

Figure 6-13 Where is Mexico City?

A: 6%

rot, attracting armies of rats and swarms of flies.

More than 3 million motor vehicles and 35,000 factories (making up half of the country's industry) spew pollutants into the atmosphere. Air pollution is intensified because the city lies in a basin surrounded by mountains and has frequent thermal inversions that trap pollutants near ground level (Figure 6-14). Between 1982 and 1990, the amount of contamination in the city's smog-choked air more than tripled.

Breathing the city's air is like smoking two packs of cigarettes a day from birth. The city's air and water pollution cause an estimated 100,000 premature deaths a year. According to a World Health Organization study, 7 out of 10 babies born in Mexico City have unsafe levels of lead in their blood — threatening to stunt the intellectual growth of an entire generation of children. These problems, already at crisis levels, will become even worse if this urban area, as projected, grows to 26.3

million people by the end of this century.

The Mexican government is industrializing other parts of the country in an attempt to stop or at least slow migration to Mexico City. Since 1993, all new cars in Mexico have catalytic converters (output devices for reducing pollution emissions), but new cars represent only about 5% of the cars on the road each year. If you were in charge of Mexico City, what would you do?

People in these illegal settlements live in constant fear of eviction by police or of having their makeshift shelters destroyed by bulldozers. When this happens, the people either move back in, relocate to another existing squatter settlement, or create a new one.

Most cities refuse to provide these settlements with adequate drinking water, sanitation, electricity, food, health care, housing, schools, and jobs. It is not only the lack of money, but also fear by officials that improving services will attract even more of the rural poor. Officials, with urging from business owners, sometimes allow illegal settlements because they provide a source of cheap labor without costing the city money for services.

Despite joblessness, squalor, overcrowding, and rampant disease, squatter and slum residents cling to life with resourcefulness, tenacity, and hope. Most urban migrants do have more opportunities and are better off than the rural poor they left behind. With better access to family planning programs, they tend to have fewer children, and the children in most cities have better access to schools than do rural dwellers. Even so, nearly half of all school-age children in urban areas of LDCs drop out before they finish the fourth grade, to work or take care of younger children.

THE U.S. SITUATION In 1800, only 5% of Americans lived in cities. Since then, three major internal population shifts have taken place in the United States:

- *Migration from rural to mostly large central cities.* Currently, about 75% of Americans live in the nation's 317 *metropolitan areas* — cities and towns with at least 50,000 people that are linked socially or

economically. Two out of three Americans live in the country's largest urban regions (Figure 6-15). Nearly half (48%) of the American people live in *consolidated metropolitan areas* with 1 million or more people. It is projected that by 1995, 83% of the U.S. population will live in urban areas.

- *Migration from large central cities to suburbs and smaller cities.* Since 1970, this type of migration has taken place mostly because of the large numbers of new jobs in such areas. Today, about 41% of the country's urban dwellers live in central cities and 59% live in suburbs.

- *Migration from the North and East to the South and West.* Since 1980, about 80% of the population increase in the United States has occurred in the South and West, particularly near the coasts. Most of this growth is due to migration from the North and East. This shift is projected to continue.

The biggest problems facing numerous cities in the United States and in other industrialized countries are deteriorating services, aging and decaying infrastructure (streets, schools, housing, sewers), budget crunches from a loss in tax revenue and rising costs, environmental degradation, inner-city decay, and neighborhood collapse.

The result is usually an increase in violence, drug traffic, drug abuse, crime, decay, and blight in parts of central cities. In these areas, the poor, the elderly, the unemployed (typically 50% or higher in economically depressed inner-city areas), the homeless (an estimated 3.5 million in the United States), the handicapped, and other people who cannot afford to leave the city are trapped in a downward spiral of poverty and degradation.

Q: How many people have been killed by motor vehicles since the first automobile was built in 1885?

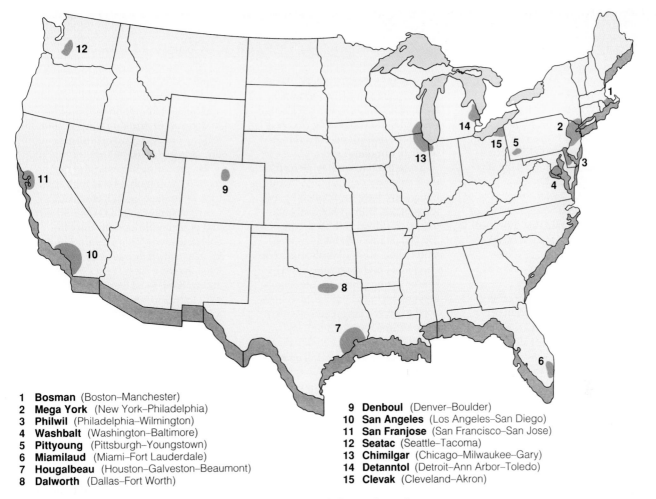

1 **Bosman** (Boston–Manchester)
2 **Mega York** (New York–Philadelphia)
3 **Philwil** (Philadelphia–Wilmington)
4 **Washbalt** (Washington–Baltimore)
5 **Pittyoung** (Pittsburgh–Youngstown)
6 **Miamilaud** (Miami–Fort Lauderdale)
7 **Hougalbeau** (Houston–Galveston–Beaumont)
8 **Dalworth** (Dallas–Fort Worth)

9 **Denboul** (Denver–Boulder)
10 **San Angeles** (Los Angeles–San Diego)
11 **San Franjose** (San Francisco–San Jose)
12 **Seatac** (Seattle–Tacoma)
13 **Chimilgar** (Chicago–Milwaukee–Gary)
14 **Detanntol** (Detroit–Ann Arbor–Toledo)
15 **Clevak** (Cleveland–Akron)

Figure 6-15 Major urban regions in the United States. (Data from U.S. Census Bureau)

POPULATION DISTRIBUTION, TRANSPORTATION SYSTEMS, AND ENERGY EFFICIENCY If suitable rural land is not available for conversion to urban land, a city grows upward, not outward; it occupies a relatively small area and develops a high population density. Most people living in such compact cities walk, ride bicycles, or use energy-efficient mass transit. Residents often live in multistory apartment buildings with fewer outside walls, reducing heating and cooling costs. Because of the lack of land, many European cities are compact and tend to be more energy-efficient than the dispersed cities of the United States and Australia, where there is often ample land for outward expansion.

A combination of cheap gasoline, a large supply of rural land suitable for urban development, and a network of highways usually results in a dispersed, car-culture city with a low population density—often called *urban sprawl*. Most people living in such a city rely on cars with low energy efficiencies for transportation (see Pro/Con on p. 130). Most people live in single-family houses, with unshared walls that lose and gain heat rapidly unless they are well insulated and airtight.

RESOURCE AND ENVIRONMENTAL PROBLEMS OF URBAN AREAS Cities are not self-sustaining. They survive only by importing large quantities of food, water, energy, minerals, and other resources from near and distant farmlands, forests, mines, and watersheds, and they produce enormous quantities of wastes that can pollute air, water, and land within and outside their boundaries (Figure 6-16).

As urban areas grow, their resource input needs and pollution outputs place increasing stress on distant sources of water, wetlands, estuaries, forests, croplands, rangelands, wilderness, and other ecosystems. In the words of Theodore Roszak:

The supercity . . . stretches out tentacles of influence that reach thousands of miles beyond its already sprawling parameters. It sucks every hinterland and wilderness into its technological metabolism. It forces rural populations off the land and replaces them with vast agroindustrial combines. Its investments and technicians bring the roar of the bulldozer and oil derrick into the most uncharted quarters. It runs its conduits of transport and communication, its lines of supply and distribution through the wildest landscapes. It flushes its wastes into every nearby river, lake,

Worldwide, there are about 550 million motor vehicles, consisting of 440 million cars and 110 million trucks—more than a tenfold increase since 1950. If this rate continues, the global motor vehicle population will reach 740 million by 2000 and 1.2 billion by 2030.

With only 4.7% of the world's people, the United States has 36% of the world's cars. In LDCs, most people cannot afford a car and travel mostly by foot, bicycle, or motor scooter. Only 8% of the world's population own cars.

In the United States, the car is now used for about 98% of all urban transportation, 86% of all travel between cities, and 84% of all travel to and from work. Over two-thirds of the cars used to go to and from work carry only one passenger. Less than 7% of Americans use public transportation, and only 6% walk or use a bicycle to get to and from work. The total distance Americans drive each year equals that of the rest of the world combined. No wonder British author J. B. Priestley remarked, "In America, the cars have become the people."

The automobile has many advantages. Above all, it offers people freedom to go where they want to go, when they want to go there. The basic purpose of a motor vehicle is to get one from point A to point B as cheaply, quickly, and safely as possible. However, to most people cars are also personal fantasy machines that serve as symbols of power, success, speed, excitement, sexiness, spontaneity, and adventure.

In addition, much of the world's economy is built on producing motor vehicles and supplying roads, services, and repairs for those vehicles. Half of the world's paychecks and resource use are auto-related. In the United States, one of every six dollars spent and one of every six nonfarm jobs are connected to the automobile or related industries, such as oil, steel, rubber, plastics, automobile services, and highway construction.

In spite of its advantages, the automobile may be the most destructive machine ever invented. Though we tend to deny it, riding in cars is one of the most dangerous things we do in our daily lives.

Since 1885, when Karl Benz built the first automobile, almost 18 million people have been killed by motor vehicles. Every year, cars and trucks worldwide kill an average of 250,000 people—as many as were killed in the atomic bomb attacks on Hiroshima and Nagasaki—and injure or permanently disable 10 million more. Half of the world's people will be involved in an auto accident at some time during their lives.

Each year in the United States, motor vehicle accidents kill around 45,000 people—more than from all other accidental deaths combined—and seriously injure at least 300,000. Since the automobile was introduced, almost 3 million Americans have been killed on the highways—about twice the number of Americans killed on the battlefield in all U.S. wars. In addition to the tragic loss of life, these accidents cost American society up to $93 billion annually in lost income and in insurance, legal, and other expenses.

Motor vehicles are the largest source of air pollution, producing a haze of damaging smog over the world's cities (Figure 6-14). In the United States, they produce at least 50% of the country's air pollution, even though U.S. emission standards are as strict as any in the world.

Motor vehicles are the major cause of oil addiction in MDCs and to a growing extent in LDCs. They account for 63% of the oil used in the United States. These vehicles generate 25% of U.S. carbon dioxide emissions, the primary greenhouse gas contributing to projected global warming. Leaky air conditioners in U.S. vehicles are the country's single largest source of CFC emissions, the primary culprits in depletion of the planet's vital ozone layer. Motor vehicle use is directly or indirectly responsible for water pollution caused by oil and gasoline spills and leakage and dumping of used engine oil and for contamination of sources of underground drinking water due to leaking underground oil and gasoline storage tanks.

By providing almost unlimited mobility, automobiles and highways have been the biggest factor leading to urban sprawl in the United States and other countries with large livable land areas. This dispersal of cities has made it increasingly difficult for subways, trolleys, buses, bicycles, and walking to be feasible alternatives to the private car.

Worldwide, at least a third of urban land is devoted to roads and parking. Half the land in an average American city is used for cars, prompting urban expert Lewis Mumford to suggest that the U.S. national flower should be the concrete cloverleaf.

Instead of reducing automobile congestion, the construction of roads has encouraged more automobiles and travel, causing even more congestion or gridlock. As economist Robert Samuelson put it, "Cars expand to fill available concrete." In 1975, some 40% of U.S. rush hour traffic was rated as congested. By 1990, that figure had risen to 77%.

If present trends continue, U.S. motorists will spend an average of two years of their lifetime in traffic jams, forced to remain in a small metal cell. The American economy loses about $100 billion a year because of time lost in traffic delays.

In 1907, the average speed of horse-drawn vehicles through the borough of Manhattan was 18.5 kilometers (11.5 miles) per hour. Today, cars and trucks with the potential power of 100 to 300 horses creep along Manhattan streets at an average speed of 8 kilometers (5 miles) per hour. In London, average auto speeds are about 13 kilometers (8 miles) per hour, and they are even lower in Paris and in Tokyo, where everyday traffic is called *tsukin jigoku*, or commuting hell. What do you think should be done?

Q: Worldwide, how many people are killed each year by motor vehicles?

Figure 6-16 Typical daily input and output of matter and energy for a U.S. city of 1 million people.

Daily Inputs

Daily Outputs

U.S. city of
1 million people

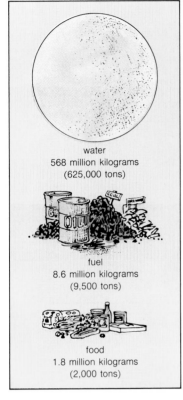

water
568 million kilograms
(625,000 tons)

fuel
8.6 million kilograms
(9,500 tons)

food
1.8 million kilograms
(2,000 tons)

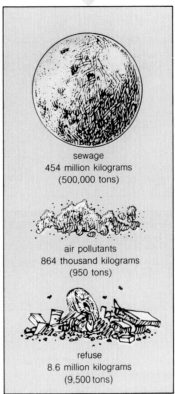

sewage
454 million kilograms
(500,000 tons)

air pollutants
864 thousand kilograms
(950 tons)

refuse
8.6 million kilograms
(9,500 tons)

and ocean or trucks them away to other areas. The world becomes its garbage can.

Some major urban resource and environmental problems are:

- Scarcity of trees, shrubs, and other natural vegetation that absorb air pollutants, give off oxygen, help cool the air as water evaporates from their leaves, muffle noise, provide wildlife habitats, and give aesthetic pleasure. As one observer remarked, "Most cities are places where they cut down the trees and then name the streets after them."

- Alteration of local and, sometimes, regional climate. Average temperatures, precipitation, fog, and cloudiness are generally higher in urban areas than in suburbs and nearby rural areas. The enormous amounts of heat generated by cars, factories, furnaces, lights, air conditioners, and people in cities creates a microclimatic effect known as an **urban heat island** in which large cities are typically like islands of heat surrounded by cooler

suburban and rural areas. This dome of heat also traps pollutants, especially tiny solid particles (suspended particulate matter), creating a **dust dome** above urban areas (Figure 6-17).

- Lack of water, requiring expensive reservoirs, aqueducts, and deep wells.

- Rapid runoff of water from asphalt and concrete. This can overload sewers and storm drains, contributing to water pollution and flooding in cities and downstream areas.

- Production of large quantities of air pollution (Chapter 9), water pollution (Chapter 11), and garbage and other solid waste (Chapter 19).

- Excessive noise (Table 6-1).

- Loss of rural land, fertile soil, and wildlife habitats as cities expand.

MAKING URBAN AREAS MORE LIVABLE AND SUSTAINABLE An important goal in coming decades should be to make existing and new urban areas more

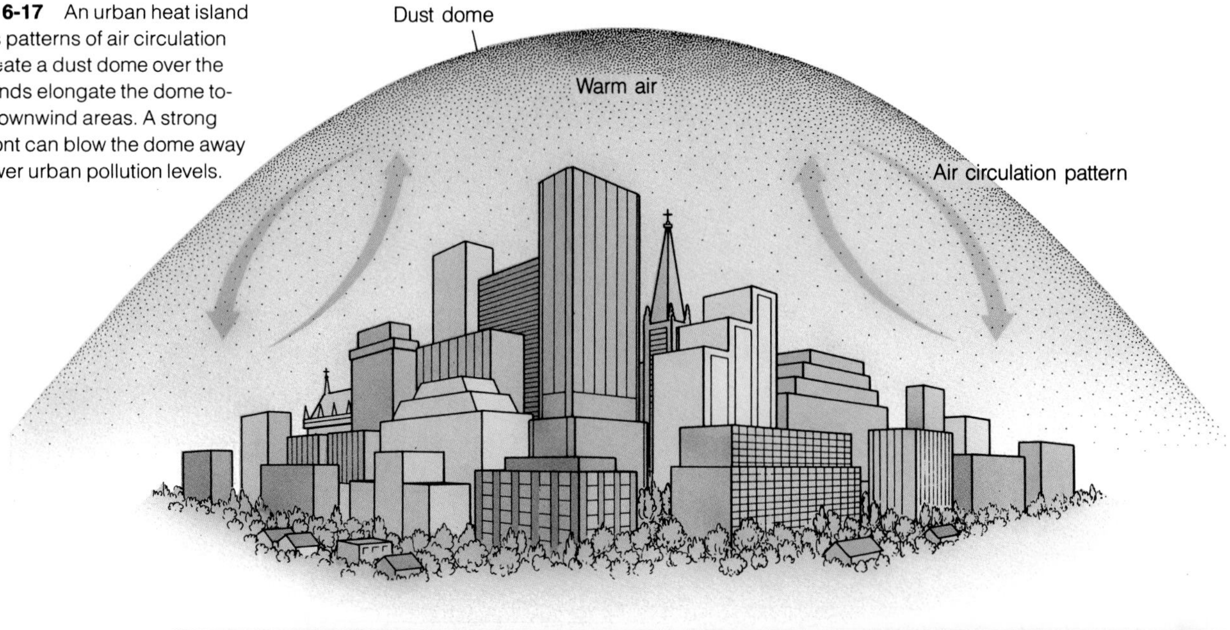

Figure 6-17 An urban heat island causes patterns of air circulation that create a dust dome over the city. Winds elongate the dome toward downwind areas. A strong cold front can blow the dome away and lower urban pollution levels.

Dust dome

Warm air

Air circulation pattern

Table 6-1 Effects of Common Sounds		
Example	Sound Pressure (dbA)	Effect from Prolonged Exposure
Jet takeoff (25 meters away*)	150	Eardrum rupture
Aircraft carrier deck	140	
Armored personnel carrier, jet takeoff (100 meters away), earphones at loud level	130	
Thunderclap, textile loom, live rock music, jet takeoff (161 meters away), siren (close range), chain saw	120	Human pain threshold
Steel mill, riveting, automobile horn at 1 meter, "jam box" stereo held close to ear	110	
Jet takeoff (305 meters away), subway, outboard motor, power lawn mower, motorcycle at 8 meters, farm tractor, printing plant, jackhammer, garbage truck	100	
Busy urban street, diesel truck, food blender, cotton spinning machine	90	Hearing damage (8 hours), speech interference
Garbage disposal, clothes washer, average factory, freight train at 15 meters, dishwasher, blender	80	Possible hearing damage
Freeway traffic at 15 meters, vacuum cleaner, noisy office or party, TV audio	70	Annoying
Conversation in restaurant, average office, background music, chirping bird	60	Intrusive
Quiet suburb (daytime), conversation in living room	50	Quiet
Library, soft background music	40	
Quiet rural area (nighttime)	30	
Whisper, rustling leaves	20	Very quiet
Breathing	10	
	0	Threshold of hearing

*To convert meters to feet, multiply by 3.3.

Q: How much of the air pollution in the United States is produced by motor vehicles?

Davis, California (Figure 6-18) has ample sunshine, a flat terrain, and about 38,000 people. Its citizens and elected officials have committed themselves to making it an ecologically sustainable city.

The city's building codes encourage the use of solar energy to provide space heating and hot water and require all new homes to meet high standards of energy efficiency. When any existing home is sold, it must be inspected and the buyer must bring it up to the energy conservation standards for new homes. The community also has a master plan for planting deciduous trees, which provide shade and reduce heat gain in the summer and allow solar gain during the winter.

The city has adopted several policies that discourage the use of automobiles and encourage the use of bicycles. Some streets are closed to automobiles, and people are encouraged to work at home.

A number of bicycle paths and lanes have been built, and some city employees are given bikes. Any new housing tract must have a separate bicycle lane. As a result, 28,000 bikes account for 40% of all in-city transportation, and much less land is needed for parking spaces. This heavy dependence on the bicycle is made possible by the city's warm climate and flat terrain.

Davis also limits the type and rate of growth and development and maintains a mix of homes for people with low, medium, and high incomes. Development of the fertile farmland surrounding the city for residential or commercial use is restricted. What things are being done to make the area where you live more sustainable?

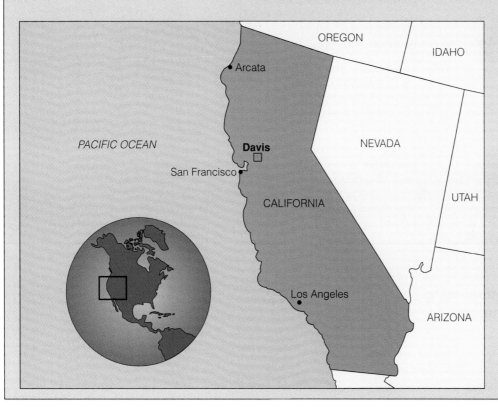

Figure 6-18 Where is Davis, California?

self-reliant, sustainable, and enjoyable places to live (see Case Study above and Individuals Matter on p. 134). As the era of cheap oil and gasoline comes to a close over the next few decades, urban sprawl and car-culture cities are likely to become unaffordable and unsustainable luxuries. Cities are likely to become more compact and less dependent on the automobile. In ecologically sustainable cities, people would walk or use a bicycle or tricycle for most short trips and walk or bike to bus, metro, or trolley stops for longer urban trips. Rapid rail transport between cities would replace many long drives and short airplane flights. In a few decades, it is likely that people in today's car-dominated cities and countries will be wondering why they allowed cars to dominate their lives and degrade the environment for so long.

Since most people now live, or will live, in urban areas, improving the quality of urban life must be one of our most urgent priorities. Ways to do this include:

Economic Development and Population Regulation

- Reduce the flow of people from rural to urban areas by increasing investments and social services in rural areas and by not giving higher food, energy, and other subsidies to urban dwellers than to rural dwellers.

- Reduce national population growth rates (Section 6-4).

- Maintain employment and plug dollar drains from local communities by setting up "buy local" programs, greatly improving energy efficiency, and instituting extensive recycling programs.

Land Use and Maintenance

- Rely on comprehensive, regional ecological land-use planning and control to regulate the speed and nature of economic development in urban areas and to protect rural and natural areas from unsustainable development.

- Give squatters legal title to land they have lived on, and provide them with support and low-cost loans to develop housing, water, sanitation, and utility systems and to plant community gardens and trees for fruit, shade, and fuel.

- Repair and revitalize existing cities.

- Stimulate the development of ecologically and economically sustainable new towns.

- Plant lawns and public areas with wildflowers and natural ground cover vegetation instead of grasses that must be drenched with water, fertilizer, and pesticides.

- Establish greenbelts of undeveloped forestland and open space within and around urban areas and preserve nearby wetlands and agricultural land.

- Plant large numbers of trees in greenbelts, on unused lots, and along streets to reduce air pollution and noise and to provide recreational areas and wildlife habitats.

Transportation

- Discourage excessive dependence on motor vehicles within urban areas by providing efficient bus and trolley service and bike lanes, charging car commuters fees to enter cities and to park their vehicles, establishing express lanes solely for cars and vans with three or more people and for buses, providing tax incentives for individuals and businesses using car and van pooling, and establishing car-free zones in some parts of downtown areas, with mass transit systems carrying people to and from the edges of these zones.

- Raise gasoline taxes and car registration fees and add sizable taxes based on fuel economy and pollutant emissions so that car owners pay the full costs of driving directly instead of paying these costs indirectly in higher income, sales, and other taxes and higher insurance and health costs. If phased in over a decade to avoid economic disruption, this would be an effective way to make cities more compact and livable, reduce noise and pollu-

6-4 Methods for Influencing Population Change

CONTROLLING MIGRATION A government can influence the size and rate of growth or decline of its population by encouraging a change in any of the three basic demographic variables: births, deaths, and migration. The governments of most countries achieve some degree of population regulation by allowing little immigration from other countries. Some governments also encourage emigration to other countries to reduce population pressures. Only a few countries, chiefly Canada, Australia, and the United States (see Case Study on p. 136), allow large annual increases in their population from immigration.

CONTROLLING BIRTHS Increasing the death rate is not an acceptable alternative for regulating population size. Thus, decreasing the birth rate is the focus of most efforts to slow population growth. Today, about 93% of the world's population and 91% of the people in LDCs live in countries with fertility reduction programs. Three general approaches to decreasing birth rates are *economic development, family planning,* and *socioeconomic change.*

The effectiveness and funding of these programs vary widely from country to country. Few governments spend more than 1% of the national budget on them. There is also controversy over whether population growth is good or bad (see Pro/Con on p. 137).

ECONOMIC DEVELOPMENT AND THE DEMOGRAPHIC TRANSITION Demographers examined the birth and death rates of western European countries that industrialized during the nineteenth century. On the basis of these data, they developed a hypothesis of population change known as the **demographic transition**. Its basic idea is that as countries become industrialized, they have declines in death rates followed by de-

Q: How much of the oil used in the United States is consumed by motor vehicles?

tion (including ozone depletion and projected global warming), greatly increase the energy efficiency of motor vehicles, and make public transport, cycling, and walking more appealing.

- Use at least half of the revenue from gasoline taxes for mass transit, bike and pedestrian paths and parking facilities, and to improve the energy efficiency of motor vehicles.

Improving Energy Efficiency

- Get more energy from locally available perpetual and renewable resources (Chapter 17).

- Enact laws that require all new cars to have fuel efficiencies of at least 17 kilometers per liter (40 miles per gallon) by 2000 and 21 kilometers per liter (50 miles per gallon) by 2010.

- Give tax rebates to businesses and individuals who use gas-sipping vehicles, and impose heavy taxes on those using gas guzzlers.

- Enact building codes that require new and existing buildings to be energy efficient and responsive to climate (Section 17-2).

- Retrofit public buildings to obtain all or most of their energy from renewable sources.

Water

- Encourage water conservation by installing water meters in all buildings and raising the price of water to reflect its true cost.

- Establish small neighborhood water-recycling plants.

- Enact building codes that require water conservation in new and existing buildings and businesses (see Individuals Matter inside the back cover).

Food

- Grow food (with emphasis on sustainable organic methods) in abandoned lots, community garden plots, small fruit-tree orchards, rooftop gardens and greenhouses, apartment window boxes, school yards, and solar-heated fish ponds and tanks, and on some of the land in greenbelts (with careful controls).

- Lower meat consumption (especially beef) to reduce deforestation, overgrazing, and health problems.

Pollution and Wastes

- Discourage industries that produce large quantities of pollution and that use large amounts of water or energy.

- Enact and enforce strict noise control laws to reduce stress from rising levels of urban noise.

- Give tax breaks and other economic incentives to businesses that recycle and reuse resources and that emphasize pollution prevention and waste reduction.

- Establish urban composting centers to convert yard and food wastes into soil conditioner for use on parks, highway medians, and other public lands.

- Recycle food wastes and effluents and sludge from sewage treatment plants as fertilizer for parks, roadsides, flower gardens, and forests.

- Recycle or reuse at least 80% of urban solid waste and some types of hazardous waste instead of burying it or burning it.

---

clines in birth rates. As a result, they move from fast growth, to slow growth, to zero growth, and eventually to a slow decline in population.

This transition takes place in four distinct phases (Figure 6-20). In the *preindustrial stage*, harsh living conditions lead to a high birth rate (to compensate for high infant mortality) and a high death rate, and the population grows slowly, if at all. The *transitional stage* begins shortly after industrialization begins. In this phase, the death rate drops, mostly because of increased food production and improved sanitation and health. However, the birth rate remains high, and the population grows rapidly (typically 2.5% to 3% a year).

In the *industrial stage*, industrialization is widespread. The birth rate drops and eventually approaches the death rate. The main reason for this is that couples in cities realize that children are expensive to raise and that having too many children hinders them from taking advantage of job opportunities in an expanding economy. Population growth continues, but at a slower

and perhaps fluctuating rate, depending on economic conditions. Most MDCs are now in this third phase.

A fourth phase, the *postindustrial stage*, takes place when the birth rate declines even further to equal the death rate, thus reaching zero population growth. Then the birth rate falls below the death rate, and total population size slowly decreases. By 1992, Japan and 21 European countries had reached or were close to ZPG. Two of these countries—Hungary and Germany—were experiencing population declines.

CAN MOST OF TODAY'S LDCS MAKE THE DEMOGRAPHIC TRANSITION? In most LDCs today, death rates have fallen much more than birth rates (Figure 6-7). In other words, these LDCs are still in the transitional phase, halfway up the economic ladder, with high population growth rates. Some economists believe that LDCs will make the demographic transition over the next few decades without increased family planning efforts.

Between 1820 and 1992, the United States admitted almost twice as many immigrants and refugees as all other countries combined. The number of legal immigrants entering the United States since 1820 has varied during different periods because of changes in immigration laws and economic growth (Figure 6-19). Between 1820 and 1960, most legal immigrants came from Europe. Since then, most have come from Asia and Latin America.

Between 1960 and 1992, the number of legal immigrants admitted per year rose sixfold, from 250,000 to 1,000,000. These figures do not include refugees, who are admitted under other regulations.

Each year, an additional 200,000 to 500,000 people enter the United States illegally, most from Mexico and other Latin American countries. This means that in 1992, legal and illegal immigrants increased the U.S. population by 1.2 million to 1.5 million people. Soon, immigration is expected to be the primary factor increasing the population of the United States.

Some have called for an annual ceiling of no more than 450,000 for all categories of legal immigration, including refugees, to reduce the intensity of some of the country's social, economic, and environmental problems and reach zero population growth sooner. Some opponents of the country's open-door policy often portray immigrants as either job stealers or welfare recipients, but recent studies indicate that this is not true. Immigrants draw very lightly on Social Security and Medicare and make virtually the same demands as other Americans do on other kinds of welfare spending. They also create jobs, sometimes helping ailing businesses stay alive.

Other analysts favor increasing the number of immigrants and changing immigration laws to give much more preference to those with valuable professional skills, high levels of education, and a knowledge of English. Some people oppose a

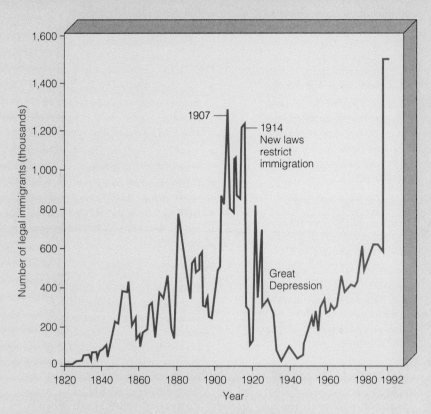

Figure 6-19 Legal immigration to the United States: 1820–1992. (Data from U.S. Immigration and Naturalization Service)

policy of immigration based primarily on skills. They argue that it amounts to a brain drain of educated and talented people from LDCs that need these important human resources. It would also diminish the historic role of the United States as a place of opportunity for the world's poor and oppressed. In 1990, Congress voted to increase the number of immigrants admitted each year because of their skills and talents from 54,000 to 140,000.

In 1986, Congress passed a new immigration law designed to help control illegal immigration. It prohibits the hiring of illegal immigrants. Employers must examine the identity documents of all new employees. Employers who knowingly hire illegal immigrants are subject to fines of $250 to $10,000 per violation, and repeat offenders can be sentenced to prison for up to six months. The bill also okayed funds to increase the border patrol by 50%,

to increase efforts to detect employers violating the new law, and to deport illegal immigrants.

Critics charge that illegal immigrants can get around the law with readily available fake documents. Employers are not responsible for verifying the authenticity of documents or for keeping copies. Besides, the Immigration and Naturalization Service does not have enough money or staff to check most employers, prosecute repeat violators, or effectively patrol more than a small fraction of the 3,140-kilometer (1,950-mile) U.S.–Mexico border.

With nearly 60% of Mexico's labor force unemployed or underemployed, many Mexicans and immigrants from other Latin American countries think being caught and sent back is a minor risk compared with remaining in poverty. What, if anything, do you think should be done about legal and illegal immigration into the United States?

Q: Worldwide, how much of urban land is devoted to roads and parking?

To most environmentalists, the data in Table 1-1 suggest that the planet already has more people than can live in comfort, happiness, and health and still leave the planet a fit place for future generations (Figure 1-12).

Critics of the view that Earth is overpopulated point out that the world now supports 5.4 billion people with an average life span longer than at any time in the past. Things are getting better, not worse, for many of the world's people.

Many of these analysts call for more population growth, arguing that people are the world's most valuable resource for finding solutions to our problems. An increase in the number of people leads to increased economic productivity by creating and applying new knowledge. These analysts are confident that the nature of the physical world combined with human ingenuity permits continued improvement in humanity's lot in the long run, even indefinitely.

Some believe that if a "birth dearth" eventually leads to a population decline in MDCs, their economic growth and power will decrease. They argue that without more babies, MDCs with declining populations will face a shortage of workers, taxpayers, scientists and engineers, consumers, and soldiers needed to maintain healthy economic growth, national security, and global power and influence.

They also contend that the aging societies in MDCs will be less innovative and dynamic. These analysts urge the governments of the United States and other MDCs to prevent this by giving tax breaks and other economic incentives to couples who have more than two children.

To these analysts, the primary cause of poverty and despair for one out of five people on Earth is not population growth. Instead, it is a lack of free and productive economic systems in LDCs.

Others opposed to population regulation feel that all people should have the freedom to have as many children as they want. To some, population regulation is a violation of their deep religious beliefs. To others, it is an intrusion into their personal privacy and freedom. To minorities, population regulation is sometimes seen as a form of genocide to keep their numbers and power from rising.

Proponents of population regulation point to the fact that we are not providing adequate basic necessities for one out of five people on Earth today who don't have the opportunity to be a net economic gain for their country. They see people overpopulation in LDCs and consumption overpopulation in MDCs (Figure 1-12) as threats to Earth's life support systems for us and other species.

These analysts recognize that population growth is not the only cause of our environmental and resource problems. They believe, however, that adding several hundred million more people in MDCs and several billion more in LDCs will intensify many environmental and social problems by increasing resource use and waste, environmental degradation, rapid climate change, and pollution. To proponents of population regulation, it is unethical for us not to encourage a sharp drop in birth rates and unsustainable forms of resource use to prevent a sharp rise in death rates and human misery and a decrease in Earth's biodiversity in the future (see Guest Essay on p. 143).

Despite promises about sharing the world's wealth, the gap between the rich and the poor has been getting larger since 1960 (see Section 7-4). Proponents of population regulation believe this is caused by a combination of population growth and unwillingness of the wealthy to share the world's wealth and resources more fairly.

Those favoring population regulation point out that technological innovation, not sheer numbers of people, is the key to military and economic power in today's world. Otherwise, England, Germany, Japan, and Taiwan, with fairly small populations, should have little global economic and military power, and China and India should rule the world. Also, as world military tensions ease, people are becoming aware that environmental security is now the key to economic and national security (see Guest Essay on p. 19).

History does not show that an older society is necessarily more conservative and less innovative than one dominated by younger people. A society with a higher average age tends to have a larger pool of collective wisdom based on experience. Indeed, the most conservative and least innovative societies in the world today are LDCs with a large portion of their populations under age 29.

Instead of encouraging births, these analysts believe that the United States and other MDCs should establish an official goal of stabilizing their populations by 2025. This would help reduce the severe environmental impact of these MDCs on the biosphere. It would also set a good example for LDCs to reduce their population growth more rapidly and adopt sustainable forms of economic development.

Proponents of population regulation believe that we should have the freedom to produce as many children as we want only as long as this does not reduce the quality of other people's lives now and in the future by impairing the ability of Earth to sustain life. Limiting individual freedom to protect the freedom of other individuals is the basis of most laws in modern societies. What do you think?

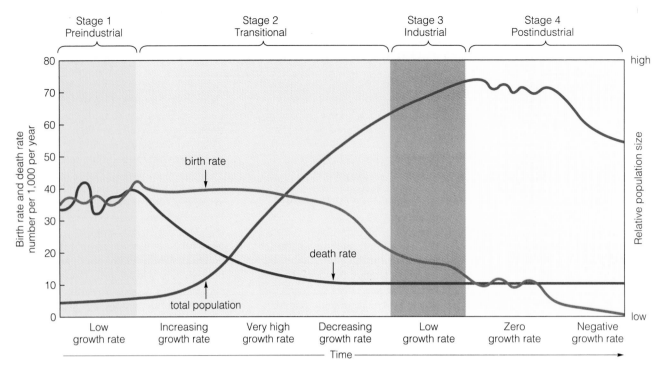

Figure 6-20 Generalized model of the demographic transition.

Many population analysts fear that the rate of economic growth in many LDCs will never exceed their high rates of population growth. Without rapid and sustained economic growth, LDCs could become stuck in the transitional stage of the demographic transition.

Furthermore, some of the conditions that allowed today's MDCs to develop are not available to today's LDCs. Even with large and growing populations, many LDCs do not have enough skilled workers to produce the high-technology products needed to compete in today's economic environment. Most low- and middle-income LDCs also lack the capital and resources needed for rapid economic development. Also, the amount of money being given or lent to LDCs—struggling under tremendous debt burdens—has been decreasing since 1980.

LDCs also face stiff competition from MDCs and recently industrialized LDCs in selling the products on which their economic growth depends; and many LDCs with the fastest rates of population growth do not have enough natural resources to support economic development similar to that in Europe and North America.

FAMILY PLANNING Recent evidence suggests that improved and expanded family planning programs may bring about a more rapid decline in the birth rate, and at a lower cost, than economic development alone. **Family planning** programs provide educational and clinical services that help couples choose how many children to have and when to have them.

Such programs vary from culture to culture; but most provide information on birth spacing, birth con-

trol (Figures 6-5), breastfeeding, and prenatal care as well as distribute contraceptives. In some cases, they also perform abortions and sterilizations, often without charge or at low rates.

Family planning saves a government money by reducing the need for various social services. It also has health benefits. In LDCs, 1 million women a year die from pregnancy-related causes. Half of these deaths could be prevented by effective family planning and health care programs. Family planning programs also help control the spread of AIDS and other sexually transmitted diseases.

Family planning has been a significant factor in reducing birth and fertility rates in highly populous China and in Indonesia, Brazil (see Case Study on p. 126), and several other LDCs with moderate to small populations. These successful programs have been based on committed leadership, local implementation, and wide availability of contraceptive services.

Family planning has had moderate to poor results in more populous LDCs such as India, Egypt, Bangladesh, Pakistan, and Nigeria. Results have also been poor in 79 less populous LDCs—especially in Africa and Latin America—where population growth rates are usually very high.

An estimated 400 million women in LDCs want to limit the number and determine the spacing of their children but lack access to such services. Extending family planning services to these women and those who will soon be entering their reproductive years could prevent an estimated 5.8 million births a year and more than 130,000 abortions a day.

Q: How many legal immigrants are admitted to the United States each year?

Family planning could be provided in LDCs to all couples who want it for about $10 billion a year—less than four days of world military spending. Currently, only about $4.5 billion is being spent. If MDCs provided half of the $10 billion, each person in the MDCs would spend only $4.00 a year to help reduce the world population by 2.7 billion.

Even the present inadequate level of expenditure for family planning is decreasing. The United States has sharply curtailed its funding of international family planning agencies since 1985, mostly as a result of political pressure by pro-life activists. Critics believe that unless the United States reverses this policy, it sends a message to the world that the United States considers mass starvation preferable to helping people prevent unwanted pregnancies.

Improved family planning can also reduce unplanned pregnancies in the United States. More than half of all American pregnancies—3.4 million out of 6 million each year—are accidental, the result of misusing contraceptives, using unreliable contraceptives, or not using any form of contraception. Mostly because of a fear of costly lawsuits, most major American pharmaceutical companies have all but abandoned research and development on new methods of birth control. As a result, Americans now have fewer contraceptive options than their counterparts in most other MDCs. Also, contraceptives are more expensive and more difficult to obtain in the United States than in some LDCs.

ECONOMIC REWARDS AND PENALTIES Some population experts argue that family planning, even coupled with economic development, cannot lower birth and fertility rates fast enough to avoid a sharp rise in death rates in many LDCs. The main reason for this is that most couples in LDCs want three or four children—well above the 2.1 fertility rate needed to bring about eventual population stabilization.

These experts call for increased emphasis on bringing about socioeconomic change to help regulate population size. They call for better basic health care and education, expanded women's rights, increased equity in land ownership, and fair prices for agricultural products.

Governments can discourage births by using economic rewards and penalties. In addition, increased rights, education, and work opportunities for women would reduce fertility rates.

About 20 countries offer small payments to individuals who agree to use contraceptives or to be sterilized. They also pay doctors and family planning workers for each sterilization they perform and each IUD they insert. In India, for example, a person receives about $15 for being sterilized, the equivalent of about two weeks' pay for an agricultural worker. Such payments, however, are most likely to attract people who already have all the children they want. In some cases, the poor feel they have to accept them in order to survive.

Some countries, such as China, penalize couples who have more than a certain number of children—usually one or two. Penalties may be extra taxes and other costs, or not allowing income tax deductions for a couple's third child (as in Singapore, Hong Kong, Ghana, and Malaysia). Families who have more children than the desired limit may also suffer reduced free health care, decreased food allotments, and loss of job choice.

Like economic rewards, economic penalties can be psychologically coercive for the poor. Programs that withhold food or increase the cost of raising children punish innocent children for the actions of their parents.

Experience has shown that economic rewards and penalties designed to reduce fertility work best if they

- Nudge rather than push people to have fewer children

- Reinforce existing customs and trends toward smaller families

- Do not penalize people who produced large families before the programs were established

- Increase a poor family's income or land

Once population growth is out of control, a country may be forced to use coercive methods to prevent mass starvation and hardship. This is what China has had to do (Section 6-5).

CHANGES IN WOMEN'S ROLES Another socioeconomic method of population regulation is to improve the condition of women. Today, women do almost all of the world's domestic work and child care, mostly without pay. They also do more than half the work associated with growing food, gathering fuelwood, and hauling water. Women also provide more health care with little or no pay than all the world's organized health services put together. As one Brazilian woman put it, "For poor women the only holiday is when you are asleep."

The worldwide economic value of women's work at home is estimated at $4 trillion annually. This unpaid work is not included in the GNP of countries, so the central role of women in an economy is unrecognized and unrewarded.

Despite their vital economic and social contributions, most women in LDCs don't have a legal right to own land or to borrow money to increase agricultural productivity. Although women work two-thirds of all hours worked in the world, they get only one-tenth of the world's income and own a mere 1% of the world's land. Many are abused or beaten by their husbands, who, in effect, own them as slaves.

At the same time, women make up about 60% of the world's almost 900 million adults who can neither read nor write. Women also suffer the most malnutrition, because men and children are usually fed first where food supplies are limited.

A: About 1 million (plus 0.2 to 0.5 million illegal immigrants)

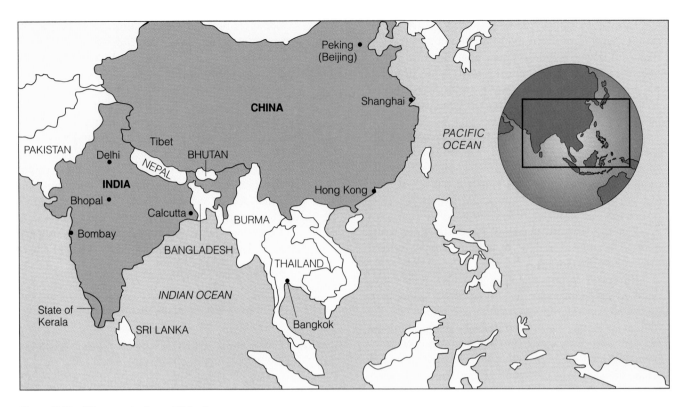

Figure 6-21 Where are India and China?

Numerous studies have shown that increased education is a strong factor leading women to have fewer children. Educated women are more likely than uneducated women to be employed outside the home rather than to stay home and raise children. They marry later, thus reducing their prime reproductive years, and lose fewer infants to death, a significant factor in reducing fertility rates.

Giving more of the world's women the opportunity to become educated and to express their lives in meaningful, paid work and social roles outside the home will require some major social changes. Making these changes will be difficult because of the long-standing political and economic domination of society by men throughout the world.

6-5 Case Studies: Population Regulation in India and China

INDIA India (Figure 6-21) started the world's first national family planning program in 1952, when its population was nearly 400 million. In 1992, after 40 years of population control effort, India was the world's second most populous country, with a population of 883 million. Although India is only about one-third as large as the United States, its population is 3.4 times greater.

In 1952, India was adding 5 million people to its population each year. In 1992, it added 18 million. According to UN projections, India's population should reach 1 billion by 2000, 1.4 billion by 2025, and 1.6 billion before leveling off early in the 22nd century. By 2030, India is projected to overtake China as the world's most populous country.

India's people are among the poorest in the world, with average income per person equivalent to less than $350 a year. Agriculture employs about 67% of the country's labor force. At least one-third of its population has an annual income per person of less than $100 a year, and 10 out of every 100 babies born die before their first birthday. To add to the problem, nearly half of India's labor force is unemployed or can find only occasional work.

Currently, India produces enough food to give its population an adequate survival diet, but widespread poverty means that many people don't have enough land to grow the food they need or enough money to buy sufficient food. Some analysts fear that hunger and malnutrition will increase in India as its population continues to grow rapidly. About 40% of India's cropland is degraded as a result of soil erosion, waterlogging, salinization, overgrazing, and deforestation; and roughly 80% of the country's land is subject to repeated droughts — often lasting two to five years.

Without its long-standing family planning program, India's numbers would be growing even faster. However, the results of the program have been disappointing. Factors contributing to this failure have been poor planning, bureaucratic inefficiency, the low status

Q: Are the widely used GNP and GNP-per-capita indicators of economic growth useful indicators of changes in life quality?

Figure 6-22 Poster encouraging couples in China to have no more than one child. Couples who comply are given economic rewards, and those who do not suffer economic penalties.

IT IS BETTER TO HAVE ONE CHILD ONLY

只生一个孩子好

United Nations

of women (despite constitutional guarantees of equality), extreme poverty, and too little administrative and financial support.

The roots of the problem are deeper. About three out of every four people in India live in 560,000 rural villages, where birth rates tend to be higher than in urban areas and where the illiteracy rate for women is typically 80% to 90%.

For years, the government has provided information about the advantages of small families; yet, Indian women still have an average of 3.9 children because most couples believe they need many children as a source of cheap labor and old-age survival insurance. Almost one-third of Indian children die before age 5, reinforcing that belief.

In 1978, the government took a new approach, raising the legal minimum age for marriage from 18 to 21 for men and from 15 to 18 for women. The 1981 census, however, showed that there was no drop in the population growth rate between 1971 and 1981. Since then, the government has increased family planning efforts and funding, with the goal of achieving 60% contraceptive use and replacement-level fertility by 2000. Whether these efforts will succeed remains to be seen.

CHINA Between 1958 and 1962, an estimated 30 million people died from famine in China (Figure 6-21). Since 1970, however, China has made impressive efforts to feed its people and bring its population growth under control. On the other hand, since 1990, the number of homeless and hungry people in China has been rising. As in India, the average income in China is equivalent to about $370 a year.

Today, China has enough grain both to export and to feed its population of 1.17 billion. Between 1972 and 1985, China achieved a remarkable drop in its crude birth rate, from 32 to 18 per 1,000 people; and its average

total fertility rate dropped from 5.7 to 2.1 children per woman. Life expectancy in China is 71 years — 12 years higher than in India.

To accomplish a sharp drop in fertility, China has established the most extensive, intrusive, and strict population control program in the world, with an outlay of about $1 per person annually. The following are its most important features:

- Strongly encouraging couples to postpone marriage (age 28 for men and 25 for women)

- Expanding educational opportunities

- Providing married couples with easy access to free sterilization, contraceptives, and abortion

- Urging couples to have no more than one child (Figure 6-22)

- Giving couples who sign pledges to have no more than one child economic rewards such as salary bonuses, extra food, larger pensions, better housing, free medical care and school tuition for their child, and preferential treatment in employment when the child grows up

- Requiring those who break the pledge to return all benefits

- Exerting pressure on women pregnant with a third child to have abortions

- Requiring one of the parents in a two-child family to be sterilized

- Using mobile units and paramedics to bring sterilization, family planning, health care, abortion, and education to rural areas

- Training local people to carry on the family planning program

- Expecting all leaders to set an example with their own family size

If you believe that population growth in MDCs and LDCs is harmful to the biosphere, push for

- The United States and other MDCs to establish policies designed to reach zero population growth by 2025
- Worldwide family planning, with generous assistance from the United States and other MDCs to raise the level of spending from the current $4.5 billion to $10 billion a year
- Making birth control information and devices available to every man and woman at little or no cost
- Forgiving the debts of LDCs that institute effective programs to regulate population growth and agree to protect unspoiled areas from unsustainable development
- Compulsory education on population dynamics and the implications of rapid population growth

in MDCs and LDCs from the third grade through college

- Greatly expanded sex education for the world's teenagers, unless this is against your religious beliefs
- Policies that will slow the flow of the rural poor to urban areas by placing more emphasis on sustainable economic development in rural areas
- Giving the world's women the opportunity to become educated, to own property, and to express their lives in meaningful, paid work and social roles outside the home
- Sharply reducing poverty to lessen unnecessary human suffering and to reduce the need for people to have a large number of children as a form of social security
- Shifting from unsustainable to sustainable economic develop-

ment in MDCs to reduce consumption overpopulation, which is undermining the planet's life-support capacity (Figure 1-12)

In addition, carefully consider how many children you want to have. Those who consider population growth to be a serious global problem call for couples throughout the world to have no more than two children and to provide every child with a high-quality childhood that is nurturing, not damaging.

Despite these efforts, there have been reversals in China's population control programs since 1985. Between 1985 and 1992, China has had a birth rate of 20 (compared with 17 in 1984), an average total fertility rate of 2.2 (compared with 2.1 in 1984), and an annual population growth rate of 1.3% (compared with 1% in 1984). The primary reasons for these increases were the large number of women moving into their childbearing years, some relaxation of the government's stringent policies, and a strong preference for male children.

China's leaders have a goal of reaching zero population growth by 2000 with a population at 1.2 billion, followed by a slow decline to a population of 0.6 billion to 1.0 billion by 2100. Achieving this goal will be very difficult, because 27% of the Chinese people are under age 15. As a result, the United Nations projects that the population of China may be around 1.2 billion by 2000, 1.6 billion by 2025, and 1.7 billion before reaching ZPG perhaps around 2100.

Most countries cannot or do not want to use the coercive elements of China's program. Other parts of this program, however, could be used in many LDCs. Especially useful is the practice of localizing the program, rather than asking the people to go to distant centers. Perhaps the best lesson that other countries can learn from China's experience is not to wait to curb population growth until the choice is between mass starvation and coercive measures. Even harshly coercive measures can fail if a country starts too late. The lesson of China also shows how rapid population growth can help lead to severe limitations on individual freedom.

CUTTING GLOBAL POPULATION GROWTH Lester Brown, president of the Worldwatch Institute, urges the leaders of countries to adopt a goal of cutting world population growth in half during the 1990s by reducing the average global birth rate from 26 to 18 per 1,000 people. The experience of some countries such as Japan and China indicates that this is a possible goal. Each of us plays an important role in controlling global population growth (see Individuals Matter above).

Short of thermonuclear war itself, rampant population growth is the gravest issue the world faces over the decades immediately ahead.

ROBERT S. MCNAMARA

Garrett Hardin

As professor of human ecology at the University of California at Santa Barbara for many years, Garrett Hardin made important contributions to the joining of ethics and biology. He has raised hard ethical questions, sometimes taken unpopular stands, and forced people to think deeply about environmental problems and their possible solutions. He is best known for his 1968 essay, "The Tragedy of the Commons," which has had significant impacts on economics, political science, and the management of potentially renewable resources. His many books include Promethean Ethics *and* Filters Against Folly: How to Survive Despite Economists, Ecologists, and the Merely Eloquent.

For many years, Angel Island in San Francisco Bay was plagued with too many deer. A few animals transplanted there early in this century lacked predators and rapidly increased to nearly 300 deer—far beyond the carrying capacity of the island. Scrawny, underfed animals tugged at the heartstrings of Californians, who carried extra plant food from the mainland to the island.

Such charity worsened the plight of the deer. Excess animals trampled the soil, ate the bark off of small trees, and destroyed seedlings of all kinds. The net effect was a lowering of the carrying capacity, year by year, as the deer continued to multiply in a deteriorating habitat.

State game managers proposed that the excess deer be shot by skilled hunters. "How cruel!" some people protested. Then the managers proposed that coyotes be imported to the island. Though not big enough to kill adult deer, coyotes can kill defenseless young fawns, thus reducing the size of the herd. However, the Society for the Prevention of Cruelty to Animals was adamantly opposed to such human introduction of predators.

In the end, it was agreed to export deer to some other area suitable for deer life. A total of 203 animals were caught and trucked many miles away. From the fate of a sample of animals fitted with radiocollars, it was estimated that 85% of the transported deer died within a year (most of them within two months) from various causes: predation by coyotes, bobcats, and domestic dogs; shooting by poachers and legal hunters; and being run over by automobiles.

The net cost (in 1982 dollars) for relocating each animal that survived for a year was $2,876. The state refused to finance the continuation of the program, and no volun-

teers stepped forward to pay future bills. Even if funding had been forthcoming, managers would soon have run out of areas suitable for deer life. Organisms reproduce exponentially like compound interest (see Spotlight on p. 4), but the environment doesn't increase at all. The moral is a simple ecological commandment: *Thou shalt not transgress the carrying capacity.*

Now let's look at the human situation. A competent physicist has placed the human carrying capacity of the globe at 50 billion—about ten times the present world population. Before you are tempted to urge women to have more babies, consider what Robert Malthus said nearly 200 years ago: "There should be no more people in a country than could enjoy daily a glass of wine and piece of beef for dinner."

A diet of grain or bread is symbolic of minimum living standards; wine and beef are symbolic of all forms of higher living standards that make greater demands on the environment. When land used for the direct production of plants for human consumption is converted into land for growing crops for wine or corn for cattle, fewer calories get to the human population. Since carrying capacity is defined as the *maximum* number of animals (humans) an area can support, using part of the area to support such cultural luxuries as wine and beef reduces the carrying capacity. This reduced capacity is called the *cultural carrying capacity.* Cultural carrying capacity is always less than simple carrying capacity.

Energy is the common coin in which all competing demands on the environment can be measured. Energy saved by giving up a luxury can be used to produce more bread and support more people. We could increase the simple carrying capacity of the earth by giving up any (or all) of the following "luxuries": street lighting, vacations, most private cars, air conditioning, and artistic performances of all sorts—drama, dancing, music, and lectures. Since the heating of buildings is not as efficient as multiple layers of clothing, space heating would be forbidden.

Is that all? By no means: To come closer to home, look at this book. The production and distribution of such an expensive treatise consumes a great deal of energy. In fact, the energy bill for the whole of higher education is very high (which is one reason tuition costs so much). By giving up all education beyond the eighth grade, we could free enough energy to sustain millions of additional human lives.

At this point a skeptic might well ask: "Does God give a prize for the maximum population?" From this brief analysis we can see that there are two choices. We can maximize the number of human beings living at the lowest possible level of comfort, or we can try to optimize the quality of life for a much smaller population.

"What is the carrying capacity of the earth?" is a scientific question. Scientifically, it may be possible to support 50 billion people at a "bread" level. Is that what we want?

(continued)

"What is the cultural carrying capacity?" requires that we debate questions of value, about which opinions differ.

An even greater difficulty must be faced. So far, we have been treating the capacity question as a *global* question, as if there were a global sovereignty to enforce a solution on all people. However, there is no global sovereignty ("one world"), nor is there any prospect of one in the foreseeable future. We must make do with nearly 200 national sovereignties. That means, as concerns the capacity problem, that we must ask how nations are to coexist in a finite global environment if different sovereignties adopt different standards of living.

Consider a redwood forest. It produces no human food. Protected in a park, the trees do not even produce lumber for houses. Because people have to travel many kilometers to visit it, the forest is a net loss in the national energy budget. However, those who are fortunate enough to wander quietly through the cathedral-like aisles of soaring trees report that the forest does something precious for the human spirit.

Now comes an appeal from a distant land where millions are starving because their population has overshot the carrying capacity. We are asked to save lives by sending food. So long as we have surpluses, we may safely indulge in the pleasures of philanthropy. But the typical population in such poor countries increases by 2.3% a year—*or more*; that is, the country's population doubles every 30 years—*or less*. After we have run out of our surpluses, then what?

A spokesperson for the needy makes a proposal: "If you would only cut down your redwood forests, you could use the lumber to build houses and then grow potatoes on the land, shipping the food to us. Since we are all passengers together on Spaceship Earth, are you not duty bound to do so? Which is more precious, trees or human beings?"

The last question may sound ethically compelling, but let's look at the consequences of assigning a preemptive and supreme value to human lives. There are at least 2 billion people in the world who are poorer than the 34

million legally "poor" in America, and they are increasing by about 40 million per year. Unless this increase is brought to a halt, sharing food and energy on the basis of need would require the sacrifice of one amenity after another in rich countries. The final result of sharing would be complete poverty everywhere on the face of the earth to maintain the earth's simple carrying capacity. Is that the best humanity can do?

To date, there has been overwhelmingly negative reaction to all proposals to make international philanthropy conditional upon the stopping of population growth by the poor, overpopulated recipient nations. Foreign aid is governed by two apparently inflexible assumptions:

- The right to produce children is a universal, irrevocable right of every nation, no matter how hard it presses against the carrying capacity of its territory.

- When lives are in danger, the moral obligations of rich countries to save human lives is absolute and undeniable.

Considered separately, each of these two well-meaning doctrines might be defended; together, they constitute a fatal recipe. If humanity gives maximum carrying capacity precedence over problems of cultural carrying capacity, the result will be universal poverty and environmental ruin. Or do you see an escape from this harsh dilemma?

Guest Essay Discussion

1. What population size do you believe would allow the world's people to have a good quality of life? What do you believe is the cultural carrying capacity of the United States? Should the United States have a national policy to establish this population size as soon as possible? Explain.

2. Do you agree with the two principles the author of this essay says are the basis of foreign aid to needy countries? If not, what changes would you make in the requirements for receiving such aid?

DISCUSSION TOPICS

1. Project what your own life may be like at ages 25, 45, and 65 on the basis of the present population age structure of the country in which you live. What changes, if any, do such projections make in your career choice and in your plans for children?

2. Why is it rational for a poor couple in India to have six or seven children? What changes might induce such a couple to think of their behavior as irrational?

3. What conditions, if any, would encourage you to rely less on the automobile? Would you regularly travel to school or work by bicycle or motor scooter, on foot, by mass transit, or by a car or van pool? Explain.

4. Should world population growth be controlled? Explain.

5. Debate the following resolution: The United States has a serious consumption overpopulation problem and should adopt an official policy to stabilize its population and reduce unnecessary resource waste and consumption as rapidly as possible.

6. a. Should the number of legal immigrants and refugees allowed into the United States each year be sharply reduced? Explain.
   b. Should illegal immigration into the United States be sharply decreased? Explain. If so, how would you go about achieving this?
   c. Should families in the United States be given financial incentives and be persuaded to have more children to prevent population decline? Explain.

*7. Survey members of your class to determine the number of children they plan to have; tally the results.

CHAPTER 7

ENVIRONMENTAL ECONOMICS AND POLITICS

General Questions and Issues

1. What is economic growth? How can it and economic systems be redirected and managed to sustain Earth's life-support systems?

2. How can economics be used to regulate resource use and reduce environmental degradation and pollution?

3. What are the main causes of poverty, and what can be done to help people escape from the poverty trap?

4. How do political decisions affect resource use and environmental quality?

5. How can we bring about change?

As important as technology, politics, law, and ethics are to the pollution question, all such approaches are bound to have disappointing results, for they ignore the primary fact that pollution is primarily an economic problem, which must be understood in economic terms.

LARRY E. RUFF

INDIVIDUALS, BUSINESSES, AND SOCIETIES make **economic decisions** about what goods and services to produce, how to produce them, how much to produce, how to distribute them, and what to buy and sell. Because producing and using anything requires resources and has some harmful impact on the environment, economic decisions affect resource use and the quality of the environment.

As the number of people and their use of resources increase, the environmental impact of their economic activities increases (Figure 1-12 and Table 1-1). The basic problem is how economic systems can be used to produce economic goods to meet human needs and wants and — at the same time — sustain, rather than degrade, Earth's finite capital, which supports all economic activities.

Politics is the process by which individuals and groups try to influence or control the policies and actions of governments, whether local, state, national, or international. Politics is concerned with the distribution of resources and benefits — who gets what, when, and how. Thus, it plays a significant role in regulating the world's economic systems and influencing economic decisions. The poor, who don't own enough land or have enough work income to meet their basic needs, are often pushed into a downward spiral of poverty and environmental degradation by economic and political decisions beyond their control (Figure 7-1).

We are at a turning point. We can reshape our economic and political systems from Earth-degrading to Earth-sustaining, based on how nature works, or nature will do the job for us with an unprecedented and unnecessary increase in human misery and loss of life.

7-1 Economic Growth and External Costs

ECONOMIC GOODS, NEEDS, AND WANTS An **economic good** is any material item or service that gives people satisfaction. The types and amounts of certain economic goods — food, clothing, water, oxygen, shelter, health care, education — that you must have to survive and to stay healthy are your **economic needs**. Anything beyond those is an **economic want**. What you believe you need and want is influenced by the customs and conventions of the society in which you live, your level of affluence, and advertising.

ECONOMIC RESOURCES The things used in an economy to produce material goods and services are called **economic resources** or **factors of production**. They are usually divided into three groups:

Figure 7-1 Extreme poverty forces hundreds of millions of people to live in slums such as this one in Rio de Janeiro, Brazil, where adequate water supplies, sewage disposal, and other services don't exist.

1. **Natural resources:** resources produced by Earth's natural processes. These forms of Earth capital include the actual area of Earth's solid surface; nutrients and minerals in the soil and deeper portions of Earth's crust; wild and domesticated plants and animals (biodiversity); water; air; and nature's dilution, waste disposal, pest control, and recycling services.

2. **Capital** or **intermediate goods:** manufactured items made from natural resources and used as inputs to produce and distribute economic goods and services bought by consumers. These include tools, machinery, equipment, factory buildings, and transportation and distribution facilities.

3. **Labor:** the physical and mental efforts and talents of workers, managers, and investors in producing and distributing economic goods and services.

ECONOMIC GROWTH AND GROSS NATIONAL PRODUCT Virtually all economies in the world today seek to enhance their **economic growth:** an increase in the capacity of the economy to provide goods and ser-

vices for final use. Such growth is accomplished by maximizing the flow of matter and energy resources (throughput) through society as fast as possible (Figure 3-21). Economic growth is seen as good, limitless, and necessary to maximize wealth and power over people and the rest of nature.

Economic growth is usually measured by an increase in a country's **gross national product (GNP):** the market value in current dollars of all goods and services produced by an economy for final use during a year. To get a better idea of how much economic output is actually growing or declining, economists use the **real GNP:** the gross national product adjusted for *inflation*—any increase in the average price level of final goods and services.

To show how the average person's slice of the economic pie is changing, economists often calculate the **real GNP per capita:** the real GNP divided by the total population. If population expands faster than economic growth, the real GNP per capita falls. The pie has grown, but the slice per person has shrunk. This is useful, but the size of the per capita slice may hide the fact that the wealthy few have an enormous slice and the many poor have only a few crumbs.

GNP, QUALITY OF LIFE, AND ENVIRONMENTAL DEGRADATION Since 1942, most governments have used real GNP and real GNP indicators as if they were measures of Gross National Quality of Life, when in fact they measure only the speed at which an economy is producing economic goods of any type. The truth is that GNP and GNP per capita are poor indicators of social well-being, environmental health, and even economic health because:

■ They hide the harmful effects an economy produces by including the production of harmful goods and services. For example, producing more cigarettes raises GNP and GNP per capita, but it also causes more cancer and heart disease, which also increase GNP and GNP per capita by increasing health and insurance costs but decrease life quality through poor health and premature death.

■ They hide or underestimate good effects. For example, an energy-efficient light bulb or car comes on the market. The electric and gasoline bills for people using these Earth-saving devices go down, but this causes a drop in the country's GNP, which economists and politicians call bad. GNP indicators also do not include the labor we put into volunteer work; health care we give loved ones; growing some of our own food; and the cooking, cleaning, and repairs we do for ourselves.

■ They tell us nothing about economic justice. They don't tell us how resources and income are distributed among the people in a country—how many people have a large slice and how many have only a few crumbs of the economic pie. UNICEF sug-

Q: Each day, how many people die prematurely from starvation, malnutrition, and poverty-related diseases?

gests that countries should not be ranked by average GNP per capita, but by the average income of the lowest 40% of their people.

- They are used to stimulate economic growth that favors production of goods and services to fulfill artificially created wants; these goods and services often add little to life quality and degrade the ecosphere.

- Depletion and degradation of natural resources, upon which all economies ultimately depend, are not subtracted from the GNP. As a result, a country can exhaust its mineral resources, erode its soils, pollute its water, cut down its forests, and deplete its wildlife and fisheries and none of that degradation and depletion shows up as a loss in the country's GNP at the time. A country can have a rapidly rising GNP while heading toward ecological bankruptcy from permanent loss of its true wealth in the form of Earth capital.

SOCIAL AND ENVIRONMENTAL INDICATORS

In 1972, economists William Nordhaus and James Tobin developed an indicator called **net economic welfare (NEW)** to estimate the annual change in quality of life in a country. They calculate the NEW by putting a price tag on pollution and other "negative" goods and services included in the GNP—those that do not improve the quality of life. The costs of these negative factors are then subtracted from the GNP to give the NEW.

The net economic welfare can then be divided by a country's population to estimate the **per capita NEW**. This indicator and net economic welfare can then be adjusted for inflation. Applying these indicators to the United States shows that, since 1940, the real NEW per capita has risen at about half the rate of the real GNP per person and that, since 1968, the gap between these two indicators has been widening.

In 1989, economist Robert Repetto and other researchers at the World Resources Institute proposed that the depletion of natural resources be included as a factor in GNP to calculate a country's *net national product (NNP)*. They have developed a fairly simple model for doing this and have successfully applied it to Indonesia.

In 1990, Herman E. Daly and John B. Cobb, Jr., developed an index of sustainable economic welfare (ISEW) and applied it to the United States. This index, the most comprehensive indicator of well-being available, shows that between 1950 and 1976, the average welfare or well-being per person in the United States rose by 46%. Since 1976, however, the ISEW has been decreasing and declined 12% between 1977 and 1988. The biggest problems with this indicator are that it has been calculated only for the United States and that it depends on information available for only a few countries. In LDCs, where such information is not available, grain consumption per person provides a rough estimate of life quality.

These social and environmental indicators are not perfect. Without such indicators, however, we know too little about what is happening to people, the environment, and the planet's natural resource base, what needs to be done, and what types of policies work. We have blindfolded ourselves so that we cannot see what we are doing at a time when we have immense power to harm ourselves and other living things.

Why aren't such indicators used? First, putting a price tag on the "bads" is difficult and controversial. Second, many elected officials prefer using the real GNP per capita because it can make people think they are better off than they are and prevent them from recognizing the need for significant economic and political change.

INTERNAL AND EXTERNAL COSTS   The price you pay for a car reflects the costs of building and operating the factory, raw materials, labor, marketing, shipping, and company and dealer profits. After you buy the car, you also have to pay for gasoline, maintenance, and repair. All these direct costs, paid for by the seller and the buyer of an economic good, are called **internal costs**.

Making, distributing, and using any economic good also involve what economists call **externalities**. These are social benefits ("goods") and social costs ("bads") not included in the market price of an economic good or service. For example, if a car dealer builds an aesthetically pleasing sales building, that is an **external benefit** to other people who enjoy the sight at no cost to them.

On the other hand, when mines, and factories producing raw materials for cars, car factories, and the cars sold emit pollutants into the environment, their harmful effects are an **external cost** passed on to society and, in some cases, to future generations. Pollution from producing cars and driving them harms people and kills some of them. As a result, car insurance, health insurance, and medical bills go up for everyone. Air pollution from cars also kills or weakens some types of trees, raising the price of lumber, paper, and this textbook. Taxes may also go up, because the public may demand that the government spend money to regulate the land, air, and water pollution and degradation caused by producing and using cars and by mining and processing the raw materials used to make them.

Because these harmful costs are external and, hence, aren't included in the market price, you don't connect them with the car or type of car you are driving. As a consumer and taxpayer, however, you pay these hidden costs sooner or later.

If you use a car, you can pass other external costs on to society. You increase those costs when you throw trash out of a car, drive a car that gets poor gas mileage and thus adds more air pollution per kilometer than a more efficient car, dismantle or don't maintain a car's air pollution control devices, drive with a noisy muffler or faulty brakes, and don't keep your motor tuned. You don't pay directly for these harmful activities, but you and others pay indirectly in the form of higher taxes, higher health costs, higher health insurance, and higher cleaning and maintenance bills.

To environmentalists, the increasing number of harmful externalities (Table 1-1) is a warning sign that our economic systems are stressing the ecosphere. To pro-growth economists, externalities (as the name implies) are minor imperfections in our economic systems that can be cured from the profits made from more economic growth.

INTERNALIZING EXTERNAL COSTS   As long as people are rewarded for polluting, depleting, degrading, and wasting resources, few are going to volunteer to change; doing so would be committing economic suicide. Suppose you own a company and believe it's wrong to pollute the environment any more than can be handled by Earth's natural processes. If you voluntarily install expensive pollution controls and your competitors don't, your product will cost more and you will be at a competitive disadvantage. Your profits will decline and, sooner or later, you will probably go bankrupt and your employees will lose their jobs.

A general way to deal with the problem of external costs is for the government to add taxes, pass laws, or use other devices to force producers to include all or most of this expense in the market price of all economic goods. Then the market price of an economic good would be its **true cost**: its internal costs plus its short- and long-term external costs. This is what economists call *internalizing the external costs*. Internalizing external costs requires government action because few people are going to increase their cost of doing business unless their competitors have to do it as well.

What would happen if we internalized enough of the external costs of pollution and resource waste to help prevent pollution and to use resources more efficiently? Economic growth would be redirected. We would increase the beneficial parts of the GNP, decrease the harmful parts, increase production of beneficial goods, raise the net economic welfare, and help sustain the earth. Pollution prevention would be more profitable than pollution control, and waste reduction, recycling, and reuse would be more profitable than waste management.

On the other hand, some things (such as powerful, fuel-inefficient cars and trucks) would not be available any more because they would cost producers so much to make that few people could afford to buy them. You would pay more for most things because their market prices would be closer to their true costs, but everything would be "up front." External costs would no longer be hidden. You would have the information you need to make informed economic decisions about the effects of your lifestyle on the planet's life-support systems.

Moreover, real market prices wouldn't always be higher. Some things could even get cheaper. Internalizing external costs stimulates producers to find ways to cut costs by inventing more resource-efficient and less harmful methods of production.

Internalizing external costs makes so much sense you might be wondering why it's not more widely done. One reason is that many producers of harmful and wasteful goods fear they would have to charge so much they couldn't stay in business or would have to give up government subsidies that have helped hide the external costs. Their philosophy is: "If it isn't broken and we are making money, why fix it?" By contrast, environmentalists believe that our throwaway economic system is broken and we don't have much time to fix it.

It's also difficult to internalize external costs because it's not easy to put a price tag on all the harmful effects of making and using an economic good. People disagree on the values they attach to various costs and benefits, but making difficult choices about resource use is what economics and politics are all about.

 7-2

Economic Approaches to Improving Environmental Quality and Conserving Resources

HOW FAR SHOULD WE GO?   Shouldn't our goal always be zero pollution? For most pollutants, economists say, the answer is no. First, nature can handle some of our wastes, as long as we don't destroy, degrade, or overload these natural processes. Exceptions are toxic products that cannot be degraded by natural processes or that break down very slowly in the environment. They should be neither produced nor used, except in small amounts with special permits.

Second, we can't afford to have zero pollution for any but the most harmful substances. Removing a small percentage of the pollutants in air, water, or soil is not too costly; but when we remove more, the price per unit multiplies. The cost of removing pollutants follows a J-shaped curve of exponential growth (Figure 7-2).

If we go too far in cleaning up, the costs of pollution control will be greater than the harmful effects of pollution. As a result, some businesses could go bankrupt. You and others could lose jobs, homes, and savings. If we don't go far enough, the harmful external effects will cost us more than it would cost to reduce the pollution to a lower level. Then you and others could get sick or even die. Getting the right balance is crucial.

How do we do this? Theoretically, we begin by plotting a curve of the estimated economic costs of cleaning up pollution and a curve of the estimated social (external) costs of pollution. Adding the two curves together, we get a third curve showing the total costs. The lowest point on this third curve is the optimal level of pollution (Figure 7-3).

Q: How many children die prematurely each year because of the debt burden of LDCs?

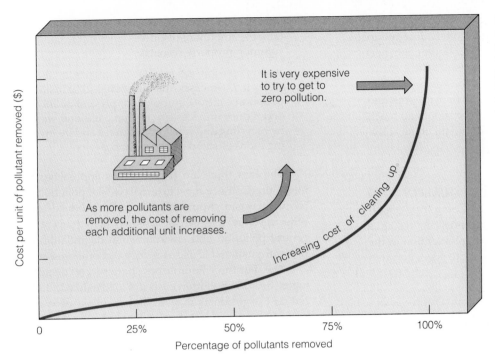

Figure 7-2 The cost of removing each additional unit of pollution rises exponentially. This explains why it's better to use an input approach that prevents a pollutant from reaching the environment or that keeps its concentration very low.

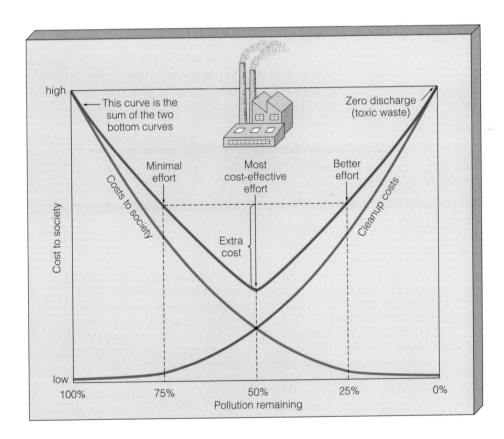

Figure 7-3 Finding the optimal level of pollution.

A: 500,000 — nearly 1,400 a day

On a graph, this looks neat and simple, but environmentalists and business leaders often disagree in their estimates of the social costs of pollution. Furthermore, the optimal level of pollution is not the same in different areas. Soils and lakes in some areas are more sensitive to acids and other pollutants than are soils and lakes in other places. Some believe we should go much further than merely establishing optimal pollution levels (see Spotlight below).

IMPROVING ENVIRONMENTAL QUALITY AND REDUCING RESOURCE WASTE Controlling or preventing pollution and reducing unnecessary resource use and waste require government intervention in the marketplace. There are four ways local, state, and federal governments can intervene.

1. *Make harmful actions illegal.* Pass and enforce laws that set pollution standards, regulate harmful activities, ban the release of toxic chemicals into the environment (see Spotlight below), and require that certain resources be conserved.

2. *Penalize harmful actions.* Levy taxes on each unit of pollution discharged into the air or water and each unit of unnecessary resource waste; require polluters to carry high levels of liability insurance; and have pollution control laws carry large automatic fines and automatic jail sentences.

3. *Market pollution rights and resource use rights.* Sell rights that allow pollution up to the estimated optimal level; sell the right to harvest or extract a sustainable amount of resources from public lands or common property resources.

4. *Reward beneficial actions.* Use tax dollars to pay subsidies to businesses and individuals that install pollution control equipment or prevent pollution and reduce unnecessary resource use and waste by recycling and reusing resources and by inventing more-efficient processes and devices.

The first three are *consumer-pays* approaches that internalize some or most external costs of pollution and resource waste. Approaches 2 and 3 produce tax or other revenue that can be used to help prevent and control pollution and environmental degradation and promote sustainable use of energy and other resources.

The first three approaches share several disadvantages. Because pollution costs are internalized, the initial cost of products may be higher unless new, more cost-effective and productive technologies are developed. This can put a country's products at a competitive disadvantage in the international marketplace. Higher initial costs also mean that the poor are penalized unless they are given tax relief or other subsidies from public funds. Also, fines and other punishments must be severe enough and enforced quickly enough to deter violations.

The fourth approach is a *taxpayer-pays* approach that does little to internalize external costs. It leads to higher-than-optimal levels of pollution and resource waste. It is not surprising that polluting industries and

---

SPOTLIGHT The Case for Low Discharge and for Assuming Chemicals Are Guilty Until Proven Innocent

Some analysts argue that setting optimal or politically acceptable levels of pollutants based on using pollution cleanup is a legalized way of justifying the killing or harming of an "acceptable" number of people. To them, that approach is ethically unacceptable.

They say that instead of spending a lot of money and time cleaning up chemicals we release into the environment (see Guest Essay on p. 33), we should sharply reduce our input of harmful chemicals into the environment. They say we should use the economic system to reward those who prevent pollution and punish those who don't. Then most of the expensive time- and talent-consuming apparatus of setting

standards and arguing over optimal levels would no longer be needed.

These environmentalists also call for reversing the present legal principle by which a chemical is assumed innocent until it is proved to have caused harm. They point out that by then it's too late, and the people who have been harmed usually don't have the money and other resources needed to establish their claims in the courts.

Instead, these environmentalists believe that a chemical should be assumed to be guilty until proven otherwise by the people proposing to make or use it. Why should chemicals be given the same legal rights as people, they ask? This standard of guilt is already applied to pharma-

ceutical chemicals, so why shouldn't it be expanded to cover all potentially harmful chemicals?

Critics of this proposal and the idea of low discharge argue that these changes would bring the production of most goods to a halt, wreck the economy, and put large numbers of people out of work. Proponents counter that not making these changes will eventually wreck the environment and thus the economy, eventually put more people out of work, kill large numbers of workers and citizens, and reduce Earth's biodiversity upon which our economies and survival depend. What do you think?

resource wasters usually prefer this approach, which has taxpayers pay them not to pollute or waste resources.

Another problem with subsidies is that often they go to those with the most political power and influence regardless of need. They reward the greedy rather than the needy. Furthermore, it's difficult to lower or withdraw a subsidy when it's no longer needed because companies with subsidies use their influence to keep them.

COST-BENEFIT ANALYSIS   One method used to help make economic decisions is **cost-benefit analysis**. It involves comparing the estimated short-term and long-term costs (losses) and benefits (gains) of an economic decision. If the estimated benefits exceed the estimated costs, the decision to produce or buy an economic good or provide a public good is considered worthwhile. You intuitively make such evaluations when you decide to buy a particular economic good or service.

More formal cost-benefit analysis is often used in evaluating whether to build a large hydroelectric dam, to clean up a polluted river, or to reduce air pollution emissions to an optimal level (Figure 7-3). However, use of cost-benefit analysis is controversial (see Pro/Con below).

| 7-3 | **Making the Transition to a Sustainable-Earth Economy** |

A SUSTAINABLE-EARTH ECONOMY   Environmentalists and a few economists have proposed that the world's countries make a transition to a **sustainable-Earth economy** (see Spotlight on p. 153). They point out that the current forms of capitalism and all other economic systems are not working well because they live parasitically on Earth capital, which belongs to future generations, and because they are based on the wrong ethics.

These economic systems are also based largely on unrealistic assumptions that make up the throwaway worldview (Section 2-2): that the human population can grow indefinitely, that enough resources will always be available, that the environment can handle all the waste we put into it, and that science and technology can solve our problems and allow us to manage and control the earth for our species. To most environmentalists and a few economists, this is fairy-tale thinking based on our complete dependence on Earth capital and little understanding of how the world really works.

PRO/CON How Useful Is Cost-Benefit Analysis?

The two main arguments for using cost-benefit analysis are that it is a useful way to gather and analyze data on a proposed project or course of action and that it can be used to find the cheapest way to do something. However, unless decision makers and citizens are also aware of its severe limitations, cost-benefit analysis can be used as a device for justifying something that should not be done or that could be done in a less harmful and less expensive way.

A great source of disagreement between environmentalists and business people is the **discount rate**: an estimate of how much economic value a resource might have in the future compared with its present value. Suppose a stand of redwood trees has a current market value of $1 million. At a zero discount rate, it will still be worth $1 million 50 years from now, while at a 10% discount rate (normally used by most businesses and the U.S. Office of Management and Budget), it would be

worth only $10,000. Thus, *the choice of discount rate is a primary factor affecting the outcome of any cost-benefit analysis.*

Proponents of high discount rates argue that inflation will make the value of their earnings less in the future than now. They also fear that innovation or changed consumer preferences will make a product or service obsolete.

Proponents also assume that economic growth through technological progress will automatically raise average living standards in the future. Why, then, should the current generation pay higher prices and taxes to benefit future generations who will be better off anyway? Environmentalists believe that this is not a reasonable assumption as long as our economic systems are based upon depleting the natural capital that supports them.

Environmentalists point out that high discount rates encourage rapid exploitation of resources and envi-

ronmental quality for immediate payoffs. This makes sustainable management of most natural resources virtually impossible by loading the economic dice in favor of rapid exploitation. Environmentalists believe that unique and scarce resources would be protected by having a 0% or a negative discount rate and discount rates of 1% to 3% would be used to make it profitable to use other resources sustainably or slowly.

Another problem is determining who gets the benefits and who is harmed by the costs. For example, suppose a cost-benefit analysis concludes that it is too expensive to meet certain safety and environmental standards in a manufacturing plant. The owners of the company benefit by not having to spend money on making the plant less hazardous. Consumers may also benefit from lower prices. However, the workers are harmed by having

(continued)

---

to work under hazardous and unhealthful conditions. On the other hand, they may lose their jobs if the plant shuts down because its owners can't or won't spend the money to meet stricter safety and environmental standards.

In the United States, for example, an estimated 100,000 Americans die each year from exposure to hazardous chemicals and other safety hazards at work. An additional 400,000 are seriously injured from such exposure. Is that a necessary or an unnecessary (and unethical) cost of doing business?

The most serious limitation of cost-benefit analysis is that many things we value cannot be reduced to dollars and cents. Some of the costs of air pollution, such as extra laundry bills, house repainting, and ruined crops, are fairly easy to estimate. But how do we put meaningful price tags on human life, good health, clean air and water, beautiful scenery, a wilderness area, whooping cranes, and the ability of natural

systems to degrade and recycle some of our wastes and replenish timber, fertile soil, and other vital potentially renewable resources?

The dollar values we assign to such items will vary widely because of different assumptions and value judgments, leading to a wide range of projected costs and benefits. For example, values assigned to a human life in various cost-benefit studies vary from nothing to about $7 million, with the most frequently assigned values ranging from $200,000 to $500,000. If you were asked to put a price tag on your life, you might say it is priceless, or you might contend that making such an estimate would be impossible or even immoral.

Although you may not want others to place a low monetary value on your life, you do so yourself if you choose to smoke cigarettes, to eat improperly, to drive without a seat belt, to drive while impaired by alcohol or some other drug, or to save money rather than buy a safer car. In

each case, you decide that the benefits — pleasure, convenience, or a lower purchase price — outweigh the potential costs — poorer health, injury, or death.

Critics of cost-benefit analysis argue that because estimates of many costs and benefits are so uncertain, they can easily be weighted to achieve the desired outcome by proponents or opponents of a proposed project or action. The experts making or evaluating such analyses have to be paid by somebody, so they often represent the point of view of that somebody.

The difficulty in making cost-benefit analyses does not mean that they should not be made or that they are not useful. They can be useful if decision makers and the public are aware that they give only rough estimates and guidelines for resource use and management based on certain assumptions and that they can easily be distorted.

To correct these serious and dangerous flaws, environmentalists and some economists call for us to move from an Earth-plundering economy based on addiction to unlimited economic growth to an Earth-sustaining economy based on cooperating with the earth and recognizing that the wealth that truly sustains us is not money or property but nature. We need to redefine what we call wealth, progress, and national and global security. We need economists, leaders, and ordinary citizens who understand that global, national, and local security depends on treasuring and putting infinite value on the air, water, soil, and wildlife that keep us all alive. Just as important, we need to see every person — especially children, who are the future of our species — as equally unique, precious, and special individuals, not primarily as workers and consumers in our economic machines.

We desperately need to rethink our economics. We can begin by downgrading the importance of economics in our thinking — recognizing that economics is a limited subsystem of the ecosphere that should not be used to dominate and degrade the earth for short-term financial gain. Our activities should not be driven mostly by *quantity*, as measured by numbers, prices,

bottom lines, and economic growth, but by the unmeasurable things such as love, caring, human dignity, beauty, cooperation, and sustaining Earth's life-support system that we call *quality*.

This new economics would recognize that on a finite planet perpetual economic growth and population growth are not only impossible but also self-destructive. It would be built around the concept of *enough*, based on meeting everyone's basic needs and providing them with quality lives.

MAKING SUSTAINING THE EARTH PROFITABLE
The exciting news is that there is a way to shift from our current Earth-degrading economy to a sustainable-Earth economy within 10 to 20 years by using the profit motive that drives the world's market-based economic systems. The way out of our current self-destructive behavior is to switch the rewards from Earth-degrading to Earth-sustaining businesses and to do this over a time period that allows companies to make the shift.

To achieve this goal, elected officials, prodded by voters, would have to announce that over the next decade, all federal, state, and local subsidies that encourage resource depletion and waste and environmental

Q: How many people are expected to be infected with the AIDS virus by 2000?

A sustainable-Earth economy discourages Earth-degrading types of economic growth and encourages Earth-sustaining activities to prevent overloading and degrading Earth's life-support systems now and in the future.

Discourages:

- Throwaway and nondegradable products, use of oil and coal, nuclear energy, deforestation, overgrazing, groundwater depletion, soil erosion, resource waste, and pollution cleanup instead of pollution prevention.

- Creation and satisfaction of wants that cause high levels of pollution, environmental degradation, and resource waste.

Does This By:

- Using taxes and marketable permits to internalize the external costs of goods and services so that market prices of all goods and services reflect their true costs.

- Removing government subsidies from highly pollution-producing, resource-depleting, and resource-wasting economic activities.

- Discouraging policies and practices that support current living standards by depleting Earth's natural resource capital for us, future generations, and other species.

- Requiring a standardized environmental audit for all economic goods from "cradle to grave" and widely publishing the results.

Encourages:

- A demographic transition to a stable world population of low birth and death rates (Figure 6-20).

- An energy transition with emphasis on high efficiency and increasing reliance on perpetual and renewable energy resources.

- An economic transition from a society devoted to satisfying the artificially created wants of a few

to one committed to providing the basic needs of all. This includes making sure that taxes and other burdens of making this transition do not fall unfairly on the poor.

- Recycling, reuse, solar energy, improving energy efficiency, education, prevention of health problems, ecological restoration, pollution prevention, appropriate technology, waste reduction, and long-lasting, reusable, easily repaired products (durability instead of disposability).

- Sustainable development that emphasizes growth in the quality of life instead of the quantity of economic goods and that does not deplete or degrade Earth's natural capital for current and future generations. Proposals made under the name of sustainable development must be evaluated carefully to be sure that they are not sanitized versions of economic growth as usual.

- Preservation of biological diversity at local, national, and global levels by setting aside and controlling the use of forests, wetlands, grasslands, soil, wildlife, and representative aquatic ecosystems.

- Use of renewable resources at a sustainable rate.

- Limiting waste discharge into the environment to the rate at which wastes can be diluted, absorbed, and degraded by natural processes with no harm to humans, other species, or the functioning of natural processes.

- Sustainable agriculture (Section 13-6) that conserves soil (Section 12-3) and water (Section 11-3), emphasizes polyculture instead of monoculture, and emphasizes use of natural fertilizers and integrated pest management (Section 14-5).

- Use of locally available matter and energy resources to reduce the loss of capital, income, and jobs from the local economy.

- Decentralization of some production facilities to reduce transportation costs, make better use of locally available resources, enhance national security by spreading out targets, increase employment, and keep money circulating in local economies.

- A transition from competitive nationalistic politics to cooperative planetary politics in which countries work together politically and economically to promote peace and sustain Earth's life-support systems for everyone now and in the future.

- A fairer distribution of the world's resources and wealth, with primary emphasis on meeting the basic needs of the poor and helping them sustain themselves (see Section 7-4).

- Breaking down trade barriers between MDCs and LDCs.

- A broadened definition of national security to include resource, environmental, and economic security and consideration of demographic issues (see Guest Essay on p. 19). In 1990, the U.S. federal government spent $330 billion on military security and only $14 billion on environmental security.

Does This By:

- Recognizing that economics is a subsystem of the ecosphere and integrating economics and ecology in decision making (the most important condition).

- Using government subsidies and taxes to encourage pollution prevention, resource conservation, and waste reduction and selling marketable permits for resource extraction.

- Increasing the aid from rich countries to poor countries that helps LDCs become more self-reliant rather than more dependent on MDCs.

(continued)

- Eliminating at least 60% of the $1.3-trillion debt that LDCs owe to MDCs and international lending agencies through debt forgiveness in exchange for agreements to improve environmental quality, education, and health care; reduce poverty; protect undeveloped areas; control population growth; and use resources sustainably.

- Requiring all international lending institutions and governments to make only loans that enhance the transition to a sustainable-Earth economy.

Determines Progress with Indicators that Measure:

- Changes in the quality of life.
- Sustainable use of renewable resources.
- Recycling and reuse of nonrenewable resources.

- Pollution prevention and waste reduction.
- Improvements in energy efficiency.
- The life-cycle environmental impacts of all goods and services.

INDIVIDUALS MATTER What You Can Do

Individual consumers are the catalyst for making the shift to an Earth-sustaining economy. By choosing what to buy and what companies to invest in, American and other consumers can also force companies and elected leaders to become more environmentally responsible.

Here are some guidelines for green consuming:

1. Begin by asking yourself if you really need this product. Recognize that green consuming is still consuming, much of it devoted to meeting harmful and unsatisfying wants.

2. When possible, buy products that are durable and reusable and used rather than new.

3. When that is not possible, buy products that are made from recycled materials or renewable resources and that are recyclable. Just because something is recyclable doesn't mean that it will be recycled unless you see that it gets to a recycling center and unless you buy recycled products to create a demand for such products.

4. Buy the product with the least packaging.

5. Boycott harmful products.*

6. Buy products that have been evaluated from cradle to grave and given the following seals of approval: Green Seal or Green Cross in the United States, Blue Angel in Germany, Environmental Choice in Canada, and Eco-Mark in Japan. Because of a lack of necessary data and funding, these new indicators are not perfect, but they are a start.

7. Help elect people to local, state, and national offices who make sustaining the earth their top priority.

Buying green and recycling a little bit (25% instead of at least 60%) may make us feel good and may buy a little time. But if that is all we do, sooner or later we will be overwhelmed by the diseases of rapid population growth, overconsumption of resources, and resource waste and by failure to modify the economic and political systems that promote those afflictions.

Try to work for or start green companies. Each year, the Council on Economic Priorities publishes a small book rating companies on their social and environmental responsibility. To reduce the hemorrhage of capital, energy, resources, and jobs from local economies, participate in, invest in, and support environmentally responsible production by locally owned, operated, and controlled enterprises.

On Earth Day 1990, millions of people signed the Earth Day Pledge, promising to honor the environment when they vote, purchase, consume, and invest. Honoring this pledge is a way of exercising the most important economic and political power we have to help sustain the earth.

*For information on boycotted products, subscribe to *National Boycott News*, 6506 28th Avenue N.E., Seattle, WA 98115 ($10.00 a year).

Q: Worldwide, how many people have malaria?

degradation would be phased out and replaced with taxes on such activities. During that same period, new government subsidies would be phased in for businesses built around resource conservation, waste reduction, recycling, reuse, pollution prevention, and use of renewable energy.

Because this shift would be well publicized and would take place over 10 years, businesses would have time to shift into these new ways to make a profit. The transition would also provide jobs because most Earth-sustaining businesses are more labor intensive than are Earth-degrading businesses. Also, managers, workers, and stockholders in these businesses would be able to feel better about what they were making and doing.

Making this transition will not be easy. Powerful economic interests making short-term profits from the present system of rewards will vigorously oppose such changes, but if voters oust officeholders who cave in to those interests, politicians will get the message loud and clear. Consumers and investors will have to exercise the enormous power they have over corporate behavior, what products are produced, and how they are produced (see Individuals Matter on p. 154).

7-4 Poverty: A Human and Environmental Tragedy

THE GLOBAL POVERTY TRAP The world's poor are caught in a poverty trap by local, national, and global forces beyond their control. **Poverty** is usually defined as not being able to meet one's basic economic needs. Most of the world's 1.2 billion desperately poor people live in LDCs.

Since 1960, the gap between the rich and the poor, as measured by GNP per capita, has grown, and it has accelerated since 1980 (Figure 7-4). For decades economists have talked of wealth produced by economic growth "trickling down" to the poor, but Figure 7-4 shows that little has trickled down. The rich have grown much richer, while the poor have stayed poor and some have grown even poorer. Today, one in five people on Earth lives in luxury. The next three get by, while the fifth is desperately poor and must constantly struggle to survive on less than $1 a day (see Spotlight on p. 156).

Poverty is also found in MDCs. In the United States, 34 million people—nearly one in seven Americans—were below the official poverty line in 1990. This burden of poverty falls most heavily on minorities, female-headed households, and the young. In 1990, one in five children and one in three blacks in the United States lived below the official poverty level.

Much poverty in MDCs is not as serious as that for the desperately poor in LDCs, but poverty anywhere represents an unnecessary degradation of human life and a failure of the world's economic and political systems. At the local level there are four parts of the poverty trap:

- Lack of access to enough land and income to meet basic needs.

- Physical weakness and poor health caused by not having enough land to grow food or enough income to buy enough food for good health. This decreases the ability of the poor to work and plunges them deeper into poverty (Figure 7-5).

- Powerlessness that can subject the poor to being tricked into signing away the little land or live-

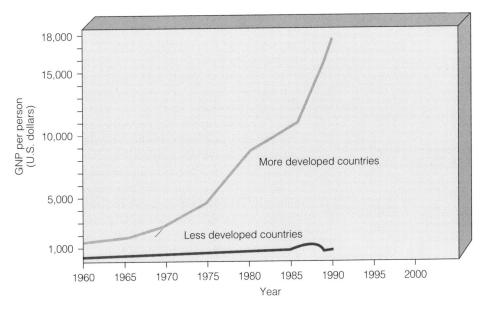

Figure 7-4 The gap in GNP per person in MDCs and LDCs has been widening since 1960 and has accelerated in the 1980s. When adjusted for inflation, this gap is even wider than shown here. (Data from United Nations)

A: 500 million (1 in every 11 people)

One of every five people on earth is desperately poor — too poor to grow or buy enough food to maintain good health or perform a job. Each year, an estimated 40 million of the world's 1.2 billion desperately poor people die unnecessarily from preventable malnutrition (lack of enough protein and other nutrients needed for good health) and diseases. Half of those who die are children under the age of 5 (Figure 1-3). Most of these children die from diarrhea and measles, which are deadly diseases for people weakened by malnutrition. *Those dying are unique human beings, not mere numbers or things.*

During your lunch hour, an estimated 4,600 people died prematurely from starvation, malnutrition, and poverty-related diseases. By the time you eat lunch tomorrow, 110,000 more will have died. This death toll is equivalent to 275 jumbo jet planes, each carrying 400 passengers, crashing every day with no survivors.

This is the most important and disturbing news taking place on the planet every day; yet, this incredibly tragic news is rarely covered by the media. Because these deaths occur every day, are spread out over the world, and happen mostly in rural areas and urban slums in LDCs away from the glare of TV cameras and reporters, they are not considered major or dramatic news. Moreover, we don't want to hear this news. We prefer to deny its harsh reality.

The bad news is that so many of the world's poor are dying every day. The good news is that most of these premature deaths could be prevented at little cost, typically only $5 per child. Such unnecessary deaths will continue until we expand the concept of national and global security to include economic and environmental security for everyone and greatly increase funding for these vital elements of our individual and collective security.

stock they own, paying such high interest rates on loans that they lose their land and livestock, and having to pay bribes to get work.

- Rapid population growth, which produces more workers than can be employed and forces wages down as the poor compete with each other for scarce work. Some people in affluent countries consider poor people ignorant for having so many children. To most poor parents, however, having many children, especially boys, makes good sense: They need children as a form of economic security to help grow food, tend livestock, work, or beg in the streets. The two or three of their children who typically survive to adulthood are also a

form of social security to help their parents survive in old age (typically their forties). This strength in numbers may lower the family's chances of escaping poverty, but it reduces their risk of starvation.

These local parts of the poverty trap are reinforced by government policies at the national level. They include national budgets that favor urban and industrial over rural development and military over social expenditures.

Additional layers of the global poverty trap are added at the international level. They include:

- The $1.3-trillion debt LDCs owe to MDC banks and governments (UNICEF blames the death of 500,000 children a year on the debt burden of the LDCs)

- Sharp declines in the income of LDCs that depend on exports of cash crops such as coffee, sugar, and cotton and raw materials such as iron ore and copper because of drops in the market prices of those commodities since 1980

- Rising trade barriers in rich countries that each year cost LDCs about $100 billion in lost sales and depressed prices

- Decreased investment in LDCs by MDCs because of the economic turmoil and uncertainty in these poor countries

- Loss of investment capital because wealthy elites in LDCs have invested or deposited much of their money abroad, where it is safe from taxation and political and economic disruptions

POVERTY AND ENVIRONMENTAL DEGRADATION Poverty is the primary cause of environmental degradation in LDCs. For the rural poor, sustaining soil fertility, forest productivity, and wildlife populations is not just an idea, but also is what keeps them alive. The poor are also the world's greatest recyclers and reusers. They can't afford to waste anything.

However, when the rural poor are faced with starvation, they are driven to knowingly overexploit their vital resource base. The result is increased deforestation, soil erosion and flooding, spreading deserts, and loss of biodiversity. The rural poor become locked into a downward spiral of increasing poverty, desperation and misery, and environmental degradation. This is a tragedy for the poor, the rich, and the earth.

In effect, LDCs are being coerced into depleting their resources to help support the wasteful, Earth-degrading lifestyles of people in MDCs and the rich in their own countries who refuse to share enough of their enormous wealth to eliminate poverty. If these LDCs don't sell off their resources at bargain basement prices, they can't pay the interest on their debts and don't have enough income to prevent economic decline. However,

Q: How many people die from malaria each year?

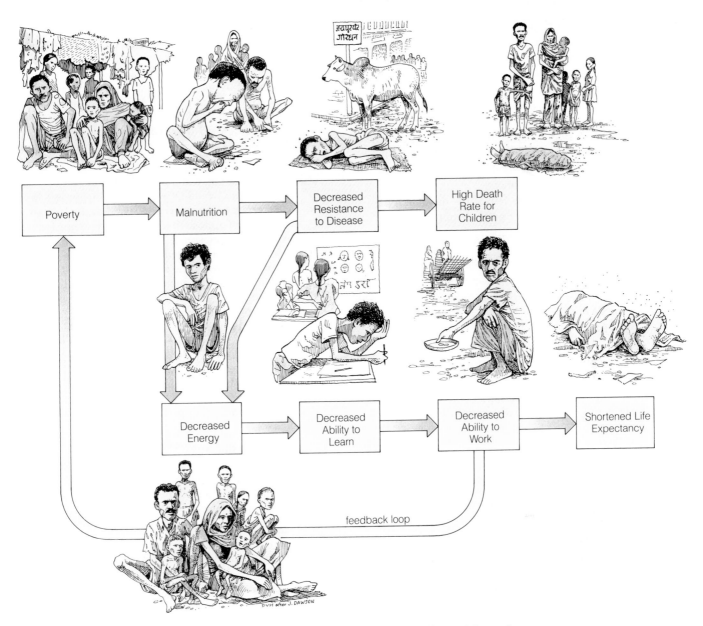

Figure 7-5 Part of the poverty trap at the local level. Interactions among poverty, malnutrition, and disease form a tragic cycle that tends to perpetuate such conditions in succeeding generations of families.

by selling off and degrading their resource base, these LDCs face an even bleaker economic and environmental future.

Without radical shifts in policies by both MDCs and LDCs, perhaps 3 billion to 5 billion people—half of humanity—could be living in absolute poverty sometime between 2050 and 2075. Another possibility is that pollution and environmental degradation by the rich and the poor will become so great that there will be a population crash (Figure 5-33b), with 2 billion to 5 billion people dying prematurely.

It is urgent that national governments and the international community recognize that population growth, poverty, and environmental degradation are interrelated and mount a crash program to deal with these crises simultaneously. Despite much controversy and foot-dragging by the United States, the United Nations Conference on Environment, held in Rio de Janeiro in June 1992, was an important event that could help shape environmental agendas for everybody.

WHAT CAN BE DONE? The solution to the global poverty–environmental degradation trap is to direct virtually all forms of aid from MDCs and from the governments of LDCs to the one out of five people on Earth without enough land or income to meet their basic needs. This is based on Mahatma Gandhi's concept of *antyodaya*: putting the poor and their environment first, not last.

A: 2.5 million (some say 5 million)

Instead of asking only experts and consultants what to do, we must also ask the poor. They know far more about poverty, survival, and environmental sustainability than do bureaucrats or experts. How many of the world's experts could survive by growing food on a steeply sloping plot or could raise and keep a family of six alive on 80 cents a day? The role of MDCs and the governments of LDCs is to give the poor enough land and job income to meet their basic needs, put them in charge, get out of their way, spotlight what works, and transfer that information to others.

The layers of the poverty trap at the national level must be dismantled by drastic and difficult changes in government policies. They include:

- Shifting more of the national budget to the rural and urban poor

- Seeing that the present trickle of aid to the poor becomes a healthy flow and that this flow is not diverted by the greedy before it reaches the needy

- Giving villages, villagers, and the urban poor title to common lands and to crops and trees they plant on common lands

- Redistributing some of the land owned by the wealthy to the poor, as has been done in South Korea and China

- Allocating much more money for education, health care, family planning, clean drinking water, and sanitation for the poor in rural villages and in urban slums, with these programs planned and run by local residents

- Greatly increasing the rights of poor women, who grow and cook most of the food, collect most of the firewood, haul most of the water, and provide most of the health care for the poor with no pay and few human rights

The local poor and the governments of LDCs cannot escape the widening jaws of the poverty–environmental degradation trap unless MDCs and the rich in LDCs dismantle their layers of this trap. Ways to dismantle those layers include

- Forgiving much (at least 60%) of the present debt owed by LDCs to MDCs and recognizing that this is a vital investment in global environmental and economic security for the rich and the poor. Much of this debt can be forgiven in exchange for agreements by the governments of LDCs to increase expenditures for rural development, family planning, health care, and education and to commit to better land redistribution, protection of remaining wilderness areas, and sustainable use of other lands and renewable resources.

- Increasing the nonmilitary aid given by MDCs to LDCs to 5% of the annual GNP of the MDCs. Currently, the United States contributes only 0.2% of its GNP as nonmilitary aid to LDCs. This aid should be given directly to the poor to help them sustain themselves. All national and international lending agencies should not lend money for projects unless a favorable environmental impact assessment has been made and strict controls are used to see that environmental controls are fully implemented. In 1979, $40 billion flowed from MDCs to LDCs. Now because of debt repayments and capital flight, a net $85 billion flows each year from LDCs to MDCs.

- Lifting trade barriers that hinder the export of commodities from LDCs to MDCs. Businesses in MDCs now being protected from cheaper foreign imports will oppose this. However, it is time for protected businesses to innovate and become more competitive instead of resisting change in the name of protecting short-term profits and keeping prices for consumers higher than they need be. They should practice the basic principle of free enterprise: If you can't compete, you shouldn't be in business. However, lifting these trade barriers should not be used by powerful multinational companies as an excuse for reducing environmental and consumer protection by reducing pollution and food safety standards to global standards decided by international bodies dominated by representatives of these companies.

- Having governments throughout the world cooperate in tracking the flight and concealment of capital from LDCs to MDCs and requiring the owners of that capital to pay taxes on it and any income it generates to their national treasuries to help finance the economic recovery of their homelands.

- Recognizing that the greatest threat to the global environment for the rich and the poor and other species are the throwaway economic systems (Figure 3-21) in MDCs and replacing them with sustainable-Earth economic systems (Figure 3-22 and Section 7-3).

- Aiding LDCs in developing new, diversified sustainable-Earth economies instead of using the throwaway economic systems of the MDCs that must now be modified and replaced because they threaten the life-support systems for everyone (Section 7-3).

7-5 Politics and Environmental and Resource Policy

INFLUENCING PUBLIC POLICY Politics is concerned with the distribution of resources and benefits — who gets what, when, and how. Decision makers in democratic governments must deal with an array of conflicting groups. Each special-interest group is asking for resources or money or relief from taxes to help purchase or control more of certain resources. Interest

Q: How many women in LDCs die each year of preventable pregnancy-related causes?

groups that are highly organized and well funded usually have the most influence.

Constitutional democracies are run by elected elites drawn largely from the upper socioeconomic strata of society. These government officials are strongly influenced by other elites running corporations, the media, educational institutions, and other organized special-interest groups. Individuals and organized groups influence and change government policies in constitutional democracies mainly by

- Voting
- Contributing money and time to candidates running for office
- Lobbying and writing elected representatives to pass certain laws, establish certain policies, and fund various programs
- Using the formal education system and the media to influence public opinion
- Filing lawsuits asking the courts to overturn, enforce, or interpret the meaning of existing laws
- Carrying out grassroots activities such as marches, mass meetings, sit-ins, hugging trees to prevent them from being cut (see Individuals Matter on p. 32), protesting the location of waste landfills and incinerators, organizing product boycotts, and using consumer buying power (see Individuals Matter on p. 154)

REACTION-TO-CRISIS PUBLIC POLITICS IN DEMOCRACIES Political systems in constitutional democracies are designed to bring about gradual or incremental change, not revolutionary change. Rapid change is difficult because of distribution of power among different branches of government, conflicts among interest groups, conflicting information from experts, and lack of money (see Case Study on p. 160).

Because tax income is limited, developing and adopting a budget is the most important thing decision makers do. Developing a budget involves answering two key questions: What resource use and distribution problems will be addressed? How much limited tax income will be used to address each problem? Someone once said that the way to understand human history is to study budgets.

Most political decisions are made by bargaining, accommodation, and compromise between leaders of competing elites or power groups within a society. Most politicians who remain in power become good at finding compromises and making trade-offs that give a little to each side. They play an important role in holding society together, preventing chaos and disorder, and making incremental changes; but these same processes hinder substantial changes and dealing with long-range problems.

U.S. ENVIRONMENTAL LEGISLATION Environmentalists, with backing from many other citizens and members of Congress, have pressured Congress to enact a number of important federal environmental and resource protection laws, as discussed throughout this text and listed on the page before the inside of the back cover. Similar laws, and in some cases even stronger laws, have been passed by most states.

These laws attempt to provide environmental protection using mainly these five approaches:

1. Setting standards for pollution levels or limiting emissions or effluents for various classes of pollutants (Federal Water Pollution Control Act and the Clean Air Act)

2. Screening new substances before they are widely used in order to determine their safety (Toxic Substances Control Act of 1976)

3. Requiring a comprehensive evaluation of the environmental impact of an activity before it is undertaken (National Environmental Policy Act)

4. Setting aside or protecting various ecosystems, resources, or species from harm (Wilderness Act and Endangered Species Act)

5. Encouraging resource conservation (Resource Conservation and Recovery Act and National Energy Act)

Most current environmental laws legalize certain levels of pollution and waste and then move these wasted resources from one part of the environment to another in a futile search for an infinite away. Instead, we should be passing and strictly enforcing a new set of laws that emphasize pollution prevention, resource reduction, and integrated pollution management that considers the effects of waste materials on all parts of the environment.

STRATEGIES OF POLLUTERS AND RESOURCE DEPLETERS It is natural that producers of pollution and resource degradation resist government regulations or taxes that require them to reduce or eliminate pollution and use resources more efficiently. Being forced to internalize some of the external costs they pass on to society (Section 7-1) costs them money and can reduce their profits.

Corporate elites use several basic strategies to ensure that government laws and regulations do little to damage corporate profit margins. They

- Make donations to the election campaigns of politicians favoring their positions.
- Establish groups of lobbyists and lawyers in national and state capitals. These corporate representatives often oppose restrictive legislation, weaken proposed laws and standards, inject loopholes and opportunities for delays and legal challenges

The writers of the U.S. Constitution wanted to develop a political system strong enough to provide security and order and to protect liberty and property, but without giving too much power to the federal government. That was done by dividing political power between the federal and state governments and within the three branches of the federal government — legislative, executive, and judicial (Figure 7-6).

These branches are connected and controlled by a series of checks and balances to prevent one branch from gaining too much power. Once federal laws are passed, they are supposed to be implemented and enforced by various bureaucratic agencies in the executive branch of the federal government and by delegation of certain responsibilities to state governments.

Actions that affect environmental quality and resource use are controlled by an elaborate network of laws and regulations at the federal, state, and local levels. Figure 7-7 summarizes the primary forces involved in environmental policy-making at the federal level. Similar factors are found at the state level.

The end result is usually a compromise that satisfies no one but that all participants hope will muddle through, mostly by making short-term incremental changes. Even if a tough environmental law is passed, the next hurdle is to see that Congress appropriates enough funds to adequately enforce the law. Some environmental laws contain glowing rhetoric about goals, but only vague, unrealistic, or indirect guidance about how those goals are to be achieved.

The details of implementation are left up to a regulatory agency such as the EPA and the courts. Fragmentation of management responsibility among many different federal and state agencies often leads to contradictory policies, duplicated efforts, and wasted funds, while prohibiting an effective integrated approach to interrelated problems.

The government established by the U.S. Constitution was designed for consensus and accommodation to promote survival and adaptation through gradual change. By staying as close to the middle of the road as possible, the government attempts to steer or muddle its way through crises. Ralph Waldo Emerson once said, "Democracy is a raft which will never sink, but then your feet are always in the water."

Despite serious shortcomings in the U.S. political system, environmental and resource conservation laws and agencies have improved the quality of the environment and reduced some forms of resource degradation. On a per capita basis, few other countries spend as much as the United States does to protect the environment.

Some analysts believe that the U.S. political-economic system is working reasonably well and no fundamental changes need to be made. "If it's not broken, don't fix it," they say.

Others think that the system must undergo changes that will improve its ability to deal with, anticipate, or prevent the growing number of regional, national, and global environmental and resource prob-

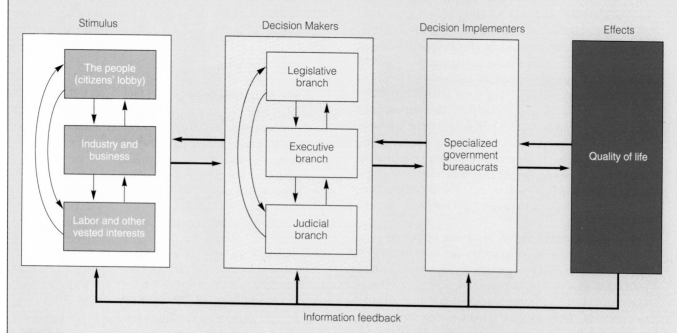

Figure 7-6 Crude model of the U.S. political system.

Q: How much of the money spent on health care in the United States is used to prevent disease?

lems we face today. They say, "Fix the system better and use it to reward pollution prevention, waste reduction, and resource conservation instead of concentrating mostly on pollution control and waste management."

We face an interlocking set of environmental, economic, and social problems that must be dealt with using integrated, comprehensive approaches. Yet most of our political institutions are compartmentalized and fragmented into specialized, narrowly focused cells that bear little relationship to the real world.

We must integrate economic and environmental policies and reorganize local, national, and global institutions to reflect the way the earth works. Otherwise many analysts believe that we will continue our Earth-degrading ways until we impoverish the planet for ourselves and many other species.

This means we must recognize four facts of life:

- The earth can easily get along without our species, which has been around for only an eye blink of the planet's existence.

- We cannot get along without the earth.

- We have done a lot of damage to the earth during our brief existence, especially during the past 200 years, but nature always bats last and has a bat that makes our bat look like a toothpick.

- We must shift from economic and political policies that rely largely on increasingly expensive and ineffective after-the-fact repair of environmental damage to those that anticipate and prevent such damage.

Writer Kurt Vonnegut has suggested a prescription for choosing leaders:

I hope you have stopped choosing abysmally ignorant optimists for positions of leadership. . . . The sort of leaders we need now are not those who promise ultimate victory over Nature, but those with the courage and intelligence to present what appear to be Nature's stern, but reasonable surrender terms:

1. *Reduce and stabilize your population.*

2. *Stop poisoning the air, the water, and the topsoil.*

3. *Stop preparing for war and start dealing with your real problems.*

4. *Teach your kids, and yourselves too, while you're at it, how to inhabit a small planet without killing it.*

5. *Stop thinking science can fix anything, if you give it a trillion dollars.*

6. *Stop thinking your grandchildren will be OK no matter how wasteful or destructive you may be, since they can go to a nice new planet on a spaceship. That is really mean and stupid.*

We have the option of choosing leaders who bring out the best in us, not the worst. If we fail to choose well, we can blame no one but ourselves.

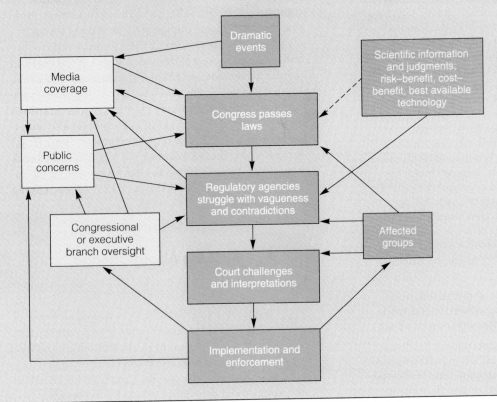

Figure 7-7
Primary forces involved in making environmental policy at the federal level in the United States.

into laws, divert attention from important issues such as pollution prevention and waste reduction, make penalties for violations trivial compared with the profits to be made by not complying with the law, and make laws so complex and full of unnecessary technical jargon that they cannot be understood even by well-educated citizens.

- Lobby elected officials to reduce the budgets of the EPA, Department of Interior, and other agencies so they do not have enough money or personnel to effectively monitor, implement, and enforce the laws passed by federal or state legislatures.

- Pressure elected officials to appoint agency heads and middle- and upper-level managers who support the position of industries threatened with environmental regulation — the "put the fox in the henhouse" approach.

- Make donations or give research grants to environmental and resource conservation organizations with the goal of diluting or influencing how far they go and withdrawing support if they go too far.

- Influence media by directly or implicitly threatening to withdraw vital advertising income if those organizations probe too deeply. If necessary, they buy up media businesses.

- Mount well-funded advertising and political campaigns to encourage support for industry positions that scare and divide people by saying that certain laws and environmental regulations will put them out of work, and to oppose tougher environmental and resource laws. Industry-funded groups in the United States with Earth-friendly names include the Responsible Industry for a Safe Environment (pesticide industry), the National Wetlands Council (oil and construction industries), the Coalition for Vehicle Choice (automobile and oil industries), U.S. Council for Energy Awareness (nuclear power industry), America the Beautiful (packaging industry), Council for Solid Waste Solutions (plastics industry), American Council on Science and Health (food and pesticides industries), Information Council on the Environment (coal companies), and the Wilderness Impact Research Foundation (mining, logging, ranching, coal, and oil industries and snowmobilers and dirt bikers wanting much greater access to public lands). At the federal level, the Council on Competitiveness has been quite effective in allowing businesses to circumvent environmental, safety, and public health laws and regulations without public scrutiny.

- Set up and highly publicize showcase environmental and resource conservation projects while continuing to do most of their business as usual.

- Adopt the latest environmental slogans such as sustainable development, pollution prevention, recycling, reuse, resource reduction, and biodegradable products, and use them to give the appearance of change while continuing to do business as usual — a tactic environmentalists call "eco-pornography."

- Fund and develop environmental curricula and video presentations for grade and high schools that promote industry positions — a growing trend.

- Decide what is most profitable to manufacture, use advertising to create a demand for mostly throwaway products, and tell people that they are the problem because businesses are merely responding to consumer demands for a throwaway society — a blame-the-victim strategy.

- Brand environmentalists as radical, anti-American terrorists who are a threat to environmental health and safety, jobs, the economy, and national security instead of people who are trying to make the planet a safer, better, and more just place to live. Because of its growth in numbers and impact, the environmental movement in the United States and other countries is increasingly being subjected to such tactics.

- Urge the federal government to prevent localities and states from passing stronger environmental laws than those at the federal level.

- Circumvent local, state, and national environmental and resource use laws and regulations by having them established by international commissions dominated by multinational companies and elites under the guise of promoting free trade.

Not all corporations follow this model, but too many do. According to a study by Amitai Etzioni of the Harvard Business School, two-thirds of the Fortune 500 companies have been charged with serious crimes, from price fixing to illegal dumping of hazardous wastes.

Some businesses, recognizing the growing political and economic power of the national and global environmental movement, are changing their ways. They realize that producing green products that help sustain the earth is an important source of future economic growth and profit. Instead of digging in their heels and adopting the philosophy that "if it isn't broken, don't fix it," innovative business leaders say "If it isn't broken, break it and fix it better." These are the companies of the future. Invest in or work for this type of Earth-sustaining company or start one of your own.

7-6 Bringing About Change

THE ROLE OF INDIVIDUALS A principal theme of this book is that individuals matter. History shows that significant change comes from the bottom up, not the top down. Leaders with vision can lead only when they have the support of the people. Leaders without vision or courage must be pushed to lead by the people.

The earth is too vital and under too much stress to be left in the hands of politicians and corporate elites alone. Without the grassroots political actions of millions of individual citizens and organized groups, the air you breathe and the water you drink today would be much more polluted. Leading leaders is not easy, but history shows that it can be done. You can make a difference.

There are three types of environmental leadership:

- *Leading by working within the system* — bringing about environmental improvement by using existing economic and political systems, often in new, creative ways

- *Leading by example* — using your own life to show others that change is possible and beneficial

- *Leading by challenging the system* — raising public awareness and building political support for far-reaching changes by challenging existing political and economic systems

All three types of leadership are needed to sustain the earth. Many lawyers, lobbyists, and technical experts are playing important roles in sustaining the earth by working within the system. They are supported, pushed, and challenged by grassroots activists who are leading by example and by challenging the system. Find the type of leadership you are most comfortable with and become such a leader or work with such leaders. Also, consider an environmental career (see Spotlight below).

THE GRASSROOTS ACTION LEVEL OF THE ENVIRONMENTAL MOVEMENT Practicing green politics means working from the bottom up to protect the earth. The base of the environmental movement in the United States and in other countries consists of thousands of grassroots groups of citizens who have organized to protect themselves from pollution and environmental degradation at the local level. In the United

---

SPOTLIGHT Environmental Careers

In addition to dedicated Earth citizens, the environmental movement needs dedicated professionals working to help sustain the earth. There is an incredible variety of jobs in the environmental field.

Examples are careers in sustainable forestry and range management, parks and recreation, environmental planning, air and water quality control, solid waste management, hazardous-waste management, urban and rural land-use planning, ecological restoration, soil conservation, water conservation, fishery and wildlife conservation and management, environmental education, environmental health and toxicology, environmental geology, ecology, conservation biology, environmental chemistry, climatology, population dynamics and regulation (demography), environmental law, environmental journalism and communication, environmental engineering, environmental design and architecture, energy conservation, energy analysis, renewable-energy technologies, hydrology, environmental consulting, environmental activism and lobby-

ing, environmental economics, the development and marketing of Earth-sustaining products, environmental law enforcement (pollution detection and enforcement teams), and running for an elected office on an environmental platform.

Most employers, who are now scrambling to hire graduates with environmental backgrounds, are looking for people who are well-rounded generalists with a marketable specialization. They are especially interested in those with science and engineering backgrounds and those with double majors (business and ecology, for example) or double minors.

For details on these careers, consult the Environmental Careers Organization (formerly the CEIP Fund), *The Complete Guide to Environmental Careers* (Covelo, Calif.: Island Press, 1990), and Nicholas Basta, *The Environmental Career Guide* (New York: John Wiley, 1991). The Environmental Careers Organization (286 Congress St., Dept. GM, Boston, MA 02110, 617-426-4375) places college students and recent college graduates as interns in short-term,

paid professional positions with corporations, consultants, government agencies, and nonprofit organizations. For a superb guide to career planning and job searches in any field, see Richard Nelson Bolles, *What Color Is Your Parachute?* (Berkeley, Calif.: Ten Speed Press, published annually).

Other sources of information on jobs in the environmental field are

- *Earth Work*, published monthly ($29.95 for one year) by the Student Conservation Association, P. O. Box 550, Charlestown, NH 03603, 603-826-4301.

- *Environmental Job Opportunities*, published 10 times a year (subscription $10.00) by the Institute for Environmental Studies, 550 North Park St., 15 Science Hall, Madison, WI 53706.

- *National Directory of Internships*, published by National Society of Internships and Experiential Education ($24.50 ppd), 3509 Haworth Drive, Suite 207, Dept. GM, Raleigh, NC 27609-7229, 919-787-3623.

The world's largest environmental group is Greenpeace. Between 1980 and 1990, membership in this organization increased from 240,000 to 1.6 million in the United States; worldwide the group has 5 million members and offices in 24 countries.

Greenpeace members have risked their lives by placing themselves in small boats between whales and the harpoon guns of whaling ships. Its members have dangled from a New York bridge to stop traffic and protest a garbage barge heading to sea; protested the dumping of toxic wastes into rivers by industries and sewage treatment plants; skydived from the smokestacks of coal-burning power plants to protest acid rain; sneaked into plants to document illegal pollution and dumping; led countless demonstrations; and helped organize local activist organizations.

Two environmental groups even more activist than Greenpeace are Earth First!, led by Dave Foreman until 1990, and the Sea Shepherd Conservation Society, headed by Paul Watson. These two organizations use aggressive tactics because its members believe that the earth can't wait for the beneficial, but much too slow, pace of change accomplished by working only within the system. Their goals are to prevent environmental destruction, increase citizen awareness, and raise the costs of business for loggers,

whalers, and others practicing planet wrecking.

They practice civil disobedience and aggressive nonviolence with the goal of battling excessive greed and evil without becoming evil. This means *absolute nonviolence* against humans and other living things and *strategic* violence against inanimate objects such as bulldozers, power lines, and whaling ships. Tactics include chaining themselves to the tops of trees to keep loggers from cutting them down; driving spikes into trees and labeling these trees (the spikes don't hurt the trees, but shatter sawblades, which could hurt loggers or millworkers, so the trees are labeled to keep them from being cut down); blocking bulldozers with their bodies (Figure 7-8); blocking or sinking illegal whaling ships; taking photos and videos of illegal or brutal commercial fishing and hunting activities; pulling up survey stakes; felling high-voltage towers; dyeing the fur of harp seals to prevent them from being killed for their furs; and sabotaging bulldozers, road graders, power shovels, and backhoes.

Members of more-militant environmental groups point to the long history of civil disobedience against laws believed to be unjust — the American Revolution, the fight to allow women to vote, the civil rights movement, the antiwar movement, and now the environmental movement. They point out that environ-

mentalists who spike trees or sink illegal whaling ships are labeled terrorists or criminals, while those who pollute the air and water, cut down irreplaceable ancient forests, and slaughter species to the point of extinction are called developers, miners, loggers, or business leaders. Benjamin White, Jr., Atlantic Director of the Sea Shepherd Conservation Society, summarizes why we must all become environmental activists:

We must begin by declaring a state of planetary emergency. . . . We must stop compromising our basic right to clean air, water, soil, and bloodstreams, and a future with wild animals and wilderness. . . . We must also be willing to take risks. If your family were threatened, would you put your life on the line? Would you go to jail if necessary? Your family is threatened. It's time to take direct action.

As Ralph Nader has said, "Pollution is violence with a seriousness of harm exceeding that of crime in the streets. . . . The first priority is to deprive the polluters of their unfounded legitimacy. Too often they assume a conservative, patriotic posture when in reality they are radical destroyers of the nation's resources and the most fundamental rights of people."

An increasing number of ordinary citizens are directly or indirectly supporting more militant

States alone there are almost 7,000 such groups. Their motto is *think globally and act locally*. It is encouraging that the percentage of Americans supporting environmental protection, regardless of cost, has risen from 45% in 1981 to 80% today.

Some Earth citizens work within the existing system to bring about change while others often risk their lives to protect various patches of the earth and various species from being devastated (see Pro/Con above). Others work to restore or rehabilitate degraded areas.

Unlike environmental organizations at the national and state levels, most grassroots organizations are un-

willing to compromise or negotiate. Instead of dealing with environmental goals and abstractions, they are fighting immediate threats to their lives and the lives of their children and grandchildren and to the value of any property they own. They want pollution stopped and prevented. They don't want themselves and their children poisoned at all in the name of economic growth, which mostly benefits the wealthy at the expense of the poor and increasingly the middle class. They are inspired by the words of ecoactivist Edward Abbey: "At some point we must draw a line across the ground of our home and our being, drive a spear into the land,

Q: What percentage of cancers are caused or promoted by environmental and lifestyle factors?

grassroots environmental groups because they fear for their children's environmental future. They are fed up with politicians who make nice speeches about protecting the environment, support a few symbolic projects, and behind the scenes allow the continuing rape of the earth in the name of short-term economic growth.

Environmentalists disagree over the use of militant tactics. Some applaud, and join or financially support, such activist groups. Some point out that leaders of mainstream environmental groups need to have more militant groups nipping at their heels to make them take stronger positions.

Other environmentalists fear that activist groups, especially if they begin using illegal or violent actions, could cause a public backlash against other environmental efforts and groups. Some worry that if environmentalists alienate the public and Congress, industry will be able to successfully lobby Congress to rewrite and weaken environmental laws. What do you think?

Figure 7-8 Earth First! activists blocking a logging road in the Siskiyou National Forest in Oregon.

and say to the bulldozers, earthmovers, and corporations, 'this far and no further.'"

The necessary political action and intervention into the marketplace that determines what we produce and how it is produced won't happen unless enough people adopt a sustainable-Earth worldview (Section 2-3), live their lives and base their consumption patterns on this worldview, and carry out political actions to bring about changes in the ways we think and act (see Guest Essay on p. 166).

This begins with the realization that the most important things that sustain us and other forms of life cannot be assigned a dollar value and that economic and military security are impossible without environmental security. It also recognizes that we live in an environmentally interdependent world, where no country can separate its actions and fate from that of the rest of the world.

There is something fundamentally wrong in treating the earth as if it were a business in liquidation.

HERMAN E. DALY

Claudine Schneider

Claudine Schneider was a five-term Congresswoman representing Rhode Island until 1990 and is now a fellow at Harvard's Institute for Policy Analysis. She has been at the forefront of national efforts to protect and promote environmental quality and has championed a wide range of legislation to protect the environment and preserve endangered species and to promote balanced use of natural resources. She was one of the leaders in the fight to stop the Clinch River breeder nuclear fission reactor. She was lead sponsor of both the Ocean Dumping Act of 1989 and the Wolpe-Schneider Hazardous Waste Reduction Act. She has been especially active in promoting improvements in energy efficiency, promoting least-cost energy planning, and developing a comprehensive plan to deal with projected global warming. These efforts include being the author and primary sponsor of the Global Warming Prevention Act of 1989.

In recent years, we have witnessed record heat waves, droughts, forest fires, hurricanes, floods, and urban pollution. These are all warnings that Mother Earth is sending us. We ignore these warnings at our own peril. The gaping annual hole in the planet's protective ozone shield [Figure 10-8] and the rapid destruction of vast regions of tropical rain forests [Section 15-2] threaten humanity's well-being, just as if someone ripped off the skin protecting our bodies.

Each of us can help heal the planet. Choked by the smog of gridlocked autos, we can buy more-efficient and less-polluting cars, or carpool and remove two or three vehicles from the road; we can take the bus or subway; or even better, we can emulate Dutch and Danish communities, where half the people bicycle to and from work, preventing the release of tons of pollutants.

The food we grow or eat, the homes and appliances we buy, the packaging we avoid, reuse, or recycle — in short, the lifestyles we lead — offer endless opportunities for healing the planet. A healthy future depends on the degree to which we practice a stewardship ethic by living as if Mother Earth mattered.

Individual changes of habit constitute an essential first step we all must take, but not a sufficient one. In an ideal world, the good stewardship actions willingly taken by each person would add up to an ecologically sustainable world economy. Unfortunately, we are far from that ideal world. Whether because of ignorance, slothful indifference, outright greed, or callous disregard, the collective actions of humans now wreak havoc on the planet. We need to alter society's habits.

The production of greenhouse gases from burning fossil fuels [Figure 10-6] has brought us numerous economic goods and services, but the benefits from producing those gases are being surpassed by their costs and risks. It is time to stop the growth of greenhouse gases and substitute safer alternatives. This will require a broad range of changes at all levels of decision making — at home, at work, through community, state, and federal governments, and by international agreements.

Individuals have a responsibility here, as well, to lobby for changing the focus of these various institutions, especially those involved in producing legislation. Just as physical exercise maintains a healthy body, so the exercise of citizen advocacy maintains a healthy politic.

The healthy politic is a potent metaphor that emerged in the 1800s. At that time, individuals mobilized to remove the scourge of diseases afflicting society that were spread from contaminated water, due in part to the lack of sanitary waste disposal options. We need to galvanize public support for sustaining this noble tradition in the face of new environmental challenges.

Any review of history shows that it takes years, decades, sometimes centuries, to effect change in monu-

DISCUSSION TOPICS

1. Some economists argue that only through unlimited economic growth will we have enough money to eliminate poverty and protect the environment. Explain why you agree or disagree with that view. If you disagree, how should we deal with these problems? For example, do you agree or disagree with the proposals for dismantling the global poverty trap listed on pages 155–158? Explain.

2. Do you believe that cost-benefit analysis should be used to make all decisions about how limited federal, state, and local government funds are to be used? Explain. If not, what decisions should not be made in this way?

3. Do you favor internalizing the external costs of pollution and unnecessary resource waste? Explain. How might it affect your lifestyle? The lifestyle of the poor? Wildlife?

4. Do you favor making a shift to a sustainable-Earth economy? Explain. How might this affect your lifestyle? The lifestyle of the poor? Wildlife?

Q: Which environmental and lifestyle factor causes the most death and suffering?

mental problems. This has been the case with democracies overthrowing dictators, with abolishing slavery, and with protecting human rights. These struggles continue in our day, and they all turn on the concern and commitment of individuals working to effect change.

Grappling with environmental problems like projected global climate change poses a no-less-daunting task. It is too easy for policymakers elected for two- to six-year terms to evade action by pushing the problem far into the future. Some have referred to this unconscionable behavior as the NIMLT syndrome: "Not in My Life Time."

Without strong, ongoing citizen advocacy for change, most policymakers will continue to support environmental deficit spending, just as they have budget deficit spending. That is to say, current policies encourage squandering the natural endowment of future generations, who will be faced with paying off our environmental debts (pollutants) with fewer capital resources (forests, topsoil, watersheds, extinct species, and so forth).

We must refuse to submit to the gloom-and-doom future implicit in the policies and practices of our time. Decades of scientific research, technical advancements, and ecological insights show us that humans can thrive on Earth in an ecologically sustainable manner. The key insight of our time is that environmental quality and economic well-being are compatible. By acting on that insight, we can eliminate the seemingly intractable problems of hunger and poverty and maintain a thriving economy for generations to come.

The greatest barrier to recognizing this insight is the way policymakers make decisions. Issues get quickly compartmentalized. Transportation, housing, health, security, energy, and the environment are dealt with separately by specialized bureaucracies, few of whom exchange ideas with their fellow specialists. So we build more highways for polluting cars instead of designing land uses to minimize the need for cars. We operate highly polluting power plants instead of installing lower-cost, energy-efficient lights, motors, and appliances in homes and factories. We contaminate soil and groundwater instead of reducing, reusing, and recycling wastes.

This fragmentary approach must be replaced by an integrated, holistic approach. This is where citizens can gain considerable leverage from their efforts. There are numerous examples of how cities and states have established advisory commissions to look at the future shape of their regions and recommend changes in public policies. When that happens, trends become more apparent, problems are more readily identified, and concerned citizens can voice alternative visions that could be further studied and duly incorporated.

Analytic tools have been developed and are available for helping citizens ensure that comprehensive planning is performed. Often, for example, half or more of the food, energy, and water services could be produced locally, saving millions of dollars for the local economy and cutting pollutants and solid wastes in half. With that kind of information base, a powerful tool is available for accelerating public policy.

A citizens' commission can serve a tremendous education function for voters in helping them identify ecologically sustainable ways to spur economic growth. Perhaps never in history have individual actions had the potential to so greatly influence the course of planetary change.

Prevention pays, and it is incumbent on all of us to capitalize upon these abundant opportunities. A healthy environment is the basis for a health economy. In promoting ecologically sound economic practices, we will not only slow global climate change but also greatly alleviate urban smog, acid rain, tropical deforestation, and a host of other social and environmental problems.

Guest Essay Discussion

1. How would you go about getting elected officials and government agencies to deal with the problems we face in an integrated, holistic manner?

2. What economically sound ecological policies would you propose for dealing with the problem of projected global warming?

---

5. **a.** Do you believe that we should establish optimal levels or zero discharge levels for most of the chemicals we release into the environment? Explain. What effects would adopting zero discharge levels have on your life and lifestyle?

   b. Do you believe that all chemicals we release or propose to release into the environment should be assumed to be guilty of causing harm until proven otherwise? Explain. What effects would adopting this legal principle have on your life and lifestyle?

6. Do you believe that activist environmental groups such as Earth First! and the Sea Shepherd Conservation Society serve a useful role? Explain.

CHAPTER 8

HAZARDS, RISK,

AND HUMAN HEALTH

General Questions and Issues

1. What are common hazards that people face, and what are their effects?

2. How can the risks and benefits associated with using a particular technology or product be estimated?

3. How can government or other agencies manage risks to protect the public?

4. What risks can lead to cancer, and how can they be reduced?

For the first time in the history of the world, every human being is now subjected to dangerous chemicals, from the moment of conception until death.

RACHEL CARSON

VERY FORM OF technology and everything we make or consume result in some pollution and degradation of the environment and involve some degree of risk to our health and the health of other species. When we evaluate the many risks we face, the key questions we need to ask are whether the risks of damage from each hazard outweigh the short- and long-term benefits and how we can reduce the hazards and minimize the risks.

8-1 Hazards: Types and Effects

COMMON HAZARDS **Risk** is the possibility of suffering harm from a hazard. A **hazard** is a source of risk and refers to any substance or action that can cause injury, disease, economic loss, or environmental damage. Most hazards come from exposure to various factors in our environment:

- *Physical hazards:* ionizing radiation (Figure 3-10), noise (Table 6-1), fires, floods (see Case Study on p. 230), drought, tornadoes, hurricanes, landslides, earthquakes, and volcanic eruptions

- *Chemical hazards:* harmful chemicals in air (Chapters 9 and 10), water (Chapter 11), soil (Chapter 12), and food (Chapters 13 and 14)

- *Biological hazards:* disease-causing bacteria and viruses (Figure 8-1), pollen, and parasites

- *Cultural hazards:* working and living conditions, smoking, diet, drugs, drinking, driving, criminal assault, unsafe sex, and poverty (Section 7-4)

CHEMICAL HAZARDS The principal types of chemical hazards are

- **Toxic substances:** chemicals that are fatal to humans in low doses or fatal to over 50% of test animals at stated concentrations. Examples are botulism toxin, potassium cyanide, heroin, chlorinated hydrocarbons (DDT, PCBs, dioxins), organophosphate pesticides (Malathion, Parathion), carbamate pesticides (Sevin, Zeneb), and various compounds of arsenic, mercury, lead, and cadmium.

- **Hazardous substances:** chemicals that can cause harm because they are flammable or explosive, irritate or damage the skin or lungs (such as strong acidic or alkaline substances), or induce allergic reactions of the immune system (allergens).

- **Carcinogens:** chemicals, ionizing radiation, and viruses that cause or promote the growth of a malignant tumor, or **cancer**, in which cells in a certain type of tissue multiply and invade the surrounding tissue. Typically, 10 to 40 years may elapse before a cancer reaches detectable size.

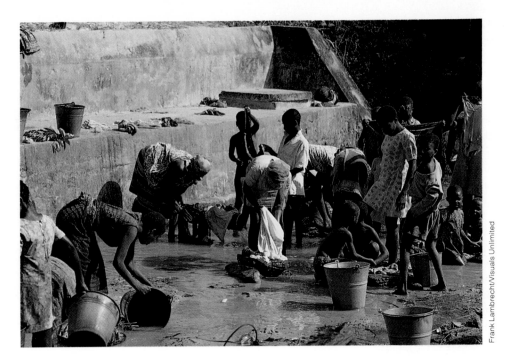

Figure 8-1 Unsafe water supply in Nigeria. Transmissible diseases from drinking contaminated water are the leading killer, especially of young children, in LDCs.

■ **Mutagens:** chemicals, ionizing radiation, and heat that cause **mutations** (inheritable changes in the DNA molecules in the genes found in chromosomes). The altered genes transmit these traits from parent to offspring. Some mutations are beneficial, but most are harmful.

■ **Teratogens:** chemicals, ionizing agents, and viruses that cause birth defects. Examples of chemicals known to cause birth defects in laboratory animals are caffeine, PCBs, and heavy metals such as arsenic, cadmium, lead, and mercury.

DETERMINING TOXICITY LEVELS Determining the toxicity levels of chemicals or ionizing radiation and the harmful effects of biological organisms is difficult, costly, and controversial. Because it is neither ethical nor practical to use people to test toxicity, it is usually determined by carrying out tests on live (*in vivo*) laboratory animals (mostly mice and rats for testing carcinogens and guinea pigs, mice, and some primates for testing harmful microorganisms), bacteria, and cell and tissue cultures.

There are several problems with animal tests. Extrapolating test animal data from high-dose to low-dose levels is uncertain and controversial. According to the *linear dose-response model*, any dose of ionizing radiation or some toxic chemical is harmful, and the harm rises as the dose increases. With the *threshold dose-response model*, there is a threshold dose below which no detectable harmful effects occur. It's very difficult to establish whether these or other models apply at low doses.

Many scientists also question the validity of extrapolating data from test animals to humans because human physiology and metabolism are different from those of the test animals. In addition, animal tests take two to five years and cost from $200,000 to $1 million per substance. Furthermore, they are coming under increasing fire from animal rights groups. As a result, scientists are trying to develop and use substitute methods where possible.

Also controversial is the effectiveness of using bacteria and cell and tissue cultures for determining harmful effects of toxic agents on humans. One of the most widely used bacterial tests, the Ames test, is considered to be an accurate predictor of substances that cause genetic mutations (mutagens) and is also quick (two weeks) and cheap ($1,000 to $1,500 per substance). However, evidence indicates that this test is not a reliable predictor of substances that cause or promote cancer (carcinogens). Cell and tissue culture tests have similar uncertainties, take several weeks to months, and cost about $18,000 per substance.

Another approach to toxicity testing and determining the agents causing diseases such as cancer is **epidemiology**—an attempt to find out why some people get sick and some do not. Typically, the health of people exposed to a particular toxic chemical or other agent from an industrial accident, people working under high exposure levels, or people in certain geographic areas is compared with the health of groups of people not exposed to these conditions to see if there are statistically significant differences.

This approach also has limitations. For many toxic agents, not enough people have been exposed to high enough levels to detect statistically significant differences. Because people are exposed to many different toxic agents and disease-causing factors throughout their lives, it is not possible to say with much certainty that an observed epidemiological effect is caused only by exposure to a particular toxic agent or to another hazardous condition. Because epidemiology can be used only to evaluate hazards to which people have already been exposed, it is rarely useful for predicting the effects of new technologies or substances.

Thus, all the methods we use to estimate toxicity levels have serious limitations. But they are all we have.

BIOLOGICAL HAZARDS: DISEASE, ECONOMICS, AND GEOGRAPHY Human diseases can be broadly classified as transmissible and nontransmissible. A **transmissible disease** is caused by living organisms such as bacteria, viruses, and parasitic worms and can be spread from one person to another by air, water (Figure 8-1), food, body fluids, and—in some cases—insects and other nonhuman transmitters (called *vectors*). Examples are malaria (see Case Study on p. 171), schistosomiasis, elephantiasis, sleeping sickness, measles, and sexually transmitted diseases, including AIDS (which is projected to infect 40 million people by the year 2000).

A **nontransmissible disease** is not caused by living organisms and does not spread from one person to another. Examples include cardiovascular (heart and blood vessel) disorders, cancer, diabetes, chronic respiratory diseases (bronchitis and emphysema), and malnutrition (see Figure 1-3). Many of these diseases have several, often unknown, causes and tend to develop slowly and progressively over time.

Fortunately, significant improvements in human health in LDCs can be made with primary preventive health care measures at a relatively low cost. These include providing

- Contraceptives (Figure 6-5), sex education, and family planning counseling.

- Better nutrition, prenatal care, and birth assistance for pregnant women. At least 500,000 women in LDCs die each year of mostly preventable pregnancy-related causes, compared with only 6,000 in MDCs.

- Greatly improved postnatal care (including the promotion of breastfeeding) to reduce infant mortality.

- Immunization against tetanus, measles, diphtheria, typhoid, and tuberculosis.

- Oral rehydration for diarrhea victims by feeding them a simple solution of water, salt, and sugar.

- Antibiotics for infections.

- Clean drinking water and sanitation facilities to the third of the world's population that lacks them.

Extending such primary health care to all the world's people would cost an additional $10 billion a year, one twenty-fifth as much as the world spends each year on cigarettes.

As a country industrializes and makes the *demographic transition* (Figure 6-20), it also makes an *epidemiologic transition*, in which the infectious diseases of childhood become less important and the chronic diseases of adulthood (heart disease and stroke, cancer, and respiratory infections) become more important in determining mortality. Generally, people in countries making this transition have a longer life expectancy at birth and a lower average infant mortality rate (Figure 6-8), although that usually does not hold true for the poorest people in such MDCs.

In MDCs, most deaths are a result of environmental and lifestyle factors rather than infectious agents invading the body. Except for auto accidents (see Pro/Con on p. 130), these deaths result from chronic diseases that take a long time to develop, have multiple causes, and are largely related to the area in which people live (urban or rural), their work environment, their diet, whether they smoke, how much exercise they get, their sexual habits, and whether they abuse alcohol or other harmful drugs.

Changing these harmful lifestyle factors could prevent 40% to 70% of all premature deaths, one-third of all cases of acute disability, and two-thirds of all cases of chronic disability. So far, about 95% of the money spent on health care in the United States is used to treat rather than prevent disease—a tragic imbalance that needs to be corrected.

8-2 Risk Analysis

RISK ANALYSIS AND ESTIMATING RISKS **Risk analysis** involves identifying hazards (Table 5-1), evaluating the nature and severity of risks (*risk assessment*), using that and other information to determine options and make decisions about reducing or eliminating risks (*risk management*), and communicating information about risks to decision makers and the public (*risk communication*).

Formal risk assessment is difficult, imprecise, and controversial. Probabilities based on past experience, animal and other tests, and epidemiological studies are used to estimate risks from older technologies and products. For new technologies and products, much more uncertain statistical probabilities, based on models rather than actual experience, must be calculated. Table 8-1 summarizes the greatest ecological and health risks identified by a panel of scientists acting as advisers to the U.S. Environmental Protection Agency.

The more complex a technological system, the more difficult it is to make realistic calculations of risks

Q: Worldwide, how many people die prematurely each year of causes related to smoking?

More than half the world's population live in malaria-prone regions in about 100 different countries in tropical and subtropical regions, especially West Africa and Central and Southeast Asia (Figure 8-2). Malaria is spread by various species of the water-breeding *Anopheles* mosquito and afflicts up to 500 million people worldwide. Each year, it kills at least 2.5 million (some sources say 5 million) people. At least half of its victims are children under the age of 5.

There are an estimated 250 million new cases each year, with the largest number of infections occurring in sub-Saharan Africa. Even in the United States, an average of four people discover they have malaria each day. Malaria's symptoms come and go; they include fever and chills, anemia, an enlarged spleen, severe abdominal pain and headaches, extreme weakness, and greater susceptibility to other diseases.

Most cases of the disease are transmitted when an uninfected female of about 60 of the 400 different species of *Anopheles* mosquito bites an infected person and then bites an uninfected person. When this happens, *Plasmodium* parasites move from the mosquito into the bloodstream, multiply in the liver, and then enter blood cells to continue multiplying (Figure 8-3). Malaria can also be transmitted when a person receives the blood of an infected donor or when a drug user shares a needle with an infected user.

During the 1950s and 1960s, the spread of malaria was sharply reduced by draining swamplands and marshes; by spraying breeding areas with DDT, dieldrin, and other pesticides; and by using drugs to kill the *Plasmodium* parasites in the bloodstream.

That strategy worked for two decades, but since 1970 malaria has made a dramatic comeback in many parts of the world. Because of repeated spraying, most of the malaria-carrying species of *Anopheles* mosquitoes have become genetically resistant to most of the insecticides used. The *Plasmodium* parasites have become genetically resistant to widely used antimalarial drugs. Irrigation ditches, which provide breeding grounds for mosquitoes, have increased in number, and budgets for malaria control have been reduced because of the mis-

(continued)

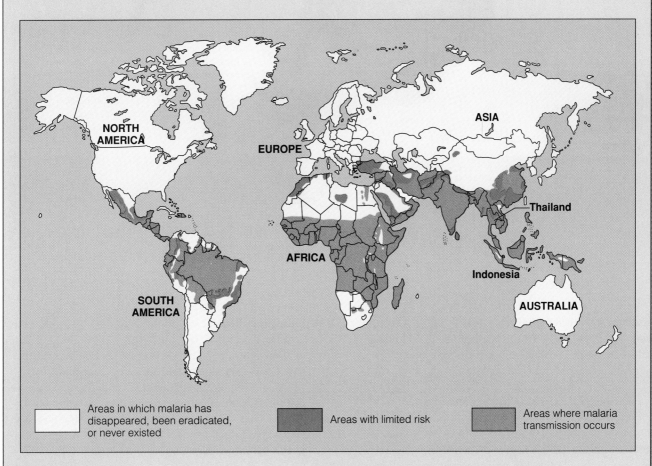

Figure 8-2 Malaria threatens half the world's population. (Data from the World Health Organization)

Areas in which malaria has disappeared, been eradicated, or never existed

Areas with limited risk

Areas where malaria transmission occurs

taken belief that the disease was under control.

Researchers are working to develop new antimalarial drugs and vaccines and biological controls for *Anopheles* mosquitoes, but such approaches are in the early stages of development, have proved to be more difficult than originally thought, and lack adequate funding. The World Health Organization estimates that only 3% of the money spent worldwide each year on biomedical research is devoted to malaria and other tropical diseases, even though more people suffer and die worldwide from these diseases than from all others combined.

Figure 8-3 The life cycle of malaria.

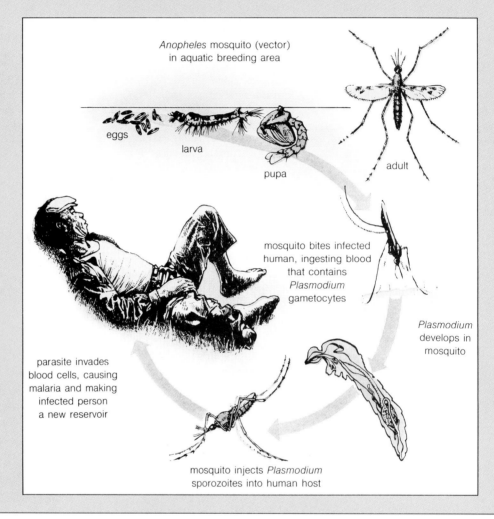

Anopheles mosquito (vector) in aquatic breeding area

eggs

larva

pupa

adult

mosquito bites infected human, ingesting blood that contains *Plasmodium* gametocytes

Plasmodium develops in mosquito

parasite invades blood cells, causing malaria and making infected person a new reservoir

mosquito injects *Plasmodium* sporozoites into human host

based on statistical probabilities of the failure of equipment and people. The total reliability of any technological system is the product of two factors:

$$\text{system reliability (\%)} = \text{technology reliability} \times \text{human reliability} \times 100$$

With careful design, quality control, maintenance, and monitoring, a high degree of technology reliability can usually be obtained in complex systems such as a nuclear power plant, the space shuttle, or an early warning system for nuclear attack. However, human reliability is almost always much lower than technology relia-

bility and virtually impossible to predict; to be human is to err.

For example, suppose that the technology reliability of a system such as a nuclear power plant is 95% (0.95) and the human reliability is 65% (0.65). Then the overall system reliability is only 62% (0.95 × 0.65 = 0.62 × 100 = 62%). Even if we could increase the technology reliability to 100% (1.0), the overall system reliability would still be only 65% (1.0 × 0.65 = 0.65 × 100 = 65%).

This crucial dependence of even the most carefully designed systems on unpredictable human reliability helps explain the occurrence of events that risk analysts

Q: How many Americans die each year because of exposure to other people's smoke (passive smoke)?

Table 8-1 Greatest Ecological and Health Risks

High-Risk Ecological Problems

Global climate change
Stratospheric ozone depletion
Wildlife habitat alteration and destruction
Species extinction and loss of biodiversity

Medium-Risk Ecological Problems

Acid deposition
Pesticides
Airborne toxic chemicals
Toxic chemicals, nutrients, and turbidity in surface waters

Low-Risk Ecological Problems

Oil spills
Groundwater pollution
Radioactive isotopes
Acid runoff to surface waters
Thermal pollution

High-Risk Health Problems

Indoor air pollution
Outdoor air pollution
Worker exposure to industrial or farm chemicals
Pollutants in drinking water
Pesticide residues on food
Toxic chemicals in consumer products

Data from Science Advisory Board, *Reducing Risks* (Washington, D.C.: Environmental Protection Agency, 1990). Items in each category are not listed in rank order.

Figure 8-4 Control room of a nuclear power plant. Watching these indicators is such a boring job that government investigators have found some operators asleep, and in one case they found no one in the control room. Most accidents at nuclear power plants have resulted primarily from human errors.

consider almost impossible. Examples are the Three Mile Island and Chernobyl nuclear power plant accidents (see Spotlight on p. 428), the tragic (and unnecessary) explosion of the space shuttle *Challenger,* and the far too frequent false alarms given by early warning defense systems on which the fate of the entire world depends.

Poor management, poor training, and poor supervision increase the chances of human errors. Maintenance workers or people who monitor warning panels in complex systems such as the control rooms of nuclear power plants (Figure 8-4) become bored and inattentive because most of the time nothing goes wrong. They may fall asleep while on duty (as has happened in control rooms at several U.S. nuclear plants); they may falsify maintenance records because they believe that the system is safe without their help; they may be distracted by personal problems or illness; or they may be told by managers to take shortcuts to increase short-term profits or to make the managers look more efficient and productive.

One way to improve system reliability is to move more of the potentially fallible elements from the hu-

man side to the technical side, making the system more foolproof or "fail-safe." But chance events such as a lightning bolt can knock out automatic control systems. No machine or computer program can replace all the skillful human actions and decisions involved in seeing that a complex system operates properly and safely. Also, the parts in any automated control system are manufactured, assembled, tested, certified, and maintained by fallible human beings.

There are other problems with risk assessment. Complex processes and effects may be oversimplified or poorly understood, and risk evaluators may have overconfidence in the reliability of current scientific and technical knowledge and models. They may also fail to see how the system as a whole functions and how different components and chemicals interact. All systems have properties that cannot be determined or predicted by understanding the properties of their parts.

RISK-BENEFIT ANALYSIS The key question is whether the estimated short- and long-term benefits of using a particular technology or product outweigh the estimated short- and long-term risks compared with other alternatives. One method for making such evaluations is **risk-benefit analysis**. It involves estimating the short- and long-term societal benefits and risks involved and then dividing the benefits by the risks to find a **desirability quotient**:

$$\text{desirability quotient} = \frac{\text{societal benefits}}{\text{societal risks}}$$

Assuming that accurate calculations of benefits and risks can be made (a big assumption), here are several possibilities:

The rapidly developing technology of genetic engineering excites some scientists and many investors. They see it as a way to increase crop and livestock yields and to produce, patent, and sell plant and livestock varieties that have greater resistance to diseases, pests, frost, and drought and that provide greater quantities of nutrients such as proteins.

They hope to develop, patent, and sell bacteria that can destroy oil spills, degrade toxic wastes, and concentrate metals found in low-grade ores as well as to develop new vaccines, drugs, and therapeutic hormones. Already, genetic engineering has produced a drug to arrest heart attacks and agents to fight diabetes, hemophilia, and some forms of cancer. It has also been used to diagnose AIDS and cancer. Genetically altered viruses have been used to manufacture more effective vaccines and human-growth hormones.

In agriculture, gene transfer has been used to develop strawberries that resist frost and smaller cows that produce more milk. Toxin-producing genes have been transferred from bacteria to plants, increasing immunity to insect attack.

Some people are horrified by the prospect of biotechnology running amok. Most of these critics recognize that it is essentially impossible to stop the development of genetic engineering, which is already well

under way, but they believe that this technology should be kept under strict control.

Genetic engineering may also reduce genetic and species diversity. Critics do not believe that people have enough understanding of how nature works to be trusted with such control over the genetic characteristics of humans and other species.

Critics also fear that unregulated biotechnology could lead to the development of "superorganisms." If such organisms were released deliberately or accidentally into the environment, they could cause unpredictable, possibly harmful, effects.

Since many organisms, especially bacteria, are capable of rapidly reproducing and spreading to new locations, any problems they cause would be widespread. For example, genetically altered bacteria designed to clean up ocean oil spills by degrading the oil might multiply rapidly and eventually degrade the world's remaining oil supplies—including the oil in cars and trucks.

Genetically engineered organisms might also mutate and change their form and behavior. Unlike defective cars and other products, living organisms can't be recalled once they are in the environment.

Critics fear that biotechnology is a potential source of such enormous profits that without strict controls, greed—not ecological wisdom and restraint—will take over.

Genetic scientists answer that it is highly unlikely that the release of genetically engineered species would cause serious and widespread ecological problems. Critics point out that this has happened many times when we have accidentally or deliberately introduced alien organisms into biological communities.

In 1989, a committee of prominent ecologists appointed by the Ecological Society of America stated that the validity of many of the assertions about the inherent safety of genetically engineered organisms varies widely with the type of organism. The committee also warned that the ecological impacts of new combinations of genetic traits from different species would be difficult to predict.

Their report calls for a case-by-case review of any proposed environmental releases. It also calls for carefully regulated, small-scale field tests before any bioengineered organism is put into commercial use.

This controversy illustrates the difficulty of balancing the actual and potential benefits of a technology with its actual and potential risks of harm. What restrictions, if any, do you believe should be placed on genetic engineering research and use? How would you enforce any restrictions?

---

1. $$\text{large desirability quotient} = \frac{\text{large societal benefits}}{\text{small societal risks}}$$

   Example: *X rays*. Use of ionizing radiation in the form of X rays to detect bone fractures and other medical problems has a large desirability quotient. This is true, however, only if X rays are not overused to protect doctors from liability suits, the dose is no larger than needed, and less harmful alternatives are not available. Other examples in this category are mining, most dams, and airplane travel. Proponents of nuclear power plants place nuclear technology in this category.

2. $$\text{very small desirability quotient} = \frac{\text{very small societal benefits}}{\text{very large societal risks}}$$

   Example: *Nuclear war*. Global nuclear war has no societal benefits (except the short-term profits made by companies making weapons and weapons defense systems) and involves totally unacceptable risks to the human species and Earth's life-support systems for all species, as discussed in Section 10-6.

3. $$\text{small desirability quotient} = \frac{\text{large societal benefits}}{\text{much larger societal risks}}$$

   Example: *Coal-burning power plants* (Section 18-2) *and nuclear power plants* (Section 18-3). Nuclear and coal-burning power plants provide society with electricity—a highly desirable benefit—but many analysts contend that the short- and long-term so-

Q: What is the role of ozone (O_3) gas in the stratosphere?

According to the National Academy of Sciences, pesticides account for 2.1% of all U.S. cancer deaths each year. That means that pesticides licensed for use in the United States legally kill about 10,000 real, but nameless, Americans a year prematurely from cancer, without the informed consent of the victims.

If you or I put a poison in a supply of public drinking water or in food bought in a grocery or restaurant and kill a number of people, we are committing premeditated murder. However, if the government allows companies to put enough poisonous chemicals in our water or food supply to kill a certain number of people, that is acceptable and not punishable by law. According to

Peter Montague (see Guest Essay on p. 33), "The explicit aim of risk assessment is to convince people that some number of citizens *must* be killed each year to maintain a national lifestyle based on necessities like Saran Wrap, throwaway cameras, and lawns without dandelions."

While risk analysis attempts to find some politically or economically acceptable level of pollution or other risk, pollution prevention aims at reducing the risk to health to the lowest possible level. If a pollutant or a risky technology is eliminated or reduced to a very low level of risk, the elaborate and uncertain system of risk assessment, standard setting, and the resulting controversy and legal challenges become irrelevant.

Proponents of risk analysis argue that anything we do has some risk and that formal risk analysis helps regulators evaluate and reduce risks. Just because risk analysis is difficult and uncertain does not mean that it should not be done or that it is not useful.

Despite the inevitable uncertainties involved, proponents argue that risk analysis is a useful way to organize available information, identify significant hazards, focus on areas that need more research, and stimulate people to make decisions about health and environmental goals and priorities. What do you think?

---

cietal risks from widespread use of these technologies outweigh the benefits. They believe that other more economically and environmentally acceptable alternatives exist for producing electricity with less-severe societal risks (see Chapter 17 and Guest Essay on p. 58).

4. $$\text{uncertain desirability quotient} = \frac{\text{large benefits}}{\text{large risks}}$$

Example: *Genetic engineering.* For many decades, humans have selected and crossbred genetic varieties of plants and animals to develop new varieties with certain desired qualities. Today, "genetic engineers" have learned how to splice genes and recombine sequences of existing DNA molecules in organisms to produce DNA with new genetic characteristics (recombinant DNA). In other words, they use laboratory techniques to transfer traits from one species to another to make new genetic combinations instead of waiting for nature to evolve new genetic combinations through natural selection. However, this is a controversial new technology (see Pro/Con on p. 174).

PROBLEMS WITH RISK ASSESSMENT Calculation of desirability quotients and other ways of evaluating or expressing risk is extremely difficult, filled with uncertainty, and controversial. Listed here are some of the problems and issues:

- Some technologies benefit one group of people (population A) while imposing a risk on another (population B). Who should decide which groups benefit and which ones are harmed?

- Some people making the estimates emphasize short-term risks, while others put more weight on long-term risks. Which type of risk should get more emphasis and who decides this?

- Who should carry out a particular risk-benefit analysis or risk assessment? Should it be the corporation or government agency involved in developing or managing the technology or some independent laboratory or panel of scientists? If it involves outside evaluation, who chooses the persons to do the study? Who pays the bill and thus has the potential to influence the outcome by refusing to give the lab, agency, or experts future business?

- Once a risk-assessment study is done, who reviews the results—a government agency, independent scientists, the general public—and what influence will outside criticism have on the final decisions?

- Should the cumulative impacts of various risks be considered, or should risks be considered separately as is usually done? For example, a pesticide might be found to have a risk of killing 1 in 1 million Americans, the acceptable death limit set by the EPA. However, the cumulative effects from 40 such pesticides may kill 40 of every 1 million Americans, far beyond the officially acceptable limit.

- Is risk analysis a useful and much-needed tool or is it, as some critics charge, a way to justify premeditated murder in the name of profit (see Pro/Con above)?

Risk Assessment

Dose-response assessment

Hazard identification

Exposure assessment

Risk characterization

Risk Management

Regulatory decision

Control options

Non-risk analyses

Figure 8-5 Summary of risk assessment and risk management. (Environmental Protection Agency)

Scientists, politicians, and the general public who must make decisions based on risk assessments should be aware of their serious limitations. They should recognize that politics, economics, and value judgments that can be biased in either direction are involved at every step of the risk-analysis process. At best, risk assessments can be expressed only as a range of probabilities and uncertainties based on different assumptions—not as the precise bottom-line numbers that decision makers want.

8-3 Risk Management

MANAGING RISK **Risk management** includes the administrative, political, and economic actions taken to decide how, and if, a particular societal risk is to be reduced to a certain level, and at what cost. It is integrated with risk assessment (Figure 8-5). Risk management involves trying to answer the following questions:

- Which of the vast number of risks facing society should be evaluated and managed with the limited funds available?

- In what sequence or priority should the risks be evaluated and managed?

- How reliable is the risk-benefit analysis or risk assessment carried out for each risk?

- How much risk is acceptable? How safe is safe enough?

- How much money will it take to reduce each risk to an acceptable level?

- How much will each risk be reduced if limited funds are available, as is usually the case?

- How will the risk management plan be communicated to the public, monitored, and enforced?

Risk managers must make difficult decisions involving inadequate and uncertain scientific data, potentially grave consequences for human health and the environment, and large economic effects on industry and consumers. Thus, each step in this process involves value judgments and trade-offs to find some reasonable compromise between conflicting political and economic interests.

So far, most risk reduction from pollutants has focused on output or end-of-pipe pollution control or cleanup techniques. Beginning with and emphasizing front-of-pipe pollution prevention instead of end-of-pipe pollution control is the key to risk reduction (Figure 8-6), but so far efforts to do this have been mostly talk, not serious action.

RISK PERCEPTION AND COMMUNICATION

Most of us are bad at assessing the risks from the hazards that surround us, and we tend to be full of contradictions. On the one hand, many people deny and shrug off high-risk activities such as driving or riding in a car, not wearing seat belts, hang gliding, smoking, and exposing themselves to the cancer-causing rays of the sun or tanning lamps to get a tan.

On the other hand, many people insist on zero or near-zero risk from things that are quite unlikely to kill them, mostly because of dramatized and well-publicized events that distort our sense of risk from various hazards. Some of us become almost paranoid about eating apples that might bear a trace of a pesticide, riding in a commercial airplane, or being killed by a burglar, a mugger, a shark, or a snake.

Being bombarded with news about people killed or harmed by various hazards distorts our sense of risk. The real news each year is that 99% of the people on Earth didn't die, but that's not considered dramatic news by the media and most of the public.

The public generally perceives that a technology or a product has a greater risk than the risk estimated by experts when it

- Is relatively new or complex (genetic engineering, nuclear power) rather than familiar (dams, automobiles).

- Is mostly involuntary (nuclear power plants, nuclear weapons, industrial pollution, food additives) instead of voluntary (smoking, drinking alcohol, driving).

- Is viewed as unnecessary or not beneficial (CFCs and hydrocarbons as propellants in aerosol spray cans, food additives used to increase sales appeal) rather than as beneficial and necessary (cars and firearms).

Q: How much air pollution is emitted into the atmosphere each year by a typical motor vehicle in the United States?

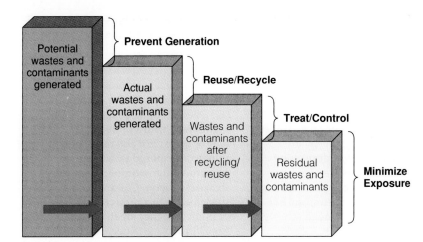

■ Involves a well-publicized large number of deaths and injuries from a single catastrophic accident (severe nuclear power plant accident, industrial explosion, or plane crash) rather than the same or a larger number of deaths spread out over a longer time (coal-burning power plants, automobiles, malnutrition in LDCs).

■ Involves unfair distribution of the risks. Citizens are outraged when government officials decide to put a hazardous-waste landfill or incinerator in or near their neighborhood under the guise of scientific analysis. This is usually viewed as politics, not science.

■ Is poorly communicated. Does the decision-making agency or company come across as trustworthy and concerned or as dishonest, unconcerned, and arrogant (as Exxon was viewed after the *Valdez* oil spill, and the Nuclear Regulatory Agency and the nuclear industry have been viewed since the Three Mile Island accident)? Does it involve the community in the decision-making process from start to finish and tell it what's going on before the real decisions are made? Does it understand, listen to, and respond to community concerns? Does it mostly let the public blow off steam at a few public meetings while decisions are made behind closed doors without serious public participation or consultation?

■ Is promoted by people who do not take into account ethical and moral concerns. Spewing out numbers and talking about cost-risk trade-offs seem very callous when the risk involves moral issues such as the health of people and other species and environmental quality.

People who believe their lives and the lives of their children are being threatened because they live near an actual or proposed chemical plant, toxic-waste dump, or waste incinerator don't care that experts say the chemical is likely to kill only 1 out of 1 million people in the general population. Only a small number of those million people live or will live near the plant, dump, or

incinerator as they do. *To those on the front lines of risk, often the poor and middle class, risk is a personal threat, not a statistical abstraction.*

Risk communicators also need to point out clearly the assumptions and uncertainties in their estimates and risk comparisons. They also must acknowledge that risk analysis is a way to help make political and economic decisions based on useful but incomplete and often controversial statistical and scientific evidence.

Some observers contend that when it comes to evaluation of large-scale, complex technologies, the public often is better at seeing the big picture than the risk-benefit specialists, who look primarily at the details. This commonsense wisdom does not usually depend on understanding or even caring about the details of risk-benefit analysis. Instead, it is based on the average person's understanding that science and technology have limits and that the people responsible for making and managing potentially hazardous technological systems and products are fallible just like everyone else.

 8-4 **Risk Factors and Cancer**

CANCER INCIDENCE AND CURE RATES Cancer will strike about 1 million Americans this year, and 1 of every 3 Americans now living will eventually have some type of cancer (see Spotlight on p. 178). About 1 person dies from cancer every 66 seconds in the United States. Worldwide, 1 of every 10 deaths is due to cancer.

The good news is that almost 50% of Americans (under age 75) who get cancer can now be cured, which is defined as being alive and cancer-free five or more years after treatment, compared with only 38% in 1960. Survival rates for some types of cancers now range from 66% to 88%. The improvement is mostly due to a combination of early detection and improved use of surgery, radiation, and drug treatments.

Nonfatal skin cancer is by far the most common form of cancer; about one in seven Americans gets it sooner or later. Cumulative exposure to ultraviolet ionizing radiation in sunlight over a number of years is the primary cause of basal-cell and squamous-cell skin cancers (Figures 8-7a and 8-7b). These two types of cancer can be cured if detected early enough, although their removal may leave disfiguring scars. I have had three basal-cell cancers on my face because of too much exposure to the sun in my younger years. I wish I had known then what I know now.

Evidence suggests that just one severe, blistering burn as a child or teenager is enough to double a person's risk of contracting deadly malignant melanoma (Figure 8-7c) later in life. Each year, it kills about 9,000 Americans and 100,000 people worldwide. Depletion of the ozone layer will lead to a sharp increase in all types of skin cancers.

Virtually anyone can get skin cancer, but those with very fair and freckled skin run the highest risk. Americans who spend long hours in the sun or in tanning booths (which are even more hazardous than direct exposure to the sun) greatly increase their chances of developing skin cancer. They also tend to have wrinkled, dry skin by age 40. Blacks are almost immune to sunburn but do get skin cancer, although at a rate one-tenth that of whites. A dark suntan also doesn't prevent skin cancer. Outdoor workers are particularly susceptible to cancer of the exposed skin on the face, hands, and arms.

The safest thing to do is to stay out of the sun and tanning booths. Avoid direct exposure between 10:00 AM and 3:00 PM when the sun's ultraviolet rays are strongest. Sitting under an umbrella does not protect against the sun because sunlight is reflected from sand, concrete, and water. Clouds are deceptive because they allow as much as 80% of the sun's harmful ultraviolet radiation to pass through.

When you are in the sun, wear tightly woven protective clothing and a wide-brimmed hat, and apply a sunscreen with a protection factor of 15 or more (25 if you have light skin) to all exposed skin. Reapply sunscreen after swimming or excessive perspiration. Children using a sunscreen with a protection factor of 15 anytime they are in the sun from birth to age 18 decrease their chance of skin cancer by 80%.

Get to know your moles, and examine your skin surface at least once a month for any changes. The warning signs of skin cancer are a change in the size, shape, or color of a mole or wart (the major sign of malignant melanoma, which needs to be treated quickly), sudden appearance of dark spots on the skin, and a sore that keeps oozing, bleeding, and crusting over but does not heal. If any of these signs are observed, you should immediately consult a doctor.

What are you doing to protect your skin and your life?

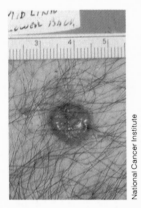

a Basal

National Cancer Institute

b Squamous

Ken Greer/Visuals Unlimited

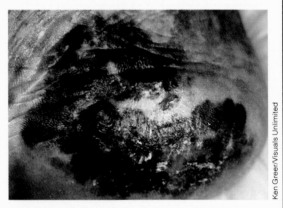

c Malignant melanoma

Ken Greer/Visuals Unlimited

Figure 8-7   Three types of skin cancer: basal (**a**), squamous (**b**), and malignant melanoma (**c**). The occurrence of these types of cancer is rising because of increased exposure to ultraviolet-B radiation, resulting from depletion of ozone gas in the stratosphere by chlorofluorocarbons (CFCs) and other chemicals containing chlorine or bromine atoms.

CANCER RISK FACTORS   According to the World Health Organization, environmental and lifestyle factors play a key role in causing or promoting 80% to 90% of cancers. Major sources of carcinogens are cigarette smoke (40% of cancers), dietary factors (25% to 30%), occupational exposure (10% to 15%), and environmental pollutants (5% to 10%). About 10% to 20% of cancers may be caused by inherited genetic factors and viruses.

The risks of developing cancer can be greatly reduced by working and living in a less hazardous environment, not smoking or being around smokers (see Case Study on p. 179), drinking in moderation (no more

Q: What are the three most dangerous indoor air pollutants in MDCs?

Smoking tobacco causes more death and suffering by far among adults than does any other environmental factor. Each cigarette smoked reduces one's average life span by about 10 minutes. Worldwide, at least 2.5 million smokers die prematurely each year from heart disease, lung cancer, other cancers, bronchitis, emphysema, and stroke—all related to smoking.

In 1989, smoking killed about 434,000 Americans—an average of 1,190 a day (Figure 8-8). This annual death toll is equal to three 400-passenger jets crashing every day with no survivors. This is almost nine times the number of Americans killed in traffic accidents each year, and eight times the number of American soldiers killed in the nine-year Vietnam War.

Nicotine is not classified as an illegal drug; yet, it kills and harms more people each year in the United States than all illegal drugs and alcohol (the second most harmful drug), automobile accidents, suicide, and homicide combined (Figure 8-8).

Numerous studies have shown that the nicotine in tobacco is a highly addictive drug that, like heroin and cocaine, can quickly and strongly hook its victims. A British government study showed that adolescents who smoke more than one cigarette have an 85% chance of becoming smokers. The typical smoker has a 200- to 400-hit-a-day legalized habit, which costs about $26,000 for a person smoking 1 pack a day for 40 years.

Some recovering heroin addicts report they had a much harder time quitting smoking than quitting heroin. About 75% of smokers who quit start smoking again within six months, about the same relapse rate as recovering alcoholics and heroin addicts.

Several studies indicate that passive smoke inhaled by nonsmokers causes at least 3,800 premature deaths of Americans a year from lung cancer and an estimated 53,000 deaths from all diseases related to smoking. According to the National Research Council, nonsmoking spouses of smokers have a 30% greater chance of contracting lung cancer than do the spouses of nonsmokers.

Tobacco's harmful costs to American society exceed its economic benefits to tobacco farmers and employees and stockholders of tobacco companies by more than two to one. In the United States, smoking costs society at least $52 billion (some estimate $95 billion) a year in premature death, disability, medical treatment, increased insurance costs, and lost productivity because of illness (accounting for 19% of all absenteeism in industry). These external costs amount to an average cost to society of at least $2.20 per pack of cigarettes sold.

The American Medical Association and numerous health experts have called for

- A total ban on cigarette advertising in the United States.

- Prohibition of the sale of cigarettes and other tobacco products to anyone under 21, with strict penalties for violations.

- A ban on all cigarette vending machines.

- Classifying nicotine as a drug and placing the manufacture, distribution, sale, and promotion of tobacco products under the jurisdiction of the Food and Drug Administration.

- Eliminating all federal subsidies to U.S. tobacco farmers and tobacco companies.

- Taxing cigarettes at about $2.20 a pack to discourage smoking and to make smokers pay for the harmful effects of smoking now borne by society as a whole.

- Prohibiting elected and appointed government officials from exerting any influence on other governments to enhance the export of tobacco from the United States to other countries. Since 1985, the federal government has threatened to impose trade sanctions against foreign countries that do not lift tariffs and other restrictions on American tobacco products. That means that the U.S. government is coercing other governments into allowing imports of a very hazardous, addictive drug from America while trying to halt the flow of illicit drugs from other countries into the United States.

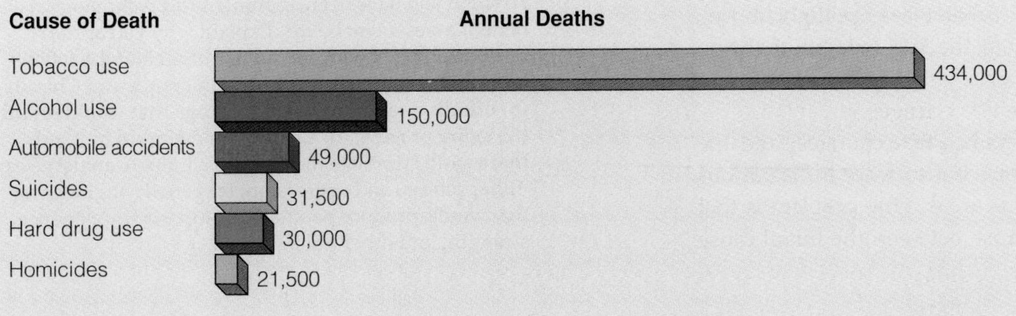

Cause of Death   **Annual Deaths**

Cause of Death	Annual Deaths
Tobacco use	434,000
Alcohol use	150,000
Automobile accidents	49,000
Suicides	31,500
Hard drug use	30,000
Homicides	21,500

Figure 8-8   Annual deaths in the United States related to tobacco use and other causes in 1989. Smoking is by far the nation's leading cause of preventable death, causing almost twice as many premature deaths each year as all the other categories shown in this figure combined. (Data from National Center for Health Statistics)

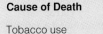

A: Cigarette smoke, radon, and formaldehyde

Improper diet plays a key role in an estimated 25% to 30% of all cancer deaths. The National Academy of Sciences and the American Heart Association advise that the risk of certain types of cancer—lung, stomach, colon, breast, and esophageal—heart disease, and diabetes can be significantly reduced by a daily diet that cuts down on certain foods and includes others. Such a diet limits

- Total fat intake to 25% or less of total calories, with no more than 10% from saturated fats and the remaining 15% divided about equally between polyunsaturated fats (like safflower oil and corn oil) and monounsaturated fats (such as olive oil)

- Protein (particularly meat protein) to 15% of total calories, or about 171 grams (6 ounces) a day (about the amount in one hamburger)

- Alcohol consumption to 15% of total caloric intake—no more than two drinks, glasses of wine, or beers a day

- Cholesterol consumption to no more than 300 milligrams a day, the goal being to keep blood cholesterol levels below 200 milligrams per deciliter

- Sodium intake to no more than 6 grams (about 1 teaspoon of salt) a day to help lower blood pressure, which should not exceed 140 over 90

We should eat more poultry, fish, beans, peas, whole grains, cereals, fruits, and vegetables and much less red meat (which recently was linked to a higher risk of colon cancer) and processed foods. Also, each of us should achieve and maintain the ideal body weight for his or her frame size and age by a combination of diet and 20 minutes of exercise a day at least three days a week.

or causes of a cancer and the appearance of detectable symptoms. Healthy high school and college students and young adults have difficulty accepting the fact that their smoking, drinking, eating, and other lifestyle habits today will be significant influences on whether they will die prematurely from cancer before they reach age 50. Denial can be deadly.

Government has an important role to play in reducing the risks from the numerous hazards we are exposed to. However, when we have a choice, changing our own lifestyles is the most effective way of reducing risks to our health and survival.

Though their health needs differ drastically, the rich and the poor do have one thing in common: both die unnecessarily. The rich die of heart disease and cancer, the poor of diarrhea, pneumonia, and measles. Scientific medicine could vastly reduce the mortality caused by these illnesses. Yet, half the developing world lacks medical care of any kind.

WILLIAM U. CHANDLER

DISCUSSION TOPICS

1. Considering the benefits and risks involved, do you believe that **(a)** nuclear power plants should be controlled more rigidly and gradually phased out? **(b)** Coal-burning power plants should be controlled more rigidly and gradually phased out? **(c)** Genetic engineering should be prohibited? **(d)** Genetic engineering should be more rigidly controlled? In each case defend your position.

2. Explain why you agree or disagree with each of the following proposals:
   a. All advertising of cigarettes and other tobacco products should be banned.
   b. All smoking should be banned in public buildings and commercial airplanes, buses, subways, and trains.
   c. All government subsidies to tobacco farmers and the tobacco industry should be eliminated.
   d. Cigarettes should be taxed at about $2.20 a pack so that smokers—not nonsmokers—pay for the health and productivity losses now borne by society as a whole.

3. Assume you have been appointed to a technology risk-benefit assessment board. Explain why you approve or disapprove of widespread use of each of the following: **(a)** abortion pills (now used in France and China); **(b)** effective sex stimulants; **(c)** drugs that would retard the aging process; **(d)** electrical or chemical methods that would stimulate the brain to eliminate anxiety, fear, unhappiness, and aggression; **(e)** genetic engineering that would produce people with superior intelligence, strength, and other traits.

than two beers, glasses of wine, or drinks a day) or not at all, adhering to a healthful diet (see Spotlight above), and shielding oneself from the sun (see Spotlight on p. 178). According to experts, 60% of all cancers could be prevented by such lifestyle changes.

Many people don't make such changes, and the poor often have little choice but to work in hazardous jobs and live in hazardous areas. One problem is that usually 10 to 40 years elapse between the initial cause

PART THREE

Air, Water, and

Soil Resources

I am utterly convinced that most of the great environmental struggles will be either won or lost in the 1990s, and that by the next century it will be too late to act.

THOMAS E. LOVEJOY

CHAPTER 9

AIR RESOURCES AND AIR POLLUTION

General Questions and Issues

1. What are the principal components of the atmosphere?

2. What are the primary types and sources of air pollutants?

3. What is smog? What is acid deposition?

4. What undesirable effects can air pollutants have on people, other species, and materials?

5. What legal and technological methods can be used to reduce air pollution?

I thought I saw a blue jay this morning. But the smog was so bad that it turned out to be a cardinal holding its breath.

MICHAEL J. COHEN

TAKE A DEEP BREATH. About 99% of the volume of air you inhaled is gaseous nitrogen and oxygen. You also inhaled trace amounts of other gases, minute droplets of various liquids, and tiny particles of various solids. Many of these chemicals are classified as air pollutants. Most come from cars, trucks, power plants, factories, cigarettes, cleaning solvents, and other sources created by human activity. Most are related to the burning of fossil fuels, with motor vehicles responsible for at least half of the air pollution in urban areas.

You are exposed to air pollutants outdoors and indoors. Repeated exposure to trace amounts of many of these chemicals can damage lung tissue, plants, fish and other animals, buildings, metals, and other materials. The nature of this damage and what we can do to prevent it are the focus of this chapter. Air pollutants emitted by our activities are also increasing the amount of the sun's harmful ultraviolet radiation reaching Earth's surface and are projected to alter local, regional, and global climates from an enhanced greenhouse effect, which is discussed in Chapter 10.

9-1 The Atmosphere

OUR AIR RESOURCES The **atmosphere**, the thin envelope of life-sustaining gases surrounding the earth, is divided into several spherical layers, much like the successive layers of skin on an onion (Figure 9-1). About 95% of the mass of Earth's air is found in the atmosphere's innermost layer, known as the **troposphere**, extending only about 17 kilometers (11 miles) above sea level. If Earth were an apple, this lower layer that contains the air we breathe would be no thicker than the apple's skin.

About 99% of the volume of clean, dry air in the troposphere consists of two gases: nitrogen (78%) and oxygen (21%). The remaining volume of air in the troposphere has slightly less than 1% argon and about 0.035% carbon dioxide. Air in the troposphere also holds water vapor in amounts varying from 0.01% by volume at the frigid poles to 5% in the humid tropics.

The atmosphere's second layer, extending from about 17 to 48 kilometers (11 to 30 miles) above Earth's surface, is called the **stratosphere** (Figure 9-1). It contains small amounts of gaseous ozone (O_3) that keeps about 99% of the harmful ultraviolet radiation (especially ultraviolet-B or UV-B) given off by the sun from reaching Earth's surface (Figure 3-4). This filtering action by the thin gauze of ozone in the stratosphere protects us from increased sunburn, skin cancer (see Spotlight on p. 178), eye cancer, eye cataracts, and damage to our immune system. This global sunscreen

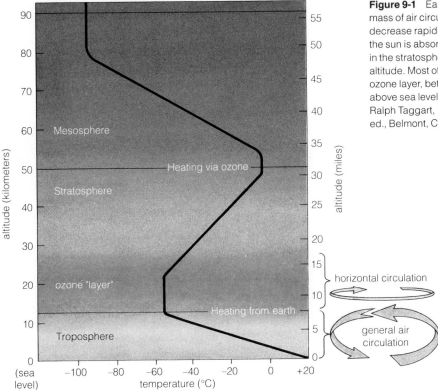

Figure 9-1 Earth's atmosphere. About 95% of the planet's mass of air circulates in the troposphere, where temperatures decrease rapidly with altitude. Most ultraviolet radiation from the sun is absorbed by small amounts of gaseous ozone (O_3) in the stratosphere, where temperatures rise with increasing altitude. Most of this ozone is found in what is called the ozone layer, between 17 and 26 kilometers (11 and 16 miles) above sea level. (Used by permission from Cecie Starr and Ralph Taggart, *Biology: The Unity and Diversity of Life*, 6th ed., Belmont, Calif.: Wadsworth, 1992)

also prevents damage to some plants and aquatic organisms.

By filtering out high-energy UV radiation, stratospheric ozone also keeps much of the oxygen in the troposphere from being converted to toxic ozone. The trace amounts of ozone that do form in the troposphere as a component of urban smog damage plants, the respiratory systems of people and other animals, and materials such as rubber.

Thus, our good health and that of many other species depends on having enough "good" ozone in the stratosphere and as little "bad" ozone as possible in the troposphere. Unfortunately, our activities are increasing the amount of ozone in the tropospheric air we must breathe and decreasing the amount in the stratosphere (see Section 10-4).

DISRUPTING EARTH'S GASEOUS BIOGEOCHEMICAL CYCLES Earth's biogeochemical cycles (Section 4-4) work fine as long as we don't disrupt them by overloading them at certain points or by removing too many vital chemicals at other points. But, in fact, our activities are disrupting the natural gaseous biogeochemical cycles, and the effects of that disruption are growing exponentially.

We produce one-fourth as much CO_2 as nature does as we burn up nature's one-time deposit of fossil fuels and clear forests to support a rapidly growing human population and to fuel unsustainable forms of economic growth. This disruption of the carbon cycle (Figure 4-

22) has the potential to warm the earth and alter global climate and food-producing regions (Section 10-2). We also disrupt natural energy flows (Figure 4-4) and produce massive heat islands and dust domes over urban areas (Figure 6-17).

By burning fossil fuels and using nitrogen fertilizers, we are releasing three times the nitrogen oxides and gaseous ammonia into the atmosphere as are natural processes in the nitrogen cycle (Figure 4-23). In the atmosphere these nitrogen oxides are converted to nitric acid (HNO_3) that returns to the earth as a component of acid deposition.

We are currently releasing twice as much sulfur into the atmosphere as are natural processes. Most of this is sulfur dioxide emitted by petroleum refining and by burning coal and oil. In the atmosphere this sulfur dioxide is converted to sulfuric acid (H_2SO_4) that returns to the earth as another component of acid deposition.

These are only a few of the chemicals we are spewing into the atmosphere. Small amounts of toxic metals like arsenic, cadmium, and lead are also circulated in the ecosphere in chemical cycles. We now inject twice as much arsenic into the atmosphere as nature does, 7 times as much cadmium, and 17 times as much lead.

These facts give you a glimpse of why many environmentalists believe that we may have only a few years to turn things around before we cause even larger-scale disruption of the gaseous and other chemical cycles and the energy flows that sustain life (Figure 4-3).

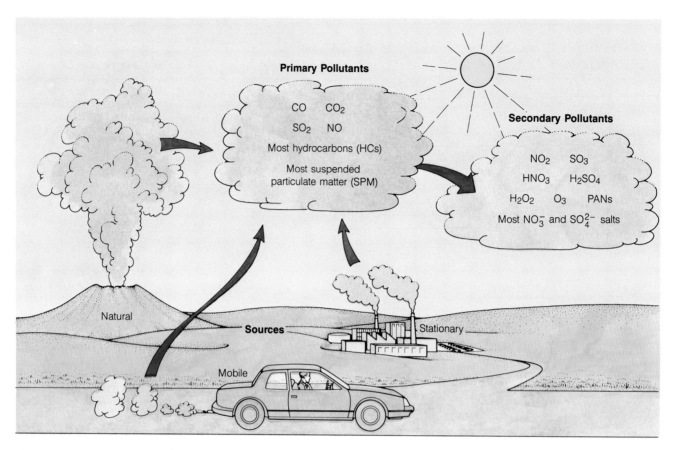

Figure 9-2 Primary and secondary air pollutants.

Outdoor and Indoor Air Pollution

TYPES AND SOURCES OF OUTDOOR AIR POLLU-TION As clean air moves across Earth's surface, it collects various chemicals produced by natural events and human activities. Once in the troposphere, these potential air pollutants mix vertically and horizontally, often reacting chemically with each other or with natural components of the atmosphere. Air movements and turbulence help dilute potential pollutants, but long-lived pollutants are transported great distances before they return to Earth's surface as solid particles, liquid droplets, or chemicals dissolved in precipitation.

Hundreds of air pollutants are found in the troposphere. However, trace amounts of nine classes of pollutants cause most outdoor (ambient) air pollution:

1. *Carbon oxides* — carbon monoxide (CO) and carbon dioxide (CO_2)

2. *Sulfur oxides* — sulfur dioxide (SO_2) and sulfur trioxide (SO_3)

3. *Nitrogen oxides* — nitric oxide (NO), nitrogen dioxide (NO_2), and nitrous oxide (N_2O). NO and NO_2 are often lumped together and labeled as NO_x

4. *Volatile organic compounds (VOCs)* — hundreds of compounds such as methane (CH_4), benzene (C_6H_6), formaldehyde (CH_2O), chlorofluorocarbons (CFCs), and bromine-containing halons

5. *Suspended particulate matter (SPM)* — thousands of different types of *solid particles* such as dust, soot (carbon), pollen, asbestos, lead, arsenic, cadmium, nitrate (NO_3^-) and sulfate (SO_4^{2-}) salts, and *liquid droplets* of chemicals such as sulfuric acid (H_2SO_4), oil, PCBs, dioxins, and various pesticides

6. *Photochemical oxidants* — ozone (O_3), PANs (peroxyacyl nitrates), hydrogen peroxide (H_2O_2), hydroxyl radicals (OH), and aldehydes, such as formaldehyde (CH_2O), formed in the atmosphere by the reaction of oxygen, nitrogen oxides, and volatile hydrocarbons under the influence of sunlight

7. *Radioactive substances* — radon-222, iodine-131, strontium-90, plutonium-239, and other radioisotopes that enter the atmosphere as gases or suspended particulate matter

8. *Heat* — produced when any kind of energy is transformed from one form to another, especially when fossil fuels are burned in cars, factories, homes, and power plants (Figure 6-17)

9. *Noise* — produced by motor vehicles, airplanes, trains, industrial machinery, construction machinery, lawn mowers, vacuum cleaners, food, sirens,

Q: What is the most dangerous indoor air pollutant in LDCs?

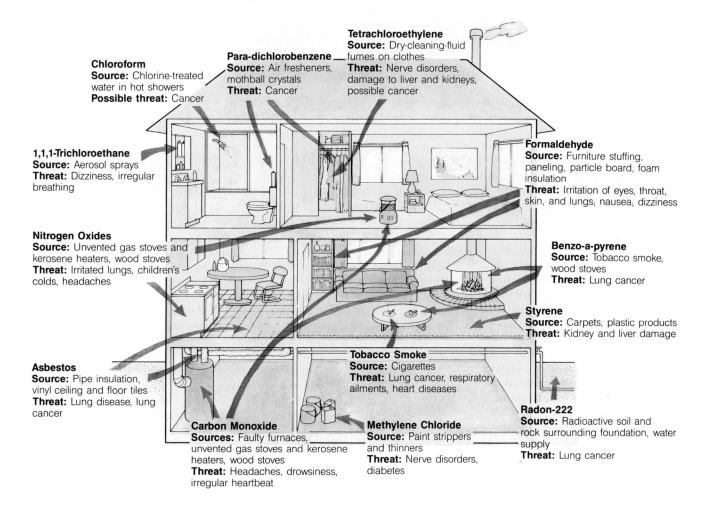

Chloroform
Source: Chlorine-treated water in hot showers
Possible threat: Cancer

Para-dichlorobenzene
Source: Air fresheners, mothball crystals
Threat: Cancer

Tetrachloroethylene
Source: Dry-cleaning-fluid fumes on clothes
Threat: Nerve disorders, damage to liver and kidneys, possible cancer

1,1,1-Trichloroethane
Source: Aerosol sprays
Threat: Dizziness, irregular breathing

Formaldehyde
Source: Furniture stuffing, paneling, particle board, foam insulation
Threat: Irritation of eyes, throat, skin, and lungs; nausea; dizziness

Nitrogen Oxides
Source: Unvented gas stoves and kerosene heaters, wood stoves
Threat: Irritated lungs, children's colds, headaches

Benzo-a-pyrene
Source: Tobacco smoke, wood stoves
Threat: Lung cancer

Styrene
Source: Carpets, plastic products
Threat: Kidney and liver damage

Asbestos
Source: Pipe insulation, vinyl ceiling and floor tiles
Threat: Lung disease, lung cancer

Tobacco Smoke
Source: Cigarettes
Threat: Lung cancer, respiratory ailments, heart diseases

Carbon Monoxide
Sources: Faulty furnaces, unvented gas stoves and kerosene heaters, wood stoves
Threat: Headaches, drowsiness, irregular heartbeat

Methylene Chloride
Source: Paint strippers and thinners
Threat: Nerve disorders, diabetes

Radon-222
Source: Radioactive soil and rock surrounding foundation, water supply
Threat: Lung cancer

Figure 9-3 Some important indoor air pollutants. (Data from Environmental Protection Agency)

earphones, radios, cassette players, and live concerts (Table 6-1)

A **primary air pollutant**, such as sulfur dioxide, directly enters the air as a result of natural events or human activities. A **secondary air pollutant**, such as sulfuric acid, is formed in the air through a chemical reaction between a primary pollutant and one or more air components (Figure 9-2).

Most of the widely recognized outdoor air pollution in the United States (and other industrialized countries) comes from five groups of primary pollutants: carbon monoxide, nitrogen oxides, sulfur oxides, volatile organic compounds (mostly hydrocarbons), and suspended particulate matter. Other key pollutants are ozone (a secondary pollutant) and lead—mostly from burning leaded gasoline, metal smelters (see photo on p. 181), and municipal waste incinerators. Each of the 198 million motor vehicles in the United States spews out an average of 0.9 metric ton (1 ton) of pollutants a year.

In MDCs, most of these pollutants are emitted into the atmosphere from the burning of fossil fuels in power and industrial plants (*stationary sources*) and in motor vehicles (*mobile sources*) (see Pro/Con on p. 130).

In LDCs, especially in rural areas where more than half of the world's people live, most air pollution is produced by the burning of wood, dung, and crop residues in inefficient crude stoves and open fires. This burning adds carbon dioxide and soot to the atmosphere, and wood gathered for fuel contributes to deforestation.

Recently, scientists have recognized that trace amounts of hundreds of *toxic outdoor air pollutants*, 60 of them known carcinogens, are legally released by industries and motor vehicles into American skies. The EPA estimates that these toxic pollutants are responsible for 2,000 excess cancer deaths a year in the United States.

TYPES AND SOURCES OF INDOOR AIR POLLUTION Because we spend 70% to 98% of our time indoors, the EPA has called indoor air quality "the most significant environmental issue we have to face." As many as 20 to 150 hazardous chemicals in concentrations 10 to 40 times those outdoors can be found in the typical American home (Figure 9-3).

The EPA estimates that indoor air pollutants in U.S. homes and offices cause as many as 6,000 cancer deaths each year and up to 20,000 more deaths from indoor inhalation of the decay products of radioactive radon gas (see Case Study on p. 186). Other air pollutants

A: Smoke from unvented or poorly vented stoves for cooking and heating

Radon-222 is a colorless, odorless, tasteless, naturally occurring radioactive gas produced by the radioactive decay of uranium-238. Small amounts of radon-producing uranium-238 are found in most soil and rock, but this isotope is much more concentrated in underground deposits of uranium, phosphate, granite, and shale.

When radon gas from such deposits seeps upward to the soil and is released outdoors, it disperses quickly in the atmosphere and decays to harmless levels. However, when the gas seeps into or is drawn into buildings through cracks, drains, hollow concrete blocks, and drains in basements, or into water in underground wells over such deposits, it can build up to high levels (Figure 9-4). Stone and other building materials obtained from radon-rich deposits can also be a source of indoor radon contamination.

Radon-222 gas quickly decays into solid particles of other radioactive elements that can be inhaled, exposing lung tissue to a large amount of ionizing radiation from alpha particles (Figure 3-10). Smokers are especially vulnerable because the inhaled radioactive particles contained in smoke tend to adhere to tobacco tar deposits in the lungs and upper respiratory tract. Repeated exposure to these radioactive particles over 20 to 30 years can cause lung cancer.

According to the EPA, average indoor radon levels in a closed house above 4 picocuries per liter are considered unsafe (Figure 9-4). Some researchers think this level is too low and recommend that corrective action be taken only if radon levels exceed 10 to 20 picocuries per liter — claims disputed by EPA scientists.

EPA indoor radon surveys indicate that there may be several million U.S. homes with annual radon levels above 4 picocuries per liter and more than 100,000 homes with levels above 20 picocuries per liter. In Pennsylvania, radon levels in the home of one family created a cancer

risk equal to having 455,000 chest X rays a year. In 1989, the EPA reported that about 54% of 130 schools tested had unsafe levels of radon.

According to studies by the EPA and the National Research Council, prolonged exposure to high levels of radon over a 70-year lifetime is estimated to cause up to 20,000 of the 136,000 lung cancer deaths each year in the United States. About 85% of these deaths are due to a combination of radon and smoking.

Water obtained from underground near radon-laden rock and then heated and used for showers and washing clothes and dishes may be responsible for at least 50 to 400 of these premature deaths. Indeed, recent research indicates that the risk from waterborne radon released indoors may be even higher than that from airborne radon.

Because radon "hot spots" can occur almost anywhere, it's impossible to know which buildings have unsafe levels of radon without carrying out tests. In 1988, the EPA and the U.S. Surgeon General's Office recommended that everyone living in a detached house, a town house, a mobile home, or on the first three floors of an apartment building test for radon.* By 1991, only 11% of U.S. households had conducted such tests, even though radon is one of the most controllable environmental hazards we face today.

Individuals can measure radon levels in their homes or other buildings with radon detection kits that can be bought in many hardware stores and supermarkets or from mail-order firms for $10 to $50. Pick one that is EPA approved and mail them to an EPA-certified testing laboratory to get the test result.

Unsafe levels can build up easily in a superinsulated or airtight home unless the building has an air-to-air heat exchanger to change indoor air without losing much heat. Some tests also indicate higher levels of ra-

*For information, see "Radon Detectors: How to Find Out If Your House Has a Radon Problem," *Consumer Reports*, July 1987.

don in houses with electric heat. Homeowners with wells should also have their water tested for radon. If testing reveals an unacceptable level (over 4 picocuries of radiation per liter of air), the EPA recommends several ways to reduce radon levels and health risks.†

In Sweden, no house can be built until the lot has been tested for radon. If the reading is high, the builder must follow government-mandated construction procedures to ensure that the house won't be contaminated.

Environmentalists urge enactment of a similar building-code program for all new construction in the United States. They also suggest that before buying a lot to build a new house, individuals have the soil and the water tested for radon.

Similarly, no one should buy an existing house unless its indoor air and its water have been tested for radon by certified personnel, just as houses must now be inspected for termites. People building a new house should insist that the contractor use relatively simple construction practices that prevent harmful buildup of radon and add only $100 to $1,000 to the construction cost. This includes using foundation materials such as solid concrete blocks or poured concrete walls and installing a heat-bonded nylon mat (called Enkavent and costing $450 to $650) under the slab of a house during construction.

Has the building where you live or work been tested for radon?

†A free copy of *Radon Reduction Methods* can be obtained from the Environmental Protection Agency, 401 M St. S.W., Washington, DC 20460. A free copy of *Radon Reduction in New Construction* is available from state radiation-protection offices or the National Association of Home Builders, Attention: William Young, 15th and M Streets N.W., Washington, DC 20005.

Q: How many Americans die prematurely each year because of air pollution?

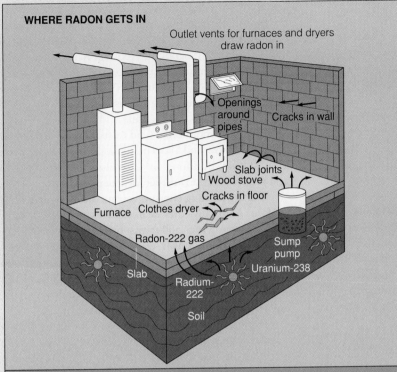

WHERE RADON GETS IN

Outlet vents for furnaces and dryers draw radon in

Openings around pipes

Cracks in wall

Slab joints
Wood stove
Cracks in floor

Furnace
Clothes dryer

Radon-222 gas

Sump pump
Uranium-238

Slab

Radium-222

Soil

POSSIBLE RISKS

Exposure (picocuries per liter of air)*	Lung-Cancer Deaths Per 1,000 People Exposed (for a lifetime of 70 years)	Comparable Lifetime Risk (70 years)	Recommended Action
200	440–470	Smoking 4 packs of cigarettes a day	**20–200 picocuries** Lower levels within several months. If higher than 200, remedy within a few weeks or move out until levels are reduced.
100	270–630	2,000 chest X rays a year	
40	120–380	Smoking 2 packs of cigarettes a day	
20	60–210	Smoking 1 pack of cigarettes a day	**4–20 picocuries** You've got a few years to make changes, but do it sooner if you're at the top of the scale.
10	30–120	5 times the lung-cancer risk of a nonsmoker	
4	13–50		
2	7–30	200 chest X rays a year	**Below 4 picocuries** Once you get around 4, it's nearly impossible to bring levels lower.
1	3–13	Same lung-cancer risk as a nonsmoker	
0.2	1–3	20 chest X rays a year	

* A picocurie is a trillionth of a curie, a standard measure of ionizing radiation.

Figure 9-4 Sources of indoor radon-222 gas and comparable risks of exposure to various levels of this radioactive gas for a lifetime of 70 years. Levels are those in an actual living area, not a basement or crawl space where levels are much higher. Smokers have the highest risk of getting lung cancer from a combination of prolonged exposure to cigarette smoke and radon-222 gas. (Data from Environmental Protection Agency)

A: At least 50,000 and perhaps up to 120,000

found in buildings produce dizziness, headaches, coughing, sneezing, nausea, burning eyes, upper respiratory problems, and flulike symptoms in many people—a health problem called the "sick building syndrome."

An estimated one-fifth to one-third of all U.S. buildings, including the EPA headquarters, are considered "sick." Each year, exposure to pollutants inside factories and businesses in the United States kills from 100,000 to 210,000 workers prematurely. According to the EPA and public health officials, cigarette smoke (see Case Study on p. 179), radioactive radon-222 gas (see Case Study on p. 186), asbestos, and formaldehyde are the four most dangerous indoor air pollutants.

While MDCs have serious indoor air pollution problems, the most severe exposure to indoor air pollution, especially particulate matter, occurs inside the dwellings of poor rural people in LDCs. In those dwellings, the burning of wood, dung, and crop residues in unvented or poorly vented stoves for cooking and heating (in temperate and cold areas) exposes the people, especially women and young children, to very high levels of indoor air pollution. Partly as a result, respiratory illnesses are the chief cause of death and illness in most LDCs.

<h2>9-3   Smog and Acid Deposition</h2>

SMOG: CARS + SUNLIGHT = TEARS **Photochemical smog** (Figure 9-5) is a mixture of dozens of primary pollutants and secondary pollutants that forms when some of the primary pollutants interact under the influence of sunlight. Virtually all modern cities have photochemical smog, but it is much more common in those with sunny, warm, dry climates and lots of motor vehicles. Cities with serious photochemical smog problems include Los Angeles, Denver, Salt Lake City, Sydney, Mexico City (Figure 6-14), and Buenos Aires. The worst episodes of photochemical smog tend to occur in summer.

Thirty years ago, cities like London, Chicago, and Pittsburgh burned large amounts of coal and heavy oil, which contain sulfur impurities, in power and industrial plants and for space heating. During winter, such cities suffered from **industrial smog**, consisting mostly of a mixture of sulfur dioxide, suspended droplets of sulfuric acid formed from some of the sulfur dioxide, and a variety of suspended solid particles. Today, coal and heavy oil are burned only in large boilers with reasonably good control or with tall smokestacks (see photo on p. 181), so industrial smog, sometimes called *gray-air smog*, is rarely a problem. However, that is not the case in China and in some eastern European countries, such as Poland and Czechoslovakia, where large quantities of coal are burned with inadequate controls.

LOCAL CLIMATE, TOPOGRAPHY, AND SMOG
The frequency and severity of smog in an area depend on the local climate and topography; the density of population and industry; and the primary fuels used in industry, heating, and transportation. In areas with high average annual precipitation, rain and snow help cleanse the air of pollutants. Winds also help sweep pollutants away and bring in fresh air but may transfer some pollutants to distant areas.

Hills and mountains tend to reduce the flow of air in valleys below and allow pollutant levels to build up at ground level. Buildings in cities also slow wind speed and reduce dilution and removal of pollutants.

During the day, the sun warms the air near Earth's surface. Normally, this heated air expands and rises, carrying low-lying pollutants higher into the troposphere. Colder, denser air from surrounding high-pressure areas then sinks into the low-pressure area created when the hot air rises (Figure 9-6a). This continual mixing of the air helps keep pollutants from reaching dangerous levels in the air near the ground.

Sometimes, however, weather conditions trap a layer of dense, cool air beneath a layer of less dense, warm air in an urban basin or valley. This is called a **temperature inversion** or a **thermal inversion** (Figure 9-6b). In effect, a lid of warm air covers the region and prevents the upward-flowing air currents that would disperse pollutants from developing. Usually, these inversions last for only a few hours; but sometimes, when a high-pressure air mass stalls over an area, they last for several days. Then air pollutants at ground level build up to harmful and even lethal levels. Thermal inversions also enhance the harmful effects of urban heat islands and dust domes that build up over urban areas (Figure 6-17).

In 1948, a lengthy thermal inversion over Donora, an industrial town in Pennsylvania, killed 20 people and made 6,000 of the town's 14,000 inhabitants sick. A prolonged thermal inversion over New York City in 1963 killed 300 people and injured thousands.

Thermal inversions occur more often and last longer over towns or cities located in valleys surrounded by mountains (Donora, Pennsylvania, and Mexico City, Figure 6-14), on the leeward sides of mountain ranges (Denver), and near coasts (New York City and Los Angeles).

A city with several million people and automobiles in an area with a sunny climate, light winds, mountains on three sides, and the ocean on the other has the ideal conditions for photochemical smog worsened by frequent thermal inversions. This describes the Los Angeles basin, which has 13.8 million people, 8.5 million cars, and thousands of factories. It also has almost daily

Q: What is the greenhouse effect?

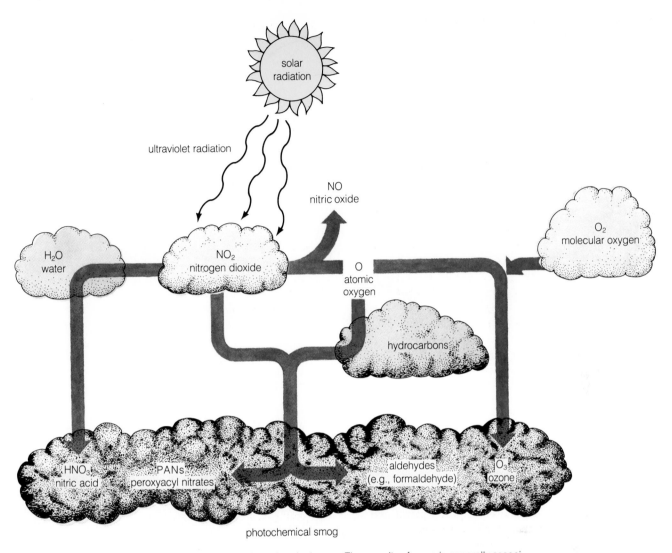

Figure 9-5 Simplified scheme of the formation of photochemical smog. The severity of smog is generally associated with atmospheric concentrations of ozone at ground level. Other harmful compounds in photochemical smog are aldehydes, peroxyacyl nitrates (PANs), and nitric acid. Traces of the secondary pollutants in photochemical smog build up to peak levels by early afternoon on a sunny day, irritating people's eyes and respiratory tracts. People with asthma and other respiratory problems, and healthy people who exercise outdoors between 11 AM and 4 PM, are especially vulnerable. The hotter the day, the higher the levels of ozone and other components of photochemical smog.

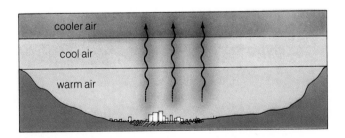

a Normal pattern

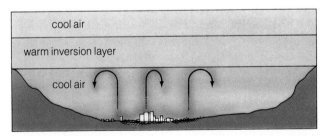

b Thermal inversion

Figure 9-6 Thermal inversion traps pollutants in a layer of cool air that cannot rise to carry the pollutants away.

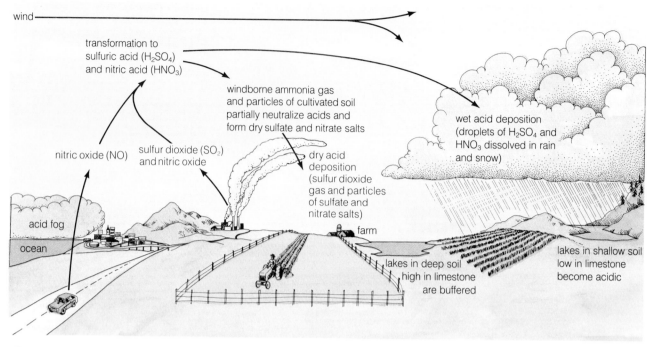

Figure 9-7 Acid deposition. It consists of acidified rain, snow, dust, or gas with a pH lower than 5.6. The lower the pH level, the greater the acidity of this wet and dry deposition, commonly called acid rain.

inversions, many of them prolonged during the summer months. Despite having the world's toughest air pollution control program, Los Angeles is the air pollution capital of the United States.

ACID DEPOSITION When electric power plants and industrial plants burn coal or oil, their smokestacks emit large amounts of sulfur dioxide, suspended particulate matter, and nitrogen oxides. To reduce local air pollution and meet government standards without having to add expensive air pollution control devices, power plants and industries began using tall smokestacks (see photo on p. 181) to spew pollutants above the inversion layer (Figure 9-6). As more power plants and industries began using this fairly cheap output approach to controlling local pollution in the 1960s and 1970s, pollution in downwind areas began to rise.

As emissions of sulfur dioxide and nitric oxide from stationary sources are transported long distances by winds, they form secondary pollutants such as nitrogen dioxide, nitric acid vapor, and droplets containing solutions of sulfuric acid and sulfate and nitrate salts (Figure 9-2). These chemicals descend to Earth's surface in wet form as acid rain or snow and in dry form as gases, fog, dew, or solid particles. The combination of dry deposition and wet deposition of acids and acid-forming compounds onto Earth's surface is known as **acid deposition**, commonly called *acid rain* (Figure 9-7). Other contributions to acid deposition come from emissions of nitric oxide from motor vehicles in large urban areas. Because water droplets and most solid particles are re-

moved from the atmosphere fairly quickly, acid deposition is a regional or continental problem rather than a global problem.

Acidity and basicity of substances in water solution are commonly expressed in terms of **pH** (Figure 9-8). A neutral solution has a pH of 7; one with a pH greater than 7 is basic, or alkaline; and one with a pH less than 7 is acidic. The lower the pH below 7, the more acidic the solution. Each whole-number decrease in pH represents a tenfold increase in acidity.

Natural precipitation varies in acidity, with an average pH of 5.0 to 5.6; but the average rain in the eastern United States is as acidic as tomato juice, with a pH of 4.3. Precipitation in some areas is more than 10 times as acidic, with a pH of 3 — as acidic as vinegar (Figure 9-8). Some cities and mountaintops downwind from cities are bathed in acid fog as acidic as lemon juice, with a pH of 2.3.

Acid deposition has a number of harmful effects, especially when the pH falls below 5.5 for aquatic systems and 5.1 in general:

- It damages statues, buildings, metals, and car finishes.

- It kills fish, aquatic plants, and microorganisms in lakes and streams.

- It is a major contributor to regional haze in the East and parts of the West, mostly from fine particles of sulfate salts in the atmosphere.

- It weakens or kills trees, especially conifers at high elevations (bathed almost continuously in very

Q: Is there doubt about the validity of the greenhouse effect?

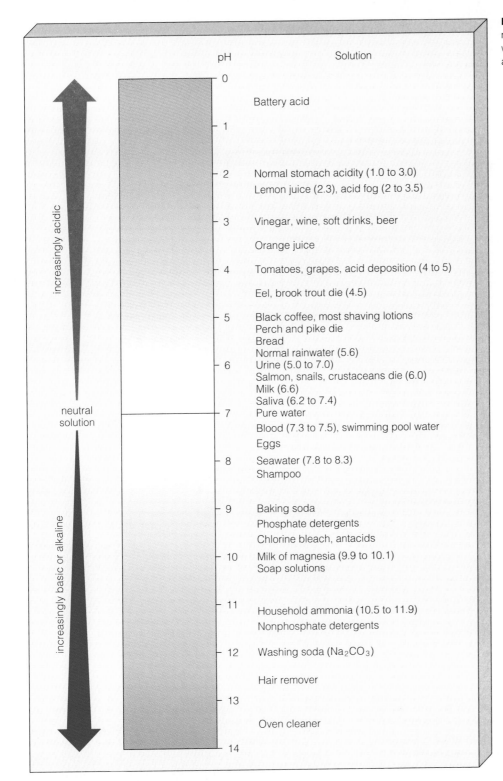

Figure 9-8 Scale of pH, used to measure acidity and alkalinity of water solutions. Values shown are approximate.

pH   Solution

0

Battery acid

1

2   Normal stomach acidity (1.0 to 3.0)
     Lemon juice (2.3), acid fog (2 to 3.5)

3   Vinegar, wine, soft drinks, beer

     Orange juice

4   Tomatoes, grapes, acid deposition (4 to 5)

     Eel, brook trout die (4.5)

5   Black coffee, most shaving lotions
     Perch and pike die
     Bread
     Normal rainwater (5.6)
6   Urine (5.0 to 7.0)
     Salmon, snails, crustaceans die (6.0)
     Milk (6.6)
     Saliva (6.2 to 7.4)
7   Pure water
     Blood (7.3 to 7.5), swimming pool water
     Eggs
8   Seawater (7.8 to 8.3)
     Shampoo

9   Baking soda
     Phosphate detergents
     Chlorine bleach, antacids
10   Milk of magnesia (9.9 to 10.1)
     Soap solutions

11   Household ammonia (10.5 to 11.9)
     Nonphosphate detergents

12   Washing soda (Na_2CO_3)

     Hair remover

13

     Oven cleaner

14

increasingly acidic

neutral solution

increasingly basic or alkaline

acidic fog and clouds), by leaching calcium, potassium, and other plant nutrients from soil (Figure 9-9).

■ It damages tree roots and kills many kinds of fish by releasing ions of aluminum, lead, mercury, and cadmium from soil and bottom sediments (Figure 9-9).

■ It makes trees more susceptible to diseases, in-

sects, drought, and fungi and mosses that thrive under acidic conditions (Figure 9-9).

■ It stunts the growth of crops such as tomatoes, soybeans, spinach, carrots, broccoli, and cotton.

■ It leaches toxic metals such as copper and lead from water pipes into drinking water.

■ It causes and aggravates many human respiratory diseases and leads to premature death.

A: No. Without it, Earth would be too cold for life as we know it to exist.

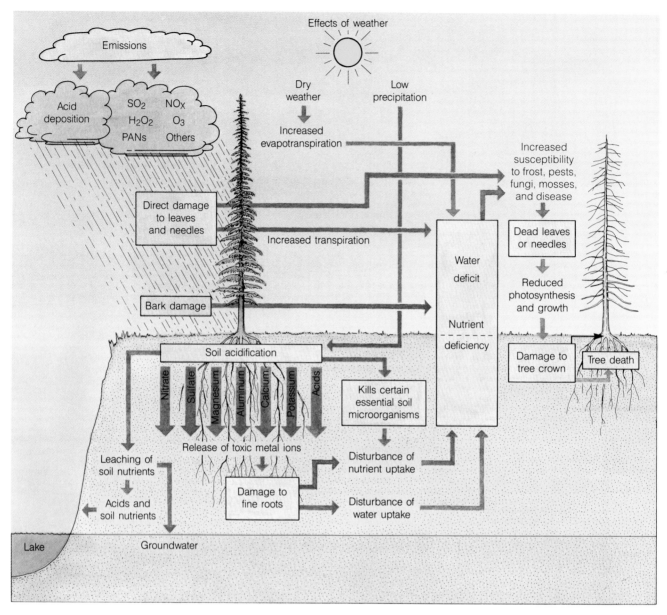

Figure 9-9 Harmful effects of air pollutants on trees.

Soils and bedrock in some areas contain limestone and other alkaline substances that easily dissolve in water and can neutralize acids. Soils in other areas are acidic and thin or have little ability to neutralize acids and so are especially sensitive to acid deposition (Figure 9-10).

Acid deposition illustrates the threshold, or the-straw-that-broke-the-camel's-back effect. Most soils, lakes, and streams contain alkaline (or basic) chemicals that can react with a certain amount of acids and thus neutralize them, but repeated exposure to acids year after year can deplete most of these acid-buffering chemicals. Then, suddenly, large numbers of trees start dying, and most fish in a lake or stream die when ex-

posed to the next year's input of acids. By that time, it's 10 to 20 years too late to prevent serious damage.

Acid deposition is already a serious problem in many areas (Figure 9-10). Estimated damage from acid deposition already costs the United States at least $6 billion a year and perhaps $10 billion a year, and costs are expected to rise sharply unless action is taken now. A 1990 study by Resources for the Future, a leading research organization, indicated that the benefits of controlling acid deposition will be worth $5 billion a year, about 50% greater than the costs of controlling acid deposition.

A large portion of the acid-producing chemicals produced in one country is exported to others by pre-

Q: Why is there concern over a potentially enhanced greenhouse effect?

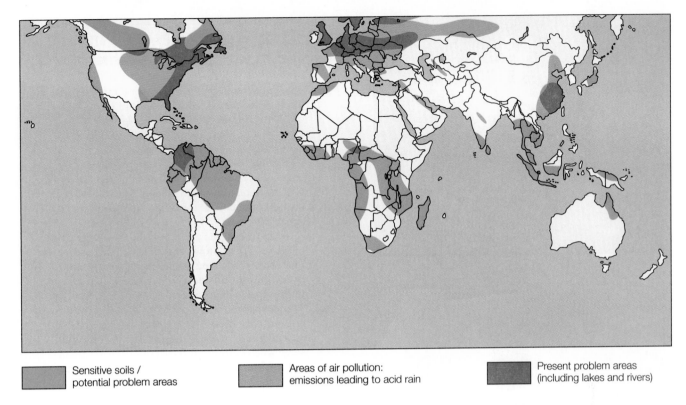

| Sensitive soils / potential problem areas | Areas of air pollution: emissions leading to acid rain | Present problem areas (including lakes and rivers) |

Figure 9-10 Areas of the world suffering from acid deposition, those with early signs of acid deposition, and those with soils sensitive to acid deposition. (Data from World Resource Institute and Environmental Protection Agency)

vailing surface winds. For example, more than three-fourths of the acid deposition in Norway, Switzerland, Austria, Sweden, the Netherlands, and Finland is blown to those countries from industrialized areas of western and eastern Europe (Figure 9-10).

More than half the acid deposition in heavily populated southeastern Canada and in the eastern United States originates from emissions from the heavy concentration of coal- and oil-burning power and industrial plants in seven central and upper midwestern states—Ohio, Indiana, Pennsylvania, Illinois, Missouri, West Virginia, and Tennessee.

A large-scale, government-sponsored research study on acid deposition in the United States in the 1980s concluded that the problem was serious but not yet at a crisis stage. Critics claim this $50 million, 10-year study was used mostly by the government to justify its denial and delay policy on controlling acid deposition during the 1980s.

Tensions between the United States and Canada over the net flow of acid deposition from the United States to southeastern Canada were eased by the Clean Air Act of 1990. It calls for a significant reduction in U.S. emissions of sulfur dioxide and a modest reduction in emissions of nitrogen oxides by the year 2000. Canada has agreed to make comparable reductions in its emissions of these air pollutants.

9-4 **Effects of Air Pollution on Living Organisms and on Materials**

DAMAGE TO HUMAN HEALTH Your respiratory system has a number of mechanisms that help protect you from air pollution. Hairs in your nose filter out large particles. Sticky mucus in the lining of your upper respiratory tract captures small particles and dissolves some gaseous pollutants. Sneezing and coughing expel contaminated air and mucus when your respiratory system is irritated by pollutants. Your upper respiratory tract is lined with hundreds of thousands of tiny, mucus-coated hairlike cell structures, called cilia. They continually wave back and forth, transporting mucus and the pollutants they trap to your mouth, where they are either swallowed or expelled.

Years of smoking (see Case Study on p. 179) and exposure to air pollutants can overload or deteriorate these natural defenses, causing or contributing to a number of respiratory diseases such as lung cancer, chronic bronchitis, and emphysema. Elderly people, infants, pregnant women, and people with heart disease, asthma, or other respiratory diseases are especially vulnerable to air pollution.

Fine particles are particularly hazardous to human health because they are small enough to penetrate the

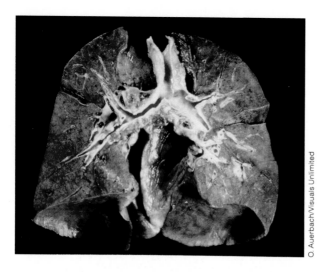

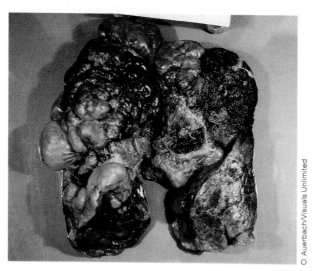

Figure 9-11 Normal appearance of human lung (top) and appearance of lung taken from a person who died from emphysema (bottom).

SPOTLIGHT The World's Most Polluted City

The air pollution capital of the world may be Cubatao, an hour's drive south of São Paulo, Brazil (Figure 6-12). This city of 100,000 people lies in a coastal valley that has frequent thermal inversions. Residents call the area "the valley of death."

In this heavily industrialized city, scores of plants spew thousands of tons of pollutants a day into the frequently stagnant air. More babies are born deformed there than anywhere else in Latin America.

In one recent year, 13,000 of the 40,000 people living in the downtown core area suffered from respiratory disease. One resident says, "On some days, if you go outside, you will vomit." The mayor refuses to live in the city.

Most residents would like to live somewhere else, but they need the jobs available in the city and cannot afford to move. The government has begun some long-overdue efforts to control air pollution, but it has far to go. Meanwhile, the poor continue to pay the price of this form of economic progress: bad health and premature death.

lungs' natural defenses. They can also bring with them droplets or other particles of toxic or cancer-causing pollutants that become attached to their surfaces. A 1991 study concluded that as many as 3% of deaths in the United States are attributable to suspended particulate matter.

Inhaling the ozone found in photochemical smog (Figure 9-5) causes coughing, shortness of breath, nose and throat irritation, and discomfort and aggravates chronic diseases such as asthma, bronchitis, emphysema, and heart trouble. Outdoor exercise in areas where ozone levels exceed safe levels (0.12 parts per million per hour) amplifies these effects. Many U.S. cities frequently exceed these levels, especially during warm weather.

Emphysema is an incurable condition that reduces the ability of the lungs to transfer oxygen to the blood, so the slightest exertion causes acute shortness of breath (Figure 9-11). Prolonged smoking and exposure to air pollutants can cause emphysema in anyone, but about 2% of emphysema cases are caused by a defective gene that reduces the elasticity of the air sacs of the lungs. Anyone with this hereditary condition, for which testing is available, should certainly not smoke and should not live or work in a highly polluted area.

The World Health Organization estimates that worldwide about 1.25 billion urban dwellers—almost one of every five people on Earth—are being exposed to health hazards from air pollutants (see Spotlight above).

The congressional Office of Technology Assessment estimates that 50,000 premature deaths occur in the United States each year from respiratory or cardiac problems caused or aggravated by current air pollution levels. The American Lung Association estimates that up to 120,000 Americans die each year as a result of air pollution.

According to the EPA and the American Lung Association, air pollution costs the United States at least $150 billion annually in health care and lost work productivity. About $100 billion of that is caused by indoor air pollution—the problem we have focused on the least—and $40 billion is caused by air pollution from motor vehicles.

DAMAGE TO PLANTS Chronic exposure of leaves and needles to air pollutants—such as sulfur dioxide, nitrogen oxides, ozone, and PANs—can break down the waxy coating that helps prevent excessive water loss

Q: What are the principal greenhouse gases?

Figure 9-12 Sulfur dioxide and other fumes from a copper smelter that operated for 52 years near Ducktown and Copperhill, Tennessee, killed the forest once found on this land and left a desert in its place. After decades of replanting, some vegetation has returned to the area, but recovery has been slow because of severe soil erosion.

Figure 9-13 Tree death and damage to coniferous trees near the top of Mt. Mitchell, North Carolina—the highest peak in the East—are believed to have been the result of long-term exposure to multiple air pollutants, which made the trees more vulnerable to disease, insects, and drought.

and damage from diseases, pests, drought, and frost. Such exposure also interferes with photosynthesis and plant growth, reduces nutrient uptake, and causes leaves or needles to turn yellow or brown and drop off. Spruce, fir, and other coniferous trees, especially at high elevations, are highly vulnerable to the effects of air pollution because of their long life spans and the year-round exposure of their needles to polluted air.

Acid deposition can also leach vital plant nutrients such as calcium, magnesium, and potassium from the soil and kill essential soil microorganisms (Figure 9-9). It also releases aluminum ions, which are normally bound to soil particles, into soil water. There they may damage fine root hairs, disrupt the ability of roots to absorb water from the soil, kill decomposers that break down organic matter and make nutrients available to plants, and make plants more vulnerable to damage or death from drought, frost, insects, fungi, mosses, and disease (Figure 9-9). This indirect damage to trees is believed to be much more threatening than the direct damage from air pollution. Prolonged exposure to high levels of multiple air pollutants can kill all trees and most other vegetation in an area (Figure 9-12).

The effects of chronic exposure of trees to multiple air pollutants may not be visible for several decades. Then, suddenly, large numbers begin dying off because of depletion of soil nutrients and increased susceptibility to pests, diseases, fungi, mosses, and drought.

That is what is happening to about 35% of the forested area in 28 European countries. The phenomenon, known as *Waldsterben* (forest death), turns whole forests of spruce, fir, and beech into stump-studded meadows. The four European countries with the highest percentages of their conifer forests damaged are Czechoslovakia (71%), Greece (64%), the United Kingdom (64%), and Germany (60%).

Similar diebacks in the United States have occurred in mostly coniferous forests on high-elevation slopes facing moving air masses. The most seriously affected areas are the Appalachian Mountains from Georgia to New England. By 1988, most spruce, fir, and other conifers atop North Carolina's Mt. Mitchell, the highest peak in the East, were dead after being damaged and weakened from being bathed in ozone and acid fog for years (Figure 9-13). The soil was so acidic that new seedlings could not survive.

Plant pathologist Robert Bruck warns that damage to mountaintop forests is an early warning that many tree species at lower elevations may soon die or be damaged by prolonged exposure to air pollution. Many scientists fear that elected officials in the United States will continue to delay establishing stricter controls on air pollution until it is too late to prevent a severe loss of valuable forest resources like that in Europe.

Air pollution, mostly by ozone, also threatens some types of crops—especially corn, wheat, soybeans, and peanuts—and is reducing U.S. crop production by 5% to 10%. In the United States, estimates of economic losses from reduced crop yields as a result of air pollution range from $1.9 billion to $5.4 billion a year.

DAMAGE TO AQUATIC LIFE Acid deposition has a severe impact on the aquatic life of freshwater lakes with low alkaline content or in areas where surrounding soils have little acid-buffering capacity (Figure 9-10). Much of the damage to aquatic life in the Northern Hemisphere is a result of *acid shock*. It is caused by the sudden runoff of large amounts of highly acidic water (along with toxic aluminum leached from the soil) into lakes and streams when snow melts in the spring or when heavy rains follow a period of drought. The alu-

A: Carbon dioxide (CO_2), CFCs, methane (CH_4), nitrous oxide (N_2), and water vapor (H_2O)

Table 9-1 Harmful Effects of Air Pollution on Materials

Material	Effects	Principal Air Pollutants
Stone and concrete	Surface erosion, discoloration, soiling	Sulfur dioxide, sulfuric acid, nitric acid, particulate matter
Metals	Corrosion, tarnishing, loss of strength	Sulfur dioxide, sulfuric acid, nitric acid, particulate matter, hydrogen sulfide
Ceramics and glass	Surface erosion	Hydrogen fluoride, particulate matter
Paints	Surface erosion, discoloration, soiling	Sulfur dioxide, hydrogen sulfide, ozone, particulate matter
Paper	Embrittlement, discoloration	Sulfur dioxide
Rubber	Cracking, loss of strength	Ozone
Leather	Surface deterioration, loss of strength	Sulfur dioxide
Textile fabrics	Deterioration, fading, soiling	Sulfur dioxide, nitrogen dioxide, ozone, particulate matter

Figure 9-14 This marble monument on a church in Surrey, England, has been damaged by exposure to acidic air pollutants.

Adrian P. Davies/Bruce Coleman Ltd.

minum leached from the soil and lake sediment kills fish by clogging their gills.

In Norway and Sweden, at least 16,000 lakes contain no fish, and an additional 52,000 have lost most of their acid-neutralizing capacity because of excess acidity. In Canada, some 14,000 lakes are almost fishless, and 150,000 more are in peril because of excess acidity.

In the United States, about 9,000 lakes are threatened with excess acidity, one-third of them seriously. Most are concentrated in the Northeast and the upper Middle West (mostly in parts of Minnesota, Wisconsin, and the upper Great Lakes), where 80% of the lakes and streams are threatened by excess acidity. Over 200 lakes in New York's Adirondack Mountains are too acidic to support fish. About 2.7% of the nation's streams are acidified.

Acidified lakes can be neutralized by treating them or the surrounding soil with large amounts of limestone. However, this approach is expensive and only a temporary Band-Aid that must be repeated. Furthermore, its long-term effects are unknown.

DAMAGE TO MATERIALS Each year, air pollutants cause billions of dollars in damage to various materials (Table 9-1). The fallout of soot and grit on buildings, cars, and clothing requires costly cleaning. Air pollutants break down exterior paint on cars and houses and deteriorate roofing materials. Irreplaceable marble statues, historic buildings, and stained-glass windows throughout the world have been pitted and discolored by air pollutants (Figure 9-14).

Q: What are the four principal sources of human emissions of greenhouse gases?

9-5 Controlling and Reducing Air Pollution

WAYS TO REDUCE POLLUTION Once a pollution control standard has been adopted, two general approaches can be used to prevent levels from exceeding the standard. One is *pollution prevention*, which prevents or reduces the severity of the problem. The other is *pollution cleanup*, which treats the symptoms. Eventually pollution cleanup is overwhelmed by increases in population and industrialization (Figure 1-12); it also creates environmental problems of its own, such as the need to dispose of the hazardous wastes removed from contaminated air and water.

The best methods for preventing or significantly reducing the total amount of pollution of any type from reaching the environment are

- Regulating population growth (Section 6-4)

- Reducing unnecessary waste of metals, paper, and other matter resources through increased recycling and reuse and by designing products that last longer and are easy to repair (Section 19-7)

- Reducing energy use (Section 18-5)

- Using energy more efficiently (Sections 17-2 and 18-5)

- Switching from coal to natural gas, which produces less pollution when burned (Section 18-1)

- Switching from fossil fuels and nuclear power (Chapter 18) to energy from the sun, wind, and flowing water (Chapter 17)

- Identifying the source of pollution in a production process, eliminating it from that process, and finding a more environmentally benign substitute

So far, these methods for preventing pollution have rarely been given serious consideration in national and international strategies for pollution control and energy use (Section 18-5).

U.S. AIR POLLUTION LEGISLATION In the United States, Congress passed the Clean Air Acts of 1970, 1977, and 1990, which gave the federal government considerable power to control air pollution. Each state is required to develop and enforce an implementation plan for attainment of these standards.

These laws required the EPA to establish *national ambient air quality standards (NAAQS)* for seven outdoor pollutants: suspended particulate matter, sulfur oxides, carbon monoxide, nitrogen oxides, ozone, hydrocarbons, and lead. Each standard specifies the maximum allowable level, averaged over a specific time period, for a certain pollutant in outdoor (ambient) air. The Clean Air Act of 1990 requires coal-burning power plants to cut their 1991 annual sulfur dioxide emissions roughly in half by 2000 or by 2005 if they switch to low-sulfur coal or other clean-coal technologies.

The Clean Air Act of 1990 uses market forces to help reduce pollution by allowing companies to buy and sell pollution rights for sulfur dioxide emissions from one another. With this *emissions trading policy*, companies that reduce their emissions below their limit would receive credit in the form of permits. They could then use those credits to avoid emission reductions in some of their existing or new facilities, or they could sell the permits to other companies. Instead of the government dictating how each company should meet its emissions target, this approach would let the marketplace determine the cheapest, most efficient way to get the job done. If this market approach works for reducing SO_2 emissions, it could be applied to other air and water pollutants.

The EPA has also established a policy of *prevention of significant deterioration (PSD)*. It is designed to prevent a decrease in air quality in regions where the air is cleaner than required by the NAAQS for suspended particulate matter and sulfur dioxide. Otherwise, industries would move into those areas and gradually degrade air quality to the national standards for these two pollutants.

The EPA is also required to establish *national emission standards* for less-common air pollutants capable of causing serious harm to human health at low concentrations. By 1990, the EPA had established emission standards for only 7 of the at-least 600 potentially toxic air pollutants scientists have identified. The Clean Air Act of 1990 requires industries to use the best available technology to reduce the industrial emissions of 189 toxic chemicals by 90% between 1995 and 2003.

Congress also set a timetable for achieving certain percentage reductions in emissions of carbon monoxide, hydrocarbons, and nitrogen oxides from motor vehicles. These standards forced automakers to build cars that emit six to eight times fewer pollutants than did the cars of the late 1960s. Although significant progress has been made, a series of legally allowed extensions has pushed deadlines for complete attainment of most of these goals into the future.

The Clean Air Act of 1990 requires reductions in auto emissions of hydrocarbons by 35% and of nitrogen oxides by 60% for all new cars by 1994. It also requires oil companies to sell cleaner-burning gasoline or other fuels in the nine dirtiest cities by 1995 and sell at least 150,000 electric or other clean-fuel vehicles in California by 1996.

TRENDS IN OUTDOOR AIR QUALITY There is still a long way to go, but since 1975 the United States has achieved significant progress in reducing outdoor air pollution from major outdoor pollutants: lead, carbon monoxide, ozone, sulfur dioxide, and suspended particulate matter. According to the Council on Environmental Quality, the Clean Air Act of 1970 has saved 14,000 lives and $21 billion in health, property, and other damages each year since 1970. Without the 1970 standards, emissions of major outdoor air pollutants would be 130% to 315% higher today.

However, most U.S. air pollution control laws are based on pollution cleanup rather than pollution prevention. Pollution cleanup is better than doing nothing, but the increase in new vehicles and other emission sources gradually overwhelms pollution control efforts. This, plus relaxing fuel efficiency standards and decreasing budgets for enforcement of air pollution laws during the 1980s, explains why levels of ozone and suspended particulate matter increased and nitrogen dioxide levels have stayed roughly the same since 1986. According to the EPA, more than half the people in the United States lived in communities polluted by too much smog in 1989.

The only air pollutant with a sharp drop (91%) in its atmospheric level was lead, which was virtually banned in gasoline. This shows the effectiveness of the pollution prevention approach. If the current 4% annual growth in the distance vehicles travel in the United States continues, annual emissions of nitrogen dioxide, carbon monoxide, and hydrocarbons will rise about 40% by 2009.

In the 1970s, most western European countries, Canada, Australia, Japan, and South Korea established automobile emissions standards similar to those in the United States, although some European countries lag behind. Brazil will have similar standards by 1997. Little, if any, attempt is made to control vehicle emissions in India, Mexico (Figure 6-14), Argentina, China, the CIS, and eastern European countries. Switzerland and Austria have the world's toughest air pollution control laws.

CONTROL OF SULFUR DIOXIDE EMISSIONS FROM STATIONARY SOURCES In addition to the general prevention methods mentioned at the beginning of this section, the following approaches can lower sulfur dioxide emissions or reduce their effects:

Prevention

1. *Burn low-sulfur coal.* Especially useful for new power and industrial plants located near deposits of such coal.

2. *Remove sulfur from coal.* Fairly inexpensive; present methods remove only 20% to 50% but new methods being tested may remove most of the sulfur.

3. *Convert coal to a gas or liquid fuel.* Low net energy yield (Figure 3-20).

4. *Remove sulfur during combustion by fluidized-bed combustion (FBC) of coal* (Figure 9-15). Removes up to 90% of the SO_2, reduces CO_2 by 20%, and increases energy efficiency by 5%; should be com-

mercially available for small to medium plants in the mid-1990s.

5. *Remove sulfur during combustion by limestone-injection multiple burning (LIMB).* Still in the development and testing stage.

Dispersion or Cleanup

1. *Use smokestacks tall enough (see photo on p. 181) to pierce the thermal inversion layer* (Figure 9-6). Can decrease pollution near power or industrial plants, but increases pollution levels in downwind areas.

2. *Remove pollutants after combustion by using flue gas scrubbers* (Figure 9-16d). Removes up to 95% of SO_2 and 99.9% of suspended particulate matter (but not the more harmful fine particles); can be used in new plants and added to most existing large plants, but is expensive; leaves *slurry*, a sludge that must be disposed of safely or converted into chemicals for use as fertilizers, catalysts, and construction materials.

3. *Remove SO_2 after combustion by using an organic amine scrubber.* Removes 95% of SO_2 and is about one-third cheaper than flue gas scrubbing; organic amine salt can be regenerated by heating, resulting in virtually no waste disposal problem.

4. *Add a tax on each unit emitted.* Encourages development of more efficient and cost-effective methods of emissions control; opposed by industry because it costs more than tall smokestacks and requires polluters to bear more of the harmful cost passed on to society (Section 7-2).

By 1985, the former Soviet Union and 21 European countries had signed a treaty agreeing to reduce their annual emissions of sulfur dioxide from 1980 levels by at least 30% by 1993; 4 countries agreed to 70% cuts. While that is an important step, ecologists believe that SO_2 emissions must be cut by about 90% to prevent continuing serious ecological damage. Between 1983 and 1989, the former West Germany cut power plant emissions of sulfur dioxide by 90%, and Switzerland and Austria reduced their emissions by more than 90%. The United States and Great Britain refused to participate in this historic but moderate agreement, citing the need for more research on the harmful effects of sulfur dioxide.

CONTROL OF EMISSIONS OF NITROGEN OXIDES FROM STATIONARY SOURCES About half the mass of emissions of nitrogen oxides in the United States comes from the burning of fossil fuels at stationary sources, primarily electric power and industrial plants. The rest comes mostly from motor vehicles.

So far, little emphasis has been placed on reducing emissions of nitrogen oxides from stationary sources because control of sulfur dioxide and particulates was considered more important. Now it is clear that nitro-

Q: What greenhouse gas is being emitted to the atmosphere in the largest quantity as a result of human activities?

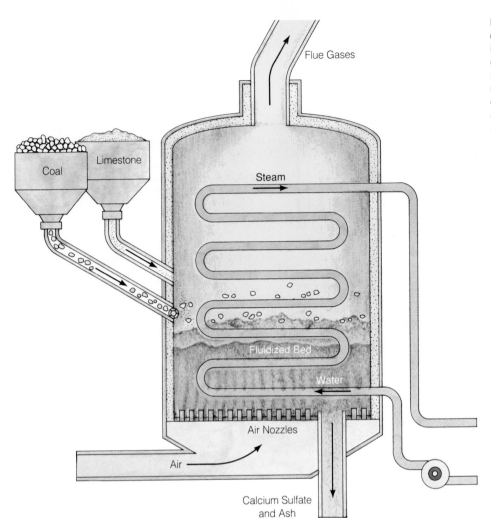

Figure 9-15 Fluidized-bed combustion (FBC) of coal. A stream of hot air is blown into a boiler to suspend a mixture of powdered coal and crushed limestone. This removes most of the sulfur dioxide, sharply reduces emissions of nitrogen oxides, and burns coal more efficiently and cheaply than do conventional combustion methods.

gen oxides are a major contributor to acid deposition and that they increase tropospheric levels of ozone and other photochemical oxidants that can damage crops, trees, and materials. The following approaches can be used to decrease emissions of nitrogen oxides from stationary sources:

Prevention

1. *Remove nitrogen oxides during fluidized-bed combustion (Figure 9-15). Removes 50% to 75%.*

2. *Remove during combustion by limestone-injection multiple burning. Removes 50% to 60%, but is still being developed.*

3. *Reduce by decreasing combustion temperatures.* Well-established technology that reduces production of these gases by 50% to 60%.

Dispersion or Cleanup

1. *Use tall smokestacks.*

2. *Add a tax for each unit emitted.*

3. *Remove after combustion by reburning.* Removes 50% or more, but is still under development for large plants.

4. *Remove after burning by reacting with isocyanic acid (HCNO). Removes up to 99% and breaks down into harmless nitrogen and water; will not be available commercially for at least 10 years.*

5. *Remove after combustion in flue gas scrubbers (Figure 9-16d) by adding phosphorus.* The effectiveness of this new technology is being evaluated.

In 1988, representatives from 24 countries, including the United States, signed an agreement that would freeze emissions of nitrogen oxides at 1987 levels by 1995. Twelve western European countries agreed to cut emissions of nitrogen oxides by 30% between 1987 and 1997. Environmentalists applaud these efforts but believe that a 90% reduction in these emissions is needed to prevent continuing serious ecological damage.

Figure 9-16 Four commonly used methods for removing particulates from the exhaust gases of electric power and industrial plants. The wet scrubber is also used to reduce sulfur dioxide emissions.

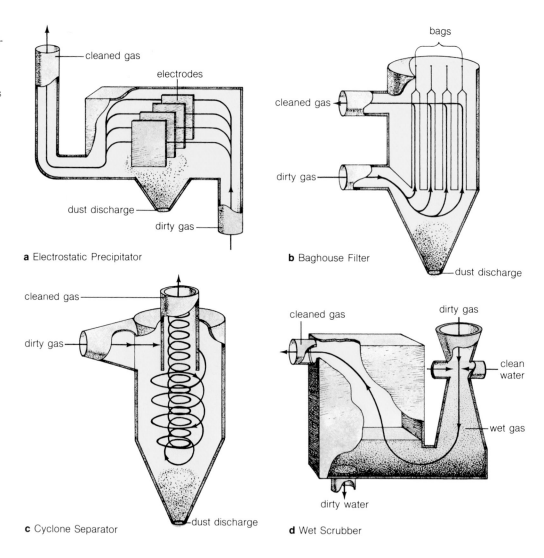

a Electrostatic Precipitator

b Baghouse Filter

c Cyclone Separator

d Wet Scrubber

CONTROL OF PARTICULATE MATTER EMISSIONS FROM STATIONARY SOURCES The only way to prevent emissions of suspended particulate matter is to convert coal into a gas or liquid (Section 18-2), a method that is expensive and low in net energy yield (Figure 3-20). The following cleanup approaches can be used to decrease emissions of suspended particulate matter from stationary sources:

Dispersion or Cleanup

1. *Use tall smokestacks.*

2. *Add a tax on each unit emitted.*

3. *Remove particulates from stack exhaust gases.* This approach is widely used in electric power and industrial plants. Several methods are in use: **(a)** electrostatic precipitators (Figure 9-16a); **(b)** baghouse filters (Figure 9-16b); **(c)** cyclone separators (Figure 9-16c); and **(d)** wet scrubbers (Figure 9-16d). Except for baghouse filters, none of these methods removes many of the more hazardous fine parti-

cles; all produce hazardous solid waste or sludge that must be disposed of safely; except for cyclone separators, all methods are expensive.

CONTROL OF EMISSIONS FROM MOTOR VEHICLES The following are other methods for decreasing emissions from motor vehicles:

Prevention

1. *Rely more on mass transit, bicycles, and walking.*

2. *Shift to less-polluting automobile engines.* Examples are the stratified charge engine, engines that run on hydrogen gas (Section 17-8), or electric motors (if the additional electricity needed to charge batteries is not produced by fossil-fuel-burning power plants or by expensive and potentially dangerous nuclear power plants). The government could overcome the auto industry's resistance to producing such engines by specifying smog-free engines on the $5 billion worth of vehicles it buys each year.

Q: What percentage of current CO_2 emissions is caused by burning fossil fuels?

3. *Shift to less-polluting fuels.* Examples are natural gas (Section 18-1), alcohols (Section 17-6), and hydrogen gas (Section 17-8).

4. *Improve fuel efficiency.* The quickest and most cost-effective approach (Section 17-1), which unfortunately is not being used (Section 18-5).

5. *Modify the internal combustion engine to reduce emissions.* Burning gasoline using a lean, or more air-rich, mixture reduces carbon monoxide and hydrocarbon emissions but increases emissions of nitrogen oxides; a new lean-burn engine that reduces emissions of nitrogen oxides by 75% to 90% may be available in about 10 years.

6. *Raise annual registration fees on older, more-polluting, gas-guzzling (petro-pig) cars, or offer owners an incentive to retire such cars.*

7. *Add a charge on all new cars based on the amount of the key pollutants emitted by the engine according to EPA tests.* This would prod manufacturers to reduce emissions and encourage consumers to buy less-polluting cars.

8. *Give subsidies to carmakers for each low-polluting, energy-efficient car they sell.* This would allow consumers to pay less for this type of vehicle and much more for polluting gas guzzlers.

9. *Give buyers federally subsidized rebates when they buy low-polluting, energy-efficient cars and charge them fees when they buy more-polluting, energy-inefficient cars.* Revenues from the fees would be used to provide the rebates.

10. *Restrict driving in downtown areas.*

Cleanup

1. *Use emission control devices.* Most widely used approach, with a new car today emitting 95% fewer pollutants than an uncontrolled car; engines must be kept well tuned for such devices to work effectively; current catalytic converters increase carbon dioxide emissions, which can enhance global warming; three-way catalytic converters now being developed can decrease pollutants further and should be available within a few years.

2. *Require car inspections twice a year and have drivers exceeding the standards pay an emission charge based on the grams of pollutants emitted per kilometer and the number of kilometers driven since the last inspection.* This would encourage drivers not to tamper with emission control devices and to keep them in good working order. Currently, the emission control systems on about 50% of the U.S. car and light-truck fleet have been disconnected or are not working properly.

3. *Establish emission standards for light-duty trucks* (presently not effectively regulated by U.S. air pollution control laws).

CONTROL OF TROPOSPHERE OZONE LEVELS

Ozone levels in the troposphere are mostly the result of photochemical smog, which forms when nitrogen oxides and hydrocarbons interact with sunlight (Figure 9-5). Thus, decreasing ozone levels involves combining the prevention and cleanup methods already discussed for nitrogen oxides and for motor vehicles.

It also involves decreasing hydrocarbon emissions from cars, which produce half of the pollutants that cause smog, and from a variety of hard-to-control sources, such as oil-based paints, aerosol propellants, dry-cleaning plants, and gas stations, which together emit the other half.

In 1989, California's South Coast Air Quality Management District Council proposed a drastic program to reduce ozone and photochemical smog in the Los Angeles area. If approved by the state environmental agency and the EPA, this plan would require

- Outlawing drive-through facilities to keep vehicles from idling in lines

- Substantially raising parking fees and assessing high fees for families owning more than one car to discourage automobile use and encourage car and van pooling and use of mass transit

- Strictly controlling or relocating petroleum refining, dry-cleaning, auto-painting, printing, baking, and trash-burning plants and other industries that release large quantities of hydrocarbons and other pollutants

- Finding substitutes for or banning use of aerosol propellants, paints, household cleaners, barbecue starter fluids, and other consumer products that release hydrocarbons

- Gradually eliminating gasoline-burning engines over two decades by converting trucks, buses, and lawn mowers to run on electricity or on alternative fuels such as methanol, ethanol, or natural gas (Section 17-6)

- Requiring gas stations to use a hydrocarbon-vapor recovery system on gas pumps and sell alternative fuels

- Banning 70% of any fleet's trucks from streets during weekday morning and evening rush hours

The plan may be defeated by public opinion when residents begin to feel the economic pinch from such drastic changes. But proponents argue that the economic costs in health and other external costs of not carrying out such a program will cost consumers and businesses much more. Such measures are a glimpse of what most cities will have to do as people, cars, and industries proliferate.

CONTROL OF INDOOR AIR POLLUTION For most people, indoor air pollution poses a much greater threat to health than does outdoor air pollution. Yet, the EPA

The most important thing you can do to reduce air pollution and ozone depletion, slow projected global climate change, and save money is to improve energy efficiency (see Individuals Matter inside the back cover and Section 17-1).

Recycle newspapers, aluminum, and other materials. Decrease your emissions of ozone-depleting chlorofluorocarbons (Section 10-5) and greenhouse gases (Section 10-3). Lobby for much stricter national clean air laws and enforcement and for development of international treaties to slow projected global warming and reduce depletion of ozone in the stratosphere (Chapter 10).

Protect yourself from most indoor air pollutants by:

- Testing for radon and taking corrective measures as needed (see Case Study on p. 186).

- Installing air-to-air heat exchangers or regularly ventilating your house by opening windows.

- Avoiding the purchase of formaldehyde products or using "low-emitting formaldehyde" or non-formaldehyde building materials.

- Reducing indoor levels of formaldehyde and several other toxic gases by using house plants such as the spider or airplane plant (the most effective), golden pothos, syngonium, philodendron (especially the elephant-ear species), chrysanthemum, azalea, poinsettia, dieffenbachia, and Gerbera daisy. About 20 plants can help clean the air in a typical home. Plants should be potted with a mixture of soil and granular charcoal (which absorbs organic air pollutants).

- Baking unoccupied houses (especially mobile or manufactured homes) out at 38°C (100°F) for three to four days and then changing the air several times.

- Testing your house or workplace for asbestos fiber levels if it was built before 1980.

- Changing air filters regularly, cleaning air conditioning systems, emptying dehumidifier water trays frequently, and not storing gasoline, solvents, or other volatile hazardous chemicals inside a home or attached garage.

- Not using commercial room deodorizers or air fresheners (see Individuals Matter inside the back cover for safe alternatives).

- Not using any aerosol spray products.

- Not smoking or smoking outside or in a closed room vented to the outside.

- Attaching whole-house electrostatic air cleaners and charcoal filters to central heating and air conditioning equipment. Humidifiers, however, can load indoor air with bacteria, mildew, and viruses.

- Making sure that wood-burning stoves and fireplaces are properly installed, vented, and maintained. If you use a wood stove for heating, buy one of the newer, more energy-efficient models that greatly reduce indoor and outdoor pollution.

spends $200 million a year trying to reduce outdoor air pollution and only $2 million a year on indoor air pollution.

To sharply reduce indoor air pollution, it's not necessary to establish mandatory indoor air quality standards and monitor the more than 100 million homes and buildings in the United States. Instead this can be done by:

- Modifying building codes to prevent radon infiltration or requiring use of air-to-air heat exchangers or other devices to change indoor air at certain intervals

- Removing some of the hazardous materials in furniture and building materials in new and older homes, apartments, and workplaces by moving people out, baking these structures out at 38°C (100°F) for three to four days, and then using a fan to exhaust and replace the contaminated air several times

- Requiring exhaust hoods or vent pipes for stoves, refrigerators, dryers, kerosene heaters, or other appliances burning natural gas or other fossil fuel

- Setting emission standards for building materials that emit formaldehyde, such as particleboard, plywood, some types of insulation, and materials used in furniture, carpets, and carpet backing

- Finding substitutes for potentially harmful chemicals in aerosols, cleaning compounds, paints, and other products used indoors (see Individuals Matter inside the back cover) and requiring all such products to have labels listing their ingredients

- Requiring employers to provide safe indoor air for employees

In LDCs, significant reductions in respiratory illnesses would occur if governments gave rural residents and poor people in cities simple stoves that burn biofuels more efficiently (which would also reduce deforestation) and that are vented outside.

PROTECTING THE ATMOSPHERE Important progress has been made in reducing the levels of several outdoor air pollutants in the United States and many other MDCs, but much more needs to be done. Few

Q: How much must global CO_2 emissions be cut by 2030 to slow projected global warming to an acceptable rate?

LDCs have begun to tackle their air pollution problems, which are increasing as these countries become more urbanized and more industrialized.

Protecting our commonly shared atmosphere will require the following significant changes:

- Emphasizing pollution prevention rather than pollution control in both MDCs and LDCs.

- Recognizing that the burning of fossil fuels is the primary cause of air pollution, reducing use of these fuels (especially coal), and reducing unnecessary waste of these fuels (Section 17-2).

- Integrating air pollution, water pollution, and energy policies with primary emphasis on improving energy efficiency; shifting from fossil fuels to perpetual and renewable energy resources (Chapter 17 and Section 18-5); discouraging automobile use; boosting the use of public transportation; revamping transportation systems and urban design; increasing recycling and reuse; and reducing the production of all forms of waste.

- Developing air quality strategies based on the air flows and pollution sources for an entire region instead of the current piecemeal, city-by-city approach.

- Controlling population growth (Section 6-4).

- Recognizing that all nations and all individuals (see Individuals Matter on p. 202) have a responsibility to protect the atmosphere—a regional and global common property resource shared by all. There is no away.

Protecting our air supply will require major modifications in our economic systems (Sections 7-2 and 7-3). As long as most of the external costs of air pollution and other forms of pollution are not included in the market prices of goods and services, industries, utilities, and individuals will have little incentive to reduce the amount of pollution they generate. We must heed the advice that Chief Seattle gave us more than 200 years ago: "Contaminate your bed, and you will one night suffocate in your own waste." It is not too late, if we act now.

Turning the corner on air pollution requires moving beyond patchwork, end-of-pipe approaches to confront pollution at its sources. This will mean reorienting energy, transportation, and industrial structures toward prevention.

HILARY F. FRENCH

DISCUSSION TOPICS

1. Rising oil and natural gas prices and environmental concerns over nuclear power plants could force the United States to depend more on coal, its most plentiful fossil fuel, for producing electric power. Comment on this in terms of air pollution. Would you favor a return to coal instead of increased use of nuclear power? Explain.

2. Evaluate the pros and cons of the statement: "Since we have not proven absolutely that anyone has died or suffered serious disease from nitrogen oxides, present federal emission standards for this pollutant should be relaxed."

3. What topographical and climate factors either increase or help decrease air pollution in your community?

4. Should all tall smokestacks be banned? Explain.

*5. Do buildings in your college or university contain asbestos? If so, what is being done about this potential health hazard?

*6. Have dormitories and other buildings on your campus been tested for radon? If so, what were the results and what has been done about areas with unacceptable levels? If this testing has not been done, talk with school officials about having it done.

CHAPTER 10

CLIMATE, GLOBAL WARMING, OZONE DEPLETION, AND NUCLEAR WAR: ULTIMATE PROBLEMS

General Questions and Issues

1. What are the most important factors determining variations in climate?

2. How can our activities cause global warming, and what are its possible effects?

3. What can we do to delay and reduce possible global warming and adjust to its effects?

4. How are we depleting ozone in the stratosphere, and what are possible effects of doing so?

5. What can we do to slow down ozone depletion?

6. What effects might even limited nuclear war have on Earth's life-support systems for humans and many other species?

We, humanity, have finally done it: disturbed the environment on a global scale.

THOMAS E. LOVEJOY

CLIMATE IS THE PRIMARY FACTOR determining the types, distribution, and abundance of Earth's biodiversity (Figure 5-3). It is also the major factor affecting where we can grow food, have enough water, and live and is a key natural resource supporting our economic activities. We and many types of plants and other animals also survive because a thin, fragile gauze of ozone in the stratosphere (Figure 9-1) keeps much of the harmful ultraviolet radiation given off by the sun (Figure 3-4) from reaching the earth's surface.

Although our species has been on Earth for only an eyeblink of its overall existence, we are now altering the chemical content of Earth's entire atmosphere 10 to 100 times faster than its natural rate of change over the past 100,000 years (see cartoon). Projected global warming brought about by our one-time binge of fossil-fuel burning (Figure 3-7) and tropical deforestation (Section 15-2), depletion of life-sustaining ozone in the stratosphere caused by our widespread use of chlorofluorocarbons and other chemicals that we could learn to do without, and the buildup of nuclear weapons are now formidable global environmental threats.

Largely invisible and silent, these problems will continue building until we reach significant thresholds of change. When those thresholds are crossed, it will be too late to prevent the drastic, lasting, and unpredictable effects these problems have on the ecosphere that supports us and other species. There will be no place for us to escape to and no place to hide from the effects of these global changes. Dealing with these planetary emergencies to prevent the ultimate tragedy of the commons for our species and many other species will require significant changes in the way we think and act as well as international cooperation on an unprecedented scale.

10-1 Climate: A Brief Introduction

WEATHER AND CLIMATE Every moment, there are changes in temperature, barometric pressure, humidity, precipitation, sunshine (solar radiation), cloud cover, wind direction and speed, and other conditions in the troposphere (Figure 9-1). These short-term changes in the properties of the troposphere at a given place and time are what we call **weather**.

Climate is the average weather of an area. It is the general pattern of atmospheric or weather conditions, seasonal variations, and weather extremes in a region over a long period—at least 30 years. The two most important factors determining the climate of an area are the temperature with its seasonal variations and the quantity and distribution of precipitation over each year.

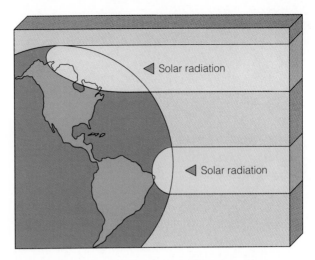

Figure 10-1 Solar energy doesn't strike all parts of Earth equally. Throughout the year, the sun's rays strike the area of Earth around the equator directly, concentrating heat and light on that part of the planet.

CLIMATE AND GLOBAL AIR CIRCULATION Several factors determine the patterns of global air circulation that in turn cause the uneven patterns of average temperature and average precipitation and thus the climates of the world (Figure 5-2). One is differences in the amount of solar energy striking parts of Earth's surface so that air is heated much more at the equator than at the poles (Figure 10-1).

The large input of heat at and near the equator warms large masses of air that rise because warm air has a lower density (mass per unit of volume) than cold air. As these warm air masses rise, they spread northward and southward, carrying heat from the equator toward the poles.

At the poles, the warm air cools and sinks downward because cool air is denser than warm air. These cool air masses then flow back near the surface to the equator to fill the void left by rising warm air masses. This general global air circulation pattern in the troposphere leads to warm average temperatures near the equator, cold average temperatures near the poles, and moderate or temperate average temperatures at the middle latitudes between the two regions (Figure 5-2).

This general north-south circulation is broken up into six huge cells of swirling air masses (three north of the equator and three south of the equator) because of forces created in the atmosphere as Earth rotates on its axis (Figure 10-2). The movement of large air masses through these cells establishes the direction of prevailing east and west winds (movements of air masses) that distribute air and moisture over Earth's surface. This distribution affects the climate, which is the primary factor determining the general types of vegetation found at different latitudes (Figures 5-3 and 5-4). Seasonal variations in climate in parts of the world away from the equator are caused by Earth's annual revolution around the sun and its daily rotation on its tilted axis (Figure 10-3), which both tip parts of Earth toward or away from the sun.

CLIMATE AND OCEAN CURRENTS Earth's rotation, the inclination of its axis, prevailing winds, and differences in water density cause ocean currents and surface drifts that generally move parallel with the equator (Figure 10-4). Trade winds blowing almost continuously from the east toward the equator push surface ocean waters westward in the Atlantic, Pacific, and Indian oceans until these waters bounce off the nearest continent. This causes several large circular water movements, called *gyres*, that turn clockwise in the Northern Hemisphere and counterclockwise in the Southern Hemisphere (Figure 10-4). These gyres move warm waters to the north and to the south of the equator.

Ocean currents and surface drifts, like air currents, redistribute heat and thus influence climate and the types of terrestrial vegetation that can be supported, especially near coastal areas. Without the warm Gulf Stream, which transports 25 times more water than all the world's rivers, the climate of northwestern Europe would be more like that of the subarctic. The mild, wet climate of the Pacific Northwest is largely a result of the California Current. Ocean currents and drifts also help mix ocean waters and distribute nutrients and dissolved oxygen needed by aquatic organisms.

CLIMATE AND THE CHEMICAL COMPOSITION OF THE ATMOSPHERE: THE GREENHOUSE EFFECT AND THE OZONE LAYER Fairly small amounts of carbon dioxide and water vapor (mostly in clouds) and trace amounts of ozone, methane, nitrous oxide, chlorofluorocarbons, and other gases in the troposphere play a key role in determining Earth's average temperatures and thus its climates.

These gases, known as **greenhouse gases**, act somewhat like the glass panes of a greenhouse or of a

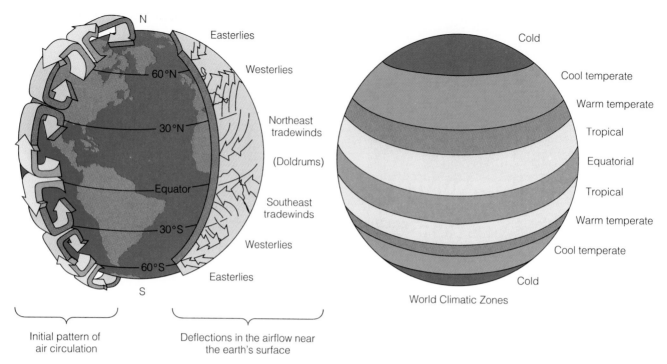

Figure 10-2 Formation of prevailing surface winds that disrupt the general flow of air from the equator, north and south to the poles, and back to the equator. As Earth rotates, its surface turns faster beneath air masses at the equator and slower below those at the poles. This deflects air masses moving north and south to the west or east, creating six huge cells in which air swirls upward through a corkscrew pathway and down toward Earth's surface at different latitudes. The direction of air movement in these cells sets up belts of prevailing winds that distribute air and moisture over Earth's surface and affect the general types of climate found in different areas.

car parked in the sun with its windows rolled up. These gases allow light, infrared radiation (heat), and some ultraviolet radiation from the sun to pass through the troposphere. Earth's surface then absorbs much of this solar energy and degrades it to infrared radiation (heat), which rises into the troposphere (Figure 4-4). Some of this heat escapes into space, and some is absorbed by molecules of greenhouse gases, thus warming the air. This heat is then radiated back toward the earth's surface. This trapping of heat in the troposphere is called the **greenhouse effect** (Figure 10-5).

Without our current heat-trapping blanket of gases, Earth's average surface temperature would be −18°C (0°F) instead of its current 15°C (59°F), and life as we know it would not exist. Thus, we and other species benefit from the right level of Earth's greenhouse effect, with only minor and slow fluctuations. Too much warming or cooling, especially if it occurs over a few decades instead of the normal hundreds to thousands of years, would be disastrous for us and many other species.

Ozone (O_3) is formed in the stratosphere as a result of the interaction between the sun's ultraviolet rays and regular oxygen molecules (O_2). In addition to filtering out harmful ultraviolet radiation, ozone in the stratosphere affects climate. Absorption of UV radiation by ozone creates warm layers of air high in the stratosphere that prevent churning gases in the troposphere from

entering the stratosphere (Figure 9-1). This thermal cap is an important factor in determining the average temperature of the troposphere and thus Earth's current climates.

Any human activities that decrease the amount of ozone in the stratosphere and increase the amount of greenhouse gases in the troposphere can have far-reaching effects on climate, human health, economic and social systems, and the health and existence of other species. Numerous measurements reveal that we are depleting ozone in the stratosphere and increasing the concentrations of various greenhouse gases in the troposphere.

PAST CLIMATE CHANGES By examining the fossil evidence of climate-sensitive organisms and the composition of rock strata and ice cores, scientists have tried to piece together a crude picture of Earth's past climatic history. This scientific detective work—which is preliminary and often speculative—suggests that the estimated average surface temperature of the earth has fluctuated considerably over geologic time. It indicates that over the past 800,000 years, there have been several great ice ages, during which much of the planet was covered with thick ice sheets. Each glacial period lasted about 100,000 years and was followed by a warmer interglacial period lasting 10,000 to 12,500 years.

Q: How many trees would each person in the world have to plant and tend each year to offset CO_2 emissions?

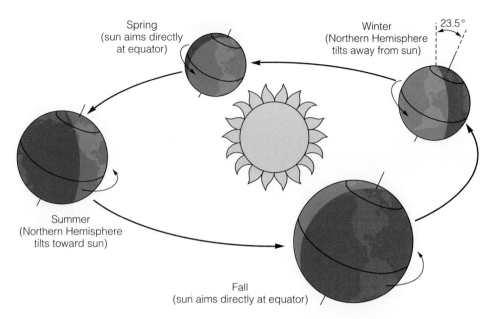

Spring
(sun aims directly
at equator)

Winter
(Northern Hemisphere
tilts away from sun)

23.5°

Summer
(Northern Hemisphere
tilts toward sun)

Fall
(sun aims directly at equator)

Figure 10-3 Seasonal changes in climate (shown here for the Northern Hemisphere only) are caused by variations in the amount of solar energy reaching various areas as Earth makes its annual revolution around the sun on an axis (an imaginary line connecting the North and South poles) tilted about 23.5 degrees. As Earth revolves around the sun, various regions are tipped toward or away from the sun.

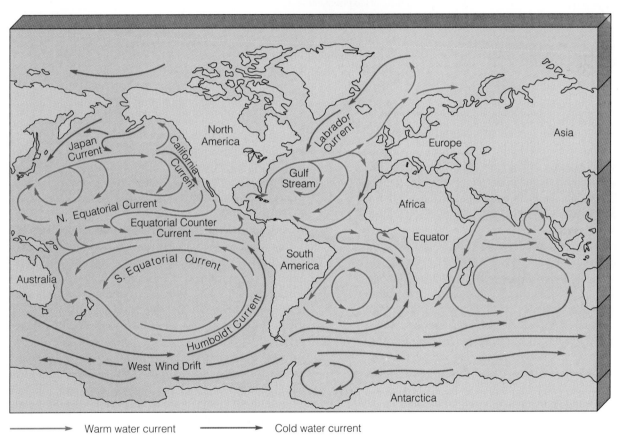

→ Warm water current   → Cold water current

Figure 10-4 The principal warm and cold surface currents of the world's oceans. These water movements are produced by Earth's winds and modified by its rotational forces (Figure 10-2). They circulate water in the oceans in great surface gyres and have profound effects on the climate of adjacent lands.

The last great ice age ended about 10,000 years ago, when agriculture began. At the coldest point of that ice age, the mean temperature of Earth's surface was only about 5°C (9°F) cooler than it is today. A fluctuation of this magnitude, up or down, is considered a significant temperature change and leads to drastic changes in cli-

mate throughout the world. As the ice melted, average sea levels rose about 100 meters (300 feet), changing the ecological face of the earth.

During the warm interglacial period we now live in, Earth's mean surface temperatures have fluctuated only moderately, typically up or down 0.5°C to 1°C

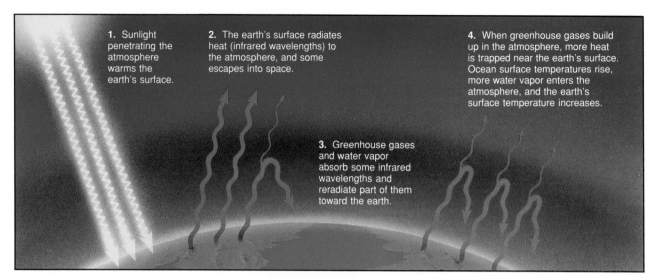

1. Sunlight penetrating the atmosphere warms the earth's surface.

2. The earth's surface radiates heat (infrared wavelengths) to the atmosphere, and some escapes into space.

3. Greenhouse gases and water vapor absorb some infrared wavelengths and reradiate part of them toward the earth.

4. When greenhouse gases build up in the atmosphere, more heat is trapped near the earth's surface. Ocean surface temperatures rise, more water vapor enters the atmosphere, and the earth's surface temperature increases.

Figure 10-5 The greenhouse effect. Without the atmospheric warming provided by this effect, Earth would be a cold and mostly lifeless planet. However, we are adding such large quantities of greenhouse gases to the atmosphere that computer models project a significant warming of the troposphere in only about 50 years—many times the rate at which changes in Earth's average atmospheric temperature have taken place during its long history. If warming (or cooling) of the planet's atmosphere should take place in such a relatively short time, places where we could grow food and have adequate water supplies would shift faster than our ability to adapt and develop new systems of food production and water distribution. Many analysts consider this the most serious environmental problem we face. (Used by permission from Cecie Starr, *Biology: Concepts and Applications*, Belmont, Calif.: Wadsworth, 1991)

(0.9°F to 1.8°F), over 100- to 200-year periods. These moderate and relatively slow fluctuations in climate have not led to drastic changes in the nature of soils and vegetation patterns throughout the world and thus have allowed large increases in food production, enabling the human population to grow to 5.5 billion in a fairly short time (Figure 1-2).

The greatest threat to human food production and economic systems and to wildlife habitats is rapid climate change, which would involve only a few degrees change (up or down) in Earth's mean surface temperature over a few decades. Conditions would change faster than some species, especially vegetation that supports animal species, could adapt or migrate to other areas. Such rapid changes in climate would shift the areas where we could grow food. Some areas would become uninhabitable because of lack of water or because of flooding from a rise in average sea levels.

10-2 Global Warming from an Enhanced Greenhouse Effect

RISING LEVELS OF GREENHOUSE GASES Until recently, most greenhouse gases were emitted and removed from the troposphere by Earth's major biogeochemical cycles without disruptive interferences from human activities. However, since the Industrial Revolution, and especially since 1950, we have been putting enormous quantities of greenhouse gases into the atmosphere (Figure 10-6), primarily from the burning of fossil fuels (57%), use of chlorofluorocarbons (17%), agriculture (15%), and deforestation (8%, although some put it as high as 30%). There is considerable concern that these gases can amplify the natural greenhouse effect and turn up the planet's thermostat fairly rapidly.

Satellite and other measurements indicate that carbon dioxide currently accounts for about 54% of the annual human-caused input of greenhouse gases, chlorofluorocarbons (CFCs) for 14%, methane for 18%, and nitrous oxide for 6%. The last three gases have a much greater warming effect per molecule than does carbon dioxide (Figure 10-6). MDCs, with only 22% of the world's population, produce more than half of all greenhouse-gas emissions, with the United States responsible for almost one-fourth of these emissions. It is followed by the CIS, European countries, China, Brazil, India, Japan, and Indonesia.

Carbon dioxide is released when carbon or any carbon-containing compound is burned. Fossil fuels provide almost 80% of the world's energy (Figure 3-6), cause about 75% of current CO_2 emissions, and produce most of the world's air pollution. The carbon dioxide level in the troposphere is now the highest it has been in at least 130,000 years, and the level is rising. The United States is by far the largest emitter of CO_2 (20% of the world's emissions), followed by the CIS. Thus, the projected global warming crisis, along with greatly increased air pollution, is largely an *energy crisis* caused

Q: What is the average amount of CO_2 each person in the United States adds to the atmosphere each year?

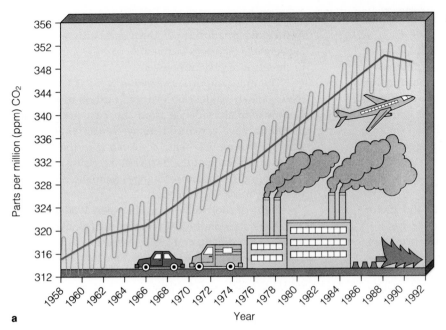

Figure 10-6 Increases in average concentrations of greenhouse gases in the troposphere, mostly because of human activities. (Data from Electric Power Research Institute. Adapted by permission from Cecie Starr and Ralph Taggart, *Biology: The Unity and Diversity of Life*, 6th ed., Belmont, Calif.: Wadsworth, 1992)

a. Carbon dioxide (CO_2) This gas is responsible for 54% of the human-caused input of greenhouse gases. The main sources are fossil-fuel burning (67%) and deforestation (33%). CO_2 remains in the atmosphere for about 500 years. Industrial countries account for about 76% of annual emissions.

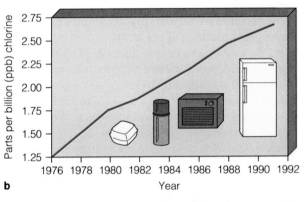

b. Chlorofluorocarbons (CFCs) These gases are responsible for 14% of the human input of greenhouse gases and by 2020 will probably be responsible for about 25% of the input. CFCs also deplete ozone in the stratosphere. The main sources are leaking air conditioners and refrigerators, evaporation of industrial solvents, production of plastic foams, and propellants in aerosol spray cans (in some countries). CFCs remain in the atmosphere for 65 to 111 years, depending on the type, and generally have 10,000 to 20,000 times the impact per molecule on global warming that each molecule of CO_2 has. However, this heating effect in the troposphere is offset somewhat by the cooling of the troposphere when CFCs deplete ozone in the stratosphere.

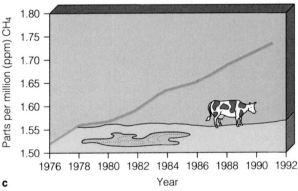

c. Methane (CH_4) This gas is responsible for about 18% of the human input of greenhouse gases. It is produced by bacteria that decompose organic matter in oxygen-poor environments. About 40% of global methane emissions come from oxygen-poor environments such as waterlogged soils, bogs, marshes, and rice paddies. A 1°C (1.8°F) warming may increase methane emissions from these sources by 20% to 30% and amplify global warming. Other sources of methane are landfills; burning of forests and grasslands; the guts of termites whose populations are expanding to digest the dead woody materials left after deforestation; and the digestive tracts of the billions of cattle, sheep, pigs, goats, horses, and other livestock. Some methane also leaks from coal seams, natural gas wells, pipelines, storage tanks, furnaces, dryers, and stoves. Natural sources produce an estimated one-third of the methane in the atmosphere, and human activities produce the rest. CH_4 remains in the troposphere for 7 to 10 years, and each molecule is about 25 times more effective in warming the troposphere than is a molecule of carbon dioxide.

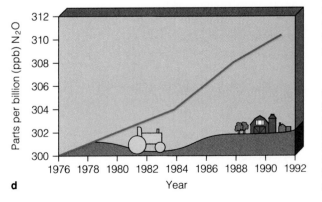

d. Nitrous oxide (N_2O) This gas is responsible for 6% of the human-caused input of greenhouse gases. It is released from nylon production, biomass burning, and the breakdown of nitrogen fertilizers in soil, livestock wastes, and nitrate-contaminated groundwater. Its average stay in the troposphere is 150 years. It also depletes ozone in the stratosphere. The global warming from each molecule of this gas is about 230 times that of a CO_2 molecule.

A: 16.7 metric tons (18 tons)—six times more than the average citizen of an LDC

by rapid, large-scale, and wasteful burning of the world's fossil fuels.

To make matters worse, we are reducing Earth's ability to remove carbon dioxide through photosynthesis by deforestation around the globe (Section 15-2) — accounting for about 20% of the increase in carbon dioxide levels. The EPA projects that unless action is taken to reduce fossil-fuel burning and deforestation, global emissions of carbon dioxide, the major greenhouse gas, will more than double between 1985 and 2025, with emissions doubling in MDCs and quadrupling in LDCs.

Modern farming, forestry, industries, and motor vehicles are also releasing other greenhouse gases — mostly methane, nitrous oxide, chlorofluorocarbons, and ozone formed in smog — into the troposphere at an accelerating rate (Figure 10-6b, c, and d). In 1992, a controversial analysis suggested that nitrogen oxides (NO and NO_2) emitted by high-flying aircraft are responsible for a small but growing input of greenhouse gases into the atmosphere.

PROJECTED GLOBAL WARMING Almost all scientists who have studied the matter agree on several points: **(1)** the greenhouse effect is real and allows most of Earth's current forms of life to exist, **(2)** concentrations of greenhouse gases in the atmosphere are increasing rapidly (Figure 10-6), **(3)** we are the cause of these increased emissions, **(4)** there is a long and mostly unknown time lag between increases in greenhouse gases and measurable climate change, **(5)** rapid climate change (warming or cooling) over a few decades is likely to be disastrous for Earth's ecosystems and for the human economy, and **(6)** we don't know enough about how the earth works to make accurate projections about the possible effects of our inputs of greenhouse gases on global and regional climates.

Because of this last factor, scientists disagree on how much average global temperature might rise as a result of our increasing inputs of greenhouse gases into the atmosphere, whether other factors in the climate system will counteract or amplify a temperature rise, how fast temperatures might climb, and what the effects will be on various areas. The reasons for these disagreements are uncertainty about the accuracy of the mathematical models and geological evidence used to project changes in climate as well as uncertainty regarding the rate at which we will consume fossil fuels and clear forests. Such controversy is a normal and healthy part of science (see Spotlight on p. 211).

Since 1880, when reliable measurements began, mean global temperatures have risen about 0.5°C (0.9°F) (Figure 10-7). But there is no strong evidence linking this recent warming to the greenhouse effect. We don't have a smoking gun because, so far, any temperature changes caused by an enhanced greenhouse effect have been too small to exceed normal short-term swings in mean atmospheric temperatures and because the time lag between increases in greenhouse gases and changes in climate is largely unknown.

The more important question is what kind of climate is likely to develop over the next 50 to 60 years. Circumstantial evidence from the past and climatic modeling have convinced many climate experts that global warming will begin accelerating in the 1990s or in the first decade of the next century, rising above the background temperature changes (climatic noise) that presently mask such an effect.

Eight of the twelve years between 1980 and 1992 were the hottest in the 110-year record of global temperature measurement, and 1990 was the hottest year during that period. We can't be certain that the warmer weather was caused by an enhanced greenhouse effect, but such years give us a glimpse of what we can expect in a warmer greenhouse world.

Current climatic models project that Earth's mean surface temperature will rise 1.5°C to 5.5°C (2.7°F to 9.9°F) over the next 60 years (by 2050) if inputs of greenhouse gases continue to rise at the current rate (Figure 10-6). By way of comparison, the typical natural variation in Earth's mean surface temperature over periods of 100 to 200 years during the interglacial period we live in has been at most 0.5°C to 1°C (0.9°F to 1.8°F).

Because of the many uncertainties in these global climate models (see Spotlight on p. 211), their developers believe their projections are accurate within a factor of two. In other words, projected global warming during the next century could be as low as 0.7°C (1.3°F) or as high as 11°C (20°F). There is about a 50% chance either way. If we keep pumping greenhouse gases into the atmosphere and continue cutting down much of the world's forests, we are flipping a coin and gambling with life as we know it on this planet.

You might be wondering why we should worry about a rise of a few degrees in the mean temperature of Earth's surface. After all, we often have that much change between June and July, or between yesterday and today. The key point is that we are not talking about the normal swings in weather from place to place. We are talking about a projected *global* change in average climate in your lifetime, with much larger changes in various parts of the world.

Current models indicate that the Northern Hemisphere will warm more and faster than the Southern Hemisphere, mostly because there is so much more ocean in the south (Figure 5-19) and water takes longer to warm than land. Temperatures at middle and high latitudes are projected to rise two to three times the average increase, while temperature increases in tropical areas near the equator would be less than the global average. The United States, the Mediterranean, and much of China in the world's heavily populated mid-latitudes could be hard hit by such climate changes.

Q: How long do CFCs stay in the atmosphere?

The main way scientists, economists, and others project (not predict) behavior of climatic, ecological, economic, and other complex systems is to develop mathematical models that simulate such systems. Then the models are run on high-speed computers. How well the results correspond to the real world depends on the design of the model and on the accuracy of the data and assumptions used.

Another way to project how climate might change is to use geological and fossil evidence to see how it has changed in the past. Such limited and often speculative evidence can be used to test and improve computer models of Earth's climate systems.

Scientists recognize that their models of Earth's climate are crude approximations at best. Current climate models generally project the same results on a global basis (Figure 10-7) but disagree widely on projected climate changes in different geographic regions. Present models do not adequately include changes in solar output; the role of cloud formation and cover on climate; differences in warming during daytime and nighttime; interactions between the atmosphere and the oceans (which contain 50 times more CO_2 than the atmosphere); how the Greenland and Antarctic ice sheets affect climate; and how soils, forests, and other ecosystems respond to changes in atmospheric temperature. Each factor could dampen or amplify global warming.

For example, global warming will increase the average surface temperatures of the world's oceans, which will increase the rate of evaporation of water into the atmosphere to form clouds. If there is a net increase in thick, low-level clouds that reflect sunlight into space, the rate of global warming will slow. On the other hand, if winds and other factors lead to a net increase in thin, high-level clouds, which act as a blanket to trap heat in the lower atmosphere, the rate of global warming will increase. We don't know the net effects of such factors or how long they take to act.

We must mount a crash research program to greatly improve our understanding of Earth's climate. Even so, we will never have the scientific certainty that decision makers want before making highly controversial decisions, such as greatly slowing down the use of fossil fuels upon which much of the world's present economy depends.

Often, those opposing change or wishing to delay decision making say that something should not be done until it has been scientifically "proved." This, however, misrepresents the results of science.

Scientific theories, models, and forecasts are based on mostly circumstantial and incomplete evidence and on statistical probabilities, not certainties (Section 3-1). All scientists can do is project that there is a low, medium, high, or very high chance of something happening. Such information is quite useful, but the only way to get conclusive, direct proof about a possible future event is to wait and see if it happens.

Many climate experts believe there is already enough circumstantial evidence to warrant immediate action to slow this warming down to a more manageable rate. Doing so will buy us precious time to do more research, shift to less harmful practices, and adapt to a warmer Earth.

They argue that if we wait for Earth's mean temperature to rise to the point where it exceeds normal climatic fluctuations, it will be too late to prevent lasting and highly disruptive social, economic, and environmental changes. Waiting to act amounts to performing a gigantic experiment on ourselves and other species — a form of global Russian roulette.

Besides, since fossil fuels (especially oil) are running out and are the leading causes of air pollution, water pollution, and land disruption, we need to drastically improve energy efficiency and shift to other energy sources as fast as possible, even if there is no threat from global warming. Similarly, since deforestation is one of the greatest threats to Earth's biodiversity, we should halt and reverse this form of environmental degradation whether the threat of global warming is serious or not.

Since 1945, the world's countries, mostly MDCs, have spent more than $12 trillion to protect us from the possibility of nuclear war. Global warming is a much more likely and an equally serious threat to national, economic, and individual security; yet, we have spent only a pittance to deal with this potentially devastating threat. The time to act is rapidly running out. What do you think should be done?

One thing is clear, however. We now have the potential to bring about disruptive climate change at a rate 10 to 100 times faster than has occurred during the past 10,000 years. By the end of the next century, the world could be warmer than at any time since the dinosaurs disappeared 65 million years ago, when alligators were found in what is now Canada and when Antarctica was ice-free. Such rapid global warming would be comparable to global nuclear war (Section 10-6) in its potential to cause sudden, unpredictable, and widespread disruption of ecological, economic, and social systems. The faster the change, the more unpredictable the results, and the harder it will be for society and the natural environment to cope with the consequences.

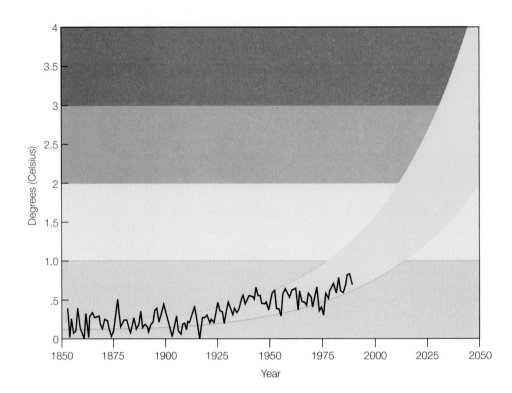

Figure 10-7 Changes in Earth's mean surface temperature between 1855 and 1990 (dark line). The yellow region shows the range of global warming predicted by various computer models of Earth's climate systems. Note that the results of the computer models roughly match the historically recorded changes in Earth's mean surface temperature between 1855 and 1990. All current models project that global warming will increase significantly between now and 2050. Scientists estimate that projections from current models could underestimate or overestimate the amount of warming by a factor of two. (Data from National Academy of Sciences and National Center for Atmospheric Research)

POSSIBLE EFFECTS ON CROP PRODUCTION, ECOSYSTEMS, AND BIODIVERSITY At first glance, a warmer average climate might seem desirable. It could lead to lower heating bills and longer growing seasons in middle and high latitudes. Crop yields might increase 60% to 80% in some areas because more carbon dioxide in the atmosphere can increase the rate of plant photosynthesis. Increased warming of the troposphere might cause some cooling in the stratosphere, thereby slowing down reactions that destroy ozone.

Other factors could offset those effects. Greater use of air conditioning would increase and contribute more heat to the troposphere. That would intensify and spread urban heat islands (Figure 6-17), causing people to use even more air conditioning. Using fossil fuels to produce more electricity to run air conditioners would add more carbon dioxide and chlorofluorocarbons (used as coolants in air conditioners) to the atmosphere, accelerating global warming and ozone depletion. That would also add more nitrogen oxides and sulfur dioxide to the troposphere, increasing ground-level ozone, photochemical smog, and acid deposition (Section 9-3).

On the other hand, recent evidence suggests that in the Northern Hemisphere temperatures have increased mainly at night—possibly because of the poorly understood effects of microscopic sulfate particles produced by the combustion of fossil fuels. Nighttime warming is relatively benign for plants because it reduces dehydration and other damage done by daytime heat and reduces harm from cold at night.

Potential gains in crop yields from increased CO_2 levels could be wiped out by increased damage from insect pests, which breed more rapidly in warmer temperatures. Higher temperatures would also increase aerobic respiration rates of plants and reduce availability of water. Recent evidence suggests that many plants have responded to past CO_2 increases by developing fewer of the pores they use to take in CO_2 and thus reducing their rate of photosynthesis. Potential increases in yields of some key crops could also be canceled out by decreased yields as a result of increases in ultraviolet radiation from depletion of ozone in the stratosphere.

Regional climate changes shift the ecological tolerance of species hundreds of kilometers horizontally and hundreds of meters vertically (Figure 5-5), with unpredictable consequences for natural systems and crops. Past evidence and computer models indicate that climate belts and thus the tolerance ranges (Figure 4-15) of plant species (including crops) would shift toward the poles by 100 to 150 kilometers (62 to 93 miles) or 150 meters (492 feet) vertically for each 1°C (1.8°F) rise in the global atmospheric temperature. If that happens, the wheat-belt climate that feeds much of the world would move northward.

Current and even improved climatic models won't be able to accurately project where such changes might occur, but the point is that there would be pronounced and unpredictable shifts in where we could grow food. The main reason we can grow so much food today is that global and regional climates have not changed much during the past 200 years.

Having to shift the location of much of our agricultural production in only a few decades would create

Q: How much of the stratospheric ozone over the Antarctic is destroyed from September to December each year?

great disruptions in food supplies and could lead to as many as 1 billion environmental refugees and mass starvation in some areas. Shifting crop production would also require huge investments in new dams, in irrigation systems, and in water-supply distribution systems, fertilizer plants, and other parts of our agricultural systems. Since the effects of rapid climate change would be largely unpredictable, we might take all the steps to shift production only to find that food-growing areas shift again if global warming accelerates or starts to drop.

In some areas, lakes, streams, and aquifers that have nourished ecosystems, cropfields, and cities for centuries could shrink or dry up altogether, forcing entire communities and populations to migrate to areas with adequate water supplies. The Gulf Stream (Figure 10-4) might stop flowing northeastward as far as Europe, leading to a much colder climate in that part of the world.

Global warming might also speed up the bacterial decay of dead organic matter in the soil. That could lead to a rapid release of vast amounts of carbon dioxide from dry soils and methane from waterlogged wetlands and rice paddies. Huge amounts of methane tied up in hydrates in soils of the arctic tundra (Figure 5-13) and in muds on the bottom of the Arctic Ocean could also be released if the blanket of permafrost covering tundra soils melts and the oceans warm. Because methane is such a potent greenhouse gas (Figure 10-6c), this release could greatly amplify global warming.

The spread of tropical climates from the equator would bring malaria (see Case Study on p. 171), encephalitis, yellow fever, and other insect-borne diseases to formerly temperate zones. Tropical skin diseases would also spread to many areas that now have a temperate climate.

In a warmer world, the frequency and intensity of highly damaging weather extremes, such as prolonged heat waves and droughts, would increase in many parts of the world. As the upper layers of seawater warm, the severity of hurricanes and typhoons would increase in some parts of the world. For example, computer models project that giant hurricanes with 50% more destructive potential than those today would hit farther north and during more months of the year.

If Earth warms, forest growth in temperate regions will move toward the poles and replace open tundra and some snow and ice. However, tree species in such forests can move only through the slow growth of new trees along their edges—typically about 0.9 kilometer (0.5 mile) a year or 9 kilometers (5 miles) per decade. If climate belts move faster than this very slow migration or if migration is blocked by cities, cropfields, highways, and other human barriers, then entire forests will wither and die. These diebacks could amplify the greenhouse effect when the decaying trees release carbon dioxide into the air. Then the increased bacterial

decay of organic matter in the warmer exposed soil would release even more CO_2. According to Oregon State University scientists, global warming could cause massive fires in up to 90% of North America, destroying forests and wildlife habitats and injecting huge amounts of carbon dioxide into the atmosphere.

Large-scale forest diebacks would also cause mass extinction of species that couldn't migrate to new areas. Fish would die as temperatures soar in streams and lakes and lower water levels concentrate pesticides.

There would be increased stress to trees from pests and disease microorganisms, which are able to adapt to climate change faster than trees are. Costly efforts to plant trees may fail when many of the new trees die.

Any shifts in regional climate caused by an enhanced greenhouse effect would pose severe threats to many of the world's parks, wildlife reserves, wilderness areas, and wetlands and would accelerate the already serious and increasing loss of Earth's biodiversity. Biologist Thomas Lovejoy of the Smithsonian Institution warns: "There will be no winners in this game of ecological chairs, for it will be fundamentally disruptive and destabilizing, and we can anticipate hordes of environmental refugees."

POSSIBLE EFFECTS ON SEA LEVELS Water expands slightly when it is heated. This fact explains why global sea levels would rise if the oceans warm, just as the fluid in a thermometer rises when heated. Additional rises would occur if the projected higher-than-average heating at the poles causes some, or even complete, melting of ice sheets and glaciers. Approximately half of the world's population lives in coastal regions that would be threatened or flooded by rising seas.

The Greenland and Antarctic ice sheets act like enormous mirrors to cool Earth by reflecting sunlight back into space. Some scientists fear that even a small temperature rise would shrink these glaciers, allowing more sunlight to hit the earth and leading to a larger rise in average sea levels than that from the thermal expansion of water. If most of the Greenland and West Antarctic ice sheets melted, as happened during a warm period 150,000 years ago, sea levels would gradually rise as much as 6 meters (20 feet) over several hundred years.

Other scientists argue that increased warming would allow the atmosphere to carry more water vapor and increase the amount of snowfall on some glaciers, particularly the Antarctic ice sheet. If snow accumulates faster than ice is lost, the Antarctic ice sheet would grow, reflect more sunlight, and help cool the atmosphere.

Current models project that an increase in the average atmospheric temperature of 3°C (5°F) would raise the average global sea level by 0.2 to 1.5 meters (1 to 5 feet) over the next 50 to 100 years. About one-third of the world's population and more than a third of the world's economic infrastructure are concentrated in coastal regions with altitudes below 1.5 meters (5 feet). If the Antarctic ice sheet grows in size because snow accumulation exceeds ice loss, the lower estimate (give or take 0.4 meter) is more likely by the year 2050.

Even a modest rise in average sea level would flood coastal wetlands and low-lying cities and croplands, flood and move barrier islands (Figure 5-27) further inland, and contaminate coastal aquifers with salt. A 0.3-meter (1-foot) rise would push shorelines back about 30 meters (98 feet) compared with 136 meters (445 feet) for a 1.5-meter (5-foot) rise in the average sea level. Only a few of the most intensively developed resort areas along the U.S. coast have beaches wider than 30 meters (78 feet) at high tide. Especially hard-hit would be North and South Carolina (Figure 5-26), where the slope of the shoreline is so gradual that a 0.3-meter (1-foot) rise in sea level would push the coastline back several kilometers.

A 1-meter (3-foot) rise would flood low-lying areas of major cities such as Shanghai, Cairo, Bangkok, and Venice and large areas of agricultural lowlands and deltas in Egypt, Bangladesh, India, and China, where much of the world's rice is grown. With a 1.5-meter (5-foot) rise, many small low-lying islands like the Marshall Islands in the Pacific, the Maldives (a series of about 1,200 islands off the west coast of India that are home to 200,000 people), and some Caribbean nations would be submerged and cease to exist, creating a multitude of environmental refugees.

Large areas of the wetlands that nourish the world's fisheries would also be destroyed (see Case Study on p. 103). According to EPA projections, even a 0.5-meter (1.6-foot) rise would result in the loss of about one-third of U.S. coastal wetlands. The salinity of streams, bays, and coastal aquifers would increase. Tanks storing hazardous chemicals along the Gulf and Atlantic coasts would be flooded. Places such as the low-lying Florida Keys and the present beaches of Malibu, California, would be covered with water. One comedian jokes that he is planning to buy land in Kansas because it will probably become valuable beachfront property.

10-3 Dealing with Global Warming

SLOWING DOWN GLOBAL WARMING We have two options for dealing with the global warming that many scientists believe we have already set in motion: slow it or adjust to its effects. Many experts believe that we must do both — with no time to lose.

The cures for this planetary crisis we have caused are controversial, difficult, and painful. If the models are correct, we are in the position of a long-time alco-

holic whose doctor tells him that if he doesn't stop drinking now he'll die.

We and many other species can learn to live under different climatic conditions, if we are given time to make the necessary changes. This need for time explains why slowing down any significant climate change — warming or cooling — caused by our activities must become the top priority of our species worldwide. Otherwise, environmental and economic security everywhere in the world could be threatened within a single generation.

The general guidelines for slowing global warming and deforestation are to reduce our use of the five deadly C's — cars, coal, cattle, chlorofluorocarbons, and chain saws — and increase our use of the Earth-saving C's — contraceptives and conservation. In 1990, the UN Intergovernmental Panel on Climate Change estimated that worldwide carbon dioxide emissions must be cut 50% to 80% by 2030 to slow projected global warming to an acceptable rate. Ways to do this include:

Prevention (Input) Approaches

- Banning all production and uses of chlorofluorocarbons and halons by 1995. This is the easiest thing we can do because we can either do without these chemicals or phase in substitutes for their essential uses. It is also the best early test of worldwide commitment to protecting the atmosphere from both global warming and ozone depletion.

- Cutting current fossil fuel use 20% by 2000, 50% by 2010, and 70% by 2030. The largest users of fossil fuels, such as the United States and the CIS, should cut their use about 35% by 2000.

- Greatly improving energy efficiency. This is the quickest, cheapest, and most effective method to reduce emissions of CO_2 and other air pollutants during the next two to three decades (see Spotlight on p. 215). According to the National Academy of Sciences, this approach alone could reduce U.S. greenhouse gas emissions by 10% to 40% at no net cost to the economy.

- Shifting, over the next 30 years, to perpetual and renewable energy resources that do not emit CO_2 (Chapter 17). Greatly increased use of perpetual and renewable energy resources can cut projected U.S. CO_2 emissions 8% to 15% by 2000 and virtually eliminate them by 2010.

- Transferring energy efficiency and renewable energy technology and pollution prevention and waste reduction technology to LDCs so they can leapfrog into a new sustainable-Earth age instead of following the energy- and matter-wasting and Earth-depleting path of today's MDCs. Studies indicate that improvements in energy efficiency over the next 10 years would allow LDCs to meet their projected energy needs while reducing their current energy use by 20% to 25% — thus saving $30

Energy expert Amory Lovins (see Guest Essay on p. 58) argues that *the remedies for slowing global warming are things we need to do now even if there were no threat of global warming or any other type of climate change*. He also argues that getting countries to sign treaties and agree to cut back their use of fossil fuels in time to reduce serious environmental effects is difficult, if not almost impossible, and very costly.

So far, the United States has called for more research rather than action to delay global warming—what environmentalists have labeled the *greenhouse denial syndrome*. Claudine Schneider, a former member of the U.S. House of Representatives (see Guest Essay on p. 166), calls this the "let's wait until the ship hits the rocks, and then figure out what to do" approach so prevalent in public policy-making today.

Such denial is what some scientists have labeled the *boiled frog syndrome* that wishes away the existence of threshold levels of change. Psychologist Robert Ornstein points out that scientists who have been alerting us to harmful effects from possible climate change (and other environmental problems, Table 1-1) get the same response as would someone trying to alert a frog to danger as it sits in a pan of water being heated on the stove. If the frog could talk, it would say, "I'm slightly warmer, but I'm doing fine." As the water gets hotter, we warn the frog that it will die, but it replies, "The temperature has been increasing for a long time, and I'm still alive and

doing well. Stop worrying." Eventually, the frog dies because it has no evolutionary experience of the lethal effects of boiling water and thus cannot perceive its situation as dangerous. Like the frog, we also face a future without precedent, and our senses are unable to pick up warnings of impending danger. Denial is deadly.

According to Lovins, the good news, among all the gloom and doom about global warming, is that improving energy efficiency is the fastest, cheapest, and surest way to sharply cut carbon dioxide emissions and emissions of most other air pollutants within two decades using existing technology (Section 17-2). This approach should also be immensely profitable, saving the world as much as a trillion dollars a year—as much as the annual global military budget.

In 1991, a report by the National Academy of Sciences urged immediate action (despite the uncertainties in predicting global climate change) to curb greenhouse-gas emission by reducing fossil-fuel consumption, promoting improvements in energy efficiency, and improving perpetual and renewable energy technologies and nuclear energy technologies. According to this report, improvements in energy efficiency alone could cut U.S. emissions of greenhouse gases by 10% to 40% from 1990 levels at little or no expense.

Moreover, reducing use of fossil fuels by improving energy efficiency reduces all forms of pollution, helps protect biodiversity, and avoids ar-

guments among governments about how CO_2 reductions should be divided up and enforced. This approach will also make the world's supplies of fossil fuel last longer, reduce international tensions over who gets the world's dwindling oil supplies, and give us more time to phase in alternatives to fossil fuels.

Industrialized countries—especially the energy-inefficient United States—will have to set a better example by committing themselves to a crash program to improve energy efficiency (Section 17-2). They will also have to lead the shift from nonrenewable fossil fuels and nuclear energy (Chapter 18) to perpetual and renewable energy sources (Chapter 17).

Existing and new technologies for improving energy efficiency and using perpetual and renewable energy must also be transferred to LDCs, which on average are nearly three times less energy-efficient than the average MDC. According to Lovins, this in principle could allow LDCs to expand their economies by about tenfold with no increase in energy use and to avoid the dirtiest stage of the industrialization process. Instead of abiding by this principle, the United States and some other industrialized countries are now exporting their least-efficient energy technologies—the ones too obsolete and costly to sell at home—to LDCs. Greatly improving energy efficiency *now* is a money-saving, life-saving, and Earth-saving offer that we must not refuse.

---

billion a year. Yet, in 1990, less than 1% of the $3.3 billion the World Bank loaned to LDCs for energy projects went to improving energy efficiency.

■ Increasing the use of nuclear power to produce electricity *if* a new generation of much safer reactors can be developed and the problem of how to store nuclear waste safely for thousands of years can be solved (Section 18-3). However, improving energy efficiency is much quicker and safer and reduces emissions of CO_2 2.5 to 10 times more

than nuclear power per dollar invested (see Pro/Con on p. 436).

■ Phasing in heavy taxes on gasoline and emissions fees on each unit of fossil fuel (especially coal) burned to reduce emissions of CO_2 and other air pollutants over a 10-year period. This tax revenue should to be used to improve the energy efficiency of dwellings and heating systems for the poor in MDCs and LDCs, to provide them with enough energy to offset higher fuel prices, and to subsidize the transition to perpetual and renewable energy resources. At the same time, large taxpayer subsidies for fossil fuels and nuclear power should be withdrawn over a 10-year period.

- Sharply reducing the use of coal, which emits 60% more carbon dioxide per unit of energy produced than does any other fossil fuel.

- Switching from coal to natural gas for producing electricity and high-temperature heat in regions such as the United States and the CIS that have ample supplies of natural gas, which emits only half as much CO_2 per unit of energy as coal. Switching to natural gas also sharply reduces emissions of other air pollutants. Because burning natural gas still emits CO_2, this is only a transitional method that helps buy time to switch to an age of energy efficiency and renewable energy.

- Capturing methane gas emitted by landfills and using it as a fuel. Burning this methane produces carbon dioxide, but each molecule of methane reaching the atmosphere causes about 25 times more global warming than does each molecule of CO_2.

- Sharply reducing beef production to reduce the fossil-fuel inputs into agriculture, carbon dioxide released because of deforestation for grazing land, and methane produced by cattle.

- Halting unsustainable deforestation everywhere by 2000 (Sections 15-2 and 15-3).

- Switching from unsustainable to sustainable agriculture (Section 13-6). Worldwide, agriculture is responsible for about 15% of the greenhouse gases we emit into the atmosphere. If LDCs increase their use of unsustainable, industrialized agriculture, this percentage could rise.

- Slowing population growth (Section 6-4). If we cut greenhouse-gas emissions in half and population more than doubles, we're back where we started.

- Dismantling the global poverty trap to reduce unnecessary deaths and human suffering and environmental degradation and to help LDCs help themselves and not follow the present unsustainable industrial path of the MDCs (Section 7-4).

Cleanup (Output) Approaches

- Developing better methods to remove carbon dioxide from the smokestack emissions of coal-burning power and industrial plants and from vehicle exhausts. If used, currently available methods would remove only about 30% of the CO_2 and would at least double the cost of electricity. This approach would eventually be overwhelmed by increased fossil-fuel use. Furthermore, the recovered CO_2 must be kept out of the atmosphere, but the effectiveness and cost of methods for doing so are unknown.

- Planting trees. This is an important form of Earth care, especially in restoring deforested and degraded cropland and rangeland. Tree planting, however, is only a stopgap measure for slowing CO_2 emissions. To absorb the carbon dioxide we are now putting into the atmosphere each year, we would have to plant and tend an average of 1,000 trees per person every year and 4,500 trees annually for each American citizen — 18,000 trees a year for a family of four.

- Removing CO_2 by photosynthesis by using tanks and ponds of marine algae or by fertilizing the oceans with iron to stimulate the growth of marine algae — an uncertain scheme rejected by a number of environmental scientists.

ADJUSTING TO GLOBAL WARMING Even if all the things just listed are done and the models are correct, we are still likely to experience some global warming, although at a more manageable rate. If we stopped adding greenhouse gases to the atmosphere now, current models project that what we have already added could warm the earth by 0.5 to 1.8°C (0.9 to 3.2°F). Since there is a good chance that many of the things we should do will either not be done or will be done too slowly, some analysts suggest that we should also begin preparing for the effects of long-term global warming. Their suggestions include:

- Increasing research on the breeding of food plants that need less water and plants that can thrive in water too salty for ordinary crops

- Building dikes to protect coastal areas from flooding, as the Dutch have done for hundreds of years

- Moving storage tanks of hazardous materials away from coastal areas

- Banning new construction on low-lying coastal areas

- Storing large supplies of key foods throughout the world as insurance against disruptions in food production

- Expanding existing wilderness areas, parks, and wildlife refuges northward in the Northern Hemisphere and southward in the Southern Hemisphere and creating new wildlife reserves in these areas

- Connecting existing and new wildlife reserves by corridors that would allow mobile species to change their geographic distributions and transplanting endangered species to new areas

- Wasting less water (see Individuals Matter inside the back cover)

We have known about the possibility of an enhanced greenhouse effect and its possible consequences for decades. We also know what needs to be done at the international, national, local, and individual levels (see Individuals Matter on p. 217).

Q: What is necessary to slow ozone depletion?

While waiting for the world's governments to adopt strategies for slowing global warming, we can take matters into our own hands.

- Be aware of your CO_2 emissions and reduce them. Each person in the United States is responsible for an average of 16.7 metric tons (18.4 tons) of CO_2 emissions a year, six times more than the average citizen in an LDC.

- Reduce your use and unnecessary waste of energy (see Individuals Matter inside the back cover). Because use and waste of fossil fuels is the primary cause of projected global warming and most other forms of pollution and environmental degradation, this is the most important thing you can do. Driving a car that gets at least 15 kilometers per liter (35 miles per gallon), using a car pool and mass transit, and walking or bicycling where possible are the best ways you can reduce your emissions of CO_2 and other air pollutants and save money.

- Don't use electricity to heat space or water (Section 3-6), and use

energy-efficient fluorescent light bulbs, refrigerators, and other appliances.

- Make your house energy-efficient and heat it and household water by using as much perpetual energy from the sun as possible. Cool it by using shade trees and available winds (Section 17-2).

- If you can't use perpetual and renewable energy to heat your house and water, use natural gas. When burned, it produces much less carbon dioxide and other air pollutants than does burning oil or using electricity generated by burning coal at a power plant.

- Plant and care for trees to help cool the globe and your house. Ask your employer to sponsor a tree-planting program by buying seedlings to be planted by children in a local school.

- Use the following priorities for all items: *No use unless necessary, reuse, recycle, and throw away only as a last resort*. In addition, buy products made from recycled materials. While it is encouraging that so many people have begun recycling, it is merely the first

baby step in the right direction. The emphasis must now shift to reuse and no or low use (of throwaway and hazardous items).

- Urge state and national legislators to sponsor bills aimed at greatly improving energy efficiency, halting the harvesting of ancient forest stands in national forests (Section 15-3), and curbing emissions of greenhouse gases and other air pollutants.

- Don't support highly unpredictable schemes such as covering the oceans with white Styrofoam chips to help reflect more energy away from Earth's surface, dumping iron into oceans to stimulate the growth of marine algae to remove CO_2 from the atmosphere (costing about $1 billion per year), unfurling a gigantic foilfaced sun shield in space, or injecting sunlight-reflecting particulate matter into the stratosphere to cool it by exploding nuclear bombs near Earth's surface or by using aircraft or rocket systems.

10-4 Depletion of Ozone in the Stratosphere

DEPLETION OF THE OZONE LAYER Ozone (O_3) is an unstable gas that breaks up quickly to form plain old two-atom oxygen (O_2). Until the ozone layer in the stratosphere formed about 500 million years ago, life on land was not possible. Ozone is destroyed and replenished in the stratosphere by natural atmospheric chemical reactions and is maintained at a fairly stable level. There is much evidence that we are upsetting this balance and reducing the levels of life-saving ozone in the stratosphere.

In 1974, chemists Sherwood Roland and Mario Molina theorized that human-made *chlorofluorocarbons (CFCs)*, also known by their DuPont trademark, as Freons, were lowering the average concentration of ozone

in the stratosphere and creating a global time bomb. The two most widely used CFCs are CFC-11 (trichlorofluoromethane) and CFC-12 (dichlorofluoromethane).

When they were developed in 1930, these stable, odorless, nonflammable, nontoxic, and noncorrosive chemicals were seen as nearly perfect human-made compounds. Soon they were widely used as coolants in air conditioners and refrigerators and as propellants in aerosol spray cans. Now they are also used as hospital sterilants and fumigants for granaries and cargo holds, and to clean electronic parts such as computer chips and to create the bubbles in polystyrene plastic foam (often called by its trade name, Styrofoam), used for insulation and packaging.

Spray cans, discarded or leaking refrigeration and air conditioning equipment, and the production and burning of plastic foam products release CFCs into the atmosphere. Depending on the type, CFCs are so unreactive that they stay intact in the atmosphere for 65 to

---

111 years. This gives them plenty of time to rise slowly through the troposphere until they reach the stratosphere (Figure 9-1). There, under the influence of high-energy UV radiation from the sun, they break down and release chlorine atoms, which speed up the breakdown of ozone into O_2 and O.

Over time, a single chlorine atom—acting somewhat like a gaseous Pac-Man—can convert as many as 100,000 molecules of O_3 to O_2. A single polystyrene cup contains over 1 billion molecules of CFCs. Although this effect was described in 1974, it took 15 years of interaction between science and politics before countries took action to begin slowly phasing out CFCs.* The primary reason is that elimination of CFCs threatened a powerful $28 billion-a-year industry.

Industrial countries account for 84% of CFC production, with the United States being the top producer, followed by western European countries and Japan. Since 1978 most uses of CFCs in aerosol cans have been banned in the United States, Canada, and most Scandinavian countries, primarily because of consumer boycotts. Despite this encouraging ban, per capita use of CFCs in the United States is six times greater than global per capita use. Vehicle air conditioners account for about three-quarters of annual CFC emissions in the United States. There is also some controversial evidence that space shuttle emissions of chlorine molecules directly into the ozone layer are an important and growing factor in ozone depletion.

Other stable chemicals also destroy ozone in the stratosphere. These include bromine-containing compounds, called *halons*, which are widely used, mostly in fire extinguishers, and methyl bromide, a crop fumigant. Each bromine atom destroys hundreds of times more ozone molecules than does a chlorine atom. Other widely used ozone-destroying chemicals are carbon tetrachloride (a highly toxic but cheap chemical used mostly as a solvent) and methyl chloroform, or 1,1,1-trichloroethane (used as a cleaning solvent for metals and in more than 160 consumer products, such as correction fluid, dry-cleaning sprays, spray adhesives, and other aerosols). Although they receive little publicity compared with CFCs, carbon tetrachloride and methyl chloroform contribute more to ozone-threatening chlorine levels than all but two of the eight CFCs and halons now partially controlled by an international treaty. Substitutes are available for virtually all uses of these two chemicals. All these compounds are also greenhouse gases that contribute to global warming during their trip through the troposphere (Figure 10-6b). However, this is partially offset by tropospheric cooling caused by stratospheric ozone depletion.

---

*For a fascinating account of how corporate stalling, politics, economics, and science interact, see Sharon Roan's *Ozone Crisis: The 15-Year Evolution of a Sudden Global Emergency* (New York: John Wiley, 1989).

" I MISS THE OZONE LAYER...."

In the 1980s, researchers were surprised to find that up to 50% of the ozone in the upper stratosphere over the Antarctic is destroyed during the antarctic spring from September through mid-October (and since 1990, into December)—something not predicted by computer models of the stratosphere (Figure 10-8). A new analysis in 1991 suggests that this already-serious loss of seasonal ozone could double in size by 2001.

Measurements indicate that this large annual decrease in ozone over the South Pole is caused when water droplets in clouds form tiny ice crystals as they enter large streams of air called polar vortices that circle the poles in wintertime in both the Antarctic and the Arctic. The surfaces of these ice crystals absorb CFCs and other ozone-depleting chemicals. This process greatly increases the rate at which these chemicals destroy ozone and leads to the sharp seasonal drop in ozone over the Antarctic.

After two to three months, the vortex breaks up and great clumps of ozone-depleted air flow northward and linger over parts of Australia, New Zealand, and the southern tips of South America and Africa for a few weeks. During this period, ultraviolet levels in these areas may increase as much as 20%. Television stations now air daily ultraviolet levels and warnings for Australians—who already have the world's highest rate of skin cancer (see Spotlight on p. 178)—to stay inside during bad spells.

Since 1988, scientists have discovered that a similar but smaller ozone hole formed over the Arctic during the two-month arctic spring, with an annual ozone loss of 15% to 25%. When this hole breaks up, clumps of ozone-depleted air flow southward and linger over parts of Europe and North America. This can produce a 5% to 10% winter and spring loss of ozone over much of the Northern Hemisphere.

Each year the news about ozone depletion seems to get worse. In 1991, the National Aeronautics and

Q: If all ozone-depleting substances were banned tomorrow, how long would it take for the ozone layer to recover?

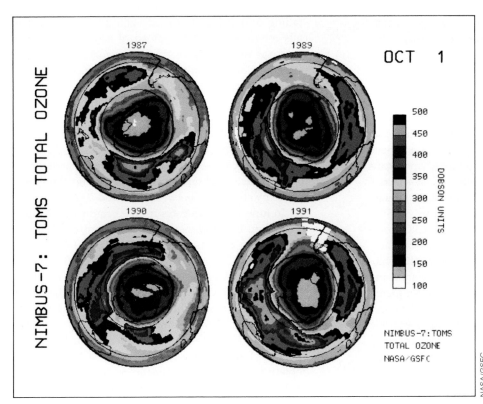

Figure 10-8 The pink and darker pink shades in these images taken by the NIMBUS-7 satellite show the annual ozone hole (area with extremely low ozone concentrations) that appeared in the upper stratosphere over the Antarctic on October 3 of 1987, 1989, 1990, and 1991. This hole, where the normal ozone level has been cut in half, is 10 times larger than the area of the continental United States. It is caused by ozone-destroying chlorofluorocarbons we have put into the atmosphere. The lower the Dobson units, shown in the scale on the right, the greater the depletion of ozone. Normal Dobson units for the stratosphere are around 350; on October 3, 1991, the level over the Antarctic fell to an all-time low of 110.

Space Administration (NASA) reported that the average annual level of stratospheric ozone over heavily populated regions of North America, Europe, and Asia had decreased at twice the rate scientists projected only a few years ago. In 1992, NASA scientists reported that ozone-depleting chemicals in the stratosphere over the Northern Hemisphere had reached record levels. They said chances are high that an increasingly larger ozone hole will open up there each winter and spring, bathing heavily populated areas of the eastern United States (especially northern New England), eastern Canada, and parts of Europe with unprecedented levels of harmful ultraviolet-B radiation.

EFFECTS OF OZONE DEPLETION With less ozone in the stratosphere, more biologically harmful ultraviolet-B radiation will reach Earth's surface. This form of UV radiation damages DNA molecules and can cause genetic defects on the outer surfaces of plants and animals, including your skin. The EPA estimates that current rates of ozone depletion would cause the following effects in the United States:

■ An extra 12 million cases of skin cancer (Figure 8-7) between 1990 and 2023, with more than 200,000 premature deaths from melanoma skin cancer (Figure 8-7c), which now kills almost 9,000 Americans each year (see Spotlight on p. 178).

■ A sharp increase in eye cataracts (a clouding of the eye that causes blurred vision and eventual blindness) and severe sunburn in people, and an increase in eye cancer in cattle.

■ Suppression of the human immune system, which would reduce our defenses against a variety of infectious diseases, an effect similar to that of the AIDS virus.

■ An increase in eye-burning photochemical smog, highly damaging ozone, and acid deposition in the troposphere (Chapter 9).

■ Decreased yields of important food crops such as corn, rice, soybeans, and wheat.

■ Reduction in the growth of ocean phytoplankton that form the base of ocean food chains and webs and that help remove carbon dioxide from the atmosphere.

■ A loss of perhaps $2 billion a year from degradation of paints, plastics, and other polymer materials.

■ Increased global warming from an enhanced greenhouse effect because of heat-trapping CFCs (Figure 10-6b) and halons in the troposphere.

■ Unpredictable effects on global climate from cooling in the stratosphere because of ozone depletion. Cooling of the stratosphere reduces the thermal lid it places on the troposphere (Figure 9-1), with unknown consequences for global climate.

In a worst-case scenario, people would not be able to expose themselves to the sun (see cartoon). Cattle could graze only at dusk without eye damage. Farmers might measure their exposure to the sun in minutes. These are quite high prices to pay for chemicals that we could do without.

10-5 Protecting the Ozone Layer

A PLAN OF ACTION Models of atmospheric processes indicate that just to keep CFCs at 1987 levels would require an immediate 85% drop in total CFC emissions throughout the world. Analysts believe that the first step toward this goal should be an immediate worldwide ban on the use of CFCs in aerosol spray cans and in producing plastic foam products. Cost-effective substitutes are already available for those uses. Nissan, Toyota, and Honda have announced that by 1995 air conditioners in their cars will no longer use CFCs.

The next step would be to phase out all other uses of CFCs, halons, carbon tetrachloride, and methyl chloroform by 1995. Substitute coolants in refrigeration and air conditioning will probably cost more, but compared with the potential economic and health consequences of ozone depletion, such cost increases would be minor. For example, the estimated harmful costs of releasing the CFCs in a single aerosol can are $12,000. The harmful costs of CFCs released from one auto air conditioner during use and repair are many times that figure.

We must be careful that substitutes don't contribute to atmospheric warming or cause other harmful effects. Currently, there are three principal types of substitutes. One consists of chemicals outside the fluorocarbon family that can be used as cleaning and blowing agents. The other two types, useful mainly as cooling agents in refrigerators and air conditioners, are hydrofluorocarbons (HFCs), which contain no chlorine or bromine atoms, and hydrochlorofluorocarbons (HCFCs), which contain fewer atoms of chlorine per molecule than conventional CFCs. A 1991 study revealed that HCFC-123, a CFC replacement already on the market for industrial refrigeration and large-building cooling systems, causes benign tumors in the pancreas and testes of male rats.

HFCs and HCFCs are decomposed more rapidly than conventional CFCs and have lower atmospheric lifetimes of 2 to 20 years, depending on the compound. But HCFCs contain some ozone-destroying chlorine atoms, and both HFCs and HCFCs are still greenhouse gases. However, their ozone-depletion potential is only 2% to 10% that of conventional CFCs, and they would contribute about 90% less per kilogram to greenhouse warming than do currently used CFCs. HFC and HCFC substitutes may help make the transition away from CFCs for essential uses such as refrigeration, but eventually these new chemicals will also have to be banned to halt ozone depletion.

HOPEFUL BUT INADEQUATE PROGRESS Some progress has been made since the discovery of the Antarctic ozone hole (Figure 10-8). That dramatic event and public pressure forced political leaders in MDCs to begin taking action after more than a decade of corporate stalling and political "foot-dragging," with repeated calls for more research instead of action. This same pattern is now being used to delay action on slowing potential global warming, improving energy efficiency, and reducing ground-level air pollution.

In 1987, 24 nations meeting in Montreal, Canada, developed a treaty—commonly known as the Montreal Protocol—to reduce production of the eight most widely used and most damaging CFCs. By 1992, 70 countries had signed this historic treaty. If carried out, it will reduce total emissions of CFCs into the atmosphere by about 35% between 1989 and 2000.

In June 1990, delegates from 93 countries meeting in London, England, expanded the Montreal Protocol and pledged to phase out all production of CFCs and halons in MDCs by 2000 and in LDCs by 2010, *if substitutes are available by then.* They also agreed on the need to phase out or reduce the use of other ozone-depleting substances such as carbon tetrachloride, methyl chloroform, and the HCFCs now being used as substitutes for some CFCs, but set no deadlines for such actions. Moreover, the effectiveness of any ban on ozone-depleting chemicals will depend on how well it is enforced and on the willingness of LDCs such as China and India to participate.

Although this treaty is a very important symbol of global cooperation, many scientists believe that it still does not go far enough in preventing significant depletion of the ozone layer and global warming. Even if all ozone-depleting substances were banned tomorrow, it would take about 100 years for the planet to recover from the present ozone depletion and that which will come from those already in the atmosphere. The key question is whether MDCs and LDCs can agree to sacrifice short-term economic gain by eliminating their use of *all* ozone-depleting chemicals within the next decade to protect life on Earth in coming decades.

Perhaps the challenges posed by global warming and ozone depletion can be a catalyst for worldwide awareness of the urgent need to get serious about sustaining the earth and learning how to deal with long-term problems that build up slowly and invisibly until they exceed threshold levels. Let's hope so and begin by sharply reducing our individual impacts on the ozone layer (see Individuals Matter on p. 221).

10-6 Climate, Biodiversity, and Nuclear War

THE ULTIMATE ECOLOGICAL CATASTROPHE Most people believe that global nuclear war is the single greatest threat to the human species and Earth's life-support systems for most species. The nuclear age began in August 1945, when the United States exploded a single nuclear fission atomic bomb over Hiroshima and

Q: What is the largest source of CFC emission in the United States?

- Avoid purchasing products containing chlorofluorocarbons, carbon tetrachloride, and methyl chloroform (1,1,1-trichloroethane on most ingredient labels). Such products include cleaning sprays for sewing machines, VCRs, and electronic equipment; spray-on cleaners and spot removers; bug killers and foggers; shoe polish sprays and other aerosols; and polystyrene foam packaging. Seek out the substitutes that are or will soon be available for these products.

- Don't buy CFC-containing polystyrene foam insulation. Types of insulation that don't contain CFCs are extended polystyrene (commonly called EPS or beadboard), fiberglass, rock wool, cellulose, and perlite.

- Don't buy halon or carbon dioxide fire extinguishers for home use. Instead, buy those using dry chemicals.

- Stop using all aerosol spray products, except in some medical sprays. Even those not using CFCs and HCFCs (such as Dymel) emit hydrocarbon or other propellant chemicals into the air. Use roll-on and hand-pump products instead.

- Pressure legislators to ban all uses of CFCs, halons, and methyl bromide by 1995, carbon tetrachloride and methyl chloroform by 2000, and HCFC and HFC substitutes by 2010.

- Pressure legislators to tax the billions of dollars in windfall profits that CFC and halon manufacturers will get from phasing out their use and to use these tax revenues for climate research, improving energy efficiency, and switching to perpetual and renewable energy resources.

- As they become available, buy new refrigerators and freezers that use vacuum insulation (as in Thermos bottles) instead of rigid-foam insulation and that use helium as a coolant instead of CFCs or HCFCs (such refrigerators are available from Cryodynamics, 1101 Bristol Road, Mountainside, NJ 07092).

- Pressure legislators to require that all products containing or requiring CFCs, halons, or other ozone-depleting chemicals for their manufacture be clearly labeled (so that consumers can consciously choose whether to use such products) and to require recovery of CFCs when refrigerators, freezers, and home and auto air conditioners are junked.

- Since leaky air conditioners in cars are the single largest source of CFC emissions in the United States, make sure your auto air conditioner is not leaking. If it needs to be recharged, take it to a shop that has the equipment to recycle its CFCs.

- Switch from electrical home and office air conditioning systems to new natural gas absorption cooling systems that use salt and water instead of CFCs or HCFCs.

- Don't fall for highly unpredictable and money-wasting schemes such as using lasers to blast CFCs out of the sky, injecting methane into the stratosphere to scavenge chlorine atoms, and building more supersonic commercial airplanes (SSTs), whose emissions could further deplete ozone in the stratosphere.

---

another over Nagasaki. These blasts killed an estimated 110,000 to 140,000 people and injured tens of thousands more.

By the end of the year 100,000 more people had died. Most of these deaths were the result of exposure to high levels of ionizing radiation from neutrons emitted by the nuclear fission chain reaction (Figure 3-12) and by radioactive isotopes (Figure 3-10) in the resulting *fallout:* dirt and debris sucked up and made radioactive by the blast and then dropped back to Earth's surface near ground zero as well as on downwind areas hundreds and even thousands of kilometers away. Other people, exposed to nonlethal doses of ionizing radiation, developed cataracts, leukemia, and other forms of lethal cancer decades later. Some are still dying today. This shows us what a small nuclear bomb can do.

Today, the world's nuclear arsenals have an explosive power equal to more than 952,000 Hiroshima-type bombs or 3,333 times all the explosives detonated during World War II. Each Trident II submarine that began coming on line in 1989 carries nuclear warheads with the explosive power of 4,570 Hiroshima bombs or more than 30 times all the explosives detonated in World War II. *Today, we live in a world with enough nuclear weapons to kill everyone on Earth 60 times.* By the end of this century, 60 countries—one of every three in the world—will have either nuclear weapons or the knowledge and capability to build them.

In addition to the health and environmental threats, the buildup of nuclear and conventional weapons drains funds and creativity that could be used to solve most of the world's population, food, health, resource, and environmental problems. For example,

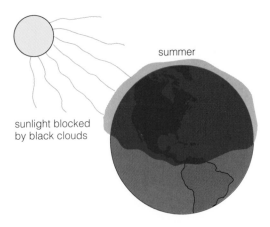

Figure 10-9 The nuclear winter or autumn effect caused by a limited nuclear war in the Northern Hemisphere.

about 40% of the world's research and development expenditures and 50% of its physical scientists and engineers are devoted to developing weapons to improve our ability to kill one another.

NUCLEAR WINTER AND NUCLEAR AUTUMN EFFECTS Since 1982, evaluation of previously overlooked calculations has suggested that even a limited nuclear war could kill 1 billion to 4 billion people — 20% to 80% of the world's current population. If such an exchange took place in the Northern Hemisphere, the direct effects of the explosions would kill an estimated 1 billion people, mostly in the Northern Hemisphere. Tens of millions more would suffer injuries.

Computer models indicate that within the next two years, another 1 billion to 3 billion people might die from starvation. Their deaths would be caused by disruption of world agricultural production, first in the Northern Hemisphere and later in the Southern Hemisphere, because of what is called the *nuclear winter* or *nuclear autumn effect* (Figure 10-9).

Depending on the extent, time, and location of the explosions, average atmospheric temperatures in temperate areas would probably drop rapidly to temperatures typical of fall or early winter. This atmospheric cooling would happen because of a reverse greenhouse effect. Enormous amounts of smoke, soot, dust, and other debris, lifted into the atmosphere as a result of the nuclear explosions and subsequent fires, would coalesce into huge smoke clouds. These dense clouds would cover large portions of the Northern Hemisphere and prevent 20% to 90% of all sunlight from reaching large areas (Figure 10-9).

The abnormally cold temperatures and reduction of sunlight would cause a sharp drop in food production in the growing season following the war. This would cause widespread starvation in the Northern Hemi-

sphere and in African and Asian countries dependent on food imports from countries such as the United States and Canada.

Food production in the Southern Hemisphere might also be affected as the smoke clouds gradually became less dense and spread southward. Drops in temperature and sunlight would be less severe than in the Northern Hemisphere. But even a slight reduction in temperature could be disastrous to agriculture in tropical and subtropical forest areas and could lead to the extinction of numerous plant and animal species. Subtropical grasslands and savannas in Africa (Figure 5-9) and South America might be the least affected of the world's ecosystems because their plants are more cold-tolerant and drought-resistant.

A cold and dark nuclear winter or autumn would not be the only cause of food scarcity. Plagues of rapidly reproducing insects and rodents — the life forms best equipped to survive nuclear war — would damage stored food and spread disease. In areas where crops could still be grown, farmers would be isolated from supplies of seeds, fertilizer, pesticides, and fuel. People hoping to subsist on seafood would find many surviving aquatic species contaminated with radioactivity, runoff from ruptured tanks of industrial liquids, and oil pouring out of damaged offshore rigs.

A limited nuclear war would also destroy 30% to 70% of the ozone layer, leading to a deadly *ultraviolet summer*. This condition would sharply decrease the ability to grow crops and harvest fish. It would also cause a huge increase in skin cancers and eye cataracts and impair immune systems so that already-weakened survivors would die from infectious diseases.

Incineration of oil in tanks and refineries, storage tanks of hazardous chemicals, rubber tires, and other materials would produce toxic smog, which would cover much of the Northern Hemisphere. Large areas might also be assaulted with extremely acid rains. High levels of radioactivity from fallout would contaminate most remaining supplies of food and water, kill many people and other warm-blooded animals, some crops, and certain coniferous trees, especially pines. Thus, people not killed outright by the nuclear explosions might find themselves choking and freezing in a smoggy, radioactive darkness with contaminated water supplies and little chance of growing food for a year or perhaps several years.

The computer models of the atmosphere used to make these calculations are crude and may overestimate or underestimate the effects of nuclear explosions. Scientists agree, however, that even if the effects are less than the models suggest, they would still cause serious disruptions in regional and global climate and thus disrupt food and water supplies.

It is encouraging that there has been a sharp reduction in tensions between the United States and the for-

Q: Nuclear weapons existing today could kill everyone in the world how many times over?

mer Soviet Union and that these countries have destroyed a small number of their nuclear missiles. However, most people are unaware that only the delivery systems have been destroyed. The fissionable bomb material has merely been removed and stored for possible future use. There is also concern over control of nuclear weapons scattered in the various independent states of what used to be the Soviet Union. The predicted spread of nuclear weapons to as many as one-third of the world's countries by the end of this century is also of concern.

Some people have wondered whether there is intelligent life in other parts of the universe. Perhaps the real question we should ask is whether there is intelligent life on Earth? If we can seriously deal with the planetary emergencies discussed in this chapter and with deforestation, discussed in Chapter 15, beginning *now*, then the answer is a hopeful yes. If we insist on decades more of discussion, research, denial, delay, and wasteful depletion of Earth's natural capital instead of concerted action, the answer is a tragic no. If that happens, civilization as we know it will end. We may even bring about the extinction of our own species — the first species to commit suicide — and take several million more species with us. The choice is ours. Not to decide is to decide.

The atmosphere is the key symbol of global interdependence. If we can't solve some of our problems in the face of threats to this global commons, then I can't be very optimistic about the future of the world.

MARGARET MEAD

DISCUSSION TOPICS

1. What consumption patterns and other features of your lifestyle directly add greenhouse gases and ozone-depleting chemicals to the atmosphere? Which, if any, of those things would you be willing to give up to slow projected global warming and reduce other forms of air pollution and to slow ozone depletion?

2. Explain why you agree or disagree with each of the proposals for **(a)** slowing down emissions of greenhouse gases into the atmosphere listed on pp. 214–216 and **(b)** adjusting to the effects of global warming listed on p. 216. Explain. What effects would carrying out these proposals have on your lifestyle and those of any children you might choose to have? What effects might not carrying out these actions have?

3. In 1989, U.S. Senator Albert Gore introduced a legislative package he calls the Strategic Environment Initiative (SEI), an ecological version of Ronald Reagan's Strategic Defense Initiative (SDI). Domestically, the SEI would focus on improving energy efficiency, developing alternative fuels, reforestation, comprehensive recycling, and drastic cuts in ozone-depleting chemicals. It would also help LDCs obtain energy-efficient technology and develop environmentally sustainable industries and agriculture. Do you support such a bill? What things, if any, would you add? What has happened to this proposal since it was first introduced in 1989?

4. Should all uses of CFCs, halons, and other ozone-depleting chemicals be banned in the United States and worldwide? Explain. Suppose this meant that air conditioning (especially in cars and perhaps in buildings) had to be banned or became five times as expensive. Would you still support such a ban?

5. Do you think that nuclear war is preventable? How?

CHAPTER 11

WATER RESOURCES

AND WATER

POLLUTION

General Questions and Issues

1. How much usable fresh water is available for human use, and how much of this supply are we using?

2. What are the most serious water resource problems in the world and in the United States?

3. How can water resources be managed to increase the supply and reduce unnecessary waste?

4. What are the principal types and sources of water pollutants?

5. What are the biggest pollution problems of streams, lakes, oceans, and groundwater aquifers?

6. What legal and technological methods can be used to prevent or reduce water pollution?

Our liquid planet glows like a soft blue sapphire in the hard-edged darkness of space. There is nothing else like it in the solar system. It is because of water.

JOHN TODD

W E LIVE ON the water planet, with this life-giving resource covering about 71% of Earth's surface (Figure 5-19). This precious film of water—most of it salt water—helps maintain Earth's climate, dilutes pollutants, and is essential to all life because you and most living things are made up mostly of water.

Earth's relatively small amount of fresh water, constantly recycled and purified by the hydrologic cycle (Figure 4-26), is a vital resource for agriculture, manufacturing, transportation, and countless other human activities. Through the global circulation of water we are all connected to each other, to other forms of life, and to the entire planet.

Despite its importance, water is one of the most poorly managed resources on earth. We waste it and pollute it. We also charge too little for making it available, encouraging even greater waste and pollution of this vital potentially renewable resource.

11-1 Supply, Renewal, and Use of Water Resources

WORLDWIDE SUPPLY, RENEWAL, AND DISTRIBUTION Only a tiny fraction of the planet's enormous supply of water is available to us as fresh water, and that is distributed very unevenly. About 97% of Earth's volume of water is found in the oceans and is too salty for drinking and growing crops and for most industrial uses, except cooling.

The remaining 3% is fresh water. Of this, more than 99% (about 2.997% of Earth's total volume) is locked up as ice at the poles and in glaciers or is groundwater that is too deep and too expensive for us to extract. Only about 0.003% of Earth's total volume of water is easily available to us as fresh water in lakes, soil moisture, exploitable groundwater, atmospheric water vapor, and streams. If the world's water supply were only 100 liters (26 gallons), our usable supply of fresh water would be only about 0.003 liter (one-half teaspoon) (Figure 11-1).

Fortunately, this supply of fresh water is continually collected, purified, and distributed in the *hydrologic cycle* (Figure 4-26). This natural recycling and purification process works and provides plenty of fresh water as long as we don't pollute the water faster than it is replenished, overload it with slowly degradable and nondegradable wastes, or withdraw it from slowly renewable underground supplies faster than it is replenished. Unfortunately, we are disrupting the water cycle by doing all of those things.

SURFACE WATER The fresh water we use comes from two sources: surface water and groundwater (Figure 11-2). Precipitation that does not infiltrate the

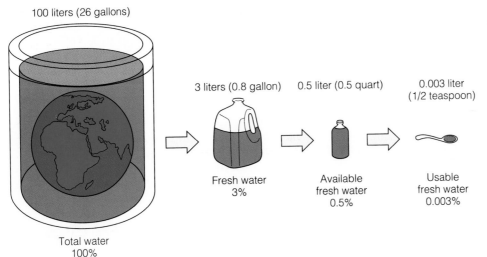

100 liters (26 gallons)

3 liters (0.8 gallon)

0.5 liter (0.5 quart)

0.003 liter (1/2 teaspoon)

Total water
100%

Fresh water
3%

Available
fresh water
0.5%

Usable
fresh water
0.003%

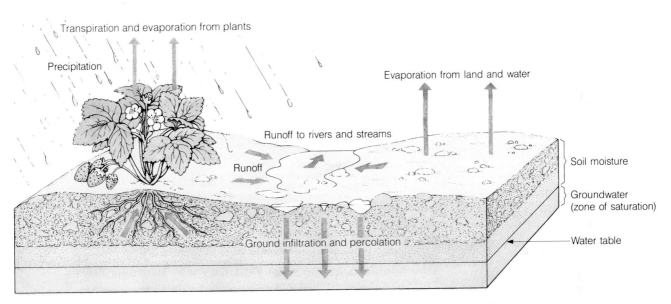

Transpiration and evaporation from plants

Precipitation

Evaporation from land and water

Runoff to rivers and streams

Runoff

Soil moisture

Groundwater
(zone of saturation)

Ground infiltration and percolation

Water table

Figure 11-2 Main routes of local precipitation: surface runoff into surface waters, ground infiltration to aquifers, and evaporation and transpiration into the atmosphere.

ground or return to the atmosphere by evaporation or transpiration is called **surface water**. It is fresh water that is on Earth's surface in streams, lakes, wetlands, and artificial reservoirs.

Watersheds, also called **drainage basins**, are those areas of land that drain runoff water into bodies of surface water. Water flowing off the land into bodies of surface water is called **surface runoff**, and water flowing in rivers to the ocean is called **river runoff**.

GROUNDWATER Some precipitation infiltrates the ground and fills pores (spaces or cracks) in soil and rock in the earth's crust. The below-ground area where all available soil and rock are filled by water is called the **zone of saturation**, and the water in these pores is called **groundwater** (Figure 11-2). The **water table** is the upper surface of the zone of saturation.

There is 40 times as much groundwater below Earth's surface as there is in all the world's streams and lakes. However, this groundwater is unequally distributed, and only a small amount of it is economically exploitable. Mining deep groundwater faster than it is recharged by the hydrologic cycle consumes potentially renewable liquid Earth capital.

A geologic formation's ability to hold water is dependent on its porosity and permeability. **Porosity** is a measure of the volume of pores per volume of soil or rock and the average distances between those spaces. **Permeability** is the rate at which water and air move from upper to lower soil layers or through the pores in rocks. For example, sand and coarse gravel are highly permeable, while clay has a very low permeability.

Underground, porous, water-saturated layers of sand, gravel, or bedrock that can yield an economically

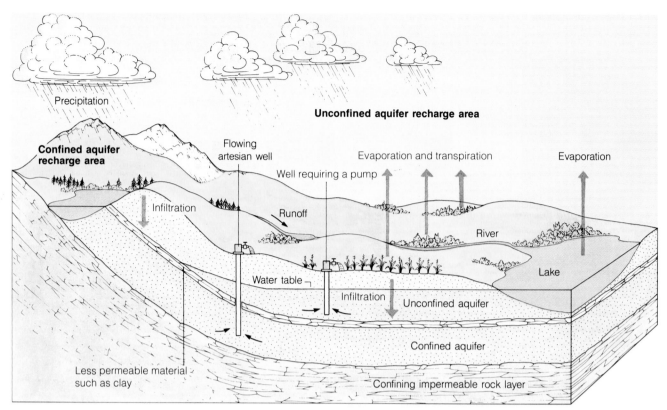

Figure 11-3 The groundwater system. An *unconfined*, or *water table*, *aquifer* forms when groundwater collects above a layer of rock or compacted clay through which water flows very slowly (low permeability). A *confined aquifer* is sandwiched between layers such as clay or shale that have a low permeability. Groundwater in this type of aquifer is confined and under pressure.

Figure 11-4 Drawdown of water table and cone of depression.

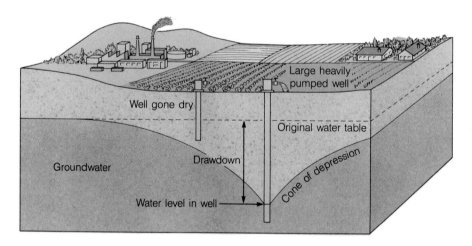

significant amount of water are called **aquifers**. Most aquifers are recharged or replenished naturally by precipitation, which percolates downward through soil and rock in what is called **natural recharge** (Figure 11-3). Any area of land allowing water to pass through it and into an aquifer is called a **recharge area**. Groundwater moves from the recharge area through an aquifer and out to a discharge area as part of the hydrologic cycle. Discharge areas can be wells, springs, lakes, geysers, streams, and oceans.

Normally, groundwater moves from points of high elevation and pressure to points of lower elevation and

pressure. This movement is quite slow, typically only a meter or so (about 3 feet) a year and rarely more than 0.3 meter (1 foot) a day. Thus, most aquifers are like huge, slow-moving underground lakes.

If the withdrawal rate of an aquifer exceeds its natural recharge rate, the water table around the withdrawal well is lowered, creating a waterless volume known as a *cone of depression* (Figure 11-4). Any pollutant discharged within the land area above the cone of depression will be pulled directly into the well and can have a devastating effect on the quality of water withdrawn from that well.

Q: How much of Earth's enormous supply of water is available to us as usable fresh water?

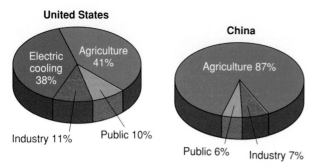

Figure 11-5 Use of water in the United States and China. (Data from Worldwatch Institute and World Resources Institute)

Some aquifers, called *fossil aquifers*, are often found deep underground, get very little recharge, and are nonrenewable resources on a human time scale. Withdrawals from fossil aquifers amount to "water mining" and eventually deplete these one-time deposits of liquid Earth capital.

WORLD AND U.S. WATER USE Two common measures of human water use are withdrawal and consumption. **Water withdrawal** involves taking water from a groundwater or surface-water source and transporting it to a place of use. **Water consumption** occurs when water that has been withdrawn is not returned to the surface water or groundwater from which it came so that it may be used again in that area, usually because the water has evaporated or transpired into the atmosphere. In arid areas, such as much of the western United States, the biggest consumptive uses of water are irrigation and lawn watering. Worldwide, about 60% of the water withdrawn is consumed.

Since 1950, global water withdrawal has increased three and a half times and per capita use has trebled, largely in response to the rapid growth in population, agriculture, and industrialization. Water withdrawals are projected to at least double in the next two decades to meet the food and other resource needs of the world's rapidly growing population.

The United States has the highest per capita water withdrawal in the world, followed by Canada, Australia, the CIS, Japan, and Mexico. Per capita water withdrawal in LDCs is typically 1% to 2% of that in the United States. If everyone on Earth had the same average per capita water withdrawal as in the United States, we would be trying to withdraw more fresh water than is available worldwide.

Uses of withdrawn water vary widely from one country to another (Figure 11-5). Averaged globally, about 63% of the water withdrawn each year is used to irrigate 18% of the world's cropland. The largest areas of irrigated land are found in the United States, the CIS, and Mexico. The percentage of withdrawn water used for irrigation can reach 80% or more in some areas, such as Egypt, where all cropland must be irrigated, and Pakistan, where 77% of the cropland is irrigated. In the western United States, irrigation accounts for about 85% of all water use.

Agriculture and manufacturing require large amounts of water (Figure 11-6). In most cases, much of that water could be used more efficiently and reused. Domestic and municipal use accounts for about 7% of worldwide withdrawals and about 13% to 16% of withdrawals in industrialized countries. Although the quantity of water required for domestic and municipal needs is not large, the quality must be high.

11-2 Water Resource Problems

TOO LITTLE WATER Droughts do more economic damage and harm more people worldwide than does any other natural hazard. During the 1970s, severe droughts affected an average of 24.4 million people per year, killed more than 23,000 a year, and created large numbers of environmental refugees—a trend that continued in the 1980s and 1990s (Figure 11-7). At least 80 arid and semiarid countries, where nearly 40% of the world's people live, experience cycles of droughts that can last several years. Areas likely to face increased water shortages in the 1990s and beyond include northern Africa, parts of India, northern China, much of the Middle East, Mexico, and parts of the western United States, Poland, and much of the CIS.

Reduced precipitation, higher-than-normal temperatures, or both usually trigger a drought; but rapid population growth and poor land use intensify its effects. The effects of drought are made worse by trying to support too many people and livestock in areas that normally have prolonged droughts and by local and regional climate changes brought about by severe loss of vegetation from deforestation (Section 15-2), overgrazing grasslands (Section 15-5), plowing prairies, and irrigating fields. In many LDCs, large numbers of poor people have no choice but to try to survive on drought-prone land.

Unless we take action now to slow down projected global warming (Section 10-2), severe droughts may occur more frequently in some areas of the world. It is also likely that irrigation systems will be poorly matched to altered rainfall patterns, jeopardizing our ability to produce enough food for the world's growing population and possibly leading to virtual abandonment of many water-starved cities built in desert areas.

Water will be the foremost foreign-policy issue for water-short countries in the 1990s and beyond. Almost 150 of the world's 214 largest river systems are shared by two countries and 50 by three to ten countries. Together, these countries contain 40% of the world's population, and they often clash over water rights (see Spotlight on p. 229).

Product   **Gallons of Water Used**
                 Agriculture

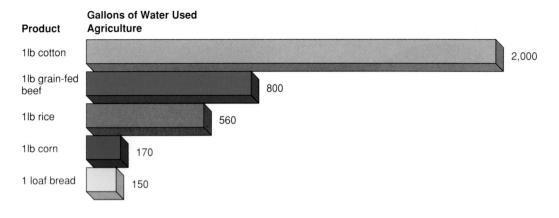

1 lb cotton — 2,000

1 lb grain-fed beef — 800

1 lb rice — 560

1 lb corn — 170

1 loaf bread — 150

Product   **Industry**

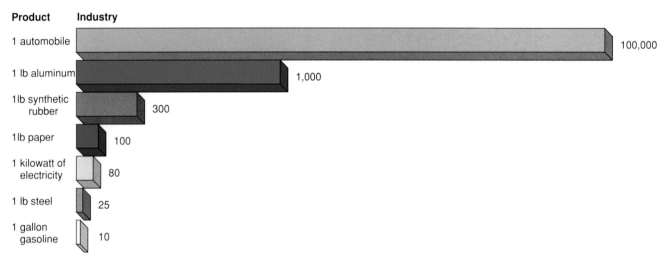

1 automobile — 100,000

1 lb aluminum — 1,000

1 lb synthetic rubber — 300

1 lb paper — 100

1 kilowatt of electricity — 80

1 lb steel — 25

1 gallon gasoline — 10

Figure 11-6 Amount of water typically used to produce various foods and products in the United States. (Data from U.S. Geological Survey)

International Development Research Center/Ottawa, Canada

Figure 11-7 Camp of drought refugees in Burkina Faso, West Africa, depicts the plight of some of the estimated 10 million people driven from their homes worldwide by environmental degradation.

Competition between cities and farmers for scarce water within countries is also escalating in areas such as California and northern China, where dozens of cities, including Beijing, already face acute water shortages. Water shortages are expected in 450 of China's 644 major cities by the turn of this century.

TOO MUCH WATER Some countries have enough annual precipitation but get most of it at one time of the year. In India, for example, 90% of the annual precipitation falls between June and September, the monsoon season. This downpour can cause flooding, waterlogging of soils, depletion of soil nutrients, and the washing away of topsoil and crops.

Hurricanes and typhoons can flood low-lying coastal areas. Prolonged rains anywhere can cause streams and lakes to overflow and flood surrounding land areas, but low-lying river basins are especially vulnerable to flooding.

During the 1970s, disastrous floods affected 15.4 million people annually, killed an average of 4,700 people a year, and caused tens of billions of dollars in property damages. This trend continued throughout the 1980s and into the 1990s.

       Q: What is the largest global use of water withdrawn from surface or groundwater sources?

Nowhere are conflicts over water supplies more serious than in the water-short Middle East (Figure 11-8). Arguments between Egypt, Ethiopia, and Sudan over access to the water from the Nile River basin are escalating rapidly. Ethiopia, which controls the headwaters of 80% of the Nile's flow, has plans to divert more of this water; so does Sudan.

Egypt, where it hardly ever rains, is almost completely desert except for a thin strip of productive land along the Nile and its delta. In 1989, Egypt's foreign minister warned: "The next war in our region will be over the waters of the Nile." Egypt's

only practical course is to sharply reduce population growth, which increases by 1 million every nine months, and reduce the enormous amount of water wasted through inefficient irrigation techniques.

Competition for water is also fierce between Jordan, Israel, and Syria, which get most of their water from the Jordan River basin (Figure 11-8). The 1967 Arab-Israeli war was fought in part over access to water from this river basin. Many towns in Jordan receive water only twice a week, and the country must double its supply over the next 20 years just to keep up with projected population growth.

Israel has been more effective at water conservation than has any other country in the world. Despite that success, Israel is now using 95% of its renewable supplies of fresh water, and supplies are projected to fall 30% short of demand by 2000.

Turkey is building a vast complex of dams on the Euphrates River. That project will drastically reduce the flow of water to Syria and Iraq, which lie downstream. Indeed, the greatest threat to Iraq is a cutoff of its water supply by Turkey and Syria. Clearly, distribution of water resources will be a key issue in any future peace processes in this highly volatile region.

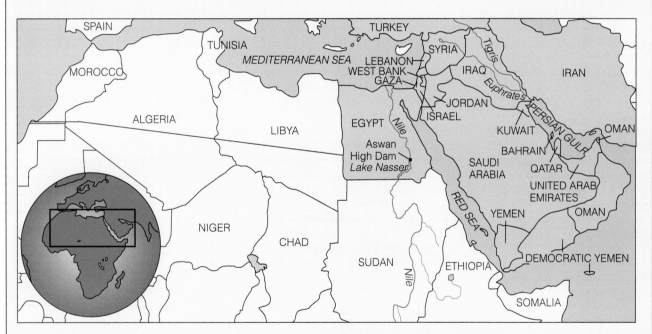

Figure 11-8 Where is the Middle East? Middle East countries have some of the highest population growth rates in the world. Because of their dry climate, food production depends on irrigation. In the 1990s and beyond, conflicts between countries over access to water supplies in this region may overshadow long-standing religious and ethnic clashes and conflicts over ownership of oil supplies.

Floods, like droughts, are usually called natural disasters, but human activities have contributed to the sharp rise in flood deaths and damages since the 1960s. Cultivation of land, deforestation (Figure 1-1), overgrazing, and mining have removed water-absorbing vegetation and soil (see Case Study on p. 230).

Urbanization also increases flooding, even with moderate rainfall. It replaces vegetation and soil with highways, parking lots, shopping centers, office build-

ings, homes, and other structures that lead to rapid runoff of rainwater. If sea levels rise during the next century as a result of projected global warming, flooding of low-lying coastal cities, wetlands, and croplands will increase dramatically.

WATER FAR FROM PEOPLE In some countries, the largest rivers, which carry most of the runoff, are far from agricultural and population centers where the

Bangladesh (Figure 6-21) is one of the world's most densely populated countries. More than 111 million people—almost half the population of the United States—are packed into an area roughly the size of Wisconsin. The country's population is projected to reach 212 million by 2025. Bangladesh is also one of the world's poorest countries, with an average per capita income of about $200 per year.

The country is located on a vast, low-lying delta of shifting islands of silt at the mouth of three rivers. Because most of the country consists of low-lying deltas and floodplains, its people are accustomed to flooding after water from annual monsoon rains in the Himalaya of India, Nepal, Bhutan, and China flows downward through rivers to Bangladesh and into the Bay of Bengal.

Bangladesh depends on this annual flooding to grow rice, its primary source of food. The annual deposit of Himalayan soil in the delta basin also helps maintain soil fertility. Thus, the people of this country are used to moderate annual flooding and need it for their survival. However, severe flooding from excessive Himalayan runoff and from storm surges caused by cyclones in the Bay of Bengal is disastrous.

In the past, great floods occurred only once every 50 years or so; but during the 1970s and 1980s, the average interval between major floods in Bangladesh was only four years. After a flood in 1974, an estimated 300,000 people died in a famine. In 1988, a disastrous flood covered two-thirds of the country's land mass for several days and leveled 2 million homes after the heaviest monsoon rains in 70 years (Figure 11-9). At least 2,000 people drowned and 30 million people—one out of four—were left homeless. Hundreds of thousands more contracted dis-

Figure 11-9 Some annual flooding in Bangladesh is necessary for growing rice, but the country now experiences more disastrous floods because other countries allow forest clearing in the watershed of the Himalaya.

eases such as cholera and typhoid fever from contaminated water and food supplies. At least a quarter of the country's crops were destroyed, costing this impoverished nation at least $1.5 billion and causing the premature deaths of thousands from starvation.

Bangladesh's flooding problems begin in the Himalayan watershed. There, a combination of rapid population growth, deforestation, overgrazing, and unsustainable farming on easily erodible steep mountain slopes has greatly diminished the ability of soil in this mountain watershed to absorb water. Instead of being absorbed and released slowly, water from the annual monsoon rain runs off the denuded foothills of the Himalaya north of Bangladesh's border. Then, heavier-than-normal monsoon rains cause severe flooding in Bangladesh. This deluge of water also carries with it the topsoil vital to the survival of people in the Himalaya.

In their struggle to survive, the poor in Bangladesh have cleared many of the country's coastal mangrove forests (Figure 5-22) for fuelwood and for growing food. This

deforestation has increased the severity of flooding because these coastal wetlands help protect the low-lying coastal areas from storm surges generated by cyclones in the Bay of Bengal. In 1970, between 200,000 and 1 million people drowned in one of these storms. Another cyclone killed an estimated 200,000 people in 1991. Flood damages and deaths in areas where protective mangrove forests still exist are much lower than in areas where they have been cleared.

The severity of this problem can be reduced only if Bangladesh, Bhutan, China, India, and Nepal all agree to cooperate in reforestation efforts and flood control measures. MDCs also have an important role to play. They must provide aid for reforestation and flood control. Equally important, they must do their part in dismantling the global poverty trap (Section 7-4) that forces the poor into unsustainable land use and makes them highly vulnerable to environmental change by having to survive on unprotected floodplains.

Q: How many people don't have a safe supply of drinking water?

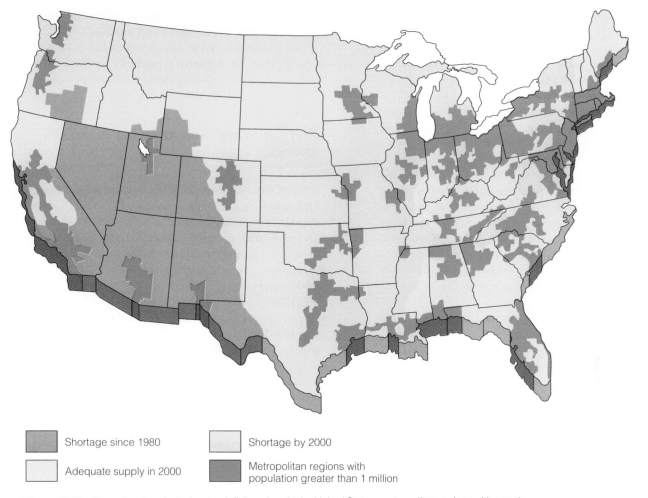

	Shortage since 1980		Shortage by 2000
	Adequate supply in 2000		Metropolitan regions with population greater than 1 million

Figure 11-10 Present and projected water deficit regions in the United States; metropolitan regions with populations greater than 1 million are superimposed. (Data from U.S. Water Resources Council and U.S. Geological Survey)

water is needed. For example, South America has the largest average annual runoff of any continent, but 60% of the runoff flows through the Amazon, the world's largest river, in areas far from where most people live (Figure 6-12).

In water-short areas, many women and children must walk long distances each day, carrying heavy jars or cans, to get a meager supply of sometimes-contaminated water for their families.

CONTAMINATED DRINKING WATER In its passage through the hydrologic cycle, water is polluted primarily by three kinds of waste: **(1)** sediment washed from the land into surface waters by natural erosion and by greatly accelerated erosion of soil from agriculture, forestry, mining, construction, and other land-clearing and disturbing activities, **(2)** organic waste from human and animal excreta and the discarded parts of harvested plants, and **(3)** the rapidly increasing volume of a variety of hazardous chemicals produced by industrialized societies. All three categories of waste are increasing because of rapid population growth, poverty, and industrialization (see the last half of this chapter).

According to the World Health Organization, 1.5 billion people don't have a safe supply of drinking water and 1.7 billion don't have adequate sanitation facilities. At least 5 million people, mostly children under age 5, die every year from waterborne diseases that could be prevented by improvements in supplies of drinking water and in sanitation. This amounts to an average death rate of 13,700 people a day.

In 1980, the United Nations called for MDCs and LDCs to spend $300 billion to supply all of the world's people with clean drinking water and adequate sanitation by 1990. The $30-billion-a-year cost of this program would be roughly equal to what the world spends every 10 days for military purposes. The actual amount spent during the 1980s was only about $1.5 billion a year, far short of the goal.

THE U.S. SITUATION Overall, the United States has plenty of fresh water, but certain regions have a shortage of water (Figure 11-10). Much of the country's annual runoff is not in the desired place, occurs at the wrong time, or is contaminated from agricultural and industrial activities. Most of the eastern half of the country usually has ample precipitation, while much of the western half has too little.

The most serious water problem in the arid and semiarid areas of the western half of the country is a shortage of runoff caused by low precipitation, high rates of evaporation, and recurring prolonged drought. About 85% of western water is used to irrigate crops. As a result, water tables are dropping rapidly as farmers and cities deplete groundwater aquifers faster than they are recharged.

Many major urban centers in the United States are located in areas that don't have enough water or are projected to have water shortages by 2000, especially in the West and Midwest (Figure 11-10). These shortages could worsen if the world's climate warms up as a result of an enhanced greenhouse effect. Because water is such a vital resource, you might find Figures 6-15 and 11-10 useful in deciding where to live in coming decades.

In many parts of the eastern United States, the most serious water problems are flooding; inability to supply enough water to some large urban areas; and pollution of streams, lakes, and groundwater. For example, 3 million residents of Long Island, New York, must draw all their water from an aquifer. This aquifer is becoming severely contaminated by industrial wastes, leaking septic tanks and landfills, and ocean water, which is drawn into the aquifer when fresh water is withdrawn faster than it is naturally recharged.

11-3 Water Resource Management

METHODS FOR MANAGING WATER RESOURCES
One way to manage water resources is to increase the supply in a particular area, mostly by building dams and reservoirs, bringing in surface water from another area, and tapping groundwater. The other approach is to improve the efficiency of water use by decreasing unnecessary use and waste.

When LDCs do not have enough water, they also rarely have the money needed to develop the water storage and distribution systems needed to increase their supply. Their people must settle where the water is.

In MDCs, people tend to live where the climate is favorable and bring in water through expensive transfers of water from one watershed to another. Some settle

---

Table 11-1 Advantages and Disadvantages of Large Dams and Reservoirs

Advantages

Reduce danger of flooding downstream by controlling stream flow.

Provide a controllable supply of water for irrigating arid and semiarid land below the dam.

Can be used to provide electric power from the energy of water flowing through turbines. Hydroelectric power plants provide 20% of the world's electricity.

Reservoirs behind large dams can also be used for outdoor recreation such as swimming, boating, and fishing.

Disadvantages

Expensive to build.

Flooding of land behind dam to form the reservoir displaces people and destroys vast areas of valuable agricultural land, wildlife habitat, and scenic natural beauty.

Storage of water behind a dam raises the water table, which often waterlogs the soil on nearby land, decreasing its crop or forest productivity.

Diversion of water into reservoir reduces aquifer recharge in the watershed above the dam.

Tremendous weight of the water impounded in reservoirs increases the likelihood of fault movement, which causes subsidence and earthquakes.

Evaporation increases the salinity of reservoir water, decreasing its usefulness for irrigation.

Reservoirs fill up with silt and become useless in 40 to 200 years, depending on local climate and land-use practices.

Can give developers and residents in a floodplain below the dam a false sense of safety from major floods, which can overwhelm the ability of a dam to control floodwaters.

Danger of collapse.

Disrupt the migration and spawning of fish, such as salmon.

Deprive downstream croplands and estuaries of vital nutrients from silt deposited by annual flooding and decrease their productivity.

Q: How many people die every year from preventable waterborne diseases?

in a desert and expect water to be brought to them at a low price. Others settle on a floodplain and expect the government to keep floodwaters away.

Increasing the water supply in some areas is important, but this approach is eventually overwhelmed by increasing population, food production, industrialization, and unpredictable shifts in water supplies from projected global warming. Thus, it makes much more sense economically and environmentally to emphasize prevention methods that increase the efficiency of the ways we use water in agriculture, industry, and homes and thus help prevent unnecessary waste of this precious resource.

CONSTRUCTING DAMS AND RESERVOIRS Rainwater and water from melting snow that would otherwise be lost can be captured and stored in large reservoirs behind dams built across streams (Figure 5-30). Large dams and reservoirs have benefits and drawbacks (see Table 11-1).

Studies have shown that large-scale dams in LDCs often tend to benefit a small minority of the well-to-do while flooding the lands and often destroying floodwater farming and fisheries that are vital to the poor majority. Building small dams, which can avoid most of

the destructive effects of large dams and reservoirs (Table 11-1), is a useful way to trap more water for irrigation.

WATERSHED TRANSFERS Water can be moved around by building dams and reservoirs to collect river runoff and then using tunnels, canals, and underground pipes to transfer water from water-rich watersheds to water-poor areas. Two of the world's largest watershed transfer projects are the California Water Project (see Case Study below) and diversion of water from rivers feeding the Aral Sea in the CIS to irrigate cropland (see Case Study on p. 234).

In 1971, construction began on a huge $50 billion, 50-year scheme, known as the James Bay Project, to harness the wild rivers that flow into the James and Hudson bays in Canada's Quebec province, to produce electric power for use by Canadian and U.S. consumers. When completed, the project will involve reversing or altering the flow of 19 major rivers, reshaping a territory the size of France, flooding boreal forest and tundra equal to the area of the state of Washington, and displacing thousands of members of the Cree Indian Nation. Its proponents call it "the engineering project of the century," while its opponents call it the "ecological and economic folly of the century."

CASE STUDY Conflict over Water Supply in California

In California, the basic water problem is that 75% of the population lives south of Sacramento, but 75% of the rain falls north of it. The California Water Project uses a maze of giant dams, pumps, and aqueducts to transport water from water-rich parts of northern California to heavily populated parts of northern California and to mostly arid and semiarid, heavily populated southern California (Figure 11-11). For decades, northern and southern Californians have been feuding over how the state's water should be allocated under this plan.

People in arid southern California say they need more water from the north for growing crops and supporting Los Angeles, San Diego, and other large and growing urban areas. Opponents in the north say that sending more water south would degrade the Sacramento River, threaten fishing, and reduce the flushing action that helps clean San Francisco Bay of pollutants.

Figure 11-11 California Water Project and Central Arizona Project for large-scale transfer of water from one watershed to another. Arrows show general direction of water flow.

(continued)

They also argue that much of the water already sent south is wasted and that an increase of only 10% in irrigation efficiency would provide enough water for domestic and industrial uses in southern California.

In California's giant Central Valley irrigation project, farmers have had to pay only 5% of what it has cost American taxpayers to supply them with this water for the last 40 years. To supply agribusiness in California and other parts of the West with such cheap water, the Bureau of Reclamation has drained major rivers, lakes, and large areas of prime wetlands; destroyed vast areas of wetland waterfowl habitat and salmon spawning habitat; and contaminated rivers and groundwater with pesticides and fertilizers.

Conservationists believe that the government should not award new long-term water contracts that give many farmers and ranchers cheap, federally subsidized water for irrigating crops — especially grass for cows and "thirsty" crops such as rice, alfalfa, and cotton — that could be grown more cheaply in rain-fed areas. They also propose that cities wanting more water should also be required to pay farmers to install water-saving irrigation technology and then have the right to use the water saved. Bringing about these changes is difficult because the political power of California's farmers greatly exceeds their contribution to the state's economy.

A related project is the federally financed $3.9 billion Central Arizona Project, which pumps water from the Colorado River uphill to Phoenix and Tucson (Figure 11-11). When the first part of this project was completed in 1985, southern California, especially the arid and booming San Diego region, began losing up to one-fifth of its water, which Arizona has a legal right to divert. Because of this project, Arizona has been able to reduce its dependence on groundwater from over 90% to about 65%.

If water supplies in California should drop sharply because of projected global warming, water delivered by this huge distribution system would drop sharply. Most irrigated agriculture in California would have to be abandoned, and much of the population of southern California might have to move to areas with more water.

Groundwater is no answer. It is already being withdrawn faster than it is being replenished throughout much of California. Improving irrigation efficiency is a much quicker and cheaper solution.

CASE STUDY The Aral Sea Ecological Disaster

Another example of large-scale watershed transfer is in the CIS republics of Kazakhstan and Uzbekistan, which have the driest climate in Central Asia. Since 1960, enormous amounts of irrigation water have been diverted from the inland Aral Sea and the two rivers that replenish its water to grow cotton and food crops.

This diversion has caused a regional ecological disaster, described by one former Soviet official as "ten times worse than the 1986 accident at the Chernobyl nuclear power plant." Since 1960, the flow of the two rivers into the Aral Sea has been reduced to a trickle. As a result, the volume of the Aral Sea — once the world's fourth largest freshwater lake — has dropped by 69%, salinity levels have risen threefold, and its surface area has shrunk by 46%.

All native fish species have disappeared, devastating the area's fishing industry, which once provided work for more than 60,000 people. Two major fishing towns are now in a desert containing graveyards of stranded fishing boats and rusting commercial ships. Roughly half of the area's species of birds and mammals have disappeared.

Salt, dust, and dried pesticide residues have also been carried by winds and deposited on towns and cropfields as far as 300 kilometers (190 miles) away. As the salt spreads, it kills crops and trees, wildlife, and pastureland.

Local farmers have turned to herbicides, insecticides, and fertilizers to keep growing some crops. Many of these chemicals have percolated downward and accumulated to dangerous levels in the groundwater used as the source of most drinking water. The area has experienced soaring rates of hepatitis (up sevenfold since 1960), typhoid fever (up 30-fold since 1960), kidney disease, birth deformities, intestinal infections, throat and other cancers, and respiratory and eye diseases. The area also has the highest infant mortality rate in the CIS.

Ways to deal with this problem include charging farmers more for irrigation water to reduce waste and encourage a shift to less-water-intensive crops, decreasing irrigation-water quotas, introducing water-saving technologies such as drip irrigation, developing a regional integrated water management plan, planting protective forest belts, improving health services, and instituting a serious family planning effort to slow the area's rapid population growth (3% a year).

In 1990, the former Soviet Union and the United Nations Environment Programme signed an agreement to save the Aral Sea. However, given the political and economic crises brought about by the breakup of the Soviet Union, the huge sums of money needed to do this will probably not be available.

Q: How much drinking water in the United States is withdrawn from groundwater?

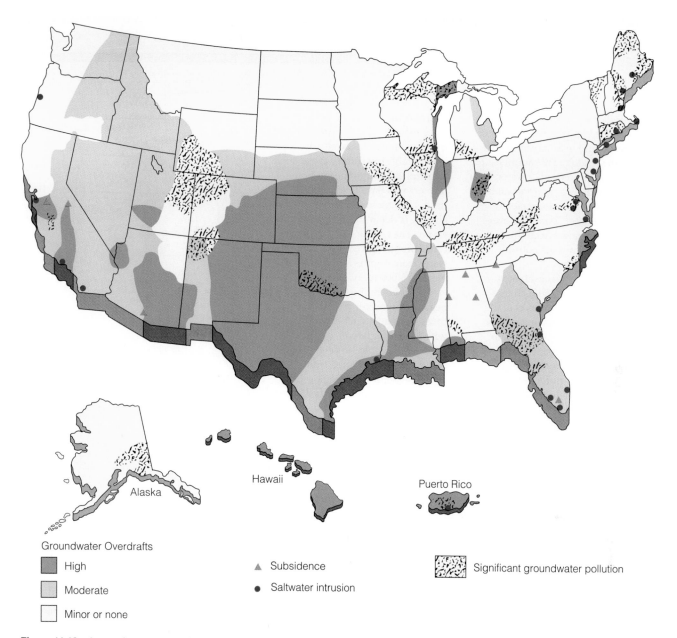

Figure 11-12 Areas of greatest aquifer depletion, subsidence, saltwater intrusion into aquifers when the water table is lowered by large-scale withdrawal of fresh water in coastal areas, and groundwater contamination in the United States. (Data from U.S. Water Resources Council and U.S. Geological Survey)

Groundwater Overdrafts

- High
- Moderate
- Minor or none

▲ Subsidence

● Saltwater intrusion

Significant groundwater pollution

There have been proposals to tow massive icebergs to arid coastal areas (such as Saudi Arabia and southern California) and pump the fresh water from the melting bergs ashore. However, the technology for doing this is not available and the costs may be too high, especially for water-short LDCs.

TAPPING GROUNDWATER In the United States, about half of the drinking water (96% in rural areas and 20% in urban areas), 40% of the irrigation water, and 23% of all fresh water used is withdrawn from groundwater. In Florida, Hawaii, Idaho, Mississippi, Nebraska, and New Mexico, more than 90% of the population depends on groundwater for supplies of drinking water.

Overuse of groundwater can cause or intensify several problems: *aquifer depletion, subsidence* (sinking of land when groundwater is withdrawn), and *intrusion of salt water into aquifers* (Figure 11-12). Groundwater can also become contaminated from industrial and agricultural activities, septic tanks, and other sources (Section 11-7).

Currently, about one-fourth of the groundwater withdrawn in the United States is not replenished. The most serious groundwater overdraft problem is in parts of the huge Ogallala Aquifer, extending under the farm belt from northern Nebraska to northwestern Texas (see Case Study on p. 236).

Aquifer depletion is also a serious problem in northern China, Mexico City (see Case Study on

A: About 50% (96% in rural areas and 20% in urban areas)

Water withdrawn from the vast Ogallala Aquifer (Figure 11-13), which underlies the arid Great Plains, is used to irrigate one-fifth of all U.S. cropland in an area too dry for rainfall farming. This aquifer contains a huge amount of water, but it is essentially a nonrenewable fossil aquifer with an extremely slow recharge rate. Today, the overall rate of withdrawal from this aquifer is eight times its natural recharge rate.

Even higher withdrawal rates, sometimes 100 times the recharge rate, are taking place in parts of the aquifer that lie beneath Texas, New Mexico, Oklahoma, and Colorado. Water resource experts project that at the present rate of withdrawal, one-fourth of the aquifer's original supply will be depleted by 2020 — much sooner in areas where it is shallow. When this water is gone, it will take thousands of years to replenish the aquifer.

Long before that happens, the high cost of pumping water from a rapidly dropping water table will force many farmers to grow crops that need much less water, instead of profitable but thirsty crops such as cotton and sugar beets. Some farmers will have to go out of business. The amount of irrigated land already is declining in five of the seven states using this aquifer because of the high cost of pumping water from depths as great as 1,830 meters (6,000 feet).

If farmers in the Ogallala region began using water conservation measures and switched to crops with low water needs, depletion of the aquifer would be delayed. Since water is being depleted from this one-time deposit to provide 40% of the beef produced in the United States, each time Americans eat hamburgers or other forms of beef, they contribute to this loss of Earth capital.

Ogallala Aquifer

Figure 11-13 Ogallala Aquifer.

p. 127), Bangkok (Thailand), and parts of India. Ways to slow groundwater depletion include reducing the amount withdrawn by wasting less irrigation water, not growing water-thirsty crops in dry areas, developing crop strains that require less water and that are more resistant to heat stress, and controlling population growth.

When groundwater in an unconfined aquifer (Figure 11-3) is withdrawn faster than it is replenished, relatively unconsolidated land overlying the aquifer can sink, or subside. This subsidence can damage pipelines, highways, railroad beds, and buildings (Figure 11-14).

When fresh water is withdrawn from an aquifer near a coast faster than it is recharged, salt water intrudes into the aquifer (Figure 11-15). Saltwater intrusion threatens to contaminate the drinking water of many towns and cities along the Atlantic and Gulf coasts (Figure 11-12) and in the coastal areas of Israel, Syria, and the Arabian Gulf states. Another growing problem in the United States and many other MDCs is groundwater contamination, discussed in Section 11-7.

DESALINATION Removing dissolved salts from ocean water or brackish (slightly salty) groundwater is an appealing way to increase freshwater supplies. Dis-

tillation and reverse osmosis are the two most widely used desalination methods. *Distillation* involves heating salt water until it evaporates and condenses as fresh water, leaving salts behind in solid form. In *reverse osmosis*, large amounts of electric power create a high pressure that forces salt water through a thin membrane whose pores allow water molecules, but not dissolved salts, to pass through.

Currently, there are about 7,500 desalination plants meeting less than 0.1% of world water use. Desalination plants in arid parts of the Middle East (especially Saudi Arabia) and North Africa produce about two-thirds of the world's desalinated water. Desalination is also used in parts of Florida. Soon, Marin County in northern California and cities in southern California such as Santa Barbara, San Diego, and Los Angeles may begin to use this expensive way to supplement their water supplies.

These desalination methods use vast amounts of energy and therefore are expensive; in addition, they produce toxic wastes. Desalination can provide fresh water for coastal cities in arid regions, such as sparsely populated and oil-rich Saudi Arabia, where the cost of getting fresh water by any method is high. But desalinated water will probably never be cheap enough to use for irrigating conventional crops or to meet much of the

Q: Worldwide, how much of the water withdrawn is unnecessarily wasted?

Figure 11-14 Subsidence in Winter Park, Florida, in May 1981. This large sinkhole developed rapidly one evening and caused $2 million in damage. By morning, it was about 80 meters (260 feet) across and had swallowed a house, parts of two businesses, portions of pavement on two streets, a large part of a municipal swimming pool, and several cars.

George Remaine

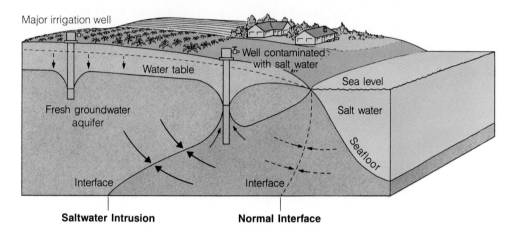

Figure 11-15 Saltwater intrusion along a coastal region. When the water table is lowered, the normal interface (dotted line) between fresh and saline groundwater moves inland (solid line).

world's demand for fresh water, unless efficient solar-powered methods can be developed.

Another problem is that even more energy and money would be needed to pump desalinated water uphill and inland from coastal desalination plants. Moreover, a vast network of desalination plants would produce large quantities of concentrated brine with high levels of salt and other minerals that must go somewhere. The easiest and cheapest solution would be to dump the concentrated brine in the ocean near the plants, but doing so would increase the salt concentration and threaten food resources in estuarine waters. Another solution is to dump these wastes on the land where they can contaminate groundwater and surface water. There is no away.

UNNECESSARY WATER WASTE Mohamed El-Ashry of the World Resources Institute estimates that *65% to 70% of the water people use throughout the world is unnecessarily wasted through evaporation, leaks, and other losses.* The United States—the world's largest user of water—does slightly better but still unnecessarily

wastes 50% of the water it withdraws. El-Ashry believes that it is economically and technically feasible to reduce water waste to 15%, which would mean we could meet most of the world's current and projected water needs.

A prime cause of water waste in the United States (and in most countries) is artificially low water prices, which discourage users from conserving water and installing water-conserving devices and processes. Low-cost water is the only reason that farmers in Arizona and southern California can grow water-thirsty crops like alfalfa in the middle of the desert. It also allows people in Palm Springs, California, to keep their lawns and 74 golf courses green in a desert area.

These and other water subsidies are paid for by all taxpayers in the form of higher taxes. Because these external costs don't show up on monthly water bills, consumers have little incentive to conserve. Raising the price of water to reflect its true cost would provide powerful incentives for reducing water waste.

In the United States, the federal Bureau of Reclamation supplies one-fourth of the water used to irrigate land in the West under long-term contracts (typically

A: 65% to 70% (50% in the United States)

Laws regulating water access and use differ in the eastern and western parts of the United States. In most of the East, water use is based on the doctrine of **riparian rights**, which gives anyone whose land adjoins a flowing stream the legal right to use water from the stream as long as some is left for downstream land-owners. However, as population and water-intensive land uses grow, there is often not enough water to meet the needs of all the people along a stream.

In the arid and semiarid West, the riparian system does not work, because large amounts of water are needed in areas far from major surface-water sources. In most of this region the principle of **prior appropriation** regulates water use. In this first-come, first-served ap-proach, the first user of water from a stream establishes a legal right for continued use of the amount origi-nally withdrawn. Some areas of the United States have a combination of riparian and prior-appropriation water rights.

To hold on to their prior-appropriation rights, users within a particular state must keep on with-drawing and using a certain amount of water even if they don't need it — a use-it-or-lose-it approach. This discourages farmers from using water-conserving irrigation meth-ods. This use-it-or-lose-it rule does not apply to water bodies shared by two or more states. Water allocation between states is determined by in-terstate compacts and court decrees.

Most groundwater use is based on common law, which holds that subsurface water belongs to whoever owns the land above such water. This means that landowners can withdraw as much as they want to use on their land. When many users tap the same aquifer, that aquifer becomes a common-property resource. The multiple users may remove water at a faster rate than it is replaced by natural re-charge. The largest users have little incentive to conserve and can de-plete the aquifer for everyone.

Environmentalists and many economists call for a change in laws allocating rights to surface and groundwater supplies, with empha-sis on *water marketing*. They believe that farmers and other users who save water through conservation or switching to less-thirsty crops should be able to sell or lease the water they save to industries and cities rather than losing their rights to this water. What do you think should be done?

40 years) at greatly subsidized prices. During the 1990s, hundreds of these long-term water contracts will come up for renewal. If Congress requires the Bureau of Rec-lamation to sharply raise the price of federally subsi-dized water to encourage investments in improving water efficiency, many of the water supply problems in the West could be eased. Outdated laws governing ac-cess and use of water resources also encourage unnec-essary water waste (see Spotlight above).

Another reason that water waste in the United States is greater than necessary is that the responsibility for water resource management in a particular wa-tershed is divided among many state and local govern-ments rather than being handled by one authority. For example, the Chicago metropolitan area has 349 water-supply systems, divided among some 2,000 local units of government over a six-county area.

In sharp contrast is the regional approach to water management used in England and Wales. The British Water Act of 1973 replaced more than 1,600 agencies with 10 regional water authorities based on natural wa-tershed boundaries. In this integrated approach, each water authority owns, finances, and manages all water-supply and waste treatment facilities in its region. The responsibilities of each authority include water pollu-tion control, water-based recreation, land drainage and flood control, inland navigation, and inland fisheries. Each water authority is managed by a group of elected local officials and a smaller number of officials ap-pointed by the national government.

REDUCING IRRIGATION LOSSES Since irrigation accounts for about 63% of water use and since almost two-thirds of that water is wasted, more efficient use of even a small amount of irrigation water frees water for other uses. Most irrigation systems distribute water from a groundwater well or a surface canal by down-slope or gravity flow through unlined field ditches (Fig-ure 11-16). This method is cheap as long as farmers in water-short areas don't have to pay the real cost of mak-ing this water available. But it provides far more water than needed for crop growth, and 40% to 50% of the water is lost by evaporation and seepage. Such overwa-tering without adequate drainage also decreases crop yields by waterlogging and the buildup of salts in the soil (Section 12-4).

Farmers could prevent seepage by placing plastic, concrete, or tile liners in irrigation canals. Lasers can also be used as a surveying aid to help level fields so that water gets distributed more evenly. Small check dams of earth and stone can be used to capture runoff from hillsides and channel this water to fields. Holding ponds can be used to store rainfall or to capture irriga-tion water for recycling to crops. Restoring deforested watersheds also leads to a more manageable flow of

Figure 11-16 Gravity-flow systems like this one in California irrigate most of the world's irrigated cropland, but only about 50% to 60% of the water actually gets to the crops.

Figure 11-17 Center-pivot irrigation systems like this one in Texas can reduce water consumed by seepage and evaporation to about 30%. Turbine pumps remove water from deep wells and feed it through huge water-propelled sprinklers that move in a huge circle and spray water on the land.

Figure 11-18 Drip irrigation greatly reduces water use and waste. A perforated pipe delivers a small volume of water close to the roots of plants in Rancho, California. For about $250, homeowners can install such a system to irrigate gardens and also add fertilizer. Plastic tubing is run to the plants, and a pressure regulator is used to reduce the flow rate. For another $50, a timer run by a computer chip and a soil-moisture sensor can be used to operate the system.

irrigation water, instead of a devastating flood (see Case Study on p. 230).

Farmers in LDCs can use inexpensive tube wells to withdraw groundwater for irrigation, watering livestock, and household use, as long as withdrawals don't exceed the natural recharge rate. In rural areas where there is no electricity, new energy-efficient pumps for these wells can be run by photovoltaic cells powered by the sun (Section 17-3).

Many farmers served by the dwindling Ogallala Aquifer have switched from gravity-flow canal systems to center-pivot sprinkler systems (Figure 11-17), which reduce water waste from 40% or more to 30%. Some farmers are switching to low-energy precision-application (LEPA) sprinkler systems. These systems cut water waste to about 25% by spraying water closer to the ground and in larger droplets than does the conventional center-pivot system. They also reduce energy use and costs by 20% to 30%. However, because of the high initial costs, sprinklers are used on only about 1% of the world's irrigated land.

In the 1960s, highly efficient trickle or drip irrigation systems were developed in arid Israel. A network of perforated piping, installed at or below the ground surface, releases a small volume of water close to the roots of plants (Figure 11-18). This minimizes evaporation and seepage and cuts water waste to 10% to 20%. These systems are expensive to install but are economically feasible for high-profit fruit, vegetable, and orchard crops and for home gardens. They would become cost-effective in most areas if water prices were raised to reflect the true cost of this resource.

Irrigation efficiency can also be improved by computer-controlled systems that monitor soil moisture and irrigate only when necessary. Farmers can switch to more water-efficient, drought-resistant, and salt-tolerant crop varieties. Also, organic farming tech-

niques produce higher crop yields per hectare and require only one-quarter of the water and fertilizer used by conventional farming. Since 1950, Israel has used many of these techniques to decrease waste of irrigation water by about 84%, while expanding the country's irrigated land by 44%.

As supplies of fresh water become more scarce and cities take over much of the water formerly used for irrigation, carefully treated urban wastewater could be used for irrigation. Effluents from sewage treatment plants are rich in plant nutrients, mostly nitrates and phosphates. Presently, these nutrients are often dumped into waterways where they overfertilize aquatic plant life, deplete dissolved oxygen, kill fish, and disrupt aquatic ecosystems. It makes more sense to return these nutrients to the land to fertilize trees, crops, and other vegetation. Israel is now using 35% of its municipal wastewater, mostly for irrigation, and plans to reuse 80% of this flow by 2000.

As long as government-subsidized water is available at low cost, farmers and other users have little incentive to conserve it. In most parts of the world, water is our most underpriced resource.

WASTING LESS WATER IN INDUSTRY Manufacturing processes either can use recycled water or can be redesigned to use and waste less water. Japan and Israel lead the world in reducing water use and waste and recycling water in industry. For example, to produce 0.9 metric ton (1 ton) of paper, a paper mill in Hadera, Israel, uses one-tenth as much water as most other paper mills do. Manufacturing aluminum from recycled scrap rather than virgin ores can reduce water needs by 97%.

Industry is the largest conserver of water. But the potential for water recycling in U.S. manufacturing has hardly been tapped because the cost of water to many industries is subsidized by taxpayers through federally financed water projects. A higher, more realistic price would greatly stimulate water reuse and conservation in industry.

WASTING LESS WATER IN HOMES AND BUSINESSES Flushing toilets, washing hands, and bathing account for about 78% of the water used in a typical home in the United States. In the arid western United States and in dry Australia, watering lawns and gardens can use up to 80% of a household's daily water expenditure. Much of this water is unnecessarily wasted.

Leaks in pipes, water mains, toilets, bathtubs, and faucets waste an estimated 20% to 35% of water withdrawn from public supplies. Because water costs so little, leaking water faucets are often not repaired, and large quantities of water are used to clean sidewalks and streets and to irrigate lawns and golf courses. Instead of being a status symbol, a green lawn in an arid or semiarid area should be viewed as a major ecological wrong (an anti-Earth activity) and should be replaced with types of low-water-use vegetation adapted to a dry climate (a form of landscaping called xeriscaping).

Many cities offer no incentive to reduce leaks and waste. In New York City, for example, 95% of the residential units don't have water meters. Users are charged flat rates, with the average family paying less than $100 a year for virtually unlimited use of high-quality water. This situation exists for one-fifth of all U.S. public water systems. Many apartment dwellers have little incentive to conserve water because their water use is included in their rent.

In Boulder, Colorado, the introduction of water meters reduced water use by more than one-third. Tucson,

Arizona, is a desert city that has city ordinances that require conserving and reusing water. On a per capita basis, Tucson now consumes half the water of Las Vegas, where water conservation is still voluntary. Ways that each of us can conserve water are listed inside the back cover.

Commercially available systems can be used to purify and completely recycle wastewater from houses, apartments, and office buildings. Such a system can be leased and installed in a small shed outside a residence or building and can be serviced for a monthly fee about equal to that charged by most city water and sewer systems. In Tokyo, all the water used in Mitsubishi's 60-story office building is purified for reuse by an automated recycling system.

11-4	**Principal Forms of Water Pollution**

MAJOR TYPES AND EFFECTS OF WATER POLLUTANTS The following are eight common types of water pollutants:

- *Disease-causing agents* — bacteria, viruses, protozoa, and parasitic worms that enter water from domestic sewage and animal wastes. In LDCs, they are the biggest cause of sickness and death, prematurely killing an average of 25,000 people each day — half of them children under five. A good indicator of the quality of water for drinking or swimming is the number of colonies of *coliform bacteria* present in a 100-milliliter sample of water. The World Health Organization recommends a coliform bacteria count of zero colonies per 100 milliliters for drinking water, and the EPA recommended maximum level for swimming water is 200 colonies per 100 milliliters.

- *Oxygen-demanding wastes* — organic wastes, which can be decomposed by aerobic bacteria that use oxygen to biodegrade organic wastes. Large populations of bacteria supported by these wastes can deplete water of dissolved oxygen gas, killing fish and other forms of oxygen-consuming aquatic life.

- *Water-soluble inorganic chemicals* — acids, salts, and compounds of toxic metals such as lead and mercury. High levels of such dissolved solids can make water unfit to drink, harm fish and other aquatic life, depress crop yields, and accelerate corrosion of equipment that uses water.

- *Inorganic plant nutrients* — water-soluble nitrate and phosphate compounds that can cause excessive growth of algae and other aquatic plants, which then die and decay, depleting water of dissolved oxygen and killing fish. Excessive levels of nitrates

Q: What percentage of U.S. toilets leak?

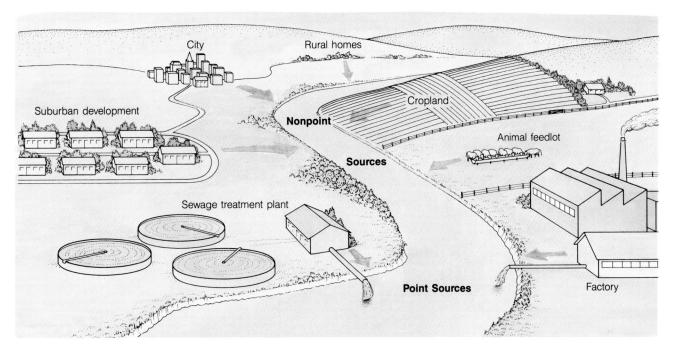

Figure 11-19 Point and nonpoint sources of water pollution.

in drinking water can reduce the oxygen-carrying capacity of the blood and kill unborn children and infants, especially those under three months old.

- *Organic chemicals* — oil, gasoline, plastics, pesticides, cleaning solvents, detergents, and many other water-soluble and insoluble chemicals that threaten human health and harm fish and other aquatic life.

- *Sediment or suspended matter* — insoluble particles of soil and other solid inorganic and organic materials that become suspended in water and that in terms of total mass are the largest source of water pollution. Suspended particulate matter clouds the water; reduces the ability of some organisms to find food; reduces photosynthesis by aquatic plants; disrupts aquatic food webs; and carries pesticides, bacteria, and other harmful substances. Sediment that settles out destroys feeding and spawning grounds of fish and clogs and fills lakes, artificial reservoirs, stream channels, and harbors.

- *Radioactive substances* — radioisotopes that are water soluble or capable of being biologically amplified to higher concentrations as they pass through food chains and webs. Ionizing radiation from such isotopes can cause birth defects, cancer, and genetic damage.

- *Heat* — excessive input of water that is heated when it is used to cool electric power plants. The resulting increase in water temperatures lowers dissolved oxygen content and makes aquatic organisms more vulnerable to disease, parasites, and toxic chemicals.

POINT AND NONPOINT SOURCES **Point sources** discharge pollutants at specific locations through pipes, ditches, or sewers into bodies of surface water (Figure 11-19). Examples include factories, sewage treatment plants (which remove some but not all pollutants), active and abandoned underground coal mines, gold mines, offshore oil wells, and oil tankers. Because point sources are at specific places (mostly in urban areas), they are fairly easy to identify, monitor, and regulate. In MDCs, many industrial discharges are strictly controlled, while in LDCs, they are largely uncontrolled.

Nonpoint sources are big land areas that discharge pollutants into surface and underground water over a large area and parts of the atmosphere where pollutants are deposited on surface waters (Figure 11-19). Examples include runoff of chemicals into surface water and seepage into the ground from croplands, livestock feedlots, logged forests, urban and suburban lands, septic tanks, construction areas, parking lots, roadways, and acid deposition (Figure 9-7).

In the United States, nonpoint pollution from agriculture — mostly in the form of sediment, commercial inorganic fertilizer, manure, salts dissolved in irrigation water, and pesticides — is responsible for 65% of the total mass of pollutants entering streams and 57% of those entering lakes. Livestock in the United States produce five times as much organic waste as humans and twice as much as industry. Little progress has been made in the control of nonpoint water pollution because of the difficulty and expense of identifying and controlling discharges from so many diffuse sources and because of government inaction.

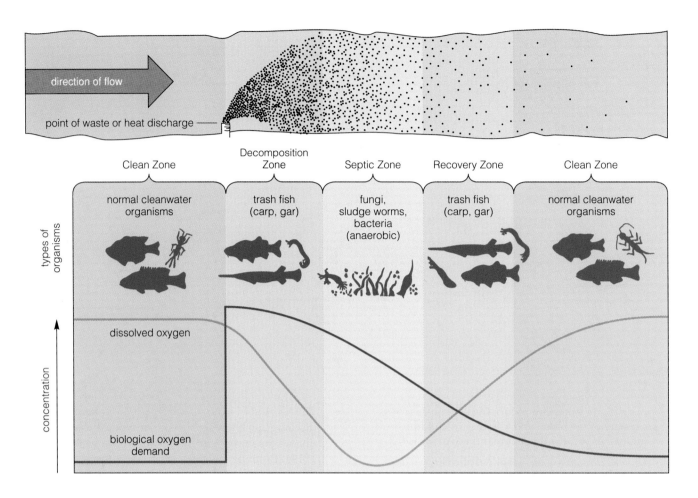

Figure 11-20 The oxygen sag curve (orange) versus oxygen demand (blue). Depending on flow rates and the amount of pollutants, streams recover from oxygen-demanding wastes and heat if given enough time and if they are not overloaded.

 Pollution of Streams and Lakes

STREAMS AND OXYGEN-CONSUMING WASTES
Because they flow, most streams recover rapidly from some forms of pollution, especially excess heat and degradable oxygen-demanding wastes (Figure 11-20). This recovery process works only as long as streams are not overloaded with degradable pollutants or heat and their flow is not reduced by drought, damming, or diversion for agriculture and industries. Slowly degradable and nondegradable pollutants are not eliminated by these natural dilution and degradation processes.

The depth and width of the *oxygen sag curve* (Figure 11-20), and thus the time and distance a stream takes to recover, depend on the stream's volume, flow rate, temperature, and pH (Figure 9-8) and on the volume of incoming degradable wastes. Similar oxygen sag curves occur when heated water from power plants is discharged into streams.

Along many streams, water for drinking is removed *upstream* from a city, and the city's industrial and sewage wastes are discharged *downstream*. This pattern might be repeated hundreds of times along the stream as it flows toward the sea, and the stream can then become overloaded with pollutants.

Requiring each city to withdraw its drinking water downstream rather than upstream would dramatically improve the quality of stream water. Each city would be forced to clean up its own waste outputs rather than pass them on to downstream areas. However, this pollution prevention approach is fought by upstream users, who have the use of fairly clean water without high cleanup costs.

STREAM WATER QUALITY   Water pollution control laws enacted in the 1970s have greatly increased the number and quality of wastewater treatment plants in the United States and in many other MDCs. Laws have also required industries to reduce or eliminate point-source discharges into surface waters. Since 1972 these efforts have enabled the United States to hold the line

Q: How much water do you waste if you let the water run while brushing your teeth?

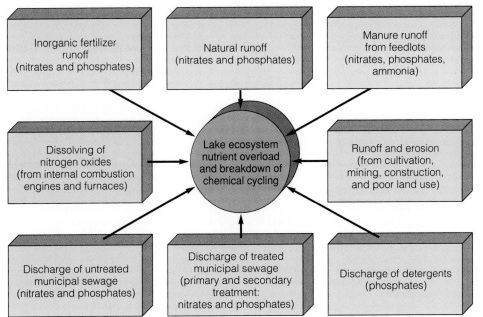

Figure 11-21 Principal sources of nutrient overload, or cultural eutrophication, in lakes, ponds, slow-flowing streams, and estuaries. The amount of nutrients from each source varies, depending on the types of human activities taking place in each airshed and watershed.

Boxes in figure:
- Inorganic fertilizer runoff (nitrates and phosphates)
- Natural runoff (nitrates and phosphates)
- Manure runoff from feedlots (nitrates, phosphates, ammonia)
- Dissolving of nitrogen oxides (from internal combustion engines and furnaces)
- Lake ecosystem nutrient overload and breakdown of chemical cycling
- Runoff and erosion (from cultivation, mining, construction, and poor land use)
- Discharge of untreated municipal sewage (nitrates and phosphates)
- Discharge of treated municipal sewage (primary and secondary treatment: nitrates and phosphates)
- Discharge of detergents (phosphates)

against increased pollution of most of its streams by disease-causing agents and oxygen-demanding wastes. That is an impressive accomplishment, considering the rise in economic activity and population since 1972.

Despite progress in improving stream quality in most MDCs, large fish kills and contamination of drinking water still occur. Most of these disasters are caused by accidental or deliberate releases of toxic inorganic and organic chemicals by industries, malfunctioning sewage treatment plants, and nonpoint runoff of pesticides from cropland.

For example, in 1986, a fire at a Sandoz chemical warehouse in Switzerland released large quantities of toxic chemicals into the Rhine River, which flows through Switzerland, France, Germany, and the Netherlands before emptying into the North Sea. The chemicals killed much aquatic life, forced temporary shutdowns of drinking-water plants and commercial fishing, and set back improvements in the river's water quality that had taken place between 1970 and 1986. The river is now making a slow comeback.

Available data indicate that pollution of streams from huge discharges of sewage and industrial wastes is a serious and growing problem in most LDCs, where waste treatment is practically nonexistent. Most of Poland's streams are severely polluted. Currently more than two-thirds of India's water resources are polluted. Of the 78 streams monitored in China, 54 are seriously polluted. In Latin America and Africa, most streams passing through urban or industrial areas are severely polluted.

POLLUTION PROBLEMS OF LAKES AND ARTIFICIAL RESERVOIRS In lakes, reservoirs, estuaries, and oceans, dilution is often less effective than in

streams because these bodies of water frequently contain stratified layers that undergo little vertical mixing (Figures 5-20 and 5-28). Stratification also reduces the levels of dissolved oxygen, especially in the bottom layer. In addition, lakes and reservoirs have little flow, further reducing dilution and replenishment of dissolved oxygen. The flushing and changing of water in lakes and large artificial reservoirs can take from 1 to 100 years, compared with several days to several weeks for streams.

Thus, lakes are usually more vulnerable than streams to contamination by plant nutrients, oil, pesticides, and toxic substances that can destroy bottom life and kill fish. Atmospheric fallout and runoff of acids into lakes is a serious problem in lakes vulnerable to acid deposition (Figure 9-7).

Cultural eutrophication from the stepped-up addition of phosphates and nitrates as a result of human activities is a serious pollution problem for shallow lakes and reservoirs, especially near urban or agricultural centers (Figure 11-21). During warm weather, this nutrient overload produces dense growths of plants such as algae, cyanobacteria, water hyacinths, and duckweed. Dissolved oxygen in the surface layer of water near the shore, and in the bottom layer, is depleted when large masses of algae die, fall to the bottom, and are decomposed by aerobic bacteria. This depletion can kill fish and other oxygen-consuming aquatic animals. If excess nutrients continue to flow into a lake, the bottom water becomes foul and almost devoid of animals, as anaerobic bacteria take over and produce smelly decomposition products such as hydrogen sulfide and methane.

About one-third of the 100,000 medium to large lakes and about 85% of the large lakes near major population centers in the United States suffer from

The five interconnected Great Lakes contain at least 95% of the surface fresh water in the United States and 20% of the world's fresh surface water (Figure 11-22). The Great Lakes basin is home for about 37 million people, making up one-third of Canada's population and one-tenth of the U.S. population. The lakes supply drinking water for 26 million people. About 40% of U.S. industry and half of Canada's industry are located in this watershed. Great Lakes tourism generates $16 billion annually, with $2 billion of that from sport fishing.

Despite their enormous size, these lakes are vulnerable to pollution from point and nonpoint sources because less than 1% of the water entering the Great Lakes flows out to the St. Lawrence River each year. The Great Lakes also receive large quantities of acids, pesticides, and other toxic chemicals by deposition from the atmosphere — often blown in from hundreds or thousands of kilometers away.

By the 1960s, many areas of the Great Lakes were suffering from severe cultural eutrophication, huge fish kills, and contamination from bacteria and other wastes. The impact on Lake Erie was particularly intense because it is the shallowest of the Great Lakes and has the smallest volume of water. Its drainage basin is heavily industrialized and has the largest human population of any of the lakes. Many bathing beaches had to be closed, and by 1970 the lake had lost nearly all its native fish.

Since 1972, a joint $20 billion pollution control program, carried out by Canada and the United States, has led to significant decreases in levels of phosphates, coliform bacteria, and many toxic industrial chemicals in the Great Lakes. Algal blooms have also decreased, and dissolved oxygen levels and sport and commercial fishing have increased. By 1988, only 8 of 516 swimming beaches around Lake Erie remained closed because of pollution.

These improvements were mainly the result of decreased point-source discharges, brought about by new or upgraded sewage treatment plants and improved treatment of industrial wastes. Also, phosphate detergents, household cleaners, and water conditioners were banned or their phosphate levels were lowered in many areas of the Great Lakes drainage basin.

The most serious problem today is contamination from toxic wastes flowing into the lakes (especially Lake Erie and Lake Ontario) from land runoff, streams, and atmospheric deposition. Children under age 16 and pregnant women are advised not to eat any salmon, trout, or other fatty fish from many areas of the Great Lakes. Other people are advised not to eat such fish more than once a week.

In 1978, the United States and Canada signed a new agreement with the goal of virtually eliminating discharges of about 360 toxic chemicals, but implementation of the agreement has been delayed by a sharp drop in federal funds for the cleanup since 1980. Furthermore, recent studies indicate that much of the input of toxic chemicals — more than 50% in Lake Superior — comes from the atmosphere, a source not covered by the agreement.

Solving these problems will be expensive and will take many years, but not dealing with the problems will cost far more. Environmentalists call for a ban on the use of chlorine as a bleach in the pulp and paper industry around the Great Lakes, a ban on all new incinerators in the area, and an immediate ban on discharges into the lakes of 70 toxic chemicals that threaten human health and wildlife.

In 1991, the U.S. government passed a law requiring accelerated cleanup of the lakes, especially of 42 toxic hot spots, and an immediate reduction of emissions of toxic air pollutants in the region. Meeting these goals and deadlines may be delayed by lack of federal and state funds.

---

some degree of cultural eutrophication (see Case Study above).

The best solution to cultural eutrophication is to use prevention methods to reduce the flow of nutrients into lakes and reservoirs and pollution cleanup methods to clean up lakes suffering from excessive eutrophication. Major prevention methods include advanced waste treatment, bans or limits on phosphates in household detergents and other cleaning agents, and soil conservation and land-use control to reduce nutrient runoff. Major cleanup methods are dredging bottom sediments to remove excess nutrient buildup, removing excess weeds, controlling undesirable plant growth with herbicides and algicides, and pumping air through lakes and reservoirs to avoid oxygen depletion (an expensive and energy-intensive method).

11-6 Ocean Pollution

THE ULTIMATE SINK The oceans are the ultimate sink for much of the waste matter we produce. This is summarized in the African proverb: "Water may flow in a thousand channels, but it all returns to the sea."

Q: What is the largest source of water pollution in the United States?

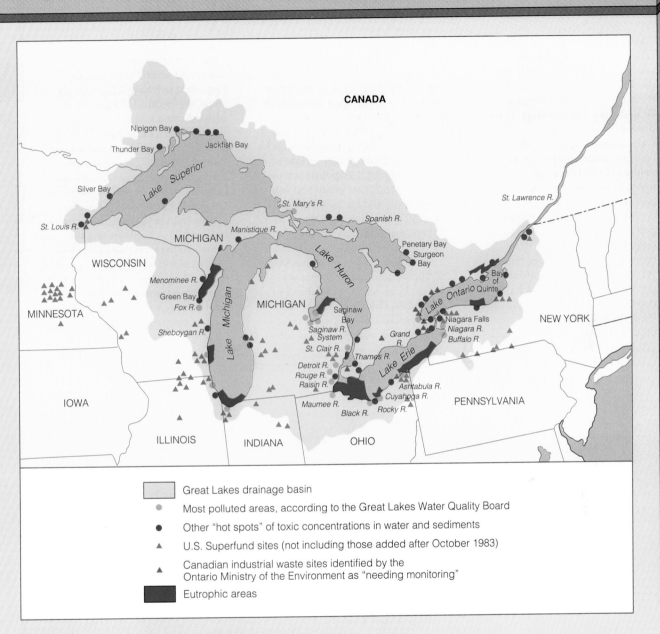

Figure 11-22 The Great Lakes basin. (Data from Environmental Protection Agency)

Legend:
- Great Lakes drainage basin
- Most polluted areas, according to the Great Lakes Water Quality Board
- Other "hot spots" of toxic concentrations in water and sediments
- U.S. Superfund sites (not including those added after October 1983)
- Canadian industrial waste sites identified by the Ontario Ministry of the Environment as "needing monitoring"
- Eutrophic areas

Oceans can dilute, disperse, and degrade large amounts of sewage, sludge, oil, and some types of industrial waste, especially in deep-water areas. Marine life has also proved to be more resilient than scientists had expected, leading some to suggest that it is much safer to dump much of the sewage sludge and various toxic and radioactive wastes into the deep ocean than to bury them on land or burn them in incinerators.

Other scientists dispute this idea, pointing out that we know less about the deep ocean than we do about outer space. They add that using the ocean to support our throwaway lifestyles will eventually overwhelm its dilution and renewal capacity. To advocate dumping

waste in the ocean would delay urgently needed pollution prevention and resource reduction and promote further degradation of this vital part of Earth's life-support system.

OVERWHELMING COASTAL AREAS Coastal areas, especially wetlands and estuaries (see Case Study on p. 246), mangrove swamps (Figure 5-22), and coral reefs (Figure 5-23) bear the brunt of our enormous inputs of wastes into the ocean and of coastal development (Figures 5-26 and 5-27). A 1986 study by the United Nations concluded that most of the world's coastal areas are polluted, with the most widespread and serious pollution

A: Agriculture (responsible for about two-thirds)

The Chesapeake Bay (Figure 11-23) on the East Coast is the largest estuary in the United States and one of the world's most productive. It is the largest source of oysters in the United States and the largest producer of blue crabs in the world. The bay is also important for shipping, boating, and sport fishing. Between 1940 and 1992, the number of people living close to the bay grew from 3.7 million to 15 million.

The estuary receives wastes from point and nonpoint sources scattered throughout a huge drainage basin that includes 9 large rivers and 141 smaller streams and creeks in parts of six states. The bay has become a huge pollution sink because it is quite shallow — with an average depth less than 7 meters (22 feet) —

and only 1% of the waste entering it is flushed into the Atlantic Ocean.

Levels of phosphate and nitrate plant nutrients have risen sharply in many parts of the bay, causing algal blooms and oxygen depletion. Studies have shown that point sources, primarily sewage treatment plants, contribute about 60% by weight of the phosphates. Nonpoint sources, mostly runoff from urban and suburban areas and agricultural activities and deposition from the atmosphere, are the source of about 60% by weight of the nitrates.

Additional pollution comes from nonpoint runoff of large quantities of pesticides from cropland and urban lawns. Point-source discharge of numerous toxic wastes by industries, often in violation of their discharge permits, is also a problem. Commercial harvests of oysters, crabs, and several commercially important fish have fallen sharply since 1960 because of a combination of overfishing and pollution.

Since 1983, more than $700 million in federal and state funds have been spent on a Chesapeake Bay cleanup program that will ultimately cost several billion dollars. Between 1980 and 1987, discharges of phosphates from point sources dropped by about 20%, but there is a long way to go to reverse severe eutrophication and oxygen depletion in many areas (Figure 11-23).

Halting the deterioration of this vital estuary will require the prolonged, cooperative efforts of citizens, officials, and industries.

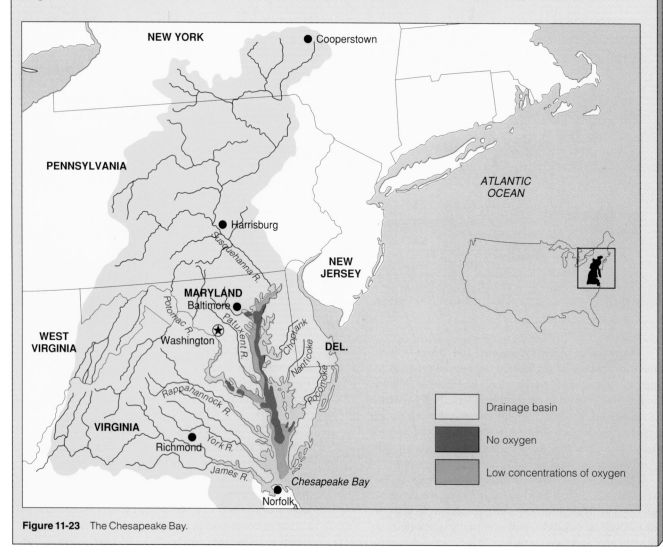

Figure 11-23 The Chesapeake Bay.

Q: How much water can be contaminated by 0.9 liter (1 quart) of oil?

Crude oil extracted from fields in Alaska's North Slope near Prudhoe Bay is carried by pipeline to the port of Valdez and then shipped by tanker to the West Coast (Figure 11-24). Just after midnight on March 24, 1989, the *Exxon Valdez*, a tanker more than three football fields long, went off course in a 16-kilometer- (10-mile-) wide channel in Prince William Sound near Valdez and hit submerged rocks on a reef. About 42 million liters (11 million gallons) of oil—22% of its cargo—gushed from several gashes in the hull, creating the worst oil spill ever in U.S. waters.

In 1990, the National Transportation Safety Board ruled that the accident was the result of drinking by the captain, a fatigued and over-worked crew, and inadequate traffic control by the Coast Guard. Since 1984, the captain had been arrested for drunken driving three times and had lost his license to drive a car, but Exxon officials still kept him in charge of one of their largest tankers, carrying a $20 million cargo.

The rapidly spreading oil slick coated at least 580,000 birds (including 144 bald eagles), up to 5,500 sea otters, 30 seals, 22 whales, and unknown numbers of fish. It also oiled more than 2,100 kilometers (1,300 miles) of shoreline, roughly the amount of shoreline from New Jersey to South Carolina. The final toll on wildlife will never be known because most of the animals killed sank and decomposed without being counted. The good news is that these animal populations are expected to recover.

Knowledge of the true damage from data collected by hundreds of scientists and projections about the rate and extent of recovery are not available to the public because of lawsuits that may take years to resolve.

In the early 1970s, conservationists predicted that a large, damaging spill might occur in these treacherous waters frequented by icebergs, submerged reefs, and violent storms. Conservationists urged that Alaskan oil be brought to the lower 48 states by pipeline over land to reduce potential damage.

Officials of Alyeska, a company formed by the seven oil companies extracting oil from Alaska's North Slope, said that a pipeline would take too long to build and that a large spill was "highly unlikely." They assured Congress that they would be at the scene of any accident within five hours and have enough equipment and trained people to clean up any spill. And in a close vote, the oil companies won.

When the Valdez spill occurred, Alyeska and Exxon officials did not have enough equipment and personnel and did too little too late. To its credit, Exxon mounted a $2.5 billion cleanup program and promptly established a claims process, even though no law required it. The federal government and the Alaskan government spent another $500 million on the cleanup.

In 1991, Exxon pleaded guilty to federal felony and misdemeanor charges and agreed to pay the federal government and the state of Alaska $1.025 billion in fines and civil damages. After tax writeoffs and inflation adjustments, Exxon will end up paying only about $500 million in fines, with the rest being absorbed by taxpayers through lost tax revenue. Exxon still faces some $59 billion in lawsuits from the Alaskan fishing industry, landowners, cannery workers, Native Americans, and other injured parties.

This $4 billion (and possibly $25 billion) accident might have been prevented if the *Exxon Valdez* had had a double hull, which would have added $22.5 million to its initial cost. In the early 1970s, Interior

(continued)

coming from disposal of untreated or poorly treated sewage and sediment from land clearing and erosion.

In 1991, a Natural Resources Defense Council survey of 10 coastal states revealed that at least 2,400 beach closings took place in 1989 and 1990. Most closings were due to bacterial contamination from inadequate and overloaded sewage treatment systems.

Regional seas such as the Baltic and Mediterranean are especially vulnerable to water pollution because their coasts are highly populated and industrialized and they have more coastline per square kilometer than the high seas do.

OIL POLLUTION Crude petroleum (oil as it comes out of the ground) and refined petroleum (fuel oil, gasoline, and other products obtained by distillation and chemical processing of crude petroleum) are accidentally or deliberately released into the environment from a number of sources. Tanker accidents and blowouts (oil escaping under high pressure from a borehole in the ocean floor) at offshore drilling rigs get most of the publicity.

However, almost half (some experts estimate 90%) of the oil reaching the oceans comes from the land when waste oil dumped onto the land by cities, individuals, and industries ends up in streams that flow into the ocean. Just 0.9 liter (1 quart) of used motor oil dumped into the environment by do-it-yourself oil changers can contaminate 940,000 liters (250,000 gallons) of water. Tanker accidents account for only 10% to 15% of the annual input of oil into the world's oceans, but concentrated spills can have severe ecological and economic impacts on coastal areas (see Case Study above). Oil can also be released as an act of environmental terrorism, as occurred during the Persian Gulf war in 1990.

A: 940,000 liters (250,000 gallons)

Secretary Rogers Morton told Congress that all oil tankers using Alaskan waters would have double hulls. Later, under pressure from oil companies, the requirement was dropped. Today, virtually all merchant ships have double hulls—except oil tankers.

According to Jay Hair, president of the National Wildlife Federation: "This is a classic example of corporate greed. Big oil, big lies. Big lie number one was, 'Don't worry, be happy; nothing's going to happen at Valdez.' Big lie number two was,

'We're doing such a good job with the environment at the North Slope we ought to be allowed into the Arctic National Wildlife Refuge, the finest arctic sanctuary for wildlife in the world, and Bristol Bay.'"

Others must also share the blame for this tragedy. State officials had been lax in monitoring Alyeska, and the Coast Guard did not effectively monitor tanker traffic because of inadequate radar equipment and personnel.

American consumers must also share some of the blame. Their un-

necessarily wasteful use of oil and gasoline (Section 17-2) is one of the driving forces for trying to find more domestic oil without adequate environmental safeguards.

This spill also highlighted the importance of pollution prevention because no spill of this magnitude can be contained or effectively cleaned up. It is estimated that even with the best technology and fast response by well-trained people, probably no more than 10% to 15% of the oil from a major spill can be recovered.

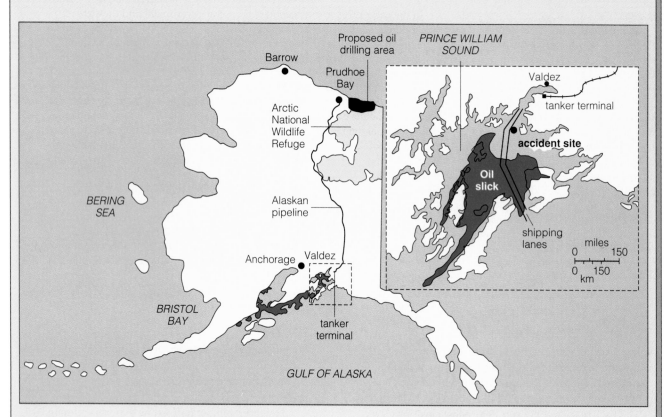

Figure 11-24   Site of the oil spill in Alaska's Prince William Sound from the tanker *Exxon Valdez* on March 24, 1989.

The effects of oil on ocean ecosystems depend on a number of factors: type of oil (crude or refined), amount released, distance of release from shore, time of year, weather conditions, average water temperature, and currents. Volatile organic hydrocarbons in oil immediately kill a number of aquatic organisms, especially in their more vulnerable larval forms. In warm waters, most of these toxic chemicals evaporate into the atmosphere within a day or two, but in cold waters this may take up to a week.

Some other chemicals remain on the surface and form floating tarlike globs or mousse. This floating oil coats the feathers of birds (Figure 11-25), especially diving birds, and the fur of marine mammals such as seals and sea otters. This oily coating destroys the animals' natural insulation and buoyancy, and many drown or die of exposure from loss of body heat.

These globs of oil are broken down by bacteria over several weeks or months, although they persist much longer in cold polar waters. Heavy oil components that

Q: What percentage of rural wells tested in the United States violate at least one federal drinking water standard?

Figure 11-25 A seabird coated with crude oil from an oil spill. Most of these birds die unless the oil is removed with a detergent solution. Many die even when the oil is removed.

sink to the ocean floor or wash into estuaries can kill bottom-dwelling organisms such as crabs, oysters, mussels, and clams or make them unfit for human consumption because of their oily taste and smell.

Research shows that most forms of marine life recover from exposure to large amounts of crude oil within three years. Recovery of marine life from exposure to refined oil, especially in estuaries, may take 10 years or longer. The effects of spills in cold waters (such as Alaska's Prince William Sound and Antarctic waters) and in shallow enclosed gulfs and bays (such as the Persian Gulf) generally last longer.

Oil slicks that wash onto beaches can have serious economic effects on coastal residents, who lose income from fishing and tourist activities. Oil-polluted beaches washed by strong waves or currents are cleaned up after about a year, but beaches in sheltered areas remain contaminated for several years. Estuaries and salt marshes (Figure 5-21) suffer the most damage and cannot effectively be cleaned up.

11-7 Groundwater Pollution and Its Control

GROUNDWATER CONTAMINATION Groundwater (Figure 11-3) is a vital source of water for drinking and irrigation in the United States and other parts of the world. This indispensable form of Earth capital is easy to deplete because it is renewed so slowly; on a human time scale, groundwater contamination can be considered permanent.

Laws protecting groundwater are weak in the United States and nonexistent in most countries. By 1992, only 38 of the several hundred chemicals found in U.S. groundwater were covered by federal water quality standards and routinely tested for in municipal drinking water supplies.

Results of limited testing of groundwater in the United States are alarming. In a 1982 survey, the EPA found that 45% of the large public water systems served by groundwater were contaminated with synthetic organic chemicals that posed potential health threats. Another EPA survey in 1984 found that two-thirds of the rural household wells tested violated at least one federal health standard for drinking water. The most common contaminants were nitrates from fertilizers and pesticides.

Crude estimates indicate that while only 2% of the volume of all U.S. groundwater is contaminated, up to 25% by volume of the usable groundwater is contaminated. In some areas, up to 75% by volume is contaminated. In New Jersey, every major aquifer is contaminated. In California, pesticides contaminate the drinking water of more than 1 million people. In Florida, where 92% of the residents rely on groundwater for drinking, over 1,000 wells have been closed; and state officials and environmentalists are worried about the increasing number of sites contaminated with the pesticides used by many citrus growers.

Groundwater can be contaminated from a number of point and nonpoint sources (Figure 11-26). A survey by the EPA found that a third of 26,000 industrial-waste ponds and lagoons in the United States have no liners to prevent toxic liquid wastes from seeping into aquifers. One-third of those sites are within 1.6 kilometers (1 mile) of one or more water-supply wells.

The EPA estimates that at least 1 million of the estimated 6 million (some say 7 million to 15 million) underground tanks used to store petroleum, gasoline, solvents, and other hazardous chemicals throughout the United States are leaking their contents into groundwater. Just as all landfills will eventually leak, so will all underground tanks.

The estimated amount of gasoline and other solvents leaking from these underground tanks each year equals the volume of oil spilled by the *Exxon Valdez* tanker (see Case Study on p. 247). A slow gasoline leak of just 4 liters (1 gallon) a day can seriously contaminate the water supply for 50,000 people. Such slow leaks usually remain undetected until someone discovers that a well is contaminated. The estimated amount of oil that has leaked from Chevron's storage tanks in El Segundo, California, is 18 times the amount released by the *Exxon Valdez* incident and 3 times the amount released into the Persian Gulf during the 1991 war against Iraq.

Environmentalists call for faster phasing in of EPA regulations governing new underground tanks and requiring much stricter training and certification for tank installers. They also believe that monitoring systems should be required for all underground tanks, not just new ones. Operators of older underground tanks should also be required to carry enough liability insurance to cover cleanup and damage costs and be liable for leaks from abandoned tanks. Twenty years ago, the

A: 66%

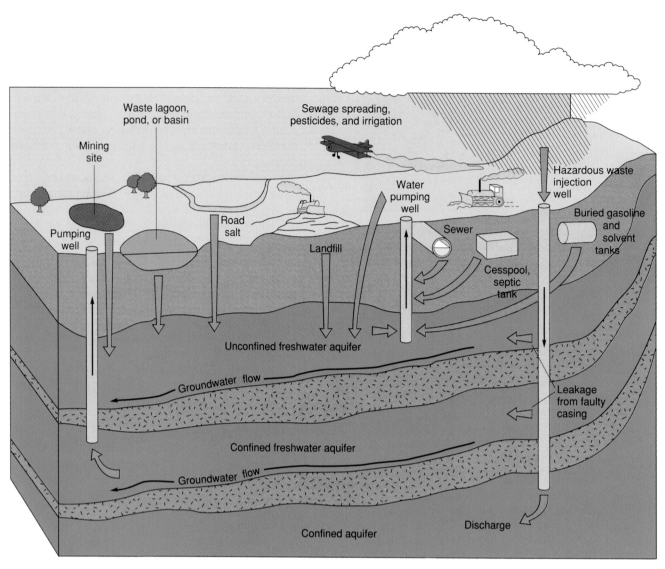

Figure 11-26 Principal sources of groundwater contamination in the United States.

former West Germany instituted such a program, which has been quite successful in reducing leaks from underground tanks. Most business owners in the United States oppose such regulations, arguing that they are too costly.

Another concern is accidental leaks into aquifers from wells used to inject an estimated 57% of the country's liquid hazardous wastes into geologic formations far beneath aquifers tapped for drinking water and irrigation. Deep-well disposal of hazardous waste is widely used because it is simple, cheap, not as visible (usually done on company-owned land), and not as carefully regulated as other disposal methods.

Laws regulating well injection are weak and poorly enforced. Reporting of the types of wastes injected is not required, and no national inventory of active and abandoned wells is kept. Operators are not required to monitor nearby aquifers and are not liable for any damages from leaks once a disposal well is abandoned and

plugged. As the public learns more about this method, it is expected to become the center of one of the biggest waste disposal fights of the 1990s.

When groundwater becomes contaminated, it does not cleanse itself. Because groundwater flows are slow and not turbulent, contaminants are not effectively diluted and dispersed. Also, there is little decomposition by aerobic bacteria, because groundwater is cut off from the atmosphere's oxygen supply and has fairly small populations of aerobic and anaerobic decomposing bacteria. The cold temperature of groundwater also slows down decomposition reactions. That means it can take hundreds to thousands of years for contaminated groundwater to cleanse itself of degradable wastes.

Because groundwater is not visible, there is little awareness of it and little public outcry against its contamination—"out of sight, out of mind"—until wells and public water supplies must be shut down. By then,

Q: In the United States, how many underground tanks that store gasoline and other hazardous chemicals are leaking?

slowly building pollution thresholds have been exceeded and it is too late.

CONTROL OF GROUNDWATER POLLUTION
Groundwater pollution is much more difficult to detect and control than surface-water pollution. Monitoring groundwater pollution is expensive (up to $10,000 per monitoring well), and many monitoring wells must be sunk.

Because of its location underground, pumping polluted groundwater to the surface, cleaning it up, and returning it to the aquifer is usually too expensive—$5 million to $10 million or more for a single aquifer. Recent attempts to pump and treat slow-flowing contaminated aquifers show that it may take decades, even hundreds of years, of pumping before all of the contamination is forced to the surface.

Thus, *preventing contamination is the only effective way to protect groundwater resources*. This will require:

- Banning virtually all disposal of hazardous wastes in sanitary landfills and deep injection wells (Figure 11-26)

- Monitoring aquifers near existing sanitary and hazardous-waste landfills, underground tanks, and other potential sources of groundwater contamination (Figure 11-26)

- Placing much stricter controls on the application of pesticides and fertilizers by millions of farmers and homeowners

- Requiring people using private wells for drinking water to have their water tested once a year

- Establishing nationwide standards for groundwater contaminants

11-8	**Controlling Surface-Water Pollution**

NONPOINT-SOURCE POLLUTION Although most U.S. surface waters have not declined in quality since 1970, they also have not improved. The primary reason has been the absence until recently of any national strategy for controlling water pollution from nonpoint sources.

The leading nonpoint source of water pollution is agriculture. Farmers can sharply reduce fertilizer runoff into surface waters and leaching into aquifers by not using excessive amounts of fertilizer and using none on steeply sloped land. They can use slow-release fertilizers and alternate between planting fields with row crops and soybeans or other nitrogen-fixing plants to reduce the need for fertilizer. Farmers should also be required to have buffer zones of permanent vegetation between cultivated fields and nearby surface water.

Farmers can also reduce pesticide runoff and leaching by applying pesticides only when needed. They can reduce the need for pesticides by using biological methods of pest control or integrated pest management (Section 14-5). Use of commercial inorganic fertilizers and pesticides on golf courses, yards, and public lands needs to be sharply reduced.

Livestock growers can control runoff and infiltration by animal wastes from feedlots and barnyards by controlling animal density, planting buffers, and not locating feedlots on land sloping toward nearby surface water. Diverting runoff of animal wastes into detention basins would allow this nutrient-rich water to be pumped and applied as fertilizer to cropland or forestland.

Critical watersheds should also be reforested. In addition to reducing water pollution from sediment, reforestation would reduce soil erosion and the severity of flooding (see Case Study on p. 230) and help slow projected global warming (Section 10-2) and loss of Earth's vital biodiversity (Chapter 16).

POINT-SOURCE POLLUTION: WASTEWATER TREATMENT In many LDCs and in some parts of MDCs, sewage and waterborne industrial wastes from point sources are not treated. Instead, most are discharged into the nearest waterway or into **wastewater lagoons**—large ponds where air, sunlight, and microorganisms break down wastes, allow solids to settle out, and kill some disease-causing bacteria. Water typically remains in a lagoon for 30 days. Then it is treated with chlorine and pumped out for use by a city or farms.

In MDCs, most wastes from point sources are purified to varying degrees. In rural and suburban areas with suitable soils, sewage from each house is usually discharged into a **septic tank** (Figure 11-27). About 24% of all homes in the United States are served by septic tanks.

In urban areas in MDCs, most waterborne wastes from homes, businesses, factories, and storm runoff flow through a network of sewer pipes to wastewater treatment plants. Some cities have separate lines for storm-water runoff, but in 1,200 U.S. cities the lines for these two systems are combined because it is cheaper. When rains cause combined sewer lines to overflow, they discharge untreated sewage directly into surface waters.

When sewage reaches a treatment plant, it can undergo up to three levels of purification, depending on the type of plant and the degree of purity desired. **Primary sewage treatment** is a mechanical process that uses screens to filter out debris such as sticks, stones, and rags. Then suspended solids settle out as sludge in a settling tank (Figure 11-28). Improved primary treatment using chemically treated polymers does a better job of removing suspended solids. **Secondary sewage treatment** is a biological process that uses aerobic bac-

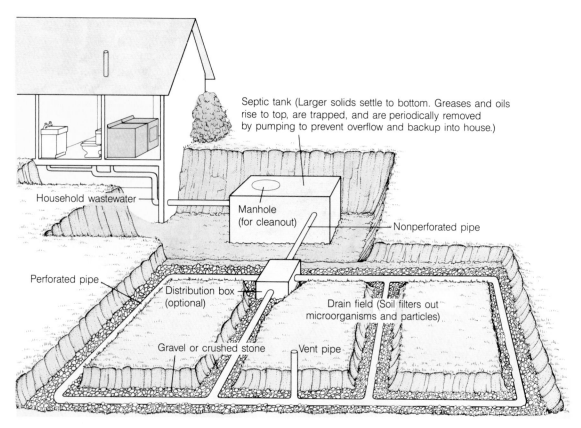

Figure 11-27 Septic tank system used for disposal of domestic sewage and wastewater in rural and suburban areas. This system traps greases and large solids and discharges the remaining wastes over a large drainage field. As these wastes percolate downward, the soil filters out some potential pollutants and soil bacteria decompose biodegradable materials. To be effective, septic tanks must not be placed too close together or too near well sites, and must be installed in soils with adequate drainage, installed properly, and pumped out when the settling tank becomes full.

Figure 11-28 Primary sewage treatment. If a combination of primary and secondary (or advanced) treatment is used, the wastewater is not disinfected until the last step.

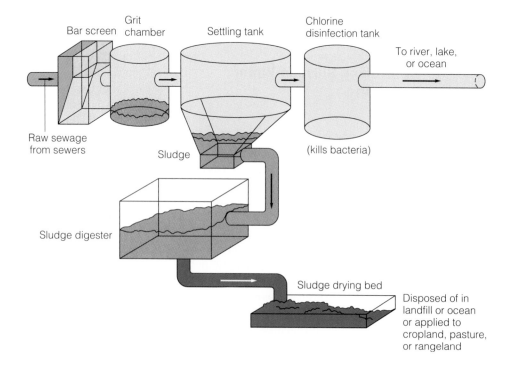

Q: What can be done when groundwater becomes contaminated?

teria as a first step to remove up to 90% of biodegradable, oxygen-demanding organic wastes (Figure 11-29).

In the United States, combined primary and secondary treatment must be used in all communities served by wastewater treatment plants. Combined primary and secondary treatment, however, still leaves about 3% to 5% by weight of the oxygen-demanding wastes, 3% of the suspended solids, 50% of the nitrogen (mostly as nitrates), 70% of the phosphorus (mostly as phosphates), and 30% of most toxic metal compounds and synthetic organic chemicals in the wastewater discharged from the plant. Virtually no long-lived radioactive isotopes nor persistent organic substances such as pesticides are removed by these two processes.

Advanced sewage treatment is a series of specialized chemical and physical processes that lower the quantity of specific pollutants still left after primary and secondary treatment (Figure 11-30). Types of advanced treatment vary, depending on the contaminants in specific communities and industries. Except in Sweden, Denmark, and Norway, advanced treatment is rarely used because the plants cost twice as much to build and four times as much to operate as secondary plants.

Before water is discharged from a sewage treatment plant, it is disinfected to remove water coloration and kill disease-carrying bacteria and some, but not all, viruses. The usual method is chlorination. However, chlorine reacts with organic materials in the wastewater or in surface water to form small amounts of chlorinated hydrocarbons, some of which cause cancers in test animals. Several other disinfectants, such as ozone and UV light, are being used in some places but are more expensive than chlorination.

Without expensive advanced treatment, effluents from primary and secondary sewage treatment plants contain enough nitrates and phosphates to contribute to accelerated eutrophication of lakes, slow-moving streams, and coastal waters (Figure 11-21). Conventional sewage treatment has helped reduce pollution of surface water, but environmentalists point out that it is a limited and flawed cleanup (output) approach that is eventually overwhelmed by more people producing more wastes. Between 1972 and 1990, Americans spent more than $75 billion on sewage treatment plants. However, by 1990, the amount of organic wastes reaching the country's surface waters was about the same as in 1972 because sewage production grew as fast as sewage treatment.

In LDCs and in many areas in MDCs, using low-tech, natural or created ecosystems may be the cheapest and best way to purify wastewater (see Case Study on p. 255).

Sewage treatment produces a toxic gooey sludge that must be disposed of or recycled as fertilizer to the land. About 42% by weight of the sludge produced in the United States is dumped in conventional landfills where it can contaminate groundwater. Another 6% is dumped into the ocean, which transfers water pollution from one part of the hydrosphere to another. The 21% of the sludge that is incinerated can pollute the air with

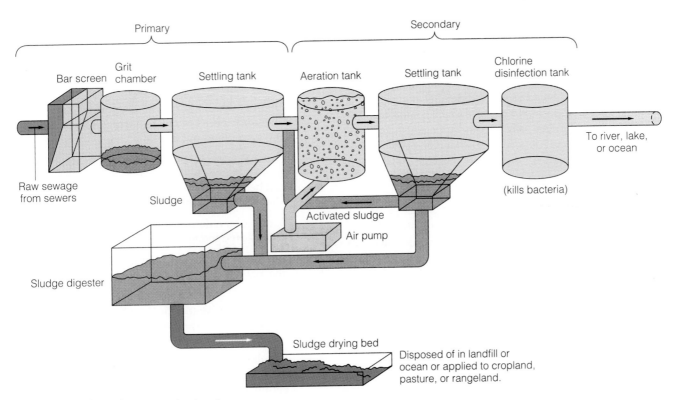

Figure 11-29 Secondary sewage treatment.

A: Usually nothing

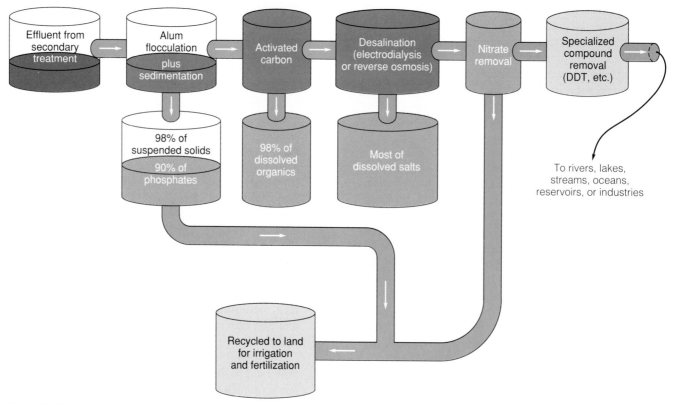

Figure 11-30 Advanced sewage treatment. This diagram shows several different types of advanced treatment. Often only one or two of these processes are used to remove specific pollutants in a particular area.

traces of toxic chemicals, and the resulting toxic ash must be disposed of, usually in landfills where it can pollute groundwater.

A better alternative is to return the nitrate and phosphate plant nutrients in sewage plant effluent and sludge to the land directly as fertilizer or to compost it and use it as a soil conditioner. In Denmark, 48% of the weight of sludge produced is used to fertilize land. In the United States, about 16% is used directly as a fertilizer and 9% is composted to produce a soil conditioner.

Before it is applied, sludge can be heated to kill harmful bacteria, as is done in Switzerland and parts of Germany, or composted. Sludge and effluents can also be treated to remove toxic metals and organic chemicals before application, but that can be expensive. Untreated sludge can be applied to land not used for crops or livestock or to land where groundwater is already contaminated or is not used as a source of drinking water. Examples include forests, surface-mined land, golf courses, lawns, cemeteries, and highway medians.

Present sewage treatment is not cost-effective compared to pollution prevention. Without massive federal subsidies, communities cannot afford to build and operate secondary sewage treatment plants. Once they are built, the huge waste treatment industry is difficult to change, and little money is available for pollution prevention and development of better methods for treating sewage (see Case Study on p. 255).

PROTECTING COASTAL WATERS The most important suggestions for preventing excessive pollution of coastal waters include the following:

Prevention Methods

■ Eliminate the discharge of toxic pollutants into coastal waters from both industrial facilities and municipal sewage treatment plants.

■ Eliminate all discharges of raw sewage from sewer-line overflows by requiring separate storm and sewer lines in cities.

■ Promote water conservation in homes and industries to reduce the flow to sewage treatment plants and hence the danger of overflow (see Individuals Matter inside the back cover).

■ Ban all ocean dumping of sewage sludge and hazardous dredged materials.

■ Enact and enforce laws and land-use practices to sharply reduce runoff from nonpoint sources in coastal areas.

■ Protect sensitive marine areas from all forms of development by designating them as ocean sanctuaries, much like protected wilderness areas.

■ Regulate the types and density of coastal development to minimize its environmental impact, and eliminate subsidies and tax incentives that encourage harmful coastal development.

Q: How many potentially harmful chemicals are found in U.S. drinking water?

In Lima, Peru, most of the sewage produced by its 7 million, mostly poor, people is discharged untreated into the Pacific Ocean. In poor areas this sewage runs to the ocean through a series of open ditches in which children often swim.

The country cannot afford to build expensive waste treatment plants. However, there are now experiments in which the sewage in some areas is channeled into holding ponds, where solids fall to the bottom. Bacteria then decompose many of the wastes. After 20 to 30 days, the water is safe to use. Some of it is used to irrigate corn fed to cattle, and some is pumped to other ponds where the remaining nutrients are used to raise fish.

Natural wetlands can also be used effectively to treat sewage, but many have been destroyed or overwhelmed by pollution (see Case Study on p. 103). An alternative is to create artificial wetlands outdoors in warm climates.

One of these systems is used in Arcata, California (Figure 6-18). In this coastal northern California town of 15,000, some 63 hectares (155 acres) of wetlands have been created in an area that was once a dump.

Arcata's approach is based on working with nature. First, the city's wastewater passes through oxidation ponds where wastes settle out and are partially broken down. Then the water moves on to be further filtered and cleansed in marshes. The water then moves on

Figure 11-31 At the Providence, Rhode Island, Solar Sewage Plant, biologist John Todd is demonstrating how ecological waste engineering takes place in a greenhouse where plants are used to purify wastewater in urban and rural areas. When working properly, such systems have produced water fit for drinking.

to irrigate and nourish other wetlands, and some is pumped into the nearby bay. The marshes are also an Audubon bird sanctuary and provide habitats for thousands of otters, seabirds, and marine animals.

Compared with sewage treatment plants, this highly effective approach is cheap and easy to maintain; however, it does require more land than the conventional approach. In colder climates, wastewater can be purified in greenhouses with rows of large tanks containing aquatic plants (Figure 11-31).

- Institute a national energy policy based on energy efficiency and renewable energy resources to reduce dependence on oil (Section 18-5).

- Collect used oils and greases from service stations and other sources and reprocess them for reuse.

- Prohibit oil drilling in ecologically sensitive offshore and nearshore areas.

- Require new oil tankers to have double hulls now and existing ones to have them within five years to lessen chances of severe leaks.

- Greatly increase the financial liability of oil companies for cleaning up oil spills, thus encouraging pollution prevention.

- Route oil tankers as far as possible from sensitive coastal areas and have Coast Guard vessels guide tankers out of all harbors and enclosed sounds and bays.

- Ban the rinsing of sludge from empty oil tankers, the dumping of sludge into the sea, and the discharge of plastic items and garbage from vessels.

A: At least 700 (with only 60 covered by federal standards by 1992)

- Sharply reduce the use of disposable plastic items (Section 19-6).

- Institute a nationwide program to collect and safely dispose of household hazardous wastes (Section 12-5), and educate consumers to use cheaper and safer alternatives to most common household chemicals (see Individuals Matter inside the back cover).

Cleanup Methods

- Greatly improve oil-spill cleanup capabilities. However, according to a 1990 report by the Office of Technology Assessment, there is little chance that large spills can be effectively contained or cleaned up.

- Upgrade all coastal sewage treatment plants to at least the degree required for inland waters (secondary treatment), or develop alternative methods for sewage treatment (see Case Study on p. 255).

U.S. WATER POLLUTION LEGISLATION Only about 54 of the world's 164 countries have safe drinking water, most in North America and Europe. In the United States, the Safe Drinking Water Act of 1974 requires the EPA to establish national drinking water standards, called *maximum contaminant levels*, for any pollutants that "may" have adverse effects on human health.

This act has helped improve drinking water in much of the United States, but there is still a long way to go. By 1991, the EPA had set maximum contaminant levels for only 60 of the at-least 700 potential pollutants found in municipal drinking water supplies. Of the chemicals found in U.S. drinking water that have been tested, 97 cause cancers, 82 cause mutations, 28 are toxic, and 23 promote tumors in test animals. By 1995, the EPA is required by Congress to set new standards for 108 drinking water contaminants.

Privately owned wells for millions of individual homes in suburban and rural areas are not required to meet federal drinking water standards. The biggest reasons are the cost of testing each well regularly (at least $1,000) and political opposition to mandatory testing and compliance by some homeowners.

A survey by the National Wildlife Federation found that only 2% of the roughly 100,000 violations of federal drinking water standards and of water testing and reporting requirements, which affected 40 million people, were subject to enforcement action and fines. In 94% of the cases, people were not notified when their drinking water either was contaminated or had not been adequately tested. The EPA's inspector general also reported that the agency was failing to enforce regulations covering 140,000 noncommunity water systems such as those in restaurants and hospitals, serving 36 million people.

Drinking quite expensive (about 700 times the price of tap water) bottled water is not always the answer. Sellers are not required to identify on their labels the source of their water (some of it tapwater) or the type of purifying equipment, if any, used.

Bottled water is regulated by the Food and Drug Administration (FDA), not the EPA, and the FDA requires bottlers to check for only 22 of the 30 chemicals tested for in tap water provided by municipalities. To be safe, consumers should purchase bottled water only from companies that belong to the International Bottled Water Association (IBWA).

Before using bottled water or buying expensive home water purifiers, consumers should have their water tested by local health authorities or private labs to find out what contaminants, if any, need to be removed, and then buy a unit that does the job. Buyers should be suspicious of door-to-door salespeople, telephone appeals, and scare tactics. They should carefully check out companies selling such equipment and demand a copy of purifying claims by EPA-certified laboratories.

The Federal Water Pollution Act of 1972, renamed the Clean Water Act of 1977 when it was amended (along with amendments in 1981 and 1987), and the 1987 Water Quality Act form the basis of U.S. efforts to control pollution of the country's surface waters. The goal of these laws is to make all U.S. surface waters safe for fishing and swimming.

These acts require the EPA to establish *national effluent standards* and to set up a nationwide system for monitoring water quality. These effluent standards limit the amounts of certain conventional and toxic water pollutants that can be discharged into surface waters from factories, sewage treatment plants, and other point sources. Each point-source discharger must get a permit specifying the amount of each pollutant that a facility can discharge.

As a result of the Clean Water Act, most U.S. cities have secondary sewage treatment made possible by over $50 billion in federal grants for building sewage treatment plants. By 1988, 87% of the country's publicly owned sewage treatment plants complied with effluent limits set by the Clean Water Act, and about 80% of all industrial dischargers were officially in compliance with their discharge permits.

In 1989, however, the EPA found that more than 66% of the nation's sewage treatment plants have water quality or public-health problems, and studies by the General Accounting Office have shown that most industries sometimes violate their permits. Also, 500 cities ranging from Boston to Key West, Florida, have failed to meet federal standards for sewage treatment plants. In 1989, 34 East Coast cities were not doing anything more to their sewage than screening out large floating objects and discharging the rest into coastal waters. According to the EPA, an additional $88 billion is needed for new wastewater treatment facilities.

Q: In tropical and temperate areas, how long does it take to renew 2.54 centimeters (1 inch) of topsoil?

FUTURE WATER QUALITY AND WATER MANAGEMENT GOALS Sustainable use of Earth's water resources involves developing an integrated approach to managing water resources and water pollution throughout each watershed and reducing or eliminating water subsidies so that the market price of water more closely reflects its true cost.

This integrated approach will require considering urbanization, population growth and control, energy use, mining, agriculture, fisheries, forests, soil conservation, and wildlife in all plans for managing water resources and water pollution. We will also have to shift the emphasis from pollution cleanup to pollution prevention and from waste management to waste reduction.

Without an integrated approach to managing water resources and all forms of pollution, we will continue to shift environmental problems from one part of the environment to another. Ultimately, this form of environmental musical chairs will fail as population and industrialization continue to grow.

To make such a shift, we must truly accept the fact that the environment that we now treat as separate parts—air, water, soil, life—is an interconnected whole. We must organize our efforts to sustain the earth on the basis of its watersheds, airsheds, and ecosystems instead of according to the neat geopolitical lines we draw on maps. This will require unprecedented cooperation between communities, states, and countries. Aquatic systems can't recover until we stop overloading their natural cleansing and renewal processes; but once we do, recovery is amazingly fast.

Individuals can contribute to bringing about this drastic change in the way we view and act in the world by reducing unnecessary water waste (see Individuals Matter inside the back cover) and preventing water pollution (see Individuals Matter below).

INDIVIDUALS MATTER What You Can Do

- Use commercial inorganic fertilizers, pesticides, detergents, bleaches, and other chemicals only if necessary and then in the smallest amounts possible.

- Use less-harmful substances for most household cleaners (see Individuals Matter inside the back cover).

- Use low-phosphate, phosphate-free, or biodegradable dishwashing liquid, laundry detergent, and shampoo.

- Don't use water fresheners in toilets.

- Contact your local Health Department about how to dispose of household hazardous and medical wastes. Don't pour products containing harmful chemicals, such as pesticides, paints, solvents, oil, and cleaning agents, down the drain or on the ground.

- Recycle old motor oil and antifreeze at an auto service center or auto parts center that has an oil recycling program. If such a program is not available, pressure local officials or businesses to start one. If disposed of improperly, the oil from one oil change can pollute 3.8 million liters (1 million gallons) of water. Each year 20 times the amount of oil spilled by the tanker *Exxon Valdez* is improperly disposed of (dumped or burned) by Americans changing their own automotive oil.

- Use manure or compost instead of commercial inorganic fertilizers (Section 12-3) to fertilize garden and yard plants.

- Use biological methods or integrated pest management (Section 14-5) instead of commercial pesticides to control garden, yard, and household pests.

- Use and waste less water (see Individuals Matter inside the back cover).

- If you get water from a private well or suspect that municipally supplied water is contaminated, have it tested by an EPA-certified laboratory for lead, nitrates, trihalomethanes, radon, volatile organic compounds, and pesticides.*

*Check with local health officials, state environmental agencies, or the EPA for a list of certified laboratories. The following labs will send you a kit to collect tap water that you mail back for analysis: National Testing Laboratories (6151 Wilson Mills Rd., Cleveland, OH 44143, 800-458-3330); Suburban Water Testing Laboratories (4600 Kutztown Rd., Temple, PA 19560, 800-433-6595); and WaterTest (33 South Commercial St., Manchester, NH 03101, 800-426-8378).

- If you have a septic tank, monitor it yearly and have it cleaned out every three to five years by a reputable contractor so that it won't contribute to groundwater pollution. Do not use septic tank cleaners. They contain toxic chemicals that can kill bacteria important to sewage decomposition in the septic system and that can contaminate groundwater if the system malfunctions.

- If you are a boater, don't dump trash overboard and discharge boat sewage only into regulated onshore facilities.

- Support ecological land-use planning in your local community.

- Get to know your local bodies of water and form community watchdog groups to help monitor, protect, and restore them.

- Support tougher water-pollution-control laws and their enforcement at the local, state, and federal levels with emphasis on pollution prevention.

A: 200 to 1,000 years, depending on climate and soil type

Water is more critical than energy. We have alternative sources of energy. But with water, there is no other choice.

EUGENE ODUM

DISCUSSION TOPICS

1. How do human activities increase the harmful effects of prolonged drought? How can these effects be reduced?

2. How do human activities contribute to flooding? How can these effects be reduced?

3. Explain why dams and reservoirs may lead to more flood damage than would have occurred if they had not been built. Should all proposed large dam and reservoir projects be scrapped? What criteria would you use in determining desirable projects?

4. Should the price of water for all uses in the United States be increased sharply to encourage water conservation? Explain. What effects might this have on the economy, on you, on the poor, on the environment?

5. List 10 major ways to conserve water on a personal level. Which, if any, of these practices do you now use or intend to use (see Individuals Matter inside the back cover)?

6. Explain why you agree or disagree with the idea that we should deliberately dump most of our wastes in the ocean because it is a vast sink for diluting, dispersing, and degrading wastes and because if it becomes polluted, we can get food from other sources.

7. Should the injection of hazardous wastes into deep underground wells be banned? Explain. What would you do with these wastes?

*8. In your community:
   a. What are the major sources of the water supply?
   b. How is water use divided among agricultural, industrial, power plant cooling, and public uses? Who are the biggest consumers of water?
   c. What has happened to water prices during the past 20 years? Are they too low to encourage water conservation and reuse?
   d. What water-supply problems are projected?
   e. How is water being wasted?
   f. How is drinking water treated?
   g. Has drinking water been analyzed recently for the presence of synthetic organic chemicals, especially chlorinated hydrocarbons? If so, were any found, and are they being removed?
   h. What are the major nonpoint sources of contamination of surface water and groundwater?

CHAPTER 12

SOIL RESOURCES AND HAZARDOUS WASTE

General Questions and Issues

1. What are the principal components and types of soil, and what properties make a soil best suited for growing crops?

2. How serious is the problem of soil erosion in the world and in the United States?

3. How can we reduce erosion and nutrient depletion in topsoil?

4. How is soil degraded by excessive salt buildup (salinization) and waterlogging?

5. How are soil and other parts of the environment degraded by hazardous chemicals?

Below that thin layer comprising the delicate organism known as the soil is a planet as lifeless as the moon.

G. Y. JACKS AND R. O. WHYTE

NLESS YOU ARE a farmer, you probably think of soil as dirt—something you don't want on your hands, clothes, or carpet. You are acutely aware of your need for air and water, but you may be unaware that your life and the lives of other organisms depend on soil, especially the upper portion known as topsoil.

The nutrients in the food we eat come from soil. To a large extent, all flesh is soil nutrients. Soil also provides you with wood, paper, cotton, and many other vital materials and helps purify the water you drink.

As long as soil is held in place by vegetation, it stores water and releases it in a nourishing trickle instead of a devastating flood. Soil's decomposer organisms recycle the key chemicals we and most other forms of life need. Bacteria in soil decompose degradable forms of garbage you throw away, although this process takes decades to hundreds of years in today's compacted, oxygen-deficient landfills. Soil is truly the base of life and civilization.

Yet, since the beginning of agriculture, we have abused this vital, potentially renewable resource. Today, we are abusing soil more than ever. Each of us must become involved in protecting the life-giving resource we call soil.

12-1 Soil: Components, Types, and Properties

SOIL LAYERS AND COMPONENTS Pick up a handful of soil and notice how it feels and looks. The **soil** you hold in your hand is a complex mixture of inorganic materials (clay, silt, pebbles, and sand), decaying organic matter, water, air, and billions of living organisms.

The components of mature soils are arranged in a series of zones called **soil horizons** (Figure 12-1). Each horizon has a distinct texture and a distinct composition that vary with different types of soils. A cross-sectional view of the horizons in a soil is called a **soil profile**. Most mature soils have at least three of the possible horizons, but some new or poorly developed soils don't have horizons.

The top layer, *surface-litter layer*, or *O-horizon*, consists mostly of freshly fallen and partially decomposed leaves, twigs, animal waste, fungi, and other organic materials. Most often, it is brown to black in color. The underlying *topsoil layer*, or *A-horizon*, is usually a porous mixture of partially decomposed organic matter (humus), living organisms, and some inorganic mineral particles. Normally it is darker and looser than deeper layers. The roots of most plants and most of a soil's organic matter are concentrated in these two upper soil layers (Figure 12-1).

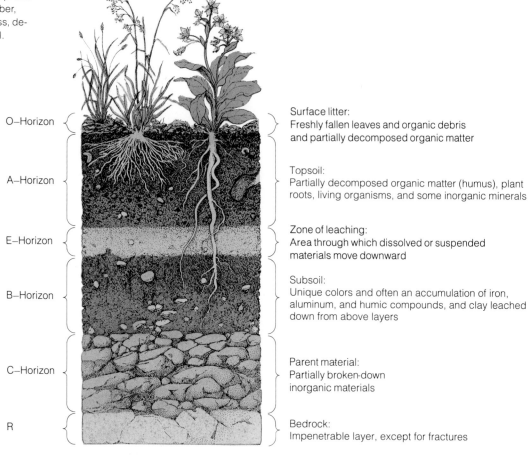

Figure 12-1 Generalized profile of soil. Layers vary in number, composition, and thickness, depending on the type of soil.

O–Horizon

A–Horizon

E–Horizon

B–Horizon

C–Horizon

R

Surface litter:
Freshly fallen leaves and organic debris and partially decomposed organic matter

Topsoil:
Partially decomposed organic matter (humus), plant roots, living organisms, and some inorganic minerals

Zone of leaching:
Area through which dissolved or suspended materials move downward

Subsoil:
Unique colors and often an accumulation of iron, aluminum, and humic compounds, and clay leached down from above layers

Parent material:
Partially broken-down inorganic materials

Bedrock:
Impenetrable layer, except for fractures

The two top layers of most well-developed soils contain vast numbers of organisms that interact in complex food webs (Figure 12-2). Most are bacteria and other decomposer microorganisms, with billions found in every handful of soil. They partially or completely break down some of the complex compounds in the upper layers of soil into simpler nutrient compounds that dissolve in soil water. Soil moisture carrying these dissolved nutrients is drawn up by the roots of plants and transported through stems and into leaves (Figure 12-3). When soil is eroded, it is the vital surface-litter and topsoil layers that are lost.

Some organic compounds in the detritus in the two top layers are broken down slowly by decomposers such as fungi and bacteria. This leaves a sticky, brown, slightly soluble residue of undigested or partially decomposed organic material called **humus**. Because humus is only slightly soluble in water, most of it remains in the topsoil layer. Humus coats the sand, silt, and clay particles in topsoil and binds them together into clumps. Humus also helps topsoil hold water and nutrients taken up by plant roots. A fertile soil, useful for growing high yields of crops, has a thick topsoil layer containing a high content of humus.

The color of the topsoil layer tells us a lot about how useful a soil is for growing crops. For example, dark-brown or black topsoil has a large amount of organic matter and is nitrogen-rich. Gray, bright-yellow, or red topsoils are low in organic matter and will require nitrogen fertilizer to increase their fertility.

The B-horizon (subsoil) and the C-horizon (parent material) contain most of a soil's inorganic matter. Most of this is broken-down rock in the form of varying mixtures of sand, silt, clay, and gravel. The C-horizon lies on a base of bedrock (Figure 12-1).

The spaces, or pores, between the solid organic and inorganic particles in the upper and lower soil layers contain varying amounts of two other key inorganic components: *air* (mostly nitrogen and oxygen gas) and *water*. The oxygen gas, concentrated in the topsoil, is used by the cells in plant roots to carry out respiration.

Some of the rain falling on the soil surface percolates downward through the soil layers and occupies many of the pores. This downward movement of water through soil is called **infiltration**. As the water seeps downward, it dissolves and picks up various soil components in upper layers and carries them to lower layers—a process called **leaching**.

Q: Worldwide, how much topsoil is eroded each year?

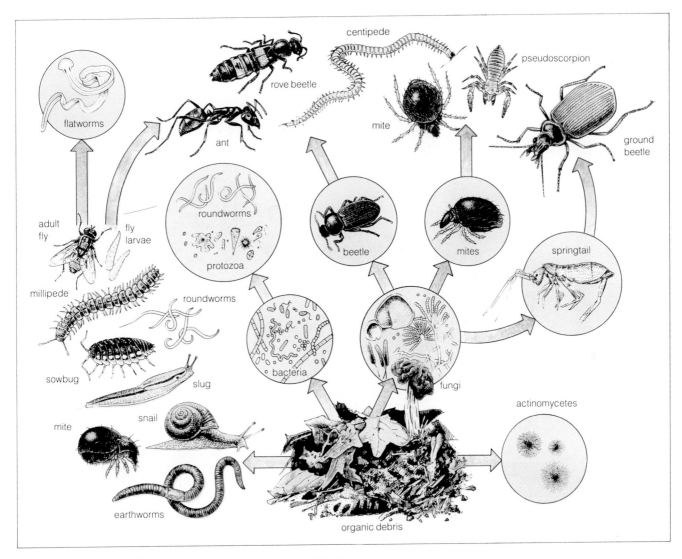

Figure 12-2 Greatly simplified food web of living organisms found in soil.

Labels in figure: centipede, pseudoscorpion, rove beetle, mite, ground beetle, flatworms, ant, roundworms, protozoa, adult fly, fly larvae, beetle, mites, springtail, millipede, roundworms, bacteria, fungi, actinomycetes, sowbug, slug, mite, snail, earthworms, organic debris

TYPES OF SOIL Mature soils in different major biomes (Figure 5-3) vary widely in color, content, pore space, acidity (pH, Figure 9-8), and depth. These differences can be used to classify soils throughout the world into 10 principal types, or orders. Five important soil types, each with a distinct soil profile, are shown in Figure 12-4. Most of the world's crops are grown on grassland soils and on soils exposed when deciduous forests (Figure 5-16) are cleared.

SOIL TEXTURE AND POROSITY Soils vary in their content of clay (very fine particles), silt (fine particles), sand (medium-size particles), and gravel (coarse to very coarse particles). The relative amounts of the different sizes and types of mineral particles determine **soil texture**. Figure 12-5 shows how soils can be grouped into textural classes according to clay, silt, and sand content. Soils containing a mixture of clay, sand, silt, and humus are called **loams**.

To get a general idea of a soil's texture, take a small amount of topsoil, moisten it, and rub it between your fingers and thumb. A gritty feel means that it contains a lot of sand. A sticky feel means that it has a high clay content, and you should be able to roll it into a clump. Silt-laden soil feels smooth like flour. A loam topsoil (Figure 12-5), best suited for plant growth, has a texture between these extremes. It has a crumbly, spongy feeling, and many of its particles are clumped loosely together.

Soil texture helps determine **soil porosity**: a measure of the volume of pores per volume of soil and the average distances between those spaces. A soil with a high porosity (many pores) can hold more water and air than can one with a lower porosity (fewer pores). The average size of the spaces or pores in a soil determines **soil permeability**: the rate at which water and air move from upper to lower soil layers.

Loams (Figure 12-5) are the best soils for growing most crops because they retain a large amount of water

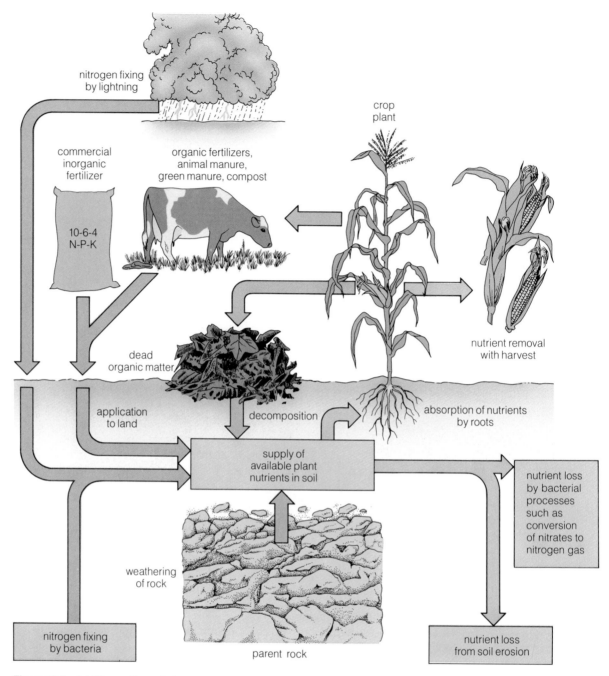

Figure 12-3 Addition and loss of plant nutrients in soils.

that is not held too tightly for plant roots to absorb. Soils with a high sand content are easy to work and have less pore space per volume of soil (lower porosity) than other soils. But water flows rapidly through sandy soils because their pores are larger than those in most other soils (high permeability). They are useful for growing irrigated crops or those without large water requirements, such as peanuts and strawberries.

The particles in clay soils are very small and easily compacted. When these soils get wet, they form large, dense clumps, explaining why wet clay is so easy to mold into bricks and pottery. Clay soils have more pore space per volume and a greater water-holding capacity than do sandy soils, but the pore spaces are so small that these soils have a low permeability. Because little water can infiltrate to lower levels, the upper layers can easily become too waterlogged to grow most crops.

SOIL ACIDITY (pH) The acidity or basicity (alkalinity) of a soil is another factor determining the types of crops it can support. Different levels of acidity and basicity of water solutions of substances are commonly expressed in terms of pH (Figure 9-8).

Q: How much of the planet's land is threatened by desertification?

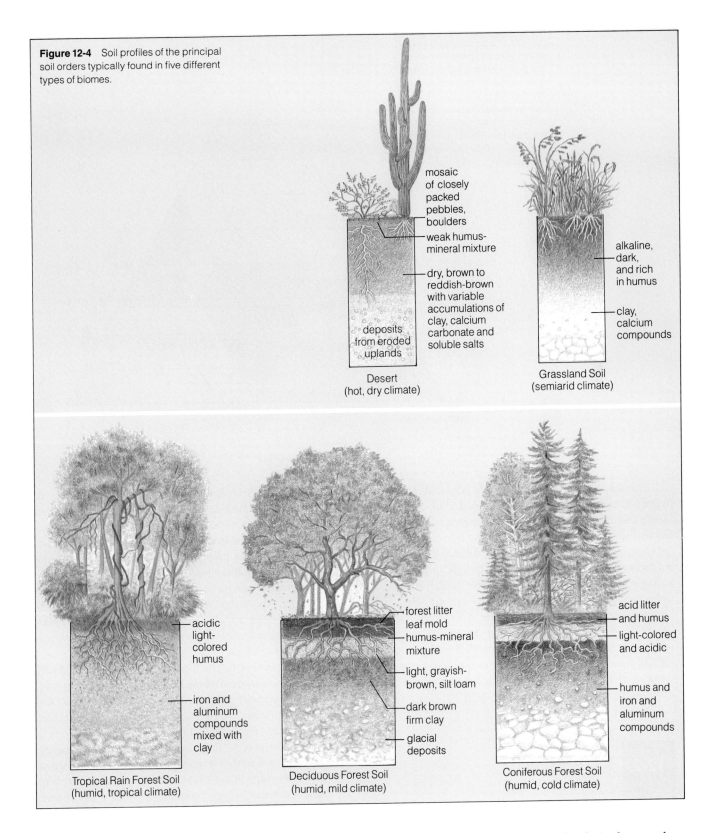

Figure 12-4 Soil profiles of the principal soil orders typically found in five different types of biomes.

mosaic of closely packed pebbles, boulders

weak humus-mineral mixture

dry, brown to reddish-brown with variable accumulations of clay, calcium carbonate and soluble salts

deposits from eroded uplands

Desert
(hot, dry climate)

alkaline, dark, and rich in humus

clay, calcium compounds

Grassland Soil
(semiarid climate)

acidic light-colored humus

iron and aluminum compounds mixed with clay

Tropical Rain Forest Soil
(humid, tropical climate)

forest litter leaf mold

humus-mineral mixture

light, grayish-brown, silt loam

dark brown firm clay

glacial deposits

Deciduous Forest Soil
(humid, mild climate)

acid litter and humus

light-colored and acidic

humus and iron and aluminum compounds

Coniferous Forest Soil
(humid, cold climate)

Soils vary in acidity (Figure 12-4), and crops vary in the pH ranges they can tolerate. For example, wheat, spinach, peas, corn, and tomatoes grow best in slightly acidic soils; potatoes and berries do best in very acidic soils; and alfalfa and asparagus do best in soils that are neutral.

When soils are too acidic for the desired crops, the acids can be partially neutralized by an alkaline substance such as lime. Because lime speeds up the undesirable decomposition of organic matter in the soil, manure or another organic fertilizer should also be added to maintain soil fertility.

Figure 12-5 Soil texture depends on the percentages of clay, silt, and sand particles in the soil. Soil texture affects soil porosity — the average number and spacing of pores in a volume of soil. Loams, made up of roughly equal mixtures of clay, sand, and silt, are the best soils for growing most crops. (Data from Soil Conservation Service)

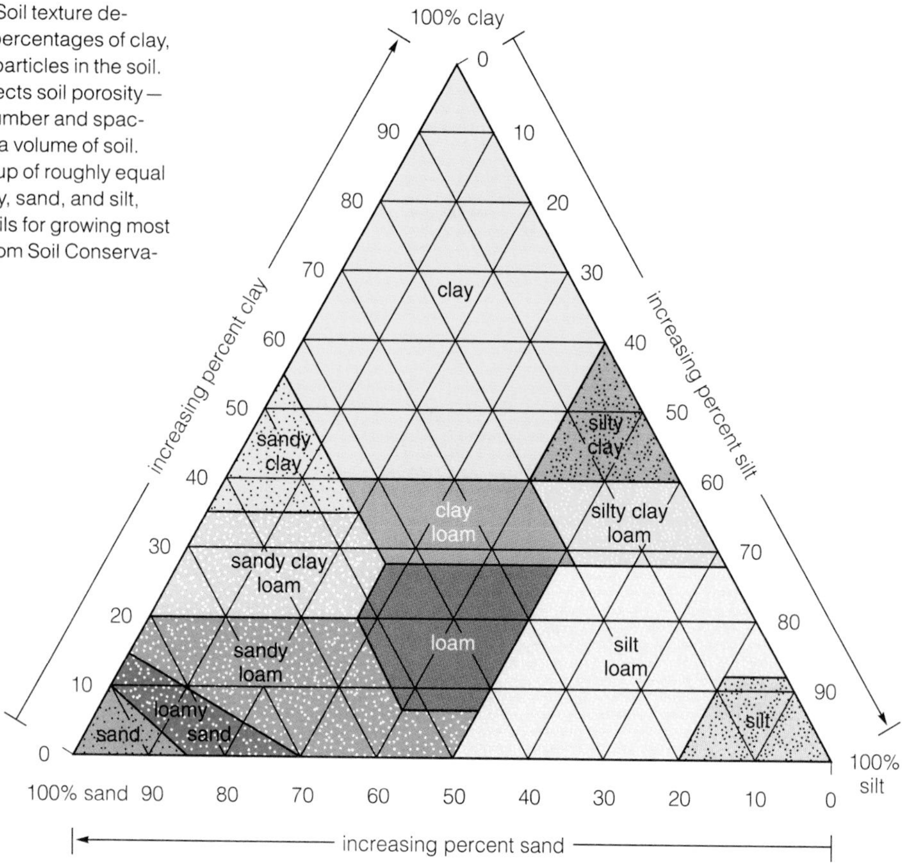

In areas of low rainfall, such as the semiarid regions in the western and southwestern United States (Figure 11-10), calcium and other alkaline compounds are not leached away. Soils in the region may be too alkaline (pH above 7.5) for some crops. If drainage is good, irrigation can reduce the alkalinity by leaching the alkaline compounds away. Adding sulfur, which is gradually converted into sulfuric acid by soil bacteria, is another way to reduce soil alkalinity.

Soils in areas affected by acid deposition are becoming increasingly acidic (Figure 9-10). This leads to a loss of soil fertility that can kill crops and trees or weaken them and make them more vulnerable to drought, disease, and pests (Figure 9-9).

12-2 Soil Erosion

NATURAL AND HUMAN-ACCELERATED SOIL EROSION Soil does not stay in one place indefinitely. **Soil erosion** is the movement of soil components, especially topsoil, from one place to another. The two main forces causing soil erosion are flowing water (Figures 12-6 and 1-1) and wind (Figure 12-7). Most soil erosion is caused by the force of moving water.

Some soil erosion always takes place because of natural water flow and winds, but the roots of plants generally protect soil from excessive erosion. Agriculture, logging, construction, off-road vehicles, and other human activities that remove plant cover increase the rate at which soil erodes.

Excessive erosion of topsoil reduces both the fertility and the water-holding capacity of a soil. The resulting sediment, the largest source of water pollution, clogs irrigation ditches, navigable waterways, reservoirs, and lakes.

Soil, especially the topsoil, is classified as a slowly renewable resource because it is continually regenerated by natural processes. However, in tropical and temperate areas, the renewal of 2.54 centimeters (1 inch) of soil takes from 200 to 1,000 years, depending on climate and soil type. If the average rate of topsoil erosion exceeds the rate of topsoil formation on a piece of land, the topsoil on that land becomes a nonrenewable resource being depleted. Annual erosion rates for agricultural land throughout the world are about 20 to 100 times the natural renewal rate (see Guest Essay on p. 283).

Soil erosion on forestland and rangeland is not as severe as erosion on cropland soil, but forest soil takes two to three times longer to restore itself than does cropland soil. Construction sites usually have the highest erosion rates by far.

Q: How much of the world's irrigated cropland has reduced yields because of soil salinization?

Figure 12-6 Water has eroded vital topsoil from this irrigated cropland in Arizona.

Figure 12-7 Wind eroding soil from farmland in Stevens County, Kansas.

Figure 12-8 Terracing of rice fields in Bali, Indonesia, reduces soil erosion. Terraces also increase the amount of usable land in steep terrain.

THE WORLD SITUATION Today, topsoil is eroding faster than it forms on about one-third of the world's cropland. In some countries, more than half the land is affected by soil erosion.

Worldwide, the estimated amount of topsoil washing and blowing into the world's streams, lakes, and oceans each year would fill a train of freight cars long enough to encircle the planet 150 times. At that rate, the world is losing about 7% of its topsoil from potential cropland each decade. The situation is worsening as farmers in MDCs and LDCs cultivate areas unsuited for agriculture to feed themselves and the world's growing population.

In mountainous areas, such as the Himalaya on the border between India and Tibet and the Andes near the west coast of South America, farmers have traditionally built elaborate systems of terraces (Figure 12-8). Terracing allowed them to cultivate steeply sloping land that would otherwise rapidly lose its topsoil.

Today, farmers in some areas cultivate steep slopes without terraces, causing a total loss of topsoil in 10 to 40 years. Although most poor farmers know that cultivating a steep slope without terracing causes a rapid loss of topsoil, they often have too little time and too few workers to build terraces. They engage in destructive cultivation practices to ward off starvation. The resultant loss of protective vegetation and topsoil also greatly increases the intensity of flooding in the lowland areas of watersheds, as has happened in Bangladesh (see Case Study on p. 230).

According to the UN Environment Programme, about 35% of Earth's land surface—on which about 1 billion people try to survive—is classified as arid or semiarid desert (Figure 5-3). The conversion of productive rangeland (uncultivated land used for animal grazing), rainfed cropland, or irrigated cropland into desertlike land with a drop in agricultural productivity of 10% or more is called **desertification**.

Moderate desertification causes a 10% to 25% drop in productivity, and *severe desertification* causes a 25% to 50% drop. *Very severe desertification* causes a drop of 50% or more and usually results in formation of huge gullies and sand dunes. Moderate, severe, and very severe desertification is a serious and growing problem in many parts of the world (Figure 12-9). Desertification often begins with small patches and then spreads outward like a skin disease.

Moderate desertification can go unrecognized. For example, overgrazing has reduced the productivity of much of the grassland of the western United States. Yet, most citizens living in many of those areas do not realize they live in an area moderately desertified by human action.

Most desertification occurs naturally near the edges of existing deserts. It is caused by dehydration of the top layers of soil during prolonged drought and increased evaporation because of hot temperatures and high winds.

Natural desertification is greatly accelerated by practices that leave topsoil vulnerable to erosion by water and wind:

- Overgrazing of rangeland as a result of too many livestock on too little land area (the major cause of desertification)
- Improper soil and water resource management that leads to increased erosion, salinization (salt buildup), and waterlogging of soil
- Cultivation of land with unsuitable terrain or soils
- Deforestation and surface mining without adequate replanting
- Soil compaction by farm machinery, cattle hoofs, and the impact of raindrops on denuded soil surfaces

These destructive practices are intensified by rapid population growth, high human and livestock population densities, poverty, and poor land management. The consequences of desertification include intensified drought and famine, declining living standards, and swelling numbers of environmental refugees whose degraded land can no longer keep them alive.

It is estimated that 810 million hectares (2 billion acres)—an area the size of Brazil and 12 times the size of Texas—have become desertified during the past 50 years (Figure 12-9). Every year, an estimated 60,000 square kilometers (23,000 square miles)—an area the size of West Virginia—of new desert are formed, and an additional 210,000 square kilometers (81,000 square miles) of land—an area the size of Kansas—are degraded by soil and nutrient loss to the point where they are no longer worth farming or grazing.

The total area of this threatened land is 33 million square kilometers (13 million square miles)—about the size of North and South America combined. If present trends continue, desertification could threaten the livelihoods of 1.2 billion people worldwide by 2000.

The only effective way to slow the march of desertification is to sharply reduce the overgrazing, deforestation, and destructive forms of crop planting, irrigation, and mining that accelerate the process. In addition to these prevention approaches, we can mount extensive reforestation programs to slow the advance of desertification and at the same time provide fuelwood and reduce the threat of global warming.

The total cost of such prevention and rehabilitation would be about $141 billion, only five and one-half times the estimated $26 billion annual loss in agricultural productivity from desertified land. Thus, once this potential productivity is restored, the costs of the program could be recouped in 5 to 10 years.

So far, however, little has been done because of inadequate efforts and funding; only about one-tenth of the amount needed has been provided. What do you think should be done?

Since the beginning of agriculture, people in tropical forests have successfully used slash-and-burn, shifting cultivation (Figure 2-4) to provide food for relatively small populations. In recent decades, growing population and poverty have caused farmers in many tropical forest areas to reduce the fallow period of their fields to as little as 2 years, instead of the 10 to 30 years needed to allow the soil to regain its fertility. The result has been a sharp increase in the rate of topsoil erosion and nutrient depletion.

Overgrazing and poor logging practices also cause heavy losses of topsoil. Intense grazing has turned many areas of North Africa from grassland to desert (see Case Study above). In Africa, soil erosion has increased 20-fold in the last three decades. Once-forested hills in many LDCs have been stripped bare of trees by poor people for firewood and by timber companies for use in MDCs. Because new trees are seldom planted in LDCs, the topsoil quickly erodes away.

In MDCs, where large-scale industrialized agriculture is practiced, many farmers have replaced traditional soil conservation practices with enormous inputs of commercial inorganic fertilizers and irrigation water. But the 10-fold increase in the use of fertilizer and the

Q: What percentage of U.S. children under age 6 have potentially dangerous levels of lead in their blood?

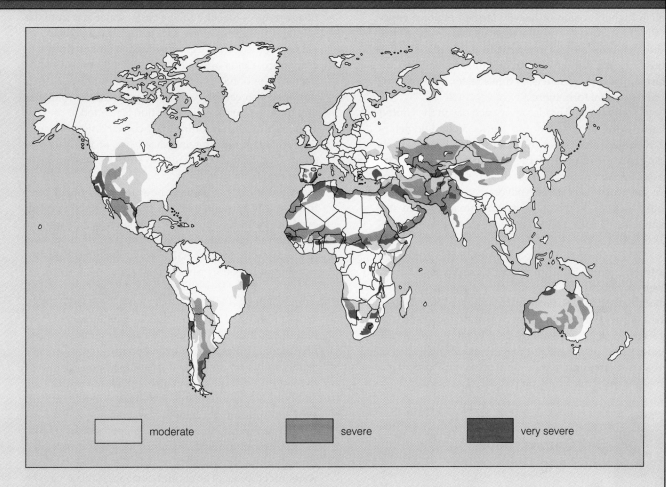

| | moderate | | severe | | very severe |

Figure 12-9 Desertification of arid and semiarid lands. (Data from UN Environment Programme and Harold E. Dregnue)

tripling of the world's irrigated cropland between 1950 and 1992 have only temporarily masked the effects of erosion and nutrient depletion.

Commercial inorganic fertilizer is not a complete substitute for naturally fertile topsoil; it merely hides for a time the gradual depletion of this vital resource. Nor is irrigation a long-term solution. Repeated irrigation of cropland without sufficient drainage eventually decreases or destroys its crop productivity as a result of waterlogging and salt buildup (Section 12-4). Even with drainage, repeated irrigation removes soil nutrients by leaching.

Severe erosion accelerated by human activities is most widespread in India, China, the CIS, and the United States, which together account for over half the world's food production and contain almost half the world's people.

THE U.S. SITUATION According to the Soil Conservation Service, about one-third of the original topsoil on U.S. croplands in use today has been washed or blown into streams, lakes, and oceans. Surveys also show that the average rate of erosion on cultivated land in the United States is about seven times the rate of natural soil formation.

This average national rate of soil erosion masks much higher erosion in heavily farmed regions, especially the corn belt and the Great Plains. Some of the country's most productive agricultural lands, such as those in Iowa, have lost about half their topsoil. In California, the erosion rate is 80 times faster than the natural rate of soil formation.

Enough topsoil erodes away each day in the United States to fill a line of dump trucks 5,600 kilometers (3,500 miles) long. Two-thirds of this soil comes from less than one-fourth of the country's cropland. The losses of plant nutrients from this erosion of Earth capital are worth at least $18 billion a year. Erosion also causes at least $4 billion a year in damages when silt, plant nutrients, and pesticides are carried into streams, lakes, and reservoirs.

Of the world's major food-producing countries, only the United States is reducing some of its soil losses. Even so, effective soil conservation is practiced on only about half of all U.S. farmland and on less than half of the country's most erodible cropland. Increased soil conservation is particularly important in the fertile midwestern plains, which are subject to high rates of erosion from high winds and occasional prolonged drought (see Case Study on p. 269).

12-3 Soil Conservation and Land-Use Control

CONSERVATION TILLAGE The practice of **soil conservation** involves using various methods to reduce soil erosion; to prevent depletion of soil nutrients; and to restore nutrients already lost by erosion, leaching, and excessive crop harvesting (Figure 12-3). Most methods used to control soil erosion involve keeping the soil covered with vegetation.

In **conventional-tillage farming**, the land is plowed, disked several times, and smoothed to make a planting surface. If plowed in the fall so that crops can be planted in the spring, the soil is left bare during the winter and early spring months, a practice that makes it vulnerable to erosion.

To lower labor costs, save energy, and reduce erosion, an increasing number of U.S. farmers are using **conservation-tillage farming**, also known as *minimum-tillage* or *no-till farming*, depending on the degree to which the soil is disturbed. Farmers using this method disturb the soil as little as possible in planting crops.

For the minimum-tillage method, special tillers break up and loosen the subsurface soil without turning over the topsoil, previous crop residues, and any cover vegetation. In no-till farming, special planting machines inject seeds, fertilizers, and weed killers (herbicides) into slits made in the unplowed soil.

In addition to reducing soil erosion, conservation tillage reduces fuel and tillage costs, water loss from the soil, and soil compaction. It can also increase the number of crops that can be grown during a season (multiple cropping). Yields are as high as or higher than yields from conventional tillage. Depending on the soil type, this approach can be used for three to seven years before more extensive soil cultivation is needed to prevent crop yields from declining. But conservation tillage is no cure-all. It requires increased use of herbicides to control weeds that compete with crops for soil nutrients (Chapter 14).

Conservation tillage is now used on about one-third of U.S. croplands and is projected to be used on over half by 2000. The USDA estimates that using conservation tillage on 80% of U.S. cropland would reduce soil erosion by at least half. So far, the practice is not widely used in other parts of the world.

CONTOUR FARMING, TERRACING, STRIP CROPPING, AND ALLEY CROPPING Soil erosion can be reduced 30% to 50% on gently sloping land by means of **contour farming**: plowing and planting crops in rows across, rather than up and down, the sloped contour of the land (Figure 12-11). Each row planted horizontally along the slope of the land acts as a small dam to help hold soil and slow the runoff of water.

Terracing can be used on steeper slopes (Figure 12-8). Some of the water running down the vegetated slope is retained by each terrace. Terracing provides water for crops at all levels and decreases soil erosion by reducing the amount and speed of water runoff. In areas of high rainfall, diversion ditches must be built behind each terrace to permit adequate drainage.

In **strip cropping**, a series of rows of one crop, such as corn or soybeans, is planted in a wide strip; then the next strip is planted with a soil-conserving cover crop, such as a grass or a grass-legume mixture, which completely covers the soil and thus reduces erosion (Figure 12-11). The alternating rows of cover crop trap soil that erodes from the row crop, catch and reduce water runoff, and help prevent the spread of pests and plant diseases from one strip to another. They also help restore soil fertility if nitrogen-rich legumes, such as soybeans or alfalfa, are planted in some of the strips.

Erosion can also be reduced by **alley cropping**, in which crops are planted in alleys between hedgerows of trees or shrubs that can be used as sources of fruits and fuelwood (Figure 12-12). The hedgerow trimmings can be used as mulch (green manure) for the crops and fodder for livestock.

GULLY RECLAMATION AND WINDBREAKS
Water runoff quickly creates gullies in sloping land not covered by vegetation (Figures 12-6 and 1-1). Such land

Q: What are the two most desirable ways to deal with hazardous waste?

The Great Plains of the United States stretch through 10 states, from Texas through Montana and the Dakotas. The region is normally dry and very windy and occasionally experiences long, severe droughts.

Before settlers began grazing livestock and planting crops in the 1870s, the extensive root systems of prairie grasses held the topsoil of these soils in place (Figure 12-4). When the land was planted in crops, the perennial grasses were replaced by annual crops (which had to be replanted each year) with less-extensive root systems.

In addition, the land was plowed up after each harvest and left bare part of the year. Overgrazing also destroyed large areas of grass, leaving the ground bare. The stage was set for crop failures during prolonged droughts, followed by severe wind erosion.

The droughts arrived in 1890 and in 1910 and again, with even greater severity, between 1926 and 1934. In 1934, hot, dry windstorms created dust clouds thick enough to cause darkness at midday in some areas. The danger of breathing this dust-laden air was revealed by the dead rabbits and birds left in its wake.

During May 1934, the entire eastern half of the United States was blanketed with a huge dust cloud of topsoil blown off the Great Plains from as far as 2,400 kilometers (1,500 miles) away. Ships 322 kilometers (200 miles) out in the Atlantic Ocean received deposits of midwestern topsoil. These events gave a

portion of the Great Plains a tragic new name: the Dust Bowl (Figure 12-10).

An area of cropland equal in size to the combined areas of Connecticut and Maryland was destroyed, and additional cropland equal in area to New Mexico was severely damaged. Thousands of displaced farm families from Oklahoma, Texas, Kansas, and other states migrated to California or to the industrial cities of the Midwest and East. Most found no jobs because the country was in the midst of the Great Depression.

In May 1934, Hugh Bennett of the U.S. Department of Agriculture (USDA) addressed a congressional hearing in Washington, pleading for new programs to protect the country's topsoil. Lawmakers took action when dust blown from the Great Plains began seeping into the hearing room.

In 1935, the United States established the Soil Conservation Service (SCS) as part of the Department of Agriculture. With Bennett as its first head, the SCS began promoting good conservation practices, first in the Great Plains and later in every state. Soil conservation districts were established throughout the country, and farmers and ranchers were given technical assistance in setting up soil conservation programs.

These efforts, however, did not completely stop human-accelerated erosion in the Great Plains. The basic problem is that the climate of much of the region makes it much

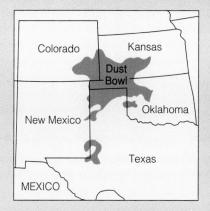

Figure 12-10 The Dust Bowl of the Great Plains, where a combination of periodic severe drought and poor soil conservation practices in the 1930s led to severe erosion of topsoil by wind.

better suited for grazing than for farming.

In 1975, the Council of Agricultural Science and Technology warned that severe drought could again create a dust bowl in the Great Plains. So far, those warnings have mostly been ignored.

Great Plains farmers, many of them debt-ridden, have continued to stave off bankruptcy by minimizing expenditures for soil conservation. Depletion of the Ogallala Aquifer is also threatening crop production and cattle raising in parts of the Dust Bowl area (see Case Study on p. 236). If projected global warming should occur, making this region even drier, farming will have to be abandoned. What do you think should be done about this situation?

can be restored by *gully reclamation*. Small gullies can be seeded with quick-growing plants such as oats, barley, and wheat to reduce erosion. In deeper gullies, small dams can be built to collect silt and gradually fill in the channels. Rapidly growing shrubs, vines, and trees can also be planted to stabilize the soil. Channels can be built to divert water from the gully and prevent further erosion.

Erosion caused by exposure of cultivated lands to high winds can be reduced by **windbreaks**, or **shelter-**

belts, long rows of trees planted to partially block wind (Figure 12-13). They are especially effective if land not under cultivation is kept covered with vegetation. Windbreaks also provide habitats for birds, pest-eating and pollinating insects, and other animals. Unfortunately, many of the windbreaks planted in the upper Great Plains following the Dust Bowl disaster of the 1930s have been destroyed to make way for large irrigation systems (Figure 11-17) and farm machinery (Figure 5-12).

Figure 12-11 On this gently sloping land in Illinois, contoured rows planted with alternating crops (strip cropping) reduce soil erosion.

Figure 12-13 Windbreaks, or shelterbelts, reduce erosion on this farm in South Dakota. They also reduce wind damage and reduce evaporation and help hold soil moisture in place, supply some wood for fuel, and provide a habitat for wildlife.

Figure 12-12 Alley cropping in Peru. Several crops are planted together in strips or alleys between trees and shrubs. The trees provide shade (which reduces water loss by evaporation) and help retain soil moisture and release it slowly.

Figure 12-14 A typical suburban housing tract in McHenry County, Illinois. Each year, about 526,000 hectares (1.3 million acres) of rural land—mostly cropland—are converted to urban development, rights-of-way, highways, and airports in the United States. This is equivalent in area to building a 1-kilometer-wide (0.6-mile-wide) highway stretching from New York City to Los Angeles each year.

LAND-USE CLASSIFICATION AND CONTROL An obvious land-use approach to reducing erosion is to prohibit the planting of crops or the clearing of vegetation on marginal land. Such land is highly erodible because of a steep slope, shallow soil structure, high winds, drought, or other factors.

Most urban areas and some rural areas use some form of **land-use planning** to decide the best present and future use of each parcel of land in the area. Because land is such a valuable economic resource, land-use planning is a complex and controversial process involving competing values and intense power struggles. Environmentalists urge communities to use comprehensive, regional **ecological land-use planning**, in which all major variables are considered and integrated into a model designed to anticipate present and future needs and problems and propose solutions for an entire region. So far, use of this approach is rare.

Once a land-use plan is developed, governments control the uses of various parcels of land by legal and economic methods. The most widely used approach

is **zoning**, in which various parcels of land are designated for certain uses. Zoning can be used to protect areas from certain types of development and to control growth.

Zoning, however, can be influenced or modified by developers because local governments depend on property taxes for revenue. Zoning often favors high-priced housing and factories, hotels, and other businesses rather than the protection of farmland and natural areas such as forests, grasslands, and wetlands.

Since World War II, the typical pattern of suburban housing development in the United States has been to bulldoze a tract of woods or farmland and build rows of houses, usually standard houses on standard lots (Figure 12-14). By removing most vegetation, this approach increases soil erosion during and after construction. Someone noted that the United States is where they cut down the trees and eliminate most of the wild-

Q: What are the three least desirable ways of handling hazardous waste?

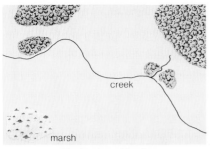  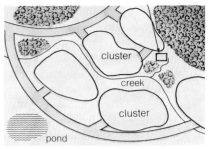

Undeveloped land   Typical Housing Development   Cluster Housing Development

Figure 12-15 Conventional and cluster developments as they would appear if constructed on the same land area. With cluster development, houses, town houses, condominiums, and two- to six-story apartments are built on only part of the tract. The rest, typically 30% of the area, is left as open space, parks, and cycling and walking paths. Parking spaces and garages can also be clustered so that cars are not used within residential areas, with access only by walking or cycling or by small electric or methane-powered golf carts.

life in an area and then name the streets and developments after them—Oak Lane, Cedar Drive, Pheasant Run, Fox Fields.

In hot climates these houses don't have natural cooling from trees. This greatly increases the use of air conditioning, raises electricity bills, and contributes to global warming and urban heat islands (Figure 6-17).

In recent years, builders have made increased use of a new pattern, known as *cluster development*, which provides areas of open space within housing developments (Figure 12-15). This approach helps reduce soil erosion by preserving medium-size blocks of open space and natural vegetation.

To encourage wise land use and reduce erosion, the Soil Conservation Service has set up a classification system for land and has established almost 3,000 soil and water conservation districts throughout the United States. It also surveys soil in these districts and classifies soils according to type and quality.

The SCS basically relies on voluntary compliance with its guidelines through the local and state soil and water conservation districts and provides technical and economic assistance through the local district offices. This means that American soil conservation policy lacks teeth. The soil conservation associations that regulate the districts are under intense local pressure to make land-use decisions based on short-term economic gains that can have harmful long-term environmental and economic impacts.

Local, state, and federal governments can take any of the following measures to protect cropland, forestland, wetlands, and other nonurban lands near expanding urban areas from degradation and ecologically unsound development:

■ Give tax breaks to landowners who agree to use land only for specified purposes, such as agriculture, wilderness, wildlife habitat, or nondestructive forms of recreation. Such agreements are called *conservation easements*.

■ Tax land on the basis of its use as agricultural land or forestland rather than its fair market value based on its economically highest potential use. This prevents farmers and other landowners from being forced to sell land to pay their tax bills.

■ Purchase and protect ecologically valuable land. Such purchases (land trusts) can be made by private groups such as the Nature Conservancy, the Audubon Society, and local and regional nonprofit, tax-exempt, charitable organizations, as well as by public agencies.

■ Purchase land development rights that restrict the way land can be used (for example, to preserve prime farmland near cities from development).

■ Assign a limited number of transferable development rights to a given area of land.

■ Require environmental impact analysis for proposed private and public projects such as roads, industrial parks, shopping centers, and suburban developments; cancel harmful projects unless they are revised to minimize harmful environmental impacts, including excessive soil erosion.

■ Give subsidies to farmers for taking highly erodible cropland out of production or eliminate subsidies for farmers who farm such land or who convert wetlands to cropland, as is being done in the 1985 Farm Act.

MAINTAINING AND RESTORING SOIL FERTILITY Organic fertilizers and commercial inorganic fertilizers can be applied to soil to partially restore and maintain plant nutrients lost by erosion, leaching, and crop harvesting and to increase crop yields (Figure 12-3). Three basic types of **organic fertilizer** are animal manure, green manure, and compost. **Animal manure** includes the dung and urine of cattle, horses, poultry, and other farm animals. In China and South Korea, human manure, sometimes called night soil, is used to fertilize crops in vegetable-growing greenbelts around cities.

A: (1) Incineration; (2) burial in deep wells, ponds, pits, or landfills; (3) ocean dumping

Chapter 12   271

Application of animal manure improves soil structure, increases organic nitrogen content, and stimulates the growth and reproduction of soil bacteria and fungi. It is particularly useful on crops of corn, cotton, potatoes, and cabbage.

Despite its effectiveness, the use of animal manure in the United States has decreased. One reason is that separate farms for growing crops and animals have replaced most mixed animal- and crop-farming operations. Animal manure is available at feedlots near urban areas, but transporting it to distant rural crop-growing areas usually costs too much. Thus, much of this valuable resource is wasted and can end up polluting nearby bodies of water (Figure 11-21). In addition, tractors and other motorized farm machinery have replaced horses and other draft animals that naturally added manure to the soil.

Green manure is fresh or growing green vegetation plowed into the soil to increase the organic matter and humus available to the next crop. It may consist of weeds in an uncultivated field, grasses and clover in a field previously used for pasture, or legumes such as alfalfa or soybeans grown for use as fertilizer to build up soil nitrogen.

Compost is a rich natural fertilizer and soil conditioner. Farmers and homeowners produce it by piling up alternating layers of carbohydrate-rich plant wastes (such as cuttings and leaves), animal manure, and topsoil (Figure 12-16). This mixture provides a home for microorganisms that aid the decomposition of the plant and manure layers.

Today, especially in the United States and other industrialized countries, farmers partially restore and maintain soil fertility by applying **commercial inorganic fertilizers**. The most common plant nutrients in these products are nitrogen (as ammonium ions, nitrate ions, or urea), phosphorus (as phosphate ions), and potassium (as potassium ions). Other plant nutrients may also be present in low or trace amounts. Farmers can have their soil and harvested crops chemically analyzed to determine the mix of nutrients that should be added.

Inorganic commercial fertilizers are easily transported, stored, and applied. Throughout the world, their use increased about 10-fold between 1950 and 1992. Today, the additional food they help produce feeds one of every three persons in the world. Without this input, world food output would plummet by an estimated 40%.

Commercial inorganic fertilizers, however, have some disadvantages. They do not add humus to the soil. Unless animal manure and green manure are added to the soil along with commercial inorganic fertilizers, the soil's content of organic matter and thus its ability to hold water will decrease. If not supplemented by organic fertilizers, inorganic fertilizers cause the soil to become compacted and less suitable for crop growth. By decreasing its porosity, inorganic fertilizers also

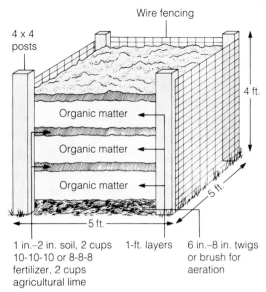

Figure 12-16 A simple home compost bin can be used to produce a mulch for garden and yard plants. A layer or two of cat litter or alfalfa meal can be used to cut down on odors. Leave a depression at the top center of the pile to collect rainwater. Turn the pile over every month or so, and cover it with a tarp during winter months. Small compost bins have been developed for use inside apartments and houses.

lower the oxygen content of soil and prevent added fertilizer from being taken up as efficiently. In addition, most commercial fertilizers do not contain many of the nutrients needed in trace amounts by plants.

Water pollution is another problem caused by the widespread use of commercial inorganic fertilizers, especially on sloped land near streams and lakes. Some of the plant nutrients in the fertilizers are washed into nearby bodies of surface water, where the resulting cultural eutrophication causes excessive growth of algae and oxygen depletion and also kills fish (Figure 11-21). Rainwater seeping through soil can leach nitrates in commercial fertilizers into groundwater. High levels of nitrate ions make drinking water drawn from wells toxic, especially for infants.

A third method for preventing depletion of soil nutrients is **crop rotation**. Crops such as corn, tobacco, and cotton remove large amounts of nutrients (especially nitrogen) from the soil and can deplete the topsoil of nutrients if planted on the same land several years in a row. Farmers using crop rotation plant areas or strips with corn, tobacco, and cotton one year. The next year they plant the same areas with legumes, whose root nodules (Figure 4-24) add nitrogen to the soil, or with crops such as oats, barley, rye, or sorghum. This method helps restore soil nutrients and reduces erosion by keeping the soil covered with vegetation. Varying the types of crops planted from year to year also reduces infestation by insects, weeds (especially if the land is planted in sorghum, which releases natural herbicides), and plant diseases.

Q: How are most hazardous wastes in the United States handled?

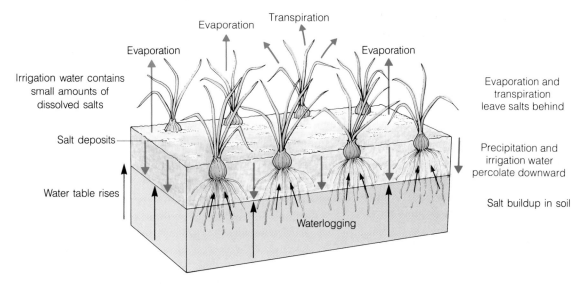

Figure 12-17 Salinization and waterlogging of soil on irrigated land without adequate drainage lead to decreased crop yields.

Soil Conservation Service

Figure 12-18 Because of high evaporation, poor drainage, and severe salinization, white alkaline salts have replaced crops that once grew in this heavily irrigated land in Colorado.

Concern about soil erosion should not be limited to farmers. At least 40% of soil erosion in the United States is caused by timber cutting, overgrazing, mining, and urban development carried out without proper regard for soil conservation.

12-4 Soil Contamination by Excess Salts and Water

SALINIZATION About 18% of the world's cropland is now irrigated, producing about one-third of the world's food. Irrigated cropland is projected to at least double by 2020.

Crop yields on irrigated land can be two to three times those from the same area of land watered only by rain, but irrigation also has some harmful side effects. Irrigation water contains various dissolved salts. In dry climates, much of the water in this saline solution is lost

to the atmosphere by evaporation, leaving behind high concentrations of salts, such as sodium chloride, in the topsoil. The accumulation of salts in soils is called **salinization** (Figure 12-17). Salt buildup stunts crop growth, decreases yields, and eventually kills crop plants and makes the land unproductive (Figure 12-18).

It is estimated that salinization is reducing yields on one-fourth of the world's irrigated cropland. In Egypt, where virtually all cropland is irrigated, half is salinized enough to reduce yields. Worldwide, it is projected that 50% to 65% of all currently irrigated cropland will suffer reduced productivity from excess soil salinity by 2000.

One way to reduce salinization is to flush salts out of the soil by applying much more irrigation water than is needed for crop growth, but that increases pumping and crop-production costs and wastes enormous amounts of water. Another method is to pump ground water from a central well and apply it with a sprinkler system that pivots around the well (Figure 11-17). This method maintains downward drainage and is especially effective at preventing salinization, but at least 30% of the water is lost by evaporation. Also, groundwater in unconfined aquifers (Figure 11-3) eventually becomes too saline for irrigation and other human uses unless expensive drainage systems are installed.

Once topsoil has become heavily salinized, the farmer can renew it by taking the land out of production for two to five years, installing an underground network of perforated drainage pipes, and flushing the soil with large quantities of low-salt water. This scheme is very expensive and only slows down the buildup of soil salinity; it does not stop the process. Flushing salts from the soil also increases the salinity of irrigation water delivered to farmers further downstream, unless the saline water can be drained into evaporation ponds rather than returned to the stream or canal.

A: Buried in deep wells (56%), ponds, pits, or landfills and incinerated

In the Indian state of Uttar Pradesh, farmers are rehabilitating tracts of salinized land by planting a saline-tolerant tree that lowers the water table by taking up water through its roots. Tube wells can also be used to lower water tables, but they are useful only in areas with an adequate groundwater supply.

WATERLOGGING   A problem often accompanying soil salinity in dry regions is **waterlogging** (Figure 12-17). To keep salts from accumulating and destroying fragile root systems, farmers often apply heavy amounts of irrigation water to leach salts deeper into the soil. If drainage isn't provided, water accumulating underground gradually raises the water table. Saline water envelops the roots of plants and kills them.

Waterlogging is a particularly serious problem in the heavily irrigated San Joaquin Valley in California, where soils contain a clay layer with a low permeability to water. Worldwide, at least one-tenth of all irrigated land suffers from waterlogging, and the problem is getting worse.

12-5 Soil and Water Contamination by Hazardous Wastes

SOIL AND GROUNDWATER POLLUTION: A GROWING THREAT   Another source of soil and groundwater contamination is hazardous wastes that are buried in landfills, injected into deep wells, or placed in surface impoundments (Figure 11-26). To this, we must add toxic chemicals discarded by households and small businesses and the vast amounts of pesticides applied to croplands, lawns, golf courses, and gardens that end up in surface waters and groundwater.

As a result, traces of toxic and hazardous chemicals (Section 8-1) are now in the groundwater supplies, rain, and food and in the blood and fat tissue of nearly every person in the United States, most MDCs, and many LDCs. The long-term results of this global chemical experiment on the human race are unknown.

WHAT IS HAZARDOUS WASTE?   According to the Environmental Protection Agency, **hazardous waste** is any discarded chemical that can cause harm because it is any of the following:

■   *Flammable* (waste oils, used organic solvents, and PCBs).

■   *Unstable* enough to explode or release toxic fumes (cyanide solvents).

■   *Corrosive* to materials such as metals or human tissue (strong acids, strong bases, Figure 9-8).

■   *Toxic* if handled in ways that release it into the environment. Examples are DDT, dioxins, PCBs

(used mostly to dissipate heat produced in electrical capacitors and transformers), and various compounds of arsenic, mercury, and lead (see Case Study on p. 275). In 1984, Congress ordered the EPA to also include chemicals that can cause cancer, genetic mutations, and birth defects in humans and test animals in the toxic category, but that has not been done.

The EPA definition of hazardous wastes is very narrow. It does not include radioactive wastes (Section 18-3), hazardous materials discarded by households, mining wastes, oil and gas drilling wastes, liquid hazardous wastes burned as fuel with little regulation in cement kilns (the fastest growing method for dealing with hazardous wastes) and industrial furnaces, cement kiln dust, municipal incinerator ash, wastes from over 930,000 small businesses and factories that generate less than 100 kilograms (220 pounds) of hazardous waste per month, and hazardous wastes generated by the military except at 116 sites so toxic that they are on the EPA's list of priority sites to be cleaned up.

Environmentalists call these omissions a form of "linguistic detoxification" designed to fool the public. They contend that these types of hazardous wastes have not been included mostly because of lobbying of elected officials and EPA regulators by the industries involved and by the Department of Defense. They urge that all excluded categories be designated as forms of hazardous waste so they can be identified and controlled under existing hazardous-waste laws.

GROWING CONCERN   There was little concern over hazardous waste in the United States and most parts of the world until 1977. Then it was discovered that hazardous chemicals leaking from an abandoned waste dump had contaminated a suburban development known as Love Canal, located in Niagara Falls, New York (see Case Study on p. 276).

HAZARDOUS-WASTE PRODUCTION: PRESENT AND PAST   The total quantity of hazardous wastes produced throughout the world, or even in one country, is impossible to determine accurately. According to the EPA, about 240 million metric tons (264 million tons)—an average of 0.9 metric ton (1 ton) per American—of federally defined hazardous waste is produced by U.S. industry each year. The American Chemical Society says the true amount is 2 to 10 times the EPA estimate.

In 1989, the EPA estimated that the annual U.S. production of hazardous and toxic waste was 5.5 billion metric tons (6 billion tons)—an average of 23 metric tons (25 tons) per American. Only 5% of this total (which is probably an overestimate) is managed under federal laws. By any of these estimates, the United States leads the world in total and per capita hazardous-waste production, and this amount is growing exponentially.

Q: How many sites in the United States contain potentially hazardous wastes?

We take in small amounts of lead in the air we breathe, the food we eat, and the water we drink. Because it does not degrade, lead is a cumulative poison.

A 1986 EPA study revealed that 88% of all U.S. children under age 6 have lead levels in their blood (equal to or greater than 10 micrograms per 0.1 liter of blood) that may retard their mental, physical, and emotional development. Fairly low levels of lead in the blood of children under age 6 can damage the brain and central nervous system, lower IQ scores, lower the ability to absorb iron and calcium and metabolize vitamin D, and cause high blood pressure, partial hearing loss, hyperactivity, irritability, and behavior problems.

Each year, 12,000 to 16,000 American children (mostly poor and nonwhite) are treated for acute lead poisoning (caused mostly by ingesting chips of lead-based paint), and about 200 die. About 30% of those who survive suffer from palsy, partial paralysis, blindness, and mental retardation. Centers for Disease Control rules announced in 1992 require that *all* U.S. children be tested for lead by age 1.

The greatest sources of lead in the United States are

- Paint in 57 million houses built before 1978, when use of lead compounds in interior and exterior paint was banned. People living in houses or apartments built before 1980 should chip off samples of paint and have them analyzed for lead by the local health department or by a private testing laboratory (cost $100 to $450).*

*If you find lead in your home, send a postcard to U.S. Consumer Product Safety Commission, Washington, DC 20207 and ask for the free pamphlet, *What You Should Know About the Lead-Based Paint in Your Home.* Two home kits for testing paint for lead are sold by HybriVet Systems (800-262-LEAD) and Frandon Enterprises (800-359-9000).

- Drinking water. According to the EPA, nearly one in five Americans (including 7 million children under age 7) drinks tap water containing excess levels of lead. Homeowners with copper pipes or joints should have the local water department or private laboratory (cost $20 to $100) test their tap water for lead. Before buying an existing house, have its water (that has been standing in pipes for at least 12 hours) and its paint tested for lead. In 1991, the EPA proposed to remove lead from municipal drinking water systems, but has given the country's largest municipalities up to 21 years to do the job.

- Lead particles in air, dust, and soil in areas with heavy traffic and where lead has been, and continues to be, released into the atmosphere by municipal solid-waste incinerators, various industrial plants, and the burning of used motor oil in unregulated boilers (the largest source of lead in U.S. air according to the EPA). Although lead has been virtually eliminated from gasoline in the United States, particles of lead deposited on the soil during the past 50 years when leaded gasoline was used are indestructible. Also, U.S. companies continue to export large amounts of highly toxic tetraethyl lead (TEL) gasoline additive to LDCs where its use is not banned. As a result, childhood lead poisoning is expected to reach epidemic proportions in many LDC cities.

- Lead solder used to seal the seams on food cans, especially in acidic foods such as tomatoes and citric juices. This type of solder has been sharply reduced in U.S. food cans but may be found in cans of imported foods.

- Imported cups, plates, pitchers, and other types of ceramicware used to cook, store, or serve food, especially acidic foods and hot liquids and foods. Expensive leaded glass crystal can leach into wine. Before using such items, consumers should test them for lead content.†

- Vegetables and fruits grown on soil contaminated for many years by lead, especially cropland or home gardens near highways, incinerators, and smelters. Careful washing should remove at least half of this lead.

- Burning certain types of paper in wood stoves and fireplaces. Homeowners should not burn comic strips, Christmas wrapping paper, or painted wood, which can be a source of lead contamination indoors and outdoors.

- Groundwater contaminated by lead leached from landfills. Lead-containing products often discarded in municipal landfills include lead-acid car batteries, TV picture tubes, electronic circuitry, and lead glass.

†A simple home test for lead content of up to 100 items of dishware is available for $24.50 from Frandon Enterprises, 511 N. 48th St., Seattle, WA 98103. Commercial testing costs about $60 per item. Contact American Council of Independent Laboratories, 1725 K Street N.W., Washington, DC 20006, 202-887-5872, for a testing lab near you.

In 1977, residents of a suburb of Niagara Falls, New York, discovered that "out of sight, out of mind" did not apply to them. Hazardous industrial waste buried decades earlier bubbled to the surface, found its way into groundwater, and ended up in backyards and basements.

Between 1942 and 1953, Hooker Chemicals and Plastics Corporation dumped almost 20,000 metric tons (22,000 tons) of toxic and cancer-causing chemical wastes (mostly in steel drums) into an old canal excavation known as the Love Canal, named for its builder William Love. In 1953, Hooker Chemicals covered the dump site with clay and topsoil and sold the site to the Niagara Falls school board for one dollar. The deed specified that the company would have no future liability for any injury or property damage caused by the dump's contents.

An elementary school, playing fields, and a housing project, eventually containing 949 homes, were built in the 10-square-block Love Canal area. Residents began complaining to city officials in 1976 about chemical smells and chemical burns received by children playing in the canal, but their complaints were ignored. In 1977, chemicals began leaking from the badly corroded steel drums into storm sewers, gardens, and basements of homes next to the canal.

Informal health surveys conducted by alarmed residents, led by Lois Gibbs (see Individuals Matter on p. 280 and Guest Essay on p. 285), revealed an unusually high incidence of birth defects; miscarriages; assorted cancers; and nerve, respiratory, and kidney disorders among people who lived near the canal. Complaints to local officials had little effect.

Continued pressure from residents and unfavorable publicity eventually led state officials to conduct a preliminary health survey and tests. They found that pregnant women in one area near the canal had a miscarriage rate four times higher than normal. They also found that the air, water, and soil of the canal area and the basements of nearby houses were contaminated with a number of toxic and carcinogenic chemicals.

In 1978, the state closed the school, permanently relocated the 238 families whose homes were closest to the dump, and fenced off the area around the canal. On May 21, 1980, after protests from the outraged 711 families still living fairly close to the landfill, President Jimmy Carter declared Love Canal a federal disaster area and had the families relocated.

Since that time, the school and 239 homes within a block and a half of the canal have been torn down and the state has purchased 570 of the remaining homes. About 60 families have remained in the desolate neighborhood, unwilling or unable to sell their houses to New York State and move.

The dump site has been covered with a clay cap and surrounded by a drain system that pumps leaking wastes to a new treatment plant. By 1990, the total cost for cleanup and relocation had reached $250 million. In June 1990, the EPA renamed the area Black Creek Village and allowed state officials to begin selling 239 remaining dilapidated and boarded-up houses at 20% below market value.

Lois Gibbs says it is "criminal to send people back in there" and has filed a lawsuit to prevent the sale. She and other environmentalists point out that the dump has not been cleaned up but only capped and fitted with a drainage system. According to Gibbs, "It isn't a matter of if the dump will leak again, but when." To her and other environmentalists, selling the houses in Love Canal sends a message from the government that "Chemical dumps make good homes for poor and middle-class Americans who can't afford to buy homes in safer neighborhoods."

No conclusive study has been made to determine the long-term effects of exposure to hazardous chemicals on former Love Canal residents. All studies made so far have been criticized on scientific grounds.

The psychological damage to evacuated families is enormous. For the rest of their lives, they will wonder whether a disorder will strike and will worry about the possible effects of the chemicals on their children and grandchildren.

In 1985, former Love Canal residents received payments from a 1983 out-of-court settlement from Occidental Chemical Corporation (which bought Hooker Chemicals in 1968), the city of Niagara Falls, and the Niagara Falls school board. The payments ranged from $2,000 to $400,000 for claims of injuries ranging from persistent rashes and migraine headaches to cancers and severe mental retardation.

In 1988, a U.S. district court ruled that Occidental Chemical must pay the cleanup costs, but the company is appealing that ruling. In 1990, a trial began in which New York State is seeking $250 million in punitive damages from Occidental Chemical.

The Love Canal incident is a vivid reminder that we can never really throw anything away, that wastes don't stay put, and that preventing pollution is much safer and cheaper than trying to clean it up.

A serious problem facing the United States and most industrialized countries is what to do with thousands of dumps like the one at Love Canal, where in the past, large quantities of hazardous wastes were disposed of in an unregulated manner. Even with adequate funding, effective cleanup is difficult because officials don't know what chemicals have been dumped and where all the sites are located.

Q: How many sites in the United States are on the EPA's list for cleanup?

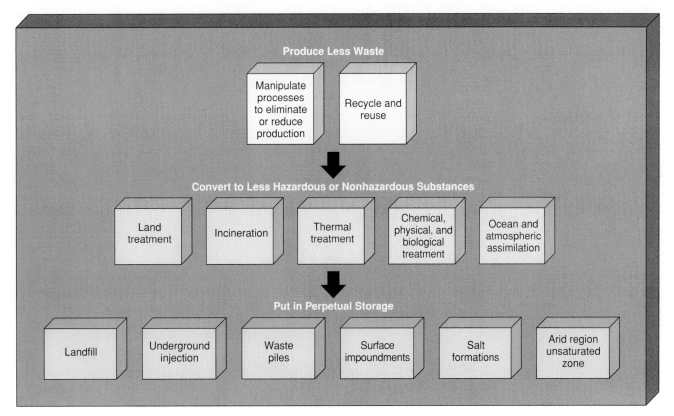

Figure 12-19 Options for dealing with hazardous waste. (National Academy of Sciences)

HOW SHOULD HAZARDOUS WASTE BE CONTROLLED AND MANAGED? There are five basic options for hazardous wastes; **(1)** don't make them in the first place; **(2)** recycle or reuse them; **(3)** detoxify them; **(4)** burn them in an incinerator or a cement kiln on land or on an incinerator ship at sea; and **(5)** hide them by putting them into a deep well, pond, pit, or landfill, or by dumping them in the ocean. According to the National Academy of Sciences (Figure 12-19), the most desirable approach is waste prevention and waste reduction (options 1 and 2).

Despite talk about waste reduction and waste prevention, the order of priorities for dealing with hazardous waste in the United States is the reverse of what prominent scientists say it should be (Figure 12-19). So far, no country has implemented an effective hazardous-waste reduction program; but countries like Denmark, the Netherlands, Germany, and Sweden are far ahead of the United States in starting to follow the priorities shown in Figure 12-19.

The EPA estimates that—using existing technology—15% to 30% of the hazardous waste produced by industry in the United States could be recycled, reused, or exchanged so that one industry's waste becomes another's raw material. Currently, however, only about 5% of such materials are managed in this manner, and the EPA devotes only a small portion of its waste management budget to waste reduction, reuse, and recycling.

Some firms have found that waste reduction and pollution prevention save them money. Since 1975, the Minnesota Mining and Manufacturing Company (3M), which makes 60,000 different products in 100 manufacturing plants, has had a program that by 1990 had cut its hazardous-waste production by two-thirds and its emissions of air pollutants by 90%, and had saved over $500 million. This achievement meant redesigning equipment and processes, using fewer hazardous raw materials, identifying hazardous chemical outputs and recycling these chemicals or selling them as raw materials to other companies, and making nonpolluting products.

Most firms have little incentive to reduce their output of waste because waste management makes up only about 0.1% of the total value of the products they ship. Placing a tax on each unit of hazardous waste generated would provide enough money to support a strong program for reducing, recycling, and reusing hazardous waste.

The second phase of a hazardous-waste management program is to convert any waste remaining after waste reduction, recycling, and reuse into less-hazardous or nonhazardous materials (Figure 12-19). Conversion methods include spreading degradable wastes on the land, burning them on land or at sea in specially designed incinerators, thermally decomposing them, using natural or bioengineered microorganisms to de-

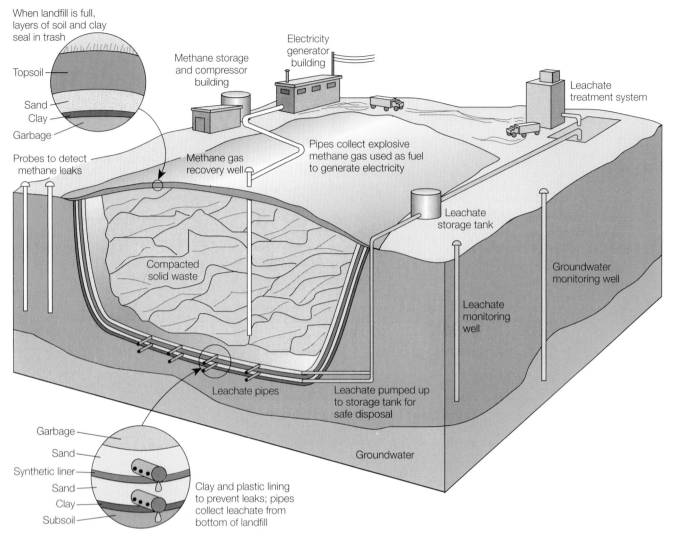

When landfill is full, layers of soil and clay seal in trash

Topsoil

Sand
Clay

Garbage

Probes to detect methane leaks

Methane storage and compressor building

Electricity generator building

Methane gas recovery well

Pipes collect explosive methane gas used as fuel to generate electricity

Leachate treatment system

Compacted solid waste

Leachate storage tank

Groundwater monitoring well

Leachate monitoring well

Leachate pipes

Leachate pumped up to storage tank for safe disposal

Groundwater

Garbage

Sand

Synthetic liner

Sand

Clay

Subsoil

Clay and plastic lining to prevent leaks; pipes collect leachate from bottom of landfill

Figure 12-20 A modern state-of-the-art landfill is designed to eliminate or minimize environmental problems that plague older landfills. Siting is restricted to geologically suitable areas. Rainwater seeping into the landfill dissolves materials from the solid waste and forms a contaminated liquid called leachate. To prevent leachate from leaking into groundwater, the bottom is covered with an impermeable liner usually made of several layers of clay, thick plastic, and an asphalt membrane. Collected leachate is pumped from the bottom of the landfill, stored in tanks, and then treated. When the landfill is full, it is covered with clay, sand, gravel, and topsoil to prevent water from seeping into its contents. Several wells are drilled around the landfill to monitor any leakage of leachate into nearby groundwater. Methane gas produced by anaerobic decomposition in the sealed landfill is collected and burned as a fuel to produce steam or electricity. Unfortunately, only a few landfills in the United States have such state-of-the-art design. Furthermore, even these landfills will eventually leak, passing contamination and cleanup costs on to the next generation.

grade specific chemicals, or treating them chemically or physically.

The Netherlands incinerates about half its hazardous waste. The EPA estimates that 60% of all U.S. hazardous waste could be incinerated. With proper air pollution controls and highly trained personnel, incineration is potentially a safe method of disposal for most types of hazardous waste, but it is also the most expensive method. The ash that is left and that must be disposed of often contains toxic metals, and the gaseous and particulate combustion products emitted can be health hazards if not controlled. In the United States, such ash is not classified as hazardous by the EPA. An-

other problem is that not all hazardous wastes are combustible. According to environmentalists, required pollution controls and operator training in the United States for hazardous-waste and municipal trash incinerators are not nearly enough to protect the public from potential harm.

Denmark, which relies almost exclusively on groundwater for drinking water, has the most comprehensive and effective program for detoxifying most of its hazardous waste. Each municipality has at least one facility that accepts paints, solvents, and other hazardous wastes from households. Toxic waste from industries is delivered to 21 transfer stations scattered through-

Q: How many hazardous-waste sites on the EPA's cleanup list have been cleaned up and removed from the list?

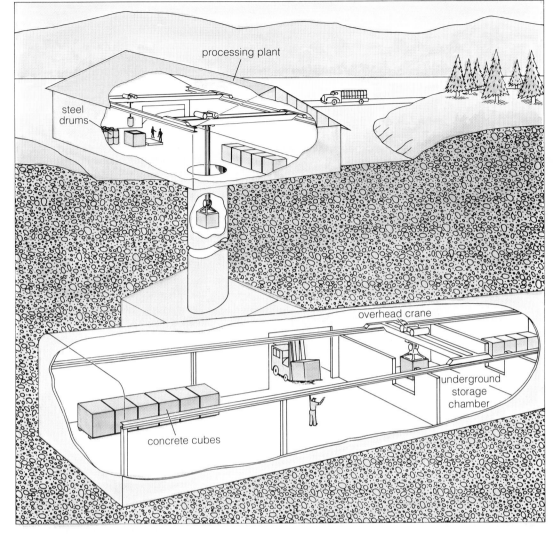

Figure 12-21 Swedish method for handling hazardous waste. Hazardous materials are placed in drums, which are stored in concrete cubes. The cubes are then placed in an underground vault.

out the country. All waste is then transferred to a large treatment facility in the town of Nyborg on the island of Fyn near the country's geographic center. There, about 75% of the waste is detoxified, and the rest is buried in a carefully designed and monitored landfill.

The third phase of waste management involves concentrating and placing any waste left after detoxification in containers and storing them in specially designed *secured landfills* (Figure 12-20) or *underground vaults* (Figure 12-21). However, according to the Office of Technology Assessment, eventually even the best-designed landfill or vault will leak and can threaten groundwater supplies.

Some engineers and environmentalists have proposed that a better solution would be to store these remaining toxic and hazardous wastes aboveground in large, two-story, reinforced concrete buildings until better technologies develop. The base of such a building would be a 0.3-meter (1-foot) thick concrete slab. The first floor would contain no wastes but would have in-

spection walkways so people could check for leaks from above. Any leachate would be collected, treated, solidified, and returned to the storage building. Such buildings would last for decades, perhaps as long as a century. This approach would be much cheaper and safer than landfills and cheaper and safer than incinerators for many wastes.

Most hazardous waste produced in the United States is disposed of in the land by deep-well injection, surface impoundments, and landfills. Deep-well disposal of hazardous waste is increasing rapidly as other methods are restricted or become too expensive. However, wastes can spill or leak at the surface and leach into groundwater, and well pipe casings can corrode and allow wastes to escape into groundwater. Inadequate or leaking seals where the well casing passes through the impervious layer of rock can allow wastes to reach aquifers. Wastes can also migrate from the porous layer of rock where they are deposited to aquifers through existing fractures or new ones caused by earth-

A: 24 (at a cost of $7 billion)

Chapter 12   **279**

One highly effective frontline activist is Lois Gibbs (see Guest Essay on p. 285), who organized residents of the Love Canal development near Niagara Falls, New York, when they discovered they were living near a leaking toxic-waste dump (see Case Study on p. 276). She then went on to form the Citizens' Clearing House for Hazardous Waste. This organization provides information and help for citizens' groups organizing **(1)** to prevent hazardous-waste dumps, landfills, waste-injection wells, and incinerators from being located in their areas and **(2)** to monitor and demand reduction of pollution and hazardous waste produced by existing waste management facilities and chemical and industrial plants.

She and other grassroots activists are not swayed by the highly profitable waste management industry's technical risk-assessment (Chapter 8) and cost-benefit studies (see Pro/Con on p. 151), slick glossy publications, promises to use state-of-the-art technology, expressions of their concern for the environment, and arguments that protesting citizens are holding up progress. Based on her experience, Lois Gibbs says, "Don't listen to them. It's all BS. The simple truth is, they're trying to kill you, to sacrifice you and your family just so they can make money."

Here are her guidelines for Earth citizens:

- Don't compromise our children's futures by cutting deals with polluters and regulators. Environmental justice cannot be bought or sold.

- Hold polluters and elected officials who go along with polluters directly and personally accountable. What they are doing is wrong, and they must be held accountable for their actions.

- Don't fall for the argument voiced by industry that protesters against hazardous-waste landfills, incinerators, and injection wells are holding up progress because we have to deal with the hazardous wastes we produce. Instead, recognize that the best way to deal with waste and pollution is not to produce so much of it. After that has been done we can decide what to do with what is left as recommended by the National Academy of Sciences (Figure 12-19).

- Oppose all hazardous-waste landfills, deep-disposal wells, and incinerators to sharply raise the cost of dealing with hazardous materials. Only in this way will waste producers and elected officials get serious about waste reduction and pollution prevention instead of talking about it while spending little money or effort to do it. The goal of politically powerful waste management companies is to have us produce even larger amounts of hazardous (and nonhazardous) waste so they can make higher profits.

- Recognize that all forms of hazardous-waste disposal (landfill, incineration, waste ponds, and deep-well disposal) ultimately contaminate the environment. There is no such thing as "safe" disposal of hazardous waste. The law of conservation of matter (Section 3-4) and the fact that hazardous chemicals we place in the ground or air don't stay put mean that we need to redefine our backyard. It is everywhere. Our goal should be to drastically reduce the production of wastes; and for especially hazardous materials, the goal should be "Not in Anyone's Backyard (NIABY)" or "Not on Planet Earth (NOPE)."

quakes. Until this method is more carefully evaluated and regulated, environmentalists believe that its use should not be allowed to increase.

Much of the country's hazardous waste is deposited into ponds, pits, or lagoons whose bottoms are supposed to be sealed with a plastic liner. Most experts consider it only a matter of time before the liners leak. According to the EPA, 70% of the pits, ponds, and lagoons used to store hazardous wastes have no liners, and as many as 90% may threaten groundwater. Major storms or hurricanes can cause overflows. Volatile compounds, such as hazardous organic solvents, can evaporate into the atmosphere and eventually return to Earth and contaminate surface and groundwater in other locations.

There is also growing concern about accidents during some of the more than 500,000 shipments of hazardous wastes in the United States each year. Between 1980 and 1990, there were 13,476 toxic-chemical accidents, causing 309 deaths, over 11,000 injuries, and evacuation of over 500,000 people. Most communities do not have the equipment and trained personnel to deal adequately with most types of hazardous-waste spills.

Increasingly, citizens are successfully opposing the location of hazardous-waste incinerators, landfills, or waste treatment plants near their communities, with the goal of protecting their health and forcing elected officials to explore and implement waste reduction and pollution prevention programs (see Individuals Matter above).

As the costs of hazardous-waste disposal have risen, waste disposal firms in the United States and several other industrialized nations have shipped hazardous wastes to other countries, especially LDCs in Asia, Africa, and Latin America (see Spotlight on p. 281).

Q: How many plants feed most of the world's people?

To save money and avoid regulatory hurdles and local opposition, cities and waste disposal companies in the United States and other MDCs legally ship vast quantities of hazardous waste to other countries. Most legal U.S. exports of hazardous wastes go to Canada and Mexico.

There is evidence of a growing trade in illegal shipments of hazardous wastes across international borders. This is fairly easy to do because customs officials in the United States and other countries are not trained to detect illegal shipments and don't have enough inspectors to examine most shipments. Sometimes exported wastes are labeled as materials to be recycled and then are dumped after reaching their destination. Hazardous wastes have also been mixed with wood chips or sawdust and shipped legally as burnable material.

Waste disposal firms can charge high prices for picking up hazardous wastes. If they can then dispose of them legally or illegally in other countries at low costs, they pocket huge profits. Officials of poor LDCs find it hard to resist the income (often in the form of bribes) from receiving these wastes. However, some countries are beginning to adopt the slogan "Not In Our Country" (NIOC) and a "return to sender" policy when illegal waste shipments are discovered.

Environmentalists and some members of Congress call for the United States to ban all exports of hazardous waste and all pesticides and drugs not approved for use in the United States. They believe that it is wrong to export Love Canals or banned pesticides and drugs to other countries and that each country and state should be responsible for the wastes it produces. Being able to export wastes to other countries (or to other states) also stimulates the throwaway mentality and discourages waste reduction.

A U.S. or worldwide ban on hazardous-waste exports would help but would not end illegal trade of these wastes. The profits to be earned are simply too great. What do you think should be done?

U.S. HAZARDOUS-WASTE LEGISLATION In 1976, the U.S. Congress passed the Resource Conservation and Recovery Act (RCRA, pronounced "rick-ra"), amending it in 1984. This law requires the EPA to identify hazardous wastes and set standards for their management; it provides guidelines and financial aid to establish state waste management programs. The law also requires all firms that store, treat, or dispose of more than 100 kilograms (220 pounds) of hazardous wastes per month to have a permit stating how such wastes are to be managed.

To reduce illegal dumping, hazardous-waste producers granted disposal permits by the EPA must use a "cradle-to-grave" manifest system to keep track of waste transferred from point of origin to approved off-site disposal facilities. EPA administrators, however, point out that this requirement is impossible to enforce effectively. The EPA and state regulatory agencies do not have enough personnel to review the documentation of more than 750,000 hazardous-waste generators and 15,000 haulers each year, let alone to verify them and prosecute offenders. If caught, however, violators are subject to large fines.

Environmentalists argue that fines for violators are too low and fail to recover amounts larger than the profits earned by illegal activity—sending polluters the clear message that crime pays. They believe that people who deliberately, or through negligence, illegally release harmful chemicals into the environment should be subject to jail terms because such crimes can kill or damage the health of many people for decades.

Operators of EPA-licensed hazardous-waste landfills must prevent leakage, continually monitor the quality of groundwater around the sites, and report any contamination to the EPA. When a landfill reaches its capacity and is closed, the operators must cover it with a leakproof cap, monitor the nearby groundwater for 30 years, and be financially responsible for cleanup and damages from leaks for 30 years. Environmentalists consider that provision a serious weakness in the law because most landfills will probably begin leaking after 30 years, passing the hazards and costs on to the next generation.

Another loophole exempts "recycled" chemical wastes from control. This includes hazardous chemical wastes burned in industrial boilers, industrial furnaces, and cement kilns, which are not required to meet the stringent permit requirements and emission standards required for EPA-licensed hazardous-waste incinerators. This rapidly growing practice of "sham recycling" pollutes the air with toxic metals and other hazardous chemicals. It also produces toxic fly ash that does not have to be disposed of in EPA-licensed hazardous-waste landfills. RCRA also allows hazardous wastes to be "recycled" into pesticides as "inert" ingredients.

In 1984, Congress amended the 1976 Resource Conservation and Recovery Act to make it national policy to minimize or eliminate land disposal of 450 regulated hazardous wastes by May 1990 unless the EPA has determined that it is an acceptable approach or the only feasible approach for a particular hazardous material. Even then, each chemical is to be treated to the fullest extent possible to reduce its toxicity before land disposal of any type is allowed.

If enforced, this policy represents a much more ecologically sound approach to dealing with hazardous wastes. However, instead of requiring treatment, EPA regulations issued in 1990 would allow industries to dilute hazardous wastes by mixing them with other wastes and then injecting the mixture into deep wells. According to environmentalists, this violates the 1984 RCRA amendments by allowing dilution to replace treatment of hazardous wastes before land disposal is allowed.

The 1980 Comprehensive Environmental Response, Compensation and Liability Act is known as the Superfund program. This law (plus amendments in 1986 and 1990) established a $16.3 billion fund, financed jointly by federal and state governments and taxes on chemical and petrochemical industries. The money is to be used for the cleanup of abandoned or inactive hazardous-waste dump sites and leaking underground tanks that are threats to human health and the environment. The EPA is authorized to collect fines and sue the owners of abandoned sites and tanks (if they can be found and held responsible) to recover up to three times the cleanup costs.

In 1989, the EPA estimated that more than 37,000 sites in the United States contain potentially hazardous wastes, but it has stopped looking for new sites. The General Accounting Office estimates that there are between 103,000 and 425,000 sites. None of these esti-

---

INDIVIDUALS MATTER What You Can Do

Here are some ways you can help protect the soil:

- Establish a soil conservation program for the land around your home.

- If you are building a home, save all the trees possible, and have the contractor set up barriers to catch any soil eroded during construction. Require the contractor to disturb as little soil as possible and to save and replace any topsoil removed instead of hauling it off and selling it. Plant any disturbed area with fast-growing native ground cover immediately after construction is completed.

- Landscape the area not used for gardening with a mix of wildflowers, herbs (for cooking and to repel insects), low-growing ground cover, small bushes, and other forms of vegetation natural to the area. This biologically diverse type of yard saves water, energy, and money and reduces infestation of mosquitoes and other damaging insects by providing a diversity of habitats for their natural predators.

- Set up a compost bin (Figure 12-16) and use it to produce mulch and soil conditioner for yard and garden plants.

- Use organic methods (no commercial fertilizers or pesticides) for growing vegetables and maintaining your yard. This in-

volves using organic fertilizers (mulch, green manure, and animal manure) and biological and cultural control of pests (Section 14-5).

- Insist that local, state, and federal elected officials establish and strictly enforce laws and policies that sharply reduce soil erosion, salinization, and waterlogging.

To reduce your inputs of hazardous waste into the environment:

- Use pesticides and other hazardous chemicals only when absolutely necessary and in the smallest amount possible.

- Use rechargeable batteries but be sure they are recycled when their useful life is over. Sanyo, for example, packages its rechargeable batteries in a tube so they can be mailed back to the company for recycling.

- Use less hazardous (and usually cheaper) cleaning products (see Individuals Matter inside the back cover).

- Take used motor oil, transmission fluid, brake fluid, and car batteries to a local auto service center or to a hazardous-waste collection center for recycling.

- Insist that local, state, and federal elected officials establish and strictly enforce laws and policies that sharply reduce soil erosion and contamination and empha-

size pollution prevention and waste reduction.

- Do not flush hazardous chemicals down the toilet, pour them down the drain, bury them, throw them away in the garbage, or dump them down storm drains.* Consult your local health department or environmental agency for safe disposal methods.

- Support changes in federal laws that would set an 80% national recycling goal for solid waste and place a 10-year moratorium on the burning of solid and hazardous wastes in incinerators, industrial boilers, and cement kilns and on placing hazardous wastes in landfills and deep injection wells to encourage pollution prevention and waste reduction. Also support bans on any shipments of hazardous waste to other countries or from one state to another.

*See the Household Hazardous Waste Wheel, Environmental Hazards Management Institute, 10 Newmarket Road, P.O. Box 932, Durham, NH 03824 ($3.75) and Earth Wise Household Inventory Sheet, P.O. Box 682, Belmar, NJ 07719 ($2.00). You can make a household inventory of hazardous and wasteful items by using the Household Inventory Worksheet: A Blueprint for Safer Homes, available for $2.00 from Earth-Ways, P.O. Box 682, Belmar, NJ 07719.

Q: How many people on average does one U.S. farmer feed?

mates includes hazardous wastes deposited in the 17,000 sites at military bases throughout the United States (called 17,000 "points of blight" by scientist Peter Montague; see Guest Essay on p. 33).

By September 1991, the EPA had placed 1,211 sites on a National Priority List for cleanup because of their threat to nearby populations, and the list is expected to reach 2,000 sites by 2000. Many of these sites are located over major aquifers and pose a serious threat to groundwater.

By 1991, after spending $7 billion of taxpayers' money, the EPA had declared only 64 sites clean and had removed only 24 from the priority list. Only $2.4 billion was spent on site-specific activities, with the rest used for administration, management, and litigation and for outside consultants. According to a 1989 report by the Office of Technology Assessment, about 75% of the cleanups are unlikely to work over the long term.

In 1985, the Office of Technology Assessment estimated that the final list could include at least 10,000 priority sites, with cleanup costs amounting to as much as $500 billion over the next 50 years, perhaps rivaling the cost of the nation's savings and loan bailout—a glaring example of why waste prevention is cheaper and more effective than pollution cleanup. Cleanup funds provided by taxes on industries that generate waste have amounted to about $1 billion a year—far short of the need.

Each of us has a role to play in seeing that soil resources are used sustainably and in reducing the input of hazardous waste into the environment (see Individuals Matter on p. 282).

Civilization can survive the exhaustion of oil reserves, but not the continuing wholesale loss of topsoil.

LESTER R. BROWN

GUEST ESSAY Land Degradation and Environmental Resources

David Pimentel

David Pimentel is professor of insect ecology and agricultural sciences in the College of Agriculture and Life Sciences at Cornell University. He has chaired the Board on Environmental Studies (1979–1981) and the Malaria Prevention and Control Panel (1990–) in the National Academy of Sciences, and the Panel on Soil and Land Degradation, Office of Technology Assessment (1978–1981). He has published over 350 scientific papers and 12 books on environmental topics including land degradation, agricultural pollution and energy use, biomass energy, and pesticides. He was one of the first ecologists to employ an interdisciplinary, holistic approach in investigating complex environmental problems.

At a time when the world's human population is rapidly expanding and its need for more land to produce food, fiber, and fuelwood is also escalating, valuable land is being degraded through erosion and other means at an alarming rate. Soil degradation is of great concern because soil re-formation is extremely slow. Under tropical and temperate agricultural conditions, an average of 500 years (with a range of 220 to 1,000 years) is required for the renewal of 2.5 cm (1 inch) of soil—a renewal rate of

about 1 metric ton (t) of topsoil per hectare (ha) of land per year (1t/ha per year). Worldwide annual erosion rates for agricultural land are about 20 to 100 times this natural renewal rate.

Erosion rates vary in different regions because of topography, rainfall, wind intensity, and the type of agricultural practices used. In China, for example, the average annual soil loss is reported to be about 40t/ha while the U.S. average is 18t/ha. In states like Iowa and Missouri, however, annual soil erosion averages are greater than 35t/ha.

Worldwide, about 10 million hectares (about the size of Virginia) of land are abandoned for crop production each year because of high erosion rates plus waterlogging of soils, salinization, and other forms of soil degradation. In addition, according to the UN Environment Programme, crop productivity becomes uneconomical on about 20 million hectares each year because soil quality has been severely degraded.

Soil erosion also occurs in forest land but is not as severe as that in the more exposed soil of agricultural land. However, soil erosion in managed forests is a primary concern because the soil reformation rate in forests is about two to three times longer than that in agricultural land. To compound this erosion problem, at least 24 million hectares of forest are being cleared each year throughout the world [Section 10-2]. About 80% of this is being cleared and planted with crops to compensate for loss of agricultural land caused by erosion and population growth. Average soil erosion per hectare increases when trees are removed and the land is planted with crops.

The effects of agriculture and forestry are interrelated in many other ways. Large-scale removal of forests without adequate replanting reduces fuelwood supplies and forces the poor in LDCs to substitute crop residue and manure for fuelwood. When these plant and animal

(continued)

wastes are burned instead of being returned to the land as ground cover and organic fertilizer, erosion is intensified and productivity of the land is decreased. These factors, in turn, increase pressure to convert more forestland into agricultural land, further intensifying soil erosion.

One reason that soil erosion does not receive high priority among many governments and farmers is that it usually occurs at such a slow rate that its cumulative effects may take decades to become apparent. For example, the removal of 1 millimeter (1/25 inch) of soil is so small that it goes undetected. But the accumulated soil loss at this rate over a 25-year period would amount to 25 mm (1 inch) — an amount that would take about 500 years to replace by natural processes.

Although reduced soil depth is a serious concern because it is cumulative, other factors associated with erosion also reduce productivity. These are losses of water, organic matter, and soil nutrients. Water is the primary limiting factor for all natural and agricultural plants and trees. When some of the vegetation on land is removed, most water is lost to remaining plants because it runs off rapidly and does not penetrate the soil. In addition, soil erosion reduces the water-holding capacity of soil because it removes organic matter and fine soil particles that hold water. When this happens, water infiltration of soil can be reduced as much as 90%.

Organic matter in soil plays an important role in holding water and in decreasing removal of plant nutrients. Thus, it is not surprising that a 50% reduction of soil organic matter on a plot of land has been found to reduce corn yields as much as 25%. When soil erodes, there is also a loss of vital plant nutrients such as nitrogen, phosphorus, potassium, and calcium. With U.S. annual cropland erosion rates of about 18t/ha, estimates are that $18 billion of fertilizer nutrients are lost annually by erosion. This use of fertilizers substantially adds to the cost of crop production.

Some analysts who are unaware of the numerous and complex effects of soil erosion have falsely concluded that the damages are relatively minor. For example, they report that an average soil loss in the United States of 18t/ha per year causes an annual reduction in crop productivity of only 0.1% to 0.5%. However, we need to consider all the ecological effects caused by erosion, including a reduction in soil depth, reduced water availability for crops, and reduction in soil organic matter and nutrients. When this is done, agronomists and ecologists report a 15% to 30% reduction in crop productivity — a key factor in increased levels of costly fertilizer and declining yields on some land despite high levels of fertilization. Because fertilizers are not a substitute for fertile soil, they can be applied only up to certain levels before crop yields begin to decline.

Reduced agricultural productivity is only one of the effects and costs of soil erosion. In the United States, water runoff is responsible for transporting about 3 billion° metric tons (3.3 billion tons) of sediment each year to waterways in the 48 contiguous states. About 60% of these sediments come from agricultural lands. Estimates show that off-site damages to U.S. water storage capacity, wildlife, and navigable waterways from these sediments cost an estimated $6 billion each year. Dredging sediments from U.S. streams, harbors, and reservoirs alone costs about $570 million each year. About 25% of new water storage capacity in U.S. reservoirs is built solely to compensate for sediment buildup.

When soil sediments that include pesticides and other agricultural chemicals are carried into streams, lakes, and reservoirs, fish production is adversely affected. These contaminated sediments interfere with fish spawning, increase predation on fish, and destroy fisheries in estuarine and coastal areas.

Increased erosion and water runoff on mountain slopes flood agricultural land in the valleys below, further decreasing agricultural productivity. Eroded land also does not hold water very well, again decreasing crop productivity. This effect is magnified in the 80 countries (with nearly 40% of the world's population) that experience frequent droughts. The rapid growth in the world's population, accompanied by the need for more crops and a projected doubling of water needs in the next 20 years, will only intensify water shortages, particularly if soil erosion is not contained.

Thus, soil erosion is one of the world's critical problems and, if not slowed, will seriously reduce agricultural and forestry production and degrade the quality of aquatic ecosystems. Solutions are not particularly difficult but are often not implemented because erosion occurs so gradually that we fail to acknowledge its cumulative impact until damage is irreversible. Many farmers have also been conditioned to believe that losses in soil fertility can be remedied by applying increasingly higher levels of fertilizer or the use of fossil-fuel energy.

The principal method of controlling soil erosion and its accompanying runoff of sediment is to maintain adequate vegetative coverage on soils [by various methods discussed in Section 12-3]. These methods are also cost-effective in preventing erosion, especially when off-site costs of erosion are included. Scientists, policymakers, and agriculturists need to work together to implement soil and water conservation practices before world soils lose most of their productivity.

Guest Essay Discussion

1. Some analysts contend that average soil erosion rates in the United States and the world are low and that this problem has been overblown by environmentalists and can easily be solved by improved agricultural technology such as no-till cultivation and increased use of commercial inorganic fertilizers. Do you agree or disagree with this position? Explain.

2. What specific things do you believe elected officials should do to decrease soil erosion and the resulting water pollution by sediment in the United States?

Q: What percentage of the commercial energy used in the United States is consumed by the agricultural system?

Lois Marie Gibbs

Lois Marie Gibbs was once a housewife living near the Love Canal toxic dump site (see Case Study on p. 276) who had never engaged in any sort of political action. Alarmed at what she saw happening to the health of her own children and those of neighbors, she organized her neighborhood and became the president and major strategist for the Love Canal Homeowners Association in their successful fight against a multimillion-dollar corporation and the New York State and federal governments to provide relief for their endangered community. This dedicated grassroots political action by "amateurs" brought hazardous-waste issues to national prominence and was a major factor leading to the development and passage of the federal Superfund legislation. Lois Gibbs then moved to Washington, D.C., and formed Citizens' Clearinghouse for Hazardous Wastes, an organization that has helped ordinary citizens in over 7,000 community grassroots organizations protect themselves from hazardous wastes. Her story is told in her autobiography, Love Canal: My Story *(State University of New York Press, 1982), and was also the subject of a CBS movie,* Lois Gibbs: The Love Canal, *which aired in 1982. She is an inspiring example of what an ordinary citizen can do to change the world.*

Just about everyone knows our environment is in danger. One of the most serious threats to our environment is the millions of metric tons of waste put into the air, water, and ground every year. All across the United States and around the world, there are thousands of places that have been, and continue to be, polluted by toxic chemicals, radioactive waste, and just plain garbage.

For generations, the main question people have asked is, "Where do we put all this waste? It's got to go somewhere." That is the wrong question, as is. This has been shown by the long series of experiments in waste disposal we have carried out to try to answer it and by the simple fact that there is no away [Section 3-4].

We tried dumping our waste in the oceans. That was wrong. We tried injecting it into deep, underground wells. That was wrong. We've been trying to build landfills that don't leak. That doesn't work. We've been trying to get rid of waste by burning it in high-tech incinerators. That only produces different types of pollution, such as air pollution and toxic ash. We've tried a broad range of

"pollution" controls. But all that does is allow legalized, high-tech pollution. Even recycling, which is a very good thing to do, suffers from the same problem as all the other methods: It addresses waste *after* it has been produced.

For many years, people have been assuming that "it's got to go somewhere," but now many people, especially young people, are starting to ask, "Why?" Why do we produce so much waste? Why do we need products and services that have so many toxic by-products? Why can't industry change the way it makes things so that it stops producing so much waste?

These are the *right* questions. When you start asking them, you start getting answers that lead to *pollution prevention* and *waste reduction* instead of simply *pollution control* and *waste management*. People, young and old, who care about pollution prevention begin challenging our use and disposal of enormous amounts of polystyrene (Styrofoam) plastic each year. They begin challenging companies to stop making products with gases that destroy the ozone layer [Section 10-4] and contribute to the threatening possibility of global warming [Section 10-2]. They begin to ask why so many goods are wrapped in excessive, throwaway packaging. They begin challenging companies that sell pesticides, cleaning fluids, batteries, and other hazardous products to either take the toxics out of those products or begin taking them back for recovery or recycling, rather than disposing of them in the environment. They begin demanding alternatives to throwaway materials in general.

Since 1988, hundreds of student groups have contacted my organization to get help and advice in taking these effective types of actions. Many of these groups begin by working to get polystyrene food packaging out of their school cafeterias and out of local fast-food restaurants.

Oregon students even took legal action to get rid of cups and plates made from bleached paper, because the paper contains the deadly poison dioxin. They were asking the right questions and gave the right answer when they demanded the school systems switch to nondisposable, reusable cups, plates, and utensils.

Dozens of student groups have joined with local environmental and grassroots organizations in their communities to get toxic-waste sites cleaned up or to stop new toxic-waste sites, radioactive-waste sites, or waste incinerators from being built.

Waste issues are not simply environmental issues. They are issues that are all tied up with economics. Our economy is geared to producing and getting rid of waste. *Somebody* is making money from every scrap of waste and has a vested interest in leaving things the way they are. Environmentalists and industry officials constantly argue about what's called "cost-benefit analysis" [Section 7-2]. Simply stated, this poses the question of whether the benefit of controlling pollution or waste will be greater than the cost. I think this is another example of the wrong

(continued)

question. Instead, I think the right question is, "Who will benefit and who will pay the cost?"

Waste issues are also issues of *justice* and *fairness*. Again, there's a lot of debate between industry officials and environmentalists, especially those in federal and state environmental agencies, about what they call "acceptable risk." Simply stated, that means that industry officials and environmentalists will decide how much exposure people will get to toxic chemicals. Unfortunately, they hardly ever ask the people who are actually going to be exposed how they feel about it. Instead, industry officials debate and ask each other how much exposure other people will be allowed to get. Again, I think this is the wrong question. I believe it's not fair to expose people to chemical poisons without their consent and, in fact, without their even being asked.

Risk analysts often say, "But there's only a one in a million chance of increased death from this toxic chemical." That may be true. But suppose I took a pistol and went to the edge of your neighborhood and began shooting. There's probably only a one in a million chance that I'd hit somebody. But would you give me permission, would you give me a license, to do that? As long as we don't stand up for our rights and demand that "bullets" in the form of hazardous chemicals not be "fired" in our neighborhoods, we are giving environmental regulators and waste producers a license to kill a certain number of us without our even being consulted.

When you study the issues of the environment, remember that they are not abstract issues that only happen somewhere else. We *all* have to live, breathe, and survive in this environment. We have all learned that decisions made for us or by us in the past have come back to haunt us. Likewise, today's decisions will affect all of us tomorrow and far into the future.

From my personal experience, I know that decisions made to dump wastes at Love Canal and in thousands of other places in the past were not made simply on the basis of the best available scientific knowledge. The same holds true for decisions made about how to manage the wastes we produce today.

Instead, the real world we live in is shaped by decisions based on money and power. If you really want to understand what's behind any given environmental issue, the first question you should ask is, "Who stands to profit from this?" Then ask, "Who is going to pay the price?" You will then be able to identify both sides of the issue, and you can decide whether you want to be part of the problem or part of the solution.

Guest Essay Questions

1. What changes would you be willing to make in your own lifestyle to prevent pollution and reduce waste?

2. What political and economic changes do you believe need to be made so that we shift from a waste production and waste management society to a pollution prevention and waste reduction society? What things are you doing to help bring about such social changes?

DISCUSSION TOPICS

1. Why should everyone, not just farmers, be concerned with soil conservation?

2. Describe briefly the Dust Bowl phenomenon of the 1930s, and explain how and where it could happen again. How would you try to prevent a recurrence?

3. Would you oppose locating a hazardous-waste landfill, treatment plant, deep injection well, or incinerator in your community? Explain. If you oppose these alternatives, how would you propose that the hazardous waste generated in your community and state be managed?

4. Give your reasons for agreeing or disagreeing with each of the following proposals for dealing with hazardous waste:
   a. Reduce the production of hazardous waste and encourage this and recycling and reuse of hazardous materials by levying a tax or fee on producers for each unit of waste generated.
   b. Ban all land disposal of hazardous waste to encourage recycling, reuse, and treatment and to protect groundwater from contamination.
   c. Provide low-interest loans, tax breaks, and other financial incentives to encourage industries that produce hazardous waste to recycle, reuse, treat, destroy, and reduce generation of such waste.
   d. Ban the shipment of hazardous waste from the United States to any other country.
   e. Ban the shipment of hazardous waste from one state to another.

*5. What hazardous wastes are produced at your school? What happens to them?

*6. As a class project, examine the land around your school to evaluate the use of natural vegetation and other methods to reduce soil erosion. Use this information to develop a soil conservation plan for your school and present it to school officials.

PART FOUR

Living Resources

It is the responsibility of all who are alive today to accept the trusteeship of wildlife and to hand on to posterity, as a source of wonder and interest, knowledge, and enjoyment, the entire wealth of diverse animals and plants. This generation has no right by selfishness, wanton or intentional destruction, or neglect, to rob future generations of this rich heritage. Extermination of other creatures is a disgrace to humankind.

WORLD WILDLIFE CHARTER

CHAPTER 13

FOOD RESOURCES

General Questions and Issues

1. How is food produced throughout the world?

2. What are the world's food problems?

3. Can increasing crop yields and cultivating more land solve the world's food problems?

4. How much food can we get from catching more fish and cultivating fish in aquaculture farms and ranches?

5. What can government policies, giving food aid, and redistributing land to the poor do to help solve world food problems?

6. How can agricultural systems in MDCs and LDCs be designed to be ecologically and economically sustainable?

Hunger is a curious thing: At first it is with you all the time, working and sleeping and in your dreams, and your belly cries out insistently, and there is a gnawing and a pain as if your very vitals were being devoured, and you must stop it at any cost. . . . Then the pain is no longer sharp, but dull, and this too is with you always.

KAMALA MARKANDAYA

AGRICULTURE USES MORE of Earth's soil, water, plant, animal, and energy resources and causes more pollution and environmental degradation than does any other human activity. By 2025, the world's population is expected to reach at least 8.5 billion. To feed these people, we must produce as much food during the next 30 years as was produced over the last 10,000 years, or since the dawn of agriculture.

Producing enough food to feed the world's population, however, is only one of a number of complex, interrelated food resource problems. Another serious problem is *food quality*—whether the food has enough proteins, vitamins, and minerals to prevent malnutrition. We must also have enough storage facilities to keep food from rotting or being eaten by pests after it is harvested. An adequate transportation and retail outlet system must be available to distribute and sell food throughout each country and the world.

There are more hungry people in the world today than at any other time in human history, and their numbers are growing. Poverty is the leading cause of hunger and of premature death from lack of food and from poor food quality. Making sure the poor have enough land or income to grow or buy enough food is the key to reducing deaths from malnutrition and to helping the poor escape the poverty trap (Section 7-4). Farmers must also have economic incentives to grow enough food to meet the world's needs.

Finally, the world's agricultural systems must be managed in sustainable ways to minimize the harm done to the soil, air, water, and wildlife by the production and distribution of food. This means that we must not deplete or degrade soil, water, and genetic resources or alter the fairly stable climate that supports the entire agricultural system.

13-1 World Agricultural Systems: How Is Food Produced?

PLANTS AND ANIMALS THAT FEED THE WORLD Although about 80,000 species of plants are edible, only about 30 crops feed the world, and fewer than 20 produce 90% of our food. Four crops—wheat, rice, corn, and potato—make up more of the world's total food production than all others combined. Those four and most other crops we depend upon are *annuals*, meaning that each year we must disturb the soil and plant new seeds. The rest of the food people eat consists mainly of fish, meat, and animal products such as milk, eggs, and cheese, obtained largely from eight species of domesticated livestock.

Grain production provides about half the world's calories, with two out of three people in the world sur-

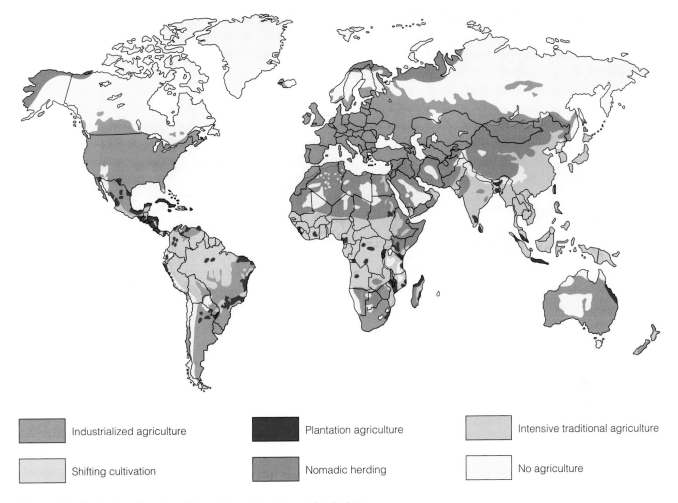

Industrialized agriculture	Plantation agriculture	Intensive traditional agriculture
Shifting cultivation	Nomadic herding	No agriculture

Figure 13-1 Generalized location of the world's principal types of agriculture.

viving on a primarily vegetarian diet. Meat and animal products are too expensive for most people, because of the loss of usable energy when an animal trophic level is added to a food chain (Figure 4-16).

As incomes rise, people consume more grain *indirectly*, in the form of meat, milk, eggs, cheese, and other products from grain-fed domesticated animals. In MDCs, almost half of the world's annual grain production (especially corn and soybeans) is fed to livestock. Thus, indirectly, the meat-eating quarter of humanity consumes nearly 40% of the world's grain. About one-third of the world's annual fish catch is converted into fish meal and fed to livestock.

PRINCIPAL TYPES OF AGRICULTURE Several types of agricultural systems are used throughout the world to grow crops and raise livestock. **Industrialized agriculture** produces large quantities of a single type of crop or livestock for sale both within the country where it is grown and to other countries. Industrialized agriculture involves supplementing solar energy with large inputs of energy from fossil fuels, mostly oil and natural

gas (used for crop drying and to produce fertilizer), water, commercial inorganic fertilizers, and pesticides.

Industrialized agriculture, which is practiced on about 25% of all cropland, is widely used in MDCs and since the mid-1960s has spread to parts of some LDCs (Figure 13-1). It is supplemented by **plantation agriculture**, in which specialized cash crops, such as bananas, coffee, and cacao, are grown in tropical LDCs mostly for sale to MDCs.

Traditional subsistence agriculture produces enough crops or livestock for a farm family's survival and, in good years, a surplus to sell or put aside for hard times. Subsistence farmers supplement solar energy with energy from human labor and draft animals. Examples are shifting cultivation of small plots in tropical forests (Figure 2-4) and nomadic herding of livestock. With **traditional intensive agriculture**, farmers increase their inputs of labor, fertilizer, and water to produce enough food to feed their families and perhaps a surplus that can be sold. These two forms of traditional agriculture are practiced by about 2.7 billion people—half the people on Earth—who live in rural areas in LDCs.

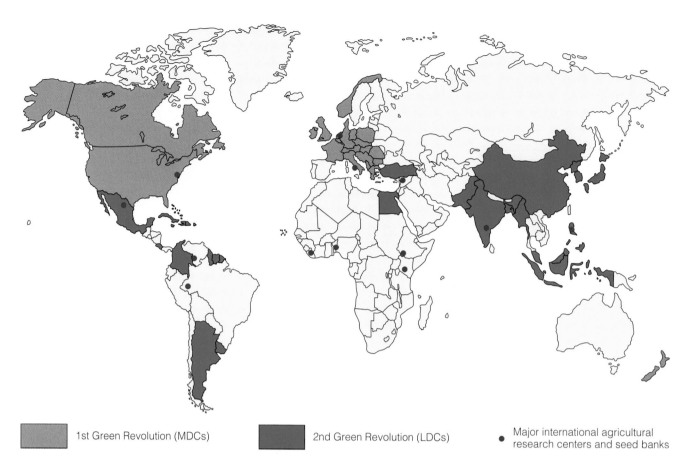

▢ 1st Green Revolution (MDCs)	▪ 2nd Green Revolution (LDCs)	● Major international agricultural research centers and seed banks

Figure 13-2 Countries achieving increases in crop yields per unit of land area during the two green revolutions. The first took place in MDCs between 1950 and 1970, and the second in LDCs with enough rainfall or irrigation capacity since 1967. Thirteen agricultural research centers and genetic storage banks play a key role in developing high-yield crop varieties.

INDUSTRIALIZED AGRICULTURE AND GREEN REVOLUTIONS Crop production is increased either by cultivating more land or by getting higher yields from existing cropland. Since 1950, most of the increase in world food production has come from increasing the yield per hectare in what is called a **green revolution**. This involves planting monocultures of scientifically bred plant varieties and applying large amounts of inorganic fertilizer, irrigation water, and pesticides.

Between 1950 and 1970, this approach led to dramatic increases in yields of major crops in the United States and most other industrialized countries, a phenomenon sometimes known as the *first green revolution* (Figure 13-2). In 1967, after 30 years of genetic research and trials, a modified version of the first green revolution began spreading to many LDCs. High-yield, fast-growing, dwarf varieties of rice and wheat, specially bred for tropical and subtropical climates, were introduced into several LDCs in what is known as the *second green revolution* (Figure 13-2).

The shorter, stronger, and stiffer stalks of the new varieties allow them to support larger heads of grain without toppling over (Figure 13-3). With large inputs

of fertilizer, water, and pesticides, the wheat and rice yields of these varieties can be two to five times those of traditional varieties. The fast-growing varieties allow farmers to grow two, and even three, consecutive crops a year (multiple cropping) on the same parcel of land.

Nearly 90% of the increase in world grain output in the 1960s, about 70% of that in the 1970s, and 80% of the increase in the 1980s can be attributed to the second green revolution. In the 1990s, at least 80% of the additional production of grains is expected to be based on improved yields of existing cropland through the use of green revolution techniques.

These increases depend heavily on fossil-fuel inputs to run machinery, produce and apply inorganic fertilizers and pesticides, and pump water for irrigation. Since 1950, agriculture's use of fossil fuels has increased fourfold, the number of tractors has quadrupled, irrigated area has tripled, use of commercial fertilizer has risen 10-fold, and use of pesticides has risen 32-fold. Green revolution agriculture, like other aspects of industrialized societies, has become addicted to oil and now uses about one-twelfth of the world's oil output. Projected increases in the price of oil, changes in global

Q: What percentage of U.S. cropland is used to produce livestock feed?

International Rice Research Institute, Manila

Figure 13-3 Two older parent strains of rice, PETA from Indonesia (center) and DGWG from China (right), were crossbred to yield IR-8 (left), a new, high-yield, semidwarf variety of rice used in the second green revolution.

climate, or both could disrupt agricultural production, cause sharp rises in food prices, and lead to mass starvation and disease.

These high inputs of energy, water, and pesticides can increase yields dramatically for a while, but plants are unable to use more than a certain amount of water and fertilizer. At some point, further inputs produce no significant increases in yield and cost more than they are worth. Experience has shown that yields also decrease because of increased soil erosion, loss of soil fertility, aquifer depletion, salinization and waterlogging, desertification, pollution of surface water and groundwater, and genetic resistance of pests to pesticides.

INDUSTRIALIZED AGRICULTURE IN THE UNITED STATES Since 1940, U.S. farmers have more than doubled crop production while cultivating about the same amount of land. They have done this through industrialized agriculture coupled with a favorable climate and some of the world's most fertile and productive soils.

Farming has become *agribusiness* as large companies and increasingly larger family-owned farms have taken control of most U.S. food production. Only about 2% of the U.S. population lives on the country's 2.1 million farms, and only about 650,000 Americans work full time at farming. Yet, these people produce enough food to feed most of their fellow citizens better and at a lower percentage of their income than do farmers in any other country. Americans spend an average of 11% to 15% of their spendable income on food.

By contrast, people in much of the world spend 40% or more of their disposable income on food. The 1 billion people making up the poorest fifth of humankind typically spend 60% to 80% of their meager income on food and still don't have an adequate diet.

In addition, U.S. farmers produce large amounts of food for export to other countries. In 1991, one U.S. farmer fed and clothed 128 persons (94 at home and 34 abroad), up from 58 persons in 1976.

About 23 million people — 9% of the population — are involved in the U.S. agricultural system in activities ranging from growing and processing food to selling it at the supermarket. In total annual sales, the agricultural system is the biggest industry in the United States — bigger than the automotive, steel, and housing industries combined. It generates about 18% of the country's GNP (2% from farming, 2% from agricultural chemicals, and 14% from processing, marketing, and retail sales) and 19% of all jobs in the private sector, employing more people than any other industry.

The amount of agricultural chemicals used to support industrialized agriculture in the United States is phenomenal. Currently, the United States uses about 18% of the commercial inorganic fertilizers and 45% of the pesticides produced worldwide each year.

The gigantic American agricultural system consumes about 17% of all commercial energy used in the United States each year (Figure 13-4). Most of this energy comes from oil, followed by natural gas used for drying and producing inorganic fertilizers.

Most plant crops in the United States provide more food energy than the energy (mostly from fossil fuels) used to grow them. However, raising animals for food requires much more fossil-fuel energy than the animals provide as food energy. To support the meat-intensive diet of Americans, 64% of U.S. cropland is used to produce livestock feed. Only 2% of U.S. cropland is used to produce fruits and vegetables.

Energy efficiency is much worse if we look at the entire U.S. food system. Counting fossil-fuel energy inputs used to grow, store, process, package, transport, refrigerate, and cook all plant and animal food, *an average of about 10 units of nonrenewable fossil-fuel energy are needed to put 1 unit of food energy on the table — an energy loss of 9 units per unit of food energy produced.* By compar-

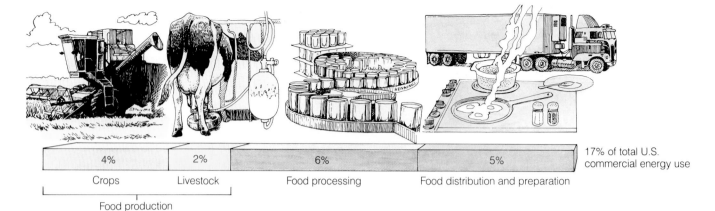

| 4% | 2% | 6% | 5% | 17% of total U.S. commercial energy use |
| Crops | Livestock | Food processing | Food distribution and preparation | |

Food production

Figure 13-4 Commercial energy use by the U.S. industrialized agriculture system. About 20% of the total energy used directly on farms to produce crops is for pumping irrigation water. On average, a piece of food eaten in the United States has traveled 2,100 kilometers (1,300 miles). Processing food also requires large amounts of energy. For example, supplying orange juice takes four times more energy than providing fresh oranges that contain the same amount of juice.

ison, every unit of energy from the human labor of subsistence farmers provides at least one unit of food energy and, with traditional intensive farming, up to 10 units of food energy.

Suppose everyone in the world ate a typical American diet consisting of food produced by industrialized agriculture. If the world's known oil reserves were used only for producing this food, those reserves would be depleted in less than 12 years. In other words, the present world population already exceeds the capacity of known supplies of cultivatable land and petroleum to provide everyone with a U.S.-type diet using industrialized agriculture.

Industrialized farming in the United States and other MDCs is truly big business and has made remarkable gains in food production and short-term economic gain. However, to many environmentalists, it is an environmentally and economically unsustainable way to produce food, built upon depleting the soil, water, and genetic Earth capital upon which the entire system depends.

EXAMPLES OF TRADITIONAL AGRICULTURE
Farmers in LDCs use various forms of traditional subsistence and intensive agriculture to grow crops on about 75% of the world's cultivated land (Figure 13-1). Many traditional farmers imitate nature by simultaneously growing a variety of crops on the same plot, a strategy called **interplanting**. This biological diversity reduces their chances of losing most or all of their year's food supply to pests, flooding, drought, or other disasters. Common interplanting strategies include

- **Polyvarietal cultivation**, in which a plot of land is planted with several varieties of the same crop.

- **Intercropping**, in which two or several different crops are grown at the same time on a plot — for

example, a carbohydrate-rich grain that depletes soil nitrogen and a protein-rich legume that adds nitrogen to the soil.

- **Agroforestry**, a variation of intercropping in which crops and trees are planted together — for example, a grain or legume crop planted around fruit-bearing orchard trees or in rows between fast-growing trees or shrubs that can be used for fuelwood or to add nitrogen to the soil.

- **Polyculture**, a more complex form of intercropping in which a large number of different plants maturing at different times are planted together. If cultivated properly, these "natural supermarkets and drugstores" can provide food, medicines, fuel, and natural pesticides and fertilizers on a sustainable basis.

13-2 World Food Problems

THE GOOD NEWS ABOUT FOOD PRODUCTION
World grain production expanded 2.6-fold between 1950 and 1984, and per capita production rose by almost 40%. During the same period, average food prices adjusted for inflation dropped by 25%, and the amount of food traded in the world market quadrupled. Most of the increase in food production since 1950 came from increases in crop yields per hectare by means of improved labor-intensive traditional agriculture in many LDCs and energy-intensive industrialized agriculture in MDCs and some LDCs (Figure 13-2).

THE BAD NEWS ABOUT FOOD PRODUCTION
The impressive improvements in world food production disguise the fact that per capita grain production declined

Q: What percentage of U.S. cropland is used to produce fruits and vegetables?

between 1950 and 1990 in 43 LDCs (22 in Africa) containing one of every seven persons on Earth. In Africa, per capita food production dropped 28% between 1960 and 1990 and is projected to drop another 30% during the next 25 years. In Latin America, it has declined 16% since 1981 and in India 24% since 1983. Most of the world's countries now require food imports from other nations, primarily the United States, Canada, Australia, Argentina, and France. Population growth is outstripping food production in areas in which about 2 billion people live.

Another disturbing trend is that the rate of increase in world per capita food production declined during each of the past three decades. It rose 15% between 1950 and 1960, 7% between 1960 and 1970, and only 4% between 1970 and 1980. Between 1984 and 1989, per capita food production fell by 14%. This trend is caused by a combination of population increase, a decrease in yields per unit of land area for some crops cultivated by industrialized agriculture, a leveling off or a drop in food production in some countries, unsustainable use of soil and water, and widespread drought in 1987 and 1988.

Projected changes in global climate (Section 10-2) could disrupt agricultural production, cause sharp rises in food prices, and lead to mass starvation and disease. Despite the successes of industrialized agriculture, agricultural success still depends on having favorable weather and a stable climate.

FOOD QUANTITY AND QUALITY: UNDERNUTRITION, MALNUTRITION, AND OVERNUTRITION

Poor people who cannot grow or buy enough food to provide them with the basic minimum number of calories (2,700 calories per day for men and 2,000 calories per day for women) suffer from **undernutrition**. For good health and immunity to infectious diseases, people also need food *quality* that provides them with the proper amounts of protein (41 grams per adult a day), carbohydrates, fats, vitamins, and minerals.

Because most poor people are forced to live on a low-protein, high-starch diet of grains such as wheat, rice, or corn, they often suffer from **malnutrition**, or deficiencies of protein and other key nutrients. Many of the world's desperately poor people suffer from both undernutrition (insufficient food quantity) and malnutrition (poor food quality).

According to the World Health Organization, about 1.3 billion people — one of every four on Earth — are underfed and undernourished because they are too poor to grow or buy the quantity and quality of food they need. Each year, it is estimated that 40 million people (some say 60 million) — half of them children under age 5 — die prematurely from undernutrition, malnutrition, or normally nonfatal infections and diseases worsened by malnutrition. The World Health Organization estimates that diarrhea alone kills at least 5 million children under age 5 each year. *Every two to five days, hunger-related causes kill as many people as the atomic bomb killed at Hiroshima.*

Adults suffering from chronic undernutrition and malnutrition are vulnerable to diseases and are too weak to work productively or think clearly. As a result, their children are also underfed and malnourished (see Spotlight on p. 294). If these children survive to adulthood, many are locked in a tragic *malnutrition-poverty cycle* that continues these conditions in each succeeding generation and traps people in the global poverty cycle (Figure 7-5).

Officials of the United Nations Children's Fund (UNICEF) estimate that between half and two-thirds of worldwide annual childhood deaths from undernutrition, malnutrition, and associated infections and diseases could be prevented at an average annual cost of only $5 to $10 per child — 10 to 19 cents a week. This lifesaving program would involve the following simple measures:

- Immunizing against childhood diseases such as measles

- Encouraging breastfeeding

- Preventing dehydration from diarrhea by giving infants a solution of a fistful of sugar and a pinch of salt in a glass of water

- Preventing blindness by giving people a small vitamin A capsule twice a year at a cost of about 75 cents per person

- Providing family planning services to help mothers space births at least two years apart

- Increasing female education, with emphasis on nutrition, sterilization of drinking water, and child care

While 15% of the people in LDCs suffer from severe undernutrition and malnutrition, about 15% of the people in MDCs suffer from **overnutrition**. This is an excessive intake of food (especially fats) that can cause obesity, or excess body fat, in people who do not suffer from glandular or other disorders that promote obesity.

Overnourished people exist on diets high in calories, cholesterol-containing saturated fats (especially from red meat), salt, sugar, and processed foods, and low in unprocessed fresh vegetables, fruits, and fiber. Partly because of these dietary choices, overweight people have significantly higher than normal risks of diabetes, high blood pressure, stroke, heart disease, kidney disease, arthritis, and some types of cancer.

Overnutrition is associated with at least two-thirds of the deaths in the United States each year. While 40 million people die each year from hunger or hunger-related diseases and 1.3 billion people suffer from chronic hunger, at least 38 million overweight Americans spend $36 billion a year on diet books, diet foods, and diet programs.

The two most widespread nutritional-deficiency diseases are marasmus and kwashiorkor. **Marasmus** (from the Greek, "to waste away") occurs when a diet is low in both total energy (calories) and protein. Most victims of marasmus are infants in poor families in which children are not breastfed or in which food quantity and quality are insufficient after the children are weaned.

A child suffering from marasmus typically has a bloated belly, a thin body, shriveled skin, wide eyes, and an old-looking face (Figure 1-3). If the child is treated in time with a balanced diet, most of these effects can be reversed.

Kwashiorkor (meaning "displaced child" in a West African dialect) occurs in infants and children 1 to 3 years old who suffer from se-

vere protein deficiency, usually after the arrival of a new baby deprives them of breast milk. The displaced child's diet changes from highly nutritious breast milk to grain or sweet potatoes, which provide enough calories but not enough protein.

Children suffering from kwashiorkor have skin swollen with fluids, a bloated abdomen, lethargy, liver damage, hair loss, diarrhea, stunted growth, possible mental retardation, and irritability. If such malnutrition is not prolonged, most of the effects can be cured with a balanced diet.

Each of us must have a daily intake of small amounts of vitamins that cannot be made in the human body. Although balanced diets, vitamin-fortified foods, and vitamin supplements have greatly reduced the number of vitamin-deficiency diseases in MDCs, millions of cases

occur each year in LDCs. For example, each year more than 500,000 children in LDCs are partially or totally blinded because their diet lacks vitamin A.

Other nutritional-deficiency diseases are caused by the lack of certain minerals, such as iron and iodine. Too little iron causes anemia. Anemia causes fatigue, makes infection more likely, increases a woman's chances of dying in childbirth, and increases an infant's chances of dying from infection during its first year of life. In tropical regions of Asia, Africa, and Latin America, iron-deficiency anemia affects about 10% of the men, more than half of the children, two-thirds of the pregnant women, and about half of the other women.

HUNGER AND POVERTY The world produces more than enough food to meet the basic calorie needs of every person on Earth. Indeed, if distributed equally, the grain currently produced in the world would provide enough calories to give 6 billion people—the projected world population for the year 1998—a subsistence diet. The world's supply of food, however, is not now produced or distributed equally among the world's people, nor will it be, because of differences in soil, climate, political and economic power, and average income throughout the world.

In contrast, if the world's food were used to give everyone the typical diet of a person in a developed country with 30% of the calories coming from meat, it would support only 2.5 billion people. That is less than half the present world population and only one-fourth of the 10 billion people projected sometime in the next century (Figure 1-2). *Thus, poverty—not lack of food production—is the chief cause of hunger, malnutrition, and premature death from hunger-related diseases throughout the world today.* This is caused by local, national, and international forces that make up the global poverty trap (Section 7-4).

Increases in worldwide total food production and food production per person often hide widespread differences in food supply and quality between and within countries, mostly because of poverty and inadequate

storage and distribution systems. For example, about one-third of the world's hungry live in India, even though it is self-sufficient in food production. Nearly half of its population is too poor to buy or grow enough food to meet basic needs, and India's population increases by 17 million a year. An estimated two-thirds of its land is threatened by erosion, water shortages, and salinization. This, coupled with population growth, may mean that India will again suffer from famine in the 1990s and beyond.

In more fertile and urbanized southern Brazil, the average daily food supply per person is high. However, in Brazil's semiarid, less fertile northeastern interior, many people are severely underfed. Overall, almost two out of three Brazilians suffer from malnutrition (see Case Study on p. 126).

Food is also unevenly distributed within families. In poor families, the largest part of the food supply goes to men working outside the home. Children (ages 1–5) and women (especially pregnant women and nursing mothers) are the most likely to be underfed and malnourished.

MDCs also have pockets of poverty and hunger. A 1985 report by a task force of doctors estimated that at least 20 million people (12 million children and 8 million adults)—1 out of every 11 Americans—were hungry, mostly because of cuts in food stamps and other forms

Q: How many units of energy are required to put one unit of food energy on the table in the United States?

Industrialized Agriculture

- Soil erosion and loss of soil fertility through poor land use, failure to practice soil conservation techniques, and too little use of organic fertilizers (Section 12-3).

- Salinization and waterlogging of heavily irrigated soils (Figure 12-18).

- Reduction in the number and diversity of nutrient-recycling soil microorganisms from heavy use of pesticides and commercial inorganic fertilizers and soil compaction by large tractors and other farm machinery.

- Air pollution caused by dust blown off cropland that is not kept covered with vegetation (Figure 12-7) and from overgrazed rangeland (Section 15-5).

- Air pollution from droplets of pesticide sprayed from planes or by ground sprayers and blown into the air from plants and soil.

- Air pollution caused by the extraction, processing, transportation, and combustion of enormous amounts of fossil fuels used in industrialized agriculture (Figure 13-4).

- Pollution of estuaries and deep ocean zones with oil from offshore wells and tankers (see Case Study on p. 247) and from improper disposal of oil, the main fossil fuel used in industrialized agriculture.

- Pollution of streams, lakes, and estuaries and killing of fish and shellfish from pesticide runoff.

- Depletion of groundwater aquifers by excessive withdrawals for irrigation (Figure 11-12).

- Pollution of groundwater caused by leaching of water-soluble pesticides, nitrates from commercial inorganic fertilizers, and salts from irrigation water (Figure 11-26).

- Overfertilization of lakes and slow-moving rivers caused by runoff of nitrates and phosphates in commercial inorganic fertilizers, livestock animal wastes, and food-processing wastes (Figure 11-21).

- Sediment pollution of surface waters caused by erosion and runoff from farm fields and animal feedlots.

- Loss of genetic diversity of plants caused by clearing biologically diverse grasslands and forests and replacing them with monocultures of single crop varieties (Figure 5-12). Expansion of agriculture accounts for about 85% of the worldwide destruction of forests each year (Chapter 15).

- Endangerment and extinction of animal wildlife from loss of habitat when grasslands and forests are cleared and wetlands are drained for farming.

- Depletion and extinction of commercially important species of fish caused by overfishing.

- Threats to human health from nitrates in drinking water and pesticides in drinking water, food, and the atmosphere.

Traditional Subsistence and Intensive Agriculture

- Soil erosion and rapid loss of soil fertility caused by clearing and cultivating steep mountain highlands without terracing (Figure 12-8), using shifting cultivation in tropical forests without leaving the land fallow long enough to restore soil fertility (Figure 2-4), overgrazing of rangeland (Section 15-5), and deforestation to provide cropland or fuelwood.

- Increased frequency and severity of flooding in lowlands when mountainsides are deforested (see Case Study on p. 230).

- Desertification caused by cultivation of marginal land with unsuitable soil or terrain, overgrazing, deforestation, and failure to use soil conservation techniques (see Case Study on p. 266).

- Air pollution caused by dust blown from cropland not kept covered with vegetation and from overgrazed rangeland.

- Sediment pollution of surface waters caused by erosion and runoff from farm fields, overgrazed rangeland, and deforested land.

- Endangerment and extinction of animal wildlife caused by loss of habitat when grasslands and forests are cleared for farming.

- Threats to human health from flooding intensified by poor land use and from human and animal wastes discharged or washed into irrigation ditches and sources of drinking water.

---

of government aid since 1980. A 1991 study revealed that one out of eight U.S. families with children under the age of 12 experiences hunger due to poverty.

In 1989, the UN World Food Commission reported that progress in fighting hunger, malnutrition, and poverty came to a halt or was reversed in many parts of the world during the 1980s — a trend that continues in the 1990s. Without a widespread increase in income and access to land, the number of chronically hungry and malnourished people in the world will increase in the 1990s and beyond.

ENVIRONMENTAL EFFECTS OF PRODUCING FOOD Both industrialized agriculture and traditional agriculture have a number of harmful impacts on the air, soil, and water resources that sustain all life (see Spotlight above).

INCREASING CROP YIELDS Agricultural experts expect most future increases in crop production to come from increased yields per hectare on existing cropland and from improvement and expansion of green revolution technology to other parts of the world. Agricultural scientists are working to create new green revolutions — *or gene revolutions* — by using genetic engineering and other forms of biotechnology (see Pro/Con on p. 174). Over the next 20 to 40 years, they hope to breed high-yield plant strains that have greater resistance to insects and disease, thrive on less fertilizer, make their own nitrogen fertilizer like legumes do (Figure 4-24), do well in slightly salty soils, withstand drought, and make more efficient use of solar energy during photosynthesis.

If even a small fraction of the research and development of genetically engineered crops and livestock is successful, the world could experience rapid and enormous increases in crop production before the middle of the next century. However, some analysts point to several factors that have limited the spread and long-term success of green and gene revolutions:

■ Without huge doses of fertilizer and water, green revolution crop varieties produce yields no higher and often lower than those from traditional strains. Without good soil, water, and weather, new genetically engineered crop strains will fail.

■ So far, plants have been far less responsive to genetic engineering than have animals. The entire process, from gene transfer to widespread planting of a new crop variety, can take as long as conventional crossbreeding (typically, 5 to 15 years).

■ Areas without enough rainfall or irrigation water or with poor soils cannot benefit from the new varieties; that is why the second green revolution has not spread to many arid and semiarid areas (Figure 13-2).

■ Increasingly larger and thus more expensive inputs of fertilizer, water, and pesticides eventually produce little or no increase in crop yields as the J-shaped curve of crop productivity reaches limits and is converted into an S-shaped curve.

■ Without careful land use and environmental controls (Section 12-3), degradation of water and soil can limit the long-term ecological and economic sustainability of green and gene revolutions.

■ The cost of genetically engineered crop strains is too high for most of the world's subsistence farmers in LDCs. Also, LDCs are not being compensated adequately for the genetic strains that scientists collect from their countries and use to produce patented seed varieties.

■ The severe and increasing loss of Earth's biological diversity from deforestation and destruction and degradation of other ecosystems, and replacement of a diverse mixture of natural crop varieties with monoculture crops, limit the potential of future green and gene revolutions.

Wild varieties of the world's most important plants can be collected and stored in gene banks, agricultural research centers (Figure 13-2), and botanical gardens; but space and money severely limit the number of species that can be preserved in those facilities. Also, many species cannot be stored successfully in gene banks, and accidents such as power failures, fires, and unintentional disposal of seeds can cause irrecoverable losses.

Because of these limitations, ecologists and plant scientists warn that the only effective way to preserve the genetic diversity of most of the world's plant and animal species is to protect large areas of representative ecosystems throughout the world from agriculture and other forms of development.

CULTIVATING MORE LAND Despite our technological cleverness, only about 11% of Earth's land area is suitable for growing crops. The rest is covered by ice, is too dry or too wet, is too hot or too cold, is too steep, or has unsuitable soils for growing crops.

Some agricultural experts have suggested that farmers could more than double the world's cropland by clearing tropical forests and irrigating arid lands, mostly in Africa, South America, and Australia (Figure 13-5). Others believe only a small portion of these lands can be cultivated because most are too dry or too remote or lack productive soils.

Even if more cropland were developed, much of it would be on marginal land that would require large and expensive inputs of fertilizer, water, and energy. Furthermore, these possible increases in cropland would not offset the projected loss of almost one-third of today's cultivated cropland from erosion, overgrazing, waterlogging, salinization, mining, and urbanization. Pollution is also reducing crop yields on existing cropland.

LOCATION, SOIL, AND INSECTS AS LIMITING FACTORS About 83% of the world's potential new cropland is in the remote rain forests of the Amazon and Orinoco river basins in South America and in Africa's rain forests. Most of this forested land is located in just two countries, Brazil (Figure 6-12) and Zaire.

Cultivation would require huge investments of capital and energy to clear the land and to transport the harvested crops to distant populated areas. The resulting deforestation would greatly increase soil erosion and enhance projected global warming through a net release of the greenhouse gases carbon dioxide and nitrous oxide (Section 10-2). It would also reduce the

Q: How many people are underfed and undernourished?

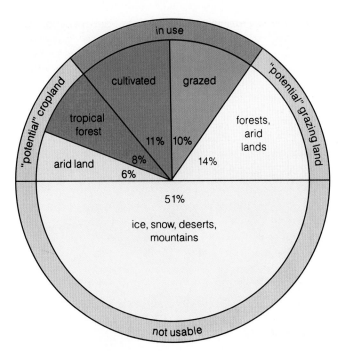

Figure 13-5 Classification of Earth's land. Theoretically, we could double the world's cropland in size by clearing tropical forests and irrigating arid lands. However, converting this marginal land into cropland would destroy valuable forest resources, reduce Earth's biodiversity, cause serious environmental problems, and usually not be cost-effective.

world's biological diversity by eliminating vast numbers of plant and animal species found only in these ecosystems.

Tropical rain forests have plentiful rainfall and long or continuous growing seasons, but their soils often are not suitable for intensive cultivation. About 90% of the plant nutrient supply is in ground litter and vegetation above the ground rather than in the soil (Figure 12-4). Clear the land and you have few soil nutrients, and most of those are eroded or leached away by heavy tropical rains.

Nearly 75% of the vast Amazon basin (Figure 6-12), roughly one-third of the world's potential new cropland, has highly acidic and infertile soils. In addition, 5% to 15% of tropical soils (4% of those in the Amazon basin), if cleared, would bake under the tropical sun into a brick-hard surface called laterite, useless for farming.

Some tropical soils can produce up to three crops of grain per year if enormous quantities of fertilizer are applied at the right time. But costs are high, and rapid runoff and leaching of soil nutrients from heavy tropical rains limit production. The warm temperatures, high moisture, and year-round growing season also support large populations of pests and diseases that can devastate monoculture crops in the tropics. Huge doses of pesticides could be used, but the same conditions that favor crop growth in the tropics also favor rapid de-

velopment of genetic resistance in pest species (Section 14-3).

In Africa, potential cropland in savanna (Figure 5-9) and other semiarid land, covering an area larger than the continental United States, cannot be used for farming or livestock grazing because it is infested by 22 species of the tsetse fly. The bite of this insect can infect people and livestock with incurable sleeping sickness and transmit the wasting disease nagana to livestock. A $120 million eradication program has been proposed, but many scientists doubt it can succeed. Others point out that if it should succeed, farming this land and overgrazing by livestock would cause depletion and extinction of many forms of wildlife, thus contributing to the planet's growing biodiversity crisis.

Researchers hope to develop new methods of intensive cultivation in tropical areas. But some scientists argue that it makes more ecological and economic sense not to use intensive cultivation in the tropics. Instead, farmers should use shifting cultivation with fallow periods long enough to restore soil fertility (Figure 2-4) and various forms of interplanting. Scientists also recommend plantation cultivation of rubber trees, oil palms, and banana trees, which are adapted to tropical climates and soils.

WATER AS A LIMITING FACTOR Much of the world's potentially cultivatable land lies in dry areas, where water shortages limit crop growth, especially in Africa. Large-scale irrigation in these areas would be very expensive, requiring large inputs of fossil fuel to pump water long distances. Irrigation systems would deplete many groundwater supplies and require constant and expensive maintenance to prevent groundwater contamination, salinization, and waterlogging (Figure 12-17).

There are signs that irrigation limits are being reached in land now under cultivation. Between 1950 and 1980, the world's irrigated cropland almost tripled, increasing the average irrigated area per person by 52%. However, during the 1980s, growth in irrigated area slowed dramatically and fell behind population growth, leading to an 8% drop in the irrigated area per person—a trend that is continuing in the 1990s.

DO THE POOR BENEFIT? Increasing per capita food production is a big task, but making sure that it reaches the hungry is a much greater one. Whether present and future green or gene revolutions reduce hunger among the world's poor depends on how the technology is applied. In LDCs, the resource most available to agriculture is human labor. When green revolution techniques are used to increase yields of traditional labor-intensive agriculture on existing or new cropland in countries with equitable land distribution, the poor benefit, as has occurred in China.

Figure 13-6 The winged bean is a protein-rich annual plant from the Philippines. It has edible flowers, seeds, seedpods, tendrils, and tubers. It is only one of many little-known and little-used plants that could become important sources of food and fuel. Other examples are the sugar apple of South America, protein-rich seeds of the grain amaranth, the groundnut (a high-protein tuber eaten by Native Americans), and cocoyam (a native plant of West Africa and Latin America that is as nutritious as the potato).

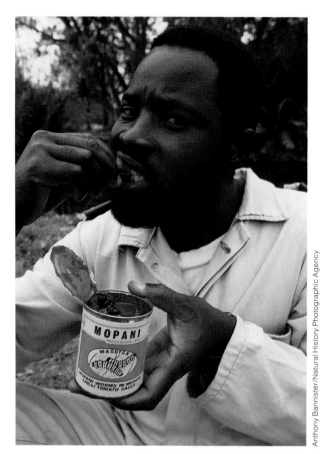

Larry Mellichamp/Visuals Unlimited

Anthony Bannister/Natural History Photographic Agency

Figure 13-7 In South Africa, "Mopani" — larvae of a species of emperor moth — is one example of a number of insects that are eaten. In the Kalahari Desert of Africa, cockroaches are consumed as food. Lightly toasted butterflies are a favorite food in Bali. French-fried ants are sold on the streets of Bogotá, Colombia, and Malaysians love deep-fried grasshoppers. Most of these insects are 58% to 78% protein by weight — three to four times that of beef, fish, or eggs.

Most poor farmers, however, don't have enough land, money, or credit to buy the seed, fertilizer, irrigation water, pesticides, equipment, and fuel that the new plant varieties need. This means that the second green revolution (Figure 13-2) has bypassed more than 1 billion poor people in LDCs.

Switching to industrialized agriculture makes LDCs heavily dependent on large, MDC-based multinational companies for expensive supplies, increasing the LDCs' foreign debts. It also makes their agricultural and economic systems more vulnerable to collapse from increases in oil and fertilizer prices and environmental degradation. In addition, mechanization displaces many farm workers, thus increasing rural-to-urban migration and overburdening the cities (Section 6-3).

UNCONVENTIONAL FOODS AND PERENNIAL CROPS Some analysts recommend greatly increased cultivation of various nontraditional plants in LDCs to supplement or replace traditional foods such as wheat, rice, and corn. One of many possibilities is the winged bean, a protein-rich legume presently used extensively only in New Guinea and Southeast Asia (Figure 13-6). Its edible winged pods, leaves, tendrils, and seeds contain as much protein as soybeans, and its edible roots contain more than four times the protein of potatoes. Indeed, this plant yields so many different edible parts that it has been called a "supermarket on a stalk." Insects are also important potential sources of protein, vitamins, and minerals (Figure 13-7).

Scientists have identified many plants and insects that could be used as sources of food. The problem is getting farmers to cultivate such crops and convincing consumers to try new foods.

Most crops we depend on are tropical annuals. Each year the land is cleared of all vegetation, dug up, and planted with the seeds of annuals. David Pimentel (see Guest Essay on p. 283) and plant scientists such as Wes and Dana Jackson of the Land Institute in Salina,

Q: How many people die each year from hunger-related causes?

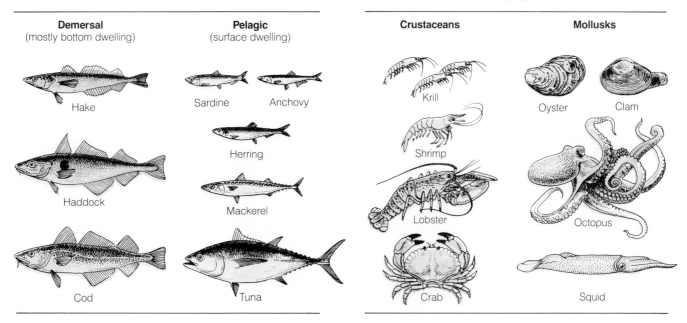

Fish		Shellfish	
Demersal (mostly bottom dwelling)	**Pelagic** (surface dwelling)	**Crustaceans**	**Mollusks**

Figure 13-8 Some major types of commercially harvested marine fish and shellfish.

Kansas, believe we should rely more on polycultures of perennial crops that are more closely adapted to regional soil and climate conditions than are most annuals. This would eliminate the need to till soil each year and would greatly reduce the amount of fossil-fuel, draft-animal, and human energy used in agriculture each year. It would also conserve water and reduce soil erosion and sediment water pollution.

Widespread use of perennials would greatly reduce the income of large agribusiness companies that sell annual seeds, fertilizers, and pesticides, explaining why they don't favor this approach. Thus, research and development of such Earth-sustaining crops must be carried out by governments and private groups.

13-4 Catching More Fish and Fish Farming and Ranching

THE WORLD'S FISHERIES Concentrations of particular aquatic species suitable for commercial harvesting in a given ocean area or inland body of water are called **fisheries**. Worldwide, people get an average of 20% of the animal protein in their food directly from fish and shellfish and another 5% indirectly from fish meal fed to livestock. In most Asian coastal and island countries, fish and shellfish supply 30% to 90% of the animal protein eaten by people.

About 87% of the annual commercial catch of fish and shellfish comes from the ocean and the rest from fresh water. Ninety-nine percent of the world marine catch is taken from plankton-rich waters (mostly estu-

aries and upwellings) within 370 kilometers (200 nautical miles) of the coast. However, this vital coastal zone is being disrupted and polluted at an alarming rate (see Case Study on p. 103).

Only about 40 of the world's 20,000 known species of fish are harvested in large quantities. Some of the commercially important species of fish in marine habitats are shown in Figure 13-8.

More than 90% of the fish and shellfish we consume is obtained by using small and large motorized fishing boats to hunt and gather these resources over a large area. Because 30% to 40% of the operating costs of motorized fishing boats is spent on fuel, energy inputs for each unit of food energy obtained from most marine species are enormous (Figure 13-9).

TRENDS IN THE WORLD FISH CATCH Between 1950 and 1970, the weight of the annual commercial fish catch grew annually by about 7% and increased more than threefold (Figure 13-10). Since then, the rate of growth has slowed down, and the global marine catch may soon reach the estimated sustainable yield.

Although the total fish catch has grown, the worldwide per capita fish catch has declined in most years since 1970 because world population has grown at a faster rate than the fish catch (Figure 13-11). Because of overfishing, pollution, population growth, and increased demand, the world catch per person is projected to drop back to the 1960 level by 2000.

Overfishing occurs when so many fish are taken that too little breeding stock is left to prevent a drop in numbers. Overfishing rarely causes biological extinction because commercial fishing becomes unprofitable

A: 40 million (some say 60 million)

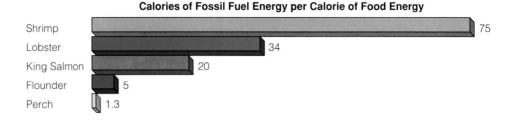

Figure 13-9 Average energy input needed to produce one unit of food energy from some commercially desirable types of fish and shellfish.

Calories of Fossil Fuel Energy per Calorie of Food Energy

Shrimp — 75
Lobster — 34
King Salmon — 20
Flounder — 5
Perch — 1.3

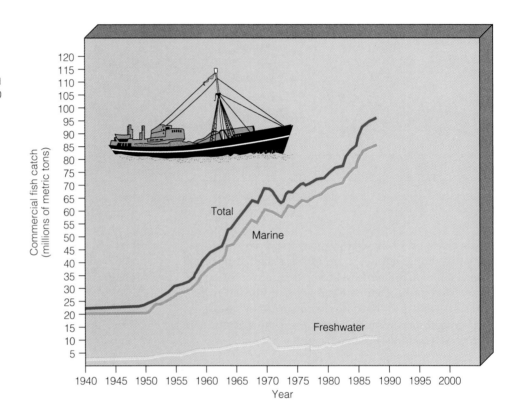

Figure 13-10 World fish catch. About one-third of the annual marine catch is used to feed animals and fertilize croplands. Scientists estimate that the sustainable yield of the world's marine fishery is 100 million metric tons (110 million tons), which may be reached or exceeded soon. If this yield is exceeded, key fish stocks will be depleted and yields will drop sharply. (Data from UN Food and Agriculture Organization)

before that point. Instead, prolonged overfishing leads to **commercial extinction**, the point at which the stock of a species is so low that it's no longer profitable to hunt and gather the remaining individuals in a specific fishery. Fishing fleets then move to a new species or to a new region, hoping that the overfished species will eventually recover.

Since the early 1980s, overfishing has caused declines in the yields of nearly one-third of the world's fisheries and the collapse of 42 valuable fisheries. Examples include cod and herring in the North Atlantic, salmon and the Alaska king crab in the northwest Pacific, and Peruvian anchovy in the southeast Pacific (see Case Study on p. 301).

The fishing industry is trying to combat the decreasing catches with more efficient fishing techniques, but some of these methods are controversial (see Spotlight on p. 302).

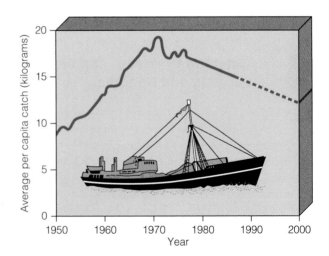

Figure 13-11 Per capita world fish catch has declined in most years since 1970 because population has grown faster than the fish catch. The per capita catch is projected to drop further by the end of this century. (Data from United Nations and Worldwatch Institute)

Q: What is the chief cause of hunger, malnutrition, and premature death from hunger-related diseases?

In 1953, Peru began fishing for anchovy in nutrient-rich upwellings off its western coast. The size of the fishing fleet increased rapidly. Factories were built to convert the small fish into fish meal for sale to MDCs for use as livestock feed. Between 1965 and 1971, harvests of the Peruvian anchovy made up about 20% of the world's annual commercial fish catch.

Between 1971 and 1978, however, the Peruvian anchovy became commercially extinct. The collapse of this fishery is an example of how biology, climate, geography, economics, and politics interact, and often clash, in fishery management.

At unpredictable intervals the productivity of the upwellings off the coast of Peru drops sharply because of a natural weather change called the El Niño–Southern Oscillation, or ENSO, which warms the normally cool water of the Humboldt Current flowing along Peru's coast. The numbers of anchovy, other fish, seabirds, and marine mammals in food webs based on phytoplankton then drop sharply.

Biologists with the UN Food and Agriculture Organization warned that during seven of the eight years between 1964 and 1971, the anchovy harvest exceeded the estimated sustainable yield. Peruvian fishery officials ignored those warnings.

Peru's fishing industry was financed largely by short-term loans. Government officials decided to risk the collapse of the fishery to pay off

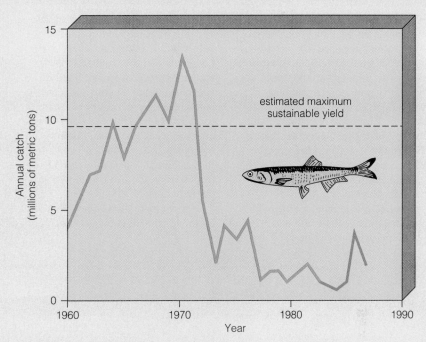

Figure 13-12 Peruvian anchovy catch, showing the combined effects of overfishing and a natural climate change that occurs every few years. (Data from UN Food and Agriculture Organization)

the loans and avoid putting thousands of people out of work. They also believed that a slight drop in the anchovy catch would be beneficial because it would cause shortages and raise the price of fish meal.

Disaster struck in 1972, when a strong ENSO arrived. The anchovy population, already at dangerously low levels because of overfishing, could not recover from the effects of the ENSO and the annual yield plummeted (Figure 13-12). By putting short-term economics above biology, Peru lost a major source of income and jobs and had to increase its foreign debt.

The country has made some economic recovery by harvesting the Peruvian sardine, which took over the niche once occupied by the anchovy. The catches of mackerel, bonito, and hake have also increased. Since 1983, the Peruvian anchovy fishery has been making a slight recovery (Figure 13-12).

AQUACULTURE **Aquaculture**, in which fish and shellfish are raised in enclosed structures for all or part of their lives, supplies about 10% of the world's commercial fish harvest. There are two basic types of aquaculture. **Fish farming** involves cultivating fish in a controlled environment, usually a pond, and harvesting them when they reach the desired size. **Fish ranching** involves holding species in captivity for the first few years of their lives and then harvesting the adults when they return to spawn. Ranching is useful for *anadromous species*, such as salmon and ocean trout, which after birth move from fresh water to the ocean and then back to fresh water to spawn.

Almost three-fourths of the world's annual aquaculture catch comes from 71 LDCs. Species cultivated in LDCs include carp, tilapia, milkfish, clams, and oysters, which feed low in food webs on phytoplankton and other forms of aquatic plants. These are usually raised in small freshwater ponds or underwater cages. Aquaculture supplies 60% of the fish eaten in Israel, 40% in China, and 22% in Indonesia.

In MDCs, aquaculture is used mostly to raise expensive fish and shellfish and to stock lakes and streams with game fish. This benefits anglers who fish for sport and is highly profitable for aquaculture farmers and companies, but it does little to increase food and

Since 1980, an estimated 1,800 fishing vessels from Japan, South Korea, and Taiwan have used *drift net fishing*, mostly in the Pacific Ocean (but also in the Atlantic and the Caribbean), to capture and kill almost anything that comes in contact with the almost invisible nets they set out each night during the fishing season (Figure 13-13). During each night of the fishing season, the entire fleet sets out enough nets to more than circle the world.

This indiscriminate marine holocaust not only depletes the sea of the intended species but also entangles and kills hundreds of thousands of dolphins, turtles, seals, sharks (see Case Study on p. 85), small whales, and other forms of marine life that become entangled in the fine mesh of the nets. Every country that has used drift nets in its own waters has eventually banned them. Environmentalists believe that it is now time to ban them in international waters. In 1992, most countries agreed to do this.

Environmentalists believe that to be sure drift net fishing is actually stopped, consumers need to mount U.S. and global boycotts of fish or fish products caught by this method. This tactic, led by the Earth Island Institute, caused companies importing or selling tuna in the United States to stop buying tuna caught by purse seine or drift net methods because they killed hundreds of thousands of dolphins each year. Consumer power works.

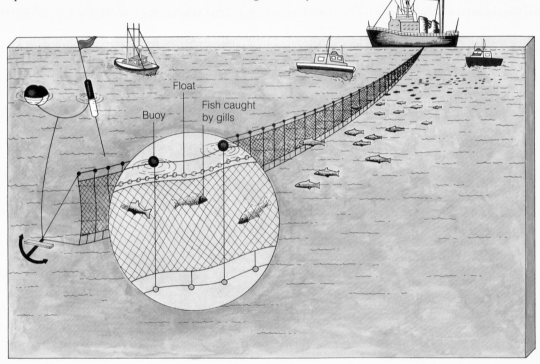

Figure 13-13 Drift net fishing by a distant-water fishing fleet. Typically, such a fleet has several huge factory ships that use sophisticated electronic detection devices, helicopters, and aerial photography to find large schools of fish. Each ship then launches 20 to 50 fast, small catcher boats to set hundreds to thousands of kilometers of drift nets, weighted down to stay at the wanted depth. After drifting overnight, the nets are hauled in by the factory ships. The catch is then processed on the ship by canning or freezing. Because these "curtains of death" can deplete target fish species and large numbers of other, nontarget species, environmentalists have been trying to have a worldwide ban imposed and enforced on this Earth-degrading type of fishing.

protein supplies for the poor. About 40% of the oysters and most of the catfish, crayfish, and rainbow trout consumed as food in the United States is supplied by U.S.-based fish farms.

Aquaculture has a number of advantages. It can produce high yields per unit of area. Large amounts of fuel are not required, so yields and profits are not closely tied to the price of oil, as they are in commercial hunting-and-gathering fishing (Figure 13-9). Also, aquaculture is usually labor-intensive and can provide much-needed jobs in LDCs.

There are problems, however. Scooping out huge ponds for fish and shrimp farming in some countries has led to widespread destruction of ecologically important mangrove forests (Figure 5-22). Fish in aquaculture ponds can be killed by pesticide runoff from nearby croplands. Bacterial and viral infections of aquatic species can also limit aquaculture yields. Without adequate pollution control, waste outputs from shrimp farming and other large-scale aquaculture operations can contaminate nearby estuaries, surface water, and groundwater.

CAN THE ANNUAL CATCH BE INCREASED SIGNIFICANTLY? Some scientists believe that the world fish catch can be expanded by harvesting more squid, octopus, Antarctic krill, and other unconventional species. But this could have unpredictable and possibly harmful effects on ocean food webs. Greatly expanded harvesting of shrimplike krill, for example, could lead to sharp declines in the populations of certain whales and other species dependent on krill (Figure 4-17). Also, food scientists have been unable to process krill into foods that taste good enough for people to eat. Currently, krill is used to make livestock feed.

Additional increases could also be brought about by a sharp decrease in the one-fifth of the annual catch now wasted, mainly from throwing back potentially useful fish taken along with desired species. More refrigerated storage at sea to prevent spoilage would also increase the catch. Experts project that freshwater and saltwater aquaculture production could be doubled during the 1990s.

Other fishery experts believe that further increases in the annual marine catch are limited by overfishing and by pollution and destruction of estuaries and aquaculture ponds. Another factor that may limit the commercial fish catch from the world's oceans is the projected rise in the price of oil—and thus of boat fuel—between 1995 and 2015. Unless more seafood is produced by aquaculture, most consumers may find seafood prices too high.

13-5	**Making Food Production Profitable, Giving Food Aid, and Distributing Land to the Poor**

GOVERNMENT AGRICULTURAL POLICIES Agriculture is an especially risky business. Whether a farmer has a good or a bad year is determined by factors over which the farmer has little control — weather, crop prices, crop pests and disease, interest rates, and the global market. Because of the variability in these factors and the need to have a reliable supply of food to prevent political unrest, most governments provide various forms of assistance to farmers.

Governments can influence crop and livestock prices, and thus the supply of food, in several ways:

- They can keep food prices artificially low. This makes consumers happy but can decrease food production by reducing profits for farmers.
- They can give farmers subsidies to keep them in business and encourage them to increase food production.
- They can eliminate price controls and subsidies, allowing market competition to determine food prices and thus the amount of food produced.

Most governments in LDCs have concentrated their limited financial resources on the cities and on industrial development, neglecting farming and rural areas. Governments in many LDCs keep food prices in cities lower than in the countryside to prevent political unrest.

Low prices, however, discourage farmers from producing enough to feed the country's population, and the government must use limited funds or go into debt to buy imported food. With food prices higher in rural areas than in cities, more rural people migrate to urban areas, aggravating urban problems and unemployment. These conditions increase the chances of political unrest, which the price control policy was supposed to prevent.

Governments can stimulate crop and livestock production by guaranteeing farmers a certain minimum yearly return on their investment. However, if government price supports are too generous and the weather is good, farmers may produce more food than can be sold. Food prices and profits then drop because of the oversupply. The resulting availability of large amounts of food for export or food aid to LDCs depresses world food prices. The low prices reduce the financial incentive for farmers to increase domestic food production. Whether government agricultural subsidies should be maintained, reduced, or eliminated is a controversial issue (see Pro/Con on p. 304).

INTERNATIONAL AID Between 1945 and 1985, the United States was the world's largest donor of nonmilitary foreign aid to LDCs. Since 1986, however, Japan has been the largest donor of such aid to LDCs. This aid is used mostly for agriculture and rural development, food relief, population planning, health, and economic development. Private charity organizations such as CARE and Catholic Relief Services and funds from benefit music concerts and record sales provide over $3 billion a year of additional foreign aid.

In addition to helping other countries, foreign aid stimulates economic growth and provides jobs in the donor country. For example, 70 cents of every dollar the United States gives directly to other countries is used to

In MDCs, government price supports and other subsidies for agriculture total more than $300 billion a year. This makes farmers and agribusiness executives happy. These supports are also popular with most consumers because they make food prices seem low. Politicians favor this approach because it increases their chances of staying in office.

What most consumers don't realize is that they are paying higher prices for their food indirectly in the form of higher taxes to provide the subsidies. There is no free lunch. A 1989 Department of Agriculture study estimated that U.S. shoppers would pay $30 to $35 more each year if federal farm subsidies were eliminated. However, the same study did not point out that those subsidies cost each U.S. taxpayer an average of $200 in 1990.

The U.S. agricultural system is too successful for its own good. It produces so much food that the government must pay farmers not to produce food on one-fourth of U.S. cropland or must buy up and store unneeded crops. This encourages farmers to produce even more, discourages the use of Earth-sustaining agriculture, wastes taxpayer dollars, and is a form of welfare for wealthy farmers.

Any phaseout of farm subsidies in the United States or any other country should be carried out gradually over several years and should be coupled with increased aid for the poor, who would suffer the most from any increase in food prices. Eliminating all price controls and agricultural subsidies and allowing market competition to determine food prices and production is not

easy to do. Farmers and owners of farm-related businesses usually have enough votes to elect congressional representatives opposed to phasing out all farm subsidies.

Instead of eliminating subsidies, some agricultural experts suggest using them to regulate crop production rather than crop acreage. This would reduce the pressure on growers to increase yields per hectare to qualify for help, thereby reducing soil erosion and excessive inputs of fertilizers, pesticides, and irrigation water. Regulations should be set up and strictly enforced so that subsidies go only to needier, but competent, small-scale farmers, not—as in the present situation—to large-scale farmers who do not need government payments to be profitable. What do you think should be done?

purchase American goods and services. Today, 21 of the 50 largest buyers of U.S. farm goods are countries that once received free U.S. food.

Despite the humanitarian benefits and economic returns of such aid, the percentage of the U.S. gross national product used for nonmilitary foreign aid to LDCs has dropped from a high of 1.6% in the 1950s to only 0.20% since 1980—an annual average of only $30 per American. Since 1980, 16 other MDCs have used a higher percentage of their GNP for nonmilitary foreign aid to LDCs than has the United States. Some people call for greatly increased food relief for starving people from government and private sources, while others question the value of such aid (see Pro/Con on p. 305).

DISTRIBUTING LAND TO THE POOR An important step in reducing world hunger, malnutrition, poverty, and land degradation is land reform. Land reform involves giving the landless rural poor in LDCs ownership or free use of enough land to produce the food they need to survive and, ideally, to produce a surplus for emergencies and for sale. China and Taiwan have had the most successful land reforms.

Such reform would increase agricultural productivity in LDCs and reduce the need to farm and degrade marginal land. It would also help reduce the flow of

poor people to overcrowded urban areas by creating employment in rural areas.

Many of the countries with the most unequal land distribution are in Latin America, especially Guatemala, Bolivia, and Brazil (see Case Study on p. 126). In Latin America, 7% of the population owns 93% of the farmland. Most of this land is used for luxury export crops or beef, products that degrade the land and do little to help the landless poor. Land reform is difficult to institute in countries where government leaders are unduly influenced by wealthy and powerful landowners.

13-6 Sustainable-Earth Agriculture

SUSTAINABLE-EARTH AGRICULTURAL SYSTEMS To environmentalists, the key to reducing world hunger and the harmful environmental impacts of industrialized and traditional forms of agriculture is to develop a variety of **sustainable-Earth agricultural systems**. This involves combining appropriate parts of existing industrialized and subsistence agricultural systems and new agricultural techniques to take advantage of local climates, soils, resources, and cultural systems. The fol-

Q: What percentage of the world's potential food supply is lost to pests?

Most people view food relief as a humanitarian effort to prevent people from dying prematurely. However, some analysts contend that giving food to starving people in countries where population growth rates are high does more harm than good in the long run. By encouraging population growth and not helping people grow their own food, food relief condemns even greater numbers to premature death in the future.

Biologist Garrett Hardin (see Guest Essay on p. 143) has suggested that we use the concept of *lifeboat ethics* to decide which countries get food aid. He starts with the belief that there are already too many people in the lifeboat we call Earth. If food aid is given to countries that are not reducing their population, this adds more people to an already-overcrowded lifeboat. Sooner or later, the boat will sink and kill most of the passengers.

Large amounts of food aid can also depress local food prices, decrease food production, and stimulate mass migration from farms to already-overburdened cities. It discourages the government from investing in rural agricultural development to enable the country to grow enough food for its population on a sustainable basis.

Another problem is that much food aid does not reach hunger victims. Transportation networks and storage facilities are inadequate, so that some of the food rots or is devoured by pests before it can reach the hungry. Typically, some of the food is stolen by officials and sold for personal profit. Some must often be given to officials as bribes for approving the unloading and transporting of the remaining food to the hungry.

Critics of food relief are not against foreign aid. Instead, they believe that such aid should be given to help countries control population growth, grow enough food to feed their population using sustainable agricultural methods (Section 13-6), or develop export crops to help pay for food they can't grow. Temporary food aid should be given only when there is a complete breakdown of an area's food supply because of natural disaster. What do you think?

---

lowing are general guidelines for sustainable-Earth agriculture:

- *Place primary emphasis on preserving and renewing the soil and on conserving water.*

- *Recognize that the marketplace cannot sustain agriculture because it does not assign an infinite value to the soil and water upon which all agriculture depends.*

- *Adapt and design the agricultural system to the environment (soil, water, climate, and pest populations) of the region.* This means maintaining vegetative cover on cropland, raising water prices to encourage water conservation, increasing the organic content of soils, limiting livestock grazing on arid and semiarid lands, and not trying to grow water-thirsty crops in arid and semiarid areas.

- *Increase intensive production of a diverse mix of fruit, vegetable, and fuelwood crops (including perennials) and livestock animals, instead of relying primarily on monoculture production of a single crop or livestock animal.*

- *Whenever possible, matter inputs should be obtained from locally available, renewable biological resources and used in ways that preserve their renewability.* Examples include using organic fertilizers from animal and crop wastes, planting fast-growing trees to supply fuelwood and add nitrogen to the soil, and building simple devices for capturing and storing rainwater for irrigating crops.

- *Greatly reduce the use of fossil fuels in agriculture by using locally available perpetual and renewable energy resources such as sun, wind, and flowing water to perform as many functions as possible (Chapter 17), and by increasing the use of animal and crop wastes as organic fertilizer.*

- *Emphasize use of biological pest control (Section 14-5), windbreaks, crop rotation, green manure, and other methods that reduce soil erosion and nutrient depletion, conserve water, encourage beneficial organisms, and discourage pests.*

- *Governments must frame agricultural development policies that include economic incentives to encourage farmers to grow enough food to meet the demand using sustainable-Earth agricultural systems.*

- *Limit population growth (Section 6-4).*

The shift to sustainable-Earth agriculture could be brought about over 10 to 20 years by:

- Greatly increasing government support of research and development of sustainable-Earth agricultural methods and equipment.

- Setting up demonstration projects in each county so farmers can see how sustainable systems work.

- Establishing training programs for farmers, county farm agents, and most Department of Agriculture personnel in sustainable-Earth agriculture.

- Look at your lifestyle to find ways to reduce your unnecessary use and waste of food, fertilizers, and pesticides. Recognize that agriculture has a greater environmental impact than any other human activity (see Spotlight on p. 295).

- Eat lower on the food chain by eliminating or reducing meat consumption, especially beef. This saves money and energy and can reduce your intake of fats, which contribute to heart disease and other disorders. It also reduces air and water pollution, water use, deforestation, soil erosion, overgrazing, species extinction, and emissions of the greenhouse gas methane produced by cattle.

- If you have a dog or a cat, don't feed it canned meat products.

- Use sustainable-Earth cultivation techniques to grow some of your own food in a backyard plot, a window planter, a rooftop garden, or a cooperative community garden.

- Fertilize your crops primarily with organic fertilizer produced in a compost bin (Figure 12-16). Use small amounts of commercial inorganic fertilizer only when supplies of certain plant nutrients are inadequate.

- Use drip irrigation (Figure 11-18) to water your crops.

- Control pests by a combination of cultivation and biological methods (Section 14-5). Use carefully selected chemical pesticides in small amounts only when absolutely necessary.

- Help reduce the use of pesticides on agricultural products by asking grocery stores to stock fresh produce and meat produced by organic methods (without the use of commercial fertilizers and pesticides). Insist that such foods have been tested to certify that they were grown by organic methods and support legislation that will set standards for labeling and certification of organic foods. Currently, about 0.5% of U.S. farmers grow about 3% of the country's crops using organic methods.

- Recognize that organically grown fruits and vegetables may have a few holes, blemishes, or frayed leaves, but they taste just as good and are just as nutritious as better-looking products (on which pesticides were used).

- Reduce unnecessary waste of food. An estimated 25% of all food produced in the United States is wasted; it rots in the supermarket or refrigerator or is thrown away off the plate in households and restaurants.

- Exert pressure on candidates for public office and elected officials to support policies designed to develop and encourage sustainable-Earth agricultural systems in the United States and throughout the world.

- Support efforts to regulate and slow down population growth (Section 6-4). Ultimately, the size of the world population will determine the need for food and the harmful environmental impacts of producing that food.

- Establishing college curricula for sustainable-Earth agriculture.

- Giving subsidies and tax breaks to farmers using sustainable-Earth agriculture and to agribusiness companies developing products for this type of farming.

Each of us has a role to play in bringing about a shift from unsustainable to sustainable agriculture at the local, national, and global levels (see Individuals Matter above).

The need to bring birthrates well below death rates, increase food production, while protecting the environment, and distribute food to all who need it is the greatest challenge our species has ever faced.

PAUL AND ANNE EHRLICH

DISCUSSION TOPICS

1. Summarize the advantages and limitations of each of the following proposals for increasing world food supplies and reducing hunger over the next 30 years: **(a)** cultivating more land by clearing tropical forests and irrigating arid lands, **(b)** catching more fish in the open sea, **(c)** producing more fish and shellfish with aquaculture, and **(d)** increasing the yield per area of cropland.

2. Should price supports and other federal subsidies paid to U.S. farmers out of tax revenues be eliminated? Explain. Try to have one or more farmers discuss this problem with your class.

3. Is sending food to famine victims helpful or harmful? Explain. Are there any conditions you would attach to sending such aid? Explain.

4. Should tax breaks and subsidies be used to encourage more U.S. farmers to switch to sustainable-Earth farming? Explain.

5. Do you eat meat? Would you be willing to go to a slaughterhouse and kill a cow or a pig?

CHAPTER 14

PROTECTING FOOD RESOURCES: PESTICIDES AND PEST CONTROL

General Questions and Issues

1. What principal types of pesticides are being used?
2. What are the advantages of using insecticides and herbicides?
3. What are the disadvantages of using insecticides and herbicides?
4. How is pesticide use regulated in the United States?
5. What alternatives are there to using pesticides?

A weed is a plant whose virtues have not yet been discovered.

RALPH WALDO EMERSON

NY UNWANTED organism that directly or indirectly interferes with human activity is called a **pest**. Pests compete with people for food, and some spread disease. Only about 100 of the at-least 1 million cataloged insect species cause about 90% of damage to food crops. In diverse ecosystems, their populations are kept in control by a variety of natural enemies—another crucial part of Earth's natural capital.

Since 1945, vast fields planted with only one crop or only a few crops, as well as homes, home gardens, and lawns, have been treated with a variety of chemicals called **pesticides** (or *biocides*): substances that can kill organisms that we consider to be undesirable. The most widely used types of pesticides are **insecticides** (insect killers), **herbicides** (weed killers), **fungicides** (fungus killers), and **rodenticides** (rodent killers).

There is controversy over whether the harmful effects of these chemicals outweigh their benefits, especially in comparison with other alternatives (see Section 14-5).

14-1 Pesticides: Types and Uses

THE IDEAL PESTICIDE The ideal pest-killing chemical would

- Kill only the target pest
- Have no short- or long-term health effects on nontarget organisms, including people
- Be broken down into harmless chemicals in a fairly short time
- Prevent the development of genetic resistance in target organisms
- Save money compared with making no effort to control pest species

Unfortunately, no known pest control method meets all those criteria.

USE OF PESTICIDES Pesticides are not a modern invention. So-called *first-generation pesticides* included mostly persistent inorganic chemicals and nonpersistent organic compounds extracted from insect poisons that were produced by plants to ward off herbivores. By the fifteenth century, inorganic compounds made from toxic metals such as arsenic, lead, and mercury were being applied to crops as insecticides. Use of those compounds continued until the late 1920s, when there were enough poisonings and fatalities to encourage a search for less-toxic substitutes.

In the mid-1800s, two additional natural pesticides were introduced. One was rotenone, extracted from the

Figure 14-1 The heads of these chrysanthemum flowers being grown in Kenya contain a natural insecticide called pyrethrum. The flower heads are harvested and ground into a powder that is used as a commercial insecticide. Since 1949, chemists have modified the natural pyrethrum molecule to produce a variety of more stable synthetic pyrethroids that are used as insecticides in homes and on crops.

Hutchison Library

root of the derris plant and other legumes that grow in tropical forests. The other natural pesticide was pyrethrum, which was obtained from the heads of chrysanthemum flowers (Figure 14-1). Other natural insecticides include red pepper (for ant control) and garlic oil and lemon oil (for use against fleas, mosquito larvae, houseflies, and other insects).

Since 1945, chemists have developed many synthetic organic chemicals for use as pesticides. Collectively, these chemicals are known as *second-generation pesticides*.

Worldwide, about 2.3 million metric tons (2.5 million tons) of these pesticides are used each year—an average of 0.45 kilogram (1 pound) for each person on Earth. About 85% of all pesticides are used in MDCs, but use in LDCs is growing rapidly.

In the United States, about 600 biologically active ingredients and 1,475 inert (presumably biologically inactive) ingredients are mixed to make some 55,000 pesticide products. Between 1964 and 1981, pesticide use in the United States almost tripled, but since then annual use has leveled off at around 500 million kilograms (1.1 billion pounds). At that rate, an average of 2.0 kilograms (4.4 pounds) of these products is used for each American each year.

Herbicides account for 69% of all pesticides used by American farmers, insecticides 19%, and fungicides 12%. Four crops—corn, cotton, wheat, and soybeans—account for about 70% of the insecticides and 80% of the herbicides used on crops in the United States. Fungicides are used primarily to treat seeds and to protect

fruits and vegetables during growth and after harvest from fungal diseases.

About 20% of the pesticides used each year in the United States are applied to lawns, gardens, parks, golf courses, and cemeteries. The average homeowner in the United States applies about five times more pesticide per unit of land area than do farmers.

PRINCIPAL TYPES OF INSECTICIDES AND HERBICIDES Most of the thousands of insecticides used today fall into one of four classes of compounds: chlorinated hydrocarbons, organophosphates, carbamates, or pyrethroids (Table 14-1). Most of these chemicals kill target and nontarget insects in the sprayed area by disrupting their nervous systems.

By the mid-1970s, DDT and most other slowly degradable, chlorinated hydrocarbon insecticides shown in Table 14-1 (except lindane) were banned or severely restricted in the United States and most MDCs. However, many of these compounds are still produced in the United States and exported to other countries, mostly LDCs, where they have not been banned.

In the United States and most MDCs, chlorinated hydrocarbon insecticides have been replaced by a number of more rapidly degradable pesticides, especially organophosphates and carbamates (Table 14-1). Some of these compounds, especially organophosphates such as parathion, are more toxic to birds, people, and other mammals than are the chlorinated hydrocarbon insecticides they replaced. They are also more likely to contaminate surface water and groundwater because they are water-soluble, whereas chlorinated hydrocarbon insecticides are insoluble in water but soluble in fats. Furthermore, to compensate for their fairly rapid breakdown, farmers usually apply nonpersistent insecticides at regular intervals to ensure more effective insect control. That means they are often present in the environment almost continuously, like the slowly degradable pesticides they replaced.

Other insecticides resulted from learning how wild plants, especially tropical species, produce chemical compounds that repel insects or inhibit their feeding. Today, synthetic pyrethroids made by altering the natural insecticide molecules in chrysanthemum flowers (Figure 14-1) and rotenoids produced by the roots of certain rain-forest legumes are widely used as insecticides in homes and on crops. Both types of compounds are biodegradable, are effective at low doses, and cause little harm to birds and mammals, including humans.

Herbicides can be placed into three classes, based on their effect on plants: contact herbicides, systemic herbicides, and soil sterilants (Table 14-2). Most herbicides are active for only a short time. In the United States and most MDCs, the use of 2,4,5-T and Silvex has been banned.

Q: What is the most serious drawback to using chemicals to control pests (especially insects)?

Table 14-1 Major Types of Insecticides

Type	Examples	Persistence
Chlorinated hydrocarbons	DDT, aldrin, dieldrin, endrin, heptachlor, toxaphene, lindane, chlordane, kepone, mirex	High (2–15 years)
Organophosphates	Malathion, parathion, monocrotophos, methamidophos, methyl parathion, DDVP	Low to moderate (normally 1–12 weeks, but some can last several years)
Carbamates	Carbaryl, maneb, priopoxor, mexicabate, aldicarb, aminocarb	Usually low (days to weeks)
Pyrethroids	Pemethrin, decamethrin	Usually low (days to weeks)

Table 14-2 Major Types of Herbicides

Types	Examples	Effects
Contact	Triazines such as atrazine and paraquat	Kills foliage by interfering with photosynthesis
Systemic	Phenoxy compounds such as 2,4-D, 2,4,5-T, and Silvex; synthetic ureas such as diuron, norea, fenuron, and other nitrogen-containing compounds such as daminozide (Alar), glyphosate	Absorption creates excess growth hormones; plants die because they cannot obtain enough nutrients to sustain their greatly accelerated growth
Soil sterilants	Trifluralin, diphenamid, dalapon, butylate	Kills soil microorganisms essential to plant growth; most also act as systemic herbicides

14-2 The Case for Pesticides

Proponents of pesticides believe that the benefits of pesticides outweigh their harmful effects. They point out the following benefits:

- *Pesticides save lives.* Since World War II, DDT and other chlorinated hydrocarbon and organophosphate insecticides have probably prevented the premature deaths of at least 7 million people from insect-transmitted diseases such as malaria (carried by the *Anopheles* mosquito, Figure 8-3), bubonic plague (rat fleas), typhus (body lice and fleas), and sleeping sickness (tsetse fly).

- *They increase food supplies and lower food costs.* Each year, about 55% of the world's potential food supply is lost to pests before (35%) and after (20%) harvest. Proponents argue that without pesticides, those losses would be much higher and food prices would increase (perhaps by 30% to 50% in the United States).

- *They increase profits for farmers.* In the United States, 37% of the annual potential food supply is destroyed by pests before and after harvest. Pesticide companies estimate that every $1 spent on pesticides leads to an increase in crop yield worth $3 to $5 to farmers.

- *They work faster and better than other alternatives.* Compared with alternative methods of pest control, pesticides can control most pests quickly and at a reasonable cost, have a relatively long shelf life, are easily shipped and applied, and are safe when handled properly. When genetic resistance occurs in pest insects and weeds, farmers can usually keep them under control by using stronger doses or switching to other pesticides.

- *The health risks of pesticides are insignificant compared with their health and other benefits.* According to Elizabeth Whelan, director of the American Council on Science and Health (ACSH), which presents positions of the pesticide industry: "The reality is that pesticides, when used in the approved regulatory manner, pose no risk to either farm workers or consumers." She and pesticide industry scientists call the pesticide health-scare stories often appearing in the media examples of scientific distortion and irresponsible reporting.

■ *Safer and more effective products are continually being developed*. Pesticide company scientists are continually developing pesticides, such as pyrethroids (Table 14-1), that are safer to use and that cause less ecological damage than older types. New herbicides are being developed that are effective at very low dosage rates. Genetic engineering also holds promise (see Pro/Con on p. 174). However, the costs for research and development and government approval for a single pesticide have risen from $6 million in 1976 to more than $40 million today, explaining why pesticide prices have risen sharply.

14-3 The Case Against Pesticides

DEVELOPMENT OF GENETIC RESISTANCE The most serious drawback to using chemicals to control pests is that most pest species, especially insects, can develop genetic resistance to a chemical poison through natural selection (Section 5-4). Most pest species — especially insects and disease organisms — can produce a large number of similarly resistant offspring in a short time. For example, the boll weevil (Figure 14-2), a major cotton pest, can produce a new generation every 21 days.

When an area is sprayed with a pesticide, a few organisms in a large population of a particular species usually survive because they have genes that make them resistant or immune to a specific pesticide. With repeated spraying, each succeeding generation contains a higher percentage of resistant organisms. Thus, eventually, widely used pesticides (especially insecticides) fail because of genetic resistance; in fact, widespread use usually leads to even larger populations of pest species, especially insects with large numbers of offspring and short generation times. In temperate regions, most insects develop genetic resistance to a chemical poison within 5 to 10 years; it happens much sooner in tropical areas. Weeds and plant-disease organisms also develop genetic resistance, but not as quickly as most insects.

Since 1950, at least 510 major insect pest species have developed genetic resistance to one or more insecticides, and at least 20 insect species are now apparently immune to all widely used insecticides. It is estimated that by 2000, virtually all major insect pest species will show some form of genetic resistance. About 80 species of the more than 500 major weed species are resistant to one or more herbicides. Because half of all pesticides applied worldwide are herbicides, genetic resistance in weeds is expected to increase significantly. Genetic resistance has also appeared in 70 species of fungi treated

Figure 14-2 In the cotton fields of the southern United States there may be as many as six generations of cotton boll weevils in one growing season. Attempts to control the cotton boll weevil account for at least 25% of the insecticides used in the United States. However, farmers are now increasing their use of natural predators and other biological methods to control this major pest.

with fungicides and in 10 species of rodents (mostly rats) treated with rodenticides.

Because of genetic resistance, most widely used insecticides no longer protect people from insect-transmitted diseases in many parts of the world, leading to even more serious outbreaks of disease. Genetic resistance is the primary reason for the almost 40-fold increase in malaria between 1970 and 1988 in 84 tropical and subtropical countries (see Case Study on p. 171).

KILLING OF NATURAL PEST ENEMIES AND ITS CONSEQUENCES Most insecticides are broad-spectrum poisons that kill not only the target pest species but also a number of natural predators and parasites that may have been maintaining the pest species at a reasonable level. Without sufficient natural enemies and with much food available, a rapidly reproducing insect pest species can make a strong comeback a few days or weeks after initially being controlled. The use of broad-spectrum insecticides also kills off the natural enemies of many minor pests. Then their numbers can increase greatly, and they become major pests.

THE PESTICIDE TREADMILL When genetic resistance develops, pesticide sales representatives usually recommend more frequent applications, stronger doses, or a switch to new (usually more expensive) chemicals to keep the resistant species under control, rather than suggesting nonchemical alternatives. That puts farmers on an accelerating **pesticide treadmill**, in which they pay more and more for a pest control program that becomes less and less effective.

Q: What percentage of U.S. crops are lost to pests?

Figure 14-3 Crop duster spraying a pesticide on grapevines south of Fresno, California. Typically, no more than 2%, and often less than 0.1%, of the chemical being applied reaches the target organisms. Aircraft are used to apply 60% of the pesticides used on cropland in the United States.

National Archives/EPA Documerica

A 1989 study by David Pimentel (see Guest Essay on p. 283), an expert in insect ecology, based on data from more than 300 agricultural scientists and economists, concluded that

- Although the amount of synthetic pesticides used in the United States has increased 33-fold since the 1940s, U.S. crop losses to pests have increased from about 31% in the 1940s to about 37% today.

- The estimated environmental, health, and social costs of pesticide use in the United States range from $4 billion to $10 billion a year.

- Use of alternative pest control practices (Section 14-5) could cut the use of chemical pesticides in the United States in half without any reduction in crop yields.

- A 50% cut in pesticide use in the United States would cause food prices to rise by only 0.6%. This rise would cost consumers $1 billion a year, but it would be more than offset by an estimated $2 billion to $5 billion reduction in environmental, health, and social costs.

MOBILITY AND BIOLOGICAL AMPLIFICATION OF PERSISTENT PESTICIDES Pesticides don't stay put. According to the U.S. Department of Agriculture, only 1% to 2% (and often less than 0.1%) of the insecticides applied to crops by aerial spraying (Figure 14-3) or ground spraying reach the target pests. Less than 5% of herbicides applied to crops reach the target weeds.

Pesticides not reaching target pests (95% to 99%) end up in the soil, air, surface water, groundwater, bottom sediment, food, and nontarget organisms, including people and even penguins in the Antarctic. Concentrations of fat-soluble, slowly degradable insecticides such as DDT, PCBs, and other chlorinated hydrocarbons (Table 14-1) can be biologically amplified thousands to millions of times in food chains and webs (see Spotlight on p. 312).

Pesticide waste can be reduced by using recirculating sprayers that catch pesticides that miss their targets the first time, placing shrouds around spray booms to reduce drift, and using rope-wick applicators that deliver herbicides directly to weeds and reduce herbicide use by 90%. Substituting such methods for aerial spraying can increase the amount of pesticide reaching target organisms by 75%.

SHORT-TERM THREATS TO HUMAN HEALTH FROM PESTICIDE USE AND MANUFACTURE The World Health Organization estimates that each year, about 3 million people are poisoned by pesticides and 5,000 to 20,600 of them die. At least half of those poisoned, and 75% of those killed, are farm workers in LDCs, where educational levels are low, warnings are few, and pesticide regulation and control methods are often lax or nonexistent. The actual number of pesticide-related illnesses among farm workers in the United States and throughout the world is probably greatly underestimated because of poor records, lack of doctors and reporting in rural areas, and faulty diagnoses.

Each year, about 45,000 cases of pesticide poisoning, most involving children, are reported in the United States, including 3,000 hospital admissions and 200 deaths. The majority of the poisonings occur because of unsafe use or storage of pesticides in and around the home.

An estimated 10,000 Americans get some form of cancer, mostly from the handling of pesticides by farmers, pesticide plant workers, pesticide applicators, crop pickers, and home gardeners, all of whom are repeatedly exposed directly to much higher levels of pesticides than the rest of society. Accidents and unsafe practices in pesticide plants can expose workers, their families, and sometimes the general public to harmful levels of pesticides or chemicals used in their manufacture (see Case Study on p. 313).

LONG-TERM THREATS TO HUMAN HEALTH According to the Food and Drug Administration, about 3% of the food bought in supermarkets has levels of residues of one or more of the active ingredients used

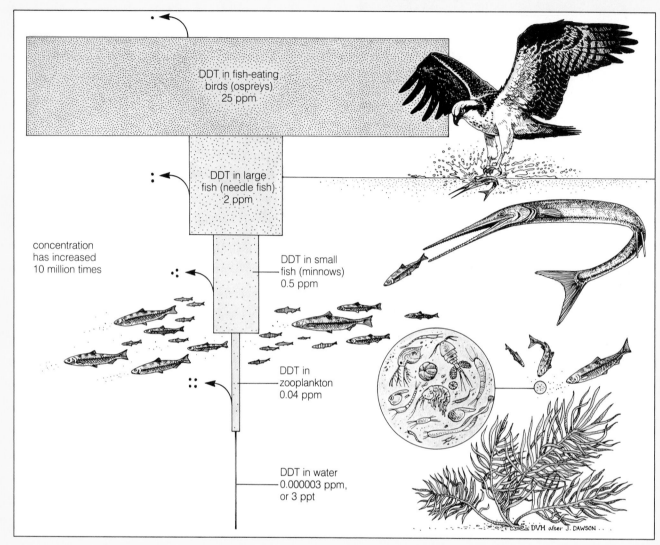

concentration
has increased
10 million times

DDT in fish-eating
birds (ospreys)
25 ppm

DDT in large
fish (needle fish)
2 ppm

DDT in small
fish (minnows)
0.5 ppm

DDT in
zooplankton
0.04 ppm

DDT in water
0.000003 ppm,
or 3 ppt

DVH after J. DAWSON

Figure 14-4 The concentration of DDT in the fatty tissues of organisms was biologically amplified about 10 million times in this food chain of an estuary adjacent to Long Island Sound near New York City. Dots represent DDT, and arrows show small losses of DDT through respiration and excretion.

in pesticides in the United States that are above the legal limit. The results of this long-term worldwide experiment, with people involuntarily playing the role of guinea pigs, may never be known because it is almost impossible to determine that a certain level of specific chemical caused a particular cancer or some other harmful effect (Section 8-1).

In 1987, the National Academy of Sciences reported that the active ingredients in 90% of all fungicides, 60% of all herbicides, and 30% of all insecticides in use in the United States may cause cancer in humans. According to the *worst-case estimate* in this study, exposure to pesticides in food causes 4,000 to 20,000 cases of cancer

a year in the United States. In 1987, the EPA ranked pesticide residues in foods as the third most serious environmental health threat in the United States (after worker exposure and indoor radon) in terms of cancer risk.

It is also argued that the long-term health risks from pesticides are too narrowly focused on pesticide exposure from food. While this is important, many people can be exposed to much higher levels of pesticides from community spraying programs used to control mosquitoes or other insect pests; pesticide-sprayed lawns, parks, golf courses, and roadsides; and living near sprayed croplands, rangelands, and forests.

Q: What percentage of insecticides applied to crops in the United States reach the target pests?

Figure 14-5 The peregrine falcon is endangered in the United States, mostly because of exposure to DDT. Only about 1,000 peregrine falcons are left in the lower 48 states. Most of them were bred in captivity and then released into the wild as a result of a $2.7-million-a-year recovery program. However, some of these birds are illegally shot or captured for sale on the black market. Peregrine falcons can also die during their annual migration to parts of South America and because of loss of habitat in these areas.

A factor affecting the survival of some individual organisms and populations of organisms is **biological amplification** (also called bioaccumulation or biological magnification). It occurs when concentrations of certain chemicals in organisms feeding at high trophic levels in a food chain or web are drastically higher than concentrations of those chemicals found in organisms feeding at lower trophic levels.

Chemicals that can be biologically amplified include synthetic organic chemicals (such as the pesticide DDT and PCBs), some radioactive materials, and some toxic mercury and lead compounds. Synthetic organic compounds that can be biologically amplified are insoluble in water, are soluble in fat, and are slowly biodegraded by natural processes. This means that they become more concentrated in the fatty tissues of organisms at successively higher trophic levels in food chains and webs.

Figure 14-4 shows the biological amplification of DDT in a five-step food chain of an estuary ecosystem. High concentrations of DDT or other slowly biodegraded, fat-soluble organic chemicals can reduce populations of species in several ways. They can directly kill the organisms, reduce their ability to reproduce, or weaken them so that they are more vulnerable to diseases, parasites, and predators.

During the 1950s and 1960s, populations of ospreys, cormorants, eastern and California brown pelicans, and bald eagles declined drastically. These birds feed mostly on fish at the top of long aquatic food chains and webs and thus ingest large quantities of biologically amplified DDT in their prey.

Populations of predatory birds such as prairie falcons, sparrow hawks, Bermuda petrels, and peregrine falcons (Figure 14-5) also dropped when they ate animal prey containing DDT. These birds control populations of rabbits, ground squirrels, and other crop-damaging small mammals.

Research has shown that these population declines occurred because DDE, a chemical produced by the breakdown of DDT, accumulated in the bodies of the affected bird species. This chemical reduces the amount of calcium in the shells of their eggs. As a result, the shells are so thin that many of them break and the unborn chicks die.

Since the U.S. ban on DDT in 1972, populations of most of these bird species have made a comeback. In 1980, however, it was discovered that levels of DDT and other banned pesticides were rising in some areas and in some species such as the peregrine falcon and the osprey.

These species may be picking up biologically amplified DDT and other chlorinated hydrocarbon insecticides in Latin American countries, where the birds live during winter. In those countries, the use of such chemicals is still legal. Illegal use of DDT and other banned pesticides in the United States may also play a role.

CASE STUDY The Bhopal Tragedy

In 1984, the world's worst industrial accident occurred at a Union Carbide pesticide plant in Bhopal, India. At least 4,000 people were killed and 300,000 more were injured (Union Carbide says 10,000) when about 36 metric tons (40 tons) of highly toxic methyl isocyanate gas, used in the manufacture of carbamate pesticides, leaked from a storage tank. About 2,800 people lost their jobs when the plant was permanently closed.

The Indian Supreme Court ordered Union Carbide to pay a $470 million settlement and dropped criminal charges against the company. The Indian government has challenged the ruling, arguing that the settlement is inadequate and that the court had no constitutional right to drop the criminal charges.

In 1991, India's Supreme Court upheld the settlement amount but allowed reopening of criminal charges against Union Carbide.

Union Carbide could probably have prevented this tragedy, which cost at least $570 million, by spending no more than $1 million to improve plant safety.

Numerous studies by the National Academy of Sciences and the General Accounting Office have shown that the weakest and most poorly enforced U.S. environmental law in the United States is the Federal Insecticide, Fungicide, and Rodenticide Act (FIFRA) of 1972 and its subsequent amendments.

This act required the EPA to reevaluate the 600 active ingredients approved for use in pesticide products before 1972 to determine whether any of them caused cancer, birth defects, or other health risks. The EPA was supposed to complete its analysis by 1975. But by 1989, the EPA had carried out preliminary assessment of only 139 of these chemicals and completed its review on only 2 of them. In 1987 Congress extended the deadline for completing this review to 1997. The EPA claims that Congress has not appropriated enough money for it to do the job.

According to the National Academy of Sciences, up to 98% of the potential risk of developing cancer from pesticide residues on food grown in the United States would be eliminated if the EPA set the same stricter standards for pesticides registered for use before 1972

as it has for those registered after 1972.

It has also become clear that many of the 1,475 so-called inert or biologically inactive ingredients in pesticide products are in fact biologically active and can cause harm to people and some forms of wildlife. The EPA plans to cancel the use of 358 of these active ingredients. At the same time, the agency allows hazardous wastes to be "recycled" into pesticides as "inert" ingredients.

This law allows the EPA to leave inadequately tested pesticides on the market and to license new chemicals without full health and safety data. It also gives the EPA unlimited time to remove a chemical when its health and environmental effects are shown to outweigh its economic benefits. The appeals and other procedures built into the law often allow a dangerous chemical to remain on the market for up to 10 years.

The EPA can immediately cancel the use of a chemical on an emergency basis. Until 1990, however, the law required the EPA to use its already severely limited funds to compensate pesticide manufacturers for

their remaining inventory and for all the costs of storing and disposing of the banned pesticide. This provision made it very difficult for the EPA to cancel a chemical quickly. For only one chemical, compensation costs could amount to more than the agency's pesticide budget for one year. Usually, therefore, the only economically feasible solution has been for the EPA to allow existing stocks of a chemical that should be banned immediately to be sold.

After 20 years of pressure from environmentalists, Congress passed several new amendments to the federal pesticide law in 1988. One of those amendments shifts some, but not all, of the costs of banning and disposing of banned pesticides from the EPA to companies making the chemicals.

Environmentalists consider the 1988 amendments better than nothing, but they point out that the law still has numerous weaknesses and loopholes. One loophole allows the sale in the United States of a number of insecticide products containing as much as 15% DDT by weight, classified as an impurity. These products, along with others illegally smuggled into the United States (mostly from

---

14-4 Pesticide Regulation in the United States

IS THE PUBLIC ADEQUATELY PROTECTED? Because of the potentially harmful effects of pesticides on wildlife and people, Congress passed the Federal Insecticide, Fungicide, and Rodenticide Act (FIFRA) in 1972. This law, which was amended in 1975, 1978, and 1988, requires that all commercial pesticides be approved for general or restricted use by the Environmental Protection Agency.

Approval is based mostly on an evaluation of the safety of the chemicals that pesticide companies designate as biologically active ingredients in their pesticide products. These data are submitted to the EPA by the companies seeking approval.

Since 1972, the EPA has used this law to ban the use, except for emergencies, of over 50 pesticides be-

cause of their potential hazards to human health. The banned chemicals include most chlorinated hydrocarbon insecticides, several carbamates and organophosphates (Table 14-1), and several herbicides, such as 2,4,5-T and Silvex (Table 14-2).

However, according to a 1988 report by the National Academy of Sciences, federal laws regulating the use of pesticides in the United States are inadequate and poorly enforced by the Food and Drug Administration (FDA) and the EPA (see Spotlight above).

14-5 Alternative Methods of Insect Control

MODIFYING CULTIVATION PROCEDURES Opponents of the widespread use of pesticides argue that there are many safer and, in the long run, cheaper and

Q: Worldwide, how many people are poisoned each year by pesticides?

Mexico), are believed to be responsible for increases in DDT levels in some vulnerable forms of wildlife and on some fruits and vegetables grown and sold in the United States (especially in California).

Also, this law is the only major environmental statute that does not provide for citizen suits against the EPA for violations in enforcing the law, an essential tool to assure government compliance with a law.

Each year the Food and Drug Administration inspectors check less than 1% (about 12,000 samples) of domestic and imported food for pesticide contamination. Furthermore, the FDA's turnaround time for food analysis is so long that about half of contaminated foods have been sold and eaten by the time the contamination is detected. Even when contaminated food is found, the growers and importers are rarely penalized. Also, FDA tests can detect fewer than half of the 600 active chemical ingredients approved for use in U.S. pesticide products.

Pesticide companies can make and export to other countries pesticides that have been banned in the United States or that have not been submitted to the EPA for approval.

The United States leads the world in pesticide exports. On average, 15 metric tons (17 tons) of pesticides banned, unregistered, or severely restricted for use in the United States are shipped to other countries *each hour*. In what environmentalists call a *circle of poison*, residues of some of these banned or unapproved chemicals return to the United States as pesticide residues on imported coffee, meats, fruits, and vegetables. More than one-fourth of the produce (fruits and vegetables) consumed in the United States is grown overseas.

Environmentalists have pressured Congress to halt all export of pesticides banned or not approved for use in the United States and to bar imports of food treated with such chemicals. They believe that it is morally wrong for the United States to export pesticides that we have determined to be a serious risk to human health to other countries and to allow food with residues of those pesticides to be imported for use by U.S. consumers.

President George Bush opposes such a ban. He argues that such a decision should be a two-way decision between the United States and

the importing country; that unilateral bans will not work; and that, since the chemicals can be purchased from other countries, the United States shouldn't lose this business. In 1990, both houses of Congress voted to ban the export of banned pesticides, but the measure was eventually scuttled in a House-Senate committee.

If the newest version of the General Agreement on Tariffs and Trade (GATT) (a treaty on international trade) goes into effect, no country or state would be able to have stricter regulations on pesticide residues on imported goods than international standards (which would be developed mostly behind closed doors by international commissions) unless it paid importers a fee to make up for their extra costs. Since many U.S. pesticide residue standards are higher than international standards, the result of the new treaty could be to lower U.S. standards.

What, if anything, do you think should be done to provide more protection for the public from contamination of food and drinking water by traces of numerous pesticides?

more effective alternatives to the use of pesticides by farmers and homeowners. For centuries, farmers have used cultivation methods that discourage or inhibit pests. Examples are

- *Crop rotation*, in which the types of crops planted in fields are changed from year to year so that populations of pests that attack a particular crop don't have time to multiply to uncontrollable sizes.

- *Planting rows of hedges or trees in and around crop fields* to act as barriers to invasions by insect pests, provide habitats for their natural enemies, and serve as windbreaks to reduce soil erosion (Figure 12-13).

- *Adjusting planting times* to ensure that most major insect pests either starve to death before the crop is available or are consumed by their natural predators.

- *Growing crops in areas where their major pests do not exist.*

- *Switching from monocultures to modernized versions of intercropping, agroforestry, and polyculture* that use plant diversity to help control pests (Section 13-1).

- *Removing diseased or infected plants and stalks and other crop residues that harbor pests.*

- *Using photodegradable plastic to prevent growth of weeds between rows of some crops.*

- *Using vacuum machines that gently remove bugs from plants.*

Unfortunately, to increase profits, qualify for government subsidies, and—in some cases—avoid bankruptcy, many farmers in MDCs such as the United States have abandoned these cultivation methods.

ARTIFICIAL SELECTION, CROSSBREEDING, AND GENETIC ENGINEERING Varieties of plants and animals that are genetically resistant to certain pest insects, fungi, and diseases can be developed. New vari-

Figure 14-6 Use of genetic engineering to reduce pest damage. Both of these tomato plants were exposed to destructive caterpillars. The foliage on the normal tomato plant on the left has been almost completely eaten, while the genetically engineered plant on the right shows few signs of damage.

eties usually take a long time (10 to 20 years) to develop by conventional methods and are costly.

However, insect pests and plant diseases can develop new strains that attack the once-resistant varieties, forcing scientists to continually develop new resistant strains. Genetic engineering techniques are now being used to develop resistant crops (Figure 14-6) and animals more rapidly (see Pro/Con on p. 174).

BIOLOGICAL CONTROL Various natural predators (Figure 14-7), parasites, and pathogens (disease-causing bacteria and viruses) can be introduced or imported to regulate the populations of specific pests. Worldwide, more than 300 biological pest control projects have been successful, especially in China. In the United States, natural enemies have been used to control about 70 insect pests, and the use of biological control is increasing rapidly as more farmers seek alternatives to conventional chemical pesticides.

Bacillus thuringiensis, a bacterial agent, is a registered pesticide sold commercially as a dry powder. By choosing which of the thousands of strains of this microorganism to use, companies selling this biological agent can tailor their products to combat a variety of pests. Sales are soaring, and by 1992, there were more than 45 of these and other biological pesticides on the market.

A gene from *Bacillus thuringiensis* has been transferred to cotton plants. These plants then produce a protein that disrupts the digestive system of pests. Insects that bite the plant die within a few hours.

Other examples of biological control include the use of

- *Guard dogs* to protect livestock from predators. Guard dogs are more effective and cost less than erecting fences and shooting, trapping, and poi-

soning predators—methods that sometimes kill nontarget organisms, including people.

- *Geese* for weeding orchards, eating fallen and rotting fruit (often a source of pest problems), and controlling grass in gardens and nurseries. Geese also warn of approaching predators or people by honking loudly.

- *Chickens* to control insects and weeds and to increase the nitrogen content of the soil in orchards or in gardens after plants have become well established.

- *Birds* to eat insects. Farmers and homeowners can provide habitats and nesting sites that attract woodpeckers, purple martins, chickadees, barn swallows, nuthatches, and other insect-eating species.

- *Spiders* to eat insects (Figure 14-7). Spiders are insects' worst enemies, devouring enough bugs worldwide in a single day to outweigh the entire human population. One type of banana spider, harmless to humans, can keep a house clear of cockroaches. Most spiders, except the brown recluse and the black widow, are harmless to humans.

- *Allelopathic plants* that naturally produce chemicals toxic to their weed competitors or that repel or poison their insect pests. For example, certain varieties of barley, wheat, rye, sorghum, and Sudan grass can be grown in gardens or orchards to suppress weeds. Peppermint can be planted around houses to repel ants and to be used as a natural mouth freshener (pull off a leaf, wash it, and chew it) and a cooking spice.

Biological control normally affects only the target species and is nontoxic to other species, including people. Once a population of natural predators or parasites is established, control of pest species is often self-perpetuating. Development of genetic resistance is minimized because both pest and predator species usually undergo natural selection to maintain a stable interaction (coevolution). In the United States, biological control has saved farmers an average of $25 for every $1 invested in conventional pesticides.

No method of pest control, however, is perfect. Typically, 10 to 20 years of research may be required to understand how a particular pest interacts with its various enemies and to determine the best biological control agent. Mass production of biological agents is often difficult, and farmers find that they are slower to act and harder to apply than pesticides.

Biological agents must be protected from pesticides sprayed in nearby fields, and there is a chance that some can later become pests themselves; others (such as praying mantises) may also devour other beneficial insects. In addition, some pest organisms can develop genetic resistance to viruses and bacterial agents used for biological control.

Q: What is the weakest environmental law in the United States?

Figure 14-7 Biological control of pests. An adult convergent ladybug is consuming an aphid (left). The wolf spider, like most spiders, is harmless to humans and plays an important role in keeping insects in check (right).

INSECT STERILIZATION Males of some insect pest species can be raised in the laboratory and sterilized by radiation or chemicals, then released in large numbers in an infested area to mate unsuccessfully with fertile wild females. If sterile males outnumber fertile males by 10 to 1, a pest species in a given area can be eradicated in about four generations, provided reinfestation does not occur.

This technique works best if the females mate only once, if the infested area is isolated so that it can't be periodically repopulated with nonsterilized males, and if the insect pest population has already been reduced to a fairly low level by weather, pesticides, or other factors. Success is also increased if only the sexiest — the loudest, fastest, and largest — males are sterilized.

Serious problems with this approach include ensuring that sterile males are not overwhelmed numerically by nonsterile males, knowing the mating times and behavior of each target insect, preventing reinfestation with new nonsterilized males, and high costs.

INSECT SEX ATTRACTANTS In many insect species, when a virgin female is ready to mate she releases a minute amount (typically about one-millionth of a gram) of a species-specific chemical sex attractant called a *pheromone*. Pheromones, extracted from an insect pest species or synthesized in the laboratory, can be used in minute amounts to lure pests into traps containing toxic chemicals or to attract natural predators of insect pests into crop fields (usually the most effective approach).

Scientists have identified sex-attractant pheromones for more than 436 insect species. Worldwide, more than 50 companies sell about 250 of these pheromones to control pests (Figure 14-8).

These chemicals work on only one species, are effective in trace amounts, have little chance of causing genetic resistance, and are not harmful to nontarget species. However, it is costly and time-consuming to identify, isolate, and produce the specific sex attractant for each pest or natural predator species. Pheromones

Figure 14-8 A lemon infested with red scale mites. Pheromones are now being used to help control populations of red scale mites.

have also failed for some pests because only adults are drawn to the traps; for most species, the juvenile forms — such as caterpillars — do most of the damage.

INSECT HORMONES Hormones are chemicals, produced in an organism's cells, that travel through the bloodstream and control various aspects of the organism's growth and development. Each step in the life cycle of a typical insect is regulated by the timely release of juvenile hormones (JH) and molting hormones (MH) (Figure 14-9).

These chemicals can be extracted from insects or synthesized in the laboratory. When applied at certain stages in an insect's life cycle (Figure 14-9), they produce abnormalities that cause the insect to die before it can reach maturity and reproduce (Figure 14-10).

Insect hormones have the same advantages as sex attractants, but they take weeks to kill an insect, are often ineffective with a large infestation, and sometimes break down before they can act. Also, they must be applied at exactly the right time in the life cycle of the target insect. They sometimes affect natural predators

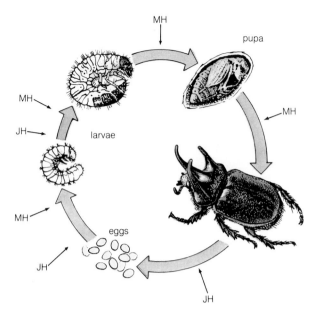

Figure 14-9 For normal growth, development, and reproduction, certain juvenile hormones (JH) and molting hormones (MH) must be present at genetically determined stages in the typical life cycle of an insect. If applied at the right time, synthetic hormones can be used to disrupt the life cycle of insect pests.

of the target insect species and other nonpest species and can kill crustaceans if they get into aquatic ecosystems. Like sex attractants, they are difficult and costly to produce.

IRRADIATION OF FOODS Exposing certain foods to various levels of ionizing radiation is being touted by the nuclear industry and the food industry as a means of killing insects and preventing them from reproducing in certain foods after harvest, extending the shelf life of some perishable foods, and destroying parasitic worms (such as trichinae) and bacteria (such as salmonellae, which infect 51,000 Americans and kill 2,000 of them each year).

Since 1986, the FDA has approved use of low doses of ionizing radiation on spices, fruits, vegetables, white potatoes, wheat and wheat flour, pork, nuts, seeds, teas, and chicken. It may soon be approved for use on seafood. Irradiated foods are already sold in 33 countries, including Japan, Canada, Brazil, Israel, and many western European countries.

Because tests show that consumers will not buy food if it is labeled as being irradiated, foods exposed to radiation sold in the United States bear a characteristic logo and a label stating that the product has been *picowaved*.

A food does not become radioactive when it is irradiated, just as being exposed to X rays does not make the body radioactive. There is controversy, however, over irradiating food (see Pro/Con on p. 319).

Agricultural Research Service/USDA

Figure 14-10 Chemical hormones can prevent insects from maturing completely and make it impossible for them to reproduce. Comparison of a stunted (left) and a normal (right) tobacco hornworm. The stunted hornworm was fed a compound that prevents its larvae from producing molting hormones (MH).

INTEGRATED PEST MANAGEMENT Pest control is basically an ecological problem, not a chemical problem. That is why using large quantities of broad-spectrum chemical poisons to kill and control pest populations eventually fails and ends up costing more than it is worth. As biologist Thomas Eisner puts it, "Bugs are not going to inherit the earth. They own it now. So we might as well make peace with the landlord."

An increasing number of pest control experts believe that in most cases the best way to control crop pests is a carefully designed **integrated pest management (IPM)** program. In this approach, each crop and its pests are evaluated as an ecological system. Then a pest control program is developed that uses a variety of cultivation, biological, and chemical methods in proper sequence and timing.

The overall aim of integrated pest management is not eradication but keeping pest populations just below the size at which they cause economic loss (Figure 14-11). Fields are carefully monitored to check whether pests have reached an economically damaging level.

Q: What is the best way to control pests?

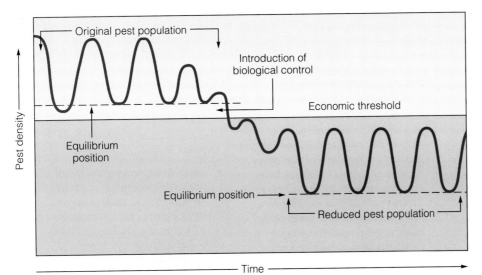

Figure 14-11 The goal of biological control and integrated pest management is to keep each pest population just below the size at which it causes economic loss.

When such a level is reached, farmers first use biological and cultivation controls. Small amounts of pesticides are applied only when absolutely necessary, and a variety of chemicals are used to retard development of genetic resistance. This approach allows farmers to escape from the pesticide treadmill and to minimize the hazards to human health, wildlife, and the environment from the widespread use of chemical pesticides.

China, Brazil, Indonesia, and the United States have led the world in the use of this approach, especially to protect cotton, soybeans, cassava, and rice. These experiences have shown that a well-designed integrated pest management program can

- Reduce inputs of fertilizer and irrigation water
- Reduce preharvest pest-induced crop losses by 50%
- Reduce pesticide use and control costs by 50% to 90%
- Increase crop yields and reduce crop production costs

However, integrated pest management requires expert knowledge about each pest-crop situation and is slower acting and more labor-intensive (but this creates jobs) than the use of conventional pesticides. Methods developed for a given crop in one area may not be applicable to another area with slightly different growing conditions. Although long-term costs are typically lower than the costs of using conventional pesticides, initial costs may be higher. Use of IPM is hindered by government subsidies of conventional chemical pesticides.

Switching to integrated pest management on a large scale in the United States is very difficult. First, it is strongly opposed by the politically and economically powerful agricultural chemical companies, who would suffer from a sharp drop in pesticide sales. They see

PRO/CON Should Food Be Irradiated?

According to the FDA and the World Health Organization, over 1,000 studies show that foods exposed to low doses of ionizing radiation are safe for human consumption. But critics of irradiation argue that not enough animal studies have been done and that evaluations of the effects of irradiated foods on people have been too few and brief to turn up any long-term effects, which typically require 30 to 40 years to be evaluated.

Opponents also point to studies suggesting that consuming irradiated food may be harmful. Irradiating food also destroys some of its vitamins and other nutrients.

Opponents also fear that more people might die of deadly botulism in irradiated foods. Present levels of irradiation do not destroy the spore-enclosed bacteria that cause this disease, but they do destroy the microbes that give off the rotten odor that warns of the presence of botulism bacteria.

Environmentalists and consumer advocates consider food irradiation a giant step backward. What Americans want and need is fresh, wholesome food, not old food made to appear fresh and healthy by irradiation or food that has reduced nutritional value. They call for consumers to pressure elected officials to halt food irradiation, strictly regulate all irradiation facilities, and require that any food product that is irradiated, or that contains irradiated ingredients, clearly state this information.

Proponents respond that irradiation of food is likely to reduce health hazards to people by decreasing the use of some potentially damaging pesticides and that its potential benefits greatly exceed the risks. What do you think?

- Pressure elected officials to significantly strengthen the Federal Insecticide, Fungicide, and Rodenticide Act to better protect human health and the environment from the harmful effects of pesticides.

- Pressure elected officials to ban exports of pesticides not approved for use in the United States.

- Pressure elected officials to ban food irradiation or require all food that is irradiated or contains irradiated projects to be clearly labeled to show that it has been irradiated (not picowaved). Also, require much stricter regulation of irradiation facilities.

- Use pesticides in your home and on your yard or garden only when absolutely necessary, and use them in the smallest amount possible.

- Dispose of any unused pesticides in a safe manner (contact your local health department or environmental agency for safe disposal methods).

- Fix all leaking pipes and faucets, because they provide moisture

that attracts ants and roaches. This also saves water and money.

- Allow plants native to an area to grow on all or most of the land around a house site not used for gardening. This type of yard reduces infestations by mosquitoes and other insects by providing a diversity of habitats for their natural predators. It also saves time, energy, and money (because there's no lawn mower and no fuel to buy and no mower repairs to be made).

- Don't cut grass below 8 centimeters (3 inches). Taller grass provides more habitats for natural predators of many pest species, shades weeds out, and holds moisture in the soil.

- If you hire a company to take care of your lawn, use one that relies only on organic methods.* If a company claims to use only

*For names of lawn companies that don't use toxic chemicals, write Lorens Tronet, Executive Director of Lake Country Defenders, Box 911, Lake Zanich, IL 60047, and the Bio-Integral Resource Center, Box 7414, Berkeley, CA 94707. Also consult *Success with Lawns Starts with Soil*, Ringer Research Corp., 6860 Flying Cloud Drive, Eden Prairie, MN 55344.

organic methods, get its claims in writing.

Use the following natural alternatives to pesticides for controlling common household pests:†

- *Ants*. Make sure firewood and tree branches are not in contact with the house; caulk common entry points, such as windowsills, door thresholds, and baseboards (also saves energy and money). Keep ants out by planting mint or onion around the outside of a house and by putting coffee grounds or crushed mint leaves around doors and windows; sprinkle cayenne, red pepper, or boric acid (with an anticaking agent) along ant trails inside your house, and wipe off countertops with vinegar. After about four days of such treatments, ants usually go somewhere else.

- *Mosquitoes*. Establish nests and houses for insect-eating birds;

†For further information on safe control of insect pests, contact the National Coalition Against the Misuse of Pesticides, 530 7th St., NE, Washington, DC 20003.

---

little profit to be made from most alternative pest control methods, except insect sex attractants, hormones, and patented genetically engineered strains of plants and animals that have increased resistance to pests.

Second, farmers get most of their information about pest control from pesticide salespeople. They also get information from U.S. Department of Agriculture county farm agents, who have supported pesticide use for decades and rarely have adequate training in the design and use of integrated pest management. The small number of integrated pest management advisers and consultants is overwhelmed by the army of pesticide sales representatives.

Third, integrated pest management methods will have to be developed and introduced to farmers by federal and state agencies because pesticide companies see little profit in this approach. Currently, however, only about 2% of the Department of Agriculture's budget is spent on integrated pest management.

Environmentalists urge the USDA to promote integrated pest management by

- Adding a 2% sales tax on pesticides and using all of these revenues to greatly expand the federal budget for integrated pest management

- Setting up a federally supported demonstration project on at least one farm in every county

- Training Department of Agriculture field personnel and all county farm agents in integrated pest management so they can help farmers use this alternative

- Providing federal and state subsidies and perhaps government-backed crop-loss insurance to farmers who use integrated pest management or other approved alternatives to pesticides

- Gradually phasing out federal and state subsidies to farmers who depend almost entirely on pesticides once effective integrated pest management methods have been developed for major pest species

Environmentalists call for a 50% reduction in the use of chemical pesticides in the United States by 2000.

Q: What percentage of Earth's land area is covered by tropical forests?

eliminate sources of stagnant water in or near your yard; plant basil outside windows and doors; use screens on all doors and windows; and use a yellow light bulb outside entryways. Reduce bites by not using scented soaps and not wearing perfumes, colognes, and other scented products outdoors during mosquito season. Repel mosquitoes by rubbing a bit of vinegar on exposed skin. Don't use No-Pest strips for control of flying insects, especially in bedrooms or areas where food is prepared or eaten, because most contain DDVP, an organophosphate that some environmentalists have been trying unsuccessfully to have banned. Don't use electric zappers to kill mosquitoes and other flying insects. These devices are noisy and waste electricity, and the light attracts insects rather than repelling them.

■ *Roaches*. Caulk or otherwise plug small cracks around wall shelves, cupboards, baseboards, pipes, sinks, and bathroom fixtures (also saves energy); eliminate folded grocery sacks and news-

papers, which are favorite hiding places for roaches; and don't leave out dirty dishes, food spills, dog or other indoor pet food, or uncovered food or garbage overnight. Kill roaches by sprinkling boric acid (or a mixture of boric acid and flour, cornmeal, or sugar) under sinks and ranges, behind refrigerators, and in cabinets, closets, and other dark, warm places. Establish populations of banana spiders.

■ *Mice*. Seal holes and keep areas free of food, as with roaches and ants. Use glass, metal, or sturdy plastic containers to store food. Trap mice remaining in the house by using spring-loaded traps baited with a small amount of peanut butter.

■ *Flies*. Dispose of garbage and clean garbage cans regularly; eat or remove overripened fruit; and don't leave moist, uneaten pet food out for more than an hour. Clean up dog manure and cat litter boxes daily. Repel flies by planting sweet basil and tansy near doorways and patios and hanging a series of polyethylene strips in front of entry doors (like

the ones you see on some grocery store coolers); grow sweet basil in the kitchen; place sweet clover in small bags made of mosquito netting and hang the bags around the room; make flypaper by applying honey to strips of yellow paper, and hang it from the ceiling in the center of rooms.

■ *Termites*. Make sure that soil around and under your home is well drained and that crawl spaces are dry and well ventilated; remove scrap wood, stumps, sawdust, cardboard, firewood, and other sources of cellulose close to your house; replace heavily damaged or rotted sills, joists, or flooring; fill voids in concrete or masonry with mortar grout. In new construction install a termite shield between the foundation and floor joists, and don't let untreated wood touch soil. Inspect for damage each year, and if infestation is discovered apply a heat lamp for ten minutes to any infested area; nematodes (tiny parasitic worms) can also be used; for a large infestation have your
(continued)

Indonesia has led the way in the pest management revolution. In 1986, the Indonesian government banned the use of 57 pesticides on rice and launched a nationwide program to switch to integrated pest management. Denmark, Sweden, the Netherlands, and the Canadian province of Ontario have passed legislation to reduce pesticide use by 50% over the next 5 to 15 years.

CHANGING THE ATTITUDES OF CONSUMERS AND FARMERS Three attitudes tend to support the widespread use of pesticides and lock us into the pesticide treadmill:

■ Many people believe that the only good bug is a dead bug.

■ Most consumers insist on buying only perfect, unblemished fruits and vegetables, even though a few holes or frayed leaves do not significantly affect the taste, nutrition, or shelf life of such produce.

■ Most people accept the argument of pesticide makers that without these chemicals, there wouldn't be enough to eat and food prices would soar. However, studies show that cutting pesticide use in half in the United States by using alternative forms of pest management would not decrease crop yields; would raise food prices only slightly; and would reduce the health, environmental, and social costs of pesticides to consumers by $2 billion to $5 billion a year.

Educating farmers and consumers to change their attitudes and pressuring elected officials to change U.S. agricultural and pesticide policies would help reduce unnecessary pesticide use and economic loss and the resulting risks to human health and wildlife (see Individuals Matter on p. 320).

We need to recognize that pest control is basically an ecological, not a chemical problem.

ROBERT L. RUDD

house treated by a professional using one of the new termicides such as Dursban, Torpedo, or Dragnet. Safer treatments that may soon be available are freezing termites to death by pouring liquid nitrogen into walls and infested areas, a growth regulator that transforms young termites into soldiers instead of workers needed to feed a colony, and antibiotics that eliminate the wood-digesting microorganisms that live inside termites.

- *Fleas.* Keep fleas off you by bathing in soaps that contain certain green dyes that repel fleas. Vacuum frequently and toss a couple of mothballs into the vacuum cleaner bag to kill fleas sucked into the bag. Dust your pet with flea powders made from eucalyptus, sage, tobacco, wormwood, bay leaf, or vetiver. Mix essential oils such as citronella, cedarwood, eucalyptus, pennyroyal, orange, sassafras, geranium, clove, or mint with water and use for dips and shampoos for pets. Do not use flea collars or flea preparations containing synthetic insecticides, which contain

chemicals that can cause cancer, nerve damage, and mutations in pets and may be a hazard to humans (especially small children).

Roaches, ants, termites, carpenter ants, and other household insect pests are now being killed by pumping air heated to more than 49°C (120°F) into infected buildings for at least half an hour.

You can reduce potential health risks from pesticide residues in food by

- Buying organically grown produce that has not been treated with synthetic fertilizers, pesticides, or growth regulators. Purchase only organic produce that is certified to be free of pesticide residues by independent testing laboratories, and urge your supermarket manager to carry only organic produce that meets those standards.‡

‡For a list of more than 100 sources of organically grown and processed fruits, vegetables, grains, and meats, send a self-addressed business envelope with 50 cents postage to Mail-Order Organic, The Center for Science in the Public Interest, 1501 16th St. NW, Washington, DC 20036.

- Not buying imported produce, which generally contains more pesticide residues than domestic fruits and vegetables. Show your concern and influence supermarket buying decisions by asking managers where their produce comes from.

- Not buying perfect-looking fruits and vegetables, which are more likely to contain higher levels of pesticide residues.

- Carefully washing and scrubbing all fresh produce in soapy water.

- Removing and not using the outer leaves of lettuce and cabbage and peeling fruits that have thick skins.

- Growing your own fruits and vegetables using organic methods.

DISCUSSION TOPICS

1. Should DDT and other pesticides be banned from use in malaria control throughout the world? Explain. What are the alternatives?

2. Environmentalists argue that because essentially all pesticides eventually fail, their use should be phased out and farmers should be given economic incentives for switching to integrated pest management. Explain why you agree or disagree with this proposal.

3. Debate the following resolution: Because DDT and the other banned chlorinated hydrocarbon pesticides pose no demonstrable threat to human health and have saved millions of lives, they should again be approved for use in the United States.

4. Should certain types of foods used in the United States be irradiated? Explain.

5. What changes, if any, do you believe should be made to the Federal Insecticide, Fungicide, and Rodenticide Act regulating pesticide use in the United States?

6. Should U.S. companies continue to be allowed to export to other countries pesticides, medicines, and other chemicals that have been banned or severely restricted in the United States? Explain.

*7. How are bugs and weeds controlled on your yard and garden and on the grounds of your school and the public schools, parks, and playgrounds where you live? Consider mounting efforts to have integrated pest management and organic fertilizers used on school and public grounds. Do the same thing for your yard and garden.

CHAPTER 15

LAND RESOURCES: FORESTS, RANGELANDS, PARKS, AND WILDERNESS

General Questions and Issues

1. Why are the world's forests such important resources?

2. Why are tropical deforestation and fuelwood shortages serious global environmental and resource problems, and how should we deal with these problems?

3. What are the principal types of public lands in the United States, and how are they used?

4. How should forest resources be managed and conserved?

5. Why are rangelands important, and how should they be managed?

6. What problems do parks face, and how should parks be managed?

7. Why is wilderness important, and how much should be preserved?

We abuse land because we regard it as a commodity belonging to us. When we see land as a community to which we belong, we may begin to use it with love and respect.

ALDO LEOPOLD

DURING THE SECOND it takes for you to snap your fingers, an area of tropical forest almost the size of two football fields was destroyed, and roughly the same area of these incredibly diverse and important biomes was degraded. Such extensive tropical deforestation is happening every second of every day. This fact explains why most of the world's remaining tropical forests, as well as most of the remaining ancient forests in the northwestern United States (Figure 15-1 and photo on p. 287) and southwest Canada, will be gone within the next 30 to 40 years.

Forests, rangelands, parks, and wilderness are key land and biological resources that are coming under increasing stress (Table 1-1) from population growth and economic development. Preventing further destruction and degradation of these vital forms of Earth capital and healing those we have degraded are urgent priorities.

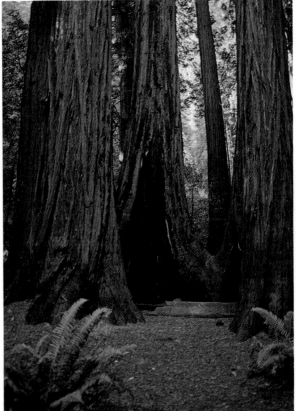

Chris Caldwell/NRDC

Figure 15-1 Sunlight filtering through a redwood forest in Muir Woods near the coast of northern California. At one time, large areas of these and other ancient forests covered much of the United States. Now most redwood forests have been cleared or have been eliminated by climate shifts. Many of the country's few remaining ancient forests, especially in the Northwest, are also being cleared rapidly for timber. At the same time, the U.S. government is urging tropical LDCs not to cut down most of their remaining ancient forests in order to protect Earth's biodiversity and to help delay projected global warming.

TYPES AND COMMERCIAL IMPORTANCE Today, about 34% of the world's land area is covered with potentially renewable forests. Principal types of these biomes include tropical rain forests (Figure 5-15), tropical deciduous forests, temperate deciduous forests (Figure 5-16), and evergreen coniferous forests (Figures 5-18 and 15-1).

Secondary forests are stands of trees resulting from secondary ecological succession (Figure 5-36). Most forests in the United States and other temperate areas are secondary forests that developed after the logging of virgin forests (forests not altered by human activity) or the abandonment of agricultural lands. About 40% of the forests in tropical areas are secondary forests.

Old-growth forests are virgin (uncut) and old second-growth forests containing massive trees that are often hundreds, sometimes thousands, of years old. Examples include forests of Douglas fir (see photo on p. 287), western hemlock, giant sequoia, and coastal redwoods (Figure 15-1) in the western United States; loblolly pine in the Southeast; and 60% of the world's tropical forests.

Forests supply us with lumber for housing, biomass for fuelwood, pulp for paper, medicines, and many other products worth more than $150 billion a year. Many forestlands are also used for mining, grazing livestock, and recreation.

ECOLOGICAL IMPORTANCE Forested watersheds act as giant sponges, slowing down runoff and absorbing and holding water that recharges springs, streams, and aquifers. Thus, they regulate the flow of water from mountain highlands to croplands and urban areas and help control soil erosion. This reduces the severity of flooding (see Case Study on p. 230) and the amount of sediment washing into streams, lakes, and artificial reservoirs.

Forests also play an important role in local, regional, and global climate. For example, about 50% to 80% of the moisture in the air above tropical forests comes from trees by transpiration and evaporation. If large areas of these forests are cleared, average annual precipitation decreases, and the region's climate gets hotter and drier so that their nutrient-poor soils (Figure 12-4) are depleted, baked, and washed away. Eventually, these changes can convert a diverse tropical forest into a sparse grassland or even a desert. Regeneration of a tropical forest on such areas may not be possible or, where it can occur, may take hundreds of years.

Figure 15-2 The cutting and burning of an area of tropical forest in Brazil's Amazon basin for growing crops.

Forests also play an important role in the global carbon cycle (Figure 4-22) and act as an important defense against projected global warming from an enhanced greenhouse effect (Figure 10-5). Through photosynthesis, trees help remove carbon dioxide from and add oxygen to the air, explaining why the world's forests have been called a key part of Earth's "lungs."

Forests provide habitats for a larger number of wildlife species than any other biome, making them the planet's principal reservoir of biological diversity (see Spotlight on p. 8). They also help buffer us against noise, absorb some air pollutants, and nourish the human spirit by providing solitude and beauty.

On a human time scale, all of Earth's remaining virgin forests should be considered nonrenewable resources. They should not be cut down, because their long-term ecological services are far more important than the short-term economic gain from removing them. According to one calculation, a typical tree provides $196,250 worth of ecological benefits in the form of oxygen, reduction of air pollution, soil fertility and erosion control, water recycling and humidity control, wildlife habitat, and protein for wildlife. Sold as timber, the same tree is worth only about $590. As long as the lasting and renewable ecological benefits of forests are assigned little or no value in the world's market-oriented economic systems (Section 7-2), we will continue to destroy and degrade these vital ecosystems.

Q: How rapidly are the world's remaining tropical forests vanishing?

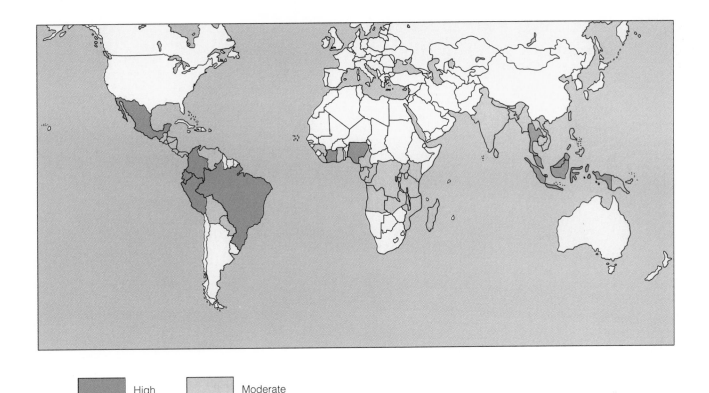

High   Moderate

Figure 15-3 Countries experiencing large annual destruction of tropical forests. (Data from UN Food and Agriculture Organization)

15-2 Tropical Deforestation, the Biodiversity Crisis, and the Fuelwood Crisis

DEFORESTATION AND DEGRADATION OF TROPICAL FORESTS Tropical forests are found near the equator in Latin America, Africa, and Asia and cover 6% to 7% of Earth's total land area (Figure 5-3). These irreplaceable storehouses of Earth's planetary biodiversity, which have existed for more than 100 million years, are being cleared and degraded for timber, cattle grazing, fuelwood, mining, and farming (Figure 15-2) at an alarming rate (Figure 15-3). The area of land now covered by tropical forests is about half what it once was, and the area of these forests cleared per year more than doubled in the 1980s. Three countries—Brazil (Figures 15-2, 15-3, and 15-4), Indonesia, and Zaire—account for 44% of the current annual loss. Brazil has more tropical forests and probably more of Earth's species than any other country.

According to the UN Food and Agriculture Organization and the World Resources Institute, satellite sensing shows that the world's tropical forests are vanishing at a rate of 171,000 square kilometers (66,000 square miles) a year—or about 37 city blocks every minute. It is estimated that an equal area of these forests is degraded every minute. For example, selective cutting

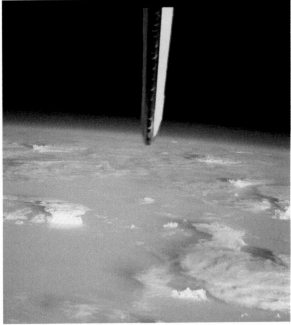

Figure 15-4 Photo taken from the space shuttle *Discovery* in September 1988 shows smoke from fires set to burn cleared areas of tropical rain forests in South America's Amazon River basin. The white areas that look like clouds are plumes of smoke. Because of international pressure and the elimination of new government subsidies to cattle ranchers, the amount of forest land cleared in Brazil dropped about 30% between 1988 and 1990.

A: 171,000 sq km (66,000 sq mi) a year—equal to about 37 city blocks a minute. An equal area is degraded.   Chapter 15   **325**

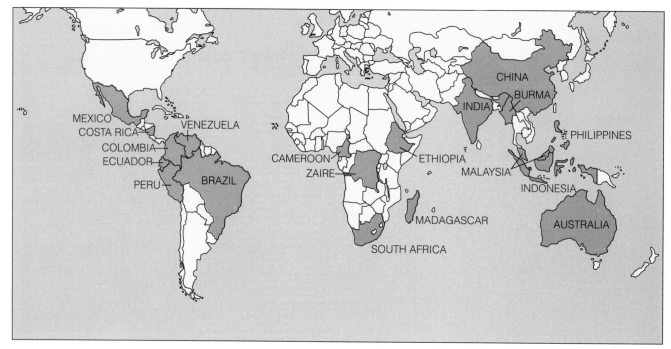

Figure 15-5 Earth's megadiversity countries. Conservationists believe that efforts should be concentrated on preserving repositories of Earth's biodiversity found in the remaining wild areas of these countries. For example, because of its astounding biological diversity, Madagascar, an island slightly smaller than Texas, is considered a crown jewel among Earth's ecosystems — a "biological superpower." The island's plant and animal species are also among the world's most endangered, mostly because of loss of habitat as a result of rapid population growth, poverty, and small-scale farming in increasingly densely populated rural areas. National and international efforts to slow the island's rapid slide into an environmental wasteland over the next 10 years can serve as a test case and a model for other areas. (Data from Conservation International and the World Wildlife Fund)

of prize trees in these dense forests is highly destructive — typically, 17 or more other trees are knocked down by logging equipment and road building for each tree removed. Reforestation in the tropics is proceeding at a snail's pace, with 10 trees cut for every 1 planted. In Africa, 29 are cut for each 1 planted.

If the current exponential rate of loss continues, all remaining tropical forests (except for a few preserved and vulnerable patches) will be gone within 30 to 50 years, and much sooner in some areas.

WHY SHOULD WE CARE ABOUT TROPICAL FORESTS? Conservationists and ecologists consider the present destruction and degradation of tropical forests one of the world's most serious environmental and resource problems (see Guest Essay on p. 353). These forests are the world's key storehouse of biological diversity — an irreplaceable genetic treasure that our present activities will destroy within a few decades unless we come to our senses. They provide homes for at least 50% (some estimate as much as 90%) of Earth's total stock of species (Figures 1-8, 15-5, 15-6, and photo on p. 1). Biologists Paul Ehrlich and Edward O. Wilson estimate that one-quarter or more of Earth's species could be eliminated within 50 years if current rates of tropical forest destruction and degradation continue.

No rate of extinction of this magnitude has occurred during the past 65 million years.

Tropical forests supply half of the world's annual harvest of hardwood. They also supply hundreds of food products, including coffee, spices, nuts, chocolate, and tropical fruits and industrial materials such as natural latex rubber, resins, dyes, and essential oils. A 1988 study by a team of scientists showed that sustainable harvesting of such nonwood products as nuts, fruits, and latex rubber tapped from trees (Figure 15-7) over 50 years would generate twice as much revenue per hectare as clearing these forests for timber and three times as much as cattle ranching.

Patches of tropical forest can also be cleared and used sustainably to raise crops by slash-and-burn and shifting cultivation (Figure 2-4). However, this method of farming is sustainable only for low-density populations of people and only if these plots are not cultivated or grazed for 10 to 30 years after their nutrient-poor soils are depleted (Figure 2-4).

The key active ingredients in one-fourth of the world's prescription and nonprescription drugs come from plants growing in tropical rain forests. Almost three-fourths of the 3,000 plants identified by the National Cancer Institute as having chemicals that fight cancer come from tropical rain forests. While you are reading this page, a plant species that can cure a type

Q: At current loss rates, when will most remaining tropical forests be gone?

Figure 15-6 The world's tropical forests are the planet's largest storehouse of biological diversity and contain between 50% and 90% of Earth's 40 to 100 million species. Two of these species are the red uakari monkey (left) in the Peruvian portion of the Amazon basin (Figure 6-12) and the keel-billed toucan in Belize, Central America (right). Most tropical forest species have specialized niches (Figure 4-28). This makes them highly vulnerable to extinction when their forest habitats are cleared or severely degraded.

Figure 15-7 Rubber tapping is a way to use tropical forests without destroying them. This photo, taken in 1987, shows Chico Mendes, leader of 70,000 Amazon rubber tappers in his Brazilian home state of Acre, making a cut on a rubber tree near the village of Xapuri. On December 22, 1988, he was murdered near his home in Xapuri by ranchers who opposed his internationally known efforts to protect Brazil's rain forests from unsustainable land clearing, colonization, and other destructive forms of development. In 1991, his assassins were convicted of murder.

of cancer, AIDS, or some other deadly disease could be wiped out forever.

Most of the original strains of rice, wheat, and corn that supply more than half of the world's food were developed from wild strains grown in the tropics. Scientists believe that undiscovered strains of these and tens of thousands of other plants that could be used as sources of new foods and genetically engineered varieties exist mostly in tropical forests.

Despite their immense potential, less than 1% of tropical forest plants have been examined for their possible use as human resources. Destroying these forests and many of the species they contain for short-term economic gain is like throwing away an unwrapped present or burning down an ancient library before you read the books.

Tropical forests are also home for 250 million people, many of whom survive by hunting and gathering

(Figure 2-3) or by slash-and-burn and shifting cultivation (Figure 2-4). Indigenous tribespeople are seeing their land bulldozed, burned, and flooded. They are being driven from their homelands and forced to adopt new ways that subject them to disease (against which they have little immunity because of their isolation from modern civilization), hunger, and cultural shock. Those who resist are often killed by ranchers, miners, and settlers.

Eliminating these people who are living gently on the earth is unethical and involves a tragic loss of ecological wisdom and cultural diversity that the rest of the world needs. These tribal people have more ecological knowledge about how to live sustainably in tropical forests and what plants can be used as foods and medicines than does anyone else, including the world's foremost tropical biologists.

Tropical forests also protect watersheds and regulate water flow for farmers, who grow food for more than 1 billion people in LDCs. The Environmental Policy Institute estimates that unless the destruction of tropical forests stops, the resulting loss of water and topsoil, along with flooding, will cause as many as 1 billion people to starve to death during the next 30 years.

Regardless of the economic, health, and ecological importance of tropical forests to us, people with a sustainable-Earth worldview (Section 2-3) believe that this destruction must be stopped because it is *wrong*. Over the next few decades, it could cause the premature extinction of at least 1 million species with as much right to exist, or struggle to exist, as we have.

CAUSES OF TROPICAL DEFORESTATION Tropical forests are being destroyed and degraded largely because of affluence, economic growth, development, profit, human dominance of the earth, and poverty. Much of the destruction and degradation of the world's tropical forests is caused by gigantic projects of multinational corporations and international lending agencies that finance resource extraction, mostly to support the affluent lifestyles of people in MDCs. These projects include

- Cattle ranches used mostly to produce raw and canned beef for export to MDCs

- Inefficient commercial logging and paper mills, with most of the logs and paper exported to MDCs

- Immense plantations of sugar cane and cash crops such as bananas and coffee, mostly for export to MDCs

- Growing of marijuana and cocaine-yielding coca, with most of these drugs smuggled into MDCs to supply the rapidly growing and highly profitable illegal drug trade

- Mining operations, with much of the extracted minerals exported to MDCs

- Dams, often used as sources of electric power for mining and smelting operations for minerals exported to MDCs

Governments of tropical countries feel driven to sell cash crops, timber, and minerals to MDCs at low prices to help finance economic growth and to pay interest on loans made by MDCs and international lending agencies controlled by MDCs (see Pro/Con on p. 329).

Since 1950, the consumption of tropical lumber has risen 15-fold, with Japan now accounting for 60% of the annual consumption. Although 68% of Japan is covered with forests, it prefers to deplete the forests of other countries (see Case Study on p. 331). Other leading importers of tropical hardwoods are the United States and Great Britain.

As the remaining supply of tropical timber in Asia is depleted in the 1990s, timber cutting in tropical forests will shift to Latin America and Africa. The World Bank estimates that of the 33 countries that are net exporters of tropical timber, only 10 will have any timber left to export by the year 2000.

Between 1965 and 1983, satellite photos showed that cattle ranches raising beef mostly for export to MDCs in Europe were responsible for 30% of the total deforestation in Brazil's portion of the Amazon basin. During the past 25 years, Central America has lost two-thirds of its tropical forests (Figure 15-3). Much of this land has been cleared and used as rangeland to raise beef for export to the United States, Canada, and western Europe. This imported beef is sold mostly to fast-food chains and food-processing companies for use in hamburgers, hot dogs, luncheon meats, chilis, stews, frozen dinners, and pet food.

The true cost of a quarter-pound hamburger made from cattle grazing on land that was once tropical forest is the destruction of half a metric ton (1,100 pounds) of the forest occupying an area roughly the size of a small kitchen (5 square meters or 54 square feet). This irreplaceable chunk of the planet's precious biodiversity and Earth's capital wealth was destroyed to save one cent on the price of a quick snack that doctors tell us is unhealthy for our hearts.

After being grazed for 5 to 10 years, tropical pastures can no longer be used for cattle. Often, torrential rains and overgrazing turn the nutrient-poor soils into eroded wastelands. Ranchers then move to another area and repeat the process. This destructive *shifting ranching* is often encouraged by government tax subsidies. Tropical forests in Latin America are also being cleared and used to grow soybeans that are exported to feed cattle in western Europe.

Environmental and consumer groups (especially the Rainforest Action Network in San Francisco) have

328

Q: What percentage of Earth's species live in tropical forests?

One-third of the world's tropical forests are found in South America's Amazon basin (Figure 6-12), which occupies an area equal in size to almost 90% of the land area of the continental United States. Although only about 10% of the tropical forests in this vast area have been destroyed, 80% of this deforestation has taken place since 1980 (Figures 15-2 and 15-3).

The Brazilian government's solution to widespread rural and urban poverty (see Case Study on p. 126) has been to send the landless poor off to chop down tropical forests in the Amazon basin, giving them title to the land they clear. These policies are supported and encouraged by wealthy landowners to help counteract political pressures for more equitable land distribution.

Much of this development is financed with loans from the World Bank and other international lending agencies (controlled by MDCs) and from MDCs, mostly for building roads and large dams. These roads open up the forests for logging, farming, ranching, mining, and other forms of development that destroy and degrade these once-inaccessible biomes. Government subsidies to ranchers, miners, and other exploiters who develop the Amazon have cost the debt-ridden Brazilian government more than $2.5 billion in lost revenue.

The more than 500,000 poor and dispossessed people who have migrated from the slums of Brazil's major cities and countryside to the Amazon in a desperate search for enough land to survive rarely improve their lives. Most contract malaria (see Case Study on p. 171). They must clear new plots every two to three years as the soil in earlier plots is depleted. Some of the new settlers are illegally driven off their land or killed by gunmen working for wealthy ranchers and cash-crop farmers trying to amass large land holdings. (The average price of a settler's life is $25.) After several years of further overexploitation, most of these lands are left in a severely de-graded state by agricultural squatters and usually end up in the hands of ranchers and cash-crop farmers.

In Brazil's Amazon territory of Roraima, the Yanomami—a Stone Age tribe of about 9,000—is fighting for its land and life. Since 1985, more than 45,000 gold miners have flooded into this remote area of Brazilian rain forest, bringing diseases that are killing off members of the Yanomami tribe. The miners have also carved more than 100 airstrips out of the rain forests, cleared and gouged out large portions of land, and poisoned nearby soil and water with toxic mercury used to extract gold from gold ore.

Conservationists, tribal people, rubber tappers (Figure 15-7), and others who believe these forests should be protected and used sustainably have mounted a global campaign to preserve 70% of the forests in the Amazon basin. They call for the government to set aside one-fourth of the Brazilian Amazon as *extractive reserves* managed by living off of nature's natural income instead of destroying Earth capital. Fruits, latexes (Figure 15-7), nuts, medicinal plants, and other valuable products would be harvested sustainably from these areas protected against cutting, mining, and other destructive forms of development. These areas would be owned by the national government but managed by local forest communities.

Environmentalists and Amazon tribal people also call for the government to set up large *indigenous reserves*, land for tribal people that would be protected from all forms of development. However, protecting land in the Amazon basin from destructive development is an uphill fight against powerful economic forces that want short-term economic gain from depleting this treasure house of potentially renewable Earth capital.

Brazilian officials argue that they must exploit the resources in these forests to help finance economic development and to help pay the interest on their huge foreign debt. They point out they are doing the same thing that the United States and other MDCs did to help finance their economic growth, including cutting down most of their native forests.

They resent being lectured by the United States and environmentalists about how they should use their resources when the United States has cleared 95% of the virgin forests that once covered its 48 lower states and is still encouraging rapid clearing of much of its remaining old-growth forests on private and public lands and replacement with tree farms (Figure 5-17). Canada, Sweden, and the CIS are doing the same thing to their old-growth northern coniferous forests.

The Brazilian government is going ahead with plans to build internationally financed highways to open up larger areas of the Amazon for development, despite objections by environmentalists and other governments. Brazilian government leaders ask, "How would Americans feel if the British or some other government told them that they should not build a highway from New York to California because it would destroy their forests? We have as much right to clear our wilderness as Americans did when they cleared most of theirs."

They point out that much of the timber, beef, and mineral resources removed from tropical forests in the Amazon basin are exported to support throwaway lifestyles in MDCs. Brazilian officials also argue that the world's MDCs are the biggest culprits behind global warming, ozone depletion, and the threat of nuclear war (Chapter 10).

In 1988, the Brazilian government temporarily suspended new subsidies and tax breaks for agricultural and ranching operations in the Amazon basin, but old subsidies remain for existing ranches and have already cost the debt-ridden government more than $2.5 billion in lost revenue. Since 1987, 14 extractive reserves covering about 0.8% of the
(continued)

Brazilian Amazon and three new national parks have been established. In 1990, the government expelled gold prospectors from Yanomami lands. Although vast areas of the Amazon are still cleared and burned, deforestation rates have slowed by about one-third since the peak year of 1987.

Environmentalists applaud these actions but fear that they are mostly window dressing to help defuse international pressures to protect much larger areas of the Amazon basin from development. Evidence for this came in 1991 when Brazil's government reinstated tax breaks for cattle ranches and other destructive developments and cut funds for identifying and setting aside indigenous and extractive reserves by 80%.

Since 1980, the Washington-based World Bank and the Inter-American Development Bank (both controlled by MDCs) have lent Brazil more than $82 billion for development of 166 hydropower dams and reservoirs, over half of them in the Amazon basin. Most of this power will be used to support mining, smelting, and other resource extraction industries, with most of the extracted resources exported to MDCs. These dams and reservoirs will displace about 500,000 people and flood vast areas of these forests.

With funding and technical advice from the World Bank, Japan, and the European community, Brazil seeks to exploit mineral deposits and encourage settlements in a mineral-rich area of the eastern Amazon twice the size of California. Smelters that will convert iron ore into pig iron will be powered by charcoal produced from wood. The cheapest way to get the charcoal is to chop down the surrounding forests and burn the trees. Environmentalists fear that this project will repeat the ecological disaster of a similar project in southeastern Brazil, where pig-iron production consumed nearly two-thirds of the area's forests.

Although tropical forests in the Amazon basin receive most of the attention, forests on Brazil's Atlantic Coast are even more threatened. As the populations of the nearby urban centers of Rio de Janeiro and São Paulo (Figure 6-12) have skyrocketed, the area of these forests has shrunk by 90%, with only a few fragments left. The 1990 war in the Middle East accelerated destruction of these forests. When the war erupted, the Brazilian government raised the price of fuel, causing many rural people to return to the use of wood (cut from Atlantic Coast forests) for cooking—another example of how everything is connected. Conservationists urge that preserving the remaining fragments should be the top priority in all of South America. What do you think should be done about economic development and forest preservation in the Amazon basin and in the rest of Brazil?

organized boycotts of hamburger chains buying beef imported from Central America and other tropical countries. Because of these efforts, many large chains claim they no longer buy beef from tropical countries, but such claims are quite difficult to verify. In some cases, cattle raised in a tropical country are imported to the United States or other MDCs and slaughtered there. This allows hamburger chains and other meat processors to claim they are using American beef.

Environmentalists call for a ban on all beef or beef products raised on cleared land in tropical forests. This would encourage tropical countries to raise beef on existing rangeland (which could double or triple meat yields with improved management) and to stop giving ranchers the subsidies needed to make raising beef on cleared tropical forestland profitable.

Tropical forests are also destroyed by the landless poor who migrate there, hoping to get enough land to survive. They are driven there by a combination of rapid population growth, the global poverty trap (Section 7-4), and ownership of much of the arable land by a few wealthy people. Their small-scale farming is the largest single cause of tropical deforestation, followed by commercial logging and cattle ranching. This mass migration of poor people to tropical forests would not be possible without the internationally financed projects that build roads and open up these usually inaccessible areas.

REDUCING THE DESTRUCTION AND DEGRADATION OF TROPICAL FORESTS Destruction of most of the world's remaining virgin tropical forests (and other virgin and ancient secondary forests) and much of their biodiversity is a devastating global biological war against ourselves, our children and grandchildren, and other species. Because in our interconnected global markets, we are all involved in the destruction of rain forests, we all have a responsibility to correct this situation. We can do so by carefully considering what we buy and promoting and supporting government policies such as those suggested in the remainder of this section.

Q: What percentage of tropical forest species have been studied for their possible use as human resources?

As Japan has developed into a leading economic power, its impact on the global environment has grown rapidly. Japan's control of industrial pollution is one of the best in the world. Its control of urban air pollution is better than that in the United States. It is also the world's most energy-efficient country.

Because of its lack of domestic resources, Japan has one of the highest resource recycling rates in the world, using a sophisticated resource recovery system. During the 1960s, Japan sharply cut its rate of population growth and now has an annual population growth rate half that of the United States.

Japan has preserved most of its forests. Like most other MDCs, however, Japan has not shown a high regard for nature outside its boundaries, causing the World Wildlife Fund in 1989 to name Japan as the world's worst *eco-outlaw*. Japan is the world's largest importer of low-cost tropical hardwoods, resulting in the deforestation of vast tracts in Asian forests. Most of this wood is used to make throwaway plywood forms for molding concrete, furniture, buildings, and about 24 billion pairs of throwaway chopsticks a year.

Because Asian tropical forests will be stripped of timber within 15 years, Japan is now shifting its operations to tropical forests in Brazil and other parts of South America. Diverse, old-growth stands of timber in U.S. national forests in the states of Washington, Oregon, and Alaska have also been clear-cut and sold to Japan at bargain prices. In 1990, two Japanese pulp-and-paper companies obtained 20-year logging rights to clear-cut 15% of the old-growth forests in Canada's province of Alberta. Japan's giant Mitsubishi Corporation has offered to pay off Brazil's entire national debt in exchange for exclusive mineral rights to the country's gold-rich land in the Amazon basin.

Japan is also the world's largest illegal consumer and importer of endangered and threatened plant and animal species. Large amounts of rare orchids and endangered ornamental plants are imported by Japan. Over the years, thousands of elephants have been slaughtered for valuable ivory imported to Japan. In 1989, Japan bowed to international pressure to support a ban on the trade of ivory obtained from African elephants (Figure 5-9). However, the Japanese then asked the Soviets to sell them ivory from the tusks of long-extinct woolly mammoths buried under permafrost in Siberia.

Recently, Japan has moved to reduce or ban imports of four endangered species. However, its government has used a provision in the Convention on International Trade of Endangered Species to exempt itself from bans on imports of 10 endangered species. Increased illegal killing (poaching) of endangered and other wildlife in the United States and other countries is fueled by Japan, Hong Kong, and South Korea (see Spotlight on p. 362). For example, black bears are killed illegally and their gallbladders are removed and sold to these countries for use as folk medicines. The paws are also cut off and used to make soups and ashtrays.

Until commercial whaling was banned from 1987 to 1992, Japan was the world's leading whaling nation. It still takes several hundred Minke whales for "scientific" purposes. Although the International Whaling Commission says this killing does not qualify for research, Japan has refused to stop the practice and works to have the ban on commercial whaling lifted. They view whales as an important source of food, the same way Americans see cattle.

Japan's huge fishing industry has been criticized for its use of large drift nets across great expanses of the Pacific Ocean (Figure 13-13). These nets — called "curtains of death" by environmentalists — are intended to catch mostly tuna and squid, but also catch and kill hundreds of thousands of dolphins, porpoises, seals, and seabirds. Their use can also deplete stocks of commercially valuable fish. Japan has agreed to stop using these nets by 1992.

Since 1990, Japan has been the world's largest donor of aid to LDCs. But most of this aid is commercially oriented; favors trading partners in Asia; provides low-interest loans rather than grants; and supports large-scale projects such as roads, dams, power plants, and mines, which have severe environmental impacts. The Japanese government has been unwilling to require that environmental impact assessments be made before these projects are approved.

A 1989 survey of 14 countries by the United Nations Environment Programme rated the Japanese people lowest in environmental concern and awareness. Japan is the only MDC that doesn't have a national-level environmental movement of any strength.

On the positive side, Japan has ratified the international treaty to protect the ozone layer, supported international efforts to slow global warming, and taken a leadership role in developing fuel-efficient cars and energy-efficient industrial processes. In 1991, Japan announced plans to become the global leader in developing environmental and renewable-energy technology and in transferring modern environmental and pollution-control technology to LDCs. If Japan uses its economic and technological power to become a major force in helping sustain the Earth, it could dominate one of the major economic-growth markets of the 1990s and beyond, turn its critics into admirers, and stimulate other MDCs to follow its lead.

In 1984, biologist Thomas Lovejoy suggested that debtor nations willing to protect some of their natural resources should be eligible for discounts or credits against some of their debts. With such **debt-for-nature swaps**, a certain amount of foreign debt is canceled in exchange for local currency investments that will improve natural resource management in the debtor country. Typically, a conservation or other organization buys a certain amount of a country's debt from a bank at a discount rate and negotiates a debt-for-nature swap.

In 1987, Conservation International, a private U.S. banking consortium, paid $100,000 to a Swiss bank to buy up $650,000 of Bolivia's $5.7 billion foreign debt. In exchange for forgiveness of this part of its debt, Bolivia agreed to protect 1.5 million hectares (3.7 million acres) of tropical forest around its existing Beni Biosphere Reserve in the Amazon basin from harmful forms of development (Figure 15-8). The government was to establish maximum legal protection for the reserve and create a $250,000 fund, with the interest to be used to manage the reserve.

This land is supposed to be a model of how conservation of forest and wildlife resources can be mixed with sustainable economic development (Figure 15-8). The core of this land is a virgin tropical forest to be set aside as a biological reserve. It will be surrounded by a protective buffer of savanna to be used for sustainable grazing of livestock.

Controlled commercial logging, as well as hunting and fishing by local natives, will be permitted in some of the forest in the tract. Logging will not be allowed in the mountain area above the tract, to protect the area's watershed and to prevent erosion.

However, by 1992, five years after the agreement was signed, the Bolivian government had not provided legal protection for the reserve. It also waited until April 1989 to contribute only $100,000 to the reserve management fund. Meanwhile, with approval from the Bolivian government, timber companies have cut thousands of mahogany trees from the area, with most of this lumber exported to the United States.

One lesson learned from this first debt-for-nature swap is that the legislative and budget requirements should be established before the swap is made. Another is that such swaps need to be carefully monitored by environmental organizations to be sure that paper proposals labeled as models of sustainable development are not ways to disguise eventually unsustainable development. Debt-for-nature swaps are an excellent idea if they lead to true protection or restoration of some of Earth's remaining natural areas.

Since 1987, a number of these arrangements have been made. This method will not solve the problem of the destruction and degradation of tropical forests and other natural systems, but it is an important tool for protecting priority areas.

Figure 15-8 Mixing economic development and conservation in a 1.5-million-hectare (3.7-million-acre) tract in Bolivia. A U.S. conservation organization arranged a debt-for-nature swap to help protect this land from harmful forms of development.

To reduce the severity of this unnecessary catastrophe, environmentalists believe that over the next 10 years we need to do a number of things:

Prevention (Input) Approaches

- Establish an international ban on imports of timber, wood products, beef, and other goods that directly or indirectly destroy or degrade existing virgin tropical forests.

- Ban the burning of tropical forests (Figure 15-4), which accounts for 75% of the deforestation and releases large amounts of carbon dioxide into the atmosphere.

- Fully fund the Rapid Assessment Program (RAP), which sends teams of highly qualified tropical biologists to gather ecological data rapidly on "hot spots," imperiled tracts of tropical forests that are the most deserving of protection.

Q: How much of the tropical forests in South America's Amazon basin have been destroyed?

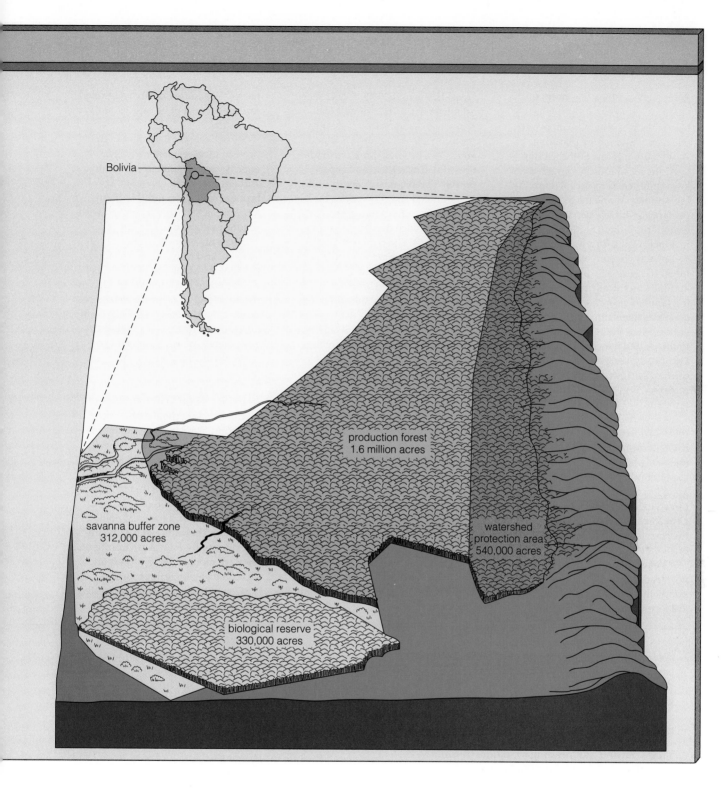

Bolivia

production forest
1.6 million acres

savanna buffer zone
312,000 acres

watershed
protection area
540,000 acres

biological reserve
330,000 acres

- Provide aid and debt relief for tropical countries that ban commercial logging, cattle ranching, and other destructive uses of virgin tropical forests and that emphasize sustainable harvesting of rubber, nuts, fruits, and other renewable resources. So far, only 0.1% of the world's area of tropical forest is managed sustainably.

- Set aside large areas of the world's tropical forests as reserves and parks protected from unsustain-

able development. The key is to get local people involved in the protection of such areas by showing them how to profit from using these areas sustainably (see Case Study on p. 332).

- Use debt-for-nature swaps and conservation easements to encourage countries to protect areas of tropical forests or other valuable natural systems. In a *debt-for-nature swap*, participating tropical countries act as custodians for protected forest

Because Costa Rica (Figure 15-9) abolished its army in 1949, it has been able to spend more on health, education, and family planning. As a result, it is one of the leading LDCs in social indicators such as lower infant and maternal mortality, higher literacy, and longer life expectancy (which is two years longer than in the United States).

Once, Costa Rica was almost completely covered with tropical forests (Figure 2-5). Between 1963 and 1983, politically powerful ranching families cleared much of the country's forests to graze cattle, with most of the beef exported to the United States and western Europe. By 1983, only 17% of the country's original tropical forest remained and soil erosion was rampant.

Many small landholders lost their land to ranchers, and rural jobs dried up because ranching requires much less labor than growing crops. Large numbers of landless poor migrated to expanding cities or were forced to farm fragile slopes or to clear forests in ways that accelerated the country's deforestation and soil erosion.

The bright note is that Costa Rica now leads all tropical countries in efforts to protect its remaining tropical forests and restore degraded areas. In the mid-1970s, Costa Rica established a system of national parks and reserves that presently protects 12% of the country's land area. Despite widespread degradation, tiny Costa Rica is a "superpower" of biological diversity, with an estimated 500,000 species of plants and animals living on a land mass only twice the size of Vermont (Figure 15-5). The country's plan is to combine conservation and sustainable economic development and to expand protected areas to 25% of the country's land by the end of this century.

A rugged mountainous region with a tropical rain forest contains the Guanacaste National Park, which has been designated an international biosphere reserve. One of the country's most visible projects is the restoration of the tropical deciduous forest in this park, the world's first project of this kind.

Daniel Janzen, professor of biology at the University of Pennsylvania in Philadelphia, has helped galvanize international support for this restoration project. Janzen is a leader in the growing field of rehabilitation and restoration of degraded ecosystems. His vision is to make the nearly 40,000 local people who live near the park an essential part of the restoration of 70,000 hectares (270 square miles) of degraded forest—a concept he calls *biocultural restoration*.

By actively participating in the project, local residents will reap enormous educational, economic, and environmental benefits. Local farmers have been hired to plant large areas with tree seeds and with seedlings started in Janzen's lab.

Students in grade schools, high schools, and universities will study the ecology of the park in the classroom and go on annual field trips in the park itself. There will also be educational programs for civic groups and tourists from Costa Rica and elsewhere. These visitors and activities will stimulate the local economy.

The project will also serve as a training ground in tropical forest restoration for scientists throughout the world. Research scientists working on the project will give guest lectures in classrooms and lead some of the field trips.

Janzen recognizes that in 20 to 40 years, these children will be running the park and the local political system. If they understand the importance of their local environment, they are more likely to protect and sustain its biological resources.

Costa Rica is making a dedicated effort to protect and sustain much

reserves in return for foreign aid or relief from some of their debt (see Case Study on p. 332). With *conservation easements*, a country, a private organization, or a consortium of countries compensates individual countries for protecting specific natural habitats selected on a priority basis.

- Phase out and halt funding for dams, tree and crop plantations, ranches, roads, colonization programs, and destructive types of tourism on any land now covered by virgin tropical forests.

- Require responsible and well-supervised logging practices and reforestation on all tropical forestlands approved for timber cutting (secondary forests and existing tree plantations), and ban all logging of virgin tropical forests.

- Reforest 5 million square kilometers (2 million square miles, about the size of the continental United States) of the 8 million square kilometers (3 million square miles) of deforested land in tropical countries with fast-growing trees. This would cost about $20 billion a year for a decade but could save much more by helping slow projected greenhouse warming and helping preserve planetary biodiversity.

- Include indigenous tribal peoples, women, and private local conservation organizations in the planning and execution of tropical forestry plans.

- Give indigenous people title to tropical forest lands that they and their ancestors have lived on sustainably for centuries, with the stipulations that these lands cannot be developed in unsustainable ways and cannot be sold. The Colombian government is giving indigenous tribes complete control of two-thirds of the country's land area in the Amazon basin with the provision that they must never sell the land.

Q: What country is the largest importer of tropical lumber?

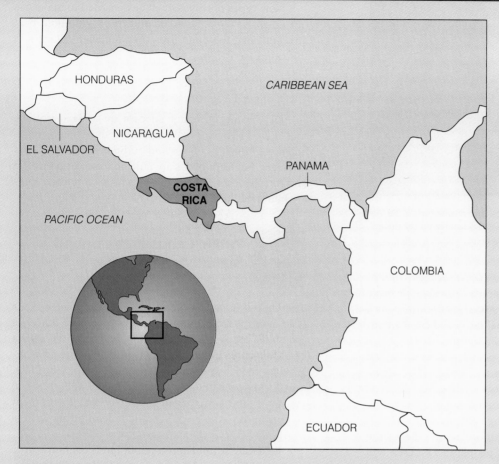

Figure 15-9 Where is Costa Rica? This country, smaller than West Virginia, has a population of 3.2 million and an annual population growth rate of 2.4%. Average total fertility is 3.3 children per woman, and population size is projected to reach 5.6 million by 2025. Annual per capita GNP is $1,910.

of its remaining storehouse of the planet's biodiversity. However, it is waging an uphill fight against the highest rate of deforestation in Latin America, rapid population growth, air and water pollution, pesticide contamination, and the ever-present pressure of wealthy individual and multinational interests to overexploit its resources for short-term profit. At the present rate of deforestation, most of the country's forests could disappear in less than 15 years.

- Require an extensive environmental impact evaluation for any proposed development project in tropical forests, and use internationally accepted standards for such studies. Carefully monitor funded projects, and halt further funding when abuse occurs.

- Prevent banks and international lending agencies from lending money for environmentally destructive projects involving tropical forests. The key is to regulate road building, the crucial step leading to the disappearance of an untouched forest.

- Exert political and consumer pressure (boycotts) on large U.S., Japanese, and British timber, paper, meat-processing, and food companies now involved in destructive development projects in tropical forests.

- Pressure elected officials to not approve portions of the international General Agreement on Tariffs and Trade (GATT) that weaken environmental protection in the name of free trade by giving transnational corporations a charter to exploit the earth with fewer controls. For example, if a government wanted to stop the export of a country's tropical hardwoods or other resources or ban the import of toxic wastes, it could be accused of violating the principles of free trade being proposed in this agreement.

- Support effective family planning and programs that attack the root causes of poverty, including unequal distribution of farmland.

Restoration (Output) Approaches

- Rehabilitate degraded tropical forests and watersheds (see Case Study on p. 334).

- Provide financial incentives to villagers and village organizations to establish fuelwood trees and tree plantations for growing fuelwood and timber on abandoned and degraded land with suitable soil.

A: Japan (followed by the United States and Great Britain)

Figure 15-10 Making fuel briquettes from cow dung in India. As fuelwood becomes scarce, more people collect and burn dung, depriving the soil of an important source of plant nutrients.

THE FUELWOOD CRISIS IN LDCS Almost 70% of the people in LDCs rely on biomass as their primary fuel for heating and cooking. About half of this comes from burning wood or charcoal produced from wood, 33% from crop residues, and 17% from dung.

By 1985, about 1.5 billion people—almost one out of every three persons on Earth—in 63 LDCs either could not get enough fuelwood to meet their basic needs or were forced to meet their needs by consuming wood faster than it was being replenished. The UN Food and Agriculture Organization projects that by the end of this century, 3 billion people in 77 LDCs will experience a fuelwood crisis.

Fuelwood scarcity leads to several harmful effects in addition to deforestation and accelerated soil erosion. It places an additional burden on the poor, especially women. Often, they must walk long distances to find and carry home bundles of fuelwood. Buying fuelwood or charcoal can take 40% of a poor family's meager income. Poor families who can't get enough fuelwood often burn dried animal dung and crop residues for cooking and heating (Figure 15-10). This keeps these natural fertilizers from reaching the soil and reduces cropland productivity, creating a vicious circle of land degradation that helps lock the poor in the poverty trap.

LDCs can reduce the severity of the fuelwood crisis by planting more fast-growing fuelwood trees such as the leucaenas and acacias, burning wood more efficiently, and switching to other fuels, such as the sun-dried roots of various common gourds and squashes. Experience has shown that planting projects are most successful when local people, especially women, are involved in their planning and implementation. Programs work best when village farmers own the land or are given ownership of any trees grown on land owned by a village. This gives them a strong incentive to plant and protect trees for their own use and for sale. The governments of China, Nepal, Senegal, and South Korea have established successful tree-planting programs at the village level in selected areas.

New types of stoves must be designed to make use of locally available materials and to provide both heat and light like the open fires they replace. Villagers in Burkina Faso in West Africa have been shown how to make a stove from mud and dung that cuts wood use by 30% to 70%. It can be made by villagers in half a day at virtually no cost.

Despite encouraging success in some countries, most LDCs suffering from fuelwood shortages have inadequate forestry policies and budgets and lack trained foresters. Such countries are cutting trees for fuelwood and forest products 10 to 20 times faster than new trees are being planted.

15-3 Public Lands in the United States: An Overview

The United States has set aside a larger portion of its land area for the public's use and enjoyment than has any other country. About 42% of all U.S. land consists of public lands owned jointly by all citizens and managed for them by federal (see Spotlight on p. 338), state, and local governments. Over one-third (35%) of the country's land is managed by the federal government (Figure 15-11). About 95% of this federal public land is in Alaska (73%) and in western states (22%).

Federally administered public lands contain a large portion of the country's commercial timber (40%), grazing land (54%), and energy resources (especially shale oil, uranium, coal, and geothermal) and most of its copper, silver, asbestos, lead, molybdenum, beryllium, phosphate, and potash. For example, $3.9 billion in minerals are mined each year from public lands with no royalty paid to the public. Each year these mining activities cause an estimated $11 billion in environmental damage. Through various laws, Congress has allowed private individuals and corporations to harvest or extract many of these resources—often at below-market prices. Because of the economic value of these resources, there has been a long and continuing history of conflict between resource extractors and conservationists over management and use of these public lands.

Since the early 1900s the American conservation movement has been split into two schools of thought, the *preservationists* and the *scientific conservationists*. Preservationists emphasize protecting large areas of public lands from mining, timbering, and other forms of economic development and environmental degradation.

In contrast, scientific conservationists see public lands as resources to be used now to enhance economic growth and national strength. They believe that the

Q: How much of the world's area of tropical forests is managed sustainably?

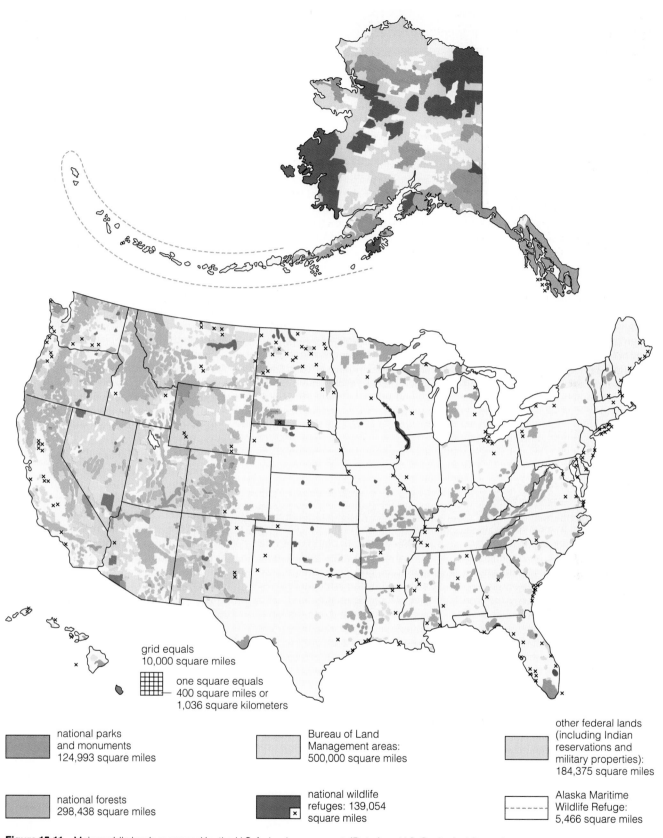

grid equals
10,000 square miles

one square equals
400 square miles or
1,036 square kilometers

national parks
and monuments
124,993 square miles

national forests
298,438 square miles

Bureau of Land
Management areas:
500,000 square miles

national wildlife
refuges: 139,054
square miles

other federal lands
(including Indian
reservations and
military properties):
184,375 square miles

Alaska Maritime
Wildlife Refuge:
5,466 square miles

Figure 15-11 Major public lands managed by the U.S. federal government. (Data from U.S. Geological Survey)

Multiple-Use Lands

National Forests The forest system includes 156 national forests and 19 national grasslands managed by the Forest Service. Excluding the 15% protected as wilderness areas, this land is supposed to be managed according to the principles of sustainable yield and multiple use. According to the *principle of sustainable yield*, a potentially renewable resource should not be harvested or used faster than it is replenished throughout the world or in a particular area. *Multiple use* means that public forests are to be managed to allow a variety of uses *on the same land, at the same time.* Currently, national forests are used for timbering, mining, grazing, agriculture, oil and gas leasing, recreation, sport hunting, sport and commercial fishing, and conservation of watershed, soil, and wildlife resources. Off-road vehicles are usually restricted to designated routes.

National Resource Lands These lands are mostly grassland, prairie, desert, scrub forest, and other open spaces located in the western states and Alaska. They are managed by the Bureau of Land Management under the *principle of multiple use.* Emphasis is on providing a secure domestic supply of energy and strategically important nonenergy minerals and on preserving the renewability of rangelands for livestock grazing under a permit system. About 10% of these lands are being evaluated for possible designation as wilderness areas.

Moderately Restricted-Use Lands

National Wildlife Refuges This system includes 456 refuges and various ranges managed by the Fish and Wildlife Service. About 24% of this land is protected as wilderness areas. The purpose of most refuges is to protect habitats and breeding areas for waterfowl and big-game animals to provide a harvestable supply for hunters. A few refuges have been set aside to save specific endangered species from extinction. These lands are not officially managed under the principles of multiple use and sustained yield. Nevertheless, sport hunting, trapping, sport and commercial fishing, oil and gas development, mining (old claims only), timber cutting, livestock grazing, and farming are permitted as long as the Secretary of the Interior finds such uses compatible with the purposes of each unit.

Restricted-Use Lands

National Parks This system consists of 359 units. They include 50 major parks (mostly in the West) and 307 national recreation areas, monuments, memorials, battlefields, historic sites, parkways, trails, rivers, seashores, and lakeshores. All are managed by the National Park Service. Its management goals are to preserve scenic and unique natural landscapes, preserve and interpret the country's historic and cultural heritage, provide protected wildlife habitats, protect wilderness areas within the parks, and provide certain types of recreation. National parks may be used only for camping, hiking, sport fishing, and motorized and nonmotorized boating. Motor vehicles are permitted only on roads, and off-road vehicles are not allowed. National recreation areas can be used for the same activities as national parks plus sport hunting, new mining claims, and new oil and gas leasing. About 49% of the land in the National Park System is protected as wilderness areas.

National Wilderness Preservation System This system includes 474 roadless areas within the national parks, national wildlife refuges, and national forests. They are managed, respectively, by the National Park Service, the Forest Service, and the Fish and Wildlife Service. These areas are to be preserved in their essentially untouched condition "for the use and enjoyment of the American people in such a manner as will leave them unimpaired for future use and enjoyment as wilderness." Wilderness areas are open only for recreational activities such as hiking, sport fishing, camping, nonmotorized boating, and, in some areas, sport hunting and horseback riding. Roads, timber harvesting, grazing, mining, commercial activities, and human-made structures are prohibited, except where such activities occurred before an area's designation as wilderness. Motorized vehicles, boats, and equipment are banned except for emergency uses such as fire control and rescue operations. However, aircraft are allowed to land in Alaskan wilderness areas.

---

government must protect these lands from degradation by managing them efficiently and scientifically for *sustainable yield* and *multiple use.*

The controversy between these two groups continues today. Since 1980, public agencies managing these lands have, little by little, yielded to pressure for more grazing, more roads, more timber cutting, more mining, more resorts in national parks, and more drilling for oil and natural gas.

Currently, a group of ranchers, loggers, oil companies, mining and land developing companies and associations, and off-road vehicle recreational associations are spearheading an anti-environmental movement known as the "wise-use or multiple-use movement." Some of their major goals are to open up Alaska's Arctic National Wildlife Refuge for oil drilling (see Pro/Con on p. 370), clear-cutting all old-growth forests and replacing them with tree farms, setting aside national forest lands exclusively for logging, building off-road vehicle trails in roadless areas of federal lands, and opening up all federal lands—including national parks and wilderness areas—for mining and energy production. Environmentalists call this movement the "multiple-abuse," "unwise-use," or "overuse movement."

Q: What percentage of the people in LDCs rely on biomass (mostly wood) for heating and cooking?

15-4 Forest Management and Conservation

TYPES OF FOREST MANAGEMENT Although crops can be harvested annually, trees take 20 to 1,000 years to mature. There are two basic forest management systems: even-aged management and uneven-aged management. With **even-aged management**, trees in a given stand are maintained at about the same age and size, harvested all at once, and replanted naturally or artificially so a new even-aged stand will grow. Growers emphasize mass production of low-quality wood with the goal of maximizing economic return on investment in as short a time as possible.

Even-aged management begins with the cutting of all or most trees from a diverse, old-growth (Figure 15-1) or secondary forest. Then the site is replanted with an even-aged stand, or *tree farm*, of a single species (monoculture) of faster-growing softwoods (Figure 5-17). Tree farms need close supervision and usually require expensive inputs of fertilizers and pesticides to protect the monoculture species from diseases and insects. Once the trees reach maturity, the entire stand is harvested and the area is replanted with seeds or seedlings. Genetic crossbreeding and genetic engineering can be used to improve both the quality and the quantity of wood produced from tree farms.

With **uneven-aged management**, trees in a given stand are maintained at many ages and sizes to permit continuous natural regeneration. Here, the goals are to sustain biological diversity, maintain long-term production of high-quality timber, provide a reasonable economic return, and allow multiple use of a forest stand. The emphasis is on selective cutting of mature trees, with clear-cutting used only on small patches of tree species that benefit from this type of harvesting.

TREE HARVESTING The method chosen for harvesting depends on whether uneven-aged or even-aged forest management is being used. It also depends on the tree species involved, the nature of the site, and the objectives and resources of the owner.

In **selective cutting**, intermediate-aged or mature trees in an uneven-aged forest are cut singly or in small groups (Figure 15-12). This reduces crowding, encourages the growth of younger trees, maintains an uneven-aged stand with trees of different species, ages, and sizes, and allows natural regeneration of trees. It also decreases the fire hazard because the volume of wood debris (slash) left after harvest is reduced. If done properly, selective cutting also helps protect the site from soil erosion and tree damage and blowdown by the wind.

Selective cutting is costly unless the value of the trees removed is high, and maintaining a good mixture of tree ages and sizes takes considerable planning and skill. It's not useful for shade-intolerant species, which require full sunlight for seedling growth. The need to reopen roads and trails periodically for selective harvests can cause erosion of certain soils.

One type of selective cutting, not considered a sound forestry practice, is *high grading*, or *creaming*—removing the most valuable trees without considering the quality or the distribution of the remaining trees needed for regeneration. Many loggers in tropical forests in LDCs use this destructive form of selective cutting. For example, 100 trees may be destroyed just to remove 1 mature mahogany tree in a tropical forest.

Some tree species do best when grown in full or moderate sunlight in forest openings or in large cleared and seeded areas. Even-aged stands or tree farms of such shade-intolerant species are usually harvested by shelterwood cutting, seed-tree cutting, or clear-cutting.

Shelterwood cutting is the removal of all mature trees in an area in a series of cuttings, typically over a period of ten years. This technique can be applied to even-aged or uneven-aged stands. In the first harvest, selected mature trees; unwanted tree species; and dying, defective, and diseased trees are removed. This cut opens up the forest floor to light and leaves the best trees to cast seed and provide shelter for growing seedlings (Figure 15-13).

After a number of seedlings have taken hold, a second cutting removes more of the remaining mature trees. Some of the best mature trees are left to provide shelter for the growing young trees. After the young trees are well established, a third cutting removes the remaining mature trees and allows the even-aged stand of young trees to grow to maturity.

This method allows natural seeding from the best seed trees and protects seedlings from being crowded out. It leaves a fairly natural-looking forest that can be used for a variety of purposes. It also helps reduce soil erosion and provides good habitat for wildlife.

Without careful planning and supervision, however, loggers may take too many trees in the initial cutting, especially the most valuable trees. Shelterwood cutting is also more costly and takes more skill and planning than clear-cutting.

Seed-tree cutting harvests nearly all the trees on a site in one cutting, leaving a few seed-producing, wind-resistant trees uniformly distributed as a source of seed to regenerate a new crop of trees (Figure 15-14). After the new trees have become established, the seed trees are sometimes harvested.

By allowing a variety of species to grow at one time, seed-tree cutting leaves an aesthetically pleasing forest, useful for recreation, deer hunting, erosion control, and wildlife conservation. Leaving the best trees for seed can also lead to genetic improvement in the new stand.

Clear-cutting is the removal of all trees from a given area in a single cutting to establish a new even-aged stand or tree farm. The clear-cut area may consist of a whole stand (Figures 15-2 and 15-15), a group, a strip, or a series of patches (Figure 15-16). After all trees are cut,

Figure 15-12 Selective cutting of ponderosa pine in Deschutes National Forest, an old-growth forest near Sisters, Oregon.

Figure 15-13 First stage of shelterwood cutting of a stand of longleaf pine in southern Alabama.

Figure 15-14 Seed trees left after the seed-tree cutting of a stand of longleaf pine in Alabama. About 10 trees per hectare are left to reseed the area.

the site is reforested naturally from seed released by the harvest, or foresters broadcast seed over the site or plant genetically superior seedlings raised in a nursery. If clear-cut areas are kept small enough, seeding may occur from trees in adjacent areas.

Currently, almost two-thirds of the annual U.S. timber production and about one-third of the cutting in national forests is harvested by clear-cutting. Clear-cutting increases the volume of timber harvested per hectare, reduces road building, often permits reforesting with genetically improved stock of fast-growing trees, and shortens the time needed to establish a new stand of trees. Timber companies prefer this method because it requires much less skill and planning than other harvesting methods and usually gives them the maximum economic return.

Large-scale clear-cutting on steeply sloped land leads to severe soil erosion, sediment water pollution, flooding from melting snow and heavy rains (see Case Study on p. 230), and landslides. The heavy logging equipment also compacts the soil and reduces its pro-

ductivity. As a result, such slopes often remain barren wastelands (Figure 1-1).

Clear-cutting leaves ugly, unnatural forest openings that take decades to regenerate (Figures 15-2 and 15-16) and reduces the recreational value of the forest. It also reduces the number and types of wildlife habitats and thus reduces biological diversity. Trees in stands bordering clear-cut areas are more vulnerable to blow-down by windstorms.

If properly done, clear-cutting can be useful for some shade-intolerant species, such as the Douglas fir. That means not clear-cutting large areas or steeply sloped sites and making sure that the area is reseeded or replanted and protected until the next harvest. The problem is that timber companies have a built-in economic incentive to use large-scale clear-cutting, often on species that could be harvested by less environmentally destructive methods.

PROTECTING FORESTS FROM PATHOGENS AND INSECTS In a healthy, diverse forest, tree diseases (especially those caused by parasitic fungi) and insect populations rarely get out of control and seldom destroy many trees. However, a tree farm of one species has few natural defenses and is vulnerable to attack by pathogens and insects.

The best and cheapest way to prevent excessive damage to trees from diseases and insects is to preserve forest biological diversity. Other methods include:

- Banning imported timber that might carry harmful parasites

- Removing infected trees and vegetation

- Clear-cutting infected areas and removing or burning all debris

- Treating diseased trees with antibiotics

- Developing disease-resistant tree species

Q: How many people cannot find or buy enough fuelwood to meet their basic needs?

Figure 15-15 Forest Service clear-cut in Oregon. All trees in the area are removed and the area is reseeded.

Figure 15-16 Patch clear-cutting and logging roads in Gifford Pinchot National Forest, Washington. This method of cutting destroys diverse ancient forests and fragments what remains into patches or islands that are often too small and too isolated to support some of the species that live in these biomes. After an area is clear-cut, the debris is burned, leaving a blackened soil, studded with tombstonelike stumps. A Forest Service ranger conceded that the clear-cut area looks "as if it had been nuked."

■ Applying insecticides and fungicides (Section 14-1)

■ Using integrated pest management (Section 14-5)

PROTECTING FORESTS FROM FIRES Occasional natural fires set by lightning are an important part of the ecological cycle of many forests. Some species, especially conifers such as pines and redwoods (Figure 15-1), have thick, fire-resistant bark and benefit from occasional fires. For example, the seeds of some conifers, such as the giant sequoia and the jack pine, are released or germinate only after being exposed to intense heat.

In evaluating the effects of fire on forest ecosystems, it's important to distinguish between three kinds of forest fires: surface, crown, and ground. **Surface fires** are low-level fires that usually burn only undergrowth and leaf litter on the forest floor (Figure 15-17). These fires kill seedlings and small trees but don't kill most mature trees. Wildlife can usually escape from these fairly slow-burning fires.

In forests where ground litter accumulates rapidly, a surface fire every five years or so burns away flammable material and helps prevent more destructive crown and ground fires. Surface fires also release and recycle valuable mineral nutrients tied up in slowly decomposing litter and undergrowth, increase the activity of nitrogen-fixing bacteria, stimulate the germination of certain tree seeds, and help control pathogens and insects. Some wildlife species, such as deer, moose, elk, muskrat, woodcock, and quail, depend on occasional surface fires to maintain their habitats and to provide food in the form of vegetation that sprouts after fires.

Crown fires are extremely hot fires that burn ground vegetation and tree tops (Figure 15-18). They usually occur in forests where all fire has been prevented for several decades, allowing the buildup of deadwood, leaves, and other flammable ground litter.

Figure 15-17 Surface fire in Ocala National Forest in Florida. Occasional fires like this burn deadwood, undergrowth, and litter and help prevent more destructive crown fires in some types of forests.

In such forests, an intense surface fire driven by a strong wind can spread to treetops. These rapidly burning fires can destroy all vegetation, kill wildlife, and lead to accelerated erosion.

Sometimes, surface fires become **ground fires**, which burn partially decayed leaves, or peat, below the ground surface. Such fires, common in northern bogs, may smolder for days or weeks before being detected. They are very difficult to extinguish.

The Smokey-the-Bear educational campaign of the Forest Service and the National Advertising Council has been successful in preventing many forest fires in the United States, saving many lives, and avoiding losses of

Figure 15-18 Destructive crown fire in Yellowstone National Park during the summer of 1988. Wildlife that can't escape are killed and wildlife habitats are destroyed. Severe erosion can occur. Since 1972, Park Service policy has been to allow most lightning-caused fires to burn themselves out, as long as they don't threaten human lives, park facilities, private property, or endangered wildlife. The Park Service's intention is to allow fire to play its important role in forest succession and regeneration. After fires raged in parts of Yellowstone National Park during the hot, dry summer of 1988, some people called for a reversal of this policy. Biologists oppose this and contend that damage was more widespread than it should have been because the earlier park policy of fighting all fires had allowed the buildup of flammable ground litter and small plants.

billions of dollars. Ecologists, however, contend that it also has caused harm by allowing litter buildup in some forests, increasing the likelihood of highly destructive crown fires (Figure 15-18). For that reason, many fires in national parks and wilderness areas are now allowed to burn as part of the natural ecological cycle of succession and regeneration.

Prescribed surface fires in some forests can be an effective method for preventing crown fires, by reducing litter buildup. They are also used to control outbreaks of tree diseases and pests. These fires are started only by well-trained personnel when weather and forest conditions are ideal for control and proper intensity of burning. Prescribed fires are also timed to keep levels of air pollution as low as possible.

PROTECTING FORESTS FROM AIR POLLUTION AND GLOBAL WARMING Forests at high elevations and forests downwind from urban and industrial cen-

ters are exposed to a variety of air pollutants that can harm trees, especially conifers (Figure 9-13). In addition to doing direct harm, prolonged exposure to multiple air pollutants makes trees much more vulnerable to drought, diseases, insects, and mosses (Figure 9-9).

The only solution is to sharply reduce emissions of the offending pollutants from coal-burning power plants, industrial plants, and cars (Section 9-5). In coming decades, an even greater threat to forests, especially temperate and boreal forests, is expected to result from projected changes in regional climate brought about by global warming (Sections 10-2 and 10-3).

SUSTAINABLE-EARTH FORESTRY To timber companies, sustainable forestry means getting a sustainable yield of commercial timber in as short a time as possible. This usually means using even-aged management in which diverse forests are cleared and replaced with intensely managed tree farms (Figure 5-17).

To environmentalists, this approach is ecologically and economically unsustainable. They call for widespread use of sustainable-Earth forestry, which recognizes that a biologically diverse forest ecosystem is the best protection against soil erosion; flooding; sediment water pollution; loss of biodiversity; and tree loss from fire, wind, insects, and diseases. Sustainable-Earth forest management emphasizes

- Growing and harvesting a diversity of high-quality timber, instead of short-term pulpwood production

- Greatly increasing paper recycling to reduce the demand for pulpwood

- Growing timber on long rotations, generally from 100 to 200 years, depending on the species and the soil quality

- Selective cutting of individual trees or small groups of most tree species (Figure 15-12)

- Extreme precautions to protect topsoil, upon which all present and future forest productivity depends

- Methods of road building and logging that minimize soil erosion and compaction

- Use of small, lightweight equipment for logging

- Clear-cutting only in small patches of less than 6 hectares (15 acres) and never on steeply sloped land (more than a 15- to 20-degree slope)

- Leaving standing dead trees and fallen timber to maintain diverse wildlife habitats and enhance nutrient recycling

- Leaving slash, treetops, and branches to help restore soil fertility, unless it causes too much buildup of dry fuel on the ground or hinders seeding of some desirable species

- Relying on natural controls to protect the forest from most diseases and pests

Q: By 2000 how many people may not be able to get enough fuelwood?

- Controlling occasional severe pest outbreaks by using natural predators (biological control) and integrated pest management (Section 14-5)

Sustainable-Earth forestry does not mean that tree farms or even-aged management should never be used, but it does mean that their use should be severely limited on public land and especially in old-growth forests. On private land, they should be regulated to prevent excessive soil erosion and water pollution from runoff of sediment, fertilizers, and pesticides.

MANAGEMENT AND CONSERVATION OF NATIONAL FORESTS IN THE UNITED STATES Today forests cover about one-third of the land area in the lower 48 states and make up 10% of the world's forested land area. However, most of the country's virgin forests have been cut (Figure 15-19), and what remains is under threat.

About 22% of the country's commercial forest area is located within the 156 national forests managed by the U.S. Forest Service (see Spotlight on p. 338). These forestlands serve as cheap grazing lands for more than 3 million cattle and sheep each year, support multimillion-dollar mining operations, contain a network of roads that is eight times longer than the entire U.S. interstate highway system, and receive more recreational visits than do any other federal public lands—more than twice as many as the National Park System.

Almost half of national forestlands are open to commercial logging. They supply about 14% of the country's total annual timber harvest—enough wood to build about 1.5 million homes—at cheap prices. Each year, private timber companies bid for rights to cut a certain amount of timber from areas designated by the Forest Service.

The Forest Service is required by law to manage national forests according to the principles of sustained yield and multiple use. But managing a public forest for balanced multiple use is difficult and sometimes impossible. Because of growing and often conflicting demands on national forest resources, the management policies of the Forest Service have been the subject of heated controversy since the 1960s.

Timber company officials complain that they aren't allowed to buy and cut enough timber on public lands, especially in remaining old-growth forests in California and the Pacific Northwest (see Case Study on p. 344). Conservationists charge that the Forest Service has made timber harvesting the dominant use in most national forests and has turned multiple use into multiple abuse (see Pro/Con on p. 345).

Conservationists point out that about 74% of the 1990 Forest Service budget was devoted directly or indirectly to the sale of timber, making it little more than a taxpayer-subsidized logging agency. By comparison, 4% of the budget was used for recreation, 2.3% for wild-

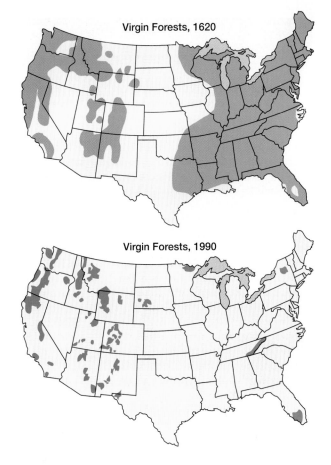

Figure 15-19 Vanishing primeval forests in the United States. Since 1620, an estimated 95% to 97% of the virgin forests that once covered much of America's lower 48 states have been cleared away. About 80% of the remaining old-growth forest in 12 national forests in the northwestern United States is slated for logging. Environmentalists believe that most of these diverse and irreplaceable ecosystems, owned by the entire American public, should not be destroyed to serve the interests of timber company owners and loggers whose jobs will soon be gone anyway because of overexploitation of this resource. (Data from the Wilderness Society and the U.S. Forest Service)

life and fish conservation, and 1.3% for soil, water, and air management. Much of any money the agency makes on a timber sale is kept by the agency, and any losses are passed on to the taxpayer. Since timbering is a way to increase its budget, the Forest Service has a powerful built-in incentive to make timber sales its primary objective.

RECYCLING WASTEPAPER The United States leads the world in consumption and waste of paper. Annual per capita consumption of paper in the United States is about 318 kilograms (699 pounds), compared with only 2.3 kilograms (5 pounds) per person in India.

Sharply increasing the recycling of paper is a key to reducing clearance and degradation of forests, solid waste, and water and air pollution. Conservationists estimate that at least 50% of the world's wastepaper

Untouched, old-growth forests once covered much of what is now the lower 48 states (Figure 15-19). Today, an estimated 95% to 97% of these virgin forests have been cleared away, with most of what is left found in the Pacific Northwest (Figures 15-1 and 15-19).

What's left of these ancient forests, often referred to as the crown jewels of America's forests, is being destroyed and fragmented at a rapid rate—much higher than the rate of destruction of the rain forests in Brazil. Each year, enough old-growth trees are taken from the Pacific Northwest to fill a convoy of logging trucks long enough to circle the entire planet. At current rates of logging, all unprotected ancient forests in western Washington and Oregon will be gone by the year 2023.

These disappearing ancient forests are not renewable on a human time scale, despite the boast of the owner of a logging company that he could "replicate the forest, redo it like a farmer growing a crop and do it better than nature."

To officials of timber companies, the giant living trees and rotting dead trees in old-growth forests are valuable resources going to waste and should not be locked up to please environmentalists.

Timber officials argue that protecting large areas of remaining old-growth forests on public lands will cause a loss of at least 26,000 jobs and hurt the economy of logging and milling towns throughout the Pacific Northwest. But studies show that between 1983 and 1989, more than 26,000 jobs were lost because of automation, Canadian timber imports, and the exporting of large volumes of unprocessed logs overseas, where millworkers in Japan, China, and South Korea, rather than in the United States, turned them into lumber, plywood, and other wood products.

The Wilderness Society estimates that another 20,800 timber-related jobs will be lost, mostly for these same reasons, during the 1990s. The result is that loggers and millwork-

ers are mostly pawns in a high-stakes game of corporate profit and greed, and the nation and the world are losing irreplaceable ancient forests. Many jobs could be created by using labor-intensive selective cutting instead of clear-cutting and by putting people to work restoring forests we have damaged.

The fate of these forests is a national issue because these forests are owned by all the American people, not just the timber industry or the residents of a region. It is a global issue because these forests are important reservoirs of threatened global biodiversity and because what the United States does with its remaining virgin forest sets a precedent for nations we are asking not to destroy their virgin forests, wetlands, coral reefs, and other vital parts of Earth's natural capital for short-term economic gain.

The endangered northern spotted owl (see front cover) has become a symbol in the struggle between environmentalists and timber company owners over the fate of unprotected old-growth forests on public lands in the Pacific Northwest. This species is vulnerable to extinction because of its low reproductive rates and the low survival of juveniles through their first five years. Only about 3,000 pairs remain. Because the owl feeds at the top trophic levels in old-growth forest food webs, it is what ecologists call an indicator species. If the owl's survival is threatened, probably dozens of other species are just as threatened.

Despite simplistic media coverage, *the controversy over cutting of ancient forests in the Pacific Northwest isn't an owl-vs.-jobs issue*. The owl and other threatened species (such as the Pacific yew tree and the marbled murrelet) in these forests are merely symbols of the broader clash between timber-company owners who want to cut most remaining old-growth stands in the national forests and environmentalists who want to protect them. The threatened owl is the best tool environmentalists have available to help

them achieve this broader goal of protecting biodiversity by protecting habitats.

Ways to reduce the destruction of remaining old-growth forests in the United States include:

- Reducing the annual sale and harvesting of timber from federal public lands by about 50%.

- Sharply raising the price of timber sold from national forests and other public lands. The bargain-basement sales of public timber discourage private owners from managing their forests more intensively.

- Giving logging and milling towns grants and interest-free loans to spur economic diversification.

- Closing loopholes in and strictly enforcing the law that bans the export of unprocessed logs from the Pacific Northwest and expanding this ban to the entire United States.

- Taxing exports of raw logs heavily, but leaving exports of lumber, plywood, and other finished wood products untaxed.

- Providing tax breaks and interest-free loans for revamping mills to cut smaller secondary-growth logs instead of large old-growth trees.

- Providing funds for extensive reforestation and restoration on denuded lands to furnish alternative jobs for unemployed loggers and millworkers.

- Allowing individuals, conservation organizations, or other groups to buy conservation easements that prevent harvesting of the timber on designated areas of old-growth forests on public lands. In such *conservation-for-tax-relief swaps*, purchasers would be allowed tax breaks for the funds they put up.

If we don't take steps like these, we won't save the jobs or remaining old-growth forests. What do you think should be done?

Q: How much of all U.S. land consists of public lands?

Conservationists are alarmed at proposals by the Forest Service to double the timber harvest on national forests between 1986 and 2030.

To accomplish this, the Forest Service has proposed the building of new roads in the national forests over the next 50 years whose overall length will be six times the length of roads in the entire interstate highway system. Conservationists charge that plans to build roads in inaccessible areas (about one-fifth of the proposed new roads) are designed to disqualify those areas from inclusion in the National Wilderness Preservation System.

Conservationists and the General Accounting Office have also accused the Forest Service of poor financial management of public forests. By law, the Forest Service must sell timber for no less than the cost of reforesting the land it was harvested from, but administrative costs and the cost of building roads to make the timber accessible are not included in this price. Thus, the main reason that logging companies want more timber from public land is that it is cheap. Taxpayers provide these companies with subsidies that pay for road building and many administrative costs when they cut on private land. Timber companies also get the timber at a low cost, another loss for taxpayers.

Studies have shown that between 1978 and 1991, national forests lost $3.9 billion from timber sales. With interest, this addition to the country's tremendous debt cost taxpayers $5.7 billion. This means that taxpayers are providing the timber industry with subsidies that average $343 million a year. Some have suggested that we would be better off if we gave the money to the logging companies and kept them out of the national forests. The Forest Service claimed it made a $628 million profit in 1990, but a former forestry expert and economist for the Congressional Research Service characterized them as absurd, mythical profits based on misleading bookkeeping.

Representatives of the timber industry argue that such subsidies help taxpayers by keeping lumber prices down. However, conservationists note that each year, taxpayers already give the lumber industry tax breaks almost equal to the cost of managing the entire National Forest System.

Forestry experts and conservationists have suggested several ways to reduce overexploitation of publicly owned timber resources and provide true multiple use of national forests as required by law:

■ Cut the present annual harvest of timber from national forests in half instead of doubling it as proposed by the timber industry.

■ Keep at least 50% of remaining old-growth timber in any national forest from being cut.

■ Pass an Ancient Forest Protection Act that would require the government to identify ecologically significant old-growth forests in the United States and protect these areas from environmentally disruptive exploitation, including logging and the building of any new roads.

■ Require that timber from national forests be sold at a price that includes the costs of roads, site preparation, and site regeneration.

■ Require that *all* timber sales in national forests yield a profit (using realistic accounting methods) for taxpayers based on the fair market value of any timber harvested.

■ Don't allow money from sales of timber in national forests to be used to supplement the Forest Service budget.

■ Use a much larger portion of the Forest Service budget to improve management and increase timber yields of the country's privately owned commercial forestland and thus take pressure off the national forests.

What do you think should be done?

(mostly newspapers, corrugated board and paperboard, office paper, and computer and copier paper) could be recycled by the end of this century. In 1991, about 33% was recycled (up from 25% in 1989). The percentage was higher in the Netherlands (53%), Japan (50%, including 90% of its newspapers and 81% of its paperboard products), Mexico (45%), Germany (41%), and Sweden (40%).

During World War II, when paper drives and recycling were national priorities, the United States recycled about 45% of its wastepaper. In 1991, only about 33% was recycled.

Product overpackaging is a major contributor to paper use and waste. Packages inside packages and over-sized containers are designed to trick consumers into thinking they're getting more for their money. Nearly $1 of every $10 spent for food in the United States goes for throwaway packaging. Junk mail also wastes enormous amounts of paper.*

Recycling the country's Sunday newspapers would save an entire forest of 500,000 trees each week. Recycling paper also saves energy because it takes 30% to

---

*You can reduce your junk mail by about 75% by writing to Mail Preference Service, Direct Marketing Association, 11 West 42nd Street, P.O. Box 3861, New York, NY 10163-3861. They will stop your name from being added to most large mailing-list companies.

64% less energy to produce the same weight of recycled paper as making the paper from trees. The U.S. paper industry is the country's third largest consumer of energy and the largest single user of fuel oil.

Recycling paper also reduces air pollution from pulp mills by 74% to 95%, lowers water pollution by 35%, conserves large quantities of water, and saves landfill space. Recycling paper also helps prevent groundwater contamination from the toxic ink left after paper eventually biodegrades in landfills over a 30- to 60-year period.

Recycling paper can also save money. In 1988, American Telephone and Telegraph earned more than $485,000 in revenue and saved $1.3 million in disposal costs by collecting and recycling office paper.

Requiring people to separate paper from other waste materials is a key to increased recycling. Otherwise, paper becomes so contaminated with other trash that wastepaper dealers won't buy it.

Unfortunately, it is difficult and costly to attain color reproduction of a quality that we find acceptable using recycled paper. That is why the publisher and I donate money each year to tree-planting organizations so that at least one tree is planted for each tree used in printing this book. To make up for the additional paper I use in writing this book, I plant 50 trees for each tree that I use. Color reproduction using recycled paper is improving, and we hope to use recycled paper in future editions.

In the United States, tax subsidies and other financial incentives make it cheaper to produce paper from trees than from recycled wastepaper. Widely fluctuating prices and a lack of demand for recycled paper products also make recycling wastepaper a risky financial venture.

For example, since 1988, the supply of recycled newspapers has exceeded the capacity of U.S. paper mills to use it, and the price for wastepaper has plummeted. Loans and tax credits to companies that invest in paper-recycling equipment could help ease this unfortunate situation that is discouraging communities from recycling paper just at a time when consumer interest in doing so has soared.

If the demand for recycled paper products increased, recycled paper would be cheaper and the price paid for wastepaper would rise. One way to increase demand is to require federal and state governments to use recycled paper products as much as possible. Half of the trash the government throws away is paper. A tax can also be added to every metric ton of virgin newsprint that is used, as is now done in Florida.

In the mid-1970s, Congress passed a law calling for federal agencies to buy as many recycled products as practical. That law has failed because it contains so many exemptions that almost nothing has to be recycled.

Simple measures like asking teachers to instruct their students to write on both sides of the paper would also reduce unnecessary paper waste and increase environmental awareness. Conservationists call for national, state, and local policies designed to recycle half of the wastepaper in the United States by 2000.

15-5 Rangelands

THE WORLD'S RANGELAND RESOURCES Almost half of Earth's ice-free land is **rangeland**: land that supplies forage or vegetation (grasses, grasslike plants, and shrubs) for grazing and browsing animals and that is not intensively managed. Most rangelands are grasslands in semiarid areas too dry for rain-fed cropland (Figure 5-3). Only about 42% of the world's rangeland is used for grazing livestock. Much of the rest is too dry, cold, or remote from population centers to be grazed by large numbers of livestock animals.

About 34% of the total land area of the United States is rangeland. Most of this is short-grass prairies in the arid and semiarid western half of the country (Figure 5-11). About 52% of the nation's rangeland is privately owned, and 43% of U.S. rangeland is owned by the general public and managed by the federal government, mostly by the Forest Service and the Bureau of Land Management (Figure 15-11). The remaining 5% is owned by state and local governments.

CHARACTERISTICS OF RANGELAND VEGETATION Most of the grasses on rangelands have deep, complex root systems (Figure 12-4). The multiple branches of their roots make these grasses hard to uproot, helping prevent soil erosion.

When the leaf tip of most plants is eaten, the leaf stops growing, but each leaf of rangeland grass grows from its base, not its tip. When the upper half of the shoot and leaves of grass is eaten, the plant can grow back quickly. However, the lower half of the plant must remain if the plant is to survive and grow new leaves. As long as only the upper half is eaten, rangeland grass is a renewable resource that can be grazed again and again.

RANGELAND CARRYING CAPACITY AND OVERGRAZING Each type of grassland has a herbivore **carrying capacity**: the maximum number of herbivores a given area can support without consuming the metabolic reserve needed for grass renewal. Carrying capacity is influenced by season, range condition, annual climatic conditions, past grazing use, soil type, kinds of grazing animals, and how long animals graze in an area.

Overgrazing occurs when too many grazing animals feed too long and exceed the carrying capacity of a grassland area. Large populations of wild herbivores

Q: What royalties do companies and individuals removing minerals from federal public lands pay to the federal government?

Figure 15-20 Overgrazed (left) and lightly grazed rangeland (right). Between 1936 and 1988, public rangeland in the United States in unsatisfactory (fair and poor) condition decreased from 84% to 68%. By 1988, 29% was in good condition, and only 3% was in excellent shape. Conservationists argue that overall estimates of rangeland condition greatly underestimate severe degradation of heavily grazed areas. Such areas are mostly *riparian zones*—thin strips of lush vegetation adjacent to streams and springs where livestock get their water. The basic problem in the western United States is that we insist on raising cattle, which need large amounts of water, in a water-poor environment.

Figure 15-21 Desertification in this arid outback region of Australia was caused by cattle overgrazing the vegetation. Livestock cropped plants so severely that the vegetation died; trampling prevented the establishment of seedlings.

can overgraze range in prolonged dry periods, but most overgrazing is caused by excessive numbers of livestock feeding too long in a particular area.

Figure 15-20 compares normally grazed and severely overgrazed grassland. Heavy overgrazing converts continuous grass cover into patches of grass and makes the soil more vulnerable to erosion, especially by wind. Then woody shrubs such as mesquite and prickly cactus invade and take over.

Severe overgrazing combined with prolonged drought can convert potentially productive rangeland into desert (Figure 15-21 and Case Study on p. 266). Dune buggies, motorcycles, and other off-road vehicles also damage or destroy rangeland vegetation.

RANGELAND MANAGEMENT The primary goal of range management is to maximize livestock productivity without overgrazing rangeland vegetation. The most widely used way to prevent overgrazing is to control the **stocking rate**—the number of a particular kind of animal grazing on a given area—so it doesn't exceed the carrying capacity.

Determining the carrying capacity of a range site, however, is difficult and costly. Even when the carrying capacity is known, it can change because of drought, invasions by new species, and other environmental factors.

Controlling the distribution of grazing animals over a range is the best way to prevent overgrazing and

undergrazing. Ranchers can control distribution by building fences to protect degraded rangeland, rotating livestock from one grazing area to another, providing supplemental feeding at selected sites, and locating water holes and salt blocks in strategic places.

A more expensive and less widely used method of rangeland management is to suppress the growth of unwanted plants by herbicide spraying, mechanical removal, or controlled burning. A cheaper and more effective way to remove unwanted vegetation is controlled, short-term trampling by large numbers of livestock.

Growth of desirable vegetation can be increased by seeding and applying fertilizer, but this method is usually too costly. On the other hand, reseeding is an excellent way to restore severely degraded rangeland.

Many ranchers still promote the use of poisons, trapping, and shooting to kill rabbits and rodents (such as prairie dogs), which compete with livestock for range vegetation. But this usually gives only temporary relief and is rarely worth the cost because these animals have high reproduction rates and their populations can usually recover in a short time.

For decades, hundreds of thousands of predators, such as coyotes (which sometimes kill sheep and goats), have been shot, trapped, and poisoned by ranchers, farmers, and federal predator control officials. However, experience has shown that killing predators is an expensive and temporary solution—one that sometimes makes matters worse.

Government agencies are required by law to manage public rangelands according to the principle of multiple use. For years, ranchers and conservationists have battled over how much ranchers should be charged for the privilege of grazing their livestock on public lands (see Pro/Con on p. 348).

The 27,000 U.S. ranchers who hold permits to graze livestock on Bureau of Land Management and National Forest Service rangelands in 16 western states pay a grazing fee for this privilege. Since 1981, grazing fees on public rangeland have been set by Congress at about one-seventh to one-fourth of the fees charged for grazing on comparable private and state lands, a subsidy that costs taxpayers about $100 million a year. Each year, the government also spends millions of dollars to manage these rangelands. Overall, the government collects only about $1 from ranchers in grazing fees for every $10 spent on range management.

Conservationists call for grazing fees on public rangeland to be raised to a fair market value for use of this land. Higher fees would reduce incentives for overgrazing and provide more money for improvement of range conditions, wildlife conservation, and watershed management. So far, repeated attempts to get Congress to sharply raise grazing fees have failed.

Because it is an ecological failure and an economic failure (for taxpayers), some conservationists call for the current grazing permit system

to be replaced with a competitive bidding system. Livestock grazing would be allowed only on range in good or excellent condition under strictly controlled conditions to prevent overgrazing. If the bids did not reflect the current market value of the forage, no permit would be issued. Permits would last for only three to five years. Failure to live up to the permit requirements would lead to automatic cancellation. Ranchers with permits would share 50-50 with the government the cost of capital improvements related to livestock grazing.

Ranchers with permits fiercely oppose higher grazing fees and competitive bidding. Grazing rights on public land raise the value of their livestock animals by $1,000 to $1,500 per head. That means that a permit to graze 500 cattle on public land can be worth $500,000 to $750,000 a year to the rancher. The economic value of a permit is included in the overall worth of the ranches and can be used as collateral for a loan.

Ranchers also argue that they must put up fences on the government land and provide water, which also benefits wildlife. Under the federal multiple-use land policy, they

must also share the land with hunters, hikers, off-road vehicle enthusiasts, and others seeking outdoor recreation.

Many of the 98% of U.S. ranchers who can't get a grazing permit favor open bidding for grazing rights on public land. They believe that the permit system gives politically influential ranchers an unfair economic advantage at the expense of taxpayers.

Some conservationists believe that all commercial grazing of livestock on public lands should be phased out over a 10- to 15-year period. Federal lands provide forage for less than 3% of the domestic cattle and sheep produced annually in the United States at a cost of about $2 billion to American taxpayers. Thus, phasing out livestock grazing on public lands would have little effect on the overall production and price of beef and lamb, save taxpayers money by eliminating what environmentalists call "cowboy welfare" to ranchers who don't need the money, and allow restoration of degraded public rangeland. What do you think should be done?

15-6 Parks: Use and Abuse

THREATS TO PARKS In 1912, Congress created the U.S. National Park System and declared that national parks are to be set aside to conserve and preserve scenery, wildlife, and natural and historic objects for the use, observation, health, and pleasure of people. The parks are to be maintained in a manner that leaves them unimpaired for future generations.

Today, there are over 1,100 national parks of more than 1,000 hectares (2,500 acres) in more than 120 countries. Together, they cover an area equal to that of Alaska, Texas, and California combined. This is an important achievement in the global conservation movement, spurred by the development of the world's first national park system in the United States. In addition

to national parks, the U.S. public has access to state, county, and city parks. Most state parks are located near urban areas and thus are used more heavily than national parks.

Throughout the world, parks and other protected areas are increasingly threatened. In MDCs, many national parks are threatened by nearby industrial development, urban growth, air and water pollution, roads, noise, invasion by alien species, and loss of natural species. Some of the most popular national parks are also threatened by overuse.

In LDCs, the problems are worse. Plant life and animal life in national parks are being threatened by local people who desperately need wood, cropland, and other resources. Poachers kill animals and sell their parts, such as rhino horns, elephant tusks, and furs. Park services in these countries have too little money and staff to fight these invasions, either through en-

Q: What percentage of timber in the United States is harvested by clear-cutting?

forcement or through public education programs. Also, most national parks in MDCs and LDCs are too small to sustain many of their natural species, especially larger animals.

U.S. NATIONAL AND STATE PARKS

The National Park System is dominated by 50 national parks found mostly in the West (Figure 15-11). These repositories of majestic beauty and biological diversity have been called America's crown jewels. They are supplemented by numerous state parks.

The biggest problems of national and state parks stem from their spectacular success. Because of more roads, cars, and affluence, annual recreational visits to National Park System units have increased more than 12-fold and visits to state parks 7-fold since 1950.

Under the onslaught of people during the peak summer season, the most popular national and state parks are often overcrowded with cars and trailers and are plagued by noise, traffic jams, litter, vandalism, poaching, deteriorating trails, polluted water, drugs, and crime (including 16 murders, 44 rapes, 147 armed robberies, and 207 serious assaults in 1990). Many visitors to heavily used parks leave the city to commune with nature and find that it's more congested, noisy, and stressful than where they came from. An increasing number of visitors to such parks ask for their entrance money back.

Park Service rangers now spend an increasing amount of their time on law enforcement instead of on resource conservation and management. Many now have to wear body armor. Since 1976 the number of federal park rangers has not changed, yet the number of visitors to park units has gone up by 65 million. It's not surprising that many overworked rangers, with an average salary less than $25,000 and substandard housing, have become discouraged. Some are leaving for better-paying jobs. Some who remain depend on food stamps, welfare, parental assistance, and second jobs to support their families.

Populations of wolves, bears, and other large predators in and near various parks have dropped sharply or disappeared because of excessive hunting, poisoning by ranchers and federal officials, and the limited size of most parks. This decline has allowed populations of remaining prey species to increase sharply, destroy vegetation, and crowd out other native animal species. The movement of alien species into parks is also a threat.

The greatest danger to many parks today is from human activities in nearby areas. Wildlife and recreational values are threatened by mining, timber harvesting, grazing, coal-burning power plants, water diversion, and urban development. Over the next 50 years, the greatest threat to many of the world's parks may be shifts in regional climate caused by a projected enhanced greenhouse effect (Section 10-2).

PARK MANAGEMENT: COMBINING CONSERVATION AND SUSTAINABLE DEVELOPMENT

Some park managers, especially in LDCs, are developing integrated management plans that combine conservation and sustainable development of the park and surrounding areas (Figure 15-8). In such a plan, the inner core and especially vulnerable areas of the park are protected from development and treated as wilderness. Controlled numbers of people are allowed to use these areas for hiking, nature study, ecological research, and other nondestructive recreational and educational activities.

In other areas, controlled commercial logging, sustainable grazing by livestock, and sustainable hunting and fishing by local people are allowed. Money spent by park visitors adds to local income. By involving local people in developing park management plans, managers help them see the park as a vital resource they need to protect and sustain rather than degrade (see Case Study on p. 332).

In most cases, however, the protected inner core is too small to sustain many of its natural species. Such plans look good on paper, but often they cannot be carried out because of a lack of funds for land acquisition, enforcement, and maintenance.

In 1988, the Wilderness Society and the National Parks and Conservation Association suggested a blueprint for the future of the U.S. National Park System that included the following proposals:

- Educate the public about the urgent need to protect, mend, and expand the system.

- Establish the National Park Service as an independent agency responsible to the president and Congress. This would make it less vulnerable to the shifting political winds of the Interior Department.

- Significantly increase the pay and number of park rangers.

- Block the mining, timbering, and other threats that are taking place near park boundaries on land managed by the Forest Service and the Bureau of Land Management.

- Acquire new parkland near threatened areas and add at least 75 new parks within the next decade. About half of the most important types of ecosystems in the United States are not protected in national parks.

- Locate most commercial park facilities (such as restaurants and shops) *outside* park boundaries.

- Raise the fees charged to private concessionaires who operate restaurants and camping, food, and recreation services inside national parks to at least 22% of their gross receipts. The present maximum return for taxpayers is only 5% and the average is only 2.5% of the $1.5 billion they take in annually. Many of the large concessionaire companies have worked out up to 30-year contracts with national park officials in which they pay the government as little as 0.75% of their gross receipts.

- Halt concessionaire ownership of facilities in national parks, which makes buying buildings back very expensive.

- Wherever feasible, place visitor parking areas outside the park areas. Use low-polluting vehicles to carry visitors to and from parking areas and for transportation within the park.

- Greatly expand the Park Service budget for maintenance and science and conservation programs. Currently, only 1% of national park funding goes for environmental research. The national parks face a $2 billion backlog of repairs.

- Make buildings and vehicles in national and state parks educational showcases for improvements in energy efficiency and the latest developments in the use of energy from the sun, wind, flowing water, and Earth's interior heat (geothermal energy).

- Require the Park Service and the Forest Service to develop integrated management plans so activities in nearby national forests don't degrade national parklands.

15-7 Wilderness Preservation

HOW MUCH WILD LAND IS LEFT? According to the Wilderness Act of 1964, **wilderness** consists of those areas "where the earth and its community of life are untrammeled by man, where man himself is a visitor who does not remain." The Wilderness Society estimates that a wilderness area should contain at least 400,000 hectares (1 million acres). Otherwise, the area can be degraded by air pollution, water pollution, and noise pollution from nearby mining, oil and natural gas drilling, timber cutting, industry, and urban development.

A 1987 survey sponsored by the Sierra Club revealed that only about 34% of Earth's land area is undeveloped wilderness in blocks of at least 400,000 hectares. About 30% of these remaining wildlands are forests. Many are in tropical forests, which are being rapidly cleared and degraded. Tundra and desert make up most of the world's remaining wildlands. Only about 20% of the undeveloped lands identified in this survey are protected by law from exploitation.

WHY PRESERVE WILDERNESS? We need wild places where we can experience majestic beauty and natural biological diversity. We need places where we can enhance our mental health by getting away from noise, stress, and large numbers of people. Wilderness preservationist John Muir advised:

Climb the mountains and get their good tidings. Nature's peace will flow into you as the sunshine into the trees. The winds will blow their freshness into you, and the storms their energy, while cares will drop off like autumn leaves.

Even if individuals do not use the wilderness, many want to know it is there, a feeling expressed by novelist Wallace Stegner:

Save a piece of country . . . and it does not matter in the slightest that only a few people every year will go into it. This is precisely its value . . . we simply need that wild country available to us, even if we never do more than drive to its edge and look in. For it can be a means of reassuring ourselves of our sanity as creatures, a part of the geography of hope.

Wilderness areas provide recreation for growing numbers of people. Wilderness also has important ecological values. It provides undisturbed habitats for wild plants and animals, maintains diverse biological reserves protected from degradation, and provides a laboratory in which we can discover more about how nature works. It is an ecological insurance policy against eliminating too much of Earth's natural biological diversity. In the words of Henry David Thoreau: "In wildness is the preservation of the world."

To sustainable-Earth conservationists, the most important reason for protecting and expanding the world's wilderness areas is an ethical one: Wilderness should be preserved because the wild species it contains have a right to exist without human interference (Section 2-3).

U.S. WILDERNESS PRESERVATION SYSTEM In the United States, preservationists have been trying to keep wild areas from being developed since 1900. On the whole, they have fought a losing battle. It was not until 1964 that Congress passed the Wilderness Act. It allows the government to protect undeveloped tracts of public land from development as part of the National Wilderness Preservation System (see Spotlight on p. 338).

Only 4% of U.S. land area is protected as wilderness, with almost two-thirds of this in Alaska. Most of the rest is in the West. Only 1.8% of the land area of the lower 48 states is protected in the wilderness system. Of the 413 wilderness areas in the lower 48 states, only 4 consist of more than 400,000 hectares. Furthermore, the present wilderness preservation system includes only 81 of the country's 233 distinct ecosystems.

There remain almost 40 million hectares (100 million acres) of public lands that could qualify for designation as wilderness. Conservationists believe all of this land should be protected as wilderness and that a vigorous effort should be mounted to rehabilitate other lands to enlarge existing wilderness areas.

The long-term goal would be to have 30% of the country's land area protected as wilderness. This would require that virtually all Forest Service and Bureau of

Q: How much of the U.S. Forest Service budget is devoted to timber sales?

Land Management public lands be reclassified as wilderness and restored as natural wildlife habitat. Wilderness recovery areas could be created by closing roads in large areas of public lands, restoring habitats, allowing natural fires to burn, and reintroducing species that have been driven from such areas. However, resource developers lobby elected officials and government agencies to build roads in areas being evaluated for inclusion in the wilderness system so that they can't be designated as wilderness and strongly oppose the idea of wilderness recovery areas.

USE AND ABUSE OF WILDERNESS AREAS Popular wilderness areas, especially in California, North Carolina, and Minnesota, are visited by so many people that their wildness is threatened. Fragile vegetation is damaged, soil is eroded from trails and campsites, water is polluted from bathing and dishwashing, and litter is scattered along trails. Instead of quiet and solitude, visitors sometimes face the noise and congestion they are trying to escape.

Wilderness areas are also being degraded by air, water, and noise pollution from nearby grazing, logging, oil and gas drilling, factories, power plants, and urban areas. If projected global warming from an enhanced greenhouse effect occurs, it is expected to be the biggest threat to wilderness, parks, forests, rangelands, croplands, estuaries, and inland wetlands over the next few decades (Section 10-2).

WILDERNESS MANAGEMENT To protect the most popular areas from damage, wilderness managers have had to limit the number of people hiking or camping at any one time. They have also designated areas where camping is allowed. Managers have increased the number of wilderness rangers to patrol vulnerable areas and enlisted volunteers to pick up trash discarded by thoughtless users.

Historian and wilderness expert Roderick Nash suggests wilderness areas be divided into three categories. The easily accessible, popular areas would be intensively managed and have trails, bridges, hiker's huts, outhouses, assigned campsites, and extensive ranger patrols. Large, remote wilderness areas would not be intensively managed. They would be used only by people who get a permit by demonstrating their wilderness skills. A third category would consist of large, biologically unique areas. They would be left undisturbed as gene pools of plant and animal species, with no human entry allowed.

NATIONAL WILD AND SCENIC RIVERS SYSTEM
In 1968, Congress passed the National Wild and Scenic Rivers Act. It allows rivers and river segments with outstanding scenic, recreational, geological, wildlife, historical, or cultural values to be protected in the National Wild and Scenic Rivers System. The only activities al-

Figure 15-22 Wangari Maathai, the first Kenyan woman to earn a Ph.D. (in anatomy) and head a department (veterinary medicine) at the University of Nairobi, organized the internationally acclaimed Green Belt Movement in 1977. The goal of this widely regarded women's self-help community action group is to plant a tree for each of Kenya's 25 million people. She recruited 50,000 women to establish tree nurseries and to help farmers raise tree seedlings. Members of the group get a small fee for each tree that survives. By 1990, more than 10 million trees had been planted. The success of this project has sparked the creation of similar programs in more than a dozen other African countries. She and members of this group are true Earth heroes.

lowed are camping, swimming, nonmotorized boating, sport hunting, and sport and commercial fishing. New mining claims, however, are permitted in some areas.

Conservationists have urged Congress to add 1,500 additional eligible river segments to the system by 2000. If that goal is achieved, about 2% of the country's unique rivers would be protected from further development. During this period, they want none of the candidate rivers to be developed in any way that might affect its ecological integrity. Conservationists also urge that a permanent federal administrative body be established to manage the Wild and Scenic Rivers System and that states develop their own wild and scenic river programs.

Sustaining existing forests, rangelands, wilderness, and parks and rehabilitating those that we have degraded are urgent tasks. They will cost a great deal of money and require strong support from the public and changes in individual lifestyles (see Individuals Matter on p. 352). But it will cost our civilization much more if we do not protect these resources from degradation and destruction and help heal those we have wounded.

Today, up to 25,000 women's self-help groups are active in Earth-sustaining activities, especially soil conservation and tree planting. In Kenya, Wangari Maathai (Figure 15-22) started the Green Belt Movement, a national effort by 50,000 women farmers and half a million school children to plant trees for firewood and to help hold the soil in place. For two decades, women and children in parts of India have gone into nearby forests, joined hands, and encircled trees to prevent commercial loggers from cutting them down (see Individuals Matter on p. 32).

The task of protecting Earth's biodiversity and restoring lands we have degraded is enormous, but it can be done if you and enough other people care. Ours is

INDIVIDUALS MATTER What You Can Do to Help Sustain the Earth's Land Ecosystems

- If you or your loved ones own forested land, develop a management and conservation plan for the sustainable use of those resources.
- Plant trees on a regular basis in your yard and in your town.* Take care of trees you plant so they survive.
- Cut down on the use of wood and paper products you don't really need, recycle paper products, and buy recycled paper products. Use washable cloth dish towels and napkins instead of throwaway paper towels and napkins. Buy toilet paper made from recycled paper fibers. Pressure your office or school to start a paper recycling program and to buy recycled paper products.
- Recycle aluminum cans, or better yet, switch to reusable glass beverage containers. Recognize that using aluminum cans or other throwaway aluminum products encourages the development of more aluminum mines and smelters in the Amazon basin, powered by dams. These dams flood large areas of tropical forests and displace indigenous people from their lands.
- Reduce or eliminate your consumption of beef, some of which is produced by clearing tropical and other forests.

*Sources of information for tree planting are Treepeople, *The Simple Act of Planting a Tree* (Los Angeles: Tarcher, 1990); Global Releaf (American Forestry Association, P.O. Box 2000, Washington, DC 20013; and the *1990 Green Front Report* (available from Friends of the Trees, P.O. Box 1466, Chelan, WA 98816). You can also get technical assistance on species and tree planting from county cooperative extension services, state forestry or conservation departments, or local parks and public works departments.

- Don't buy furniture or other items made from tropical hardwoods, such as teak, mahogany, and plywood containing mahogany. Claims that wood products do not use tropical hardwoods are almost impossible to verify. If you must buy such hardwoods, look for the Good-Wood Seal given by Friends of the Earth or consult the *Wood User's Guide* available for $7.50 plus $2.50 postage from the Rainforest Action Network (see Appendix).
- Don't buy a tropical plant or animal (including fish).
- Contribute time, money, or both to organizations devoted to forest conservation, especially of the world's rapidly disappearing tropical forests, and tree planting.†
- Engage in protests and physically help protect virgin forests from being cleared or degraded (see Pro/Con on p. 164).
- Don't cut trees at Christmas. Instead, buy a living tree in a tub for later planting outdoors.
- Help rehabilitate or restore a degraded area of forest or grassland near where you live.

†Examples are the American Forestry Association (which has a campaign to plant 100 million trees throughout the United States between 1989 and 1992), Environmental Defense Fund, Friends of the Trees, Greenpeace, Nature Conservancy, Programme for Belize (each $50 donation used to buy and protect an acre of endangered tropical forestland in Belize, a small country in Central America), Rainforest Action Network, Rainforest Alliance (each $55 donation used to buy and protect one acre of rainforest in Costa Rica's Monteverde Cloudforest Preserve, Figure 5-15), Trees for Life, and Treepeople. Addresses and other organizations are given in the Appendix.

- Don't buy products produced by companies involved in destructive development projects in tropical forests. Information on such companies can be obtained from the Rainforest Action Network, Rainforest Alliance, and Friends of the Earth (see Appendix).
- Lobby elected officials to protect all remaining virgin forests on public lands in the United States.
- If you visit a park or wilderness area, don't harm or remove anything, and don't leave anything there.
- Support efforts to protect large areas of the world's remaining undeveloped lands and wild rivers as wilderness. In the United States, lobby elected officials to protect all undeveloped public lands and wild and scenic river segments in the lower 48 states from development.
- Pressure banks and international lending agencies not to lend money for environmentally destructive projects.
- Lobby elected officials to protect ancient forests on public lands, reduce timber harvests in national forests, require that taxpayers get a fair return on all timber harvesting and livestock grazing on public lands, eliminate subsidies for cutting virgin timber, and adopt a national program for recycling half of the wastepaper in the United States by 2000.
- Support efforts to protect, expand, and mend the National Park System and get a much fairer return from concessionaires who operate services in park units.

Q: What percentage of the original virgin forests in the lower 48 states are left?

the last generation that has the opportunity to reverse the process of degradation. All significant change begins from the bottom up, not from the top down. Act — starting now!

Forests precede civilizations, deserts follow them.
FRANÇOIS-AUGUSTE-RENÉ
DE CHATEAUBRIAND

GUEST ESSAY Tropical Forests and Their Species: Going, Going . . . ?

Norman Myers

Norman Myers is an international consultant in environment and development with emphasis on conservation of wildlife species and tropical forests. He has served as a consultant for many development agencies and research organizations, including the U.S. National Academy of Sciences, the World Bank, the Organization for Economic Cooperation and Development, various UN agencies, and the World Resources Institute. Among his recent publications (see Further Readings) are The Sinking Ark *(1979),* Conversion of Tropical Moist Forests *(1980),* A Wealth of Wild Species *(1983),* The Primary Source *(1984),* The Gaia Atlas of Planet Management *(1985), and* The Gaia Atlas of Future Worlds *(1990).*

Tropical forests still cover an area roughly equivalent to the "lower 48" United States. Climatic and biological data suggest they could have once covered an area at least twice as large. So we have already lost half of them, mostly in the recent past.

Worse, remote-sensing surveys show that we are now destroying the forests at a rate of at least 1.25% a year, and we are grossly degrading them at a rate of at least another 1.25% a year — and both rates are accelerating rapidly. Unless we act now to halt this loss, within just another few decades at most, there could be little left, except perhaps a block in central Africa and another in the western part of the Amazon basin. Even those remnants may not survive the combined pressures of population growth and land hunger beyond the middle of the next century.

This means that we are imposing one of the most broad-scale and impoverishing impacts on the biosphere that it has ever suffered throughout its 4 billion years of existence. Tropical forests are the greatest celebration of nature to appear on the face of the planet since the first flickerings of life. They are exceptionally complex ecologi-

cally, and they are remarkably rich biotically. Although they now account for 6% to 7% of the earth's land surface, they still are home for half, and perhaps three-quarters or more, of all the planet's species of plant and animal life. Thus, elimination of these forests is by far the leading factor in the mass extinction of species that appears likely over the next few decades.

Already, we are certainly losing several species every day because of clearing and degradation of tropical forests. The time will surely come, and come soon, when we shall be losing many thousands every year. The implications are profound, whether they be scientific, aesthetic, ethical — or simply economic. In medicine alone, we benefit from myriad drugs and pharmaceuticals derived from tropical forest plants. The commercial value of these products worldwide can be reckoned at $20 billion each year.

By way of example, the rosy periwinkle from Madagascar's tropical forests has produced two potent drugs against Hodgkin's disease, leukemia, and other blood cancers. Madagascar has — or used to have — at least 8,000 plant species, of which more than 7,000 could be found nowhere else. Today Madagascar has lost 93% of its virgin tropical forest [Figure 15-5]. The U.S. National Cancer Institute estimates that there could be many plants in tropical forests with potential against various cancers, provided pharmacologists can get to them before they are eliminated by chain saws and bulldozers.

We benefit in still other ways from tropical forests. One critical environmental service is the famous "sponge effect," by which the forests soak up rainfall during the wet season and then release it in regular amounts throughout the dry season. When tree cover is removed and this watershed function is impaired, the result is a yearly regime of floods followed by droughts, which destroys property and reduces agricultural production. There is also concern that if tropical deforestation becomes wide enough, it could trigger local, regional, or even global changes in climate. Such climatic upheavals would affect the lives of billions of people, if not the whole of humankind.

All this raises important questions about our role in the biosphere and our relations with the natural world around us. As we proceed on our disruptive way in tropical forests, we — political leaders and the general public alike — give scarcely a moment's thought to what we are doing. We are deciding the fate of the world's tropical forests unwittingly, yet effectively and increasingly.

(continued)

A: 3% to 5%, with most remaining virgin forests in the Pacific Northwest

The resulting shift in evolution's course, stemming from the elimination of tropical forests, will rank as one of the greatest biological upheavals since the dawn of life. It will equal, in scale and significance, the development of aerobic respiration, the emergence of flowering plants, and the arrival of limbed animals, taking place over eons of time.

Whereas those were enriching disruptions in the course of life on this planet, the loss of biotic diversity associated with the destruction of tropical forests will be almost entirely an impoverishing phenomenon brought about entirely by human actions. And it will all have occurred within the twinkling of a geologic eye.

In short, our intervention in tropical forests should be viewed as one of the most challenging problems that humankind has ever encountered. After all, we are the first species ever to be able to look upon nature's work and to decide whether we should consciously eliminate it or leave much of it untouched.

So the decline of tropical forests is one of the great sleeper issues of our time. Yet, we can still save much of these forests and the species they contain. Should we not consider ourselves fortunate that we alone among all generations are being given the chance to preserve tropical forests as the most exuberant expression of nature in the biosphere — and thereby to support the right to life of many of our fellow species and their capacity to undergo further evolution without human interference?

Guest Essay Discussion

1. What obligation, if any, do you as an individual have to preserve a significant portion of the world's remaining tropical forests?

2. Should MDCs provide most of the money to preserve remaining tropical forests in LDCs? Explain.

3. What can you do to help preserve some of the world's tropical forests? Which, if any, of these actions do you plan to carry out?

DISCUSSION TOPICS

1. Explain how eating a hamburger from some U.S. fast-food chains indirectly contributes to the destruction of virgin tropical forests. What, if anything, do you believe should be done about this?

2. Explain why you agree or disagree with each of the proposals listed on pages 332–335 concerning protection of the world's tropical forests.

3. Should private companies cutting timber from national forests continue to be subsidized by federal payments for reforestation and for building and maintaining access roads ? Explain.

4. Should all cutting on remaining ancient forests in U.S. national forestlands be banned? Explain.

5. Should exports of timber cut from U.S. national forests and other public lands be banned? Explain.

6. Should fees for grazing on public rangelands in the United States be **(a)** eliminated and replaced with a competitive bidding system, or **(b)** increased to the point where they equal the fair market value estimated by the Bureau of Land Management and the Forest Service? Explain your answers.

7. Explain why you agree or disagree with each of the proposals listed on pages 349–350 concerning the U.S. National Park System.

8. Should more wilderness areas and wild and scenic rivers be preserved in the United States, especially in the lower 48 states? Explain.

*9. Investigate paper recycling in your community and by your school. Try to find answers to the following questions:
   a. What percentage of the paper used by your school is recycled?
   b. What percentage of the paper used in your community is recycled?
   c. What percentage of the newsprint in local or nearby newspapers is made from recycled materials?
   d. What percentage of the paper products bought by your school contains recycled fibers?
   e. What percentage of the paper products bought by local government agencies contains recycled fibers?

CHAPTER 16

WILD PLANT

AND ANIMAL

RESOURCES

General Questions and Issues

1. Why are wild species of plants and animals important to us and to the ecosphere?

2. What human activities and natural traits cause wild species to become depleted, endangered, and extinct?

3. How can endangered and threatened wild species be protected from premature extinction caused by human activities?

4. How can populations of large game be managed to have enough animals available for sport hunting without endangering the long-term survival of the species?

5. How can populations of species of freshwater and marine fish be managed to have enough available for commercial and sport fishing without endangering their long-term survival?

The mass of extinctions which the earth is currently facing is a threat to civilization second only to the threat of thermal nuclear war.

NATIONAL ACADEMY OF SCIENCES

N THE EARLY 1800s, Alexander Wilson, a prominent ornithologist, watched a single migrating flock of passenger pigeons darken the sky for over four hours. He estimated that this flock consisted of more than 2 billion birds and was 386 kilometers (240 miles) long and 1.6 kilometers (1 mile) wide.

By 1914, the passenger pigeon (Figure 16-1) had disappeared forever. How could the species that was once the most numerous bird in North America become extinct in only a few decades?

The answer is people. The main reasons for the extinction of this species were uncontrolled commercial hunting and the loss of habitat and food supplies as forests were cleared for farms and cities.

Passenger pigeons were good to eat, their feathers made good pillows, and they were widely used for fertilizer. They were easy to kill because they flew in gigantic flocks and nested in long, narrow colonies. People captured one pigeon alive, sewed its eyes shut, and tied it to a perch called a stool. Soon a curious flock landed beside this "stool pigeon." They were then either shot or trapped by nets that might contain more than 1,000 birds.

Beginning in 1858, the mass killing of passenger pigeons became a big business. Shotguns, fire, traps, artillery, and even dynamite were used. Birds were also suffocated by burning grass or sulfur below their roosts. Live birds were used as targets in shooting galleries. In 1878, one professional pigeon trapper made $60,000 by killing 3 million birds at their nesting grounds near Petoskey, Michigan.

By the early 1880s, commercial hunting ceased because only several thousand birds were left. Recovery of the species was essentially impossible because these birds laid only one egg per nest. Many of the remaining birds died from infectious disease and from severe storms during their annual fall migration to Central and South America.

Figure 16-1 The extinct passenger pigeon. The last known passenger pigeon died in the Cincinnati Zoo in 1914.

355

In 1896, the last major breeding colony of about 250,000 birds was tracked, and all but about 5,000 birds, which escaped, were killed by hunters. In Ohio on March 24, 1900, a young boy shot the last known passenger pigeon in the wild. The last known passenger pigeon on Earth, a hen named Martha after Martha Washington, died in the Cincinnati Zoo in 1914. Her stuffed body is now on view at the National Museum of Natural History in Washington, D.C. (Figure 16-1).

Sooner or later, all species become extinct, but we have become a primary factor in the premature extinction of an increasing number of species as a result of our relentless march across the globe. Every day at least 10 and probably 140 species become extinct because of our activities, and the loss may soon reach several hundred species a day. Reducing this enormous loss of Earth's biological diversity, protecting wildlife habitats throughout the world, and restoring species and habitats that we have helped deplete and degrade are planetary emergencies that we must deal with now.

Figure 16-2 California condor in captivity at the Los Angeles Zoo. By 1987 none of these birds was left in the wild. As a result of a $1.5-million-a-year captive breeding program, there were 52 of these birds in captivity in the Los Angeles Zoo and in the San Diego Wild Animal Park by August 1991. In January 1992, scientists returned two condor chicks to their natural habitat north of Los Angeles, where the species existed for 600,000 years until we began killing them and crowding them out. This species is especially vulnerable to extinction because of its low reproduction rate, long period (7 years) needed to reach reproductive age, failure of parents to hatch chicks when they are scared away from the nest by noise or human activities, and the need for a large, undisturbed habitat.

16-1 Why Preserve Wild Species?

WHY NOT LET THEM DIE? Species extinction over Earth's long history is a natural phenomenon, so why should we be concerned about losing a few more? Does it make any difference that the California condor (Figure 16-2), the black rhinoceros (Figure 4-31), or some plant in a tropical forest becomes extinct mostly because of our activities? The answer is yes, for a number of reasons.

ECONOMIC AND MEDICAL IMPORTANCE Wild species that are actually or potentially useful to people are called **wildlife resources**. They are potentially renewable resources, if not driven to extinction or near extinction by our activities.

Most of the plants that supply 90% of the world's food today were domesticated from wild plants found in the tropics. Existing wild plant species, most of them still unclassified and unevaluated, will be needed by agricultural scientists and genetic engineers to develop new crop strains (Section 13-3), and many of them may become important sources of food (Figure 13-6). Wild plants and plants domesticated from wild species are also important sources of rubber (Figure 15-7), oils, dyes, fiber, paper, lumber, and other important products.

About 75% of the world's population relies on plants or plant extracts as sources of medicines. Roughly half of the prescription and nonprescription drugs used in the world, and 25% of those used in the United States today, have active ingredients extracted from wild organisms or are synthetic versions of compounds found in wild organisms. Worldwide, medicines from wild species are worth $40 billion a year. Only about 5,000 of the world's estimated 250,000 plant species have been studied thoroughly for their possible medical uses. A recent analysis shows that 10% of the U.S. gross national product is derived directly from wildlife resources.

Many wild animal species are used to test drugs, vaccines, chemical toxicity, and surgical procedures and to increase our understanding of human health and disease (Section 8-1 and Figure 16-3). However, animal rights and welfare advocates are protesting the use of animals in medical and biological research and teaching. Bacteria, cell and tissue cultures, and computer models are now used as alternatives for the use of animals, but researchers point out that such techniques cannot replace all animal research (Section 8-1).

AESTHETIC AND RECREATIONAL IMPORTANCE Wild plants and animals are a source of beauty, wonder, joy, and recreational pleasure for large numbers of people. Wild **game species** provide recreation in the form of hunting and fishing. Each year, almost 50% of the American people and 84% of the Canadian population participate in bird watching, photographing, and other nondestructive forms of outdoor recreational activity involving wildlife.

Wildlife tourism, sometimes called eco-tourism, is important to the economy of some LDCs, such as Kenya

Q: Between 1978 and 1991, how much have taxpayers lost from timber sales in national forests?

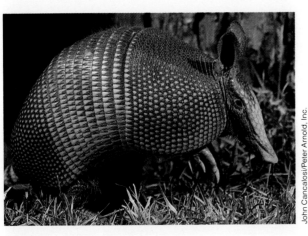

Figure 16-3 The nine-banded armadillo is used in research to find a cure for leprosy.

and Tanzania. One wildlife economist estimated that one male lion living to seven years of age in Kenya leads to $515,000 of expenditures by tourists. If the lion were killed for its skin, it would be worth only about $1,000. Intensive use of favorite spots for eco-tours, however, can damage ecosystems and disrupt species. Environmentalists call for strict guidelines governing nature tours in sensitive areas.

ECOLOGICAL IMPORTANCE Wild species perform vital ecosystem services for us and other species. They supply us and other species with food from the soil and the sea, recycle nutrients essential to agriculture, and help produce and maintain fertile soil. They also produce and maintain oxygen and other gases in the atmosphere, moderate Earth's climate, help regulate water supplies, and store solar energy as chemical energy in food, wood, and fossil fuels. Moreover, they detoxify poisonous substances, decompose organic wastes, control potential crop pests and carriers of disease, and make up a vast gene pool of biological diversity from which we and other species can draw.

ETHICAL IMPORTANCE So far, the reasons given for preserving wildlife are based on the actual or potential usefulness of wild species as resources for people. Many ecologists and conservationists believe that wild species will continue to disappear at an alarming rate until we replace this *human-centered (anthropocentric)* view of wildlife and the environment either with a *life-centered (biocentric)* view or with an *ecosystem-centered (ecocentric)* view.

According to the *biocentric worldview*, each wild species has an inherent right to exist, or at least the right to struggle to exist, equal to that of any other species. Thus, it is ethically wrong for us to hasten the extinction of any species. Some go further and believe that each individual wild creature — not just a species — has a

right to survive without human interference, just as each human being has the right to survive.

Some distinguish between the survival rights of plants and those of animals. The poet Alan Watts once commented that he was a vegetarian "because cows scream louder than carrots." Many people make ethical distinctions among various types of animals. For instance, they think little about killing a fly, a mosquito, a cockroach, or a sewer rat, or about catching and killing fish they don't eat. Unless they are strict vegetarians, they also think little about having others kill cattle, calves, lambs, and chickens in slaughterhouses to provide them with meat, leather, and other animal products. The same people, however, might deplore the killing of game animals such as deer, squirrels, or rabbits for sport or for food.

The *ecocentric worldview* stresses the importance of preserving biodiversity by preserving, or not degrading, entire ecosystems, rather than focusing only on individual species or on an individual organism. It recognizes that saving wildlife means saving the places where they live. This view is based on Aldo Leopold's ethical principle that something is right when it tends to maintain Earth's life-support systems for us and other species and wrong when it tends otherwise. The *sustainable-Earth worldview* is a combination of the biocentric and ecocentric worldviews (Section 2-3).

16-2 How Species Become Depleted and Extinct

THE RISE AND FALL OF SPECIES Extinction is a natural process (Section 5-4). As the planet's surface and climate have changed over its 4.6 billion years of existence, species have disappeared and new ones have evolved to take their places. This rise and fall of species has not been smooth. Evidence indicates that over the past 500 million years, there have been several periods when mass extinctions have reduced Earth's biodiversity and other periods, called radiations, when the diversity of life has increased and spread.

EXTINCTION OF SPECIES TODAY Imagine you are driving on an interstate highway at a high speed. You notice that your two passengers are passing the time by using wrenches and screwdrivers to remove various bolts, screws, and parts of your car on a random basis and throwing them out the window. How long will it be before they remove enough parts to cause a breakdown or a crash?

This urgent question is one that we as a species should be asking ourselves. As we tinker with the only home for us and other species, we are rapidly removing parts of Earth's natural biodiversity upon which we and other species depend in ways we know little about. We are not heeding Aldo Leopold's warning: "To keep every cog and wheel is the first precaution of intelligent tinkering."

Past mass extinctions took place slowly enough to allow new forms of life to arise as adaptations to an ever-changing world. This process began changing about 40,000 years ago when the latest version of our species came on the scene. Since agriculture began about 10,000 years ago, the rate of species extinction has increased sharply as human settlements have expanded worldwide.

It is hard to document extinctions, since most go unrecorded. Using available data, biologists estimate that during 1992 at least 4,000 and possibly 51,000 species became extinct mostly because of our activities, and the number is rising. These scientists warn that if deforestation (especially of tropical forests), desertification, and destruction of wetlands and coral reefs continue at their present rates, within the next few decades we could easily cause the loss of at least 2% and perhaps 25% of Earth's species forever. This will rival some of the great natural mass extinctions of the past.

There are three important differences between the present mass extinction and those in the past:

- The present extinction crisis is being brought about by us—the first one to be caused by a single species.

- The current wildlife holocaust is taking place in only a few decades rather than over thousands to millions of years. Such rapid extinction cannot be balanced by speciation because it takes between 2,000 and 100,000 generations for new species to evolve.

- Plant species are disappearing as rapidly as animal species, thus threatening many animal species that otherwise would not become extinct at this time. The fate of our species and millions of others is likely to depend on the survival of numerous known and unknown species of plants, insects that pollinate plants, and decomposers. It is estimated that over the next several decades 25% of Earth's plant species may become extinct because of our activities—most of these species never examined to determine their roles in the ecosphere and their potential usefulness to us as sources of food, fiber, fuel, medicines, and other products.

ENDANGERED AND THREATENED SPECIES TODAY Species heading toward extinction can be classified as either endangered or threatened. An **endangered species** is one having so few individual survivors that the species could soon become extinct over all or most of its natural range. Examples are the Javan rhino (60 left), the California condor (Figure 16-2) in the United States (only two in the wild), the giant panda in central China (1,000 left), the snow leopard in central

Figure 16-4 This endangered shallowtail butterfly was almost pushed to extinction in Great Britain but is now hanging on, mostly in protected nature reserves.

Asia (2,500 left), and the rare shallowtail butterfly (Figure 16-4).

A **threatened species** is still abundant in its natural range but is declining in numbers and likely to become endangered. Examples are the bald eagle (Figure 16-5) and the grizzly bear.

Many wild species are not in danger of extinction, but their populations have been sharply reduced locally or regionally. They may be a better sign of the condition of wildlife and entire ecosystems than endangered and threatened species. They can serve as early warnings so that we can prevent species extinction rather than responding mostly to emergencies.

HABITAT LOSS AND DISTURBANCE The greatest threat to most wild species is destruction, fragmentation, and degradation of their habitats, especially on land where most of Earth's species (possibly 90%) exist. Such disruption of natural communities threatens wild species by destroying migration routes, breeding areas, and food sources. Deforestation, especially of tropical forests (Section 15-2), is the greatest cause of the decline in global biological diversity by habitat loss and degradation, followed by destruction of coral reefs (Figure 5-23) and wetlands (see Case Study on p. 103 and Spotlight on p. 104), and plowing of grasslands (Figure 5-12).

Since Europeans first settled North America, 98% of the tall-grass prairies (Figure 5-10) in the United States have been destroyed, half of the wetlands have been lost (see Spotlight on p. 104), 98% of virgin and old-growth forests have been cut (Figure 15-19), overall forest cover has been reduced by 33%, and at least 500 native species have become extinct. Furthermore, much of the remaining wildlife habitat is being fragmented and polluted at an alarming rate.

Loss or degradation of habitat is the key factor in the extinction of American bird species such as the

Q: How much of the world's wastepaper was recycled in 1991?

Figure 16-5 An estimated 250,000 American bald eagles were found in the United States when this bird became the national symbol in 1782. During the late 1960s and early 1970s, the number of American bald eagles in the lower 48 states declined because of loss of habitat, illegal hunting, poisoning, and reproductive failure caused by pesticides in fish, their primary diet. Federal protection has led to recovery in many areas. In 1990, there were about 37,500 to 40,000 bald eagles in the wild, with 7,500 to 10,000 in the lower 48 states and about 30,000 in Alaska. In 1989, the U.S. Fish and Wildlife Service spent $3.9 million on this recovery program.

Figure 16-6 The whooping crane, shown in its winter refuge in Texas, is an endangered species in North America. Once, it lived throughout most of North America, but its low reproduction rates and fixed migration pattern make it vulnerable to extinction. Mostly because of illegal shooting and loss of habitat, the number of whooping cranes in the wild dropped to only 16 by 1941. Because of a $5-million-a-year habitat protection and captive breeding program directed by the U.S. Fish and Wildlife Service, about 217 birds survive today, including 142 in the wild. By the mid-1990s, wildlife officials hope to release 15 to 20 captive birds annually into the wild.

heath hen and the near extinction of Atwater's prairie chicken, the California condor (Figure 16-2), and the whooping crane (Figure 16-6).

Many rare and threatened plant and animal species live in vulnerable, specialized habitats, such as islands (Figure 16-7) or single trees in tropical forests. Madagascar — a megadiversity country (Figure 15-5) — is a prime example of an island where hundreds of species found nowhere else are threatened with extinction. Human alterations of terrestrial areas fragment wildlife habitats into patches, or "habitat islands," which are often too small to support the minimum number of individuals needed to sustain a population. Most national parks and other protected areas are habitat islands.

Many species of insect-eating, migratory songbirds in North America are being threatened with extinction, with population drops of 25% to 45% between 1978 and 1987. The main reasons for these population declines are destruction and fragmentation of tropical forests in their winter habitats in Central and South America and fragmentation of their summer habitat in North America, which provides easier access for predators and parasites.

Thus, the primary reason for our current and escalating extinction crisis is that we are using 40% of Earth's terrestrial net primary productivity. This eliminates or severely limits places where terrestrial wild species can live. What will happen to wildlife and the services they provide for us if our population doubles in the next 40 years and we use as much as 80% of the planet's terrestrial net primary productivity?

Figure 16-7 Island species are especially vulnerable to extinction. The endangered *Symphonia* clings to life on the island of Madagascar, where 90% of the original vegetation has been destroyed.

COMMERCIAL HUNTING AND POACHING There are three main types of hunting: subsistence, sport, and commercial. The killing of animals to provide enough food for survival is called **subsistence hunting**. **Sport hunting** is the hunting of animals for recreation and in some cases for food. **Commercial hunting** involves killing animals for profit from sale of their furs or other parts. Illegal commercial hunting or fishing is called **poaching**.

Today, subsistence hunting has declined sharply in most parts of the world because of the decrease in hunting-and-gathering societies. Sport hunting is now closely regulated in most countries. Game species

A: About 33% (33% in the United States)

When European explorers discovered North America in the late 1400s, various tribes of Native Americans depended heavily on bison for survival. The meat was their staple diet. The skin was used for tepees, moccasins, and clothes. The gut made their bowstrings, and the horns their spoons. Even the dried feces, called buffalo chips by English-speaking settlers, were used for fuel.

In 1500, before European settlers came to North America, between 60 million and 125 million grass-eating American bison roamed the plains, prairies, and woodlands over most of the continent (Figure 16-8). Single herds covered thousands of square kilometers of land. Their numbers were so large they were thought to

be inexhaustible. By 1906, however, the once-extensive range of the American bison was reduced to a tiny area, and the species was nearly driven to extinction, mostly because of overhunting and loss of habitat.

As settlers moved west after the Civil War, the sustainable balance between Native Americans and bison was upset. Native Americans of the plains traded bison skins to settlers for steel knives and firearms, and they began killing bison in larger numbers.

Much greater depletion of this potentially renewable resource was caused by other factors. First, as railroads spread westward in the late 1860s, railroad companies hired professional bison hunters to supply construction crews with meat. The

well-known bison hunter "Buffalo Bill" Cody killed an estimated 4,280 bison in only 18 months — surely a world record. Passengers also gunned down bison from train windows, purely for sport, leaving the carcasses to rot.

As farmers settled the plains, they shot bison because the animals destroyed crops. Ranchers killed them because they competed with cattle and sheep for grass and knocked over fences, telegraph poles, and sod houses.

An army of commercial hunters shot millions of bison for their hides and for their tongues, which were considered a delicacy. Instead of being eaten, however, most of the meat was left to rot. "Bone pickers"

(continued)

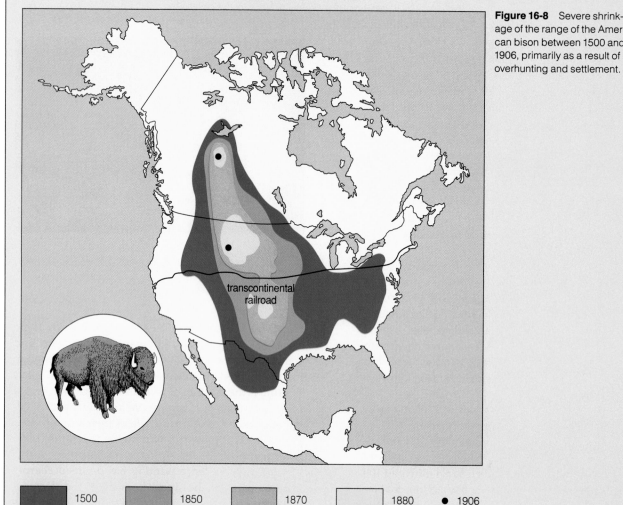

Figure 16-8 Severe shrinkage of the range of the American bison between 1500 and 1906, primarily as a result of overhunting and settlement.

transcontinental railroad

| 1500 | 1850 | 1870 | 1880 | ● 1906 |

Q: How much of the world's wastepaper could be recycled by 2000?

then collected the bleached bones that whitened the prairies and shipped them east for use as fertilizer.

Finally, after the Civil War, the U.S. Army began to subdue plains tribes of Native Americans and take over their lands by killing off their primary source of food. At least 2.5 million bison were slaughtered each year between 1870 and 1875 in this form of biological warfare.

By 1890, only one herd of about 1 million bison was left. Commercial hunters and skinners descended on this herd, and by 1892, only 85 bison were left. They were given refuge in Yellowstone National Park and protected by an 1893 law against the killing of wild animals in national parks.

In 1905, 16 people formed the American Bison Society to protect and rebuild the captive population of the animal. In the early 1900s, the federal government established the National Bison Range near Missoula, Montana. Since then, captive herds on this federal land and other herds mostly on privately owned land scattered throughout the West have been protected by law.

Today, there are about 100,000 bison in the United States — one-fifth of them on the National Bison Range. Some captive bison are crossbred with cattle to produce hybrids, called beefalo. Their meat is tasty and they grow faster and are easier to raise than cattle, with no need for expensive grain feed.

---

are endangered by such sport hunting only when protective regulations do not exist or are not enforced. No animal in the United States, for instance, has become extinct or endangered because of regulated sport hunting.

In the past, legal and illegal commercial hunting has led to the extinction or near extinction of many animal species, such as the American bison (see Case Study on p. 360). This continues today. It's not surprising that Bengal tigers face extinction, since a coat made from their fur sells for $100,000 in Tokyo. A mountain gorilla is worth $150,000; an ocelot skin, $40,000; an Imperial Amazon macaw, $30,000; a snow leopard skin, $14,000; rhinoceros horn, up to $28,600 per kilogram (Figure 16-9); and tiger meat, $286 per kilogram ($130 per pound).

Elephants are slaughtered by poachers for their valuable ivory tusks (Figure 16-10). In 1970, there were about 4.5 million African elephants (Figure 5-9). By 1990, there were only about 650,000 left. If widespread poaching is not halted, the African elephant could be wiped out within 10 years. In January 1990, members of a 119-nation convention (CITES) devoted to protecting endangered and threatened species banned all international trade in African elephant products. Although seven countries exempted themselves from the ban, the bottom dropped out of the worldwide ivory market within a short time after the ban. Conservationists now fear that poachers will begin killing large numbers of Alaska's population of walrus for their ivory tusks (Figure 16-11).

Even if the poacher is caught, the economic incentive far outweighs the risk of paying a small fine and the much smaller risk of serving time in jail. As more of the world's species become endangered, their economic

Figure 16-9 All five species of rhinoceros (Figure 4-31), one of the world's oldest mammals, are threatened with extinction because of poachers, who kill them for their horns, and loss of habitat. In parts of the Middle East, such as Yemen, rhino horns are carved into ornate dagger handles, which sell for $500 to $12,000. In the Middle East, Asian rhino horns, the most prized, can fetch as much as $28,600 a kilogram ($13,000 a pound). In China and other parts of Asia, the powder of ground rhino horns is used for medicinal purposes and as an aphrodisiac, although its effectiveness has not been established. Efforts to protect these species from extinction are under way; however, only about 12,000 rhinos remain in the wild.

As wildlife habitats in other parts of the world have disappeared, the United States has become a target for poachers. Much of this is taking place in national parks and wilderness areas in the western half of the country and in Alaska.

Some of the poaching involves outfitters who charge large fees to help wealthy hunters kill an endangered species or other prized trophy species and a few renegade hunters who violate hunting laws. Much of the killing and trapping is done by networks of professional poachers tied to markets in China, Japan, Korea, Hong Kong, and Taiwan.

According to the U.S. Fish and Wildlife Service, a poached gyrofalcon sells for $120,000; a bighorn sheep head, $10,000 to $60,000; a large saguaro cactus (Figure 4-5), $5,000 to $15,000; a peregrine falcon (Figure 14-5), $10,000; a polar bear, $6,000; a grizzly bear, $5,000; an elk head, $5,000 to $10,000; a mountain goat, $3,500; a bald eagle, $2,500; and a bear gallbladder (used in Asia for medicinal purposes), up to $800 a gram ($363,000 per pound).

Walruses are decapitated for their ivory tusks (Figure 16-11). Thousands of night-roosting robins are captured illegally by nets and used

to make Cajun gumbo. In Alaska, poachers shoot wolves, polar bears (for their furs and gallbladders) and bald eagles from airplanes. They also catch sturgeon and rare paddlefish and sell their eggs for caviar.

Most poachers are not caught. There are more police officers in New York City than wildlife protection officers in the entire United States. Only 22 agents cover one-third of the country where extensive poaching occurs. Despite a 94% conviction rate for those caught in the United States, most are fined much less than the profits they make and few are sent to jail.

Figure 16-10 Vultures feeding on the carcass of a male elephant in Tanzania. The poachers who killed it cut off its ivory tusks. The valuable ivory is used for jewelry, piano keys, ornamental carvings, and art objects. African elephants play several important ecological roles. Their dung spreads seeds of the fruit they eat. In Central and West Africa, their trampling of underbrush and uprooting of small trees create open spaces in dense rain forest that allow growth of vegetation favored by gorillas and hoofed plant eaters. In East Africa, these same activities convert woodland into savanna (Figure 5-9), increasing the habitat for hoofed grazers such as gazelles, wildebeests, and zebras. However, when elephants are forced into a small area of habitat, they can destroy most of the vegetation and also food crops.

Figure 16-11 Increasing numbers of bull walruses found in the Bering Sea off the coast of Alaska are being killed illegally, mostly by Alaska's native Inuits (Eskimos) for their ivory tusks. A pair of these tusks is worth $800 to $1,500 on the black market. The ivory-tusked male walruses are easy to kill because they spend the summer on ice floes. Hunters in small boats shoot the slow-moving mammals; use the liver, the heart, and other parts for food (legally allowed if this slaughter is not done in an excessive and wasteful manner); sever the head with a chain saw; and illegally sell the tusks. With an estimated 250,000 walruses remaining in the Pacific, this species is not endangered now, but it may soon be if excessive and wasteful hunting continues.

value and the demand for them on the black market rise sharply, hastening their extinction. Poaching is also increasing in the United States (see Spotlight above).

PREDATOR AND PEST CONTROL Extinction or near extinction can also occur when people attempt to exterminate pest and predator species that compete

with humans for food and game. Fruit farmers exterminated the Carolina parakeet in the United States around 1914 because it fed on fruit crops. The species was easy to wipe out because when one member of a flock was shot, the rest of the birds hovered over its body, making themselves easy targets.

As animal habitats have shrunk, farmers have killed large numbers of African elephants (Figure 5-9)

Q: How much of the money taken in by private concessionaires in national parks is paid to the government in user fees?

Figure 16-12 The Utah prairie dog is a threatened species in the United States, mostly because of widespread poisoning by ranchers and government agencies since 1929.

Figure 16-13 The black-footed ferret is nearly extinct in North America because most of the once-abundant prairie dogs (Figure 16-12) that made up 90% or more of its diet have been eliminated. By 1985, none of these animals were left in the wild. Between 1985 and 1992, the population of black-footed ferrets in captivity grew from 18 to 325. In 1991, biologists released 49 of these captively bred animals to a favorable habitat in north-central Wyoming. Over the next decade, there are plans to reintroduce more ferrets, with the goal of eventually building a wild population of 1,500 at nine sites throughout the West.

to keep them from trampling and eating food crops. Since 1929, ranchers and government agencies have poisoned prairie dogs because horses and cattle sometimes step into the burrows and break their legs. This poisoning has killed 99% of the prairie dog population in North America (Figure 16-12). It has also led to the near extinction of the black-footed ferret (Figure 16-13), which preyed on the prairie dog.

PETS AND DECORATIVE PLANTS Each year, large numbers of threatened and endangered animal species are smuggled into the United States, Great Britain, Germany, and other countries (Figure 16-14). Most are sold as pets.

Some species of exotic plants, especially orchids and cacti, are also endangered because they are gath-

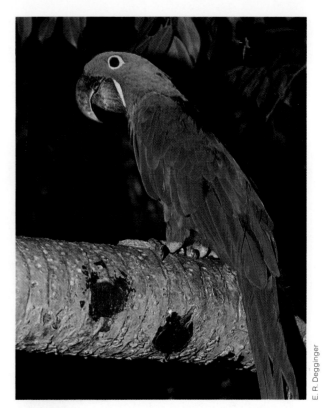

Figure 16-14 Collectors of exotic birds may pay $10,000 for a threatened hyacinth macaw smuggled out of Brazil. These high prices help doom such species to eventual extinction. Worldwide, more than 3.5 million live wild birds are captured and sold legally each year, and 2.5 million more are captured and sold illegally. For every bird that reaches a pet shop legally or illegally, at least one other dies in transit. After purchase, many of these animals are mistreated, killed, or abandoned by their owners.

Figure 16-15 The black lace cactus is one of the many U.S. plants that are endangered, mostly because of development and collectors.

ered, often illegally (Figure 16-15). They are then sold to collectors and used to decorate houses, offices, and landscapes. A collector may pay $5,000 for a single rare orchid.

A single prize specimen such as a rare mature crested saguaro cactus can earn cactus rustlers as much

The fast-growing water hyacinth is native to Central and South America. In 1884, a woman took one of these plants from an exhibition in New Orleans and planted it in her backyard in Florida. Within 10 years, the plant, which can double its population in weeks, was a menace.

Unchecked by natural enemies and thriving on Florida's nutrient-rich waters, water hyacinths rapidly displaced native plants. They also clogged waterways in many ponds, streams, canals, and rivers in Florida and in other parts of the southeastern United States (Figure 16-16).

Since 1898, mechanical harvesters and a variety of herbicides have been used to keep the plant in check, with little success. Large numbers of Florida manatees, or sea cows (Figure 16-17), can control the growth and spread of water hyacinths in inland waters more effectively than mechanical or chemical methods. However, these gentle and playful herbivores are threatened with extinction, mostly from being slashed by powerboat propellers, becoming entangled in fishing gear, or being hit on the head by oars.

In recent years, scientists have introduced other alien species that feed on water hyacinths to help control its spread. They include a weevil imported from Argentina, a water snail from Puerto Rico, and the grass carp, a fish brought in from the then Soviet Union. These species can help, but the water snail and the grass carp also feed on other, desirable aquatic plants.

There is some good news in this story. Preliminary research indicates that water hyacinths can be used in several beneficial ways. They can be introduced in sewage treatment lagoons to absorb toxic chemicals.

Figure 16-16 The fast-growing water hyacinth was intentionally introduced into Florida from Latin America in 1884. Since then, this plant, which can double its population in only two weeks, has taken over waterways in Florida and other southeastern states.

Heather Angel/Biofotos

Florida Marine Research Institute/Florida Department of Natural Resources

Figure 16-17 The Florida manatee, or sea cow, one of America's most endangered species, is a dying breed in a vanishing habitat. It feeds on aquatic weeds and could help control the growth and spread of the water hyacinth in Florida. Only about 1,000 of these gentle animals are left in their habitats in the sluggish bays and rivers of southern and central Florida. They may not exist much longer because of loss of habitat, water pollution, injury or death from boat propellers, and their low reproductive rate.

They can be converted by fermentation into a biogas fuel similar to natural gas, added as a mineral and protein supplement to cattle feed, and applied to the soil as fertilizer. They can also be used to clean up polluted ponds and lakes — if their numbers can be kept under control.

as $15,000. To reduce losses from cactus rustlers, Arizona has put 222 species under state protection with penalties of up to $1,000 and jail sentences up to one year. However, only seven people are assigned to enforce this law over the entire state, and the fines are too small to discourage poaching.

POLLUTION AND CLIMATE CHANGE Toxic chemicals degrade wildlife habitats, including wildlife refuges, and kill some plants and animals. Slowly degradable pesticides, especially DDT and dieldrin, have caused populations of some bird species to decline (see Spotlight on p. 312).

Q: How much of all U.S. land area is protected as wilderness?

Table 16-1 Damage Caused by Plants and Animals Imported into the United States

Name	Origin	Mode of Transport	Type of Damage
Mammals			
European wild boar	Russia	Intentionally imported (1912), escaped captivity	Destruction of habitat by rooting; crop damage
Nutria (cat-sized rodent)	Argentina	Intentionally imported, escaped captivity (1940)	Alteration of marsh ecology; damage to levees and earth dams; crop destruction
Birds			
European starling	Europe	Intentionally released (1890)	Competition with native songbirds; crop damage; transmission of swine diseases; airport interference
House sparrow	England	Intentionally released by Brooklyn Institute (1853)	Crop damage; displacement of native songbirds
Fish			
Carp	Germany	Intentionally released (1877)	Displacement of native fish; uprooting of water plants with loss of waterfowl populations
Sea lamprey	North Atlantic Ocean	Entered via Welland Canal (1829)	Destruction of lake trout, lake white-fish, and sturgeon in Great Lakes
Walking catfish	Thailand	Imported into Florida	Destruction of bass, bluegill, and other fish
Insects			
Argentine fire ant	Argentina	Probably entered via coffee shipments from Brazil (1918)	Crop damage; destruction of native ant species
Camphor scale insect	Japan	Accidentally imported on nursery stock (1920s)	Damage to nearly 200 species of plants in Louisiana, Texas, and Alabama
Japanese beetle	Japan	Accidentally imported on irises or azaleas (1911)	Defoliation of more than 250 species of trees and other plants, including many of commercial importance
Plants			
Water hyacinth	Central America	Intentionally introduced (1884)	Clogging waterways; shading out other aquatic vegetation
Chestnut blight (fungus)	Asia	Accidentally imported on nursery plants (1900)	Destruction of nearly all eastern American chestnut trees; disturbance of forest ecology
Dutch elm disease, *Cerastomella ulmi* (fungus)	Europe	Accidentally imported on infected elm timber used for veneers (1930)	Destruction of millions of elms; disturbance of forest ecology

From *Biological Conservation* by David W. Ehrenfeld. Copyright © 1970 by Holt, Rinehart & Winston, Inc. Modified and reprinted by permission.

Wildlife in even the best-protected and best-managed wildlife reserves throughout the world may be depleted in a few decades because of climatic change caused by projected global warming (Section 10-2).

INTRODUCTION OF ALIEN SPECIES As people travel around the world, they sometimes pick up plants and animals intentionally or accidentally and introduce them to new geographical regions. Many of these alien species have provided food, game, and beauty and have helped control pests in their new environments.

Some alien species have no natural predators and competitors in their new habitats. That allows them to dominate their new ecosystem and reduce the populations of many native species (see Case Study on p. 364). Such aliens can cause the extinction, near extinction, or displacement of native species (Table 16-1).

POPULATION GROWTH, AFFLUENCE, AND POVERTY The underlying causes of extinction and population reduction of wildlife are population growth of humans, affluence, and poverty. As the human popu-

Table 16-2 Characteristics of Extinction-Prone Species

Characteristic	Examples
Low reproduction rate	Blue whale, polar bear, California condor, Andean condor, passenger pigeon, giant panda, whooping crane
Specialized feeding habits	Everglades kite (eats apple snail of southern Florida), blue whale (krill in polar upwelling areas), black-footed ferret (prairie dogs and pocket gophers), giant panda (bamboo), Australian koala (certain types of eucalyptus leaves)
Feed at high trophic levels	Bengal tiger, bald eagle, Andean condor, timber wolf
Large size	Bengal tiger, African lion, elephant, Javan rhinoceros, American bison, giant panda, grizzly bear
Limited or specialized nesting or breeding areas	Kirtland's warbler (nests only in 6- to 15-year-old jack pine trees), whooping crane (depends on marshes for food and nesting), orangutan (now found only on islands of Sumatra and Borneo), green sea turtle (lays eggs on only a few beaches), bald eagle (prefers habitat of forested shorelines), nightingale wren (nests and breeds only on Barro Colorado Island, Panama)
Found in only one place or region	Woodland caribou, elephant seal, Cooke's kokio, and many unique island species
Fixed migratory patterns	Blue whale, Kirtland's warbler, Bachman's warbler, whooping crane
Preys on livestock or people	Timber wolf, some crocodiles
Certain behavioral patterns	Passenger pigeon and white-crowned pigeon (nest in large colonies), redheaded woodpecker (flies in front of cars), Carolina parakeet (when one bird is shot, rest of flock hovers over body), key deer (forages for cigarette butts along highways — it's a "nicotine addict")

lation grows, it occupies more land and clears and degrades more land to supply food, fuelwood, timber, and other resources.

Increasing affluence and economic growth lead to greatly increased average resource use per person, which is a prime factor in destruction and degradation of wildlife habitat (Figure 1-12). In LDCs, the combination of rapid population growth and poverty push the poor to cut forests, grow crops on marginal land, overgraze grasslands, and poach endangered animals.

CHARACTERISTICS OF EXTINCTION-PRONE SPECIES Some species have natural traits that make them more vulnerable than others to premature extinction (Table 16-2). Each animal species has a critical population density and size, below which survival may be impossible because males and females have a hard time finding each other. Once the population reaches its critical size, it continues to decline, even if the species is protected, because its death rate exceeds its birth rate. The remaining small population can easily be wiped out by fire, flood, landslide, disease, or some other catastrophic event. Extinctions are more likely to occur in terrestrial ecosystems than in marine ecosystems.

Some species, such as bats, are vulnerable to extinction for a combination of reasons (see Case Study on p. 367).

16-3 Protecting Wild Species from Extinction

METHODS FOR PROTECTING AND MANAGING WILDLIFE There are three basic approaches to wildlife conservation and management.

1. *The species approach:* Protect endangered species by identifying them, giving them legal protection, preserving and managing their critical habitats, propagating species in captivity, and reintroducing species in suitable habitats.

2. *The ecosystem approach:* Preserve balanced populations of species in their native habitats, establish legally protected wilderness areas and wildlife reserves, and eliminate alien species from an area.

3. *The wildlife management approach:* Manage species, mostly game species, for sustained yield by using laws to regulate hunting, establishing harvest quotas, developing population management plans, and using international treaties to protect migrating game species such as waterfowl.

THE SPECIES APPROACH: TREATIES AND LAWS Several international treaties and conventions help protect wild species. One of the most far-reaching treaties

Q: How much of the U.S. gross national product is derived from wildlife resources?

Despite their variety (950 species) and worldwide distribution, bats have several traits that make them vulnerable to extinction from human activities. They reproduce very slowly compared with other mammals, and many nest in huge breeding colonies in accessible places, where people can easily destroy them by blocking the entrances.

Bats play important ecological roles and are also of great economic importance to humans. Bats help control many insects that damage human crops and other pest species, such as mosquitoes and rodents (Figure 16-18). About 70% of all bat species feed on various night-flying insects, making them the primary predators of night-flying insects.

Other species of bats feed on certain types of pollen nectar, and still others feed on certain types of fruit. Because of this specialized feeding, these bat species are the chief pollinators for many types of trees, shrubs, and other plants and also disperse plants throughout tropical forests by excreting undigested seeds. If these keystone species are eliminated from an area, dependent plants would disappear.

If you enjoy bananas, cashews, dates, figs, avocados, or mangos, you can thank bats. Likewise, you can thank bats if you have benefited from surgical bandages or life preservers filled with kapok, hemp fibers for rope, and hundreds of other commercially important materials.

G. B. Barker/A.N.T. Photo Library

Figure 16-18 Endangered ghost bat carrying a mouse in tropical northern Australia. This carnivorous bat feeds at night and is harmless to people. Bats are considered keystone species in many ecosystems because of their roles in pollinating plants, dispersing seeds, and controlling insect and rodent populations.

Research involving bats has contributed to the development of birth control and artificial insemination methods, drug testing, studies of disease resistance and aging, production of vaccines, and development of navigational aids for the blind.

People kill bats in large numbers because of fears based on misinformation, vampire movies, and folklore and because of lack of knowledge about their important ecological roles. Bats are not dirty, aggressive, rabies-carrying, bloodsucking creatures. Most bat species are harmless to people, livestock, and crops.

In all of Asia, Europe, Australia, and the Pacific Islands, only two people have been suspected of dying from bat-transmitted rabies. No people in these areas are known to have died of any other bat-

transmitted disease. By comparison, in India alone, some 15,000 people die each year from rabies transmitted by other animals, mostly dogs.

In the United States, only 10 people have died of bat-transmitted disease in four decades of record keeping. More Americans die each year from dog attacks or falling coconuts. Only three species of bats (none of them found in the United States) feed on blood, drawn mostly from cattle or wild animals. These bat species can be serious pests to domestic livestock but rarely affect humans.

We need to see bats as valuable allies — not enemies — before we destroy them and lose their important benefits. Educating people about the nature and importance of bats and building barriers to exclude people from bat caves will help.

is the 1975 Convention on International Trade in Endangered Species (CITES). This treaty, now signed by 119 countries, lists 675 species that cannot be commercially traded as live specimens or wildlife products because they are endangered or threatened.

However, enforcement of this treaty is spotty, violators often pay only small fines, and member countries can exempt themselves from protection of any listed species. Also, much of the $1- to $2-billion-a-year illegal trade in wildlife and wildlife products goes on in countries, such as Singapore, that have not signed the treaty.

The United States controls imports and exports of endangered wildlife and wildlife products with two im-

portant laws. One is the Lacey Act of 1900, which prohibits transporting live or dead wild animals or their parts across state borders without a federal permit. The other law is the Endangered Species Act of 1973, including amendments in 1982 and 1988 (see Spotlight on p. 368).

Funds for state game management programs are provided by the sale of hunting and fishing licenses and federal taxes on hunting and fishing equipment. Two-thirds of the states also have checkoffs on state income tax returns that allow individuals to contribute money to state wildlife programs. Only 10% of all federal and state wildlife dollars are spent to study or benefit the

The Endangered Species Act of 1973 is one of the world's toughest environmental laws. This act makes it illegal for the United States to import or to carry on trade in any product made from an endangered or threatened species unless it is used for an approved scientific purpose or to enhance the survival of the species.

All commercial shipments of wildlife and wildlife products must enter or leave the country through one of nine designated ports, but many illegal shipments of wildlife slip by. The 60 Fish and Wildlife Service inspectors are able to physically examine only about one-fourth of the 90,000 shipments that enter and leave the United States each year (Figure 16-19). Permits have been falsified, and some government inspectors have been bribed. Even if caught, many violators are not prosecuted, and convicted violators often pay only a small fine.

The law also provides protection for endangered and threatened species in the United States and abroad. It authorizes the National Marine Fisheries Service (NMFS) to identify and list endangered and threatened ma-

Figure 16-19 Confiscated products derived from endangered species. Because of a lack of funds and too few inspectors, probably no more than one-tenth of the illegal wildlife trade in the United States is discovered. The situation is much worse in most other countries.

rine species. The Fish and Wildlife Service (FWS) identifies and lists all other endangered and threatened species. These species cannot be hunted, killed, collected, or injured in the United States.

Any decision by either agency to add or remove a species from the list must be based only on biological grounds without economic considerations. The act also prohibits federal agencies from carrying out, funding, or authorizing projects that would jeopardize an endangered or threatened species or destroy or modify its critical habitat —

Figure 16-20 The first national wildlife refuge was set up off the coast of Florida in 1903 to protect the brown pelican from extinction. In the 1960s, this species was threatened with extinction when exposure to DDT and other persistent pesticides in the fish it eats caused reproductive losses. Now it is making a comeback.

nongame species that make up nearly 90% of the country's wildlife species.

THE SPECIES APPROACH: WILDLIFE REFUGES

In 1903, President Theodore Roosevelt established the first U.S. federal wildlife refuge at Pelican Island on the east coast of Florida to protect the endangered brown pelican (Figure 16-20). By 1992, the National Wildlife Refuge System had 456 refuges (Figure 15-11). About 85% of the area included in these refuges is in Alaska.

Over three-fourths of the refuges are wetlands for protection of migratory waterfowl. Most of the species on the U.S. endangered list have habitats in the refuge system and some refuges have been set aside for specific endangered species. These have helped the key deer, the brown pelican of southern Florida (Figure 16-20), and the trumpeter swan to recover. Conservationists complain there has been too little emphasis on establishing refuges for endangered plants.

Congress has not established guidelines (such as multiple use or sustained yield) for management of the

Q: How many of Earth's species are believed to become extinct each year because of human activities?

the land, air, and water necessary for its survival.

Between 1970 and 1992, the number of species found only in the United States that have been placed on the official endangered and threatened list increased from 92 to 639. Also on the list are 508 species found in other parts of the world.

Once a species is listed as endangered or threatened in the United States, the FWS or the NMFS is supposed to prepare a plan to help it recover. However, because of a lack of funds, recovery plans have been developed and approved for only about 61% of the endangered or threatened species native to the United States, and half of those plans exist only on paper. Only a handful of species have recovered sufficiently to be removed from protection.

The current annual federal budget for endangered species is $8.4 million—equal to the cost of about 25 Army bulldozers. This helps explain why, at the current budget level, it will take the Fish and Wildlife Service 38 to 48 years to evaluate the more than 3,500 species now under consideration for listing. Wildlife experts estimate that 10% or more of these species will become extinct.

In 1990, Manuel Lujan, the secretary of the interior (who is responsible for wildlife protection), proposed that the Endangered Species Act, which was up for renewal in 1992, be weakened. He suggested that economic factors should be considered when deciding whether to include a species on the list of endangered and threatened species or when deciding whether to approve federally funded projects that might threaten the critical habitats of endangered or threatened species. There are those who support these proposed changes to the law, believing that economic interests must be balanced against ecological interests; they often frame the debate as a choice between jobs and wildlife.

However, these proposals are seen by many conservationists as a misguided attack on the law, and they and many members of Congress vigorously oppose these changes. They believe the jobs-versus-wildlife dichotomy obscures the real issue, which is that biological diversity must be protected. They argue that to protect this diversity we need to make wildlife protection stronger—not weaker—by

- Giving federal officials deadlines for developing and implementing recovery plans for ecosystems containing threatened, endangered, and candidate species

- Requiring officials to develop conservation plans for whole ecosystems to help prevent future declines in species not yet listed as threatened or endangered

- Allowing citizens to file lawsuits immediately if an endangered species faces serious harm or extinction

- Greatly increasing funding for federal endangered species programs

What do you think should be done?

National Wildlife Refuge System, as it has for other public lands. As a result, the Fish and Wildlife Service has allowed many refuges to be used for hunting, fishing, trapping, timber cutting, livestock grazing, farming, oil and gas development, mining, waste dumping, military air and land exercises, power boating, air boats, and off-road vehicles. Currently, more than 50% of the refuges are open to hunting, 89% to trapping, and 56% to fishing.

Development of oil, gas, and mineral resources can destroy or degrade wildlife habitats in refuges through road building, well and pipeline construction, oil and gas leaks, and pits filled with brine or drilling muds (see Pro/Con on p. 370).

Pollution is also a problem in a number of wildlife refuges. A 1986 study by the Fish and Wildlife Service estimated that one in five federal refuges is contaminated with toxic chemicals. Most of this pollution comes from old toxic-waste dump sites (including military bases) and runoff from nearby agricultural land. For example, massive waterfowl deaths in the Kesterson National Wildlife Refuge in California's San Joaquin Valley in 1982 have been blamed on runoff of selenium-tainted irrigation water.

THE SPECIES APPROACH: GENE BANKS, BOTANICAL GARDENS, AND ZOOS Botanists preserve genetic information and endangered plant species by storing their seeds in gene banks—refrigerated environments with low humidity. Gene banks of most known and many potential varieties of agricultural crops and other plants now exist throughout the world (Figure 13-2). Scientists have urged that many more be established, especially in LDCs; but some species can't be preserved in gene banks, and maintaining gene banks is very expensive.

The world's 1,500 botanical gardens and aboreta hold about 90,000 plant species and also help preserve some of the genetic diversity found in the wild. However, these sanctuaries have too little storage capacity and too little money to preserve most of the world's rare and threatened plants.

The Arctic National Wildlife Refuge on Alaska's North Slope is the second largest in the system (Figure 16-21), covering an area the size of South Carolina. This fragile, ecologically valuable area contains more than one-fifth of all the land in the U.S. wildlife refuge system and has been called the crown jewel of the system.

Its coastal plain, the most biologically productive part of the refuge, is the only stretch of Alaska's arctic coastline that has not been been opened by Congress to oil and gas development. Energy companies hope to change this because they believe that the area *might* contain oil and natural gas deposits that would increase their profits and also reduce U.S. reliance on foreign oil. Since 1985, they have asked Congress to open 607,000 hectares (1.5 million acres) of the coastal plain of the refuge to drilling for oil and natural gas, a proposal the Bush administration has supported.

President Bush went further by asking Congress to approve opening *all* federal land (except national parks)—including national forests, wildlife refuges, and the continental shelf—to oil and gas development whenever oil imports exceed 50% of the country's oil use (Figure 1-10).

The Bush administration would also like to lift the ban on export of Alaskan crude oil to other countries. Oil companies favor lifting this ban because they could get a higher price for this American oil by selling it to oil refiners in Japan, Taiwan, and Korea.

Conservationists oppose these proposals and want Congress to designate the entire coastal plain as wilderness. They point to Interior Department estimates that there is only a 19% chance of finding oil equal to about as much as the United States consumes every six months. If the oil exists, the earliest it could be developed is 2000, and at best it would reduce projected oil imports by only a few percentage points for a short time.

Even if such a deposit of oil is found there, conservationists do not believe that it's worth the potential degradation of this priceless and irreplaceable wilderness area when simple energy conservation measures would save far more oil—faster and at a much lower cost. For example, boosting auto fuel-efficiency standards 40% in the next decade could save 10 times as much oil as the refuge *might* produce.

Conservationists also oppose allowing oil from Alaska to be sold to other countries so that energy companies can make bigger profits. They accuse energy companies of saying we need to develop more oil in Alaska to reduce U.S. oil imports and then asking for permission to export this oil so they can make more money.

Officials of oil companies claim they have developed Alaska's Prudhoe Bay oil fields without significant harm to wildlife. However, the 1989 huge oil spill from the tanker *Exxon Valdez* in Alaska's Prince William Sound cast serious doubt on such claims (see Case Study on p. 247).

A study leaked from the Fish and Wildlife Service in 1988 revealed that oil drilling at Prudhoe Bay has

---

Zoos and animal research centers are increasingly being used to preserve a representative number of individuals of critically endangered animal species. Two techniques for preserving such species are egg pulling and captive breeding.

Egg pulling involves collecting eggs produced in the wild by the remaining breeding pairs of a critically endangered bird species and hatching them in zoos or research centers. In 1983, scientists began an egg-pulling program to help save the critically endangered California condor (Figure 16-2).

For *captive breeding*, some or all of the individuals of a critically endangered species still in the wild are captured and placed in zoos or research centers to breed in captivity. Scientists hope that after several decades of captive breeding and egg pulling, the captive population of an endangered species will be large enough that some individuals can be successfully reintroduced into protected wild habitats.

Captive breeding programs at zoos in Phoenix, San Diego, and Los Angeles saved the nearly extinct Arabian oryx (Figure 16-22). This large antelope species once lived throughout the Middle East. By the early 1970s, it had disappeared from the wild after being hunted by people using jeeps, helicopters, rifles, and machine guns. Since 1980, small numbers of these animals bred in captivity have been returned to the wild in protected habitats in the Middle East. Endangered U.S. species now being bred in captivity include the California condor (Figure 16-2), the peregrine falcon (Figure 14-5), and the black-footed ferret (Figure 16-13).

Keeping populations of endangered animal species in zoos and research centers is limited by lack of space and money. The captive population of each species must number 100 to 500 to avoid extinction through accident, disease, or loss of genetic variability through inbreeding. Moreover, caring for and breeding captive animals is very expensive.

Q: If current trends continue, what percentage of Earth's species could become extinct by 2050?

caused much more air and water pollution than was estimated before drilling began in 1972. According to this study, oil development in the coastal plain could cause the loss of 20% to 40% of the area's 180,000-member caribou herd, 25% to 50% of the musk oxen still left, 50% or more of the wolverines, and 50% of the snow geese that live there part of the year. A 1988 EPA study found that "violations of state and federal environmental regulations and laws are occurring at an unacceptable rate" in the Prudhoe Bay area.

Do you think that oil and gas development should be allowed in the Arctic National Wildlife Refuge? Do you believe that oil extracted from Alaska should be exported to other countries? Relate your answers to your own use and waste of oil and gasoline.

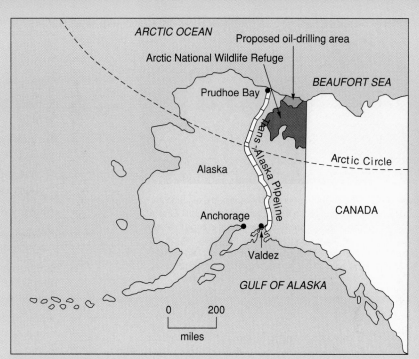

Figure 16-21 Proposed oil-drilling area in Alaska's Arctic National Wildlife Refuge. Some believe that looking for and extracting oil from the coastal plain of this refuge could be one solution to U.S. dependence on foreign oil. Conservationists oppose threatening this protected area of precious biodiversity, believing government estimates that there is only a one in five chance of finding enough oil there to meet all U.S. oil needs for six months. (Data from U.S. Fish and Wildlife Service)

The world's zoos now contain only 20 endangered species of animals with populations of 100 or more individuals. It is estimated that today's zoos and research centers have space to preserve healthy and sustainable populations of only 925 of the 2,000 large vertebrate species that could vanish from the planet. It is doubtful that the more than $6 billion needed to take care of these animals for 20 years will be available.

Because of limited money and trained personnel, however, only a few of the world's endangered and threatened species can be saved by treaties, laws, wildlife refuges, and zoos. That means that wildlife experts must decide which species out of thousands of candidates should be saved. Many experts suggest that the limited funds for preserving threatened and endangered wildlife be concentrated on those species that **(1)** have the best chance for survival, **(2)** have the most ecological value to an ecosystem, and **(3)** are potentially useful for agriculture, medicine, or industry.

THE ECOSYSTEM APPROACH: PROTECTING HABITATS Most wildlife biologists believe that the best way to prevent the loss of wild species is to establish and maintain a worldwide network of reserves, parks, wildlife sanctuaries, and other protected areas. By 1992, there were about 7,000 nature reserves, parks, and other protected areas throughout the world—occupying about 4.9% of Earth's land surface. That is an important beginning, but it is only one-third of the minimum 10% of the world's land area that conservationists say is needed to protect much of Earth's biodiversity. Furthermore, many of the world's 193 biogeographical types have not been included in reserves, or reserves are too small to protect their populations of wild species. In addition, many current protected areas exist only on paper and receive little protection.

Conservationist Norman Myers (see Guest Essay on p. 353) proposes extending all key parks and reserves northward in the northern hemisphere (and

Figure 16-22 The Arabian oryx barely escaped extinction in 1969 after being overhunted in the deserts of the Middle East in Oman and Jordan. Captive breeding programs in zoos in Arizona and California have been successful in saving this antelope species from extinction. Some have been reintroduced into the wild in the Middle East, with the wild population now about 120.

southward in the southern hemisphere) and providing a network of corridors, or "green lanes," to allow migration of animal species and some plant species if global warming occurs as projected (Section 10-2). Otherwise, he argues that existing parks and reserves will become death traps instead of sanctuaries.

This ecosystem approach would prevent many species from becoming endangered by human activities and would also be cheaper than managing endangered species one by one. An international fund to help LDCs protect and manage biosphere reserves would cost $100 million a year—about what the world spends on arms every 90 minutes. Since there won't be enough money to protect enough of the world's biodiversity, conservationists believe that efforts should be focused on megadiversity countries, which contain the largest concentrations of Earth's threatened biodiversity (Figure 15-5).

In the United States, conservationists urge Congress to pass an Endangered Ecosystems Act as an important step toward preserving the country's biodiversity. Such an act would also require environmental impact studies to assess the effects of any federal activity on biological diversity. It would also make conservation the prime goal (including budget expenditures) of the U.S. Forest Service, the Bureau of Land Management, and the National Wildlife Refuge System.

WORLD CONSERVATION STRATEGY In 1980, the International Union for the Conservation of Nature and Natural Resources (IUCN), the UN Environment Programme, and the World Wildlife Fund developed the

World Conservation Strategy, a long-range plan for conserving the world's biological resources. This plan was expanded in 1991. Its primary goals are to

- Maintain essential ecological processes and life-support systems on which human survival and economic activities depend, mostly by combining wildlife conservation with sustainable development (see Case Study on p. 332)

- Preserve species diversity and genetic diversity

- Ensure that any use of species and ecosystems is sustainable

- Include women in the development of conservation plans

- Include indigenous people in the development of conservation plans

- Monitor the sustainability of development

- Promote an ethic that includes protection of plants and animals as well as people

- Encourage recognition of the harmful environmental effects of armed conflict and economic insecurity

- Encourage rehabilitation of degraded ecosystems upon which humans depend for food and fiber

So far, 40 countries have planned or established national conservation programs. The United States has not established such a program. If MDCs provide enough money and scientific assistance, this conservation strategy offers hope for slowing the loss of much of the world's biological diversity. Ultimately, however, no system of reserves will be able to protect the planet's biodiversity unless governments act to reduce poverty, control population growth, slow global warming, and reduce the destruction and degradation of tropical and old-growth forests, wetlands, and coral reefs.

16-4 Wildlife Management

MANAGEMENT APPROACHES **Wildlife management** is the manipulation of wildlife populations (especially game species) and habitats for their welfare and for human benefit, the preservation of endangered and threatened wild species, and wildlife law enforcement.

The first step in wildlife management is to decide which species or groups of species are to be managed in a particular area. This is a source of much controversy. Ecologists stress preservation of biological diversity. Wildlife conservationists are concerned about endangered species. Bird watchers want the greatest diversity of bird species. Hunters want large populations of game species for harvest each year during hunt-

Q: What is the greatest threat to wild species?

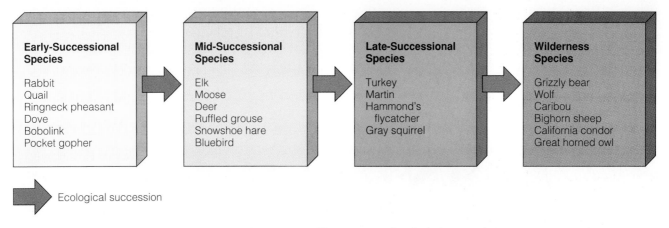

Early-Successional Species

Rabbit
Quail
Ringneck pheasant
Dove
Bobolink
Pocket gopher

Mid-Successional Species

Elk
Moose
Deer
Ruffled grouse
Snowshoe hare
Bluebird

Late-Successional Species

Turkey
Martin
Hammond's
 flycatcher
Gray squirrel

Wilderness Species

Grizzly bear
Wolf
Caribou
Bighorn sheep
California condor
Great horned owl

Ecological succession

Figure 16-23 Preferences of some wildlife species for habitats at different stages of ecological succession.

ing season. In the United States, most wildlife management is devoted to the production of harvestable surpluses of game animals and game birds.

After goals have been set, the wildlife manager must develop a management plan. Ideally, the plan should be based on principles of ecological succession (Section 5-5); wildlife population dynamics (Section 5-4); and an understanding of the cover, food, water, space, and other habitat requirements of each species to be managed. The manager must also consider the number of potential hunters, their success rates, and the regulations available to prevent excessive harvesting.

This information is difficult, expensive, and time-consuming to get. Often it is not available or reliable. That is why wildlife management is as much an art as a science. In practice, it involves much guesswork and trial and error. Management plans must also be adapted to political pressures from conflicting groups and to budget constraints.

MANIPULATION OF HABITAT VEGETATION AND WATER SUPPLIES Wildlife managers can encourage the growth of plant species that are the preferred food and cover for a particular animal species by controlling the ecological succession of vegetation in various areas (Figure 5-36).

Animal wildlife species can be classified into four types according to the stage of ecological succession at which they are most likely to be found: wilderness, late-successional, mid-successional, and early-successional (Figure 16-23). *Early-successional species* find food and cover in weedy pioneer plants. These plants invade an area that has been cleared of vegetation for human activities and then abandoned, as well as areas devastated by mining, fires, volcanic lava, and glaciers.

Mid-successional species are found around abandoned croplands and partially open areas. Such areas

are created by the logging of small stands of timber; controlled burning; and clearing of vegetation for roads, firebreaks, oil and gas pipelines, and electrical transmission lines. Such openings of the forest canopy promote the growth of vegetation favored as food by mid-successional mammal and bird species. They also increase the amount of edge habitat, where two communities such as a forest and a field come together. This transition zone allows animals such as deer to feed on vegetation in clearings and quickly escape to cover in the nearby forest.

Late-successional species need old-growth and mature forest habitats to produce the food and cover on which they depend. These animals require the establishment and protection of moderate-size, old-growth forest refuges.

Wilderness species flourish only in fairly undisturbed, mature vegetational communities, such as large areas of old-growth forests, tundra, grasslands, and deserts. Their survival depends largely on the establishment of large state and national wilderness areas and wildlife refuges.

Various types of habitat improvement can be used to attract a desired species and encourage its population growth. Improvement techniques include artificial seeding, transplanting certain types of vegetation, building artificial nests, and setting prescribed burns. Wildlife managers often create or improve ponds and lakes in wildlife refuges to provide water, food, and habitat for waterfowl and other wild animals.

POPULATION MANAGEMENT BY CONTROLLED SPORT HUNTING The United States and most MDCs use sport hunting laws to manage populations of game animals. These laws

■ Require hunters to have a license

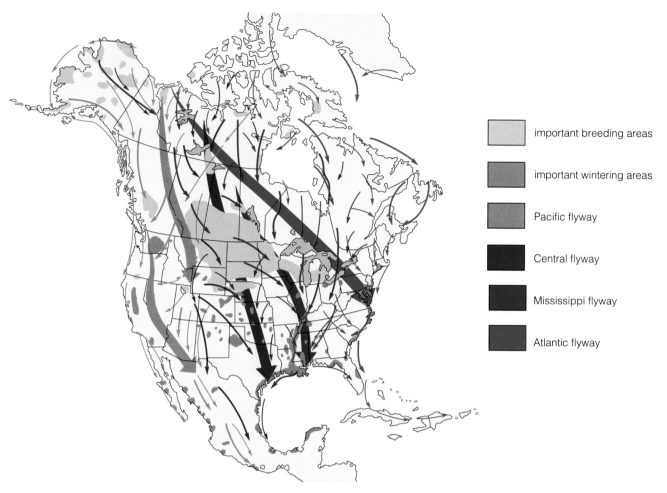

	important breeding areas
	important wintering areas
	Pacific flyway
	Central flyway
	Mississippi flyway
	Atlantic flyway

Figure 16-24 Principal breeding and wintering areas and fall migration flyways used by migratory waterfowl in North America.

- Allow hunting only during certain months of the year to protect animals during mating season

- Allow hunters to use only certain types of hunting equipment, such as bows and arrows, shotguns, and rifles, for a particular type of game

- Set limits on the size, number, and sex of animals that can be killed and on the number of hunters allowed in a game refuge

But close control of sport hunting is often not possible. Accurate data on game populations may not exist and may cost too much to get. People in communities near hunting areas, who benefit from money spent by hunters, may push to have hunting quotas raised. On the other hand, some individuals and conservation groups are opposed to sport hunting and exert political pressure to have it banned or sharply curtailed.

MANAGEMENT OF MIGRATORY WATERFOWL In North America, migratory waterfowl such as ducks, geese, and swans nest in Canada during the summer. During the fall hunting season they migrate to the United States and Central America along generally fixed routes called **flyways** (Figure 16-24).

Canada, the United States, and Mexico have signed agreements to prevent habitat destruction and overhunting of migratory waterfowl. However, since 1969 the estimated breeding populations of ducks in North America have declined by 30%. The primary reasons for this decrease are prolonged drought in key breeding areas and degradation and destruction of wetland and grassland breeding habitats by farmers.

The remaining wetlands are used by dense flocks of ducks and geese. This crowding makes them more vulnerable to diseases and predators such as skunks, foxes, coyotes, minks, raccoons, and hunters. Water-

Q: How much of the original tall-grass prairies in the United States has been destroyed?

fowl in wetlands near croplands are also exposed to pollution from pesticides and other chemicals in the irrigation runoff they drink.

Wildlife officials manage waterfowl by regulating hunting, protecting existing habitats, and developing new habitats. More than 75% of the federal wildlife refuges in the United States are wetlands used for migratory birds. Other waterfowl refuges have been established by local and state agencies and private conservation groups such as Ducks Unlimited, the Audubon Society, and the Nature Conservancy.

Building artificial nesting sites, ponds, and nesting islands is another method of establishing protected habitats for breeding populations of waterfowl. Solar-powered electric fences are being used in some areas to keep predators away from nesting waterfowl.

In 1986, the United States and Canada agreed on a plan to spend $1.5 billion over a 16-year period, with the goal of almost doubling the continental duck-breeding population. The key elements in this program will be the purchase, improvement, and protection of an additional waterfowl habitat in five priority areas.

Since 1934, the Migratory Bird Hunting and Conservation Stamp Act has required waterfowl hunters to buy a duck stamp each season they hunt. Revenue from these sales goes into a fund to buy land and easements for the benefit of waterfowl.

16-5 Fishery Management

FRESHWATER FISHERY MANAGEMENT The goals of freshwater fish management are to encourage the growth of populations of desirable commercial and sport fish species and to reduce or eliminate populations of less-desirable species. A number of techniques are used:

- Regulating the timing and length of fishing seasons
- Establishing the minimum-size fish that can be taken
- Setting catch quotas
- Requiring that commercial fishnets have a large enough mesh to ensure that young fish are not harvested
- Building reservoirs and farm ponds and stocking them with game fish
- Fertilizing nutrient-poor lakes and ponds with commercial fertilizer, fish meal, and animal wastes
- Protecting and creating spawning sites and cover spaces

- Protecting habitats from buildup of sediment and other forms of pollution and removing debris
- Preventing excessive growth of aquatic plants to prevent oxygen depletion
- Using small dams to control water flow
- Controlling predators, parasites, and diseases by habitat improvement, breeding genetically resistant fish varieties, and using antibiotics and disinfectants
- Using hatcheries to restock ponds, lakes, and streams with species such as trout and salmon

MARINE FISHERY MANAGEMENT The history of the world's commercial marine fishing and whaling industry is an excellent example of the tragedy of the commons—the overexploitation of a potentially renewable resource (see Spotlight on p. 10). As a result, many species of commercially valuable fish (see Case Study on p. 301) and whales in international and coastal waters have been overfished to the point of commercial extinction. At that point, the stock of a species is so low that it's no longer profitable to hunt and gather the remaining individuals in a specific fishery.

Managers of marine fisheries can use several techniques to prevent commercial extinction and allow depleted stocks to recover. Fishery commissions, councils, and advisory bodies with representatives from countries using a fishery can be established. They can set annual quotas for harvesting fish and marine mammals and establish rules for dividing the allowable annual catch among the countries participating in the fishery.

These groups may also limit fishing seasons and regulate the type of fishing gear that can be used to harvest a particular species. Fishing techniques such as dynamiting and poisoning are outlawed. Fishery commissions may also enact size limits that make it illegal to keep fish below a certain size, usually the average length of the particular fish species when it first reproduces.

As voluntary associations, however, fishery commissions don't have any legal authority to compel member states to follow their rules. Nor can they compel all countries fishing in a region to join the commission and submit to its rules. It is also very difficult to estimate the sustainable yields of various marine species.

International and national laws have been used to extend the offshore fishing zone of coastal countries to 370 kilometers (200 nautical miles or 230 statute miles) from their shores. Foreign fishing vessels can take certain quotas of fish within such zones, called *exclusive economic zones*, only with government permission.

Ocean areas beyond the legal jurisdiction of any country are known as the *high seas*. Any limits on the use of the living and mineral common-property re-

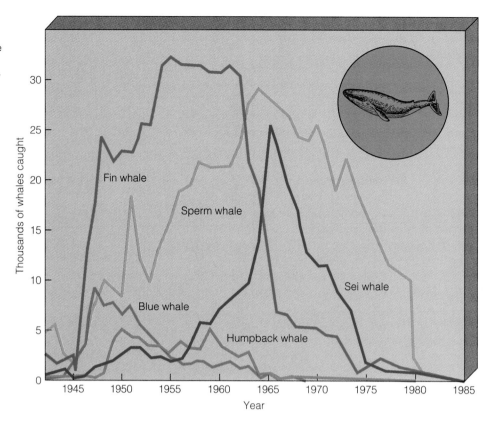

Figure 16-25 Whale harvests, showing the signs of overharvesting. After continued protests since the 1960s, the International Whaling Commission banned commercial whaling in 1986 until 1991. In 1992, the ban was extended for another 5 years. (Data from International Whaling Commission)

sources in these areas are set by international maritime law and international treaties.

DECLINE OF THE WHALING INDUSTRY In 1900, an estimated 4.4 million whales swam the ocean. Today only about 1 million are left. Overharvesting has caused a sharp drop in the populations of almost every whale species of commercial value (Figure 16-25). The populations of 8 of the 11 major species of whales once hunted by the whaling industry have been reduced to commercial extinction. This devastation has happened because of the tragedy of the commons and because whales are more vulnerable to biological extinction than are fish species (see Case Study on p. 377).

In 1946, the International Whaling Commission (IWC) was established to regulate the whaling industry. Since 1949, the IWC has set annual quotas to prevent overfishing and commercial extinction. But these quotas often were based on inadequate scientific information or were ignored by whaling countries. Without any powers of enforcement, the IWC has been unable to stop the decline of most whale species (Figure 16-25).

In 1970, the United States stopped all commercial whaling and banned all imports of whale products, mostly because of pressure from conservationists and the general public. Since then, conservation groups and the governments of many countries, including the United States, have called for a permanent ban on all commercial whaling.

After years of meetings and delays, the IWC established a five-year halt on commercial whaling, beginning in 1986 and ending in 1991. Between 1986 and 1991, Japan, Norway, and Iceland killed an estimated 13,000 whales for "scientific" purposes (mostly for sale as meat in Japan), despite being refused permits to do this by the IWC. In 1991, the IWC banned commercial whale hunting for another five years, but allowed Japan, Norway, and other countries to kill an undetermined number of whales each year for scientific purposes. Conservationists believe that the allowed killing of whales for scientific purposes is a sham and should be banned and vigorously enforced.

INDIVIDUAL ACTION We are all involved, at least indirectly, in the destruction of wildlife any time we buy or drive a car, build a house, consume almost anything, and waste electricity, paper, water, or any other resource. All those activities contribute to the destruction or degradation of wildlife habitats or to the killing of one or more individuals of some plant or animal species.

Modifying our consumption habits is a key goal in protecting wildlife, the environment, and ourselves (see Individuals Matter on p. 377). This also involves sup-

Q: How much money is made each year from illegal trade in wildlife?

The blue whale is the world's largest animal and bigger than any dinosaur that ever roamed the earth. Fully grown, it's more than 30 meters (100 feet) long—longer than three train boxcars—and weighs 136 metric tons (150 tons)—more than 25 elephants. The adult has a heart as big as a Volkswagen "Beetle" car, and some of its arteries are so big that a child could swim through them. Its brain weighs four times more than yours, its tongue is as large as the size of an adult elephant, and this mammal shows signs of great intelligence.

Blue whales spend about eight months of the year in antarctic waters. There they find an abundant supply of shrimplike krill, which they filter from seawater (Figure 4-17). During the winter months, they migrate to warmer waters where their young are born.

Once, an estimated 200,000 blue whales roamed the antarctic waters. Today the species has been hunted to near biological extinction for its oil, meat, and bone (Figure 16-25).

This decline was caused by a combination of prolonged overfishing and certain natural traits of the blue whale. Their huge size made them easy to spot. They were caught in large numbers because they grouped together in their antarctic feeding grounds. Also, they take 25 years to mature sexually and have only one offspring every two to five years. This low reproduction rate makes it hard for the species to recover once its population has been reduced to a low level.

Blue whales haven't been hunted commercially since 1964 and are classified as an endangered species. Despite this protection, some marine experts believe that not enough blue whales are left for the species to recover. Fewer than 1,000 blue whales may be left today. Within a few decades the blue whale could disappear forever.

INDIVIDUALS MATTER What You Can Do

- Improve the habitat on a patch of the earth in your immediate environment, such as backyards, abandoned city lots, campus areas, and streams clogged with debris.

- Develop a wildlife protection and management plan for any land that you own, emphasizing the promotion of biological diversity.

- Don't buy furs, ivory products, reptile-skin goods, tortoiseshell jewelry, and imported tropical fish, rare orchids or cacti, and imported exotic birds such as parrots, canaries, parakeets, cockatoos. If enough people joined this boycott, the illegal trade in endangered and threatened species would dry up and the legal trade in wild species that results in much unnecessary killing would be sharply reduced.

- Consider reducing or eliminating your consumption of meat (especially beef) and not using products made from leather or other materials obtained from domesticated animals raised with little regard for their well-being.

- Don't buy brands of tuna fish unless the cans say they were caught by dolphin-safe methods and boycott all fish products caught using drift nets (Figure 13-13).

- Support efforts to ensure that test animals are treated humanely and to reduce their use to a minimum.

- If you have a dog or a cat as a pet, have it spayed or neutered. Each year, U.S. pounds and animal shelters have to kill about 15 million unwanted dogs and cats because of pet overpopulation. That is 75 times the number of dogs and cats killed each year in the United States for research and teaching purposes. Most of these test animals are obtained from animal shelters, where they would have to be killed anyway because of our throwaway attitude toward pets.

- Leave wild animals in the wild. Consider not buying exotic birds, fish, and other pets imported from tropical and other areas. Typically, one or more animals die for each one that reaches a pet shop. Also, most of these pets die prematurely because they are killed, abandoned, or cared for improperly by their owners.

- Reduce habitat destruction and degradation by recycling paper, cans, plastics, and other house-

(continued)

hold items. Better yet, reuse items and sharply reduce your use of throwaway items.

- Support efforts to sharply reduce the destruction and degradation of tropical forests (Section 15-2) and old-growth forests (Section 15-3), slow global warming (Section 10-3), and reduce ozone depletion in the stratosphere (Section 10-5).

- Pressure elected officials to pass laws requiring much larger fines and longer prison sentences for wildlife poachers and to provide more funds and personnel for wildlife protection.

- Pressure Congress to pass a national biological diversity act and to develop a national conservation program as part of the World Conservation Strategy.

- Encourage the development of an international treaty to preserve biological diversity.

porting efforts to reduce deforestation, global warming, ozone depletion, population growth, and poverty—the greatest threats to Earth's wildlife and the human species.

During our short time on this planet we have gained immense power over what species—including our own—live or die. We named ourselves the wise (*sapiens*) species. In the next few decades, we will learn whether we are indeed a wise species. If not, millions of years from now, some new and truly wise species that might take our place may look back and change the name of our extinct species to *Homo unsapiens unsapiens*. If we eliminate ourselves and take millions of other species down with us, we will be mourned by no one, and what's left will go cycling on without us.

Biological diversity must be treated as a global resource to be indexed and used, and above all preserved.

E. O. WILSON

DISCUSSION TOPICS

1. Discuss your gut-level reaction to this statement: "It doesn't really matter that the passenger pigeon is extinct and the blue whale, the whooping crane, the California condor, the rhinoceros, the grizzly bear, and a number of other plant and animal species are endangered mostly because of human activities." Be honest about your reaction, and give arguments for your position.

*2. Make a log of your own consumption and use of food and other products for a single day. Relate your consumption to the increased destruction of wildlife and wildlife habitats in the United States, in tropical forests, and in aquatic ecosystems.

3. a. Do you accept the ethical position that each *species* has the inherent right to survive without human interference, regardless of whether it serves any useful purpose for humans? Explain.
   b. Do you believe that *each individual* of an animal species has an inherent right to survive? Explain. Would you extend such rights to individual plants and microorganisms? Explain.

4. Do you believe that the use of animals, mostly mice and rats, to test new drugs and vaccines and the toxicity of chemicals should be banned? Explain. What are the alternatives? Should animals be used to test cosmetics?

5. Are you for or against sport hunting? Explain.

PART FIVE

Energy and Mineral Resources

Our entire society rests upon—and is dependent upon—our water, our land, our forests, and our minerals. How we use these resources influences our health, security, economy, and well-being.

JOHN F. KENNEDY

CHAPTER 17

PERPETUAL AND RENEWABLE ENERGY RESOURCES

General Questions and Issues

1. How can we evaluate present and future energy alternatives?

2. What are the advantages and disadvantages of improving energy efficiency?

3. What are the advantages and disadvantages of capturing and using direct solar energy to heat buildings and water and to produce electricity?

4. What are the advantages and disadvantages of using flowing water and solar energy stored as heat in water for producing electricity?

5. What are the advantages and disadvantages of using wind to produce electricity?

6. What are the advantages and disadvantages of burning plants and organic waste for heating buildings and water, for producing electricity, and for transportation?

7. What are the advantages and disadvantages of using geothermal energy?

8. What are the advantages and disadvantages of using hydrogen gas to produce electricity, to heat buildings and water, and to propel vehicles?

If the United States wants to save a lot of oil and money and increase national security, there are two simple ways to do it: stop driving Petropigs and stop living in energy sieves.

AMORY B. LOVINS

A MAJOR THEME OF THIS book is that energy is the thread sustaining and integrating all life and supporting all economies. That's why it's so important that we understand the nature and the implications of the two energy laws that govern all energy use. I suggest that you review Sections 3-4, 3-6, 3-7, and 3-8 before studying this and the next chapter.

What types of energy we use and how we use them are the major factors determining how much we abuse the life-support systems for all species on Earth. Our current dependence on nonrenewable fossil fuels is the primary cause of air and water pollution, land disruption, and projected global warming.

Most analysts agree that the era of cheap oil is coming to an end (see Case Study on p. 12). Some analysts argue that to reduce the threat of projected global warming (Section 10-2) and air and water pollution, we must reduce our current use of all fossil fuels 50% by 2010 and 70% by 2030 (Section 10-3).

What is our best option for reducing dependence on oil and other fossil fuels? Cut out unnecessary energy waste by improving energy efficiency (see Guest Essay on p. 58). What is our next best energy option? There is disagreement about that.

Some say we should get more of the energy we need from the sun, wind, flowing water, biomass, heat stored in Earth's interior, and hydrogen gas (see Guest Essay on p. 58) by making the transition to a new *solar-hydrogen economy*. These energy choices, based on using Earth's underutilized perpetual and renewable energy resources, are evaluated in this chapter.

Others say we should burn more coal and synthetic liquid and gaseous fuels made from coal. Some believe natural gas is the answer, at least as a transition fuel to a new solar-hydrogen energy era built around improved energy efficiency and perpetual and renewable energy. Others think nuclear power is the answer. These choices, based on using more of Earth's nonrenewable energy resources, are evaluated in the next chapter.

17-1 Evaluating Energy Resources

Experience has shown that it takes 50 to 60 years to develop and phase in new supplemental energy resources on a large scale (Figure 3-7). In deciding which combination of energy alternatives we should use in the future, we need to plan for three time periods: the short term (1994 to 2004), the intermediate term (2004 to 2014), and the long term (2014 to 2044).

First, we must decide how much we need, or want, of different kinds of energy, such as low-temperature heat, high-temperature heat, electricity, and fuels for transportation. This involves deciding what type and quality of energy can best perform each energy task (Figure 3-9). Then, we must decide which energy sources can meet our needs at the lowest cost and with the least environmental impact by answering four questions about each alternative.

1. How much will probably be available during the short term, intermediate term, and long term?

2. What is the estimated net useful energy yield (Figure 3-20)?

3. How much will it cost to develop, phase in, and use?

4. What are its potentially harmful environmental, social, and security impacts, and how can they be reduced?

The most important question decision makers and individuals should ask is: What energy choices will do the most to sustain the earth for us, for future generations, and for the other species living on this planet? Despite its importance, this ethical question is rarely considered by government officials, energy company executives, and most other people. Changing this situation is probably the most important and difficult challenge we face (Section 2-3).

17-2 Improving Energy Efficiency: Doing More with Less

REDUCING ENERGY WASTE: AN OFFER WE CAN'T AFFORD TO REFUSE The easiest, quickest, and cheapest way to make more energy available with the least environmental impact is to reduce or eliminate unnecessary energy use and waste (Figure 3-15). There are two general ways to achieve this goal.

1. *Reduce energy consumption by changing energy-wasting habits.* Examples include walking or riding a bicycle for short trips, using mass transit instead of cars, wearing a sweater indoors in cold weather to allow a lower thermostat setting, turning off unneeded lights, and reducing our use of throwaway items, which require energy for raw materials, manufacture, and disposal.

2. *Improve energy efficiency by using less energy to do the same amount of work.* Examples of doing more with less include adding more insulation to houses and buildings, keeping car engines tuned, and switching to, or developing, more energy-efficient cars, houses, heating and cooling systems, appliances, lights, and industrial processes (Figure 3-16).

Improving energy efficiency has the highest net useful energy yield of all energy alternatives. It reduces the environmental impacts of using energy because less

of each energy resource is used to provide the same amount of energy. It adds no carbon dioxide to the atmosphere and is the best, cheapest, and quickest way to slow projected global warming because it reduces wasteful use of fossil fuels and the need for costly and politically unacceptable nuclear power. It does not mean freezing in the dark or having to drive small, unsafe vehicles.

Reducing the amount of energy we use and waste makes domestic and world supplies of nonrenewable fossil fuels last longer and buys time for phasing in perpetual and renewable energy resources. It also reduces international tensions and improves national and global military and economic security by decreasing dependence on oil imports (50% in the United States) and the need for military intervention to protect sources of oil, especially in the unstable Middle East, which has 65% of the world's oil reserves (compared with 4% in the United States).

Improving energy efficiency saves money and usually provides more jobs and promotes more economic growth per unit of energy than do other energy alternatives. According to energy expert Amory Lovins (see Guest Essay on p. 58), cumulative savings from efficiency improvements since the first Arab oil embargo in 1973 total nearly $1 trillion, and if the world *really* got serious about improving energy efficiency, it would save $1 trillion a year. He also points out that we could use existing technology to run the present U.S. economy on one-fifth the oil now used; the cost of saving each barrel of oil would be less than $5.

The only serious disadvantage of improving energy efficiency is that replacing houses, industrial equipment, and cars, as they wear out, with more energy-efficient ones takes a long time. For example, replacing most buildings and industrial equipment takes several decades, and replacing most older cars on the road with new ones takes 10 to 12 years.

Improvements in energy efficiency have saved the world more than $300 billion worth of energy every year since 1973, but these improvements have only scratched the surface (see Spotlight on p. 382).

IMPROVING INDUSTRIAL ENERGY EFFICIENCY Industrial processes consume 36% of the energy used in the United States. Today, American industry uses 70% less energy to produce the same amount of goods as it did in 1973, but it still wastes enormous amounts of energy. Since 1983, overall U.S. industrial energy efficiency has scarcely improved. Japan has the highest overall industrial energy efficiency in the world, followed closely by the western part of Germany and Sweden.

Industries that use large amounts of both high-temperature heat or steam and electricity can save energy and money by installing *cogeneration units*. They recover some of the wasted two-thirds of energy in a

As the world's largest energy user and waster, the United States has more impact on fossil-fuel depletion, water pollution, projected global warming, acid deposition, and other forms of air pollution than does any other country. At least 43% of all energy used in the United States is *unnecessarily* wasted (Figure 3-15). That waste equals all the energy consumed by two-thirds of the world's population.

The largest and cheapest untapped supplies of energy in the United States are in its energy-wasting buildings, factories, and vehicles, not in Alaska or offshore areas. This vast source of energy can be found almost everywhere, can be exploited cheaply and quickly, strengthens rather than weakens the economy and national security, creates jobs, improves rather than damages the environment, and leaves little or no harmful waste.

The untapped energy available from improving energy efficiency in the United States at a low cost is more than three times that available from developing remaining nonrenewable energy resources (fossil fuels and nuclear power) at a very high cost (Figure 17-1). Had the United States vigorously pursued a least-cost, high-energy-efficiency energy policy since 1973, instead of its high-cost, mostly fruitless search for significant new domestic deposits of oil, the country would have no need to import any oil today — something that would have greatly reduced the need to engage in any war in the Middle East. Furthermore, enough money would have been saved to pay off the entire national debt.

The good news is that since 1979, the United States has gained more than seven times as much energy from improvements in energy efficiency as from all net increases in the supply of all forms of energy, with little help from federal and state governments. This reduction of energy waste has cut the country's annual energy bill by about $160 billion — about equal to the cur-

rent annual national deficit. Those savings of $630 per year for each citizen ($2,520 a year for a family of four) have also reduced emissions of carbon dioxide, sulfur dioxide, and nitrogen oxides 40% below what they otherwise would have been.

Using today's best available technology in transportation, in buildings, and in industry could save 80% of all the oil used in the United States, while providing the same or better services at lower life-cycle costs. To unhook from Middle East oil, the United States would need to capture only 15% of these savings.

The bad news is that energy efficiency in the United States is still half what it could be and has not improved much since 1985. Average gas mileage for new cars and for the entire fleet of cars is below that in most other MDCs. Most U.S. houses and buildings are still underinsulated and leaky. Although electric resistance heating is the most wasteful and expensive way to heat a home (Figure 3-17), it is installed in over half the new homes in the United States, mostly because it saves builders money. Buyers are then left with the high heating bills.

Bringing about a low-cost, energy-efficiency revolution by investing about $50 billion a year would stimulate the economy, cut carbon dioxide emissions in half, reduce urban smog and acid deposition, and save $250 billion annually between 1994 and 2004 — enough to pay off the entire national debt. It would also create many jobs, reduce the cost of producing goods and services, and make the United States more competitive in the international marketplace. For example, the United States spends about 11% of its GNP to obtain energy, while Japan uses only 5%. That gives Japanese goods an average 6% cost advantage over American goods. If the United States were as energy-efficient as Japan, France, or Sweden, it would need no imported oil.

Why isn't the United States pursuing an energy strategy that makes economic and environmental sense?

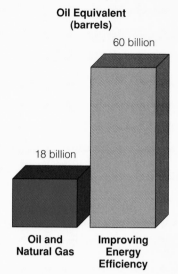

Oil Equivalent (barrels)

60 billion

18 billion

Oil and Natural Gas   **Improving Energy Efficiency**

Figure 17-1 Improving energy efficiency in the United States using available technologies would produce more than three times as much energy by 2020 at a low cost as would finding and developing at a very high cost all new oil and natural gas deposits believed to exist in the United States. (Data from Natural Resources Defense Council and Rocky Mountain Institute)

There are several reasons. One is the political influence of companies controlling the use of nonrenewable fossil fuels and nuclear power and their emphasis on short-term profits regardless of the long-term economic and environmental consequences. Other reasons include a temporary glut of low-cost fossil fuels, failure of elected officials to require that the external costs of using fossil and nuclear fuels be included in their market prices, and sharp cutbacks in federal support for improvements in energy efficiency and development of perpetual and renewable resources since 1980.

Such short-sighted policies will continue until enough citizens demand that elected officials make improvements in energy efficiency and a shift to renewable energy resources the cornerstones of U.S. energy and economic policy. What do you think should be done?

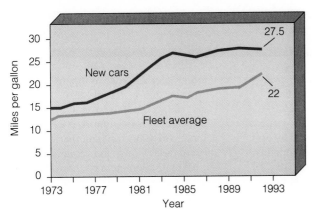

Figure 17-2 Increase in average fuel efficiency of new cars and the entire fleet of cars in the United States between 1973 and 1992. Average fuel efficiency of new cars dropped or stayed about the same between 1984 and 1992 because Congress relaxed standards set in the 1970s and has refused to enact higher standards since then. (Data from U.S. Department of Energy and Environmental Protection Agency)

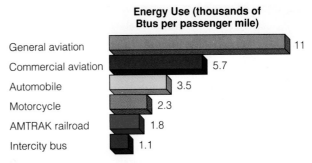

Figure 17-3 Energy efficiency of various types of domestic transportation.

conventional boiler and use it to produce both heat and electricity. The town of Vesterås, Sweden, uses cogeneration to meet all of its electricity and space-heating needs. Cogeneration has the potential to produce more electricity than all the nuclear power plants in the United States by 2000 at a much lower cost.

About 70% of the electricity used in U.S. industry and 60% of the electricity generated in the United States drives electric motors. Most of those motors run at full speed, and their output is "throttled" to match the task they perform—like driving with one foot pushing the gas pedal to the floor and the other foot on the brake to slow you down. Each year a heavily used electric motor consumes 10 times its purchase cost in electricity, equivalent to using $120,000 worth of gasoline each year to fuel a $12,000 car. According to a study by energy expert Amory Lovins, it would be cost-effective to scrap virtually all standard-efficiency motors now in use and replace them with new high-efficiency motors. Within a year, the extra costs would be paid back.

Switching to high-efficiency lighting is another way to save energy in industry. Industries can also use computer-controlled energy management systems to turn off lighting and equipment in nonproduction areas and make adjustments during periods of low production.

Another significant way to save energy in industry is to reduce the production of throwaway products—by increasing recycling and reuse and by making products that last longer and are easy to repair and recycle (Section 19-7). Despite the potential for major energy savings, federal support for research and development to improve industrial energy efficiency was cut by almost 60% between 1981 and 1991.

IMPROVING TRANSPORTATION ENERGY EFFI-CIENCY One-fourth of the commercial energy consumed in the United States is used to transport people and goods. Americans have one-third of the world's automobiles and drive about as many kilometers each year as the rest of the world combined. About one-tenth of the oil consumed in the world each day is used by American motorists on their way to and from work, 69% of them driving alone.

Today, transportation consumes 63% of all oil used in the United States—up from 50% in 1973. Burning gasoline and other transportation fuels accounts for about 33% of total U.S. emissions of carbon dioxide, and the air conditioners in cars and light trucks are responsible for 75% of the country's annual ozone-destroying CFC emissions. Thus, the best way to reduce world oil consumption, to slow ozone depletion in the stratosphere and projected global warming, and to reduce air pollution is to improve the fuel efficiency of vehicles (Figure 17-2), make greater use of mass transit (Figure 17-3), and haul freight more efficiently.

Between 1973 and 1985, the average fuel efficiency of new American cars doubled, and the average fuel efficiency of all the cars on the road increased by 54% (Figure 17-2). The modest $200 to $400 that this added to the price of the average car was more than made up for by savings in gasoline purchases. During that period, improvements in fuel efficiency saved American consumers about $285 billion in fuel costs and now save about 5 million barrels of oil a day. That important gain saves Americans nearly $40 billion a year, but it is well below what is achievable with existing technology. Moreover, since 1985, there have been no gains in U.S. fuel efficiency and even a slight decline for new cars (Figure 17-2).

According to the U.S. Office of Technology Assessment, new cars produced in the United States could easily average between 16 and 23 kilometers per liter (kpl) (38 to 55 mpg) within five years and 22 to 33 kpl (52 to 78 mpg) within ten years. The additional cost would be about $500 per car, but the gasoline savings

---

A: As of this writing, the U.S. Endangered Species Act

"Fuel-efficient cars will take decades to develop, and will be sluggish, small, and unsafe." Wrong! Average fuel economy for new cars produced from 1990 on could have been at least 26 kilometers per liter (61 mpg). These cars could have carried four or five people in comfort and could have been as safe as, or safer than, and at least as peppy as the average new car today.

Why can't we buy these cars today? Elected officials in the United States, influenced by the powerful American automobile companies, did not raise fuel efficiency standards in 1981 to accomplish this goal. Had the higher standards been enacted in 1981, the United States would not have had to import any oil from the Middle East in 1990 when the war with Iraq began (with a major goal of protecting U.S. oil imports from Saudi Arabia). After

the war with Iraq started, environmentalists pushed again to have standards enacted that would double the fuel efficiency of new cars by 2000, but they were defeated by opposition from the Bush administration and the automobile industry.

Since 1985, at least 10 automobile companies, including Volvo, Volkswagen, Renault, Peugeot, Honda, Mazda, and Toyota, have had prototype cars that carry four or five passengers, are nimble and peppy, meet or exceed current safety and pollution standards, and have fuel efficiencies of 29 to 59 kpl (67 to 138 mpg).

One example of such eco-cars is Volvo's LCP 2000, which could be in production today had there been sufficient consumer demand for fuel-efficient cars. This car averages 28 kpl (65 mpg). Because of better design and use of stronger but

lighter materials (such as magnesium, aluminum, and plastics), it exceeds U.S. crash standards. It carries four passengers in comfort, is quiet, is more corrosion-resistant than most of today's cars, and accelerates from 0 to 97 kilometers per hour (0 to 60 miles per hour) in 11 seconds — better than average.

This car also meets California's air pollution emission standards — the most stringent in the world. Over its lifetime, it is estimated that this car would use half the energy of a conventional car of the same size and would add 15 metric tons (17 tons) less carbon dioxide to the atmosphere. It can run on several different fuels, including diesel fuel and vegetable oil. The Volvo LCP 2000 is also designed for easy assembly and for recycling of its materials when it is taken off the road.

would total at least $2,000 over the life of the car. The fuel efficiency of new light trucks—pickup trucks, minivans, and 4-wheel-drive sport vehicles—could be increased from 8.5 kpl (20 mpg) to 14 kpl (33 mpg) within ten years.

Making these improvements in fuel efficiency would raise the fuel efficiency of the entire U.S. automotive fleet from its current 8 kpl (19 mpg) to 14.5 kpl (34 mpg), eliminate the need to import any oil, and save consumers more than $50 billion a year in fuel costs. Consumers buying new fuel-efficient cars would get back any extra costs involved through fuel savings in about a year. From then on, they would be saving money by driving their cars instead of cars that get only 9 to 15 kpl (22 to 35 mpg).

Fuel efficiency will not increase in the United States unless elected officials set and enforce greatly increased gas mileage standards. But they won't act unless voters pressure them enough to overcome the political influence of the American automobile industry. Higher gasoline taxes are a weak incentive to buy an energy-efficient car because gasoline costs are one-fifth that of the nonfuel costs of owning and running a car. Furthermore, without additional aid, politically unpopular gasoline taxes would hurt low- and middle-income families.

Japan and some western European countries have increased their research on fuel efficiency. They want to

have fuel-efficient cars ready when the oil crisis, expected to occur sometime during the next two decades, replaces the current oil glut. In 1992, consumers could buy cars such as Chevrolet's Geo Metro XFi, built in Japan by Suzuki with a fuel efficiency of 25 kpl (58 mpg) for highway driving and 22 kpl (53 mpg) for city driving, and the Honda Civic HB VX, which averages 23 kpl (55 mpg) on the highway and 20 kpl (48 mpg) in city driving. The technology has existed since the mid-1980s to build cars that are even larger, safer, and much more fuel-efficient than those models (see Spotlight above).

The American automobile industry has tried to scare consumers and sell more-profitable larger cars by claiming that using smaller, lighter cars decreases safety. However, traffic fatalities in the United States fell by 40% from 1975 to 1991, while fuel efficiency doubled and the average weight of a new car dropped by about 454 kilograms (1,000 pounds). Furthermore, new lightweight materials and improved safety standards could significantly improve vehicle safety.

Electric cars might help out, especially for urban commuting and short trips. All major American car companies have developed prototype electric cars and minivans, some of which might be available by 1995. They are extremely quiet, require little maintenance, and produce no air pollution except that emitted indirectly when the electricity needed to recharge their bat-

Q: What is the best way to prevent wildlife extinction from human activities?

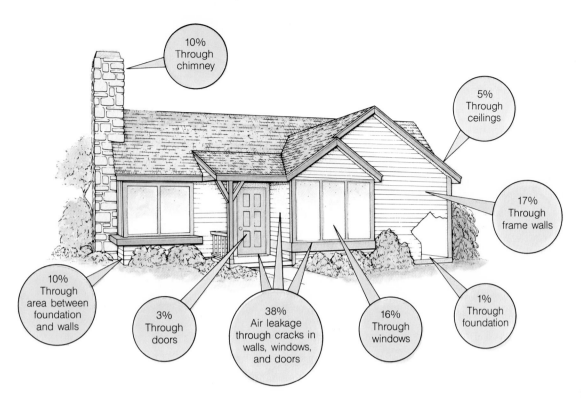

Figure 17-4 Typical ranch-style homes built throughout the United States are heated with energy-wasting electricity and are so full of leaks that up to 85% of this expensive heat is rapidly lost. Such heat loss is equivalent to having a large, window-size hole in the wall of such houses.

teries is produced. Batteries can be recharged each night at off-peak load hours when rates are lower. If solar cells can be used for recharging, the environmental impacts from producing electricity at coal or nuclear power plants to recharge the batteries would be eliminated.

But the batteries in current electric cars have to be replaced about every 40,000 kilometers (25,000 miles) at a cost of about $1,500. This requirement and the electricity costs for daily recharging mean that current prototypes cost about twice as much to operate as does a gasoline-powered car. If new and cost-effective types of batteries that last longer and hold a higher charge density were developed, the operating costs would be reduced and performance would increase.

Another way to make the world's diminishing supply of oil last longer is to shift more freight from trucks and airplanes to trains and ships. General Motors has developed a new truck trailer that can easily be converted to a railcar and then back to a truck, without having to be unloaded. Using this truck-rail combination would use 80% less fuel than truck transport alone for hauls of more than 322 kilometers (200 miles). Truck companies can reduce waste by not allowing trucks to return empty after reaching their destination (but not by carrying garbage or toxic materials on the initial run and food on the return run, as has happened in some cases).

Boeing's new 777 jet will use about half the fuel per passenger seat of a 727. Existing advanced diesel engine technology could improve the fuel efficiency of ships by 30% to 40% over the next few decades.

Although increasing fuel efficiency is crucial, improvements in energy efficiency can eventually be overwhelmed by increases in population and the number and use of vehicles (Figure 1-12). For example, while the fuel consumed in the United States decreased by 15% between 1970 and 1991, the total number of motor vehicles increased by 70% and total motor vehicle use (as measured by distance traveled) rose by 40%.

IMPROVING THE ENERGY EFFICIENCY OF COMMERCIAL AND RESIDENTIAL BUILDINGS Sweden and South Korea have the world's toughest standards for energy efficiency in homes and other buildings. The average home in Sweden consumes about one-third as much energy as an average American home of the same size (Figure 17-4).

A monument to energy waste is the 110-story, twin-towered World Trade Center in Manhattan, which uses as much electricity as a city of 100,000 people. Windows in its walls of glass cannot be opened to take advantage of natural warming and cooling. Its heating and cooling systems must run around the clock, chiefly to take away heat from its inefficient lighting.

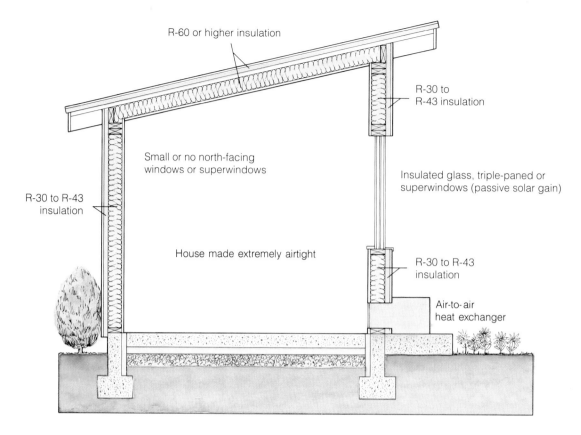

Figure 17-5 Major features of a superinsulated house.

R-60 or higher insulation

R-30 to R-43 insulation

Small or no north-facing windows or superwindows

Insulated glass, triple-paned or superwindows (passive solar gain)

R-30 to R-43 insulation

House made extremely airtight

R-30 to R-43 insulation

Air-to-air heat exchanger

By contrast, Atlanta's 17-story Georgia Power Company building uses 60% less energy than conventional office buildings. The largest surface of the building is oriented to capture solar energy. Each floor extends over the one below, allowing heating by the low winter sun and blocking out the higher summer sun to reduce air conditioning costs. Energy-efficient lights focus on desks rather than illuminating entire rooms. Employees working at unusual hours use an adjoining three-story building so that the larger structure doesn't have to be heated or cooled when few people are at work.

With existing technology, the United States could save 40% to 60% of the energy used in existing buildings and 70% to 90% of the energy used in new buildings (see Spotlight on p. 387). Building a **superinsulated house** is a superb way to improve the efficiency of residential space heating and cooling by more than 75% and save on lifetime energy costs (Figure 17-5). Such a house is heavily insulated and made extremely airtight. Heat from direct solar gain, people, and appliances warms the house, which requires little or no auxiliary heating. An air-to-air heat exchanger prevents buildup of humidity and indoor air pollution.

Most home buyers look only at the initial price, not the more meaningful lifetime cost. A superinsulated house costs about 5% more to build than a conventional house, but this extra cost is paid back by energy savings within five years and can save a home owner $50,000 to $100,000 over a 40-year period. Sadly, this type of house

accounts for less than 1% of new home construction in the United States, mostly because of a lack of consumer demand.

To keep the initial cost for buyers down, developers and builders routinely construct inefficient buildings and stock them with inefficient heating and cooling systems and appliances. When lifetime costs are considered, however, such energy-inefficient houses cost buyers 40% to 50% more. Builders and owners of rental housing have little incentive to pay slightly more to make their units energy-efficient, when renters pay the fuel and electricity bills.

Requiring all buildings to meet higher energy-efficiency standards and requiring a building's estimated annual and lifetime energy consumption to be revealed to buyers would help correct these problems. Rebates for buying high-efficiency appliances and houses (and cars), reduced hookup fees for gas or electric service, and requiring reduced electricity rates for energy-efficient buildings would also help.

The federal government is the nation's single largest energy consumer. According to a 1991 study by Congress's Office of Technology Assessment, the federal government could save at least 25% ($800 million) of the $3.5 billion worth of energy used in federal buildings annually with no sacrifice of comfort or productivity.

Many energy-saving features can be added to existing homes, a process called *retrofitting*. Simply increasing insulation above ceilings can drastically reduce

Q: How many unwanted dogs and cats are killed by U.S. animal shelters each year because of pet overpopulation?

Energy experts Amory and Hunter Lovins have built a large passively heated, superinsulated, partially earth-sheltered home and office (used by 40 people) in Old Snowmass, Colorado, where winter temperatures can drop to $-40°C$ ($-40°F$). This structure, which also houses the research center for the Rocky Mountain Institute, gets 99% of its space heating and water heating and 95% of its daytime lighting (from superwindows) from the sun, uses one-tenth the normal amount of electricity, and uses less than half the normal amount of water for a structure of comparable size. Total energy savings repaid the added cost of its energy-saving features after 10 months and are projected to pay off the cost of the entire facility over about 40 years.

In energy-efficient houses of the near future, microprocessors will monitor indoor temperatures, sunlight angles, and the location of people, and will then send heat or cooled air where it is needed. Some will automatically open and close windows and insulated shutters to take advantage of solar energy and breezes and to reduce heat loss from windows at night and on cloudy days. Sensors can turn off lights in unoccupied rooms or dim lights when sunlight is available.

Researchers have developed "smart windows" that automatically change electronically from clear, which allows sunlight and heat in on cold days, to reflective, which deflects sunlight when the house gets too hot. Superinsulating windows (R-8 to R-10), already available, mean that a house can have as many windows as the owner wants in any climate without much heat loss. Insulating windows with R-12 or better should be available in the near future. Thinner insulation material will allow roofs to be insulated to R-100 and walls to R-43, far higher ratings than are found in today's best superinsulated houses (Figure 17-5).

Small-scale cogeneration units that run on natural gas or LPG (liquefied petroleum gas) are already available. They can supply a home with all its space heat, hot water, and electricity needs. The units are no larger than a refrigerator and make less noise than a dishwasher. Except for an occasional change of filters and spark plugs, they are nearly maintenance-free. Typically, this home-size power and heating plant will pay for itself in four to five years.

Soon, homeowners may be able to get all the electricity they need from rolls of solar cells attached like shingles to a roof or applied to window glass as a coating, already developed by a Japanese and a German firm.

A German firm (Bomin) has developed a solar-powered hydrogen system that can meet all energy needs of a home, an apartment building, or a small village or housing development at an affordable price. This system should be available within a few years.

In 1989, Albers Technologies Corporation of Arizona patented a home air conditioner that uses water, not CFCs or HCFCs, as a coolant, draws half the electricity of a conventional unit, and costs about the same as conventional models with the same cooling capacity. A Saudi Arabian company plans to build 25,000 units every year beginning in 1992, with 20,000 units a year being imported to the United States.

---

heating and cooling loads (Figure 17-4). The homeowner usually recovers initial costs in two to six years and then saves money each year. Caulking and weatherstripping around windows, doors, pipes, vents, ducts, and wires save energy and money quickly.

One-third of the heat in U.S. homes and buildings escapes through closed windows (Figure 17-6) — an energy loss equal to the energy found in all the oil flowing through the Alaskan pipeline every year. During hot weather these windows also let in large amounts of heat, greatly increasing the use of air conditioning. This loss and gain of heat occurs because a single-pane glass window has an insulating value of only R-1. The R-value of a material is a measure of its resistance to heat flow and thus its insulating ability. Even double-glazed windows have an insulating value of only R-2, and a typical triple-glazed window has an insulating value of R-4 to R-6.

Two U.S. firms now sell "superinsulating" R-8 to R-10 windows, about the insulating value of a normal outside wall (R-11), that pay for themselves in lower fuel bills within two to four years and then save money every year for decades. If everyone in the United States used these windows, it would save more oil and natural gas each year than Alaska now supplies. The energy savings are equal to buying oil at $2 to $3 a barrel.

Building codes can be changed to require that all new houses use 80% less energy than conventional houses of the same size, as has been done in Davis, California (see Case Study on p. 133). Laws can require that any existing house be insulated and weatherproofed to certain standards before it can be sold, as required in Portland, Oregon, for example. That, plus use of the latest energy-saving designs, could double the energy efficiency of U.S. buildings by 2010, cut carbon emissions in half, and save $100 billion a year.

Figure 17-6 Infrared photo shows heat loss around the windows, doors, roofs, and foundations (red, white, and yellow colors) of houses and stores in Plymouth, Michigan. The average U.S. house has heat leaks and air infiltration equivalent to leaving a typical window wide open during the heating season. Because of energy-inefficient design, most existing office buildings and houses in the United States unnecessarily waste about half of the energy used to heat and cool them. This wastes about $300 billion a year—more than the entire annual military budget.

Using the most energy-efficient appliances available can also save energy and money.* About one-third of the electricity generated in the United States and other industrial countries is used to power household appliances.

One-fifth of the electricity produced in the United States is used for lighting—about equal to the output of 100 large (1,000-megawatt) power plants or half of all coal burned by the nation's electric utilities. Since conventional incandescent bulbs are only 5% efficient, they waste enormous amounts of energy and add to the heat load of houses during hot weather. About half the air conditioning used in a typical U.S. office building is used to remove the internal heat gain from inefficient lighting.

Socket-type fluorescent light bulbs (Figure 3-16) and new E-lamp bulbs use one-fourth the electricity of conventional bulbs. Although they cost about $10 to $20 a bulb, they last 10 to 13 times longer than conventional bulbs, save three times more money than they cost, and emit light indistinguishable from that of incandescents. Over their lifetime, 15 of these new bulbs will save a homeowner $400 to $900. Switching to these bulbs and other improved lighting equipment would save one-third of the electric energy now produced by all U.S. coal-fired plants or eliminate the need for all electricity produced by the country's 111 nuclear power plants.

Residential refrigerators consume about 7% of the electricity used in the United States—roughly the output of 30 large (1,000-megawatt) power plants. If all U.S. households had the most efficient typical frost-free refrigerator now available, they would save enough electricity to eliminate the need for 18 existing large nuclear or coal-fired power plants.

A SunFrost refrigerator, now produced by a small California company, costs $1,550 and uses 85% less electricity than the average model. By spending $550 more on such a refrigerator, a consumer saves about $2,550 in its lifetime cost. Meanwhile, consumers can reduce the energy use of an existing refrigerator by taping about $25 worth of foil-faced rigid insulation to its sides and doors, with a payback time of about one year.

Similar savings are possible with high-efficiency models of other energy appliances such as stoves, water heaters, and air conditioners. Microwave ovens can reduce electricity use for cooking by 25% to 50% (but not if they are used for defrosting food). New microwave and heat-pump clothes dryers being developed use 15% to 60% less energy than do conventional electric-resistance heating models. Front-loading clothes washers use 50% to 60% less energy than top-loading models and cost no more than top loaders. Increasing the spin speed of a washer is 70 times more efficient than using heat in a dryer to remove water from laundry. If the most energy-efficient appliances now available were installed in all U.S. homes over the next 20 years, the savings in energy would equal the energy content of all the oil produced by Alaska's North Slope fields over their 25-year lifetime.

Energy expert Amory Lovins (see Guest Essay on p. 58) carries around a small briefcase that contains examples of fluorescent light bulbs, a low-flow shower head, superinsulated window glass, and other devices

---

*Each year, the American Council for an Energy-Efficient Economy (ACEEE) publishes a list of the most energy-efficient major appliances mass-produced for the U.S. market. For a copy, send $3 to the council at 1001 Connecticut Ave., NW, Suite 530, Washington, D.C. 20036. Each year, they also publish *A Consumer Guide to Home Energy Savings*, available in bookstores or from the ACEEE for $8.95.

Q: How much money could be saved if the United States got serious about improving energy efficiency?

that save energy and money (Figure 17-7). Using these devices throughout the United States would save energy equal to the output of 200 large electric power plants. This would also save enough money to pay off the national debt, create many jobs, eliminate the need to import any oil, sharply reduce pollution and environmental degradation, and slow projected global warming.

DEVELOPING A PERSONAL ENERGY CONSERVATION PLAN Each of us can develop an individual plan for saving energy and money and helping sustain the earth (see Individuals Matter inside the back cover). Here are four basic guidelines:

1. Don't use electricity to heat space or water (Figure 3-9).

2. Insulate new or existing houses heavily, caulk and weatherstrip to reduce air infiltration and heat loss, and use energy-efficient windows.

3. Get as much heat and cooling as possible from natural sources — especially sun, wind, geothermal energy, and trees (windbreaks and natural shading).

4. Buy the most energy-efficient homes, lights, cars, and appliances available, and evaluate them only in terms of lifetime cost.

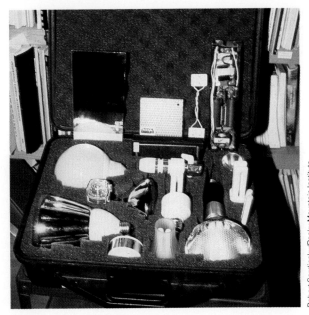

Figure 17-7 Amory Lovins's briefcase of available energy-saving lights, superinsulating window glass, water-flow restrictors, and other devices. Using these throughout the United States would save energy equal to that from 200 large electric power plants, save hundreds of billions of dollars, and sharply reduce pollution and environmental degradation.

17-3 Direct Solar Energy for Producing Heat and Electricity

THE UNTAPPED POTENTIAL OF PERPETUAL AND RENEWABLE ENERGY RESOURCES The largest, mostly untapped sources of energy for all countries are perpetual and renewable energy from the sun, wind, flowing water, biomass, and Earth's internal heat (Figure 17-8). Developing these untapped resources could meet 50% to 80% of projected U.S. energy needs by 2030, or sooner, and virtually all energy needs if coupled with improvements in energy efficiency (Figure 17-1).

Such development would save money, create jobs, eliminate the need for oil imports, produce less pollution and environmental degradation per unit of energy used, and increase economic, environmental, and military security. In the United States, geothermal power plants, wood-fired (biomass) power plants, wind farms, and solar-thermal power plants can produce electricity more cheaply than can new nuclear power plants with far fewer subsidies from the federal government (Figure 17-9).

If coal's harmful effects on the biosphere were included as part of its overall price, it would be so expensive that utilities would use it only as a last resort and replace it with much cheaper perpetual and renewable energy resources and even cheaper improvements in energy efficiency. Although renewable energy resources are regionally concentrated, they are far less so than oil, where two-thirds of the world's proven reserves are in the politically unstable Persian Gulf area.

With an aggressive program to develop perpetual and renewable energy resources, these forms of energy could meet 30% to 45% of the world's projected energy demand by 2050 and bring about enough reduction in greenhouse gases to stabilize projected climate changes. The rest of this chapter evaluates the various perpetual and renewable energy resources available to us.

PASSIVE SOLAR SYSTEMS FOR SPACE HEATING AND COOLING A **passive solar heating system** captures sunlight directly within a structure and converts it into low-temperature heat for space heating (Figure 17-10). Superwindows, greenhouses, and sunspaces face the sun to collect solar energy by direct gain. Thermal mass (heat-storing capacity), such as walls and floors of concrete, adobe, brick, stone, salt-treated timber, or tile, stores collected solar energy as heat and releases it slowly throughout the day and night. Some designs also store heat in water-filled glass or plastic columns, black-painted barrels filled with water, and panels or cabinets containing heat-absorbing chemicals.

A: $1 trillion a year

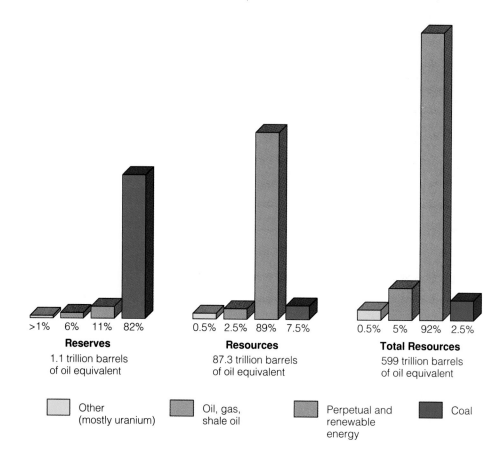

Figure 17-8 U.S. energy resource estimates. The estimated total resources (reserves plus resources) available from perpetual and renewable energy sources is more than 10 times that from domestic supplies of coal, oil, natural gas, shale oil, and uranium. Perpetual and renewable energy resources — primarily hydropower and biomass — already supply 20% of the world's energy and 8% of the commercial energy used in the United States. With a worldwide development program supported by greatly increased government efforts, these largely untapped sources of energy could supply 50% to 80% of the world's projected energy needs within a few decades. (Data from U.S. Department of Energy)

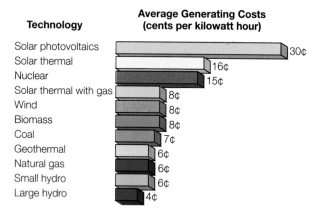

Figure 17-9 Generating costs of electricity per kilowatt-hour by various technologies in 1989. By 2000, costs per kilowatt-hour for wind are expected to fall to 5¢, solar thermal with gas assistance to 6¢, and solar photovoltaic to 10¢. Costs for other technologies are projected to remain about the same. (Data from U.S. Department of Energy, Council for Renewable Energy Education, and Investor Responsibility Research Center)

Besides collecting and storing solar energy as heat, passive systems must also reduce heat loss in cold weather and heat gain in hot weather. Such structures are usually heavily insulated and caulked. Superwindows or movable, insulated shutters or curtains on windows reduce heat loss at night and on days with little sunshine.

Buildup of moisture and indoor air pollutants is minimized by an air-to-air heat exchanger, which supplies fresh air without much heat loss or gain. A small backup heating system may be used, but it is not necessary in a well-designed passively heated and superinsulated house in most climates.

Today, over 250,000 homes and 17,000 nonresidential buildings in the United States have passive solar designs, including earth-sheltered homes (Figure 17-11), and get 30% to 100% of their energy from the sun. However, that is a small number compared with the 80 million homes in the United States and the roughly 3 million new ones built each year. Recently, engineer and builder Michael Sykes has developed an Enertia house design that is passively heated and cooled by solar energy and the earth beneath it and that doesn't need a backup heating or cooling system in most areas (see Spotlight on p. 393).

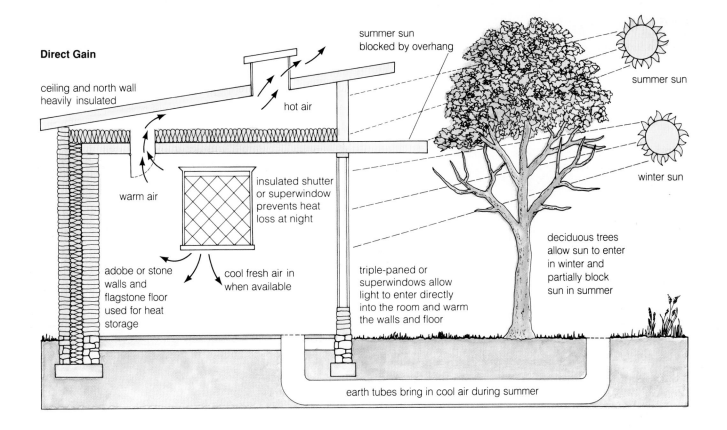

Direct Gain

ceiling and north wall heavily insulated

hot air

summer sun blocked by overhang

summer sun

winter sun

warm air

insulated shutter or superwindow prevents heat loss at night

deciduous trees allow sun to enter in winter and partially block sun in summer

adobe or stone walls and flagstone floor used for heat storage

cool fresh air in when available

triple-paned or superwindows allow light to enter directly into the room and warm the walls and floor

earth tubes bring in cool air during summer

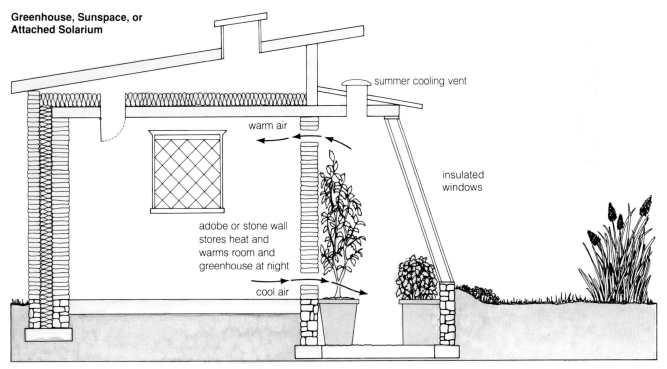

Greenhouse, Sunspace, or Attached Solarium

summer cooling vent

warm air

insulated windows

adobe or stone wall stores heat and warms room and greenhouse at night

cool air

Figure 17-10 Three examples of passive solar design.

(continued)

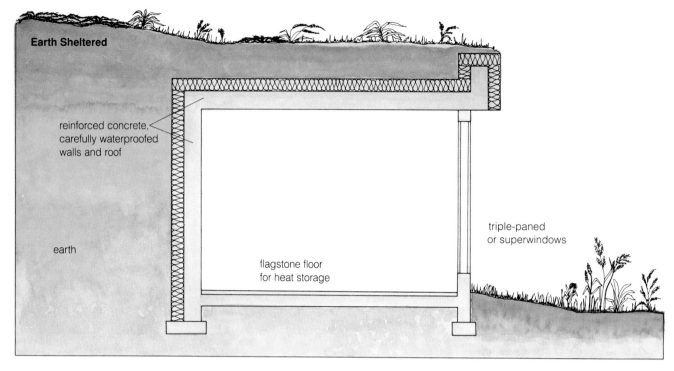

Earth Sheltered

reinforced concrete, carefully waterproofed walls and roof

earth

flagstone floor for heat storage

triple-paned or superwindows

Figure 17–10 (continued)

Pat Armstrong/Visuals Unlimited

Figure 17-11 Exterior of an earth-sheltered house in Will County, Illinois. The interior can look like that of any ordinary house. Passive solar design and skylights can provide more daylight than is found in most conventional houses. On a lifetime-cost basis, earth-sheltered houses are cheaper than conventional aboveground houses of the same size because of reduced heating and cooling costs, no exterior maintenance and painting, and lower fire insurance rates. These structures also provide more privacy, quiet, and security from break-ins, fires, hurricanes, earthquakes, tornadoes, and storms than do conventional homes. Across the United States, about 13,000 families have built earth-sheltered houses.

Roof-mounted passive solar water heaters can also supply all or most of the hot water for a typical house (Figure 17-13). The most promising model, called the Copper Cricket, is produced by Sage Advance Company in Eugene, Oregon, and sells for $2,200.

In hot weather, passive cooling can be provided by blocking the high summer sun with deciduous trees, window overhangs, or awnings (Figure 17-10). Windows and fans take advantage of breezes and keep air moving. A reflective insulating foil sheet can be suspended in the attic to block heat from radiating down into the house.

At a depth of 3 to 6 meters (10 to 20 feet), the temperature of the earth stays about 13°C (55°F) all year long in cold northern climates and about 19°C (67°F) in warm southern climates. Earth tubes buried at this depth can pipe cool and partially dehumidified air into an energy-efficient house at a cost of several dollars a summer (Figure 17-10). For a large space, two or three of these geothermal cooling fields running in different directions from the house should be installed. When the added heat degrades the cooling effect from one field, homeowners can switch to another field. People allergic to pollen and molds should add an air purification system, but they would also need to do that with a conventional cooling system.

In areas with a dry climate, such as the southwestern United States, evaporative coolers can remove interior heat by evaporating water. Solar-powered air conditioners have been developed but so far are too expensive for residential use. In Reno, Nevada, some buildings stay cool throughout the hot summer without air conditioning; large, insulated tanks of water chilled by cool nighttime air keep indoor temperatures comfortable during the day. In 1992, Sanyo began producing a room air conditioner powered mostly by solar cells.

Q: How much of the oil consumed in the United States is for transportation?

Michael Sykes's solar envelope house is heated and cooled passively by solar energy and the slow storage and release of energy by massive timbers and the earth beneath the house (Figure 17-12). The front and back sides of this house contain two walls of heavy timber impregnated with salt to provide immense thermal storage capacity. The space between these two walls plus the basement form a convection loop or envelope that surrounds the inner shell of the house.

Solar energy entering through windows or a greenhouse on the front side of the house facing the sun circulates around the loop, is stored in the heavy timber, and is released slowly during daylight and at night. In summer, a roof vent re-leases heated air in the convection loop throughout the day. At night, these roof vents, with the aid of a fan, draw air into the loop, which cools the inner shell of the house passively.

The interior temperature of the house typically stays within 2 degrees of 21°C (70°F) year-round, without the need for a conventional cooling or heating system. In areas with a cold climate or a fair number of cloudy days, a small wood stove or vented natural gas heater can be placed in the basement portion of the loop and used as a backup to heat the air in the convection loop.

Because of the large amount of timber involved, the initial costs are high. However, they are recovered severalfold by not having to install a conventional heating and cooling system and by heating and cooling energy savings over the lifetime of the house. All timber comes precut with a detailed guidebook, which allows quick assembly. Buyers can save money by erecting the inner and outer shells themselves, which requires little experience and few tools. Michael plants 50 trees for each one used in providing builders with his timber kits. For his design, he has received the Department of Energy's Innovation Award and the North Carolina Governor's Energy Achievement Award.

Figure 17-12 Solar envelope house that is heated and cooled passively by solar energy and Earth's thermal energy. This patented Enertia design needs no conventional heating or cooling system in most areas. It comes in a precut kit engineered and tailored to the buyer's design goals.

Figure 17-13 Active and passive solar water heaters.

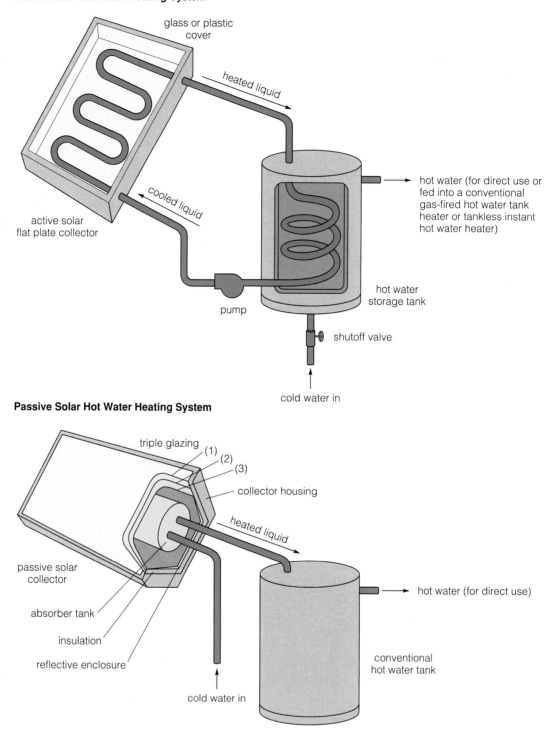

Active Solar Hot Water Heating System

glass or plastic cover

heated liquid

active solar flat plate collector

cooled liquid

hot water (for direct use or fed into a conventional gas-fired hot water tank heater or tankless instant hot water heater)

hot water storage tank

pump

shutoff valve

cold water in

Passive Solar Hot Water Heating System

triple glazing

(1)
(2)
(3)

collector housing

heated liquid

passive solar collector

absorber tank

insulation

reflective enclosure

cold water in

hot water (for direct use)

conventional hot water tank

ACTIVE SOLAR SYSTEMS FOR HEATING SPACE AND WATER In an **active solar heating system**, specially designed collectors concentrate solar energy, with a fan or a pump used to supply part of a building's space-heating or water-heating needs. Several connected collectors are usually mounted on a roof with an unobstructed exposure to the sun (Figure 17-13). In middle and high latitudes with cold winter temperatures and moderate levels of sunlight (Figure 17-14), a small backup heating system is needed during prolonged cold or cloudy periods.

Active solar collectors can also supply hot water. Over 1.3 million active solar hot-water systems have been installed in the United States, especially in Cali-

Q: How could the United States eliminate all oil imports from the Middle East?

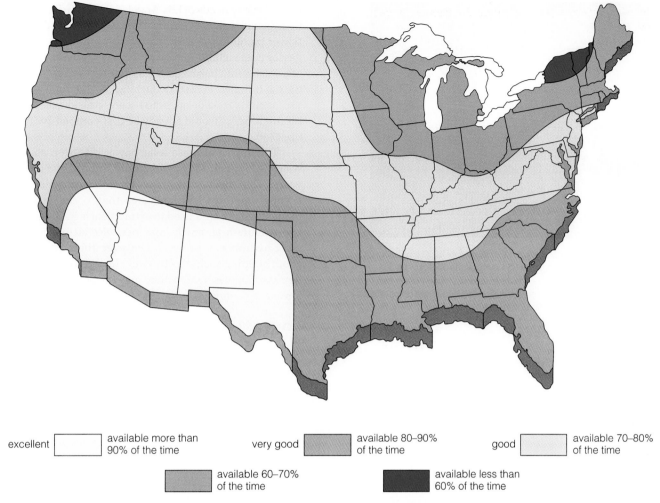

excellent □ available more than 90% of the time   very good ▤ available 80-90% of the time   good ▤ available 70-80% of the time

▤ available 60-70% of the time   ■ available less than 60% of the time

Figure 17-14 Availability of solar energy during the day in the continental United States. (Data from U.S. Department of Energy and National Wildlife Federation)

fornia, Florida, and southwestern states with ample sunshine. The main barrier to their widespread use in the United States is an initial cost of $1,800 to $5,000.

In Cyprus, Jordan, and Israel, active solar water heaters supply 25% to 65% of the hot water for homes. About 12% of the houses in Japan and 37% in Australia use such systems.

PROS AND CONS OF USING SOLAR ENERGY FOR HEATING SPACE AND WATER The energy supply for active or passive systems to collect solar energy for low-temperature heating of buildings is free and is naturally available on sunny days, and the net useful energy yield is moderate (active) to high (passive). The technology is well developed and can be installed quickly. No carbon dioxide is added to the atmosphere, and environmental impacts from air pollution and water pollution are low. Land disturbance is also low because passive systems are built into structures and active solar collectors are usually placed on rooftops.

On a lifetime-cost basis, good passive solar and superinsulated design is the cheapest way to provide 40% to 100% of the space heating for a home or a small building in regions with enough sunlight (Figure 17-14). Such a system usually adds 5% to 10% to the construction cost, but the lifetime cost of operating such a house is 30% to 40% lower than that of conventional houses.

Active systems cost more than passive systems on a lifetime basis because they require more materials to build, they need more maintenance, and eventually they deteriorate and must be replaced. However, retrofitting an existing house with an active solar system is often easier than adding a passive system.

There are disadvantages. Higher initial costs discourage buyers not used to considering lifetime costs and buyers who move every few years. With present technology, active solar systems usually cost too much for heating most homes and small buildings, but better design and mass-production techniques could change

Figure 17-15 The world's largest solar power facility in California's Mojave Desert produces 354 megawatts of electricity by using 810 hectares (2,000 acres) of parabolic collectors to concentrate solar energy. Mirrored troughs focus sunlight on oil-filled tubes that use the concentrated heat absorbed by the oil to produce steam, which is used to run an electricity-generating turbine. Small natural gas turbines are used to run the facility when the sun is not shining. This solar–natural gas fuel mix produces less than one-sixth as much carbon dioxide per kilowatt-hour of electricity as does a normal coal-fired plant. This plant, which began operating in 1989, produces enough electricity to meet the residential needs of 750,000 people at a cost lower than that for electricity from a new nuclear power plant (Figure 17-9) and should be cost-competitive with coal by 2000.

that. Some people also believe that active solar collectors sitting on rooftops or in yards are ugly.

Most passive solar systems require that owners open and close windows and shades to regulate heat flow and distribution, but this can be done by cheap microprocessors. Owners of passive and active solar systems also need laws that prevent others from building structures that block a user's access to sunlight. Such legislation is often opposed by builders of high-density developments.

CONCENTRATING SOLAR ENERGY TO PRODUCE HIGH-TEMPERATURE HEAT AND ELECTRICITY
Huge arrays of computer-controlled mirrors, called heliostats, can track the sun and focus sunlight on a central heat-collection point atop a tall tower or on oil-filled pipes running through the middle of curved solar collectors (Figure 17-15). This concentrated sunlight can produce temperatures high enough for industrial processes or for making high-pressure steam to run turbines and produce electricity. Molten salt can be used to store the sun's heat to produce electricity at night or on cloudy days.

The main use of these plants is supplying reserve power to meet daytime peak electricity loads, especially in sunny areas with large air conditioning demands. It is estimated that solar-thermal plants occupying less than 1% of the area of the Mojave Desert could supply the electricity needs of Los Angeles. They can be backed up by small turbines burning natural gas. Solar-thermal power plants could also be used to produce hydrogen gas for use as a fuel (Section 17-8) and to convert hazardous wastes into harmless or less-harmful substances. If the environmental costs of burning coal (about 1.5 cents to 2 cents per kilowatt hour) were considered, solar thermal energy would already be cost-competitive (Figure 17-9).

The impact of these solar power plants on air and water is low, and they can be built in only one or two years. They need large areas for solar collection but occupy one-third less land area than a coal-burning plant when the land used to extract coal is included and one-twentieth as much land per kilowatt-hour as do most hydropower projects. However, there is concern about building such structures in arid, ecologically fragile desert biomes, where there may not be enough water for use in cooling towers to recondense spent steam.

CONVERTING SOLAR ENERGY DIRECTLY TO ELECTRICITY: PHOTOVOLTAIC CELLS
Solar energy can be converted by **photovoltaic cells**, commonly called **solar cells**, directly into electrical energy. Most solar cells consist of layers of purified silicon, which can be made from inexpensive, abundant sand. Trace amounts of other substances (such as gallium arsenide or cadmium sulfide) are added so that the resulting semiconductor emits electrons and produces a small amount of electrical current when struck by sunlight (Figure 17-16).

Today, solar cells supply electricity for at least 30,000 homes worldwide (20,000 in the United States) and for villages in a number of LDCs, including 6,000 villages in India. Most of these homes and villages are in remote areas where it costs too much to bring in electric power lines. Solar cells are also used to switch railroad tracks and to supply power for water wells, irrigation pumping, battery charging, calculators, portable laptop computers, ocean buoys, lighthouses, and offshore oil-drilling platforms in the sunny Persian Gulf.

Because the amount of electricity produced by a single solar cell is very small, many cells must be wired together in a panel to provide 30 to 100 watts of electric power (Figure 17-16). Several panels are wired together and mounted on a roof, or on a rack that tracks the sun, to produce electricity for a home or a building.

Massive banks of such cells can also produce electricity at a small power plant (Figure 17-17). By 2030, the projected price of producing electricity in this way is expected to reach 4 cents per kilowatt-hour, making it cost-competitive with all other methods of producing electricity. In 1991, Texas Instruments and Southern California Edison announced plans to produce a new type of solar cell that costs half as much to manufacture as existing models.

Q: What is the best way to save oil, slow ozone depletion and global warming, and reduce air pollution?

Single Solar Cell

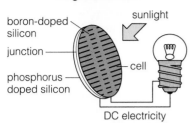

boron-doped silicon

sunlight

junction

cell

phosphorus doped silicon

DC electricity

Panel of Solar Cells

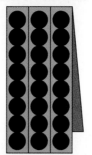

Figure 17-16 Use of photovoltaic (solar) cells to provide DC electricity for an energy-efficient home; any surplus can be sold to the local power company. Prices should be competitive sometime in the 1990s. In 1990, a Florida builder began selling tract houses that get all of their electricity from roof-mounted solar cells. Although the solar-cell systems account for about one-third of the cost of each house, the savings in electric bills will pay this off over a 30-year mortgage period. Sanyo, a Japanese company, has incorporated solar cells into roof shingles.

Array of Solar Cell Panels on a Roof

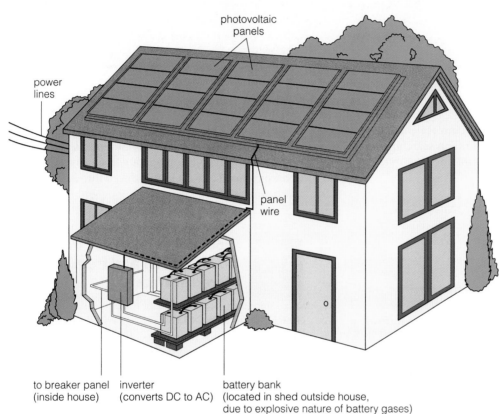

photovoltaic panels

power lines

panel wire

to breaker panel (inside house)   inverter (converts DC to AC)   battery bank (located in shed outside house, due to explosive nature of battery gases)

By 2010, solar cells could supply as much of the world's electricity as nuclear power does today at a lower cost and with much less risk of environmental harm. The U.S. Solar Energy Research Institute estimates that solar cells are capable of supplying more than half of projected U.S. electricity needs four or five decades from now.

Despite their enormous potential, the U.S. federal research and development budget for solar cells was cut by 76% between 1981 and 1990, and the U.S. share of the worldwide solar-cell market fell from 75% to 32%. During that same period, Japanese government expenditures in this area tripled, and Japan's share of the worldwide solar-cell market grew from 15% to 37%. In 1989, a U.S. company (Arco) that was the world's largest manufacturer of solar cells was sold to a German company.

Federal and private research efforts on photovoltaics in the United States need to be increased sharply. Otherwise, the United States will lose out on a huge global market (at least $100 billion a year) and may find much of its capital being drained to pay for imports of photovoltaic cells from Japan, Germany, Italy, and other countries that are investing heavily in this promising technology.

If the federal government were to order $500 million worth of solar cells, the industry could expand. Because of the assured sales and resulting mass-production cost efficiencies, the price of these cells would drop about 90% and become cost-competitive in most parts of the

Figure 17-17 This power plant in Sacramento, California, uses solar-powered photovoltaic cells to produce electricity. The nuclear power plant in the background has been closed down. By 1991, at least two dozen U.S. utility companies were using photovoltaic cells in their operations. As the price of electricity from solar cells continues to fall, such use will increase dramatically.

U.S. Department of Energy

country within a few years. Such an investment of tax-payer dollars would be much better than searching for more oil, burning more coal, or building new nuclear power plants.

PROS AND CONS OF PHOTOVOLTAIC CELLS

If present projections are correct, solar cells could supply 20% to 30% of the world's electricity — half of that in the United States — sometime between 2030 and 2050. That would eliminate the need to build large-scale power plants of any type and would allow many existing nuclear and coal-fired power plants to be phased out.

Solar cells are reliable and quiet, have no moving parts, and should last 30 years or more if encased in glass or plastic. They can be installed quickly and easily and need little maintenance other than occasional washing to prevent dirt from blocking the sun's rays. Small or large solar-cell packages can be built, and they can be easily expanded or moved as needed. Suitable locations for solar cells include deserts, marginal lands, alongside interstate highways, yards, and rooftops. Solar-cell (Figure 17-17) and other solar energy systems (Figure 17-15) need less space to produce a megawatt of electricity than does coal-fired power when the land used for coal mining is included.

Most solar cells are made from silicon, the second most abundant element by weight in the earth's crust. They do not produce carbon dioxide during use. Air and water pollution during operation is low, air pollution from manufacture is low, and land disturbance is very low for roof-mounted systems. The net useful energy yield is fairly high and rising with new designs.

The present costs of solar-cell systems are high, but are projected to become competitive in 7 to 15 years. Additionally, some people feel that racks of solar cells on rooftops or in yards are unsightly; potential limits

could be placed on their use by an insufficient amount of gallium or cadmium; and absence of effective pollution control could allow moderate levels of water pollution from chemical wastes introduced through the manufacturing process.

17-4 Producing Electricity from Moving Water and from Heat Stored in Water

TYPES OF HYDROELECTRIC POWER In *large-scale hydropower projects*, high dams are built across large rivers to create large reservoirs (Figure 5-30). The stored water is then allowed to flow through huge pipes at controlled rates, spinning turbines and producing electricity.

In *small-scale hydropower projects*, a low dam with no reservoir, or only a small one, is built across a small stream. The renewable natural water flow is used to generate electricity, but electricity production can vary with seasonal changes in stream flow.

Falling water can also be used to produce electricity in *pumped-storage hydropower systems*, used mostly to supply extra power during times of peak electrical demand. When electricity demand is low, usually at night, pumps using electricity from a conventional power plant pump water uphill from a lake or a reservoir to another reservoir at a higher elevation, usually on top of a mountain. When a power company temporarily needs more electricity than its plants can produce, water in the upper reservoir is released. On its downward trip to the lower reservoir, the water flows through turbines and generates electricity, but this is an expensive way to produce electricity. Much cheaper alterna-

Q: How much of the heat in U.S. homes and other buildings escapes through closed windows?

tives, such as natural gas turbines, are available. Another possibility may be the use of solar-powered pumps to raise water to the upper reservoir.

PRESENT AND FUTURE USE OF HYDROPOWER

In 1989, hydropower supplied 20% of the world's electricity and 6% of the world's total commercial energy. Hydropower supplies Norway with essentially all its electricity, Switzerland 74%, Austria 67%, and LDCs 50%.

Much of the hydropower potential of North America and Europe has been developed, but Africa has tapped only 5% of its hydropower potential, Latin America 8%, and Asia 9%. Many large-scale hydroelectric dams are being built or planned in Brazil, China, India, and other LDCs. By 2000, China, with one-tenth of the world's hydropower potential, is likely to become the world's largest producer of hydroelectricity. China has also built almost 100,000 small dams to produce electricity for villages. Brazil has identified 136 potential hydropower sites, of which 70 are in the Amazon—already threatened with deforestation (see Pro/Con on p. 329).

Currently, the United States is the world's largest producer of electricity from hydropower, which supplies 10% to 14% of the electricity and 5% to 8% of all commercial energy used by the United States, with the amount varying with rain and snowfall patterns. However, the era of building large dams is drawing to a close in the United States because of high construction costs, lack of suitable sites, and opposition from conservationists. Any new large supplies of hydroelectric power in the United States will be imported from Canada, which gets more than 70% of its electricity from hydropower.

According to the U.S. Army Corps of Engineers, retrofitting abandoned small and medium-size hydroelectric sites and building new small-scale hydroelectric plants on suitable sites could supply the United States with electricity equal to that of 47 large power plants. However, since 1985, the development of small-scale hydropower in the United States has fallen off sharply because of low oil prices, loss of federal tax credits, and opposition to some projects from local residents and conservationists.

PROS AND CONS OF HYDROPOWER

Many LDCs have large, untapped potential hydropower sites, although many are far from where the electricity is needed. Hydropower has a moderate to high net useful energy yield and fairly low operating and maintenance costs.

Hydroelectric plants rarely need to be shut down, and they produce no emissions of carbon dioxide or other air pollutants during operation. Their reservoirs have life spans 2 to 10 times those of coal and nuclear plants. Large dams also help control flooding and sup-

ply a regulated flow of irrigation water to areas below the dam.

Developing small-scale hydroelectric plants by rehabilitating existing dams has little environmental impact, and once rebuilt, the units have a long life. Only a few people are needed to operate them, and they need little maintenance.

However, construction costs for new large-scale systems are high, and few suitable sites are left in the United States and Europe. The reservoirs of large-scale projects flood huge areas, destroy wildlife habitats, uproot people, decrease natural fertilization of prime agricultural land in river valleys below the dam, and decrease fish harvests below the dam (Table 11-1). Without proper land-use control, large-scale projects can greatly increase soil erosion and sediment water pollution near the reservoir above the dam. This reduces the effective life of the reservoir.

By reducing stream flow, small hydroelectric projects threaten recreational activities and aquatic life, disrupt wild and scenic rivers, and destroy wetlands. During drought periods, these plants produce little if any power. Most of the electricity produced by these projects can be supplied at a lower cost and with less environmental impact by industrial cogeneration and by improving the energy efficiency of existing big dams.

TIDAL OR MOON POWER   Twice a day, a large volume of water flows in and out of bays and estuaries along the coast as a result of high and low tides caused by the gravitational attraction of the moon. In a few places, tides flow in and out of a bay with an opening narrow enough to be obstructed by a dam with turbines to produce electricity.

If the difference in water height between high and low tides is large enough, the kinetic energy in these daily tidal flows based on moon power can be used to spin turbines to produce electricity, but only about two dozen places in the world have these conditions. Currently, only two large tidal energy facilities are operating, one at La Rance, France, and the other in Canada in the Bay of Fundy. The Chinese government has built several small tidal plants.

The energy source (tides from gravitational attraction) is free, operating costs are low, and the net useful energy yield is moderate. No carbon dioxide is added to the atmosphere, air pollution is low, and little land is disturbed.

Most analysts, however, expect tidal power to make only a tiny contribution to world electricity supplies. There are few suitable sites, and construction costs are high. The output of electricity varies daily with tidal flows, so there must be a backup system. The dam and power plant can be damaged by storms, and metal parts are easily corroded by seawater. The disruption of normal tidal flows may also disturb aquatic life in coastal estuaries.

WAVE POWER The kinetic energy in ocean waves, created primarily by wind, is another potential source of energy. Japan, Norway, Great Britain, Sweden, the United States, and the former Soviet Union have built small experimental plants to evaluate this form of hydropower. None of these plants has produced electricity at a competitive price, but some designs show promise.

Most analysts expect wave power to make little contribution to world electricity production, except in a few coastal areas with the right conditions. Construction costs are moderate to high, and the net useful energy yield is moderate. Equipment could be damaged or destroyed by saltwater corrosion and severe storms.

OCEAN THERMAL ENERGY CONVERSION

Ocean water stores huge amounts of heat from the sun, especially in tropical areas. Japan and the United States have been conducting experiments to evaluate the technological and economic feasibility of using the large temperature differences between the cold deep waters and the sun-warmed surface waters of tropical oceans to produce electricity in *ocean thermal energy conversion* (OTEC) plants anchored to the bottom of tropical oceans in suitable sites. Although scientists have been working on this method for producing electricity for over 50 years, the technology is still in the research and development stage.

The source of energy for OTEC is limitless at suitable sites, and a costly energy storage and backup system is not needed. No air pollution except carbon dioxide is produced during operation, and the floating power plant requires no land area. Nutrients brought up when water is pumped from the ocean bottom might be used to nourish schools of fish and shellfish.

However, most energy analysts believe that the large-scale extraction of energy from ocean thermal gradients may never compete economically with other energy alternatives. Construction costs are high—two to three times those of comparable coal-fired plants. Operating and maintenance costs are also high because of corrosion of metal parts by seawater and fouling of heat exchangers by algae and barnacles. Plants could also be damaged by hurricanes and typhoons.

Other problems include a limited number of sites and a low net useful energy yield; possible disruption of coral reef communities (Figure 5-23) and other aquatic life by pumping large volumes of deep-ocean water to the surface; and the release of large quantities of dissolved carbon dioxide into the atmosphere.

SOLAR PONDS *Saline solar ponds* can be used to produce electricity and are usually located near inland saline seas or lakes, in areas with ample sunlight. The bottom layer of water in such ponds stays on the bottom when heated because it has a higher salinity and density (mass per unit volume) than the top layer. Heat accumulated during daylight in the bottom layer can be used to produce steam that spins turbines, generating electricity.

Such ponds can also be built by digging a hole, lining it with black plastic, and filling it with salt and water, or brine. An experimental saline solar-pond power plant on the Israeli side of the Dead Sea has been operating successfully for several years. By 2000, Israel plans to build several plants around the Dead Sea to supply electricity for air conditioning and for desalinating water. Several experimental saline solar ponds have been built in the United States, Australia, India, and Mexico.

Freshwater solar ponds can be used as a source of hot water and space heating. A shallow hole is dug, lined with concrete, and covered with insulation. A number of large, black plastic bags, each filled with several centimeters of water, are placed in the hole. The top of the pond is then covered with fiberglass panels, which let sunlight in and keep most of the heat stored in the water during daylight from being lost to the atmosphere. When the water in the bags has reached its peak temperature in the afternoon, a computer turns on pumps to transfer hot water from the bags to large, insulated tanks for distribution as hot water or for space heating.

Saline and freshwater solar ponds have the same advantages as OTEC systems. In addition, they have a moderate net useful energy yield, have moderate construction and operating costs, and need little maintenance. Freshwater solar ponds can be built in almost any sunny area. They may be useful for supplying hot water and space heating for large buildings and small housing developments.

Saline solar ponds are feasible in areas with moderate to ample sunlight, especially ecologically fragile deserts. Operating costs can be high because of saltwater corrosion of pipes and heat exchangers. Unless lined, the ponds can become ineffective when compounds leached from bottom sediment darken the water and reduce transmission of sunlight. With adequate research-and-development support, solar ponds could supply 3% to 4% of U.S. energy needs within 10 years.

17-5 Producing Electricity from Wind

WIND POWER Worldwide, by 1991, there were over 20,000 wind turbines, grouped in clusters called *wind farms* (see photo on p. 379), which fed power to a utility grid. They produced electricity equal to that from 1.6 large (1,000-megawatt) nuclear or coal-burning power plants. Most of these are in California (17,000 machines) and Denmark, located in windy mountain passes and along coastlines. Sweden has installed an offshore wind power plant. In 1991, new wind-farm projects were announced in northern Germany and in Iowa.

Q: How much money does switching from an incandescent bulb to a fluorescent bulb save?

In 1991, California wind farms produced enough electricity to meet the residential power needs of San Francisco. The state could potentially use wind to produce electricity equal to that from 6 to 31 large power plants by 2000, and California is only the 14th windiest state in the country. The island of Hawaii gets about 8% of its electricity from wind, and the use of wind power is spreading to the state's other islands.

The cost of producing electricity with wind farms is about half that of a new nuclear power plant (Figure 17-9) and should be cost-competitive with coal by 1995. Wind power experts project that by the middle of the next century, wind power could supply more than 10% of the world's electricity and 10% to 25% of the electricity used in the United States. U.S. government studies indicate that one-fourth of the country's current electric power could be supplied by wind farms installed on the windiest 1.5% of the land area of the continental United States, and much of this land could still be used to graze livestock below the wind turbines.

Development of this energy resource in the United States has slowed since 1986, when federal tax credits and most state tax credits for wind power were eliminated. Also, the federal budget for research and development of wind power was cut by 90% between 1981 and 1990. Today, Danish companies, with tax incentives and low-interest loans from their government, have taken over the global market for manufacturing wind turbines from the United States.

PROS AND CONS OF WIND POWER Wind power is an unlimited source of energy at favorable sites, and large wind farms can be built in only three to six months. With a moderate to fairly high net useful energy yield, these systems emit no carbon dioxide or other air pollutants during operation; they need no water for cooling; and their manufacture and use produce little water pollution. The land occupied by wind farms can be used for grazing and other purposes, and the leases can provide extra income for farmers and ranchers. Wind power (with much lower subsidies) has a significant cost advantage over nuclear power and should become competitive with coal in many areas sometime in the 1990s (Figure 17-9).

However, wind power can be used only in areas with sufficient winds. Backup electricity from a utility company or from an energy storage system is necessary when the wind dies down, but that is not a problem at sites where the wind blows almost continuously. Backup could also be provided by linking wind farms with a solar-cell or hydropower system or by using efficient turbines fueled by natural gas.

Building wind farms in mountain passes and along shorelines can cause visual pollution. Noise and interference with local television reception have been problems with large turbines, but that can be overcome with improved design and use in isolated areas. Large wind farms might also interfere with the flight patterns of migratory birds in certain areas.

17-6 Energy from Biomass

RENEWABLE BIOMASS AS A VERSATILE FUEL

Biomass is organic plant matter produced by solar energy through photosynthesis. It includes wood, agricultural wastes, and garbage. Some of this plant matter can be burned as solid fuel or converted into more convenient gaseous or liquid *biofuels* (Figure 17-18). In 1989, biomass, mostly from the burning of wood and manure to heat buildings and cook food, supplied about 15% of the world's supplemental energy (4% to 5% in Canada and the United States) and about half of the energy used in LDCs.

Various types of biomass can be used in solid, liquid, and gaseous forms for space heating, water heating, producing electricity, and propelling vehicles. It is a renewable energy resource as long as trees and plants are not harvested faster than they grow back—a requirement that is not being met in most places (Section 15-2).

No net increase in atmospheric levels of carbon dioxide occurs as long as the rate of removal and burning of trees and plants and loss of below-ground organic matter does not exceed the rate of replenishment. Burning of biomass fuels adds much less sulfur dioxide and nitric oxide to the atmosphere per unit of energy produced than does the uncontrolled burning of coal, and thus it requires fewer pollution controls.

However, it takes a lot of land to grow biomass fuel—about 10 times as much as solar cells to provide the same amount of electricity. Without effective land-use controls and replanting, widespread removal of trees and plants can deplete soil nutrients and cause excessive soil erosion, water pollution, flooding, and loss of wildlife habitat. Biomass resources also have a high moisture content (15% to 95%), which lowers their net useful energy. The added weight of the moisture makes collecting and hauling wood and other plant material fairly expensive. Each type of biomass fuel has other specific advantages and disadvantages.

BURNING WOOD AND WOOD WASTES About 80% of the people living in LDCs heat their dwellings and cook their food by burning wood or charcoal made from wood. However, at least 1.1 billion people in LDCs cannot find, or are too poor to buy, enough fuelwood to meet their needs; and that number may increase to 2.5 billion by 2000.

In MDCs with adequate forests, the burning of wood, wood pellets, and wood wastes to heat homes

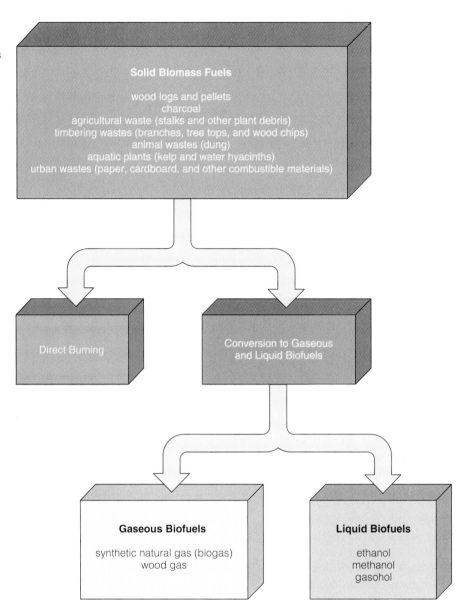

Figure 17-18 Principal types of biomass fuel. Biomass is any plant matter that stores the sun's energy through photosynthesis.

Solid Biomass Fuels

wood logs and pellets
charcoal
agricultural waste (stalks and other plant debris)
timbering wastes (branches, tree tops, and wood chips)
animal wastes (dung)
aquatic plants (kelp and water hyacinths)
urban wastes (paper, cardboard, and other combustible materials)

Direct Burning

Conversion to Gaseous and Liquid Biofuels

Gaseous Biofuels

synthetic natural gas (biogas)
wood gas

Liquid Biofuels

ethanol
methanol
gasohol

and produce steam and electricity in industrial boilers increased rapidly during the 1970s because of price increases in heating oil and electricity. Sweden leads the world in using wood as an energy source, mostly for district heating plants.

In the United States, small wood-burning power plants (Figure 17-19) located near sources of their fuel can produce electricity at about half the price of a new nuclear power plant and at about the same cost as burning coal (Figure 17-9). Wood-fired power plants provide 23% of the electricity used in Maine. The National Wood Energy Association estimates that burning the wood wastes from paper and lumber mills, agriculture, urban land clearing, and tree trimming in the United States could provide electricity equal to that from 200 large (1,000-megawatt) power plants.

The forest-products industry (mostly paper companies and lumber mills) consumes almost two-thirds of the fuelwood used in the United States. Homes and

small businesses burn the rest, with wood providing all the heating needs of 5.6 million U.S. homes and supplementary heat in an additional 21 million. The largest use of fuelwood is in New England, where wood is plentiful.

Wood has a moderate to high net useful energy yield when collected and burned directly and efficiently near its source. However, in urban areas where wood must be hauled from long distances, it can cost homeowners more per unit of energy produced than oil and electricity. Burning wood produces virtually no emissions of sulfur dioxide.

Harvesting and burning wood can cause accidents. Each year in the United States over 10,000 people are injured by chain saws, and several hundred people are killed in house fires caused by improperly located or poorly maintained or operated wood stoves.

A typical wood stove without pollution controls emits 1,000 times as much particulate matter (soot) as a

Q: How much will a person save by paying about $550 more for the most energy-efficient refrigerator?

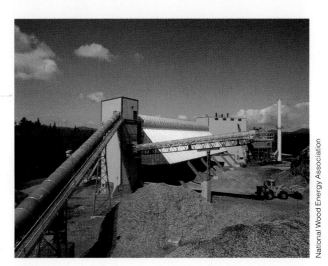

Figure 17-19 This small, 16-megawatt biomass power plant in Whitefield, New Hampshire, is operated by Thermo Electron Energy. Nearby forest residue is burned to generate electricity.

gas furnace. According to the EPA, wood burning causes as many as 820 cancer deaths a year in the United States.

In 1991, an analysis of fireplace ash and smoke from wood-burning factories and stoves revealed that they contained significant levels of radioactive isotopes of cesium and strontium, presumably taken up by trees decades earlier as a result of fallout from nuclear weapons testing. If unregulated wood ash, some of which is being used in fertilizers, were subject to the same regulations as nuclear waste, it would cost wood burners more than $30 billion a year to safely dispose of such ash.

The outdoor air pollution can be reduced 75% by a $100 to $250 catalytic combustion chamber in the stove or stovepipe. These units also increase the energy efficiency of a typical airtight wood stove from 55% to as high as 81% and reduce the need for chimney cleaning and the chance of chimney fires. But these devices must be replaced every four years at a cost of about $100. Recently, wood stoves have been developed that are 65% efficient, don't use catalytic combustion, and emit 90% less air pollution than conventional wood stoves.

Many people consider fireplaces cozy and romantic. They can also be used for heating but are so inefficient that they result in a net loss of energy from a house. The draft of heat and gases rising up the fireplace chimney exhausts warm air and pulls in cold air from cracks and crevices throughout a house. Fireplace inserts with glass doors and blowers help but still waste energy compared with an efficient wood-burning stove. If you must have a fireplace, shut the room it is in off from the rest of the house. Then crack a window in that room so that the fireplace won't draw much heated air from other rooms, or run a small pipe into the front of the fireplace so it can get the air it needs during combustion from the outside.

In London, South Korean cities, and some areas of Colorado, wood fires have been banned to reduce air pollution. Since 1990, the EPA has required all new wood stoves sold in the United States to emit at least 70% less particulate matter than earlier models. Some new stoves meet these standards by using catalytic combustion devices, others by better design or by using cleaner-burning wood pellets for fuel. Anyone owning an older wood stove should add a catalytic converter or replace it with a newer model that meets government air pollution standards.

ENERGY PLANTATIONS One way to produce biomass fuel is to plant large numbers of fast-growing trees (especially cottonwoods, poplars, sycamores, and leucaenas), shrubs, or grasses in *biomass-energy plantations* to supply fuelwood. Plantations of oil palms and varieties of Euphorbia plants, which store energy in hydrocarbon compounds (like those found in oil), can also be established. After these plants are harvested, their oil-like material can be extracted and either refined to produce gasoline or burned directly in diesel engines. Both types of energy plantations can be established on semiarid land not needed to grow crops, although lack of water can limit productivity.

This industrialized approach to biomass production usually requires heavy use of pesticides and fertilizers, which can pollute drinking water supplies and harm wildlife. It also requires large areas of land.

Conversion of large forested areas into monoculture energy plantations reduces biodiversity. In some areas, biomass plantations might compete with food crops for prime farmland. To produce enough liquid fuels to replace all of the gasoline and diesel fuel currently consumed each year in the United States would require planting energy crops on more land than the country now devotes to agriculture. Furthermore, these crops are likely to have low or negative net useful energy yields, as do most conventional crops grown by industrialized agricultural methods.

BURNING AGRICULTURAL AND URBAN WASTES In agricultural areas, crop residues (the unharvested parts of food crops) and animal manure can be collected and burned (Figure 17-18) or converted into biofuels. By 1985, Hawaii was burning a residue (called *bagasse*) left after sugarcane harvesting and processing to supply almost 10% of its electricity (58% on the island of Kauai and 33% on the island of Hawaii). Other crop residues that could be burned include coconut shells, peanut and other nut hulls, and cotton stalks. Brazil gets 10% of its electricity by burning bagasse and plans to use this crop residue to produce 35% of its electricity by 2000.

This approach makes sense when residues are burned in small power plants located near areas where the residues are produced (Figure 17-19). Otherwise, it

Figure 17-20 This biogas digester converts animal dung into a methane-rich gas that can be burned for cooking, space heating, and other purposes.

takes too much energy to collect, dry, and transport the residues to power plants. Also, ecologists argue that it makes more sense to use crop residues to feed livestock, retard soil erosion, and fertilize the soil.

An increasing number of cities in Japan, western Europe, and the United States have built incinerators that burn trash and use the heat released to produce electricity or to heat nearby buildings (Section 19-6). However, this approach may be limited by opposition from citizens concerned about emissions of toxic gases and what to do with the resulting toxic ash. Some analysts argue that more energy is saved by composting or recycling paper and other organic wastes than by burning them (Section 19-7).

CONVERTING SOLID BIOMASS INTO GASEOUS BIOFUELS Plants, organic wastes, sewage, and other forms of solid biomass can be converted by bacteria and various chemical processes into gaseous and liquid biofuels (Figure 17-18). Examples are *biogas* (a mixture of 60% methane and 40% carbon dioxide), *liquid methanol* (methyl, or wood, alcohol), and *liquid ethanol* (ethyl, or grain, alcohol).

In China, anaerobic bacteria in an estimated 7 million *biogas digesters* convert organic plant and animal wastes into methane fuel for heating and cooking. After the biogas has been separated, the solid residue is used as fertilizer on food crops or, if contaminated, on trees. India has about 750,000 biogas digesters in operation, half of them built since 1986 (Figure 17-20).

When they work, biogas digesters are very efficient. However, they are slow and unpredictable. Development of new, more reliable models could change this, and biomass-derived methane could become an affordable alternative to natural gas before 2000.

Methane fuel is also produced by underground decomposition of organic matter in the absence of air (anaerobic digestion) in landfills. This gas can be collected by pipes inserted into landfills, separated from other gases, and burned as a fuel (Figure 12-20). Eighty-two

U.S landfills currently recover methane, but 2,000 to 3,000 large U.S. landfills have the potential for large-scale methane recovery. Burning this gas instead of allowing it to escape into the atmosphere helps slow projected global warming because methane is 25 times more effective in causing atmospheric global warming per molecule than carbon dioxide (Figure 10-6).

Methane can also be produced by anaerobic digestion of manure produced by animal feedlots and sludge produced at sewage treatment plants. However, conservationists believe that in most cases, recycling manure to the land instead of using commercial inorganic fertilizer, which requires large amounts of natural gas to produce, would probably save more natural gas than is saved by burning the manure.

CONVERTING SOLID BIOMASS INTO LIQUID BIOFUELS Some analysts believe that methanol and ethanol can be used as liquid fuels to replace gasoline and diesel fuel when oil becomes too scarce and expensive. Both alcohols can be burned directly as fuel without requiring additives to boost octane ratings.

Currently, emphasis is on using ethanol as an automotive fuel. It can be made from sugar and grain crops (sugarcane, sugar beets, sorghum, and corn) by fermentation and distillation. Pure ethanol can be burned in today's cars with little engine modification. Gasoline can also be mixed with 10% to 23% ethanol to make *gasohol*. It burns in conventional gasoline engines and is sold as super unleaded or ethanol-enriched gasoline.

Since 1987, ethanol made by fermentation of surplus sugarcane has accounted for about half the automotive fuel consumption in Brazil. Bagasse, a by-product of the production of ethanol from sugarcane, can be burned to produce electricity or steam for industrial processes. The use of ethanol has helped Brazil cut its oil imports and created an estimated 575,000 full-time jobs, but the government has spent $8 billion to subsidize the country's ethanol industry. In recent years, ethanol production has been curtailed because of financial difficulties.

Super unleaded gasoline containing 90% gasoline and 10% ethanol now accounts for about 8% of gasoline sales in the United States — 25% to 35% in Illinois, Iowa, Kentucky, and Nebraska. The ethanol used in gasohol is made mostly by fermenting corn in 150 ethanol production plants built between 1980 and 1985. Excluding federal taxes, it costs about $1.60 to produce a gallon of ethanol, compared with about 50 cents for a gallon of gasoline; but new, energy-efficient distilleries are lowering the production cost. Soon this fuel may be able to compete with other forms of unleaded gasoline without federal tax breaks.

Ethanol produces 25% less carbon monoxide and 15% fewer nitrogen oxides per unit of energy than conventional gasoline and is a better antiknock fuel. How-

Q: How much of projected U.S. energy needs by 2030 could be provided by perpetual and renewable energy resources?

ever, without catalytic converters, cars burning ethanol fuels produce more aldehydes and PANs (peroxyacyl nitrates) that kill plants and cause more eye irritation than do cars burning gasoline. Ethanol also has less energy per liter than gasoline, so cars require larger fuel tanks or more frequent fill-ups. Ethanol produces less carbon dioxide per unit of energy than gasoline, but total CO_2 impact depends on the energy source used in the distillation process and whether the crops are grown using energy-intensive industrialized agriculture.

The distillation process to make ethanol produces large volumes of a waste material (swill), which kills fish and aquatic plants if allowed to flow into waterways. Also, the net useful energy yield from producing ethanol fuel is low in older distilleries fueled by oil or natural gas. However, the yield is moderate at new distilleries powered by coal, wood, or solar energy.

Some experts are concerned that growing corn or other grains to make alcohol fuel could cause competition for cropland needed to grow food. It takes nine times more cropland to fuel one average U.S. automobile with ethanol for one year than it does to feed one American per year. About 40% of the entire U.S. annual harvest of corn would be needed to make enough ethanol to meet just 10% of the country's demand for automotive fuel. However, ethanol production uses only the starch portion of the corn, leaving a high-protein by-product that makes an excellent animal feed when supplemented with some carbohydrates. Ethanol's future may depend on learning how to make it economically from wood or agricultural wastes.

Another alcohol, methanol, can be produced from wood, wood wastes, agricultural wastes (such as corncobs), sewage sludge, garbage, coal, or natural gas at a cost of about $1.10 per gallon—almost twice the cost of producing gasoline. High concentrations of methanol corrode some metals and embrittle rubber and some plastics, but in a properly modified engine methanol burns cleanly without any problems.

A fuel of 85% methanol and 15% unleaded gasoline (called M85) could reduce emissions of ozone-forming hydrocarbons 20% to 50% but may produce more nitrogen oxides than burning gasoline. Cars burning pure methanol would reduce those emissions by 85% to 95% and carbon monoxide emissions by 30% to 90%. But, cars burning pure methanol emit 2 to 5 times more cancer-producing formaldehyde, a suspected carcinogen, than do cars burning gasoline.

Methanol-powered cars emit less carbon dioxide than gasoline-powered cars, but producing the methanol from coal would double carbon dioxide emissions. Methanol also has less energy per liter than gasoline, so cars require larger tanks or more refuelings. It is also more flammable than gasoline and can cause blindness if spilled on the skin or splashed into the eyes. Cars running on methanol would cost about $300 to $500 more than gasoline-powered cars.

EXTRACTING ENERGY FROM THE EARTH'S INTERIOR Heat contained in underground rocks and fluids is an important source of energy. At various places in the earth's crust, this **geothermal energy** from the earth's interior (Figure 4-2) is transferred over millions of years to underground concentrations of dry steam (steam with no water droplets), wet steam (a mixture of steam and water droplets), and hot water trapped in fractured or porous rock (Figure 3-5).

If these geothermal sites are close enough to the earth's surface, wells can be drilled to extract the dry steam, wet steam (Figure 17-21), or hot water trapped in rocks and fluids beneath Earth's crust. This thermal energy can be used for space heating and to produce electricity or high-temperature heat for industrial processes.

Geothermal reservoirs can be depleted if heat is removed faster than it is renewed by natural processes. Thus, geothermal resources are nonrenewable on a human time scale, but the potential supply is so vast that it is often classified as a potentially renewable energy resource. However, recent depletion of geothermal sites in California at about twice the expected rate may lead to the classification of some types of geothermal resources as nonrenewable. In 1991, the U.S. Geological Survey estimated that the amount of heat trapped in California's rock that could be extracted for power generation was about half the amount estimated in 1978.

Currently, about 20 countries are extracting energy from geothermal sites and supplying enough heat to meet the needs of over 2 million homes in a cold climate and enough electricity for over 1.5 million homes. The United States accounts for 44% of the electricity generated worldwide from geothermal energy. Figure 17-22 shows that most accessible, high-temperature geothermal sites in the United States lie in the West, especially in California and the Rocky Mountain states. Iceland, Japan, and Indonesia are among the countries with the greatest potential for tapping geothermal energy.

Dry-steam reservoirs are the preferred geothermal resource, but they are also the rarest. A large dry-steam well near Larderello, Italy, has been producing electricity since 1904 and is an important source of power for Italy's electric railroads. Two other large dry-steam sites are the Matsukawa field in Japan and the Geysers steam field about 145 kilometers (90 miles) northwest of San Francisco. Currently, 28 plants tapping energy from the Geysers field supply more than 6% of northern California's electricity. Largely without government subsidies, that is enough to meet all the electrical needs of a city the size of San Francisco at less than the cost of electricity from a new coal plant and one-fourth the cost of

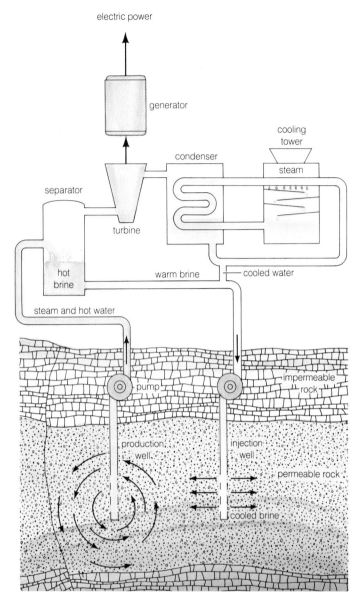

electric power

generator

cooling tower

condenser

steam

separator

turbine

hot brine

warm brine

cooled water

steam and hot water

impermeable rock

pump

production well

injection well

permeable rock

cooled brine

Figure 17-21 Tapping the earth's heat or geothermal energy in the form of wet steam to produce electricity.

electricity from a new nuclear plant (Figure 17-9). New units can be added every 2 to 3 years (compared with 6 years for a coal plant and 10 to 12 years for a nuclear plant). However, there is evidence that this field has been overdeveloped and may produce declining yields.

Wet-steam reservoirs are more common than dry-steam reservoirs but harder and more expensive to convert to electricity. The world's largest wet-steam power plant is in Wairaki, New Zealand. Others operate in Mexico, Japan, El Salvador, Nicaragua, and the CIS. Four small-scale wet-steam demonstration plants in the western United States are producing electricity at a cost equal to paying $40 a barrel for oil.

Hot-water reservoirs are more common than dry-steam and wet-steam reservoirs. Almost all the homes,

buildings, and food-producing greenhouses in Reykjavik, Iceland, a city with a population of about 85,000, are heated by hot water drawn from deep geothermal wells under the city. In Paris, France, the equivalent of 200,000 dwellings are heated by tapping such reservoirs. At 180 locations in the United States, mostly in the West, hot-water reservoirs have been used for years to heat homes and farm buildings and to dry crops.

A fourth potential source of nonrenewable geothermal energy and natural gas is *geopressurized zones*. These are underground reservoirs of water at a high temperature and pressure, usually trapped deep under continental shelf beds of shale or clay. With present drilling technology, they would supply geothermal energy and natural gas at a cost equal to paying $30 to $45 a barrel for oil.

There are also three types of vast, virtually perpetual sources of geothermal energy: *molten rock* (magma) found near Earth's surface; *hot dry-rock zones*, where molten rock that has penetrated Earth's crust from below heats subsurface rock to high temperatures; and low- to moderate-temperature *warm-rock reservoir deposits*, useful for preheating water and running geothermal heat pumps for space heating and air conditioning. According to the National Academy of Sciences, the amount of potentially recoverable energy from such reservoirs would meet U.S. energy needs at current consumption levels for 600 to 700 years.

The problem is developing methods to extract this energy economically. Several experimental projects are in progress, but so far none has been able to produce energy at a cost competitive with other energy sources.

PROS AND CONS The biggest advantages of geothermal energy include a vast and sometimes renewable supply of energy for areas near reservoirs, moderate net useful energy yields for large and easily accessible reservoir sites, and far less carbon dioxide per unit of energy than fossil fuels. The cost of producing electricity in geothermal plants is cheaper than it is in coal-burning plants and much cheaper than in new nuclear plants (Figure 17-9).

A serious limitation of geothermal energy is the scarcity of easily accessible reservoir sites. Geothermal reservoirs must also be carefully managed or they can be depleted within a few decades. Geothermal development in some areas can destroy or degrade forests or other ecosystems. In Hawaii, for example, environmentalists are fighting the construction of a large geothermal project, located mostly in the only lowland tropical rain forest left in the United States.

Without pollution control, geothermal energy production causes moderate to high air pollution from hydrogen sulfide, ammonia, mercury, boron, and radioactive materials. It also causes moderate to high water pollution from dissolved solids (salinity) and runoff of toxic compounds of heavy metals such as arsenic and

Q: How much of projected U.S. electricity needs could be supplied by solar cells within 40 to 50 years?

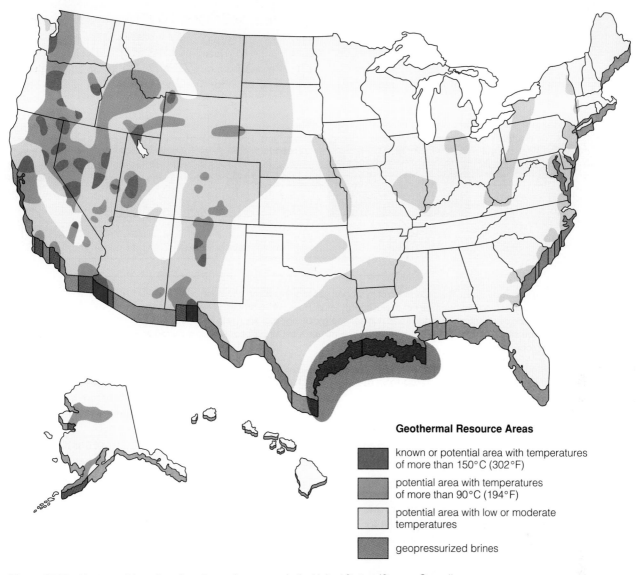

Geothermal Resource Areas

known or potential area with temperatures of more than 150°C (302°F)

potential area with temperatures of more than 90°C (194°F)

potential area with low or moderate temperatures

geopressurized brines

Figure 17-22 Most promising sites of geothermal resources in the United States. (Source: Council on Environmental Quality)

mercury. Noise, odor, and local climate changes can also be problems. Without proper controls, the expansion of geothermal energy could lead to increased water pollution from the hazardous wastes produced. With proper controls, most experts consider the environmental effects of geothermal energy to be less, or no greater, than those of fossil-fuel and nuclear power plants.

17-8 Hydrogen as the Fuel of the Future

THE SOLAR-HYDROGEN REVOLUTION Hydrogen gas (H_2) is an extremely attractive fuel that could be used in place of oil and other fossil fuels and nuclear power. When hydrogen burns, it combines with oxygen gas in the air and produces harmless water vapor clean enough to condense and drink (Figure 17-23). A small amount of nitric oxide (NO) is also produced when the nitrogen and oxygen gases in air combine at the high temperatures reached during the burning of hydrogen (or any other) fuel. Unlike the burning of fossil fuels and biomass fuel, the burning of hydrogen releases no heat-trapping carbon dioxide into the atmosphere. Hydrogen has about 2.5 times the energy by weight of gasoline, making it an especially attractive aviation fuel.

Once hydrogen gas is produced by passing electrical current through water, it can be collected and stored in tanks at high pressures and distributed by pipeline like natural gas or stored in tanks for use in homes, factories, or cars. Hydrogen gas is much easier to store

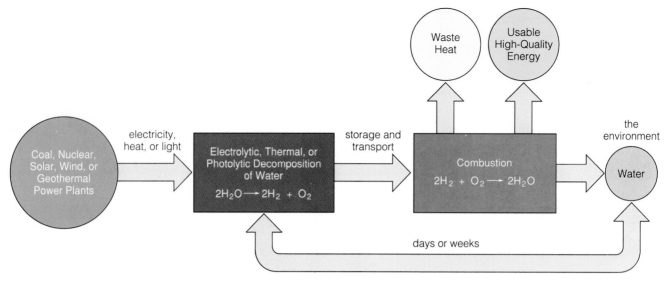

Figure 17-23 The hydrogen energy cycle. The production of hydrogen gas requires electricity, heat, or solar energy to decompose water, thus leading to a negative net useful energy yield. However, hydrogen is a clean-burning fuel that can be used to replace oil and other fossil fuels and nuclear energy. Using solar energy to produce hydrogen from water could provide an antidote to our fossil-fuel addiction, eliminate most air pollution, and greatly reduce the threat from projected global warming.

than electricity. It can be stored in a pressurized tank or in metal hydrides, metal powders that absorb gaseous hydrogen and release it when heated for use as a fuel in a car, a furnace, or an electricity-producing fuel cell. Years' worth of hydrogen could be stored in depleted oil or gas wells or other underground areas.

Unlike gasoline, the solid metallic hydrogen compounds would not explode or burn if the tank were ruptured in an accident. Several experimental cars and a bus in Utah have been running on hydrogen fuel for a number of years. Hydrogen can also be phased in gradually by mixing it with natural gas as reserves of this fuel are gradually depleted and prices rise in the early decades of the next century. The sunny U.S. Southwest could supply much of the country with electricity produced by solar power or with hydrogen produced by solar power. The gas could then be carried by pipeline to areas where it is needed. Small industrial hydrogen pipelines have been used for decades in several countries.

Switching to hydrogen as our primary fuel and using solar energy to produce the hydrogen—known as the *solar-hydrogen revolution*—would change the world as dramatically as the Agricultural and Industrial revolutions did. Burning hydrogen would eliminate most air pollution and water pollution caused by extracting, transporting, and burning fossil fuels and would greatly reduce the projected threat of enhanced global warming. It would also reduce the threat of conventional and nuclear wars between countries fighting over dwindling supplies of oil and faced with economic depression from rapidly escalating oil prices.

Nuclear power could be phased out. We would also have a versatile fuel based on using perpetual energy

from the sun and produced from abundant water. Individuals would also be able to produce most, if not all, of their own energy, instead of having to rely on oil and utility companies.

The greatest problem with hydrogen as a fuel is that only trace amounts of the gas occur in nature. Producing it uses high-temperature heat or electricity from another energy source—such as nuclear fission, direct solar power, or wind—to decompose water (Figure 17-23). Currently, it would cost about $1.40 to produce hydrogen gas with the energy found in 3.8 liters (1 gallon) of gasoline. But the current price of gasoline does not include its numerous pollution and health costs, which add at least $1 a gallon to its true cost. Thus, even today, hydrogen is cheaper than gasoline and other fossil fuels when the overall societal costs are considered.

Because of the first and second energy laws (Section 3-6), hydrogen production by any method will take more energy than is released when it is burned. Thus, its net useful energy yield will always be negative. That means that its widespread use depends on having an abundant and affordable supply of some other type of environmentally acceptable energy.

The key to the spread of the solar-hydrogen revolution is the development of effective and affordable ways of using solar energy to produce electricity that can be passed through water to make hydrogen gas. If this can be accomplished, we can make the transition to a *solar-hydrogen* economy over the next 30 years, using natural gas to help us make the transition. Using fossil fuels (especially coal and oil) or nuclear fuels to produce hydrogen in large quantities is too expensive and leaves us with the serious environmental problems associated with those fuels.

I am writing this book deep in the midst of some beautiful woods in Eco-Lair, a structure that Peggy, my wife and earthmate, and I designed to work with nature. This ongoing experiment is designed as a low-tech, low-cost example of sustainable-Earth design and living.

First, in 1980, we purchased a 1954 school bus from a nearby school district for $200 and sold the tires for the same price that we paid for the bus. We built an insulated foundation, rented a crane for two hours to lift and set the gutted bus on the foundation, placed heavy insulation around the bus, and added a wooden outside frame. The interior is paneled with wood, some of it obtained from the few trees we carefully selected for removal (Figure 17-24). Most people who visit us don't know the core of the structure is a school bus unless we tell them.

We attached a solar room—a passive solar collector with double-paned conventional sliding glass windows (for ventilation)—to the entire south side of the bus structure (Figure 17-24). Thick concrete floors and filled concrete blocks on the lower half of the interior wall facing the sun absorb and slowly release solar energy collected during the day. The solar room serves as a year-round sitting and work area and contains a small kitchen with a stove and a heavily insulated refrigerator that run on liquefied petroleum gas (LPG). I plan to replace the windows with new superinsulated windows, which were not available at the time of construction.

The room collects enough solar energy to meet about 60% of the space heating needs during the cold months. The rest of the heat is provided by a continuous loop system of water preheated by solar collectors and, when necessary, heated further by a tankless instant water heater fueled by LPG (Figure 3-19).

During sunny days, active solar collectors store heat in an insulated tank, which can be a discarded conventional hot water tank that is wrapped with thick insulation. A pump connected to the water tank circulates heated water in well-insulated pipes through the instant hot water heater and from there to a heat exchanger before the water is returned to the tank. A fan transfers the heat in the water to air, which is blown through well-insulated ducts as in a conventional heating system. Some of the heat is recovered for use in the next stage when the heated water returns to the insulated tank. Indoor temperatures are controlled by a conventional thermostat. A valve on the input of the instant water heater senses water temperature and bypasses the heater when the solar-heated water has a high enough temperature to provide the necessary space heating.

During the summer, all hot water can be supplied by the roof-mounted active solar collectors (Figure 17-24), which I plan to replace with a Copper Cricket passive collector. In winter, the water heated by these collectors is heated further as needed by a second tankless instant heater fueled by LPG. Our compact fluorescent light bulbs last an average of six years and use about 70% less electricity than conventional bulbs.

For the time being, we are buying electricity from the power company, but we plan to get our electricity from roof-mounted panels of photovoltaic cells (Figure 17-16) within the next few years. Present electricity bills run around $30 a month (with $18 of this a base charge regardless of how much electricity is used), compared with $100 or more for conventional structures of the same size.

In moderate weather, cooling is provided by opening windows to capture breezes. During the hot and humid North Carolina summers, additional cooling is provided by earth tubes (Figure 17-10).

Four plastic pipes, with a diameter of 10 centimeters (4 inches) were buried about 5.5 meters (18 feet) underground, extending down a gently sloping hillside until their ends emerged some 31 meters (100 feet) away. The other ends of the tubes come up into the foundation of the bus and connect to a duct system containing a small fan with rheostat-controlled speed. When the fan is turned on, outside air at a temperature of 35°C (95°F) is drawn slowly through the buried tubes (which are surrounded by earth at about 16°C or 60°F), entering the structure at about 22°C (72°F). This natural air conditioning costs about $1 per summer for running the fan.

Several large oak trees and other deciduous trees in front of the solar room give us additional passive cooling during summer and drop their leaves to let the sun in during winter. A used conventional central air conditioning unit (purchased for $200) is used as a backup. It can be turned on for short periods (typically no more than 15 to 30 minutes a day) when excessive pollen or heat and humidity overwhelm our immune systems and the earth tubes. Life always involves some trade-offs.

Eco-Lair is surrounded by natural vegetation, including flowers and low-level ground cover adapted to the climate of the area. This means there is no grass to cut and no lawn mower to repair, feed with gasoline, and listen to. Plants that repel various insects have also been added, so we have few insect pest problems. The surrounding trees and other vegetation also provide habitats for various species of insect-eating birds. When ants, mice, and other creatures find their way inside, we use natural alternatives to repel and control them (see Individuals Matter on p. 320).

Water use has been reduced by installing water-saving faucets, a water-saving shower head, and a low-flush toilet. We have also experimented with a waterless composting toilet that gradually converts waste and garbage scraps into a dry, odorless powder that can be used as a soil conditioner.

Kitchen wastes are composted and recycled to the soil. Paper and nonrefillable glass bottles we use are carried to a local recycling center, along with most of the small amount of plastics we use. We try to never use energy-intensive aluminum cans and plastic bags and instead use refillable bottles and

(continued)

Evan Kruppenbach

Evan Kruppenbach

Figure 17-24   Eco-Lair is where I work. It is a low-tech, low-cost ongoing experiment in saving energy and money. A south-facing solar room (shown in the photo on the left) collects solar energy passively and distributes it to a well-insulated, recycled 1954 school bus. The solar room also contains a compact, energy-efficient kitchen. Backup heat and hot water are provided by two solar-assisted, tankless instant water heaters fueled by LPG (Figure 3-19). Active solar collectors are shown on the left, and a passive solar water heater is shown near the ground on the right. The photo on the right shows the interior of the recycled school bus. The computer and desk at the far end are located where the hood and motor of the bus used to be. The large cabinet on the left folds down and serves as a double bed. The bus windows on the right can be opened as needed to allow heat collected in the attached solar room to flow into the bus space.

reusable cloth bags; reuse and waste reduction are much better than recycling and using throwaway items. Extra furniture, clothes, and other items we have accumulated or salvaged over the years are stored in three other old school buses and recycled to family, friends, and people in need. For most household chemicals we use more Earth-friendly substitutes (see Individuals Matter inside the back cover). We use recycled toilet paper made from post-consumer paper waste and recycled paper for my office.

Because I work at home, I do little driving. Our primary car is a four-door, automatic transmission (Peggy has back problems that prevent use of the even more energy-efficient manual shift model) version of a Geo Metro that gets 18 kpl (42 mpg). It is peppy and has more interior room than most mid-size cars and is the most exciting and rewarding car we have ever had. This is backed up by a much less fuel-efficient 4-wheel-drive vehicle needed for occasional travel on the 1.6-kilometer (1-mile) dirt road leading to Eco-Lair when the weather is bad.

We wish cars like the Volvo LCP 2000 were available. If the technol-ogy becomes available and economically feasible in the future, we hope to purchase a vehicle that runs on hydrogen gas produced by solar photovoltaic cells that decompose water into hydrogen and oxygen gas. We think increasing energy efficiency, using solar energy, and helping promote the exciting solar-hydrogen revolution are key ways to help sustain the earth and save money.

We get most of our food from the grocery store rather than growing it ourselves. For health and environmental reasons, we have greatly reduced our meat consumption. I have reduced my consumption of beef and pork by 99% and my overall consumption of meat (mostly chicken and fish) by 60%. For ethical reasons, we should be strict vegetarians, but so far, we have been unwilling to go quite that far.

We feel a part of the piece of land we live on and love. To us, ownership of this land means that we are ethically driven to defend and protect it from degradation. We feel that the trees, flowers, deer, squirrels, hummingbirds, songbirds, and other forms of wildlife we often see are a part of us and we are a part of them. As temporary caretakers of this small portion of the biosphere, we feel obligated to pass it on to future generations with its ecological integrity and sustainability preserved.

Each year we plant several trees on our land and I donate money to organizations to plant at least 10 trees for each tree I use in writing this and other books. The publisher and I also join together in donating money to tree-planting and land-preserving organizations to offset the paper used in printing this book.

Most of our political activities involve thinking globally but acting locally. We also financially support numerous environmental and conservation organizations working at local, state, national, and global levels.

Working with nature gives us great joy and a sense of purpose. It also saves us money. Our attempt to work with nature is imperfect and is in a rural area, but people in cities can also have high-quality lifestyles that conserve resources and protect the environment (see Further Readings).

Currently, large-scale government funding of such research is generally opposed by powerful fossil-fuel companies, electric utilities, and automobile manufacturers, because a hydrogen revolution is a severe threat to their existence and short-term economic well-being. Earth's people and other species, however, would benefit from an Earth-sustaining solar-hydrogen revolution.

Phasing in the widespread use of hydrogen over several decades would also allow fossil-fuel, utility, car, and other companies to shift to producing and selling hydrogen fuel and the motors, furnaces, fuel cells, and other devices that burn this fuel. Supporting the necessary research and providing the subsidies needed to phase in hydrogen fuel will require considerable political pressure by individuals to counteract the powerful economic interests temporarily threatened by such a change.

Sometime in the 1990s, a German firm plans to market solar-hydrogen systems that can be used to meet all the heating, cooling, cooking, refrigeration, and electrical needs of a home and also provide hydrogen fuel for one or more cars. Within a few years, BMW plans to introduce hydrogen-powered automobiles, with the hydrogen produced by home generators leased from the company. Germany has also built a 193-kilometer (120-mile) pipeline that transports hydrogen produced from fossil fuels for use in industry. In 1992, Mazda unveiled a prototype car that runs on hydrogen released slowly from metal-hydrides heated by the car's radiator coolant. By 2000, a photovoltaic-hydrogen car could be cost-competitive with the gasoline car if gas prices rise to about 53¢ per liter ($2 a gallon).

Scientist John O'M Bockris of Texas A & M University calculated that energy-related pollution costs the United States $450 billion per year, or $1,800 a person. He estimates that phasing in a solar-hydrogen energy base over 25 years, which would eliminate most of this pollution, would cost only $120 per person annually. Like improving energy efficiency, it is an undertaking we dare not refuse.

The solar-hydrogen revolution has begun and, with proper support, we could be living in a hydrogen age within two or three decades. Despite the enormous potential of hydrogen as a fuel, U.S. government research and development funding for hydrogen was only a minuscule $4 million in 1991. During that same year, the government of Japan spent $30 million on hydrogen research and development and a joint industry-government program in Germany spent $58 million.

TAKING ENERGY MATTERS INTO YOUR OWN HANDS While elected officials, energy company executives, and conservationists argue over the key components of a national energy strategy, many individuals have become fed up and have taken energy matters into their own hands. With or without tax credits, they are insulating, weatherizing, and making other improvements to improve energy efficiency and save money.

Some are building passively heated and cooled solar homes. Others are building superinsulated dwellings or are adding passive or active solar heating to existing homes. Each of us can develop a personal energy strategy that improves personal and national security and saves money (see Individuals Matter inside the back cover and Spotlight on p. 409).

Countries that have the vision to change from an unsustainable to a sustainable energy strategy will be rewarded with increased security — not just military security but also economic, energy, and environmental security. Those that do not will experience unnecessary economic and environmental hardships and increased human suffering.

In the long run, humanity has no choice but to rely on renewable energy. No matter how abundant they seem today, eventually coal and uranium will run out. The choice before us is practical: We simply cannot afford to make more than one energy transition within the next generation.

DANIEL DEUDNEY AND CHRISTOPHER FLAVIN

DISCUSSION TOPICS

1. What are the 10 most important things an individual can do to save energy in the home and in transportation (see Individuals Matter inside the back cover)? Which, if any, of these do you do? Which, if any, do you plan to do? When?

2. Should the United States institute a crash program to develop solar photovoltaic cells and solar-produced hydrogen fuel? Explain.

3. Explain why you agree or disagree with the ideas that the United States can get most of the electricity it needs by (a) developing solar power plants, (b) using direct solar energy to produce electricity in photovoltaic cells, (c) building new, large hydroelectric plants, (d) building ocean thermal electric power plants, (e) building wind farms, (f) building power plants fueled by wood, crop wastes, trash, and other biomass resources, (g) tapping dry-steam, wet-steam, and hot-water geothermal deposits, (h) tapping molten rock (magma) geothermal deposits, and (i) improving energy efficiency by 50%.

4. Explain why you agree or disagree with the following propositions:
   a. The United States should cut average per capita energy use by at least 50% between 1993 and 2013.
   b. A mandatory energy conservation program should form the basis of any U.S. energy policy to provide economic, environmental, and military security.
   c. To solve world and U.S. energy supply problems, all we need do is recycle some or most of the energy we use.

*5. Make an energy-use study of your school and use the findings to develop an energy-efficiency improvement program.

CHAPTER 18

NONRENEWABLE

ENERGY RESOURCES

General Questions and Issues

1. What are the advantages and disadvantages of using oil and natural gas as energy resources?

2. What are the advantages and disadvantages of using coal as an energy resource?

3. What are the advantages and disadvantages of using conventional nuclear fission, breeder nuclear fission, and nuclear fusion to produce electricity?

4. What are the best present and future energy options for the United States?

We are an interdependent world and if we ever needed a lesson in that, we got it in the oil crisis of the 1970s.

ROBERT S. MCNAMARA

S INCE 1950, OIL, COAL, and natural gas have supported most of the world's economic growth. Their use is also responsible for much of the world's pollution and environmental degradation. Nuclear energy was supposed to be providing much of the world's electricity by 2000. However, high costs (even with enormous government subsidies), safety concerns, and failure to find an economically and politically acceptable solution for storing long-lived radioactive wastes have led many countries to sharply scale back or eliminate their plans to build new nuclear power plants.

How long might various fossil fuels last? How can we reduce their environmental impact? What role should nuclear energy play in the future? What should be the energy strategy of the United States? These important and controversial issues are discussed in this chapter.

18-1 Oil and Natural Gas

CONVENTIONAL CRUDE OIL Petroleum, or **crude oil**, is a gooey liquid consisting mostly of hydrocarbon compounds and small amounts of compounds containing oxygen, sulfur, and nitrogen. Crude oil and natural gas are often trapped together deep within Earth's crust on land and beneath the seafloor (Figure 3-5). The crude oil is dispersed in pores and cracks in rock formations.

Primary oil recovery involves drilling a well and pumping out the oil that flows by gravity into the bottom of the well. Thicker, slowly flowing heavy oil is not removed. After the flowing oil has been removed, water can be injected into adjacent wells to force some of the remaining thicker crude oil into the central well and push it to the surface. This is known as **secondary oil recovery**. Usually, primary and secondary recovery remove only one-third of the crude oil in a well.

For each barrel removed by primary and secondary recovery, two barrels of *heavy oil* are left in a typical well. As oil prices rise, it may become economical to remove about 10% of the heavy oil by **enhanced**, or **tertiary**, **oil recovery**. One method is to force steam into the well to soften the heavy oil so that it can be pumped to the surface. Carbon dioxide gas can also be pumped into a well to force some of the heavy oil into the well cavity for pumping to the surface.

The problem is that enhanced oil recovery is expensive. The net useful energy yield is low because it takes energy equivalent to that in one-third of a barrel of oil to soften and pump each barrel of heavy oil to the surface. Additional energy is needed to increase the flow rate and to remove sulfur and nitrogen impurities before the heavy oil can be pumped through a pipeline to an oil refinery. Recoverable heavy oil from known U.S. crude oil reserves could supply all U.S. oil needs for only about seven years at current usage rates.

Once it is removed from a well, most crude oil is sent by pipeline to a refinery. There it is heated and distilled to separate it into gasoline, heating oil, diesel oil, asphalt, and other components. Because these components boil at different temperatures, they are removed at different levels of giant distillation columns (Figure 18-1).

Some components and products called **petrochemicals** are used as raw materials in industrial chemicals, fertilizers, pesticides, plastics, synthetic fibers, paints, medicines, and many other products. Petrochemical production accounts for about 3% of the crude oil extracted throughout the world and 7% of the oil used in the United States. That explains why the prices of many items we use go up after crude oil prices rise.

HOW LONG WILL SUPPLIES OF CONVENTIONAL CRUDE OIL LAST? **Reserves** are identified deposits of a nonrenewable fossil fuel or mineral resource from which the resource can be extracted profitably at present prices with current technology. Almost two-thirds of the world's oil reserves are in just five countries: Saudi Arabia, Kuwait, Iran, Iraq, and the United Arab Emirates. OPEC countries have 67% of these reserves, with Saudi Arabia having 25%. Geologists believe that the Middle East (Figure 11-8) also contains most of the world's undiscovered oil. Therefore, OPEC is expected to have long-term control over world oil supplies and prices.

Various countries making up the Commonwealth of Independent States presently are the world's largest oil extractors, with an annual output triple that of Saudi Arabia. The United States, the world's second largest oil extractor, has only 4% of the world's oil reserves but uses nearly 30% of the oil extracted each year. Transportation uses 63% of the 17 million barrels of oil consumed each day in the United States. The rest is used by industry (24%), residences and commercial buildings (8%), and electric utilities (5%).

Although the United States is the world's most intensely drilled petroleum region, the U.S. oil extraction rate has been declining since 1970. More than half of the country's biggest oil fields are 80% depleted.

Most sources of oil in the Middle East are large and the oil cheaply extracted; most sources in the United States are small and the oil more expensive to tap. Therefore, it has generally been cheaper for the United States to buy oil from other countries than to extract it from its own deposits. In 1991, almost 50% of this oil was imported, and dependence on imports is projected to rise (Figure 1-10) unless the country gets serious about improving energy efficiency and phasing in a variety of perpetual and renewable energy resources (Chapter 17).

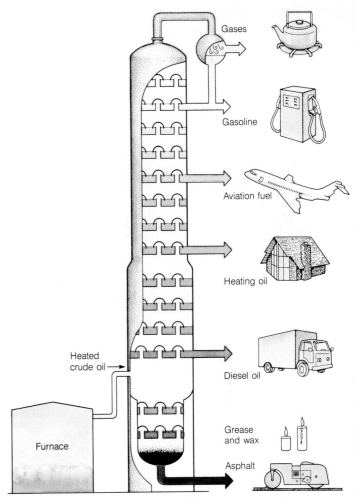

Figure 18-1 Refining of crude oil. Components are removed at various levels, depending on their boiling points, in a giant distillation column.

U.S. oil imports from Arab OPEC countries cost at least $100 a barrel (compared with a market price of around $20 per barrel) when the military costs of ensuring the flow of oil from the Persian Gulf are included. That estimate does not even include the additional costs of military intervention and the continuing American presence in the Middle East.

The Alaska oil pipeline is a much greater threat to U.S. national security than is the inability to move oil by tankers through the Persian Gulf. There are now other oil suppliers and several alternative ways to get oil from the Middle East, but there is only one way to get oil from Alaska. Sabotage of the highly vulnerable Alaska oil pipeline could disrupt the entire American economy. The Department of Defense admits that it is impossible to protect this pipeline.

Figure 18-2 shows the locations of the largest crude oil and natural gas fields in the United States. U.S. oil extraction has declined steadily since 1970 despite

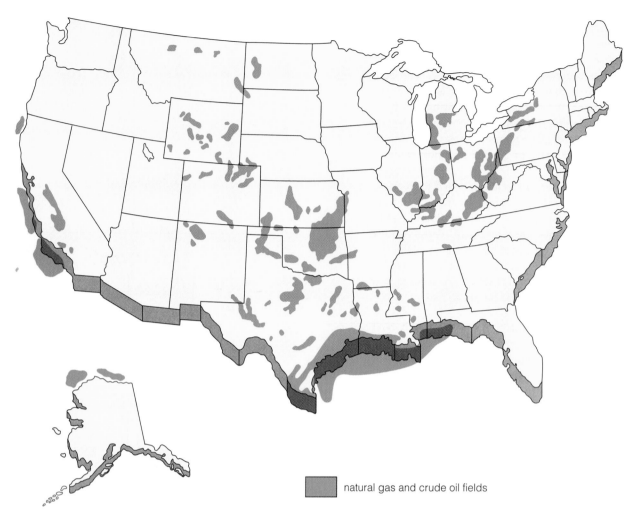

natural gas and crude oil fields

Figure 18-2 Locations of the largest occurrences of natural gas and crude oil in the United States. The oil and natural gas industries have about 15% of the total U.S. land area under lease. Relatively little new oil and natural gas is expected to be found in the United States. For example, if oil is found by drilling in the Arctic National Wildlife Refuge, the most optimistic projection is that within 10 years it would supply only 300,000 barrels of expensive oil a day for only 20 years. However, increasing the fuel efficiency of new cars to 17 kpl (40 mpg) would reduce U.S. oil consumption by 2.5 million barrels a day within 10 years. (Source: Council on Environmental Quality)

greatly increased exploration and test drilling. The net useful energy yield for most new oil is low, and by as early as 1995, it could take more energy to explore for and extract oil in the United States than the wells will produce.

At present exponential consumption rates, world crude oil reserves will be economically depleted in 35 years. U.S. reserves will be economically depleted by 2018 at the current consumption rate and by 2010 if oil use from these reserves increases exponentially by 2% a year.

Some analysts argue that higher oil prices will stimulate the discovery and extraction of large new crude oil resources. They also believe we can extract and upgrade heavy oils from oil shale and tar sands and can enhance recovery from existing wells at affordable prices.

Some believe that the earth's crust may contain 100 times more oil than usually thought. Such oil, if it exists, lies 10 kilometers (6 miles) or more below Earth's surface—about twice the depth of today's deepest wells. Most geologists do not believe this oil exists.

Other analysts argue that people who make optimistic projections about future oil supplies don't understand the arithmetic and the consequences of exponential growth in the use of any nonrenewable resource (see Spotlight on p. 4). Consider the following facts about the world's exponential growth in oil use, assuming that we continue to use crude oil at the current rate instead of the projected higher rates. If the following supplies of oil were the only source:

- Saudi Arabia, with the world's largest known crude oil reserves, could supply all the world's oil needs for only 10 years.

Q: What is the most promising fuel for replacing oil and other fossil fuels?

- Mexico, with the world's sixth largest crude oil reserves, could supply the world's needs for only about 3 years.

- The estimated crude oil reserves under Alaska's North Slope — the largest ever found in North America — would meet world demand for only 6 months or U.S. demand for 3 years.

- The oil that oil companies have only a one-in-five chance of finding by drilling in Alaska's Arctic Wildlife Refuge could meet world demand for only 1 month and U.S. demand for 6 months (see Pro/Con on p. 370).

- All estimated, undiscovered, recoverable deposits of oil in the United States could meet world demand for only 1.7 years and U.S. demand for 10 years.

- Those who believe that new discoveries will solve world oil supply problems must figure out how to discover the equivalent of a new Saudi Arabian supply *every 10 years* just to keep on using oil at the current rate.

The ultimately recoverable supply of crude oil is estimated to be three times today's proven reserves. Suppose all that new oil is found and developed — which most oil experts consider unlikely — and sold at a price of $50 to $95 a barrel, compared with the 1991 price of about $20 a barrel. About 80% would be depleted by 2073 at the current consumption rate and by 2037 if oil use increased 2% a year.

We can see why most experts expect little of the world's affordable crude oil to be left by the 2059 bicentennial of the world's first oil well. Over the next 50 years we will have to replace virtually every oil- or gasoline-burning device in the world with those that use a more sustainable form of energy. The less oil we waste, the longer we will have for this transition.

Oil company executives have known for a long time that oil is running out, which explains why oil companies have become diversified energy companies. To keep making money after oil runs out, these international companies now own much of the world's natural gas, coal, and uranium reserves and have bought many of the companies producing solar collectors and solar cells.

PROS AND CONS OF OIL Oil has been, and still is, cheap (Figure 1-9), can easily be transported within and between countries, and has a high net useful energy yield (Figure 3-20). It is a versatile fuel that can be burned to propel vehicles, heat buildings and water, and supply high-temperature heat for industrial processes and electricity production.

The crucial disadvantage of oil is that affordable supplies are expected to be depleted within 40 to 80 years. Its burning also releases carbon dioxide gas, which could alter global climate, and other air pollu-

Figure 18-3 Sample of oil shale and the shale oil extracted from it. Big oil shale projects have now been canceled in the United States because of excessive cost.

tants such as sulfur oxides and nitrogen oxides, which damage people, crops, trees, fish, and other wild species. Oil spills and leakage of toxic drilling muds cause water pollution (see Case Study on p. 247), and the brine solution injected into oil wells can contaminate groundwater.

If all the harmful environmental effects of using oil were included in its market price and current government subsidies were removed, oil would be too expensive to use and would be replaced by a variety of less harmful and cheaper perpetual and renewable energy resources. We are addicted to using and wasting oil because governments keep its market price artificially low, mostly for political reasons.

HEAVY OIL FROM OIL SHALE **Oil shale** is a fine-grained rock (Figure 18-3) that contains varying amounts of a solid, waxy mixture of hydrocarbon compounds called **kerogen**. After being removed by surface or subsurface mining, the shale is crushed and heated to a high temperature to vaporize the kerogen (Figure 18-4). The kerogen vapor is condensed, forming a slow-flowing, dark-brown, heavy oil called **shale oil**. Before shale oil can be sent by pipeline to a refinery, it must be processed to increase its flow rate and heat content and to remove sulfur, nitrogen, and other impurities.

It is estimated that the potentially recoverable heavy oil from oil shale deposits in the United States — mostly on federal lands in Colorado, Utah, and Wyoming — could meet the country's crude oil demand for 41 years if consumption remains at the current level, and for 32 years if consumption rises 2% a year. Large oil shale deposits are also found in Canada, China, and the CIS.

Environmental problems may limit shale oil production. Shale oil processing requires large amounts of water, which is scarce in the semiarid areas where the

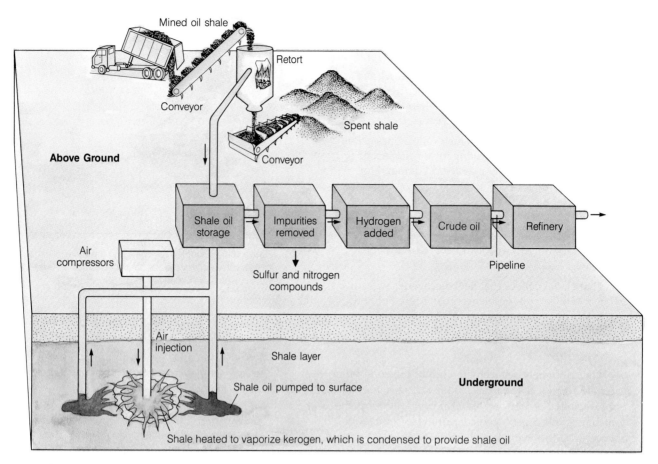

Figure 18-4 Aboveground and underground (*in situ*) methods for producing synthetic crude oil from oil shale.

richest deposits are found. Converting kerogen to processed shale oil and burning the shale oil release more carbon dioxide per unit of energy than do processing and burning conventional oil. Nitrogen oxides and sulfur dioxide are also released. If shale is extracted above ground, there is severe land disruption from the mining and disposal of large volumes of shale rock, which breaks up and expands like popcorn when heated. Various salts, cancer-causing substances, and toxic metal compounds can be leached from the processed shale rock into nearby water supplies.

One way to avoid some of these environmental problems is to extract oil from shale underground, known as *in situ* (in-place) *processing* (Figure 18-4). However, this method is too expensive with present technology and produces more sulfur dioxide emissions than surface processing.

The net useful energy yield of shale oil is much lower than that of conventional oil because the energy equivalent of almost one-half a barrel of conventional crude oil is needed to extract, process, and upgrade one barrel of shale oil (Figure 3-20). Furthermore, shale oil does not refine as well as crude oil and yields fewer useful products.

HEAVY OIL FROM TAR SAND **Tar sand** (or oil sand) is a deposit of a mixture of clay, sand, water, and varying amounts of **bitumen**, a gooey, black, high-sulfur, heavy oil. Tar sand is usually removed by surface mining and heated with steam at high pressure to make the bitumen fluid enough to float to the top. The bitumen is removed and then purified and chemically upgraded into a synthetic crude oil suitable for refining (Figure 18-5). So far, it is not technically or economically feasible to remove deeper deposits of tar sand by underground mining or to remove bitumen by underground extraction.

The world's largest known deposits of tar sands lie in a cold, desolate area in northern Alberta, Canada — the Athabasca Tar Sands. Heavy oil in these deposits is estimated to exceed the proven oil reserves of Saudi Arabia. Other large deposits are in Venezuela, Colombia, and the CIS. Smaller deposits exist in the United States, mostly in Utah. If all U.S. deposits were developed, they would supply all U.S. oil needs at the current usage rate for only about three months at a price of $48 to $62 a barrel.

Since 1985, two plants have been supplying almost 12% of Canada's oil demand by extracting and process-

Q: What is the best way to make the transition to a solar-hydrogen energy age?

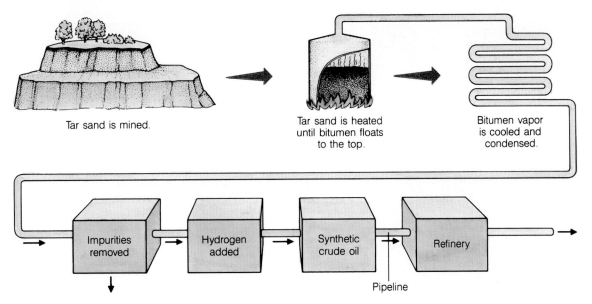

Figure 18-5 Generalized summary of how synthetic crude oil is produced from tar sand.

ing heavy oil from tar sands at a cost of $12 to $15 a barrel—below the average world oil price between 1986 and 1991. Economically recoverable deposits of heavy oil from tar sands can supply all of Canada's projected oil needs for about 33 years at the current consumption rate. These deposits are an important source of oil for Canada, but they would meet the world's present oil needs for only about 2 years.

The net useful energy yield from producing synthetic crude oil from tar sands is low because it takes the energy equivalent of almost one-half a barrel of conventional oil to extract and process one barrel of bitumen and upgrade it to synthetic crude oil before it can be sent to an oil refinery. Other problems include the need for large quantities of water for processing and the release of air and water pollutants. Upgrading bitumen to synthetic crude oil releases sulfur dioxide, hydrogen sulfide, and particulates of toxic metals.

Environmentalists charge that synthetic crude oil is produced from tar sand at a low price in Canada only because the tar sand processing plants are not required to control air pollution emissions. The plants have also created huge waste disposal ponds. Cleaning up these toxic waste dump sites is another external cost not included in the price of crude oil produced from Canadian tar sand.

NATURAL GAS In its underground gaseous state, **natural gas** is a mixture of 50% to 90% by volume of methane gas (CH_4) and smaller amounts of heavier gaseous hydrocarbon compounds such as propane (C_3H_8) and butane (C_4H_{10}). *Conventional natural gas* lies above most occurrences of crude oil (Figure 3-5). Some of this is burned off and wasted when the primary goal is oil

extraction (Figure 18-6). *Unconventional natural gas* is found by itself in other underground occurrences.

When a natural gas field is tapped, propane and butane gases are liquefied and removed as **liquefied petroleum gas (LPG)**. LPG is stored in pressurized tanks for use mostly in rural areas not served by natural gas pipelines. The rest of the gas (mostly methane) removed from the field is dried to remove water vapor, cleaned of hydrogen sulfide and other impurities, and pumped into pressurized pipelines for distribution.

At a very low temperature, natural gas can be converted to **liquefied natural gas (LNG)**. This highly flammable liquid form of natural gas can then be shipped to other countries in refrigerated tanker ships.

HOW LONG WILL NATURAL GAS SUPPLIES LAST? Countries making up the CIS have 40% of the world's natural gas reserves and are the world's largest extractors of natural gas. Other countries with large proven natural gas reserves are Iran (14%), the United States (5%), Qatar (4%), Algeria (4%), Saudi Arabia (3%), and Nigeria (3%). Geologists expect to find more deposits of conventional natural gas, especially in LDCs that have not been widely explored for this resource. They believe that China may have enough undiscovered natural gas to eliminate its current heavy dependence on coal.

Most U.S. reserves of natural gas are located with the country's occurrences of crude oil (Figure 18-2). About 95% of the natural gas used in the United States comes from domestic sources; the other 5% is imported by pipeline from Canada. Algeria and some of the countries making up the CIS use pipelines to supply

A: Use natural gas coupled with greatly increased energy efficiency

Chapter 18

Figure 18-6 Large quantities of energy are wasted when natural gas that is found with oil is sometimes burned off, as in this oil field in Saudi Arabia. This is done because collecting and using the natural gas cost more than it can be sold for in the oil-rich Middle East. Burning this high-quality fuel also adds carbon dioxide and other pollutants to the atmosphere, but that causes less projected global warming than allowing the methane to escape into the atmosphere.

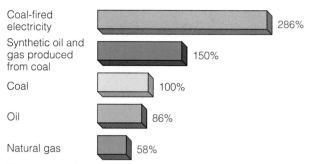

Coal-fired electricity		286%
Synthetic oil and gas produced from coal		150%
Coal		100%
Oil		86%
Natural gas		58%

Figure 18-7 Carbon dioxide emissions per unit of energy produced by other fossil fuels shown as percentages of those produced by coal.

many eastern and western European countries with natural gas and are planning more pipelines.

In 1991, about 82% of the natural gas consumed in the United States was used for space heating of residential and commercial buildings and for drying and other purposes in industry. The rest was used to produce electricity (15%) and as a vehicle fuel (3%).

Conventional supplies of natural gas are larger and better distributed than those of crude oil. Known reserves and undiscovered, economically recoverable occurrences of conventional natural gas in the United States are projected to last 60 years and world supplies at least 80 years at present consumption rates.

As the price of natural gas from conventional sources rises, it may become economical to get natural gas from unconventional sources. Such sources include coal seams, Devonian shale rock, deep underground deposits of tight sands, and deep geopressurized zones that contain natural gas dissolved in hot water. New technology for extracting gas from these resources is being developed rapidly.

In 1988, the Department of Energy estimated that technically recoverable natural gas from both conventional and unconventional sources in the lower 48 states would meet domestic needs for 50 years at current usage rates. Worldwide, conventional supplies of natural gas and unconventional supplies available at higher prices would last about 200 years at the current rate and 80 years if use rose 2% a year. If these estimates are correct, natural gas could serve as a transition fuel to greatly increased dependence on perpetual and renewable energy resources and help usher in the solar-hydrogen energy era.

PROS AND CONS OF NATURAL GAS Natural gas burns hotter and produces less air pollution than does any other fossil fuel. Burning it produces virtually no sulfur dioxide and particulate matter and only about one-sixth as many nitrogen oxides per unit of energy as does burning coal, oil, or gasoline. Burning natural gas produces carbon dioxide, but the amount per unit of energy produced is much lower than that of other fossil fuels (Figure 18-7). Extracting natural gas causes much less environmental damage than extracting coal. Methane, the primary component of natural gas, is a greenhouse gas that is 25 times more effective per molecule than is carbon dioxide in causing global warming (Figure 10-6). Little of the methane in the atmosphere comes from extraction and use of natural gas.

So far, the price of natural gas has remained low (equivalent to buying oil at about $9 a barrel). Natural gas is more abundant and more widely distributed around the world than is oil. It can be transported easily over land by pipeline and has a high net useful energy yield. It is a versatile fuel that can be burned cleanly and efficiently in furnaces, stoves, water heaters, dryers, boilers, incinerators, motor vehicles (with more than 1 million vehicles on the road), fuel cells, heat pumps, air conditioners, and refrigerators.

New natural-gas-burning turbines, working like jet engines, can be used to produce electricity. Compared to coal-fired systems equipped with the latest pollution-control devices, these turbines cost 50% less to build and 25% less to operate, can be put into operation

Q: At present consumption rates, how long will the world's proven reserves of oil last?

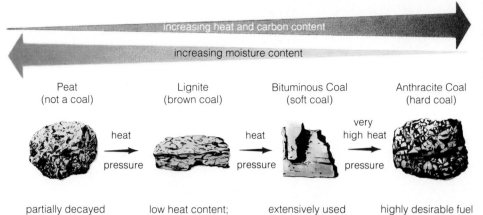

Figure 18-8 Stages in the formation of coal over millions of years. Peat is a humus soil material. Lignite and bituminous coal are sedimentary rocks, and anthracite is a metamorphic rock (Figure 19-3).

increasing heat and carbon content

increasing moisture content

| Peat (not a coal) | Lignite (brown coal) | Bituminous Coal (soft coal) | Anthracite Coal (hard coal) |

heat / pressure → heat / pressure → very high heat / pressure

partially decayed plant and animal matter in swamps and bogs; low heat content

low heat content; low sulfur content; limited supplies in most areas

extensively used as a fuel because of its high heat content and large supplies; normally has a high sulfur content

highly desirable fuel because of its high heat content and low sulfur content; supplies are limited in most areas

within 12 to 18 months, are much more energy-efficient, and emit 65% to 85% fewer nitrogen oxides and 65% less carbon dioxide. Natural gas can also be burned cleanly and efficiently in cogenerators to produce high-temperature heat and electricity, and small amounts can be burned with coal in boilers to reduce emissions of nitrogen oxides by 50% to 75%.

One problem is that natural gas must be converted to liquid natural gas before it can be shipped by tanker from one country to another. Shipping LNG in refrigerated tankers is expensive and dangerous. Huge explosions could kill many people and cause much damage in urban areas near LNG loading and unloading facilities. Conversion of natural gas into LNG also reduces the net useful energy yield by one-fourth.

If large amounts of natural gas can be extracted from nonconventional deposits at affordable prices, natural gas will be a key option for making an orderly transition to solar, hydrogen, and other energy options as oil, coal, and nuclear energy are phased out over the next 50 years. Hydrogen gas produced from water by solar-generated electricity (Section 17-8) can be mixed gradually with natural gas to make a smooth shift to a sustainable-Earth, solar-hydrogen economy.

18-2 Coal

TYPES AND DISTRIBUTION **Coal** is a solid formed in several stages as the remains of plants are subjected to intense heat and pressure over millions of years. It is a complex mixture of organic compounds with 30% to 98% carbon by weight, plus varying amounts of water and small amounts of nitrogen and sulfur.

Three types of coal are formed at different stages: lignite, bituminous coal, and anthracite (Figure 18-8).

Peat, which is the first stage of coal formation, is not a coal. It is burned in some places but has a low heat content. Low-sulfur coal produces less sulfur dioxide when burned than does high-sulfur coal. The most desirable type of coal is anthracite because of its high heat content and low sulfur content.

About 60% of the coal extracted in the world and 80% in the United States is burned in boilers to produce steam for generating electrical power. The rest is converted to coke used to make steel and burned in boilers to produce steam used in various manufacturing processes. Coal is burned to generate 44% of the world's electricity and is used in the production of 75% of the world's steel. In 1991, coal was burned to supply 56% of the electricity generated in the United States. The rest was produced by nuclear energy (20%), natural gas (11%), hydropower (9%), oil (3%), and geothermal and solar energy (1%).

Coal is the world's most abundant fossil fuel. About 68% of the world's proven coal reserves and 85% of the estimated undiscovered coal deposits are located in the United States, the Commonwealth of Independent States, and China. Coal-burning now provides 76% of China's commercial energy, making China the world's third largest emitter of carbon dioxide (after the United States and the CIS).

Most U.S. coalfields are located in 17 states (Figure 18-9). Anthracite, the most desirable form of coal, makes up only 2% of U.S. coal reserves. About 45% is high-sulfur, bituminous coal with a high fuel value. It is found mostly in the East, primarily in Kentucky, West Virginia, Pennsylvania, Ohio, and Illinois.

About 55% of U.S. coal reserves are found west of the Mississippi River. Most of these are deposits of low-sulfur bituminous and lignite coal. Unfortunately, these deposits are far from the heavily industrialized and populated East, where most coal is consumed.

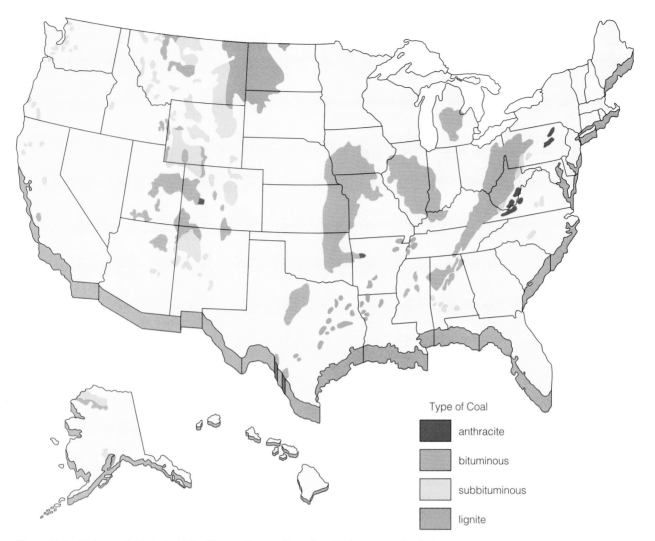

Figure 18-9 Major coalfields in the United States. (Source: Council on Environmental Quality)

Type of Coal

- anthracite
- bituminous
- subbituminous
- lignite

EXTRACTING COAL Surface mining is used to extract almost two-thirds of the coal used in the United States. Most surface-mined coal is removed by area strip mining or contour strip mining, depending on the terrain (Figure 3-5).

Area strip mining is used where the terrain is fairly flat. It involves stripping away the overburden and digging a cut to remove a mineral deposit, in this case coal (Figure 18-10). After the coal deposit is removed from the cut, the trench is filled with overburden. The power shovel removing coal then digs a cut parallel to the previous one. This process is repeated for the entire deposit. If the land is not restored, this type of mining leaves a wavy series of highly erodible hills of rubble called *spoil banks* (Figure 18-11).

Contour strip mining is a form of surface mining used in hilly or mountainous terrain. A power shovel cuts a series of terraces into the side of a hill or a mountain (Figure 18-12). An earthmover removes the overburden and a power shovel extracts the coal, with the over-

burden from each new terrace dumped onto the one below. Unless the land is restored, a wall of dirt is left in front of a highly erodible bank of soil and rock called a *highwall*. In the United States, contour strip mining is used mostly for extracting coal in the mountainous Appalachian region. If the land is not restored, this type of surface mining has a devastating impact. (Figure 18-13 shows land restored after mining.) Sometimes, giant augers are used to drill horizontally into a hillside to extract underground coal.

Subsurface mining is used to remove coal too deep to be extracted by surface mining (Figure 3-5). Miners dig a deep vertical shaft, blast subsurface tunnels and rooms to get to the deposit, and haul the coal or ore to the surface. In the *room-and-pillar method*, as much as half of the coal is left in place as pillars to prevent the mine from collapsing. In the *longwall method*, a narrow tunnel is created and then supported by movable metal pillars. After a cutting machine has removed the coal or ore from part of the mineral seam, the roof supports are

Q: How long could *all* known and projected oil deposits in the United States supply the world and the United States?

Figure 18-10 Area strip mining of coal in Decker, Montana. This type of surface mining is used on flat or gently rolling terrain.

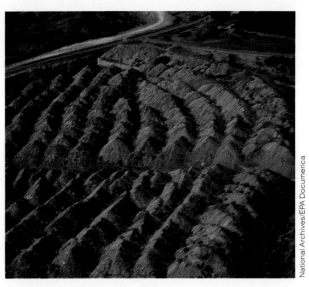

Figure 18-11 Effects of area strip mining of coal near Mulla, Colorado. Restoration of newly strip-mined areas is now required in the United States, but many previously mined areas have not been restored. In arid areas, full restoration isn't possible, and enforcement of surface mining laws is often lax.

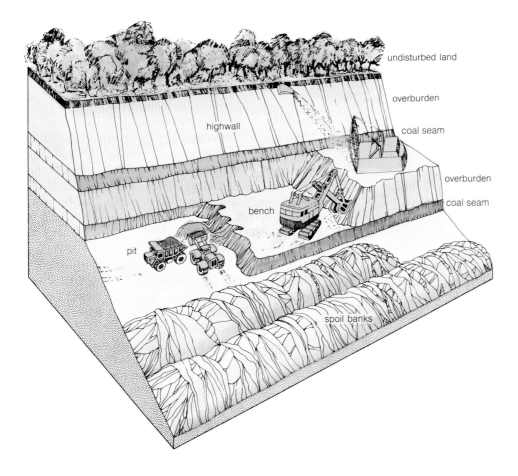

Figure 18-12 Contour strip mining of coal. This type of surface mining is used in hilly or mountainous terrain.

undisturbed land

overburden

coal seam

highwall

overburden

coal seam

bench

pit

spoil banks

Figure 18-13 With the land returned to its original contour and grass planted to hold the soil in place, it is hard to tell that this was once a surface coal-mining site in Grantsville, Maryland. However, about three-fourths of the coal in the United States that can be surface-mined is in the West, in arid and semiarid regions (Figure 18-9). There the climate and the soil usually prevent full restoration of surface-mined land.

moved forward, allowing the earth behind the supports to collapse. No tunnels are left behind after the mining operation has been completed.

HOW LONG WILL SUPPLIES LAST? Identified world reserves of coal should last about 220 years at current consumption and 65 years if consumption rises 2% a year. The world's unidentified coal resources are projected to last about 900 years at the current rate and 149 years if use increases 2% a year.

Identified coal reserves in the United States should last about 300 years at the current usage rate. Unidentified U.S. coal resources could extend those supplies at the current rate for perhaps 100 years, at a much higher average cost.

PROS AND CONS OF SOLID COAL   Coal is the most abundant conventional fossil fuel in the world and in the United States. It also has a high net useful energy yield for producing high-temperature heat for industrial processes and for generating electricity (Figure 3-20). In countries with adequate coal supplies, burning solid coal is the cheapest way to produce high-temperature heat and electricity. However, the low costs do not include requiring the best air pollution control equipment on all plants and requiring effective reclamation of all land surface-mined for coal (Figure 18-13). *If all of coal's harmful environmental costs were included in its market price and government subsidies were removed, coal would be too expensive to use and would be replaced by cheaper and less environmentally harmful perpetual and renewable energy resources.*

Since 1900, underground mining in the United States has killed more than 100,000 miners and permanently disabled at least 1 million. At least 250,000 retired U.S. miners suffer from black lung disease, a form of emphysema caused by prolonged breathing of coal dust and other particulate matter. Moreover, mining safety laws in most countries are much weaker than those in the United States. Underground mining also causes subsidence when a mine shaft partially collapses during or after mining. Over 800,000 hectares (2 million acres) of land, much of it in central Appalachia, has subsided because of underground coal mining.

Surface mining causes severe land disturbance (Figures 18-10 and 18-11) and soil erosion, and surface-mined land in arid and semiarid areas can be only partially restored. Surface and subsurface mining of coal can cause severe pollution of nearby streams and groundwater from acids and toxic metal compounds (Figure 18-14). Once coal is mined, it is expensive to move from one place to another; and it cannot be used in solid form as a fuel for cars and trucks.

Coal is the dirtiest fossil fuel to burn. Without expensive air pollution control devices, burning coal produces larger amounts of sulfur dioxide, nitrogen oxides, and particulate matter than does burning other fossil fuels. These pollutants contribute to acid deposition, corrode metals, and harm trees, crops, wild animals, and people.

Each year, these and other air pollutants emitted when coal is burned kill about 5,000 people in the United States. They also cause 50,000 cases of respiratory disease and several billion dollars in property damage each year. Burning coal also produces more carbon dioxide per unit of energy than do other fossil fuels (Figure 18-7). That means that burning more coal to meet energy needs can accelerate projected global warming (Section 10-2). This problem by itself may prevent much of the world's coal reserves from being mined and burned. Coal burning in the United States accounts for 22% of global CO_2 emissions. Coal burning is responsible for 42% of the world's carbon dioxide emissions from fossil fuels.

New ways have been developed to burn coal more cleanly and efficiently. One is *fluidized-bed combustion*, which also sharply reduces emissions of sulfur dioxide and nitrogen oxides (Figure 9-15). Successful small-scale fluidized-bed combustion plants have been built in Great Britain, Sweden, Finland, the CIS, Germany, and China. In the United States, commercial fluidized-bed combustion boilers are expected to begin replacing conventional coal boilers in the mid-1990s.

SYNFUELS: CONVERTING SOLID COAL INTO GASEOUS AND LIQUID FUELS   Besides being used in solid form, coal can also be converted into gaseous or liquid fuels, called **synfuels**. They are more useful than solid coal in heating homes and powering vehicles,

Q: How much new oil must be discovered and developed to continue using oil at the current rate?

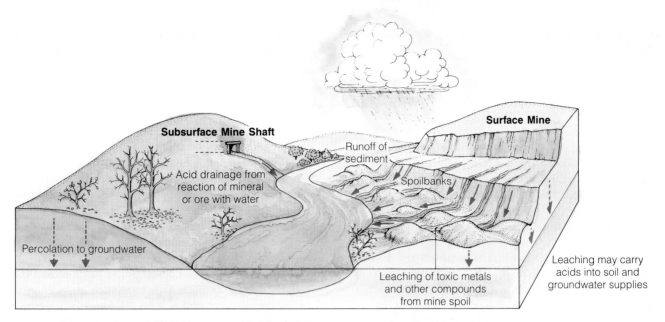

Figure 18-14 Degradation and pollution of a stream and groundwater by runoff of acids — called *acid mine drainage* — and toxic chemicals from surface and subsurface mining operations. These substances can kill fish and other forms of aquatic life. In the United States, acid mine drainage has damaged over 26,000 kilometers (16,100 miles) of streams, mostly in Appalachia and the western United States.

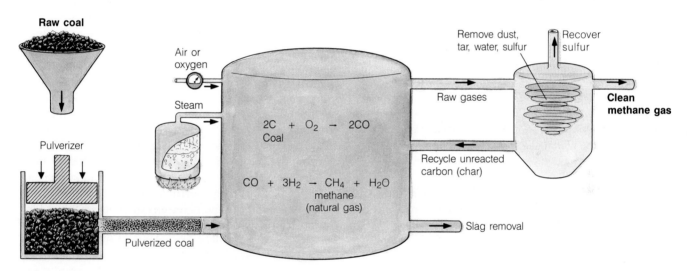

Figure 18-15 Coal gasification. Generalized view of one method for converting solid coal into synthetic natural gas (methane).

and burning them produces much less air pollution than does burning solid coal.

Coal gasification (Figure 18-15) is the conversion of solid coal into synthetic natural gas (SNG). **Coal liquefaction** is the conversion of solid coal into a liquid hydrocarbon fuel such as methanol or synthetic gasoline. A $2 billion commercial coal liquefaction plant supplies 10% of the liquid fuel used in South Africa at a cost equal to paying $35 a barrel for oil. When two new plants are completed, the country will be able to meet half of its oil needs from this source. Engineers hope to get the cost down to $25 a barrel.

Synfuels can be transported through a pipeline, burn more cleanly than solid coal, and are more versatile than solid coal. Besides being burned to produce high-temperature heat and electricity as solid coal does, synfuels can be burned to heat houses and water and to propel vehicles.

However, a synfuel plant costs much more to build and run than an equivalent coal-fired power plant fully equipped with air pollution control devices. Synfuels also have low net useful energy yields (Figure 3-20). The widespread use of synfuels would accelerate the depletion of world coal supplies because 30% to 40% of the energy content of coal is lost in the conversion process. It would also lead to greater land disruption from surface mining because producing a unit of energy from synfuels uses more coal than does burning solid coal.

Producing synfuels requires huge amounts of water, and burning synfuels releases larger amounts of carbon dioxide per unit of energy than does burning coal (Figure 18-7). Converting coal into SNG underground would solve the water problem, but underground coal gasification is not now competitive with conventional coal mining and aboveground coal gasification.

The biggest factor holding back large-scale production of synfuels in the United States is their high cost, compared with conventional oil and natural gas. Producing synfuels with current technology is the equivalent of buying oil at $38 a barrel. The U.S. Department of Energy has a goal of supporting development of new processes that will reduce the cost to $25 per barrel by 1995, but most analysts expect synfuels to play only a minor role as an energy resource in the next 30 to 50 years.

18-3 Conventional Nuclear Fission

A CONTROVERSIAL AND FADING DREAM By the end of this century, 1,800 nuclear power plants were supposed to supply 21% of the world's supplemental energy and 25% of that used in the United States. These rosy forecasts turned out to be an example of unrealistic high-tech intoxication.

By 1991, after 44 years of development and enormous government subsidies, about 428 commercial nuclear reactors in 26 countries were producing only 19% of the world's electricity — equal to only about 5% of the world's supplemental energy. Little additional construction is expected after the roughly 160 plants still being built are completed. These new plants will not replace the almost 250 older plants scheduled for retirement between 1990 and 2010.

The percentage of the world's electricity produced by nuclear power will probably drop between 1990 and 2010 as aging nuclear plants are retired faster than new ones are built. By 2000, nuclear power will supply less than one-tenth of the electricity it was projected to produce.

Industrialized countries such as Japan and France, which have few fossil-fuel resources, believe that using nuclear power is the best way to reduce their dependence on imported oil. For example, France (with 55 nuclear power plants) got 75% of its electricity from nuclear power in 1991 and plans to get 90% sometime in the 1990s. In 1991, Japan's 39 commercial nuclear reactors supplied 26% of the country's electricity. By early next century, reactors now planned or under construction are expected to provide 50% of Japan's electricity.

However, both Japan and France already are producing more electricity than they can use (see Guest Essay on p. 58). France has been forced to sell electricity to neighboring countries at bargain prices and run its plants at partial capacity. The cumulative debt of the government-owned company that builds and runs the country's nuclear plants is now more than $50 billion — a sum greater than France's entire income tax receipts in 1988. In addition, there are growing complaints that nuclear power was developed in France by the government with very little public input or debate.

Japan's reliance on nuclear power helps reduce its reliance on coal imports and, to a much lesser extent, on oil imports, but makes it totally dependent on uranium imports. Also, according to a 1991 poll, 99% of the Japanese people feel uneasy about nuclear power and 46% think it is not safe.

Since the Chernobyl nuclear accident in 1986 (see Spotlight on p. 428), many countries have scaled back or eliminated their plans to build nuclear power plants. Since 1975, no new nuclear power plants have been ordered in the United States, and 120 previous orders have been canceled. In 1991, the 111 licensed commercial nuclear plants in the United States generated about 20% of the country's electricity, and this percentage is expected to decline over the next two decades when more than 60% of the current reactors are scheduled for retirement.

What happened to nuclear power? The answer is that the nuclear industry has been crippled by high and uncertain costs of building and operating plants, billion-dollar cost overruns, frequent malfunctions, false assurances and cover-ups by government and industry officials, overproduction of electricity in some areas, poor management, and lack of public acceptance because of mistrust and concerns about safety, cost, radioactive waste disposal, and the proliferation of nuclear weapons. To better understand some of the problems with nuclear power, we need to know how a nuclear power plant works.

HOW DOES A NUCLEAR FISSION REACTOR WORK? When the nuclei of atoms such as uranium-235 and plutonium-239 are split by neutrons, energy is released and converted mostly into high-temperature heat in a nuclear fission chain reaction (Figure 3-12). The rate at which this happens can be controlled in the nuclear fission reactor in a nuclear power plant, and the heat released can be used to spin a turbine and produce electrical energy.

Light-water reactors (LWRs) now generate about 85% of the electricity generated worldwide (98% in the

Q: How long will proven reserves of natural gas last at current consumption rates?

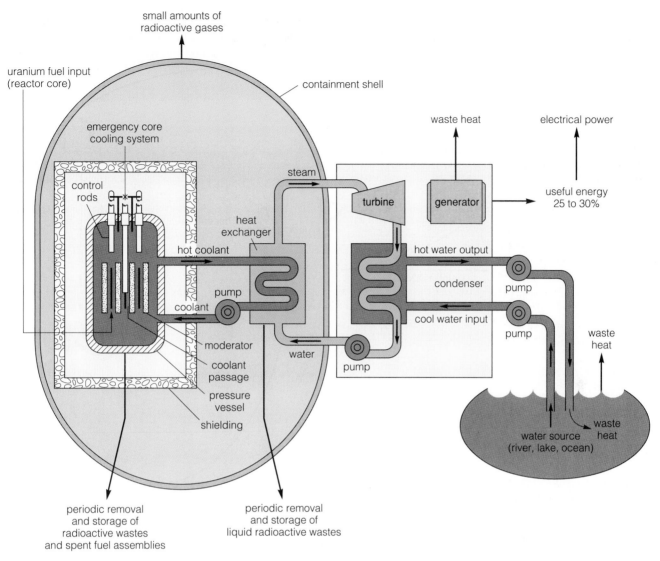

Figure 18-16   Light-water-moderated-and-cooled nuclear power plant with a pressurized water reactor.

small amounts of
radioactive gases

uranium fuel input
(reactor core)

containment shell

emergency core
cooling system

waste heat

electrical power

control
rods

steam

turbine

generator

useful energy
25 to 30%

heat
exchanger

hot coolant

hot water output

condenser

pump

pump

coolant

moderator

pump

cool water input

pump

coolant
passage

water

waste
heat

pressure
vessel

pump

shielding

waste
heat

water source
(river, lake, ocean)

periodic removal
and storage of
radioactive wastes
and spent fuel assemblies

periodic removal
and storage of
liquid radioactive wastes

United States) by nuclear power plants. Key parts of an LWR are the core, fuel assemblies, fuel rods, control rods, moderator, and coolant (Figure 18-16). The core of an LWR typically contains about 40,000 long, thin fuel rods bundled in 180 fuel assemblies of around 200 rods each. Each fuel rod is packed with pellets of uranium oxide fuel the size of a pencil eraser.

About 97% of the uranium in each fuel pellet is uranium-238, an isotope that is nonfissionable. The other 3% is uranium-235, which is fissionable. Uranium ore contains 97% uranium-238 by weight and only 0.7% of the fissionable uranium-235 (Figure 3-2). Enrichment separates some of the uranium-238 from the ore, increasing the concentration of uranium-235 from 0.7% to 3% by weight. This enriched ore can be used as a fuel in a fission reactor. The uranium-235 in each fuel rod produces energy equal to that of three

railroad carloads of coal over a lifetime of about three to four years.

When the fuel in the rods can no longer sustain nuclear fission, the intensely radioactive spent fuel rods are removed. If the fuel pellets in the rods are processed to remove plutonium and other very long-lived radioactive isotopes, the remaining radioactive waste must be safely stored for at least 10,000 years. Otherwise, the rods must be stored safely for at least 240,000 years—about six times longer than our species has been around.

Control rods are made of materials such as boron or cadmium that absorb neutrons. The rods are moved in and out of the reactor core to regulate the rate of fission and the amount of power the reactor produces. All reactors place or circulate some type of material between the fuel rods and the fuel assemblies. This

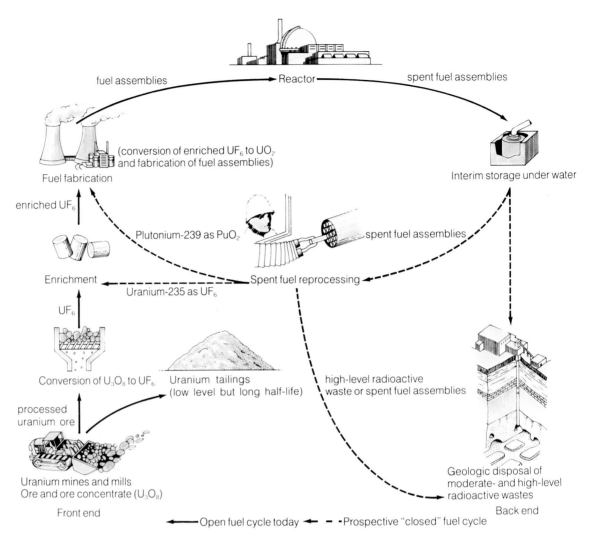

Figure 18-17 The nuclear fuel cycle.

material, known as a *moderator*, slows down the neutrons emitted by the fission process so that the chain reaction can be kept going.

Some 75% of the world's commercial reactors use ordinary water, called light water, as a moderator. Thus, the interior of most commercial reactors is somewhat like a swimming pool with a large number of movable vertical fuel rods and control rods hanging in it. The moderator in about 20% of the world's commercial reactors (50% of those in the CIS, including the ill-fated Chernobyl reactor) is solid graphite, a form of carbon. Graphite-moderated reactors can also be used to produce fissionable plutonium-239 for use in nuclear weapons.

A coolant circulates through the reactor's core. It removes heat to keep fuel rods and other materials from melting and to produce steam that spins generators to produce electricity. Most water-moderated and graphite-moderated reactors use water as a coolant; a few gas-cooled reactors use an unreactive gas such as helium or argon for cooling.

A typical light-water reactor has an energy efficiency of only 25% to 30%, compared with 40% for a coal-burning plant. Graphite-moderated, gas-cooled reactors are more expensive to build and operate but are more energy-efficient (38%) than LWRs because they operate at a higher temperature.

Nuclear power plants, each with one or more reactors, are only one part of the nuclear fuel cycle necessary for using nuclear energy to produce electricity (Figure 18-17). *In evaluating the safety and economy of nuclear power, we need to look at the entire cycle, not just the nuclear plant itself.*

After about three to four years in a reactor, the concentration of fissionable uranium-235 in a fuel rod becomes too low to keep the chain reaction going, or the rod becomes damaged from exposure to ionizing radiation. Each year, about one-third of the spent fuel assemblies in a reactor are removed and stored in large, concrete-lined pools of water at the plant site.

After they have cooled for several years and lost some of their radioactivity, the spent fuel rods could be

Q: How much of the world's electricity is produced by burning coal?

sealed in shielded, supposedly crash-proof casks and transported by truck or train to storage pools away from the reactor or to a nuclear waste repository or dump.

A third option is to send spent fuel to a fuel-reprocessing plant (Figure 18-17). There, remaining uranium-235 and plutonium-239 produced as a by-product of the fission process are removed and sent to a fuel fabrication plant. Such plants would also handle and ship bomb-grade plutonium-239 that could be used to make nuclear weapons.

Two small commercial fuel-reprocessing plants in operation (one in France and one in Great Britain) have had severe operating and economic problems. Two others are under construction—one in Japan and one in Germany. The United States has delayed development of commercial fuel-reprocessing plants because of technical difficulties, high construction and operating costs, and adequate domestic supplies of uranium.

The fission products produced in a nuclear reactor give off radioactivity by radioactive decay and heat, even after control rods have been inserted to stop all nuclear fission in the reactor core. To prevent a *meltdown* of the fuel rods and the reactor core after a reactor is shut down, huge amounts of water must be kept circulating through the core. A meltdown could release enormous quantities of highly radioactive materials into the environment.

HOW SAFE ARE NUCLEAR POWER PLANTS? To greatly reduce the chances of a meltdown and other serious reactor accidents, commercial reactors in the United States (and most countries) have many safety features:

- Thick walls and concrete and steel shields surrounding the reactor vessel

- A system for automatically inserting control rods into the core to stop fission under emergency conditions

- A steel-reinforced concrete containment building to keep radioactive gases and materials from reaching the atmosphere after an accident

- Large filter systems and chemical sprayers inside the containment building to remove radioactive dust from the air and further reduce chances of radioactivity reaching the environment

- Systems to condense steam released from a ruptured reactor vessel and prevent pressure from rising beyond the holding power of containment building walls

- An emergency core-cooling system to flood the core automatically with huge amounts of water within one minute to prevent meltdown of the reactor core

- Two separate power lines servicing the plant, and several diesel generators to supply backup power for the huge pumps in the emergency core-cooling system

- X ray inspection of key metal welds during construction and periodically after the plant goes into operation to detect possible sources of leaks from corrosion

- An automatic backup system to replace each major part of the safety system in the event of a failure

Such elaborate safety systems make a complete reactor core meltdown very unlikely. However, a partial or complete meltdown is possible through a series of equipment failures, operator errors, or both. In 1979, a reactor at the Three Mile Island plant in Pennsylvania underwent a partial meltdown because of equipment failures and operator errors (see Spotlight on p. 428). Most of the 42 nuclear reactors scattered throughout the former Soviet Union and most reactors in Eastern Europe do not have many of these safety features and are viewed by nuclear experts as catastrophic accidents waiting to happen.

Many studies of nuclear safety have been made since 1957 when the first commercial nuclear power plant began operating in the United States. However, there is still no officially accepted study of just how safe or unsafe these plants are and no study of the safety of the entire nuclear fuel cycle. Even if engineers can make the hardware 100% reliable, human reliability can never reach 100% (Section 8-2).

The Nuclear Regulatory Commission estimated that there is a 15% to 45% chance of a complete core meltdown at a U.S. reactor during the next 20 years. The commission also found that 39 U.S. reactors have an 80% chance of containment failure from a meltdown or a tremendous gas explosion. Scientists in Germany and Sweden project that, worldwide, there is a 70% chance of another serious core-damaging accident within the next 5.4 years.

A 1982 study by the Sandia National Laboratory estimated that a possible, but highly unlikely, *worst-case accident* in a reactor near a large U.S. city might cause 50,000 to 100,000 immediate deaths, 10,000 to 40,000 later deaths from cancer, and $100 billion to $150 billion in damages. Most citizens and businesses suffering injuries or property damage from a major nuclear accident would get little if any financial reimbursement. Since the beginnings of commercial nuclear power in the 1950s, insurance companies have refused to cover more than a small part of the possible damages from an accident.

In 1957, Congress enacted the Price-Anderson Act, which limited insurance liability from a nuclear accident in the United States. In 1988, Congress extended the law for 20 years and raised the insurance liability to $7 billion—only 7% of the estimated damage from a worst-case accident. Without this law, the U.S. nuclear power industry would never have developed. Critics charge that the law is an unfair subsidy of the nuclear

■ **Winter 1957** Perhaps the worst nuclear disaster in history occurred in the then Soviet Union in the southern Ural Mountains near the city of Kyshtym, believed to be the center of plutonium production for Soviet nuclear weapons at that time. The cause of the accident and the number of people killed and injured remain a secret. However, in 1989, government officials admitted that several hundred square kilometers were contaminated with radioactivity when a tank containing radioactive wastes exploded and that 10,000 people were evacuated. The names of 30 towns and villages in the region disappeared from official maps. Today, the area is deserted and sealed off.

■ **October 7, 1957** A water-cooled, graphite-moderated reactor used to produce plutonium for nuclear weapons north of Liverpool, England, caught fire as the Chernobyl nuclear plant did 29 years later. By the time the fire was put out, 516 square kilometers (200 square miles) of countryside had been contaminated with radioactive material. Exposure to high levels of radiation caused an estimated 33 people to die prematurely from cancer.

■ **March 22, 1975** Against regulations, a maintenance worker used a candle to test for air leaks at the Brown's Ferry commercial nuclear reactor near Decatur, Alabama. That set off a fire that knocked out five emergency core-cooling systems. Although the reactor's cooling water dropped to a dangerous level, backup systems prevented any radioactive material from escaping into the environment. At the same plant, in 1978, a worker's rubber boot fell into a reactor and led to an unsuccessful search costing $2.8 million. Such incidents, caused mostly by unpredictable human errors, are common in most nuclear plants.

■ **March 29, 1979** The worst accident in the history of U.S. commercial nuclear power happened at the Three Mile Island (TMI) nuclear plant near Harrisburg, Pennsylvania (Figure 18-18). One of its two reactors lost its coolant water because of a series of mechanical failures and human operator errors not anticipated in safety studies. The reactor's core became partially uncovered. At least 70% of the core was damaged, and about 50% of it melted and fell to the bottom of the reactor. Unknown amounts of ionizing radiation escaped into the atmosphere, and 144,000 people were evacuated. Investigators

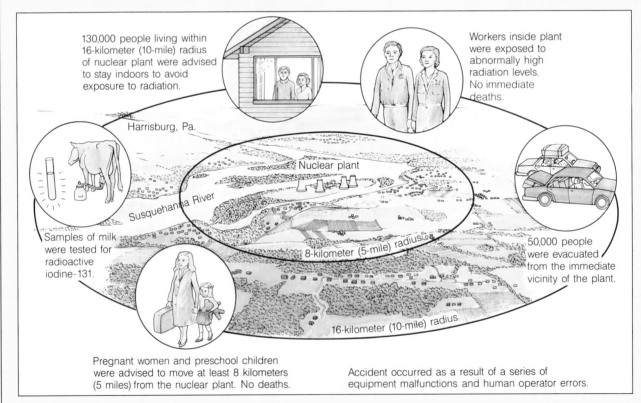

130,000 people living within 16-kilometer (10-mile) radius of nuclear plant were advised to stay indoors to avoid exposure to radiation.

Workers inside plant were exposed to abnormally high radiation levels. No immediate deaths.

Harrisburg, Pa.

Nuclear plant

Susquehanna River

Samples of milk were tested for radioactive iodine-131.

8-kilometer (5-mile) radius

50,000 people were evacuated from the immediate vicinity of the plant.

16-kilometer (10-mile) radius

Pregnant women and preschool children were advised to move at least 8 kilometers (5 miles) from the nuclear plant. No deaths.

Accident occurred as a result of a series of equipment malfunctions and human operator errors.

Figure 18-18 Three Mile Island (TMI) in eastern Pennsylvania, where a nuclear accident occurred on March 29, 1979.

found that if a stuck valve had stayed open for just another 30 to 60 minutes, there would have been a complete meltdown. No one is known to have died because of the accident, but its long-term health effects on workers and nearby residents are still being debated because data published on the radiation released during the accident are contradictory and incomplete.

Partial cleanup of the damaged TMI reactor will cost more than $1 billion, more than the $700 million construction cost of the reactor. In addition, about $187 million of taxpayers' money has been spent by the Department of Energy on the TMI cleanup. Plant owners have also paid out $25 million to over 2,100 people who filed lawsuits for damages. When the partial cleanup is completed, the plant will be sealed and some radioactive debris will be left in the plant for 20 to 90 years.

Confusing and misleading statements about the accident issued by Metropolitan Edison (which owned the plant) and by the Nuclear Regulatory Commission (NRC) eroded public confidence in the safety of nuclear power. Critics of nuclear power contend that it is mostly luck that has prevented the TMI accident and hundreds of serious incidents since then from leading to a complete meltdown and breach of a reactor's containment building. U.S. nuclear industry officials claim that a catastrophic accident has not happened because the industry's multiple-backup safety systems work.

■ **April 26, 1986** At 1:23 AM there were two huge explosions inside one of the four graphite-moderated, water-cooled reactors at the Chernobyl nuclear power plant north of Kiev in the then Soviet Union. These blasts blew the 909-metric-ton (1,000-ton) roof off the reactor building, set the graphite core on fire, and flung radioactive debris high into the air (Figure 18-19). Over the next several days, winds carried some of those radioactive materials over parts of the then Soviet Union and much of eastern and western Europe as far as 2,000 kilometers (1,250 miles) from the plant. The accident happened when engineers turned off most of the reactor's automatic safety and warning systems to keep them from interfering with an unauthorized safety experiment (Figure 18-19). It is likely that little radioactivity would have been released had the reactor been built with a

(continued)

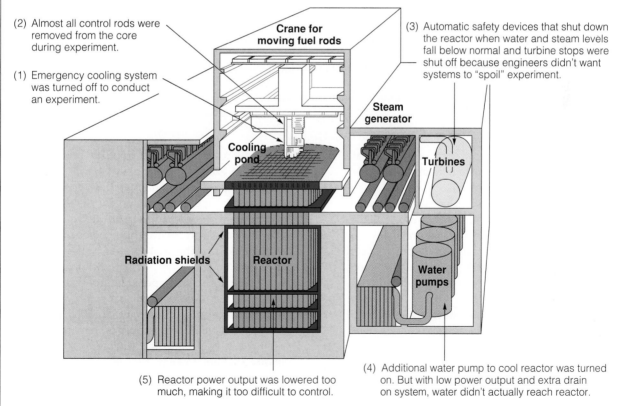

(2) Almost all control rods were removed from the core during experiment.

(1) Emergency cooling system was turned off to conduct an experiment.

Crane for moving fuel rods

(3) Automatic safety devices that shut down the reactor when water and steam levels fall below normal and turbine stops were shut off because engineers didn't want systems to "spoil" experiment.

Steam generator

Cooling pond

Turbines

Radiation shields

Reactor

Water pumps

(5) Reactor power output was lowered too much, making it too difficult to control.

(4) Additional water pump to cool reactor was turned on. But with low power output and extra drain on system, water didn't actually reach reactor.

Figure 18-19 Major events leading to the Chernobyl nuclear power plant accident on April 26, 1986, in the then Soviet Union.

strong containment dome like those found on commercial nuclear reactors in the United States and most other countries (Figure 18-16).

About 135,000 people living within 29 kilometers (18 miles) of the plant were eventually evacuated by an armada of 1,100 buses and trucks. According to government officials, most, perhaps all, of those people will never be able to return to their contaminated homes and farms.

Exposure to high levels of ionizing radiation at the accident site killed 31 plant workers, fire fighters, and rescuers. An additional 237 people were hospitalized with acute radiation sickness. Many of those people will probably die prematurely from cancer in coming years. Estimates of future premature deaths from the accident range from thousands to tens of thousands.

Government officials have compiled a list of 576,000 potential health victims who may contract cancers, thyroid tumors, and eye cataracts, and become sterile. Some 300,000 citizens per year are being treated for radiation exposure. Some top govern-

ment officials think exposure to ionizing radiation will affect at least 4 million people, most in the western portion of the CIS, but some as far away as Germany and Sweden. The immediate and later death tolls would have been much higher if the accident had happened during the day, when people were not sheltered in houses, and if the wind had been blowing toward Kiev and its 2.4 million people.

According to a 1990 government study, the total cost of the accident, including lost electricity production from plants closed down as a result of the incident, will reach $358 billion — almost 90 times the original estimate and about five times larger than the revenues generated in the entire history of the former Soviet Union's nuclear industry. The report concluded that the country would have been better off economically if it had not built any nuclear reactors.

Records of radiation levels have been classified top secret, casting doubt on whether the true effects of the accident will ever be known. Official estimates indicate that the accident released

300 to 400 times more radioactive particles into the atmosphere than did the atomic bombing of Hiroshima. Some government officials and scientists charge that the accident released 20 times more radiation than the government has admitted, with 300 people killed in the explosion, fire, and immediate nuclear fallout.

Because of recent measurements of radioactive contamination, CIS officials plan to move 200,000 more people to other areas. According to some estimates, as many as 2.2 million residents may need to be moved. Today, the reactor is entombed in concrete and metal.

In 1987, the United States permanently shut down a Chernobyl-type military reactor at Hanford, Washington; 54 serious safety violations had occurred at the plant during 1985 and 1986. The Chernobyl accident eroded public support for nuclear power worldwide and showed people that they need to be concerned about the safety of nuclear plants within and outside the borders of their countries.

industry and that if nuclear power plants are not safe enough to operate with adequate insurance, then they are not safe enough to operate at all.

Nuclear critics also contend that nuclear accident and evacuation plans in the United States are inadequate. A serious problem is that areas around many U.S. reactors are up to 10 times more densely populated than those around most reactors in the former Soviet Union. Many urban areas near U.S. reactors would be impossible to evacuate; most Americans would get into their cars and clog exit routes. At Chernobyl, few people had cars.

The U.S. nuclear industry has been pushing the NRC to *reduce* the evacuation area around reactors to as low as 1.6 kilometers (1 mile). Environmentalists charge that the industry wants to reduce the size of evacuation zones to prevent state and local governments from blocking the licensing of new nuclear plants with inadequate evacuation plans.

In 1988, just before leaving office, President Reagan signed an executive order allowing the NRC to issue operating permits for nuclear power plants without state or local approval of emergency evacuation plans, which many believe to be inadequate. Critics of this executive decision believe that the people in a democracy should have the final say over events that can affect their lives.

There is also widespread lack of confidence in the NRC's ability to enforce nuclear safety. In 1989, NRC documents revealed that four out of five licensed U.S. reactors had failed to make all the new safety changes required in 1979 after the TMI accident. None of those plants was shut down by the NRC. According to a 1987 General Accounting Office report, the NRC has also allowed plants to continue operating even after a record of repeated safety violations.

Congressional hearings in 1987 uncovered evidence that high-level NRC staff members have de-

Q: How long will the world's proven reserves of coal last at current consumption rates?

stroyed documents and obstructed investigations of criminal wrongdoing by utilities, suggested ways utilities can evade commission regulations, and provided utilities and their contractors with advance notice of surprise inspections. Some NRC field supervisors have also harassed and intimidated lower-level NRC inspectors who cite utilities for too many violations.

In 1986, U.S. citizens learned that most of the 14 nuclear weapons production facilities in 13 states supervised by the Department of Energy have been operated with gross disregard for the safety of their workers and people in nearby areas. Since 1957, these facilities have released huge quantities of radioactive particles into the air and dumped tons of potentially cancer-inducing radioactive waste and toxic substances into flowing creeks and leaking pits without telling local residents. Numerous serious incidents were kept secret while government officials repeatedly assured local residents that there was no danger from radioactive contamination. Ohio's Senator John Glenn summed up the situation: "We are poisoning our own people in the name of national security."

The General Accounting Office and the Department of Energy estimate that it will cost taxpayers $84 billion to $270 billion over 60 years to get these facilities cleaned up and in safe working order. The EPA has cited various federal nuclear facilities for violations of hazardous-waste handling, but has not been authorized by Congress to enforce cleanup regulations or levy fines. The Department of Energy claims it is exempt from hazardous-waste laws that apply to private businesses. Without loud and constant pressure from citizens, Congress may not appropriate enough money to do the job and change laws to insure that rigid safety standards are required at all government nuclear facilities.

DISPOSAL AND STORAGE OF RADIOACTIVE WASTES

Each part of the nuclear fuel cycle (Figure 18-17) for military and commercial nuclear reactors produces solid, liquid, and gaseous radioactive wastes. Some of these, called *low-level radioactive wastes*, give off small amounts of ionizing radiation, usually for a long time. Others are *high-level radioactive wastes*, which give off large amounts of ionizing radiation for a short time and small amounts for a long time.

From the 1940s to 1970, most low-level radioactive waste produced in the United States (and most other countries) was dumped into the ocean in steel drums. Since 1970, low-level radioactive wastes from military activities have been buried at government-run landfills. Three of these have been closed because of leakage. Great Britain and Pakistan still dump their low-level radioactive wastes into the ocean.

Low-level waste materials from commercial nuclear power plants, hospitals, universities, industries, and other producers are put in steel drums and shipped to regional landfills run by federal and state governments.

By 1990, three of the six commercial landfills had been closed because of radioactive contamination of groundwater and nearby property. Attempts to build new regional dumps for low-level radioactive waste in 12 states have met with fierce public opposition.

In June 1990, the Nuclear Regulatory Commission caused a shockwave of opposition from environmentalists and the EPA when it proposed that most of the country's low-level radioactive waste be removed from federal regulation. These wastes would then be handled like ordinary trash and dumped in landfills, incinerated, reused, or recycled into consumer products. According to the NRC, exposure to radiation from these unregulated wastes would kill 2,500 Americans — 1 out of every 100,000 citizens. Other estimates show as many as 12,412 more cancer deaths per year.

The NRC contends that this loss of life is acceptable because it would save the nuclear power industry at least $1 billion over the next 20 years. This decision was made despite several recent studies showing that the hazards to humans from exposure to low-level radiation is at least 30 times higher than previously estimated. In 1990, several environmental groups filed a suit to overturn the NRC policy.

Most high-level radioactive wastes are spent fuel rods from commercial nuclear power plants and an assortment of wastes from nuclear weapons plants. After 35 years of research and debate, scientists still don't agree on a safe method of storing these wastes (see Case Study on p. 432). Regardless of the storage method, most U.S. citizens strongly oppose the location of a low- or high-level nuclear waste disposal facility anywhere near them (see Case Study on p. 434).

DECOMMISSIONING NUCLEAR POWER PLANTS AND WEAPONS FACILITIES

The useful operating life of today's nuclear power plants is hoped to be 30 to 40 years, but many plants are aging faster than expected. Because the core and many other parts contain large amounts of radioactive materials, a nuclear plant cannot be abandoned or demolished by a wrecking ball like a worn-out, coal-fired power plant. Most of the radioactivity decays within 50 years, but it takes 3 million years for an abandoned plant to become no more radioactive than its original uranium fuel.

Decommissioning nuclear power plants and nuclear weapons plants is the last step in the nuclear fuel cycle. Three ways have been proposed.

1. *Immediate dismantlement:* removing spent fuel, decontaminating and taking the reactor apart after shutdown, and shipping all radioactive debris to a radioactive-waste burial facility. This method promptly rids the plant site of radioactive materials and is the least expensive option, but it exposes work crews to the highest level of radiation and results in the largest volume of radioactive waste.

Some scientists believe that the long-term safe storage or disposal of high-level radioactive wastes is technically possible. Others disagree, pointing out that it is impossible to show that any method will work for the 10,000 years of fail-safe storage needed for reprocessed wastes and the 240,000 years needed for wastes not reprocessed. Following are some of the proposed methods and their possible drawbacks:

1. *Bury it deep underground.* The currently favored method is to package unreprocessed spent fuel rods and bury them in a deep underground salt, granite, or other stable geological formation that is earthquake-resistant and waterproof (Figure 18-20). A better method would be to reprocess the waste to remove very long-lived radioactive isotopes and convert what is left into a dry solid. The solid would then be fused with glass or a ceramic material and sealed in metal canisters for burial. This would reduce burial time from 240,000 years to 10,000 years, but it is expensive. Some geologists question the idea of burying nuclear wastes.

They argue that the drilling and tunneling to build the repository might cause water leakage and weaken resistance to earthquakes. They also contend that with present geological knowledge, scientists cannot make meaningful 10,000- to 240,000-year projections about earthquake probability and paths of groundwater flows in underground storage areas. According to a 1990 report by the National Academy of Sciences, "Use of geological information — to pretend to be able to make very accurate prediction of long-term site behavior — is scientifically unsound."

2. *Shoot it into space or into the sun.* Costs would be very high, and a launch accident, such as the explosion of the space shuttle *Challenger*, could disperse high-level radioactive wastes over large areas of the earth's surface.

3. *Bury it under the Antarctic ice sheets or the Greenland ice caps.* The long-term stability of the ice sheets is not known. They could be destabilized by heat from the wastes, and retrieval of the

wastes would be difficult or impossible if the method failed.

4. *Dump it into descending subduction zones in the deep ocean.* Wastes could eventually be spewed out somewhere else by volcanic activity. Waste containers might leak and contaminate the ocean before being carried downward, and retrieval would be impossible if the method did not work.

5. *Change it into harmless, or less harmful, isotopes.* Right now, there is no way to do this. Even if a method were developed, costs would probably be extremely high. Resulting toxic materials and low-level, but very long-lived, radioactive wastes would have to be disposed of safely.

6. *Use it in shielded batteries to run small electric generators.* Researchers claim that a wastebasket-size battery using spent fuel could produce enough electricity to run five homes for 28 years or longer at about half the current price of electricity. However, leakage could contaminate homes and communities. Dispersing high-level radioactive waste through-

---

2. *Mothballing:* removing spent fuel, putting up a barrier, and setting up a 24-hour security guard system to keep out intruders for 30 to 100 years before dismantlement. This permits short-lived radioactive isotopes to decay, which reduces the threat to dismantlement crews and the volume of contaminated waste.

3. *Entombment:* removing spent fuel, covering the reactor with reinforced concrete, and putting up a barrier to keep out intruders. This allows for radioactive decay but passes a dangerous legacy to future generations.

Each method involves shutting down the plant, removing the spent fuel from the reactor core, draining all liquids, flushing all pipes, and sending all radioactive materials to an approved waste storage site yet to be built.

Worldwide, more than 21 commercial reactors (5 in the United States) have been retired and are awaiting

decommissioning. Another 228 large commercial reactors (66 in the United States) are scheduled for retirement between 2000 and 2010.

Utility company officials estimate that dismantlement of a typical large reactor should cost about $170 million and mothballing $225 million. Most analysts consider the dismantlement figure too low and estimate that the decommissioning of existing U.S. nuclear power plants could cost about $1 billion per reactor — roughly equal to the initial construction cost. Decommissioning costs will add to the already high price of electricity produced by nuclear fission. Politicians and nuclear industry officials in the United States and other countries may be tempted to mothball retired plants and pass dismantlement costs and problems on to the next generation.

In 1991, the NRC, under pressure from nuclear industry officials and others, approved a rule under which nuclear reactors whose 40-year operating licenses are

Q: How long will proven reserves of coal in the United States last at current consumption rates?

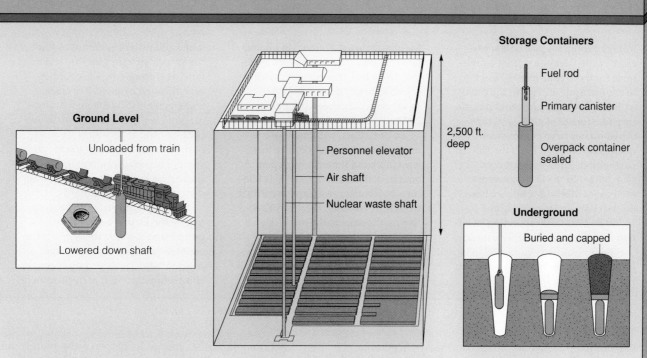

Storage Containers

Fuel rod

Primary canister

Overpack container sealed

Ground Level

Unloaded from train

Lowered down shaft

2,500 ft. deep

Personnel elevator

Air shaft

Nuclear waste shaft

Underground

Buried and capped

Figure 18-20 Proposed general design for deep underground permanent storage of high-level radioactive wastes from commercial nuclear power plants in the United States. (Source: U.S. Department of Energy)

out a country would probably be politically unacceptable. Besides, this method would use only a small portion of the nuclear waste.

Critics of nuclear power are appalled that, after decades, there has been so little effort to solve the serious problem of what to do with nuclear waste while the industry has

plunged ahead and built hundreds of nuclear reactors and weapons facilities. What do you think should be done?

expiring may apply for renewals of up to 20 years. Environmentalists call this proposal a wasteful and potentially dangerous financial bailout of the ailing nuclear power industry, which cannot compete with other energy alternatives on an even economic playing field.

PROLIFERATION OF NUCLEAR WEAPONS Since 1958, the United States has been giving away and selling to other countries various forms of nuclear technology. Today at least 14 other countries sell nuclear technology in the international marketplace.

For decades, the U.S. government denied that the information, components, and materials used in the nuclear fuel cycle could be used to make nuclear weapons. In 1981, however, a Los Alamos National Laboratory report admitted: "There is no technical demarcation between the military and civilian reactor and there never was one" — something environmentalists had been saying for years.

Today, 135 countries have signed the 1968 Nuclear-Nonproliferation Treaty. They have agreed to forgo building nuclear weapons in return for help with commercial nuclear power. The International Atomic Energy Agency (IAEA) was established to monitor compliance.

However, nuclear facilities belonging to India, Israel, South Africa, Argentina, Brazil, Pakistan, and other countries that have not signed the treaty are not monitored. Nuclear facilities in countries such as China, France, Great Britain, the CIS, and the United States that have signed the treaty are generally not monitored by the IAEA.

There is clear evidence that the governments of Israel, South Africa, Pakistan, and India have made almost 200 nuclear weapons, mostly by diverting weapons-grade fuel from research reactors and commercial power plants. It takes only about 10 kilograms (22 pounds) of plutonium to make a Nagasaki-size nu-

In 1982, Congress passed the Nuclear Waste Policy Act. It set a timetable for the Department of Energy to choose a site and build the country's first deep underground repository for storage of high-level radioactive wastes from commercial nuclear reactors. In 1985, the Department of Energy announced plans to build the first repository, at a cost of at least $10 billion, based on the design shown in Figure 18-20. By 1992, after spending $2 billion, little progress had been made.

The repository is supposed to be built in a type of volcanic rock called tuff on federal land in the Yucca Mountain desert region, 161 kilometers (100 miles) northwest of Las Vegas, Nevada. Construction was supposed to begin in 1998, and the facility was scheduled to open by 2003.

In 1990, the Department of Energy put off the opening date to at least 2010, but it may never open. A young, active volcano is only 11 kilometers (7 miles) away, and according to DOE's own data, there are 32 active earthquake faults on the site itself. Nevada ranks just behind Alaska and California in frequency of earthquakes.

Yucca Mountain's many geologic faults and its large amount of fractured rock also suggest that water flowing through the site could escape through a network of cracks. Some geologists estimate that water carrying leached radioactive wastes could move 5 kilometers (3.1 miles) or more from the site in 400 to 500 years. This would automatically make it ineligible as a repository under current federal standards.

Since 1988, Nevada has refused to give the Department of Energy permission to study the site, but the state was overruled by a federal court in 1991. Two-thirds of Nevada's citizens are opposed to development

clear bomb. At least six other countries—Argentina, Brazil, Libya, Syria, Iraq, and Iran—are actively seeking to make nuclear weapons or to buy them from black market sources. A typical 1,000-megawatt nuclear reactor generates about 15 bombs' worth of plutonium a year.

Sophisticated terrorist groups can also make a small atomic bomb by using about 2.2 kilograms (5 pounds) of plutonium or uranium-233, or about 5 kilograms (11 pounds) of uranium-235. Such a bomb could blow up a large building or a small city block and would contaminate a much larger area with radioactive materials for centuries. For example, a crude 10-kiloton nuclear weapon placed properly and detonated during working hours could topple the World Trade Center in New York City. This explosion could easily kill more people than those killed by the atomic bomb the United States dropped on Hiroshima in 1945.

Spent reactor fuel is so highly radioactive that theft is unlikely, but plutonium separated at commercial and military reprocessing plants (Figure 18-17) is much less radioactive and can be handled fairly easily. Although plutonium shipments are heavily guarded, plutonium could be stolen from nuclear weapons or reprocessing plants, especially by employees. Each year, about 3% of the 142,000 people working in 127 U.S. nuclear weapons facilities in 23 states are fired because of drug use, mental instability, or other security risks. By the mid-1990s, hundreds of shipments of plutonium separated from reprocessing facilities in France, Great Britain, Germany, Japan, and India will be traveling by land, sea, and air within and between countries.

Those who would steal plutonium need not bother to make atomic bombs. They could simply use a conventional explosive charge to disperse the plutonium into the atmosphere from atop any tall building. Dispersed in that way, 1 kilogram (2.2 pounds) of plutonium oxide powder theoretically would contaminate 8 square kilometers (3 square miles) with dangerous levels of radioactivity for several hundred thousand years.

One way to reduce the diversion of plutonium fuel from the nuclear fuel cycle is to contaminate it with other substances that make it useless as weapons material. So far, no one has come up with a way to do this, and most nuclear experts doubt that it can be done.

The best ways to slow down the spread of bomb-grade material are to abandon civilian reprocessing of power plant fuel, develop substitutes for highly enriched uranium in research reactors, and tighten international safeguards.

SOARING COSTS After the United States dropped atomic bombs on Hiroshima and Nagasaki, ending World War II, the scientists who developed the bomb and the elected officials responsible for its use were determined to show the world that the peaceful uses of atomic energy would outweigh the immense harm it had done. One part of this "Atoms for Peace" program was to use nuclear power to produce electricity. American utility companies were skeptical but began ordering nuclear power plants in the late 1950s for four reasons.

1. The Atomic Energy Commission and builders of nuclear reactors projected that nuclear power would produce electricity at a very low cost compared with using coal and other alternatives.

2. The nuclear industry projected that nuclear reactors would have an 88% *capacity factor*—a measure

of the repository. President Bush's 1991 energy plan calls for states to lose their authority in the selection of radioactive waste sites. In 1991, the nuclear industry began a three-year, $9 million public relations and advertising campaign to neutralize public opposition to the Yucca Mountain repository.

The DOE has also asked Congress to allow it to begin immediate construction of an aboveground interim storage facility for high-level radioactive wastes — a sort of halfway house for wastes awaiting permanent disposal. Some critics fear the temporary facility could become the permanent site, with DOE declaring the problem solved. Others believe that aboveground storage may be safer than uncertain underground storage.

Citizens in cities and states along the proposed routes for transporting these highly radioactive wastes to the Nevada repository are becoming increasingly concerned about the possibility of accidents that would release radioactive materials. Many cities are passing laws to ban shipments of radioactive materials through their areas, but such laws may be overridden by the federal government — circumventing the rights of citizens to decide the risks they are willing to accept.

In 1991, the Department of Energy proposed that the handling of nuclear waste be turned over to the private sector, arguing that this would reduce government accountability and regulation and lower budget expenditures. This passing of a hot political potato to the private sector would also limit public access to information about nuclear waste by avoiding disclosure requirements faced by government agencies. What do you think should be done?

---

of the time a reactor would operate each year at full power.

3. The first round of commercial reactors was built with the government paying about one-fourth of the cost and with the reactors provided to utilities at a fixed cost with no cost overruns allowed. (The builders lost their shirts but knew they could make big profits on later rounds of plants.)

4. Congress passed the Price-Anderson Act, which protected the nuclear industry and utilities from significant liability to the general public in case of accidents.

It was an offer utility company officials could not resist. Today many wish they had.

Experience has shown that nuclear power is a very expensive way to produce electricity, even when it is heavily subsidized and enjoys partial protection from free market competition with other energy sources. According to the Department of Energy, commercial nuclear power received over $1 trillion in research and development and other federal subsidies between 1952 and 1991 — an average of $9 billion per reactor. Yet, after four decades of subsidies and development, commercial nuclear reactors in the United States now deliver less of the country's energy than is provided by wood and crop wastes with hardly any subsidies.

New nuclear power plants produce electricity at an average of about 15¢ per kilowatt-hour — equal to buying oil at $247 per barrel. These already-high costs do not include most of the costs of storing radioactive wastes and decommissioning worn-out plants. Nuclear cost analyst, Charles Komanoff, has calculated that including these and other environmental and social costs of nuclear power would add about 9¢ per kilowatt-hour to its already-high price. All other methods of producing electricity in the United States, except solar voltaic and solar thermal, have average costs below those of new nuclear power plants (Figure 17-9). By 2000, solar photovoltaics (Figure 17-17) and solar-thermal with natural gas backup (Figure 17-15) are expected to be cheaper than nuclear power for producing electricity.

Operating costs of nuclear plants have been higher than projected because U.S. pressurized water reactors (PWRs) operate at an average of only about 60% of their full-time, full-power capacity — far below the 88% capacity projected by proponents of nuclear power in the 1950s. The average capacity factor for PWRs in the United Kingdom is only 51% and those in Sweden 54%. Those in other countries are higher — Japan and Canada (71%), France (74%), the former West Germany (82%), and Switzerland (87%) — mostly because of standardized design and better management.

New nuclear plants in France and Japan cost about half as much per kilowatt of power to build as those in the United States because they are better planned and use standardized designs. But France ran up an enormous $50 billion debt to finance its nuclear industry, and France and Japan now produce more electricity than they need.

In the United States, where there are 81 different designs among the country's 111 operating reactors, poor planning and management and stricter safety regulations since the TMI accident have increased costs and lengthened construction time. Currently, new nuclear power plants cost three times as much to build as equivalent coal-fired plants with the latest air pollution control equipment.

A: Coal would be too expensive to use and would be phased out.

Since the Three Mile Island accident, the U.S. nuclear industry and utility companies have financed a vigorous advertising campaign by the U.S. Council for Energy Awareness. This $20-million-a-year public relations campaign is designed to improve the industry's image, resell nuclear power to the American public, and downgrade the importance of solar energy, conservation, geothermal energy, wind, and hydropower as alternatives to nuclear power.

The campaign's magazine and television ads do not tell readers and viewers that the ads are paid for by the nuclear industry. Most ads use the argument that more nuclear power is needed in the United States to reduce dependence on imported oil and improve national security.

The truth is that since 1979, only about 5% (3% in 1991) of the electricity in the United States has been produced by burning oil, and 95% of that is residual oil that can't be used for other purposes. Thus, *building more nuclear plants will not save the United Sates any significant amount of domestic or imported oil*. Even if all electricity in the United States came from nuclear power—requiring about 500 nuclear plants—this would reduce U.S. oil consumption by less than 5%. The nuclear industry also does not point out that half of the uranium used for nuclear fuel in the United States is imported.

The nuclear industry claims that nuclear power, unlike coal burning, does not add any carbon dioxide to the atmosphere. Supporters argue that replacing coal-burning power plants with nuclear plants would help delay projected climate changes from an enhanced greenhouse effect. It is true that nuclear power plants don't release carbon dioxide, but the fuel cycle involved in using nuclear power does produce some carbon dioxide, mainly in the processing of uranium fuel (Figure 18-17). However, the amount of carbon dioxide produced per unit of electricity is only one-sixth that produced by a coal-burning plant.

If the use of nuclear power soared, uranium would have to be extracted from increasingly lower-grade ores. This could result in the release of as much or nearly as much CO_2 to generate one unit of electricity from a nuclear power plant as from a coal-burning plant.

The nuclear industry hopes to persuade governments and utility companies to build hundreds of new "second-generation" plants using standardized designs. They are supposed to be safer and quicker to build (3 to 5 years); they would supposedly operate at full power 85% of the time and last 60 years. Some nuclear experts believe that we can make nuclear power acceptably safe and that we have little choice but to take the risks involved in doing this.

Nuclear advocates call the new designs, still only on drawing boards, *inherently safe*. However, Robert Pollard, a former safety engineer with the NRC, points out that any scheme for fissioning atoms is inherently dangerous. You can build new reactors that are safer than existing ones, but you can't make them inherently safe.

Scientists disagree about which of the proposed new designs to pursue, and it would take at least 30 years and trillions of dollars for a new type of reactor to begin supplying 10% of U.S. electricity. According to *Nucleonics Week*, an important nu-

Banks and other lending institutions have become skeptical about financing new U.S. nuclear power plants. The Three Mile Island accident showed that utility companies could lose $1 billion or more of equipment in an hour and at least $1 billion more in cleanup costs, even without any known harmful effects on public health. Abandoned reactor projects have cost U.S. utility investors at least $12 billion since the middle 1970s. The business magazine *Forbes* has called the failure of the U.S. nuclear power program "the largest managerial disaster in U.S. business history." It involves perhaps $1 trillion in wasted investments, cost overruns, and unnecessarily high electricity costs, as well as production of more electricity than the country needs. Abandoned and cost-ineffective nuclear power plants in the United States have generated at least $10 billion of losses for utilities' stockholders. No U.S. utility company is planning the construction of any new nuclear power plants because it is no longer cost-effective.

Is nuclear power dead in the United States and most other MDCs? You might think so because of its high costs and tremendous public opposition, but powerful economic and political forces strive to maintain and expand the world's nuclear power industry (see Pro/Con above). Also, the U.S. Department of Energy and energy agencies in many other MDCs are heavily staffed with officials who continue to push for nuclear power instead of other, safer, and more cost-effective alternatives.

PROS AND CONS OF CONVENTIONAL NUCLEAR FISSION Nuclear plants don't release particulate matter, sulfur dioxide, or nitrogen oxides into the atmosphere, as do coal-fired plants. Water pollution and disruption of land are low to moderate if the entire nuclear fuel cycle operates normally. Multiple safety systems greatly decrease the likelihood of a catastrophic accident releasing deadly radioactive material into the environment.

On the other hand, nuclear power produces electricity, which cannot be used to run vehicles without the development of affordable, long-lasting batteries to

Q: What would happen if the price of oil included its environmental costs and all subsidies were removed?

clear industry publication, "experts are flatly unconvinced that safety has been achieved—or even substantially increased—by the new designs." In addition, construction costs will probably be higher than for conventional nuclear power plants of the same size.

None of the new designs solves the problem of what to do with nuclear waste and the problem of the use of nuclear technology and fuel to build nuclear weapons. Indeed, these problems would become more serious as the number of nuclear plants increased to the many thousands needed to slow global warming only a little.

If half of the U.S. use of coal burned to produce electricity was displaced by building 200 large new nuclear plants at a cost of $1.2 trillion or more, the global emissions of CO_2 would be reduced by only 2%. Just to make that small dent in the carbon dioxide problem would require completing a new large nuclear reactor in the United States every 6 days for the next 20 years. To do that worldwide, we would have to build *one reactor every 4 days* for 20 years at a total cost of $23 trillion!

Improvements in energy efficiency—especially requiring all new cars to get at least 21 kilometers per liter (50 miles per gallon) of gasoline—would save energy and result in much greater and faster reductions of carbon dioxide emissions at a small fraction of the cost of building new nuclear plants. According to the Rocky Mountain Institute, *if we hope to reduce carbon dioxide emissions using the least-cost methods, then investing in energy efficiency and renewable energy resources are at the top of the list and nuclear power is at the bottom* (see Guest Essay on p. 58 and Spotlight on p. 215).

Indeed, the full costs of heavily subsidized nuclear power are rising while those of perpetual and renewable energy resources, which have received only small subsidies, are decreasing (Figure 17-9). Using the least-cost approach not only is more effective but also frees capital for reforestation and other activities that will reduce projected greenhouse warming.

Despite the significant economic and other drawbacks of nuclear power compared with other alternatives, President Bush's 1991 energy

plan called for building more nuclear power plants and drilling for more oil while putting little emphasis on improving energy efficiency and development of perpetual and renewable energy resources. Bush's energy plan calls for reducing the licensing of nuclear plants (involving public hearings) from two steps to one step. This would speed up plant construction and help the ailing nuclear industry but would greatly reduce public input into the process.

President Bush also proposed that aging nuclear plants be renovated to extend their useful lives another 20 years—a proposal environmentalists believe is both costly and dangerous. Another proposal is that states would be cut out of the approval process in selecting sites for the storage of nuclear waste. Critics call these proposals a dangerous example of the undue influence of an elitist nuclear industry—persuading government to override the rights of citizens to determine the risks they are willing to accept. What do you think?

propel electric cars. Construction and operating costs for nuclear power plants in the United States and most countries are high and rising, even with enormous government subsidies.

Standardized design and mass production can bring costs down, but electricity can still be produced by safer methods at a cost equal to, or lower than, that of nuclear power. Although large-scale accidents are infrequent, a combination of mechanical failure and human errors, sabotage, or shipping accidents could again release deadly radioactive materials into the environment.

The net useful energy yield of nuclear-generated electricity is probably low (Figure 3-20), especially if the entire nuclear fuel cycle (Figure 18-17) is included. Scientists disagree over how high-level radioactive wastes should be stored, and some doubt that an acceptably safe method can ever be developed. Also, some carbon dioxide is released as part of the nuclear fuel cycle.

Today's military and commercial nuclear energy programs commit future generations to storing danger-

ous radioactive wastes for thousands of years even if nuclear fission power is abandoned tomorrow. The existence of nuclear power technology also helps spread knowledge and materials that can be used to make nuclear weapons. For these reasons, many people feel that it is unethical, uneconomic, and unnecessary to use nuclear power to produce electricity.

 Breeder Nuclear Fission and Nuclear Fusion

NONRENEWABLE BREEDER NUCLEAR FISSION Some nuclear power proponents urge the development and widespread use of breeder nuclear fission reactors that generate nuclear fuel to start up other breeders. Conventional fission reactors use fissionable uranium-235, which makes up only 0.7% of natural uranium ore. At the present rate of use in conventional reactors, the

A: Oil would be too expensive to use and would be phased out.

Chapter 18   **437**

world's supply of uranium should last for at least 100 years and perhaps 200 years.

Breeder nuclear fission reactors convert nonfissionable uranium-238 into fissionable plutonium-239. Since breeders would use over 99% of the uranium in ore deposits, the world's known uranium reserves would last 1,000 years and perhaps several thousand years.

Under normal operation, a breeder reactor is considered by its proponents to be much safer than a conventional fission reactor. However, if the reactor's safety system should fail, the reactor could lose some of its liquid sodium coolant. This could cause a runaway fission chain reaction and perhaps a small nuclear explosion with the force of several hundred kilograms of TNT. Such an explosion could blast open the containment building, releasing a cloud of highly radioactive gases and particulate matter. Leaks of flammable liquid sodium also can cause fires, as has happened with all experimental breeder reactors built so far.

Since 1966, small experimental breeder reactors have been built in the United Kingdom, the CIS, Germany, Japan, and France. In December 1986, France began operating a $3 billion commercial-size breeder reactor. It cost three times the original estimate to build. The little electricity it has produced is twice as expensive as that generated by France's conventional fission reactors. In 1987, shortly after the reactor began operating at full power, it began leaking liquid sodium coolant and was shut down. Repairs could be so expensive that the reactor might not be put back into operation.

Tentative plans to build full-size commercial breeders in Germany, the CIS, the United Kingdom, and Japan have been canceled because of the excessive cost of France's reactor and an excess of electric generating capacity. Also, experimental breeders built so far produce only about one-fourth of the plutonium-239 each year needed to replace their own fissionable material. If this serious problem is not solved, it would take 100 to 200 years at best for breeders to begin producing enough plutonium to fuel a significant number of other breeders.

NUCLEAR FUSION Scientists hope someday to use controlled nuclear fusion (Figure 3-13) to provide an almost limitless source of energy for producing high-temperature heat and electricity. For 45 years, research has focused on the D-T nuclear fusion reaction in which two isotopes of hydrogen—deuterium (D) and tritium (T)—fuse at about 100 million degrees, 10 times as hot as the sun's interior.

Another possibility is the D-D fusion reaction, in which the nuclei of two deuterium atoms fuse together at much higher temperatures. If developed, it would run on virtually unlimited heavy-water (D_2O) fuel obtained from seawater at a cost of about 10¢ a gallon.

After 45 years of research, high-temperature nuclear fusion is still at the laboratory stage. Deuterium

and tritium atoms have been forced together by using electromagnetic reactors the size of 12 locomotives, 120-trillion-watt laser beams, and bombardment with high-speed particles. So far, none of these approaches has produced more energy than it uses.

If researchers eventually can get more energy out than they put in, the next step would be to build a small fusion reactor and then scale it up to commercial size. This task is considered one of the most difficult engineering problems ever undertaken. The estimated cost of a commercial fusion reactor is several times that of a comparable conventional fission reactor.

In 1989, two chemists claimed to have brought about some D-D nuclear fusion at room temperature using a simple apparatus. But subsequent experiments could not substantiate their claims.

If everything goes right, a commercial nuclear fusion power plant might be built as early as 2030. Even if everything goes right, energy experts don't expect nuclear fusion to be a significant source of energy until 2100, if then. Meanwhile, several other quicker, cheaper, and safer ways can produce and save more electricity than we need.

18-5 Developing an Energy Strategy for the United States

OVERALL EVALUATION OF U.S. ENERGY ALTERNATIVES Table 18-1 summarizes the biggest advantages and disadvantages of the energy alternatives discussed in this and the preceding chapter, with emphasis on their potential in the United States. Energy experts argue over these and other projections, and new data and innovations may change some information in this table. However, it does provide a useful framework for making decisions based on presently available information. Four basic conclusions can be drawn:

1. The best short-term, intermediate, and long-term alternatives for the United States and other countries are a combination of improved energy efficiency and greatly increased use of both perpetual and renewable energy resources (Chapter 17).

2. Total systems for future energy alternatives in the world and the United States will probably have low to moderate net useful energy yields and moderate to high development costs. Since there is not enough financial capital to develop all energy alternatives, projects must be chosen carefully. Otherwise, limited capital will be depleted on energy alternatives that yield too little net useful energy or prove to be economically or environmentally unacceptable.

3. We cannot and should not depend mostly on one nonrenewable energy resource like oil, coal, natural gas, or nuclear power. Instead, the world and

Q: What would happen if the price of nuclear power included its environmental costs and all subsidies were removed?

the United States should rely more on improving energy efficiency and developing a mix of perpetual and renewable energy resources.

4. We should decrease dependence on coal and nuclear power to produce electricity at large, centralized power plants. Individuals, communities, and countries should get more of their heat and electricity from locally available renewable and perpetual energy resources. This would give individuals more control over the energy they use. It would also enhance national security by eliminating large, centralized energy facilities that would be easy to knock out.

ECONOMICS AND NATIONAL ENERGY STRATEGY Cost is the biggest factor determining which commercial energy resources are widely used by consumers. Governments throughout the world use three basic economic and political strategies to stimulate or dampen the short- and long-term use of a particular energy resource:

1. *Not attempting to control the price*, so that its use depends on open, free-market competition (assuming all other alternatives also compete in the same way)

2. *Keeping prices artificially low* to encourage its use and development

3. *Keeping prices artificially high* to discourage its use and development

Each approach has advantages and disadvantages.

FREE-MARKET COMPETITION Leaving it to the marketplace without any government interference is appealing, in principle. However, a free market rarely exists in practice because business people are in favor of it for everyone but their own companies.

Most energy industry executives work hard to get control of supply, demand, and price for their particular energy resource, while urging free-market competition for any competing energy resources. They try to influence elected officials and help elect those who will give their businesses the most favorable tax breaks and other government subsidies. Such favoritism distorts and unbalances the marketplace.

Currently, in the United States and most other countries, the marketplace is greatly distorted by huge government subsidies that make the prices of fossil fuels and nuclear power artificially low. Between 1980 and 1990, federal energy R & D funding for renewable energy and improving energy efficiency was slashed 90%.

Despite this grossly unequal economic playing field, many solar technologies already can produce electricity (and other forms of energy) more cheaply than can heavily subsidized nuclear energy and fossil fuels;

and these prices are coming down (Figure 17-9). If current energy alternatives had to compete in a true free market that included their external costs to society (Section 7-2), significant use of nuclear power and fossil fuels (especially coal) would disappear within two decades or less.

An equally serious problem with the open marketplace is its emphasis on today's prices to enhance short-term economic gain. This inhibits long-term development of new energy resources, which can rarely compete in their development stages without government support.

KEEPING ENERGY PRICES ARTIFICIALLY LOW: THE U.S. STRATEGY Many governments give tax breaks and other subsidies, pay for long-term research and development, and use price controls to keep prices for particular energy resources artificially low. This is the main approach used by the United States and the one that was used by the former Soviet Union.

This approach encourages the development and use of those energy resources getting favorable treatment. It also helps protect consumers (especially the poor) from sharp price increases, and it can help reduce inflation. Because keeping prices low is popular with consumers, this practice often helps leaders in democratic societies get reelected and helps keep leaders in nondemocratic societies from being overthrown.

However, this approach also encourages waste and rapid depletion of an energy resource (such as oil) by making its price lower than it should be, compared with its true value and projected long-term supply. This strategy discourages the development of those energy alternatives not getting at least the same level of subsidies and price control.

Once energy industries, such as the fossil-fuel and nuclear power industries, get government subsidies, they usually have enough clout to maintain that support long after it becomes unproductive. They often successfully fight efforts to provide equal or higher subsidies for the development of new energy alternatives that would allow more nearly equal competition in the marketplace.

According to Harold Hubbard, former director of the Solar Energy Research Institute, government subsidies in 1990 were $26 billion for fossil fuels, $19 billion for nuclear power, and only $5 billion for renewable energy and energy conservation. Furthermore, many of the harmful pollution and health costs of using fossil fuels and nuclear power are not included in their market prices. A 1990 study by the American Solar Energy Society estimated that these hidden costs in the United States amount to at least $109.2 billion a year. Thus, the marketplace is heavily distorted in favor of fossil fuels and nuclear power.

Yet, according to the Department of Energy, reserves and potential supplies of perpetual and renew-

Energy Resources	Estimated Availability			Estimated Net Useful Energy of Entire System	Projected Cost of Entire System	Actual or Potential Overall Environmental Impact of Entire System
	Short Term (1994–2004)	Intermediate Term (2004–2014)	Long Term (2014–2044)			
Nonrenewable Resources						
Fossil fuels						
Petroleum	High (with imports)	Moderate (with imports)	Low	High but decreasing	High for new domestic supplies	Moderate
Natural gas	High (with imports)	Moderate (with imports)	Moderate (with imports)	High but decreasing	High for new domestic supplies	Low
Coal	High	High	High	High but decreasing	Moderate but increasing	Very high
Oil shale	Low	Low to moderate	Low to moderate	Low to moderate	Very high	High
Tar sands	Low	Fair (imports only)	Poor to fair (imports only)	Low	Very high	Moderate to high
Synthetic natural gas (SNG) from coal	Low	Low to moderate	Low to moderate	Low to moderate	High	High (increases use of coal)
Synthetic oil and alcohols from coal and organic wastes	Low	Moderate	High	Low to moderate	High	High (increases use of coal)
Nuclear energy						
Conventional fission (uranium)	Low to moderate	Low to moderate	Low to moderate	Low to moderate	Very high	Very high
Breeder fission (uranium and thorium)	None	None to low (if developed)	Moderate	Unknown, but probably moderate	Very high	Very high
Fusion (deuterium and tritium)	None	None	None to low (if developed)	Unknown, but may be high	Very high	Unknown (probably moderate to high)
Geothermal energy	Low	Low	Low	Low to moderate	Moderate to high	Moderate to high
Perpetual and Renewable Resources						
Improving energy efficiency	High	High	High	Very high	Low	Decreases impact of other sources
Water power (hydroelectricity)						
New large-scale dams and plants	Low	Low	Very low	Moderate to high	Moderate to very high	Low to moderate
Reopening abandoned small-scale plants	Moderate	Moderate	Low	High	Moderate	Low

Q: Has a scientifically and politically acceptable method for the long-term disposal of nuclear waste been developed?

| Energy Resources | Estimated Availability | | | Estimated Net Useful Energy of Entire System | Projected Cost of Entire System | Actual or Potential Overall Environmental Impact of Entire System |
	Short Term (1994–2004)	Intermediate Term (2004–2014)	Long Term (2014–2044)			
Perpetual and Renewable Resources (continued)						
Tidal energy	None	Very low	Very low	Unknown (probably moderate)	High	Low to moderate
Ocean thermal gradients	None	Low	Low to moderate (if developed)	Unknown (probably low to moderate)	Probably high	Unknown (probably moderate)
Solar energy						
Low-temperature heating (for homes and water)	High	High	High	Moderate to high	Moderate	Low
High-temperature heating	Low	Moderate	Moderate to high	Moderate	High initially, but probably declining fairly rapidly	Low to moderate
Photovoltaic production of electricity	Low to moderate	Moderate	High	Fairly high	High initially but declining fairly rapidly	Low
Wind energy						
Neighborhood turbines and wind farms	Low	Moderate	Moderate to high	Fairly high	Moderate	Low
Large-scale power plants	None	Very low	Probably low	Low	High	Low to moderate?
Geothermal energy (low heat flow)	Very low	Very low	Low to moderate	Low to moderate	Moderate to high	Moderate to high
Biomass (urban wastes for incineration)	Low	Moderate	Moderate	Low to fairly high	High	Moderate to high
Biomass (burning of wood, crop, food, and animal wastes)	Moderate	Moderate	Moderate to high	Moderate	Moderate	Variable
Biofuels (alcohols and natural gas from plants and organic wastes)	Low to moderate?	Moderate	Moderate to high	Low to fairly high	Moderate to high	Moderate to high
Hydrogen gas (from coal or water)	None	Low to moderate	Moderate	Variable	Variable	Variable, but low if produced by using solar energy

able energy resources make up 92% of the total energy resources potentially available to the United States and could meet up to 80% of the country's projected energy needs by 2010 (Figure 17-8). In 1980, the United States was the major developer and exporter of renewable energy technologies. By 1990, it was a net importer of renewable energy technologies and had lost its leadership role in this crucial area.

If the current short-sighted national energy policy is not corrected during the 1990s, within a few decades the United States will lose out on the huge global market for renewable energy resources and will have to import most of its wind turbines, hydroelectric generators, hydrogen-fuel systems, and solar cells from Japan, Germany, and other countries, including several LDCs. This will drain the country's economic resources, increase the already-enormous national debt, and cause the loss of tens of thousands of jobs—another example of short-term economic gain leading to long-term economic and environmental grief.

Environmentalists are alarmed that an increasing share of the Department of Energy's annual budget is being used to develop nuclear weapons instead of new energy alternatives. Between 1981 and 1991, the share of the DOE's budget used for making nuclear weapons and developing new ones increased from 38% to 63%. Thus, almost two-thirds of the DOE budget is actually a thinly disguised addition to the Defense Department's budget. Critics call for these activities to be shifted from the Department of Energy to the Department of Defense.

KEEPING ENERGY PRICES ARTIFICIALLY HIGH: THE WESTERN EUROPEAN STRATEGY Governments keep the price of an energy resource artificially high by withdrawing existing tax breaks and other subsidies or by adding taxes on its use. This encourages improvements in energy efficiency, reduces dependence on imported energy, and decreases use of an energy resource (like oil) that has a limited future supply.

Increasing taxes on energy use, however, contributes to inflation and dampens economic growth. It also puts a heavy economic burden on the poor unless some of the energy tax revenues are used to help low-income families offset increased energy prices and to stimulate labor-intensive forms of economic growth, such as improving energy efficiency. High gasoline and oil import taxes have been imposed by many European governments. That is one reason why those countries use about half as much energy per person and have greater energy efficiency than the United States.

One popular myth is that higher energy prices would wipe out jobs. Actually, low energy prices increase unemployment because farmers and industries find it cheaper to substitute machines run on cheap energy for human labor. On the other hand, raising energy prices stimulates employment because building

solar collectors, adding insulation, and carrying out most other forms of improving energy efficiency are labor-intensive activities.

WHY THE UNITED STATES HAS NO COMPREHENSIVE LONG-TERM ENERGY STRATEGY After the 1973 oil embargo, Congress was prodded to pass a number of laws (see page opposite the inside back cover) to deal with the country's energy problems. Most energy experts agree, however, that those laws do not represent a comprehensive energy strategy. Indeed, analysis of the U.S. political system reveals why the United States has not been able, and will probably never be able, to develop a coherent energy policy.

One reason is the complexity of energy issues as revealed in this and the preceding chapter, but the biggest problem is that the American political process produces laws, not policies, and is not designed to deal with long-term problems. Each law reflects political pressures of the moment and a maze of compromises between competing groups representing industry, environmentalists, and consumers. Once a law is passed, it is difficult to repeal or modify drastically until its long-term harmful consequences reach crisis proportions.

This means that energy policy in the United States will have to be developed from the bottom up by individuals and communities taking energy matters into their own hands (see Individuals Matter inside the back cover). Across the country, people are realizing that paying for energy is bleeding them to death economically, with 80% to 90% of the money they spend on energy leaving the local economy forever, much of it ending up in the hands of wealthy Saudi Arabians and Texas oil barons (see Case Study on p. 443).

A SUSTAINABLE ENERGY FUTURE FOR THE UNITED STATES Citizens will have to exert intense pressure on elected officials to develop a national energy policy based on improvements in energy efficiency and a transition to a mix of perpetual and sustainable energy resources. The most important components of such a policy are

- Doubling the contribution of perpetual and renewable energy resources to the country's domestic energy production from 10% in 1990 to 20% by 2000 and to at least 40% by 2010 (Figure 17-8).

- Reducing the use of coal and oil by 50% by 2010 and using natural gas as an interim fuel during the transition toward cleaner, sustainable energy resources.

- Building no new nuclear reactors and accelerating the retirement of existing plants. Fund a modest research and development program for building and testing a few prototype advanced nuclear reactors in case they are needed after 2020. Put off any decision to build commercial versions of such

Q: Can switching to increased use of nuclear power in the United States save much oil?

Simple improvements in energy efficiency can stimulate local economies and save utilities enormous amounts of money. During the last 16 years, Osage, Iowa (population about 4,000), has become the energy efficiency capital of the United States.

It began in 1974 when Wes Birdsall, head of Osage's municipal utility, initiated a program to get the townspeople to save energy and reduce their electric and natural gas bills and save the utility money by not having to buy more oil and generators. He launched a highly successful nine-year program to insulate houses and plug heat losses, control electricity loads at peak periods, turn down the temperature on water heaters and enclose them in jackets of insulation (provided free by the utility company), switch from electric to gas water heaters and clothes dryers, and install energy-efficient light bulbs (Figure 17-7), low-flow shower heads, and other devices. No new houses could be hooked up to the utility company's natural gas line unless they met certain minimum energy-efficiency standards.

He got people interested in adding insulation, installing energy-saving windows, and plugging air leaks by using an infrared scanner to take a free picture of every house in the community (Figure 17-6). When homeowners could see the energy (and money) flowing out of their houses, they took action to waste less energy. The town now uses 25% less energy than the average U.S. town or city.

There were also enormous financial benefits. The outlay saved the utility company enough money to prepay all its debt, accumulate a cash surplus, and cut inflation-adjusted electricity rates by a third. Furthermore, each household received more than $1,000 in savings per year, with this money recirculating in the local economy. Before the changes, this money, amounting to $1.2 million a year, had gone out of town, and usually out of state, to buy energy. What are your local utility and community doing to improve energy efficiency and stimulate the local economy?

---

plants until 2010 when the effectiveness of improving energy efficiency and greatly increased reliance on perpetual and renewable energy can be evaluated — if they have been made the foundation of a national energy strategy.

■ Phasing out most government subsidies for fossil fuels and nuclear energy and phasing in such subsidies for improvements in energy efficiency and greatly increased use of perpetual and renewable energy resources during the 1990s. Improvements in energy efficiency would serve as the bridge to a renewable-energy economy over the next two to three decades.

■ Adding taxes on fossil fuels (especially coal) that reflect their true health and environmental external costs to society, with the tax revenues used to improve energy efficiency, encourage use of perpetual and renewable energy resources, and provide energy assistance to poor and lower-middle-class Americans. The public might accept these higher taxes if income taxes were lowered as carbon taxes were raised.

■ Giving tax credits or government rebates for purchase of energy-efficient vehicles and adding high taxes on gas guzzlers. Similar tax credits or rebates could be given for those building and buying energy-efficient buildings and those buying energy-efficient appliances. This could be accomplished by using *freebates*, a self-financing mechanism that charges fees to purchasers of inefficient products and uses those funds to provide rebates to buyers of energy-efficient products. This approach relies on market forces and requires no new government taxes or subsidies.

■ Requiring all federal and state facilities to meet the highest feasible standards for energy efficiency.

■ Greatly increasing fuel efficiency standards for cars and trucks.

■ Strengthening federal energy efficiency standards for commercial and residential appliances and establishing energy-efficient building standards for all new and existing buildings.

■ Buying renewable-energy systems for government facilities.

■ Requiring that all energy systems supported by government funds be based on least-cost analysis, including the harmful environmental costs of each alternative. Such analysis would be based on lifetime costs of each system and would include estimates of all major external costs. Government subsidies would be subtracted from estimated costs so that energy resources could be compared on an equal economic basis.

■ Modifying electric-utility regulations so that the utilities are required to produce electricity on a least-cost basis, can earn money for their shareholders by reducing electricity demand, and are allowed rate increases based primarily on improvements in energy efficiency. Then the goal of utility companies would be to maximize production of what Amory Lovins calls energy- and money-saving "negawatts" instead of megawatts.

A: No. In 1991, burning oil supplied only 3% of the country's electricity.

Energy experts estimate that implementing these policies now would save oil and money, slow projected global warming, and sharply reduce air and water pollution. This sustainable-energy path would also double the percentage of energy obtained from perpetual and renewable energy resources in the United States to 15% by 2000 and to as high as 50% by 2020. This path to a sustainable-energy future will happen only if individuals change their own energy lifestyles and elect, or keep in office, officials who pledge to support these policies.

A few countries and states are leading the way in making the transition from the age of oil to the age of energy efficiency and renewable energy. Sweden leads the world in energy efficiency, followed by Japan. Brazil and Norway get more than half their energy from hydropower, wood, and alcohol fuel. Israel, Japan, the Philippines, and Sweden plan to rely on renewable and perpetual sources for most of their energy. California has become the world's showcase for solar and wind power. By 1991, the state got 42% of its energy from renewable resources, largely from hydropower. But 12%—virtually all of it developed since 1980—came from biomass, wind (see photo on p. 379), geothermal, and solar energy (Figures 17-15 and 17-17). What are you, your local community, and your state doing to save energy and money, use renewable and perpetual energy, and help sustain the earth?

Nuclear fission energy is safe only if a number of critical devices work as they should, if a number of people in key positions follow all their instructions, if there is no sabotage, no hijacking of the transport, if no reactor fuel processing plant or repository anywhere in the world is situated in a region of riots or guerrilla activity, and no revolution or war—even a "conventional" one—takes place in these regions. No acts of God can be permitted.

HANNES ALFVEN (NOBEL LAUREATE, PHYSICS)

DISCUSSION TOPICS

1. Explain why you agree or disagree with the ideas that the United States can get **(a)** all of the oil it needs by extracting and processing heavy oil left in known oil wells, **(b)** all of the oil it needs by extracting and processing heavy oil from oil shale deposits, **(c)** all of the oil it needs by extracting heavy oil from tar sands, **(d)** all the natural gas it needs from unconventional sources.

2. Coal-fired power plants in the United States cause an estimated 5,000 deaths a year, mostly from atmospheric emissions of sulfur oxides, nitrogen oxides, and particulate matter. These emissions also damage many buildings and some forests and aquatic systems.
   a. Should air pollution emission standards for *all* new and existing coal-burning plants be tightened significantly? Explain.

   b. Do you favor a U.S. energy strategy based on greatly increased use of coal-burning plants to produce electricity? Explain. What are the alternatives?

3. Explain why you agree or disagree with each of the following proposals made by the nuclear power industry:
   a. The licensing time of new nuclear power plants in the United States should be halved (from an average of 12 years) so they can be built at less cost and compete more effectively with coal and other energy alternatives.
   b. A large number of new, better-designed nuclear fission power plants should be built in the United States to reduce dependence on imported oil and slow down projected global warming.
   c. Large federal subsidies (already totaling $1 trillion) should continue to be given to the commercial nuclear power industry so it does not have to compete in the open marketplace with other energy alternatives receiving no, or smaller, federal subsidies.
   d. A comprehensive program for developing the nuclear breeder fission reactor should be developed and funded largely by the federal government to conserve uranium resources and keep the United States from being dependent on other countries for uranium supplies.

4. Explain why you agree or disagree with the following propositions suggested by various energy analysts:
   a. Federal subsidies for all energy alternatives should be eliminated so that all energy choices can compete in a true free-enterprise market system.
   b. All government tax breaks and other subsidies for conventional fuels (oil, natural gas, coal), synthetic natural gas and oil, and nuclear power should be removed and replaced with subsidies and tax breaks for improving energy efficiency and developing solar, wind, geothermal, and biomass energy alternatives.
   c. Development of solar and wind energy should be left to private enterprise with little or no help from the federal government, but nuclear energy and fossil fuels should continue to receive large federal subsidies (present U.S. policy).
   d. To solve present and future U.S. energy problems, all we need to do is find and develop more domestic supplies of conventional and unconventional oil, natural gas, and coal and increase our dependence on nuclear power (present U.S. policy).
   e. The United States should not worry about heavy dependence on foreign oil imports because they improve international relations and help prevent depletion of domestic supplies (the "don't drain America first" approach).
   f. A heavy federal tax should be placed on gasoline and imported oil used in the United States.
   g. Between 2000 and 2020, the United States should phase out all nuclear power plants.

*5. How is electricity used in your community produced? How has the cost of electricity in your community changed since 1970? Do your community and your campus have an energy conservation plan? If so, what is this plan and how much money has it saved during the past 10 years? If there is no plan, develop an energy plan for your school and community and present it to the appropriate officials.

CHAPTER 19

NONRENEWABLE MINERAL RESOURCES AND SOLID WASTE

General Questions and Issues

1. How are minerals formed and distributed?

2. How are mineral resources found and extracted from the earth's crust?

3. What are the harmful environmental impacts from mining, processing, and using minerals and other crustal resources?

4. How long will affordable supplies of key minerals last for the world and the United States?

5. How can we increase the supplies of key minerals?

6. How can we make supplies of key minerals last longer by reducing the production of solid waste?

Mineral resources are the building blocks on which modern society depends. Knowledge of their physical nature and origins and the web they weave between all aspects of human society and the physical earth can lay the foundations for a sustainable society.

ANN DORR

WHAT DO CARS, SPOONS, glasses, dishes, beverage cans, coins, electrical wiring, bricks, and sidewalks have in common? Few of us stop to think that these products and many others we use every day are made from nonrenewable minerals we have learned to extract from Earth's solid crust (Figure 4-2).

If LDCs are to become MDCs, the supplies of nonfuel minerals vital to industry and modern lifestyles will have to increase dramatically, and we will have to greatly increase the recycling and reuse of these nonrenewable resources. We will also have to reduce the environmental impact from mining, processing, and using more of these resources.

19-1 Geologic Processes and Mineral Resources*

THE DYNAMIC EARTH   Over billions of years, Earth's interior has separated into three major, concentric zones that geologists identify as the core, the mantle, and the crust (Figure 4-2). The outer zone of the earth is called the **crust**. It consists of the *continental crust* that underlies the continents (including the continental shelves extending into the oceans) and the *oceanic crust* that underlies the ocean basins.

Earth's crust, which is still forming in various places, is composed of minerals and rocks and is the source of virtually all the nonrenewable resources—fossil fuels, metallic minerals, and nonmetallic minerals—we use (Figure 1-7). It is also the source of soil and the elements that make up our bodies and those of other living organisms.

A **mineral** is an element or an inorganic compound that occurs naturally and is solid. Some minerals consist of a single element, such as gold, silver, diamond (carbon), and sulfur. However, most of the over 2,000 identified minerals occur as inorganic compounds formed by various combinations of the eight elements that make up 98.5% by weight of Earth's crust (Figure 19-1). A **rock** is any material that makes up a large, natural, continuous part of Earth's crust. Rock usually consists of two or more minerals; sometimes, however, it consists of only one, and a few rocks are made of nonmineral material.

Over millions of years various geological, physical, and chemical processes have concentrated certain minerals in deposits or veins in Earth's upper crust. That part of a metal-yielding material that can be economically and legally extracted at a given time is called an **ore**.

---

*Portions of this section were written by or with the help of **Kenneth J. Van Dellen**, professor of geology and environmental science, Macomb Community College.

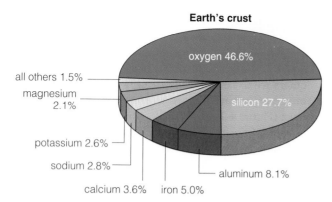

Earth's crust

oxygen 46.6%

silicon 27.7%

all others 1.5%

magnesium 2.1%

potassium 2.6%

sodium 2.8%

calcium 3.6%

iron 5.0%

aluminum 8.1%

Figure 19-1 Composition by weight of Earth's crust. Various combinations of only eight elements make up the bulk of most minerals. Because of separation processes as the interior of Earth has cooled, the crust is richer in the lighter elements than is the average of the whole planet.

Earth's core is surrounded by a thick, solid zone called the **mantle**. This largest zone of Earth's interior is rich in the elements iron (its major constituent), silicon, oxygen, and magnesium. Most of the mantle is solid rock, but under its rigid outermost part there is a zone of very hot, partly melted rock that flows like soft plastic. This plastic region of the mantle is called the *asthenosphere*.

The inner zone of the earth is called the **core** and is composed mostly of iron and probably some nickel. The core has a solid inner part, surrounded by a liquid core of molten material.

INTERNAL EARTH PROCESSES: PLATE TECTONICS A map of Earth's earthquakes and volcanoes shows that most of these phenomena are not random but occur along certain lines or belts on Earth's surface (Figure 19-2a). The areas of Earth outlined by these major belts are called **plates** (Figure 19-2b). They are composed of the crust and the rigid, outermost part of the mantle outside the asthenosphere, a combination called the **lithosphere**. They slowly move, carried around on the flowing asthenosphere like large pieces of ice floating on the surface of a lake during the spring breakup. Some plates move faster than others, but a typical speed is about as fast as fingernails grow.

The theory that explains the movements of the plates and the processes that occur at their boundaries is called **plate tectonics**. Plate motion is responsible for producing mountains (including volcanoes), ocean trenches and ridges, and other features of Earth's surface. Natural hazards such as earthquakes and volcanoes are likely to be found at places where plates interact (Figure 19-2a). Perhaps most importantly, plate movements and interactions concentrate many of the minerals we extract and use.

Internal lithosphere processes are driven by the flow of heat from Earth's core to the mantle and crust. Some of this is residual heat from the formation of Earth that is still being given off as the inner core cools and the outer core both cools and solidifies. Continued decay of radioactive elements in the crust, especially the continental crust, adds to the flow of heat from within Earth.

Three types of boundaries occur between the lithosphere's moving plates: divergent, convergent, and transform fault. At a **divergent plate boundary**, the plates move apart in opposite directions; for example, one plate might go east and the other west ($\leftarrow | \rightarrow$). They occur mostly where hot and partially molten rock material (magma) pushes up between two plates, cools, and solidifies to form new ocean floor that pushes the plates apart. Mountain chains, called *oceanic ridges*, are formed along the ocean floor where the two plates diverge. Divergent plate boundaries can also occur on continents. A good example is found at the East African rift valleys.

Where the tops of heated solid rock flow toward each other, the lithospheric plates are pushed together ($\rightarrow | \leftarrow$). This produces a **convergent plate boundary**. At most convergent plate boundaries, oceanic lithosphere is carried downward (subducted) under an island arc or the continent at a **subduction zone**. An oceanic trench ordinarily forms at the boundary between the two converging plates.

The third type of plate boundary, called a **transform fault**, occurs where plates move in opposite but parallel directions along a fracture (fault) in the lithosphere. This slipping of plates horizontally past one another can trigger earthquakes, mostly on the ocean floor. For example, the San Andreas fault in California is a parallel boundary between two of the lithosphere's plates.

Some commercially important ore deposits are formed where magma intrudes into crustal rock or extrudes onto Earth's surface as lava at all three types of plate boundaries. For example, along divergent plate boundaries, magma moving upward from the mantle interacts with seawater that enters these fractures in the seafloor, known as *hydrothermal* (hot water) *vents*.

Figure 19-2 Earthquakes and volcanoes occur mostly along lithospheric plate boundaries (**a**). According to the *theory of plate tectonics*, the rigid lithosphere consists of various-size plates that move apart (diverge), move toward one another (converge), and slide past one another with parallel motion at transform faults (**b**). Divergent plate boundaries are marked by oceanic ridge segments and rift valleys. Convergent plate boundaries are marked by volcanic island chains or folded mountain belts and usually trenches. Transform faults connect the other two types of plate boundaries. (A few examples on this map are marked with black arrows.)

Q: How many nuclear power plants would have to be built to reduce global emissions of carbon dioxide by 2% within 20 years?

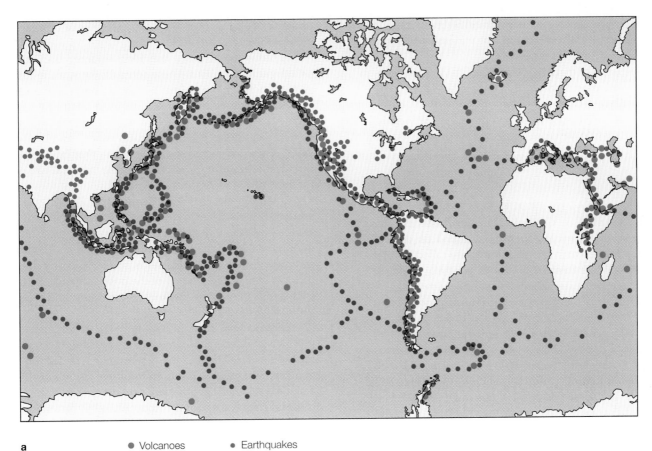

a   ● Volcanoes   ● Earthquakes

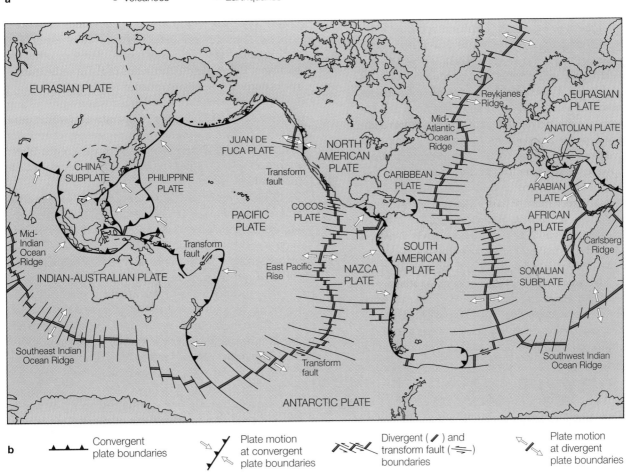

b   ⊥⊥⊥⊥ Convergent plate boundaries   Plate motion at convergent plate boundaries   Divergent (／) and transform fault (≡) boundaries   Plate motion at divergent plate boundaries

Through a complex series of chemical reactions, sulfide ores, made up of combinations of various metals and sulfur, form around these vents.

Deposits of metallic ores can also be found at convergent plate boundaries. Some metallic elements are released when the descending plate partially melts. This metal-rich fluid is then concentrated in the magma, which rises into the crust, cools, and solidifies as metal-rich rock.

EXTERNAL EARTH PROCESSES: EROSION AND MASS WASTING Geological changes based directly or indirectly on energy from the sun and on gravity, instead of on heat in Earth's interior, are called *external processes*. While internal processes generally build up Earth's surface, external processes tend to lower it.

Erosion is the process or group of processes by which earth materials, loose or consolidated, are dissolved, loosened, or worn away, and removed from one place and deposited in another. One of the subprocesses of erosion is **weathering**, in which solid rock exposed at Earth's surface is changed to separate solid particles and dissolved material that can then be moved to another place as *sediment*. Various types of *soil* are the ultimate products of weathering plus interactions with various forms of life (Figure 12-4). Wind, flowing water, and moving ice (glaciers) remove, transport, and redeposit sediments over parts of Earth's surface by erosion. Human activities, particularly those that destroy vegetation, accelerate erosion (Section 12-2).

Weathering and erosion also concentrate some resources in ores. For example, in some places gold and diamonds are weathered out of their host rock and become mixed with gravel and streambeds to form sedimentary deposits called *placers*. In other cases, minerals dissolved out of rock by weathering precipitate from groundwater or seawater to form ore deposits.

Weathering and erosion can sometimes expose *bed rock,* the solid rock mass of Earth. Usually, however, bed rock is under a blanket of unconsolidated material called *regolith*. Regolith or rock masses newly detached from underlying material may move downslope in various ways under the influence of gravity, without being carried in, on, or under a glacier, stream, or other agent of erosion. This transport of material is called *mass wasting*. The names used to classify the types of mass wasting, such as rockfall, rockslide, slump, creep, earthflow, and mudflow, often give clues to their characteristics.

ROCK TYPES AND THE ROCK CYCLE Based on its origin and formation, a rock is placed in one of three broad classes: igneous, sedimentary, or metamorphic. **Igneous rock** forms when molten rock material (magma) wells up from Earth's upper mantle or deep crust, cools, and hardens into rock.

Igneous rock masses that form underground are called *igneous intrusions*. These generally form at sites of volcanic activity, which are mostly at convergent and divergent plate boundaries (Figure 19-2). *Extrusive igneous rocks* are formed when lava erupts from volcanoes or cracks in the earth's surface, cools rapidly, and hardens. *Lava* is the term used for magma that has been extruded onto Earth's surface and is also a general name for the igneous rocks that form from it.

Igneous rocks are the most abundant type of rock and are the main source of many nonfuel mineral resources we use. Granite and its relatives are used for monuments and as decorative stone in buildings, basalt as crushed stone where gravel is scarce, and volcanic rocks in landscaping. Many of the popular gemstones, such as diamonds, tourmaline, garnet, ruby, and sapphire, are found in igneous rocks.

Sedimentary rock forms from the accumulated products of erosion and, in some cases, from the compacted shells, skeletons, and other remains of dead organisms. Gravel, sand, silt, and clay are the results of chemical weathering, abrasion, and other erosion processes. When transported and deposited by water, ice, and wind, they may become compacted and cemented into layers of solid rock such as sandstone and shale.

Other sedimentary rocks are precipitated from solution. Rock salt, gypsum, and several limestones form this way. Some limestones are composed of essentially nothing but the skeletons of corals, clams, or other organisms. Lignite and bituminous coal are sedimentary rocks derived from plant remains (Figure 18-8).

Metamorphic rock is produced when a preexisting rock is subjected to high temperatures (which may cause it to melt partially), high pressures, chemically active fluids, or a combination of those agents. Slate, marble, and anthracite (Figure 18-8) are important metamorphic rocks.

Earth's rocks are constantly being exposed to changes in the pressure, temperature, or chemical environment that over time can change them from one type of rock to another. The interaction of processes that change rocks of Earth from one type to another is called the **rock cycle** (Figure 19-3).

The rock cycle concentrates and disperses Earth's minerals. We know how to find and mine more than 100 minerals concentrated by the rock cycle. We convert these minerals into many everyday items we use and then discard, reuse, or recycle. When we return these materials to the rock cycle in diluted form, they are further dispersed by earth processes. Once this dispersion process has taken place, the resource may not be concentrated again for millions of years. This is why these minerals are classified on a human time scale as nonrenewable resources.

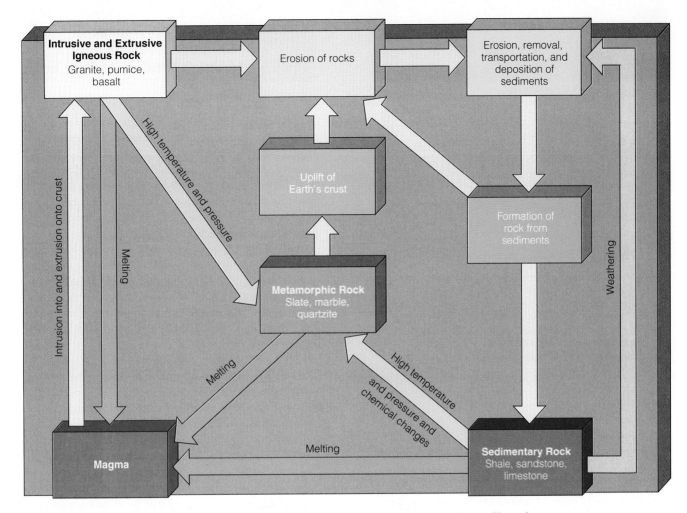

Figure 19-3 The rock cycle, the slowest of Earth's cyclic processes. Earth materials are recycled over millions of years by three processes: melting, erosion, and metamorphism. These processes produce igneous, sedimentary, and metamorphic rocks, respectively. Rock of any of the three classes can be converted to rock of either of the other two classes or can even be recycled within its own class.

19-2 Locating and Extracting Crustal Resources

FINDING AND MINING CRUSTAL RESOURCE DEPOSITS A **mineral resource** is a concentration of naturally occurring solid, liquid, or gaseous material, in or on Earth's crust, in such form and amount that its extraction and its conversion into useful materials or items are currently or potentially profitable. Key mineral resources are *energy resources* (coal, oil, natural gas, uranium, and geothermal energy; Figure 3-5), *metallic mineral resources* (iron, copper, and aluminum), and *nonmetallic mineral resources* (salt, gypsum, clay, sand, phosphates, water, and soil; Figure 1-7).

Mining companies use several methods to find promising mineral deposits. Geological information about plate tectonics (Figure 19-2) and mineral formation helps mining companies find areas for closer study.

Photos taken from airplanes or images relayed by satellites sometimes reveal geological features such as rock formations often associated with deposits of certain minerals. Other instruments on aircraft and satellites can detect deposits of minerals by effects on Earth's magnetic or gravitational fields.

Deposits of nonfuel minerals and rock and coal near the earth's surface are removed by **surface mining**. Mechanized equipment strips away the overlying layer of soil and rock, known as **overburden**, and vegetation. Surface mining is used to extract about 90% by weight of the mineral and rock resources and more than 60% by weight of the coal in the United States (Figure 3-5).

The type of surface mining used depends on the type of crustal resource and the local topography. In **open-pit mining**, machines dig holes and remove ore deposits, such as iron and copper (Figure 19-4). This method is also used to remove sand and gravel, and building stone such as limestone, sandstone, slate, granite, and marble.

Don Green/Kennecott Copper Corporation (now owned by British Petroleum)

Figure 19-4 This open-pit copper mine in Bingham, Utah, the largest human-made hole in the world, is 4.0 kilometers (2.5 miles) in diameter and 0.8 kilometer (0.5 mile) deep. It produces 227,000 metric tons (250,000 tons) of copper a year, along with fairly large amounts of gold, silver, and molybdenum and releases enormous amounts of toxic chemicals. The amount of material removed from this mine is seven times the amount moved to build the Panama Canal.

Strip mining is surface mining in which bulldozers, power shovels, or stripping wheels remove large chunks of Earth's surface in strips. It is used mostly for removing coal (Figures 18-10 and 18-12) and some phosphate rock, especially in Florida, North Carolina, and Idaho. Another form of surface mining is **dredging**, in which chain buckets and draglines scrape up sand, gravel containing placer deposits, and other surface deposits covered with water.

Some deposits of crustal resources lie so deep that surface mining is impractical. These deposits of metal ores and coal are removed by **subsurface mining** (Figure 3-5). In most cases, miners dig a deep vertical shaft or horizontal adits and blast tunnels and rooms to reach the ore or coal. Then the resource is extracted and hauled to the surface.

Often the desired mineral in an ore makes up only a small percentage by weight of the rock mass that is removed by mining. This means that massive amounts of rock must be removed from the ground and processed to separate the desired mineral from the host rock.

Most metals in ores are combined chemically with other elements such as oxygen (oxide ores) or sulfur (sulfide ores). To get the desired metal, such ores must be broken down chemically through smelting (see photo on p. 181) or refining processes. These processes require large amounts of energy and produce solid, liquid, and gaseous (especially sulfur dioxide and particulate matter) waste products that must be disposed of.

ENVIRONMENTAL IMPACT AND ECONOMICS

The extracting, processing, and use of fuel or nonfuel mineral resources requires enormous amounts of energy, causes land disturbance, erosion, air pollution, water pollution, and the production of solid and hazardous wastes (Figure 19-5). The degree to which these harmful effects are reduced depends mostly on whether their costs are included in the market prices we pay for items (Section 7-2).

Mining companies and manufacturers have little incentive to find ways to reduce resource waste and pollution as long as they can pass many of the harmful environmental costs of their production on to society. Internalizing these external costs is a major way to reduce pollution, environmental degradation, and resource waste (Section 7-2).

The greatest danger from high levels of resource consumption may not be the exhaustion of resources but the damage that their extraction and processing impose on the environment. Much of this environmental damage is not seen, so most people know little about it.

MINING IMPACTS

Mining involves removing material from Earth's crust and dumping unwanted rock and other waste materials somewhere else — usually near the mining site. Mining is one of the most environmentally damaging activities carried out by humans.

In the United States, nonfuel mining produces at least six times more solid waste material than the total amount of garbage produced by all U.S. towns and cities. Abandoned and unrestored metal and coal surface mines in the United States cover an estimated 90,000 square kilometers (34,700 square miles) — an area about the size of Indiana. That figure does not include the probably larger area of abandoned quarries, pits, and mines used for extracting sand, gravel, and stone.

Although mining uses only a small amount of Earth's surface, it has a severe local (and sometimes regional) environmental impact on the land, air, and water. Bare land, created when vegetation and topsoil are removed by surface mining, and the waste rock and other materials from mining are eroded by wind and water (Figures 18-10 and 18-12). In addition, harmful materials run off into nearby streams; and some toxic compounds in mining wastes percolate into groundwater (Figure 18-14). The air can be contaminated with dust and toxic substances. In the United States, 48 of the 1,211 sites on the EPA's Superfund hazardous-waste cleanup list are former mineral operations.

Subsurface mining disturbs less than one-tenth as much land as surface mining and usually produces less waste material. However, it leaves much of the resource

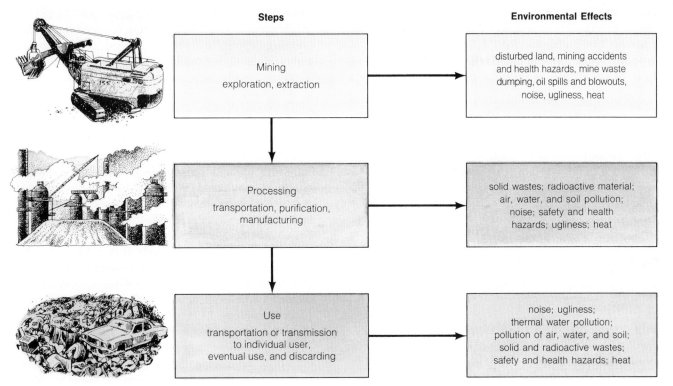

Steps		Environmental Effects
Mining exploration, extraction	→	disturbed land, mining accidents and health hazards, mine waste dumping, oil spills and blowouts, noise, ugliness, heat
Processing transportation, purification, manufacturing	→	solid wastes; radioactive material; air, water, and soil pollution; noise; safety and health hazards; ugliness; heat
Use transportation or transmission to individual user, eventual use, and discarding	→	noise; ugliness; thermal water pollution; pollution of air, water, and soil; solid and radioactive wastes; safety and health hazards; heat

Figure 19-5 Some harmful environmental effects of resource extraction, processing, and use. The energy used to carry out each step causes further pollution and environmental degradation. This harm could be minimized by requiring that the full costs of the pollution and environmental degradation caused by mining, processing, and manufacturing companies be included in the price of their products. Many of these "external" costs are passed on to society, but they are in the form of poorer health, increased health and insurance costs, and increased taxes to deal with pollution and environmental degradation.

in the ground and is more dangerous and expensive than surface mining. Roofs and walls of underground mines collapse, trapping and killing miners. Explosions of dust and natural gas kill and injure them. Prolonged inhalation of mining dust causes lung diseases. Much energy is needed for ventilation and sometimes for pumping water.

Surface mining disrupts the landscape more than subsurface mining. One way to reduce the severe environmental impact of surface mining is to pass, and strictly enforce, laws that require mining companies to restore land after minerals have been removed (Figure 18-13). However, when minerals are removed by surface mining in arid and semiarid regions, full restoration is rarely possible. There is too little rainfall for growth of enough vegetation to prevent continuing soil erosion by rain when it does fall.

Another environmental problem of mining, especially subsurface mining, is *acid mine drainage*, which occurs when aerobic bacteria produce sulfuric acid from iron sulfide minerals in spoils from coal mines and some ore mines. Rainwater seeping through the mine or mine wastes may carry the acid to nearby streams, destroying aquatic life and contaminating water supplies (Figure 18-14). It may also infiltrate the ground.

PROCESSING IMPACTS Processing extracted mineral deposits to remove impurities produces huge quantities of waste rock and other waste materials. Usually these wastes are piled on the ground or dumped into ponds near mining and processing sites. Unless covered and stabilized, particles of dust and toxic metals in these wastes blow into the air, and water leaches toxic and radioactive substances into nearby surface water or groundwater (Figure 19-5).

As lower-grade ores are mined and processed, the quantity of mining waste rises sharply. Most ore minerals do not consist of pure metal, so **smelting** is done to separate the metal from the other elements in the ore mineral. Without effective pollution control equipment, smelters emit enormous quantities of air pollutants (see photo on p. 181) that damage vegetation and soils in the surrounding area. Pollutants include sulfur dioxide (8% of global emissions), soot, and tiny particles of arsenic, cadmium, lead, and other toxic elements and compounds found in many ores.

Decades of uncontrolled sulfur dioxide emissions from copper-smelting operations near Copperhill and Ducktown, Tennessee, killed all vegetation over a large area around the smelter (Figure 9-12). Another "dead zone" or environmental disaster area has been created around the Sudbury, Ontario, nickel smelter in Canada (see photo on p. 181). New dead zones are being created in parts of Eastern Europe, the CIS, and Chile. Smelters also cause water pollution and produce liquid and solid hazardous wastes that must be disposed of safely. Workers in some smelting industries have an increased risk of cancer.

RESOURCE USE IMPACTS The burning of fossil fuels, the manufacture of items from mineral resources, and the use and discarding of many of these items produce air pollution (Chapters 9 and 10), water pollution (Chapter 11), hazardous waste (Chapter 12), and solid waste (Section 19-6).

19-4 Will There Be Enough Mineral Resources?

WILL THERE BE ENOUGH? Experts disagree about whether there will be enough affordable supplies of key nonfuel minerals to meet the projected needs of the world's MDCs and LDCs. Geologists and environmentalists tend to view Earth's supply of minerals as finite because of the uneven concentrations of key minerals in Earth's crust and the two laws of energy (Section 3-6), which impose lower limits on the grades of ore that can be processed without spending more money than they are worth and causing unacceptable environmental damage (Figure 19-5).

Economists, by contrast, tend to view the supply of minerals as essentially infinite because of our ability to develop improved technologies for finding and processing minerals or for finding substitutes.

Many LDCs fear that most of the world's resources will continue to be used to sustain increasingly greater economic growth by the MDCs, thus preventing many LDCs from becoming developed countries.

HOW MUCH IS THERE? The U.S. Geological Survey divides mineral resources into two broad categories, identified and undiscovered, based on degree of geologic understanding and certainty that the resource exists (Figure 19-6). **Identified resources** are deposits of a particular mineral-bearing material that have a known location, quantity, and quality or that are estimated from direct geological evidence and measurements. **Reserves** are identified resources from which a usable mineral can be extracted profitably at present prices with current mining technology (Figure 19-6).

Undiscovered resources are potential supplies of a particular mineral believed to exist on the basis of geologic knowledge and theory, though specific locations, quality, and amounts are unknown. The term **resources** refers to the rest of the estimated total resources of a particular fuel or nonfuel mineral (Figure 19-6).

HOW FAST ARE SUPPLIES BEING DEPLETED? Worldwide, demand for mineral commodities is increasing exponentially because of increasing population and rising per capita consumption (Figure 1-12). The future supply of a nonrenewable mineral resource depends on two factors: its actual or potential supply and how rapidly the supply is being depleted.

We never completely run out of any mineral. Instead of becoming physically depleted, a mineral becomes *economically depleted* when finding, extracting, transporting, and processing the remaining lower-quality deposits cost more than the minerals in these deposits are currently worth. When that economic limit is reached, we have four choices: recycle or reuse what has already been extracted, cut down on unnecessary waste of the resource, find a substitute, or do without.

Most published estimates of particular mineral resources refer only to reserves. Reserves can be increased when exploration reveals undiscovered, economic resources. They can also be increased when identified, subeconomic resources become economic because of new technology or higher prices (which can encourage development of new technology). In recent decades, reserves for most nonfuel minerals have grown at least as fast as mineral production. Many of the best reserves are now found in LDCs.

Depletion time is the time it takes to use a certain portion—usually 80%—of the known reserves of a mineral at an assumed rate of use. Resource experts project depletion times and plot them on a graph by making certain assumptions about the resource supply and its rate of use (Figure 19-7).

We get one estimate of depletion time by assuming that the resource is not recycled or reused, that its estimated reserves will not increase, and that its price increases over time (curve A, Figure 19-7). A longer depletion time estimate is obtained by assuming that recycling will extend the life of existing reserves and that improved mining technology, price rises, and new discoveries will expand present reserves by some factor, say two (curve B, Figure 19-7). An even longer depletion time estimate is obtained by assuming that new discoveries will expand reserves even more, perhaps five or ten times, and that recycling, reuse, and reduced consumption will extend supplies (curve C, Figure 19-7).

Finding a substitute for a resource cancels all these curves and requires a new set of depletion curves for the new resource. Figure 19-7 shows why experts disagree over projected supplies of nonrenewable nonfuel and fuel resources. We get optimistic or pessimistic projections of the depletion time for a nonrenewable resource by making different assumptions.

Generally we use the more accessible and higher-grade mineral and energy resources first. As they are depleted, it takes more money, energy, water, and other materials to get resources of lower quality. As a result, oil wells must be drilled deeper and larger quantities of

Q: How much of the Department of Energy budget is used to develop nuclear weapons?

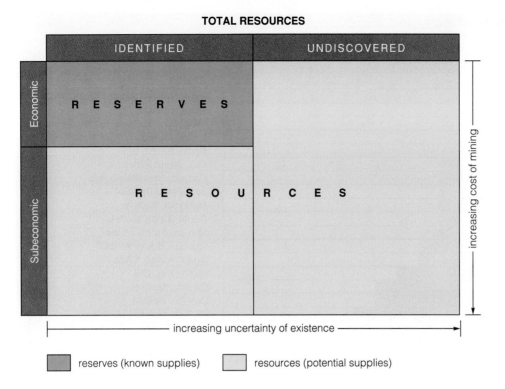

TOTAL RESOURCES

Figure 19-6 General classification of mineral resources by the U.S. Geological Survey. Reserves are resources that are both identified and economic. Other resources are either undiscovered, subeconomic, or both. This is *not* an area graph depicting abundance of reserves relative to other resources.

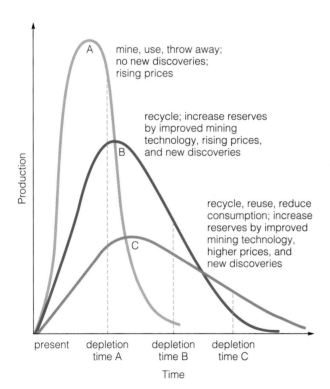

Figure 19-7 Depletion curves for a nonrenewable resource, such as aluminum or copper, using three sets of assumptions. Dashed vertical lines show when 80% depletion occurs.

rock must be processed to meet increased mineral demands from rising population and affluence. That increases the energy and water required and the environmental impacts from mineral extraction, processing, and use (Figure 19-5).

Some minerals are more important than others, although importance can change as new technologies and substitutes are developed. Minerals essential to the economy of a country are called **critical minerals**, and those necessary for national defense are called **strategic minerals**.

WHO HAS THE WORLD'S NONFUEL MINERAL RESOURCES? The Commonwealth of Independent States, the United States, Canada, Australia, and South Africa supply most of the 20 minerals that make up 98% by weight of all nonfuel minerals consumed in the world today. No industrialized country is self-sufficient in fuel and nonfuel mineral resources, although the CIS comes close and is a principal exporter of critical and strategic minerals. The United States, Japan, and western European countries are heavily dependent on imports for most of their critical nonfuel minerals.

THE U.S. SITUATION Many people do not realize, or they deny the reality, that the era of abundant high-grade energy and mineral resources in the United States is gone forever. This unsustainable depletion of Earth capital has also been responsible for the loss of millions of jobs. Even though the United States is the world's largest producer of nonfuel mineral resources, it is highly dependent on imports from 25 other countries for 50% or more of 24 of its 42 most critical and strategic nonfuel minerals. Some of these minerals are imported into the United States because they are consumed more rapidly than they can be produced from domestic supplies. Others are imported because other countries have

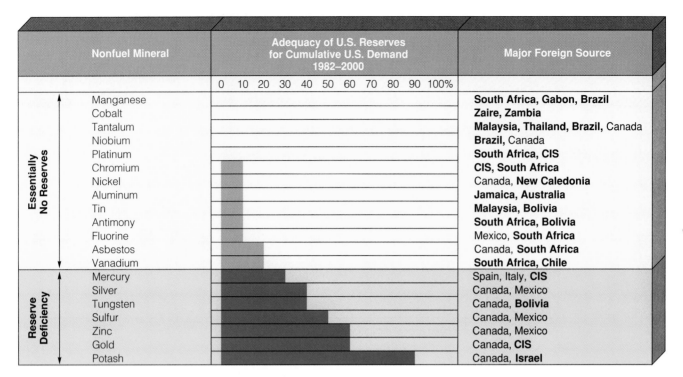

Nonfuel Mineral	Adequacy of U.S. Reserves for Cumulative U.S. Demand 1982–2000	Major Foreign Source
Essentially No Reserves	0 10 20 30 40 50 60 70 80 90 100%	
Manganese		**South Africa, Gabon, Brazil**
Cobalt		**Zaire, Zambia**
Tantalum		**Malaysia, Thailand, Brazil,** Canada
Niobium		**Brazil,** Canada
Platinum		**South Africa, CIS**
Chromium		**CIS, South Africa**
Nickel		Canada, **New Caledonia**
Aluminum		**Jamaica, Australia**
Tin		**Malaysia, Bolivia**
Antimony		**South Africa, Bolivia**
Fluorine		Mexico, **South Africa**
Asbestos		Canada, **South Africa**
Vanadium		**South Africa, Chile**
Reserve Deficiency		
Mercury		Spain, Italy, **CIS**
Silver		Canada, Mexico
Tungsten		Canada, **Bolivia**
Sulfur		Canada, Mexico
Zinc		Canada, Mexico
Gold		Canada, **CIS**
Potash		Canada, **Israel**

Figure 19-8 Estimated deficiencies of selected nonfuel mineral elements in the United States, 1982–2000, and major foreign sources of these minerals. Foreign sources subject to potential interruption of supply by political, economic, or military disruption are shown in boldface print. (Data from U.S. Geological Survey)

higher-grade ore deposits that are cheaper to extract than remaining lower-grade U.S. reserves.

Figure 19-8 shows the projected deficiency in U.S. reserves for 20 critical nonfuel minerals to 2000 and the major foreign sources of these minerals. Most U.S. mineral imports come from reliable and politically stable countries. There is particular concern, however, over embargoes or sudden cutoffs of supplies of four strategic minerals—manganese, cobalt, platinum, and chromium—for which the United States has essentially no reserves and depends on imports from the CIS or potentially unstable African countries (South Africa, Zambia, Zaire).

The United States has stockpiles of most of its critical and strategic minerals to cushion against short-term supply interruptions and sharp price rises. These stockpiles are supposed to be large enough to last through a three-year conventional war, after subtracting the amounts available from domestic sources and secure foreign sources, but stockpiles for most of these minerals are far below that level.

19-5 Increasing Mineral Resource Supplies: The Supply-Side Approach

ECONOMICS AND RESOURCE SUPPLY According to standard economic theory, a competitive free market should control the supply and demand of goods and services. If a resource becomes scarce, its price rises. If there is an oversupply, the price falls. Some analysts believe that increased demand will raise mineral prices and stimulate new discoveries and development of more-efficient mining technology. Rising prices will also make it profitable to mine ores of increasingly lower grades and stimulate the search for substitutes.

Many economists argue that this theory does not currently apply to nonfuel mineral resources in most MDCs. In the United States and many other MDCs, industry and government have gained so much control over supply, demand, and prices of mineral raw materials and mineral products that a competitive free market does not exist.

Most mineral prices are artificially low because many countries subsidize development of their domestic mineral resources by providing mining companies generous tax exemptions called depletion allowances. Taxing rather than subsidizing production of virgin materials would create incentives for more efficient use of minerals, encourage recycling and reuse, and provide governments wth considerable revenue.

Another problem is that the costs of nonfuel mineral resources make up only a small part of the total cost of most final goods. As a result, scarcities of nonfuel minerals do not raise the market price of products very much. Low mineral prices, caused by failure to include the external costs of mining and processing (Figure 19-5), also encourage resource waste, faster depletion, and more pollution and environmental degradation.

Q: What is the largest source of solid waste in the United States?

In the United States, the outdated Mining Law of 1872 encourages mineral extraction on public lands (see Spotlight on p. 338) almost free of charge. Since 1872, individuals or companies have been able to buy public land for $2.50 to $5.00 an acre simply by spending $500 to improve the land for mineral development and filing a claim. Then the owners can extract minerals, pay no royalty to the government (in contrast to the situation with fossil fuels and timber found on public land), and ravage the land and dump toxic chemicals into the environment with little chance of being required by the government to clean up or reclaim the land they have disrupted. Owners can also sell the public land they bought for almost nothing at prices ranging from $200 to $200,000 an acre. According to Senator Dale Bumpers, "The 1872 mining law is a license to steal and the biggest scam in America."

Under this law, miners annually remove $4 billion worth of mineral resources from public lands at taxpayers' expense and have caused at least $300 million in damages to the land with the tab to be picked up by taxpayers. Environmentalists have fought without success to require mining companies to pay fair market values for public land and to pay royalties on minerals removed from such land. They would also be responsible for restoring the land and paying for environmental cleanups resulting from their mining activities.

FINDING NEW LAND-BASED MINERAL DEPOSITS Geologic exploration guided by better geologic knowledge and satellite surveys and other new techniques will increase present reserves of most minerals. In MDCs and many LDCs, however, most of the easily accessible, high-grade deposits have already been discovered. Thus, geologists believe that most new concentrated deposits will be found in unexplored areas in LDCs.

Exploration for new resources requires a large capital investment and is a risky financial venture. Typically, if geologic research identifies 10,000 sites where a deposit of a particular resource might be found, only 1,000 sites are worth costly exploration; only 100 justify even more costly drilling, trenching, or tunneling; and only 1 out of the 10,000 will probably be a producing mine. Even if large new supplies are found, no nonrenewable mineral supply can stand up to continued exponential growth in its use.

IMPROVING MINING TECHNOLOGY AND MINING LOW-GRADE ORE Some analysts assume that all we have to do to increase supplies of any mineral is to mine increasingly lower grades of ore. They point to the development of large earth-moving equipment, techniques for removing impurities, and other advances in mining and processing technology during the past few decades.

For example, these and other technological changes have allowed the average grade of copper ore mined in the United States to fall from about 5% copper by weight in 1900 to 0.4% today, with a drop in the inflation-adjusted copper price. Technological improvements also led to a 500% increase in world copper reserves between 1950 and 1980.

Future advances may increase our ability to extract metals from lower-grade ores. One possibility is the use of microorganisms for in-place (*in situ*) mining, which would remove desired metals from ores while leaving the surrounding environment relatively undisturbed. That would reduce land disturbance and the air and water pollution associated with the smelting of metal ores (Figure 19-5).

Other analysts point out that several factors limit the mining of lower-grade ores. As increasingly poorer ores are mined, energy costs increase sharply. We eventually reach a point where it costs more to mine and process such resources than they are currently worth, unless we have a virtually inexhaustible source of cheap energy.

Available supplies of fresh water also may limit the supply of some mineral resources, because large amounts of water are needed to extract and process most minerals. Many areas with significant mineral deposits are poorly supplied with fresh water.

Finally, exploitation of lower grades of ore may be limited by the environmental impact of waste material produced during mining and processing (Figure 19-5). At some point, the costs of land restoration and pollution control exceed the current value of the minerals.

GETTING MORE MINERALS FROM SEAWATER AND THE OCEAN FLOOR Ocean resources are found in three areas: seawater, sediments and deposits on the shallow continental shelf, and sediments and nodules on the deep-ocean floor. Only magnesium, bromine, and sodium chloride are abundant enough in seawater to be extracted profitably at present prices with current technology.

Continental shelf deposits and placer deposits are already significant sources of sand, gravel, phosphates, and nine other nonfuel mineral resources. Offshore wells also supply large amounts of oil and natural gas (Figure 3-5).

The deep-ocean floor at various sites may be a future source of manganese and other metallic minerals. There are also deposits of metal sulfides of iron, manganese, copper, and zinc around hydrothermal vents found at certain locations on the deep-ocean floor. But concentrations of metals in most of these deposits are too low to be valuable mineral resources.

Environmentalists recognize that seabed mining would probably cause less harm than mining on land. They are concerned, however, that removing seabed mineral deposits and dumping back unwanted material will stir up ocean sediments. That could destroy sea-floor organisms and have unknown effects on poorly understood ocean food webs. Surface waters might also be polluted by the discharge of sediments from mining ships and rigs.

At a few sites on the deep-ocean floor, manganese-rich nodules have been found in large quantities. These cherry- to potato-size rocks contain 30% to 40% by weight manganese, used in certain steel alloys. They also contain small amounts of other strategically important metals, such as nickel, copper, and cobalt. These nodules could be sucked up from the muds of the ocean floor by pipe or scooped up by a continuous cable with buckets and be transported to a mining ship above.

However, most of these nodules are found in seabed sites in international waters. Development of these resources has been put off indefinitely because of squabbles between countries over who owns them.

FINDING SUBSTITUTES Some analysts believe that even if supplies of key minerals become very expensive or scarce, human ingenuity will find substitutes. They point out that new developments by scientists are already leading to a materials revolution in which materials made of silicon and other abundant elements (Figure 19-1) are being substituted for most scarce metals.

For example, ceramic materials are being used in engines, knives, scissors, batteries, and artificial limbs. Ceramics are harder, stronger, lighter, and longer-lasting than many metals. They withstand enormous temperatures, and they do not corrode. Because they can burn fuel at higher temperatures than metal engines, ceramic engines can boost fuel efficiency by 30% to 40%. The cutting edge of ceramic technology is found in Japan.

High-strength plastics and composite materials strengthened by carbon and glass fibers are likely to transform the automobile and aerospace industries. Many of these new materials are stronger and lighter than metals. They cost less to produce because they require less energy, don't need painting, and can easily be molded into any shape.

Substitutes can probably be found for many scarce mineral resources, but finding or developing a substitute is costly, and phasing it into a complex manufacturing process requires a long lead time. While an increasingly scarce mineral is being replaced, people and businesses dependent on it may suffer economic hardships as the price rises sharply.

Finding substitutes for some key materials may be extremely difficult, if not impossible. Examples are helium, phosphorus for phosphate fertilizers, manganese for making steel, and copper for wiring motors and generators.

Another problem is that some substitutes are inferior to the minerals they replace. For example, aluminum could replace copper in electrical wiring, but the energy cost of producing aluminum is much higher than that of producing copper. Aluminum wiring is also more of a fire hazard than copper wiring.

19-6 Wasting Resources: Solid Waste and the Throwaway Approach

SOLID WASTE U.S. residents (followed closely by Canadians) are the most wasteful people on the planet. With only 4.6% of the world's population, the United States produces 33% of the world's **solid waste**: any unwanted or discarded material that is not a liquid or a gas.

While garbage produced directly by households and businesses is a significant problem, about 98.5% of the solid waste in the United States comes from mining, oil and natural gas production, and industrial activities. Although individuals don't generate this waste directly, they generate it indirectly through the products they consume. *Reducing this indirectly produced solid waste, rarely seen by the public, is the real waste crisis caused by a throwaway society.* So far, reduction of this waste has received little public attention.

MUNICIPAL SOLID WASTE The remaining 1.5% of the mass of solid waste produced in the United States is **municipal solid waste** from homes and businesses in or near urban areas. The estimated 168 million metric tons (185 million tons) of municipal solid waste—often referred to as garbage—produced in the United States in 1991 would fill a bumper-to-bumper convoy of garbage trucks that would encircle the earth almost six times.

U.S. consumers throw away enough aluminum to rebuild the country's entire commercial airline fleet every three months. Enough glass bottles are thrown away to fill the 412-meter- (1,350-foot-) high towers of the New York World Trade Center every two weeks. If laid flat, the 247 million tires thrown away each year in the United States would circle the earth almost three times. Each hour, Americans throw away more than 2.5 million nonreturnable plastic bottles. Each year American babies use enough disposable diapers to stretch to the moon and back seven times. Americans receive 60 billion pieces of junk mail a year, most of it tossed away.

The average amount of municipal solid waste thrown away per person in the United States is two to five times that in most other MDCs and is growing. The United States also recycles far less than most other MDCs. Only about 13% of the municipal solid waste produced in the United States is recycled or composted

Q: How much of the world's solid waste is produced by the United States?

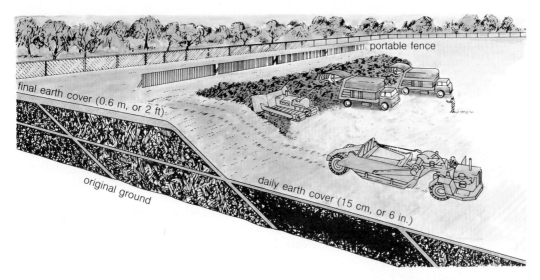

Figure 19-9 A sanitary landfill. Wastes are spread in a thin layer and then compacted with a bulldozer. A scraper (foreground) covers the wastes with a fresh layer of clay or plastic foam at the end of each day. Portable fences catch and hold windblown debris. The world's largest landfill is in Fresh Kills on Staten Island. It is as big as 16,000 baseball diamonds and is the final resting place for 80% of New York City's trash. It is as tall as a 15-story building. When it reaches its capacity, probably around 2005, it will be as tall as a 50-story building. It has no liner, and each day 3.8 million liters (1 million gallons) of contaminated leachate oozes into groundwater beneath Fresh Kills. Fortunately, Staten Island residents do not rely on groundwater for their water supply.

(a form of recycling). The other 87% is hauled away and dumped or burned at a cost of about $6 billion a year.

Litter is also a source of solid waste. For example, helium-filled balloons are released into the atmosphere at sporting events and celebrations. When the helium escapes or the balloons burst, the balloons fall back to Earth as long-lasting litter. Fish, turtles, seals, whales, and other aquatic animals die when they ingest balloons falling into oceans and lakes. This practice also suggests that it is acceptable to litter, waste helium (a scarce resource) and energy used to separate helium from air, and kill wildlife (even if we switched to balloons that biodegraded within six weeks).

WAYS TO DEAL WITH SOLID WASTE There are two basic approaches to dealing with the mountains of solid waste we produce in mining, processing, manufacturing, and using resources. The first is a *throwaway* or *high-waste approach* in which solid wastes are left where they are produced, are buried, or are burned. This temporary output approach is based on using the economic system to encourage waste production and then attempting to manage the wastes in ways that will reduce environmental harm—mostly by removing it from one part of the environment and putting it in another part. We rely primarily on this wasteful and hazardous approach because we use economic systems to reward those who produce and manage waste instead of those who try to use fewer resources and produce less waste.

The second way to deal with solid waste is a *prevention* or *low-waste approach*, based on recycling, reuse,

and waste reduction. This input approach views solid wastes as wasted solids that we should be recycling, reusing, or—in many cases—not producing. With this approach, the economic system is used to discourage waste production.

BURYING SOLID WASTE IN LANDFILLS About 75% by weight of the municipal solid waste in the United States is buried in sanitary landfills, compared with 98% in Australia, 93% in Canada, 90% in Great Britain, 54% in France, 44% in Sweden, 18% in Switzerland, and 16% in Japan. A **sanitary landfill** is a garbage graveyard in which wastes are spread out in thin layers, compacted, and covered with a fresh layer of clay or a plastic foam each day (Figure 19-9).

No open burning is allowed, odor is seldom a problem, and rodents and insects cannot thrive. Sanitary landfills should be located so as to reduce water pollution from leaching, but that is often not done.

A sanitary landfill can be put into operation quickly, has low operating costs, and can handle a huge amount of solid waste. After a landfill has been filled, the land can be graded, planted with grass, and used as a park, a golf course, a ski hill, an athletic field, a wildlife area, or some other recreation area.

While landfills are in operation, there is much traffic, noise, and dust; and most also emit toxic gases. As a result, most people don't want a landfill nearby.

Paper and other biodegradable wastes break down very slowly in today's compacted and water-deficient landfills. Newspapers dug up from some landfills are

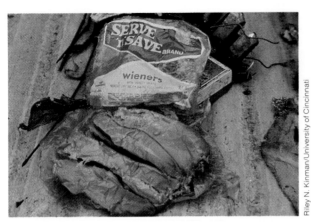

Figure 19-10 Hot dogs after 10 years in a sanitary landfill. The idea that a landfill is a large compost pile in which things biodegrade fairly rapidly is a myth. Decomposition in modern landfills is slow because the garbage is tightly packed and exposed to little moisture and essentially no light. The biggest component in U.S. landfills is paper, which makes up 38% of the volume of waste. That is followed by plastic (18%), metals (14%), yard waste (11%), food (4%), glass (2%), and other materials (13%).

still readable after 30 or 40 years. After 10 years, hot dogs, carrots, and chickens that have been dug up have not been degraded (Figure 19-10). New, expensive biodegradable plastics will take decades to degrade in landfills, are largely a waste of money, and discourage recycling of plastics and reduction in the use of plastics.

The underground anaerobic decomposition of organic wastes at landfills produces explosive methane gas, toxic hydrogen sulfide gas, and smog-forming volatile organic compounds that are emitted into the atmosphere. This problem can be prevented by equipping landfills with vent pipes to collect these gases (Figure 12-20). Besides saving energy, collecting and burning methane gas to produce steam or electricity from all large landfills worldwide would lower atmospheric emissions of methane and help reduce projected global warming from greenhouse gases (Figure 10-6).

When rain filters through a landfill it leaches out inks, water-soluble metal compounds, and other toxic materials. This produces a contaminated leachate that seeps from the bottom of unlined landfills or cracks in the lining of lined landfills. Contamination of groundwater and nearby surface water is a serious problem, especially for thousands of older filled and abandoned landfills that did not have liners.

Modern state-of-the-art landfills (Figure 12-20) can handle municipal waste more safely, but few of them are in operation. Only about 15% of existing landfills in the United States are lined, only 5% collect leachate, and only 25% monitor groundwater.

Sooner or later, even the best-designed landfills leak wastes into water supplies because of liner failure. State-of-the-art landfills *delay* the release of toxic leachate into groundwater below landfills but do not *prevent* it.

Once groundwater is contaminated it is extremely difficult—often impossible—to clean up (Section 11-7). The best landfills merely pass today's garbage and water pollution problems on to the next generation, while avoiding the difficult and necessary choice to emphasize recycling, reuse, and waste reduction and prevention.

Within the next 5 to 10 years, half of the 6,500 landfills in the United States, especially those in the East and the Midwest, will be filled and closed. Few new landfills are being built. Either there are no acceptable sites, costs to build or upgrade landfills to new stricter federal standards (Figure 12-20) are too high ($10 million or more per landfill), or construction is prevented by citizens who want their trash hauled away but don't want a landfill anywhere near them. Forty percent of the municipal landfills in Canada will be filled within 10 years.

Some cities without enough landfill space are shipping their trash to other states or other countries, especially LDCs. However, some states and LDCs are rebelling against becoming the dumping grounds for other people's wastes (Figure 19-11).

BURNING SOLID WASTE Incinerating solid waste kills disease-carrying organisms (pathogens), reduces the volume of waste going to landfills by about 60% (not the 90% usually cited), reduces the need for landfill space, and does not require changes in the throwaway habits of consumers, manufacturers, or waste haulers. Also, once the waste is burned, the original producer of the waste escapes liability.

Proponents call incineration a form of waste reduction. However, instead of reducing the total amount of waste, it puts some of it into the air as gaseous pollutants and produces toxic fly ash and bottom ash that must be landfilled. Although the amount of material to be buried is greatly reduced, its toxicity is increased.

In *trash-to-energy incinerators*, trash is burned and the energy released is used to produce steam or electricity that can be sold or used to run the incinerator. Most are *mass-burn incinerators*, which burn mixed trash without separating out hazardous materials (such as batteries) and noncombustible materials that can interfere with combustion conditions and cause excessive air pollution. Denmark and Sweden burn 50% of their solid waste to produce energy, compared with 15% in the United States.

In the United States, many existing municipal incinerators have been shut down because of numerous air pollution violations and excessive costs. In 1991, there were 128 refuse-to-energy incinerators in operation in the United States and 20 under construction. Since 1985, over 73 new incinerator projects have been blocked, delayed, or canceled because of citizen opposition and high costs. Of the 70 plants still in the planning stage, most face stiff opposition and may not be built as communities are discovering that recycling and

Q: How much municipal solid waste is produced in the United States?

Figure 19-11 There is no away. In 1987, the barge *Mobro* tried to dump 2,900 metric tons (3,190 tons) of garbage picked up from Islip, Long Island. It was refused permission to unload its cargo in North Carolina, Florida, Louisiana, the Bahamas, Mexico, and Honduras. After 164 days and a 9,700-kilometer (6,000-mile) journey, it came back to New York City where it was barred from docking. After remaining in the harbor for three months, its garbage was incinerated in Brooklyn, leaving 364 metric tons (400 tons) of ash, which was shipped back to Islip for burial in a local landfill. The publicity from this event catalyzed Islip into developing a recycling program, and by 1989 the town was recycling 35% of its solid waste. This has saved the community $2 million a year and extended the life of the landfill.

waste reduction are cheaper, safer, and more politically acceptable alternatives.

Incinerators are very expensive to build, operate, and maintain, and they create very few long-term jobs once they are built. Even with advanced air pollution control devices, incinerators emit small amounts of hydrochloric acid, highly toxic dioxins and furans, and tiny particles of nondegradable lead, cadmium, mercury, and other toxic substances into the atmosphere. Without continuous maintenance and good operator training and supervision, the air pollution control equipment on incinerators often fails and exceeds emission standards.

In Japan, incinerator plant operations and emissions are carefully monitored, and violations of air standards are punishable by large fines, plant closings, and—in some cases—jail sentences for company officials. Japanese incinerator workers spend 6 to 18 months learning how the incinerator works, must have an engineering degree, and undergo closely supervised on-site training.

In the United States, monitoring of incinerators is not as strict, and punishment for violations is much less severe. Also, U.S. incinerator workers get far less training and are not required to have engineering degrees. Incineration in the United States is plagued by faulty equipment and errors by human operators that have exposed workers and people in surrounding areas to dangerous levels of air pollution.

Incinerators produce a residue of toxic ash, consisting of toxic *fly ash* (lightweight particles removed from smokestack emissions by air pollution control devices, Figure 9-16) and less toxic *bottom ash*. Usually, the two types of ash are mixed and disposed of in leak-prone ordinary landfills. In the United States, the ash is usually contaminated with hazardous substances such as dioxins and nondegradable lead, cadmium, mercury, and other toxic metals that can cause cancers and nervous system disorders.

Environmentalists have pushed Congress to classify incinerator ash as hazardous waste and allow it to be disposed of only in landfills designed to handle hazardous waste, as is done in Japan. This has not been done, largely because waste management companies say it would make incineration too expensive and put them out of the incineration business. Environmentalists counter that if they aren't willing to properly dispose of the toxic ash they produce, they shouldn't be in the incineration business.

Environmentalists oppose heavy dependence on incinerators because it encourages people to continue tossing away paper, plastics, and other burnable materials rather than looking for ways to conserve, recycle, and reuse those resources and to reduce waste production. Once they are built, incinerators hinder recycling, reuse, and waste reduction because, to be profitable, they must be fueled with a large volume of trash every day. Many existing incinerators have 20- to 30-year contracts with cities to supply them with a certain volume of trash, a procedure that makes it financially difficult for these cities to switch to large-scale recycling.

Incinerators, especially trash-to-energy incinerators, will play a role in a waste management system, because not everything can be recycled. However, environmentalists believe that no new incinerators should be built until a community is recycling *at least 60%* of its municipal solid waste. This allows a much smaller incinerator to be built and saves the community money.

Incinerator and landfill sites are hard to find because of citizen opposition (see Individuals Matter on p. 280). To reduce opposition, waste management companies have targeted poor areas and Native American reservations as sites for landfills and hazardous-waste incinerators—a practice called *toxic racism*.

One of the biggest environmental struggles in the 1990s is between citizens and environmentalists demanding pollution prevention and waste reduction and elected federal officials, the EPA, and waste management companies pushing large-scale incinerators and landfills. Environmentalists charge that these large waste management companies (many of them run or staffed by former EPA officials) have enough economic and political power to keep the country too dependent on end-of-pipe, output approaches to waste management, which hinders the shift to reuse, recycling, and waste reduction.

19-7 Extending Resource Supplies: Recycle, Reuse, Reduce, Rethink

THE LOW-WASTE APPROACH Environmentalists believe we should begin shifting from the high-waste, throwaway approach (Figure 3-21) to a low-waste, sustainable-Earth approach to dealing with nonfuel solid resources (Figure 3-22). This would require much greater emphasis on composting, recycling, reuse, and waste reduction, and much less emphasis on dumping, burying, and burning.

Japan has the world's most comprehensive waste management and recycling program, in which 50% of its municipal solid waste is recycled. About 34% is incinerated, 16% is disposed of in landfills, and 0.2% is composted. In Japan half the paper, 55% of the glass bottles, and 66% of food and beverage cans are recycled. From their earliest school years on, Japanese children are taught about recycling and waste management. They often tour their local recycling centers and incinerators.

COMPOSTING Biodegradable solid waste from slaughterhouses, food-processing plants, and kitchens and yard waste, manure from animal feedlots, and municipal sewage sludge can be mixed with soil and decomposed by aerobic bacteria to produce **compost**, a sweet-smelling, dark-brown humus material that is rich in organic matter and soil nutrients. It can be used as an organic soil fertilizer or conditioner, as topsoil, and as a landfill cover.

Compost can be produced from biodegradable solid waste in large plants, bagged, and sold. This approach is used in many European countries, including the Netherlands, Germany, France, Sweden, and Italy, and in states such as Minnesota and Oregon. Odor problems can be reduced by enclosing the facilities and using filters to deodorize the air inside, but residents near large composting plants complain of unacceptable odors. In 1991, a $30 million composting plant accepting

mixed solid waste built by Agripost in Dade County, Florida, was forced to close because of odor problems.

Households can use backyard compost bins (Figure 12-16) to compost food and yard wastes. Apartment dwellers can compost by using indoor bins in which a type of earthworm converts food waste into humus.

Composting yard waste would reduce the amount of solid waste in the United States by almost 18%. Currently, only 1% of the mass of solid waste in the United States is composted. Locating a city compost heap next to a landfill would reduce the waste going to the landfill and extend its life. The compost can then be applied as landfill cover and used for fertilizing golf courses, parks, forests, roadway medians, and the grounds around public buildings.

HIGH-TECH RESOURCE RECOVERY Resources can be recycled by using high- or low-technology approaches. In *high-technology resource recovery plants*, machines shred and automatically separate mixed urban waste to recover glass, iron, aluminum, and other valuable materials (Figure 19-12). These materials are then sold to manufacturing industries as raw materials for recycling. The remaining paper, plastics, and other combustible wastes are recycled or incinerated. The heat given off is used to produce steam or electricity to run the recovery plant; it can also be sold to nearby industries or residential developments.

Currently, the United States has only a few plants that recover some iron, aluminum, and glass for recycling. The plants are expensive to build and maintain. Once trash is mixed it takes a lot of money and energy to separate it. It makes much more sense economically to have consumers separate trash into recyclable categories before it is picked up.

LOW-TECH RESOURCE RECOVERY With *low-technology resource recovery*, homes and businesses place various kinds of waste materials—usually glass, paper, metals, and plastics—into separate containers. Studies have shown that once people start doing this, it takes no more time than putting garbage into one container. Compartmentalized city collection trucks, private haulers, or volunteer recycling organizations pick up the segregated wastes and sell them to scrap dealers, compost plants, and manufacturers.

A comprehensive low-technology recycling program could save 5% of annual U.S. energy use—more than the energy generated by all U.S. nuclear power plants at perhaps one-hundredth of the capital and operating costs. By contrast, burning all combustible urban solid waste in trash-to-energy plants would supply only 1% of the country's annual energy use.

The low-technology approach produces little air and water pollution, reduces litter, and has low start-up costs and moderate operating costs. It also saves more energy, provides more jobs for unskilled workers than

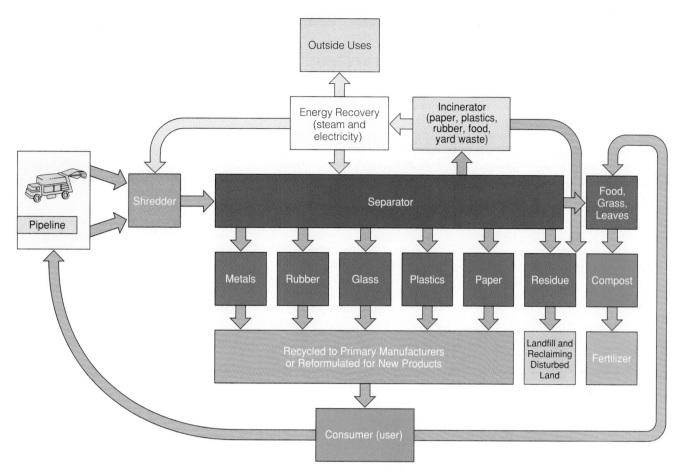

Figure 19-12 Generalized urban resource recovery system used to separate mixed wastes for recycling and burning to produce energy. Very few resource recovery plants of this type exist today. This high-tech approach is much more expensive and wasteful of energy than having consumers separate garbage into categories for recycling. Because resource recovery plants depend on high inputs of trash to be economical, they discourage reuse and waste reduction. For the same reason, trash-to-energy incinerators discourage the recycling of paper, plastics, and other combustible items.

do high-technology resource recovery plants, and creates three to six times more jobs per unit of material than do landfilling or incineration. Another advantage is that collecting and selling aluminum cans (see Case Study on p. 462), paper, plastics (see Case Study on p. 463), and other materials for recycling is an important source of income for volunteer service organizations and for many people, especially the homeless and the poor in MDCs and LDCs.

Many communities are switching to low-tech recycling programs because it can save them money. Ideally, a community should set up one or more materials recovery centers. Each center would have a reuse and repair center, a place for consumers to take household toxic wastes and used motor oil, a composting area, a section for handling commercial waste, and a section in which separated household paper, aluminum, plastics, and iron and other metallic wastes are upgraded and marketed as sources of income for the community.

There are two types of recycling. The most desirable type is *primary* or *closed-loop recycling*, in which a

product such as an aluminum can or a glass bottle is recycled to produce new products of the same type — newspaper into newspaper and cans into cans, for example.

The second and less desirable type, called *secondary* or *open-loop recycling*, occurs when waste materials such as plastics are converted into different products for which uses must be found. Secondary recycling does not reduce the use of resources as much as does primary recycling. For example, primary recycling reduces the use of virgin materials in making a product by 20% to 90%, while the reduction with secondary recycling is 0% to 25%. Paper recycling (Section 15-4) involves a mix of these two methods, depending on the type of paper product produced.

In 1991, Germany enacted the world's toughest packaging law, designed to reduce the amount of waste being landfilled or incinerated. By 1993, companies must take back and recycle all packaging. Incineration of packaging, even if it is used to generate power, is not allowed.

Recycling aluminum produces 95% less air pollution and 97% less water pollution and requires 95% less energy than mining and processing aluminum ore. In the United States, the recycling rate for all aluminum in 1990 was 29%.

In 1990, about 64% of the new aluminum beverage cans used in the United States were recycled at more than 10,000 recycling centers set up by the aluminum industry, other private interests, and local governments.

People who returned the cans got about a penny a can for their efforts, earning about $900 million. Within six weeks, the average recycled aluminum can has been melted down and is back on the market as a new can.

Despite this progress, about 38% of the 83 billion aluminum cans produced in 1990 in the United States were still thrown away; more aluminum is in discarded cans than most countries use for all purposes. If the aluminum cans Americans throw away in one year were laid end-to-end, the cans would wrap around the earth more than 120 times.

Recycling aluminum cans is great, but many environmentalists see the aluminum can as a glaring example of an unnecessary and harmful product, regardless of how many are recycled. They believe that all aluminum cans could be replaced by reusable glass bottles that would be collected, washed, and filled by a nationwide network of local bottlers. That would keep money and jobs in local communities rather than in a few centralized production plants and distributors and would also reduce transportation and energy processing costs.

Placing a heavy tax on each aluminum can and no tax on reusable glass bottles would help correct this situation. Meanwhile, consumers can refuse to buy anything packaged in aluminum cans (or plastic bottles, which are also an unnecessary item) and can buy reusable glass containers when they are available.

BEVERAGE CONTAINER DEPOSIT BILLS Beverage container deposit laws can be used to decrease litter and encourage recycling of nonrefillable glass, metal, and plastic containers. Consumers pay a deposit (usually five or ten cents) on each beverage container they buy. The deposits are refunded when empty containers are turned in to retailers, redemption centers, or reverse vending machines, which return cash when consumers put in empty beverage cans and bottles.

Container deposit laws have been adopted in Sweden, Norway, the Netherlands, the CIS, Ecuador, and parts of Australia, Canada, and Japan. Such laws have been proposed in almost every state in the United States but have been enacted in only 10, with about one-fourth of the U.S. population. Maine has the toughest law. Studies by state and federal agencies show that such laws decrease litter, reduce the use of mineral resources, extend the life of landfills, increase recycling, save energy, reduce air and water pollution, and create jobs.

Environmentalists believe a nationwide deposit law should be passed by Congress. Surveys have also shown that a national container deposit law is supported by 73% of the Americans polled. So far, such a law has been effectively opposed in all but 10 states by a well-funded lobby of steel, aluminum, and glass companies, metalworkers' unions, supermarket chains, and most major brewers and soft-drink bottlers.

Ad campaigns financed by Keep America Beautiful and other groups opposing deposit laws have helped prevent passage of such laws in a number of states. These groups favor litter-recycling laws, which levy a tax on industries whose products may end up as litter or in landfills. Revenues from the tax are used to set up and maintain statewide recycling centers. By 1992, seven states, containing about 14% of the U.S. population, had this type of law.

Environmentalists point out that litter laws are waste management (output) approaches that provide some money to clean up litter. By contrast, container deposit laws are waste reduction (input) approaches that reward consumers who return containers and that can make people aware of the need to shift to refillable containers. This is a main reason that companies making nonrefillable containers oppose such laws.

OBSTACLES TO RECYCLING IN THE UNITED STATES Several factors hinder recycling in the United States. One is that Americans have been conditioned by advertising and example to accept a throwaway lifestyle. Another is that many of the environmental and health costs of items are not reflected in their market prices, so consumers have little incentive to recycle, reuse, or reduce their use of throwaway products.

Another serious problem is that primary mining and energy industries get huge tax breaks, depletion allowances, and other tax-supported federal subsidies to encourage them to get virgin resources out of the ground as fast as possible. In contrast, recycling industries get few tax breaks and other subsidies so there is an uneven economic playing field. In addition, the lack of large, steady markets for recycled materials also makes recycling a risky business. It is a boom-and-bust financial venture that attracts little investment capital.

OVERCOMING THE OBSTACLES In 1988, the EPA set a goal of recycling 25% by weight of municipal solid waste by 1992—a step in the right direction but not

Q: How many tires do Americans throw away each year?

Plastics are synthesized from petrochemicals (chemicals produced from oil). The plastics industry is a leading producer of hazardous waste.

Plastics now account for about 8% of the weight and 20% of the volume of municipal solid wastes in the United States. Most plastics used today are nondegradable or take 200 to 400 years to degrade. In landfills, toxic cadmium and lead compounds used as binders and for other purposes can leach out of plastics and ooze into groundwater and surface water in unlined landfills or ones in which the liners have failed. When plastics are thrown away, they can harm wildlife (Figure 19-13).

Scientists have developed *photodegradable plastics* that disintegrate after a few weeks of exposure to sunlight. *Partially biodegradable plastics* are made with a combination of plastic and cornstarch. The cornstarch can be broken down in the soil by aerobic bacteria and moisture, leaving behind a fine powder of plastic. Instead of being biodegraded, the plastic in these products is merely converted into a plastic dust. Biodegradable plastics take decades to partially decompose in landfills because of a lack of oxygen and moisture. We also need to know more about what degradable plastics degrade to. The chemicals they are broken down to could contaminate groundwater supplies and may be

Figure 19-13 Some of the plastic items we throw away harm wildlife. This Hawaii monk seal was slowly being choked to death by a discarded yoke from a beverage can six-pack before it was saved when the yoke was removed. Before disposing of such yokes, cut each of the holes. Maine has banned plastic yokes.

Doris Alcorn/National Marine Fisheries

hazardous to animals that ingest them.

To environmentalists, it makes good sense to recycle plastics instead of burying slowly degradable plastics in landfills, and it makes even better sense to reduce the amount of plastic we use. In theory, nearly all plastics could be recycled; but currently, less than 2% by weight of all plastic wastes and 5% of plastic packaging used in the United States are recycled.

When the label says that a plastic product is degradable or recyclable, this statement is true, but it is also highly misleading. Plastics degrade very slowly in landfills, and 98% of all plastic waste is not recycled.

With proper economic and political incentives, about 43% by weight of the plastic wastes produced in the United States could be recycled by

2000. Since most of the raw materials used to make plastics come from petroleum and natural gas, recycling would help reduce unnecessary waste of these energy resources.

The $140-billion-a-year U.S. plastics industry has set up the Council for Solid Waste Solutions, which runs ads promoting plastics recycling and has helped set up plastics recycling programs in more than 3,700 U.S. communities. But the main purpose of this organization is to keep us buying more plastics.

To environmentalists, the best solution is simply to use much less plastic in the first place, especially in throwaway items, and to pressure elected officials to ban the use of plastics in products for which other, less-harmful alternatives are available.

enough to reach the 60% recycling level that would bring about a nationwide shift from waste management to waste reduction. By 2000, the United States could recycle and reuse 60% by weight of the municipal solid waste resources it now throws away by instituting the following measures:

- Issue no permits for landfills or incinerators until a community or state has achieved a 60% recycling rate and a program for waste reduction that reduces waste output per person by 20%.

- Enact a national beverage container law.

- Require that all beverage containers have several standardized sizes, forms, and colors so that any bottler can refill bottles produced by other manufacturers.

- Ban use of disposable plastic items and disposable metal, glass, and plastic beverage containers.

- Establish a virgin materials tax.

- Tax manufacturers on the amount of waste they generate by having them pay a tax or fee equal to the cost of landfilling or incineration.

- Include a waste disposal fee in the price of all disposable items (especially batteries, tires, cars, and appliances) so that market prices of items directly reflect what it costs to dispose of those items.

- Require labeling of products made with recycled materials and show the percentages used.

- Require manufacturers to design products to facilitate reuse and primary recycling.

- Provide federal and state subsidies and tax credits for secondary-materials industries and for municipal recycling and waste reduction programs.

- Decrease federal and state subsidies for primary-materials industries.

- Guarantee a large market for recycled items and stimulate the recycling industry by encouraging federal, state, and local governments to require the highest feasible percentage of recycled materials in all products they purchase.

- Use advertising and education to discourage the throwaway mentality.

- Require consumers to sort household wastes for recycling, or give them financial incentives for recycling.

- Establish national standards for calculating and comparing municipal recycling rates (so figures are difficult to inflate).

- Encourage municipal composting and backyard composting by banning the disposal of yard wastes in landfills.

REUSE Recycling is an important first step, but it is still a way of reinforcing the throwaway society — use more and more of Earth's resources but try to recycle some of them. A much more important step is reuse, in which a product is used again and again in its original form. For example, glass beverage bottles can be collected, washed, and refilled by local bottling companies (often as many as 50 or more times) under a system that has now been largely dismantled in the United States.

Today, only 10 states even have returnable bottles. We need to go back to refillable bottles, collected and filled at local bottling plants to reduce transportation and energy costs. This system also creates local jobs and improves the local economy.

To encourage use of refillable bottles, Ecuador has a beverage container deposit fee that is 50% higher than the cost of the drink. This has been so successful that bottles as old as 10 years continue to circulate. Sorting is not a problem because there are only two sizes of glass bottles allowed. In Finland, 95% of the soft drink, beer, wine, and spirits containers are refillable, and in Germany 73% are refillable.

Another reusable container is the metal or plastic lunchbox that most workers and school children once used. Today, many people carry their lunches in paper or plastic bags that are thrown away. At work, people can have their own Earth-care kit consisting of a reusable glass, coffee cup, plate, knife, fork, spoon, cloth napkin, and cloth towel, and they can encourage others to have them as well. These kits can also be taken to fast-food restaurants.

Also reusable are plastic or metal garbage cans and wastebaskets, which we should teach everyone to start

calling *resource containers*. Using these containers to separate wastes for recycling and rinsing them out as needed would eliminate the need to throw any garbage away in plastic bags, which waste oil (because they are made from petrochemicals) and are themselves an unnecessary form of waste. Lining these containers with throwaway plastic bags is an expensive, unnecessary waste of matter and energy resources.

Reuse extends resource supplies and reduces energy use and pollution even more than recycling. Refillable glass bottles are the most energy-efficient beverage containers on the market. Denmark has led the way by banning all beverage containers that can't be reused.

Reuse is much easier if containers for products that can be packaged in reusable glass are available in only a few sizes. In Norway and Denmark, fewer than 20 sizes of reusable containers for beer and soft drinks are allowed. A popular bumper sticker reads: "Recyclers do it more than once." A better version would be "Recyclers do it more than once, but reusers do it the most."

WASTE REDUCTION: REDUCE AND RETHINK

Reducing unnecessary waste of nonrenewable mineral resources, plastics, and paper can extend supplies even more dramatically than recycling and reuse and is the key to making the transition to a sustainable-Earth society. Reducing waste generally saves more energy and virgin resources than recycling and reduces the environmental impacts of extracting, processing, and using resources (Figure 19-5). Table 19-1 compares the throwaway resource system of the United States, a resource recovery and recycling system, and a sustainable-Earth, or low-waste, resource system. Ultimately, a sustainable-Earth resource system is based on this principle: "If you can't recycle or reuse something, don't make it."

Manufacturers can conserve resources by using less material per product and by redesigning manufacturing processes to use fewer resources and produce less waste. Lighter cars, for example, save nonfuel mineral resources as well as energy and can still meet, or exceed, the safety standards required for all cars. Solid-state electronic devices and microwave transmissions greatly reduce materials requirements. Optical fibers drastically reduce the demand for copper wire in telephone transmission lines.

One of the best ways to reduce municipal solid waste is to cut down on unnecessary packaging, which makes up about 50% of the volume and 30% of the weight of municipal waste. Packaging accounts for 50% of all paper produced in the United States, 90% of all glass, 11% of all aluminum, and 3% of all energy used. Americans and Canadians use twice as much packaging per person as in European countries with equal or higher average standards of living.

Packaging should be minimal and, where possible, should be returnable, refillable, reusable. If that is not

Table 19-1 Three Systems for Handling Discarded Materials

Item	For a High-Waste Throwaway System	For a Moderate-Waste Resource Recovery and Recycling System	For a Low-Waste Sustainable-Earth System
Glass bottles	Dump or bury	Grind and remelt; remanufacture; convert to building materials	Ban all nonreturnable bottles. Reuse bottles
Bimetallic "tin" cans	Dump or bury	Sort, remelt	Limit or ban production. Use returnable bottles
Aluminum cans	Dump or bury	Sort, remelt	Limit or ban production. Use returnable bottles
Cars	Dump	Sort, remelt	Sort, remelt. Tax cars lasting less than 15 years and getting less than 17 kilometers per liter (40 miles per gallon)
Metal objects	Dump or bury	Sort, remelt	Sort, remelt. Tax items lasting less than 10 years
Tires	Dump, burn, or bury	Grind and revulcanize or use in road construction; incinerate to generate heat and electricity	Recap usable tires. Tax or ban all tires not usable for at least 96,000 kilometers (60,000 miles)
Paper	Dump, burn, or bury	Incinerate to generate heat	Compost or recycle. Tax all throwaway items. Eliminate overpackaging
Plastics	Dump, burn, or bury	Incinerate to generate heat or electricity	Limit production; use returnable glass bottles instead of plastic containers; tax throwaway items and packaging
Yard wastes	Dump, burn, or bury	Incinerate to generate heat or electricity	Compost; return to soil as fertilizer; use as animal feed

feasible, then the packaging should be recyclable and made from the greatest possible amount of recycled materials. Many products in hardware, grocery, and clothing stores need no packaging.

Another low-waste approach is to make products that last longer. The economies of the United States and most industrial countries are built on the principle of *planned obsolescence* so people will buy more things to stimulate the economy and raise short-term profits, even though that can eventually lead to economic and environmental grief. Many consumers can empathize with Willy Loman in Arthur Miller's *Death of a Salesman:* "Once in my life I would like to own something outright before it's broken! I'm always in a race with the junkyard."

Manufacturers should design products that are easy to reuse, recycle (primary), and repair. Today, many items are intentionally designed to make repair, reuse, or recycling impossible or too expensive. Manufacturers should adopt the principle of modular design, which allows circuits in computers, television sets, and other electronic devices to be replaced easily and quickly without replacing the entire item. We also need to develop remanufacturing industries that would disassemble, repair, and reassemble used and broken items.

To accomplish these goals we must *rethink* the whole idea of a consumer or throwaway society that equates economic growth and well-being with ever-increasing consumption and waste. Such a society is based on depleting Earth capital (Section 2-2).

Adopt the four Rs of Earth care: Reduce, Reuse, Recycle, Rethink. Think of recycling as a first and important baby step in helping sustain the earth. Then move to reuse as part of environmental adolescence. Finally, reach environmental maturity and adopt a sustainable-Earth worldview by sharply reducing the amount of waste you produce; break the trap of defining yourself by your possessions and seeking satisfaction in unneeded things (see Individuals Matter on p. 466).

We will always produce some wastes, but the amount we produce can be greatly reduced by not using wasteful or hazardous products and by redesigning manufacturing processes. To do that, we must force elected officials to get serious about preventing most waste (especially hazardous waste) from being produced or from reaching the environment. So far, less than 1% of the U.S. government's environmental spending goes for pollution prevention and waste reduction.

The end-of-pipe methods for managing wastes that we now depend on merely move potential pollutants from one part of the environment to another and are

- As your top priority, make a conscious effort to produce less waste, mostly by not using disposable paper, plastic, or metal products when other alternatives are available. Before you buy anything, ask yourself whether you really need that product.

- If they are available, buy refillable glass containers for beverages instead of cans or throwaway bottles.

- Use plastic or metal lunchboxes and metal or plastic garbage containers without plastic throwaway bags as liners. Wrap sandwiches in biodegradable wax paper or, better, put them in small reusable plastic containers. Use reusable containers to store food in refrigerators instead of wrapping food in aluminum foil or plastic wrap.

- Use unbleached paper coffee filters to reduce your exposure to toxic dioxins leached out of bleached paper filters. A much better and cheaper solution is to find cloth filters that can be reused or permanent metal filters for drip coffee makers. After use, they should be rinsed and stored in a glass of water in a refrigerator to prevent buildup of rancid coffee oils.

Seventh Generation

Figure 19-14 An example of good earthkeeping. A reusable string bag can be used to carry groceries and other purchases and avoid the use of throwaway paper and plastic bags, both of which are environmentally harmful even if they are recycled. Cloth or canvas bags can also be used.

- Use rechargeable batteries. Manufacturing a standard disposable battery uses 50 times more electricity than the battery generates. The 2.5 billion disposable batteries thrown away each year in the United States are a significant source of toxic metals, such as lead and cadmium, that can leak from landfills.

- Carry groceries and other items in a reusable basket, a canvas or string bag (Figure 19-14), or a small cart. BYOC (bring your own container) is one reason why Europeans, Africans, and Asians produce so much less solid waste per person than most people in the United States. Tell store clerks and managers why

---

eventually overwhelmed by more people producing more wastes. To prevent pollution and reduce waste, we must understand and live by three key principles: Everything is interconnected; there is no away for the wastes we produce; and dilution is not the solution to most pollution.

We can send a powerful message by refusing to buy high-waste, Earth-degrading products and emphasizing purchase of things we truly need. This will catalyze companies into making low-waste, longer-lasting, Earth-sustaining products. This is using the buying power you have to help change the world.

Solid wastes are only raw materials we're too stupid to use.

ARTHUR C. CLARKE

DISCUSSION TOPICS

1. Give some of the ways, positive and negative, that plate tectonics is important to you.

2. Debate each of the following propositions:
   a. The competitive free market will control the supply and demand of mineral resources.
   b. New discoveries will provide all the raw materials we need.
   c. The ocean will supply all the mineral resources we need.
   d. We will not run out of key mineral resources because we can always mine lower-grade deposits.
   e. When a mineral resource becomes scarce, we can always find a substitute.
   f. When a nonrenewable resource becomes scarce, all we have to do is recycle it.

Q: What happens to municipal solid waste in the United States?

you are doing this and increase their sensitivity to unnecessary waste. Ideally, stores would not provide paper or plastic bags, or would charge for them, as is done in the Netherlands.

- Skip the bag when you buy only a quart of milk, a loaf of bread, or anything you can carry out with your hands. Tell store clerks and managers why you are doing this.

- Use washable cloth napkins and dish towels and sponges instead of paper ones.

- Don't use throwaway paper and plastic plates and cups, eating utensils, razors, pens, lighters, and other disposable items when reusable or refillable versions are available.

- Buy recycled goods, especially those made by primary recycling and then recycle them.

- Recycle all newspapers, glass, and aluminum and any other items accepted for recycling in your community.

- If you plan to build a house, consider building highly energy-efficient and less costly earth-ships built mostly from discarded tires, aluminum cans, bottles, and clay as pioneered by architect Michael Reynolds of Taos, New Mexico.

- Buy repairable items and ones that last for a long time.

- Just say no to throwaway plastic items.

- Reduce the amount of junk mail you get by writing to Mail Preference Service, Direct Marketing Association, 11 West 42nd St., P.O. Box 3681, New York, NY 10163-3861, or by calling (212) 768-7277, asking that your name not be sold to large mailing-list companies.

- Push for mandatory trash-separation and recycling programs in your community and schools.

- Support legislation that would ban the transport of garbage from one state or one country to another as a key way to promote recycling, reuse, and waste reduction and make individuals more responsible for and aware of the wastes they produce.

- Push for use of washable, reusable dishes and silverware in school and business cafeterias.

- Ask stores, communities, and colleges to install reverse vending machines that give you cash for each reusable or recyclable container you put in.

- Buy food items in large cans or in bulk to reduce packaging.

- Choose items that have the least packaging or, better yet, no packaging ("nude products").

- Don't buy helium-filled balloons, and urge elected officials and university administrators to ban balloon releases except for atmospheric research and monitoring. Mass releases of helium balloons are now banned in Florida, Connecticut, Tennessee, and Virginia.

- Compost your yard and food wastes (Figure 12-16), and pressure local officials to set up a community composting program.

- Share, barter, trade, or donate items you no longer need.

- Pressure managers of businesses and schools to recycle computer and other office paper and to set up an easy system to encourage in-office recycling.

- Ask heads of companies to switch their letterhead and paper stock to recycled products.

- Copy and write on both sides of the page.

- Consider going into the recycling business as a way to make money.

- Don't litter.

3. Use the second law of energy (thermodynamics) to show why the following options are usually not profitable without subsidies:
   a. Extracting most minerals dissolved in seawater
   b. Recycling minerals that are widely dispersed
   c. Mining increasingly lower-grade deposits of minerals
   d. Using inexhaustible solar energy to mine minerals
   e. Continuing to mine, use, and recycle minerals at increasing rates
   f. Building high-tech resource recovery plants (Figure 19-12) to separate mixed wastes for recycling

4. Explain why you support or oppose the following:
   a. Eliminating all tax breaks and depletion allowances for extraction of virgin resources by mining industries
   b. Passing a national beverage container deposit law

   c. Requiring that all beverage containers be reusable
   d. Requiring all households and businesses to sort recyclable materials for curbside pickup in separate containers
   e. Requiring consumers to pay for plastic or paper bags at grocery and other stores to encourage the use of reusable shopping bags (Figure 19-14)

*5. Determine whether (a) your school and your city have recycling programs; (b) your school sells soft drinks in throwaway cans or bottles; (c) your school bans release of helium-filled balloons at sporting events and other activities; and (d) your state has, or is contemplating, a law requiring deposits on all beverage containers.

EPILOGUE

ACHIEVING A SUSTAINABLE-EARTH SOCIETY

AVOIDING SOME COMMON TRAPS Sustaining the earth requires each of us to make a personal commitment to live an environmentally ethical life. We must do this not because it is required by law but because it is right. It is our responsibility to ourselves, our children and grandchildren, our neighbors, and the earth.

Start by being sure you have not fallen into some common traps or excuses that lead to indifference and inaction:

■ *Gloom-and-doom pessimism:* the belief that the world is doomed by nuclear war or environmental catastrophe, so we should enjoy life while we can.

■ *Blind faith in experts and leaders:* the belief that someone is in charge who knows what to do and will do it without continual pressure and help from ordinary citizens. Usually, the people are far ahead of their political and economic leaders in understanding what must be done and so must organize and lead the leaders.

■ *Blind technological optimism:* the belief that human ingenuity will always be able to come up with technological advances to solve our problems. This most seductive and dangerous trap is something that we would like to believe.

■ *Fatalism:* the belief that whatever will be will be, and we have no control over our actions and the future.

■ *"Why bother?" syndrome:* the belief that even if I do my share, nobody else will, so why should I waste my time and energy trying to make the world a better place?

■ *Extrapolation to infinity:* the belief that "if I can't change the entire world quickly, I won't try to change any of it." This rationalization is reinforced by modern society's emphasis on instant gratification and quick results with as little effort as possible.

All of these traps represent various forms of *denial* that enable us to avoid facing up to problems and the need for change. With our present power to destroy ourselves and most other species, denial is a recipe for disaster. It's like jumping off the top of a tall skyscraper and, as we hurtle past the twentieth floor, proclaiming, "So far, so good. Some new technological breakthrough will save me before I hit the ground."

GROWING UP AS A SPECIES Our species is still in its adolescent phase of development. We can no longer remain at this stage. We must face reality, accept our responsibility to sustain and heal the earth, and become a mature species. That means we can no longer view the world in terms of "we" and "they." Instead, there is only "us"—a diverse, global community of interacting and interdependent individuals, cultures, and species.

This begins by recognizing that the earth's environment is not only around us it is also within us. We live in the environment and it lives in us. We are made of it. We eat, drink, and breathe it. Because of our complete dependence on and oneness with nature, we must leave the earth undiminished for ourselves, our children and grandchildren, and all other creatures. To do this means that we must rethink everything we do in our daily lives.

Instead of succumbing to despair and denial, we should rejoice that this generation can make a planetary transformation and avoid environmental disaster by abandoning our aggression against each other and the planet. No future generation will have this chance; if we don't do the job now, future humans and other species will have to exist on an earth that we have impoverished.

BECOMING EARTH CITIZENS: THE EARTH SUSTAINING DOZEN The good news is that we can sustain the earth and lead more meaningful and joyful lives. Begin yourself by doing 12 things.

1. **Evaluate the way you think the world works and sensitize yourself to your local environment.** Look around, experience what is going on in the environment around you, compare what is with what could and should be. Where do the water you drink and the air you breathe come from? What kind of soil is around where you live? Where does your garbage go? What forms of wild plants and animals live around you? Which species have become extinct in your area, and which ones are threatened with extinction? What is the past history of land use in your area and what are the

projected future uses of this land? What are your environmental bad habits? What is your world-view? How does your worldview influence the way you act?

2. **Become ecologically informed.** Immerse yourself in sustainable-Earth thinking by looking for connections between everything we do and Earth's ecological health and sustainability for us and other species. Specialize in one particular area of environmental knowledge and awareness, relate it to sustainable-Earth thinking, and share your knowledge and understanding with others (networking). Consider going into an environmental profession (see Spotlight on p. 163) or starting or working in an environmentally responsible business, buy green products (see Individuals Matter on p. 154), and invest only in green companies. Keep in mind Norman Cousins' statement: "The first aim of education should not be to prepare young people for careers, but to enable them to develop respect for life."

3. **Become emotionally involved in caring for the earth by experiencing nature directly and by trying to find a place that you love and must defend because you are part of it and it is part of you.** Intellectual ecological knowledge of how the world works is vitally important. However, it will not be enough to bring about a change in the way you live unless it is combined with a sense of place — a feeling of oneness and rootedness with, and thankfulness for, some piece of the earth that you experience, love, and respect. Care for one piece of land — a yard, a neighborhood lot or park, a stream. Poet-philosopher Gary Snyder urges us to "find our place on the planet, dig in, and take responsibility from there."

4. **Choose a simpler lifestyle by reducing resource consumption and waste and pollution production.** Distinguish between your true needs and your wants and use trade-offs. For every high-energy, high-waste, or highly polluting thing you do (buying a car, living or working in an air-conditioned building), give up a number of other things. Such a lifestyle based on voluntary simplicity (not forced poverty) will be less expensive and should bring you joy as you learn how to walk more gently on the earth.

5. **Focus especially on energy use and energy waste.** Recognize that energy — the integrating theme of this book — is the currency of life for us and other species. People in MDCs have achieved their higher standards of living primarily by increasing their use of energy (Figure 2-1). At the same time, our rapid depletion of Earth's one-time deposit of fossil fuels is the primary cause of most air pollution, water pollution, land degradation, and international tension over control of dwindling oil supplies. Fossil fuels also give us more energy to rapidly clear forests and degrade other ecosystems that are homes for Earth's vital biodiversity. These

fuels are also used to produce petrochemicals that in turn are used to produce the plastics, pesticides, solvents, chlorofluorocarbons, and thousands of other hazardous, and often slowly degradable, chemicals and products we are dumping into the environment.

Thus, any effective efforts to sustain and heal the earth must be built around two things that must be carried out at the individual, local, national, and global levels within your lifetime. First, we must waste as little energy as possible. By doing this we are expressing our love of and connection to current and future life on Earth. One of the most serious threats to the earth is that American society unnecessarily wastes at least half of the energy it uses. Second, we must shift from lifestyles and economies built around the use of nonrenewable fossil and nuclear fuels to ones built around perpetual and renewable energy from the sun, wind, falling and flowing water, sustainable burning of biomass, and Earth's interior heat.

6. **Become more self-sustaining by trying to unhook yourself from dependence on large, centralized systems for your water, energy, food, and livelihood.** You can do this in the country or in the city. Use organic, intensive gardening techniques to grow some of your own food in a small plot, roof garden, or window box planter. Get as much of your energy as possible from renewable sources such as the sun, wind, water, or biomass. Move closer to work or try to work at home.

7. **Remember that environment begins at home.** Before you start trying to convert others, begin by changing your own living patterns. If you become an Earth citizen, be prepared to have everyone looking for, and pointing out, your own environmental sins. Your actions force people to look at what they are doing — a threatening process that disrupts the denial syndrome. People are most influenced by what we do, not by what we say.

8. **Become politically involved on local and national levels.** Start or join a local environmental group, and also join and financially support national and global environmental and conservation organizations whose causes you believe in (see Appendix). Work to elect sustainable-Earth leaders and to influence officials once they are elected to public office. Remember that change takes place from the bottom up based on actions by ordinary citizens.

9. **Do the little things based on thinking globally and acting locally.** Environmental problems are caused by quadrillions of small, unthinking actions by billions of people. They'll be cured by quadrillions of small, environmentally beneficial actions that you and others substitute for the thoughtless and wasteful ones. Recycle and, better yet, reuse things; don't waste energy (see Individuals Matter inside the back cover); improve the energy efficiency of your house; don't use electricity to heat space or household water; drive a car that

gets at least 17 kilometers per liter (40 miles per gallon); join a car pool; use mass transit; ride a bicycle to work; replace incandescent lights with new energy-efficient light bulbs; turn off unnecessary lights; plant trees; have a compost pile; help restore a damaged part of the earth; eat lower on the food chain by reducing or eliminating your consumption of meat (especially beef and pork); grow food organically; shop at farmers' markets and food co-ops instead of relying on packaged and prepared foods; don't waste water (see Individuals Matter inside the back cover); choose to have no more than one or, at most, two children, and teach any child you have to sustain the earth; write on both sides of a piece of paper; don't discard useful clothing and other items and buy new ones just to be fashionable; don't buy overpackaged products; distinguish between your needs and your wants before you buy anything; reduce use of, recycle, and reuse matter resources; buy products from, invest in, or work for companies that are working to sustain the earth.

Each of these small measures sensitizes you to Earth-sustaining acts and leads to more such acts. Each of these individual actions is also a small-scale economic and political decision that, when coupled with actions of others, leads to larger-scale political and economic changes.

10. **Work on the big polluters and big problems, primarily through political action, economic boycotts, and selective consumption.** Individual actions help reduce pollution and environmental degradation, give us a sense of involvement, and help us develop a badly needed Earth consciousness. Our awareness must then expand to recognize that large-scale pollution and environmental degradation are caused by industries, governments, and big agriculture driven by overemphasis on short-term economic gain that eventually leads to economic and environmental grief for us and premature extinction for many other species. Recognize that Love Canal, Bhopal, Chernobyl, and the *Exxon Valdez* spill are forms of pollution and environmental degradation that could have been prevented by spending a relatively small amount of money. Earth care is self-care. The ethic of the international Greenpeace movement is "not only to personally bear witness to atrocities against life; it is to take direct nonviolent action to prevent them."

11. **Start a movement of awareness and action.** You can change the world by changing the two people next to you. For everything, big or little, that you decide to do to help sustain the earth, try to persuade two others to do the same thing, and encourage them in turn to persuade two others. Carrying out this doubling or exponential process only 24.5 times would persuade everyone in the United States, and doing it 28.5 times would persuade everyone in the world. However, only about 5% to 10% of the people in a community, a state, a country, or the world need to be actively involved to bring about change. Get involved and become a part of the solution instead of a part of the problem.

12. **Don't make people feel guilty.** If you know people who are overconsuming or carrying out environmentally harmful acts, don't make them feel bad. Instead, lead by example and find the things that others are willing to do to sustain the earth. There is plenty to do, and no one can do everything. Use positive rather than negative reinforcement. We need to nurture, reassure, understand, and love, rather than to threaten, one another.

It is not too late. There is time to deal with the complex, interacting problems we face and to make an orderly rather than catastrophic transition to a sustainable-Earth society, if enough of us really care. It's not up to "them," it's up to "us." Don't wait.

Make a difference by caring. Care about the air, water, soil. Care about wild plants, wild animals, wild places. Care about people—young, old, handicapped, black, white, brown—in this generation and generations to come. Let this caring be your guide for doing. Live your life caring about the earth and you will be fulfilled.

Envision the world as made up of all kinds of matter cycles and energy flows. See these life-sustaining processes as a beautiful and diverse web of interrelationships—a kaleidoscope of patterns and rhythms whose very complexity and multitude of potentials remind us that cooperation, honesty, humility, and love must be the guidelines for our behavior toward one another and the earth.

When there is no dream, the people perish.

PROVERBS 29:18

470

PUBLICATIONS, ENVIRONMENTAL ORGANIZATIONS, AND FEDERAL AND INTERNATIONAL AGENCIES

Publications

The following publications can help you keep well informed and up to date on environmental and resource problems. Subscription prices, which tend to change, are not given.

Ambio: A Journal of the Human Environment Royal Swedish Academy of Sciences, Box 50005, S-104 05 Stockholm, Sweden.

American Forests American Forestry Association, 1516 P St. NW, Washington, DC 20005.

American Journal of Alternative Agriculture 9200 Edmonston Rd., Suite 117, Greenbelt, MD 20770.

Amicus Journal Natural Resources Defense Council, 122 E. 42nd St., New York, NY 10168.

Annual Review of Energy Department of Energy, Forrestal Building, 1000 Independence Ave. SW, Washington, DC 20585.

Audubon National Audubon Society, 950 Third Ave., New York, NY 10022.

Audubon Wildlife Report National Audubon Society, 950 Third Ave., New York, NY 10022. Published every two years.

Biologue National Wood Energy Association, 1730 North Lynn St., Suite 610, Arlington, VA 22209

Bioscience American Institute of Biological Sciences, 730 11th St. NW, Washington, DC 20001.

Buzzworm P.O. Box 6853, Syracuse, NY 13217-7930.

The CoEvolution Quarterly P.O. Box 428, Sausalito, CA 94965.

Conservation Biology Blackwell Scientific Publications, Inc., 52 Beacon St., Boston, MA 02108.

Demographic Yearbook Department of International Economic and Social Affairs, Statistical Office, United Nations Publishing Service, United Nations, NY 10017.

Earth Island Journal Earth Island Institute, 300 Broadway, Suite 28, San Francisco, CA 94133.

Earth Journal: Environmental Almanac and Resource Directory Buzzworm, Inc., 2305 Canyon Blvd., Suite 206, Boulder, CO 80302. Published annually.

The Ecologist MIT Press Journals, 55 Hayward St., Cambridge, MA 02142.

Ecology Ecological Society of America, Dr. Duncan T. Patten, Center for Environmental Studies, Arizona State University, Tempe, AZ 85281.

E Magazine P.O. Box 5098, Westport, CT 06881.

Environment Heldref Publications, 4000 Albemarle St. NW, Washington, DC 20016.

Environment Abstracts Bowker A & I Publishing, 245 W. 17th St., New York, NY 10011. In most libraries.

Environmental Action 6930 Carroll Park, 6th Floor, Takoma Park, MD 20912.

Environmental Almanac Annual compilation by the World Resources Institute. Published by Houghton Mifflin (Boston).

Environmental Engineering News School of Civil Engineering, Purdue University, West Lafayette, IN 47907.

Environmental Ethics Department of Philosophy, University of North Texas, Denton, TX 76203.

The Environmental Professional Editorial Office, Department of Geography, University of Iowa, Iowa City, IA 52242.

EPA Journal Environmental Protection Agency. Order from Government Printing Office, Washington, DC 20402.

Everyone's Backyard Citizens' Clearinghouse for Hazardous Waste, P.O. Box 926, Arlington, VA 22216.

The Futurist World Future Society, P.O. Box 19285, Twentieth Street Station, Washington, DC 20036.

Garbage: The Practical Journal for the Environment P.O. Box 56520, Boulder, CO 80321-6520.

Greenpeace Magazine Greenpeace USA, 1436 U St. NW, Washington, DC 20009.

In Context Box 11470, Bainbridge Island, WA 98110.

International Environmental Affairs University Press of New England, 17½ Lebanon St., Hanover, NH 03755.

Issues in Science and Technology National Academy of Sciences, 2101 Constitution Ave. NW, Washington, DC 20077-5576.

Journal of Environmental Education Heldref Publications, 4000 Albemarle St. NW, Suite 504, Washington, DC 20016.

Journal of Environmental Health National Environmental Health Association, 720 S. Colorado Blvd., Suite 970, Denver, CO 80222.

Journal of Pesticide Reform P.O. Box 1393, Eugene, OR 97440.

National Geographic National Geographic Society, P.O. Box 2895, Washington, DC 20077-9960.

National Parks and Conservation Magazine National Parks and Conservation Association, 1015 31st St. NW, Washington, DC 20007.

National Wildlife National Wildlife Federation, 1400 16th St. NW, Washington, DC 20036.

Natural Resources Journal University of New Mexico School of Law, 1117 Stanford NE, Albuquerque, NM 87131.

Nature 711 National Press Building, Washington, DC 20045.

The New Farm Rodale Research Center, Emmaus, PA 18049.

New Scientist 128 Long Acre, London, WC 2, England.

Newsline Natural Resources Defense Council, 122 E. 42nd St., New York, NY 10168.

Not Man Apart Friends of the Earth, 530 Seventh St. SE, Washington, DC 20003.

One Person's Impact P.O. Box 751, Westborough, MA 01581.

Organic Gardening & Farming Magazine Rodale Press, Inc., 33 E. Minor St., Emmaus, PA 18049.

Orion Nature Quarterly P.O. Box 2130, Knoxville, IA 50198-7130.

Pollution Abstracts Cambridge Scientific Abstracts, 7200 Wisconsin Ave., Bethesda, MD 20814. Found in many libraries.

Population Bulletin Population Reference Bureau, 1875 Connecticut Ave. NW, Suite 520, Washington, DC 20009.

Rachel's Hazardous Waste News Environmental Research Foundation, P.O. Box 73700, Washington, DC 20056-3700.

Renewable Energy News Solar Vision, Inc., 7 Church Hill, Harrisville, NH 03450.

Renewable Resources 5430 Grosvenor Lane, Bethesda, MD 20814.

Rocky Mountain Institute Newsletter 1739 Snowmass Creek Rd., Snowmass, CO 81654.

Science American Association for the Advancement of Science, 1333 H St. NW, Washington, DC 20005.

Science News Science Service, Inc., 1719 N St. NW, Washington, DC 20036.

Scientific American 415 Madison Ave., New York, NY 10017.

Sierra 730 Polk St., San Francisco, CA 94108.

State of the World Worldwatch Institute, 1776 Massachusetts Ave. NW, Washington, DC 20036. Published annually.

Statistical Yearbook Department of International Economic and Social Affairs, Statistical Office, United Nations Publishing Service, United Nations, New York, NY 10017.

Technology Review Room E219-430, Massachusetts Institute of Technology, Cambridge, MA 02139.

Transition Laurence G. Wolf, ed., Department of Geography, University of Cincinnati, Cincinnati, OH 45221.

The Trumpeter Journal of Ecosophy P.O. Box 5883 St. B, Victoria, B.C., Canada V8R 6S8.

Vegetarian Journal P. O. Box 1463, Baltimore, MD 21203.

Wilderness The Wilderness Society, 1400 I St. NW, 10th Floor, Washington, DC 20005.

Wildlife Conservation New York Zoological Society, 185th St. and Southern Boulevard, Bronx, NY 10460.

World Rainforest Report Rainforest Action Network, 300 Broadway, Suite 298, San Francisco, CA 94133.

World Resources World Resources Institute, 1735 New York Ave. NW, Washington, DC 20006. Published every two years.

World Watch Worldwatch Institute, 1776 Massachusetts Ave. NW, Washington, DC 20036.

Worldwatch Papers Worldwatch Institute, 1776 Massachusetts Ave. NW, Washington, DC 20036.

Yearbook of World Energy Statistics Department of International Economic and Social Affairs, Statistical Office, United Nations Publishing Service, United Nations, New York, NY 10017.

Environmental and Resource Organizations

For a more detailed list of national, state, and local organizations, see Conservation Directory, *published annually by the National Wildlife Federation, 1400 16th St. NW, Washington, DC 20036;* Your Resource Guide to Environmental Organizations *(Irvine, CA: Smiling Dolphin Press, 1991); and* World Directory of Environmental Organizations, *published by the California Institute of Public Affairs, P.O. Box 10, Claremont, CA 91711.*

Acid Rain Foundation 1410 Varsity Dr., Raleigh, NC 27606.

African Wildlife Foundation 1717 Massachusetts Ave. NW, Washington, DC 20036.

Alan Guttmacher Institute 2010 Massachusetts Ave. NW, 5th Floor, Washington, DC 20036.

Alliance for Chesapeake Bay 6600 York Rd., Baltimore, MD 21212.

Alliance to Save Energy 1925 K St. NW, Washington, DC 20006-1401.

American Cetacean Society P.O. Box 2639, San Pedro, CA 90731-0943.

American Council for an Energy Efficient Economy 1001 Connecticut Ave. NW, Suite 535, Washington, DC 20013.

American Forestry Association 1516 P St. NW, Washington, DC 20005.

American Geographical Society 156 Fifth Ave., Suite 600, New York, NY 10010.

American Institute of Biological Sciences, Inc. 730 11th St. NW, Washington, DC 20001.

American Rivers 801 Pennsylvania Ave. SE, Suite 303, Washington, DC 20003.

American Society for the Prevention of Cruelty to Animals (ASPCA) 441 E. 92nd Street, New York, NY 10128.

American Solar Energy Society 859 W. Morgan St., Raleigh, NC 27603.

American Water Resources Association 5410 Grosvenor Lane, Suite 220, Bethesda, MD 20814.

American Wilderness Alliance 7500 E. Arapahoe Rd., Suite 114, Englewood, CO 80112.

American Wildlife Association 1717 Massachusetts Ave. NW, Washington, DC 20036.

American Wind Energy Association 1730 N. Lynn St., Suite 610, Arlington, VA 22209.

Appropriate Technology International 1331 H St. NW, Washington, DC 20005.

Bat Conservation International P.O. Box 162603, Austin, TX 78716.

Bio-Integral Resource Center P.O. Box 8267, Berkeley, CA 94707.

Bioregional Project (North American Bioregional Congress) Turtle Island Office, 1333 Overhulse Rd. NE, Olympia, WA 98502.

Carrying Capacity 1325 G St. NW, Washington, DC 20005.

Center for Conservation Biology Department of Biological Sciences, Stanford University, Stanford, CA 94305.

Center for Marine Conservation 1725 DeSales St. NW, Suite 500, Washington, DC 20036.

Center for Science in the Public Interest 1501 16th St. NW, Washington, DC 20036.

Chipko P.O. Silyara via Ghansale, Tehri-Garwhal, Utar Pradesh, 249155 India.

Citizens' Clearinghouse for Hazardous Waste P.O. Box 926, Arlington, VA 22216.

Clean Water Action 317 Pennsylvania Ave. SE, Washington, DC 20003.

Conservation Foundation 1250 24th St. NW, Suite 500, Washington, DC 20037.

Council for Economic Priorities 30 Irving Pl., New York, NY 10003.

Council for Solid Waste Solutions 275 K St. NW, Suite 400, Washington, DC 20005.

Cousteau Society 930 W. 21st St., Norfolk, VA 23517.

Critical Mass Energy Project 215 Pennsylvania Ave. SE, Washington, DC 20003.

Cultural Survival 11 Divinity Ave., Cambridge, MA 02138.

Defenders of Wildlife 1244 19th St. NW, Washington, DC 20036.

Ducks Unlimited One Waterfowl Way, Long Grove, IL 60047.

Earth First! 305 N. Sixth St., Madison, WI 53704.

Earth Island Institute 300 Broadway, Suite 28, San Francisco, CA 94133.

Earthsave 706 Frederick St., Santa Cruz, CA 95062-2205.

Earthscan 1717 Massachusetts Ave. NW, Washington, DC 20036.

Earthwatch 680 Mt. Auburn St., Box 403N, Watertown, MA 02272.

Elmwood Institute P.O. Box 5805, Berkeley, CA 94705.

Energy Conservation Coalition 1525 New Hampshire Ave. NW, Washington, DC 20036.

Environmental Action, Inc. 6930 Carroll Park, 6th Floor, Takoma Park, MD 20912.

Environmental Defense Fund, Inc. 257 Park Ave. South, New York, NY 10010.

Environmental Law Institute 1616 P St. NW, Suite 200, Washington, DC 20036.

Environmental Policy Institute 218 D St. SE, Washington, DC 20003.

Food First (Institute for Food and Development Policy) 145 Ninth St., San Francisco, CA 94103.

Friends of Animals P.O. Box 1244, Norwalk, CT 06856.

Friends of the Earth 218 D St. SE, Washington, DC 20003.

Friends of the Trees P.O. Box 1466, Chelan, WA 98816.

Fund for Animals 200 W. 57th St., New York, NY 10019.

Global Greenhouse Network 1130 17th St. NW, Suite 530, Washington, DC 20036.

Global Tomorrow Coalition 1325 G St. NW, Suite 915, Washington, DC 20005.

Greenhouse Crisis Foundation 1130 17th St. NW, Suite 630, Washington, DC 20036.

Greenpeace, USA, Inc. 1436 U St. NW, Washington, DC 20009.

Green Seal 1733 Connecticut Ave. NW, Washington, DC 20009.

Humane Society of the United States, Inc. 2100 L St. NW, Washington, DC 20037.

INFORM 381 Park Ave. South, New York, NY 10016.

Institute for Alternative Agriculture 9200 Edmonston Rd., Suite 117, Greenbelt, MD 20770.

Institute for Local Self-Reliance 2425 18th St. NW, Washington, DC 20009.

International Alliance for Sustainable Agriculture 1201 University Ave. SE, Suite 202, Minneapolis, MN 55414.

International Planned Parenthood Federation 105 Madison Ave., 7th Floor, New York, NY 10016.

Izaak Walton League of America 1401 Wilson Blvd., Level B, Arlington, VA 22209.

Land Institute Route 3, Salina, KS 67401.

League of Conservation Voters 2000 L St. NW, Suite 804, Washington, DC 20036.

League of Women Voters of the U.S. 1730 M St. NW, Washington, DC 20036.

National Audubon Society 950 Third Ave., New York, NY 10022.

National Clean Air Coalition 801 Pennsylvania Ave. SE, Washington, DC 20003.

National Coalition Against the Misuse of Pesticides 530 Seventh St. SE, Washington, DC 20001.

National Environmental Health Association 720 S. Colorado Blvd., Suite 970, Denver, CO 80222.

National Geographic Society 17th and M Sts. NW, Washington, DC 20036.

National Parks and Conservation Association 1015 31st St. NW, 4th Floor, Washington, DC 20007.

National Recreation and Park Association 3101 Park Center Dr., 12th Floor, Alexandria, VA 22302.

National Recycling Coalition 1101 30th St. NW, Suite 304, Washington, DC 20007.

National Solid Waste Management Association 1730 Rhode Island Ave. NW, Suite 100, Washington, DC 20036.

National Toxics Campaign 29 Temple Pl., 5th Floor, Boston, MA 02111.

National Wildlife Federation 1400 16th St. NW, Washington, DC 20036.

National Wood Energy Association 1730 N. Lynn St., Suite 610, Arlington, VA 22209.

Natural Resources Defense Council 40 W. 20th St., New York, NY 10011, and 1350 New York Ave. NW, Suite 300, Washington, DC 20005.

Nature Conservancy 1814 N. Lynn St., Arlington, VA 22209.

New Alchemy Institute 237 Hatchville Rd., East Falmouth, MA 02536.

Nuclear Information and Resource Service 1424 16th St. NW, Suite 601, Washington, DC 20036.

The Oceanic Society 218 D St. SE, Washington, DC 20003.

Permaculture Association P.O. Box 202, Orange, MA 01364.

Permaculture Institute of North America 4649 Sunnyside Ave. N, Seattle, WA 98103.

Planetary Citizens 325 Ninth St., San Francisco, CA 94103.

Planet/Drum Foundation P.O. Box 31251, San Francisco, CA 94131.

Planned Parenthood Federation of America 810 Seventh Ave., New York, NY 10019.

Population Crisis Committee 1120 19th St. NW, Suite 530, Washington, DC 20036-3605.

Population-Environment Balance 1325 G St. NW, Washington, DC 20005

Population Institute 110 Maryland Ave. NE, Suite 207, Washington, DC 20036.

Population Reference Bureau 1875 Connecticut Ave. NW, Suite 520, Washington, DC 20009-5728.

Public Citizen 215 Pennsylvania Ave. SE, Washington, DC 20003.

Rainforest Action Network 300 Broadway, Suite 29A, San Francisco, CA 94133.

Rainforest Alliance 270 Lafayette St., Suite 512, New York, NY 10012.

Renewable Natural Resources Foundation 5430 Grosvenor Lane, Bethesda, MD 20814.

Renew America 1001 Connecticut Ave. NW, Suite 719, Washington, DC 20036.

Resources for the Future 1616 P St. NW, Washington, DC 20036.

Rocky Mountain Institute 1739 Snowmass Creek Rd., Snowmass, CO 81654.

Rodale Research Center 222 Main St., Emmaus, PA 18098.

Save America's Forests 4 Library Court SE, Washington, DC 20003.

Scientists' Institute for Public Information 355 Lexington Ave., New York, NY 10017.

Sea Shepherd Conservation Society P.O. Box 7000-S, Redondo Beach, CA 90277.

Sierra Club 730 Polk St., San Francisco, CA 94109, and 408 C St. NE, Washington, DC 20002.

Smithsonian Institution 1000 Jefferson Dr. SW, Washington, DC 20560.

Social Investment Forum C.E.R.E.S. Project, 711 Atlantic Ave., Boston, MA 02111.

Society of American Foresters 5400 Grosvenor Lane, Bethesda, MD 20814.

Soil and Water Conservation Society 7515 N.E. Ankeny Rd., Ankeny, IA 50021.

Student Conservation Association, Inc. P.O. Box 550, Charlestown, NH 03603.

Student Environmental Action Coalition (SEAC) 217 A Carolina Union, University of North Carolina, Chapel Hill, NC 27599.

Tree People 12601 Mulholland Dr., Beverly Hills, CA 90210.

Union of Concerned Scientists 26 Church St., Cambridge, MA 02238.

U.S. Public Interest Research Group 215 Pennsylvania Ave. SE, Washington, DC 20003.

The Wilderness Society 900 17th St. NW, Washington, DC 20006.

Windstar Foundation 2317 Snowmass Creek Rd., Snowmass, CO 81654.

Work on Waste 82 Judson St., Canton, NY 13617.

World Future Society 4916 St. Elmo Ave., Bethesda, MD 20814.

World Resources Institute 1735 New York Ave. NW, Washington, DC 20006.

Worldwatch Institute 1776 Massachusetts Ave. NW, Washington, DC 20036.

World Wildlife Fund 1250 24th St. NW, Suite 500, Washington, DC 20037.

Zero Population Growth 1400 16th St. NW, 3rd Floor, Washington, DC 20036.

Addresses of Federal and International Agencies

Agency for International Development State Building, 320 21st St. NW, Washington, DC 20523.

Bureau of Land Management U.S. Department of Interior, 18th and C Sts., Room 3619, Washington, DC 20240.

Bureau of Mines 2401 E St. NW, Washington, DC 20241.

Bureau of Reclamation Washington, DC 20240.

Congressional Research Service 101 Independence Ave. SW, Washington, DC 20540.

Conservation and Renewable Energy Inquiry and Referral Service P.O. Box 8900, Silver Spring, MD 20907, (800) 523-2929.

Consumer Product Safety Commission Washington, DC 20207.

Council on Environmental Quality 722 Jackson Pl. NW, Washington, DC 20006.

Department of Agriculture 14th St. and Jefferson Dr. SW, Washington, DC 20250.

Department of Commerce 14th St. between Constitution Ave. and E St. NW, Washington, DC 20230.

Department of Energy Forrestal Building, 1000 Independence Ave. SW, Washington, DC 20585.

Department of Health and Human Services 200 Independence Ave. SW, Washington, DC 20585.

Department of Housing and Urban Development 451 Seventh St. SW, Washington, DC 20410.

Department of the Interior 18th and C Sts. NW, Washington, DC 20240.

Department of Transportation 400 Seventh St. SW, Washington, DC 20590.

Environmental Protection Agency 401 M St. SW, Washington, DC 20460.

Federal Energy Regulatory Commission 825 N. Capitol St. NE, Washington, DC 20426.

Fish and Wildlife Service Department of the Interior, 18th and C Sts. NW, Washington, DC 20240.

Food and Agriculture Organization (FAO) of the United Nations 101 22nd St. NW, Suite 300, Washington, DC 20437.

Food and Drug Administration Department of Health and Human Services, 5600 Fishers Lane, Rockville, MD 20852.

Forest Service P.O. Box 96090, Washington, DC 20013.

Government Printing Office Washington, DC 20402.

Inter-American Development Bank 1300 New York Ave. NW, Washington, DC 20577.

International Whaling Commission The Red House, 135 Station Rd., Histon, Cambridge CB4 4NP England 02203 3971.

Marine Mammal Commission 1625 I St. NW, Washington, DC 20006.

National Academy of Sciences Washington, DC 20550.

National Aeronautics and Space Administration 400 Maryland Ave. SW, Washington, DC 20546.

National Cancer Institute 9000 Rockville Pike, Bethesda, MD 20892.

National Center for Appropriate Technology 3040 Continental Dr., Butte, MT 59701.

National Center for Atmospheric Research P.O. Box 3000, Boulder, CO 80307.

National Marine Fisheries Service U.S. Dept. of Commerce, NOAA, 1335 East-West Highway, Silver Spring, MD 20910.

National Oceanic and Atmospheric Administration Rockville, MD 20852.

National Park Service Department of the Interior, P.O. Box 37127, Washington, DC 20013.

National Science Foundation 1800 G St. NW, Washington, DC 20550.

National Solar Heating and Cooling Information Center P.O. Box 1607, Rockville, MD 20850.

National Technical Information Service U.S. Department of Commerce, 5285 Port Royal Rd., Springfield, VA 22161.

Nuclear Regulatory Commission 1717 H St. NW, Washington, DC 20555.

Occupational Safety and Health Administration Department of Labor, 200 Constitution Ave. NW, Washington, DC 20210.

Office of Ocean and Coastal Resource Management 1825 Connecticut Ave., Suite 700, Washington, DC 20235.

Office of Surface Mining Reclamation and Enforcement 1951 Constitution Ave. NW, Washington, DC 20240.

Office of Technology Assessment U.S. Congress, 600 Pennsylvania Ave. SW, Washington, DC 20510.

Organization for Economic Cooperation and Development (U.S. Office) 2001 L St. NW, Suite 700, Washington, DC 20036.

Soil Conservation Service P.O. Box 2890, Washington, DC 20013.

Solar Energy Research Institute 1617 Cole Blvd., Golden, CO 80401.

United Nations 1 United Nations Plaza, New York, NY 10017.

United Nations Environment Programme Regional North American Office, United Nations Room DC2-0803, New York, NY 10017, and 1889 F St. NW, Washington, DC 20006.

U.S. Geological Survey 12201 Sunrise Valley Dr., Reston, VA 22092.

World Bank 1818 H St. NW, Washington, DC 20433.

FURTHER READINGS

Chapter 1 Population, Resources, Environmental Degradation, and Pollution

Asimov, Isaac, and Frederick Pohl. 1991 *Our Angry Earth.* New York: St. Martin's Press.

Bender, David L., and Bruno Leone, eds. 1990. *Environment: Opposing Viewpoints.* Vol. I. San Diego: Greenhaven.

Brown, Lester R., et al. Annual. *State of the World.* New York: W. W. Norton.

Buzzworm **Magazine Editors. Annual.** *Earth Journal: Environmental Almanac and Resource Directory.* Boulder, Colo.: Buzzworm Books.

Catton, William R., Jr. 1980. *Overshoot: The Ecological Basis of Revolutionary Change.* Chicago: University of Illinois Press.

Commoner, Barry. 1990. *Making Peace with the Planet.* New York: Pantheon.

Council on Environmental Quality. Annual. *Environmental Quality.* Washington, D.C.: Government Printing Office.

Ehrlich, Paul R., and Anne H. Ehrlich. 1990. *The Population Explosion.* New York: Doubleday.

Ehrlich, Paul R., and Anne H. Ehrlich. 1991. *Healing the Planet.* Reading, Mass.: Addison-Wesley.

Global Tomorrow Coalition. 1990. *The Global Ecology Handbook: What You Can Do About the Environmental Crisis.* Boston: Beacon Press.

Gordon, Anita, and David Suzuki. 1991. *It's a Matter of Survival.* Cambridge, Mass.: Harvard University Press.

Hardin, Garrett. 1968. "The Tragedy of the Commons," *Science,* vol. 162, 1243-1248.

Kirdon, Michael, and Ronald Segal. 1991. *The New State of the World Atlas.* 4th ed. New York: Simon & Schuster.

Lehr, J., ed. 1992. *Rational Readings on Environmental Concerns.* New York: Van Nostrand Reinhold.

Meadows, Donella. 1991. *The Global Citizen.* Covelo, Calif.: Island Press.

Meadows, Donella H., et al. 1992. *Beyond the Limits: Confronting Global Collapse, Envisioning a Sustainable Future.* Post Mills, Vt.: Chelsea Green.

Myers, Norman. 1990. *The Gaia Atlas of Future Worlds.* New York: Anchor/Doubleday.

Myers, Norman, ed. 1984. *Gaia: An Atlas of Planet Management.* Garden City, N.Y.: Anchor Press/Doubleday.

Porritt, Jonathan. 1991. *Save the Earth.* Atlanta, Ga.: Turner Publishing.

Repetto, Robert. 1986. *World Enough and Time: Successful Strategies for Resource Management.* New Haven, Conn.: World Resources Institute.

Ruchlis, Hy, and Sandra Oddo. 1990. *Clear Thinking.* New York: Prometheus Books.

Wilson, E. O., ed. 1988. *Biodiversity.* Cambridge, Mass.: Harvard University Press.

World Resources Institute. Annual. *The Information Please Environmental Almanac.* Boston: Houghton Mifflin.

World Resources Institute and International Institute for Environment and Development. Published every two years. *World Resources.* New York: Basic Books.

Chapter 2 Cultural Changes, Worldviews, Ethics, and Environment

Berry, Thomas. 1988. *The Dream of the Earth.* San Francisco: Sierra Club Books.

Berry, Wendell. 1990. *What Are People For?* Berkeley: North Point Press.

Brown, Lester R., et al. 1991. *Saving the Planet: How to Shape an Environmentally Sustainable Global Economy.* New York: W. W. Norton.

Cahn, Robert. 1978. *Footprints on the Planet: A Search for an Environmental Ethic.* New York: Universe Books.

Clark, M. E. 1989. *Ariadne's Thread: The Search for New Models of Thinking.* New York: St. Martin's Press.

Cohen, Michael J. 1988. *How Nature Works: Regenerating Kinship with Planet Earth.* Walpole, N.H.: Stillpoint.

Devall, Bill, and George Sessions. 1985. *Deep Ecology: Living As If Nature Mattered.* Salt Lake City: Gibbs M. Smith.

Earth Works Group. 1990. *50 Simple Things You Can Do to Save the Earth.* Berkeley: Earthworks Press.

Gore, Al. 1992. *Earth in the Balance: Ecology and the Human Spirit.* Boston: Houghton Mifflin.

Hardin, Garrett. 1978. *Exploring New Ethics for Survival.* 2nd ed. New York: Viking Press.

Hargrove, Eugene C. 1989. *Foundations of Environmental Ethics.* Englewood Cliffs, N.J.: Prentice-Hall.

IUCN, UNEP, WWF. 1991. *Caring for the Earth: A Strategy for Sustainable Living.* London: Earthscan.

Johnson, Warren. 1985. *The Future Is Not What It Used to Be: Returning to Traditional Values in an Age of Scarcity.* New York: Dodd, Mead.

Klenig, John. 1991. *Valuing Life.* Princeton, N.J.: Princeton University Press.

Leopold, Aldo. 1949. *A Sand County Almanac.* New York: Oxford University Press.

MacEachern, Diane. 1990. *Save Our Planet: 750 Everyday Ways You Can Help Clean Up the Earth.* New York: Dell.

Milbrath, Lester W. 1989. *Envisioning a Sustainable Society.* Albany: State University of New York Press.

Naar, Jon. 1990. *Design for a Liveable Planet.* New York: Harper & Row.

Naess, Arne. 1989. *Ecology, Community, and Lifestyle.* New York: Cambridge University Press.

Nash, Roderick. 1988. *The Rights of Nature: A History of Environmental Ethics.* Madison: University of Wisconsin Press.

Norton, Bryan G. 1991. *Toward Unity Among Environmentalists.* New York: Oxford University Press.

Orr, David. 1992. *Ecological Literacy.* Ithaca: State University of New York Press.

Rifkin, Jeremy, ed. 1990. *The Green Lifestyle Handbook: 1001 Ways You Can Heal the Earth.* New York: Henry Holt.

Robbins, John, and Ann Mortifee. 1992. *In Search of Balance: Discovering Harmony in a Changing World.* Los Angeles: H. J. Kramer.

Rolston, Holmes, III. 1988. *Environmental Ethics: Duties to and Values in the Natural World.* Philadelphia: Temple University Press.

Roszak, Theodore. 1978. *Person/Planet.* Garden City, N.Y.: Doubleday.

Sale, Kirkpatrick. 1990. *Conquest of Paradise.* New York: Alfred A. Knopf.

Schumacher, E. F. 1973. *Small Is Beautiful: Economics As If People Mattered.* New York: Harper & Row.

Starke, Linda. 1990. *Signs of Hope: Working Towards Our Common Future.* New York: Oxford University Press.

Chapter 3 Matter and Energy Resources: Types and Concepts

Bauer, Henry H. 1992. *Scientific Literacy and the Myth of the Scientific Method.* Urbana: University of Illinois Press.

Berry, R. Stephen. 1991. *Understanding Energy: Energy, Entropy, and Thermodynamics for Everyman.* River Edge, N.J.: World Scientific.

Carrying Capacity, Inc. 1987. *Beyond Oil.* New York: Ballinger.

Christensen, John W. 1990. *Global Science: Energy, Resources, and Environment.* 3rd ed. Dubuque, Iowa: Kendall/Hunt.

Colorado Energy Research Institute. 1976. *Net Energy Analysis: An Energy Balance Study of Fossil Fuel Resources.* Golden, Colo: Colorado Energy Research Institute.

Lovins, Amory B. 1977. *Soft Energy Paths.* Cambridge, Mass.: Ballinger.

Lovins, Amory B., and L. Hunter Lovins. 1986. *Energy Unbound: Your Invitation to Energy Abundance.* San Francisco: Sierra Club Books.

Miller, G. Tyler, Jr., and David G. Lygre. 1991. *Chemistry: A Contemporary Approach.* 3rd ed. Belmont, Calif.: Wadsworth.

Odum, Howard T., and Elisabeth C. Odum. 1981. *Energy Basis for Man and Nature.* 3rd ed. New York: McGraw-Hill.

Rifkin, Jeremy. 1989. *Entropy: Into the Greenhouse World: A New World View.* New York: Bantam.

Rothman, Milton, A. 1992. *The Science Gap: Dispelling the Myths and Understanding the Reality of Science.* New York: Prometheus Books.

Chapter 4 Ecosystems: What Are They and How Do They Work?

Bradbury, Ian. 1991. *The Biosphere.* New York: Belhaven Press.

Burton, Robert, ed. 1991. *Animal Life.* New York: Oxford University Press.

Colinvaux, Paul A. 1978. *Why Big Fierce Animals Are Rare.* Princeton, N.J.: Princeton University Press.

Ehrlich, Paul R. 1986. *The Machinery of Life: The Living World Around Us and How It Works.* New York: Simon & Schuster.

Ehrlich, Paul R., Anne H. Ehrlich, and John P. Holdren. 1977. *Ecoscience: Population, Resources and Environment.* New York: W. H. Freeman.

Kormondy, Edward J. 1984. *Concepts of Ecology.* 3rd ed. Englewood Cliffs, N.J.: Prentice-Hall.

Moore, D. M., ed. 1991. *Plant Life.* New York: Oxford University Press.

Odum, Eugene P. 1990. *Ecology and Our Endangered Life-Support Systems.* Sunderland, Mass.: Sinauer.

Rickleffs, Robert E. 1989. *Ecology.* 3rd ed. New York: W. H. Freeman.

Smith, Robert L. 1990. *Elements of Ecology.* 4th ed. New York: Harper & Row.

Starr, Cecie, and Ralph Taggart. 1992. *Biology: The Unity and Diversity of Life.* 6th ed. Belmont, Calif.: Wadsworth.

Tudge, Colin, 1991. *Global Ecology.* New York: Oxford University Press.

Watt, Kenneth E. F. 1982. *Understanding the Environment.* Newton, Mass.: Allyn & Bacon.

Chapter 5 Ecosystems: What Are the Major Types and What Can Happen to Them?

Attenborough, David, et al. 1989. *The Atlas of the Living World.* Boston: Houghton Mifflin.

Berger, John J. 1986. *Restoring the Earth.* New York: Alfred A. Knopf.

Botkin, Daniel. 1990. *Discordant Harmonies: A New Ecology for the Twenty-First Century.* New York: Oxford University Press.

Brown, J. H., and A. C. Gibson. 1983. *Biogeography.* St. Louis: C. V. Mosby.

Clapham, W. B., Jr. 1984. *Natural Ecosystems.* 2d ed. New York: Macmillan.

Goldsmith, Edward, et al. 1990. *Imperiled Planet: Restoring Our Endangered Ecosystems.* Cambridge, Mass.: MIT Press.

Hardin, Garrett. 1985. "Human Ecology: The Subversive, Conservative Science," *American Zoologist,* vol. 25, 469–476.

Lovelock, James E. 1988. *The Ages of Gaia: A Biography of Our Living Earth.* New York: W. W. Norton.

Maltby, Edward. 1986. *Waterlogged Wealth.* Washington, D.C.: Earthscan.

Pilkey, Orin H., Jr., and William J. Neal, eds. 1987. *Living with the Shore.* Durham, N.C.: Duke University Press.

Teal, J., and M. Teal. 1969. *Life and Death of a Salt Marsh.* New York: Ballantine.

Wallace, David. 1987. *Life in the Balance.* New York: Harcourt Brace Jovanovich.

Wilson, E. O. 1984. *Biophilia.* Cambridge, Mass.: Harvard University Press.

Wilson, E. O., ed. 1988. *Biodiversity.* Washington, D.C.: National Academy Press.

Chapter 6 Human Population Dynamics: Growth, Urbanization, and Regulation

Berg, Peter, et al. 1989. *A Green City Program.* San Francisco: Planet/Drum Foundation.

Bouvier, Leon F. 1992. *Peaceful Invasions: Immigration and Changing America.* Lanham, Md.: University Press of America.

Bouvier, Leon F., and Carol J. De Vita. 1991. "The Baby Boom—Entering Midlife," *Population Bulletin,* vol. 6, no. 3, 1–35.

Brown, Lester R., and Jodi Jacobson. 1986. *Our Demographically Divided World.* Washington, D.C.: Worldwatch Institute.

Brown, Lester R., and Jodi Jacobson. 1987. *The Future of Urbanization: Facing the Ecological and Economic Restraints.* Washington, D.C.: Worldwatch Institute.

Cadman, D., and G. Payne, eds. 1990. *The Living City: Towards a Sustainable Future.* London: Routledge.

Ehrlich, Paul R., and Anne H. Ehrlich. 1990. *The Population Explosion.* New York: Doubleday.

Formos, Werner. 1987. *Gaining People, Losing Ground: A Blueprint for Stabilizing World Population.* Washington, D.C.: Population Institute.

Grant, James P. Annual. *The State of the World's Children.* New York: Oxford University Press.

Grant, Lindsey. 1992. *Elephants in the Volkswagen: Facing the Tough Questions About Our Overcrowded Country.* New York: W. H. Freeman.

Haupt, Arthur, and Thomas T. Kane. 1985. *The Population Handbook: International.* 2nd ed. Washington, D.C.: Population Reference Bureau.

Lowe, Marcia D. 1990. *Alternatives to the Automobile: Transport for Living Cities.* Washington, D.C.: Worldwatch Institute.

Lowe, Marcia D. 1991. *Shaping Cities: The Environmental and Human Dimensions.* Washington, D.C.: Worldwatch Institute.

McFalls, Joseph A., Jr. 1991. "Population: A Lively Introduction," *Population Bulletin,* vol. 46, no. 2, 1–43.

McHarg, Ian L. 1969. *Design with Nature.* Garden City, N.Y.: Natural History Press.

Nadis, Stephen, and James MacKenzie. 1992. *Car Trouble.* Washington, D.C.: World Resources Institute.

Population Reference Bureau. 1990. *World Population: Fundamentals of Growth.* Washington, D.C.: Population Reference Bureau.

Population Reference Bureau. Annual. *World Population Data Sheet.* Washington, D.C.: Population Reference Bureau.

Renner, Michael. 1988. *Rethinking the Role of the Automobile.* Washington, D.C.: Worldwatch Institute.

Ryn, Sin van der, and Peter Calthorpe. 1986. *Sustainable Communities: A New Design Synthesis for Cities, Suburbs, and Towns.* San Francisco: Sierra Club Books.

Simon, Julian L. 1989. *Population Matters: People, Resources, Environment, and Immigration.* New Brunswick, N.J.: Transaction.

Todd, John, and George Tukel. 1990. *Reinhabiting Cities and Towns: Designing for Sustainability.* San Francisco: Planet/Drum Foundation.

United Nations Population Fund. 1991. *The State of the World's Population, 1991.* New York: United Nations Population Fund.

Weber, Susan, ed. 1988. *USA by Numbers: A Statistical Portrait of the United States.* Washington, D.C.: Zero Population Growth.

Zero Population Growth. 1990. *Planning the Ideal Family: The Small Family Option.* Washington, D.C.: Zero Population Growth.

Zuckerman, Wolfgang. 1991. *End of the Road: The World Car Crisis and How We Can Solve It.* Post Mills, Vt.: Chelsea Green.

Chapter 7 Environmental Economics and Politics

Andersen, Terry, and Donald R. Leal. 1991. *Free-Market Environmentalism.* Boulder, Colo.: Westview Press.

Anderson, Bruce, ed. 1990. *Ecologue: The Environmental Catalogue and Consumer's Guide for a Safe Earth.* Englewood Cliffs, N.J.: Prentice-Hall.

Basta, Nicholas. 1991. *The Environmental Career Guide: Job Opportunities with the Earth in Mind.* New York: Wiley.

Bennett, Steven J. 1991. *Ecopreneuring: The Green Guide to Small Business Opportunities from the Environmental Revolution.* New York: John Wiley.

Borman, F. H., and Stephen R. Kellert, eds. 1992. *Ecology, Economics, Ethics.* New Haven, Conn.: Yale University Press.

CEIP Fund. 1989. *The Complete Guide to Environmental Careers.* Washington, D.C.: CEIP Fund.

Constanza, Robert, ed. 1991. *Ecological Economics: The Science and Management of Sustainability.* New York: Columbia University Press.

Co-op America. 1991. *Directory of Socially and Environmentally Responsible Businesses.* Washington, D.C.: Co-op America.

Court, T. de la. 1990. *Beyond Bruntland: Green Development in the 1990s.* London: Zed Books.

Dahlberg, Kenneth A., et al. 1985. *Environment and the Global Arena.* Durham, N.C.: Duke University Press.

Daly, Herman E. 1991. *Steady-State Economics.* 2nd ed. Covelo, Calif.: Island Press.

Daly, Herman E., and John B. Cobb, Jr. 1989. *For the Common Good: Redirecting the Economy Toward Community, the Environment, and a Sustainable Future.* Boston: Beacon Press.

Day, David. 1990. *The Environmental Wars: Reports from the Front Line.* New York: St. Martin's Press.

Durning, Alan T. 1989. *Poverty and the Environment: Reversing the Downward Spiral.* Washington, D.C.: Worldwatch Institute.

Durning, Alan T. 1992. *How Much Is Enough? The Consumer Society and the Earth.* New York: W. W. Norton.

Elkington, John, et al. 1990. *The Green Consumer.* New York: Penguin Books.

Foreman, Dave. 1991. *Confessions of an Eco-Warrior.* New York: Harmony Books.

Hall, Bob. 1990. *Environmental Politics: Lessons from the Grassroots.* Durham, N.C.: Institute for Southern Studies.

Henderson, Hazel. 1988. *The Politics of the Solar Age.* Chicago, Ill.: Knowledge Systems.

Henning, Daniel H., and William R. Mangun. 1989. *Managing the Environmental Crisis.* Durham, N.C.: Duke University Press.

Hirschorn, Joel S., and Kirsten U. Oldenberg. 1990. *Prosperity Without Pollution: The Prevention Strategy for Industry and Consumers.* New York: Van Nostrand Reinhold.

Johnson, R. J. 1990. *Environmental Problems: Nature, Economy, and State.* New York: Belhaven Press.

Mathews, Jessica Tuchman. 1989. "Redefining Security," *Foreign Affairs,* Spring, 162–177.

Matthews, Christopher. 1988. *Hardball: How Politics Is Played—Told by One Who Knows the Game.* New York: Summit Books.

Montague, Peter. 1989. "What We Must Do—A Grass-Roots Offensive Against Toxics in the 1990s," *The Workbook,* vol. 14, no. 3, 90–113.

Ophuls, William, and A. S. Boyan, Jr. 1992. *Ecology and the Politics of Scarcity.* 2nd ed. New York: W. H. Freeman.

Paehlke, Robert C. 1989. *Environmentalism and the Future of Progressive Politics.* New Haven, Conn.: Yale University Press.

Pearce, Fred. 1991. *Green Warriors: The People and Politics Behind the Environmental Revolution.* Cornwall, England: WEC Books.

Renner, Michael. 1989. *National Security: The Economic and Environmental Dimensions.* Washington, D.C.: Worldwatch Institute.

Renner, Michael. 1991. *Jobs in a Sustainable Economy.* Washington, D.C.: Worldwatch Institute.

Repetto, Robert, et al. 1989. *Wasting Assets: Natural Resources in the National Income Accounts.* Washington, D.C.: World Resources Institute.

Rifkin, Jeremy. 1991. *Biosphere Politics: A New Consciousness for a New Century.* New York: Crown.

Rosenbaum, Walter A. 1990. *Environment, Politics, and Policy.* 2nd ed. Washington, D.C.: Congressional Quarterly.

Schumacher, E. F. 1973. *Small Is Beautiful: Economics As If the Earth Mattered.* New York: Harper & Row.

Smart, Bruce, ed. 1992. *Beyond Compliance: A New Industry View of the Environment.* Washington, D.C.: World Resources Institute.

Tietenberg, Tom. 1992. *Environmental and Resource Economics.* 3rd ed. Glenview, Ill.: Scott, Foresman.

World Commission on the Environment and Development. 1987. *Our Common Future.* New York: Oxford University Press.

Chapter 8 Hazards, Risk, and Human Health

Bernarde, Melvin A. 1989. *Our Precarious Habitat: Fifteen Years Later.* New York: John Wiley.

Douglas, Mary, and Aaron Wildavsky. 1982. *Risk and Culture.* Berkeley: University of California Press.

Environmental Protection Agency. 1987. *Unfinished Business: A Comparative Assessment of Environmental Problems.* Washington, D.C.: Environmental Protection Agency.

Environmental Protection Agency. 1990. *Reducing Risk: Setting Priorities and Strategies for Environmental Protection.* Washington, D.C.: Environmental Protection Agency.

Environmental Protection Agency. 1991. *The Environmental Challenge of the 1990s.* Washington, D.C.: Environmental Protection Agency.

Harte, John, et al. 1992. *Toxics A to Z: A Guide to Everyday Pollution Hazards.* Berkeley: University of California Press.

Lappé, Marc. 1991. *Chemical Deception: The Toxic Threat to Health and Environment.* San Francisco: Sierra Club Books.

National Academy of Sciences. 1989. *Diet and Health: Implications for Reducing Chronic Disease Risk.* Washington, D.C.: National Academy Press.

Olson, Steve. 1989. *Shaping the Future: Biology and Human Values.* Washington, D.C.: National Academy Press.

Ottobon, M. Alice. 1991. *The Dose Makes the Poison: A Plain-Language Guide to Toxicology.* New York: Van Nostrand Reinhold.

Piller, Charles. 1991. *The Fail-Safe Society.* New York: Basic Books.

Rifkin, Jeremy. 1985. *Declaration of a Heretic.* Boston: Routledge & Kegan Paul.

Suzuki, David, and Peter Knudtson. 1989. *Genethics: The Clash Between the New Genetics and Human Values.* Cambridge, Mass.: Harvard University Press.

U.S. Department of Health and Human Services. 1988. *The Surgeon General's Report on Nutrition and Health.* Washington, D.C.: Government Printing Office.

U.S. Department of Health and Human Services. Annual. *The Health Consequences of Smoking.* Washington, D.C.: Government Printing Office.

Wilson, Richard, and E.A.C. Crouch. 1987. "Risk Assessment and Comparisons: An Introduction," *Science,* vol. 236, 267–270.

Chapter 9 Air Resources and Air Pollution

Bridgman, Howard. 1991. *Global Air Pollution: Problems for the 1990s.* New York: Belhaven Press.

Brookins, Douglas G. 1990. *The Indoor Radon Problem.* Irvington, N.Y.: Columbia University Press.

Coffel, Steve, and Karyn Feiden. 1991. *Indoor Pollution.* New York: Random House.

Environmental Protection Agency. 1988. *The Inside Story: A Guide to Indoor Air Quality.* Washington, D.C.: Environmental Protection Agency.

EPA Journal, vol. 17, no. 1, 1991. *Entire issue devoted to 1990 Clean Air Act.*

French, Hilary F. 1990. *Clearing the Air: A Global Agenda.* Washington, D.C.: Worldwatch Institute.

Geller, H., et al. 1986. *Acid Rain and Energy Conservation.* Washington, D.C.: American Council for an Energy-Efficient America.

Hunter, Linda Mason. 1989. *The Healthy House: An Attic-to-Basement Guide to Toxin-Free Living.* Emmaus, Penn.: Rodale Press.

MacKenzie, James J., and Mohamed T. El-Ashry. 1990. *Air Pollution's Toll on Forests and Crops.* Washington, D.C.: World Resources Institute.

National Academy of Sciences. 1988. *Air Pollution, the Automobile, and Human Health.* Washington, D.C.: National Academy Press.

Regens, James L., and Robert W. Rycroft. 1988. *The Acid Rain Controversy.* Pittsburgh: University of Pittsburgh Press.

Wark, K., and C. F. Warner. 1986. *Air Pollution: Its Origin and Control.* 3rd ed. New York: Harper & Row.

Chapter 10 Climate, Global Warming, Ozone Depletion, and Nuclear War: Ultimate Problems

Ausubel, Jesse H. 1991. "A Second Look at the Impacts of Climate Change," *American Scientist*, vol. 79, 210–221.

Bates, Albert K. 1990. *Climate in Crisis: The Greenhouse Effect and What We Can Do.* Summertown, Tenn.: Book Publishing Company.

Benedick, Richard Eliot. 1991. *Ozone Diplomacy: New Directions in Safeguarding the Planet.* Cambridge, Mass.: Harvard University Press.

Dotto, Lydia. 1986. *Planet Earth in Jeopardy: Environmental Consequences of Nuclear War.* New York: John Wiley.

Dotto, Lydia. 1990. *Thinking the Unthinkable: Civilization and Rapid Climate Change.* Waterloo, Ontario: Wilfrid Lanier University Press.

Environmental Protection Agency. 1988. *The Potential Effects of Global Climate Change on the United States.* Washington, D.C.: Environmental Protection Agency.

Environmental Protection Agency. 1989. *Policy Options for Stabilizing Global Climate.* Washington, D.C.: Environmental Protection Agency.

Fisher, David E. 1990. *Fire and Ice: The Greenhouse Effect, Ozone Depletion, and Nuclear Winter.* New York: Harper & Row.

Fishman, Albert, and Robert Kalish. 1990. *Global Alert: The Ozone Pollution Crisis.* New York: Plenum.

Flavin, Christopher. 1989. *Slowing Global Warming: A Worldwide Strategy.* Washington, D.C.: Worldwatch Institute.

Graedel, T. C., and Paul J. Cutzen. 1992. *Atmospheric Change.* New York: W. H. Freeman.

Greenhouse Crisis Foundation. 1990. *The Greenhouse Crisis: 101 Ways to Save the Earth.* Washington, D.C.: Greenhouse Crisis Foundation.

Lovins, Amory B., et al. 1989. *Least-Cost Energy: Solving the CO_2 Problem.* 2nd ed. Snowmass, Colo.: Rocky Mountain Institute.

Lyman, Francesca, et al. 1990. *The Greenhouse Trap: What We're Doing to the Atmosphere and How We Can Slow Global Warming.* Washington, D.C.: World Resources Institute.

McKibben, Bill. 1989. *The End of Nature.* New York: Random House.

Mintzer, Irving, and William R. Moomaw. 1991. *Escaping the Heat Trap: Probing the Prospects for a Stable Environment.* Washington, D.C.: World Resources Institute.

Mintzer, Irving, et al. 1990. *Protecting the Ozone Shield: Strategies for Phasing Out CFCs During the 1990s.* Washington, D.C.: World Resources Institute.

National Academy of Sciences. 1989. *Ozone Depletion, Greenhouse Gases, and Climate Change.* Washington, D.C.: National Academy Press.

National Academy of Sciences. 1991. *Policy Implications of Greenhouse Warming.* Washington, D.C.: National Academy Press.

National Academy of Sciences. 1992. *Global Environmental Change.* Washington, D.C.: National Academy Press.

Office of Technology Assessment. 1991. *Changing by Degrees: Steps to Reduce Greenhouse Gases.* Washington, D.C.: Government Printing Office.

Oppenheimer, Michael, and Robert H. Boyle. 1990. *Dead Heat: The Race Against the Greenhouse Effect.* New York: Basic Books.

Peters, Robert L., and Thomas E. Lovejoy, eds. 1992. *Global Warming and Biological Diversity.* New Haven, Conn.: Yale University Press.

Ray, Dixie Lee. 1990. *Trashing the Planet.* Washington, D.C.: Regnery Gateway.

Roan, Sharon L. 1989. *Ozone Crisis: The 15-Year Evolution of a Sudden Global Emergency.* New York: John Wiley.

Rowland, F. Sherwood. 1989. "Chlorofluorocarbons and the Depletion of Stratospheric Ozone," *American Scientist*, vol. 77, 36–45.

Schneider, Stephen. 1989. *Global Warming: Are We Entering the Greenhouse Century?* New York: Random House.

Schotterer, Ulrich, and Peter Andermatt. 1992. *Climate — Our Future?* Duluth: University of Minnesota Press.

Shea, Cynthia Pollock. 1988. *Protecting Life on Earth: Steps to Save the Ozone Layer.* Washington, D.C.: Worldwatch Institute.

Weiner, Jonathan. 1990. *The Next One Hundred Years: Shaping the Fate of Our Living Earth.* New York: Bantam.

Chapter 11 Water Resources and Water Pollution

Ashworth, William. 1982. *Nor Any Drop to Drink.* New York: Summit Books.

Ashworth, William. 1986. *The Late, Great Lakes: An Environmental History.* New York: Alfred A. Knopf.

Borgese, Elisabeth Mann. 1986. *The Future of the Oceans.* New York: Harvest House.

Bullock, David K. 1989. *The Wasted Ocean.* New York: Lyons & Burford.

Colborn, Theodora E., et al. 1989. *Great Lakes, Great Legacy?* Washington, D.C.: Conservation Foundation.

Davidson, Art. 1990. *In the Wake of the Exxon Valdez.* San Francisco: Sierra Club Books.

El-Ashry, Mohamed, and Diana C. Gibbons, eds. 1988. *Water and Arid Lands of the Western United States.* Washington, D.C.: World Resources Institute.

Environmental Protection Agency. 1990. *Citizen's Guide to Ground-Water Protection.* Washington, D.C.: Environmental Protection Agency.

Gabler, Raymond. 1988. *Is Your Water Safe to Drink?* New York: Consumer Reports Books.

Goldsmith, Edward, and Nicholas Hidyard, eds. 1986. *The Social and Environmental Effects of Large Dams.* 3 vols. New York: John Wiley.

Hansen, Nancy R., et al. 1988. *Controlling Nonpoint-Source Water Pollution.* New York: National Audubon Society and The Conservation Society.

Horton, Tom, and Wiliam Eichbaum. 1991. *Turning the Tide: Saving the Chesapeake Bay.* Covelo, Calif.: Island Press.

Ives, J. D., and B. Messeric. 1989. *The Himalayan Dilemma: Reconciling Development and Conservation.* London: Routledge.

Jefferies, Michael, and Derek Mills. 1991. *Freshwater Ecology: Principles and Applications.* New York: Belhaven Press.

Jorgensen, Eric P., ed. 1989. *The Poisoned Well: New Strategies for Groundwater Protection.* Covelo, Calif.: Island Press.

Keeble, John. 1991. *Out of the Channel: The Exxon Valdez Oil Spill in Prince William Sound.* New York: HarperCollins.

Kotlyakov, V. M. 1991. "The Aral Sea Basin: A Critical Environmental Zone," *Environment*, vol. 33, no. 1, 4–9, 36–39.

Marquardt, Sandra, et al. 1989. *Bottled Water: Sparkling Hype at a Premium Price.* Washington, D.C.: Environmental Policy Institute.

Mitchell, Bruce, ed. 1990. *Integrated Water Management.* New York: Belhaven Press.

National Academy of Sciences. 1986. *Drinking Water and Health.* Washington, D.C.: National Academy Press.

Natural Resources Defense Council. 1989. *Ebb Tide for Pollution: Actions for Cleaning Up Coastal Waters.* Washington, D.C.: Natural Resources Defense Council.

Office of Technology Assessment. 1989. *Coping with Oiled Environments.* Washington, D.C.: Government Printing Office.

Postel, Sandra. 1992. *The Last Oasis: Facing Water Scarcity.* New York: W. W. Norton.

Reisner, Marc, and Sara Bates. 1990. *Overtapped Oasis: Reform or Revolution for Western Water.* Covelo, Calif.: Island Press.

Rocky Mountain Institute. 1990. *Catalog of Water-Efficient Technologies for the Urban/Residential Sector.* Old Snowmass, Colo.: Rocky Mountain Institute.

Simon, Anne W. 1985. *Neptune's Revenge: The Ocean of Tomorrow.* New York: Franklin Watts.

Waggoner, Paul E., ed. 1990. *Climate Change and U.S. Water Resources.* New York: John Wiley.

Chapter 12 Soil Resources and Hazardous Waste

Agency for Toxic Substances and Disease Registry. 1988. *The Nature and Extent of Lead Poisoning in Children in the United States.* Atlanta: U.S. Department of Health and Human Services.

Brady, Nyle C. 1989. *The Nature and Properties of Soils.* 10th ed. New York: Macmillan.

Brown, Lester R., and Edward C. Wolf. 1984. *Soil Erosion: Quiet Crisis in the World Economy.* Washington, D.C.: Worldwatch Institute.

Cohen, Gary, and John O'Connor. 1990. *Fighting Toxics: A Manual for Protecting Family, Community, and Workplace.* Covelo, Calif.: Island Press.

Commoner, Barry. 1990. *Making Peace with the Planet.* New York: Pantheon.

Connett, Paul. 1989. *Waste Management As If the Future Mattered.* Canton, N.Y.: Work on Waste.

Dadd, Debra Lynn. 1990. *Nontoxic, Natural & Earthwise.* Los Angeles: Jeremy Tarcher.

Environmental Defense Fund. 1985. *To Burn or Not to Burn.* New York: Environmental Defense Fund.

Environmental Protection Agency. 1987. *The Hazardous Waste System.* Washington, D.C.: Environmental Protection Agency.

Gibbs, Lois. 1982. *The Love Canal: My Story.* Albany: State University of New York Press.

Gordon, Ben, and Peter Montague. 1989. *Zero Discharge: A Citizen's Toxic Waste Manual.* Washington, D.C.: Greenpeace.

Grainger, Alan. 1983. *Desertification: How People Make Deserts, How People Can Stop and Why They Don't.* Washington, D.C.: Earthscan.

Kenworthy, Lauren, and Eric Schaeffer. 1990. *A Citizen's Guide to Promoting Toxic Waste Reduction.* New York: INFORM.

Moyers, Bill. 1990. *Global Dumping Ground: The International Traffic in Hazardous Waste.* Cabin John, Md.: Seven Locks Press.

National Academy of Sciences. 1986. *Soil Conservation.* (2 vols.). Washington, D.C.: National Academy Press.

Office of Technology Assessment. 1986. *Serious Reduction of Hazardous Waste.* Washington, D.C.: Government Printing Office.

Office of Technology Assessment. 1987. *From Pollution to Prevention: A Progress Report on Waste Reduction.* Washington, D.C.: Government Printing Office.

Piasecki, Bruce, and Gary Davis. 1987. *America's Future in Toxic Waste Management: Lessons from Europe.* New York: Quorum Books.

Pollack, Stephanie. 1989. "Solving the Lead Dilemma," *Technology Review*, October, 22–31.

Postel, Sandra. 1987. *Defusing the Toxics Threat: Controlling Pesticides and Industrial Waste.* Washington, D.C.: Worldwatch Institute.

Water Pollution Control Federation. 1989. *Household Hazardous Waste: What You Should and Shouldn't Do.* Alexandria, Va.: Water Pollution Control Federation.

Whelan, Elisabeth M. 1985. *Toxic Terror.* Ottawa, Ill.: Jameson Books.

Wilson, G. F., et al. 1986. *The Soul of the Soil: A Guide to Ecological Soil Management.* 2nd ed. Quebec, Canada: Gaia Services.

Chapter 13 Food Resources

Bartholomew, Mel. 1987. *Square Foot Gardening.* Emmaus, Pa.: Rodale Press.

Berry, Wendell. 1990. *Nature as Measure.* Berkeley, Calif.: North Point Press.

Brown, Lester R., and John E. Young. 1990. "Feeding the World in the Nineties." In Lester R. Brown, et al., *State of the World 1990*, pp. 59–78. Washington, D.C.: Worldwatch Institute.

Crosson, Pierre R., and Norman J. Rosenberg. 1989. "Strategies for Agriculture," *Scientific American*, September, 128–135.

Dover, Michael J., and Lee M. Talbot. 1988. "Feeding the Earth: An Agroecological Solution," *Technology Review*, Feb./Mar., 27–35.

Doyle, Jack. 1985. *Altered Harvest: Agriculture, Genetics, and the Fate of the World's Food Supply.* New York: Viking Press.

Dunning, Alan B., and Holly W. Brough. 1991. *Taking Stock: Animal Farming and the Environment.* Washington, D.C.: Worldwatch Institute.

The Ecologist, vol. 21, no. 2, 1991. Entire issue devoted to world hunger.

Gordon, R. Conway, and Edward R. Barbier. 1990. *After the Green Revolution: Sustainable Agriculture for Development.* East Haven, Conn.: Earthscan.

Granatstein, David. 1988. *Reshaping the Bottom Line: On-Farm Strategies for a Sustainable Agriculture.* Stillwater, Minn.: Land Stewardship Project.

Jackson, Wes. 1980. *New Roots for Agriculture.* San Francisco: Friends of the Earth.

Jacobson, Michael, et al. 1991. *Safe Food: Eating Wisely in a Risky World.* Washington, D.C.: Planet Earth Press.

Lappé, Francis M., et al. 1988. *Betraying the National Interest.* San Francisco: Food First.

League of Women Voters, 1991. *U.S. Farm Policy: Who Benefits? Who Pays? Who Decides?* Washington, D.C.: League of Women Voters.

McGoodwin, Russell. 1990. *Crisis in the World's Fisheries: People, Problems, and Politics.* Stanford, Calif.: Stanford University Press.

Mollison, Bill. 1990. *Permaculture: A Practical Guide for a Sustainable Future.* Covelo, Calif.: Island Press.

National Academy of Sciences. 1989. *Alternative Agriculture.* Washington, D.C.: National Academy Press.

Pimentel, David, and Carl W. Hall. 1989. *Food and Natural Resources.* Orlando, Fla.: Academic Press.

Rifkin, Jeremy. 1992. *Beyond Beef: The Rise and Fall of the Cattle Culture.* New York: Dutton.

Robbins, John. 1987. *Diet for a New America.* Walpole, N.H.: Stillpoint Publishing.

Rodale Press. 1984. *The Encyclopedia of Organic Gardening.* Emmaus, Penn.: Rodale Press.

Schell, Orville. 1984. *Modern Meat: Antibiotics, Hormones, and the Pharmaceutical Farm.* New York: Random House.

Soil and Water Conservation Society. 1990. *Sustainable Agricultural Systems.* Ankeny, Iowa: Soil and Water Conservation Society.

Tarrant, J. R., ed. 1991. *Farming and Food.* New York: Oxford University Press.

Tudge, Colin. 1988. *Food Crops for the Future: Development of Plant Resources.* Oxford, England: Blackwell.

United Nations World Food Commission. 1989. *The Global State of Hunger and Malnutrition.* New York: United Nations.

Wolf, Edward C. 1986. *Beyond the Green Revolution: New Approaches for Third World Agriculture.* Washington, D.C.: Worldwatch Institute.

Yang, Linda. 1990. *The City Gardener's Handbook: From Balcony to Backyard.* New York: Random House.

Chapter 14 Protecting Food Resources: Pesticides and Pest Control

Bogard, William. 1989. *The Bhopal Tragedy: Language, Logic, and Politics in the Production of a Hazard.* Boulder, Colo.: Westview Press.

Bosso, Christopher. 1987. *Pesticides and Politics.* Pittsburgh: University of Pittsburgh Press.

Carson, Rachel. 1962. *Silent Spring.* Boston: Houghton Mifflin.

Dover, Michael J. 1985. *A Better Mousetrap: Improving Pest Management for Agriculture.* Washington, D.C.: World Resources Institute.

Flint, Mary Louise. 1990. *Pests of the Garden & a Small Farm: A Grower's Guide to Using Less Pesticide.* Oakland, Calif.: ANR Publications.

Friends of the Earth. 1990. *How to Get Your Lawn and Garden Off Drugs.* Ottawa, Ontario: Friends of the Earth.

Gips, Terry. 1987. *Breaking the Pesticide Habit.* Minneapolis: IASA.

Heylin, Michael, ed. 1991. "Pesticides: Costs Versus Benefits," *Chemistry & Engineering News,* 7 January, 27–56.

Horn, D. J. 1988. *Ecological Approach to Pest Management.* New York: Guilford Press.

Hynes, Patricia. 1989. *The Recurring Silent Spring.* New York: Pergamon Press.

Kourik, Robert. 1990. "Combatting Household Pests Without Chemical Warfare," *Garbage,* March/April, 22–29.

League of Women Voters. 1989. *America's Growing Dilemma: Pesticides in Food and Water.* Washington, D.C.: League of Women Voters.

Marco, G. J., et al. 1987. *Silent Spring Revisited.* Washington, D.C.: American Chemical Society.

Marquardt, Sandra. 1989. *Exporting Banned Pesticides: Fueling the Circle of Poison.* Washington, D.C.: Greenpeace.

National Academy of Sciences. 1986. *Pesticide Resistance: Strategies and Tactics for Management.* Washington, D.C.: National Academy Press.

Pimentel, David, et al. 1991. "Environmental and Economic Effects of Reducing Pesticide Use," *BioScience,* vol. 41, no. 6, 402–409.

Schultz, Warren. 1989. *The Chemical-Free Lawn.* Emmaus, Penn.: Rodale Press.

Van den Bosch, Robert. 1978. *The Pesticide Conspiracy.* Garden City, N.Y.: Doubleday.

Yepsen, Roger B., Jr. 1987. *The Encyclopedia of Natural Insect and Pest Control.* Emmaus, Penn.: Rodale Press.

Chapter 15 Land Resources: Forests, Rangelands, Parks, and Wilderness

Allin, Craig W. 1982. *The Politics of Wilderness Preservation.* Westport, Conn.: Greenwood.

Anderson, Patrick. 1989. "The Myth of Sustainable Logging: The Case for a Ban on Tropical Timber Imports," *The Ecologist,* vol. 19, no. 5, 166–168.

Barber, Chip. 1991. *Cutting Our Losses: Policy Reform to Sustain Tropical Forest Resources.* Washington, D.C.: World Resources Institute.

Burger, Julian. 1990. *The Gaia Atlas of First Peoples.* New York: Anchor Books.

Collins, Mark, ed. 1990. *The Last Rainforests: A World Conservation Atlas.* Emmaus, Penn.: Rodale Press.

Eckholm, Erik, et al. 1984. *Fuelwood: The Energy Crisis That Won't Go Away.* Washington, D.C.: Earthscan.

Ervin, Keith. 1989. *Fragile Majesty: The Battle for North America's Last Great Forest.* Seattle: The Mountaineers.

Foreman, Dave, and Howie Wolke. 1989. *The Big Outside.* Tucson: Nedd Ludd Books.

Fritz, Edward. 1983. *Sterile Forest: The Case Against Clearcutting.* Austin, Texas: Eakin Press.

Frome, Michael. 1974. *The Battle for the Wilderness.* New York: Praeger.

Frome, Michael. 1983. *The Forest Service.* Boulder, Colo.: Westview Press.

Goodland, Robert, ed. 1990. *Race to Save the Tropics: Ecology and Economics for a Sustainable Future.* Covelo, Calif.: Island Press.

Gradwohl, Judith, and Russell Greenberg. 1988. *Saving the Tropical Forests.* Covelo, Calif.: Island Press.

Hartzog, George B., Jr. 1988. *Battling for the National Parks.* New York: Moyer Bell.

Hendee, John, et al. 1991. *Principles of Wilderness Management.* Golden, Colo.: Fulcrum Publishing.

Hunter, Malcolm L., Jr. 1990. *Wildlife, Forests, and Forestry: Principles of Managing Forests for Biodiversity.* Englewood Cliffs, N.J.: Prentice-Hall.

International Union for Conservation of Nature and Natural Resources (IUCN). 1992. *Tropical Deforestation and Extinction of Species.* Gland, Switzerland: IUCN.

Jolly, Alison, and Frans Lanting. 1990. *Madagascar: A World Out of Time.* New York: Aperture.

Kelly, David, and Gary Braasch. 1988. *Secrets of the Old Growth Forest.* Salt Lake City: Peregrine Smith.

Leopold, Aldo. 1949. *A Sand County Almanac.* New York: Oxford University Press.

Maser, Chris. 1989. *Forest Primeval.* San Francisco: Sierra Club Books.

Miller, Kenton, and Laura Tangley. 1991. *Trees of Life: Saving Tropical Forests and Their Biological Wealth.* Washington, D.C.: World Resources Institute.

Myers, Norman. 1984. *The Primary Source: Tropical Forests and Our Future.* New York: W. W. Norton.

Nash, Roderick. 1982. *Wilderness and the American Mind.* 3rd ed. New Haven, Conn.: Yale University Press.

National Parks and Conservation Association. 1988. *Blueprint for National Parks* (9 vols.). Washington, D.C.: National Parks and Conservation Association.

Newman, Arnold. 1990. *The Tropical Rainforest: A World Survey of Our Most Valuable Endangered Habitats.* New York: Facts on File.

Norse, Elliot A. 1990. *Ancient Forests of the Pacific Northwest.* Covelo, Calif.: Island Press.

Oelschlager, Max. 1991. *The Idea of Wilderness from Prehistory to the Age of Ecology.* New Haven, Conn.: Yale University Press.

O'Toole, Randal. 1987. *Reforming the Forest Service.* Covelo, Calif.: Island Press.

Postel, Sandra, and Lori Heise. 1988. *Reforesting the Earth.* Washington, D.C.: Worldwatch Institute.

Repetto, Robert. 1990. "Deforestation in the Tropics," *Scientific American,* vol. 262, no. 4, 36–42.

Revkin, Andrew. 1990. *The Burning Season: The Murder of Chico Mendes and the Fight for the Amazon.* Boston: Houghton Mifflin.

Robinson, Gordon. 1987. *The Forest and the Trees: A Guide to Excellent Forestry.* Covelo, Calif.: Island Press.

Runte, Alfred. 1987. *National Parks: The American Experience.* 2nd ed. Lincoln: University of Nebraska Press.

Rush, James. 1991. *The Last Tree: Reclaiming the Environment in Tropical Asia.* Boulder, Colo.: Westview Press.

Ryan, John C. 1992. *Life Support: Conserving Biological Diversity.* Washington, D.C.: Worldwatch Institute.

Shanks, Bernard. 1984. *This Land Is Your Land.* San Francisco: Sierra Club Books.

Simon, David J., ed. 1988. *Our Common Lands: Defending the National Parks.* Washington, D.C.: Island Press.

Society of American Foresters. 1981. *Choices in Silviculture for American Forests.* Washington, D.C.: Society of American Foresters.

Stoddard, Charles H., and Glenn M. Stoddard. 1987. *Essentials of Forestry Practice.* 4th ed. New York: John Wiley.

Tree People. 1990. *The Simple Act of Planting a Tree.* Los Angeles: Jeremy Tarcher.

Valentine, John E., ed. 1990. *Grazing Management.* San Diego: Academic Press.

Wellner, Pamela, and Eugene Dickey. 1991. *The Wood Users Guide.* San Francisco: Rainforest Action Network.

Wilcove, David S. 1988. *National Forests: Policies for the Future.* Vols. 1 & 2. Washington, D.C.: Wilderness Society.

Wilderness Society. 1988. *Ancient Forests: A Threatened Heritage.* Washington, D.C.: Wilderness Society.

Wilson, E. O., ed. 1988. *Biodiversity.* Cambridge, Mass.: Harvard University Press.

Zaslowsky, Dyan, and The Wilderness Society. 1986. *These American Lands.* New York: Henry Holt.

Zuckerman, Seth. 1991. *Saving Our Ancient Forests.* Federalsburg, Md.: Living Planet Press.

Chapter 16 Wild Plant and Animal Resources

Boo, Elizabeth. 1990. *Ecotourism: The Potential and the Pitfalls.* Vols. 1, 2. Washington, D.C.: World Wildlife Fund.

Credlund, Arthur G. 1983. *Whales and Whaling.* New York: Seven Hills Books.

DeBlieu, Jan. 1991. *Meant to Be Wild: The Struggle to Save Endangered Species Through Captive Breeding.* New York: Fulcrum Publishing.

DiSilvestro, Roger L. 1990. *Fight for Survival.* New York: John Wiley.

Durrell, Lee. 1986. *State of the Ark: An Atlas of Conservation in Action.* Garden City, N.Y.: Doubleday.

Ehrlich, Paul, and Anne Ehrlich. 1981. *Extinction.* New York: Random House.

Elliot, David K. 1986. *Dynamics of Extinction.* New York: John Wiley.

Gilbert, Frederick F., and Donald G. Dodds. 1987. *The Philosophy and Practice of Wildlife Management.* Malabar, Fla.: Robert E. Krieger.

Hargrove, Eugene C. 1992. *The Animal Rights/ Environmental Ethics Debate.* Ithaca: State University of New York Press.

International Union for Conservation of Nature and Natural Resources. 1985. *Implementing the World Conservation Strategy.* Gland, Switzerland: IUCN.

Kohm, Kathryn A., ed. 1990. *Balancing on the Brink of Extinction: The Endangered Species Act and Lessons for the Future.* Covelo, Calif.: Island Press.

Koopowitz, Harold, and Hilary Kaye. 1983. *Plant Extinctions: A Global Crisis.* Washington, D.C.: Stone Wall Press.

Livingston, John A. 1981. *The Fallacy of Wildlife Conservation.* Toronto: McClelland and Stewart.

Luoma, Jon. 1987. *A Crowded Ark: The Role of Zoos in Wildlife Conservation.* Boston: Houghton Mifflin.

McNeely, Jeffery A., et al. 1989. *Conserving the World's Biological Resources: A Primer on Principles and Practice for Development Action.* Washington, D.C.: World Resources Institute.

Myers, Norman. 1983. *A Wealth of Wild Species: Storehouse for Human Welfare.* Boulder, Colo.: Westview Press.

Nash, Roderick F. 1988. *The Rights of Nature: A History of Environmental Ethics.* Madison: University of Wisconsin Press.

Office of Technology Assessment. 1989. *Oil Production in the Arctic National Wildlife Refuge.* Washington, D.C.: Government Printing Office.

Oldfield, Margery L., and Janis B. Alcorn, eds. 1992. *Biodiversity: Culture, Conservation, and Ecodevelopment.* Boulder, Colo.: Westview Press.

Pringle, Laurence. 1989. *The Animal Rights Controversy.* New York: Harcourt Brace Jovanovich.

Reagan, Tom. 1983. *The Case for Animal Rights.* Berkeley: University of California Press.

Reid, Walter V. C., and Kenton R. Miller. 1989. *Keeping Options Alive: The Scientific Basis for Conserving Biodiversity.* Washington, D.C.: World Resources Institute.

Roe, Frank G. 1970. *The North American Buffalo.* Toronto: University of Toronto Press.

Shaw, J. H. 1985. *Introduction to Wildlife Management.* New York: McGraw-Hill.

Soulé, Michael E. 1986. *Conservation Biology: Science of Scarcity and Diversity.* Sunderland, Mass.: Sinauer.

Tudge, Colin. 1988. *The Environment of Life.* New York: Oxford University Press.

Tuttle, Merlin D. 1988. *America's Neighborhood Bats: Understanding and Learning to Live in Harmony with Them.* Austin: University of Texas Press.

Wallace, David Rains. 1987. *Life in the Balance.* New York: Harcourt Brace Jovanovich.

Western, David, and Mary Pearl, eds. 1989. *Conservation for the Twenty-First Century.* New York: Oxford University Press.

Wilson, E. O., ed. 1988. *Biodiversity.* Washington, D.C.: National Academy Press.

Wolf, Edward C. 1987. *On the Brink of Extinction: Conserving the Diversity of Life.* Washington, D.C.: Worldwatch Institute.

World Resources Institute. 1992. *Global Biodiversity Strategy: Guidelines for Action to Save, Study, and Use Earth's Biotic Wealth Sustainably and Equitably.* Washington, D.C.: World Resources Institute.

Chapter 17 Perpetual and Renewable Energy Resources

Also see readings for Chapter 3.

American Council for an Energy Efficient Economy. 1988. *Energy Efficiency: A New Agenda.* Washington, D.C.: American Council for an Energy Efficient Economy.

Blackburn, John O. 1987. *The Renewable Energy Alternative: How the United States and the World Can Prosper Without Nuclear Energy or Coal.* Durham, N.C.: Duke University Press.

Brower, Michael. 1990. *Cool Energy: The Renewable Solution to Global Warming.* Cambridge, Mass.: Union of Concerned Scientists.

Davidson, Joel. 1987. *The New Solar Electric Home.* Ann Arbor, Mich.: Aatec Publications.

Flavin, Christopher, and Alan B. Durning. 1988. *Building on Success: The Age of Energy Efficiency.* Washington, D.C.: Worldwatch Institute.

Flavin, Christopher, and Rock Piltz. 1990. *Sustainable Energy.* Washington, D.C.: Renew America.

Gever, John, et al. 1986. *Beyond Oil.* Cambridge, Mass.: Ballinger.

Goldenberg, Jose, et al. 1988. *Energy for a Sustainable World.* New York: John Wiley.

Kozloff, Keith, and Roger C. Dower. 1992. *Energy Policies for the 1990s and Beyond.* Washington, D.C.: World Resources Institute.

Ogden, Joan M., and Robert H. Williams. 1989. *Solar Hydrogen: Moving Beyond Fossil Fuels.* Washington, D.C.: World Resources Institute.

Oppenheimer, Michael, and Robert H. Boyle. 1990. *Dead Heat: The Race Against the Greenhouse Effect.* New York: Basic Books.

Pimentel, David, et al. 1984. "Environmental and Social Costs of Biomass Energy," *BioScience,* Feb., 89–93.

Rader, Nancy, et al. 1989. *Power Surge: The Status and Near-Term Potential of Renewable Energy Technologies.* Washington, D.C.: Public Citizen.

Renner, Michael. 1988. *Rethinking the Role of the Automobile.* Washington, D.C.: Worldwatch Institute.

Rocky Mountain Institute. 1991. *Practical Home Energy Savings.* Old Snowmass, Colo.: Rocky Mountain Institute.

Scientific American. 1990. *Energy for Planet Earth,* entire Sept. issue.

Wade, Herb. 1983. *Building Underground: The Design and Construction Handbook for Earth-Sheltered Houses.* Emmaus, Penn.: Rodale Press.

Chapter 18 Nonrenewable Energy Resources

See also the readings for Chapter 3.

Chernousenko, Vladimir M. 1991. *Chernobyl: Insight from the Inside.* New York: Springer-Verlag.

Clark, Wilson, and Jake Page. 1983. *Energy, Vulnerability, and War.* New York: W. W. Norton.

Cohen, Bernard L. 1990. *The Nuclear Energy Option: An Alternative for the 90s.* New York: Plenum.

Flavin, Christopher. 1988. "The Case Against Reviving Nuclear Power," *World Watch,* July/Aug., 27–35.

Flavin, Christopher. 1992. "Building a Bridge to Sustainable Energy," in Lester Brown, et al., *State of the World 1992,* pp. 27–55. New York: W. W. Norton.

Ford, Daniel F. 1986. *Meltdown.* New York: Simon & Schuster.

Fund for Renewable Energy and the Environment. 1987. *The Oil Rollercoaster.* Washington, D.C.: Fund for Renewable Energy and the Environment.

Golay, Michael W., and Neil E. Todreas. 1990. "Advanced Light-Water Reactors," *Scientific American,* April, 82–89.

Heede, H. Richard, et al. 1985. *The Hidden Costs of Energy.* Washington, D.C.: Center for Renewable Resources.

Hubbard, Harold H. 1991. "The Real Costs of Energy," *Scientific American,* vol. 265, no. 4, 36–41.

Hughes, Barry B., et al. 1985. *Energy in the Global Arena: Actors, Values, Policies, and Futures.* Durham, N.C.: Duke University Press.

Jasper, James M. 1990. *Nuclear Politics: Energy and the State in the United States, Sweden, and France.* Princeton, N.J.: Princeton University Press.

League of Women Voters Education Fund. 1985. *The Nuclear Waste Primer.* Washington, D.C.: League of Women Voters.

Lenssen, Nicholas. 1991. *Nuclear Waste: The Problem That Won't Go Away.* Washington, D.C.: Worldwatch Institute.

Lovins, Amory B., and L. Hunter Lovins. 1982. *Brittle Power: Energy Strategy for National Security.* Andover, Mass.: Brick House.

Medvedev, Grigori. 1990. *The Truth About Chernobyl.* New York: Basic Books.

Morone, Joseph G., and Edward J. Woodhouse. 1989. *The Demise of Nuclear Energy?* New Haven, Conn.: Yale University Press.

Murray, Raymond L. 1989. *Understanding Radioactive Waste.* 3rd ed. Columbus, Ohio: Batelle Press.

National Academy of Sciences. 1990. *Energy: Production, Consumption, and Consequences.* Washington, D.C.: National Academy Press.

National Academy of Sciences. 1991. *Nuclear Power: Technical and Institutional Options for the Future.* Washington, D.C.: National Academy Press.

Office of Technology Assessment. 1991. *Complex Cleanup: The Environmental Legacy of Nuclear Weapons Production.* Washington, D.C.: Government Printing Office.

Oppenheimer, Ernest J. 1990. *Natural Gas, the Best Energy Choice.* New York: Pen & Podium.

Patterson, Walter C. 1984. *The Plutonium Business and the Spread of the Bomb.* San Francisco: Sierra Club Books.

President's Commission on the Accident at Three Mile Island. 1979. *Report of the President's Commission on the Accident at Three Mile Island.* Washington, D.C.: Government Printing Office.

Reddy, Amulya K. N., and Jose Goldenberg. 1990. "Energy for the Developing World," *Scientific American,* September, 111–118.

Rosenbaum, Walter A. 1987. *Energy, Politics, and Public Policy.* 2nd ed. Washington, D.C.: Congressional Quarterly.

Schobert, Harold H. 1987. *Coal: The Energy Source of the Past and Future.* Washington, D.C.: American Chemical Society.

Shea, Cynthia Pollock. 1989. "Decommissioning Nuclear Plants: Breaking Up Is Hard to Do," *World Watch,* July/August, 10–16.

Sierra Club. 1991. *Kick the Oil Habit: Choosing a Safe Energy Future for America.* San Francisco: Sierra Club Books.

Squillace, Mark. 1990. *Strip Mining Handbook.* Washington, D.C.: Friends of the Earth.

Union of Concerned Scientists. 1990. *Safety Second: The NRC and America's Nuclear Power Plants.* Bloomington: Indiana University Press.

U.S. Department of Energy. 1988. *An Analysis of Nuclear Power Operating Costs.* Washington, D.C.: Government Printing Office.

Watson, Robert K. 1988. *Fact Sheet on Oil and Conservation Resources.* New York: Natural Resources Defense Council.

Weinberg, Alvin M. 1985. *Continuing the Nuclear Dialogue.* La Grange Park, Ill.: American Nuclear Society.

Winteringham, F.P.W. 1991. *Energy Use and the Environment.* Boca Raton, Fla.: Lewis Publishers.

Yeargin, Daniel. 1990. *The Prize: The Epic Quest for Oil, Money, and Power.* New York: Simon & Schuster.

Chapter 19 Nonrenewable Mineral Resources and Solid Waste

Blumberg, Louis, and Robert Gottlieb. 1988. *War on Waste—Can America Win Its Battle with Garbage?* Covelo, Calif.: Island Press.

Borgese, Elisabeth Mann. 1985. *The Mines of Neptune: Minerals and Metals from the Sea.* New York: Abrams.

Boyd, Susan, et al., eds. 1988. *Waste: Choices for Communities.* Washington, D.C.: CONCERN.

Connett, Paul. 1989. *Waste Management As If the Future Mattered.* Canton, N.Y.: Work on Waste.

Dorr, Ann. 1984. *Minerals—Foundations of Society.* Montgomery County, Md.: League of Women Voters of Montgomery County, Maryland.

Earth Works Group. 1990. *The Recycler's Handbook: Simple Things You Can Do.* Berkeley: Earth Works Press.

Environmental Protection Agency. 1989. *Solid Waste Disposal in the United States.* Washington, D.C.: Government Printing Office.

Keller, Edward D. 1988. *Environmental Geology.* 5th ed. Columbus, Ohio: Charles E Merrill.

Kirshner, Dan, et al. 1988. *To Burn or Not to Burn.* New York: Environmental Defense Fund.

Newsday. 1989. *Rush to Burn: Solving America's Garbage Crisis?* Covelo, Calif.: Island Press.

Office of Solid Waste. 1989. *Recycling Works! State and Local Solutions to Solid Waste Management.* Washington, D.C.: Environmental Protection Agency.

Office of Technology Assessment. 1989. *Facing America's Trash: What's Next for Municipal Solid Waste.* Washington, D.C.: Government Printing Office.

Platt, Brenda, et al. 1991. *Beyond 40 Percent: Record-Setting Recycling and Composting Programs.* Covelo, Calif.: Island Press.

Pollock, Cynthia. 1987. *Mining Urban Wastes: The Potential for Recycling.* Washington, D.C.: Worldwatch Institute.

Reynolds, Michael. 1991. *Earthship,* vols. 1 & 2. Taos, N.M.: Survival Press.

Seldman, Neil, and Bill Perkins. 1988. *Designing the Waste Stream.* Washington, D.C.: Institute for Local Self-Reliance.

Young, John E. 1991. *Discarding the Throwaway Society.* Washington, D.C.: Worldwatch Institute.

Young, John E. 1992. "Mining the Earth," in Lester R. Brown, et al., *State of the World 1992,* pp. 99–118. New York: W. W. Norton.

Youngquist, Walter. 1990. *Mineral Resources and the Destinies of Nations.* Portland, Ore.: National Book.

GLOSSARY

abiotic Nonliving. Compare *biotic*.

absolute resource scarcity Situation in which there are not enough actual or affordable supplies of a resource left to meet present or future demand. Compare *relative resource scarcity*.

acclimation Adjustment to slowly changing new conditions. Compare *threshold effect*.

acid deposition The falling of acids and acid-forming compounds from the atmosphere to Earth's surface. Acid deposition is commonly known as acid rain, a term that refers only to wet deposition of droplets of acids and acid-forming compounds.

acid solution Any water solution that has more hydrogen ions (H^+) than hydroxide ions (OH^-); any water solution with a pH less than 7. Compare *basic solution, neutral solution*.

active solar heating system System that uses solar collectors to capture energy from the sun and store it as heat for space heating and heating water. A liquid or air pumped through the collectors transfers the captured heat to a storage system such as an insulated water tank or rock bed. Pumps or fans then distribute the stored heat or hot water throughout a dwelling as needed. Compare *passive solar heating system*.

advanced sewage treatment Specialized chemical and physical processes that reduce the amount of specific pollutants left in wastewater after primary and secondary sewage treatment. This type of treatment is usually expensive. See also *primary sewage treatment, secondary sewage treatment*.

aerobic organism Organism that needs oxygen to stay alive. Compare *anaerobic organism*.

aerobic respiration Complex process that occurs in the cells of most living organisms in which nutrient organic molecules such as glucose ($C_6H_{12}O_6$) combine with oxygen (O_2) and produce carbon dioxide (CO_2), water (H_2O), and energy. Compare *photosynthesis*.

age structure (age distribution) Percentage of the population, or the number of people of each sex, at each age level in a population.

Agricultural Revolution Gradual shift from small, mobile hunting-and-gathering bands to settled agricultural communities, where people survived by learning how to breed and raise wild animals and to cultivate wild plants near where they lived. It began 10,000 to 12,000 years ago. Compare *Industrial Revolution*.

agroforestry Planting trees and crops together.

air pollution One or more chemicals in high enough concentrations in the air to harm humans, other animals, vegetation, or materials. Excess heat or noise can also be considered as forms of air pollution. Such chemicals or physical conditions are called air pollutants. See *primary air pollutant, secondary air pollutant*.

alien species See *immigrant species*.

alley cropping Planting of crops in strips with rows of trees or shrubs on each side.

alpha particle Positively charged matter, consisting of two neutrons and two protons, that is emitted as a form of radioactivity from the nuclei of some radioisotopes. See also *beta particle, gamma rays*.

altitude Height above sea level. Compare *latitude*.

ambient Outdoor.

anaerobic organism Organism that does not need oxygen to stay alive. Compare *aerobic organism*.

ancient forest See *old-growth forest*.

animal manure Dung and urine of animals that can be used as a form of organic fertilizer. Compare *green manure*.

animals Eukaryotic, multicelled organisms such as sponges, jellyfishes, arthropods (insects, shrimp, lobsters), mollusks (snails, clams, oysters, octopuses), fish, amphibians (frogs, toads, salamanders), reptiles (turtles, lizards, alligators, crocodiles, snakes), birds, mammals (kangaroos, bats, cats, rabbits, elephants, whales, porpoises, monkeys, apes, humans). See *carnivores, herbivores, omnivores*.

aquaculture Growing and harvesting of fish and shellfish for human use in freshwater ponds, irrigation ditches, and lakes, or in cages or fenced-in areas of coastal lagoons and estuaries. See *fish farming, fish ranching*.

aquatic Pertaining to water. Compare *terrestrial*.

aquifer Porous, water-saturated layers of sand, gravel, or bed rock that can yield an economically significant amount of water. See *confined aquifer, unconfined aquifer*.

arable land Land that can be cultivated to grow crops.

area strip mining Cutting deep trenches to remove minerals such as coal and phosphate found near the earth's surface in fairly flat terrain. Compare *contour strip mining, open-pit mining*.

arid Dry. A desert or other area with an arid climate has little precipitation.

atmosphere The whole mass of air surrounding the earth. See *stratosphere, troposphere*.

atomic number Number of protons in the nucleus of an atom. Compare *mass number*.

atoms Minute units made of subatomic particles that are the basic building blocks of all chemical elements and thus all matter; the smallest unit of an element that can exist and still have the unique characteristics of that element. Compare *ion, molecule*.

autotroph See *producer*.

bacteria Prokaryotic, one-celled organisms. Some transmit diseases. Most act as decomposers and get the nutrients they need by breaking down complex organic compounds in the tissues of living or dead organisms into simpler inorganic nutrient compounds.

basic solution Water solution with more hydroxide ions (OH^-) than hydrogen ions (H^+); water solution with a pH greater than 7. Compare *acid solution, neutral solution*.

beta particle Swiftly moving electron emitted by the nucleus of a radioactive isotope. See also *alpha particle, gamma rays*.

bioconcentration Accumulation of a harmful chemical in a particular part of the body. Compare *biological amplification*.

biodegradable pollutant Material that can be broken down into simpler substances (elements and compounds) by bacteria or other decomposers. Paper and most organic wastes such as animal manure are biodegradable but can take decades to biodegrade in modern landfills. Compare *degradable pollutant, nondegradable pollutant, slowly degradable pollutant*.

biodiversity See *biological diversity*.

biofuel Gas or liquid fuel (such as ethyl alcohol) made from plant material (biomass).

biogeochemical cycle Natural processes that recycle nutrients in various chemical forms from the nonliving environment, to living organisms, and then back to the nonliving environment. Examples are the carbon, oxygen, nitrogen, phosphorus, sulfur, and hydrologic cycles.

biological amplification Increase in concentration of DDT, PCBs, and other slowly degradable, fat-soluble chemicals in organisms at successively higher trophic levels of a food chain or web.

biological community See *community*.

biological diversity Variety of different species (*species diversity*), genetic variability among individuals within each species (*genetic diversity*), and variety of ecosystems (*ecological diversity*).

biological evolution See *evolution*.

biological oxygen demand (BOD) Amount of dissolved oxygen needed by aerobic decomposers to break down the organic materials in a given volume of water at a certain temperature over a specified time period.

biological pest control Control of pest populations by natural predators, parasites, or disease-causing bacteria and viruses (pathogens).

biomass Organic matter produced by plants and other photosynthetic producers; total dry weight of all living organisms that can be supported at each trophic level in a food chain; dry weight of all organic matter in plants and animals in an ecosystem; plant materials and animal wastes used as fuel.

biome Terrestrial regions inhabited by certain types of life, especially vegetation. Examples are various types of deserts, grasslands, and forests.

biosphere Zone of Earth where life is found. It consists of parts of the atmosphere (the troposphere), hydrosphere (mostly surface water and groundwater), and lithosphere (mostly soil and surface rocks and sediments on the bottoms of oceans and other bodies of water) where life is found. See also *ecosphere*.

biotic Living. Living organisms make up the biotic parts of ecosystems. Compare *abiotic*.

biotic potential Maximum rate at which the population of a given species can increase when there are no limits of any sort on its rate of growth. See *environmental resistance*.

birth rate See *crude birth rate*.

bitumen Gooey, black, high-sulfur, heavy oil extracted from tar sand and then upgraded to synthetic fuel oil. See *tar sand*.

breeder nuclear fission reactor Nuclear fission reactor that produces more nuclear fuel than it consumes by converting nonfissionable uranium-238 into fissionable plutonium-239.

calorie Unit of energy; amount of energy needed to raise the temperature of 1 gram of water 1°C. See also *kilocalorie*.

cancer Group of more than 120 different diseases—one for each type of cell in the human body. Each type of cancer produces a tumor in which cells multiply uncontrollably and invade surrounding tissue.

capital goods Tools, machinery, equipment, factory buildings, transportation facilities, and other manufactured items made from natural resources and used to produce and distribute consumer goods and services. Compare *labor, natural resources*.

carbon cycle Cyclic movement of carbon in different chemical forms from the environment, to organisms, and then back to the environment.

carcinogen Chemicals, ionizing radiation, and viruses that cause or promote the growth of cancer. See *cancer, mutagen, teratogen*.

carnivore Animal that feeds on other animals. Compare *herbivore, omnivore*.

carrying capacity (K) Maximum population of a particular species that a given habitat can support over a given period of time. See *consumption overpopulation, people overpopulation*.

cell Smallest living unit of an organism. See *eukaryotic cell, prokaryotic cell*.

CFCs See *chlorofluorocarbons*.

chain reaction Multiple nuclear fissions taking place within a certain mass of a fissionable isotope that release an enormous amount of energy in a short time.

chemical One of the millions of different elements and compounds found naturally and synthesized by humans. See *compound, element.*

chemical change Interaction between chemicals in which there is a change in the chemical composition of the elements or compounds involved. Compare *physical change.*

chemical reaction See *chemical change.*

chemosynthesis Process in which certain organisms (mostly specialized bacteria) extract inorganic compounds from their environment and convert them into organic nutrient compounds without the presence of sunlight. Compare *photosynthesis.*

chlorinated hydrocarbon Organic compound made up of atoms of carbon, hydrogen, and chlorine. Examples are DDT and PCBs.

chlorofluorocarbons (CFCs) Organic compounds made up of atoms of carbon, chlorine, and fluorine. An example is Freon-12 (CCl_2F_2), used as a refrigerant in refrigerators and air conditioners and in making plastics such as Styrofoam. Gaseous CFCs can deplete the ozone layer when they slowly rise into the stratosphere and their chlorine atoms react with ozone molecules.

chromosome A grouping of various genes and associated proteins in plant and animal cells that carry certain types of genetic information. See *genes.*

clear-cutting Method of timber harvesting in which all trees in a forested area are removed in a single cutting. Compare *selective cutting, seed-tree cutting, shelterwood cutting.*

climate General pattern of atmospheric or weather conditions, seasonal variations, and weather extremes in a region over a long period — at least 30 years; average weather of an area. Compare *weather.*

climax community See *mature community.*

coal Solid, combustible mixture of organic compounds with 30% to 98% carbon by weight, mixed with varying amounts of water and small amounts of sulfur and nitrogen. It is formed in several stages as the remains of plants are subjected to heat and pressure over millions of years.

coal gasification Conversion of solid coal to synthetic natural gas (SNG).

coal liquefaction Conversion of solid coal to a liquid hydrocarbon fuel such as synthetic gasoline or methanol.

coastal wetland Land along a coastline, extending inland from an estuary that is covered with salt water all or part of the year. Examples are marshes, bays, lagoons, tidal flats, and mangrove swamps. Compare *inland wetland.*

coastal zone Relatively warm, nutrient-rich, shallow part of the ocean that extends from the high-tide mark on land to the edge of a shelflike extension of continental land masses known as the continental shelf. Compare *open sea.*

coevolution Evolution when two or more species interact and exert selective pressures on each other that can lead each species to undergo various adaptations. See *evolution, natural selection.*

cogeneration Production of two useful forms of energy such as high-temperature heat or steam and electricity from the same fuel source.

commensalism An interaction between organisms of different species in which one type of organism benefits, while the other type is neither helped nor harmed to any great degree. Compare *mutualism.*

commercial extinction Depletion of the population of a wild species used as a resource to a level where it is no longer profitable to harvest the species.

commercial hunting Killing of wild animals for profit from sale of their furs, meat, or other parts.

See *poaching.* Compare *sport hunting, subsistence hunting.*

commercial inorganic fertilizer Commercially prepared mixtures of plant nutrients such as nitrates, phosphates, and potassium applied to the soil to help restore fertility and increase crop yields. Compare *organic fertilizer.*

common-property resource Resource that people are normally free to use; each user depletes or degrades the available supply. Most are potentially renewable and are owned by no one. Examples are clean air, fish in parts of the ocean not under the control of a coastal country, migratory birds, gases of the lower atmosphere, and the ozone content of the upper atmosphere. See *tragedy of the commons.*

community Populations of all species living and interacting in an area at a particular time.

competition Two or more individual organisms of a single species (*intraspecific competition*) or two or more individuals of different species (*interspecific competition*) attempting to use the same scarce resources in the same ecosystem.

competitive exclusion principle No two species can occupy exactly the same fundamental niche indefinitely in a habitat where there is not enough of a particular resource to meet the needs of both species. See *ecological niche, fundamental niche, realized niche.*

compost Partially decomposed organic plant and animal matter that can be used as a soil conditioner or fertilizer.

compound Combination of atoms, or oppositely charged ions, of two or more different elements held together by attractive forces called chemical bonds. See *inorganic compound, organic compound.* Compare *element.*

concentration Amount of a chemical in a particular volume or weight of air, water, soil, or other medium.

confined aquifer Aquifer between two layers of relatively impermeable Earth materials, such as clay or shale. Compare *unconfined aquifer.*

coniferous trees Cone-bearing trees, mostly evergreens, that have needle-shaped or scalelike leaves. They produce wood known commercially as softwood. Compare *deciduous plants.*

conservationists People who believe resources should be used, managed, and protected so they will not be degraded and unnecessarily wasted and will be available to present and future generations.

conservation-tillage farming Crop cultivation in which the soil is disturbed little (minimum-tillage farming) or not at all (no-till farming) to reduce soil erosion, lower labor costs, and save energy. Compare *conventional-tillage farming.*

constancy Ability of a living system, such as a population, to maintain a certain size. See *homeostasis.* Compare *inertia, resilience.*

consumer Organism that cannot synthesize the organic nutrients it needs and gets its organic nutrients by feeding on the tissues of producers or other consumers; generally divided into *primary consumers* (herbivores), *secondary consumers* (carnivores), *tertiary and higher consumers, omnivores,* and *detritivores* (decomposers and detritus feeders). In economics, one who uses economic goods.

consumption overpopulation Situation in which people in the world or in a geographic region use resources at such a high rate and without sufficient pollution prevention and control that significant pollution, resource depletion, and environmental degradation occur. Compare *people overpopulation.*

continental shelf Submerged part of a continent.

contour farming Plowing and planting across the changing slope of land, rather than in straight lines, to help retain water and reduce soil erosion.

contour strip mining Cutting a series of shelves or terraces along the side of a hill or mountain to remove a mineral such as coal from a deposit found near the earth's surface. Compare *area strip mining, open-pit mining.*

contraceptive Physical, chemical, or biological method used to prevent pregnancy.

conventional-tillage farming Making a planting surface by plowing land, disking it several times to break up the soil, and then smoothing the surface. Compare *conservation-tillage farming.*

convergent plate boundary Area where Earth's lithospheric plates are pushed together. See *subduction zone.* Compare *divergent plate boundary, transform fault.*

core Inner zone of the earth. It consists of a solid inner core and a liquid outer core. Compare *crust, mantle.*

cost-benefit analysis Estimates and comparison of short-term and long-term costs (losses) and benefits (gains) from an economic decision. If the estimated benefits exceed the estimated costs, the decision to buy an economic good or provide a public good is considered worthwhile.

critical mass Amount of fissionable nuclei needed to sustain a branching nuclear fission chain reaction.

critical mineral A mineral necessary to the economy of a country. Compare *strategic mineral.*

crop rotation Planting a field, or an area of a field, with different crops from year to year to reduce depletion of soil nutrients. A plant such as corn, tobacco, or cotton, which removes large amounts of nitrogen from the soil, is planted one year. The next year a legume such as soybeans, which add nitrogen to the soil, is planted.

crown fire Extremely hot forest fire that burns ground vegetation and tree tops. Compare *ground fire, surface fire.*

crude birth rate Annual number of live births per 1,000 persons in the population of a geographical area at the midpoint of a given year. Compare *crude death rate.*

crude death rate Annual number of deaths per 1,000 persons in the population of a geographical area at the midpoint of a given year. Compare *crude birth rate.*

crude oil Gooey liquid consisting mostly of hydrocarbon compounds and small amounts of compounds containing oxygen, sulfur, and nitrogen. Extracted from underground accumulations, it is sent to oil refineries, where it is converted to heating oil, diesel fuel, gasoline, tar, and other materials.

crust Solid outer zone of the earth. It consists of oceanic crust and continental crust. Compare *core, mantle.*

cultural eutrophication Overnourishment of aquatic ecosystems with plant nutrients (mostly nitrates and phosphates) because of human activities such as agriculture, urbanization, and discharges from industrial plants and sewage treatment plants. See *eutrophication.*

DDT Dichlorodiphenyltrichloroethane, a chlorinated hydrocarbon that has been widely used as a pesticide.

death rate See *crude death rate.*

debt-for-nature swap Agreement in which a certain amount of foreign debt is canceled in exchange for local currency investments that will improve natural resource management or protect certain areas from harmful development in the debtor country.

deciduous plants Trees, such as oaks and maples, and other plants that survive during dry seasons or cold seasons by shedding their leaves. Compare *coniferous trees, succulent plants.*

decomposer Organism that digests parts of dead organisms and cast-off fragments and wastes of living organisms by breaking down the complex organic molecules in those materials into simpler inorganic compounds and absorbing the soluble nutrients. Most of these chemicals are returned to the soil and water for reuse by producers. Decomposers consist of various bacteria and fungi. Compare *consumer, detritivore, producer*.

deforestation Removal of trees from a forested area without adequate replanting.

degradable pollutant Potentially polluting chemical that is broken down completely or reduced to acceptable levels by natural physical, chemical, and biological processes. Compare *biodegradable pollutant, nondegradable pollutant, slowly degradable pollutant*.

degree of urbanization Percentage of the population in the world, or a country, living in areas with a population of more than 2,500 people (higher in some countries). Compare *urban growth*.

demographic transition Hypothesis that countries, as they become industrialized, have declines in death rates followed by declines in birth rates.

demography Study of characteristics and changes in the size and structure of the human population in the world or other geographical area.

depletion time How long it takes to use a certain fraction — usually 80% — of the known or estimated supply of a nonrenewable resource at an assumed rate of use. Finding and extracting the remaining 20% usually costs more than it is worth.

desalination Purification of salt water or brackish (slightly salty) water by removing dissolved salts.

desert Biome where evaporation exceeds precipitation and the average amount of precipitation is less than 25 centimeters (10 inches) a year. Such areas have little vegetation or have widely spaced, mostly low vegetation. Compare *forest, grassland*.

desertification Conversion of rangeland, rainfed cropland, or irrigated cropland to desertlike land, with a drop in agricultural productivity of 10% or more. It is usually caused by a combination of overgrazing, soil erosion, prolonged drought, and climate change.

desirability quotient A number expressing the results of risk-benefit analysis by dividing the estimate of the benefits to society of using a particular product or technology by its estimated risks. See *risk-benefit analysis*. Compare *cost-benefit analysis*.

detritivore Consumer organism that feeds on detritus, parts of dead organisms and cast-off fragments and wastes of living organisms. The two principal types are *detritus feeders* and *decomposers*.

detritus Parts of dead organisms and cast-off fragments and wastes of living organisms.

detritus feeder Organism that extracts nutrients from fragments of dead organisms and their cast-off parts and organic wastes. Examples are earthworms, termites, and crabs. Compare *decomposer*.

deuterium (D: hydrogen-2) Isotope of the element hydrogen, with a nucleus containing one proton and one neutron and a mass number of 2. Compare *tritium*.

dieback Sharp reduction in the population of a species when its numbers exceed the carrying capacity of its habitat. See *carrying capacity, consumption overpopulation, overshoot, people overpopulation*.

differential reproduction Ability of individuals with adaptive genetic traits to produce more living offspring than individuals without such traits. See also *natural selection*.

discount rate How much economic value a resource will have in the future compared with its present value.

dissolved oxygen (DO) content (level) Amount of oxygen gas (O_2) dissolved in a given volume of water at a particular temperature and pressure, often expressed as a concentration in parts of oxygen per million parts of water.

divergent plate boundary Area where Earth's lithospheric plates move apart in opposite directions. Compare *convergent plate boundary, transform fault*.

DNA (deoxyribonucleic acid) Large molecules in the cells of organisms; carries genetic information in living organisms.

doubling time The time it takes (usually in years) for the quantity of something growing exponentially to double. It can be calculated by dividing the annual percentage growth rate into 70. See *rule of 70*.

drainage basin See *watershed*.

dredging Type of surface mining in which chain buckets and draglines scrape up sand, gravel, and other surface deposits covered with water. It is also used to remove sediment from streams and harbors to maintain shipping channels.

drift-net fishing Catching fish in huge nets that drift in the water.

drip irrigation Using small tubes or pipes to deliver small amounts of irrigation water to the roots of plants.

drought Condition in which an area does not get enough water because of lower than normal precipitation, higher than normal temperatures that increase evaporation, or both.

dust dome Dome of heated air that surrounds an urban area and traps and keeps pollutants, especially suspended particulate matter. See also *urban heat island*.

Earth capital Earth's natural resources and processes that sustain us and other species.

ecological diversity The variety of forests, deserts, grasslands, oceans, streams, lakes, and other biological communities interacting with one another and with their nonliving environment. See *biological diversity*. Compare *genetic diversity, species diversity*.

ecological land-use planning Method for deciding how land should be used; development of an integrated model that considers geological, ecological, health, and social variables.

ecological niche Total way of life or role of a species in an ecosystem. It includes all physical, chemical, and biological conditions a species needs to live and reproduce in an ecosystem. See *fundamental niche, realized niche*.

ecological succession Process in which communities of plant and animal species in a particular area are replaced over time by a series of different and usually more complex communities. See *primary succession, secondary succession*.

ecology Study of the interactions of living organisms with one another and with their nonliving environment of matter and energy; study of the structure and functions of nature.

economic decision Choosing what to do with scarce resources; deciding what goods and services to produce, how to produce them, how much to produce, and how to distribute them to people.

economic depletion Exhaustion of 80% of the estimated supply of a nonrenewable resource. Finding, extracting, and processing the remaining 20% usually costs more than it is worth; may also apply to the depletion of a potentially renewable resource, such as a species of fish or trees.

economic good Any service or material item that gives people satisfaction.

economic growth Increase in the real value of all final goods and services produced by an economy; an increase in real GNP.

economic needs Types and amounts of certain economic goods — food, clothing, water, oxygen, shelter — that each of us must have to survive and to stay healthy. See also *poverty*. Compare *economic wants*.

economic resources Natural resources, capital goods, and labor used in an economy to produce material goods and services. See *capital goods, labor, natural resources*.

economics Study of how individuals and groups make decisions about what to do with economic resources to meet their needs and wants.

economic wants Economic goods that go beyond our basic economic needs. These wants are influenced by the customs and conventions of the society we live in and by our level of affluence. Compare *economic needs*.

ecosphere Earth's collection of living organisms (found in the biosphere) interacting with one another and their nonliving environment (energy and matter) throughout the world; all of Earth's ecosystems. See also *biosphere*.

ecosystem Community of different species interacting with one another and with the chemical and physical factors making up its nonliving environment.

efficiency Measure of how much output of energy or of a product is produced by a certain input of energy, materials, or labor. See *energy efficiency*.

electromagnetic radiation Forms of kinetic energy traveling as electromagnetic waves. Examples are radio waves, TV waves, microwaves, infrared radiation, visible light, ultraviolet radiation, X rays, and gamma rays. Compare *ionizing radiation, nonionizing radiation*.

electron (e) Tiny particle moving around outside the nucleus of an atom. Each electron has one unit of negative charge ($^-$) and almost no mass.

element Chemical, such as hydrogen (H), iron (Fe), sodium (Na), carbon (C), nitrogen (N), or oxygen (O), whose distinctly different atoms serve as the basic building blocks of all matter. There are 92 naturally occurring elements. Another 15 have been made in laboratories. Two or more elements combine to form compounds that make up most of the world's matter. Compare *compound*.

emigration Migration of people out of one country or area to take up permanent residence in another country or area. Compare *immigration*.

endangered species Wild species with so few individual survivors that the species could soon become extinct in all or most of its natural range. Compare *threatened species*.

energy Capacity to do work by performing mechanical, physical, chemical, or electrical tasks or to cause a heat transfer between two objects at different temperatures.

energy conservation Reduction or elimination of unnecessary energy use and waste. See *energy efficiency*.

energy efficiency Percentage of the total energy input that does useful work and is not converted into low-quality, usually useless, heat in an energy conversion system or process. See *energy quality, net useful energy*.

energy quality Ability of a form of energy to do useful work. High-temperature heat and the chemical energy in fossil fuels and nuclear fuels is concentrated high-quality energy. Low-quality energy such as low-temperature heat is dispersed or diluted and cannot do much useful work. See *high-quality energy, low-quality energy*.

enhanced oil recovery Removal of some of the heavy oil left in an oil well after primary and secondary recovery. Compare *primary oil recovery, secondary oil recovery*.

environment All external conditions and factors, living and nonliving (chemicals and energy), that affect an organism or other specified system during its lifetime.

environmental degradation Depletion or destruction of a potentially renewable resource such as soil, grassland, forest, or wildlife by using it at a faster rate than it is naturally replenished. If such use continues, the resource can become nonrenewable on a human time scale or nonexistent (extinct). See also *sustainable yield*.

environmentalists People who are primarily concerned with preventing pollution and degradation of the air, water, soil, and Earth's biodiversity. See *conservationists*.

environmental resistance All the limiting factors jointly acting to limit the growth of a population. See *biotic potential, limiting factor*.

environmental science Study of how we and other species interact with each other and with the nonliving environment of matter and energy. It is a holistic science that uses and integrates knowledge from physics, chemistry, biology (especially ecology), geology, resource technology and engineering, resource conservation and management, demography (the study of population dynamics), economics, politics, and ethics.

EPA Environmental Protection Agency; responsible for managing federal efforts in the United States to control air and water pollution, radiation and pesticide hazards, environmental research, and solid waste disposal.

epidemiology Study of the patterns of disease or other harmful effects from toxic exposure within defined groups of people to find out why some people get sick and some do not.

erosion Process or group of processes by which earth materials, loose or consolidated, are dissolved, loosened, and worn away, removed from one place and deposited in another. See *weathering*.

estuarine zone Area near the coastline that consists of estuaries and coastal saltwater wetlands, extending to the edge of the continental shelf.

estuary Partially enclosed coastal area at the mouth of a river where its fresh water, carrying fertile silt and runoff from the land, mixes with salty seawater.

ethics What we believe to be right or wrong behavior.

eukaryotic cell Cell containing a *nucleus*, a region of genetic material surrounded by a membrane. Membranes also enclose several of the other internal parts found in a eukaryotic cell. Compare *prokaryotic cell*.

eutrophication Physical, chemical, and biological changes that take place after a lake, an estuary, or a slow-flowing stream receives inputs of plant nutrients — mostly nitrates and phosphates — from natural erosion and runoff from the surrounding land basin. See *cultural eutrophication*.

eutrophic lake Lake with a large or excessive supply of plant nutrients — mostly nitrates and phosphates. Compare *mesotrophic lake, oligotrophic lake*.

evaporation Physical change in which a liquid changes into a vapor or gas.

even-aged management Method of forest management in which trees, usually of a single species in a given stand, are maintained at about the same age and size and are harvested all at once so a new stand may grow. Compare *uneven-aged management*.

even-aged stand Forest area where all trees are about the same age. Usually, such stands contain trees of only one or two species. See *even-aged management, tree farm*. Compare *uneven-aged management, uneven-aged stand*.

evergreen plants Plants that keep some of their leaves or needles throughout the year. Examples are ferns, and cone-bearing trees (conifers) such as firs, spruces, pines, redwoods, and sequoias. Compare *deciduous plants, succulent plants*.

evolution Changes in the genetic composition (gene pool) of a population exposed to new environmental conditions as a result of differential reproduction. Evolution can lead to the splitting of a single species into two or more different species. See also *differential reproduction, natural selection, speciation*.

exhaustible resources See *nonrenewable resources*.

exponential growth Growth in which some quantity, such as population size or economic output, increases by a fixed percentage of the whole in a given time period; when the increase in quantity over time is plotted, this type of growth yields a curve shaped like the letter J. Compare *linear growth*.

external benefit Beneficial social effect of producing and using an economic good that is not included in the market price of the good. Compare *external cost, internal cost, true cost*.

external cost Harmful social effect of producing and using an economic good that is not included in the market price of the good. Compare *external benefit, internal cost, true cost*.

externalities Social benefits ("goods") and social costs ("bads") not included in the market price of an economic good. See *external benefit, external cost*. Compare *internal cost, true cost*.

extinction Complete disappearance of a species from the earth. This happens when a species cannot adapt and successfully reproduce under new environmental conditions or evolves into one or more new species. See also *endangered species, threatened species*. Compare *speciation*.

factors of production See *economic resources*.

family planning Providing information, clinical services, and contraceptives to help individuals or couples choose the number and spacing of children they want to have.

famine Widespread malnutrition and starvation in a particular area because of a shortage of food, usually caused by drought, war, flood, earthquake, or other catastrophic event that disrupts food production and distribution.

feedlot Confined outdoor or indoor space used to raise hundreds or thousands of domesticated livestock. Compare *rangeland*.

fertilizer Substance that adds inorganic or organic plant nutrients to soil and improves its ability to grow crops, trees, or other vegetation. See *commercial inorganic fertilizer, organic fertilizer*.

first law of ecology We can never do merely one thing. Any intrusion into nature has numerous effects, many of which are unpredictable.

first law of energy See *first law of thermodynamics*.

first law of thermodynamics (energy) In any physical or chemical change, no detectable amount of energy is created or destroyed, but in these processes energy can be changed from one form to another; you can't get more energy out of something than you put in; in terms of energy quantity, you can't get something for nothing (there is no free lunch). This law does not apply to nuclear changes, where energy can be produced from small amounts of matter. See also *second law of thermodynamics*.

fishery Concentrations of particular aquatic species suitable for commercial harvesting in a given ocean area or inland body of water.

fish farming Form of aquaculture in which fish are cultivated in a controlled pond or other environment and harvested when they reach the desired size. See also *fish ranching*.

fish ranching Form of aquaculture in which members of a fish species such as salmon are held in captivity for the first few years of their lives, released, and then harvested as adults when they return from the ocean to their freshwater birthplace to spawn. See also *fish farming*.

fissionable isotope Isotope that can split apart when hit by a neutron at the right speed and thus undergo nuclear fission. Examples are uranium-235 and plutonium-239.

floodplain Flat valley floor next to a stream channel. For legal purposes, the term is often applied to any low area that has the potential for flooding, including certain coastal areas.

flyway Generally fixed route along which waterfowl migrate from one area to another at certain seasons of the year.

food chain Series of organisms, each eating or decomposing the preceding one. Compare *food web*.

food web Complex network of many interconnected food chains and feeding relationships. Compare *food chain*.

forage Vegetation eaten by animals, especially grazing and browsing animals.

forest Biome with enough average annual precipitation (at least 76 centimeters, or 30 inches) to support growth of various species of trees and smaller forms of vegetation. Compare *desert, grassland*.

fossil fuel Products of partial or complete decomposition of plants and animals that occur as crude oil, coal, natural gas, or heavy oils as a result of exposure to heat and pressure in Earth's crust over millions of years. See *coal, crude oil, natural gas*.

Freons See *chlorofluorocarbons*.

frontier worldview See *throwaway worldview*.

fundamental niche The full potential range of the physical, chemical, and biological factors a species can use, if there is no competition from other species. See *ecological niche*. Compare *realized niche*.

fungi Eukaryotic, mostly multicelled organisms such as mushrooms, molds, and yeasts. As decomposers, they get the nutrients they need by secreting enzymes that break down the organic matter in the tissue of other living or dead organisms. Then they absorb the resulting nutrients.

fungicide Chemical that kills fungi.

Gaia hypothesis Proposal that Earth is alive and can be considered a system that operates and changes by feedbacks of information between its living and nonliving components.

game species Type of wild animal that people hunt or fish for sport and recreation and sometimes for food.

gamma rays A form of ionizing, electromagnetic radiation with a high energy content emitted by some radioisotopes. They readily penetrate body tissues.

gasohol Vehicle fuel consisting of a mixture of gasoline and ethyl or methyl alcohol — typically 10% to 23% ethanol or methanol by volume.

gene pool All genetic (hereditary) information contained in a reproducing population of a particular species.

generalist species Species with a broad ecological niche. They can live in many different places, eat a variety of foods, and tolerate a wide range of environmental conditions. Examples are flies, cockroaches, mice, rats, and human beings. Compare *specialist species*.

genes Segments of various DNA molecules that control hereditary characteristics in organisms.

genetic adaptation Changes in the genetic makeup of organisms of a species that allow the species to reproduce and gain a competitive advantage under changed environmental conditions. See *differential reproduction, evolution, natural selection*.

genetic diversity Variability in the genetic makeup among individuals within a single species. See *biodiversity*. Compare *ecological diversity, species diversity*.

geosphere Earth's interior core, mantle, and crust (containing soil and rock). Compare *atmosphere, biosphere, ecosphere, hydrosphere, lithosphere*.

geothermal energy Heat transferred from the earth's underground concentrations of dry steam (steam with no water droplets), wet steam (a mixture of steam and water droplets), or hot water trapped in fractured or porous rock.

GNP See *gross national product*.

grassland Biome found in regions where moderate annual average precipitation (25 to 76 centimeters, or 10 to 30 inches) is enough to support the growth of grass and small plants but not enough to support large stands of trees. Compare *desert, forest*.

greenhouse effect A natural effect that traps heat in the atmosphere (troposphere) near Earth's surface. Some of the heat flowing back toward space from Earth's surface is absorbed by water vapor, carbon dioxide, ozone, and several other gases in the atmosphere and then reradiated back toward the earth's surface. If the atmospheric concentrations of these greenhouse gases rise, the average temperature of the lower atmosphere will gradually increase.

greenhouse gases Gases in Earth's lower atmosphere (troposphere) that cause the greenhouse effect. Examples are carbon dioxide, chlorofluorocarbons, ozone, methane, water vapor, and nitrous oxide.

green manure Freshly cut or still-growing green vegetation that is plowed into the soil to increase the organic matter and humus available to support crop growth. Compare *animal manure*.

green revolution Popular term for introduction of scientifically bred or selected varieties of grain (rice, wheat, maize) that, with high enough inputs of fertilizer and water, can greatly increase crop yields.

gross national product (GNP) Total market value in current dollars of all goods and services produced by an economy for final use during a year. Compare *per capita GNP, per capita real NEW, real GNP*.

gross primary productivity See *primary productivity*.

ground fire Fire that burns decayed leaves or peat deep below the ground surface. Compare *crown fire, surface fire*.

groundwater Water that sinks into the soil and is stored in slowly flowing and slowly renewed underground reservoirs called aquifers; underground water in the zone of saturation, below the water table. See *confined aquifer, unconfined aquifer*. Compare *runoff, surface water*.

habitat Place or type of place where an organism or a population of organisms lives. Compare *ecological niche*.

hazard Something that can cause injury, disease, economic loss, or environmental damage.

hazardous substance Chemical that can cause harm because it is flammable or explosive or that can irritate or damage the skin or lungs (such as strong acidic or alkaline substances) or cause allergic reactions of the immune system (allergens).

hazardous waste Any solid, liquid, or containerized gas that can catch fire easily, is corrosive to skin tissue or metals, is unstable and can explode or release toxic fumes, or has harmful concentrations of one or more toxic materials that can leach out. See also *toxic waste*.

heat Total kinetic energy of all the randomly moving atoms, ions, or molecules within a given substance, excluding the overall motion of the whole object. This form of kinetic energy flows from one body to another when there is a temperature difference between the two bodies. Heat always flows spontaneously from a hot sample of matter to a colder sample of matter. This is one way to state the second law of thermodynamics. Compare *temperature*.

heavy oil Black, high-sulfur, tarlike oil found in deposits of crude oil, tar sands, and oil shale.

herbicide Chemical that kills a plant or inhibits its growth.

herbivore Plant-eating organism. Examples are deer, sheep, grasshoppers, and zooplankton. Compare *carnivore, omnivore*.

heterotroph See *consumer*.

high-quality energy Energy that is organized or concentrated and has great ability to perform useful work. Examples are high-temperature heat and the energy in electricity, coal, oil, gasoline, sunlight, and nuclei of uranium-235. Compare *low-quality energy*.

high-quality matter Matter that is organized, concentrated, and contains a high concentration of a useful resource. Compare *low-quality matter*.

homeostasis A dynamic steady state in which internal processes change in response to changes in external environmental conditions to maintain constant internal conditions. See *constancy, inertia, resilience*.

host Plant or animal upon which a parasite feeds.

humus Slightly soluble residue of undigested or partially decomposed organic material in topsoil. This material helps retain water and water-soluble nutrients, which can be taken up by plant roots.

hunter-gatherers People who get their food by gathering edible wild plants and other materials and by hunting wild animals and fish.

hydrocarbon Organic compound of hydrogen and carbon atoms.

hydroelectric power plant Structure in which the energy of falling or flowing water spins a turbine generator to produce electricity.

hydrologic cycle Biogeochemical cycle that collects, purifies, and distributes the earth's fixed supply of water from the environment, to living organisms, and back to the environment.

hydropower Electrical energy produced by falling or flowing water. See *hydroelectric power plant*.

hydrosphere Earth's liquid water (oceans, lakes and other bodies of surface water, and underground water), Earth's frozen water (polar ice caps, floating ice cap, and ice in soil known as permafrost), and small amounts of water vapor in the atmosphere.

identified resources Deposits of a particular mineral-bearing material of which the location, quantity, and quality are known or have been estimated from direct geological evidence and measurements. Compare *total resources, undiscovered resources*.

igneous rock Rock formed when molten rock material (magma) wells up from Earth's interior, cools, and solidifies into rock masses. See *rock cycle*. Compare *metamorphic rock, sedimentary rock*.

immature community Community at an early stage of ecological succession. It usually has a low number of species and ecological niches and cannot capture and use energy and cycle critical nutrients as efficiently as more complex, mature ecosystems. Compare *mature community*.

immigrant species Species that migrate into an ecosystem or that are deliberately or accidentally introduced into an ecosystem by humans. Some of these species are beneficial, while others can take over and eliminate many native species. Compare *indicator species, keystone species, native species*.

immigration Migration of people into a country or area to take up permanent residence. Compare *emigration*.

indicator species Species that serve as early warnings that a community or an ecosystem is being degraded. Compare *immigrant species, keystone species, native species*.

industrialized agriculture Using large inputs of energy from fossil fuels (especially oil and natural gas), water, fertilizer, and pesticides to produce large quantities of crops and livestock for domestic and foreign sale. Compare *subsistence farming*.

Industrial Revolution Uses of new sources of energy from fossil fuels and later nuclear fuels and use of new technologies to grow food and manufacture products.

industrial smog Type of air pollution consisting mostly of a mixture of sulfur dioxide, suspended droplets of sulfuric acid formed from some of the sulfur dioxide, and a variety of suspended solid particles. Compare *photochemical smog*.

inertia Ability of a living system to resist being disturbed or altered. Compare *constancy, resilience*.

infant mortality rate Number of babies out of every 1,000 born each year that die before their first birthday.

infiltration Downward movement of water through soil.

inland wetland Land away from the coast, such as a swamp, marsh, or bog, that is covered all or part of the year with fresh water. Compare *coastal wetland*.

inorganic compound Any compound not classified as an organic compound. Compare *organic compound*.

inorganic fertilizer See *commercial inorganic fertilizer*.

input pollution control See *pollution prevention*.

insecticide Chemical that kills insects.

integrated pest management (IPM) Combined use of biological, chemical, and cultivation methods in proper sequence and timing to keep the size of a pest population below the size that causes economically unacceptable loss of a crop or livestock animal.

intercropping Growing two or more different crops at the same time on a plot. For example, a carbohydrate-rich grain that depletes soil nitrogen and a protein-rich legume that adds nitrogen to the soil may be intercropped. Compare *monoculture, polyculture, polyvarietal cultivation*.

intermediate goods See *capital goods*.

internal cost Direct cost paid by the producer and the buyer of an economic good. Compare *external cost*.

interplanting Simultaneously growing a variety of crops on the same plot. See *agroforestry, intercropping, polyculture, polyvarietal cultivation*.

interspecific competition Members of two or more species trying to use the same limited resources in an ecosystem. See *competition, competitive exclusion principle, intraspecific competition*.

intraspecific competition Two or more individual organisms of a single species trying to use the same limited resources in an ecosystem. See *competition, interspecific competition*.

inversion See *thermal inversion*.

invertebrates Animals that have no backbones. Compare *vertebrates*.

ion Atom or group of atoms with one or more positive (⁺) or negative (⁻) electrical charges. Compare *atom, molecule*.

ionizing radiation Fast-moving alpha or beta particles or high-energy radiation (gamma rays) emitted by radioisotopes. They have enough energy to dislodge one or more electrons from atoms they hit, forming charged ions in tissue that can react with and damage living tissue.

isotopes Two or more forms of a chemical element that have the same number of protons but different mass numbers due to different numbers of neutrons in their nuclei.

J-shaped curve Curve with a shape similar to that of the letter J; represents exponential growth.

kerogen Solid, waxy mixture of hydrocarbons found in oil shale rock. When the rock is heated to high temperatures, the kerogen is vaporized. The vapor is condensed and purified and then sent to a refinery to produce gasoline, heating oil, and other products. See also *oil shale, shale oil*.

keystone species Species that play roles affecting many other organisms in an ecosystem. Compare *immigrant species, indicator species, native species*.

kilocalorie (kcal) Unit of energy equal to 1,000 calories. See *calorie*.

kilowatt (kw) Unit of electrical power equal to 1,000 watts. See *watt*.

kinetic energy Energy that matter has because of its motion and mass. Compare *potential energy*.

kwashiorkor Type of malnutrition that occurs in infants and very young children when they are weaned from mother's milk to a starchy diet low in protein. See also *marasmus*.

labor Physical and mental talents of people used to produce, distribute, and sell an economic good. Labor includes entrepreneurs, who assume the risk and responsibility of combining the resources of land, capital goods, and workers who produce an economic good. Compare *capital goods, natural resources*.

lake Large natural body of standing fresh water formed when water from precipitation, land runoff, or groundwater flow fills a depression in the earth created by glaciation, earth movement, volcanic activity, or a giant meteorite. Compare *reservoir*. See *eutrophic lake, mesotrophic lake, oligotrophic lake*.

landfill See *sanitary landfill*.

land-use planning Process for deciding the best present and future use of each parcel of land in an area. See *ecological land-use planning*.

latitude Distance from the equator. Compare *altitude*.

law of conservation of energy See *first law of thermodynamics*.

law of conservation of matter In any physical or chemical change, matter is neither created nor destroyed, but merely changed from one form to another; in physical and chemical changes, existing atoms are rearranged into either different spatial patterns (physical changes) or different combinations (chemical changes).

law of conservation of matter and energy In any nuclear change, the total amount of matter and energy involved remains the same. Compare *first law of thermodynamics, law of conservation of matter*.

law of pollution prevention If you don't put something into the environment, it isn't there.

law of tolerance The existence, abundance, and distribution of a species in an ecosystem are determined by whether the levels of one or more physical or chemical factors fall within the range tolerated by the species. See *threshold effect*.

LDC See *less developed country*.

leaching Process in which various chemicals in upper layers of soil are dissolved and carried to lower layers and, in some cases, to groundwater.

less developed country (LDC) Country that has low to moderate industrialization and low to moderate GNP per person. Most are located in the Southern Hemisphere in Africa, Asia, and Latin America. Compare *more developed country*.

life-cycle cost Initial cost plus lifetime operating costs of an economic good.

life expectancy Average number of years a newborn infant can be expected to live.

limiting factor Single factor that limits the growth, abundance, or distribution of the population of a species in an ecosystem. See *limiting factor principle*.

limiting factor principle Too much or too little of any abiotic factor can limit or prevent growth of a population of a species in an ecosystem, even if all other factors are at or near the optimum range of tolerance for the species.

linear growth Growth in which a quantity increases by some fixed amount during each unit of time. Compare *exponential growth*.

liquefied natural gas (LNG) Natural gas converted to liquid form by cooling to a very low temperature.

liquefied petroleum gas (LPG) Mixture of liquefied propane and butane gas removed from natural gas.

lithosphere Outer shell of the Earth composed of the crust and the rigid, outermost part of the mantle outside of the asthenosphere; material found in Earth's plates. See *crust, geosphere, mantle, plates, plate tectonics*.

loams Soils containing a mixture of clay, sand, silt, and humus. Good for growing most crops.

low-quality energy Energy that is disorganized or dispersed and has little ability to do useful work. An example is low-temperature heat. Compare *high-quality energy*.

low-quality matter Matter that is disorganized, dilute or dispersed, or contains a low concentration of a useful resource. Compare *high-quality matter*.

LPG See *liquefied petroleum gas*.

magma Molten rock below the earth's surface.

malnutrition Faulty nutrition. Caused by a diet that does not supply an individual with enough proteins, essential fats, vitamins, minerals, and other nutrients needed for good health. See *kwashiorkor, marasmus*. Compare *overnutrition, undernutrition*.

mantle Zone of the earth's interior between its core and its crust. See *lithosphere*. Compare *core, crust*.

manure See *animal manure, green manure*.

marasmus Nutritional-deficiency disease caused by a diet that does not have enough calories and protein to maintain good health. See *kwashiorkor, malnutrition*.

mass The amount of material in an object.

mass number Sum of the number of neutrons and the number of protons in the nucleus of an atom. It gives the approximate mass of that atom. Compare *atomic number*.

mass transit Buses, trains, trolleys, and other forms of transportation that carry large numbers of people.

matter Anything that has mass (the amount of material in an object) and takes up space. On Earth, where gravity is present, we weigh an object to determine its mass.

matter quality Measure of how useful a matter resource is based on its availability and concentration. See *high-quality matter, low-quality matter*.

matter-recycling society Society that emphasizes recycling the maximum amount of all resources that can be recycled. The goal is to allow economic growth to continue without depleting matter resources and without producing excessive pollution and environmental degradation. Compare *sustainable-Earth society, throwaway society*.

mature community Fairly stable, self-sustaining community in an advanced stage of ecological succession; usually has a diverse array of species and ecological niches; captures and uses energy and cycles critical chemicals more efficiently than simpler, immature communities. Compare *immature community*.

maximum sustainable yield See *sustainable yield*.

MDC See *more developed country*.

meltdown The melting of the core of a nuclear reactor.

mesotrophic lake Lake with a moderate supply of plant nutrients. Compare *eutrophic lake, oligotrophic lake*.

metabolic reserve Lower half of rangeland grass plants; can grow back as long as it is not consumed by herbivores.

metamorphic rock Rock produced when a preexisting rock is subjected to high temperatures (which may cause it to melt partially), high pressures, chemically active fluids, or a combination of these agents. See *rock cycle*. Compare *igneous rock, sedimentary rock*.

mineral Any naturally occurring inorganic substance found in the earth's crust as a crystalline solid. See *mineral resource*.

mineral resource Concentration of naturally occurring solid, liquid, or gaseous material, in or on Earth's crust, in such form and amount that its extraction and conversion into useful materials or items is currently or potentially profitable. Mineral resources are classified as metallic (such as iron and tin ores) or nonmetallic (such as fossil fuels, sand, and salt).

minimum-tillage farming See *conservation-tillage farming*.

mixture Combination of one or more elements and compounds.

molecule Combination of two or more atoms of the same chemical element (such as O_2) or different chemical elements (such as H_2O) held together by chemical bonds.

monoculture Cultivation of a single crop, usually on a large area of land. Compare *polyculture*.

more developed country (MDC) Country that is highly industrialized and has a high GNP per person. Compare *less developed country*.

multiple use Principle of managing public land, such as a national forest, so it is used for a variety of purposes, such as timbering, mining, recreation, grazing, wildlife preservation, and soil and water conservation. See also *sustainable yield*.

municipal solid waste Solid materials discarded by homes and businesses in or near urban areas. See *solid waste*.

mutagen Chemical, or form of ionizing radiation, that causes inheritable changes in the DNA molecules in the genes found in chromosomes (mutations). See *carcinogen, mutation, teratogen*.

mutation An inheritable change in the DNA molecules in the genes found in the chromosomes. See *mutagen*.

mutualism Type of species interaction in which both participating species generally benefit Compare *commensalism*.

native species Species that normally live and thrive in a particular ecosystem. Compare *immigrant species, indicator species, keystone species*.

natural capital see *Earth capital*.

natural gas Underground deposits of gases consisting of 50% to 90% by weight methane gas (CH_4) and small amounts of heavier gaseous hydrocarbon compounds such as propane (C_3H_8) and butane (C_4H_{10}).

natural ionizing radiation Ionizing radiation in the environment from natural sources.

natural radioactivity Nuclear change in which unstable nuclei of atoms spontaneously shoot out particles (usually alpha or beta particles), energy (gamma rays), or both at a fixed rate.

natural recharge Natural replenishment of an aquifer by precipitation, which percolates downward through soil and rock. See *recharge area*.

natural resources Area of the earth's solid surface, nutrients and minerals in the soil and deeper layers of the earth's crust, water, wild and domesticated plants and animals, air, and other resources produced by the earth's natural processes. See *Earth capital*. Compare *capital goods, labor*.

natural selection Process by which some genes and gene combinations in a population of a species are reproduced more than others when the population is exposed to an environmental change or stress. When individual organisms in a population die off over time because they cannot tolerate a new stress, they are replaced by individuals whose genetic traits allow them to cope better with the stress. When these better-adapted individuals reproduce, they pass their adaptive traits on to their offspring. See also *differential reproduction, evolution*.

net economic welfare (NEW) Measure of annual change in quality of life in a country. It is obtained by subtracting the value of all final products and services that decrease the quality of life from a country's GNP. See *per capita NEW*.

net energy See *net useful energy*.

net primary productivity Rate at which all the plants in an ecosystem produce net useful chemical energy; equal to the difference between the rate at which the plants in an ecosystem produce useful chemical energy (primary productivity) and the rate at which they use some of that energy through cellular respiration. Compare *primary productivity*.

net useful energy Total amount of useful energy available from an energy resource or energy system over its lifetime minus the amount of energy used (the first energy law), automatically wasted (the second energy law), and unnecessarily wasted in finding, processing, concentrating, and transporting it to users.

neutral solution Water solution containing an equal number of hydrogen ions (H^+) and hydroxide ions (OH^-); water solution with a pH of 7. Compare *acid solution, basic solution*.

neutron (n) Elementary particle in the nuclei of all atoms (except hydrogen-1). It has a relative mass of 1 and no electric charge.

NEW See *net economic welfare*.

niche See *ecological niche*.

nitrogen cycle Cyclic movement of nitrogen in different chemical forms from the environment, to organisms, and then back to the environment.

nitrogen fixation Conversion of atmospheric nitrogen gas into forms useful to plants, by lightning, bacteria, and cyanobacteria; it is part of the nitrogen cycle.

nondegradable pollutant Material that is not broken down by natural processes. Examples are the toxic elements lead and mercury. Compare *biodegradable pollutant, degradable pollutant, slowly degradable pollutant*.

nonionizing radiation Forms of radiant energy such as radio waves, microwaves, infrared light, and ordinary light that do not have enough energy to cause ionization of atoms in living tissue. Compare *ionizing radiation*.

nonpersistent pollutant See *degradable pollutant*.

nonpoint source Large or dispersed land areas such as crop fields, streets, and lawns that discharge pollutants into the environment over a large area. Compare *point source*.

nonrenewable resource Resource that exists in a fixed amount (stock) in various places in the earth's crust and has the potential for renewal only by geological, physical, and chemical processes taking place over hundreds of millions to billions of years. Examples are copper, aluminum, coal, and oil. We classify these resources as exhaustible because we are extracting and using them at a much faster rate than the geological time scale on which they were formed. Compare *perpetual resource, potentially renewable resource*.

nontransmissible disease A disease that is not caused by living organisms and that does not spread from one person to another. Examples are most cancers, diabetes, cardiovascular disease, and malnutrition. Compare *transmissible disease*.

no-till farming See *conservation-tillage farming*.

nuclear change Process in which nuclei of certain isotopes spontaneously change, or are forced to change, into one or more different isotopes. The three principal types of nuclear change are natural radioactivity, nuclear fission, and nuclear fusion. Compare *chemical change*.

nuclear energy Energy released when atomic nuclei undergo a nuclear reaction such as the spontaneous emission of radioactivity, nuclear fission, or nuclear fusion.

nuclear fission Nuclear change in which the nuclei of certain isotopes with large mass numbers (such as uranium-235 and plutonium-239) are split apart into lighter nuclei when struck by a neutron. This process releases more neutrons and a large amount of energy. Compare *nuclear fusion*.

nuclear fusion Nuclear change in which two nuclei of isotopes of elements with a low mass number (such as hydrogen-2 and hydrogen-3) are forced together at extremely high temperatures until they fuse to form a heavier nucleus (such as helium-4). This process releases a large amount of energy. Compare *nuclear fission*.

nucleus Extremely tiny center of an atom, making up most of the atom's mass. It contains one or more positively charged protons and one or more neutrons with no electrical charge (except for a hydrogen-1 atom, which has one proton and no neutrons in its nucleus).

nutrient Any element an organism needs to live, grow, and reproduce.

oil See *crude oil*.

oil shale Underground formation of a fine-grained rock containing varying amounts of kerogen, a solid, waxy mixture of hydrocarbon compounds. Heating the rock to high temperatures converts the kerogen into a vapor that can be condensed to form a slow-flowing heavy oil called shale oil. See *kerogen, shale oil*.

old-growth forest Virgin and old second-growth forests containing trees that are often hundreds, if not thousands, of years old. Examples include forests of Douglas fir, western hemlock, giant sequoia, and coastal redwoods in the western U.S. Compare *secondary forest, tree farm*.

oligotrophic lake Lake with a low supply of plant nutrients. Compare *eutrophic lake, mesotrophic lake*.

omnivore Animal organism that can use both plants and other animals as food sources. Examples are pigs, rats, cockroaches, and people. Compare *carnivore, herbivore*.

open-pit mining Removal of materials such as iron and copper by digging them out of the earth's surface and leaving a large depression or pit. See also *area strip mining, contour strip mining*.

open sea The part of an ocean that is beyond the continental shelf. Compare *coastal zone*.

ore Part of a metal-yielding material that can be economically extracted at a given time. An ore typically contains two parts: the ore mineral, which contains the desired metal, and waste mineral material (gangue).

organic compound Molecule that contains atoms of the element carbon, usually combined with each other and with atoms of one or more other elements such as hydrogen, oxygen, nitrogen, sulfur, phosphorus, chlorine, and fluorine. Compare *inorganic compound*.

organic farming Producing crops and livestock naturally by using organic fertilizer (manure, legumes, compost) and natural pest control (bugs that eat harmful bugs, plants that repel bugs, and environmental controls such as crop rotation) instead of using commercial inorganic fertilizers and synthetic pesticides and herbicides.

organic fertilizer Organic material such as animal manure, green manure, and compost, applied to cropland as a source of plant nutrients. Compare *commercial inorganic fertilizer*.

organism Any form of life.

output pollution control See *pollution cleanup*.

overburden Layer of soil and rock overlying a mineral deposit; removed during surface mining.

overconsumption Situation where some people consume much more than they need at the expense of those who cannot meet their basic needs and at the expense of Earth's present and future life-support systems.

overfishing Harvesting so many fish of a species, especially immature ones, that there is not enough breeding stock left to replenish the species so it is not profitable to harvest them.

overgrazing Destruction of vegetation when too many grazing animals feed too long and exceed the carrying capacity of a rangeland area.

overnutrition Diet so high in calories, saturated (animal) fats, salt, sugar, and processed foods, and so low in vegetables and fruits that the consumer runs high risks of diabetes, hypertension, heart disease, and other health hazards. Compare *malnutrition, undernutrition*.

overpopulation State in which there are more people than can live on Earth or in a geographic region in comfort, happiness, and health and still leave the planet or region a fit place for future generations. It is a result of growing numbers of people, growing affluence (resource consumption), or both. See *carrying capacity, consumption overpopulation, dieback, overshoot, people overpopulation*.

overshoot Condition in which population size of a species temporarily exceeds the carrying capacity of its habitat. This leads to a sharp reduction in its population. See *carrying capacity, consumption overpopulation, dieback, people overpopulation*.

oxygen cycle Cyclic movement of oxygen in different chemical forms from the environment, to organisms, and then back to the environment.

oxygen-demanding wastes Organic materials that are usually biodegraded by aerobic (oxygen-consuming) bacteria, if there is enough dissolved oxygen in the water. See also *biological oxygen demand*.

ozone layer Layer of gaseous ozone (O_3) in the stratosphere that protects life on Earth by filtering out harmful ultraviolet radiation from the sun.

PANs Peroxyacyl nitrates. Group of chemicals found in photochemical smog.

parasite Consumer organism that lives on or in and feeds on a living plant or animal, known as the host, over an extended period of time. The parasite draws nourishment from and gradually weakens its host. This may or may not kill the host.

particulate matter Solid particles or liquid droplets suspended or carried in the air.

parts per billion (ppb) Number of parts of a chemical found in one billion parts of a particular gas, liquid, or solid.

parts per million (ppm) Number of parts of a chemical found in one million parts of a particular gas, liquid, or solid.

passive solar heating system System that captures sunlight directly within a structure and converts it into low-temperature heat for space heating or for heating water for domestic use without the use of mechanical devices. Compare *active solar heating system*.

pathogen Organism that produces disease.

PCBs See *polychlorinated biphenyls*.

people overpopulation Situation in which there are more people in the world or a geographic region than available supplies of food, water, and other vital resources can support. It can also occur where the rate of population growth so exceeds the rate of economic growth, or the distribution of wealth is so inequitable, that a number of people are too poor to grow or buy enough food, fuel, and other important resources. Compare *consumption overpopulation*.

per capita GNP Annual gross national product (GNP) of a country divided by its total population. See *gross national product, real GNP per capita*.

per capita NEW Annual net economic welfare (NEW) of a country divided by its total population. See *net economic welfare, per capita real NEW*.

per capita real NEW Per capita NEW adjusted for inflation. See *net economic welfare, per capita NEW*.

permafrost Permanently frozen underground layers of soil in tundra.

permeability The degree to which underground rock and soil pores are interconnected with each other and thus a measure of the degree to which water can flow freely from one pore to another. Compare *porosity*.

perpetual resource Resource, such as solar energy, that is virtually inexhaustible on a human time scale. Compare *nonrenewable resource, potentially renewable resource*.

persistence See *inertia*.

persistent pollutant See *slowly degradable pollutant*.

pest Unwanted organism that directly or indirectly interferes with human activities.

pesticide Any chemical designed to kill or inhibit the growth of an organism that people consider to be undesirable. See *fungicide, herbicide, insecticide*.

pesticide treadmill Situation in which the cost of using pesticides increases while their effectiveness decreases, mostly because the pest species develop genetic resistance to the pesticides.

petrochemicals Chemicals obtained by refining (distilling) crude oil. They are used as raw materials in the manufacture of most industrial chemicals, fertilizers, pesticides, plastics, synthetic fibers, paints, medicines, and many other products.

petroleum See *crude oil*.

pH Numeric value that indicates the relative acidity or alkalinity of a substance on a scale of 0 to 14, with the neutral point at 7. Acid solutions have pH values lower than 7, and basic or alkaline solutions have pH values greater than 7.

phosphorus cycle Cyclic movement of phosphorus in different chemical forms from the environment, to organisms, and then back to the environment.

photochemical smog Complex mixture of air pollutants produced in the atmosphere by the reaction of hydrocarbons and nitrogen oxides under the influence of sunlight. Especially harmful components include ozone, peroxyacyl nitrates (PANs), and various aldehydes. Compare *industrial smog*.

photosynthesis Complex process that takes place in cells of green plants. Radiant energy from the sun is used to combine carbon dioxide (CO_2) and water (H_2O) to produce oxygen (O_2) and carbohydrates (such as glucose, $C_6H_{12}O_6$), and other nutrient molecules. Compare *aerobic respiration, chemosynthesis*.

photovoltaic cell (solar cell) Device in which radiant (solar) energy is converted directly into electrical energy.

physical change Process that alters one or more physical properties of an element or a compound without altering its chemical composition. Examples are changing the size and shape of a sample of matter (crushing ice and cutting aluminum foil) and changing a sample of matter from one physical state to another (boiling and freezing water). Compare *chemical change*.

phytoplankton Small, drifting plants, mostly algae and bacteria, found in aquatic ecosystems. Compare *plankton, zooplankton*.

pioneer community First integrated set of plants, animals, and decomposers found in an area undergoing primary ecological succession. See *immature community, mature community*.

pioneer species First hardy species, often microbes, mosses, and lichens, that begin colonizing a site as the first stage of ecological succession. See *ecological succession, pioneer community*.

plankton Small plant organisms (phytoplankton) and animal organisms (zooplankton) that float in aquatic ecosystems.

plantation agriculture Growing specialized crops such as bananas, coffee, and cacao in tropical LDCs, primarily for sale to MDCs.

plants Eukaryotic, mostly multicelled organisms such as algae (red, blue, and green), mosses, ferns, flowers, cacti, grasses, beans, wheat, rice, and trees. These organisms use photosynthesis to produce organic nutrients for themselves and for other organisms feeding on them. Water and other inorganic nutrients are obtained from the soil for terrestrial plants and from the water for aquatic plants.

plates Various-sized areas of Earth's lithosphere that move slowly around on the mantle's flowing asthenosphere. Earthquakes and volcanoes occur around the boundaries of these plates. See *lithosphere, plate tectonics*.

plate tectonics Theory of geophysical processes that explains the movements of Earth's plates and the processes that occur at their boundaries. See *lithosphere, plates*.

poaching Illegal commercial hunting or fishing.

point source A single identifiable source that discharges pollutants into the environment. Examples are the smokestack of a power plant or an industrial plant, the drainpipe of a meat-packing plant, the chimney of a house, or the exhaust pipe of an automobile. Compare *nonpoint source*.

politics Process by which individuals and groups try to influence or control the policies and actions of governments that affect the local, state, national, and international communities.

pollution An undesirable change in the physical, chemical, or biological characteristics of air, water, soil, or food that can adversely affect the health, survival, or activities of humans or other living organisms.

pollution cleanup Device or process that removes or reduces the level of a pollutant after it has been produced or has entered the environment. Examples are automobile emission control devices and sewage treatment plants. Compare *pollution prevention*.

pollution prevention Device or process that prevents a potential pollutant from forming or from entering the environment or that sharply reduces the amounts entering the environment. Compare *pollution cleanup*.

polychlorinated biphenyls (PCBs) Group of 209 different toxic, oily, synthetic chlorinated hydrocarbon compounds that can be biologically amplified in food chains and webs.

polyculture Complex form of intercropping in which a large number of different plants maturing at different times are planted together. See also *intercropping*. Compare *monoculture, polyvarietal cultivation*.

polyvarietal cultivation Planting a plot of land with several varieties of the same crop. Compare *intercropping, monoculture, polyculture*.

population Group of individual organisms of the same species living within a particular area.

population crash Large number of deaths over a fairly short time, brought about when the number of individuals in a population is too large to be supported by available environmental resources.

population density Number of organisms in a particular population found in a specified area.

population distribution Variation of population density over a particular geographical area. For example, a country has a high population density in its urban areas and a much lower population density in rural areas.

population dynamics Major abiotic and biotic factors that tend to increase or decrease the population size and age and sex composition of a species.

population size Number of individuals making up a population's gene pool.

porosity The pores (crack and spaces) in rocks or soil, or the percentage of the rock's or soil's volume not occupied by the rock or soil itself. Compare *permeability*.

potential energy Energy stored in an object because of its position or the position of its parts. Compare *kinetic energy*.

potentially renewable resource Resource that theoretically can last indefinitely without reducing the available supply because it is replaced more rapidly through natural processes than are nonrenewable resources. Examples are trees in forests, grasses in grasslands, wild animals, fresh surface water in lakes and streams, most groundwater, fresh air, and fertile soil. If such a resource is used faster than it is replenished, it can be depleted and converted into a nonrenewable resource. See also *environmental degradation*. Compare *nonrenewable resource, perpetual resource*.

poverty Inability to meet basic needs for food, clothing, and shelter.

ppb See *parts per billion*.

ppm See *parts per million*.

precipitation Water in the form of rain, sleet, hail, and snow that falls from the atmosphere onto the land and bodies of water.

predation Situation in which an organism of one species (the predator) captures and feeds on parts or all of an organism of another species (the prey).

predator Organism that captures and feeds on parts or all of an organism of another species (the prey).

predator-prey relationship Interaction between two organisms of different species in which one organism called the predator captures and feeds on parts or all of another organism called the prey.

prescribed burning Deliberate setting and careful control of surface fires in forests to help prevent more destructive crown fires and to kill off unwanted plants that compete with commercial species for plant nutrients; may also be used on grasslands. See *crown fire, ground fire, surface fire*.

prey Organism that is captured and serves as a source of food for an organism of another species (the predator).

primary air pollutant Chemical that has been added directly to the air by natural events or human activities and occurs in a harmful concentration. Compare *secondary air pollutant*.

primary consumer Organism that feeds directly on all or part of plants (*herbivore*) or other producers. Compare *detritivore, omnivore, secondary consumer*.

primary oil recovery Pumping out the crude oil that flows by gravity or under gas pressure into the bottom of an oil well. Compare *enhanced oil recovery, secondary oil recovery.*

primary productivity The rate at which an ecosystem's producers capture and store a given amount of chemical energy as biomass in a given length of time. Compare *net primary productivity.*

primary sewage treatment Mechanical treatment of sewage in which large solids are filtered out by screens and suspended solids settle out as sludge in a sedimentation tank. Compare *advanced sewage treatment, secondary sewage treatment.*

primary succession Sequential development of communities in a bare area that has never been occupied by a community of organisms. Compare *secondary succession.*

principle of multiple use See *multiple use.*

prior appropriation Legal principle by which the first user of water from a stream establishes a legal right to continued use of the amount originally withdrawn. Compare *riparian rights.*

producer Organism that uses solar energy (green plant) or chemical energy (some bacteria) to manufacture the organic compounds it needs as nutrients from simple inorganic compounds obtained from its environment. Compare *consumer, decomposer.*

prokaryotic cell Cell that doesn't have a distinct nucleus. Other internal parts are also not enclosed by membranes. Compare *eukaryotic cell.*

protists Eukaryotic, mostly single-cell organisms such as diatoms, amoebas, some algae (golden brown and yellow-green), protozoans, and slime molds. Some protists produce their own organic nutrients through photosynthesis. Others are decomposers and some feed on bacteria, other protists, or cells of multicellular organisms.

proton (p) Positively charged particle in the nuclei of all atoms. Each proton has a relative mass of 1 and a single positive charge.

public land resources Land that is owned jointly by all citizens, but is managed for them by an agency of the local, state, or federal government. Examples are state and national parks, forests, wildlife refuges, and wilderness areas. Compare *common-property resource.*

pyramid of energy flow Diagram representing the flow of energy through each trophic level in a food chain or food web. With each energy transfer, only a small part (typically 10%) of the usable energy entering one trophic level is transferred to the organisms at the next trophic level.

radiation Fast-moving particles (particulate radiation) or waves of energy (electromagnetic radiation). See *ionizing radiation, nonionizing radiation.*

radioactive decay Change of a radioisotope to a different isotope by the emission of radioactivity.

radioactive isotope See *radioisotope.*

radioactive waste Radioactive waste products of nuclear power plants, research, medicine, weapons production, or other processes involving nuclear reactions. See *radioactivity.*

radioactivity Nuclear change in which unstable nuclei of atoms spontaneously shoot out "chunks" of mass, energy, or both, at a fixed rate. The three principal types of radioactivity are gamma rays and fast-moving alpha particles and beta particles.

radioisotope Isotope of an atom that spontaneously emits one or more types of radioactivity (alpha particles, beta particles, gamma rays).

range condition Estimate of how close a particular area of rangeland is to its potential for producing vegetation that can be consumed by grazing or browsing animals.

rangeland Land that supplies forage or vegetation (grasses, grasslike plants, and shrubs) for grazing and browsing animals and that is not intensively managed. Compare *feedlot.*

range of tolerance Range of chemical and physical conditions that must be maintained for populations of a particular species to stay alive and grow, develop, and function normally. See *law of tolerance.*

real GNP gross national product adjusted for inflation. Compare *gross national product, per capita GNP, real GNP per capita.*

real GNP per capita Per capita GNP adjusted for inflation. See *per capita GNP.*

realized niche Parts of the fundamental niche of a species that are actually used by a species. See *ecological niche, fundamental niche.*

recharge area Any area of land allowing water to pass through it and into an aquifer. See *aquifer, natural recharge.*

recycling Collecting and reprocessing a resource so it can be made into new products. An example is collecting aluminum cans, melting them down, and using the aluminum to make new cans or other aluminum products. Compare *reuse.*

reforestation Renewal of trees and other types of vegetation on land where trees have been removed; can be done naturally by seeds from nearby trees or artificially by planting seeds or seedlings.

relative resource scarcity Situation in which a resource has not been depleted but there is not enough available to meet the demand because of unbalanced distribution; can be caused by a war, a natural disaster, or other events that disrupt the production and distribution of a resource, or by deliberate attempts of its producers to lower production to drive prices up. Compare *absolute resource scarcity.*

renewable resource see *potentially renewable resource.*

replacement-level fertility Number of children a couple must have to replace themselves. The average for a country or the world is usually slightly higher than 2 children per couple (2.1 in the the United States and 2.5 in some LDCs) because some children die before reaching their reproductive years. See also *total fertility rate.*

reproductive age Ages 15 to 44, when most women have all their children.

reserves (economic resources) Resources that have been identified and from which a usable mineral can be extracted profitably at present prices with current mining technology. Compare *resources.*

reservoir Human-created body of standing fresh water; often built behind a dam. Compare *lake.*

resilience Ability of a living system to restore itself to original condition after being exposed to an outside disturbance that is not too drastic. See also *constancy, inertia.*

resource Anything obtained from the living and nonliving environment to meet human needs and wants.

resource partitioning Process of dividing up resources in an ecosystem so species with similar requirements (overlapping ecological niches) use the same scarce resources at different times, in different ways, or in different places. See *ecological niche, fundamental niche, realized niche.*

resource recovery Salvaging usable metals, paper, and glass from solid waste and selling them to manufacturing industries for recycling or reuse.

resources All undiscovered resources and the portion of identified resources that can't be recovered profitably with present prices and technology. Some of these materials may be converted into reserves when prices rise or mining technology improves. Compare *reserves.*

reuse To use a product over and over again in the same form. An example is collecting, washing, and refilling glass beverage bottles. Compare *recycling.*

riparian rights System of water law that gives anyone whose land adjoins a flowing stream the right to use water from the stream as long as some is left for downstream users. Compare *prior appropriation.*

risk The probability that something undesirable will happen from deliberate or accidental exposure to a hazard. See *risk assessment, risk-benefit analysis, risk management.*

risk analysis Identifying hazards, evaluating the nature and severity of risks (*risk assessment*), using this and other information to determine options and make decisions about reducing or eliminating risks (*risk management*), and communicating information about risks to decision makers and the public (*risk communication*).

risk assessment Process of gathering data and making assumptions to estimate short- and long-term harmful effects on human health or the environment from exposure to hazards associated with the use of a particular product or technology. See *risk, risk-benefit analysis.*

risk-benefit analysis Estimate of the short- and long-term risks and benefits of using a particular product or technology. See *desirability quotient, risk.* Compare *cost-benefit analysis.*

risk communication Communicating information about risks to decision makers and the public. See *risk, risk analysis, risk-benefit analysis.*

risk management Using risk assessment and other information to determine options and make decisions about reducing or eliminating risks. See *risk, risk analysis, risk-benefit analysis, risk communication.*

river runoff Water flowing in rivers to the ocean. Compare *surface runoff.*

rock Any material that makes up a large, natural, continuous part of Earth's crust. See *mineral.*

rock cycle Largest and slowest of the earth's cycles, consisting of geologic, physical, and chemical processes that form and modify rocks and soil in the earth's crust over millions of years.

rodenticide Chemical that kills rodents.

rule of 70 Method for calculating the doubling time in years for a quantity that is growing exponentially. This involves dividing the annual percentage growth rate of a quantity into 70 (70/percentage growth rate = doubling time in years).

runoff Fresh water from precipitation and melting ice that flows on the earth's surface into nearby streams, lakes, wetlands, and reservoirs. See *river runoff, surface runoff, surface water.* Compare *groundwater.*

rural area Geographical area in the United States with a population of less than 2,500 people per unit of area. The number of people used in this definition may vary in different countries. Compare *urban area.*

salinity Amount of various salts dissolved in a given volume of water.

salinization Accumulation of salts in soil that can eventually make the soil unable to support plant growth.

saltwater intrusion Movement of salt water into freshwater aquifers in coastal and inland areas as groundwater is withdrawn faster than it is recharged by precipitation.

sanitary landfill Waste disposal site on land in which waste is spread in thin layers, compacted, and covered with a fresh layer of clay or plastic foam each day.

scavenger Organism that feeds on dead organisms that either were killed by other organisms or died naturally. Examples are vultures, flies, and crows. Compare *detritivore.*

science Attempts to discover order in nature and then use that knowledge to make predictions about what will happen in nature. See *scientific data, scientific hypothesis, scientific law, scientific methods, scientific theory.*

scientific data Facts obtained by making observations and measurements. Compare *scientific hypothesis, scientific law, scientific theory.*

scientific hypothesis An educated guess that attempts to explain a scientific law or certain scientific observations. Compare *scientific data, scientific law, scientific theory.*

scientific law Summary of what scientists find happening in nature over and over in the same way. See *first law of thermodynamics, second law of thermodynamics, law of conservation of matter.* Compare *scientific data, scientific hypothesis, scientific theory.*

scientific methods The ways scientists gather data and formulate and test scientific laws and theories. See *scientific data, scientific hypothesis, scientific law, scientific theory.*

scientific theory A well-tested and widely accepted scientific hypothesis. Compare *scientific data, scientific hypothesis, scientific law.*

secondary air pollutant Harmful chemical formed in the atmosphere when a primary air pollutant reacts with normal air components or with other air pollutants. Compare *primary air pollutant.*

secondary consumer Organism that feeds only on primary consumers. Most secondary consumers are animals, but some are plants. Compare *detritivore, omnivore, primary consumer.*

secondary forest Stands of trees resulting from secondary ecological succession. Compare *ancient forest, old-growth forest, tree farm.*

secondary oil recovery Injection of water into an oil well after primary oil recovery to force out some of the remaining, usually thicker, crude oil. Compare *enhanced oil recovery, primary oil recovery.*

secondary sewage treatment Second step in most waste treatment systems, in which aerobic bacteria break down up to 90% of degradable, oxygen-demanding organic wastes in wastewater. This is usually done by bringing sewage and bacteria together in trickling filters or in the activated sludge process. Compare *advanced sewage treatment, primary sewage treatment.*

secondary succession Sequential development of communities in an area in which natural vegetation has been removed or destroyed but the soil is not destroyed. Compare *primary succession.*

second law of ecology Everything is connected to and intermingled with everything else.

second law of energy See *second law of thermodynamics.*

second law of thermodynamics In any conversion of heat energy to useful work, some of the initial energy input is always degraded to a lower-quality, more-dispersed, less-useful energy, usually low-temperature heat that flows into the environment; you can't break even in terms of energy quality. See *first law of thermodynamics.*

sedimentary rock Rock that forms from the accumulated products of erosion and in some cases from the compacted shells, skeletons, and other remains of dead organisms. See *rock cycle.* Compare *igneous rock, metamorphic rock.*

seed-tree cutting Removal of nearly all trees on a site in one cutting, with a few seed-producing trees left uniformly distributed to regenerate the forest. Compare *clear-cutting, selective cutting, shelterwood cutting.*

selective cutting Cutting of intermediate-aged, mature, or diseased trees in an uneven-aged forest stand, either singly or in small groups. This encourages the growth of younger trees and maintains an uneven-aged stand. Compare *clear-cutting, seed-tree cutting, shelterwood cutting.*

septic tank Underground tank for treatment of wastewater from a home in rural and suburban areas. Bacteria in the tank decompose organic wastes and the sludge settles to the bottom of the tank. The effluent flows out of the tank into the ground through a field of drain pipes.

shale oil Slow-flowing, dark brown, heavy oil obtained when kerogen in oil shale is vaporized at high temperatures and then condensed. Shale oil can be refined to yield gasoline, heating oil, and other petroleum products. See *kerogen, oil shale.*

shelterbelt See *windbreak.*

shelterwood cutting Removal of mature, marketable trees in an area in a series of partial cuttings to allow regeneration of a new stand under the partial shade of older trees, which are later removed. Typically, this is done by making two or three cuts over a decade. Compare *clear-cutting, seed-tree cutting, selective cutting.*

shifting cultivation Clearing a plot of ground in a forest, especially in tropical areas, and planting crops on it for a few years (typically 2 to 5 years) until the soil is depleted of nutrients or until the plot has been invaded by a dense growth of vegetation from the surrounding forest. Then a new plot is cleared and the process is repeated. The abandoned plot cannot successfully grow crops for 10 to 30 years. See also *slash-and-burn cultivation.*

slash-and-burn cultivation Cutting down trees and other vegetation in a patch of forest, leaving the cut vegetation on the ground to dry, and then burning it. The ashes that are left add nutrients to the nutrient-poor soils found in most tropical forest areas. Crops are planted between tree stumps. Plots must be abandoned after a few years (typically two to five years) because of loss of soil fertility or invasion of vegetation from the surrounding forest. See also *shifting cultivation.*

slowly degradable pollutant Material that is slowly broken down into simpler chemicals or reduced to acceptable levels by natural physical, chemical, and biological processes. Compare *biodegradable pollutant, degradable pollutant, nondegradable pollutant.*

sludge Gooey mixture of toxic chemicals, infectious agents, and settled solids, removed from wastewater at sewage treatment plant.

smelting Process in which a desired metal is separated from the other elements in an ore mineral.

smog Originally a combination of smoke and fog, but now used to describe other mixtures of pollutants in the atmosphere. See *industrial smog, photochemical smog.*

soil Complex mixture of inorganic minerals (clay, silt, pebbles, and sand), decaying organic matter, water, air, and living organisms.

soil conservation Methods used to reduce soil erosion, to prevent depletion of soil nutrients, and to restore nutrients already lost by erosion, leaching, and excessive crop harvesting.

soil erosion Movement of soil components, especially topsoil, from one place to another, usually by exposure to wind, flowing water, or both. This natural process can be greatly accelerated by human activities that remove vegetation from soil.

soil horizons Horizontal zones that make up a particular mature soil. Each horizon has a distinct texture and composition that varies with different types of soils.

soil permeability Rate at which water and air move from upper to lower soil layers.

soil porosity See *porosity.*

soil profile Cross-sectional view of the horizons in a soil.

soil texture Relative amounts of the different types and sizes of mineral particles in a sample of soil.

soil water Underground water that partially fills pores between soil particles and rocks within the upper soil and rock layers of the earth's crust, above the water table. Compare *groundwater.*

solar cell See *photovoltaic cell.*

solar collector Device for collecting radiant energy from the sun and converting it into heat. See *active solar heating system, passive solar heating system.*

solar energy Direct radiant energy from the sun and a number of indirect forms of energy produced by the direct input. Principal indirect forms of solar energy include wind, falling and flowing water (hydropower), and biomass (solar energy converted into chemical energy stored in the chemical bonds of organic compounds in trees and other plants).

solar pond Fairly small body of fresh water or salt water from which stored solar energy can be extracted, because of temperature difference between the hot surface layer exposed to the sun during daylight and the cooler layer beneath it.

solid waste Any unwanted or discarded material that is not a liquid or a gas. See *municipal solid waste.*

Spaceship-Earth worldview Earth is viewed as a spaceship — a machine that we can understand, control, and change at will by using advanced technology. Compare *sustainable-Earth worldview, throwaway worldview.*

specialist species Species with a narrow ecological niche. They may be able to live in only one type of habitat, tolerate only a narrow range of climatic and other environmental conditions, or use only one or a few types of food. Compare *generalist species.*

speciation Formation of new species from existing ones through natural selection, in response to changes in environmental conditions; usually takes thousands of years. Compare *extinction.*

species Group of organisms that resemble one another in appearance, behavior, chemical makeup and processes, and genetic structure. Organisms that reproduce sexually are classified as members of the same species only if they can actually or potentially interbreed with one another and produce fertile offspring.

species diversity Number of different species and their relative abundances in a given area. See *biological diversity.* Compare *ecological diversity, genetic diversity.*

spoils Unwanted rock and other waste materials produced when a material is removed from the earth's surface or subsurface by mining, dredging, quarrying, and excavation.

sport hunting Finding and killing animals, mostly for recreation. Compare *commercial hunting, subsistence hunting.*

S-shaped curve Leveling off of an exponential, J-shaped curve when a rapidly growing population exceeds the carrying capacity of its environment and ceases to grow in numbers. See also *overshoot, population crash.*

stability Ability of a living system to withstand or recover from externally imposed changes or stresses. See *constancy, inertia, resilience.*

stocking rate Number of a particular kind of animal grazing on a given area of grassland.

strategic mineral A fuel or a nonfuel mineral vital to the industry and defense of a country. Ideally, supplies are stockpiled to cushion against supply interruptions and sharp price rises.

stratosphere Second layer of the atmosphere, extending from about 17 to 48 kilometers (11 to 30 miles) above the earth's surface. It contains small amounts of gaseous ozone (O_3), which filters out about 99% of the incoming harmful ultraviolet (UV) radiation emitted by the sun. Compare *troposphere.*

stream Flowing body of surface water. Examples are creeks and rivers.

strip cropping Planting regular crops and close-growing plants, such as hay or nitrogen-fixing legumes, in alternating rows or bands to help reduce depletion of soil nutrients.

strip mining Form of surface mining in which bulldozers, power shovels, or stripping wheels remove large chunks of the earth's surface in strips. See *surface mining.* Compare *subsurface mining.*

subatomic particles Extremely small particles — electrons, protons, and neutrons — that make up the internal structure of atoms.

subduction zone Area in which oceanic lithosphere is carried downward (subducted) under the island arc or continent at a convergent plate boundary. A trench ordinarily forms at the boundary between the two converging plates. See *convergent plate boundary.*

subsidence Slow or rapid sinking down of part of Earth's crust that is not slope related.

subsistence farming Supplementing solar energy with energy from human labor and draft animals to produce enough food to feed oneself and family members; in good years there may be enough food left over to sell or put aside for hard times. Compare *industrialized agriculture.*

subsistence hunting Finding and killing wild animals to get enough food and other animal material for survival. Compare *commercial hunting, sport hunting.*

subsurface mining Extraction of a metal ore or fuel resource such as coal from a deep underground deposit. Compare *surface mining.*

succession See *ecological succession.*

succulent plants Plants, such as desert cacti, that survive in dry climates by having no leaves, thus reducing the loss of scarce water. They store water and use sunlight to produce the food they need in the thick fleshy tissue of their green stems and branches. Compare *deciduous plants, evergreen plants.*

superinsulated house House that is heavily insulated and extremely airtight. Typically, active or passive solar collectors are used to heat water, and an air-to-air heat exchanger is used to prevent buildup of excessive moisture and indoor air pollutants.

surface fire Forest fire that burns only undergrowth and leaf litter on the forest floor. Compare *crown fire, ground fire.*

surface mining Removal of soil, subsoil, and other strata, and then extracting a mineral deposit found fairly close to the earth's surface. See *area strip mining, contour strip mining, open-pit mining.* Compare *subsurface mining.*

surface runoff Water flowing off the land into bodies of surface water. Compare *river runoff.*

surface water Precipitation that does not infiltrate the ground or return to the atmosphere by evaporation or transpiration. See *river runoff, runoff, surface runoff.* Compare *groundwater.*

sustainable agriculture See *sustainable-Earth agricultural system.*

sustainable development See *sustainable economic development.*

sustainable-Earth agricultural system Method of growing crops and raising livestock based on organic fertilizers, soil conservation, water conservation, biological control of pests, and minimal use of nonrenewable fossil fuel energy.

sustainable-Earth economy Economic system in which the number of people and the quantity of goods are maintained at some constant level. This level is ecologically sustainable over time and meets at least the basic needs of all members of the population.

sustainable-Earth society Society based on working with nature by recycling and reusing discarded matter; by pollution prevention; by conserving matter and energy resources through reducing unnecessary waste and use; by not degrading renewable resources; by building things that are easy to recycle, reuse, and repair; by not allowing population size to exceed the carrying

capacity of the environment; and by preserving biodiversity. See *sustainable-Earth worldview.* Compare *matter-recycling society, throwaway society.*

sustainable-Earth worldview Belief that Earth is a place with finite room and resources, so continuing population growth, production, and consumption inevitably put severe stress on natural processes that renew and maintain the resource base of air, water, and soil. To prevent environmental overload, environmental degradation, and resource depletion, people should work with nature by controlling population growth, reducing unnecessary use and waste of matter and energy resources, and not causing the premature extinction of any other species. Compare *Spaceship-Earth worldview, throwaway worldview.*

sustainable economic development Forms of economic growth and activities that do not deplete or degrade natural resources upon which present and future economic growth depend.

sustainable yield (sustained yield) Highest rate at which a potentially renewable resource can be used without reducing its available supply throughout the world or in a particular area. See also *environmental degradation.*

synergistic interaction Interaction of two or more factors so the net effect is greater than that expected from adding together the independent effects of each factor.

synfuels Synthetic gaseous and liquid fuels produced from solid coal or sources other than natural gas or crude oil.

synthetic natural gas (SNG) Gaseous fuel containing mostly methane produced from solid coal.

tailings Rock and other waste materials removed as impurities when waste mineral material is separated from the metal in an ore.

tar sand Deposit of a mixture of clay, sand, water, and varying amounts of a tarlike heavy oil known as bitumen. Bitumen can be extracted from tar sand by heating. It is then purified and upgraded to synthetic crude oil. See *bitumen.*

temperature Measure of the average speed of motion of the atoms, ions, or molecules in a substance or combination of substances at a given moment. Compare *heat.*

temperature inversion See *thermal inversion.*

teratogen Chemical, ionizing agent, or virus that causes birth defects. See *carcinogen, mutagen.*

terracing Planting crops on a long, steep slope that has been converted into a series of broad, nearly level terraces with short vertical drops from one to another that run along the contour of the land to retain water and reduce soil erosion.

terrestrial Pertaining to land. Compare *aquatic.*

tertiary (and higher) consumers Animals that feed on animal-eating animals. They feed at high trophic levels in food chains and webs. Examples are hawks, lions, bass, and sharks. Compare *detritivore, primary consumer, secondary consumer.*

tertiary oil recovery See *enhanced oil recovery.*

tertiary sewage treatment See *advanced sewage treatment.*

thermal inversion Layer of dense, cool air trapped under a layer of less dense warm air. This prevents upward-flowing air currents from developing. In a prolonged inversion, air pollution in the trapped layer may build up to harmful levels.

third law of ecology Any substance we produce should not interfere with any of Earth's natural biogeochemical cycles.

threatened species Wild species that is still abundant in its natural range but is likely to become endangered because of a decline in numbers. Compare *endangered species.*

threshold effect The harmful or fatal effect of a small change in environmental conditions that exceeds the limit of tolerance of an organism or population of a species. See *law of tolerance.*

throwaway society The situation in most advanced industrialized countries, in which ever-increasing economic growth is sustained by maximizing the rate at which matter and energy resources are used, with little emphasis on pollution prevention, recycling, reuse, reduction of unnecessary waste, and other forms of resource conservation. Compare *matter-recycling society, sustainable-Earth society.*

throwaway worldview Belief that Earth is a place of unlimited resources. Any type of resource conservation that hampers short-term economic growth is unnecessary because if we pollute or deplete resources in one area, we will find substitutes; control the pollution through technology; and, if necessary, get resources from the moon and asteroids in the "new frontier" of space. Compare *Spaceship-Earth worldview, sustainable-Earth worldview.*

total fertility rate (TFR) Estimate of the average number of children that will be born alive to a woman during her lifetime if she passes through all her childbearing years (ages 15–44) conforming to age-specific fertility rates of a given year. In simpler terms, it is an estimate of the average number of children a woman will have during her childbearing years.

total resources Total amount of a particular resource material that exists on Earth. Compare *identified resources, reserves, resources.*

toxic substance Chemical that is fatal to humans in low doses, or fatal to over 50% of test animals at stated concentrations. Most are neurotoxins, which attack nerve cells. See *carcinogen, hazardous substance, mutagen, teratogen.*

toxic waste Form of hazardous waste that causes death or serious injury (such as burns, respiratory diseases, cancers, or genetic mutations). See *hazardous waste.*

traditional intensive agriculture Producing enough food for a farm family's survival and perhaps a surplus that can be sold. This type of agriculture requires higher inputs of labor, fertilizer, and water than traditional subsistence agriculture. See *traditional subsistence agriculture.*

traditional subsistence agriculture Production of enough crops or livestock for a farm family's survival and, in good years, a surplus to sell or put aside for hard times. Compare *traditional intensive agriculture.*

tragedy of the commons Depletion or degradation of a resource to which people have free and unmanaged access. An example is the depletion of commercially desirable species of fish in the open ocean beyond areas controlled by coastal countries. See *common-property resource.*

transform fault Area where Earth's lithospheric plates move in opposite but parallel directions along a fracture (fault) in the lithosphere. Compare *convergent plate boundary, divergent plate boundary.*

transmissible disease A disease that is caused by living organisms such as bacteria, viruses, and parasitic worms and that can spread from one person to another by air, water, food, body fluids, or in some cases by insects or other organisms. Compare *nontransmissible disease.*

transpiration Process in which water is absorbed by the root systems of plants, moves up through the plant, passes through pores (stomata) in their leaves or other parts, and then evaporates into the atmosphere as water vapor.

tree farm Site planted with one or only a few tree species in an even-aged stand. When the stand matures, it is usually harvested by clear-cutting and replanted. Normally used to grow rapidly growing tree species for fuelwood, timber, or pulpwood. See *even-aged management.* Compare *uneven-aged management, uneven-aged stand.*

tritium (T: hydrogen-3) Isotope of hydrogen with a nucleus containing one proton and two neutrons, thus having a mass number of 3. Compare *deuterium*.

trophic level All organisms that are the same number of energy transfers away from the original source of energy (e.g., sunlight) that enters an ecosystem. For example, all producers belong to the first trophic level and all herbivores belong to the second trophic level in a food chain or a food web.

troposphere Innermost layer of the atmosphere. It contains about 95% of the mass of Earth's air and extends about 17 kilometers (11 miles) above sea level. Compare *stratosphere*.

true cost Cost of a good when its internal costs and its short- and long-term external costs are included in its market price. Compare *external cost, internal cost*.

unconfined aquifer Collection of groundwater above a layer of Earth material (usually rock or clay) through which water flows very slowly (low permeability). Compare *confined aquifer*.

undernutrition Consuming insufficient food to meet one's minimum daily energy requirement, for a long enough time to cause harmful effects. Compare *malnutrition, overnutrition*.

undiscovered resources Potential supplies of a particular mineral resource, believed to exist because of geologic knowledge and theory, though specific locations, quality, and amounts are unknown. Compare *resources, reserves*.

uneven-aged management Method of forest management in which trees of different species in a given stand are maintained at many ages and sizes to permit continuous natural regeneration. Compare *even-aged management*.

uneven-aged stand Stand of trees in which there are considerable differences in the ages of individual trees. Usually, such stands have a variety of tree species. See *uneven-aged management*. Compare *even-aged stand, tree farm*.

upwelling Movement of nutrient-rich bottom water to the ocean's surface. This occurs along certain steep coastal areas where the surface layer of ocean water is pushed away from shore and replaced by cold, nutrient-rich bottom water.

urban area Geographic area with a population of 2,500 or more people. The number of people used in this definition may vary, with some countries setting the minimum number of people at 10,000 to 50,000.

urban growth Rate of growth of an urban population. Compare *degree of urbanization*.

urban heat island Buildup of heat in the atmosphere above an urban area. This heat is produced by the large concentration of cars, buildings, factories, and other heat-producing activities. See also *dust dome*.

urbanization See *degree of urbanization*.

vertebrates Animals with backbones. Compare *invertebrates*.

wastewater lagoon Large pond where air, sunlight, and microorganisms break down wastes, allow solids to settle out, and kill some disease-causing bacteria. Water typically remains in a lagoon for 30 days. Then it is treated with chlorine and pumped out for use by a city or spread over cropland.

water consumption Water that is not returned to the surface water or groundwater from which it came, mostly because of evaporation and transpiration. As a result, this water is not available for use again in the area from which it came. See *water withdrawal*.

water cycle See *hydrologic cycle*.

waterlogging Saturation of soil with irrigation water or excessive precipitation, so the water table rises close to the surface.

water pollution Any physical or chemical change in surface water or groundwater that can harm living organisms or make water unfit for certain uses.

watershed Land area that delivers the water, sediment, and dissolved substances via small streams to a major stream (river).

water table Upper surface of the zone of saturation in which all available pores in the soil and rock in the earth's crust are filled with water.

water withdrawal Removing water from a groundwater or surface water source and transporting it to a place of use. Compare *water consumption*.

watt Unit of power, or rate at which electrical work is done. See *kilowatt*.

weather Short-term changes in the temperature, barometric pressure, humidity, precipitation, sunshine (solar radiation), cloud cover, wind direction and speed, and other conditions in the troposphere at a given place and time. Compare *climate*.

weathering Physical and chemical processes in which solid rock exposed at Earth's surface is changed to separate solid particles and dissolved material, which can then be moved to another place as sediment. See *erosion*.

wetland Land that is covered all or part of the year with salt water or fresh water, excluding streams, lakes, and the open ocean. See *coastal wetland, inland wetland*.

wilderness Area where the earth and its community of life have not been seriously disturbed by humans and where humans are only temporary visitors.

wildlife All free, undomesticated species. Sometimes the term is used to describe only free, undomesticated species of animals.

wildlife management Manipulation of populations of wild species (especially game species) and their habitats for human benefit, the welfare of other species, and the preservation of threatened and endangered wildlife species.

wildlife resources Species of wildlife that have actual or potential economic value to people. See also *game species*.

windbreak Row of trees or hedges planted to partially block wind flow and reduce soil erosion on cultivated land.

wind farm Cluster of small to medium-size wind turbines in a windy area to capture wind energy and convert it into electrical energy.

work What happens when a force is used to move a sample of matter over some distance or to raise its temperature. Energy is defined as the capacity to do such work.

worldview How individuals think the world works and what they think their role in the world should be. See *Spaceship-Earth worldview, sustainable-Earth worldview, throwaway worldview*.

zero population growth (ZPG) State in which the birth rate (plus immigration) equals the death rate (plus emigration) so the population of a geographical area is no longer increasing.

zone of saturation Area where all available pores in soil and rock in the earth's crust are filled by water. See *water table*.

zoning Regulating how various parcels of land can be used.

zooplankton Animal plankton. Small floating herbivores that feed on plant plankton (phytoplankton). Compare *phytoplankton*.

INDEX

Note: Page numbers appearing in **boldface** indicate where definitions of key terms can be found in the text; these terms also appear in the glossary. Page numbers in *italics* indicate illustrations, tables, and figures.

MAJOR U.S. RESOURCE CONSERVATION AND ENVIRONMENTAL LEGISLATION

General

National Environmental Policy Act of 1969 (NEPA)
International Environmental Protection Act of 1983

Energy

National Energy Act of 1978, 1980
National Appliance Energy Conservation Act of 1987

Water Quality

Water Quality Act of 1965
Water Resources Planning Act of 1965
Federal Water Pollution Control Acts of 1965, 1972
Ocean Dumping Act of 1972
Ocean Dumping Ban Act of 1988
Safe Drinking Water Act of 1974, 1984
Water Resources Development Act of 1986
Clean Water Act of 1977, 1987

Air Quality

Clean Air Act of 1963, 1965, 1970, 1977, 1990

Noise Control

Noise Control Act of 1965
Quiet Communities Act of 1978

Resources and Solid Waste Management

Solid Waste Disposal Act of 1965
Resource Recovery Act of 1970
Resource Conservation and Recovery Act of 1976
Marine Plastic Pollution Research and Control Act of 1987

Toxic Substances

Hazardous Materials Transportation Act of 1975
Toxic Substances Control Act of 1976
Resource Conservation and Recovery Act of 1976
Comprehensive Environmental Response, Compensation, and Liability (Superfund) Act of 1980, 1986
Nuclear Waste Policy Act of 1982

Pesticides

Federal Insecticide, Fungicide, and Rodenticide Control Act of 1972, 1988

Wildlife Conservation

Anadromous Fish Conservation Act of 1965
Fur Seal Act of 1966
National Wildlife Refuge System Act of 1966, 1976, 1978
Species Conservation Act of 1966, 1969
Marine Mammal Protection Act of 1972
Marine Protection, Research, and Sanctuaries Act of 1972
Endangered Species Act of 1973, 1982, 1985, 1988
Fishery Conservation and Management Act of 1976, 1978, 1982
Whale Conservation and Protection Study Act of 1976
Fish and Wildlife Improvement Act of 1978
Fish and Wildlife Conservation Act of 1980 (Nongame Act)

Land Use and Conservation

Taylor Grazing Act of 1934
Wilderness Act of 1964
Multiple Use Sustained Yield Act of 1968
Wild and Scenic Rivers Act of 1968
National Trails System Act of 1968
National Coastal Zone Management Act of 1972, 1980
Forest Reserves Management Act of 1974, 1976
Forest and Rangeland Renewable Resources Act of 1974, 1978
Federal Land Policy and Management Act of 1976
National Forest Management Act of 1976
Soil and Water Conservation Act of 1977
Surface Mining Control and Reclamation Act of 1977
Antarctic Conservation Act of 1978
Endangered American Wilderness Act of 1978
Alaskan National Interests Lands Conservation Act of 1980
Coastal Barrier Resources Act of 1982
Food Security Act of 1985

Bathroom (65% of typical residential water use; 40% for toilet flushing)

- For existing toilets, reduce the amount of water used per flush by putting a tall plastic container weighted with a few stones into each tank, or buy and insert a toilet dam. Ask school officials to install toilet dams.

- In new houses, install water-saving toilets that use no more than 6 liters (1.6 gallons) per flush (now required for all new residences in Massachusetts and in Phoenix, Arizona).

- Flush toilets only when necessary, using the advice found on a bathroom wall in a drought-stricken area: "If it's yellow, let it mellow—if it's brown, flush it down."

- Take short showers (less than five minutes) instead of baths. Shower by wetting down, turning off the water while soaping up, and then rinsing off.

- Install water-saving shower heads and flow restrictors on all faucets. Ask school officials to install these devices.

- Check frequently for water leaks, and repair them promptly. A pinhole-sized leak can waste up to 640 liters (170 gallons) per month. A toilet must be leaking more than 940 liters (250 gallons) *a day* before you can hear the leak. To test for toilet leaks, add some water-soluble dye to the water in the tank but don't flush. If you have a leak, some color will show up in the bowl's water within a few minutes.

- Don't keep water running while brushing teeth, shaving, or washing.

Laundry Room (15%)

- Wash only full loads; use the short cycle and fill the machine to the lowest possible water level. Use a dryer powered by natural gas, not energy- and money-wasting electricity. Better yet, let the sun dry your clothes or use the dryer's unheated air or fluff cycle for drying.

- When buying a new washer, choose one that uses the least amount of water and fills up to different levels for loads of different sizes. Front-loading clothes washers use less water and energy than comparable top-loading models.

- Check for leaks frequently, and repair all leaks promptly.

Kitchen (10%)

- Use an automatic dishwasher only for full loads; use the short cycle and let dishes air-dry to save energy and money.

- When washing many dishes by hand, don't let the faucet run. Instead, use one filled dishpan for washing and another for rinsing.

- Keep a reusable jug of water in the refrigerator rather than running water from a tap until it gets cold enough to drink.

- Check for leaks frequently, and repair all leaks promptly.

- Don't use a garbage disposal system—a large user of water. Instead, compost your food wastes (Figure 12-18).

Outdoors (10%, higher in arid and semiarid areas)

- Don't wash your car, or wash it less frequently. Wash the car from a bucket of soapy water; use the hose only for rinsing. Use a commercial car wash that recycles its water.

- Sweep walks and driveways instead of hosing them off.

- Reduce evaporation losses by watering lawns and gardens in the early morning or in the evening, rather than in the heat of midday or when windy. Better yet, landscape with native plants adapted to local average annual precipitation so that watering is unnecessary. Think of a conventional grass lawn, which must be frequently watered, fertilized, and protected with pesticides, as a glaring example of unnecessary Earth degradation. Botanists in Florida are experimenting with a disease-resistant hybrid grass that remains lush with just four waterings a year and also repels chinch bugs and several other types of insects.

- Use drip irrigation systems and mulch on home gardens to improve irrigation efficiency and reduce evaporation.

- To irrigate plants, install a system to capture rainwater or collect, filter, and reuse normally wasted gray water from bathtubs, showers, sinks, and the clothes washer.

Chemical	Alternative
Deodorant	Sprinkle baking soda on a damp wash cloth and wipe skin.
Oven cleaner	Baking soda and water paste, scouring pad.
Toothpaste	Baking soda.
Drain cleaner	Pour ½ cup salt down drain, followed by boiling water; or pour 1 handful baking soda and ½ cup white vinegar and cover tightly for one minute.
Window cleaner	Add 2 teaspoons white vinegar to 1 quart warm water.
Toilet bowl, tub, and tile cleaner	Mix a paste of borax and water; rub on and let set one hour before scrubbing. Can also scrub with baking soda and a brush.
Floor cleaner	Add ½ cup vinegar to a bucket of hot water; sprinkle a sponge with borax for tough spots.
Shoe polish	Polish with inside of a banana peel, then buff.
Silver polish	Clean with baking soda and warm water.
Air freshener	Set vinegar out in an open dish. Use an opened box of baking soda in close areas such as refrigerators and closets. To scent the air, use pine boughs or make sachets of herbs and flowers.

Chemical	Alternative
General surface cleaner	Mixture of vinegar, salt, and water.
Bleach	Baking soda or borax.
Mildew remover	Mix ½ cup vinegar, ½ cup borax, and warm water.
Disinfectant and general cleaner	Mix ½ cup borax in 1 gallon of hot water.
Furniture or floor polish	Mix ½ cup lemon juice and 1 cup vegetable or olive oil.
Carpet and rug shampoos	Sprinkle on cornstarch, baking soda, or borax and vacuum.
Detergents and detergent boosters	Washing soda or borax and soap powder.
Spray starch	In a spray bottle, mix 1 tablespoon cornstarch in a pint of water.
Fabric softener	Add 1 cup white vinegar or ¼ cup baking soda to final rinse.
Dishwasher soap	1 part borax and 1 part washing soda.
Pesticides (indoor and outdoor)	Use natural biological controls.